Director® 6 Bible

Jonathan Bacon
Kurt Cagle
Deborah Miller

IDG Books Worldwide, Inc.
An International Data Group Company

Foster City, CA ✦ Chicago, IL ✦ Indianapolis, IN ✦ Southlake, TX

Director® 6 Bible

Published by
IDG Books Worldwide, Inc.
An International Data Group Company
919 E. Hillsdale Blvd., Suite 400
Foster City, CA 94404
www.idgbooks.com (IDG Books Worldwide Web site)

Copyright © 1998 IDG Books Worldwide, Inc. All rights reserved. No part of this book, including interior design, cover design, and icons, may be reproduced or transmitted in any form, by any means (electronic, photocopying, recording, or otherwise) without the prior written permission of the publisher.

Library of Congress Catalog Card No.: 97-70131

ISBN: 0-7645-4012-2

Printed in the United States of America

10 9 8 7 6 5 4 3 2 1

1E/RV/QR/ZY/FC

Distributed in the United States by IDG Books Worldwide, Inc.

Distributed by Macmillan Canada for Canada; by Transworld Publishers Limited in the United Kingdom; by IDG Norge Books for Norway; by IDG Sweden Books for Sweden; by Woodslane Pty. Ltd. for Australia; by Woodslane Enterprises Ltd. for New Zealand; by Longman Singapore Publishers Ltd. for Singapore, Malaysia, Thailand, and Indonesia; by Simron Pty. Ltd. for South Africa; by Toppan Company Ltd. for Japan; by Distribuidora Cuspide for Argentina; by Livraria Cultura for Brazil; by Ediciencia S.A. for Ecuador; by Addison-Wesley Publishing Company for Korea; by Ediciones ZETA S.C.R. Ltda. for Peru; by WS Computer Publishing Corporation, Inc., for the Philippines; by Unalis Corporation for Taiwan; by Contemporanea de Ediciones for Venezuela; by Computer Book & Magazine Store for Puerto Rico; by Express Computer Distributors for the Caribbean and West Indies. Authorized Sales Agent: Anthony Rudkin Associates for the Middle East and North Africa.

For general information on IDG Books Worldwide's books in the U.S., please call our Consumer Customer Service department at 800-762-2974. For reseller information, including discounts and premium sales, please call our Reseller Customer Service department at 800-434-3422.

For information on where to purchase IDG Books Worldwide's books outside the U.S., please contact our International Sales department at 415-655-3200 or fax 415-655-3295.

For information on foreign language translations, please contact our Foreign & Subsidiary Rights department at 415-655-3021 or fax 415-655-3281.

For sales inquiries and special prices for bulk quantities, please contact our Sales department at 415-655-3200 or write to the address above.

For information on using IDG Books Worldwide's books in the classroom or for ordering examination copies, please contact our Educational Sales department at 800-434-2086 or fax 817-251-8174.

For press review copies, author interviews, or other publicity information, please contact our Public Relations department at 415-655-3000 or fax 415-655-3299.

For authorization to photocopy items for corporate, personal, or educational use, please contact Copyright Clearance Center, 222 Rosewood Drive, Danvers, MA 01923, or fax 508-750-4470.

LIMIT OF LIABILITY/DISCLAIMER OF WARRANTY: AUTHOR AND PUBLISHER HAVE USED THEIR BEST EFFORTS IN PREPARING THIS BOOK. IDG BOOKS WORLDWIDE, INC., AND AUTHOR MAKE NO REPRESENTATIONS OR WARRANTIES WITH RESPECT TO THE ACCURACY OR COMPLETENESS OF THE CONTENTS OF THIS BOOK AND SPECIFICALLY DISCLAIM ANY IMPLIED WARRANTIES OF MERCHANTABILITY OR FITNESS FOR A PARTICULAR PURPOSE. THERE ARE NO WARRANTIES WHICH EXTEND BEYOND THE DESCRIPTIONS CONTAINED IN THIS PARAGRAPH. NO WARRANTY MAY BE CREATED OR EXTENDED BY SALES REPRESENTATIVES OR WRITTEN SALES MATERIALS. THE ACCURACY AND COMPLETENESS OF THE INFORMATION PROVIDED HEREIN AND THE OPINIONS STATED HEREIN ARE NOT GUARANTEED OR WARRANTED TO PRODUCE ANY PARTICULAR RESULTS, AND THE ADVICE AND STRATEGIES CONTAINED HEREIN MAY NOT BE SUITABLE FOR EVERY INDIVIDUAL.

Trademarks: All brand names and product names used in this book are trade names, service marks, trademarks, or registered trademarks of their respective owners. IDG Books Worldwide is not associated with any product or vendor mentioned in this book.

 is a trademark under exclusive license to IDG Books Worldwide, Inc., from International Data Group, Inc.

Director 6 Bible

ABOUT IDG BOOKS WORLDWIDE

Welcome to the world of IDG Books Worldwide.

IDG Books Worldwide, Inc., is a subsidiary of International Data Group, the world's largest publisher of computer-related information and the leading global provider of information services on information technology. IDG was founded more than 25 years ago and now employs more than 8,500 people worldwide. IDG publishes more than 275 computer publications in over 75 countries (see listing below). More than 60 million people read one or more IDG publications each month.

Launched in 1990, IDG Books Worldwide is today the #1 publisher of best-selling computer books in the United States. We are proud to have received eight awards from the Computer Press Association in recognition of editorial excellence and three from *Computer Currents'* First Annual Readers' Choice Awards. Our best-selling ...For Dummies® series has more than 30 million copies in print with translations in 30 languages. IDG Books Worldwide, through a joint venture with IDG's Hi-Tech Beijing, became the first U.S. publisher to publish a computer book in the People's Republic of China. In record time, IDG Books Worldwide has become the first choice for millions of readers around the world who want to learn how to better manage their businesses.

Our mission is simple: Every one of our books is designed to bring extra value and skill-building instructions to the reader. Our books are written by experts who understand and care about our readers. The knowledge base of our editorial staff comes from years of experience in publishing, education, and journalism — experience we use to produce books for the '90s. In short, we care about books, so we attract the best people. We devote special attention to details such as audience, interior design, use of icons, and illustrations. And because we use an efficient process of authoring, editing, and desktop publishing our books electronically, we can spend more time ensuring superior content and spend less time on the technicalities of making books.

You can count on our commitment to deliver high-quality books at competitive prices on topics you want to read about. At IDG Books Worldwide, we continue in the IDG tradition of delivering quality for more than 25 years. You'll find no better book on a subject than one from IDG Books Worldwide.

John Kilcullen
CEO
IDG Books Worldwide, Inc.

Steven Berkowitz
President and Publisher
IDG Books Worldwide, Inc.

Eighth Annual
Computer Press
Awards ≥1992

Ninth Annual
Computer Press
Awards ≥1993

Tenth Annual
Computer Press
Awards ≥1994

Eleventh Annual
Computer Press
Awards ≥1995

IDG Books Worldwide, Inc., is a subsidiary of International Data Group, the world's largest publisher of computer-related information and the leading global provider of information services on information technology. International Data Group publishes over 275 computer publications in over 75 countries. Sixty million people read one or more International Data Group publications each month. International Data Group's publications include: **ARGENTINA:** Buyer's Guide, Computerworld Argentina, PC World Argentina; **AUSTRALIA:** Australian Macworld, Australian PC World, Australian Reseller News, Computerworld, IT Casebook, Network World, Publish, Webmaster; **AUSTRIA:** Computerwelt Osterreich, Networks Austria, PC Tip Austria; **BANGLADESH:** PC World Bangladesh; **BELARUS:** PC World Belarus; **BELGIUM:** Data News; **BRAZIL:** Anuário de Informática, Computerworld, Connections, Macworld, PC Player, PC World, Publish, Reseller News, Supergamepower; **BULGARIA:** Computerworld Bulgaria, Network World Bulgaria, PC & MacWorld Bulgaria; **CANADA:** CIO Canada, Client/Server World, ComputerWorld Canada, InfoWorld Canada, NetworkWorld Canada, WebWorld; **CHILE:** Computerworld Chile, PC World Chile; **COLOMBIA:** Computerworld Colombia, PC World Colombia; **COSTA RICA:** PC World Centro America; **THE CZECH AND SLOVAK REPUBLICS:** Computerworld Czechoslovakia, Macworld Czech Republic, PC World Czechoslovakia; **DENMARK:** Communications World Danmark, Computerworld Danmark, Macworld Danmark, PC World Danmark, Techworld Denmark; **DOMINICAN REPUBLIC:** PC World Republica Dominicana; **ECUADOR:** PC World Ecuador; **EGYPT:** Computerworld Middle East, PC World Middle East; **EL SALVADOR:** PC World Centro America; **FINLAND:** MikroPC, Tietoverkko, Tietoviikko; **FRANCE:** Distributique, Hebdo, Info PC, Le Monde Informatique, Macworld, Reseaux & Telecoms, WebMaster France; **GERMANY:** Computer Partner, Computerwoche, Computerwoche Extra, Computerwoche FOCUS, Global Online, Macwelt, PC Welt; **GREECE:** Amiga Computing, GamePro Greece, Multimedia World; **GUATEMALA:** PC World Centro America; **HONDURAS:** PC World Centro America; **HONG KONG:** Computerworld Hong Kong, PC World Hong Kong, Publish in Asia; **HUNGARY:** ABCD CD-ROM, Computerworld Szamitastechnika, Internetto online Magazine, PC World Hungary, PC-X Magazin Hungary; **ICELAND:** Tolvuheimur PC World Island; **INDIA:** Information Communications World, Information Systems Computerworld, PC World India, Publish in Asia; **INDONESIA:** InfoKomputer PC World, Komputek Computerworld, Publish in Asia; **IRELAND:** ComputerScope, PC Live!; **ISRAEL:** Macworld Israel, People & Computers/Computerworld; **ITALY:** Computerworld Italia, Macworld Italia, Networking Italia, PC World Italia; **JAPAN:** DTP World, Macworld Japan, Nikkei Personal Computing, OS/2 World Japan, SunWorld Japan, Windows NT World, Windows World Japan; **KENYA:** PC World East African; **KOREA:** Hi-Tech Information, Macworld Korea, PC World Korea; **MACEDONIA:** PC World Macedonia; **MALAYSIA:** Computerworld Malaysia, PC World Malaysia, Publish in Asia; **MALTA:** PC World Malta; **MEXICO:** Computerworld Mexico, PC World Mexico; **MYANMAR:** PC World Myanmar; **NETHERLANDS:** Computer! Totaal, LAN Internetworking Magazine, LAN World Buyers Guide, Macworld Netherlands, Net, WebWereld; **NEW ZEALAND:** Absolute Beginners Guide and Plain & Simple Series, Computer Buyer, Computer Industry Directory, Computerworld New Zealand, MTB, Network World, PC World New Zealand; **NICARAGUA:** PC World Centro America; **NORWAY:** Computerworld Norge, CW Rapport, Datamagasinet, Financial Rapport, Kursguide Norge, Macworld Norge, Multimediaworld Norge, PC World Ekspress Norge, PC World Nettverk, PC World Norge, PC World ProduktGuide Norge; **PAKISTAN:** Computerworld Pakistan; **PANAMA:** PC World Panama; **PEOPLE'S REPUBLIC OF CHINA:** China Computer Users, China Computerworld, China InfoWorld, China Telecom World Weekly, Computer & Communication, Electronic Design China, Electronics Today, Electronics Weekly, Game Software, PC World China, Popular Computer Week, Software Weekly, Software World, Telecom World; **PERU:** Computerworld Peru, PC World Profesional Peru, PC World SoHo Peru; **PHILIPPINES:** Click!, Computerworld Philippines, PC World Philippines, Publish in Asia; **POLAND:** Computerworld Poland, Computerworld Special Report Poland, Cyber, Macworld Poland, Network World Poland, PC World Komputer; **PORTUGAL:** Cerebro/PC World, Computerworld/Correio Informático, Dealer World Portugal, Mac*In/PC*In Portugal, Multimedia World; **PUERTO RICO:** PC World Puerto Rico; **ROMANIA:** Computerworld Romania, PC World Romania, Telecom Romania; **RUSSIA:** Computerworld Russia, Mir PK, Publish, Seti; **SINGAPORE:** Computerworld Singapore, PC World Singapore, Publish in Asia; **SLOVENIA:** Monitor; **SOUTH AFRICA:** Computing SA, Network World SA, Software World SA; **SPAIN:** Communicaciones World España, Computerworld España, Dealer World España, Macworld España, PC World España; **SRI LANKA:** Infolink PC World; **SWEDEN:** CAP&Design, Computer Sweden, Corporate Computing Sweden, Internetworld Sweden, it.branschen, Macworld Sweden, MaxiData Sweden, MikroDatorn, Nätverk & Kommunikation, PC World Sweden, PCaktiv, Windows World Sweden; **SWITZERLAND:** Computerworld Schweiz, Macworld Schweiz, PCtip; **TAIWAN:** Computerworld Taiwan, Macworld Taiwan, NEW VISION/Publish, PC World Taiwan, Windows World Taiwan; **THAILAND:** Publish in Asia, Thai Computerworld; **TURKEY:** Computerworld Turkiye, Macworld Turkiye, Network World Turkiye, PC World Turkiye; **UKRAINE:** Computerworld Kiev, Multimedia World Ukraine, PC World Ukraine; **UNITED KINGDOM:** Acorn User UK, Amiga Action UK, Amiga Computing UK, Apple Talk UK, Computing, Macworld, Parents and Computers UK, PC Advisor, PC Home, PSX Pro, The WEB; **UNITED STATES:** Cable in the Classroom, CIO Magazine, Computerworld, DOS World, Federal Computer Week, GamePro Magazine, InfoWorld, I-Way, Macworld, Network World, PC Games, PC World, Publish, Video Event, THE WEB Magazine, and WebMaster; online webzines: JavaWorld, NetscapeWorld, and SunWorld Online; **URUGUAY:** InfoWorld Uruguay; **VENEZUELA:** Computerworld Venezuela, PC World Venezuela; and **VIETNAM:** PC World Vietnam. 3/24/97

Credits

Acquisitions Editors
Juliana Aldous
Andy Cummings

Development Editors
Carol Henry
Tracy Thomsic

Technical Editor
Michael D. Miller

Copy Editors
Carol Henry
Timothy Borek

Production Coordinator
Susan Parini

Quality Control Specialist
Mark Schumann
Mick Arellano

Graphics and Production Specialists
Mario Amador
Doris Figgemeier
Linda Marousek
Christopher Pimentel
Dina F Quan
Trevor Wilson

Illustrator
Greg Maxson

Proofreader
Mary C. Barnack

Indexer
Liz Cunningham

About the Authors

Jonathan Bacon

Jonathan Paul Bacon serves as Director of the Educational Technology Center at Johnson County Community College in Overland Park, Kansas. The Center seeks to encourage and support the use of instructional technology in the College's curriculum. Jonathan and his staff developed a Web Wizard Workshop series in 1996 that has trained over 175 JCCC faculty and staff to create interactive media assets and Web documents for instructional purposes. Since the mid-eighties, he has written 16 books and dozens of training manuals covering a variety of application software, including Macromedia Director, Adobe Photoshop, Netscape Navigator, DOS, Windows, Microsoft Word, Lotus 1-2-3, and WordPerfect. A sample of his work can be viewed at the Ed Tech Center's site at
www.johnco.cc.ks.us/acad/etc.

In 1997 Jonathan developed credit courses in Interactive Media Concepts and Interactive Media Assets, for JCCC's advanced certificate and degree programs in Interactive Media. He is a frequent consultant, speaker, conference presenter, and workshop facilitator on topics related to the future of instructional materials, the impact of technology on higher education, instructional uses of technology, and computer-coordinated genealogical research. Jonathan can be reached at jbacon@johnco.cc.ks.us. Comments, questions, and suggestions are always welcome.

Deborah Miller

The ever-expanding realm of possibilities has been the basis for Deborah's 30-year career as a graphic designer and illustrator. Trained in the traditional tools of drawing boards and airbrushes, she moved to computers several years ago, during the days of programming sprites in Basic. Today her tools are far more sophisticated as she explores the worlds of CorelDRAW, Macromedia Director, 3D animation, the World Wide Web, and multimedia development. The co-author and author of several books on computer graphics, and illustrator of anything that does not move fast enough, her goal is to make graphics software *understandable*. She believes that users should not have to be techie wizards to create computer graphics.

Having escaped the city, she resides in the hills of Tennessee with her husband Mike, her family, and an assortment of cats, dogs, a wolf, and a black snake named Gertrude. When she's not working, she can be found haunting the undernet of IRC, or creating sculptures from the dead computers she's notorious for pushing beyond their endurance.

Kurt Cagle

Kurt Cagle is President of Cagle Communications, a multimedia and Internet database development firm located in Olympia, Washington. He edits the *Macromedia User Journal,* a monthly newsletter for developers working with Director, Authorware, and other Macromedia products. Involved in multimedia design and production since 1982, when he worked on a training management system for General Motors, over the years Kurt has produced applications, kiosks, and Web/Internet and intranet sites for companies as diverse as Microsoft, AT&T, Gametek, Ericsson, Starwave, and many others. Attendees at several Comdexes and Macromedia User Conferences have heard him speak. Kurt has specialized in advanced programming solutions with Lingo and Visual Basic. At his Web site (http://www.onlingo.com) he maintains tips and techniques for Director behaviors and related Lingo programming issues.

Kurt can be reached at cagle@olywa.net, as can his daughter if you don't mind e-mail messages returned in crayon.

The serious writer must hate his work enough to let perfect strangers destroy and then recreate it. We want to dedicate this book to the all the people who have contributed in small, medium, and large ways to the resurrection of this tome.

To Mary Ellen Masterson, who guides by example and compassion the steps and careers of strangers and friends alike.

To Paul J. Bacon, who is loved beyond words by his eldest son.

To Jeannine (Bacon) Wagner, Jan Bacon, and Roseanne Bacon, for teaching me to assemble something marvelous out of scrap lumber, old bricks, and marbles.

To Jennifer Anne (Bacon) Harvey and Jodi Elizabeth Bacon: How beautiful is life when our children both honor and love us despite what we have and have not done. My love for you cannot be expressed in words or deeds.

Thanks to the one woman on the face of the earth who understands me — and still loves and supports me. To my extraordinary partner and cheerleader Joan, for surviving this book with me, I owe you at least another 28-year adventure.

— Jonathan Paul Bacon

To my wife, Anne, and my daughter, Katie, for their love and patience.

— Kurt Cagle

Preface

Here's a want ad for a multimedia producer. Are you interested?

> **Wanted**: *Talented multimedia professional capable of creating CD-ROMs, animations, Web pages, games, and more, with little or no budget, no schedule, and as few resources as can be made available. Such an individual must be skilled in illustration, graphic design, animation, programming, digital video production, audio production, Internet technology, photography, and interface design. Must be willing to work insane hours and subsist on pepperoni and mushroom pizza.*

Though the job description sounds like a sure recipe for an early ulcer, creating multimedia can be rewarding both emotionally and financially, especially with the right tools at hand.

And one of the best tools out there for putting together a multimedia masterpiece is Macromedia Director. It is the tool of choice for hundreds of thousands of developers around the world. Director 6 offers the simplicity of being useful right out of the box along with the power to create complex, interactive applications. Furthermore, Director's Shockwave component—because of its cross-platform capabilities and support for Web-based media—has become the standard for making Internet applications that can work in nearly every browser currently in use.

Yet, with all of Director's power, like any other tool it works best in the hands of people who know how to use it to its best advantage. The book you are holding is your means of learning how to do that. Written by veteran multimedia developers with decades of experience in their craft, *Director 6 Bible* will take you step-by-step through the process of making animations, games, portfolio pieces, and more. It's your ticket to mastering the premiere multimedia application, Macromedia Director 6.

Who Should Read This Book?

Director is a flexible and diverse program that can be used to author projects for a variety of uses. Similarly, the variety of users is nearly as diverse. This book is designed to span the power of Director as well as the range of people who use Director. You're an ideal candidate for reading the *Director 6 Bible* if you

- ✦ Need a guide to creating animated presentations and projects in Director 6
- ✦ Are an educator and/or are creating interactive learning modules
- ✦ Want to create interactive kiosks and catalogs
- ✦ Are a multimedia developer who needs a comprehensive reference to Director 6 and Lingo
- ✦ Are new to creating multimedia programs and want to learn more
- ✦ Are proficient in Director but want to become familiar with the changes introduced with Director 6
- ✦ Want to learn to use Lingo, Director's scripting language
- ✦ Plan to develop powerful Web-based Shockwave projects
- ✦ Are well-versed in Lingo but want to know more about object-oriented programming in Director
- ✦ Have interest in the latest Xtras, including database support, alpha-channel creation, and 3D virtual reality

Because this book was developed as part of IDG's comprehensive Bible series, your own particular experience and proficiency with Director won't matter. Novice users will discover how to add sophisticated behaviors into their programs—without having to do any coding. People familiar with Director but wanting to learn about Lingo will find sample scripts and ample information here. Even advanced developers will come away with a more complete understanding about how Director works in general, and Director 6 in particular. The *Director 6 Bible* is intended to take you from your first tentative steps to complete mastery, all within a mere 1,000 pages.

What Hardware and Software Do You Need?

If you don't have your own copy of Macromedia Director 6, a demo version is available on this book's CD-ROM. *Director 6 Bible* is written to be platform independent and covers both Macintosh and Windows 95/NT versions of Director 6.

According to Macromedia, the *minimum* requirements for a Macintosh developer's workstation include the following:

- ✦ A 68040 Macintosh or faster
- ✦ 16MB RAM minimum

- ✦ A 13", 8-bit color monitor supporting a minimum of 256 colors (8-bit) and 640 x 480 resolution
- ✦ Approximately 30–40MB of free hard disk space
- ✦ Macintosh System 7.1 or later
- ✦ The latest version of the QuickTime extension
- ✦ A double-speed or faster CD-ROM drive to install Director and to play the companion CD-ROM that accompanies this book

According to Macromedia, the *minimum* requirements for a Windows developer's workstation include the following:

- ✦ A 66MHz 486 PC, with Pentium or Pentium Pro preferred (but if you want to get work done in this lifetime, you'd better have a 90MHz Pentium or Pentium Pro)
- ✦ 16MB RAM minimum (but get 32MB RAM to avoid those nasty crashes)
- ✦ A 15", 8-bit color monitor supporting a minimum of 256 colors and 640 x 480 resolution
- ✦ Approximately 30–40MB of free hard disk space
- ✦ SoundBlaster-compatible sound card and speakers
- ✦ The latest drivers for QuickTime for Windows or Video for Windows
- ✦ A double-speed or faster CD-ROM drive to install Director and to play the companion CD-ROM that accompanies this book
- ✦ Windows 95/Windows NT 4.0 or later

You cannot author using a Windows 3.*x* system. You must have Windows 95/Windows NT 4.0 or later.

How This Book is Organized

In theory, you could read this book cover to cover, but you will probably find that you'll focus on one section at a time, gaining mastery and understanding by running through the clear and well-documented examples. Several chapters have sample files, available on the CD-ROM, that you can use as the basis of your own applications. In addition, a comprehensive set of behaviors is included on the companion CD-ROM that accompanies this book, which you can use to spice up your own multimedia extravaganzas.

This book is organized into the following five parts:

Part I: Getting to Know Director

The chapters in Part I introduce you to the Director program and many of the core concepts, including sprites, cast members, movies, and the Score. This part also instructs you on using the Paint window and other tools for creating media assets.

Chapter 1 discusses the basics of the Director environment and in Chapter 2 you'll learn how to use Director's Paint window and work with imported images. In Chapter 3 you'll learn fundamental techniques for manipulating sprites on the Stage and in the Score. Text and shapes are discussed in Chapter 4, and in Chapter 5 you'll get "The Big Picture"— even more basic knowledge to send you on your way to working with multimedia projects in Director.

Part II: Bringing Life to Director

In these chapters, you'll explore techniques for adding digital video and audio, transitions, tempo changes, and related elements. You'll also learn how to take advantage of Director's behaviors (Chapter 6). Information about the sound and video elements of your movies is presented in Chapters 7 and 8, including advice on choosing formats, working with sound Xtras, and how to add, manage, and export digital videos. So you can see how it comes together, Chapter 9 discusses guidelines for pulling Director's elements into an interactive resumé; it covers designing, organizing, and distributing the project.

Part III: Speaking the Lingo

Part III instructs you in Director's scripting language, Lingo. Your pilgrimage to the interactive temple of Lingo features an exploration of keywords, script creation, manipulating text, moving sprites around, and handling mouse and keyboard events.

Chapter 10 teaches you how to work with scripts; it's your introduction to using Lingo. The chapter describes the basic ingredients of a movie: events, messages, and handlers. Chapter 11 discusses all the fundamental constructs — Lingo programming building blocks — necessary to master Lingo scripting. Definitions as well as demonstrations are here for the commands, expressions, functions, properties, and variables of Lingo.

Chapter 12, "Writing Handlers," is about just that. Using the construction of a better button as the teaching vehicle, you learn to initiate an action depending on the last sprite clicked, and build handlers that react when the mouse pointer enters, leaves, or rests within the area of a sprite. In Chapters 13, 14, 15, and 16, you put more Lingo to work. You'll find out how to make sprites dance to your script, manipulate text and its appearance, incorporate and control sound, and import and control digital video — all with the Lingo language.

Part IV: Behavioral Science

In Part IV you focus on using Lingo's more advanced features: lists, parent scripts and child objects, and advanced text handling. You also see how to work with menus, custom dialog boxes, and movies in a window (MIAWs).

Chapter 17 describes the advantages of using lists over variables that store a single item. You learn the difference between linear and property lists, how to sort lists, and how to use a list to create a simple menu system. Chapter 18 is your introduction to object-oriented programming (OOP) as it relates to Director. Chapter 19 describes the single most powerful feature of Director: Xtras, which extend and enhance Lingo's native power. Chapter 20, "Lingo Troubleshooting," is the cure for a perfectly awful code day. You'll see how to use Director's built-in troubleshooting features (the Message window, the Watcher window, and the Debugger window) to help locate and solve syntax errors and errors of logic. Chapter 21 is all about using movies in a window (MIAWs) to create modular projects. In Chapter 22 you find out how to create a menu system for your applications. And finally, Chapter 23 discusses memory considerations critical to the success of Director movies.

Part V: Onto the Web

This final part of the book examines advanced Director issues, including making your applications both Internet-aware and highly Internet-ready (with Shockwave), and working with 3D graphics and virtual reality worlds.

Chapter 24 is your introduction to Shockwave and NetLingo. Beginning with a brief history, the chapter progresses from a discussion of installing the ActiveX control and the Shockwave plug-in, to embedding a Shockwave movie on a Web page, to using specific network related Lingo commands for starting, stopping, and evaluating operations over the Internet. Chapter 25 covers the principles of alpha channels and 3D technology and using them in Director movies.

Part VI: Appendixes

This book's appendixes offer important supplemental information for Director users. Here you'll find instructions for installing and configuring your Director environment, a handy summary of Lingo statements, shortcuts to improve your productivity, and a healthy batch of additional resources to keep at hand. And of course there's a description of everything that's on the CD-ROM that accompanies this book.

Conventions Used in This Book

The following conventions are used throughout this book.

Mac and Windows Conventions: When the keystrokes are different on a Macintosh and a Windows system, the differences are noted. For instance, the Command key on the Macintosh is equivalent to the Ctrl key on a Windows system. In an instruction like this:

> Press Command+C (Ctrl+C)

the first instruction is for Mac users (to press the Command and the C key in combination); and the instruction in parentheses is for Windows users (to press the Ctrl key and the C key in combination).

Key-Combinations: When you are instructed to press a key-combination (that is, to hold down the first key while pressing the second and then release both), the key-combination is separated by a plus sign. For example:

> Command+2 (Ctrl+2)

tells you to hold down the Command key (or Ctrl key on a Windows system), press the 2 key once, and then release the Command (Ctrl) key.

Mouse Instructions:

✦ When instructed to "point" the mouse, you must move the mouse so that the mouse pointer moves over your screen until it touches or passes over the specified target item.

✦ When instructed to "click" an item, you must move the mouse pointer to the specified item and click the mouse button once. (If you are a Windows user, click the *left* mouse button unless instructed otherwise.) "Double-click" means to click the mouse button twice in rapid succession.

✦ When instructed to "click and drag," you must click and hold down the left mouse button while moving the mouse to a new location. This process is used typically to select text and to drag an object from one location to another.

Menu Commands: When instructed to select a command from a menu, you will see the menu and the command separated by an arrow symbol. For example, when instructed to execute the Open command from the File menu, you will see the notation: File➪Open.

Typographical Conventions: *Italic* type is used for new terms and for emphasis. **Boldface** type is used for text that you need to type directly at the computer keyboard.

Code: A special typeface is used to indicate information that will appear on your screen, such as the text of scripts and handlers, error messages, screen prompts, and so on. As an example, the following pseudocode is in the special font:

```
on startThisBook
    Read
    Enjoy
    Learn
end
```

This special typeface is also used within paragraphs to designate Director terms such as `put the member of sprite 10` and `on mouseUp`, and commands such as `set`, `put`, and `go to`.

The (¬) character at the end of a line means you should type the next line of code before pressing the Return (Mac) or Enter (PC) key.

Navigating Through This Book

Because of the size and scope of *Director 6 Bible,* and the number of processes described, it's important that you're aware of the various signposts we've placed throughout the book to help guide you.

Each chapter begins with an overview of the information it contains, and ends with a quick summary of what you learned.

Icons occur throughout the text to indicate something important or especially helpful. Here's a list of these icons and what they represent:

Tips provide you with the extra knowledge that separates the novice from the veteran. Make use of the Tips spread throughout this book to get the most out of your hardware and software.

Notes along the way provide additional information or technical data on the subject at hand.

The Caution icon is your warning of a potential problem, usually encountered during a process.

The CD icon indicates that a sample file is available on the enclosed CD, giving the appropriate folder/directory and filename.

> ### Sidebars
>
> You'll also encounter sidebars throughout the book that offer more extensive background information on particular topics. These sidebars often provide an expanded discussion and insight for the topic under discussion. Some sidebars are technical in nature; others are anecdotal.

New Director users tend to find the program intimidating. Indeed there is much to learn to use all of Director's power. Director doesn't have to be the Goliath application it seems, however. The building-block progression of Director 6 Bible chapters will guide you through the process of creating your own movies, and you'll soon find that you have harnessed the substantial power of this versatile program.

Acknowledgments

To bend a phrase from H. L. Mencken, book publishing is "the triumph of imagination over intelligence." We wish to acknowledge all the people at IDG Books whose concerted, sustained efforts forced this book through the birthing process.

We would like to especially thank Juliana Aldous and Andy Cummings, who entrusted us with this galactic undertaking. Many thanks to IDG staffers who have worked with us at various stages in the development of this five-pound tome, including Tracy Thomsic, Ellen Camm, Tracy Cramer, Michael Koch, and Amy Thomas. Special thanks to a wonderful editor, Carol Henry, to whom we are eternally grateful for her sharp-eyed editing, gentle prodding, and editorial leadership. For his wry and devious sense of humor and his cyber-friendship (in addition to some darn fine technical editing), thanks to Mike Miller of Miller Graphics Consulting.

We would be remiss if we did not recognize and thank the many kind folks at Macromedia who assisted us with timely information and support: John Dowdell, John Embow, Keigo Kiyohara, Carrie Myers, and Suzanne Porta to name a few.

Special thanks to Kurt Ackman of Apple Computer for reviewing the material on QuickTime, to Pat and David Lovejoy for their photographic contributions, to Robert Sindt for his programming support, to Jeffrey E. Jones for his musical MIDI contributions, and to Dale Monaghen (the fotoman) and his models (Amanda Thweatt, Lisa Sato, Tammie Schneider, and Stan) for their grafitti-cal offerings.

Thanks to my staff at Johnson County Community College's Educational Technology Center, who challenge me to keep pace with their talent and ever-expanding expertise: Rosemary Bates, Saul Epstein, Vickie Frost, Aaron Fry, Brandon Henry, Jeff Jones, Jeff Kosko, Pat Lovejoy, Daniel Neath, Mike Needham, Eileen O'Neill, Beth Ramirez, Robert Sindt, Linda Stewart, John Swezey, Rory Ann Webb, and Don Wright. And thanks to Mel Cunningham, whose support and leadership mean everything to me.

Sincere thanks to all the folks who assisted by providing tools, utilities, and media for the accompanying CD-ROM: Colin Adams and Brett Kapilik of Indigo Rose Corp.; Chris Anderson of JASC Inc.; Stacy Bartlett of ClickArt Inc.; Charlie Conquest of The Fresh Music Library; James Dawson of Image Farm Inc.; Genevieve Doyon of Integration New Media Inc.; Dan French of Innovative Media Corp.; Dana Giles of Terran Interactive Inc.; Steve Justice of Dynamic Graphics, Inc.; Roger Kennerly of Kennerly Music Productions; Lenny Kissell and Jasmine White of ArtBeats;

Jim Larkin of Nico Mak Computing, Inc.; Jennifer Lyng of Aladdin Systems; Tom Meadows of Prosonus/Big Fish Productions; Lyna Miller of Classic PIO Partners; Mark Monrean of Tri-Digital Software Inc.; Dave Palo of Equilibrium; Mauricio Piacentini of Tabuleiro da Baiana Multimedia; Carol Reid of Digital Stock Corporation; and Don Wieshlow of the Image Club.

— Jonathan Paul Bacon

Writing a book about power is a unique experience—and make no mistake about it—Director is about power. It's a software program that provides the raw power necessary to create projects in a vast and rapidly expanding world of interactivity. What authors and publishers know, but readers rarely see, is the scope of what's required to write such a book. The image of a solitary author pounding out page after page of manuscript is largely a myth. This book, and others like it, required the teamwork and dedication of numerous people, mixed with a sense of humor, to become a reality. I would like to extend my personal thanks to everyone who touched this book in an effort to make it happen. My personal experience with this book involved many 4 a.m. moments, for which I'm eternally grateful to anyone who's ever picked a coffee bean, my family who tolerates me, and my friends who like me anyway.

— Deborah Miller

This book has seen an extraordinary number of writers, editors, and other contributors. Two IDG Acquisition Editors—those people who steer the book through the intricate maze from concept to final production—have put their stamp on this book: Andy Cummings and Juliana Aldous. The Development Editors, Carol Henry and Tracy Thomsic, steered the direction of the contents and art, insuring that the material was up to a high standard of quality.

Macromedia has helped considerably with the *Director 6 Bible*. Jane Chuey served as Macromedia's author liaison, coordinating much of the paperwork on that end. Leesa Lee, Project Manager for Macromedia Director, provided some technical support, and several of the engineers and developers at Macromedia gave suggestions and corrections to code in progress. Additional help and support came from Apple Computers; Tabuleiro da Baiana Multimedia; g/matter; Media Lab, Inc.; Component Software Industries; and RealSpace, Inc.

Finally, I want to recognize the families of the respective authors. Writing and programming are both solitary professions, and the combination of the two tends to make for many empty beds at night.

— Kurt Cagle

Contents at a Glance

Part I: Getting to Know Director 1
Introducing Director 3
Working with Graphics 23
Working with the Stage, Sprites, and Score 63
Using Text and Shapes in Director 113
The Big Picture 139

Part II: Bringing Life to Director 173
Sound Advice 223
Video Advice 255
Pulling It All Together 285

Part III: Speaking the Lingo 321
Scripting From Scratch 323
Lingo Programming Building Blocks 367
Writing Handlers 399
Controlling Sprites From Lingo 437
Text Manipulation with Lingo 485
Sound Lingo 539
Video Lingo 585

Part IV: Behavioral Science 629
Parent Scripts and Child Objects 675
Xtras and File Manipulation 709
Lingo Troubleshooting 747
Movies in a Window (MIAWs) 771
Designing for Memory Management 835

Part V: Onto the Web 851
Incorporating NetLingo and Shockwave 853
Into the Third Dimension 905

Part VI: Appendixes 947

Appendix A: Installing and Configuring Director 949
Appendix B: Summary of Lingo Statements 959
Appendix C: Shortcuts 971
Appendix D: Resources 979
Appendix E: What's on the CD-ROM 985

Glossary 999
Index 1013
License Agreement 1029
CD-ROM Installation Instructions 1035

Contents

Part I: Getting to Know Director — 1

Introducing Director — 3
Lights! Camera! Author! — 3
Migrating from Director 5 to Director 6 — 5
    So what else is new? — 6
The Director 6 Theater — 8
    The Score editor — 8
    The Cast editor — 9
    The other editors — 10
    Toolbar buttons and tooltips — 10
    The floating Tool Palette — 12
    Pop-up menus — 13
    The menu bar — 14
Xternal Resources — 15
    Adding Xtras to your system — 15
    Using Xtras — 16
    Cast libraries — 16
SOS (Save Our Software?) — 17
    Using context-sensitive help — 18
    Surfing for help — 19
On the Flip Side — 20
Summary — 21

Working with Graphics — 23
An Animated Discussion — 23
    Creating a concept — 24
    Planning your presentation — 25
Working in the Paint Window — 26
    Pulling out your brushes and paints — 26
    Painting with light and shadow: the ink effects — 33
Basic Painting Techniques — 36
    Drawing the graphic — 36
    Painting the graphic — 39
    Techniques for selecting the graphic — 46
    Moving, copying, cutting, and pasting selections — 49
    Design and production techniques — 49
Importing Images — 51

       Specifying options for imported images 53
       Into the depths (of color, that is) 55
   Casting Call 58
       Moving and duplicating cast members 59
       Sorting cast members 60
   Summary 62

Working with the Stage, Sprites, and Score 63

   Meeting Your Sprites 63
       Setting the Stage 65
       Settling a Score 67
       Anatomy of a sprite in Director 6 69
       Creating a moving performance 73
       Extending, splitting, and joining sprites 79
   Casting Call: Creating Animations 82
       Getting your cast members ready 83
       Using Auto-Distort to generate cast members 84
       Onion skinning and registration 87
       Working with film loops 94
   Using Step and Real-time Recording 97
       Animating with the Step Recording command 97
       Animating with the Real-time Recording command 100
   Bringing Sprites to Life 102
       Exchanging cast members 102
       Changing a single frame of a sprite 106
   Drawing Sprites upon the Stage: Blends and Inks 106
       Inking the contracts 109
   Summary 111

Using Text and Shapes in Director 113

   Working with Text in Director 113
       The text cast member 114
       Creating a text cast member 116
   Using the Text Window 120
       Specifying formatting options 121
       Specifying text properties 123
       Placing text cast members in your movie 125
   Importing Text 128
   The Shape of Things to Come 128
       Creating QuickDraw shapes 129
       Using patterns 130
       Patterns within patterns 132
       In the spotlight 134
   Summary 137

The Big Picture 139
Changing the Tempo...139
    Operating the Control Panel...140
    Specifying tempo settings in the Score window 142
Working with Transitions..145
    Choosing a transition 146
    Applying and controlling a transition 148
Working with Color Palettes...150
    First, a little color theory..150
    Mapping images to palettes 151
    Modifying palettes..155
    Creating effects with palettes 158
Building Projectors 161
    Creating a projector 161
    Distributing a projector 165
Shocking Your Movies 165
    Designing for the Web 165
    Creating a Shockwave movie 169
Designing for Success...170
    Planning ahead 170
    Storyboarding 170
Summary 171

Part II: Bringing Life to Director — 173

Be on Your Best Behavior... 175
What Are Behaviors?..175
    Predefined Director 6 behaviors 176
    Attaching predefined behaviors to objects 178
Building a Better Movie..179
    Pushing all the right buttons 180
    Using navigation behaviors to build buttons....................................181
Using the Behavior Inspector..185
    Viewing the script behind a behavior 186
    Adding behaviors using the Behavior Inspector 189
    Removing behaviors from a sprite 189
    Reordering behaviors attached to a sprite 190
    Using the gestures behaviors 194
    Creating your own basic behaviors 196
Making a Custom Button with the Button Editor.....................................204
    Building the custom button from scratch 205
Where Did That Behavior Come From? 209

Cast libraries	210
Using a behavior to make a timer	210
Changing the properties of a behavior	214
Navigating with Custom Buttons	215
Adding markers to your movie	215
Responding to custom events	220
Summary	221

Sound Advice 223

Sound Basics	224
Importing sounds	224
Using internal versus external sounds	226
Choosing a sound format	227
Editing sounds externally	228
Sampling rates, recording modes, and other issues	230
Obtaining sounds for your movies	232
Adding and Editing Sounds	232
Placing sounds in the Score	233
Using channels effectively	236
Managing Sounds	237
Using cue points in a movie	238
Tempo, sounds, and interactivity	239
Looping sounds	240
Setting the volume for a movie	242
Working with Sound Xtras	245
Using sound behaviors	245
Using Shockwave Audio (SWA)	247
Understanding Shockwave compression	248
Summary	253

Video Advice 255

Working with Digital Video	256
Determining an effective frame rate	256
Working with image dimensions	257
Considering color depth	257
Controlling file size and choosing compression	261
Selecting an image quality	262
Adding Digital Videos to Your Movies	262
Understanding Direct to Stage mode	265
Scaling and cropping a digital video	267
Setting looping and controller preferences	269
Specifying an external video editor	270
Managing Video Cast Members	272
Working with behaviors	273
Using widgets	275
Specifying tempo settings	277

Exporting Digital Video 279
Summary 283

Pulling It All Together 285

Creating an Interactive Resume 286
    Designing the interface...286
    Gathering the cast members 287
    Animating a portfolio...293
    Using navigation 299
    Adding finishing touches..310
Working as a Team..314
    Using in-house versus contract sources 315
    Distributing the work...316
Understanding Copyright Issues 316
    What can be protected by copyright?..317
    Fair use for educational purposes 318
    As a developer, what should you do? 319
Summary 320

Part III: Speaking the Lingo   321

Scripting From Scratch 323

Event Handling for Fun and Profit 324
Director's Four Types of Scripts 324
    Scripting terminology...325
    Getting to know the script types 330
    Which script has priority?..334
    Whose territory is this, anyway?..337
Composing Your Own Scripts 337
    Creating a cast member script 338
    Creating a sprite script...339
    Creating a frame script..340
    Creating a movie script..341
Creating an Interactive Movie 342
    A Director slideshow 343
    Creating navigational buttons 343
    Resizing a button on the Stage...344
    Changing the text on the face of a button 344
    Changing other button properties 345
    Deleting a button 346
    Assigning scripts to buttons...346
Understanding Basic Navigation..347
    Lingo navigation commands..349
    Using the play command to branch within the digital album 361
A Few Closing Thoughts 365
Summary 366

Lingo Programming Building Blocks 367
Learning the Lingo 368
    Scripts 368
    Commands 368
    Expressions 369
    Functions 369
    Variables and constants 370
Getting to Know the Message Window 375
    Using the Message window 375
    Working in the Message window 376
    Getting a jump start on Lingo syntax 381
Smooth Operators 384
    Arithmetic operators 385
    Comparison operators 386
    Logical operators 388
    Other operators 389
    When numbers aren't just numbers 392
    Let us be precise 394
Summary 397

Writing Handlers 399
There Go the Property Values 399
Wanted: "Real" Navigational Buttons 402
    What to expect from a polite button 403
Creating Well-Behaved Buttons 404
    Using puppetSprites in Director 404
    Swapping cast members using Lingo 405
    Adding expected button behaviors 410
Reusing Code for Greater Efficiency 421
    Identifying the current cast member 421
    Using the clickOn function to identify the current channel 425
    Creating your own handlers 428
Using Director 6's New Mouse Events 431
    Building an on mouseWithin handler 431
    Building an on mouseEnter handler 431
    Building an on mouseLeave handler 432
    Uses for the New Mouse event handlers 432
Summary 435

Controlling Sprites From Lingo 437
Dancing with puppetSprites 438
    Using Lingo to make moveable sprites 438
    Saving keystrokes and code with another type of loop 441

Where Are You Moving That Sprite? 443
    Understanding screen coordinates...443
    Using the intersect function 444
    Setting the location of a moveable sprite 445
    Simplifying with the loc of sprite property 445
    Substituting global variables to shorten code............................447
    Using cast placement to save code 453
Dancing in Tight (Constrained) Shoes...455
    Constraining movement within a specific area of the Stage 456
    Restricting the vertical or horizontal movement of a sprite 458
    Matching the sprite location to the mouse pointer location...............463
Adding puppetTransitions..466
Using Standard Cursors 471
    Choosing a cursor for a sprite 471
    Changing the cursor for an entire movie.....................................473
Using Custom Cursors..473
    Creating custom cursors..474
    Invoking a custom cursor 474
    Creating custom cursors in the Paint window............................476
    Creating a mask for a custom cursor 479
Changing the Visible to Invisible 480
    Fine-tuning the fish 482
    Making a sprite invisible with the click of a mouse 483
    Making a sprite visible on rollover 483
Summary..484

Text Manipulation with Lingo 485

Understanding the Properties of Text..487
    Setting the foreground color 488
    Setting the font size 490
    Setting the typeface 491
    Setting the style 493
Using Chunk Expressions to
Change Parts of the Whole...494
    Understanding text strings 494
    Guidelines for working with text strings.....................................495
    Using chunk expressions 497
Using Other Chunky Activities..504
    Establishing the text string in a field..504
    Counting words in a field 508
    Transferring text from one field to another 508
    Deleting text from text fields 513
    Joining text strings...514
Simulating Hypertext in Director..515
    Planning for a hypertext field 516

More Control of Text Fields 526
    Scrolling through a field 526
    Highlighting selected text 529
    Making fields editable..530
    Controlling font substitutions 531
Some Final Thoughts on Fields and Hypertext..536
Summary 537

Sound Lingo 539

Controlling Sound Using Lingo..539
    Using puppet sounds 540
    Triggering sound using Lingo 542
    Review: Attaching sound to sprites and buttons 544
    Stopping sound..545
    Additional Lingo controls for digital sound 548
    Creating sound on and sound off buttons 553
    Playing random sounds..562
    Playing a list of sounds in one frame 563
    Playing sound when the user goes to sleep 566
    Playing linked files with Lingo 568
Controlling the Sound Volume 570
    Using the soundLevel property..570
    Using the volume of sound property 572
    Controlling fade-in/fade-out 574
Using Cue Points Stored in Imported Sounds 576
    Setting cue points in an AIFF sound file......................................576
    Using a cue point in the Tempo channel 578
Preloading and Unloading Cast Members 579
Summary 584

Video Lingo 585

Understanding Digital Video 585
    The trade-off: file size vs. quality..586
A Few Incarnations of Digital Video 588
    What is QuickTime?..588
    What is Video for Windows?..592
    What is MPEG?..593
Adding a Digital Video Cast Member 595
    Importing digital video..596
    Setting digital video options 596
    Placing and playing a digital video cast member 601
Using Lingo to Control Digital Video Properties 608
    Setting the video of member property..608
    Setting the sound of member property..608

Pausing at the beginning of a video using Lingo 608
Setting the loop of member property..609
Cropping and centering video using Lingo..609
Playing a video direct to the Stage using Lingo................................609
Displaying a controller using Lingo..610
Establishing the frame rate for digital video using Lingo 610
Enabling the preload of video using Lingo..611
Using Lingo to Create Other Controls..611
Setting the volume 611
Adding step-forward and step-backward controls 611
Creating a fast-forward control..612
Getting rid of annoying artifacts..616
From Director to Digital Video 617
Exporting Director movies to digital video..618
Digital Video for Cross-Platform Projects...621
Flattening QuickTime movies for playback on Windows 622
Converting digital video between QuickTime and AVI 623
Other Resources for Digital Video Information 625
Closing Thoughts on Digital Video..626
Summary 627

Part IV: Behavioral Science   629

Linear Lists and Property Lists 631

Using Lists..631
What Is a Linear List?..632
Understanding the List-Related Commands..633
Retrieving list items 635
Using list-related functions 636
Retrieving a list item's position..638
Adding items to a list..639
Setting list values 639
Deleting items from lists 640
Sorting lists 641
Transferring and duplicating lists..647
Processing with Lists..648
Checking whether an item exists 648
Converting a list to a string..648
Converting items to a list..649
Converting a list to items..651
The Principles of Property Lists 653
What is a property list?..654
Property list commands..656
Duplicating property lists 658

Working with Property List Attributes 659
    Adding an item to a property list 660
    Setting and retrieving, revisited 661
    Getting property information 662
    Removing properties 663
    Searching a dictionary list 665
Creating a Simple Menu System Using Objects in a List 667
Summary 673

Parent Scripts and Child Objects 675

What Is Object Oriented Programming? 675
How OOP and Director Work Together 677
    The basics: parent scripts and child objects 677
    Why use OOP with Director? 678
    Getting the OOP into Lingo 679
    Comparisons between Lingo OOP and C++ 680
The Components of OOP Programming in Director 682
    The parent 682
    The child 682
    The ancestor 683
    Creating a parent script 684
    Creating child objects 687
Using the actorList 696
Creating Multiple Child Objects 702
Summary 708

Xtras and File Manipulation 709

Xtending the Power of Director 709
What Is an Xtra? 710
    Why use Xtras? 710
    Types of Xtras 711
    Xtras that come with Director 6 715
Using Xtras in Director 716
    How does Director know an Xtra exists? 717
    Installing new Xtras 718
Using Xtra-Related Lingo Commands 721
    Creating a new instance of an Xtra 721
    Listing the messages you can send to an Xtra 722
Using Xtra-Specific Methods 723
    Opening a file using the fileIO Xtra 723
    Closing a file using the fileIO Xtra 724
    Displaying an Open dialog box 724
    Using the fileIO Xtra filterMask 725
    Accessing data in a file 727
More fileIO Methods 732
    Displaying a Save dialog box 732

    Creating a new disk file 733
    Writing a disk file..735
    Knowing the current position within a file 736
  Packaging Xtras in Your Projectors..739
    Xtras available in Director 6 740
    Selecting Xtras to package 742
  Summary 745

Lingo Troubleshooting 747

  Troubleshooting Your Scripts 747
    Locating the problem 748
    Identifying syntax and spelling errors..748
    Correcting errors of logic 751
  Debugging in the Message Window..752
    Testing commands directly in the Message window 756
    Using the showGlobals command 758
  Using the Watcher Window 758
    Designating variables to watch 759
  Using the Debugger Window 762
    Setting breakpoints within your scripts 763
    Ignoring all breakpoints 763
    Running through your script in the Debugger window.................................764
    An exercise with the Debugger window...765
  Summary 769

Movies in a Window (MIAWs)..771

  What's Different about MIAWs? 771
    MIAWs versus imported movies 772
    Achieving interactivity between windows..774
  Creating a Movie with an MIAW 775
    Writing scripts to create an MIAW 775
  Controlling MIAWs 782
    Specifying transitions with MIAWs 784
    Working with palettes...786
    Adjusting the tempo with an MIAW 787
    Setting the visibility of a window..787
  Managing MIAWs 788
    Creating multiple MIAWs..788
    Preloading MIAWs 790
    Moving windows to the front or back 790
    Removing an MIAW 791
    Selecting the location on Stage for the MIAW 795
  In Your Interface: Menus and Dialogs 803
  Making Manic Menus...803

Creating Your Own Pull-Down Menu System 804
    Creating a menu using a field cast member 805
    Installing a menu 808
    Finishing the job 810
    A menu by any other name is still a menu 816
Establishing a Dialog 821
    Getting basic information with MUI 822
    Abort, retry, or ignore 825
Before You Exit This Chapter 830
    Using exitLock 830
    Running a program or opening a file from the movie 831
    Swapping cast members 832
Summary 833

Designing for Memory Management   835

Understanding Memory 835
    Determining memory requirements 837
    Testing to avoid memory problems 839
Preloading Cast Members 839
    Specifying SWA preload values 840
    Using Lingo to specify preload values 842
Setting Purge Priorities 843
Designing Movies for Memory Considerations 845
    Guidelines for saving memory 846
Optimizing for CD-ROM 847
    Building a virtual image 847
    CD-ROM basics 848
    Single or multisession recording? 849
Summary 850

Part V: Onto the Web   851

Incorporating NetLingo and Shockwave   853

Director and the Internet 854
    Clients and servers 854
    Plug-ins, Java, and ActiveX 855
    Distributed object models 857
    Where is Macromedia in all of this? 858
What Is Shockwave? 859
    The Shockwave compression engine 860
    The Shockwave plug-in 861
Overview for Creating a Shockwave Movie 864
    Placement of movie elements in a Shockwave movie 865
    Make that streaming, please 865

Director Authoring Issues and Constraints...868
    Beware of the speed bumps in Web delivery...868
    Losing some Director features 869
    Limitations and opportunities of Web-delivered movies 870
Adding a Director Movie to Your Web Document 872
    Using the <EMBED> tag...872
    Using the <OBJECT> tag..875
    Some notes on Web terminology 877
    Exercise: Putting a movie in a Web page 880
Working with NetLingo 887
    Commands that start network operations 888
    Functions that evaluate the status of network operations 890
    Functions that retrieve the results of network operations 891
    Canceling a partially complete network operation 892
    Commands and functions that interact with the browser 893
Placing Your Movies on a Web Server 897
    Where to place your files 898
    Copying files to your Web server...898
    Changing access rights to the Web documents....................................900
Creating the Ideal Shockwave Movie 900
Summary 903

Into the Third Dimension...905

Making 3D Come Alive in 2D 905
    Boxing at shadows 906
    Prerendered worlds 908
    Rendering landscapes and environments...909
    Flight of the avatar 911
    Creating avatars 912
    Working with props..913
    Putting 2D/3D presentations together...914
Understanding 3D Technologies 915
    Concentrating on coordinates..915
    Rendering with meshes 918
    Material witnesses 920
    Playing meta-balls 921
    Implementing 3D systems 922
Using QuickDraw 3D Sprites..922
    Manipulating QuickDraw 3D on the screen 931
    QuickDraw 3D and Lingo..931
    Uses for QuickDraw 3D...940
    From sprites to worlds 941
Creating Virtual Reality 941
    The rise of VRML...942
    Reviewing the RealVR Xtra 944
    Quizzing QuickTime VR...944
Summary 945

Part VI: Appendixes — 947

Appendix A: Installing and Configuring Director 949

Appendix B: Summary of Lingo Statements 959

Appendix C: Shortcuts 971

Appendix D: Resources 979

Appendix E: What's on the CD-ROM 985

Glossary 999

Index 1013

License Agreement 1029

CD-ROM Installation Instructions 1035

Getting to Know Director

P A R T

I

✦ ✦ ✦ ✦

In This Part

Chapter 1
Introducing Director

Chapter 2
Working with Graphics

Chapter 3
Working with the Stage, Sprites, and Score

Chapter 4
Using Text and Shapes in Director

Chapter 5
The Big Picture

✦ ✦ ✦ ✦

Introducing Director

CHAPTER 1

In This Chapter

Getting to know Director 6

Looking at windows, menus, and shortcuts

Setting basic preferences

Working with the Director Help system

Welcome to the wild, woolly world of multimedia programming with Director 6. By taking on this challenge you will have the benefits of eating stale pizza and drinking Dr. Pepper at three in the morning, spending a lot of time wondering about the similarities between *interface* and *in your face,* and learning to think of your computer as your best friend and worst enemy. Oh, and you'll have an incredible amount of fun doing it . . .

Lights! Camera! Author!

There is this curious mystique surrounding the creation of software. The stereotypical programmer is the nerdy kid from high school with the horn-rims and the bad complexion, the one that went on to MIT (and occasionally the one who made a gazillion dollars with his own software company). We have indeed met a few programmers like that, but most by and large are ordinary people, often people you wouldn't expect to have those interests. What they all had in common was the discovery of the great secret of programming: Programming is actually not only easy, but fun. It doesn't take a rocket scientist to do it (although a brief stint studying rocket science briefly in college convinced one of the authors that rocket science doesn't take a rocket scientist either — just a pretty good programmer).

For the past several years, Macromedia Director has served as the catalyst for many people to learn the art of programming. It's a unique product — easy and intuitive enough that many people can create a reasonably impressive application the first time they sit down at the computer to use the program, yet powerful enough to let developers put together sophisticated multimedia applications with 3D interfaces, database access, and Internet connectivity. Director is heavily graphics-oriented, making it an ideal tool for graphic designers and illustrators. But it also contains a scripting language called *Lingo* that gives you precision control over every aspect of the program — the ultimate in a left-brain/right-brain tool.

Director accomplishes all this by borrowing from a metaphor that's remarkably well suited to the creation of multimedia: the world of film and animation. When you are authoring multimedia — just like directing a film — you are integrating sound and images, movements across a stage, transitions, pacing, and special effects. In Director (and what else would you call a program with such obvious cinematic ties?), even the terminology resembles the theatrical world rather than dry programming jargon. A Director file is called a *movie*. The rectangle where the final animation or interactive application is displayed is called the *Stage* (although technically, it's a window). *Sprites* (see Figure 1-1), the actors in movie, follow actions contained in *scripts,* not modules of code. The various resources used in the program are collectively known as *cast members* (though we can't say we've ever seen a Director cast party). The overall positions of the sprites can be viewed through the *Score*, which is closely analogous to an animator's score. And the sprites are drawn upon the Stage using various *inks*.

Figure 1-1: A perhaps slightly too literal interpretation of a sprite. Director sprites are the actors that perform upon the Stage.

Fortunately for those developers who've had to work with the product over the years, this theatrical metaphor is slowly disappearing from Director. Like most metaphors, it works best for people new to the product but can become cumbersome for advanced users. Still, enough of Director's resemblance to filmmaking and animation remains that even people who have never worked with the software will quickly grasp most of the basic features just on the strength of its terminology.

Migrating from Director 5 to Director 6

If you have worked with Director before, you will discover that Director 6 has undergone some significant modifications, both on the surface and under the hood. Sprites — the graphical and sound elements placed upon the Stage — have evolved from just graphics locations to intelligent entities in their own right. They are able to respond to a whole host of new events; for example, they can detect when the mouse enters and leaves their boundaries, a capability that Director developers have been demanding for years. In addition, the sprites can remember custom information, can set themselves up when they first appear, and can remove themselves from memory when no longer needed.

Perhaps even more exciting, sprites can be scripted into *behaviors*, scripts of code that can then be used over and over without needing revision for each individual case. With such canned behaviors, Director 6 now provides what could be described as *codeless development*. You can now create sophisticated controls, custom scroll bars, gravity-sensitive sprites, and more — simply by dragging a behavior onto a sprite. Older methods still work, but the behaviors feature alone makes Director 6 a quantum leap more powerful than Director 5. For the professional developer, this translates into a significant savings in development time, something that's always at a premium in the software industry.

No one can deny the Internet's impact on software creation. Most of today's cutting-edge multimedia work touches upon the World Wide Web in some manner. Director 6 gives you some amazing new tools to connect to the Net. It can load images and download text from any Web site, regardless of whether the program is running as a stand-alone application or as a movie running within a browser. (A director movie can communicate more effectively with a browser if it is being displayed there.) Improvements in audio now let Director stream voice and music off the Web without significant download times.

Of course, Director is still fully cross-platform, from Macintosh OS/8 to Windows 95, from Netscape Navigator to Internet Explorer. Since Director can be displayed as an ActiveX control, any programming environment that uses this technology (such as Visual Basic) can also play Director movies. This exciting feature makes it possible to create sophisticated visual interfaces that still have access to the power and flexibility of a fully functional programming language (see Figure 1-2).

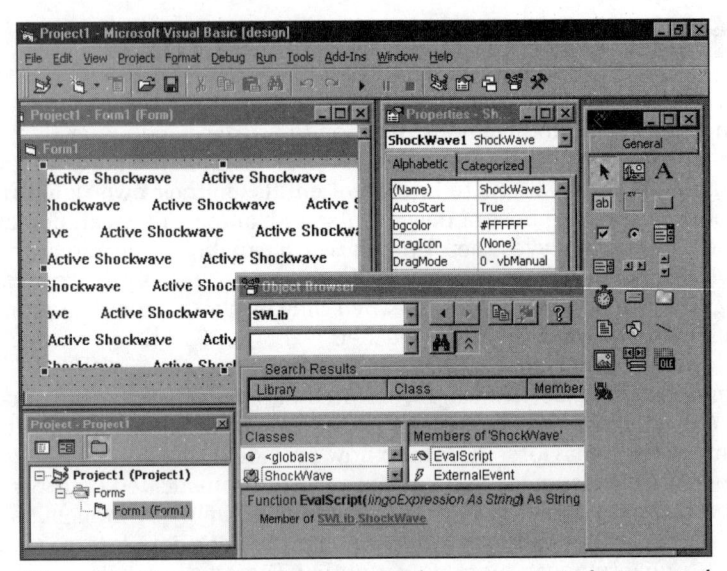

Figure 1-2: Because Director can now be run as an ActiveX control, any ActiveX-capable programming environment, such as Visual Basic, can play Director files.

So what else is new?

All Director 5 movies will work in Director 6, although they must first be run through a conversion program built into Director. In the latest version of Director, enough is different that it may be worth rewriting some of your Director 5 code rather than relying on the converter. Cast member references, parent scripts, Xtras, and other elements of Director are identical to their Director 5 counterparts.

The menu structure has not changed (and thankfully neither have the keyboard shortcuts, although a host of new ones have been added).

Lingo written in Director 5 will in all likelihood work in Director 6, although Director 4 legacy code probably won't. Finally, note that if you open up a Director 5 movie and save it, it will be saved in Director 6 format and will no longer work under 5. It's a wise move, before you begin, to archive any Director 5 source code should you discover that a movie runs fine under Director 5 but not version 6. You can also save a renamed version of an older Director 5 file with the Director 6 changes, using File ⇨ Save As.

Table 1-1 is a summary of all the changes in Director 6.

Table 1-1
Director 6's New Features and Improvements

Feature	What's New or Improved
Sprites	The number of sprites has been increased from 48 to 120.
Informative Score	The control window for animations (the Score) provides much more information. Additionally, you can now zoom into and out of the Score.
Behaviors	These self-contained scripts can be used to give sprites expanded abilities.
Internet support	Stand-alone Director applications can now make use of Internet-based Shockwave for retrieving online files, graphics, and more.
Enhanced graphics importing	Director can now import JPEG and GIF files as well as Photoshop images, although GIF89a transparencies and animations aren't yet supported.
Sprite overlays	Sprites give information about their animation paths, locations, and other properties right on the Stage.
Event and error handling	In earlier versions of Director, if an error occurred, it would stop the program and display a dialog box, even when the error was harmless. Director 6 now incorporates a mechanism to intercept and fix errors before they bring the system crashing down.
Streaming audio	Director now incorporates audio that can be streamed off a CD or the Internet and offers cue points for improved synching.
Compatible with both Microsoft Internet Explorer and Netscape Navigator browsers	Using Shockwave, you can play Director movies in both Netscape or Microsoft browsers; you can also use a Director movie as an ActiveX control. Director can now communicate via JavaScript with the browser, making such movies considerably more interactive than their predecessors.
Custom dialog boxes	Director can now create complex, custom dialog boxes that don't eat up a significant amount of memory.
Food-processing extensions	And that's not all! With the specialized attachments, Director can also slice, dice, and make julienne fries. Note that these are nonstandard extensions.

The Director 6 Theater

Doing a production, whether theatrical or multimedia, demands that you become familiar with its framework. A traditional theater is more than just a stage. A good director needs to understand the theater's acoustics and lighting, what kind of backstage facilities are available, how many people can be seated, and what the view looks like from every seat, even down to how the curtains will open and close.

Multimedia is much the same: Your theater in this case is Director 6, and its supporting structures are the dialogs, windows, menu items, and other elements that make up the program itself. You need to get to know it even before you start building your own world from it.

Director is undeniably a complex program. Although using any of its features is not difficult, there are plenty of features to use. Indeed, most of the first part of this book covers nothing but the various dialogs and windows that Director uses. This multiplicity is the result of Director's role as an *integrating* program. Its primary purpose is to bring a number of different kinds of elements together into one package, and each element has its own particular characteristics and gotchas that require special handling.

Most of the windows in Director fall into one of two categories:

- *Modal* dialog boxes, where the dialog demands immediate attention and won't let you do anything else until you dismiss it. The dialog boxes answer the question "how?" How fast does the movie play? How do images get imported? How much should a graphic be resized?

- *Modeless* editors, which generally control the action of the movie or allow you to edit resources. The editors deal with "what" issues: What elements are being used? What do they look like? What frame or point in the movie is being displayed?

When Director first starts up, it remembers the last editor windows that were up in a previous session. In the very first session, Director displays two critical editors: the *Score* and the *Cast window*.

The Score editor

The *Score,* shown in Figure 1-3, is analogous to an animator's score — it displays from left to right the time of the movie as measured in frames. *Frames* can best be described as the individual views of the movie each time it changes. They are roughly similar to the frames of a filmstrip, where one frame may vary by just a little bit from the previous frame (but this can be somewhat deceptive due to the introduction of interactivity into the movie). Typically, a movie may have between 10 and 30 frames per second, although this rate — known as the *tempo* — could vary dramatically, from one frame every several seconds to one frame every 1/60 of a second.

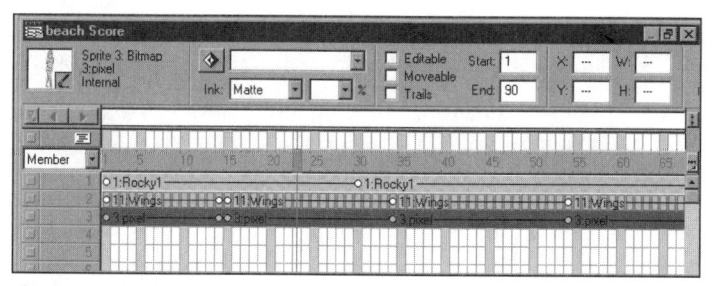

Figure 1-3: The Score is Director's cockpit, showing where all the sprites are at any given time and providing detailed information at a mouse click.

The Score is divided into 126 *sprite channels*. The 120 numbered channels are graphic channels and show the positions of different elements and their relationships to one another on the Stage at each frame of the movie. The other six channels are special-purpose channels that control the palette, sound, tempo, and store the scripts in your movie. A *sprite* occupies a sprite channel. You can think of the sprite channel as one layer in a multilayered animation: the far background, distant mountains, nearer mountains, nearby trees, a house, a character in front of a house, and so on. Each of these elements could move or be switched to a different graphic, but they roughly correspond to discrete sets of objects.

Sprites are drawn in the order that they appear in the Score. So a sprite in sprite channel 1 (let's say it's the sky sprite) will appear behind the far mountains in sprite 2, which will appear behind the near mountains in sprite 3, and so forth.

Sprites make up a significant part of Director's mechanics and are discussed in detail in Chapter 3.

The Cast editor

The *Cast* window, shown in Figure 1-4, contains the actual graphics that are used by each of the sprites, as well as sounds, digital video, scripts, and any other resources that are used by Director. Each resource is known as a *cast member*.

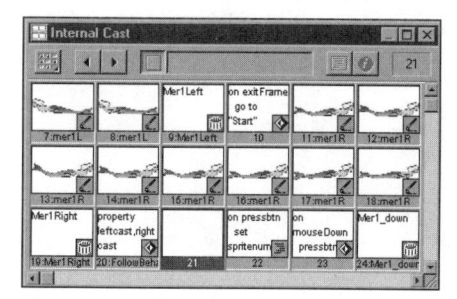

Figure 1-4: The Cast window serves as the central repository for all the resources in the movie.

One way to think of the distinction between cast members and sprites is to return to the theatrical metaphor: The sprite is a *role*, like a character in the play or movie; and the cast member is the *actor* who plays that role. The role will remain pretty constant for a given movie, but there may be any number of actors that take on that role. Shakespeare's Hamlet is a sprite (all right, a depressed sprite, but a sprite nonetheless); Sir Laurence Olivier, Sir John Gielgud, and yes, even Mel Gibson are all cast members who have played that sprite. To take the analogy one step farther, remember the school play you did in first grade. Were you the tree? Maybe a rock or a butterfly? Your role in that skit might not have been quite as distinguished as that of a fine Shakespearean actor, but the metaphor is probably a little bit closer to the truth.

The Cast and the cast members are discussed in greater detail in Chapter 2.

The other editors

Director also includes a graphics editor of limited capability. It is more a true editor of media rather than something you would use to create assets in the first place. The graphics editor gets a thorough (and withering) examination in Chapter 2.

Because text is so important in multimedia, Director can actually edit text in three different ways, as well as use externally generated text. The three text editors are considered in Chapter 4.

Finally, Director supports external editors for most types of media — graphics (see Chapter 2), sound (Chapter 7), and video (Chapter 8).

Toolbar buttons and tooltips

Starting with Director 5, Macromedia began developing a certain look and feel for the program's user interface, borrowing what was already working for both the Macintosh and Windows. One of the more useful Windows interface tools is the toolbar, shown in Figure 1-5, which presents icon shortcuts to common functions and operations. Table 1-2 gives a quick summary of the shortcut icons in Director 6.

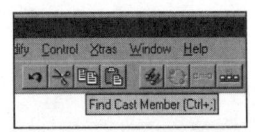

Figure 1-5: The Director 6 toolbar now supports tooltips. Hold the pointer over a button, and its name will pop up.

Table 1-2
Director 6 Toolbar

Icon	Tool	Function
	New Movie	Opens a new movie.
	New Cast	Opens a new cast library.
	Open	Opens an existing movie or cast library.
	Save	Saves the movie or cast library.
	Print	Displays the print dialog box.
	Import	Imports media.
	Undo	Undoes the last action.
	Cut	Cuts the selected object and places it on the Clipboard.
	Copy	Copies the selected object and places it on the Clipboard.
	Paste	Pastes the object on the clipboard into the selected space.
	Find Cast Member	Lets you locate a specific cast member quickly.
	Exchange Cast Member	Swaps the cast member on the Stage for the selected cast member in the cast library.
	Extend Sprite	Extends the currently selected sprite.
	Align	Aligns all the selected sprites.
	Rewind	Moves to the first frame of the movie.
	Stop	Stops the movie if it is currently playing.
	Play	Plays the movie if it is currently stopped.
	Cast Window	Opens the Cast window.
	Score Window	Opens the Score window.
	Paint Window	Opens the Paint window.
	Text Window	Opens the Text Inspector. If a text or field cast member is not currently selected, creates a text cast member.
	Behavior Inspector	Opens the Behavior Inspector.
	Script Window	Opens the currently selected script, or opens a new script if one isn't selected.
	Help Pointer	Sets the cursor to context-sensitive Help mode. Clicking any element will display help for that item if it exists.

Tip: Don't worry, you don't have to memorize all these toolbar icons right away. Director makes use of another Windows convention: *tooltips*. When you place your mouse pointer over an icon, button, or similar interface element for more than half a second, Director displays a small text box that contains a one- or two-word description of the item.

The floating Tool Palette

Many of the tools you are likely to need most frequently are assembled in a conveniently arranged package known as the Tool Palette (Figure 1-6). The Tool Palette, when turned on, "floats" above the Stage so you can move it around the workspace as needed to aid you in working with objects in Director. Use these tools to quickly add text, buttons, fields, lines, QuickDraw (vector) shapes, and pattern fills, and to change the foreground and background colors. You can turn the Tool Palette on and off by selecting Window ⇨ Tool Palette from the Director menus, or pressing Command+7 (Ctrl+7).

Figure 1-6: The floating Tool Palette gives you quick access to a handy collection of often-used tools.

See Table 1-3 for a summary of the functions available in the Tool Palette.

Table 1-3
Floating Tool Palette Functions

Icon	Tool	Function
▶	Arrow	Allows the selection of objects (active by default when the Tool Palette is opened).
A	Text	Inserts text directly on the Stage.
╲	Line	Draws straight lines directly on the Stage.

Icon	Tool	Function
■	Filled Rectangle	Draws a rectangle filled with the selected foreground color.
□	Rectangle	Draws an empty (unfilled) rectangle on the Stage. The border color is the foreground color selected in the Tool Palette.
●	Filled Round Rectangle	Draws a rectangle with rounded corners, filled with the selected foreground color.
○	Round Rectangle	Draws an empty (unfilled) rectangle with rounded corners. Border of the rounded rectangle is the selected foreground color.
●	Filled Ellipse	Draws circles and elliptical shapes, filled with the selected foreground color, on the Stage.
○	Ellipse	Draws empty circles and elliptical shapes. The border of the ellipse is the selected foreground color.
☒	Check Box	Adds a check-box style button.
◉	Radio Button	Creates a round radio button.
[Field]	Field	Creates editable text fields on the Stage.
[Button]	Push Button	Creates a customizable push-style button on the Stage. The size of the button is dependent on the amount and size of the text entered into the button.
◰	Foreground/ Background Colors	Allows selection of the foreground and background colors. Foreground = top-left color chip. Background = bottom-right color chip. Clicking either color chip opens the Color Palette of color choices.
▨	Pattern	Selects the pattern fill to be used with the Tool Palette's filled shapes. Foreground and background colors of the pattern are selected in the Foreground/Background Color Selector.
☰	Line Weight Selector	Selects the line weight to be used by the Tool Palette's various drawing tools. Choose from No Line, One Pixel Line, Two Pixel Line, and Three Pixel Line.

Pop-up menus

Another trick in the Director 6 interface arsenal is the deployment of those handy context-sensitive pop-up menus. Pop-ups can be activated for most elements in Director — cast members, sprites, behaviors, scripts, even the toolbar. A pop-up menu contains operations that are only appropriate for the selected item.

On the Macintosh, pop-up menus are brought to life by holding down the Control key and clicking the mouse. In Windows, you right-click the item in question. The pop-ups for various Director elements are often shown with the appropriate items in this book.

The menu bar

Director uses a fairly complicated set of menus, submenus, and related dialog boxes, in an arrangement that mirrors Macromedia's user interface guidelines across its product line. The idea is, of course, that someone familiar with FreeHand or Authorware can adapt to Director fairly quickly.

We will cover menus and their contents as they become relevant. Table 1-4 summarizes the contents of each menu in the menu bar.

Table 1-4
The Director Menus

Menu Name	Functions Handled
File	Opening, saving, and printing of files. Creating projectors (run-time version) and Shockwave movies. Setting preferences, sending e-mail, and terminating the program.
Edit	Clipboard operations (cut, copy, paste) and various kinds of selection. Searching and replacing text. Launching external resource editors.
View	Offers various ways of looking at the Score (the window that controls where animation sprites are placed). Also controls onion skinning in the Cast window.
Insert	Insertion and deletion of keyframes and animation frames into the Score. Serves as an alternate way of inserting media cast members into the Cast window (the library of resources that Director uses).
Modify	Changing properties for the movie, individual cast members (resources), sprites, and the Score. Also provides a means of editing text in a text field, modifying scripts (interpreted code), rearranging the order of cast members on the Stage, and converting cast members to different bit depths.
Control	Playback of Director, moving from frame to frame, setting volume, handling sprite recording, debugging features, and recompiling scripts.
Xtras	Gives information and access to Xtras (Director plug-ins) and graphic filter Xtras. Protecting and updating older versions of Director movies.
Window	Calls up any of the control windows used in Director, such as the Score, the Cast window, the Bitmap editor, the Behavior and Text Inspectors, and others.
Help	Accesses Director Help, which provides a detailed help and indexing system for all sorts of Director and Lingo problems. Also calls up Help tutorials. Accesses registration information and links to Macromedia's Web site.

Xternal Resources

No program is an island, though some try very hard to be. For a multimedia program to be useful, it has to have some way of adding functionality whenever new technology comes on the scene. With Director 5, Macromedia realized this, abandoning the rather haphazard Xobjects — which relied principally upon a ten-year-old Macintosh programming specification that was almost universally ignored. Instead, some serious work was invested in developing an *open architecture* (see Chapter 19 for the gory details of what this really means). This architecture enabled developers to create new support programs called *Xtras,* which added significantly to the capabilities of Director.

Xtras are analogous to plug-ins for browsers, and to filters for programs like Photoshop and 3D Studio. Some Xtras — such as filter Xtras that let you import Photoshop or JPEG images, and the fileIO Xtra that adds file reading and writing capabilities — are produced by Macromedia itself. Others are produced by third-party software designers. Some of these are for adding functionality to Director (such as Component Software Industries's FileFlex, which is an integrated database specifically designed for Director, and g/Matter's PrintOMatic, giving more sophisticated printing capability than Director's). Others are designed to open up access to system capabilities (such as Apple's QuickDraw3D Xtra, which lets you use the QuickDraw3D Extensions on the Macintosh to create real-time 3D graphics).

Director 5 may have introduced the concept, but Director 6 is well and truly built on Xtras. A great deal of the new functionality inherent in version 6 has been introduced using Xtras rather than built into the main program. One of the real advantages this offers is easier updating. In all versions of Director up to 5, it was necessary to download a single, huge update package when a bug was found or new functionality was needed; now you can simply replace one Xtra with another. Updating Director becomes a continuous process, rather than having to wait six months until enough bugs have been found to justify releasing an upgrade.

Adding Xtras to your system

The same folder that holds your Director program contains a folder or directory called Xtras. This folder is the repository for every Xtra in use by the program. If you want to add a new Xtra (or remove a troublesome one), then you simply need to add (or remove) the file that contains the Xtra. When Director starts up, it inventories every Xtra it finds in the Xtras folder or in subfolders of that folder; and if it can use it, Director registers the Xtra internally.

When you create your own applications, you will need to distribute these Xtras as well (although Director 6 includes an option for integrating the Xtras directly into the application file itself). As long as the Xtras folder is in the same directory as the application, it will be added.

> **Note:** Although Director itself is cross-platform, Xtras frequently are machine-specific. For example, there are Xtras that only work (and only make sense) on the PC side, such as an Xtra that reads system-level information.

Using Xtras

There are four types of Xtras:

- **Cast Member Xtras**—Increase the assets and media available for use in a movie
- **Transition Xtras**—Control the appearance of transitions from one frame to the next
- **Script Xtras**—Add Lingo commands to the language
- **Tools Xtras**—Provide development resources for code creation and debugging
- **Import Xtras**—Include the code necessary to import a specific type of media

How you invoke an Xtra, then, is dependent upon its type.

Cast Member Xtras are for adding new cast member types. For example, AlphaMania, a Cast Member Xtra produced by Media Labs, helps you create graphical cast members with partial transparency, making such things as shadows ridiculously simple to pull off. You would use Insert ⇨ Media ⇨ AlphaMania to insert such a graphic. On the other hand, a Photoshop filter would be accessed from the Xtras ⇨ Filter Bitmap command, which would then list all of the available filters currently in the Xtras folder. Many other Xtras, as well, are resident in the Xtras menu, in addition to Tool Xtras that provide a service, such as setting up the Score in different configurations.

Transitions have their own dialog box (see Chapter 5 for details), and any transition Xtra will be found there. Often, these Xtras have options beyond what are provided by the native Director transitions, which are also available through the Transitions dialog box.

Cast libraries

The evolution of Director seems to have been driven by the expansion of a pretty fair animation engine into a full-blown application development tool. One standard component of many other such environments (such as Microsoft's Visual Basic and MetroWorks's Code Warrior) is the capability of using common resource and code files.

Especially given the size and complexity of some Director projects, it might seem odd that the principle of common resources has only been recently incorporated into the program. Let's see why this is so. Because many movies share common elements — navigational bars, sound controls, general code — it's useful to place these elements into a shared resource file. Director 4 implemented one such file, but it had profound limitations — the file always had to be called Shared.dir, it had to be in the same folder as the startup movie, and it couldn't be changed. Moreover, the Shared.dir folder occupied part of the cast member slots allocated to the other movies using the shared resource. This meant some of the cast members would be overwritten if there were enough cast members in the base folder.

With Director 5, Macromedia introduced *cast libraries*. In essence, a cast library contains nothing but resources — code, bitmaps, sounds, and so forth — but no Score or sprite information. A Director movie can have, practically speaking, any number of cast libraries open at any given time, making it possible to have one library that exclusively contains common bitmaps (such as navigational elements), a second that contains nothing but behaviors and utility code, a third that has only sounds, and so forth . . . although there's nothing to stop you from mixing these resources together, as well.

Cast libraries can be linked to a movie by using the Modify➪Movie➪Casts command. Having a linked file of any sort means that the information about that file is kept in a separate file rather than within the Director movie itself. For example, if we linked a bitmap image, every time Director started up it would load that image from the disk, rather than from its own internal resources. This approach has the advantage of making it easier to work with *dynamic files* — pictures that change on a regular basis. The disadvantage comes from the location of the file; since the picture (or other resource) isn't already in a form that Director can handle, it has to be *processed* into a Director bitmap cast member. Depending upon the size and type of the image, this can involve an appreciable wait — something that might not be appropriate in a mission-critical environment (although why anyone would use Director for any mission-critical tasks is beyond us).

For more details on bitmap images, cast libraries, and resource linking, see Chapters 2, 3, and 6, respectively.

SOS (Save Our Software?)

The operation of a program as complex and feature-rich as Director cannot be assimilated in one afternoon. There are several hundred commands, properties, keywords, and related terms used just by Lingo, not to mention the dozens of menu commands, dialog boxes, and other related bits of the Director interface. With its new behaviors and other improvements, Director is now easier to use than ever before — but that doesn't mean that it won't seem overwhelming to even seasoned users. And it especially doesn't mean that keeping track of obscure syntax or seldom-used functions is a piece of cake for higher-end programmers using Director.

Fortunately, the designers of Director have provided assistance with the program's complexity in the form of a remarkably comprehensive help system. It will aid everyone from beginners to advanced professionals. In essence, much of what is available echoes the books that come with Director (*Using Director, Using Lingo,* and the *Lingo Dictionary*), although in all likelihood the online Help is probably more current.

You access the help system by selecting Help ➪ Director Help from the menu bar or by pressing the F1 key. (Actually, almost every selection in the Help menu will bring up the Help dialog box, but the F1 or Help menu route is Director Help's front door.) From here, you can go get help on most basic concepts in Director, including Lingo scripting and incorporating Director movies into Web pages (see Figure 1-7).

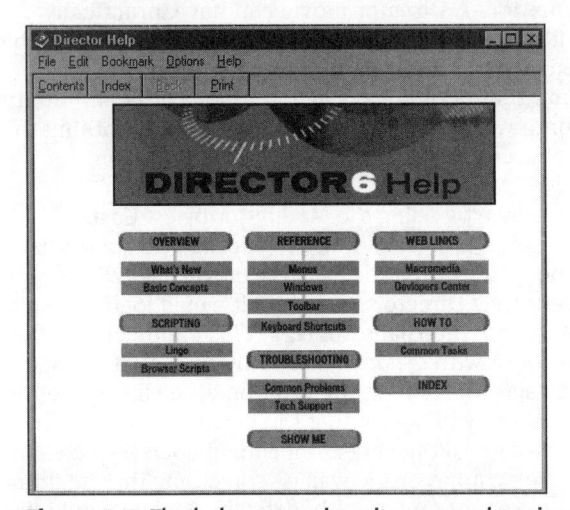

Figure 1-7: The help system is quite comprehensive, providing useful information about most aspects of Director programming, including customized Show Me movies.

Using context-sensitive help

Director also offers context-sensitive help, which gives you detailed information about a specific item or keyword. To summon context-sensitive help, follow these simple steps:

1. Move the cursor over the button or interface element you're curious about, or select the words in a script about which you need more information.
2. Press Shift+F1 to bring up the help information.

Tip: Especially with scripts, it is useful to select portions of the help screen text by clicking at the start of the text and dragging to the end, and then copy the selected text to the Clipboard. From there, the scripts can be pasted into your own scripts or into a text box for reference.

Director also offers additional shortcuts and mnemonic tips, especially for writing Lingo. These are explored in Chapter 10.

Surfing for help

One of the truly useful aspects of Director 6 is that much of its core functionality is no longer provided by a single monolithic program, but rather by lots of smaller components called *Xtras*. A benefit of this scheme is that it's now much easier to upgrade parts of Director without upgrading the entire thing. However, this comes at the price of making the help system obsolete.

Enter the Web. Macromedia posts updates to any part of the help system (or for that matter, updates to Xtras themselves) to more closely reflect the current state of the program. Director has the ability to bring up a browser if one is installed on your system, and from there can launch to a specific Web page. If you select Help ⇨ Web Links, Director will launch the Director support page at the Macromedia Web site. Clicking the link will launch the selected default browser, which can be set in the Network preferences (File ⇨ Preferences ⇨ Network). Of course, you'll need a live Internet connection for this feature to work.

Getting a second opinion (or third or fourth)

Macromedia's Web site is fairly comprehensive, but it's only a small part of the total collection of Web sites, mailing lists, newsgroups, and newsletters available to the Director developer. Many of these sites include downloadable Xtras, tips and techniques, and working examples. Of equal importance, these Internet resources also facilitate your connections with other Director users — an especially welcome capability when you're in the middle of a project and discover that you don't know how to get past a thorny problem.

The programming faculty at the Maricopa Community College in New Mexico maintain one of the most exhaustive sites devoted to Director and Authorware, at `http://www.mcli.dist.maricopa.edu/director/`. The college also maintains the Direct-L mailing list, which is an ongoing e-mail list where developers can talk over problems and quirky happenings, and find out about getting together at conferences and conventions. Check the Web site itself for details if you wish to subscribe. We recommend getting the Digest, but bear in mind that the list is very busy and can easily generate a thousand messages in a few days.

(continued)

(continued)

Pinnacle Publishing produces the *Macromedia User's Journal*, edited by Kurt Cagle (yup, that's the same Kurt who's one of this book's authors). Every month the *MUJ* covers features from the various Macromedia product lines, with a special emphasis on Director, Authorware, and Shockwave. Contact Kurt Cagle at `cagle@pinpub.com` for subscription information, or visit the Web site at `http://www.pinpub.com/muj`.

We also recommend Tab Julius's *Lingo User's Journal*. This superb publication concentrates on Lingo issues and can be viewed online at `http://www.pinpub.com`.

For a more extensive listing of Web sites that provide Director support, see Appendix D.

On the Flip Side

Is Director the perfect multimedia tool? At the risk of offending the sensibilities of the Macromedia engineers, we have to give a qualified "no." Director 6 has some significant limitations that keep it from being perfect:

- Its graphics editor, while sufficient for the task of creating animations, still has some serious deficiencies, is difficult to work with, and hasn't improved significantly in seven years.

- The support that Director offers for external editors has improved but remains less than ideal.

- Printing and file handling are still handled by external resources; they should have been integrated into the program years ago.

- Director 6 does not yet support alpha channels natively, although there are third-party Xtras that give limited support.

- Lingo in version 6 is much more object oriented but needs to be more tightly encapsulated. Furthermore, its existing support for inheritance is definitely nonstandard.

- Director for Windows doesn't support ActiveX controls — odd, given that Director's sister product, Authorware, does. On the other hand, it is possible to embed a Director movie into an ActiveX container, which can get around at least a couple of the problems.

All in all, the list of things not to like about Director is fairly short and, to be fair, borders on the esoteric. It may not be the perfect multimedia tool, but it's one of the best around.

Summary

What Director 6 *does* offer is some of the most exciting capabilities of any development environment out there. Director enables your ability to make dynamic Internet applications. You can create objects with a high degree of "intelligence" and "self-awareness." And you can enter Director development as a nonprogrammer, an intermediate programmer, or a systems-level guru — with equal ease. These are the things that make Director 6 really RAD! (That's Rapid Application Development, for you nongeeks in the crowd!)

- Director 6 slices, dices, and makes julienne fries (but only with the proper Xtensions).

- Director is a powerful tool for creating animations, mock-ups, multimedia presentations, games, resumés, advertisements, demos, embedded Internet controls, and browsers.

- Nearly every function in Director has a floating window associated with it, including bitmap editing (the Paint window), text creation (the Text window and the Field window), shapes (the Tool Palette), sprites (the Score), and navigation (the Control Panel).

- Every sprite and window, and nearly every button has a pop-up menu of the most common tasks, such as copying and pasting, importing resources, selecting/deselecting items, and more. Pop-up menus can be summoned by Control-clicking the item you're working with (or right-clicking in Windows 95).

- Holding the mouse over any interface element in Director for about a second brings up a tooltip identifying that element.

- To get Director Help, press F1 or select any of the items in the Help menu. Pressing Shift+F1 brings up context-sensitive help appropriate to the item under the pointer.

✦ ✦ ✦

Working with Graphics

CHAPTER 2

♦ ♦ ♦ ♦

In This Chapter

Planning animations

Working in the Paint window

Importing images

Taking a closer look at Director's "cast" concept

♦ ♦ ♦ ♦

The art of world-building — that's what multimedia is all about. Every time you create a multimedia product, you are creating the illusion of a completely self-contained world that can be as detailed as *Myst* or as colorful as Mercer Mayer's *Just Grandma and Me*. To pull off this trick, you need images and graphics — for buttons, backgrounds, and characters — that can take on the expressiveness of actors. With Director you can build and integrate these pictures into an incredible array of possibilities: documentaries, cartoons, even three-dimensional extravaganzas where the graphics seem to pop from the page.

An Animated Discussion

In order to take advantage of Director's imaging possibilities, you first have to create the images, which involves a rather incredible amount of work. Fortunately, Director has long recognized the fact that 90% of the process of creating a multimedia presentation involves making the graphics for it. What Director offers you for this colossal task are a serviceable (if not exactly spectacular) paint program, as well as several options for integrating already existing artwork, photographs, and other graphical resources into your movies.

Creating a concept

If you're like us, you probably find it very difficult to just sit down at a computer and start drawing without giving some thought to the result you want in the end. Director can be dangerously seductive. With all that power at your fingertips, it's really tempting to just sit down and "create," taking off without giving any forethought to your ultimate creative destination. Unfortunately, what you come up with in this case usually has to be abandoned halfway through. The upshot to all of this: Even with a simple animation that doesn't require any programming, you should still *plan everything* ahead of time.

Kurt Cagle, one of the authors, in a previous life worked as a freelance illustrator for comic books and games, and as such developed a distinct taste for dabbling in fantasy illustrations. When it came time to design a logo for his Web site, it seemed only appropriate that the logo be a Shockwave animation. Moreover, one of the primary elements in Director is the sprite, which of course led to the creation of a true sprite — a thespian pixie that Kurt named Pixel (see Figure 2-1).

Figure 2-1: Macromedia's designers may not have had Ms. Pixel in mind when they called their actor controls sprites, but . . .

Actually, part of the reason for our using such a character as Pixel is to illustrate how to design and create some very complex animations in which two or more sprites can be used together. For example, Pixel has distinct components: the figure herself, and her wings. The wings should flutter independently from the figure, and the figure should be able to assume a number of different stances for which the wings are pretty much secondary.

A winged figure flies, of course, and the animation should feature that prominently. To keep the resources down, the whole animation is set against a static backdrop with a landscape scene rendered in KPT Bryce. Pixel flies in from the upper-right, and lands on a stretch of ground in the lower-left foreground. With a wave of her hand, she makes the logo appear in a whirl of magic dust. Satisfied, she curtsies, then flies off the way she came, leaving the logo there as a static image.

The animation itself consists of four different sprite layers: the figure portion of pixel, the wings, the logo, and the background. These are the pieces we will concentrate on in this chapter. Then in Chapter 3 we'll work on implementing the animation.

Planning your presentation

A good theatrical director should know the dimensions of the stage that he or she has to work with, and multimedia work is no different in that respect. A fairly standard size for the Director Stage is 320 x 240, which is exactly one-quarter the size of the lowest screen resolution that a computer can display (640 x 480). The one-quarter Stage size also happens to be optimal for digital video, since it approximately mimics the *aspect ratio* (the ratio of the width to the height of a graphic or screen) of a television screen.

Because setting the Stage size is more relevant for sprites than for cast members, this topic is covered in detail in Chapter 3. However, let's take a quick look at the numbers now, simply to help in the creation of the graphics. Since Pixel is in the foreground, she'll occupy roughly half the height of the screen. The logo element will be about the same height and about 180 pixels wide. A good idea at this point would be to draw a preliminary sketch showing the pieces in place at various points in the animation. This technique, called *storyboarding,* is an invaluable tool for developing a convincing animation. Figure 2-2 shows an example of a storyboard for an animation.

Figure 2-2: A storyboard is a comic-book-like sequence showing where all of the pieces are at various times in the animation.

Storyboards highlight one of the basic principles for designing computer projects: You should not fail to use your special analog model number 2, wireless data development device with the semiautomated Undo feature — also known as a pencil. Pencil and paper haven't completely disappeared from design processes (thankfully), in great part because the very process of drawing or painting with a computer forces you into a computer-oriented design mode. And in that mode it's hard not to think more about the tools you're using than about the concepts you're trying to explain. So blocking out your concepts with squares and circles — even if you're not a good artist — will make a world of difference in the fluidity of the final animation.

The other purpose of the storyboard is to give you an idea about how many particular pieces will be needed for an animation. In Pixel's case, the animations will require a certain amount of hand drawing (with the exception of the wings, which can be created once and then warped within Director to the appropriate shape, as explained in the Chapter 3 section on tweening). The storyboard can be used to pick the major poses and determine how many intermediate steps will be necessary to ensure smooth movement of the figure.

Working in the Paint Window

Director's graphics editor, the Paint window, has been a part of the program since its earliest days. Though not as full featured as many commercial paint programs, the Paint window has been optimized for use as an animation editor. Creating successive frames of an animation is relatively easy to do with the Paint window, and it offers several unique tools such as *onion skinning* and *registration* to help you.

Pulling out your brushes and paints

The Paint window can be opened at any time within Director by pressing Command+5 (Ctrl+5) or selecting Window ⇨ Paint from the menu bar. If no cast member was selected, then the Paint window automatically creates a fresh pane on which to paint. (Cast members are discussed in the "Casting Call" section later in this chapter.) If you did select a cast member before opening the Paint window, it will open with that cast member at the ready; for example, see Figure 2-3. Unless your images use an external editor (another subject that's covered later), you can also double-click a bitmap cast member to open it up in the Paint window.

The various brushes and other tools sported by the Paint window will likely be familiar to anyone who's used another paint program. They are represented by the double vertical column of buttons in the tools palette at the left side of the Paint window. These tools are summarized in Table 2-1.

Figure 2-3: The Paint window opens with the current cast member if you select it first.

Table 2-1
Paint Window Tools Palette

Tool Icon	Tool Name	Paint Operation
	Lasso	Free-form selection tool. Used to select irregularly shaped areas. Also can be set to Shrink, in order to exclude background colors.
	Marquee	Rectangular selection tool. This is the required selection mode for most special effects. Can be set to Shrink, in order to exclude background colors.
	Registration Point	Determines the "registration point" of the graphic when drawn on the Stage. Double-click this button to set the registration point to the center of the graphic.
	Eraser	Paints the graphic with the selected background color. Double-clicking the button erases the whole screen.
	Hand	Used to move the graphic around. Especially useful with the Zoom tool.

(continued)

Table 2-1 *(continued)*

Tool Icon	Tool Name	Paint Operation
	Magnifying Glass	Doubles the current magnification of the image, up to 8 times. If the Shift key is held down, clicking the image with this tool active zooms back out 50%, to the original size of the image.
	Eyedropper	Sets the foreground color to the color under the Eyedropper's tip.
	Paint Bucket	Fills all contiguous pixels of the same color and pattern with the foreground color and pattern.
	Text	Places text into the graphic. This text can only be edited while the insertion point is active; after that it becomes part of the graphic.
	Pencil	Draws a line one pixel wide. If any color but the foreground color is selected, the line is drawn in the foreground color; otherwise, the background color is used.
	Air Brush	Creates a random pattern of dots of varying sizes. Can be used for texturing effects, but otherwise pretty useless — unless you happen to be a three-year-old.
	Brush	Paints the graphic with the foreground color, using the selected ink (explained in an upcoming section). By clicking and holding this button, you can select an alternate brush.
	Arc	Draws an arc, using the currently selected line width to draw the curve. Click and drag to establish the starting tangent, then drag to the end point.
	Line	Draws a line. Click to establish the line, then drag to pull it to its full length.
	Filled Rectangle	Paints a filled rectangle using the current foreground color and pattern. If a nonzero line width is selected, the rectangle will have a border of that width.
	Rectangle	Paints a hollow rectangle using the current foreground color and line width.
	Filled Ellipse	Paints a filled oval using the current foreground color and If a nonzero line width is selected, the oval will have a border of that width.
	Ellipse	Paints a hollow oval using the current foreground color and line width.

Tool Icon	Tool Name	Paint Operation
▨	Filled Polygon	Paints a filled polygon using the current foreground color, pattern, and line width. Click once at each vertex of the polygon, and then double-click to complete the shape.
▱	Polygon	Paints a hollow polygon using the current foreground color and line width. Click at each vertex of the polygon, then double-click to complete the shape.

Colors and gradients

The collection of paint swatches, patterns, and lines at the bottom of the tools palette can be a little bewildering at first. Take a look at Figure 2-4, and let's find out what all these buttons are for.

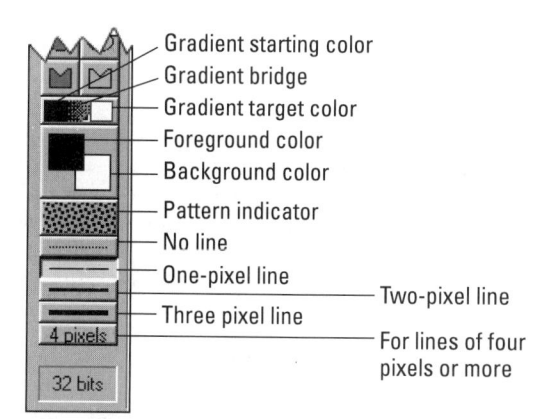

Figure 2-4: You can select colors, patterns, and gradients from the swatches and buttons at the bottom of the tools palette.

Start with the two large color squares that overlap. These are your primary work colors: the top-left one gives you the *foreground* color, and the bottom-right square shows your *background* color. If you've never worked with paint programs before, here is what these concepts actually mean:

✦ The foreground color is what you can think of as your primary paint color — when you're painting an area in the canvas, you will generally use this color.

✦ The background color, on the other hand, is the color used for erasing. This color has the most influence in terms of the Pencil tool. When you activate the Pencil tool and start drawing with it, the default color laid down will be the foreground color. However, if you start drawing on a part of the bitmap that already has the foreground color, then Director will automatically replace it with the background color. In this way, you can "erase" the color you're working with simply by starting on a foreground pixel. Usually, you will want to keep the background color set at the default, which is white.

> **Note** You'll be working with foreground and background colors fairly extensively in Director. Often you'll see them referred to in Director literature as the *forecolor* and *backcolor*.

Director has a number of basic gradient tools that are covered a little later in this chapter. For now, let's just get familiar with the gradient switches, which live just above the foreground and background color squares. The left swatch in the gradient will always be the same as the foreground color. The right swatch can take on any color, and it represents the other extreme of the gradient. If you click the area between the two swatches — the *gradient bar* or *gradient bridge* — you'll get a small pop-up list showing the various types of gradients that you can use.

Setting the color of the foreground, background, or gradient target swatch is as simple as clicking and holding the swatch. When you do this, a palette of colors pops up: 256 if you are running in 8-bit color depth or higher; 16 if you are running in a lower color depth. These colors come from the current system palette, the details of which are covered in much greater detail in Chapter 5. For now, you can select any color to have it replace the current color swatch, just by clicking the palette color that you want.

Patterns

Below the foreground/background color swatches is a larger button that probably seems right now to be the same as the foreground color. This is the *pattern swatch*. If you click and hold this button, an array of 64 possible patterns pops up. For each pattern, the black pixels represent the foreground color and the white pixels are the background color. Select a pattern, and your paintbrush will paint in two colors, reproducing the pattern as the brush moves over the Cast window.

You can also select more exotic patterns, called *tiles*, from the bottom of the pattern palette. The last eight patterns contain full-color chips that are useful for introducing tiled backgrounds into your movie. The eight tiles that are supplied can be used for general effects, but in all likelihood you'll want to create new color tiles for yourself from cast members.

Creating Tiles from Cast Members

1. Using a paint program, (such as Photoshop, Paint Shop Pro, or xRes), create a rectangular graphic with sides that measure 16, 32, 64, or 128 pixels. (That is, the image can be sized in any combination of these measurements — 32 x 128 or 16 x 32 or whatever you want, as long as you use those four dimensions.) This image should preferably be tiled so that there are no seams where the top and bottom, or left and right, meet.

2. Import the image into Director.

   You'll learn how to import images later in this chapter. For now, you can use the tiles.dir movie in the following steps. This movie already includes several imported graphics (based on 16x32a.pct, 16x32b.pct, 64x32a.pct, 64x32b.pct, 64x32c.pct, and 64x32d.pct). The entire file is on the companion CD-ROM in the exercise:ch02 (exercise\ch02) folder.

3. Slect the imported image in the cast, and open the Paint window. Click the Pattern button in the Tools palette. This brings up a pop-up palette of all the patterns, as well as two other selections: Pattern Settings and Tile Settings. See Figure 2-5.

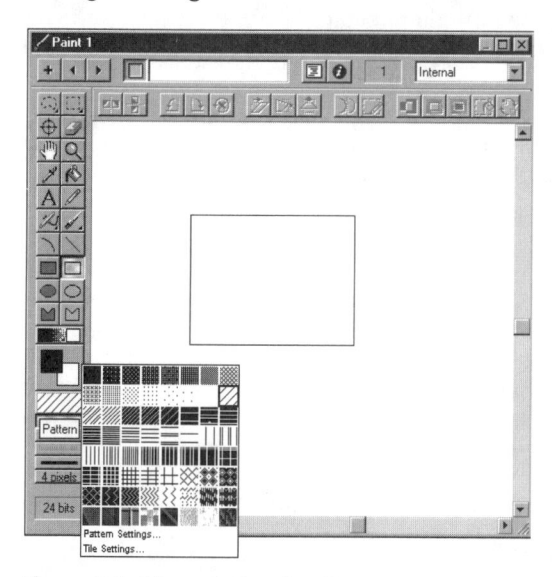

Figure 2-5: The palette of patterns

4. Choose Tile Settings. The Tile Settings dialog box appears (Figure 2-6).

5. In the Tile Settings dialog, you can select Cast Member or Built-In as the source of the image to tile. Choose Cast Member to use the graphic you just imported. Click the left and right arrows to step through all of the graphics to find the one you want.

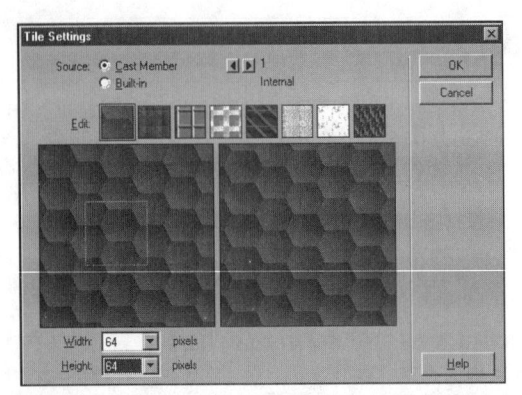

Figure 2-6: Choosing settings for a tile

6. Set the width and height of the boundary box by clicking the drop-down list and choosing any one of the values (16, 32, 64, or 128). The boundary box rectangle used for selecting the tile will change size to match those dimensions. Be sure you use settings that match the imported image's dimensions.

7. You can also drag the bounding rectangle around the graphic. This can be used to select different portions of the graphic to be used as your tile. Once you have the tile you want, click OK.

8. Once you've created the tile, you can select it from the pattern palette and paint with it, using the Paintbrush or Fill tool. Be sure to click the New Cast Member button before using the pattern. You must create a new cast member to use the pattern.

Tip

Building effective tiles takes some practice, but the results are worth it. If you have chosen an icon to repeat as a tile, the smaller sizes (16 or 32 pixels) work out best as the tile size. On the other hand, if you are trying for the illusion of a continuous field (such as water, grass, or a rocky beach) then you may want to make your tile as large as possible, since the eye is remarkably adept at seeing patterns in graphics.

Caution

You can edit any of the eight custom tiles shown at the top of the Tile Settings dialog box. To reset a swatch you've changed, select the swatch and then click the Source: Built-in radio button. This returns the swatch to Director's built-in pattern.

Line widths

Below the Pattern button are the line-width indicators. These work in conjunction with the Rectangle, Oval, and Polygon tools, regular and filled, to set the border width of these shapes. The first button, showing a dotted line, is a little deceptive — rather than a dotted line, it actually indicates that no line will be drawn. (There's no easy way to draw a dotted line, unfortunately.) The next four line-width buttons draw lines 1, 2, 3, and 4 pixels wide, respectively. If you need a border of a different width, double-click the button for 4 pixels to bring up the Paint Preferences dialog, and change the width with the appropriate slider.

Painting with light and shadow: the ink effects

One of the things we like about computer graphics is that the definition of a computer paint is so . . . well . . . *fluid*. Director has dozens of different paints, some for making washes or blends, some for painting opaque layers on top of other colors, and a few that paint with the colors of the previous cast member or paint only the lighter of two colors.

In Director (as with most "paint" programs), the inks are essentially miniprograms that instruct the current brush on how to interact with the color directly underneath the brush in the Paint window. Normal paint, for example, will just cover the image with the foreground color and the applied pattern. Transparent ink, on the other hand, will let the background of a pattern or text show through.

The ink effects list is placed (rather awkwardly) at the bottom-left of the Paint window frame; unfortunately, this corner is usually difficult to access on smaller screens. The ink effects that are available will change depending upon which tool is currently selected. The Paintbrush, for example, will have the full complement of effects, while the Pencil will be much more limited.

Tip

As you'll find out later, you can switch between several different brushes. In addition to changes in shape and size, each brush retains its own ink settings. In other words, if you change brushes, make sure that your ink effect, as well, gets changed to the one you want to use.

Table 2-2 lists all of the possible ink effects, although they won't all be available for every tool.

Table 2-2
Ink Effects

Ink Name	Effect
Normal	This is the default ink. It paints the current forecolor on top of the background, using the currently active pattern.
Transparent	This makes the backcolor of a selection transparent. Especially useful for working with text for buttons.
Reverse	This converts a white or colored image to black, and black to white. A useful ink for making masks.

(continued)

Table 2-2 (continued)

Ink Name	Effect
Ghost	This draws using the background color.
Gradient	This creates a smooth transition from one color to another. The properties of the gradient can be set by clicking the gradient bridge between the gradient start and end colors.
Reveal	Reveals the contents of the previous graphical cast member.
Cycle	Each time the brush moves, the color is changed to the next color in the palette.
Switch	Uses the gradient target color (the color at the right end of the gradient bar) as the replacement color whenever the brush passes over the forecolor. This is one way of cutting down on the halo of near-white colors resulting from images produced in xRes, Photoshop, and other paint programs. See the sidebar "Tarnished halos" later in the chapter.
Blend	Blends the current foreground color with what's already been painted on the screen. Select File ⇨ Preferences ⇨ Paint to set the blend value between 0% and 100%.
Darkest	Compares the foreground color and the pixels in the background, then chooses the darker of the two colors to paint the screen.
Lightest	Compares the foreground color and the pixels in the background, then chooses the lighter of the two colors to paint the screen.
Darken	Ignores the foreground color, darkening the background image at the rate shown in the Paint dialog box (File ⇨ Preferences ⇨ Paint).
Lighten	Ignores the forecolor, lightening the background image at the rate shown in the Paint dialog box (File ⇨ Preferences ⇨ Paint).
Smooth	Smoothes or blurs the pixels of the background image, ignoring the forecolor.
Smear	Pushes around the pixels of the background image, ignoring the forecolor. The effect is much like smearing fingerpaints.
Smudge	Combines Smoothing and Smearing into one operation.
Spread	Picks up and paints with the colors directly under the brush.
Clipboard	This can be used to turn a brush into a "stamp." Select a region with the Marquee or Lasso tool and save that to the Clipboard (using Edit ⇨ Copy or Edit ⇨ Cut). When you change the ink selector to this effect, the saved image can then be used like a brush. See "Custom brushes" later in this chapter.

Using Reveal and other "special" inks

Animation is the process of creating the illusion of movement, through (mostly) very tiny adjustments in position. Especially with computer animation, it's often more useful to retain most of an image and just draw what's changed from one frame to the next. This is where the Reveal ink comes in handy.

Reveal uses the previous bitmap cast member in the cast library as its "paint." When you set the ink to Reveal and then paint with that, whatever is "under" the current graphic will be added to the picture. For example, a centaur walking at a canter is for the most part static above the legs. With the Reveal ink you can paint the portion of the horse that doesn't move, then change the position of the legs afterward. This technique works especially well with the onion skinning feature of Director, which lets you see the previous layer as a transparent image beneath the current layer. (See Chapter 3 for more details about how to use the Onion Skin window and Reveal.)

The Clipboard ink is another powerful effect, although it comes with a few significant limitations. You can select a portion of a graphic using either the Marquee or the Lasso tool, and copy the selection to the Clipboard, either by pressing Command+C (Ctrl+C) or by selecting Edit ⇨ Copy. Choose the Clipboard ink (with the Paintbrush tool only), and the item you selected will then be drawn as a "stamp" — each time you click in the Paint window, a copy of the image is rendered there.

The one major problem with the Clipboard ink is that you can't make the ink transparent. That is, you can't create an irregularly shaped "stamp," only a rectangular one. If you need the latter capability, you should use the Lasso tool and the Paste feature instead.

The Cycle ink is perhaps one of the most complicated inks to use successfully. Once you take the time to understand this ink, however, it can be used to create some eye-catching special effects. The trick to using Cycle is to create a gradient in the gradient bridge. The foreground color should be the first color in the cycle, and the gradient target (the right end of the gradient bridge) should be the last color in the cycle. Then, each time you hold down the mouse button and move the mouse over the picture, the next color in the color palette will be drawn by the brush, and then the next, until you come to the last color. When the drawn color reaches the last color in the cycle, it either jumps back to the first color or the previous color in the palette, depending upon which option you have set in the Paint Preferences dialog.

On its own, the Cycle ink is good for creating "pipes" — in which overlapping colors seem to move closer to the viewer, providing a quick-and-dirty solution to making something "pop out of the screen." In addition, you can actually (in some situations) create animation effects by turning on color cycling, as discussed in Chapter 5. By cycling through a limited range in the color palette, you can make your cycled colors seem to pulse and writhe eerily.

Basic Painting Techniques

Having all these tools at hand is a prerequisite for painting a picture, but unless you know some basic painting techniques, no tool in the world is going to actually create your artwork for you. Some people find that they can sit down at a computer with a mouse and drawing program and create from scratch. Others need to draw their original concepts on paper and then either scan in the images or use them as references for new work.

Note: Director doesn't provide direct support for scanners. However, you can use other paint programs or scanner utilities to scan your sketches and then import them into Director as files. More about this later, in the section "Importing Images."

Drawing the graphic

In a beginning drawing class, the instructor will typically start you out drawing fruit, or draped cloth, or something similarly inanimate. This is not because you need to become proficient in drawing oranges and apples, but because you need to become familiar with your tools: pencil, paper, paint brushes, inks, and whatever else you are using. Painting with a computer is no different. Director has some very powerful painting utilities, but if you don't know where they are and what they're for, they simply add to "hard-drive bloat."

The following exercises show some techniques for creating artwork within Director. Although the tools that Director offers in the Paint window aren't as versatile as image editing programs such as Photoshop, they do offer some advantages for creating artwork for animation, especially in conjunction with the program's onion skin techniques.

Creating an Outline Drawing

1. Before you begin, it might be worth sketching out the concept on paper. This will give you a clearer idea of what you want to work with.

   On the CD-ROM: For practice drawing images in this chapter, you can use the pixtels.dir movie on the CD-ROM in the exercise:ch02 (exercise\ch02) folder. This file includes several drawings that you can copy.

   Tip: Another way to go about this is to scan in a drawn image, and then use the onion skin technique (covered in Chapter 3) to view a ghost of the image.

2. Create or activate a bitmap cast member, by doing one of the following things:

   ✦ To create a new bitmap cast member, select an empty cast member in the current cast library, and press Command+5 (Ctrl+5) to launch the Paint window.

♦ Edit an existing cast member by selecting it in the Cast window and pressing Command+5 (Ctrl+5), or by double-clicking the cast member's icon in the Cast window or the Score.

♦ If you are editing an existing bitmap, you can create a new one by pressing the New Cast Member (+) button in the Paint window's main toolbar to create an empty cast member.

3. In the Cast Member Name box at the top of the Paint window, enter a descriptive name for the graphic. This makes the cast member much easier to use with Lingo commands, and also makes it easier to distinguish between cast members when you're looking at them from the Cast window.

4. Select your outline color (most often, this will be black) as the foreground color. To set a foreground color, click and hold the foreground color square (the topmost of the two overlapping squares) until the color palette pops up. Then click on the sketching color you want.

Tip

In choosing outline color, it's often a good idea to try to closely match the final colors you anticipate for your backgrounds. Dark blues, grays, dark greens, or greenish browns work well because they have a neutral appearance against most colors.

5. Click the Pencil tool. This gives you a one-pixel-wide line to draw with. Normally, the Pencil will draw in the foreground color. However, if the first pixel that the pencil encounters is the shade of the foreground color, then Director automatically swaps to using the background color. Keep this in mind as a quick way to erase simple mistakes without having to change tools.

6. Check for broken outlines. At this stage it's best to work with outlines only, and leave solid shading to later in the process. But in preparation for future shading, you'll want to be extremely careful to make sure that all lines enclosing the regions of your work are unbroken. Even one pixel missing from a line will cause any paint that you add later to spill through to the outside.

7. If you need a sense of scale, you can display the rulers set in pixels using the View ⇨ Rulers command or by pressing Command Shift+Option I R (Ctrl+Shift+Alt+R). Change the default ruler measurement setting by clicking the word *Pixel* at the conjunction of the horizontal and vertical rulers (see Figure 2-7). This indicator will cycle through Inches and Centimeters before returning to Pixels.

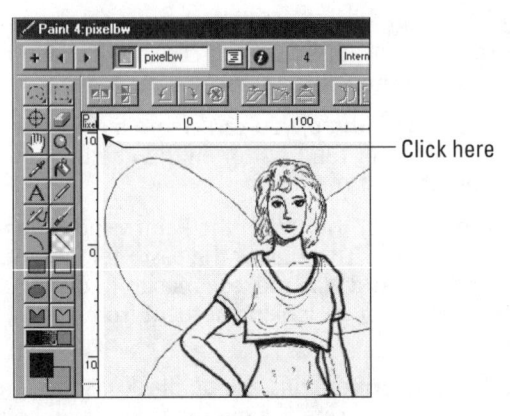

Figure 2-7: You can set the rulers to Pixels, Inches, or Centimeters.

8. Once you have the basic figure drawn (see Figure 2-8 for an example), save your movie using the File ⇨ Save command (Command+S or Ctrl+S).

Figure 2-8: Before you begin painting your figure, make sure its outline is unbroken.

9. In addition to taking the precaution of saving your movie at this early stage, you may also want to keep a duplicate of the sketch. Chances are good that you'll change your mind at least once about the direction in which your work is going. Or you may need a basic template for future images. Press Command+D (Ctrl+D) to create a duplicate of the cast member in the next open cast member slot.

10. Notice that the cast member number in the title of the Paint window changes. You are now working on the duplicated image, not the original sketch. It's a good idea to change the name of the duplicate, as well.

This preliminary drawing will provide a fundamental canvas for you to work with in the next few exercises. It gives you boundaries and regions, to fill with colors and gradients. You'll be able to flesh out your animation more quickly than if you had introduced color from the outset.

Painting the graphic

Once your "sketch" is done, you can start painting. In general, computer painting tends to follow its analog counterpart: You start by painting in the broadest strokes and work your way toward the details. Again, a little planning will go a long way.

Painting Your Figure

1. Click the Paint Bucket tool.

2. Display the color palette, by clicking the foreground color swatch. The palette represents the range of colors that you can use for your bitmaps. (Chapter 5 will take you through an in-depth study of working with colors and the color palette.)

   Tip: You may want to make some notes (mental or otherwise) at this point about which colors you will use for the overall categories of objects in your project — flesh tones, primary colors for clothing, landscape colors for plants and trees, the sky color, and so forth. That way, multiple pieces of artwork featuring the same character or object won't have colors changing unexpectedly from one frame to the next.

3. Click within the region you want filled with color (see Figure 2-9). Be careful — before you click the mouse, make sure that the cursor is not over part of the outline. If you do accidentally fill the outline, or if your graphic had a break in the outline that causes the fill to overflow, press Command+Z (Ctrl+Z) and start over.

Caution

If you want to fill an area with a solid color, be sure the pattern indicator in the tools palette is set to solid black.

If you want to modify more than one cast member in the Paint window, you can move between cast members without having to close the Paint window. Click the Previous or Next Cast Member buttons at the top of the Paint window.

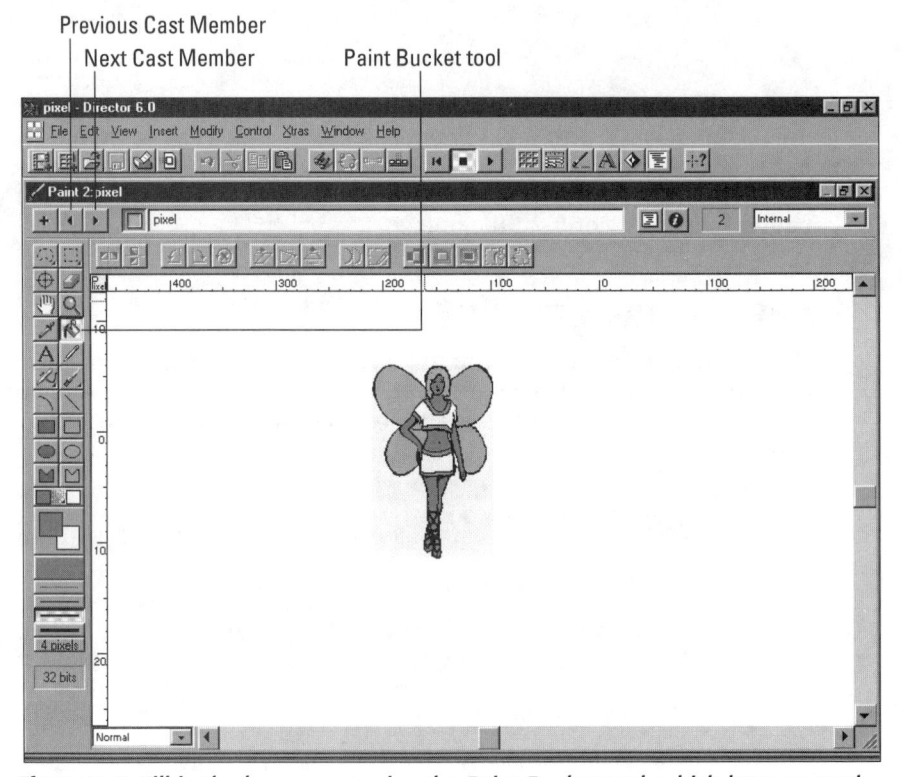

Figure 2-9: Fill in the large areas using the Paint Bucket tool, which lets you work quickly and provide uniformity between images.

4. Once you have filled the object(s) with the selected color, you can either select another color to fill another object or close the Paint window. Your work will be immediately visible in the cast menu and on the Stage, if the cast member you were modifying has been placed on the Stage.

Now, for some texture, let's see how to introduce color gradients.

Using Gradients

1. Double-click the Paint Bucket tool to bring up the Gradient Settings dialog box (Figure 2-10). Here you will choose the various settings for a gradient.

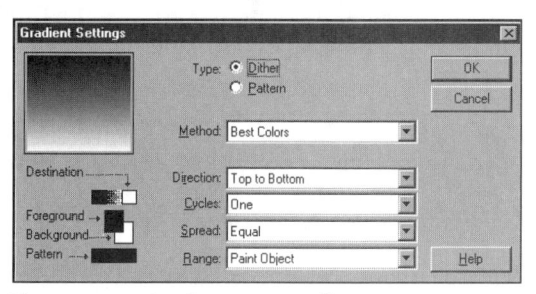

Figure 2-10: Setting up a gradient

2. Click the Foreground swatch to choose the Foreground color. This is the starting color for the gradient.

3. Click the Destination swatch to choose the Destination color, which is the color into which the forecolor will blend.

4. Click the Direction field and choose the particular form or "flow" that you want the gradient to use. You can choose one of the preset directions (Top to Bottom, Left to Right, and so on). Or choose the Direction option; this lets you draw a "rubber-band" line indicating the direction and length of the gradient fill. Click OK to close the dialog box.

5. Next, select one of the Paint window's tools that can use the gradient (Paint Brush, Paint Bucket, Filled Ellipse, Filled Polygon, or Filled Rectangle tool).

6. In the ink pop-up, select the Gradient ink option. (As explained earlier in the chapter, the ink pop-up is at the bottom-left of the Paint window.)

7. Use the selected tool to draw an object on the Paint window canvas.

Take a look at the other settings in the Gradient Settings dialog:

+ Unless you're planning on using color cycling, you'll probably want to keep the Method set to Best Colors, as this provides the smoothest gradient.

+ The Cycles setting lets you create multiple cycles of a gradient. An example of this can be seen in the curtains shown in the Pixel-on-Stage image in Figure 2-1. Here, a gradient with four cycles from dark maroon to a rich red gives the illusion of hanging drapery.

✦ You can control the progression of the colors' sliding into one another by changing the Spread setting to More Foreground, More Middle, or More Destination. This setting, in turn, controls the "tightness" of the gradient at boundary points.

Tip: For some really wild effects, try changing the Pattern setting in the Gradient Settings dialog. This is an inexpensive way to get checkered gradients, scales, rivers of parallel lines, and so forth.

Even with color gradients, the figures you have now are fairly flat. This may very well serve your purposes if you're looking for a cartoonlike effect. More realistic imagery, however, requires a certain amount of tweaking, which can be accomplished with the Paint window's Brush tool. The "brush" actually provides five distinct brushes, each of which you can customize to a different size, shape, and painting effect.

Choosing a Brush

1. To paint with the currently selected brush, simply click once briefly on the Brush tool and start painting the graphic. The area of the graphic is being painted with the foreground color in the size and shape of the selected brush.

2. Try some of the other brushes. Click and hold the Brush tool icon until the list of five brushes pops up, and then click the brush you want to use.

3. You can also modify the characteristics of the brushes. In the Brush tool pop-up, choose a brush to customize, and then double-click the Brush tool again. Or choose Settings from the Brush tool pop-up; this brings up the Brush Settings dialog box (Figure 2-11).

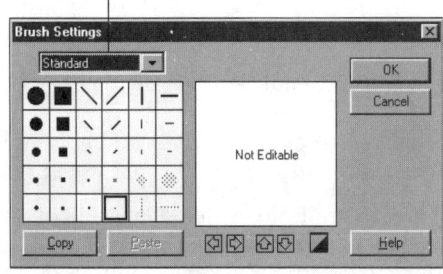

Figure 2-11: Use the Brush Settings dialog to select a brush shape or to create your own.

4. Click any one of the 30 standard brush shapes on the left of the dialog. Try one or two now.

Tip

Most of the time, you'll probably want to use the circular or square brush shapes for painting, but some of the others can produce some interesting and amusing results. The angled brushes, for instance, can be used for calligraphy if you move the brush very slowly to avoid breaking up the lines. The dotted brushes in the lower-right of the palette make for interesting non-uniform textures, especially when used in conjunction with patterns (discussed earlier in this chapter).

Custom brushes

With some effort, you can also make a new custom brush shape in the large designing panel of the Brush Settings dialog, but this technique is not for the faint of heart. To create a custom brush, you first have to select a portion of the image with the Marquee or Lasso tool (see the upcoming section) and copy it to the Clipboard. The following exercise will show you how it is done.

Creating a Custom Brush from Scratch

1. In the Cast window, select an empty cast member slot.
2. Open the Paint window by either selecting the Paint Window button on the main toolbar or by pressing Command+5 (Ctrl+5).
3. In the Paint window, make sure black is the foreground color.
4. Select the Filled Rectangle tool and draw a small rectangle.
5. Click the Marquee tool and select the No Shrink option.
6. With the Marquee tool, select the entire small rectangle and some of the white area around it.
7. Copy the selection to the Clipboard, using the Edit ⇨ Copy Bitmap command or Command+C (Ctrl+C).
8. Double-click the Brush tool to open the Brush Settings dialog box. Open the drop-down list at the top and select Custom.
9. When you select Custom, all the standard brushes shown in the left pane are available for editing. In this exercise, however, you are creating a custom brush from scratch. So click the Paste button, and the standard brushes in the left pane will be replaced by the area of the rectangle that you selected with the Marquee tool in step 6.
10. Notice that when you click in the left-hand pane of the Brush Settings dialog box, you are navigating around the black rectangle — which appears

in the right pane of the dialog. When you click in the right pane, pixels in your custom brush are turned on and off. (A click on a black pixel turns it white, so it *won't* paint when you use the custom brush. A click on a white pixel turns it black, so it *will* paint.)

11. You can also navigate around the custom brush using the Scroll Right/Left and Scroll Up/Down buttons (see Figure 2-12). Try this.

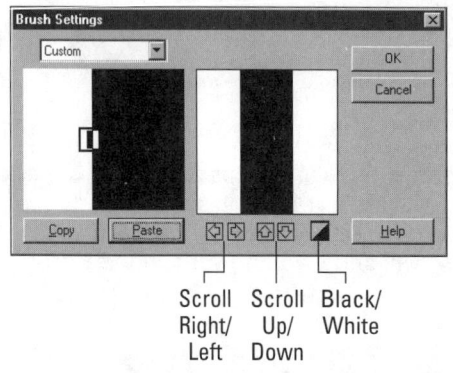

Figure 2-12: Using the arrow buttons at the bottom of the Brush Settings dialog, you can isolate a selection to modify when building your custom brush.

12. You can select an area use the left pane and then completely invert that section of the custom brush (from black to white or vice versa) using the Black/White button (see Figure 2-12). Try this.

13. Now use these tools to change the shape of your custom brush to approximate the image in Figure 2-13. Once you have the brush shaped the way you want it, click OK.

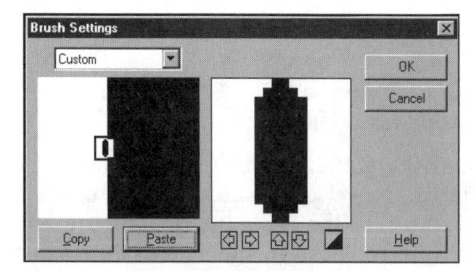

Figure 2-13: A completed custom brush

14. As you move your cursor around on the Paint window, it will have the shape of the brush you just created and will paint strokes to match its shape.

15. Don't get "stuck" using only your custom brush. You can choose another brush shape. Simply click and hold the Brush tool and select a brush from Brush 1 through Brush 5. (You can also reassign the brush shape for one of these brushes. Just select it, double-click the Brush tool, choose Standard in the list box at the top of the dialog, and assign a new brush shape by selecting one of the 30 standard shapes shown in Figure 2-11. Then click OK.

Note: The Paint window in Director supports pressure-sensitive digitizer tablets such as the ArtZ from Wacom. The more pressure applied to the tip of the digitizer, the bolder the stroke. Lessen the pressure, and you get a lighter stroke. This same effect is simulated when using a mouse. The more slowly you move the mouse, the closer together the points are placed from the brush, and vice versa. It may take some practice, and more than a little patience, to get the hang of this feature.

Using the paint (ink) effects

Each brush in the Brush tool's list retains not only its own shape information, but also the paint (ink) style that is currently used for that brush. Once you've chosen a brush, you can set this paint style in the pop-up Paint Effects list at the lower-left of the Paint window (see Figure 2-14). The ink effects were listed earlier in Table 2-2.

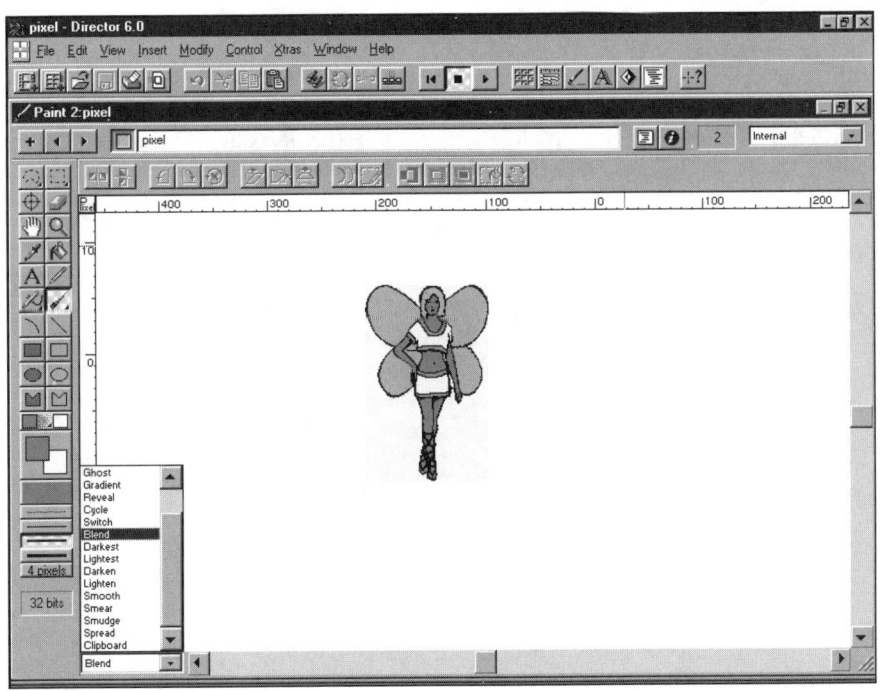

Figure 2-14: The Paint pop-up provides a wide variety of painting (ink) effects.

The paint styles provide a wide range of effects. For example, you can retain the black lines of your underdrawing by selecting the color you wish to paint with and the ink effect called Darken. This will paint the area you're working in with a 10% saturation of black. Every time you click and drag the brush over the area that has a Darken ink effect, it darkens in additional increments of 10% per stroke. The Lighten ink does the same thing, lightening in increments of 10% per stroke.

You can use the Smooth, Smear, and Smudge effects to soften internal lines in your drawing. But watch out — unless your graphic is going to be playing against a white background, you should avoid smearing the outer edges. This prevents problems with jagged edges (known as aliasing) and stray pixels appearing outside the edge of the graphic.

Techniques for selecting the graphic

With electronic media, you have a number of advantages over the traditional paints and pencils and ink-soaked pens. Perhaps the most significant innovation to come from the world of pixels is the concept of the *selection*. A selection is a piece of an image (or, for that matter, a piece of just about any kind of file) that can be moved from one place to another on the desktop, copied multiple times, distorted out of all recognition, flipped, rotated, and otherwise transformed. Selections play an integral part in animations, especially because animations by their very nature are subtle transformations from one state to another.

We'll cover the tools for fundamental selection tasks here in this section. In Chapter 3, you'll get a look at other tools for modifying and otherwise working with your selections.

First, let's see how to zoom in closer to get a better look at what we need to select. Quite frequently, you will need to get a closer look at a graphic, especially if your screen is set to 1024 x 768 or higher. The Magnifying Glass in the tools palette helps you do just that.

Zooming In and Out

1. Click the Magnifying Glass icon on the tools palette and then click the image you have displayed. The point where you click becomes the center of a magnified view of the image, with the image in its normal size displayed in a window at the upper-right (see Figure 2-15). By clicking repeatedly on the tool, you can go to an 8:1 scale.

Chapter 2 ✦ **Working with Graphics**   47

Hand tool

Figure 2-15: Zoom in and out with the Magnifying Glass, and use the Hand tool to adjust your viewpoint of the image in the Paint window.

2. You'll likely want to move around in the magnified view of your image, to make selections, apply paint, and so forth. Use the Hand tool for this. Try it now: Click and drag to change your viewpoint of the image within the Paint window. Once you've zoomed in, you can use the Hand tool to move the "canvas" right, left, up, or down, to get a better look at the portion of the image you're working on.

3. You can return to the normal image size by clicking with the Hand tool on the floating inset window at the upper-right.

4. When you've finished experimenting, set your on-screen image at the perspective you want to use for continuing these exercises.

If your hand is steady, the Lasso tool is easily the most versatile selection tool. With it, you can draw a path around or within a graphic, and everything within the path becomes the selection. The area thus selected will have a marquee that conforms with the path you drew around the area. The Lasso actually has three possible states: No Shrink, Shrink, and See Thru Lasso.

Selecting with the Lasso

1. Try the Lasso tool's No Shrink option first. Click and hold the mouse on the Lasso tool to display the pop-up, and select No Shrink. Then draw the selection path, and it will exactly correspond to the shape you created. If you don't return to the starting point in your path, the rest of the selection will be a straight line between the starting and ending points.

2. Try the Shrink option. This is useful for "lazy selection." You draw a selection path around an object with the Lasso, and the selection then shrinks in to select just the object. The Shrink option makes the Lasso wrap to the smallest possible boundary around the image, essentially eliminating any part of the selection that uses the background color.

3. Next, try See Thru Lasso. It works the same way as the Shrink option but also cuts out holes in the image where the background color is used. This option is especially useful for selecting text, which usually has "enclosed bowls" and other shapes that can retain background color when you don't want it.

4. Here's another helpful technique that you can use with the Lasso. With the Lasso tool selected, hold down the Option (Alt) key, and click at one point, then click a second point. The selection expands to include the line between the two points. To complete the selection, you need to click the starting point. In this way, you can quickly capture parts of an object that have straight edges but aren't rectangular.

Next, practice with the Marquee tool. It can be used for selecting rectangular regions, and has some additional useful functionality beyond that. This tool offers four options: No Shrink, Shrink, Lasso, and See Thru Lasso.

Selecting with the Marquee Tool

1. Like the Lasso tool, you display the Marquee tool's pop-up menu by clicking and holding the tool button. Do this now, and select the No Shrink option. Click and drag to select, and you'll find that it creates a rectangular selection that is exactly the size that you drag.

2. Next, try the Shrink option. When you work with this option, it shrinks down to the smallest bounding box that will encompass the entire image.

   Many of the transformation tools (the buttons in the Effects toolbar that runs along the top of the Paint window) require that either a No Shrink or Shrink Marquee be selected. Most of these tools won't work if your selection is irregular or created with the Lasso tool. You'll start working with the transformation tools in Chapter 3.

3. Before you stop experimenting with the Marquee tool, try the Marquee Lasso See Thru option. It works exactly as it does for the Lasso tool, wrapping to fit the boundaries of the image as tightly as possible. The only real difference is that the Marquee tool's initial shape is rectangular.

Tip

Here's a handy trick when you need to transform a number of graphics. Double-clicking the Marquee tool automatically draws a Shrink Marquee boundary around the entire graphic in the Paint window. (Be sure you do a fast double-click, or Director will think you want the Marquee options pop-up instead — which can throw off your rhythm when you're trying to warp 39 objects in the same movie!)

Caution

The Marquee tool's See Thru Lasso option really switches to the Lasso tool in See Thru mode. It is an excellent tool for grabbing text.

Moving, copying, cutting, and pasting selections

To move a selection, you have a couple of options. If you just drag it, then the region behind it will become white. On the other hand, if you hold down the Option (Alt) key while dragging the selection, Director automatically makes a copy of the selection and moves the copy. The original is unchanged.

If you cut or copy a selected region to the Clipboard, Director retains positional information with the copied graphic. So you can create a new cast member with the New Cast Member (+) button, and then paste the graphic into that new cast member. It will be exactly aligned with the previous cast member.

Floating and pasted selections are sensitive to the Paint characteristics. Typically, the Normal paint is the active one, and the pasted image will completely cover the background. However, you can change the paint (ink) characteristic to Transparent, Blend, or any other of the effects in the pop-up at the lower-left of the Paint window.

Tip

If you pick up and move a rectangle of text that's on a white background, you can select the Transparent ink to let anything that is behind the background of the text (the white area that is now made transparent) show through. Blend will make the selection translucent, showing a percentage of the background behind it. You can set the percent showing by altering the Blend property in the Paint preferences (File ⇨ Preferences ⇨ Paint).

Design and production techniques

You probably already know how important it is to get familiar with your tools before you try to use them — especially before you attempt to create serious (or even comical) works in Director. The program's powerful tools have some idiosyncrasies that can wreck the best of intentions. And once you do understand Director's features, here are a few tips on design and production that will help you make your graphics the best they can be:

- Even if you are planning "painterly" graphics, you should start out with a line drawing. This serves several purposes: It lets you lay down broad swaths of paint, fills, or gradients without having to fiddle with painting individual pixels. It lets you make easy alterations to animated figures without losing quality. And it helps prevent ghosting along the edges.

- When you work with a scanned image, you're probably better off tracing the image instead of using the scanned image itself. In this way you can simplify the drawing down to a set of enclosed regions without having to worry about pale but not white pixels corrupting your work.

- Cartoons work best when your images have variation in their line widths, as is typical in comic books. Let the weight of the line suggest the shading. This technique gives flat color images more depth than they would have with uniform line weights, cutting down on the amount of shading you'll need to do in the paint phase.

- Try to work at full size if at all possible. If you're tempted to work zoomed in and then shrink the resulting image, remember that it often comes at an aggravating cost in cleaning up edges and boundaries.

- Early on, establish a working color palette that specifies the colors to be used by major portions of the image. It helps to print out the palette on a color printer, and then mark on the printout the various roles for each color.

- If your final images are going to be 256-color indexed (8-bit) graphics, then you should set your monitor to 8-bit color when you paint these graphics. At higher resolution, Director will introduce colors that fall outside of your current palette. (There's more on color coming up, and in Chapter 5 as well.)

- Beware of adding too much detail too early. Once the underdrawing is done, add the fill colors, the paint colors for the larger brushes, and gradients — *before* you add fine detail. This rule becomes especially important when you have a number of nearly identical cast members, as is usually the case with animation.

- Keep an eye out for places where you can add patterns. Patterns can simulate colors that aren't in your palette, but they also can be used to add texture without the cost of painting in the texture by hand.

Director's Paint window works best for creating graphics that have flat colors and strongly delineated boundaries. If you are in need of more realistic images, use Photoshop, Painter, scanned images, or a 3D rendering package instead, and then import the images into Director. Its quicker, easier, and far more effective. The following section introduces you to the process of importing images for use in Director.

Importing Images

For all that the Paint window is a fair editor for creating basic animations, it does have some profound limitations. The paint tools lack subtleties — as noted earlier, they are reasonably good for creating hard-edged graphics with flat fills but don't work terribly well for creating more realistic images. Also lacking is the ability to save selections for later use, which is a staple of such products as xRes or Photoshop. And though a primitive sort of layering can be constructed using the Onion Skin window (see Chapter 3), this workaround doesn't provide the mixing modes of most modern paint editors.

Because of these limitations, and because we encounter media from more sources than just Director's Paint window, the program has long supported the capability of importing a wide variety of graphical formats. Indeed, the list is quite extensive: Macintosh PICT formats, Microsoft BMP bitmaps, JPEGs, CompuServe GIF images, most TIF formats, and PCX images. What's more, with the help of special import filter Xtras to bring in nearly every file format, Director can now support multilayer files like those produced by Macromedia xRes and Adobe Photoshop (although the images are flattened within Director).

Importing a file into Director requires a few steps but is not unduly complicated.

Note

Before opening Director, make sure your monitor is set to the color depth at which you want the imported images to appear. This will save you from having to convert them later. See the sidebar, "How Director handles color."

Importing Images into Director

On the CD-ROM

As you practice importing images in this chapter, you can use several graphic images that we've built for you — or use images that you have created, scanned, or (legally!) borrowed. The files on the CD-ROM are coolidge.pct, milton.pct, mount1.png, voteflag.bmp, dark.png, heart1.png, and heart2.png in the exercise:ch02 (exercise\ch02) folder.

1. Launch Director; then select File ➪ Import or press Command+R (Ctrl+R). The Import Files dialog box appears (Figure 2-16).

2. Click the Show button (Mac) or the Files of Type list box (Windows) and choose Bitmap Image. Selecting this format will filter out any files that Director doesn't consider to be bitmapped images.

3. Use the file navigation controls at the top of the box to locate the file you wish to import. Select the file by clicking it. To import several files, click Add after you select each file. To add every image in the entire folder, click Add All.

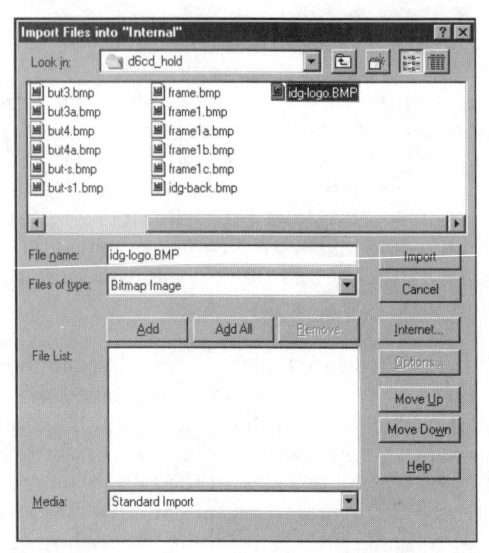

Figure 2-16: The Import Files dialog gives you an extensive set of options for specifying how your image gets imported.

4. The File List box in the lower part of the dialog contains the files in the order they will be imported into Director. If you want to change that order, select the file you want to move and click Move Up or Move Down to shift the order of the files.

   You can also import a file from the Internet by clicking the Internet button in the Import Files dialog. This brings up another dialog where you can type the URL of the file. This is particularly handy for Shockwave movies, which contain images that may change over time.

5. In the Media drop-down list, set to Standard Import by default, select a medium for storing the imported image. The four options available are explained in Table 2-3.

6. When you have all of the files arranged the way that you want, click Import to begin the actual importing of the files.

Table 2-3
Import Media Types

Media Option	Import and Storage Process
Standard Import	The complete graphic is stored within the movie's internal cast library. The graphic can be edited using the Paint window and is no longer directly connected to its source file.
Link to External File	Loads a temporary version of the graphic into Director's cast library, but when the movie is later opened and run, the graphic is reloaded from the external file rather than from the internal cast. This option is useful when the source graphic is subject to change, comes from the Internet, or is generated through a third-party utility. *Note:* If the source graphic is a QuickTime still, then it *must* be imported using this option because QuickTime resources use streaming to load images.
Include Original Data for Editing	Like the Link to External File option, this creates an external link, but it also retains internal information about how the file was defined. This enables editing of layered images such as those created in Photoshop. *Note:* In order to use an external editor, the imported file format must have an associated editor defined in the Editor Preferences dialog box (File ⇨ Preferences ⇨ Editors).
Import PICT File as PICT	PICTs are the native format that Director uses on the Macintosh. They will play slightly faster if imported into this format, but are slightly unpredictable when played on a Windows platform.

Specifying options for imported images

Director offers a multitude of options for determining how your imported images will look in their new environment.

Note

There's a certain amount of redundancy in Director. The program offers two ways of transforming images. One way is to work with them when they are first imported, using the Image Options dialog that appears after you press the Import button in the Import Files dialog. Or you can use the Transform Bitmap dialog. For mapping to palettes or dithering, you're probably better off using the Import Options dialog. Resizing images, on the other hand, can only be done with the Transform Bitmap dialog. It's your choice; both techniques are covered in this section.

Once you select all of your files for import, you will need to designate how you want imported images converted into native Director format. After you press the Import button in the Import Files dialog, you next see the Image Options dialog box. Here you designate how the files are stored internally in Director, and specify if you want to dither the images and/or convert them to a different color palette. Table 2-4 outlines these options.

Table 2-4
Import Image Options

Option	Description
Color Depth	This determines the number of bits that are used for each pixel in the image. See the sidebar "How Director Handles Color" for more information on color depth and palettes.
Palette: Import	Imports an 8-bit color palette with the imported image. (This option is grayed out if movie's color depth is not 8-bit and image isn't an 8-bit indexed color image.) Director will import the palette for the image and store it as a cast member separate from the image.
Palette: Remap To	Remaps image to one of the 8-bit color system palettes (System-Win, System-Mac, and so on) available within Director. Use the field following the radio button to select the desired system palette.
Color Depth	This determines the number of bits that are used for the image. See the sidebar "How Director Handles Color" for more information on color depth and palettes.
Dither	If Dither is turned on, Director attempts to approximate the colors in the image using mixes of the colors in the current palette. Otherwise, Director maps the colors with no mixing. If the colors in the palette closely match those in the image, this is usually the preferable method; otherwise, you should dither the image.
Same Settings for Remaining Images	If more than one image was selected in the Import Files dialog box, then the images imported after the current one will use the same palette and color depth settings as the current image. Otherwise, the Import Options dialog will appear for each image.

How Director handles color

Director — and for that matter, any computer program — doesn't work with images as groups of light and darkness, color and intensity. To Director, images are files containing numbers. Internally, each pixel (each point of color on the screen) is stored as a set of values that vary depending upon the color mode (or color depth) of the image.

In 16- and 24-bit color mode, the computer stores the relative intensity of the three primary colors (red, green, and blue); these values in combination can create nearly all of the colors visible to the human eye. In 24-bit mode, each of the primary colors can assume one of 256 possible levels of intensity, from completely off (black) to completely on (bright red, blue, or green respectively). Those 256 values can be stored in 8 bits (1 byte). So with 24-bit color, each pixel is represented as 3 bytes (24 bits/8 bits per color). To get a dark maroon, then, the intensities would be 90% red (i.e., 230 out of 256), 5% green (13 out of 256), and 30% blue (77 out of 256).

In 16-bit color mode, the principle is the same, but only 5 bits (32 possible values) are used. This is used to get realistic color on some older computers, but gradients especially will appear banded because fewer subtle shades of color are available in 16-bit mode. *High color* (another name for 16-bit graphics) has a few other drawbacks, as well. One of the most troublesome is that animation of 8-bit graphics in this color mode becomes erratic. Also, the implementation of high color on the Macintosh has long been a source of performance problems, artifacts (bits of the graphic not properly erased from the screen), and poor palette mapping.

Things become complex with 8-bit color. Older PCs (and many Macintoshes) had neither the speed nor the memory to pump even 16-bit color images onto a typical screen (the smallest size of which is 640 pixels by 480 pixels high) at an acceptable refresh rate. Because of this, video card manufacturers created what's known as an *indexed color* mode. With indexed color, a pixel was assigned a value between 0 and 255 (whatever can be achieved in 1 byte or 8 bits). This value was then used to reference a 24-bit color that was stored in a *color look-up table,* also known as a *palette.* In theory, any color at all could be displayed this way, but only 256 colors could be shown together at any one time.

Although 256 colors may seem like a lot, it's actually a fairly limited sample. Images that use predominantly the same tone may approximate the original graphic or photographs, but images with a wide variety of tones often become heavily banded or, worse, map illogically to colors. To help mitigate this effect, most 8-bit images are *dithered*: They use dots of differing hues to fool the eye into seeing colors that aren't there.

Director offers a number of dithering techniques, although the algorithms used don't always give good results. In general, if you work with many images that need to be mapped to a single 8-bit palette, use a tool such as Equilibrium's DeBabelizer, which specializes in palette manipulation.

Into the depths (of color, that is)

Especially with imported images, it may happen that you need to map an image to a different palette, change the color depth of the graphic, or resize it. Director gives you an easy-to-use utility for doing just that, with the Modify Transform Bitmap command.

Transforming Bitmaps

On the CD-ROM

If you want to practice these next steps and transform the color depth of specific images, you can use the "bunny" or "house" cast members in the pixtel.dir movie. Try changing their color depth to 1 bit, and you'll see minimal differences. On the other hand, if you transform the "egghead" cast member to 1-bit, you'll see a significant difference — because the existing "egghead" cast member's palette includes only black and white. The pixtel.dir movie is on your companion CD-ROM in the exercise:ch02 (exercise\ch02) folder.

1. Open the Cast window and click the image in the Cast window. Or, to select multiple images, Command-click (Ctrl+click) on the images you wish to transform.

2. Select Modify ⇨ Transform Bitmap to open the Transform Bitmap dialog box (see Figure 2-17).

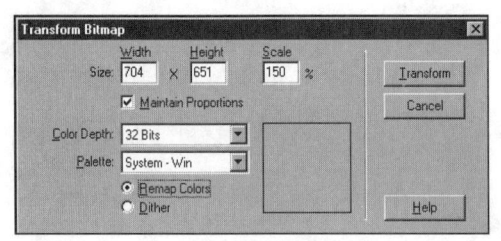

Figure 2-17: The Transform Bitmap dialog box lets you resize an image, and set its color depth and palette.

3. To scale the image to a specific size, you can type the new percentage size in the Scale text box; or you can change the width or the height, which will proportionally change the other dimension. If you wished to resize the graphic in one dimension only, uncheck the Maintain Proportions check box.

4. To set color depth, choose the appropriate entry in the Color Depth drop-down list box.

5. To change the palette of an 8-bit image, select the new palette you want in the Palette list box. This list will include not only the standard Macintosh and Windows palettes but also a variety of specialized palettes (including metallic colors, for instance); it will also include any cast member palettes that may have been imported.

6. Select Remap Colors if you want Director to find colors within the new palette that most closely match the previous colors of the image. If you have two palettes that are almost identical this may be the preferred option. For palettes that are distinctly different, you will probably want to turn on Dither instead.

7. When you have all your options set, click Transform to start processing the images.

Caution

Be careful: This last step — clicking Transform — is destructive to the cast member. You can't undo a transform change with Command+Z (Ctrl+Z).

Tarnished halos

In religious iconography, halos are considered signs of perfection and holiness. For the Director developer, however, halos are a major nuisance. Especially when an image is created in an external paint program with an airbrush that really works, the graphic may have pixels along its outer edge that appear white to the naked eye but aren't quite. When the image is imported and used with a Background Transparent or Matte ink effect on the Stage (see Chapter 3 for details), the near-white pixels appear as an unsightly pixellated halo. Take a look at Figure 2-18.

You can fix halos with a number of techniques, but the following ones work best:

- If you create a graphic in another program that has a rubylith feature (which uses a red mask to control areas that are painted), then select the region outside the graphic you're importing and switch to the mask view. This will show you areas that are "near misses" around the image.

- If the program you're using lets you resize the mask or lasso selection, reduce the size by one pixel. This works only reasonably well, however. It tends to strip the depth of border colors, making them appear jagged.

- If your Director background has a dominant color, you can use that color as a fill around the graphic while you're working in it, and then remove just the one shade of the background color. This might make your image appear to have a nonwhite halo, but the graphic will be relatively seamless on the Stage. If the background is complex, think about using a midrange gray, brown, or green for the background color. These colors tend to blend in well.

- If you're working in Photoshop, create a selection around your graphic, and then choose Select ⇨ Matting ⇨ Defringe. (The border may look a little irregular.)

- If you can, convert images with a higher color depth to 8-bit color, prior to importing them into Director. Then load the image with its associated palette. This method helps avoid remapping or dithering, both of which contribute to halos.

- Once in Director, if you still have halos, use the Paint Bucket tool to fill the background of a graphic cast member with a color not found in the graphic (bright greens work really well for this). You'll be able to see pinhole pixels that can then be removed by running the Pencil tool over them with the same bright color. When done, select the whole region by double-clicking the marquee box (you have to do this quickly, since otherwise it brings up the Marquee pop-up menu instead). Then click the Switch Colors button in the Effects toolbar to map the image back to white.

- Alpha channel effects, which assign partial levels of transparency to different parts of the graphic, work well for special effects, but they can also be used to give a smooth edge to irregularly shaped graphics. There are a few third-party Xtras that support alpha channels (including AlphaMania, a demo version of which ships with the Director CD).

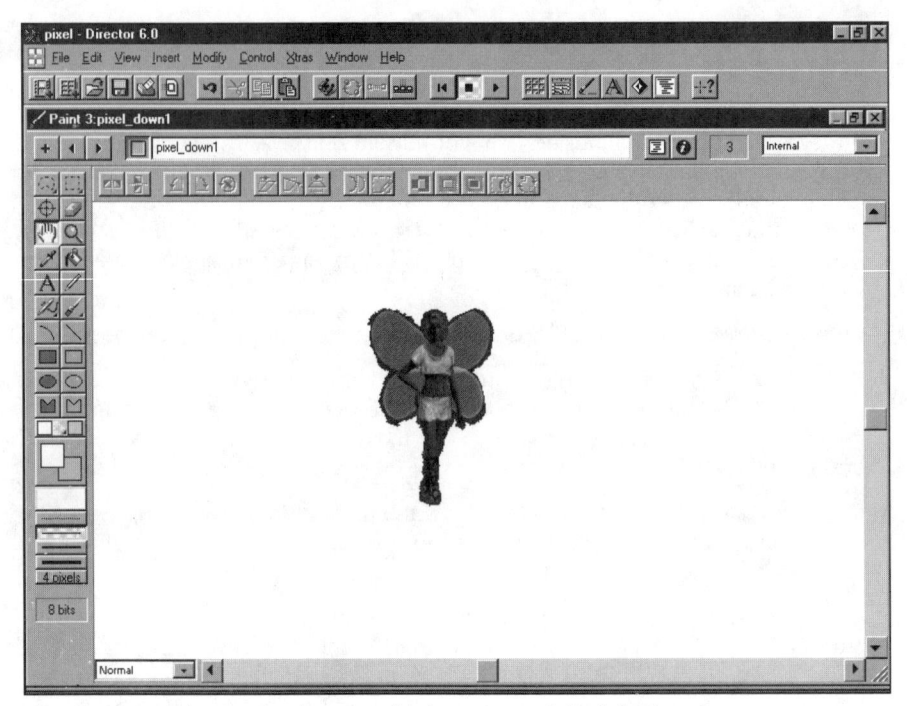

Figure 2-18: Halos can make even the best artwork look bad.

Casting Call

You've already worked a bit in Director's Cast window without a lot of explanation as to what exactly it is. In simplest terms, a *cast* is a repository of resources. It's Director's answer to integrating media with application.

Macintosh programmers have traditionally worked with a *fork* model: One section of a program contains all of the code that determines the actions of the program, and the other section of the program contains the resources (graphics, sounds, menus, dialogs, and other "pieces" of the program). Windows programmers, on the other hand, work with a *flat* model: There is no explicit process separating the code from the pictures or sounds.

When Director was initially designed, it was accepted that a multimedia program must, because of its elemental connection with media elements, provide a mechanism for storing the media and examining it quickly. In Director, this mechanism is the *cast*. A cast is a collection of individual cast members, each having a number of properties, some of which are contingent upon the media that the cast member contains.

Technically speaking, a cast member is not the media it contains. For example, if cast member 3 holds a picture and cast member 4 holds a sound, they still contain certain common properties — a name or a number for example — and can be moved about within the Cast window regardless of their differing media types. More appropriately, they can be thought of as pointers to these resources, whether the graphics and sounds are contained internally within the Director movie or are located in external files.

Moving and duplicating cast members

This distinction between cast members and media can help you understand a little better why and how you can move cast members within the Cast window. Let's say you create a number of cast members and then decide that one of them is out of place in the Cast window. (Perhaps you have accidentally created a cast member out of sequence in an animation.) You can move this out-of-place cast member to the proper position simply by dragging it over the cast member position in the Cast window and letting go. The cast member is placed in the correct slot, and every other cast member is pushed to the next cast member position.

Tip

This flexibility is, by the way, one of the reasons that you want to avoid referring to a cast member by its number, since a cast member number can be changed so unpredictably. You're much better off using names.

You can also use the standard copy, cut, and paste operations with cast members. If you select one or more cast members — holding down the Shift key to select contiguous cast members, or the Command (Ctrl) Option key to select several nonadjecent cast members — then you can copy or cut them to the Clipboard, click a new location in the cast, and paste them in.

Caution

Some care should be taken in using cut and copy, especially for cast members that are used in sprites (which most are). Sprites maintain internal references to cast members themselves, rather than to what the cast members hold. As a consequence, if you cut a cast member to the Clipboard and then paste it elsewhere, the sprite doesn't realize that the cast member no longer contains any media — and will probably end up crashing the system when it needs to draw on what it expects to be there. Usually a better choice is to move the cast member by dragging it, because it allows Director to keep track of the changes. Director automatically shifts the references because it has a clear idea of both where the cast member came from and where it's going to — which is definitely *not* the case with cutting and pasting. Essentially, you should only cut a cast member from the cast if you know for a certainty that no sprite is based on it.

Here's another way to duplicate cast members: Select the cast members that you wish to duplicate, and select Edit ⇨ Duplicate or type Command+D (Ctrl+D) to make the copies.

Note that when a cast member is duplicated, the name is also duplicated — so if you plan to use a cast member as the basis for an entire animated sequence, you may want to just use a stub name for the "base" character (for example, "wing" instead of "wing1"). This lets you rename the new cast members with a minimum of fuss and bother, by simply adding sequential numbers to the end of the stub.

Sorting cast members

As you work on your own applications, at some point you will probably discover that your cast has become unwieldy. Cast members that you've deleted leave holes in the Cast window. New cast members may end up occupying these blanks as they are filled with bitmaps, scripts, or other resources. For a small animation this isn't a major issue, but if you have more than maybe 30 cast members, the importance of keeping some sort of order for the cast escalates. A large multimedia project might have as many as forty or fifty thousand cast members, and the absence or misplacement of even one of those might be enough to crash your program.

With its Modify ⇨ Sort command, Director gives you the option of sorting selected cast members in any given cast library, or part of it. The various sorting options are summarized in Table 2-5.

Note

The Sort feature will help you organize your cast resources, but in general you should combine Sort with an aggressive naming campaign for both cast members and cast libraries.

Table 2-5
Sort Options

Option	Results
Usage in Score	Orders the cast members in the order they appear in the Score (the cast member of sprite 1 in frame 1, the cast member of sprite 2 in frame 1, and so forth). Director doesn't rely on cast order for retrieving resources, so this option won't make your movie more efficient. However, it will give you a pretty good clue about when specific cast members are called.
Media Type	Orders the cast members by media type (bitmaps, then scripts, then text members, and so on). For example, if you have three bitmaps followed by a sound followed by another bitmap, then sorting by media type will move the bitmaps together and put the sound at the end, without otherwise changing the order. This is *not* an alphabetical sort.
Name	Orders the cast members by name, in alphanumeric order. Unnamed cast members appear at the end of the list, in the order they're found in the cast.

Option	Results
Size	Orders the cast members by size, based on the number of bytes in the member, from largest to smallest. This is a handy way to determine whether a given bitmap is taking up an inordinate amount of disk space and memory.
Empty at End	Retains the current order, but removes any empty cast members from the cast selection, compacting the cast in the cast library.

You can sort any cast members that are currently selected. Selecting Modify⇨Sort from the menu will bring up the Sort dialog box (Figure 2-19), from which you can choose any of the radio button options that are listed in Table 2-5. One of the more useful techniques in sorting is to sort twice: first by alphabetical order, then by media type. This will give you blocks of alphabetically sorted bitmaps, followed by blocks of alphabetically sorted sounds, and so forth.

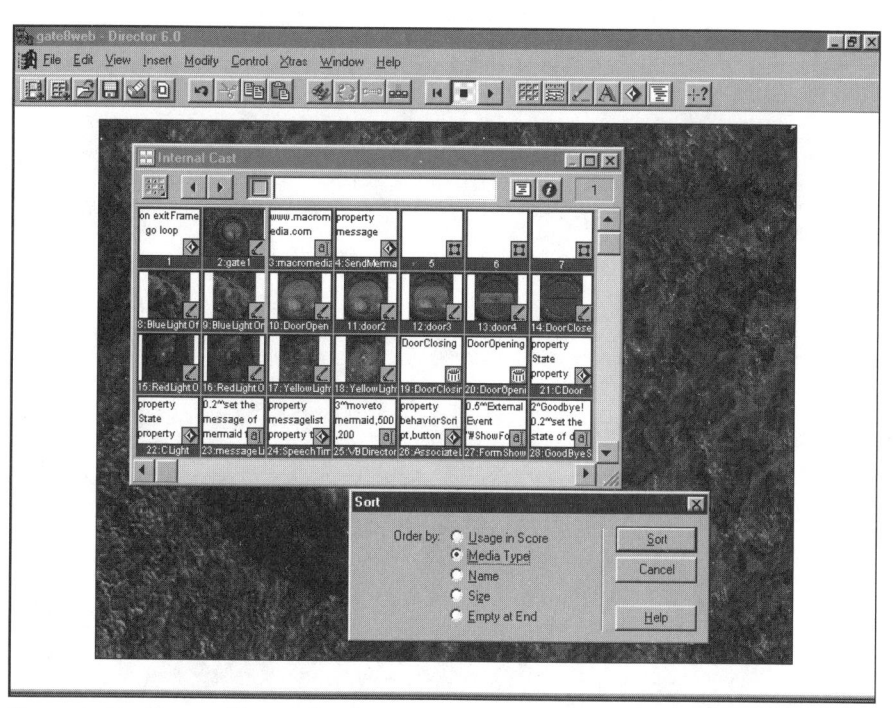

Figure 2-19: Along with an effective naming convention for your cast member, the Sort dialog will help keep your cast library in order.

Summary

Regardless of whether you import your graphics or build them from scratch, Director gives you some powerful options for integrating graphics in your productions.

- ✦ Animations form the heart of Director productions, and because of this the program is especially optimized for creating animation.
- ✦ Director includes a Paint window that can be used to create graphics.
- ✦ You can import graphics into Director and then edit them, either internally in the Paint window, or with an external media editor.
- ✦ Images are kept within cast libraries, and can be moved, sorted, and saved for later retrieval.

Of course, what you've learned about animations in this chapter is only half the battle. In Chapter 3, you will see how to put these newly created cast members into sprites that can be maneuvered across the screen.

✦ ✦ ✦

Working with the Stage, Sprites, and Score

CHAPTER 3

In This Chapter

Understanding sprites

Creating animations

Working with cast members

Using blends and inks

Writing a technical book is always a bit of a challenge, because sometimes it's necessary to hint at something you need to cover but don't want to yet in your presentation. It's that way with sprites. In Chapters 1 and 2 there were a few hints here and there about what a sprite is, but it's time now to lay the groundwork now before we can discuss sprites in detail.

Meeting Your Sprites

What exactly is a sprite? In simplest terms, a cast member becomes a sprite when you place it on the Stage. A sprite is not actually the graphic that appears in the Cast window, but rather a clone of a cast member when it's moved to the Stage. You can place multiple copies or clones of the cast member on the Stage. Changes you make to a cast member affect its associated sprite, but changes you make to a sprite do not affect the cast member. A sprite can move across the Stage and have attributes independent of its associated cast member.

Unlike the Cast window, where you can have up to 32,000 cast members in a single movie, Director only accommodates a maximum of 120 sprites on the Stage at any given time. As the number of sprites on the Stage increases, the amount of time it takes for the image or scene to render to screen increases.

Warning: Keeping the number of active sprites on the Stage to a minimum helps reduce the file size of your movie and ensures smoother playback. As the number of sprites increases, it becomes more difficult for a computer with limited resources to play your movie, and more likely that the computer will crash.

Suggestions for reducing the number of sprites on the Stage

Any Director movie contains sprites that move or are interactive, and sprites that remain in a static position. You can reduce the amount of resources required to render your scene, by incorporating into a single image sprites that don't animate. Never include buttons, fields, or scripted elements in a merged bitmap image.

For example, if you have props or other elements that are part of the background image, and other sprites don't animate behind them, you can make the props part of your background and thus reduce the number of sprites on the Stage. Even if they become part of a 640 x 480 image, it costs less in resources to load one image than to load the background plus several sprites. You can use either the Paint window or an external editor to merge the elements into a single image, and then use the Edit ⇨ Exchange Cast Members command (Command+E or Ctrl+E) to replace the background image. You can change the background image later if the elements change.

By thinking in terms of layers of activity and scenery, you'll become more adept at reducing the number of sprites on the Stage while maintaining the interactivity you want.

Each sprite occupies a *sprite channel*. Sprite channels have a specific order on the Stage, arranged from back to front. In other words, elements in channel 1 appear *behind* those in channel 2, and so forth. If you had sprites in channels 1–20, the sprite in channel 20 would appear closest to you. Sprites actually exist in a four-dimensional space. They can be positioned anywhere along the horizontal and vertical axes of the Stage, and they have a specific hierarchy that defines their distance from the viewer.

Sprites also have a life span measured in *frames*. A frame is a variable amount of time and is the smallest unit of time Director recognizes. Director maintains an internal clock that describes how often it redraws the screen. Since the actual number of frames per second can change, you can't define a frame as a specific amount of time. The concept is similar to the frames of a film. As the film progresses, each frame describes a scene that is slightly different from the previous and subsequent frames. For example, in the space of a frame, a car will move fractionally, or a neon sign will switch from on to off.

The Score in Director 6 contains a great deal of information, but its function is still the same as it was in previous versions. The Score displays each sprite's order on the Stage, its life span, and any sprite scripts you've attached to the sprite. In addition, the Score displays any effects you've placed in your movie. At first look, the Score resembles a spreadsheet. The rows represent sprite channels, and the columns represent frames (see Figure 3-1).

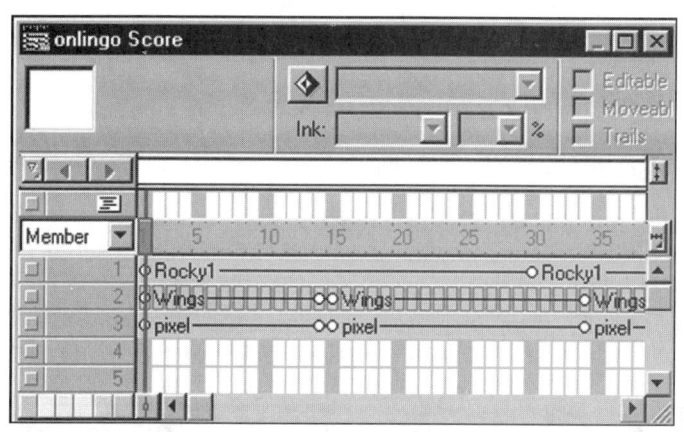

Figure 3-1: The Score resembles a spreadsheet with rows and columns.

The Score arranges the sprites from back to front in a hierarchy of sprite channels from 1 to 120, and in frames from left to right horizontally across the Score window. While this arrangement makes it easy to see and manipulate sprites using the Score, it can complicate the job of making a sprite move past other sprites toward or away from you. Let's take a closer look at how this works.

Setting the Stage

Understanding how sprites work on the Stage is one of the first steps to creating movies in Director. Director provides you with two basic methods of placing a cast member on the Stage. You can drag the cast member from the Cast window to the Stage, or you can drag it to the Score window and place it in a channel. If you drag a cast member to the Score window, the sprite of the cast member automatically appears centered on the Stage. As you drag the cast member from the Cast window, the thumbnail image of the cast member changes to a small dashed box. When you release the mouse button, the image appears on the Stage.

You can change the size of the Stage and its position in Director's main window. Normally, it's a good idea to work with the Stage centered, because it gives you a better visual sense of the space your movie occupies. Since projectors are displayed in the center of the screen, it's important to establish this mental frame of reference regarding space, during development and before you create a projector of a finished movie.

In the next exercise, you'll place a cast member on the Stage to create the backdrop for a movie. The placement of the backdrop is important, because it moves to give the illusion of scrolling.

> **Tip**
> Throughout the exercises in this chapter, you'll be reminded to save your movie. It's important that you save the movie to your hard disk, because this same movie is used again in Chapter 5.

Placing a Sprite on the Stage

On the CD-ROM

1. In Director, open the onlingo.dir movie that you created in Chapter 2. A copy of the file is on your companion CD-ROM in the exercise:ch03 (exercise\ch03) folder.

2. Select Modify ➪ Movie ➪ Properties or press Command+Shift+D (Ctrl+Shift+D) to display the Movie Properties dialog box (see Figure 3-2).

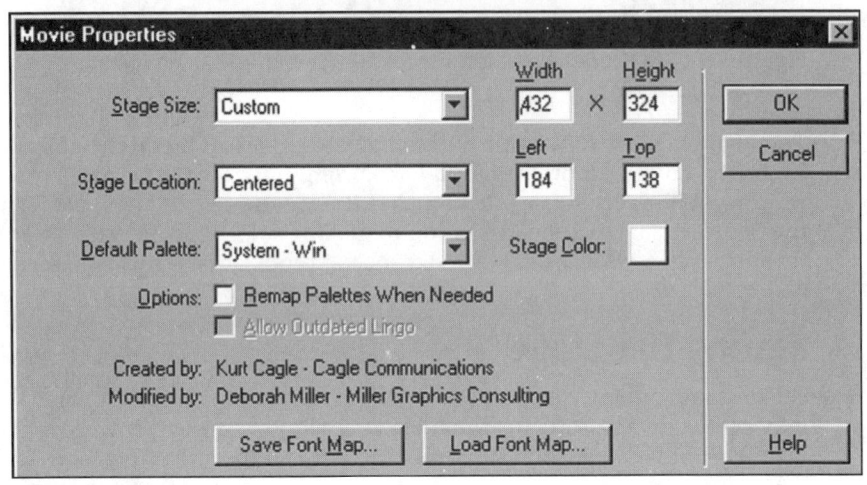

Figure 3-2: You can set a variety of movie and Stage properties in the Movie Properties dialog box.

3. In the Stage Size Width and Height boxes, set the width to **432** and the height to **324**.

4. Click the down arrow to open the Stage Location list and choose Centered.

5. Click OK to complete the operation and return to Director's main window.

6. Open the Cast window by selecting Window ➪ Cast or pressing Command+3 (Ctrl+3). If the Cast window is already open, this command closes the window. All the Window commands are toggles.

7. In the Cast window, select rocky1, and drag it onto the Stage. This is a large graphic that is over 1,000 pixels wide by 324 pixels high, and it won't fit entirely on the Stage.

8. Position the sprite on the Stage so that the upper-left corner of the sprite is flush with the upper-left corner of the Stage (see Figure 3-3). Alternatively, you can select Modify ⇨ Sprite ⇨ Properties and set the Stage Location Left and Top boxes both to 0.

9. Save your movie to your hard disk as **onlingo2.dir**.

Figure 3-3: The sprite is positioned flush against the upper-left corner of the Stage.

Congratulations, you've just created your first sprite. Take a look at the box (the Sprite Overlay) in the lower-left corner of the graphic (see Figure 3-3). This Sprite Overlay contains relevant information about the sprite, including the sprite number, the cast member that currently occupies the sprite, its location and dimensions, and script information. Clicking either the Sprite Info icon or the Cast Info icon will bring up those boxes for more information.

Tip

If you find the information box distracting, you can turn it off by selecting View ⇨ Sprite Overlay and clicking the Show Info toggle command, or pressing Command+Shift+Option+O (Ctrl+Shift+Alt+O). To make the information box visible, reselect the command. A check mark beside Show Info indicates that the information box is active and visible on the Stage.

Settling a Score

The Stage is where everything takes place. It provides you with the visual result of your actions, but it doesn't tell you much about the overall schema or organization that you're using. One way of looking at the Score is to consider it an alternate method of viewing the same movie.

To open the Score window, select Window ⇨ Score or press Command+4 (Ctrl+4). As you can see in Figure 3-4, you can tell at a glance that there is only one sprite currently on the Stage, that the sprite extends for 28 frames, and that the sprite is in channel 1.

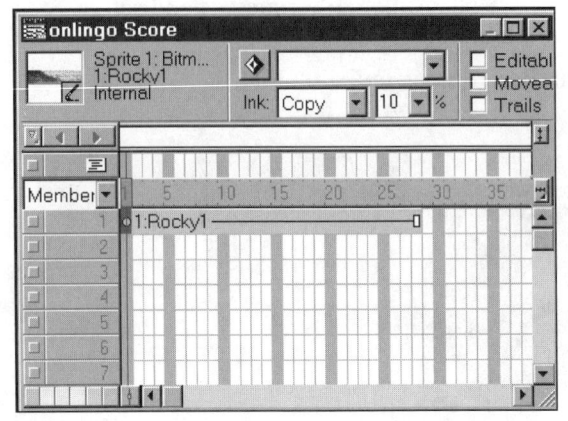

Figure 3-4: The Score shows at a glance which sprites are active on the page.

When you first start Director, the default number of sprite frames is set to 28. Every sprite you place on the Stage or in the Score window spans 28 frames initially. You can adjust the sprite interactively to span more or fewer frames by clicking the handle in the last frame and dragging it to another frame. There are times when you'll want a sprite to span a single frame. Spanning several frames allows you to specify keyframes within the span, and generally gives you some room to work. (*Keyframes* are frames that control the other frames in the sprite.)

You can choose the number of frames you want to use as the default for all your movies. This default is a matter of personal preference based upon the way you work and the types of animations you create most often. For example, if you use a lot of film loops in your movies, 28 frames will be much too long. In fact, ideally, you'll want a sprite to span a single frame while you're creating a film loop. (More information about creating film loops appears later in this chapter.) Specifying a higher number of frames, such as 60, may mean you have to scroll the view of the Score window to work on a single section of your movie. This is inconvenient; you'll spend too much time continually scrolling back and forth through your movie.

The Sprite Preferences dialog contains other choices you can make for your Score, such as having the sprite span the visible width of the Score window, or stop when it encounters a marker in the Score window.

Specifying the Default Number of Frames for a Sprite

1. Select File ➪ Preferences ➪ Sprite to display the Sprite Preferences dialog box (Figure 3-5).

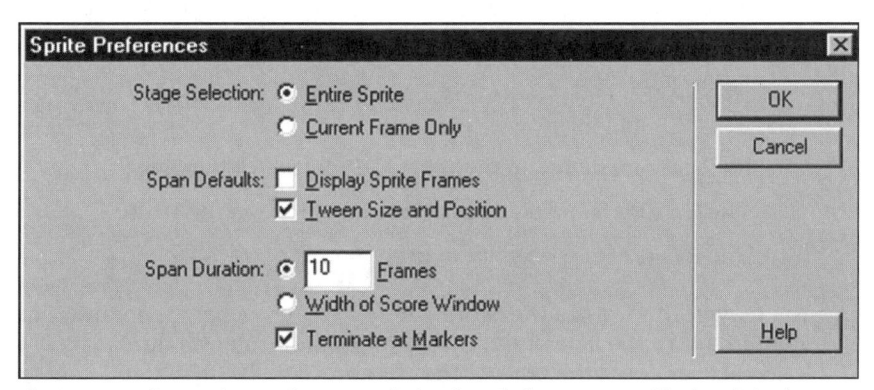

Figure 3-5: The Sprite Preferences dialog box helps you specify the default number of frames that you want a sprite to span.

2. Click the Span Duration radio button and enter the number of frames you want a sprite to span by default.

3. Click OK to complete the operation and return to Director's main window.

The span duration value you specify remains in effect from one movie to the next, until you change the value. As you work with Director, you'll discover the span duration that works best for you.

Anatomy of a sprite in Director 6

When you first create a sprite in the Score window, it has several attributes in addition to those gained from its associated cast member. Initially, a sprite that spans multiple frames has a head, body, and tail. The head (or first frame) of the sprite is a keyframe, as indicated by the large dot at the beginning of the channel. The body of a sprite is the central (tweened) portion of the sprite between the head and tail. The tail of the sprite is the end frame, which designates the end of the sprite's life span on the Stage.

When you select a sprite in the Score window, the top of the window displays information about the sprite relative to the active frame. If the sprite is a graphic element, a thumbnail of the image appears in the upper-left corner. The sprite information identifies

- The type of sprite
- The sprite's cast library
- A description of any associated behaviors or scripts
- Its x and y orientation on the screen (relative to the upper-left corner of your monitor)
- Its width and height
- Its location relative to the upper-left corner of the Stage
- The location in pixels of the right-hand side of the sprite
- The location in pixels of the bottom side of the sprite

You may need to resize the Score window to view all of the information. Just move your cursor to the side of the window until it becomes a double-headed arrow, and then click and drag the edge of the window to resize it.

Director 6's approach to sprites is different from earlier versions of the program. In previous versions, when you created a sprite in the Score window, it occupied a single frame. In order to extend the sprite to multiple frames, you needed to copy the sprite to the location where you wanted the sprite to end, and then tween between the starting and ending sprite. Although you created a tween, the in-between sprites weren't linked in any way to the starting and ending sprite.

Director 6 uses *dynamic linking* to link the tween portion of a sprite to the starting and ending frames of the sprite. When you click anywhere in the center of the sprite, the entire sprite is selected. This indicates the dynamically linked relationship of the sprite, and enables you to apply changes to the entire sprite as a unit. Dynamic linking also allows the sprite to be responsive. If you change or move either the starting or ending sprite, the rest of the sprite responds to the change. Extending a sprite has been simplified, as well, in Director 6. By clicking the tail of the sprite and selecting a new ending frame, you can extend a sprite using the Modify ⇨ Extend Sprite command.

The sprite you placed on the Stage in the last exercise is too wide for the Stage. In the following exercise you'll take advantage of a sprite's dynamic linking to extend the sprite and pan the background to the left. You could click and drag the sprite on the Stage to the left, but that would cause the image to jiggle — as if you were trying to use a video camera from a moving car on a bumpy road. Instead of dragging it, you'll use Director's Tweak feature to move the sprite. The Tweak feature enables you to move sprites with precision.

Panning a Sprite

1. Open onlingo2.dir in Director, if it's not already open. If necessary, open the Score window with Command+4 or Crtl+4.
2. In the Score window, click the tail of the rocky1 sprite in channel 1 (frame 28) to select it.
3. Hold down the Shift key and click the frame bar in frame 55 (see Figure 3-6).

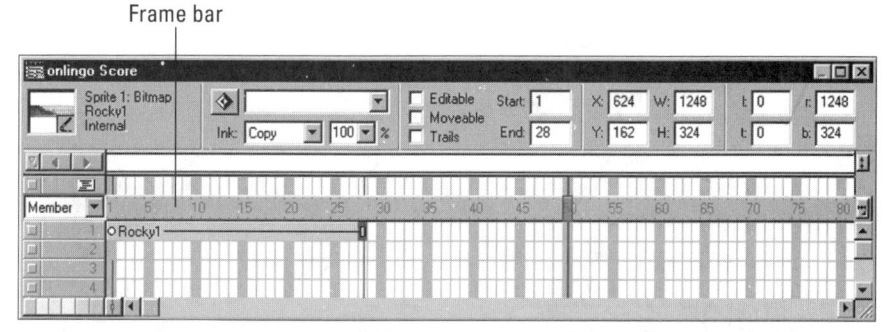

Figure 3-6: Select the tail of the sprite and the frame bar in the Score window.

4. Select Modify ⇨ Extend Sprite or press Command+B (Ctrl+B). The sprite extends to frame 55 in channel 1 of the Score window (see Figure 3-7).

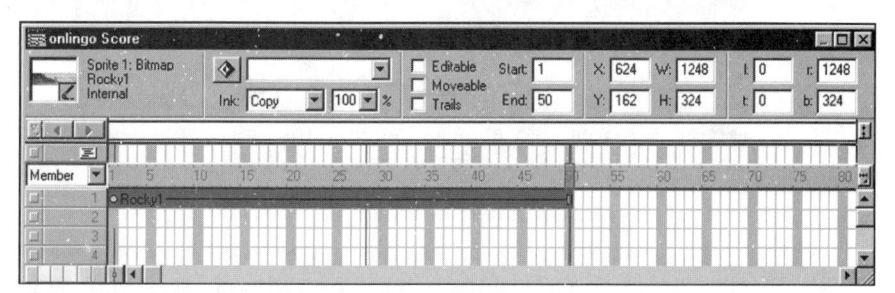

Figure 3-7: The sprite has been extended through frame 55.

5. Again, click the tail of rocky1 sprite in the Score window to select it.
6. Select Modify ⇨ Tweak or press Command+Shift+K (Ctrl+Shift+K) to display the Tweak window (Figure 3-8).

Figure 3-8: The Tweak window enables you to move sprites with precision.

7. In the Tweak window, enter **–816** (as shown in Figure 3-8) and press Enter. Next, click the Tweak button. This moves the tail of the image to the left. Note that the image on the Stage has changed, as shown in Figure 3-9.

Figure 3-9: Your view appears to pan to the right as the background moves to the left, ending in this view of the background.

8. Close the Tweak window, or drag it out of your way.

9. On the toolbar, click the Rewind button to rewind your movie; then click the Play button to test the panning background. When you're done testing, stop the movie.

10. Save the movie again as onlingo2.dir.

The animation may seem a bit jerky at this point, but for now you've created the background for the rest of your animation. You'll learn how to smooth an animation sequence in the upcoming section, "Creating a moving performance."

Take another look at Figure 3-9. A horizontal line with dots appears in the image. This line isn't visible when you play your movie, but when you stop your movie it will show up, to indicate the animation path of a selected sprite. The dots on the line are tweening stages spaced evenly along the line, between the head and tail of the sprite. A second exercise in the upcoming section shows you how to convert the tweening stages into keyframes and change the direction of an animation sequence.

Look at the Score, and you'll also notice that both the head and tail of the sprite are now keyframes. When you select the tail of a sprite and move it to animate the sprite, Director automatically converts the tail to a keyframe.

Creating a moving performance

Keyframes are critical to describing the movement of sprites in a Director movie. In the previous exercise you created a sprite with two keyframes, which basically describes linear motion. By adding keyframes to a motion path, you can describe any type of motion to give objects a realistic touch. In addition to providing realism, adding keyframes smoothes the animation sequence.

Director sees every graphic element in terms of the bounding box in which it fits. The bounding shape is always rectangular. When you place a rectangular object on the Stage, the object's background isn't an issue, since the background isn't visible. Most objects will have an irregular shape, however, so there will be areas where the white background behind the object is visible (see Figure 3-10). By default, Director applies a *copy ink* effect to cast members placed on the Stage, and the copy ink effect leaves the white background, creating this unacceptable appearance. Using other ink effects in the Score window, you can make this background invisible.

Figure 3-10: Irregularly shaped objects have a visible white background until you apply an ink effect.

Changing the Ink Effect of a Sprite

1. Open onlingo2.dir in Director, if it's not already open.
2. In the Score window, select frame 1 of channel 2. This is the beginning location for the new sprite.
3. Move the Score window out of the way to the bottom of the main window, and open the Cast window.
4. Select the cast member Pixel (cast member slot 12), and drag her onto the Stage (see Figure 3-11).

Figure 3-11: Pixel on the background in her starting position.

5. Drag the Score window back to where you can view the new sprite in channel 2. With Pixel still selected on the Stage and in the Score, close the Cast window.
6. Press the Command key (Ctrl key) and click the sprite on the Stage. A pop-up menu appears that lists Director's ink effects (see Figure 3-12).
7. Select Matte from the pop-up menu. When you release the mouse button, Pixel's background becomes transparent.
8. Save the movie as **onlingo3.dir**.

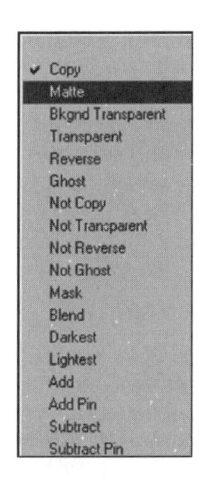

Figure 3-12: Pressing the Command key (Ctrl key) while clicking a sprite displays the ink pop-up menu.

Tip

Another way to apply inks to selected sprites is by clicking the down arrow (called a *pop-up list button*) next to Ink in the Score window, and selecting an ink.

The next step in building the onlingo movie is to select the character Pixel on the Stage and create the animation path she follows. By placing keyframes at points along the animation path, you can modify the animation path to describe an arcing (or, in Pixel's case, flying) path. When you add a keyframe to a sprite in the Score window, the sprite's appearance changes. As shown in Figure 3-13, a dot is added for each keyframe, making it easy to idenitify the keyframes of your movie.

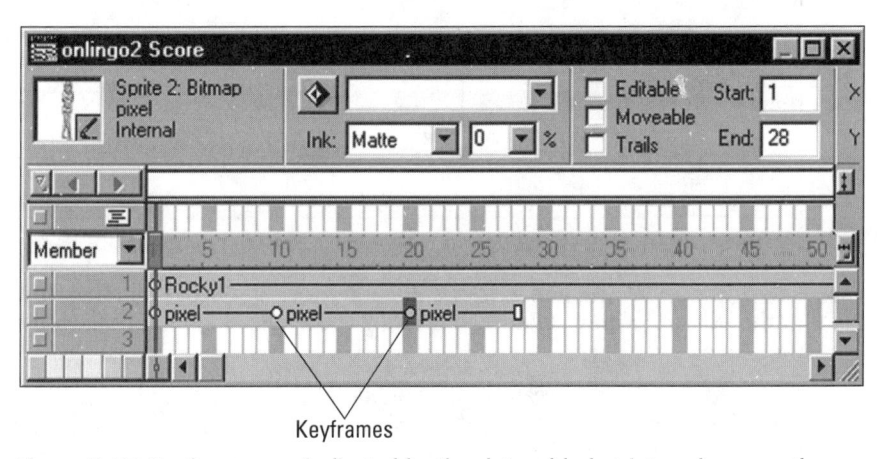

Figure 3-13: Keyframes are indicated by the dots added at intervals across the span of the sprite.

The placement of keyframes affects the speed of an animation sequence. If they are placed at regular intervals spanning the length of the sprite in the Score window, the speed remains consistent. You can use this to your advantage to create motion that seems to slow in places and speed up in others. For example, if you add a keyframe five frames from the start of a sprite and then put the sprite into a substantially different position on the Stage, the sprite appears to jump rapidly to the new location. Conversely, if you increase the number of frames between the keyframes but decrease the distance the object moves on Stage in that span, the object appears to move slowly to that location.

Creating a Nonlinear Motion Path

1. Open onlingo3.dir in Director, if it's not already open. The movie is available on the CD-ROM in the exercise:ch03 (exercise\ch03) folder.

2. Open the Score window, and scroll until frame 60 is visible on the stage.

3. Drag the tail of the sprites in channels 1 and 2 to frame 60.

4. While pressing the Control key, click the sprite in channel 2 at frame 20 (for PC users, right-click the sprite), and select Insert Keyframe. Repeat for frames 40 and 60. The keyframes are indicated by dots in their respective frames (see Figure 3-14).

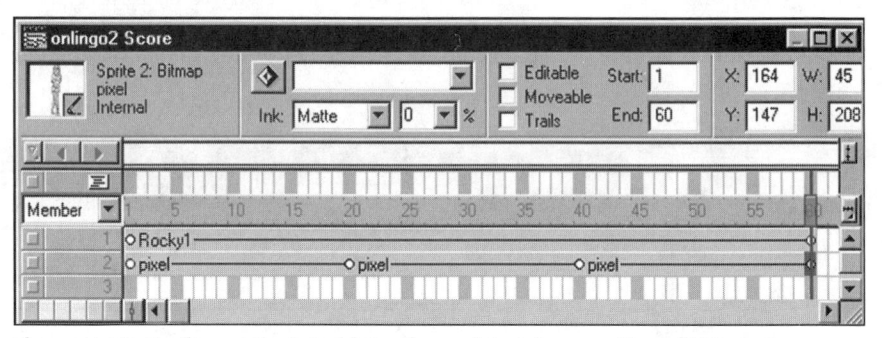

Figure 3-14: Keyframes inserted into channel 2 at frames 40 and 60.

5. Select the cell at channel 2, frame 20, and move the Score window down to the bottom of the screen and out of the way. Pixel appears selected on the Stage.

6. Click and drag Pixel upward to the middle of the Stage (see Figure 3-15). Note that a line of dots tracks the movement of the sprite. The small dots are tween frames; the keyframes are indicated by the large dots at both ends of the animation path.

7. Move the Score window back to where it's visible, and select the cell at channel 2, frame 40.

Figure 3-15: Pixel in her new position in the middle of the Stage.

8. Drag the Score window out of the way, and drag Pixel to the left on the Stage. When you drag Pixel, you create a looping animation path (see Figure 3-16). Pixel's position on Stage is actually at the same location in both keyframes 0 and 60.

Figure 3-16: When Pixel is dragged to the left, a looping animation path is created.

9. Save your movie as **onlingo4.dir**.
10. Rewind your movie, and click the Play button on the toolbar to view the animation sequence.

Animation is mostly a matter of illusion. In the preceding exercise, you created a looping animation path that moves up, to the left, and back to the sprite's original location. Pixel, however, appears to move to the right, winding up back on the beach. The illusion occurs because the background is also moving to the left at the same time as Pixel. Since the background moves a much greater distance, this gives Pixel the illusion of moving in the other direction.

At this point, the animation sequence moves at a consistent pace. Pixel is an ethereal creature, however, not a superheroine. As such, she should float rather than jolt to her beach landing. In the next exercise, you'll adjust the keyframes in the Score window and in the Sprite Tweening dialog box, to change Pixel's landing speed. When you move a keyframe, the intermediate tween frames are evenly redistributed between the keyframes on either side. The Sprite Tweening dialog box enables you to specify settings that further refine the motion of an animation sequence.

Adjusting the Speed of Animation Change

1. Open onlingo4.dir in Director, if it's not already open.
2. Open the Score window.
3. Click the keyframe in channel 2, frame 20, and drag it to frame 10.
4. Click the keyframe in channel 2, frame 40, and drag it to frame 30.
5. With the keyframe in channel 2, frame 30 still selected, select Modify ⇨ Sprite ⇨ Tweening or press Command+Shift+B (Ctrl+Shift+B) to display the Sprite Tweening dialog box (Figure 3-17). A thumbnail of the animation path appears in the upper-left corner of the dialog box.

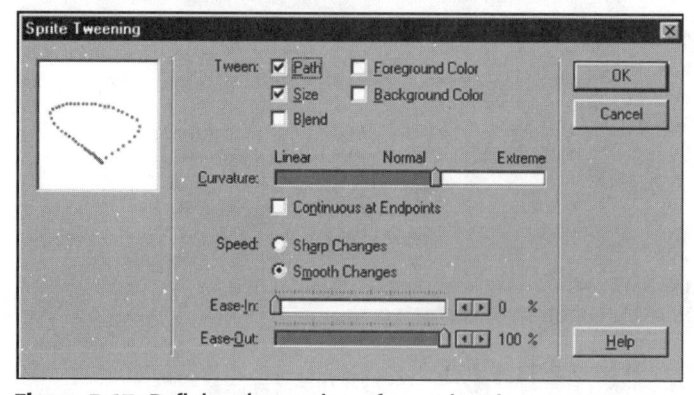

Figure 3-17: Refining the motion of an animation sequence

6. Click the Smooth Changes radio button to alter the motion to halfway between Normal and Extreme.

7. Move the Ease-Out slider to 100%, and adjust the Curvature setting to round out the direction changes of the path. The thumbnail in the upper-left corner displays the changes you make.

8. Click OK to complete the operation and return to Director's main window.

9. Save your movie as **onlingo5.dir**.

10. Rewind your movie, and click the Play button on the toolbar to play the animation sequence.

The Ease-In and Ease-Out values tell Director what percentage of the tween frames should be devoted to increasing or decreasing the speed of the path, respectively. The higher the ease rate, the more gradual the acceleration or deceleration. By increasing the Ease-Out rate to 100%, you specified the maximum deceleration rate for the path, thus slowing Pixel's landing to a float. Increasing the curvature and specifying smooth changes modified the path slightly to smooth the animation sequence.

Keyframes and tweening

Despite all the fancy bells and whistles, Director is at its heart an animation program, deriving a great deal of its architecture from traditional animation methods. The terms *keyframe* and *tweening* are cases in point.

In traditional animation, a *keyframe* is an animation cell (or image) that is drawn by an artist for setting a pose or a mood in an animation sequence. These keyframes typically occur at points where action changes. For example, in order to be convincing, Pixel's flight could be broken into several keyframes: standing, hunching down, preparing to spring, the final shot of her spring as she leaves the ground, a flying pose up, turning to bank, preparing to land, compressing as she lands, and recovering. In theory, the keyframes should be able to tell the whole story.

Tween cells, on the other hand, are the intermediate steps added to create smooth movement — changes in position from one keyframe to the next. Tween cells can also be used as intermediate steps for fades, color changes, and other effects.

Extending, splitting, and joining sprites

The way the onlingo2 scene is currently set up, Pixel takes off immediately at the beginning of the movie. It would be nice to have her pause before she springs into flight, to establish her presence in a staging shot. However, there's no way of changing the existing sprite so that she just stands there. The best way to create this staging shot is to add another sprite to channel 2 and then join it to the existing sprite.

Joining Sprites

1. Open onlingo2.dir in Director, if it's not already open.
2. Open the Score window and scroll until frame 75 is visible.
3. While holding down the Shift key, click the sprites in channels 1 and 2 to select them. Click in the middle of each sprite to select the entire sprite.
4. Drag the selected sprites to the right, so that they end in frame 75. The first 15 frames of channels 1 and 2 should now be empty (see Figure 3-18).

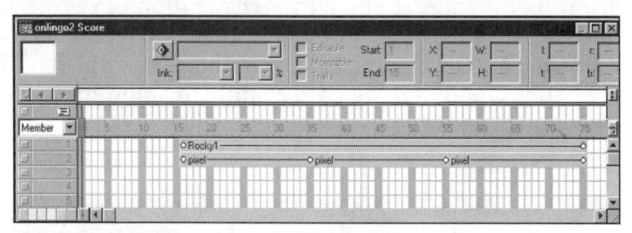

Figure 3-18: The sprites in channels 1 and 2 have been moved over to leave the first 15 frames of both channels empty.

5. Deselect the sprites, and then hold down the Command (Ctrl) key and select the first frame of the sprites in channels 1 and 2 — frame 16. Only the beginning frames of the two sprites should be selected. Press Command+C (Ctrl+C) to copy them to the Scrapbook (Clipboard).
6. Select channel 1, frame 1 and press Command+V (Ctrl+V) to paste the sprites. They appear in channels 1 and 2, as shown in Figure 3-19.

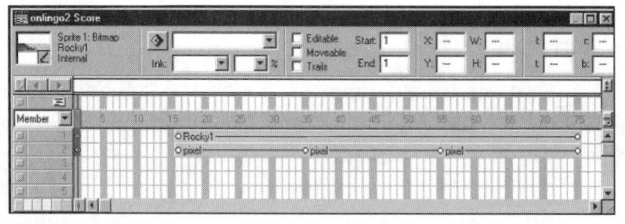

Figure 3-19: The sprites have been pasted into channels 1 and 2, frame 1 of the Score window.

7. With the sprites still selected, hold down the Shift key and click the frame bar at frame 15, and then select Modify⇨Extend Sprite or press Command+B (Ctrl+B). The sprites are extended through frame 15 (Figure 3-20).

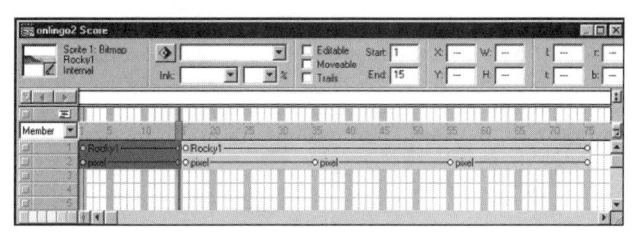

Figure 3-20: The sprites in channels 1 and 2 are extended from frame 1 through frame 15.

8. Hold down the Shift key and click both of the sprites in channel 1 to select them. Alternatively, you can select the entire channel by clicking in the gray area immediately to the left of the channel number 1.

9. Select Modify⇨Join Sprites or press Command+J (Ctrl+J) to join the two selected sprites.

10. Repeat steps 8 and 9 for the sprites in channel 2.

11. Save your movie as **onlingo.dir**.

12. Rewind your movie, and click the Play button on the toolbar to view your movie.

Joining sprites makes it possible to deal with sprites as a single unit. This is useful when you need to move the contents of one channel to another, because it reduces the possibility of associated sprites being separated in the Score window. You can also split sprites at keyframes. The ability to split sprites makes it possible to create the illusion of a sprite's becoming closer or farther away from the viewer.

For example, you could create the illusion of Pixel appearing at the beginning from behind the rocks, moving to her staging location, and then flying to the beach. To create this illusion, you would split the background and Pixel sprites near the beginning of the movie, and swap the channels occupied by the small split sections. In other words, a small part of Pixel would be in channel 1, while the rest of her sprite was in channel 2. The inverse would be true for the background sprite. A small part of the background sprite would be in channel 2, and most of the background sprite would be in channel 1 (see Figure 3-21).

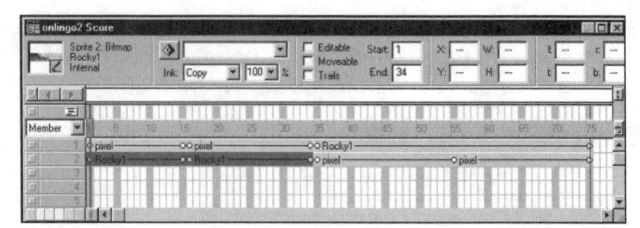

Figure 3-21: Splitting sprites enables you to change their channel, without affecting their motion path.

When you split a sprite, each section of the split retains the motion path that fell within that span of frames. This makes it easy to bring sprites closer or farther away without affecting any motion path that's been assigned to them.

Casting Call: Creating Animations

Part of any convincing animation involves the user's perception and expectation of reality. For example, in the previous exercises, you created an animation sequence in which the character Pixel flew from one scene to the next, landing on a beach. Although this is not a bad animation sequence, it lacks elements of reality that would make it more convincing. Pixel is somewhat rigid. She doesn't crouch to launch into flight, but rather maintains her model's pose throughout the sequence. Nothing indicates that she's flying, let alone how she's managing to fly, other than her movement across the Stage.

Adding elements to a movie that lend reality to an animation sequence involves creating a collection of cast members that describe motion. In the cartooning industry, the creation of these cast members is called *cel animation*. Each subsequent image in the collection is slightly different from the previous image. As the sequence plays, an image replaces the previous image at a speed that tricks the *mind's eye* into mentally drawing the intermediate steps; this creates the illusion of smooth movement. The trick to creating a successful sequence is twofold: First the sequence has to have enough images to produce the desired effect. Secondly, the images depend upon precise alignment known as *registration* to complete the effect.

In Pixel's case, adding flapping wings would improve her credibility as a creature of flight. It's a relatively simple task to create the wings images and ensure their correct registration, but you're going to run into a problem. The number of frames required to make Pixel's wings move realistically will exceed the number of frames in your movie. The result is that the wings will animate too slowly to be convincing.

If you extend the frames of your movie to allow for the animation of the wings, you also need to increase the number of frames for the other sprites. This only serves to make the motion of the entire animation sequence more ponderous.

Fortunately, Director provides a solution for making the wings animate more authentically. The solution is to create the animation sequence of the wings separately from the rest of the movie, and then covert them into a film loop. By placing the film loop of the wings into the Score window, the animation sequence is more believable.

Getting your cast members ready

Creating the cast members for a film loop requires that you transform a bitmap. You can transform bitmaps in the Paint window or in a third-party imaging application. The advantage of transforming bitmaps in the Paint window is that you can automate much of the process by using the Auto-Distort command. Director provides a variety of tools in the Paint window for transforming bitmaps. As shown in Table 3-1, these include stretching, scaling, skewing, flipping, and rotating the bitmap to change its orientation or manipulate its overall shape.

In addition to the transformation effects that are available using the toolbar buttons in the Paint window, you can also scale and stretch bitmaps using the Marquee selection tool. In the next exercise, you'll create the various stages of Pixel's wings, using Auto-Distort.

Note Don't confuse transforming bitmaps in the Paint window with the Transform Bitmap command found in the Modify menu. Although you can perform some of the same functions with both of them, transforming bitmaps in the Paint window is a different process.

Table 3-1
Transforming Bitmaps

Button	Action	Description
	Flip Horizontal	Flips the selected image horizontally.
	Flip Vertical	Flips the selected image vertically.
	Rotate Left	Rotates the selected image 90° counterclockwise.
	Rotate Right	Rotates the selected image 90° clockwise.
	Free Rotate	Enables you to rotate the selected image as desired.
	Skew	Enables you to skew the selected image as desired.
	Warp	Enables you to distort the selected image by changing the length of the sides.

(continued)

Button	Action	Description
		Table 3–1 *(continued)*
	Perspective	Applies perspective effects to a selected image.
	Smooth	Softens or dithers the edges of the selected artwork by adding pixels of blended color to the artwork's edges, giving the fill a smoother appearance.
	Trace Edges	Creates an outline around the edges of the selected artwork. The outline is the same color as the selected line, if the line is a solid color. If the original line is multicolored, an outline is created for each section of the line. Repeated use of this effect adds multiple outlines, creating a ripple effect. The Fill of the object traced is not copied.
	Invert	Reverses the colors of the selected area. For 2-, 4-, and 8-bit cast members, the inverted color is the color at the opposite end of the palette; e.g., in an 8-bit palette, color 2 is inverted as color 254. For 16- and 32-bit cast members, a true RGB complement of each color is shown. For black-and-white graphics, black changes to white and vice versa.
	Lighten	Increases the brightness (which has the effect of lightening) of anything in the selection rectangle.
	Darken	Reduces the brightness (which has the effect of darkening) of the selected artwork.
	Fill	Fills a selected area with the current foreground color and pattern. This gets the same result as using the Paint Bucket tool.
	Switch Colors	Changes every pixel that is the current foreground color to the current background color. Note: This command only works for images of 8-bit color depth or less.

Using Auto-Distort to generate cast members

If you drop a tennis ball to the ground, it will stay perfectly round until it hits the ground. At that point, however, it doesn't simply change direction. The energy of the collision distorts the ball, making the ball flatter along its direction of motion and spreading it out along the other two axes. As the ball rebounds, it regains its shape.

This principle has been known to animators for years as *squash and stretch*. A character preparing for a leap doesn't just jump up; the body has to crouch to tighten the muscles of the legs, then releases that tension as she stretches up into the sky. Director can be used to create those intermediate steps, using Auto-Distort. Any animation that requires a change in the dimensions of a graphic over several cast members is a prime candidate for the Auto-Distort technique.

For example, let's continue to work with the Pixel we've been drawing. So far, Pixel is without wings. We want to animate those independently by creating a film loop. Since the wings have been drawn separately, we can create the illusion of the wings flapping by shrinking them horizontally and using Auto-Distort to create the intermediate cast members.

Creating an Animation Sequence Using Auto-Distort

1. Open onlingo6.dir in Director, if it's not already open.

2. Open the Cast window by selecting Window ⇨ Cast or pressing Command+3 (Ctrl+3).

3. Before creating an animation sequence with Auto-Distort, you need to create space in the Cast window for the new cast members. Later, it'll be important to have all the wing cast members in adjacent cast member slots. Click on cast member slot 37 to select it (it's immediately after the last slot that has a cast member). Then hold down the Shift key and click cast member slot 43. When all seven slots are selected, click and drag them until they're over cast member slot 3 — and drop them right in! You now have seven empty cast member slots between Wings1 in slot 2, and the "On Lingo" text cast member in slot 10.

4. Double-click the cast member Wings1 to open it in the Paint window.

5. Click the Marquee selection tool, and hold down the mouse button briefly to display the pop-up menu. Select Shrink from the menu.

6. In the Paint window, click and drag to create a rectangular bounding box that completely surrounds the wings. When you release the mouse button, the wings will appear selected, with the bounding box hugging the maximum dimensions of the wings (see Figure 3-22).

7. Holding down the Command key (Ctrl key), click one side of the bounding box and drag toward the center of the wings. Reduce the width of the wings to approximately one-fourth of the original width (see Figure 3-23).

8. With the wings still selected, select Xtras ⇨ Auto Distort to display the Auto-Distort dialog box (Figure 3-24).

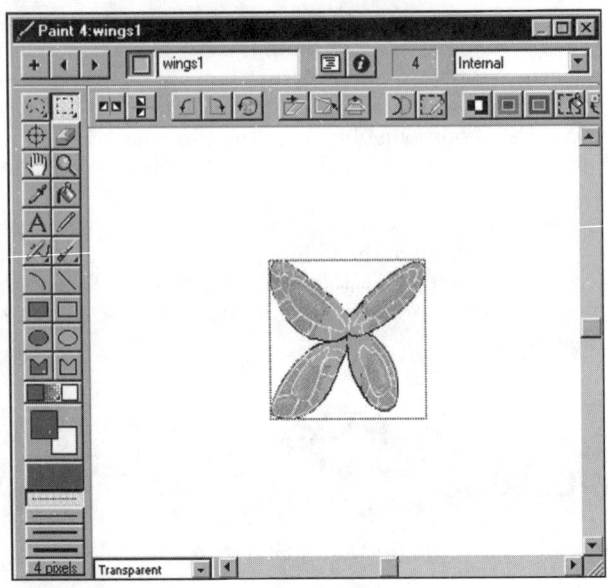

Figure 3-22: The wings have been selected with the Marquee selection tool set to Shrink.

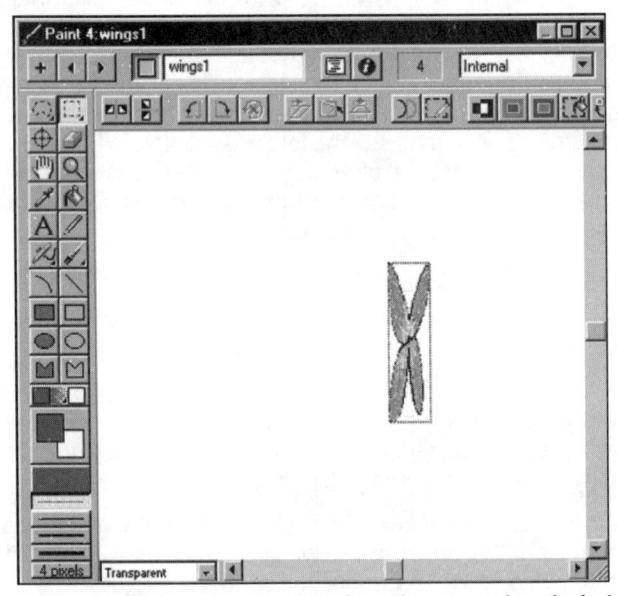

Figure 3-23: The wings, reduced to about one-fourth their original width

Figure 3-24: Telling Auto-Distort how many cast members you want Director to automatically generate

9. Enter **6** as the number of new cast members you want to generate, and click the Begin button. In a few moments, Director generates the cast members you've requested and places them in the Cast window.

10. Close the Paint window, and notice that in the Cast window the new wings now fill all but one of the empty cast member slots. Later you'll use the new "wing" cast members to create a film loop in the empty cast member slot 9.

11. Save the movie as **onlingo7.dir.**

12. Once Director is finished creating the new cast members, they appear in the Cast window with the same name as the original cast member. This can be confusing, causing you to make the wrong choices when you refer to a specific cast member in a script. It's a good idea to rename the new members. To do this, click a cast member to display the name at the top of the Cast window, and rename the new cast members as **Wing2**, **Wing3**, and so on.

13. Save the movie again as onlingo7.dir.

> **Tip:** When a script specifies a cast member in the Cast window, Director searches the Cast for the correct cast member. If multiple cast members with the same name are found, the program uses the first instance of the cast member. This might not be the cast member you intended to use, in which case the results might be less than desirable. Giving each cast member a unique name prevents this problem from occurring.

Onion skinning and registration

Traditional animators have long relied upon onion skinning to create animations. *Onion skinning* derives its name from the strong translucent paper traditional animators use to create animation cells. Onion skin allows the animator to view images below the image in progress. This enables the animator to faithfully reproduce the image, while adding the slight variation necessary to create a smooth animation. A successful animation requires many sequential frames, each slightly different from its predecessor, to create realistic movement.

Note: To give you an example of the quantity of images involved in an animation sequence, consider that the average cartoon animation plays at 15 frames per second (fps). One minute of animation requires 900 frames. The original version of Snow White was approximately 82 minutes long, or 73,800 frames! (They needed a computer.)

Using Director's Onion Skin window

Like traditional animation, the ability to create keyframes and tween frames is at the heart of animation in Director. After the Onion Skin window first made its appearance in Director 5, the process of creating realistic movement became immensely easier. When you have a cast member open in the Paint window, the Onion Skin window lets you view up to 99 cast members, both preceding and following the active cast member. The active cast member appears normally in the Paint window. Each successive cast member appears gradually fainter as its order in the Cast window becomes more distant from the active image (see Figure 3-25).

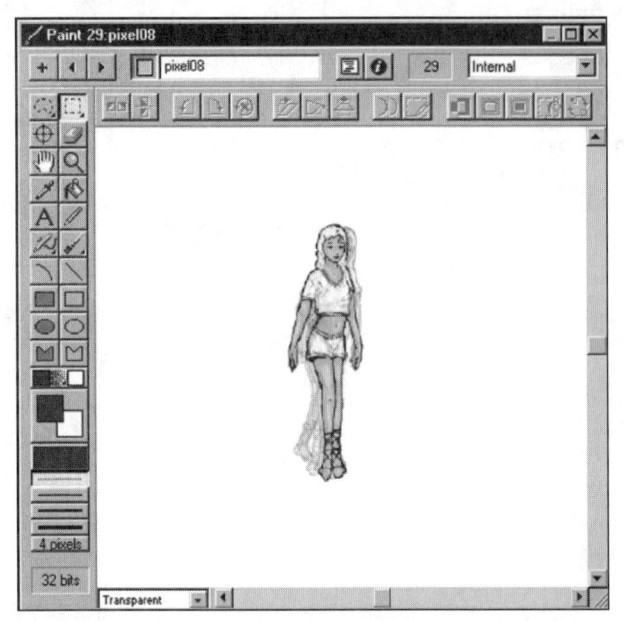

Figure 3-25: Cast members appear fainter as their distance from the active image in the Paint window increases, as determined by their order in the Cast window.

The Onion Skin window helps you create new cast members that differ slightly from their predecessors, and to align graphic elements by setting their registration points. Open the Onion Skin window now by selecting View ⇨ Onion Skin. Notice that the buttons in the window are grayed out. The Onion Skin window only becomes active when the Paint window is open and onion skinning is enabled (see Figure 3-26).

When the Onion Skin window is active, you can specify the number of preceding and subsequent cast members you want to view. You can also specify a background image upon which to base subsequent cast members and track the background. Table 3-2 describes the function of each of the buttons in the Onion Skin window.

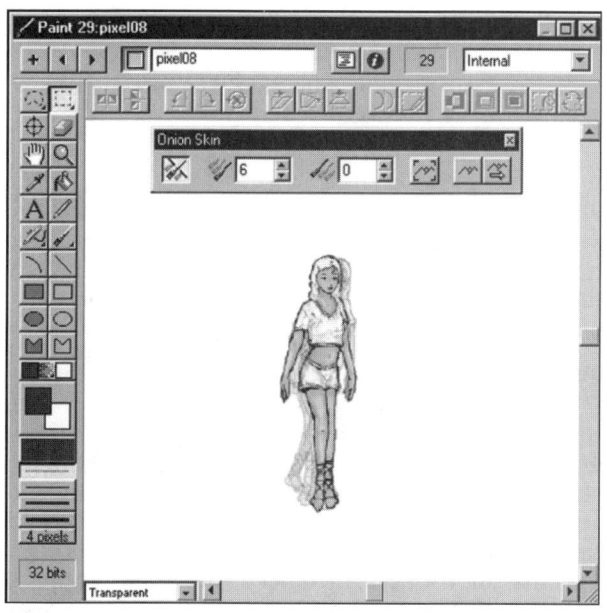

Figure 3-26: Once the Paint window is open and onion skinning enabled, the buttons in the Onion Skin window become active.

Table 3-2
Onion-Skinning Functions

Button	Action	Description
	Toggle Onion Skinning	Turns onion skinning on and off
6	Preceding Cast Members	Specifies how many cast members you want to be visible *before* the active image
6	Following Cast Members	Specifies how many cast members you want to be visible *after* the active image

(continued)

Table 3-2

Button	Action	Description
	Set Background	Sets the current image in the Paint window as the background image
	Show Background	Hides or displays the active background image you specified
	Track Background	Registers, tracks, and maintains the relative position in the Cast window of the active foreground image and background image, updating the background image as needed

There's more to this small window than meets the eye: It provides the tools to make sequential animation much easier, by enabling you to control the display in the Paint window. You can readjust the settings in the Onion Skin window as you work. The changes you make are reflected immediately in the Paint window.

A word about background tracking

Background tracking is one of the most useful yet least understood features of the Onion Skin window. Once a background image is specified and you change to another cast member as the foreground image, clicking the Track Background button registers the relative positions of both cast members in the Cast window. If you change to another foreground cast member, the background image changes to maintain the same relative position in the Cast window. For example, say you set the active background image as cast member 10. With cast member 13 active, if you click the Track Background button Director will register the relative positions of the cast members. If you then display cast member 15 in the Paint window, cast member 12 will be displayed as the visible background when Show Background is enabled.

Tracking the background image is useful when you need to create keyframe cast members, because you can set the Onion Skin window to display only the keyframes. By setting the background image as one keyframe and then turning on tracking while displaying another keyframe, you can skip displaying the images in between the two images by specifying 0 cast members in both the Preceding and Following boxes. Note that for this method to work, you must enable Show Background.

In the following exercise, you'll work with Pixel to create tween frames for the animation sequence, giving the character more life. The base images to create the animation sequence are in the onlingo2.dir Cast window. Open onlingo2.dir in Director, if it's not already open, and display the Cast window by selecting Window ⇨ Cast. Scroll down through the Cast window to view Pixel1 through Pixel8. Notice that two cast member spaces have been left between each pair of the images. By working with registration in the Paint window, you will create the additional cast members to fill those spaces. When selecting a registration point for cast members, try to choose a location that remains static from one image to the next.

> **Tip**
>
> By default, Director sets the registration at the center point of a bitmap. If you change the registration point and later want to reset it to the center, open the bitmap in the Paint window and double-click the Registration tool.

Using Registration to Create Tween Cast Members

> **On the CD-ROM**
>
> For this exercise, you need the onlingo7.dir movie that you created in the last exercise, or from the companion CD-ROM in the exercise:ch03 (exercise\ch03) folder.

1. With onlingo7.dir open, double-click Pixel01 in the cast window to open the image in the Paint window.

2. Select the Registration tool from the Paint window toolbar, and click Pixel's navel to set the registration point (see Figure 3-27). Use the Zoom tool, if needed, to ensure accurate placement of the registration point. For the first few images, her navel will be the only point that remains consistently in the same location.

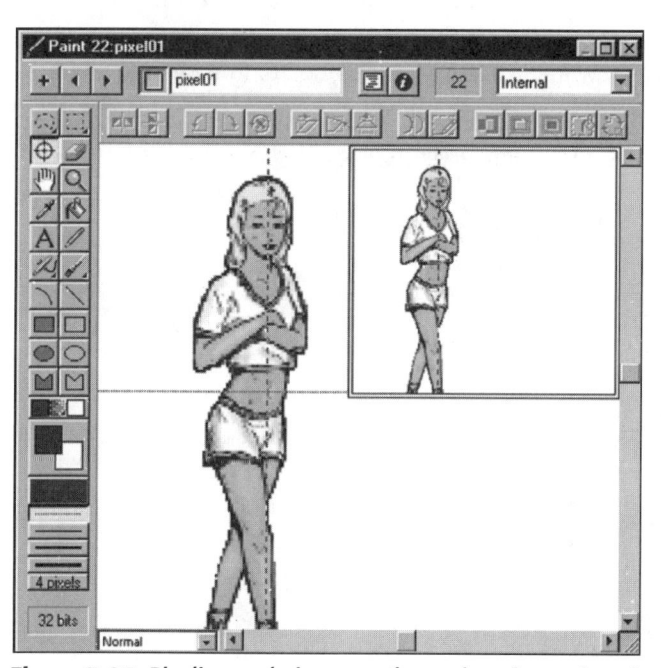

Figure 3-27: Pixel's navel gives you the registration point of the first cast member in the animation sequence.

3. Click the Next Cast Member button to move to the next view of Pixel. Note that Director skips blank cast member slots and moves on to the next graphic image it finds in the Cast window.

4. Using the Registration tool, click to set the registration point at Pixel02's navel.

5. Repeat steps 3 and 4 for the remaining six views of Pixel. You will be moving some of these registration points again slightly later on, but right now you are establishing a starting point for the registration of the cast members.

6. In the Paint window, click the Previous Cast Member button until Pixel01 is redisplayed in the Paint window.

7. From the Director menu, select View ⇨ Onion Skin to display the Onion Skin window.

8. Click the Toggle Onion Skinning button in the Onion Skin window, the on/off toggle, to turn on the onion-skinning feature. Set the Preceding Cast Members value to 3, and the Following Cast Members value to 2.

9. With Pixel01 visible in the Paint window, press Command+D (Ctrl+D) to duplicate Pixel01 as a new cast member. In the cast member name box at the top of the Paint window, rename Pixel01 to **Pixel01b**.

10. Using the Marquee selection tool, set to Shrink, select Pixel1b and press the right-arrow key twice on your keyboard, to move the character two pixels to the right. Press the down-arrow key twice to move her two pixels down. This changes the registration slightly, to create an intermediate step between Pixel01 and Pixel02 (see Figure 3-28).

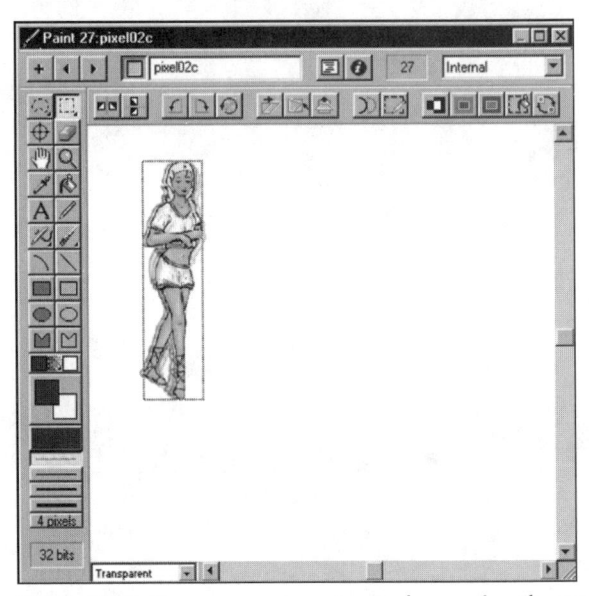

Figure 3-28: You can move cast members using the cursor arrow keys on your keyboard to create intermediate steps between images.

Note: When creating intermediate cast members, onion skinning enables you to see previous and subsequent cast members, so that you can use them as a guide.

11. Press Command+D (Ctrl+D) again to duplicate Pixel01b and create a new cast member. Rename the new cast member **Pixel01c**.

12. Repeat step 10 to move Pixel down and to the right, creating the final intermediate stage between Pixel01 and Pixel02.

13. Repeat steps 9 and 10 to create new cast members in cast member slots 26–27, 29–30, 32–33, 35–36, 38–39, 41–42, and 44–45. Each pair of empty cells should be filled with a duplicate cast member based on the version of Pixel in the cell just prior to the blank cells.

14. When done, close the Paint window and save your movie as **onlingo8.dir**.

By adjusting the number of preceding and subsequent cast members in the Onion Skin window, you can use the view in the Paint window to adjust the registration of successive cast members. As shown in the preceding exercise, you Marquee-select the successive cast members, duplicate them, and adjust the registration to make Pixel crouch and then spring up into the air. In reality, you are changing the registration, by moving the cast member in relation to the registration point you set earlier.

Another way to reset the registration points is to use the Registration tool. Unless you have a very steady hand, though, using the Registration tool to adjust the registration in small amounts is difficult. You can also modify the registration on the Stage, much as you can in the Paint window, by selecting the sprite and using the cursor arrows to move it. Setting the registration on the Stage doesn't allow you to concurrently view preceding and following cast members, as you can in the Paint window. In this situation, where you are moving the registration slightly, it's easier to perform the task in the Paint window.

Tip: While onion skinning is enabled, you don't turn it off if you close the Onion Skin window Once onion skinning is turned on with the on/off toggle in the Onion Skin window, it remains available while the Paint window is active. Toggling the Onion Skin window off is useful if you have a lot of windows open and need more screen real estate. To disable onion skinning, you need to reopen the Onion Skin window, and click the Toggle Onion Skinning button.

Once you've created and registered the cast members for the animation sequence, you're ready to place them in your movie. Like the series of images you created for the flapping wings, it's easier to place a large number of successive cast members in your movie as a film loop.

In the next exercise, you'll create the film loop for Pixel and then repeat the steps to create a film loop of the wings. You don't need to set the registration for the wings, because when Auto-Distort creates cast members, Director automatically sets the registration at the default centered location for each successive cast member. Since the wings themselves don't change their position relative to Pixel, the center registration point is ideal for this type of animation.

Working with film loops

With film loops, you can replace several cast members with a single cast member. In addition to creating smoother animations that span fewer frames, film loops also help you keep the Score tidy and compact, thereby reducing the file size of your movie.

Creating a film loop isn't difficult, but it is somewhat awkward. Film loops are generated from the Score window, so you need to temporarily move the cast members to an empty sprite channel in the Score window. The move is temporary because after you create the film loop, you no longer need the cast members in the Score window and will need to remove them.

Creating a Film Loop

1. Open onlingo8.dir in Director, if it's not already open.
2. In the Cast window, select Pixel01. Then press the Shift key and click the last cast member in the sequence, Pixel08c.
3. In the Score window, click the first frame in an empty channel.
4. Select Modify ⇨ Cast to Time. Director places the entire sequence into the Score window as sprites (see Figure 3-29). Access the pop-up ink menu and choose Matte.

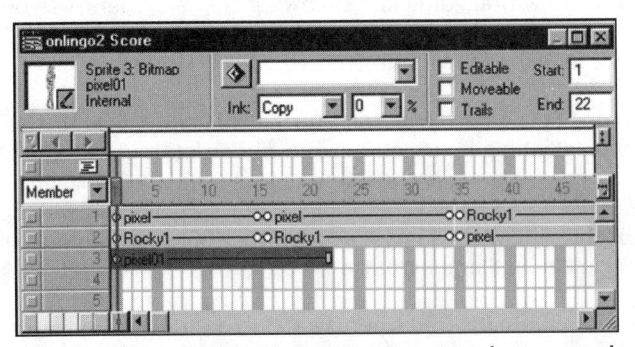

Figure 3-29: Using the Cast to Time command, you can place selected cast members sequentially into the Score window.

Note: When Director places cast members in the Score in response to Modify ⇨ Cast to Time, the order in which the cast members appear in the Cast window is used to determine their placement in the Score. Be sure the cast members are in the desired sequence *before* you execute Cast to Time.

5. With the sprites still selected, select Insert ⇨ Film Loop. In a few moments, Director prompts you to name your film loop; enter the name **Pixelfly** and then click OK to complete the operation (see Figure 3-30). Director creates a film loop of the sequence and places it in the Cast window.

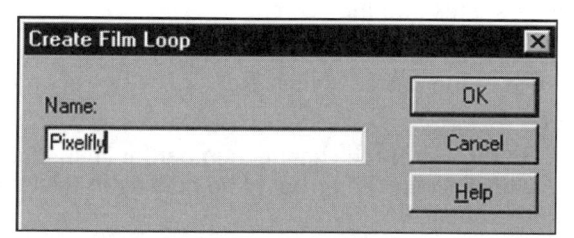

Figure 3-30: Director prompts you to name your film loop.

6. Delete the sprites from channel 3 of the Score window, by pressing the Delete key on your keyboard.

7. Save your movie as **onlingo9.dir**.

Next, you'll do the steps for creating the flapping-wings sequence. These steps are similar to what you did when you created the wing sequence using Auto Distort — with a slight twist. Before, the cast members that were generated showed the wings closing. In order to complete the sequence, you need to make them open again, using the Reverse Sequence command. Then you can make a film loop of the resulting sprite.

Using Reverse Sequence

1. Open the onlingo9.dir movie in Director. Open the Cast window.

2. Before you create the animated wings, you must set the desired registration point for each bitmap cast member used in the film loop. Double-click on the Wings1 cast member. When the Paint window opens, select the Registration tool and click to move the crosshair to the junction of the four wing segments. When set, click the Next Cast Member button and repeat the process for Wings2 through Wings7. Close the Paint window.

3. Save the movie as **onling10.dir**.

4. In the Cast window, select Wings1. Then hold down the Shift key and select Wings7. This selects the entire wing sequence in the Cast window.

5. In the Score window, select the first frame of channel 3.

6. Select Modify ⇨ Cast to Time to place the sequence in the Score, and choose Matte from the pop-up ink menu.

7. With the sequence still selected, press Command+C (Ctrl+C) to copy the sequence to the Scrapbook (Clipboard).

8. In the Score window, select frame 8 of channel 3, and press Command+V (Ctrl+V) to paste the sprites into the Score.

9. With the pasted sprites still selected, select Modify ⇨ Reverse Sequence to reverse the sequence of the pasted sprites. Now the wings open up in addition to closing.

10. Click the gray area to the left of the channel number for channel 3, to select the entire channel. *Note:* There should be nothing in this channel other than the wing sequence.

11. Select Insert ⇨ Film Loop, and when prompted, name the film loop **WingLoop.** Click OK in the Create Film Loop dialog box to complete the operation. Director creates a film loop of the wings and places it in Cast member slot 9.

12. Select the sprites in channel 3 and delete them from the Score window, by pressing the Delete key on your keyboard.

13. Save the movie again as onling10.dir.

Film loops save space in the Score and smooth the animation of your movie. They also offer another advantage: grouping or bundling elements together. Film loops may be invaluable for animation sequences, but they are also an important tool for grouping together static images that appear in sequential channels in the Score. Like other sprites, you can extend a film loop to the length you need for your movie.

In the last two exercises you created two film loops. You need to create one more. Just as you used the reversing technique in the previous exercise to enhance the wing-flapping animation, Pixel's launch sequence can be reversed to create a landing sequence. You can do this on your own; the steps are the same. Name the new film loop **PixelLand,** and be sure to save your movie. This film loop is already built into the onlingo11.dir movie. Later you'll place these film loops in your movie using the Exchange Cast Member command.

> ### Cast window housekeeping
>
> A film loop doesn't actually contain the cast members it represents. It contains pointers; these pointers call the cast members in sequence and then display them on the Stage. In other words, you can't delete the associated cast members. If you delete them, your film loop won't work, and the movie will fail.
>
> As your movie grows, these cast members accumulate and clutter up the Cast window, making it more difficult to find specific cast members. So what do you do with all those extra cast members floating about the Cast window? Though you can't delete them, you can move them to another cast. Simply create a new cast with File ➪ New ➪ Cast and give it a name that identifies its purpose. To ensure that this associated cast doesn't accidentally become separated from your movie, it's a good idea to specify that the cast is internal rather than a linked external cast. Once you've created the new Cast window, select the cast members you want to move from the original cast. Drag them to an open cast member slot in the new cast, and release the mouse button. The moved cast members are out of the way but are still available for use in your movie. After moving the cast members, you can close the new Cast window. It's still attached to your movie as an internal cast, and Director updates the pointers for the film loops when you next save your movie.

Using Step and Real-time Recording

The Cast to Time command is not the only method Director offers you for animating sprites. You could also have used either Step Recording or real-time recording to animate Pixel. Each of these methods has advantages and disadvantages when compared to Cast to Time as an animation method.

- ✦ Step recording is the most precise method of animating a sprite. The sprite is animated one frame at a time, and you have total control over the placement in each frame. It's a time-consuming procedure, however, if you have to reposition a sprite across a large span of frames.
- ✦ Real-time recording is useful for quickly creating a rough path for your sprite to follow, but lacks the precision of either Cast to Time or step recording.

Animating with the Step Recording command

Step Recording offers precision that's unavailable with the Cast to Time command or the Real-time recording option (explained shortly). Step Recording is useful for creating an animation in which the sprite needs to follow an irregular or precise path. When you are using step recording to animate a sprite, you can stretch the sprite, exchange cast members, or change any of the sprite's properties, such as its ink property.

If you move the sprite by any method other than moving its position, the recording process stops. This means you can't rewind or play your movie while in Step Recording mode, unless you are finished recording the sprite's motion. In addition, moving the playback head or moving back a frame will also stop the recording process.

Using Step Recording

On the CD-ROM

In this exercise and the next, you can practice recording an animation using the onlingo.dir movie. Just drag any of the images of Pixel to the Stage, and use her as the object of your animation. The onlingo.dir movie is on the CD-ROM in the exercise:ch03 (exercise\ch03) folder.

1. Open the Control Panel by selecting Window ⇨ Control Panel. The Control Panel will let you step through your animation one frame at a time.

2. Position the sprites on the Stage at the location where you want the recording to begin, and select all the sprites you want to animate.

3. In the Score window, click the frame bar at the location where you want the animation to begin.

4. Select Control ⇨ Step Recording. The recording indicator (a red, right-triangle icon) appears next to the channels in which you are recording sprite movement (see Figure 3-31).

5. Click the Step Forward button on the Control Panel to move to the next frame of the animation. If you reach the end of the movie, Director extends the sprites into a new frame so you can continue to record the motion.

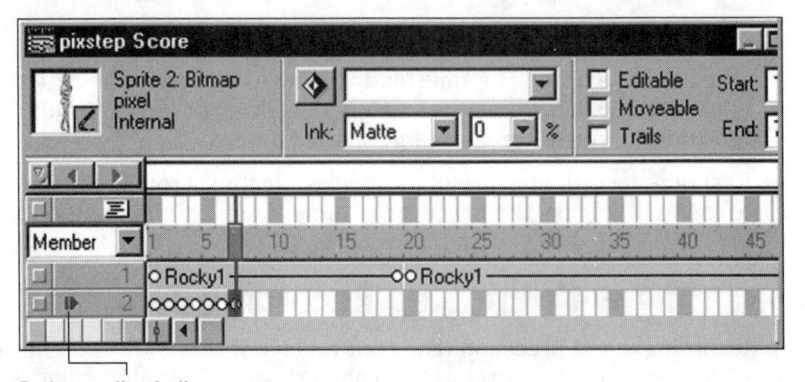

Red recording indicator

Figure 3-31: The red recording indicator appears beside the channel numbers where recording is in process.

Chapter 3 ✦ **Working with the Stage, Sprites, and Score** 99

6. Click and drag the sprites to reposition them. You can also use the Tweak command or keyboard arrow keys to move the sprites as desired.

7. Repeat steps 5 and 6, until you've completed recording the sequence. As you record the sequence, the motion paths of the sprites appear on the Stage, indicating the changes you've made (see Figure 3-32).

Figure 3-32: The motion path you are creating for the selected sprite appears on the Stage.

8. Select Control ⇨ Step Recording again, to stop recording the animation. You can also stop the movie by rewinding it, or by selecting a new frame in the Score.

If you need to stop recording, it's easy to resume. Just select the last frames of the recorded sprites, and then reselect Control ⇨ Step Recording. Pausing and restarting is useful if you want to add or remove sprites from the recording process, or if you want to test your animation.

Tip

Director's Score window underwent a makeover for version 6. If you prefer, you can switch back to the version 5 Score. Select File ⇨ Preferences ⇨ Score and choose the Director 5 Style Score Display check box.

Animating with the Real-time Recording command

When you create a real-time recording of an animation, Director records the motion of the sprite as it's being moved across the Stage. Real-time recording is thus as steady as your hand. In order for this method to work well, you need to be able to move the sprite smoothly at a consistent pace.

Because of these restrictions, real-time recording is best suited to creating rough motion paths that you intend to refine later. When using real-time recording, it's a good idea to slow the frame rate of your movie in the Control Panel to a rate slower than you anticipate using as the playback speed. This helps you to better control the movement of the sprite on Stage. You can also specify the number of frames you want to record; do this by selecting the frames in the Score window and then clicking the Selected Frames Only button in the Control Panel. If you don't specify Selected Frames Only, the recording continues as long as you hold down the mouse button.

Tip: Obtaining smooth results in real-time recording is easier if you use a digitizer pad instead of a mouse.

Using Real-time Recording

1. Open the Control Panel by selecting Window ⇨ Control Panel. Reset the frame rate to a slow speed, such as 5 fps, or click the Selected Frames Only button if you want to record a limited number of frames.

2. Open the Cast window and select the cast member you want to animate. Drag the cast member to an empty channel in the Score window.

3. Adjust the frame span of the sprite so that it occupies only a single frame. This ensures the best recording results.

4. With the sprite selected in the Score window, select Control ⇨ Real-time Recording. The sprite appears on Stage with a heavy red, rectangular bounding box, and a red dot appears beside the recording channel in the Score window (see Figure 3-33).

5. Click and drag the sprite across the Stage to describe the desired path. Notice that recording begins the moment you click the sprite on the Stage, so be prepared to move the sprite as soon as you select it on the Stage.

   Tip: It takes practice to move your hand in a smooth motion while doing real-time recording. You'll need to try it a couple times to achieve the results you want.

6. When you're ready, release the mouse button to stop recording the movement of the sprite. The path you've created appears on the Stage, and the animation sequence appears in the Score window (see Figure 3-34).

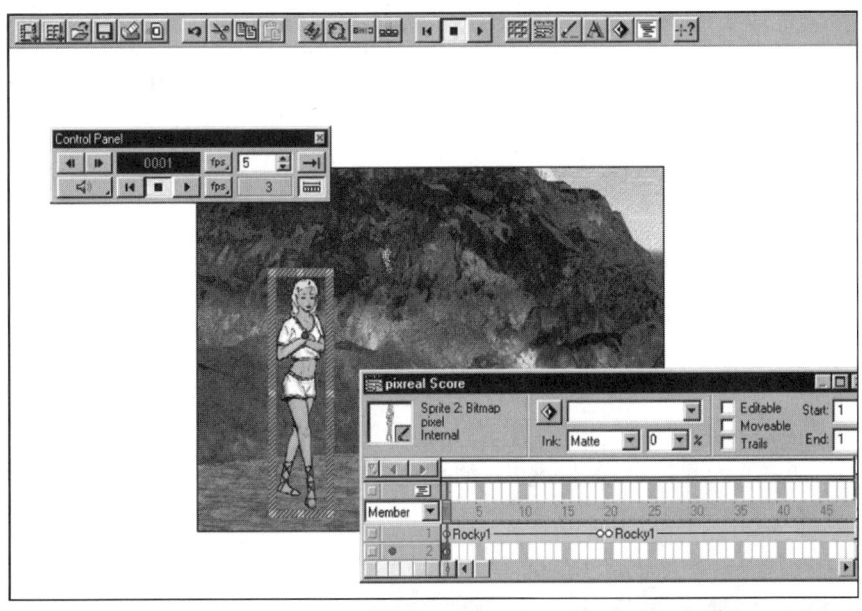

Figure 3-33: When real-time recording is active, you see a heavy (red on your screen) bounding box on the Stage and a dot beside the channel number.

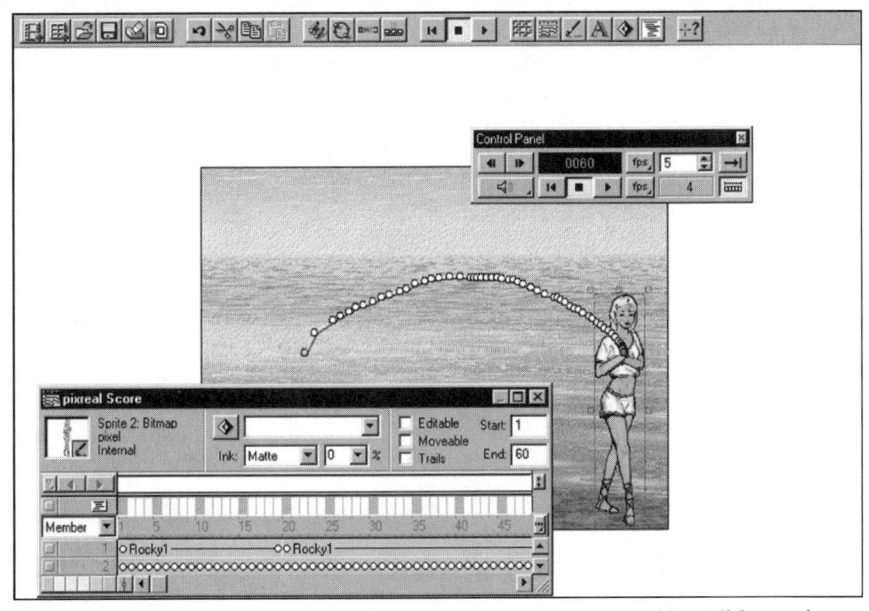

Figure 3-34: When you stop recording, the path you've created is visible on the Stage, and the animation sequence appears in the Score window.

Real-time recording requires some patience and practice, but this method can give you some great effects. For instance, consider animating a pen using real-time recording with a script font and mask to simulate handwriting (see Figure 3-35).

Figure 3-35: Use real-time recording to animate a pen, creating the effect of handwriting on the Stage.

Bringing Sprites to Life

One of Director's major strengths is the ability to create movies in a modular fashion, and edit the movies to refine their appearance and performance. Movies aren't necessarily created in a linear fashion. As you discovered when you animated the wing, takeoff, and landing sequences, some parts are created separately for later addition to a movie. Director's editing commands make the process easier, by enabling you to replace the sprites in the Score and edit individual sprite frames as well as entire sprites.

Exchanging cast members

Using the onlingo.dir movie you animated both the background and the character, Pixel. She's missing her wings, however. Obviously the wings must follow the same motion path as the character. Trying to reproduce such a path manually would be something between difficult and impossible. But there's help available with the Exchange Cast Member command, which lets you quickly apply the path to a new sprite. When you use the Exchange Cast Member command, any animation paths that exist for the selected cast member are applied to the new cast member.

Using the Exchange Cast Member Command

1. In this exercise you can use the onling10.dir file, if you added the PixelLand film loop. If you didn't, use the onling11.dir movie, which is available on the CD-ROM in the exercise:ch03 (exercise\ch03) folder. Open one of these movies now.

2. In the Score window, click the gray area to the left of channel 2, to select the entire channel.
3. Press Command+C (Ctrl+C) to copy the contents of the channel to the Scrapbook (Clipboard).
4. Select the first frame in channel 3, and press Command+V (Ctrl+V) to paste the sprite into the channel.
5. Reselect channel 2 again. Then open the Cast window by selecting Window ⇨ Cast. (If the Cast window is already open, click on it to activate it.)
6. Click the cast member WingLoop to select it.
7. Select Edit ⇨ Exchange Cast Members. As shown in Figure 3-36, the wings appear behind the character Pixel on the Stage, approximately where they belong.
8. Be sure the sprite in channel 2 (the now-winged sprite) is selected, and press the up-arrow key on the keyboard about 15 times, to move the wings up slightly.
9. Save the movie as **onling12.dir**.
10. Rewind your movie, and click the Play button to test the animation sequence.

Figure 3-36: With Exchange Cast Member, you've replaced a sprite in the Score while retaining any animation paths associated with the original sprite.

As you can see, the Exchange Cast Member command is extremely powerful. The new cast member assumes the registration and path of the old cast member. In most cases, when the new cast member takes the place of the old one, retaining the registration means that the sprite is perfectly aligned. Film loops are a bit different, however. The individual images in the film loop may have one alignment, but when Director creates a film loop, alignment is returned to the default at the center of the cast member. Generally, though, the sprite will be in approximately the correct location and will require only minor editing for repositioning.

Placing Pixel's takeoff and landing sequences in the movie isn't quite as straightforward as adding her wings. You need to split the Pixel sprite into segments, replace the segments, and then edit the alignment to ensure smooth motion. Following are the steps.

Editing the Score

1. Open onlingo12.dir in Director, if it's not already open.

2. Both the takeoff and landing sequences take about 20 frames to complete. In the Score window, click the sprite in channel 3 at frame 11; then select Modify ⇨ Split Sprite using Command+Shift+J (Ctrl+Shift+J).

3. Repeat step 2 to split the sprite in channel 3 at frames 31 and 56 (see Figure 3-37). This creates the segments you'll need to replace in order to create the takeoff and landing segments of the movie.

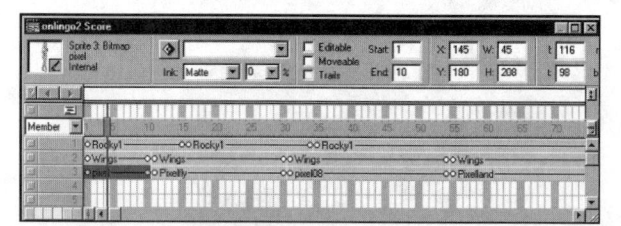

Figure 3-37: The sprite in channel 3 is split to create segments.

4. Channel 2 contains the wing animation. You need to split this channel to make sure that any position editing you do later will replicate that of the sprites in channel 3. Repeat step 2 again, this time to split the sprite in channel 2 at frames 11, 31, and 56.

5. Select the sprite in channel 3 between frames 11 and 31; then open the Cast window.

6. Select the cast member Pixelfly. Then select Edit ⇨ Exchange Cast Member, to swap the film loop for the original sprite.

7. With the sprite still selected, click the frame bar in frame 10, then in frame 11. Note that the position of the sprite in frame 10 is different from that in frame 11. Click the sprite in frame 10 of channel 3 to select the last keyframe of the first segment.

8. Pressing the Command (Ctrl) key, click between frames 11 and 31 in channels 2 and 3, to add the new sprite and its associated wing animation to the selection (see Figure 3-38).

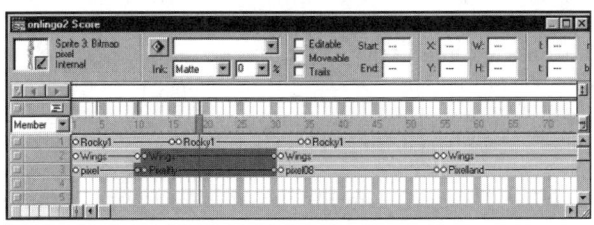

Figure 3-38: These selected segments will be aligned with the last keyframe in the first segment of channel 3.

Note

The order in which you select elements is important, because subsequent selections are aligned with the first element selected.

9. Select Modify ⇨ Align (Command+K or Ctrl+K) to display the Align window. Specify Align Tops as the horizontal alignment, and No Change as the vertical alignment.

10. Click Align to take the sprite that's in the segment between frames 11 and 31 and align it with the last keyframe of the first segment.

11. Click the sprite between frames 31 and 56 in channel 3, to select the middle segment of the movie.

12. Select Pixel8 in the Cast window. Then select Edit ⇨ Exchange Cast Member to replace the sprite in the middle segment of your movie.

13. Click the sprite between frames 56 and 75 in channel 3, to select the middle segment of the movie.

14. Select Pixelland in the Cast window. Then select Edit ⇨ Exchange Cast Member to replace the sprite in the end segment of your movie.

15. Use the same process oulined in steps 8-10 to align the segments in channels 2 and 3, between frames 56 and 75, with the keyframe in frame 55 of channel 3.

16. Rewind your movie, and click the Play button to test the animation sequence.

17. Adjust the position of the sprite segments if needed, by selecting them and using the arrow keys on your keyboard to nudge the elements into place.

18. Save your movie as **onling13.dir**.

Aligning film loops that replace regular cast members can take time. By clicking the frame bar in the last frame of one segment, and the first frame of the next segment, you get a visual guide to assist you in fine-tuning the alignment.

Changing a single frame of a sprite

The default setup for Director 6 is to select the entire sprite when you click the middle of a sprite. Editing entire sprites or sprite segments enables you to make sweeping changes in a relatively short period of time. Occasionally, though, you'll want to edit a single frame within a sprite — to make minor adjustments in a path, change a cast member, or adjust the sprite's properties.

You can edit individual frames by clicking the cell in the Score window that you want to edit, and then selecting Edit⇨Edit Sprite Frames. Alternatively, you can Command-click (right-click) the sprite, and then select Edit Sprite Frames from the pop-up menu. The view of the Score window will change to reflect that you are in frame-editing mode, by displaying the selected sprites as individual cells in the Score (see Figure 3-39). To return to editing an entire sprite, select Edit⇨Edit Entire Sprite.

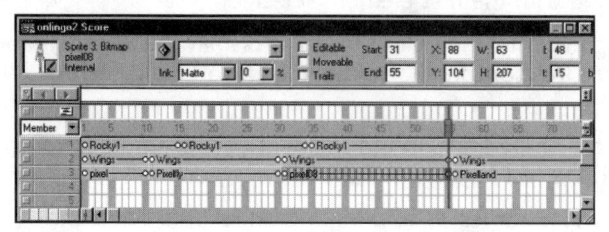

Figure 3-39: When you are in frame-editing mode, selected sprites are displayed as individual cells.

Drawing Sprites upon the Stage: Blends and Inks

The animation you've been working with in this chapter's exercises borrows more than a bit from fantasy, and as such it could benefit from a few special effects. For example, it might be nice as a final transition for Pixel to fade away once she lands, as would be appropriate for a supernatural entity. Doing such a fade using cast members can get dicey, though. You'd need to know the exact spot on the background where she lands, and if you so much as bumped the background or moved the pixel by so much as . . . well, a pixel . . . then the illusion breaks.

One attribute added to Director with version 4.0 was the Blend property for sprites. This capability blends the foreground sprite and the background image together, and can be set to any value between 0 (where only the background shows) to 100 (where the sprite is completely opaque). Any value in between will give the sprite some level of transparency, which serves as the basis for any number of special effects.

The Blend property can be set from the Sprite Properties dialog. To display this dialog, first select the sprite in the Score window; then select Modify⇨Sprite⇨ Properties or press Command+Shift+I (Ctrl+Shift+I). Alternatively, if you have the sprite information display active on Stage, you can click the Information icon in the sprite display.

Creating Fade Effects

1. Open onling13.dir in Director, if it's not already open.
2. Open the Score window, and scroll until frame 75 is visible.
3. Holding down the Command (Ctrl) key, select the last frame of the sprites in all three channels.
4. Press Command+C (Ctrl+C) to copy the cells to the Scrapbook (Clipboard).
5. Click in frame 76 of channel 1, and press Command+V (Ctrl+V) to paste the sprites into the channels.
6. With the sprites still selected, click the frame bar in frame 90, and select Modify⇨Extend Sprite to extend the sprites through frame 90 (see Figure 3-40).

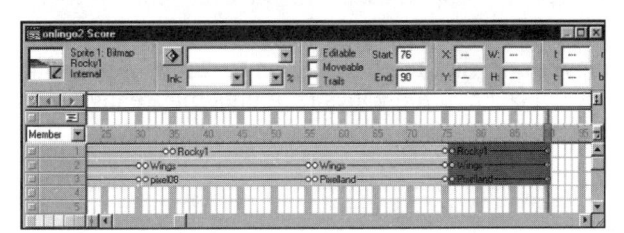

Figure 3-40: The sprites extended through frame 90.

7. Select the sprite in channel 2 between frames 76 and 90, and then open the Cast window.
8. Select Wings1. Then select the Edit⇨Exchange Cast Member command to replace the film loop with a static image.
9. Repeat steps 7 and 8 for channel 3, using Pixel01 as the replacement cast member.
10. Adjust the alignment of the sprites in channels 2 and 3 between frames 76 and 90 as needed to ensure they are directly superimposed over each other (see Figure 3-41). When the sprites are properly aligned, there appears to be a single sprite.
11. Press the Command (Ctrl) key, and select the last frame in channels 2 and 3.

Figure 3-41: Adjust the alignment of the sprites in channels 2 and 3.

12. With the frames selected, select Modify ⇨ Sprite ⇨ Properties and ensure the Blend is set at 0%. Click OK to complete the operation and return to Director's main window. The sprites in frame 90 are now invisible.

13. Press the Command (Ctrl) key, and select frame 76 in channels 2 and 3.

14. Select Modify ⇨ Sprite ⇨ Properties. Be sure the Blend is set to 100% and click OK.

15. Rewind the movie, and click the Play button to test your animation. At the end of the movie, Pixel and the wings fade until they're invisible.

16. Save your movie as **onling14.dir**.

Creating a faded blend provides you with another technique for making a smooth transition. By adjusting the frame span of the fade, you can adjust the speed at which the selected sprites change from opaque to transparent. You can also select a degree of transparency, if you don't want the sprites to disappear entirely. This is useful when you want to place text or other elements below the transparency and have them show through the other elements.

Caution

Rendering faded blends to screen is resource intensive, because each pixel must be calculated individually. On machines with limited resources this sort of expenditure can be problematic. You can reduce the impact on resources by limiting the frame span of the effect.

Inking the contracts

Throughout the exercises in this and other chapters, you've been directed to apply an ink to selected sprites in the Score window, but very little has been said about the inks themselves. Similar to cast member inks that you apply in the Paint window, *sprite inks* tell Director how you want a sprite displayed in relationship to other sprites beneath it.

For example, when you first place a sprite in the Score window, by default Director displays the sprite using a Copy ink. Copy ink is totally opaque and is suited to rectangular shapes. If the shape is irregular, however, a white rectangle will appear in the background behind colored portions of the sprite. Earlier in the chapter, when you moved Pixel to the Score, you selected a Matte ink in order to turn the background behind the colored portion of the sprite transparent. Director provides a variety of other inks that are useful for creating various effects in your movies. Each of the inks has attributes that make it suitable for a specific purpose (see Table 3-3).

When working with inks, it's important to remember that some inks are more costly than others in terms of resource consumption. The amount of memory required to render an ink on the screen depends upon the effect, and how many pixels must be individually computed for the rendering. As a result, some inks render faster than others. On a high-end computer with substantial resources, the difference between one ink and the next may not be noticeable; but on a computer with limited resources, the difference may be prohibitive. It's critical to consider the resource impact of any inks you apply in your movies.

Table 3-3
Sprite Inks and Their Effects

Ink Number	Ink Name	Description
0	Copy	Copies the contents of the cast member to the Stage, including the bounding box. This is the fastest ink to render, but it requires that you match your elements with the background exactly.
36	Background Transparent	If a pixel in the cast member has the background color (the bottom swatch in the Tool Palette, as explained in Chapter 4), then it becomes transparent; any other color remains opaque. This is easily one of the most useful inks, especially for irregular shapes with "holes."
1	Transparent	White pixels become transparent, while black pixels remain black. Useful primarily with 1-bit graphics.

continued

Table 3-3 *(continued)*

Ink Number	Ink Name	Description
2	Reverse	White pixels become transparent, while black pixels show the complementary color of the background pixel beneath it. Useful primarily with 1-bit graphics.
8	Matte	For an irregularly shaped cast member, this ink finds the boundary of the shape and then masks off everything outside that boundary. Thus anything inside the boundary is drawn, and anything outside of that boundary shows the background. This is the only ink that can alter the way Director handles mouse clicks on a sprite.
3	Ghost	Any black pixel becomes white, while any white pixel becomes transparent. Useful primarily with 1-bit graphics.
4	Not Copy	Works like the Copy ink, except that each pixel is the complementary color of the original graphic (e.g., white becomes black, red becomes cyan, and so forth).
5	Not Transparent	Every white pixel maps to black, while every black pixel becomes transparent. Useful primarily with 1-bit graphics.
6	Not Reverse	Maps every white pixel to the complement of the background pixel, while every black pixel becomes transparent. Useful primarily with 1-bit graphics.
7	Not Ghost	Takes the complement of the ghost ink; white becomes black and black becomes transparent.
9	Mask	If the cast member immediately following the selected cast member is a 1-bit (black-and-white), then the sprite appears only where the 1-bit graphic is black. This is a very useful ink and will be covered in detail in Chapter 4.
32	Blend	Ensures that the sprite uses the blend percentage specified in the Sprite Properties dialog box.
33	Add Pin	All colors are made up of red, green, and blue components (see Chapter 2). The Add Pin ink adds the color of each pixel in the graphic to the color of each pixel in the background; if the value exceeds 100% for each component, then the color is leveled off at 100%. This lightens a graphic.
34	Add	Unlike Add Pin, the Add ink takes the sum of the foreground and background colors, so that if any component exceeds 100%, the darkest color is substituted.

Ink Number	Ink Name	Description
35	Subtract Pin	Subtract Pin subtracts the foreground color from the background color, leveling out at 0 if the result is less than that. This is useful for darkening a graphic.
37	Lightest	Compares the color values of foreground and background pixels, and returns the lighter of the two colors.
38	Subtract	Subtracts the foreground color from the background color. Unlike Subtract Pin, Subtract doesn't bottom out at 0, but rather cycles back up from the lightest values.
39	Darkest	Compares the color values of foreground and background pixels, and returns the darker of the two colors.

Summary

In the next chapter, you'll discover how to add text for all occasions to your Director movies. Before moving on, let's review some of the things you've learned in Chapter 3.

- ✦ A sprite is a copy of a cast member once it's placed on the Stage and in the Score.
- ✦ A sprite is a self-contained object with a definite life span, which can be extended or shortened by dragging the end of the sprite in the Score window.
- ✦ Keyframes in Director control the changes in position, transparency, size, and other contiguous sprite properties.
- ✦ Tween frames are generated by Director; they form the intermediate steps between keyframes.
- ✦ Sprites can be extended, split, joined, and edited — as whole entities and as individual frames.
- ✦ Changes in cast members generally don't form keyframes, although a cast member change may be on a keyframe.
- ✦ Film loops are a powerful tool for creating animations without having to position each cast member individually.
- ✦ The transparency of a sprite can be set through the Blend property.
- ✦ Inks are used to control how the sprite is drawn on the screen. The most useful inks are Copy, Matte, and Background Transparent.

✦ ✦ ✦

Using Text and Shapes in Director

CHAPTER 4

In This Chapter

Working with text in Director

Using the editing tools in the Text window

Creating scrollable text

Bringing text into your Director movies

Creating basic lines and shapes, and using them to advantage

Creating patterns for use in shapes

For all that a multimedia application employs pictures and other graphics, the truth remains that almost any production you create will involve the use of words. Titles, explanatory text, scrolling fields containing the contents of external files, even an occasional "Open the pod door, HAL..." is likely to appear in your works. Used wisely, text becomes an integral part of the design, and augments graphics and other elements within a movie. To that end, the support that Director offers for text needs to be both good and extensive — and after six iterations of the product, Director 6.0 can truly be said to meet both of those requirements.

Working with Text in Director

Indeed, Director offers not just one way of producing and displaying text, but *three*. Each form has its strengths and weaknesses, and you'll probably find that the combination of all three will give you excellent flexibility while still offering you the best-looking formats possible.

Specifically, Director defines the following text elements:

✦ *Text* cast members for showing text at its best

✦ *Field* cast members that aren't as pretty but take much less memory and are far more functional

✦ *Painted* text that is actually a feature of the Paint window

The text cast member

Text in any program can prove to be a problem, and because of cross-platform issues and installation limitations, text in Director is more of a challenge than it is on most other programs.

In addition to the contents of a block of text, Director has to retain the attributes that define how the text is displayed. These attributes are the font, size, style, and formatting you apply to the text. You may already be familiar with fonts, which are specific styles of text like those illustrated in Figure 4-1. For example, Times Roman Bold Italic is one font. Times Roman Bold is an entirely different font, although it is in the same font family.

Arial (A San Serifed Font)

Book Antiqua (A Serifed Font)

Copperplate (A Script Font)

Figure 4-1: The font of a text element determines its general shape and other characteristics.

Most text attributes transfer easily from one system or platform to the next. Font information, however, is system specific. The set of fonts installed on your system may be entirely different from that of anyone else who will be running your movie. Since you can't guarantee that every system or platform will have the same fonts, font considerations are critical issues when creating a Director movie.

Finding compatible fonts when creating a cross-platform movie is nearly impossible. You can use *font mapping* (see Chapter 14) to create a font substitution list, but this is frequently an inadequate answer to the problem. *Every* font will respond differently to formatting and other attributes, such as boldface specifications. The result is that one font may take up more or less space on the page than another, and you may not wind up with the effect you want in your movie.

Another issue is readability. For a Director movie to be successful, the font you select must be easy to read. Allowing random font substitution when you're transferring a movie from one system to the next can result in hard-to-read text.

The advantages and drawbacks of rich text format

In response to these text-related issues, Director supports RTF (rich text format) text as its internal text format. In addition to being accepted cross-platform, rich text has a number of useful characteristics:

- ✦ A text cast member can be edited while in design mode, and then stored internally as a bitmap once the movie starts running (or a projector is created). This bitmap is no longer font dependent. It can be transferred between a machine that has the font to one that doesn't, without the text changing in the slightest.
- ✦ The text cast member is displayed *anti-aliased* (see Figure 4-2). Text can look aliased (jagged) if only black-and-white pixels are used. Anti-aliasing smoothes the edges of fonts and other objects by interpolating the edges of the text or object with objects behind it. For example, if you had black text on a white background, anti-aliasing would apply a fine border of gray to the edge of the text to smooth the appearance.
- ✦ A text cast member can be scrolled, or you can limit the portion of the text information that's displayed on-screen at one time.
- ✦ Because it can be edited in design mode, the text cast member is easier to edit than text created in the Paint window.

Figure 4-2: Anti-aliased fonts (top row) use intermediate shades of gray to soften the edges, making most fonts easier to read.

Bear in mind, however, that the obvious benefits of rich-text cast members come at a fairly steep price:

- ✦ A text cast member is unchangeable once it's in run-time mode, in a projector, or in a Shockwave movie. In other words, it can't be used for any text that needs to be updated on-the-fly or in situations where you want the text to be editable by the user.
- ✦ The text cast member takes up a significant amount of memory, since it stores its own bitmap (and a bitmap mask) with the text data.
- ✦ Text cast members aren't terribly well suited for animation. They take a long time to render and can slow down an animation sequence by a noticeable amount.

For these reasons, text cast members should be used with care. In a title, or for scrollable text that doesn't change content, text is generally pretty useful. But elements such as a digital clock or a marquee or a list box cannot make use of rich text's benefits.

Creating a text cast member

You have several options for creating text cast members. Each method of adding text to your movie has advantages that recommend it for a specific application. You can

- ✦ Add text directly on Stage
- ✦ Enter text in the Text window
- ✦ Import text
- ✦ Create bitmapped text in the Paint window

The Text tool in Director's Tool Palette (see Figure 4-3) enables you to add text directly on Stage, in the location you choose. The Text tool method of creating text is ideal when you need small amounts of text, such as a title, that is precisely placed on Stage. When you create text using this method, the text attributes must be edited using the Text Inspector, with which you'll get some practice in the upcoming exercise, "Using the Text Tool."

The Text tool

Figure 4-3: The Text tool, located in the floating Tool Palette, helps you add text directly onto the Stage.

When you need larger blocks of text, importing the text or using the Text window is a better choice. The Text window, like most word processors, enables you to format text as it's being created — this includes applying size, style, and alignment attributes to the text. Text created in the Text window can be edited at any time to change the attributes, formatting, or the text itself, and you can do this either on the Stage or in the Text editing window.

Text created in the Paint window is unique in that it can only be edited while you are creating the text. Once you stop editing by clicking off the text object, by changing the visible cast member, or by closing the Paint window itself, the text becomes a bitmap cast member. As a bitmap cast member, it gets treated by Director like any other graphic element in your movie. Formatting options that are available with other methods of creating text are not available in the Paint window. In addition, if you want to change the text, you'll have to re-create it.

Chapter 4 ✦ **Using Text and Shapes in Director** 117

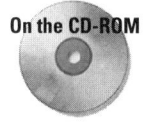

On the CD-ROM In the following exercise, you'll use the Text tool to add a title with a drop shadow to the onlingo2.dir file that you created in Chapter 3. You can also find this file on your companion CD-ROM in the exercise:ch04 (exercise/ch04) folder. After adding the title, you'll use the Text Inspector to change the text attributes.

Using the Text Tool

1. Open nolingo.dir in Director.
2. Open the Score window, and scroll over until frame 91 is visible. Click frame 91 in channel 4 to select it; then move the Score window so that the Stage is visible.
3. Open the floating Tool Palette, by selecting Window ➪ Tool Palette or pressing Command+F7 (Ctrl+F7).
4. Click the Text tool to select it. Your cursor changes to a crosshair when you move back over the Stage.
5. Click near the upper-left corner of the Stage to specify a text insertion point (see Figure 4-4). A text entry box appears on Stage.
6. Click the foreground color swatch near the bottom of the Tool Palette and choose a royal blue as the foreground color.

Figure 4-4: Click the Text tool on Stage to specify an insertion point for your text.

7. Type **On Lingo** in the text box.
8. Select Window ➪ Inspectors ➪ Text to display the Text Inspector (see Figure 4-5).

Figure 4-5: The Text Inspector helps you change the text attributes of selected text.

9. Select the text you just created, by clicking and dragging in the text box to highlight the text. Alternatively, you can triple-click the text box to select all the text in the box.
10. Select any font from the font list in the Text Inspector.
11. Choose point size 36 from the Font Size list box at the lower-left of the Text Inspector. Click the B button to specify a bold font style.
12. Click outside the text box to indicate you're finished editing the text.
13. If the text wraps to a second line, click the text box again to display the sizing handles. Drag the right-side handle to adjust the width of the text box so the text doesn't wrap.
14. In the Cast window, select cast member 10, which is a text cast member. Press Command+C (Ctrl+C) to copy the cast member to the Clipboard.
15. Select cast member slot 11 and press Command+V (Ctrl+V) to paste the cast member from the Clipboard into the empty slot. Drag the new cast member in slot 11 to channel 5, frame 91. Then shorten both sprites (in channels 4 and 5) so that they end in frame 96.
16. Notice that the new sprite, based on cast member 11, is centered on the Stage. Now you need to make the bounding box for both sprites transparent, so you can align one on top of the other. Press the Shift key and click both sprites in the Score (channels 4 and 5, spanning frames 91 through 96).
17. Choose Background Transparent from the Ink pop-up menu in the Score window. This renders the white background rectangle transparent behind the two text sprites.
18. On the Stage, click off the two text sprites to deselect them, and then double-click the text sprite closest to the center of the Stage.

19. Click the Foreground color swatch on the floating Tool Palette and set the color to bright yellow.
20. Deselect the yellow text sprite, and then click it once to display its handles. Drag the sprite until it completely overlaps the blue lettering sprite located in the upper-left corner of the Stage.
21. Once the yellow letters cover the blue, press the up-arrow key twice and then the left-arrow key twice. This offsets the yellow text by two pixels toward the upper-left of the Stage. As shown in Figure 4-6, you now have a drop shadow.

Figure 4-6: Using your cursor arrow keys, you can move the text to create a drop shadow.

22. Save your movie as **nolingo1.dir**.

You probably noticed that the Text Inspector also contains the familiar buttons for left, centered, right, and justified alignment of the text. In addition to the font, size, style, and alignment of text, you can also specify the amount of *leading* (the space between lines) and *kerning* (the space between pairs of characters) in the Text Inspector. The quality of computer fonts has increased to the point that for most purposes you don't need to alter the default kerning and leading values for your text. You may want to adjust the values, however, for precise layout and design. As you increase the values in the kerning and leading value boxes, the space between characters or lines increases.

> ### Leading the pack: a few typographic terms
>
> Printing is, in the parlance of Silicon Valley, a *very* mature technology. Indeed, when comparing printing to computer technologies in the broadest possible terms, printing has been around ten times as long. Because of this, a number of terms have made their way from traditional printing to desktop publishing:
>
> **Font** — In pre-electronic days, a *font* was a complete set of leaded type in a given style *and* size. The term *typeface* was used to describe the font family, including its various styles and point sizes. Digitized fonts have come into prominence in the last 15 years for use on computers. Today, computerization of type design and photomechanical printing techniques have almost entirely replaced metal type.
>
> **Point Size** — A *point* is a printer's unit, and was originally 1/72.72 of an inch. Computer point sizes are fractionally smaller. Typically, the point size is measured as the baseline height of the lowercase *x*, and as such is also known as the *x-height*.
>
> **Leading** — In the days of cold-press type, printers used bars made of lead to increase the space between lines when laying out a page. A slight shift in usage occurred with desktop publishing. Today leading is the distance between the baseline heights — that is, from the bottom of one *x* character to the bottom of another *x* character, one line down.
>
> **Kerning** — A *kern* is a lead slug that cold-press printers placed between letters to adjust the spacing between pairs of letters. Today kerning is the spacing between a pair of letters. The default amount of kerning applied to any pair of characters varies depending on the font and style of the characters. Kerning is normally expressed as a percentage of a space.

Using the Text Window

The Text window (Figure 4-7) enables you to create and format blocks of text. It's actually a small word processor and contains features for formatting text as well as applying text attributes. Though probably not suitable for large, multipage documents such as books, the Text window works well for creating blocks of text to use in your movies. You might require a couple of paragraphs, for example, to describe your products or services. Since Director uses RTF as its internal text format, you can use more than one font, style, or color within a single text block, as illustrated in Figure 4-7. In addition, the Text window supports Scrapbook (Clipboard) functions, with which you can paste text from other applications into your Director movies.

Tip The active foreground color shown in the Tool Palette is the color of your text. If you keep the Tool Palette open while you are entering text, you can change the color of the text as you are creating it by changing the foreground color in the Tool Palette.

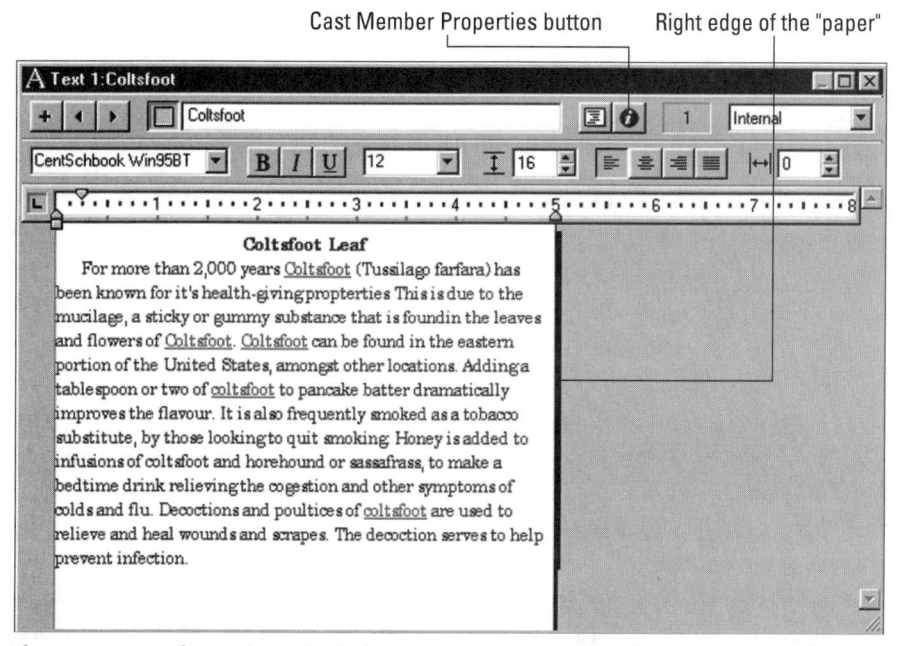

Figure 4-7: In Director's Text window you can apply more than one font, style, color, or other attributes within a single block of text.

You can edit a text cast member at any time during the development of your movie. In addition to the format or the text itself, you can also specify text *properties,* which tell Director how you want to display your text. Creating a text cast member in the Text window is a simple matter of opening the Text window and entering the text you want to use.

To open the Text window, select Insert ⇨ Media Element ⇨ Text, or select Window ⇨ Text (Command+6 or Ctrl+6). You can apply text attributes at any time during the editing process.

Specifying formatting options

Before entering the text you want to use, it's a good idea to prepare the Text window for the text you're creating. By taking the time to specify the page size, margins, tab stops, and other formatting and font options, you can save editing time later. Table 4-1 shows the buttons and other options available in the Text window and describes how to use them.

Table 4-1
Text Window Options for Text Formatting

Button or Box	Name	Description
Coltsfoot	Cast Member Name	Click to create an insertion point, and enter the name of your text cast member. The name is reflected in this box.
CentSchbook Win95BT	Font	Click the arrow button to open the list box and choose a font. This list reflects available fonts installed on your system.
B	Bold	Click to assign a bold style for your text. Keyboard alternative: Command+Option+B (Ctrl+Alt+B)
I	Italic	Click to assign an italic style for your text. Keyboard alternative: Command+Option+I (Ctrl+Alt+I)
U	Underline	Click to assign underlining attribute to your text. Keyboard alternative: Command+Option+U (Ctrl+Alt+U)
12	Font Size	Click the arrow button to open the list box and choose a preset font size, or select the entry in the box and enter a new value.
16	Line Spacing	Specifies the amount of space between lines of text. Click the up- and down-arrows to increase or decrease the space. Or you can select the entry in the box and enter a new value.
	Align Left	Click the button to align selected text flush with the left margin.
	Align Center	Click the button to center selected text between the margins.
	Align Right	Click the button to align selected text flush with the right margin.
	Justify	Click the button to align selected text between both margins. Space will be added between words and kerning will automatically be adjusted.

Button or Box	Name	Description
↔ 0	Kerning	Adjusts the space between pairs of characters. the up- and down-arrows to increase or decrease the space. Or you can select the box and enter a new value.
(ruler marker)	Left Margin and Indent Markers	Click and drag the left margin marker (bottom) to adjust the left margin. Click the indent marker (top) to indent the first line of text in each paragraph by the specified amount.
(ruler marker)	Right Margin Marker and Ruler	Click and drag the marker to adjust the right margin and drag the right edge of the "paper" to adjust the width of the paper (See figure 4-7).
L	Tab Well	Click the tab well to display the type of tab you want to use; then click the ruler to set the tab location. You can choose from the following alignment options: left, right, center, or decimal centered.

> **Tip:** Control-click (right-click) the ruler in the Text window to specify the unit of measurement you want to use. Choose inches (the default), centimeters, or pixels.

Specifying text properties

Once you've specified the formatting and entered your text, you can specify the framing and anti-aliasing options you want to use for the text. Click the Cast Member Properties button (see Figure 4-7) in the Text window to display the Text Cast Member Properties dialog box (Figure 4-8). Using this dialog, you can enter or change the name of your text cast member and set the framing and anti-alaising for the cast member.

Figure 4-8: In this dialog box you can select framing and anti-aliasing options for your text.

Framing options

To select framing options, click the arrow button and choose Adjust to Fit, Scrolling, or Cropped. Each framing option has advantages that recommend it for a particular application:

- ✦ **Adjust to Fit** — The default, Adjust to Fit, expands or contracts the text box to accommodate the amount of text you create. If you edit the text, it re-adjusts to the correct size. Adjust to Fit is useful if you think you want all the text visible on the Stage at one time.

- ✦ **Scrolling** — The Scrolling text option enables you to limit the size of the window. When the cast member is placed on Stage, a scroll bar is added on the right side of the text window. Scrolling text is a good option when you have a limited amount of Stage space in which to display a large block of text. If you add a wait statement to the Score, the user can scroll through the text at his or her own pace. (See "Waiting for user intervention" in Chapter 5.)

- ✦ **Cropped** — When you choose Cropped, the text is truncated to fit the size of the text box you create. You can enlarge the text box to display all of the text, or reduce it to display limited amounts of the text. The Cropped framing option is useful for creating effects where the display of a line or portion of the text is paced across a span of frames.

Tip

You can edit a text cast member at any time during the development of your movie, by double-clicking the cast member in the Cast window. This opens the cast member in the Text window for editing.

Using anti-aliasing

Anti-aliasing is a two-edged sword. Under ideal circumstances, anti-aliasing creates a clean, smooth edge on the text and bitmapped objects to which it's applied. Smooth curves or rounded shapes are an illusion, however, when you are dealing with bitmapped images. The nature of bitmaps is that pixels are tiny rectangles. When they are combined to create images, the result when they encounter a curved area is a series of tiny stair-steps (called *jaggies*). As the size of a text character increases, the jagged effect becomes more noticeable.

Anti-aliasing creates the illusion of a smooth curve by interpolating the color of the edge pixels with that of the background to add pixels of a color between the object and the background. Figure 4-9 shows two versions of the letter *G*. The character on the left has no anti-aliasing applied to it. The character on the right is anti-aliased, and its edges appear much smoother.

Figure 4-9: Anti-aliasing smoothes the edges of bitmapped characters.

The problem with anti-aliasing on text is that most text is created on a white background. When you apply a Background Transparent ink to the text, the white pixels are made transparent. The edge of the text is not really white, though, but a pale shade of color — and it remains with the text. The result is that on a colored background, the text appears to have a ghost around its edges, and this may be even more unattractive than a slightly rougher appearance.

The anti-aliasing options in the Text Cast Member Properties dialog box can be changed to apply anti-aliasing to all text, or just to text over a size that you specify; or you can specify no anti-aliasing at all.

Tip

It's a good idea to consider the background image in your movie, as well as the size of the text, to determine whether you want to apply anti-aliasing. You can change the option, of course, so any choice you make is not permanent. Try the various settings to determine what looks best in your movie.

Placing text cast members in your movie

Text cast members are placed in a movie much as other cast members are, by clicking and dragging them from the Cast window to either the Score or the Stage. You can then add transitions, inks, and other effects to the text sprites, just as you would to other cast members. You can also edit the text on Stage by double-clicking the text sprite. In the following exercise, you'll place several text cast members in the nolingo1.dir movie you created earlier in the chapter. To allow the user enough time to read the material in the text sprites, you'll add a wait-for-the-mouse-click effect to the Score, and then add a transition to ensure a smooth change between text cast members.

Adding Text to Your Movie

On the CD-ROM

1. Open onlingo1.dir in Director, if it's not already open. You'll need the movie you created earlier in the chapter, or the file nolingo1.dir on the CD-ROM, in the exercise:ch04 (exercise\ch04) folder.

2. Open the Score window, and scroll until frame 91 is visible. Click in frame 91 of channel 6 to set an insertion point in the Score.

3. Holding down the Option (Alt) key, click and drag the text1 cast member to frame 91, channel 6. Release the mouse button and then release the Option (Alt) key. This method causes Director to add a sprite that only scans a single frame.

4. Repeat step 3 to drop the text2 cast member on frame 92, channel 6. Then use the same method to drop text3 on frame 93, text4 on frame 94, and text5 on frame 95 in channel 6. Be sure that each sprite spans only a single frame.

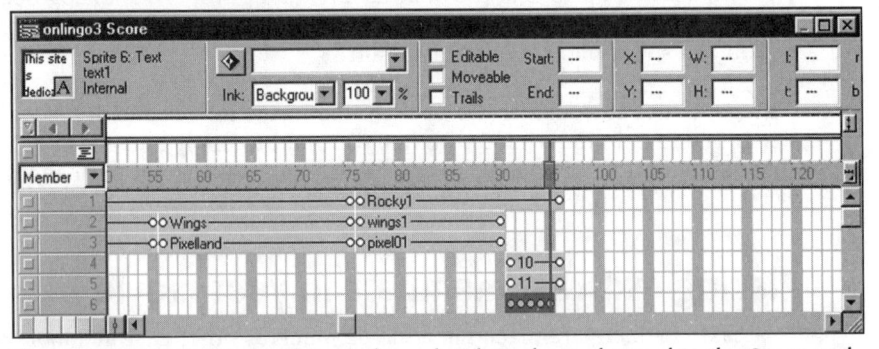

Figure 4-10: Text cast members 1 through 5 have been dragged to the Score and placed into channel 6, frame 91.

5. Select the text sprites and choose Background Transparent from the pop-up ink menu in the Score.

6. With the sprites selected, click and drag the text sprites down and to the right on Stage (see Figure 4-11). This repositions the sprites while maintaining their alignment to one another.

7. Click the Hide/Show Effects Channels button (idenfitied in Figure 4-10) to expand the Score and display the Special Effects channels. Then select cast member 17 in the Cast window, and drag it to the transition channel, in frame 91. This sets a transition between the text frames; the transition moves from one text frame to the next using diagonal stripes. Extend the sprite through frame 96.

Figure 4-11: The text sprites after clicking and dragging to reposition them on Stage

8. Double-click the Tempo channel (the first or top Special Effects channels) in frame 91, and choose Wait for Mouse Click or Key Press. Click OK to return to Director's main window. Extend the sprite through frame 96.

9. Save your movie as **nolingo2.dir.**

10. Rewind your movie, and click the Play button. When the "On Lingo" text appears, click the Stage to move to the next frame. If the text is too high and overlaps the "On Lingo" text, stop the movie and make the necessary adjustments.

> **Note**
>
> Be sure to save the onlingo movie, as you'll be using it again in Chapter 5 to create a projector. When you are creating a series of text cast members that need to be aligned on Stage, it's easier to create them all and then move them as a collection to the Score. This method ensures they are aligned in relation to one another. Then you can reposition them on Stage together rather than separately, to maintain the alignment.

Importing Text

The Text window, though certainly adequate for creating blocks of text for your movies, is not nearly as robust as full-featured word processors such as Microsoft Word and Corel WordPerfect. These powerful programs contain essential formatting features not found in the Text window. In addition, they frequently support RTF text, which can be imported into Director with its formatting intact. Director also recognizes ASCII text files (called "plain text") containing no formatting instructions beyond tabs or carriage returns. Every word processor can create a text-format document.

The *Rich Text Format* document was a standard developed by Microsoft to facilitate transferring files between applications. To create an RTF file, you need only create the document in your current word processor and then save it as a Rich Text file. (Select File➪Save As to display the program's Save dialog, and choose either Rich Text or Textured Formatting as the type of document. The name of the format will depend on which application you use.)

Importing either plain text or formatted text is as easy as importing a graphic. Select File➪Import or press Command+R (Ctrl+R) to bring up the Import box, and then navigate to the text in question. Director doesn't yet support in-place editing of text in external text editors (such as Microsoft Word), so you should always import the text in Standard Import mode.

A quick word about field cast members

Field cast members aren't as pretty as text cast members, but they are dynamic — their content can be changed at run time. Because of this, they are the controls of choice for data entry or display, status fields, marquees, digital clocks, and any other situations where text will be changing on a regular basis. Our exploration of field cast members begins in Chapter 6, where we study interactivity and behaviors in Director movies. You'll find additional coverage of fields in Chapter 14.

The Shape of Things to Come

Bitmap graphics are useful for a great number of things, but there are times when all you need is a simple shape: a rectangle, a circle, or a line. Director provides support for creating basic shapes and lines. These shapes are useful as masks more than anything else, although at the end of this chapter we'll look at one really cool thing that can be done with shapes combined with patterns.

Creating QuickDraw shapes

The QuickDraw shapes derive their name from the Macintosh Toolbox, although you can create shapes on both Macintosh and Windows-based machines, using the drawing tools from the Tool Palette. These shapes are vector based, rather than bitmaps in which each pixel has a specific color. Unlike bitmap images, vector images are drawn using precise mathematics to describe the shape. The result is a shape that has a smooth appearance regardless of the size or resolution of the device displaying the shape.

Because information is stored as a set of instructions for the creation of the shape rather than the state and location of each pixel, vector images have smaller file sizes than bitmaps. Vector images also render to screen faster, and are less costly in terms of resources than bitmapped images.

Creating a Director Shape

1. Open nolingo2.dir in Director, if it's not already open.
2. Make sure you are in frame 1 of the movie.
3. Open the Tool Palette by selecting Window ⇨ Tool Palette (Command+7 or Cntrl+7). Click the color swatch and choose a bright yellow.
4. Select the largest line width (4 pixels) at the bottom of the Tool Palette, and then select the Unfilled Rectangle tool.
5. Click the upper-left corner of the Stage, and drag downward to the lower-right corner of the Stage. This adds a yellow border to your movie, which starts in frame 1, channel 4 (see Figure 4-12). Drag the sprite in the Score until it is in channel 7, frames 1 through 28.

Figure 4-12: You can quickly add a border to your movie using the Unfilled Rectangle tool in the Tool Palette.

6. With the border rectangle you've created still selected, click the frame bar in frame 96, and extend the border sprite by pressing Command+B (Ctrl+B).

7. Save your movie as **nolingo3.dir**.

8. Rewind your movie, and click the Play button to test it.

You've seen in these exercises that, using the shape and line tools in the Tool Palette, you can quickly add vector (QuickDraw) shapes to your movie. Keep in mind as you work with shapes that although you can edit them on Stage, you cannot edit them in the Paint window. These shapes are different from bitmap graphics in two other important ways, as well:

+ Unlike bitmaps, in which the registration point is changeable and automatically set to the center of the image, a QuickDraw shape's registration point is set for the upper-left corner of the shape and can't be altered.

+ Another difference is that vector shapes can't be converted to bitmaps within Director.

Using patterns

You can apply patterns to shapes on Stage much as you can to bitmaps in the Paint window. A *pattern* in Director 6.0 is a graphic of fixed size that is tiled until the square or circle or other shape is filled. When Director was first released, the computer market was offering machines capable of displaying 1-bit graphics (black-and-white) or 4-bit graphics (16 colors) and that was about it. Very few computers were capable of displaying even 8-bit (256-color) graphics. The result was that a great deal of work was done in black-and-white, since it was small, fast, and easily loaded.

The black-and-white patterns can still be used for special effects — especially since it's possible to set the foreground and background colors of a sprite, which then maps to the black or the white, respectively, of the pattern. In addition, you can use a set of full-color patterns, discussed in the next section. First, though, let's get acquainted with the process of setting black-and-white patterns in Director.

Changing a Shape's Fill from a Solid Color to a Pattern

1. Select the sprite for which you want to set the pattern. (Or deselect all sprites, to ensure that you don't accidentally set this property for the wrong sprite.)
2. In the floating Tool Palette, set the foreground color swatch to black and the background swatch to white.
3. Click and hold the Pattern button near the bottom of the floating Tool Palette to bring up the patterns (see Figure 4-13) and choose a pattern.

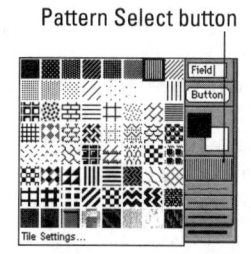

Figure 4-13: Director has a large variety of patterns from which to choose.

4. Get ready to draw a rectangle. First, select the Filled Rectangle tool in the floating Tool Palette. Then set the width of the border line to 0 by clicking the No Line button at the bottom of the Tool Palette. (You can change the border width of a rectangle by clicking the line-width buttons.)

   Note: The border conventions are a little counterintuitive. The border color will be the same as the pattern color — which is why using a completely filled pattern with a border doesn't appear to make any difference to the appearance of the cast member.

5. Draw the rectangle. At this stage, the rectangle will be filled with the pattern you selected and will use the foreground and background colors you set.
6. Set the ink of the rectangle to Background Transparent. The image beneath the rectangle shows through the white areas of the pattern.

   Tip: You can use patterns to create grayed-out areas behind text or other images (see Figure 4-14).

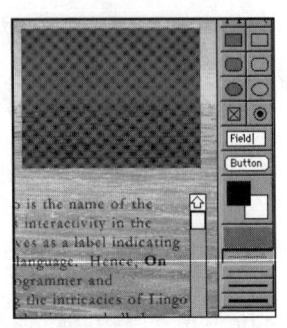

Figure 4-14: By combining a 50% gray screen with Background Transparent ink, you can "darken" a rectangular area far more efficiently than you could with darken ink.

Clicking the Cast window Information icon, Command+I (Ctrl+I), brings up the Cast Information dialog box, which we can use to demonstrate one of the principal differences between bitmap cast members and QuickDraw cast members. That is, you can set the *shape* of the QuickDraw cast member even after the cast member has been created. The permissible shapes are Rectangle, Round Rectangle, Oval, and Line. This option suggests the possibility of creating a primitive button that starts out as a grayed rectangle and when depressed becomes a grayed round rectangle. (See Figure 4-15.)

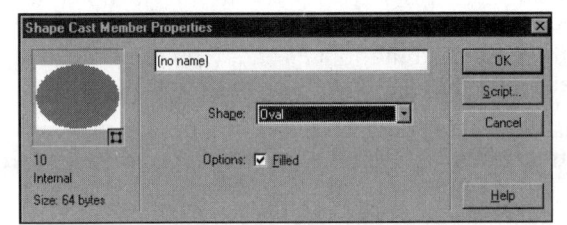

Figure 4-15: You can set the shape of a shape cast member on-the-fly, turning a rectangle into a line or a circle, for example.

Patterns within patterns

Easily the coolest part of working with shapes (which are otherwise fairly pointless) is a hidden little feature that many advanced developers don't even know about: The ability to fill patterns with *tiles*. If you have ever seen a Web page with a seamless repeating pattern as the background, you've seen tiles in action. Director gives you the ability to paint tiles into shape cast members and — even better — enables you to change these tiles on-the-fly.

If you are planning to bring your Director creation to the Web, you can use shape and tiling effects as tiled backgrounds for your Web pages, without the size limitations of using a full-screen bitmap. A shape and its associated pattern together use up approximately 3K for a full-size screen. The equivalent full-screen bitmap would take up 900K. That's not an insignificant savings! It could make the difference between your Shockwave movie zipping onto the page or stalling for ten minutes as it completes its download.

Using the color tiles works exactly the same way as using the black-and-white patterns. However, since you're unlikely to actually need any of the color tile patterns that Director displays as options, you will need to know how to make your own custom patterns. If you own a program such as Photoshop, you can create your own patterns for use in Director.

For a tile to be effective, it should be square and should appear to wrap. "Wrap" means that if the tile is repeated horizontally or vertically, the borders where tiles meet should flow from one to the next or be indiscernible. Ideally, your created pattern should be 16, 32, 64, or 128 pixels square. These sizes produce the best results when tiles are to be used as object fills.

Note

When you want to use a custom pattern (or a color), be sure to select the tool from the floating Tool Palette first and then select the pattern or color. Your selection "sticks" to the tool until you change it.

Creating Custom Patterns

1. In a paint program (such as Photoshop), create an image that will work as a tile pattern according to the guidelines stated in the preceding section and in Chapter 2. Save the image.

2. Import the image you created, or one of the images on the companion CD-ROM, into your movie in Director. The image appears in your Cast window.

3. Click the Pattern button in the floating Tool Palette. In the Patterns window that appears, click the option at the bottom that says Tile Settings.

4. The Tile Settings dialog box (similar to Figure 4-16) offers eight custom tiles and gives you the option of selecting a cast member in place of one of the custom tiles. Select the Cast Member option button, then cycle through the cast members that are available until the paper bitmap appears.

5. Specify the height and width for your tile. (Refer to the guidelines earlier in this section and in Chapter 2.)

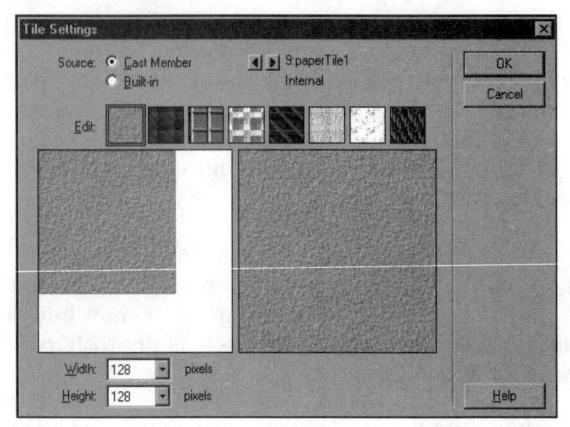

Figure 4-16: The Tile Settings dialog box enables you to edit Director's available tiles.

6. Close this dialog box. If you click the Pattern button now, you'll see your pattern as one of the eight custom patterns. You can now create shapes that will use this pattern.

Tip

The procedure in this exercise can also be used to make a box with a border in a different color than the fill color. Create a solid-color pattern of only 16 x 16 pixels, and then set the foreground color to the border color you want. This would be especially handy for dialog boxes in colorful applications (such as children's games).

In the spotlight

A good magic trick should be simple to perform, and sometimes the most magical effects require the least amount of actual work. Take, for example, creating a spotlight. Imagine a spotlight moving over a darkened (but not black) surface. As the spotlight sweeps over the ground and illuminates it, otherwise obscure details stand out. To create this illusion, you could in theory create cast members for each position in the spotlight — but the cost impact on both development and performance would be prohibitive.

The solution is so simple that it doesn't even require writing any Lingo code. The background is tiled with one pattern: a darkened, detail-poor background that repeats every 128 pixels. The spotlight is also tiled, using a pattern that showed the background lit and well detailed.

Tiles work by creating an offscreen buffer to draw the tiling pattern, then getting the position and form of the shape cast member and using that to create a mask. The tile pattern itself stays fixed relative to the upper-left corner of the screen. If you create patterns that are similar and exactly aligned, you can make one static (in this example, the dark background) and one moving (our spotlight). Then the moving pattern (the spotlight) will appear to illuminate that portion of the background that matches its shape. This is a little complex, so it's worth looking at an example.

On the CD-ROM For the following exercise, you will use several files available on your Companion CD. The files paper.pct and spackle.pct are in the exercise:ch04 (exercise\ch04) folder. The file tex0028.pct is in the goodies:digitals (goodies\digitals) folder. The files sea2568.pct and oak2568.pct are in the goodies:artbeats (goodies\artbeats) folder. The file if09033.tif is in the goodies:imagefrm (goodies\imagefrm) folder.

Making a Spotlight

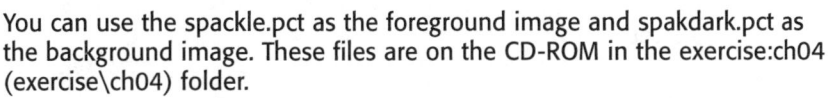

1. In an external editor, create your foreground and background tiles. The background should be a darker version of the foreground pattern.

    On the CD-ROM You can use the spackle.pct as the foreground image and spakdark.pct as the background image. These files are on the CD-ROM in the exercise:ch04 (exercise\ch04) folder.

2. Import the images into Director.

3. Go to the Tile Settings dialog box. Select your imported background image for the first tile pattern, and the imported foreground image for a second tile pattern. Specify a size of 128 pixels square to get the largest possible image.

4. Close the Tile Editor and set the pattern to the background tile. Create a borderless rectangle with the dimensions of the screen.

5. Select the Filled Ellipse tool, and create a spotlight graphic that's less than 128 pixels wide.

6. With the ellipse still selected, set the pattern of the spotlight circle to the foreground pattern.

7. Finally, open up the Score and select the whole spotlight graphic. At the top of the Score, turn on the Moveable option so the sprite can be dragged around the Stage.

8. Choose Control ⇨ Loop Playback from the menu bar and be sure the option is selected (preceded by a check mark). This ensures the movie will loop again once it reaches the end.

9. Save the movie as **spotlite.dir**.
10. Run the movie. Click and drag on the spotlight, and you'll see it as a flashlight beam on a dark wall.
11. Stop the movie, select the spakdark bitmap cast member, and open the Paint window.
12. Select the Eyedropper tool and click on a dark-brown portion of the image. If you get a light green, try again. This picks up the color and makes it the new foreground color.
13. Click the New Cast Member button to go to a clean canvas in the Paint window.
14. Double-click the Text tool to open the Font dialog box. Select a 24-point bold font (Arial or Helvetica). Click OK to close the dialog.
15. Click the middle of the canvas and type the following text with the line breaks exactly as shown.

    You are

    reading

    a secret

    message.

16. Close the Paint window and drag the new bitmap cast member to the Score in channel 3, frame 1.
17. With the new sprite still selected in the Score, use the Ink field to set the object's ink to Background Transparent.
18. Save the movie again as spotlite.dir, rewind, and play it. Drag the spotlight around the Stage and you'll see it illuminate the message.

On the CD-ROM A completed version of the spotlite.dir movie is on the companion CD-ROM in the exercise:ch04 (exercise\ch04) folder.

The 128-pixel limitation can prove troublesome, but the spotlight is still one of the more useful techniques you can do from Director without having to write any real code.

Tip This effect can be used to good effect in a number of ways. With a little bit of coding, for example, you can create an "X-ray" box that seems to see inside a person. The tiles are changed programmatically such that when you enter into a certain region, you can have the spotlight illuminate an animated character.

Summary

- Director supports three types of text: bitmapped text (see Chapter 3), rich text, and text fields (see Chapters 6 and 14).

- Rich text generates a bitmap that is stored with the field. When the program is moved to a different platform which does not support the same fonts, Director will draw the image from the bitmap. This helps you get around the limitations of needing to import fonts.

- Rich text can be set to anti-alias, letting you remove or reduce the stair-step "jaggies" effect that often occurs with black-and-white text.

- Rich text can be imported from RTF or text files.

- QuickDraw shapes occupy relatively little space but aren't as flexible as bitmaps.

- Shapes can be tiled, significantly cutting down on the space needed to display a repeating graphic.

- Sprites can be made moveable, so that they can be dragged across the screen by the mouse.

✦ ✦ ✦

CHAPTER 5

The Big Picture

Fine-tuning your Director project can make the difference between a successful project and one that lacks that certain polish that distinguishes your movie from others. Adjusting the tempo, adding transitions between scenes, and animating palettes to add polish to your movie are all refinements that help make your Director projects successful.

Once you've added the finishing touches to your movie, you can create a *projector* or a Shockwave movie of your Director project. The success of your projector or Shockwave movie starts long before you get to that point, however. A successful project depends upon the planning stages that occur before you even start Director. In this chapter you'll learn how to apply finishing touches and how to prepare your movies for distribution. You'll also get some design tips for creating a successful project.

Changing the Tempo

The human eye can see minute differences in objects and motion. This capability is tempered, however by perception. What we see and what we *perceive* are not the same thing. We mentally filter images to meet our perception of reality, based upon what we've learned to expect. The mind fills in gaps between events and skews the perception, to better understand the images it receives. For you to create animation, it's not necessary to become an expert on perception. It is helpful, though, if you understand that you can make perception work for you when you are creating an animation project.

In This Chapter

Changing the tempo

Working with transitions

Color palettes

Building projectors

Shocking your movies

Designing for success

The tempo of a Director movie has a great deal to do with perception of motion. *Tempo* is the frame rate at which an animation sequence moves. NTSC (National Television Standards Committee) video or broadcast-quality video displays at a rate of 30 fps (frames per second). PAL (Phase Alternation Line) and SECAM (Sequential Couleur Avec Mémoire) display at 25 fps. Although it might seem ideal for your Director movies to display at these frame rates or even at 60 fps, it's unrealistic and unnecessary for them to do so. Because of the way we perceive motion, if a Director movie is well designed it's doubtful most people would notice the difference between a movie at 15 fps and one at 60 fps.

It takes a computer with substantial resources to render images at 60 fps or even 30 fps. High-end computers with fast processors, large amounts of RAM, and fast video adapters might be able to render images at this rate. These machines are generally found on the desks of computer professionals, however, and don't represent the average user. The average home computer can reasonably expect to render images at a rate between 10 fps and 15 fps.

Director provides three ways to adjust the frame rate of a movie: through the Control Panel, in the Score window, and using Lingo commands (this last method is discussed in Chapter 12). Regardless of which method you use to adjust the frame rate of your movies, it's important to understand that the frame rate is a theoretical maximum. For example, if you were to set the frame rate of a movie to 60 fps, it wouldn't mean your movie would display at that speed. The actual speed of the movie would automatically drop to whatever frame rate the computer was capable of displaying.

Operating the Control Panel

The Control Panel operates much like a VCR. Using the Control Panel's controls, you can view and control the playback of your movie. Select Window⇨Control Panel, or Command+2 (Ctrl+2) to display the Control Panel (see Figure 5-1).

Each of the buttons and windows on the Control Panel has a specific function (see Table 5-1) to help you quickly adjust a variety of playback options. Changes you make using the Control Panel are global changes. Any settings you make here affect the entire movie, and can only be overwritten by settings made in the Score window or using Lingo.

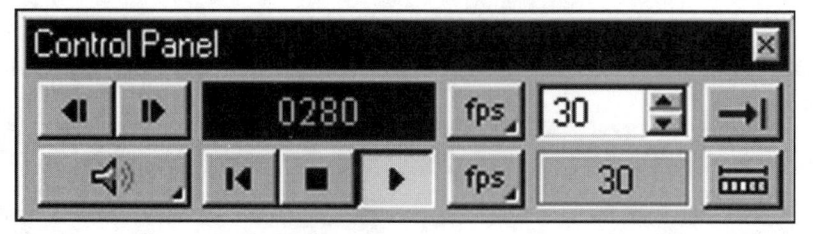

Figure 5-1: The Control Panel enables you to view and control the playback of your movie.

Table 5-1
Control Panel Functions

Control	Description
◀	Steps back one frame.
▶	Steps forward one frame.
0280	Frame counter: Displays the current frame.
fps	Allows you to choose whether to display frame rate as fps (frames per second) or seconds per frame. Click the corner arrow to make your selection.
30	Frame rate control: Allows you to adjust the frame rate of your movie. Click the up and down arrows to select a frame rate, or type a new frame rate into the box.
→▮	In this position, the Loop Playback button is toggled to play a movie to the end and then stop.
↻	In this position, the Loop Playback button is toggled to play a movie to the end, loop back to the beginning, and play it again.
🔊	Volume control: Click the corner arrow in the lower-right corner, and choose a volume level.
⏮	Rewinds your movie.
■	Pauses or stops your movie.
▶	Plays your movie or the selected range of frames.
30	Displays the current frame rate.
▭	In this position the Selected Frames Only button is toggled to play only the selected frames of a movie.
▭	In this position the Selected Frames Only button is toggled to play all frames of a movie.

> **Tip**
>
> *Checking for consistency:* One of the most valuable items on the Control Panel is the display of the current frame rate of your movie during playback. While you're testing a movie, it's a good idea to keep the Control Panel open and compare the current frame rate with the animation on the screen. Ideally, the frame rate of your movie should be consistent. The animation should move smoothly and at a consistent pace. Watch for fluctuations in the frame rate: Small ones are normal, but a dramatic change could indicate that you need to make an adjustment.

Specifying tempo settings in the Score window

Tempo is a design consideration whenever you create a Director movie. You may be aiming for anything from the relaxed pace of a slideshow presentation, to the "warp" speed of a starship racing across the galaxy. By specifying tempo settings in the Score window, you can

- Determine the maximum speed for your movie
- Pause your movie for a specified period of time
- Tell Director to wait for user interaction before continuing the movie
- Wait for a cue point in a digital video or sound file (Cue points are discussed in Chapters 7 and 8.)

The tempo in a Director movie can be changed as often as is necessary. It's a good idea to set the base tempo at the start of your movie, however. This helps you to control the frame rate and reduce fluctuations in the playback of your movie. If you don't specify a tempo at the beginning, Director plays the movie at the maximum default frame rate of 30 fps. This can cause some significant fluctuations in the actual frame rate, depending on the available resources of the computer used to play the movie and the complexity of the movie. Though you can't completely eliminate fluctuations in the frame rate, you can minimize their visual impact in your movie by slowing the frame rate of more complex animation sequences.

Compensating for a slow playback

When you create an animation sequence in Director, you use a set of keyframes to describe the major movements of the object being animated. Suppose you are animating the movement of the minute hand on a clock. By creating images that display the minute hand at the 12 o'clock, 3, 6, and 9 o'clock positions, you can then use these images as keyframes for the animation sequence. Tweening between the keyframes will simulate the movement of the minute hand.

When the tempo of your movie slows, animation sequences can become jerky. It may not be appropriate or possible to increase the frame rate, but you can compensate for jerky animation using one of two methods: adding more tween steps, or increasing the number of keyframes. In our clock example, increasing the number of tween steps between the keyframes of the animation will smooth the motion of the minute hand. A smoother motion can also be obtained by creating keyframes every ten minutes instead of every fifteen minutes.

Specifying a frame rate

Controlling tempo is always important — and sometimes critical — to your movie. A polka would sound very strange if it were played to a disco beat. Similarly, if you are trying to build a suspenseful moment in your movie, you might want to slow the tempo of your movie over a selected range of frames.

As mentioned earlier, to help ensure a consistent tempo throughout your movie you can select a median frame rate at the beginning of your movie. In this first exercise, you'll do just that.

Note: Whenever you specify a tempo setting, that tempo setting remains in effect until you change it.

Setting the Base Tempo

1. Open your movie in Director, if it's not already open.
2. Select Window ⇨ Score, to display the Score window.
3. Click the Hide/Show Effects Channels button to expand the Score window to display the Effects channels, if necessary.
4. Double-click the Tempo channel in the first frame of your movie (the Tempo channel is the one with a small clock icon). This displays the Frame Properties: Tempo dialog box (Figure 5-2). You can also select Modify ⇨ Frame ⇨ Tempo to get this dialog.

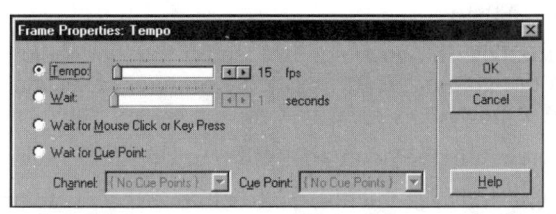

Figure 5-2: The Frame Properties: Tempo dialog box is used to specify the frame rate for your movie.

5. Select the Tempo radio button, and click the left and right arrows to slow down or speed up the frame rate for your movie. A frame rate of 15 fps is a good median rate.
6. Click OK to complete the operation and return to Director's main window. The frame rate will stay at 15 fps (or whatever setting you selected) until you change it.

You can create a dramatic moment in your movie by slowing the frame rate to 2–4 fps in the frames where you want the slowdown. Suppose you want to show a heavy weight being hoisted to the top of a building and then dropping to the ground. By slowing the frame rate during the frames in which the weight is rising to the top of the building, you reinforce the illusion of weight. The drama of the event is further enhanced when the weight falls at the normal frame rate back to the ground.

Tip: Tempo settings don't affect the duration of any transitions you've set in the transition channel, and they don't control the speed at which a sound plays. They control the maximum speed at which the playback head moves from frame to frame.

Pausing a movie

Pausing a movie for a specified period of time is a useful technique if you are creating a presentation, when you want to stop the movie briefly while the user views the contents of the frame. A typical use for a tempo pause would be a noninteractive kiosk presentation of a product line. During the three- to five-second pause while each product is displayed on the screen, the viewer gets to see an entire product line in a slideshow presentation.

Specifying a Pause in Your Movie

1. Open your movie in Director, if it's not already open.
2. In the Score window, double-click the Tempo channel in the frame where you want to insert a pause.
3. In the Frame Properties: Tempo dialog box, select the Wait radio button, and click the left or right arrows to specify the number of seconds you want your movie to pause.
4. Click OK to complete the operation and return to Director's main window.
5. Rewind your movie, and click the Play button to test the pause time.

Tip: If you want to duplicate your pause setting in another frame, you can quickly copy the tempo cell in the Score window using Command+C (Ctrl+C). Then click the the other frame and paste the tempo using Command+V (Ctrl+V).

You might need to test and change the pause time to get the right pause length. What you're aiming for in this case is to allow the user long enough to view the contents of the frame, without making the wait too long before the movie continues. Generally a pause of three seconds is more than adequate for viewing a graphic. If you are creating a pause for a frame that contains text, you'll need to specify a longer time. It's a good idea to have the frame reviewed by someone who's unfamiliar with the text. You probably know the text well and may as a result be inclined to set an insufficient pause time. Getting another point of view will reduce the risk of this happening, and it allows for the variation in the speed at which people read.

Waiting for user intervention

Another tempo consideration is when you want to allow the user to control the pace. You can arrange for user control of a range of frames using a *wait setting* in the Frame Properties: Tempo dialog box. A wait setting pauses your movie until the user presses a key or clicks the mouse. Wait settings are especially useful if you need to display multiple frames with text and want the user to control the pace.

> ## Specifying a Wait Setting
>
> 1. Open your movie in Director, if it's not already open.
> 2. Double-click the Tempo channel in the frame where you want to specify a wait setting.
> 3. In the Frame Properties: Tempo dialog box, select Wait for Mouse Click or Key Press.
> 4. Click OK to complete the operation and return to Director's main window.
> 5. Rewind your movie and click the Play button to test your wait setting.

One of the drawbacks to specifying a wait setting in the Score window is that the user can click anywhere on the screen or press any key to continue the movie. If you want the user to click a special button or a specific key, you'll need to create a Lingo script. For more information about using Lingo scripting to specify a wait setting, see Chapters 10 and 11.

Working with Transitions

Very few things can startle the viewer of a movie more than an abrupt change from one scene to the next. You can eliminate this problem by creating a *transition* between the frames. A transition is a technique by which some sort of passage connects two sequential frames in a movie. Figure 5-3 illustrates a transition; it shows two intermediate images that make up part of the passage between the starting and ending image. The transition in the figure uses a Dissolve effect, to create a blend of the two images as the intermediary stages in the passage. Like many other elements in your Director movies, transitions are represented both in the Score window and as cast members in the Cast window.

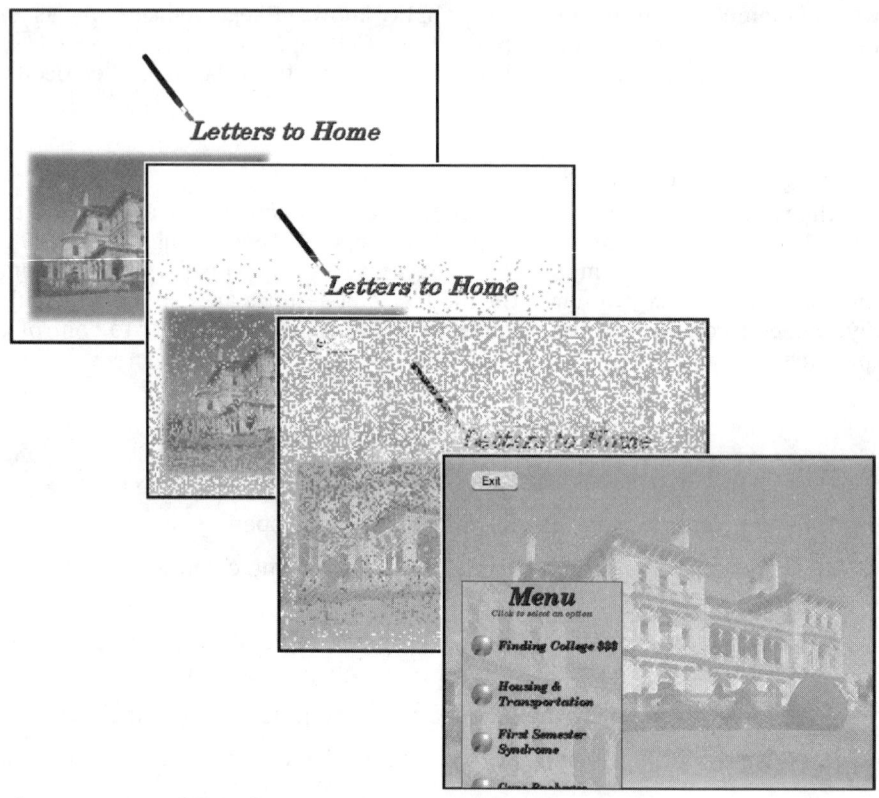

Figure 5-3: Transition effects transform one image into another.

Choosing a transition is mostly a matter of aesthetics. You can choose from a variety of transitions that range from the subtle to the dramatic.

Choosing a transition

Although a complete transition effect takes only the span of a single frame in a Director movie, you can specify the amount of time for the transition and the smoothness of the transformation. You choose the effect you want to use from the library of transitions included with Director (see Table 5-2). Transitions in Director are grouped by category for ease of selection and use, but each transition is unique in the way it appears. In addition, some transitions — such as Dissolve and those in the Other category — consume more of the computer's resources than other transitions do. Because they require more memory to render the images to the screen, they can cause performance problems if your entire movie is resource intensive overall, or if your movie is being played on a computer with limited resources.

Table 5-2
Transition Effects

Transition Category	Description and Available Options
Cover	Covers the first image with the image in the subsequent frame by sliding the image over it. You can specify the direction of the transition, the smoothness, amount of time, and whether the transition applies to the changing area only or the entire Stage.
Dissolve*	Dissolves from one image to the image of the subsequent frame, with a pixelated transition. You can choose the type of pixelation, smoothness, amount of time, and whether the transition applies to the changing area only or the entire Stage.
Other	Uses one of a miscellaneous collection of transitions, including checkerboard, random columns, random rows, blinds, and zoom effects, to change from one image to the image in the subsequent frame. You can choose the type, smoothness, amount of time, and whether the transition applies to the changing area only or the entire Stage.
Push	Pushes one image from view using the image from the subsequent frame. You can choose the type, smoothness, amount of time, and whether the transition applies to the changing area only or the entire Stage.
Reveal	Strips away one image to reveal the image in the subsequent frame. You can choose the direction, smoothness, amount of time, and whether the transition applies to the changing area only or the entire Stage.
Strips	Removes one image a strip at a time to reveal the image in the subsequent frame. You can choose the direction, smoothness, amount of time, and whether the transition applies to the changing area only or the entire Stage.
Wipe	Smoothly wipes one image away to reveal the image in the subsequent frame. You can choose the direction, smoothness, amount of time, and whether the transition applies to the changing area only or the entire Stage.

* Dissolve transitions have a different appearance on the Macintosh and Windows. If you are creating a cross-platform movie, test the transition on both platforms.

In addition to the transitions packaged with Director, a number of third-party vendors offer additional transitions that you can add to Director as Xtras. Xtra transitions are indicated with special icons in the Frame Properties: Transitions dialog box. You install Xtra transitions by placing them in the Xtras folder in the Director application folder (see Chapter 19 for more information). After they are used in the Score's transition channel, they appear in the Cast window just like any other cast member.

Tip: Transition Xtras, like other Xtras, must be included with your movie when it's distributed.

Applying and controlling a transition

Transitions — like tempos, palettes, and sounds — have a channel set aside for them in the Score and are placed in the frame where you want the transition to begin. Before you select the frame in which you want to set a transition, it's important to understand how transitions work.

Note: A transition always takes place between the end of the current frame and the beginning of the frame where the transition is set. If you want to add a transition between two scenes, you must place the transition in the first frame of the second scene, *not* in the last frame of the first scene.

Tip: If you want to use sound during a transition, place the sound in a frame earlier than where the transition is placed. This gives the sound time to decompress and load prior to the rendering of the transition. It makes for a smoother transition.

When you apply a transition, there are a variety of options you can set that affect the appearance of the transition. Each transition has a particular set of options; only the options available for a specific transition will be available in the Frame Properties: Transition dialog box. (The Description column of Table 5-2 includes the options available for each category of transition.)

Following are descriptions of the available controls in the Frame Properties: Transition dialog:

- **Duration** — You can specify the amount of time, in seconds, over which you want the transition to render to screen. Shorter transition duration creates more abrupt changes; longer duration creates gradual changes and is more resource intensive.

- **Smoothness** — By adjusting the smoothness, you can control the *chunk size* of the transition. Chunk size is the number of pixels affected at a time. (Although the Smoothness slider in the Frame Properties: Transitions dialog doesn't reflect numbers, you can choose a chunk size between 1 pixel and 128 pixels.) You adjust the Smoothness slider to the right to reduce the number of pixels and increase the smoothness of your transition. Adjust the slider to the left to increase the number of pixels in the chunk size. Smoother transitions use up more resources and render slower than transitions that use a larger chunk size.

- **Affects: Entire Stage** — This option changes the entire Stage. Although this is a slower and more resource-intensive transition, it is more attractive when the background is a bitmap image.

- **Affects: Changing Area Only** — This option changes only that portion of the Stage that actually changes. It is a good choice when transitioning to a digital video, or when changing text on the Stage.

Tip: To increase the speed of a transition, consider enlarging the chunk size of the transition instead of reducing the duration. The number of pixels has more impact on speed than does the number of seconds for the transition.

In addition to these options, others may be available if you are using an Xtra as a transition. If an Xtra has other options, the Options button will be highlighted in the Frame Properties: Transition dialog.

Adding a Transition

1. Open your movie in Director, if it's not already open.
2. Open the Score window by selecting Window ⇨ Score.
3. Double-click the Transition channel in the frame in which you want to place a transition. The Frame Properties: Transition dialog box appears (Figure 5-4).
4. Choose the transition category and transition you want to use. If you click All in the Categories list box, all of the available transitions appear in alphabetical order in the Transitions list.
5. Set the Duration, Smoothness, and Affects options.

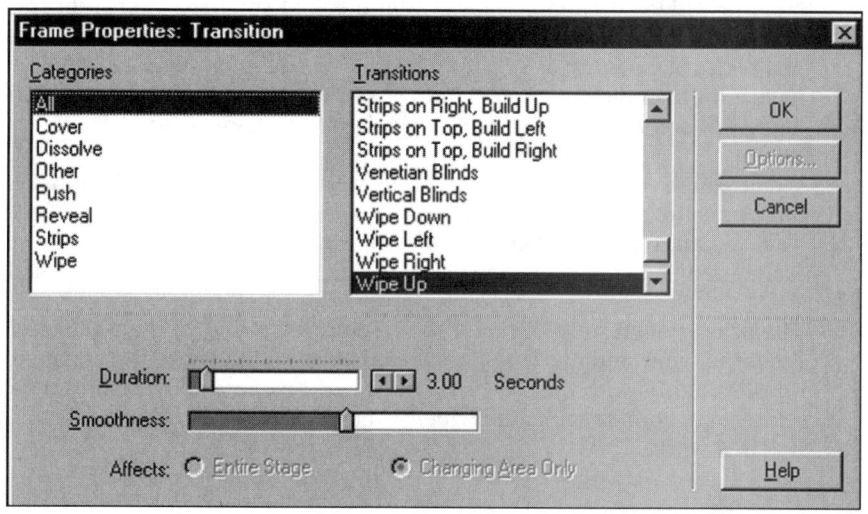

Figure 5-4: You select and control transitions in the Frame Properties: Transition dialog box.

6. Click OK to complete the operation and return to Director's main window.

7. Rewind your movie, and click the Play button to test your transition. If you want to change the transition, double-click the transition in the Score, and make any changes you want.

Once you set a transition, it appears in the Cast window as well as the Score. If you want to reuse the transition later in your movie, simply drag the transition from the Cast window to the Transition channel of the frame in which you want the transition to start.

Caution

Transitions may not be preserved if you are exporting your file to digital video, and they are ignored when used with *movies in a window* (MIAWs). To ensure the successful distribution of your movie, test your transitions carefully to make sure they function in a digital video. For more information about transitions and MIAWs, see Chapter 21.

Working with Color Palettes

Color is one of the most complex and most misunderstood topics in computer graphics. Among the myriad color issues that affect Director, one of the most critical is cross-platform color shifting. The bad news is that every platform, monitor, video adapter, computer, and piece of software interprets color just a little differently from the rest. The result can be like trying to find identical snowflakes in a blizzard. So what is a computer graphic designer supposed to do? You don't have a lot of choice. All you can do is accept the reality, and try to minimize the impact of color shifting by carefully selecting a color palette.

When you're working with color, other issues of almost equal importance are image quality and memory management. Graphics can be real resource hogs. The files are typically large and require a lot of memory to render to screen. Maintaining a balance between quality and resources is a valuable skill.

The primary determining factor for all color issues is your audience. By accurately assessing your audience, color issues become a matter of matching color considerations with the viewers' needs and resources. To begin the process of addressing your specific audience, you must first understand how color and color palettes work.

First, a little color theory

Computers read data in bits. A bit is the smallest unit of binary data. At its simplest level, a computer interprets color as either 0 (off), or 1 (on), or 1-bit color. Normally 1-bit color is black-and-white. In reality, all color is described in 0s and 1s — 2-bit color, for example, creates four possible color choices: black, white, and two shades of gray.

Color is created by translating and interpreting each bit using a color table of possible colors. As the number of bits increases, there is geometric growth in the permutations of colors that can be achieved. Director supports a variety of color depths, as listed in Table 5-3.

Table 5-3
Color Depths and Supported Colors

Color Depth	Number of Colors Supported
1-bit	2 colors (black and white)
2-bit	4 colors (usually black, white, and two grays)
4-bit	16 colors
8-bit	256 colors
16-bit	64,000 colors
24-bit	16.7 million colors
32-bit	6.8 billion colors

The file size of an image grows in proportion to increases in the color depth and the number of colors. If file size is an issue, reducing the color depth of a bitmap can represent huge savings in storage space, as well as improve the screen refresh rate of your movie. Large files take longer to import, load, and render to screen. They may also be unnecessarily larger than what is required for optimum output. A 32-bit or 24-bit color image looks wonderful, but if you intend to use it in a Director movie or on a Web page, the price in file size and download time is enormous.

Tip: When you are creating a Director movie, it's a good idea to consider the least common denominator where color is concerned. Most of the computers in use today are capable of displaying a minimum of 8-bit color without straining the resources of the computer or video adapter. If you are looking to reach the broadest audience base, you should use 8-bit color exclusively within your movies.

Mapping images to palettes

Palettes are far more than virtual boxes of crayons. Frequently, palettes are designed and intended for a specific purpose. The NTSC palette, for example, was designed to provide a standardized palette for the broadcast video industry. Other palettes, such as the system palettes for Macintosh and Windows, are the default palettes for those platforms.

Director allows you to map your images to a palette when you import the image. If your image was created using a custom (adaptive) palette and you choose not to remap the image, the palette is imported with the image and placed in the Cast window. We don't recommend the use of custom or adaptive palettes, however. When Director encounters a custom palette in a frame of your movie, it remaps *all* of the active Stage elements to that palette. A palette that was perfect for one element in your movie might look positively horrid when applied to other elements. If you want to use a custom palette, be sure to test it thoroughly with the other elements in your movie, as well as on the anticipated target platforms.

> **Caution**
> Director can only display a single palette in any given frame of your movie. If the elements of your movie use different palettes, you run the risk of conflicts. Your movie may crash if a palette conflict occurs due to multiple palettes in a frame.

Macintosh or Windows or both?

Macintosh and Windows don't display color in the same way. If you are creating a cross-platform movie, you'll notice a dramatic difference between the way your movie looks on the Macintosh versus the way it looks in Windows. The Macintosh system palette is mellower and may appear faded as compared with the sharp vibrant colors in Windows. Although you can't change the way the two platforms differ in color interpretation, you can minimize the impact to your movies.

When you are creating a cross-platform movie, it's a good idea to select one palette and use it on both the Macintosh and Windows version of your movie. At the risk of starting a platform war, we generally think it's best to use the Macintosh system palette. The reasoning behind this choice is simple: Windows is more forgiving in the way it displays color palettes. The result is that the Macintosh system palette is represented more faithfully in Windows, than the Windows system palette is on the Macintosh. Moreover, selecting a single palette enables you to create your movie with less concern about color translation when you transfer your movie to the other platform.

Color palettes and the Web

When playing in a Web browser, Shockwave movies don't control the color palette of a user's system as projectors do. Shockwave remaps the colors in Director movies to the most similar colors in the active palette of the user's system. Generally, the active palette is that of the user's browser. You can get the best color results from your Shockwave movies if you map all the images in your movie to the Netscape palette or the MSN palette included with Director. Select the Xtras⇨Palette command to open the cast of included palettes, and choose either the Netscape or MSN palette.

Remapping Images When Importing

1. Open your movie in Director, if it's not already open.
2. Select File➪Import to display the Import Files dialog box (Figure 5-5) or click the Import button on Director's toolbar.
3. Select the files you want to import and click the Add button to move them to the File List. You can also double-click a filename to automatically add it to the File List.
4. Click Import. The Import Options dialog box appears (Figure 5-6).
5. Choose the palette options you want to use. If you want to remap your image to a specific palette, choose the palette from the drop-down palette list, and click the Remap to radio button.
6. If you want all of the images to be imported using the same options, check the Same Settings for Remaining Images check box.
7. Click OK to import the images and return to Director's main window.

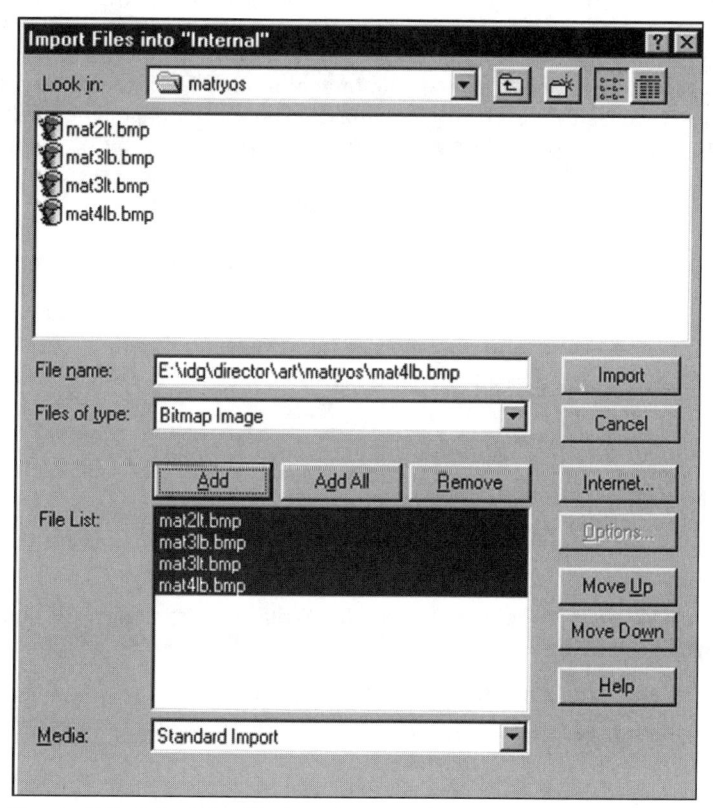

Figure 5-5: Select the files you want to import.

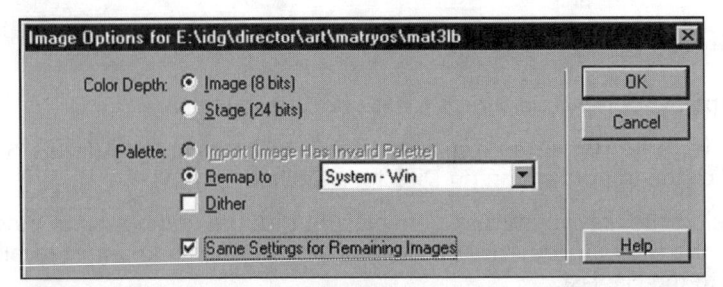

Figure 5-6: Select the import options you want to use.

Tip   Notice that the color depth of the Stage in Figure 5-6 is 24-bit color. If your movie is intended for the broadest distribution, use 8-bit color. The easiest method of accomplishing this is to set your screen color depth to 8-bit; then you can remap all imported images to the Stage's color depth, which will be 8-bit color.

Remapping images on import enables you to quickly change the palette for bitmap images before they are placed in the Cast window. You can also change the palette of existing bitmap cast members, using the Transform Bitmap command. With this command you can choose to remap the image or specify dithering. If you choose Dither, Director tries to match the existing colors of the image as closely as possible to the existing palette by interspersing pixels from the new palette. In addition to changing the palette an image uses, the Transform Bitmap command allows you to change the color depth and size of the image.

Caution   The Transform Bitmap can't be undone. If you are unhappy with the results, you'll need to reimport the image into the cast.

Transforming Bitmaps

1. Open your movie in Director, if it's not already open.
2. Select Window ⇨ Cast to display the Cast window.
3. In the Cast window, select the bitmap cast members you want to transform.
4. Select Modify ⇨ Transform Bitmap, to display the Transform Bitmap dialog box (Figure 5-7).
5. Select a palette from the Palette list.
6. Click either the Remap Colors or Dither radio button.

7. To resize your image, either enter a new value in the Scale percentage box, or type new values into the Width and Height boxes. If you check Maintain Proportions, you only need to enter one value; Director will calculate the other (width or height) values to maintain the aspect ratio of the image.

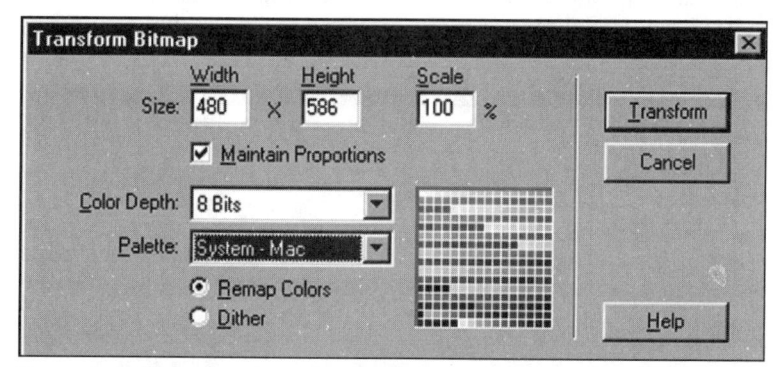

Figure 5-7: Changing the color depth, size, and palette for your image

8. Click OK to transform the bitmap. A warning box appears telling you that the operation is irreversible, and asking you to confirm your command. Click OK to continue or Cancel to quit.

The Transform Bitmap command is useful for quickly modifying your bitmap images. If you're reducing the size of an image by a small percentage (25% or less), Transform Bitmap is an effective choice. It doesn't do resampling, however, and changing the size of a bitmap without resampling degrades the quality of the image. If you need to make larger changes or enlarge an image, put the image in an external editor, such as Adobe Photoshop, for resampling.

Modifying palettes

In addition to the standard palettes that come with Director, you can duplicate existing palettes and then modify them, to create your own custom palettes. This is useful when a movie's cast members use only a few out of a range of colors. For example, if the cast members are using only 24 solid colors out of the 256-color palette, you could create a custom palette, remap all of the cast members to the new palette, and thus reduce the rendering time and file size of the entire movie. One cautionary note: This technique doesn't work as well for images containing gradient fills.

Note You can't modify or edit any of Director's standard palettes.

Creating a Modified Palette

1. Select Window➪Color Palettes or press Command+Option+7 (Ctrl+Alt+7). This displays the Color Palettes window, with the active platform palette in the palette window. In Figure 5-8, you see the Windows system palette.

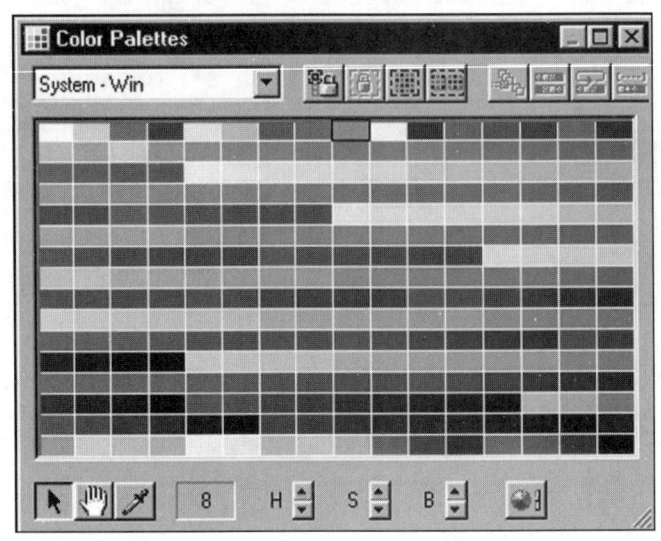

Figure 5-8: The Color Palettes window allows you to modify color palettes.

2. To modify the colors in the palette, select a color square and use the up- and down-arrow buttons at the bottom of the window to change the color's HSB (Hue, Saturation, Brightness).

3. A dialog box appears, allowing you to rename the palette (see Figure 5-9). Enter a new name — it's a good idea to enter a name that is associated with the cast members in your movie. That makes it easier to remember the palette's use later.

Figure 5-9: Enter a name for your new color palette in the Create Palette dialog box.

4. Click OK to return to the Color Palettes window. The new palette appears with the name displayed at the top of the window (see Figure 5-10).

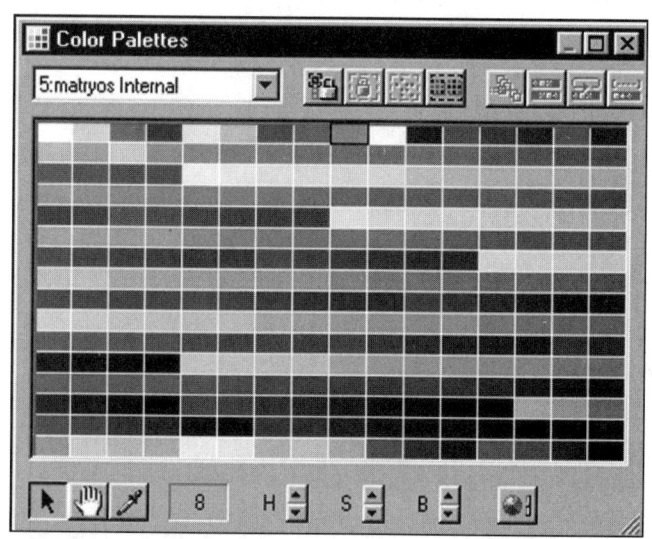

Figure 5-10: Modified color palette's name is displayed at the top of the Color Palettes window.

5. You can repeat step 2 and modify any other colors in the custom palette.

6. After modifying a palette, be sure to save your movie to preserve the changes you've made to the palette.

You've now created the basis for a modified palette. You can edit the palette as needed in a variety of ways, using the tools and command buttons in the Color Palettes window. Table 5-4 describes these tools and their functions in editing your color palettes.

Caution

You can map cast members to your modified palette as you would to one of Director's standard palettes. Be cautious when remapping cast members to a palette, as these changes are irreversible.

Table 5-4
Tools and Functions in the Color Palettes Window

Icon	Description	Function
	Reserve Selected Colors	Reserves selected colors and prevents their use. Useful for restricting effects such as cycling colors to a selected group of colors.
	Select Reserved Colors	Selects colors you have reserved in the active color palette.
	Select Used Colors	Scans the cast members to select just those colors used by the cast.
	Invert Selection	Reverses the selection. For example, if the selected colors in the palette are those used by your cast, this option will reverse that selection and select the colors that were *not* used by the cast.
	Sort	Allows you to sort colors by Hue, Saturation, or Brightness. Select a range of colors, and then click the Sort button and choose the desired parameter from the dialog that appears.
	Reverse Sequence	Reverses the order of the selected colors in the Color Palettes window.
	Cycle	Cycles selected colors one square to the left. Creates an effect similar to color cycling. **Note:** This option is only available for 256-color palettes.
	Blend	Creates a blend of a selected range of colors. Useful for creating a range of blended colors for use as a gradient. Select a range of colors and click the Blend button to create the blended range.
	Arrow tool	Used to select colors and options in the Color Palettes window. Click a color to select it. Click and drag to select a range of colors.
	Hand tool	Allows you to click and drag colors and rearrange their order in the Color Palettes window.
	Eyedropper	Allows you to replace a color in the Color Palettes window, by selecting the color and then clicking and dragging the Eyedropper to the desired color on the Stage.
	Color Picker	Allows you to select colors from the Color dialog box.

Creating effects with palettes

You can create effects with palettes much as you can with other sprites in your movie. For instance, using settings in the Frame Properties: Palette dialog box, you can fade a palette to black or white. Fading to black or white is useful for adding closure scenes to your movies. Instead of abruptly ending the movie, the scene gradually fades away.

You can also create color-cycling effects. Color cycling works well for a variety of uses, such as making a cartoon character blush by degrees from pink to red, or for creating a headline banner that cycles through several colors.

Note that palette fading and color-cycling effects are only available if you are using an 8-bit, 256-color palette. You can't create these effects with other color depths.

On the CD-ROM Let's try both of these effects in the next two exercises. You'll use the statue.dir movie in both sets of steps. The image stored in the bitmap cast member is from a collection of photographs by Sherri and Joe Mulvihill (of Kodak) taken while on assignment in Japan. The statue.dir movie is on your companion CD-ROM in the exercise:ch05 (exercise\ch05) folder.

Creating a Fade to Black or White

1. Open the statue.dir movie.
2. To add a palette fade at the end of the movie (from frame 40 to frame 60), click once in the Palettes channel in frame 40. Hold down the Shift key and click in frame 60; this selects all frames between 40 and 60.
3. Select Modify ⇨ Frame ⇨ Palette to display the Frame Properties: Palette dialog box (Figure 5-11).

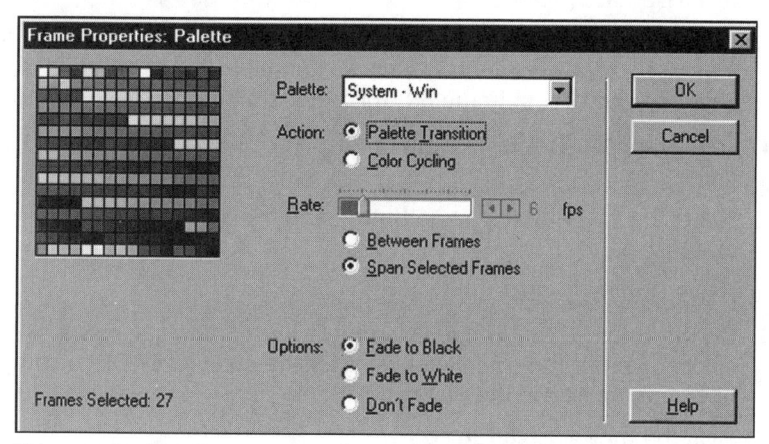

Figure 5-11: The Frame Properties: Palette dialog box lets you set up various palette effects.

4. Select the Palette Transition radio button and the Span Selected Frames radio button.
5. In the Options area at the bottom of the dialog, choose either Fade to Black or Fade to White.
6. Click OK to complete the operation and return to Director's main window.

7. Save the movie as **statue1.dir**.
8. Be sure the Loop Playback button on the Control panel is turned off so the movie doesn't recycle.
9. Rewind the movie, click the Play button, and watch the palette fade.

Although not specifically a transition like those available through the Frame Properties: Transition dialog box, you can use palette fades to create color transitions both at the end of your movie and between scenes in your movie.

Now let's work with color cycling.

Cycling Colors in Your Movie

Caution

Remember that color cycling, like the palette fade, only works when using an 8-bit, 256-color palette. Furthermore, if your monitor is set to use a high-color (16-bit) or true-color palette (24-bit or 32-bit), these effects are *not* displayed.

1. Open the statue.dir movie from the CD-ROM in the exercise:ch05 (exercise\ch05) folder.
2. To add a palette color cycle at the end of the movie (from frame 40 to frame 60), click once in the Palettes channel in frame 40. Hold down the Shift key and click in frame 60. This selects all frames between 40 and 60.
3. Select Modify ⇨ Frame ⇨ Palette to display the Frame Properties: Palette dialog box.
4. Select the Color Cycling radio button and the Span Selected Frames radio button.
5. Leave Options set to Loop.
6. On the color palette in the dialog box, click and drag across a range of colors to select the colors you want for the cycle. Click OK to complete the operation and close the dialog box.
7. Save the movie as **statue2.dir**.
8. Be sure the Loop Playback button on the Control panel is turned off so the movie doesn't recycle.
9. Rewind the movie, click the Play button, and watch the palette cycle.

Color cycling can create effects from muted to spectacular, depending on the colors you select to cycle.

Tip: To quickly highlight and call attention to text in your movie, consider selecting two contrasting colors for the text, and cycle between them with Color Cycling enabled in the Frame Properties: Palette dialog box.

Building Projectors

Once you've created a Director movie, you can play it in Director or share it with others who have Director installed on their computers. None of the available media players support Director movies, however. If you want to distribute your Director movie for others to use, you need to create a *projector* of your movie. A projector is a Director movie packaged with all of the elements required for playing it on a given platform. Director doesn't need to be installed for the projector to play.

Caution: Projectors are platform specific. A projector created on a Macintosh won't run in Windows. A projector created in Windows 95 won't run on a Macintosh or in Windows 3.*x*. On the other hand, Windows 95 can play projectors created in Windows 3.*x*. If you're creating a movie for cross-platform distribution, you'll need to create the projector on the platform for which it's designed to play. This means it's possible to create three projectors: one for each platform.

Projectors are distinct files that bundle your movie, sounds, Xtras, filters, and the run-time engine into one file. Unlike the original Director movies from which they are created, projectors are executable files, which means that the movie starts when you double-click the filename.

Caution: *Windows users:* Note that projector files have an .exe extension. The Macintosh OS doesn't routinely put extensions on files, so you should be careful not to overwrite your Director movie by giving your projector the same name as your Director movie.

Projector movies are by their nature larger than their original Director movies. The reason for the difference in size has to do with the number and types of files included in a projector. It's not uncommon for a projector to be two to three times the size of its associated Director movie.

Creating a projector

Before creating a projector, it's a good idea to play your movie one last time to check all the elements of your movie. Although your original Director movie isn't altered when you create a projector, you can't edit the projector itself.

When you create a projector, Director asks you to add the movies you want associated with the projector. You can choose to add one or more movies to the list. In addition, you can add cast libraries, Xtras, and other files needed in association with the projector. You can even create a projector that runs several movies in a sequence.

Caution: Be careful when adding several movies and files to the projector list. Movies are played in the same order in which they're listed. This point is especially critical for projectors with MIAWs, in which the host movie calls other movies to play. If the order is incorrect, your MIAW will finish playing before its host movie starts, causing the projector to fail.

You can specify a variety of options when you create a projector. These options, accessed through the Options button in the Create Projector dialog box, determine the appearance of the projector and the way the projector is stored for distribution. Table 5-5 lists and describes the various options for creating a projector.

Table 5-5
Options for Creating a Projector

Option	Description
Create For	Allows you to choose the platform for which you want to create a projector.
Playback: Play Every Movie	When you're creating a projector that contains multiple movies, choosing this option ensures that every movie will play in turn; otherwise, only the first movie plays. **Note:** For a projector of an MIAW, do *not* select this option. If you do, the child movie will be left on the screen when the projector has finished playing.
Playback: Animate in Background	Plays your projector regardless of what other applications are active. If you don't select this option, when you start another application the projector will pause until you click it to restart it.
Options: Full Screen	Blanks out the screen of all other applications and plays the projector full screen.
Options: In a Window	Plays your projector in a window the size of the movie's Stage.
Show Title Bar	If you select this option and your projector is playing in a window, the projector displays a title bar with the projector's name.
Stage Size: Use Movie Settings	Causes each movie in the projector to be displayed at its creation size (when the projector contains multiple movies).
Stage Size: Match First Movie	Causes successive movies to be resized to match the Stage size of the first movie in the play order. Be careful when you use this option because it can cause distortion in your movies. This option is most effective when the Stage size for all movies is the same.
Center	Centers the movie on the screen.

Chapter 5 ✦ **The Big Picture** 163

Option	Description
Media: Compress (Shockwave Format)	Compresses projectors for use on the Internet. This keeps the file size as small as possible for downloading, but it increases the load time because the file has to decompress before playing. Shockwave compression can be used for any projector to reduce its size.
Xtras: Include Network Xtras	Select this option if your projector is going to be used on the Internet. This option ensures that the Xtras required for Internet use are included in your projector.
Xtras: Check Movies for Xtras	Causes Director to search the movies included in the projector to make sure all of the essential Xtras are included with the projector.

Creating a Projector

On the CD-ROM

1. Open onlingox.dir in Director. You can find it on the companion CD-ROM in the exercise:ch05 (exercise/ch05) folder.

2. Select File ➪ Create Projector to display the Create Projector dialog box (Figure 5-12).

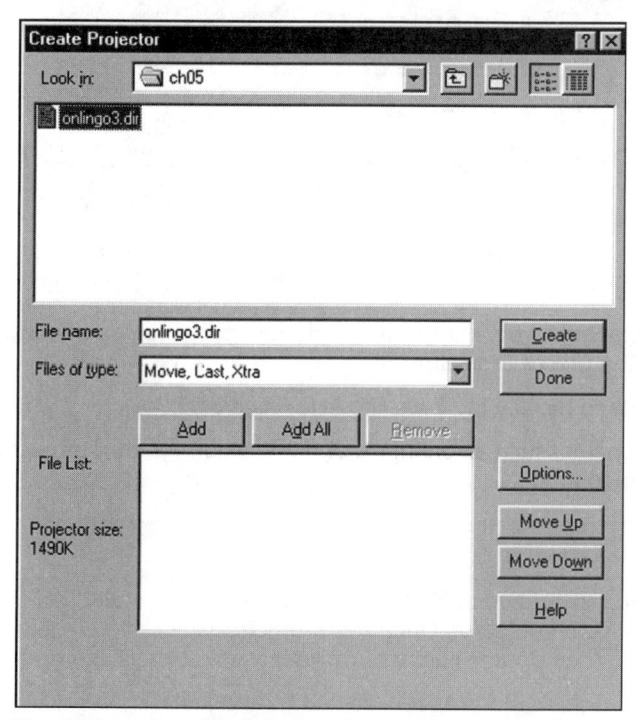

Figure 5-12: Use the Create Projector dialog box to specify the movies and options you want to include in a projector.

3. Navigate to and select onlingox.dir, and click the Add button to add it to the File List at the bottom of the dialog box.

4. If you are making a projector for more than one movie, you must verify the order in which the movies appear in the File List box. Click the Move Up or Move Down buttons as needed to reposition selected movies in the list. Remember that movies have to be listed in the order in which you want them to play.

5. Click the Options button to display the Projector Options dialog box (Figure 5-13).

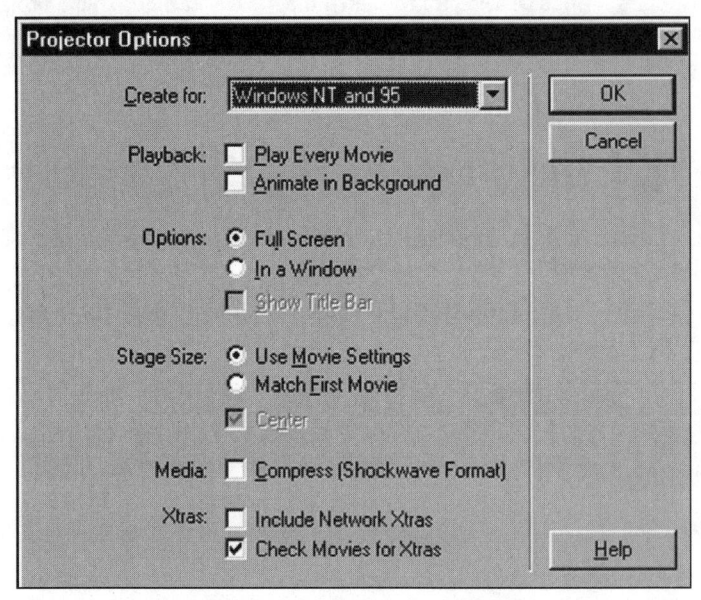

Figure 5-13: The Projector Options dialog box allows you to select the options you want to use with your projector.

6. Select the options you want to use with your projector, and click OK to return to the Create Projector dialog.

7. Click Create to display the Save Projector As dialog box.

8. Enter a filename, such as onlingox, and a location for your projector, and click OK to continue.

Depending on the size and complexity of your movie, it may take Director a couple minutes to create your projector. Once the projector is completed, minimize or close Director and then double-click your projector file to test the projector.

Distributing a projector

Projectors tend to be large — even a small projector file is usually larger than will fit on a single floppy disk. Although you can use a compression utility such as StuffIt or PKZip to compress and store your projector on multiple disks, we don't recommend it. A projector movie contains many component parts but is basically considered a single file, and it's not a good policy to span a single file across multiple disks. If a single archive disk fails, then your projector becomes worthless.

A variety of storage media can be used to distribute your projectors. Only two of them are practical, however. You can either distribute the projector via the Internet as a download, or you can create a CD-ROM containing the projector. If you choose to distribute your projector over the Internet, be aware that the user will have to download the file and play it off line. The only way the user can view your movies on line is if you create a Shockwave movie (see the upcoming section). A CD-ROM capable of holding almost 650MB of data may seem like overkill if you have a 3MB projector, but the potential audience — given the number of people who own CD-ROM drives — may warrant using that media for distribution. CD-ROM recorders and media are becoming fairly inexpensive and are reasonably easy to operate.

Shocking Your Movies

Shockwave — one of the fastest growing technological advances to hit the Internet — helps Web authors add animation and interactivity to Web pages. Shockwave is not actually a single product but rather a group of products, designed by Macromedia to provide an interactive interface for presenting high-end graphics on the Web. Until recently, each flavor of Shockwave was designed to work with a specific Macromedia product. Now the Shockwave player is distributed as a single engine, and a single plug-in that works with the three Macromedia products that can create Shockwave media (Director, Authorware, and Flash). Still, when people think of Shockwave they think of Director or the movies that you can create in Director.

Designing for the Web

Before you create a Shockwave movie, it's a good idea to check with your ISP (Internet service provider) to be sure that the Shockwave file format is supported. The server at your ISP must be able to send information to a user's Web browser telling the browser how to deal with files. If your provider doesn't support the Director or Shockwave MIME-type, users won't be able to view your movie on line. (For more information about Shockwave and the Internet, see Chapter 24.)

Caution: The Internet and World Wide Web don't support multiple windows. For that reason, you can't use MIAWs in a Web page.

A Shockwave movie can be presented using either Netscape Navigator (2.x and later) or Internet Explorer (3.x and later). Each of these browsers embeds files a bit differently. When you embed a Shockwave movie in a Web page, you need to create code specific to one or both of these browsers. Table 5-6 describes the HTML and parameter tags you might use in embedding your Shockwave movie.

Table 5-6
Coding Tags for Embedding a Shockwave Movie into a Web Page

Tag	Netscape Navigator	Internet Explorer (ActiveX)	Description
CLASSID	No	Yes	Identifies the Shockwave ActiveX control to Internet Explorer. If you are familiar with ActiveX controls in Windows 95, the CLASSID is a GUID. For Director Shockwave, the CLASSID is always CLASSID= "clsid: 166B1BCA-3F9C-11CF-8075-444553540000".
CODEBASE	No	Yes	Tells Internet Explorer where to load the ActiveX plug-in if it's not currently on the end-user's computer.
WIDTH	Yes	Yes	The width of a Shockwave window in pixels. You should enter a width that matches that of the movie. If it's larger than the movie, the background will show; if it's smaller, the movie will be cropped to fit.
HEIGHT	Yes	Yes	The height of a Shockwave window in pixels. You should enter a height that matches that of the movie. If it's larger than the movie, the background will show; if it's smaller, the movie will be cropped to fit.
ID	No	Yes	Identifies a movie to a browser. This isn't important for simple animations, but it's extremely important for JavaScript or VBScript.
NAME	Yes	Yes	Used with forms (see Chapter 24). Also, used in Netscape Navigator in lieu of the ID tag.
PLUGINSPAGE	Yes	No	Refers to the location from which the Shockwave plug-in can be downloaded (for Netscape Navigator-compatible browsers). If you don't state this property, it defaults to the Netscape plug-ins page.

Tag	Netscape Navigator	Internet Explorer (ActiveX)	Description
PALETTE	Yes	Yes*	Tells whether to use the Shockwave palette (PALETTE=foreground) or the browser's palette (PALETTE=background), which is the default. *Internet Explorer doesn't support foreground palettes.
SRC	Yes	Yes	Provides the URL for the Shockwave movie. Can be entered relative to the URL of the page, or as an absolute URL starting with http:. Note that Netscape Navigator sees SRC as a Java-style parameter.

If you are unfamiliar with Internet terminology or how to build an HTML page, you may want to look ahead to Chapter 24, which includes a short lesson on HTML with an emphasis on plug-ins and ActiveX technology.

Note that HTML is not case-sensitive except when it encounters text strings or filenames enclosed by quotes. HTML also ignores returns or spaces in the code. You could actually write the code as one long string. Inserting returns is mostly to make the code readable. Tags are also normally entered in all caps for ease of identification.

Caution

Though HTML isn't case-sensitive, UNIX definitely is. Since most ISP servers run a type of UNIX, be cautious when naming files for use on the Web. References to files in your code must specify filenames that match exactly, including capitalization. It's a good idea when naming files for use on the Web to always use lowercase letters in the name. This helps reduce the possibility of broken links due to misnamed file references and mismatches due to inconsistent letter case.

The HTML code for Netscape Navigator 2.x or later would look something like the following:

```
<EMBED SRC="onlingo.dcr" WIDTH=432 HEIGHT=324
PALETTE=foreground
PLUGINSPAGE="http://www.macromedia.com/shockwave/">
```

The code to embed a Shockwave movie into a Web page for Internet Explorer looks a bit different from that of Navigator's code:

```
<OBJECT
CLASSID="clsid:166B1BCA-3F9C-11CF-8075-444553540000"
CODEBASE="http://active.macromedia.com/director/cabs/
sw.cab#version=6,0,1,0"
WIDTH="432" HEIGHT="324"
```

(continued)

```
ID="MYMOVIE"
SRC="onlingo.dcr">
</OBJECT>
```

The problem with using these commands to embed Shockwave movies is that Internet Explorer may or may not read code for Netscape Navigator, and vice versa. This leaves you with two options. You can insert the code for Internet Explorer into that of Navigator's (as shown just below), or you can create JavaScript that senses which browser the user has and loads the correct code. The problem with the first solution is that the page may load a bit more slowly as the code is sorted out. The problem with using JavaScript is that you basically have to create two copies of the Web page that loads the movie: one encoded for Navigator, and one encoded for Internet Explorer.

If you decide to embed the code for Internet Explorer into Navigator code, the result would look something like this:

```
<EMBED
WIDTH="432" HEIGHT="324"
ID="MYMOVIE"
NAME="MYMOVIE"
PLUGINSPAGE="http://www.macromedia.com/shockwave"
PALETTE=foreground>
<PARAM NAME="SRC" VALUE="onlingo.dcr">
<OBJECT
CLASSID="clsid:166B1BCA-3F9C-11CF-8075-444553540000"
CODEBASE="http://active.macromedia.com/director/cabs/sw.cab#version=6,0,1,0"
WIDTH="432" HEIGHT="324"
ID="MYMOVIE"
SRC="onlingo.dcr">
</OBJECT>
</EMBED>
```

If you decide to let Java determine which browser is in use and load the correct version of the index page, you'll need JavaScript similar to the following in the HTML code for your Web page:

```
<SCRIPT LANGUAGE="JavaScript"><! —
var ver = navigator.appVersion;
if (ver.indexOf("MSIE") != -1)
{
window.location.href="page1.html"
}else
window.open("page2.html", target="_self")
// — ></SCRIPT>
```

Note: JavaScript is case sensitive. It also is sensitive to space characters and return characters that you place in the code. You must be precise for the code to work. This book is not intended to be a complete guide to HTML or Java scripting, however. Several excellent books have been written on these topics. If you have questions or need more assistance, refer to one of these sources.

Creating a Shockwave movie

Once you've prepared your movies for Web use, you're ready to create a Shockwave movie. Be sure to play your movies "one more time" to check for errors before creating a Shockwave movie — just as you do before creating a projector.

Also, it's a good idea to back up your movie to another folder, even though creating a Shockwave movie doesn't affect your original Director movie. You don't want to lose hours of work if something goes wrong.

Saving Your Director Movie as a Shockwave Movie

1. In Director, open the movie from which you want to create a Shockwave movie.

2. Select File ⇨ Save As Shockwave Movie to display the dialog box shown in Figure 5-14.

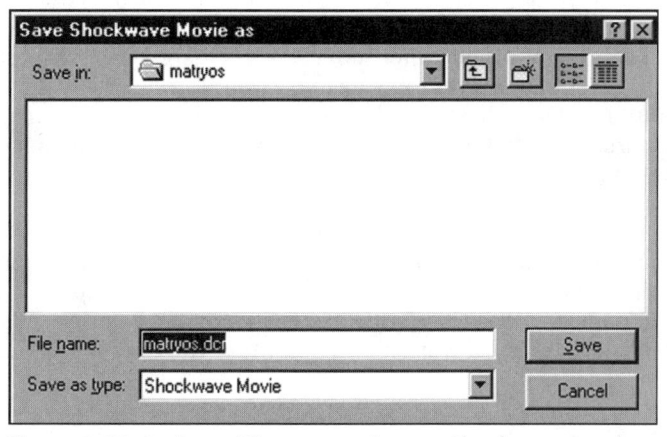

Figure 5-14: Saving a Director movie as a Shockwave movie

3. Enter a filename for your movie, and click Save to complete the operation and return to Director's main window.

   By default, Director saves your Shockwave movie using the same filename as the original Director movie — except it adds a .dcr extension. Be sure to check Chapter 24 for a more extensive discussion of building Director movies for Web distribution.

Once you've saved your movie as a Shockwave movie, you can embed it into your HTML document and upload it to the Internet. For specific instructions about uploading Web pages to the Internet, consult your ISP.

Designing for Success

In some respects, animation is one of the most challenging forms of storytelling, regardless of whether the animation is done for a multimedia presentation or for a video production. As an animator, you're responsible for bringing an entire world to life: the characters, the background behind them, and any props they use. In the world of animation, the laws of physics are malleable, at the whim of the animator.

One of the dangers of using computers in the beginning stages of animation development is that it's easy to just start putting the pieces of the animation together without considering the overall scheme. Like any other complex project, however, producing a quality animation or Director movie requires advance planning. The time to decide you want to switch directions is *not* when you are halfway through a project to which you've devoted hours and days.

Planning ahead

Planning your presentation well in advance is critical to the success of a Director movie. Although the Director movie plays back from one frame to the next, you can insert loops, branch out for other movies, and create a web of interactivity, sound, and animation that's as complex as you want it to be. Planning includes identifying your audience, assessing their probable computer resources, and plotting the course of action you want to take. Other considerations include budget and the method of distribution.

Perhaps you work with a development team. If you do, you enjoy the ability to share the planning of and responsibility for your Director project. If you are an independent designer, however, you are *the* author, technical expert, artist, writer, and director of your movie. Even a small project can yield a variety of surprises, which translates into hours of work if you don't take the time to plan ahead.

Storyboarding

One of the easiest and best methods of planning a Director movie is sitting down with paper and pencils or pens and creating a flowchart and storyboard for your project. The flowchart can contain notes about art, sounds, and video segments. Using the flowchart you can track the branching of your movie by creating simple rectangles that contain the blocks of information for your project. You don't need to be an artist to create a flowchart, and it'll help you stay on track. The flowchart also makes it easier to spot and anticipate potential problems as you move through your project.

After you've created a flowchart defining the "flow" of your project, consider creating storyboards of the various animation sequences. A storyboard is a panel of rough sketches depicting the plot, action, and characters in the sequential scenes of a film, an animated cartoon, a television show, or a filmed advertisement. You should note that the operative word here is *rough*. If you're not an artist and will be using art from a third-party source, don't be concerned. All that matters is that you know what's going on in your animations. Once your planning is complete, you are ready to start creating your Director project.

Summary

In Director, a variety of techniques are at your disposal to add the finishing touches to a project:

- Changing the tempo of your movie helps create smooth animation sequences and adds dramatic pacing in your movie.
- The Control Panel provides you with a quick method of controlling the playback and frame rate of your movie.
- You can pause a movie to wait for the user to click the mouse or press a key.
- Adding transitions to the movie helps it to move smoothly from one scene to the next.
- You can remap graphic elements in your movie to existing or custom palettes.
- By adding fades and using color cycling, you can create transitional effects with color palettes.
- Projectors enable others who don't own Director to see your movies.
- You can create Shockwave movies to distribute your projects on the Web.
- Advance planning helps ensure the success of your Director projects.

✦ ✦ ✦

Bringing Life to Director

PART

II

In This Part

Chapter 6
Be On Your Best Behavior

Chapter 7
Sound Advice

Chapter 8
Video Advice

Chapter 9
Pulling It All Together

Be On Your Best Behavior

CHAPTER 6

In This Chapter

Introducing Director's new prepackaged behaviors

Creating interactive Director movies without scripting

Using the Behavior Inspector to attach, create, and edit behaviors

Creating custom buttons with the Button Editor

Attaching external casts to use third-party behaviors

Interactivity is critical to multimedia — without it, a program is little more than a self-running slideshow. Director 6.0 introduces a powerful new tool for adding interactivity to your movies: the *behavior*. Whether encapsulated in the new Button Editor Xtra, or implemented via Lingo using the Behavior Inspector, behaviors will make your buttons click crisply, liven up your scroll bars, and even keep time for you.

What Are Behaviors?

With the introduction of behaviors in Director 6, you can now add interactivity to a movie without Lingo scripting. Later, in Chapter 10, you'll begin to learn about writing scripts from scratch. You'll create a few simple scripts in Lingo, to

- ✦ Jump to a target frame
- ✦ Loop on the current frame
- ✦ Move the playback head forward one frame
- ✦ Move the playback head back one frame
- ✦ Jump to a target marker (you'll learn about markers here in this chapter)

When you create these scripts in Chapter 10, you'll actually be creating behaviors — because a behavior is nothing more than a script or a page of code that includes *handlers* (or subroutines) for events that occur in your movie. Director's standard events are listed later in Table 6-2, and discussed in detail in Chapters 10 and 11.

Each of the scripted actions listed just above are simple examples of what you can accomplish with behaviors.

Fortunately, you can postpone learning Lingo by using the 30-plus prescripted behaviors that are shipped with Director 6; they're all in an external cast named Behavior Library.cst. These prepackaged behaviors enable you to add interactivity to objects in your movie, just by clicking, dragging, and responding to a few simple prompts.

> **Note**
>
> A well-written behavior doesn't require modifications to its code in order to make it work in your program. So you can attach behaviors to objects without writing a single line of code.

Predefined Director 6 behaviors

The behaviors included in Behavior Library.cst are grouped into seven categories: Controls, Gestures, Media, Media Preload, Messaging, Navigation, and Video. The behaviors shipped with Director 6 are listed in Table 6-1. You will work with several of these behaviors in this chapter. In each case, the action listed in the Action column occurs when a specified event occurs. When you set up the use of a behavior, you get to specify the event that triggers it.

Table 6-1
The Behavior Library Cast

Behavior Category	Behavior Name	Action
Controls	UI Radio Group Item	Causes a sprite to behave as a radio button.
Controls	UI Pushbutton	Causes a sprite to behave as a push button.
Controls	UI Toggle Button	Causes a sprite to behave as a toggle button.
Gestures	UI Pointer Change	Changes the image used for the mouse pointer.
Gestures	UI Rollover Change Pointer	Changes the mouse pointer over a specific sprite.
Gestures	UI Pointer Animate	Animates the mouse pointer.
Gestures	UI Rollover and Mouse Down Change Pointer	Changes the mouse pointer when the pointer is over the current sprite, and defines a different pointer image to display when the current sprite is clicked.
Gestures	UI Rollover Change Member	Changes the cast member upon which the sprite is based when the mouse pointer rolls over the sprite.
Gestures	UI Drag Snap to Sprite	Snaps a sprite's registration point to a specific Stage location.

Behavior Category	Behavior Name	Action
Gestures	UI Drag Snap to Sprite List	Snaps a sprite's registration point to any of a list of objects on the Stage.
Media	Sound Beep	Issues a system beep.
Media	Sound Play Castmember	Plays an internal sound cast member.
Media	Sound Play File	Plays an external (linked) sound.
Media	Image Switch Cast Members	Swaps one cast member for another on the Stage.
Media	Image Cycle Cast Members	Cycles through a range of adjacent cast members in the Cast window.
Media Preload	Net Show Proxy	Displays placeholder while media is loaded.
Media Preload	Net Hold Until Frame Ready	Loops on the current frame until media in a specified frame range is loaded into memory.
Media Preload	Net Get Text	Loads text from a specified URL (address on the Internet or a network).
Media Preload	Net Preload Net Thing	Preloads a file from the Internet or network into disk cache.
Messaging	Message All Sprites	Sends a message to all sprites in the current frame.
Messaging	Message Sprite	Sends a message to a single sprite.
Messaging	Message Movie in a Window	Sends a message to a movie in a window (MIAW; see Chapter 21).
Navigation	Hold on Current Frame	Loops to the current frame.
Navigation	Go to Frame	Jumps to a specific frame.
Navigation	Go to Marker	Jumps to a specific marker in the movie (a marker identifies a specific frame in the movie that is named using a label, such as "Start").
Navigation	Go to Previous Marker	Jumps to the previous marker.
Navigation	Go to Next Marker	Jumps to the next marker.
Navigation	Go to Movie	Jumps to a specified movie.
Navigation	Go to Net Page	Loads a designated HTML (Web) page.
Navigation	Open Movie in a Window	Opens a movie in a window (MIAW; see Chapter 21).

(continued)

Table 6-1 *(continued)*

Behavior Category	Behavior Name	Action
Navigation	Play Done	Returns the playback head to the frame where the `play` command is issued (discussed in Chapter 10).
Video	Video Play	Plays a digital video clip.
Video	Video Rewind	Rewinds a digital video clip.
Video	Video Stop	Stops a digital video clip.
Video	Video Control	Provides digital video controls, including Play, Pause, Rewind, and Stop buttons.
Video	Video Slider	Controls digital video play time control using a slider.

Attaching predefined behaviors to objects

To use a behavior from the Behavior Library.cst requires just a few steps.

1. First, open the Behavior Library (an external cast) using the Xtras ⇨ Behavior Library command. The Behavior Library Cast window appears (Figure 6-1) and includes Director 6's predefined behaviors.

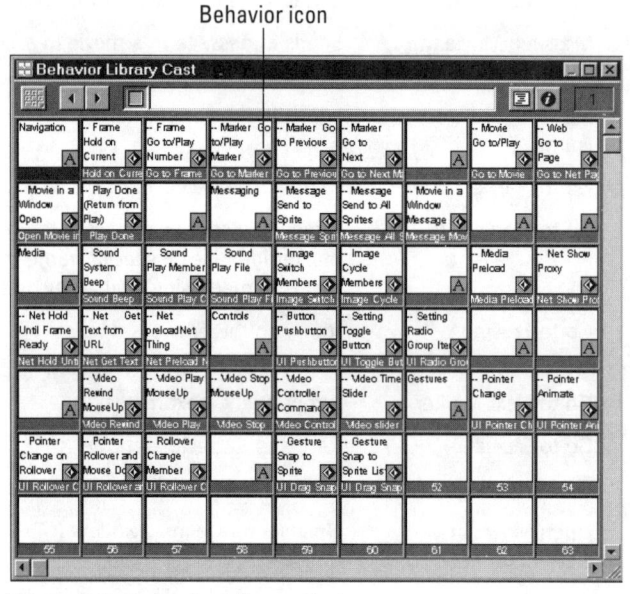

Figure 6-1: Behavior Library Cast

> **Note:** You'll learn more about Xtras in Chapter 19. For now, just be aware that for the Behavior Library to appear on the Xtra menu, the cast library file (identified with a .cst extension) must be placed in the Xtras folder. On the Macintosh, the path to this folder is typically Macintosh HD:Director 6:Xtras. On the Windows side, the path to the folder is typically C:\Program Files\Macromedia\Director 6\Xtras\.

2. Identify and select the behavior that you want to attach to a sprite (a Behavior icon is identified in Figure 6-1).

3. Drag and drop the behavior onto a sprite (on the Stage) or onto the target cell (in the Score window's script channel).

4. Some behaviors require parameters, called *properties*, which define the action or designate a target for the behavior's action. For instance, you can attach a behavior to a button that causes the playback head to jump to a specific frame. To make the jump, the behavior must be told the name or number of the target frame. If such additional information is required, a Parameters For dialog box appears, in which you enter the properties for the behavior.

A behavior can only be attached to either a sprite on the Stage, or a frame in the Score window. Behaviors that are dropped onto a sprite are called *sprite scripts*. You can attach several behaviors to a single sprite on the Stage to create a more complex action. Behaviors dropped onto a cell in the Score window are considered *frame scripts*. You can only attach a single behavior to a frame's script channel. Behaviors that are placed in the script channel cannot include properties.

> **Note:** In their most essential form, behaviors are Score scripts. Score scripts, as well as other types of scripts, are discussed in Chapter 10.

Building a Better Movie

Director is the hands-down favorite among graphic designers for creating portfolios, resumés, and promotional pieces. And version 6 of the program is sure to increase its popularity, because it offers so many code-free options for creating a highly interactive presentation.

Over the course of the next four chapters, you'll see how to incorporate behaviors, sounds, and video into an effective yet simple presentation. Eventually, in Chapter 9, you'll see the results of these tasks as you create an interactive resumé: a collection of skills and experience for presentation to a prospective employer. This chapter concentrates on using the abundant supply of behaviors that Macromedia makes available to you to add interactivity — without scripting — to your movies.

Pushing all the right buttons

When you get right down to it, creating an interactive interface boils down to building lots of buttons and then telling the program what to do when someone clicks them. It is these buttons, in fact, that make the interaction between user and application possible. With buttons, the GUI becomes more than simply a picture on the screen — it becomes a tactile experience. A good button screams "Push me!" and serves to take the program's illusion of reality one notch higher (see Figure 6-2).

Figure 6-2: Perhaps not all buttons are as explicit as this one, but a good button should give the impression of being eminently clickable.

The exact definition of a button can vary widely but for the most part includes the following characteristics:

- ✦ A button is an object or spot on the screen that, when clicked, causes something to happen.

- ✦ A button typically simulates a real-life physical button like those on an electronic appliance or computer — that is, when you click the mouse button on it, the button will look different (raised or depressed). When the mouse button is clicked again, the button will return to its former state (depressed or not depressed). This kind of button essentially transfers the physical action of the mouse click to the virtual action of a button click.

- ✦ When the cursor moves over a button, it may become highlighted (brighter on the screen) or animated, with or without the depressed appearance.

- ✦ A button can be rendered inactive, so that it does not react at all to the mouse, and then be made active again when some external event takes place.

Even though buttons are a staple of multimedia, they have always been notoriously difficult to pull off well in Director. This has changed (and how!) in Director 6.0. Now you can implement buttons in five different ways: by using the new Button Editor (covered later in this chapter), by employing standard system buttons on the Tool Palette (covered in Chapter 10), by using prepackaged behaviors (as shown in the next section), by using the Widget Wizard (discussed in Chapter 8), or by writing a navigational handler using Lingo (Chapter 10).

Using navigation behaviors to build buttons

In the next few sections, you use Director's predefined behaviors to accomplish some of the tasks that required Lingo scripting prior to version 6. To give the user control over the flow of a movie, you must be able to put the playback head in a holding pattern on a specific frame and attach buttons that, when clicked, forward the playback head to the next frame or a designated frame. The Behavior Library cast includes behaviors that you can drag and drop onto frames and sprites, to accomplish these tasks.

To demonstrate this, you'll use the gears.dir movie in the next exercise. In its current form the gears.dir movie's cast includes 22 cast members. The cast members that you'll use in the next few exercises include Background (a bitmap cast member in cast slot 1), Techno (a sound cast member in slot 2), Click (a sound cast member in slot 3), Next (a bitmap button image in cast slot 4), Sound (a bitmap button image in cast slot 5), and Ford (a bitmap cast member in slot 6). In later exercises, you also use Gear 1 Loop and Gear 2 Loop (in cast member slots 14 and 22, respectively). Most of these cast members are already placed on the Stage.

Note that when you look at the Score window, it is difficult to verify the names of cast members upon which each sprite is based, because almost all sprites in the movie are one frame in duration. To display the name for each sprite, make the Score the active window and move the mouse pointer over the sprite in question. If you leave the pointer there momentarily, a label appears with the sprite's name. You can also determine the name and appearance of a sprite by clicking its cell in the Score window. This causes a thumbnail of the cast member to appear in the upper-left corner of the Score window along with the sprite's name, as shown later in Figure 6-3.

In the following exercise, you'll initially test the movie to determine that it plays from the first frame to the last without pausing. Next, you'll open the Behavior Library with prescripted behaviors and add a behavior that causes the movie to pause and loop on frame 1.

Side Dish: Visually tasty gears

The images used in gears.dir are from the Industrial Backgrounds & Objects CD-ROM, a collection of 130 photographic images, available from Image Farm, Inc. 110 Spadina Ave. #309, Toronto, Ontario, Canada M5V 2K4. In the initial gears.dir movie, we used image 1F09090 for Gear 1, 1F09088 for Gear 2, and 1F09003 (after applying two different Adobe Photoshop filters) for the background images (Sketch and Ford). All Image Farm images are copyright 1996 by Image Farm, Inc.

(continued)

(continued)

For more information on Image Farm products, you can contact them at 800-GET-FARM, or visit their Web site at

`http://www.imagefarm.com`

To create the Sketch cast member, we applied the Sketch➪Graphic Pen filter in Photoshop 4.0 to the entire image. To create the background for the Ford cast member, we applied the Artistic➪Poster Edges filter to the image and then selected the Image➪Adjust➪Brightness/Contrast command and increased the Brightness setting to 80+.

On the CD-ROM In the next exercise, you will use a partially complete Director movie (gears.dir) available on your companion CD-ROM in the exercise:ch06 (exercise\ch06) folder. You will also use predefined behaviors that are automatically installed with Director 6.

Using a Behavior to Loop on the Current Frame

1. Open the gears.dir movie in Director.
2. Be sure the Cast and Score windows are visible. The Score will appear as shown in Figure 6-3.

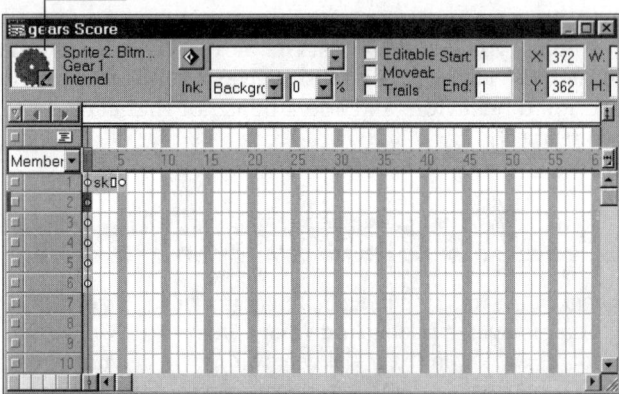

Figure 6-3: Score window with Sprite thumbnail

3. Rewind and play the movie. It plays from start to finish without stopping — and may loop, if the Control Panel Loop Playback button is selected.

4. Stop the movie and rewind it.

5. In the next few steps, you'll display the Behavior Library cast so you can drag and drop a behavior onto one of the movie's sprites. Select the Xtras command on the menu bar. (You'll learn more about Xtras, which extend the capabilities of Director, in Chapter 19.)

6. On the list of available Xtras, select the Behavior Library option.

7. When the Behavior Library Cast window appears, enlarge it so you can see all the behavior cast members while still viewing the Stage. As you examine the Behavior Library cast, you'll see cast members such as Hold on Current Frame, Go To Frame, Go To Marker, and so on.

8. Locate the Hold on Current Frame behavior in the Behavior Library Cast window. This behavior causes the movie to loop on the current frame when it plays.

9. Drag and drop the Hold on Current Frame behavior onto the script channel in frame 1.

10. Click the Score window to make it active, and then save the movie as **gears1.dir.**

11. Rewind the movie, close all open windows, and play the movie.

   > **Tip**
   >
   > You can temporarily close all windows and play a movie if you hold down the Shift key and press Enter on the numeric keypad.

   The gears1.dir movie includes a bitmap text image (Ford) in frame 5. If it appears on the Stage, the Hold on Current Frame behavior was *not* successfully attached to frame 1. If the movie stays on frame 1 with the Gear Up Now text, the attachment of the Hold on Current Frame behavior was successful. You can click the Next and Sound buttons, but nothing happens in your movie . . . yet!

12. Stop the movie and rewind it.

The Hold on Current Frame behavior accomplishes a single task. It causes the playback head to loop on the current frame until another event instructs the playback head to move on. Though there is no need to get into the "dirty little secrets" of scripting with Lingo at this juncture, it can be instructive to examine the script that causes this behavior to function. You'll do that later in this chapter.

At this point, the gears1.dir movie is spinning its gears and looped eternally on frame 1. In the following steps, you attach the Go to Frame behavior to the Next button and thus enable the playback head to escape from the frame 1 loop.

Attaching a Behavior to Jump to a Specific Frame

1. Be sure the gears1.dir movie and the Behavior Library Cast window are open.

2. Locate the Go to Frame behavior in the Behavior Library Cast window (it's in cast slot 3).

3. Drag and drop the Go to Frame behavior on the Next button sprite on the Stage. Because this behavior (unlike Hold on Current Frame) includes properties, the Parameters For dialog box appears, as shown in Figure 6-4.

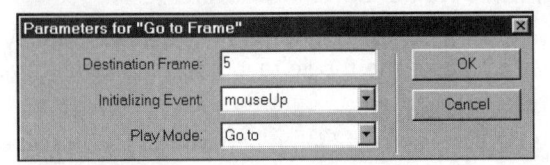

Figure 6-4: Parameters For dialog box

4. Set the Destination Frame to 5.

5. Leave the Initializing Event pop-up menu set to the default setting, mouseUp.

6. Leave the Play Mode pop-up menu set to the default setting, Go to. Click OK.

7. Watch out: Make sure the Score or (internal) Cast window is active, and *not* the Behavior Library Cast window. If the Behavior Library is the active window when you save your movie, any changes to the Behavior Library cast, whether inadvertent or intended, are saved to disk.

8. Save the movie as **gears2.dir,** rewind, and play the movie.

9. Click the Next button, to test the Go To Frame behavior. If the Loop Playback button on the Control Panel is turned off (so the movie does not loop), the Ford bitmap background will be displayed for a brief moment and then the movie ends. If the Loop Playback button is turned on, after the Ford bitmap appears the movie returns to the first frame with the Next button.

10. To cause the movie to loop on frame 5 rather than automatically terminating, drag and drop the Hold on Current Frame behavior to the script channel in frame 5.

11. Save the movie again as gears2.dir, rewind, and play the movie. After testing the Next button, stop the movie.

Using the Behavior Inspector

You can add, delete, and view the behaviors that are attached to a sprite by using the Behavior Inspector shown in Figure 6-5. The Behavior Inspector provides easy access to information about the behavior, including the behavior's script, the cast library where the behavior is located, and the names and values of any parameters (properties) associated with the behavior.

The Behavior Inspector is built upon a series of panes that can be collapsed or expanded as needed. In its default state, these panes are hidden. You click the two right-pointing triangles on the left side of the Inspector to expand the panes.

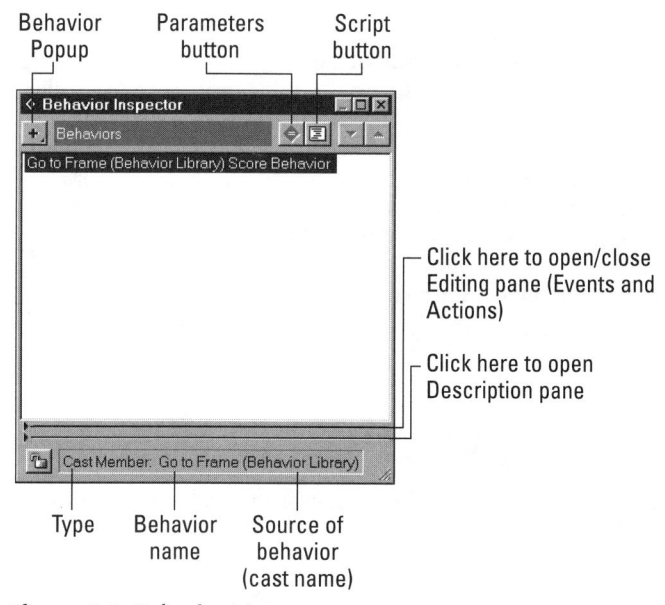

Figure 6-5: Behavior Inspector

You'll get a good look at these panes as you work through these sections. The Editing pane contains the Events and Actions Popup button. The Description pane displays a description of what the behavior does; this may include information about properties and their roles, events that the behavior generates, and copyright information.

At the top of the Behavior Inspector is the diamond-shaped Parameters button that opens the behavior's Parameters For dialog box. From it, you can change the behavior's properties. At the bottom of the Behavior Inspector you'll see the name of the behavior, its type, and the name of the cast in which it is stored.

Viewing the script behind a behavior

In Chapter 10 we'll explore the Script window and begin introducing the basics of programming using Lingo, Director's scripting language. For now, it's helpful to glimpse behind the facade of the behavior and simply be aware that it's just a series of instructions.

By default, when you double-click a behavior in the Cast window (either an internal or external cast), the Behavior Inspector opens so you can edit it. You can change the default setting so the Script window pops up rather than the Behavior Inspector. As you become proficient in Lingo scripting, you may prefer to have the Script window appear instead of the Behavior Inspector — for now, however, the Behavior Inspector is more useful as you learn and experiment with codeless programming.

To change which window appears for viewing or editing a behavior, you can select the File ⇨ Preferences ⇨ Editors command. Once the Editors Preferences dialog box appears, select Behavior from the list and click the Edit button. When the Select Editor for Behaviors dialog box appears, you can choose either Script window or Behavior Inspector. Click OK, and then click OK again to close the Editors Preferences dialog. For the duration of this chapter, we'll assume that you have established the Behavior Inspector as the default editor for behaviors.

You can open the Behavior Inspector using several methods.

- Use the shortcut keys Command+Option+Semicolon (;) on the Macintosh or Ctrl+Alt+Semicolon (;) for Windows.
- Click the Behavior button at the top center of the Score window (see Figure 6-6) or on the Director toolbar.
- If the Sprite Overlay is visible, click the Behavior Inspector icon (identified in Figure 6-6) to display the Behavior inspector.

Tip What's the Sprite Overlay? When you click a sprite to make it active, the Sprite Overlay appears with the three icons identified in Figure 6-6. You can turn Sprite Overlay on and off with the View ⇨ Sprite Overlay command. This feature provides a summary of information on the currently selected sprite.

Caution Dissecting someone else's script or behavior can help you learn Lingo, but don't try to change the behaviors until you understand what you are doing. Even a small change can make a behavior misbehave!

In the next exercise, you'll open a behavior and display its "guts" using the Script window.

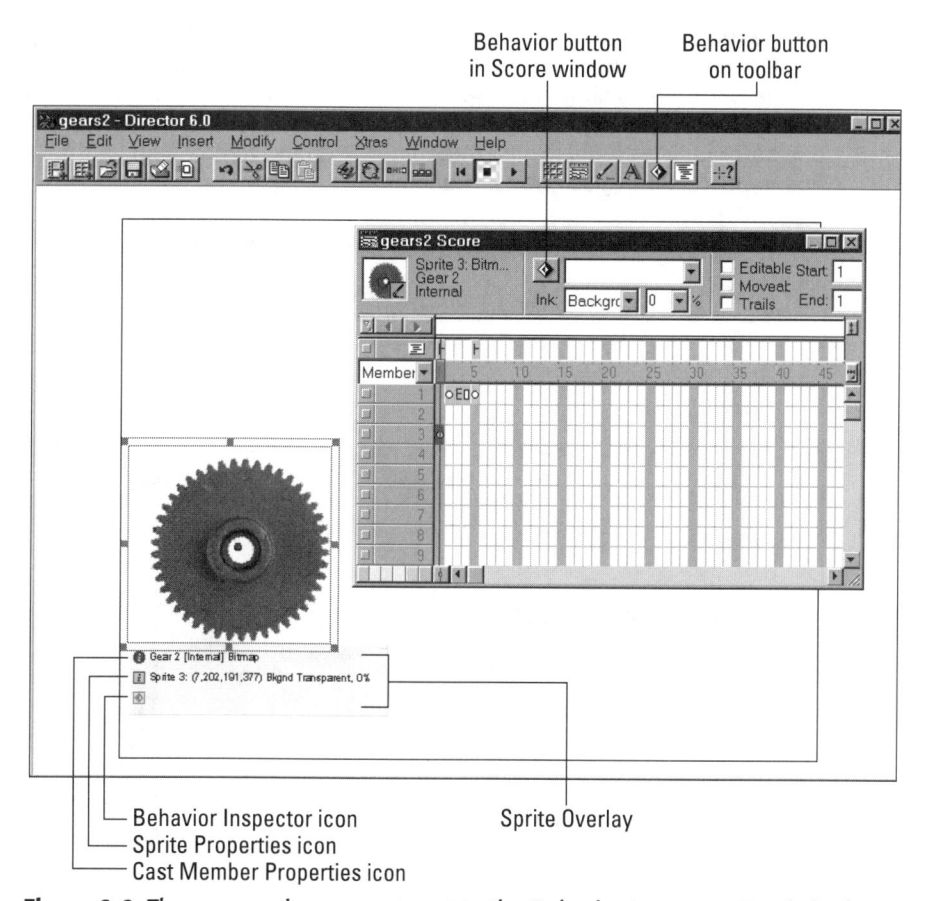

Figure 6-6: There are various ways to get to the Behavior Inspector. One is in the Sprite Overlay.

Examining the Hold on Current Frame Behavior

1. Open the gears2.dir movie that you modified in the last exercise.
2. Double-click the Hold on Current Frame behavior in the Behavior Library cast; either the Script window or the Behavior Inspector will appear. If you get the Behavior Inspector, click the Script button (see Figure 6-5) to display the Script window.
3. Use the scroll bar to scroll to the top of the script.

4. Review the script — and don't panic over its complexity. Most of the script is composed of comments; these are the lines of text preceded by the double dash (--) as shown in Figure 6-7. The behavior itself is identified as a navigational behavior ("Nav") and it does not require any parameters. This behavior is essentially just three lines, with its "heart" being a `go the frame` instruction (discussed in Chapter 10).

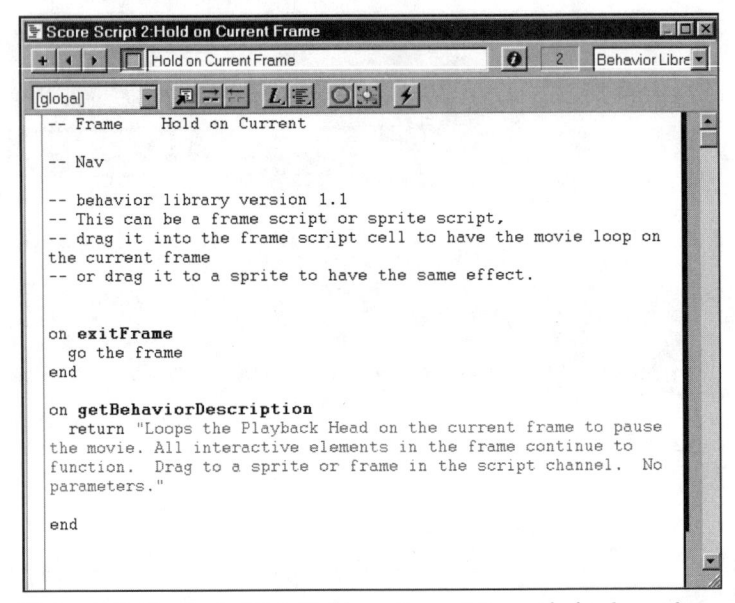

```
-- Frame     Hold on Current

-- Nav

-- behavior library version 1.1
-- This can be a frame script or sprite script,
-- drag it into the frame script cell to have the movie loop on
the current frame
-- or drag it to a sprite to have the same effect.


on exitFrame
  go the frame
end

on getBehaviorDescription
  return "Loops the Playback Head on the current frame to pause
the movie. All interactive elements in the frame continue to
function. Drag to a sprite or frame in the script channel. No
parameters."

end
```

Figure 6-7: The text of the Hold on Current Frame behavior script, with the `getBehaviorDescription` instruction indicating that no parameters are required for this behavior.

5. Close the Script window and the Behavior Inspector.

> **Caution**
>
> The Behavior Library cast is an external cast and is stored as a separate file on your hard disk. If you modify it and save those changes, the original cast of predefined behaviors is overwritten and cannot be retrieved without reinstalling Director. When you work with any external cast (especially Behavior Library.cst), be sure to make the Score or internal Cast window active before saving your movie, unless you specifically intend to alter and save the external cast.

Adding behaviors using the Behavior Inspector

You already know how to drop and drag a behavior onto a sprite, but you can also add a behavior using the Behavior Inspector. To do so, you'll need to complete these steps:

1. Open the Behavior Library cast using the Xtras ⇨ Behavior Library command.
2. Select Windows ⇨ Inspectors ⇨ Behavior to open the Behavior Inspector. You can also click the Behavior button on the toolbar or on the Score window, shown earlier in Figure 6-6.
3. Select the sprite on the Stage to which you want to add a behavior.
4. Click the Behavior Popup button (see Figure 6-5) and select the behavior you want to add. (You can also select the New Behavior option on the Behavior pop-up and create a new behavior. We'll cover that process later in this chapter.)
5. If the behavior has properties, click the Parameters button (see Figure 6-5) to open the Parameters For dialog box and establish the settings for the behavior. Then close the dialog box.

Note

The fields of the Parameters For dialog may include text entry boxes, sliders, and check boxes — based on the characteristics of each behavior. The purpose of these controls is always the same, however: to set the initial conditions that the behavior will use when it runs.

While the Behavior Inspector is open, you can repeat this process and attach additional behaviors, if appropriate, to the selected sprite on the Stage. Then continue as needed, selecting another sprite on the Stage to edit, and then add behaviors to it. When you've completed all your behavior tasks, you can close the Behavior Inspector or simply leave it "floating" open on your desktop.

Removing behaviors from a sprite

If you change you mind, you can also remove one or more behaviors using the Behavior Inspector. Here are steps to delete a behavior:

1. Open the Behavior Inspector.
2. On the Stage, locate and select the sprite from which you want to remove a behavior.
3. In the Behavior Inspector, highlight the behavior in the Behavior List pane as shown in Figure 6-8.
4. Press the Backspace or Del key.

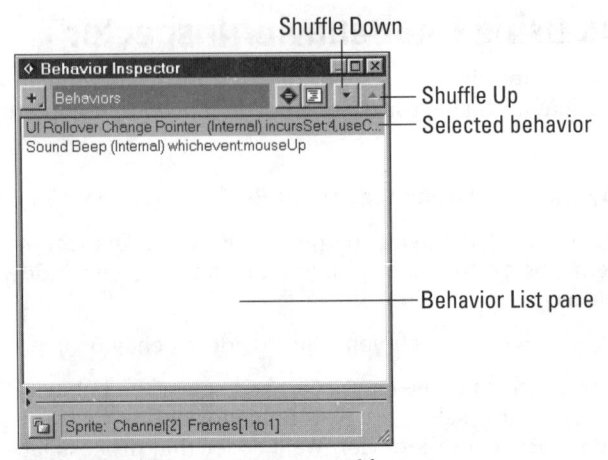

Figure 6-8: Behavior Inspector with two behaviors listed

Reordering behaviors attached to a sprite

Behaviors are executed in the order in which they were originally attached to the sprite, unless you specifically change the order. To modify the execution order, you need to change the order in which behaviors are listed in the Behavior List pane in the Behavior Inspector.

Here are the steps to change the order of execution:

1. Open the Behavior Inspector.
2. On the Stage, locate and select the sprite that includes behaviors that you want to reorder.

   To view the behaviors attached to a specific sprite, you can select the sprite on the Stage and then open the Behavior Inspector. If the Behavior Inspector is already open, you can simply select a sprite on the Stage. The Inspector will show you the behaviors already attached to that sprite.

3. In the Behavior List pane, highlight the behavior that you want to reorder, and click the Shuffle Up or Shuffle Down arrows (see Figure 6-8) to arrange the behaviors as desired.

In the following exercise, you'll add a second behavior to the Next button in the gears2.dir movie and then reorder the sequence in which the behaviors are executed.

On the CD-ROM The file gears2.dir is on your companion CD-ROM in the exercise:ch06 (exercise\ch06) folder, or you can use the gears2.dir movie that you created earlier in this chapter. You'll also use predefined behaviors that are automatically installed with Director 6.

Adding Media Behaviors to a Movie

1. Open the gears2.dir movie.
2. Click the Behavior Inspector button on the toolbar to open the Behavior Inspector.
3. Be sure the Behavior Library Cast window is open so that all behaviors in the library are accessible. If the Behavior Library Cast window is not open, you can only access and attach behaviors that have already been added to the sprites in your movie or behaviors stored in one of the movie's internal casts.
4. Click to select the Next button on the Stage.
5. Click the Behavior Pop-up button on the Behavior Inspector and select the Sound Beep behavior.
6. Save the movie as **gears3.dir**, rewind and play it. Click the Next button. You will not hear the system beep because the first behavior (go to frame 5) is executed before the second behavior's actions can occur (Sound Beep).
7. Stop and rewind the movie.
8. Select the Next button on the Stage and open the Behavior Inspector, if it is not already open. The inspector should display two behaviors attached to the Next button sprite.
9. In the Behavior Inspector, highlight the Sound Beep behavior and then click the Shuffle Up arrow. The Sound Beep behavior is now the first behavior listed in the Behavior List pane.
10. Save the movie again as gears3.dir, rewind, and play it.
11. Click the Next button and you'll hear a system beep.
12. Stop the movie.

In the next few steps, you'll remove the behavior that plays a system beep, and replace it with a behavior that plays an internal sound cast member (Click). You'll use the Behavior Inspector to accomplish these tasks.

Note

Chapters 7 and 15 provide details on importing sound, using sound channels, and controlling sound using Lingo. For now, enjoy the simplicity of using a behavior to add a sound to your movie.

Attaching and Deleting Media-Control Behaviors Using the Behavior Inspector

1. Open the gears3.dir movie that you created in the last exercise, and rewind it to frame 1, if necessary.

2. Select the Next button and open the Behavior Inspector, which displays the two behaviors previously attached to the Next button sprite.

3. Click to activate the Behavior Inspector, and highlight the Sound Beep behavior.

4. Press Del or Backspace to remove Sound Beep.

5. Click the Behavior Pop-up button and then select the Sound Play Castmember behavior.

   Caution: Do not select the Sound Play File behavior. It is used to play external sounds, not internal cast members.

6. With the Sound Play Castmember behavior still selected, click the Shuffle Up arrow so the behavior is listed (and executed) first.

7. Next, click the Parameters button in the Behavior Inspector to display the Parameters For dialog (Figure 6-9).

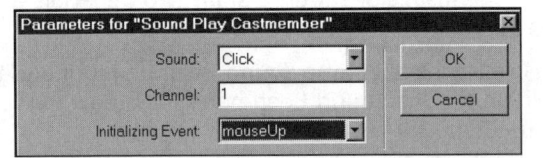

Figure 6-9: Choosing parameters for the Sound Play Cast member

8. The movie's internal cast includes two sounds (Click and Techno). By default, the sound parameter is the Click cast member, which is the first sound cast member in your movie. If you open the Sound list in the Parameters For dialog, you'll see all the sound cast members available in the current movie. Leave the Sound set to use Click.

9. Leave the Channel set to 1, and the Initializing Event set to mouseUp. (Your options in the Parameters dialog include activating the sound on mouseUp, mouseDown, prepareFrame, enterFrame, exitFrame, and initPlayMember. These events are discussed in Chapter 10.)

10. Click OK to accept the current parameters and attach the behavior to the Next button sprite.

11. Close the Behavior Inspector and save the movie as **gears4.dir**.

12. Close all windows, rewind, and play the movie.

13. Click the Next button and you'll hear the Click sound cast member play.
14. Stop the movie and rewind it.

In the following exercise, you'll use drag-and-drop to attach the Sound Play Castmember behavior to the Sound button on the Stage. Any of the behaviors in the Behavior Library Cast can be attached using drop-and-drag. This method has the advantage of automatically prompting you for parameters when needed.

Side Dish: Fresh media for grinding gears

The Techno sound cast member used in gears.dir is from The Fresh Music Library, a full-buy-out library of over 40 CDs of production music. When you purchase/license buyout music, you own the right to synchronize any and all themes, as many times as you need, forever. You don't need to pay license or "drop" fees, and you never have to report usage.

Techno is an excerpt from Techno Facto, one of 11 music cuts from the *Techno Industrial* CD (which is available from Fresh, The Music Library, 34 S. Main Street, Hanover, NH 03755). Techno Facto is the exclusive property of Fresh Music Library (copyright 1997). This clip may only be used by the owner of this book for practice/learning activities and cannot be used in other productions unless licensed from the Fresh Music Library. For more information on licensing, you can contact Fresh, The Music Library, at 800-545-0688 or visit their Web site at

    www.freshmusic.com

The Fresh Music Library also offers SearchTrack, a searchable CD-ROM index containing essential versions of every theme in the 45-disk Fresh Music Library. SearchTrack allows users to quickly search and preview themes by emotion, style, and usage attributes. SearchTrack is available for Power Macintosh and Windows 95 and is free from Fresh Music.

Dragging and Dropping a Media Behavior on a Sprite

1. Open the gears4.dir that you created in the last exercise.
2. With the Behavior Library Cast window open, locate the Sound Play Castmember behavior. Drag and drop it onto the Sound button on the Stage.
3. When the Parameters For dialog box appears, specify the following settings. For Sound, select the Techno sound. Leave Channel set to 1 and Initializing Event set to mouseUp.
4. Click OK to finish setting the parameters for the behavior attached to the Sound button sprite.

5. Save the movie as **gears5.dir**.

   Tip: If the Save button or the File ⇨ Save command is grayed out, click anywhere on the Stage to make the current movie active (rather than the external cast); otherwise, you cannot save the modified movie.

6. Close all windows, rewind, and play the movie. Click the Sound button, and the Techno cast member plays.

7. While Techno plays, click the Next button. The sound stops immediately because only one sound can play in a channel at a time.

8. Stop the movie and rewind it.

Using the gestures behaviors

In addition to navigational and media behaviors, Director 6 includes prescripted gestures behaviors (see Table 6-1). These behaviors alter the appearance of sprites on the Stage.

In the following exercise, you add the UI Rollover Change Member behavior to the gears5.dir movie; this behavior changes the appearance of a specific sprite when the mouse pointer rolls over it. In this example, a stationary gear is replaced by an animated, rotating gear. You can use this same behavior to cause a button to change its appearance from an "up" state to a "down" state when the mouse pointer rolls over it.

Note: *UI* refers to User Interface. With the UI predefined behaviors in the Behavior Library cast, you can add special effects to the user interface of your movie.

On the CD-ROM: The file gears5.dir is on your companion CD-ROM in the exercise:ch06 (exercise\ch06) folder. Or you can use the gears5.dir movie that you created in the last exercise in this chapter. You'll also use predefined behaviors that are automatically installed with Director 6.

Adding a Behavior That Swaps One Sprite for Another

1. Open the gears5.dir movie and rewind it.

2. Be sure the Behavior Library Cast window is open, and then locate the UI Rollover Change Member behavior. (It's grouped with the other gestures behaviors in the Behavior Library Cast window.) Click the behavior, and then check the Name field at the top of the Score to be sure you have selected the correct behavior.

3. Drag and drop the UI Rollover Change Member behavior onto the Gear 1 sprite on the Stage, identified in Figure 6-10.

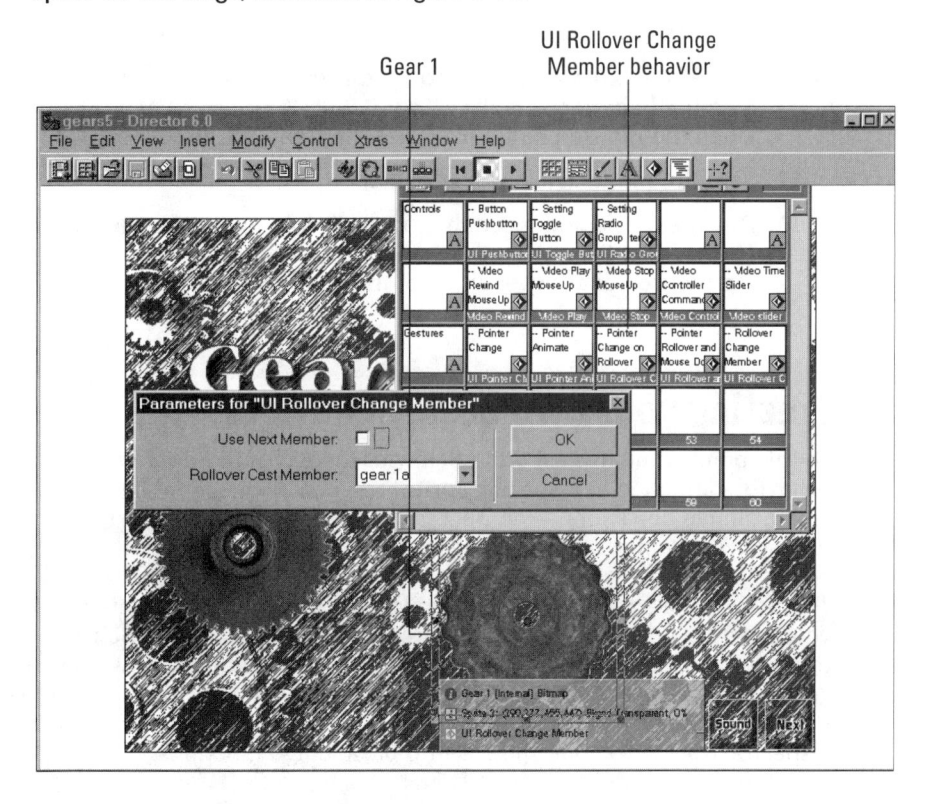

Figure 6-10: Setting up UI Rollover Change Member

4. When the Parameters For dialog box appears, *turn off* the Use Next Member check box, and in the Rollover Cast Member pop-up choose the Gear 1 Loop option.

   Tip

   If we had placed the replacement cast member (Gear 1 Loop) in the cast member slot one number higher than the original cast member (Gear 1), we could leave the Use Next Member check box selected and Director would automatically make the substitution.

5. Click OK to close the Parameters For dialog and finish attaching the behavior.

6. Click anywhere on the Stage, and save the movie as **gears6.dir**.

7. Close all windows, rewind, and play the movie.

8. Move the mouse pointer over the Gear 1 sprite (the gear image) and watch the sprite's behavior.

9. Stop the movie.

10. Repeat the process (steps 3 to 5), this time using the UI Rollover Change Member behavior to replace Gear 2 with the Gear 2 Loop cast member when the mouse pointer rolls over the Gear 2 sprite.

11. Save the movie again as gears6.dir.

12. Play the movie and move the mouse pointer over the two gear sprites (Gear 1 and Gear 2) on the Stage. The gears will animate when you move the mouse pointer over either of the sprites.

Creating your own basic behaviors

To this point, you have used the Behavior Inspector to add, remove, and view the behaviors attached to a specific sprite. You can also use the Behavior Inspector to create simple behaviors — another way to escape having to script or program interactivity from scratch.

Tip

The Behavior Inspector operates similar to a macro editor, where specific choices you make are converted to the required code. As you use the Behavior Inspector to create new behaviors, you may be tempted to examine the Lingo scripts that are generated. That's a very good learning technique — but you may want to read Chapter 10 first. Then you can learn even more by observing how the Behavior Inspector translates your choices into basic Lingo functions.

The steps needed to create a new behavior vary, depending on the nature of the behavior. In general, you must do the following:

1. Open the Behavior Inspector.

2. Click the Behavior Popup button and select the New Behavior option.

3. In the Name Behavior dialog box (Figure 6-11), enter a descriptive name for the behavior.

Figure 6-11: Naming a behavior

> **Note:** When you create a new behavior, it is stored either in the currently selected empty cast slot, or in the next empty cast position if the current slot is occupied.

4. In the Behavior Inspector, click the top arrow (see Figure 6-8) to expand the Editing pane. In Figure 6-12, you see both the Editing pane and the Description pane expanded. The Editing pane displays the events and actions included in the current behavior. No events or actions appear when you first begin to create a new behavior.

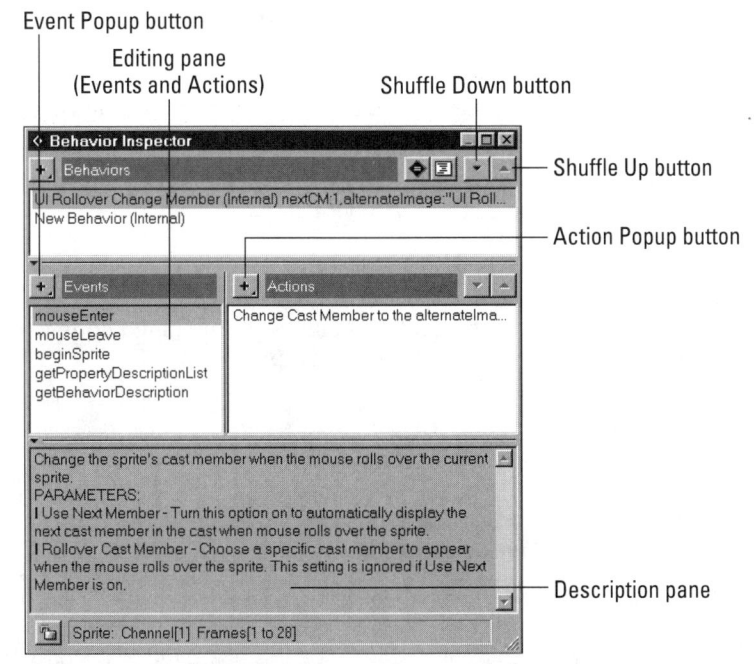

Figure 6-12: Behavior Inspector with expanded Editing pane and Description pane

5. At this point, you can add events to the behavior using the Event Popup button, and add actions using the Action Popup button (see Figure 6-12). Each time you add an event, you must add a corresponding action that occurs in response to the event. *You can assign more than one action to each event.* Each event/action combination serves as a basic building block from which you can construct a simple or complex behavior.

✦ The events available from the Event pop-up menu are listed in Table 6-2.

✦ The Actions available from the Action pop-up menu are grouped into six categories: Navigation, Wait, Sound, Frame, Sprite, and Cursor. A seventh option, New Event, enables you to create a new user-defined event. To use this feature requires that you know how to script using Lingo (see Part III of this book).

Tip

You can use a similar process to edit events and actions assigned to an existing behavior. Simply highlight the behavior, select the event from the list, and then add and delete actions as needed in the Actions list. (To delete an event or action, select it and then press the Del or Backspace key.)

6. You can alter the sequence of actions within a behavior using the Shuffle Up and Shuffle Down arrows just above the Editing pane (see Figure 6-12).

7. When you're done adding events and their corresponding actions, you can close the Behavior Inspector (or leave it open) and save your movie — which now includes the newly defined behavior.

Note

As you become familiar with Lingo (starting in Chapter 10), you'll discover that the Behavior Inspector provides a transparent way of creating Lingo code. The syntax of event names in the Behavior Inspector is similar to the Lingo code used for these behaviors (Mouse Up = mouseUp for example).

Table 6-2
Standard Events

Event	Action That Generates the Event
Mouse Up	Occurs when the left mouse button is released after being depressed (clicked). It is called only once, and only if the mouse button is released while within the active area of a sprite (see Mouse Within).
Mouse Down	Occurs when the left mouse button is pressed (clicked) but not released. Generally, it's better to assume that the user has not made a selection (such as clicking a menu item or button) until the mouse button is released. This gives users a chance to move the mouse pointer off an object if they have inadvertently pressed the mouse button over the wrong object.
Mouse Within	Occurs repeatedly while the cursor is within the active area of a sprite — that is, in the sprite's bounding rectangle, unless the sprite is displayed with Matte ink. The actions generated by this event should be short and to the point, because when you write a script that *traps* (responds to) this event it can slow down system performance if the mouse stays within a sprite's area for a prolonged period of time.

Event	Action That Generates the Event
Mouse Enter	Occurs when the cursor moves into the active area of a sprite. This event is generated only once upon each entry into the sprite, after which Mouse Within events are generated. This is a good point at which to display highlight states for a button, write out status messages, call up pop-up menus, and so forth.
Mouse Leave	The cursor moves out of the active area of a sprite; this is the only time this event is called. It's a good point at which to set highlight states for buttons back to their base states, revert status messages to the background message, hide pop-up menus, and so forth.
Key Up	Occurs every time a key is pressed and released. Works only for controls that have text field components, and only if the control currently has the focus. See Chapter 14 for more information about text fields.
Key Down	Occurs every time a key is pressed but not yet released. Only works for controls that have text field components, and only if the control currently has the focus. See Chapter 14 for more information about text fields.
Right Mouse Up	Occurs when the right mouse button is released. This obviously applies primarily to Windows-based machines, since Macintosh mice only have one button. To simulate a mouse right-click on the Macintosh, press Control+click.
Right Mouse Down	Occurs when the right mouse button is depressed. This obviously applies primarily to Windows-based machines, since Macintosh mice have only one button. To simulate a mouse right-click on the Macintosh, press Control+click.
Prepare Frame	Occurs after the playback head exits one frame and prior to the next frame being painted on the screen. This is a good place to check to see if a visible sprite needs to be invisible and vice versa.
Exit Frame	Called after the frame has been drawn and all sprites have been tested for events. This is a good point for navigating to different frames.
New Event	Gives you the ability to create a customized event handler for the behavior. To use this feature requires that you know how to script using Lingo and create a user-defined handler, which is explained in Chapter 10.

In the following exercise, you'll create a new behavior and then attach it to the Sound button in the gears5.dir movie (after deleting a prepackaged behavior that plays a click sound when you click the button). The new behavior applies the Lightest ink to its sprite when the mouse clicks it, and then reverses the ink back to the Copy ink when the mouse button is released. The new behavior also plays the Click sound.

On the CD-ROM The file gears6.dir is on your companion CD-ROM in the exercise:ch06 (exercise\ch06) folder, or you can use the version that you created in the last exercise.

Creating a New Behavior

1. Open the gears6.dir movie and rewind it.
2. Click an empty cell in frame 1 to deselect all sprites in the movie, or click an empty slot in the Internal Cast window. If a sprite is selected when you create a new behavior, the behavior will be automatically attached to the sprite.
3. Open the Behavior Inspector. If the Editing pane is not expanded, click the top arrow to expand it. The Behavior Inspector's panes should be empty.

Tip You can resize the panes of the Behavior Inspector. To do so, move the mouse pointer to the horizontal lines (pane dividers) that divide the panes. When the cursor changes to a double-headed arrow (a resizing cursor) click and drag up or down to resize the pane.

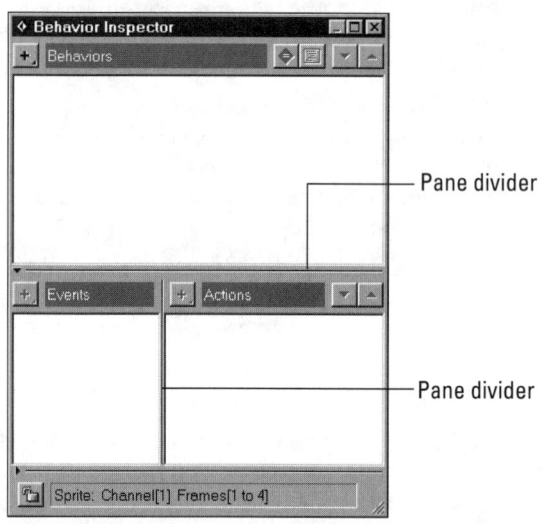

Figure 6-13: You can click and drag the pane dividers to resize the panes of the Behavior Inspector.

4. Click the Behavior Popup button and select the New Behavior option.
5. When the Name Behavior dialog box appears, change the default behavior name to **Better Button** and click OK.
6. Click the Events Popup button and select the Mouse Down option. The Events pane should match Figure 6-14.

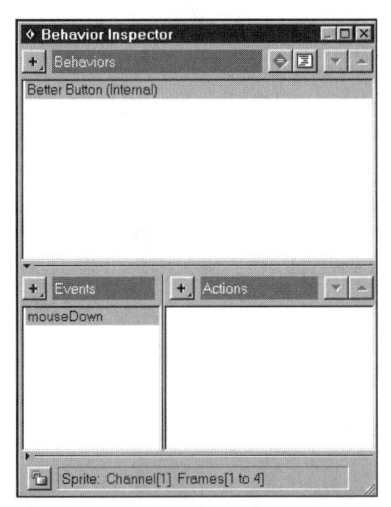

Figure 6-14: Attaching the Mouse Down event to the Better Button behavior

7. Click the Action Popup button, select Sprite, and choose Change Ink.
8. In the Specify Ink dialog box, scroll down in the Change Ink To list and select Lightest, as shown in Figure 6-15. Click OK to close the dialog box.

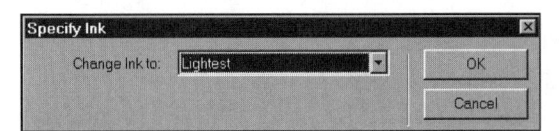

Figure 6-15: Choose Lightest for the Change Ink action.

9. To add a second action to the Mouse Down event, click the Action Popup button and select the Sound ⇨ Play Castmember option.
10. When the Specify Sound Cast Member dialog box appears, set the Play Sound setting to Click, as shown in Figure 6-16. Click OK to close the dialog box.

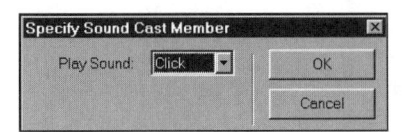

Figure 6-16: Choose Click for the sound cast member.

11. In the next few steps, you'll add a new event/action to the behavior that causes the button's ink to change to Copy when the user releases the mouse button (on the Mouse Up action). Click the Events Popup button and select the Mouse Up option.
12. Click the Action Popup button and select Sprite ⇨ Change Ink.

13. In the Specify Ink dialog box, be sure Change Ink To is set to Copy. Click OK to close the dialog box.
14. With the Behavior Inspector still open, select the Sound button sprite on the Stage. Then click the Behavior Popup button and select the Better Button property.
15. Save the movie as **gears7.dir,** rewind, and play it. Click the Sound button, and watch the ink change and listen to the Click sound play.
16. Stop the movie. With the Behavior Inspector still open, select the Next button sprite on the Stage.
17. In the Behavior List pane, select the Sound Play Castmember behavior and delete it.
18. Click the Behavior Popup button, and select the Better Button behavior to attach it to the Next button.
19. Shuffle the Better Button behavior so it is first in the list of behaviors attached to the Next button. The Behavior Inspector should look like Figure 6-17.
20. Save the movie again as gears7.dir, rewind, and play it. Click the Next button and notice the change in ink, the click sound, and that the playback head advances to frame 5.

You have attached both a predefined behavior (Go to Frame) and a user-defined behavior (Better Button) to the same sprite.

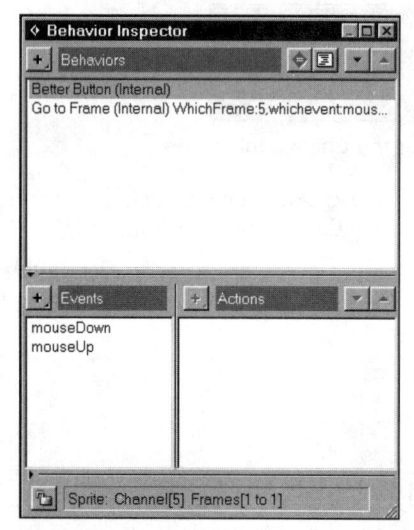

Figure 6-17: Modified Behavior Inspector for the Better Button

The new behavior still lacks some behaviors commonly associated with a "well-behaved button." In the next exercise, you'll add two more events/actions to the Better Button that provide a visual cue to users when the mouse pointer moves over an active area on the Stage. You'll add an action that changes the cursor (mouse pointer) to a pointing finger when it moves over a button to which the behavior is attached. Also, in Director as in life, whatever is done must eventually be undone, so you'll also add a second behavior that restores the cursor to its normal state when the mouse pointer is not within the bounding box of the sprite to which the behavior is attached.

Adding Actions to Your User-Defined Behavior

1. With gears7.dir and the Behavior Inspector still open from the last exercise, select the Better Button behavior in the Behavior List pane.
2. Click the Events Popup button and select the Mouse Within option.
3. Click the Action Popup button, and select the Cursor ⇨ Change Cursor option as shown in Figure 6-18.

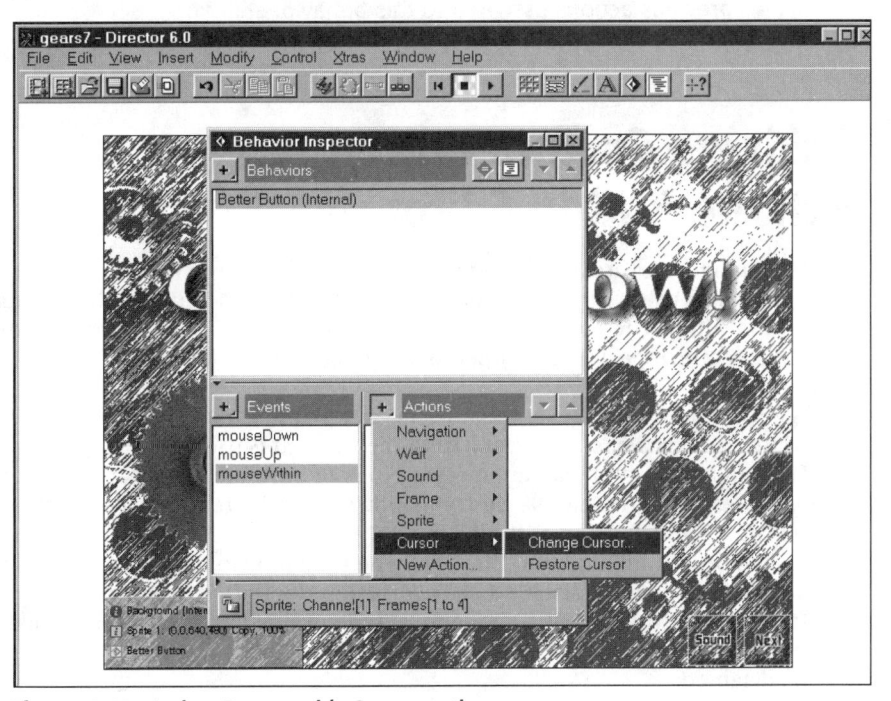

Figure 6-18: Action Popup with Cursor options

4. When the Specify Cursor dialog box appears, change the Change Cursor To setting to Finger (Figure 6-19), and click OK.

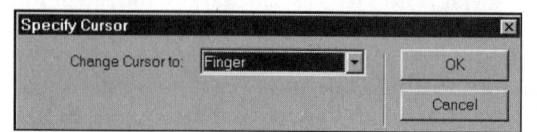

Figure 6-19: Specifying the Finger action for the cursor

5. To add a fourth event/action to the Better Button behavior, be sure it is still selected in the Behavior List pane.
6. Click the Events Popup button and select the Mouse Leave option.
7. Click the Action Popup button and select the Cursor ⇨ Restore Cursor option.
8. Save the movie as **gears8.dir,** rewind, and play it. Move the mouse pointer over the Sound and Next buttons (both have the Better Button behavior attached). Notice the change in the cursor when it is over the two buttons, as compared to when it is not. Click both buttons and notice that all the previous actions assigned to this behavior still work.

Making a Custom Button with the Button Editor

Beginning with Director 6, you have a new tool for creating interactive buttons (in addition to using Director's floating Tool Palette or behaviors that change a button's ink). The custom button is perhaps one of the most useful additions yet to the Director repertoire, and perhaps the most eagerly awaited.

A custom button is a cast member in exactly the same way that a graphic, sound, or text field is a cast member. Using the Custom Button builder (Insert ⇨ Control ⇨ Custom button) you can create two types of buttons: a regular push button that activates when the mouse button is pressed, and a toggle that switches between two states (such as on and off). In addition, custom buttons support both a "rolled-over" (highlighted) state for when the mouse rolls over a button but hasn't yet clicked it, and a disabled state for when the button governs an action that can't take place at the current time. An example of this latter situation would be a button that launches a browser; when no browser is available, the button would be disabled.

Highlights in the life of a button

The *highlight button* has of late become standard fare for multimedia developers. A highlight button changes from its base state (the state it holds when it first appears on the screen) to a more noticeable form whenever the mouse moves over the button. Simple forms of this include buttons that start out partially transparent and then become opaque when they're rolled over — essentially, a gray image becomes colored. A more sophisticated form of the highlight button might be a button in the shape of a closed book. When you roll over the book, the book opens and you can begin leafing through the pages. Clicking the book button will then cause the book to open completely and the animation to stop.

Building the custom button from scratch

Creating a custom button is less than completely straightforward, so let's start at the beginning.

First, you must decide the *states* that you want represented by your button. You'll need to design one button graphic for each state. Using the Custom Button feature, you can establish up to four states as shown in Figure 6-20: up (Normal), down (Pressed), highlighted (Roll Over), and unavailable (Disabled). Notice that the dialog box presents you with eight possible slots: four slots on the left are the states for a standard push button, and four slots on the right are for toggle-style buttons.

Note

The Custom Button Cast Member Properties dialog box (Figure 6-20) is frequently called the Button Editor, so we'll use that name from now on.

These buttons can be designed in any program, but should all be pretty much the same size. The four states for the button in the buttons.dir movie were created in Photoshop.

Once you create the bitmap images representing the desired button states, you must get them into Director. Open the Button Editor (Insert ⇨ Control ⇨ Custom Button) and click the Bitmaps tab. You can use two methods to bring in the button states:

+ Cut and paste each image, one at a time, from a graphics program (such as Photoshop or xRes) into the desired slots on the Bitmap tab of the Button Editor.

+ Import the images into Director and then cut and paste them from the Cast window into the Custom Button Cast Member Properties dialog box.

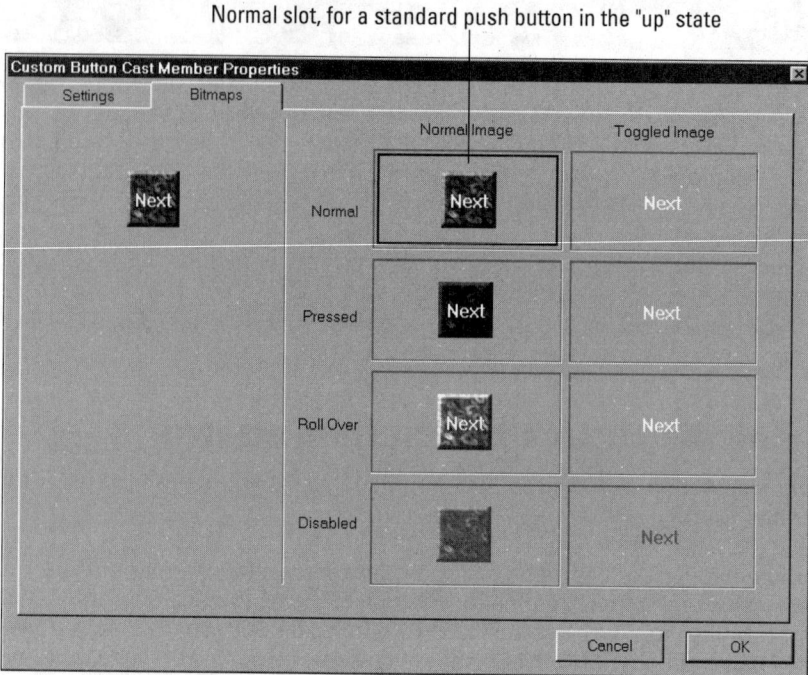

Figure 6-20: The "Button Editor" is the common name for this Custom Button Cast Member Properties dialog box.

The latter method is very tedious — you must select a bitmap cast member in the Cast window, copy it to the Clipboard (Command+C or Ctrl+C), open the Button Editor, switch to the Bitmaps tab, select the state for which you want to use the image (Normal, Pressed, Roll Over, Disabled), and paste the image from the Clipboard (Command+V or Ctrl+V) into the designated slot. Then you must close the dialog and repeat the process for each state. This procedure is necessary because you cannot import directly into the Button Editor, and you can't jump between the Button Editor and the Cast window without closing the Button Editor.

> **Caution**
>
> It's important to have the images properly placed on the Bitmaps tab of the Button Editor. Otherwise, your button may appear highlighted when you want it to appear pressed, pressed when you want it in a normal state, and so on.

In addition to adding the bitmap images to the Bitmaps tab, you must use the Settings tab at the top of the Button Editor to finish setting parameters for the multistate button. As shown in Figure 6-21, you can

- ✦ Add a text label for the button, if desired.
- ✦ Using the Font options, set the font, font size, style, color, kerning, and spacing for the button label.

✦ Specify either a Push Button (releasing the mouse returns the button to its previous state, like a key on a keyboard) or a Toggle Button (clicking the button changes its state, like turning a light switch on or off).

✦ Set the button to be enabled (available for use) immediately whenever it is used in a movie. In this case, leave the Enabled check box selected. If you deselect the check box, the button is initially disabled until you enable it using Lingo.

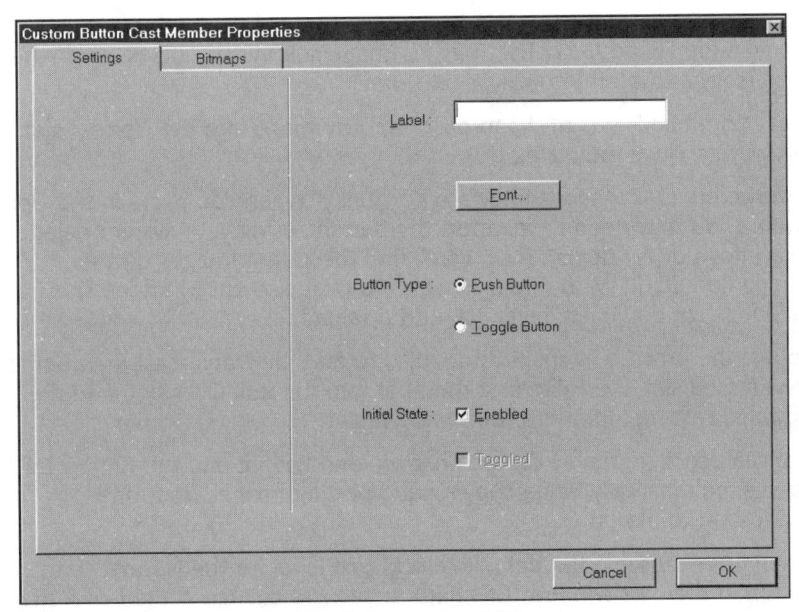

Figure 6-21: The Settings tab of the Button Editor

Once you complete these settings, close the dialog box, and the multistate button will exist as a single cast member in the Cast window. You can test this process in the next exercise.

Creating Custom Buttons

1. Open the buttons.dir movie. In its current condition, the movie includes four bitmap cast members: Up, Down, Hilite, and Disabled.

2. To construct the custom button, select the Insert ⇨ Control ⇨ Custom Button command. The Custom Button Cast Member Properties dialog box (Button Editor) appears.

3. In the Settings tab of the Button Editor (Figure 6-21), type **Next** in the Label field. Leave the font set to its default value (don't use the Font button). Director will automatically use the System font for the button label.

4. Be sure the Push Button radio button is selected, and leave the Enabled check box selected. Click OK.

5. Select the Up cast member in the Cast window and copy it to the Clipboard with Command+C (Ctrl+C).

6. Right-click the Next button (cast slot 5) and select the Edit Cast Member option from the pop-up.

7. In the Button Editor, click the Bitmaps tab.

8. Click the Normal slot in the Normal Image (not the Toggled Image), as identified in Figure 6-21. The Toggled Image column of slots is used when you create a toggle button.

9. Press Command+V (Ctrl+V) to paste the Up image into the Normal slot. Click OK to close the dialog box.

   If the colors for Director's interface go "funky" when you paste in the Up button, you may need to reimport the buttons using your system palette (Macintosh or Windows). If so, you'll find these four images on the companion CD-ROM in the exercise:ch06 (exercise\ch06) folder. They're called up.pct, down.pct, hilite.pct, and disabled.pct.

10. Repeat the process (steps 5 through 9) to add the Down cast member to the Pressed slot, the Hilite cast member into the Roll Over slot, and the Disabled cast member into the Disabled slot.

    You can use any graphic design program and keep it and the Button Editor open simultaneously while copying and pasting images from one application to the other.

11. When done, observe the default (black) text label for the Normal state button in the Cast window. (It's hard to see.) To change it, right-click the Next button (cast member 5) and select the Edit Cast Member option to open the Button Editor.

12. In the Settings tab, click the Font button, click the Color chip, and select white.

13. Click OK to close the Font dialog box. Examine the Next button in the Button Editor and you'll see the label is more readable.

14. Close the Button Editor.

15. Drag the new custom button from the Cast window to the Stage.

16. Save the movie as **myButton.dir,** rewind, and play it. Your button will detect when you click it, when the mouse rolls over it, and when you move the mouse away from it.

    You cannot use the disabled state of your custom button without using Lingo to change `the enabled of member` property. Properties are discussed in Chapter 12.

> **Tip**
>
> If you use imported bitmap cast members from the Cast window to build a multistate button in the Button Editor, once they are pasted into the Editor, you can delete them and save disk space. Bitmap images used in the Button Editor need not reside in a separate cast slot — unless you chose to use them as separate graphics within your movie.

You now have a visually responsive button, but clicking it does nothing. You'll see shortly how to attach behaviors to the button so it'll perform an action when you click it.

As a final note on the Button Editor, it does have a few problems. It works differently from any other control in Director, and it is more than a little awkward. It does not allow importing graphics short of pasting them in. The button's text content or position can't be changed from state to state. And setting the registration for the graphics pasted in is difficult — which is why the graphics should all be the same size, as we mentioned earlier. The Button Editor is fairly useless for working with any button shapes other than uniform rectangles. All in all, however, it's a fair-enough tool for creating quick-and-dirty buttons. For real control over button actions, however, you'd be better off using a behavior with a separate series of cast members representing the different button states.

Where Did That Behavior Come From?

As mentioned earlier, behaviors are *scripts* (and you'll learn a great deal more about scripts in Chapter 10). Unlike many other development languages, Director's scripts are actually kept as a resource. Specifically, the script is a cast member that contains the text of the script, as well as the internal code that stores the script when played at run-time. From the standpoint of the developer, a script is an autonomous entity, and behaviors are especially independent.

The independent nature of scripts and behaviors means they can be collected together in a cast and used in a variety of projects. An *external cast* can really include any kind of cast member (bitmap, text, script, video, and so on). The Behavior Library cast is one such example of an external cast, and you already know it includes 30-plus behaviors. It is installed automatically in Director's Xtras folder so you can access it from the Xtras menu.

A number of behaviors were developed specifically for this book, although they will be useful to you in a wide variety of circumstances. These behaviors are all contained in the cast file *genutils.cst*. You can link them to your own movies and use them royalty-free, although you should read the comments included as part of the text of the scripts, for more details.

> **On the CD-ROM**
>
> The genutils.cst file is an external cast that is available on the accompanying CD-ROM in the Xtras exercise:ch06 (exercise\ch06) folder.

Cast libraries

In traditional programming languages such as C and C++, creating an application is sometimes a real challenge. Many developers manage the overall project by breaking it up into distinct tasks — that is, by separating the application into modules. Director originally didn't support this method — everything had to be contained in a single movie, and that typically meant a lot of duplication if one movie needed to have the same resources as another.

In Director 4.0, Macromedia introduced the concept of the shared cast, which allowed every movie in a given folder to share a set of cast members. Unfortunately, this implementation left some things to be desired, especially since the spaces reserved for the shared movie ate up anything above a specific cast member number.

Cast libraries were Director 5.0's answer to the demands of developers for a more efficient container of resources. A cast library is a separate and discrete entity. It has its own cast numbers and can be used to store any cast members that the normal *internal* cast can use. There's no real limit to the number of cast libraries a movie can open (although certainly system limitations will keep the number down to four or five).

Resources such as behaviors and *widgets* are stored and transported in cast libraries. (Widgets are interface elements such as buttons and scroll bars that might be controlled by behaviors. See Chapter 8.) By using behaviors created by third-party developers, you can expand your codeless scripting options.

Using a behavior to make a timer

Ever thought of adding a digital timer to your application? In Director 5, a timer was a remarkably complicated thing to implement — you needed to know all about such things as stepframes, time display structures, event-driven programming, and the actorlist. In Director 6, adding a timer involves copying a behavior onto a sprite. That's it.

The timer behavior used in the following exercise is one of the behaviors included in the genutils.cst on the CD-ROM. Before you begin the exercise and study how the timer behavior can be used, you must link the genutils.cst to your movie. When you *link* a cast library, you essentially make all of the cast members in the library available to your program. You can link as many cast libraries as you need (there's probably a limit somewhere, but we don't expect you'll ever run into it).

On the CD-ROM In the next exercise, you will use a partially complete Director movie, timer.dir, available on your companion CD-ROM in the exercise:ch06 (exercise\ch06) folder.

Linking Cast Libraries to Movies

1. Copy the genutils.cst external cast from the accompanying CD (in the Xtras folder) to a personal folder (where you save your Director movies) on your local hard drive. The genutils.cst file is also available in exercise:06 (exercise\ch06).
2. Open the timer.dir movie.
3. From the menu, choose Modify ⇨ Movie ⇨ Casts or press Command+Shift+C (Ctrl+Shift+C) to display the Movie Casts dialog box (Figure 6-22).

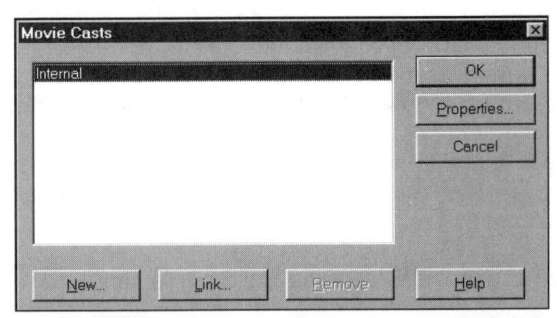

Figure 6-22: The Movie Casts dialog box enables you to link cast libraries into your current movie.

4. Click the Link button. This displays an Open (file) dialog, where you can select a cast library (any file with the .cst or .cxt extension). Locate the genutils.cst external cast, and double-click to link it to the current movie. Once the cast is linked, you can access it through the Cast window.
5. Click OK to close the dialog box.
6. If the Cast window is not visible, open it using Command+3 (Ctrl+3).
7. Click the Choose Cast button (see Figure 6-23) and a list of the active cast libraries for the current movie appears.

Figure 6-23: Clicking the Choose Cast button brings up a list of all of the current cast libraries.

8. Select genutils to make the library and all its behaviors available to you.

9. Click the Choose Cast button again and set the cast back to Internal, which is the default cast for a movie. This ensures that any new cast members you add will be added to the internal cast rather than to the imported (genutils) cast.

10. Save the movie as **timer1.dir.**

Another way of accessing cast members of a library is to place the cast library in the Xtras folder, which is located in a subfolder of the folder containing your copy of Director. This technique makes the cast available from the Xtras menu. For example, if you drag the genutils.cst into the Xtras folder, you'll see a genutils entry in the Xtras menu. Note, however, that the cast is *not* actually linked to the file. You'll have to physically drag one or more cast members from the cast into your movie's internal cast to make them work. If you use this method, Director prompts you whether to link the external cast or just transfer the selected cast members to the internal cast.

Once you have the genutils cast linked, adding the timer is simple.

Adding the Timer Behavior

1. The movie to which you linked the genutils cast should still be open. Press Command+7 (Ctrl+7) to open the Tool Palette and select the Field button.

2. Click the Stage in the center rectangle (a placeholder for the timer) and drag to create a field cast member. The internal cast now includes an unnamed field cast member in cast member slot 1.

3. Use the Choose Cast button to make genutils the active cast.

4. Locate the timerBehavior cast member in the genutils cast. You may need to scroll through the Cast window or expand it to locate this custom behavior — meaning it is not a standard behavior distributed with Director 6. All the behaviors in genutils were created specifically for you, the reader of this book!

5. Click the unnamed field sprite so it is selected and easy to locate on the Stage.

6. Click the timerBehavior cast member and drag it on top of the field sprite you just created. This is the most common way to associate a behavior with a given sprite.

7. As soon as you release the timerBehavior cast member over the field on the Stage, the Parameters For "TimerBehavior" dialog box pops up, as shown in Figure 6-24, and displays several options for controlling the actions of the clock. By default, the timer counts down a specified number of units established using the Start Time field. The units of measure (seconds or minutes) are set using the Starting Time Units field. The How Is Timer Displayed? field establishes the countdown increments.

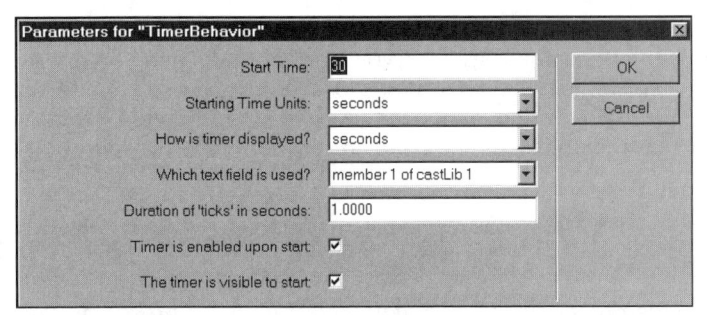

Figure 6-24: The parameters for timerBehavior include how long the timer runs, what units of time are displayed, whether the timer starts out enabled, and so on.

8. Leave the default settings, as shown in Figure 6-24. Click OK to retain the default parameters and close the Parameters For dialog box.

   Note: If your settings on the Parameters For dialog box do not match Figure 6-24, you may have dropped the behavior on the Stage rather than the sprite. Click the Cancel button and try again.

9. Click the Stage to make it active (rather than the genutils cast), and save the movie again as timer1.dir.

10. Rewind and play the movie. You will see the field cast member start its countdown, updating every second. When it reaches 0, it will stop.

11. Stop the movie.

The timerBehavior was written completely in Director using Lingo. However, you didn't have to write a single line of code to use it. The capabilities offered by behaviors are revolutionary in Director 6.

Changing the properties of a behavior

You already know that a behavior can have specific properties that control some aspect of its behavior. For example, the clockBehavior behavior, which is available in genutils.cst, includes settings that control the format used to display the time and date. These properties are initially set on the Parameters For dialog that appears when you first drag the behavior to a sprite. Once you assign a behavior to a sprite, there will likely be situations in which you want to change the parameters of the behavior. To do this, you need to invoke the Behavior Inspector. In our earlier discussion of the Behavior Inspector, you learned that when you use it to add a behavior to a sprite, you must set the properties (if there are any to set) on the Parameters For dialog which is invoked using the Parameters button. This same method is used to modify existing behavior properties in the following exercise.

Using the Behavior Inspector to Change Properties

1. Open the timer1.dir movie that you created in the preceding exercise.
2. Select the field sprite on the Stage. It's based on cast member 1.
3. When you select the sprite, the Sprite Overlay appears and indicates that there is one behavior already attached to the sprite — the timerBehavior (see Figure 6-25). Open the Behavior Inspector. (Just a reminder: You can do this by clicking the Behavior button in the Sprite Overlay or on the Director toolbar; or press Command+Shift+; (semicolon) or Ctrl+Shift+; for Windows users.)

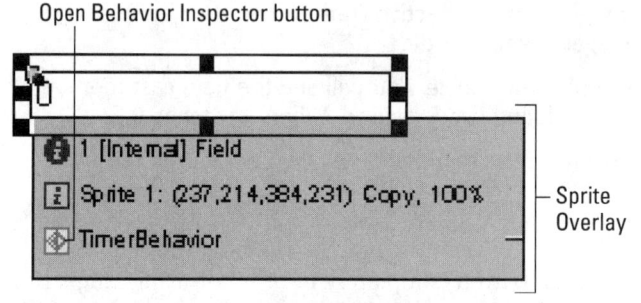

Figure 6-25: The Sprite Overlay lists the behaviors attached to the selected sprite.

4. At the top of the Behavior Inspector, click the diamond-shaped Parameters button to display the behavior's Parameters For dialog.
5. Change the Start Time field to **60** (meaning 60 seconds).
6. Open the pop-up list for the How Is Timer Displayed? field and select the minutes setting (as shown in Figure 6-26) to display the time in 1:00 format.

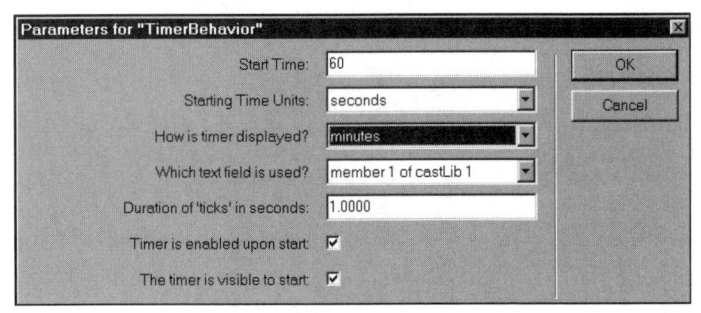

Figure 6-26: You can edit the behavior's properties even after you've assigned the behavior to a sprite, by opening the Parameters For dialog from the Behavior Inspector.

7. Click OK to close the dialog box, and close the Behavior Inspector.
8. Save the movie again as timer1.dir and run it. It now starts counting at 60 seconds and counts down from 1:00, to :59, to :58, and so on.

> **Note:** Another way to modify behavior properties and to call behavior functions is by using Lingo, as will be explored in Part III.

Navigating with Custom Buttons

Earlier we mentioned that custom buttons are far more useful if they actually do something when you click them. Fortunately, Director gives you an abundant collection of options as to what these buttons can do. One of the simplest and most useful roles for a custom button is providing the ability to jump to a different location in the Score.

Once you begin scripting behaviors (in Chapter 10), you'll discover that a simple instruction can direct the playback head to a frame number or a marker.

Adding markers to your movie

Most of Director's basic navigational commands and navigational behaviors make use of markers within a movie. Markers are labels that you attach to specific frames. The steps to adding a marker include the following:

1. In the Score window, locate the Markers channel. As shown in Figure 6-27, the Markers channel is immediately above the Effects channels.

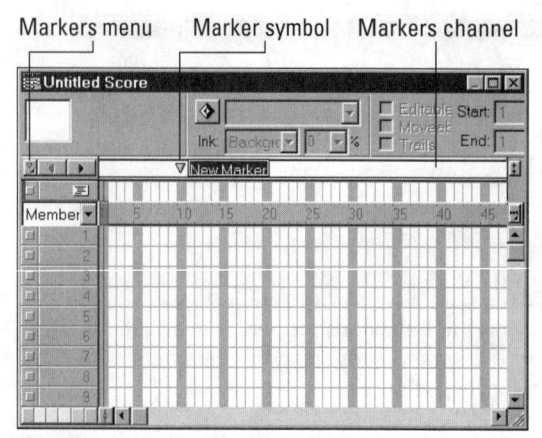

Figure 6-27: The Markers channel in the Score window

2. Click in the Markers channel above the frame where you want to add a marker. A symbol appears for the marker, as shown in Figure 6-27, along with a default marker name (New Marker).

3. You will typically want to use a more specific marker name, such as **Start**. Just type it in, and the name you type replaces the default name.

4. To delete a marker, click the triangular marker symbol and drag it off the Markers channel.

You can choose from three different methods to display a list of all the markers in your movie:

✦ Select the Window ➪ Markers command. In the Markers window, a double-click on a marker name jumps the playback head to that marker.

✦ Press Command+Shift+M (Ctrl+Shift+M).

✦ Click the Markers menu button (see Figure 6-27) to display a pop-up menu of all markers. On the Markers menu, click the desired marker name to jump to that marker in your movie.

With markers, you can control the flow of your movie. You can combine button behaviors with frame and marker navigation to really enliven your interactive presentations. In the next series of exercises, you'll use all the tools you learned in this chapter. First, you'll use the Button Editor to build a custom button.

Building an Interactive Button: Making It

1. Open the goboom.dir movie, which is available on the accompanying CD in the exercise:ch06 (exercise\ch06) folder.

2. Select the TimerBtn cast member and copy it to the Clipboard using Command+C (Ctrl+C).

3. Select the Insert⇨Control⇨Custom Button command. In the Button Editor, leave the default settings on the Settings tab. (Because this set of buttons already has a text label included in the graphic image, you don't need to use the Label field on the Settings tab.)

4. Open the Bitmaps tab. Select the Normal slot in the Normal Image column, and paste the image from the Clipboard using Command+V (Ctrl+V).

   Tip

   If the colors for Director's interface and cast members go "funky" when you paste in the TimerBtn cast member, you can fix them by doing the following. (In fact, these steps can be used whenever a movie shows "bad color.") Cancel out of the Button Editor and select File⇨Revert. Select the first bitmap cast member (slot 1). Select Modify⇨Transform Bitmap, and set Palette to use the system palette for your computer (System-Win or System-Mac). Set Color Depth to 8 bits and turn on the Dither option. Click the Transform button. When the alert box appears (warning you that you cannot undo this operation), click OK. If this trick doesn't work, you can use the File⇨Revert command to undo any changes made since you last saved your movie. Repeat these steps for each bitmap cast member (2–5 and 8–9).

5. Click OK to close the dialog. The new custom button appears in cast member slot 6.

6. Select the TimerBtn_down cast member and copy it to the Clipboard.

7. Right-click cast member 6 (the custom button), select the Edit Cast Member option, and click the Bitmaps tab.

8. Select the Pressed slot in the Normal Image column, paste the image, and close the dialog.

9. Repeat the process (steps 6 through 8) to copy and paste the TimerBtn_hi cast member into the Roll Over slot in the Normal Image column, and then close the dialog.

10. Drag the custom button, cast member 6, to the upper-left corner of the Stage, as shown in Figure 6-28.

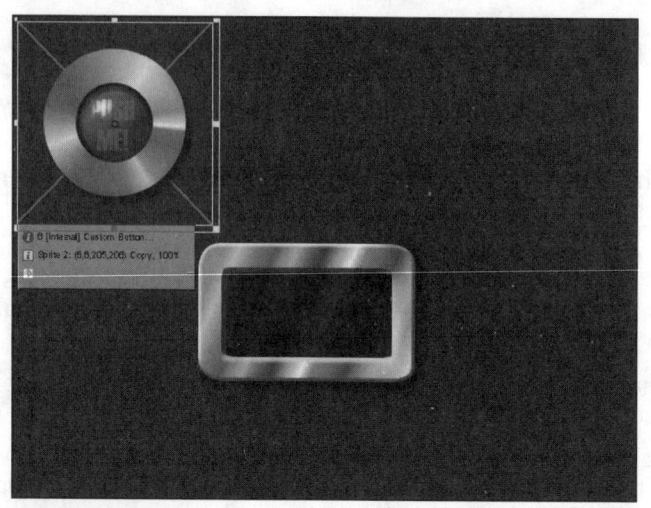

Figure 6-28: Placement of the Push Me! button on the Stage of the goboom.dir movie

11. Select the custom button in cast member slot 6. Click in the cast member name field, type **Push Me,** and press Enter to name the cast member.

12. Select the Xtras ⇨ Behavior Library command to open the cast of prescripted Director 6 behaviors.

13. Drag and drop the Hold on Current Frame behavior onto frame 1.

14. Click the Stage and save the movie as **goboom1.dir.**

15. Rewind the movie and play it. While the movie loops on frame 1, move the mouse pointer over the custom button and click it. It responds as a button should, but takes no action. You'll change that shortly.

Next, you want to give the playback head someplace to go when the user clicks the custom button. In this exercise, you add markers to target with behaviors.

Building an Interactive Button: Adding Markers

1. Be sure the goboom1.dir movie that you created in the preceding exercise is open.

2. Click the Markers channel immediately above frame 1.

3. The default marker name, New Marker, appears. Type **Start** and press Enter to rename the marker.

4. Repeat steps 2 and 3 to add a new marker in frame 2. Name it **CountDown.**

> **Tip**
> You probably won't be able to click exactly on the Markers channel over frame 2 because Director thinks you're trying to select the Start marker. If you need to, create the marker further to the right (over frame 10 or 11) and then drag it back to frame 2.

5. Repeat steps 2 and 3 to add a new marker over frame 15. Name it **Boom**.
6. Locate the Go To Next Marker behavior (*not* GoTo Marker) in the Behavior Library cast and drag it onto the Push Me button.
7. When the Parameters For dialog appears, leave the default mouseUp setting and click the OK button.
8. Click the Stage and save the movie as **goboom2.dir**.
9. Rewind the movie and play it. With the movie playing, click the Push Me button. A red number 20 appears in the timer window on the Stage, but nothing else occurs. Click the Push Me button again. The playback head jumps to the next marker (Boom), and you see the explosion on Stage.
10. Stop the movie.

In the next exercise, you'll attach an external cast (genutils.cst) to your movie, attach a behavior from the cast, and then set the properties for the new behavior.

Building an Interactive Button: Adding Behaviors

1. Be sure the goboom2.dir movie that you created in the preceding exercise is open.
2. Select the Modify ⇨ Movie ⇨ Casts command. When the Movie Cast dialog box appears, click the Link button.
3. Locate the genutils.cst file (either on your local hard drive or on the CD-ROM) and double-click the filename.
4. Click OK to close the Movie Cast dialog.
5. Use the Choose Cast button on the Internal Cast window to switch to the genutils cast.
6. Select the Timer sprite (based on the Timer cast member) in channel 4 of the Score. This sprite does not appear on the Stage until frame 2.
7. Locate timerBehavior in the genutils cast and drag it onto the Timer sprite, which is selected on the Stage.
8. When the Parameters For dialog box appears, set the Start Time to 20. Use the default settings for all other properties. Click OK to close the dialog box.
9. Use the Choose Cast button to switch back to the internal cast, and save the movie as **goboom3.dir**.

10. Rewind and play the movie. Click the Push Me button. The playback head moves to frame 2, where the TimerBehavior behavior is executed and the countdown starts. When the timer reaches 0, it stops. You can click the Push Me button again to see the explosion — but we can accomplish that without a button click with the addition of another behavior.

11. Stop the movie.

Responding to custom events

Perhaps one of the most exciting features of Director behaviors is the capability of using behaviors to create and respond to custom (user-defined) events. For example, when our timer reaches zero, it appears to do nothing at all. In truth, however, a little miracle is taking place: An event called timerDone is sent out by the timer object, and this event can be intercepted by any object at all, as long as it has a TimerDone event handler.

> **Note**
>
> If you examine the description of the TimerBehavior in the Description pane of the Behavior Inspector, you'll see that "The timer raises an event which can be trapped by any other sprite." Later in the notes, the timer is identified as TimerDone.

In the case of the goboom.dir movie, the timerDone event can be added to the behavior of any other sprite that shares frames with the timer. In fact, you can even have the Timer cast member intercept the TimerDone event that it generates! In the next exercise, you'll create a new behavior with a custom event and then drag it into the Timer sprite. When the timerDone event occurs, the new behavior will intercept it and move the playback head to the next marker in the movie.

Building an Interactive Button: Adding a Custom Event

1. Be sure the goboom3.dir movie that you created in the last exercise is open.
2. Click the next vacant cast member slot in the movie's internal cast.
3. Open the Behavior Inspector.
4. Click the Behavior Popup button and select the New Behavior option.
5. When the Name Behavior dialog box appears, type **Boom** and click OK.
6. If it's not already open, open the Editing pane by clicking the triangle below the Behaviors list.
7. With the new behavior selected in the Behaviors list, click the Event Popup button. Select New Event, and when the Name Event dialog box appears, type **timerDone**. Click OK to close the dialog box.

8. With the timerDone event selected, click the Action Popup button and select Navigation ⇨ Go To Marker.

9. When the Specify Marker dialog box appears, select the Boom marker.

   Tip: If you type **B** when the Specify Marker dialog box appears, Director replaces the default marker name with the first marker that starts with the letter *B* — which is the Boom marker.

10. Click OK to close the dialog and close the Behavior Inspector.

11. Drag the new Boom behavior onto the Timer sprite.

12. Save the movie as **goboom4.dir,** rewind, and play the movie. You'll see the button highlight when you roll over it, and depress when you click it. When you release the mouse to release the button, the timer starts counting down from 20. When it reaches zero, the screen explodes. Stop the movie when you're done testing it.

Tip: The Timer is quite a useful behavior. A timer doesn't need to be visible to work (in fact, you can turn the visibility off to begin with). Nor does it have to run at one-second intervals. By setting the interval length (in the Parameters For dialog) to 0.1, you can make it count in tenths of seconds instead of full seconds. The TimerDone event is automatically fired even if the timer itself is invisible. So you can use TimerBehavior to time slideshow displays, for instance, by setting the interval length to a longer span, say 4.0 seconds, and writing the TimerDone event to reset and restart the timer sprite.

Summary

In the next chapter, you'll discover how to add sound to your movies. Before moving on, let's review some of the things you learned in this chapter.

✦ Director incorporates a Custom Button editor that can be used to quickly create simple buttons.

✦ You can add basic interactivity within your program by using behaviors.

✦ Many canned behaviors and widgets are available in Director and on this book's CD-ROM, as well as from plenty of other resources. These behaviors save you time and energy when you're trying to add basic functionality (such as timers and buttons) to your application.

✦ Behaviors are a collection of event handlers, and each handler contains one or more actions. The Behavior Inspector is used to translate these behaviors, events, and actions into scripts, handlers, and statements.

✦ ✦ ✦

Sound Advice

CHAPTER 7

Sounds add another dimension — an important one — to Director movies. Aside from putting dazzle into your movie, when you add sounds you fulfill one of the key concepts of multimedia: to provide information in a format that maximizes the impact of the presentation. Multimedia is a multisensual method of relaying information to an audience. Whether you are creating a simple animated cartoon sequence or an elaborate interactive application, you essentially are teaching your audience about the topic of your movie. The mechanisms of learning are complex, but one simple axiom is always true: The more ways you present information, the better your chance of reaching your audience with positive results.

Director supports a variety of digitized sound file formats that you can use to enhance your movies. In this chapter you'll learn how to choose a sound format. You'll also learn the basics of importing and editing sounds for Director movies. When you understand sound theory and how Director deals with sound files, you'll have taken an important step toward using sound effectively with your audience in mind.

In This Chapter

Importing sounds into movies

Digitized sound formats

Adding sounds to your movies

Editing sounds outside of Director

File sizes and sampling considerations

Using and editing sounds efficiently

Working with sound Xtras

Sound Basics

Sounds can take a movie from the mundane to the spectacular. They can inform, guide, and stimulate the interest of the user. Understanding Director sound basics provides the foundation you need for using sounds creatively and efficiently in your movies:

When working with Director and sounds, two key concepts should be behind every sound decision you make.

- ✦ The first concept is to *remember your audience*. A sound should enhance the movie while at the same time balancing the needs and resources of the user.
- ✦ The second concept is actually more than that; it's a law. Two types of files can bring a computer to its knees in nearly the blink of an eye: complex graphics files and sound files. Sound files can be huge, requiring significant resources to store and play them. So the law is to *choose and edit sounds carefully, to balance creativity and file size*.

This section tells you about importing sounds; discusses the difference between internal and external sounds; helps you choose among sound formats; and explains how sounds are edited externally.

Importing sounds

As the author of a Director movie, you need to make a number of decisions regarding a series of issues that affect the final movie. One of these key issues, as mentioned just above, is your audience. The audience is especially critical if your movie is going to contain sounds. Your audience may not have the system resources you have, and thus balancing file size and quality factors with the goals of your movie becomes essential to the movie's success.

In selecting sounds for your project, you'll need to consider three factors: file format, sampling rate, and file compression. If you are developing a movie that's designed for both PC and Macintosh platforms, you can save a significant amount of time if you take file format into consideration before creating the movie. Choosing a sound format that is supported by both platforms is one way of ensuring that you don't need to author the movie twice. As your movies grow in size, finding individual sprites and cast members when you want them can become a tedious task. It's easy to miss a single cast member and cause your movie to fail, especially if you have to swap a number of cast members to conform to a specific platform. When you choose a sound for use in a Director movie, you should also be aware of the sampling rate and file compression.

The basics of importing a sound file into Director are the same regardless of the sound format you choose. When you import a sound file into Director, it becomes a cast member that you can place in the Effects section of the Score. Unlike other types of cast members, sound cast members aren't placed on the Stage.

Importing a Sound File into Director

1. Select File⇨Import or press Command+R (Ctrl+R) to display the Import Files dialog box (see Figure 7-1)..

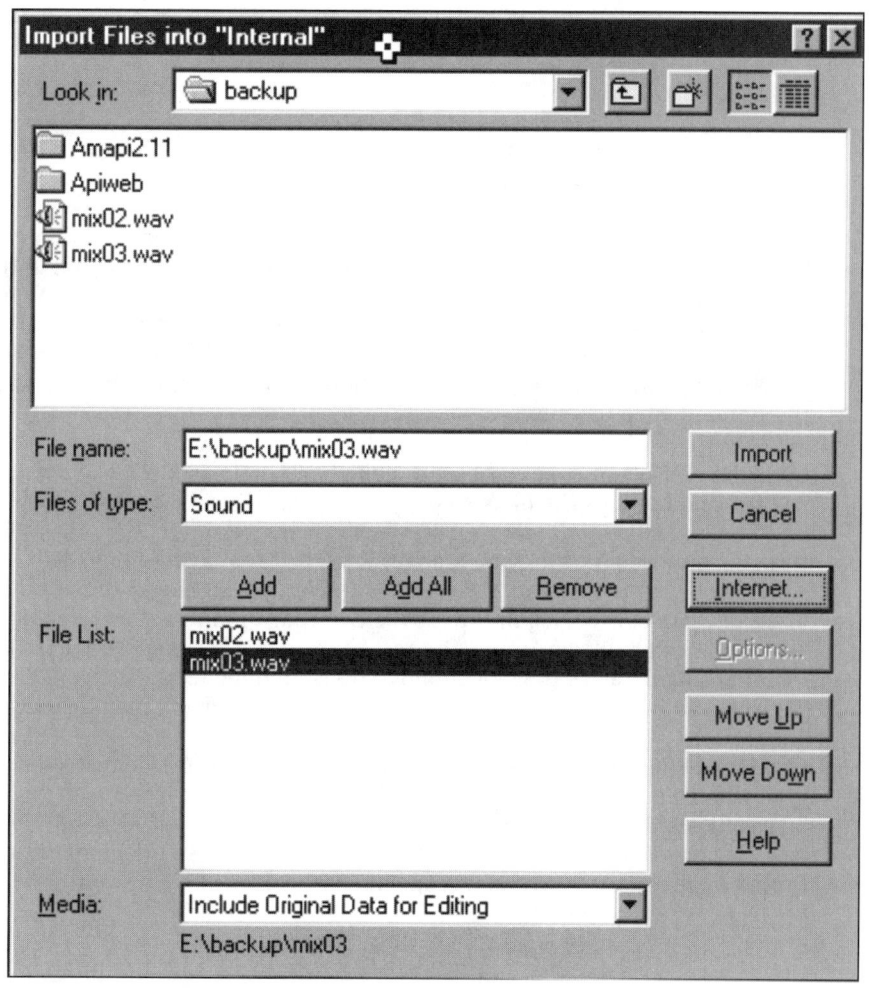

Figure 7-1: Use the Import Files dialog to select sound files and add them as cast members.

2. Choose the folder containing the sound file you want to import into Director, and select the file. You can select multiple files by pressing the Shift key while clicking the files. Click the Add button to move the selected filenames into the File List.

3. Click the Media Field. From the pop-up list, choose Include Original Data for Editing if you want to use an external sound editor. This option enables you to quickly edit and update the sound in your movie, by launching the external editor when you double-click the cast member.

4. When you have selected all the files you want to import and added them to the File List, click the Import button to complete the operation and return to the Director window. The sound files you selected will appear in the Cast window.

Using internal versus external sounds

Internal and external sounds are stored differently, and managed differently by Director as well. When you import a sound into Director, it's placed in the cast and considered an *internal sound*. (Note that the cast can be either an internal or external cast.) The sound information is saved with the cast or movie, which also increases the file size of the movie. *External sounds,* on the other hand, are linked by Director, which allows you to store the sound file separately from the movie, thereby reducing the movie's file size.

Tip Consider storing large sound files in linked external casts. This allows the sound to stream, and reduces the file size of your movie.

Director preloads internal sounds into RAM before playing them. Although this works well for small sound files such as beeps, storing larger music sound files internally can cause a lag in the movie. External sound files are *streamed*. This means they start playing while the rest of the file is loading. The drawback to external sound files is that if you move the sound file to another location, the link is broken and must be reestablished before the sound will play in your movie.

Tip Creating a folder to contain all of the elements of your movie can save you a lot of grief when it's time to output the movie. When files are stored using this method, all the files required for the movie are in the same location, which reduces the risk of losing a critical file. This storage method also reduces the amount of time it takes for Director to search for a specific file.

OLE and sound files: a bad match

Director supports *OLE* functions. OLE (Object Linking and Embedding) is a difficult concept for many people, but it's not as complicated as it seems. What OLE does is allow you to easily share and edit elements between two OLE-compliant applications, without having to worry about import and export filters. The shared objects are transferred via the Windows Clipboard, from one application (known as the *server* application) to another application (the *client* application). OLE is primarily a Windows function, although a Mac OLE SDK (Software Developers Kit) exists and can be used to add OLE functions to Macintosh applications.

When you use OLE, you can choose to either *link* or *embed* the object in the client application. Linking the element means that the element is stored separately from its associated document. Every time you open the associated document, the application searches for the object and moves it into the document. So if you change the object, it will be updated when it appears in the client application. Embedding an object means it's stored with the receiving document and isn't updated each time you open that document. Both linking and embedding allow you to quickly edit the object and return to your document.

It's important to understand that OLE is designed to transfer text and graphics — not sounds — between applications. Director basically sees every OLE object, text and graphics both, in terms of a bitmap. OLE is not intended for the transfer of sound files, and sounds may become corrupted if this method is used to place them in documents. Some OLE-compliant graphics applications include sound editors, but you should never use OLE to place these files.

Choosing a sound format

Another audience issue when you're working with sound files concerns resources. Sound file sizes typically range from large to humongous. These large files can bloat your movie, causing longer load times. And if the end-user has a system with limited resources, these files can also cause the movie to crash. The choice of file format is therefore an important one.

Director 6 supports AIFF (Audio Interchange File Format) and WAV (Waveform Audio File) sounds, as well as Macintosh System 7 sounds. If you are authoring a movie for a single platform, you can afford to use the sound format native to the platform. Use the following information to choose a sound format.

WAV Files. WAV sound files are primarily Windows files. Although some Macintoshes are capable of playing WAV files, this capability can vary from one computer to the next. WAV files support a variety of compression schemes to reduce file size. Director supports WAV files compressed with IMA-ADPCM compression (Interactive Multimedia Association - Adaptive Differential Pulse Code Modulation). You should be aware, however, that any compressed file must be uncompressed (expanded) before it can be used. Compressed files are good for storage purposes, but they can take longer to load.

AIFF Files. Though they don't support compression, AIFF files have the advantage of being multiplatform. Both PCs and Macintosh machines can play AIFF sound files. This format is not a native format for the PC, but Director and a variety of other software programs support AIFF on the PC without the use of external software.

Macintosh System 7 Files. If you are authoring your movie on a Macintosh, you can record sounds from within Director by selecting Insert ⇨ Media Element ⇨ Sound. You'll need to have an audio input or microphone connected to your Macintosh. This feature is for Macintosh only and is not supported in the Windows version of Director.

Regardless of the format you choose, you'll want the assistance of a good sound editor to help you adjust the length and effects within your sound file. Optimizing sounds within your sound editor can help keep the file size small without compromising the quality of your movie.

Editing sounds externally

Director doesn't provide the ability to edit sounds within the program. Director does allow you to specify an audio editor in the program's preferences, however. Once you've specified an editor, you can edit a selected sound cast member by choosing Edit ⇨ Launch External Editor or by double-clicking the cast member in the Cast window.

Specifying an External Sound Editor

1. Select File ⇨ Preferences ⇨ Editors to display the Editors Preferences dialog box (see Figure 7-2).

2. Scroll through the list to choose the type of sound file for which you want to select an editor. In this example the WAV file type is selected.

3. Click the Edit button. The dialog that's displayed next reflects your choice of file type in the title bar; in this example you see the Select Editor for WAVE Sound dialog (Figure 7-3).

4. Click the Browse button to locate the editor on your hard drive. Select it, and it appears in the list window. Click Open to accept this choice. Click OK to close the Select Editor dialog box and return to the Editors Preferences dialog box.

5. If you want to select more sound editors, repeat steps 2 through 4. If you select more than one editor at this time, you will have to specify which one you want to be the active editor for your movie by highlighting the name. When you are satisfied with the settings, click OK to return to Director's main window.

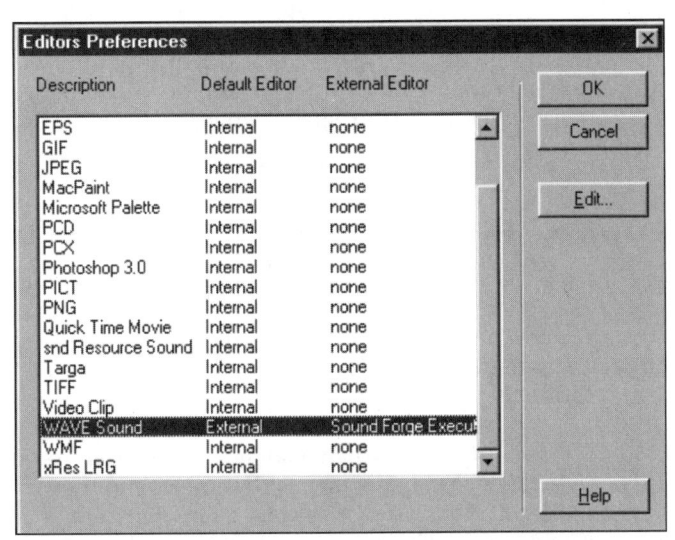

Figure 7-2: The Editors Preferences dialog box allows you to select an external editor for your sound files.

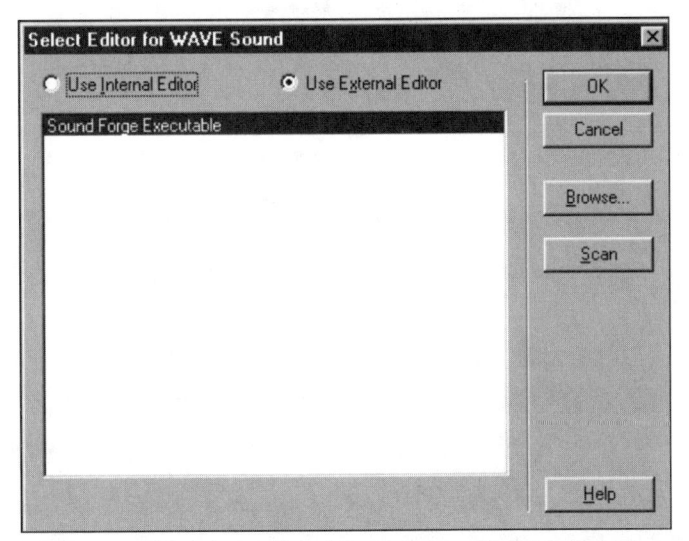

Figure 7-3: The Select Editor for WAVE Sound dialog box allows you to specify the editor you want to use for editing your sound files.

Choosing a sound editor provides you with a quick bridge to editing your sound files. Instead of having to exit Director and open another program, you can simply launch the external editor from within Director. In addition, the changes you make are automatically incorporated into your movie, which reduces the need to delete and reimport cast members.

Sampling rates, recording modes, and other issues

Understanding a bit about a sound's file size and quality will help you when you're using an audio editor to balance these elements of any sound. Factors that affect the size of a sound file are the sampling rate, recording mode (stereo or mono), bit depth, and compression method. These factors are determined during the initial recording, or later during the editing process.

The *sampling rate* is the frequency at which a sound is converted to digital format. A sampling rate of 44.1KHz, for example, means that the sound was sampled 44,100 times each second the sound lasts. In most cases, a sampling rate of 11.025KHz is good for voice recording, and 22.05KHz is fine for music-quality recording. Higher sampling rates result in a better recording. If you wish to have a CD-quality recording, use a 44.1KHz sampling rate.

Note: CD quality is not required for most multimedia projects. The files take too long to load, and they strain the memory resources of lower-end computers.

Choosing mono recording mode rather than stereo is another way to yield a smaller file. Mono recording mode uses a single channel for the sampling, whereas stereo mode uses two channels to improve the quality of the sound. Figure 7-4 shows the same WAV file in both a stereo and mono format as represented in an audio editor.

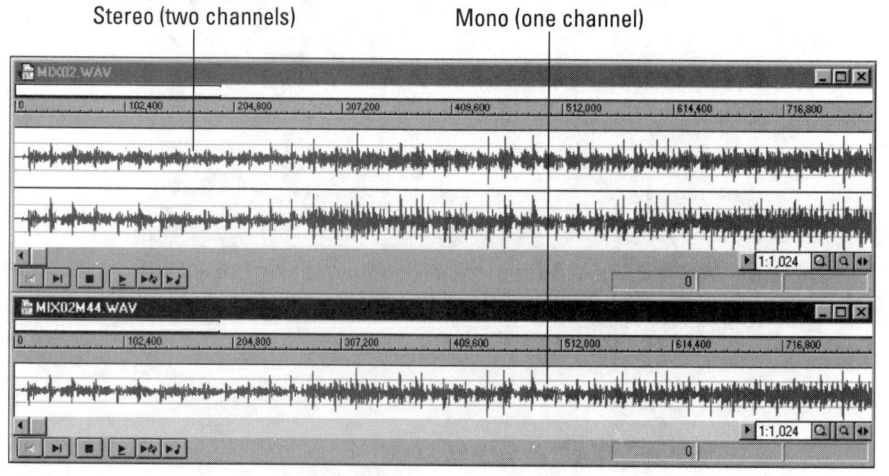

Figure 7-4: Stereo and mono sounds in an audio editor

Sounds are frequently resampled from 16-bit to 8-bit to save storage space. Typically, 8-bit sounds are *lossy*, which means information is lost in the translation from a higher bit depth, resulting in a poorer sound quality. If your sound editor supports the removal of silent bits of information and dynamic compression, you can edit a 16-bit file prior to converting it to 8-bit. This editing improves the quality of the sound when it's resampled to 8-bit. (For more information, see the documentation for your sound editor.)

Tip You'll find that 8-bit samples are noisier than 16-bit samples. You'll get better quality if you lower the frequency from 22.5KHz to 11.25KHz and use a 16-bit sample, than if you use an 8-bit sound sampled at 22.5KHz — even though the file size is approximately the same.

Table 7-1 compares the file sizes that result when applying various sampling rates and recording modes to a sound file in the humongous range. We chose a 74-second file has been used for comparison because the differences between the file sizes were so dramatic; most sound files aren't this long. You probably won't need to use sound files this long in your movies.

Later in this chapter we'll discuss looping sound, which allows you to give the illusion of a longer sound file without straining the resources of a computer.

Table 7-1
File Size Comparison for Different Sampling Rates/Recording Modes

Sampling Rate	16-bit Stereo	16-bit Mono	8-bit Stereo	8-bit Mono
44.1KHz w/compression WAV file format	3.15MB	1.57MB	1.57MB	812KB
22.5KHz w/compression WAV file format	1.58MB	812KB	812KB	412KB
11.25KHz w/compression WAV file format	818KB	412KB	412KB	376KB
44.1KHz WAV file format	12.5MB	6.29MB	6.29MB	3.14MB
22.5KHz WAV file format	6.29MB	3.14MB	3.14MB	1.57MB
11.25KHz WAV file format	3.14MB	1.57MB	1.57MB	805KB
44.1KHz AIFF file format (AIFF does not support compression)	17.9MB	8.95MB	8.95MB	4.47MB

Obtaining sounds for your movies

Your first step in obtaining sounds for your movies is to determine the type of sound files you need. Some multimedia projects require voice-overs; others require special-effects sounds (SFX) such as a bell or thunder.

If your sound card supports audio input, you can record your own sounds, either by using a microphone directly connected to your sound card or transferring sounds from tape to your computer. A variety of sound sources can be found on the World Wide Web and through companies that market sound clips. Some of these sound files are considered public domain, which means you can use them freely. Others are protected by copyright laws and licensing agreements. If you have questions regarding these laws and/or the licensing information for a particular sound file, contact the source *before* including the sound file in any project.

With a clear idea of what you need and a little research in the available sources, you can incorporate any sound you can imagine into your project.

Tip

A year or so ago, one of this book's authors created a bilingual multimedia presentation that required a voice-over. He wasn't fluent in the second language, so he hired a voice talent to create a tape with the words and phrases needed. Some of the phrases took several takes to get the inflection and sound just right. If he had used direct input via the sound card and a microphone, it would have required several gigabytes of hard disk space to produce the sounds. We suggest you avoid recording directly to your computer. It's far better to record to a high-quality tape and then transfer the sounds to your computer as they are needed.

Adding and Editing Sounds

Let's say you want to make a sphinx talk. Think it'll be easy? Here's what happened to us: First of all, we had to shanghai the right victim to play the part of the sphinx — we wanted a deep, mystical, somewhat eerie voice. Then we wrote a script, which our hired voice talent wanted to rewrite. Finally, after several hours and numerous takes, we had a tape containing the required voice-overs. Then we had to digitize, mix, and import the sound files into Director as internal cast members. And that task isn't just a matter of dropping the sound cast members into the Score and expecting a miracle. The sounds must be placed at the correct location in the Score. Oh, and the sphinx was to be animated, by the way: We wanted his lips to move. So the sounds and lip movements had to be synchronized so that the animation and sound started and ended at the same time.

Sure — none of this was terribly complicated, but it required time and patience. It also required knowing how to manage a sound and use sound channels once the sound was in the movie. That's what we'll tackle in the next few sections.

Placing sounds in the Score

Once your sounds have been imported as cast members, you are ready to place them in your movie.

Placing a Sound Cast Member in the Score

1. Start by opening the movie into which you want to place a sound.

2. Director allows you to hide or show the Effects channels in the Score (by default, they're hidden). To turn the Effects channels off and on, click the Hide/Show Effects Channels button in the Score window, as shown in Figure 7-5.

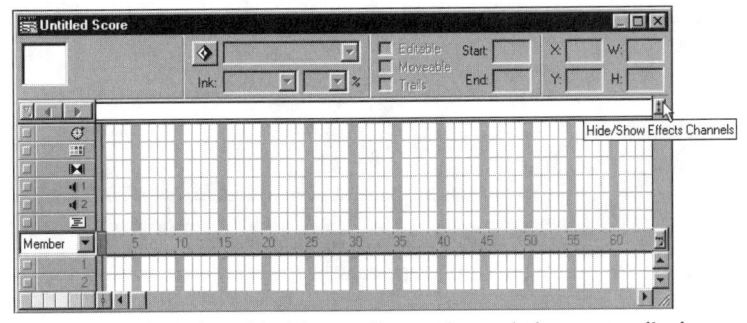

Figure 7-5: Click the Hide/Show Effects Channels button to display or hide the Effects channels.

3. Click the location in one of the Sound channels where you want the sound to start.

   Note: The Score displays two channels for sound. Although Windows technically only supports one, Director supports multiple sound channels and allows you to place sounds in both of the visible sound channels in the Score. This is accomplished by mixing the two sound channels together to produce a single channel on Windows-based machines. Additional channels beyond the visible two are accessible only through Lingo or via digital video.

4. Click and drag the sound cast member from the Cast window to the location you selected in the Score (see Figure 7-6). When you release the mouse button, the sound cast member appears in the Score in the location you selected. Alternatively, you can drag the sound cast member to the Stage. Director places the sound in the first available sound channel for the current frame, and it becomes a sound sprite.

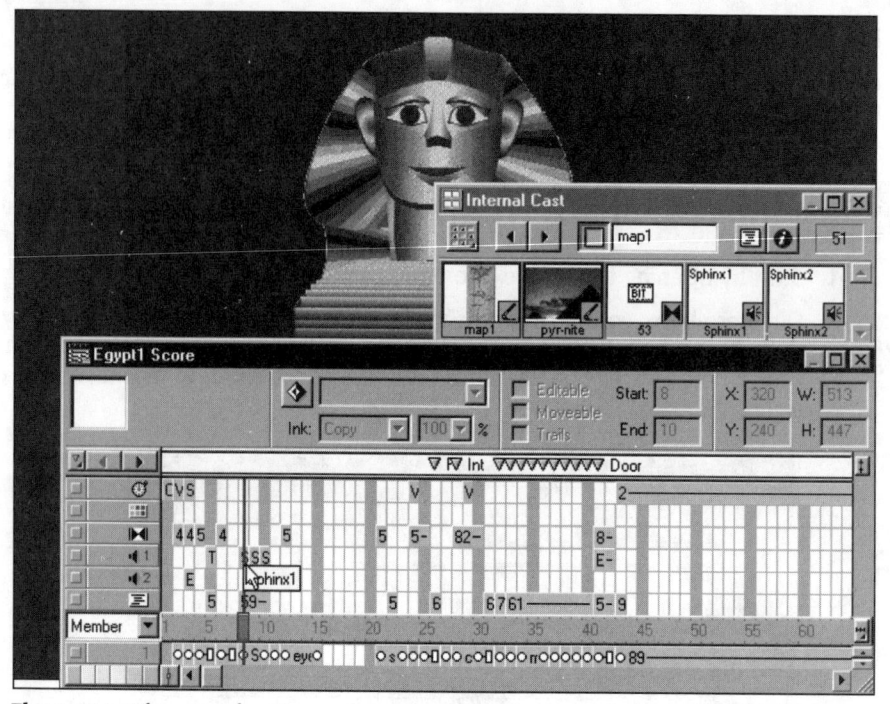

Figure 7-6: The sound cast member appears in the sound channel at the location you specified in the Score.

When you create a new sound sprite, Director assigns it a default length (28 frames). You may need to adjust the length of an individual sprite (by extending it in the Score) to ensure that the sound plays completely. If you find that this occurs frequently, you may want to adjust the Span Duration amount in the Sprite Preferences dialog (File ⇨ Preferences ⇨ Sprite), so that you aren't constantly having to change the length of sprites.

Changing the Default Length for Sprites

1. Select File ⇨ Preferences ⇨ Sprite to display the Sprite Preferences dialog box (Figure 7-7).

2. In the Sprite Duration section of the dialog box, enter a new value in the Frames field.

3. Click OK to return to Director's main window.

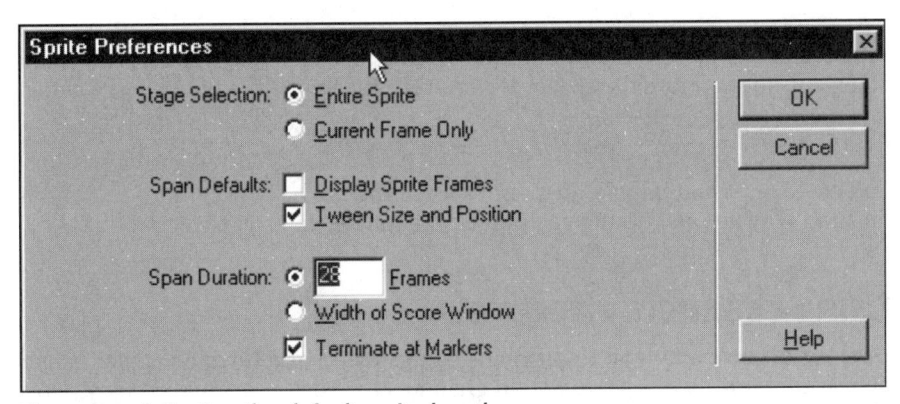

Figure 7-7: Adjusting the default sprite length

Setting a default length for sprites is a good policy, but any given cast member may require more or fewer frames.

Adjusting the Length of Individual Sound Sprites

1. In the Score window, click and drag the last frame of the sound sprite you want to adjust. To make the sound sprite longer, drag to the right (see Figure 7-8); to make the sprite shorter, drag to the left. As you drag, you can see the sound sprite extending or contracting in length.

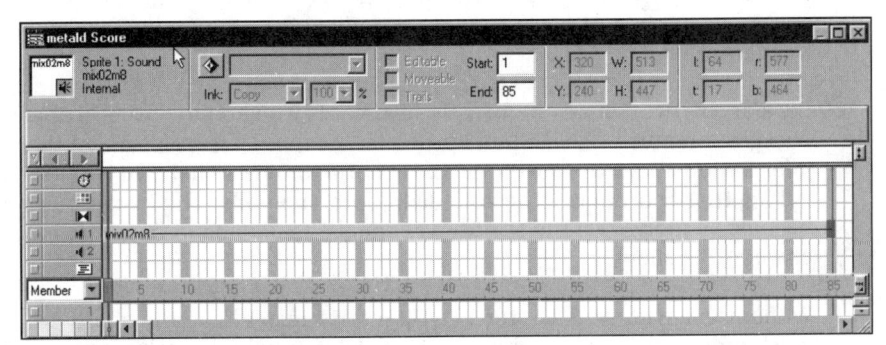

Figure 7-8: Adjust the length of a sprite by clicking and dragging the end of the sprite.

2. Rewind the movie and play it. Continue adjusting in the same way until you are satisfied with the length of the sound.

Tip: In order to keep your movie compact, adjust the frame length of sprites to be sufficient but no more than what is required to achieve the effect you want.

Note: You can also set a tempo statement to force the movie to wait until a sound is finished playing (see "Using cue points in a movie" later in this chapter).

Using channels effectively

Director doesn't limit you to playing a single sound at a time. As explained just above, Director displays two Sound channels for your use. You can play two sounds at the same time; in addition, you can add more Sound channels by using Lingo commands (see Chapter 15).

The ability to play multiple sounds is useful if you are creating a complex multimedia project and need to gather a variety of sounds together. For example, in a movie about a jungle expedition, you might want sounds of birds, animals, people talking, native drums, and perhaps background music. It would be difficult to pull all those sounds together into a single audio file. You can have *all* those sounds by alternating sounds in Director's two Sound channels.

Caution: Windows will not simultaneously play a sound in a Sound channel with a sound embedded in a digital video. If the sound in the Sound channel starts to play first, it overrides the sound in the digital video and prevents that sound from playing *even after the sound in the Sound channel has stopped playing*. If the digital video starts playing first, it overrides any sounds in the sound channels and prevents them from playing.

Look at the two Sound channels in Figure 7-9. The sound sprite in channel 2 is background music. The sound sprites in channel 1 are voice-overs that provide information about the current activity in the movie. What you can't see is the editing that coordinates the sounds in both channels. The background music becomes softer when the sprite in channel 1 is playing; it becomes louder when channel 1 is silent.

Without using Lingo (Chapter 15), Director doesn't have the ability to independently alter the volume of a single channel. The volume editing for this example was done in Sound Forge. You can create similar effects in Sound Edit Pro or other sound editors.

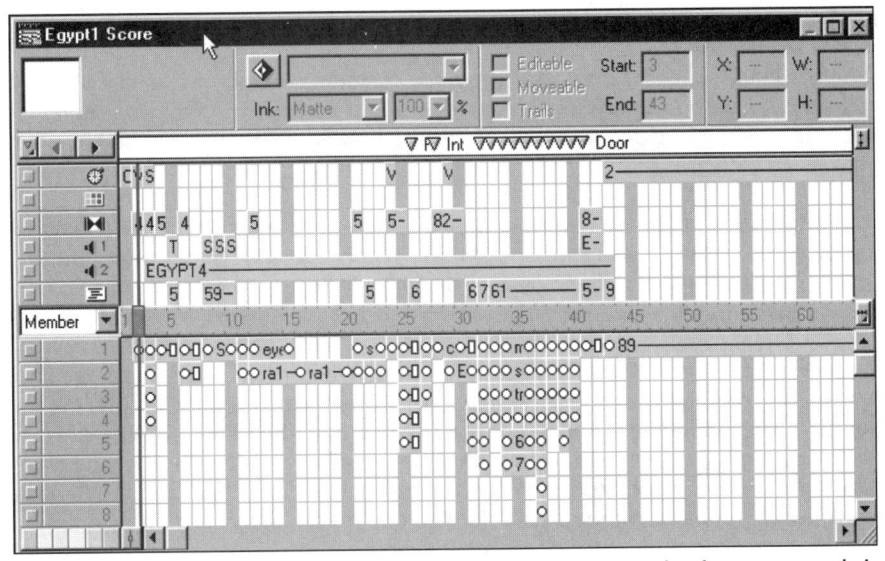

Figure 7-9: Using both Sound channels, you can simultaneously play two sounds in your movie.

In addition to volume changes, you can add other mixing effects such as echoes and fades. By carefully editing your sound files, you can customize the sounds to fit the mood or theme of your movie.

Managing Sounds

Adding sound to a short and simple movie is a process of simply dragging the sound cast member to the Score. The sound starts to play when the playhead reaches the beginning frame of the sound, and plays to the end of its allotted number of frames. What happens though, as your movies become more complex and lengthy, containing several sounds and not just one or two? Managing these sounds involves several tasks: You control when a sound plays, whether it repeats, and whether the movie pauses for the sound. Good sound management not only enhances your movie; it can be critical to the success of your movie.

Note

For more information about using Lingo commands to start sounds, stop them, and face them in and out, see Chapter 15.

Using cue points in a movie

Director makes it easy to control the pace of your movie by using *cue points* in audio files. Cue points are used to mark a position at which you want an event to occur in an audio or digital video. Macromedia's SoundEdit 16 is used to place cue points in audio and digital video files.

Note: SoundEdit 16 is made for the Macintosh. Although there isn't a Windows version of the program, you can use it to specify cue points for AIFF, Shockwave Audio, and QuickTime digital video files, for use on both platforms. You can't place cue points in AVI files.

Suppose you want to create an animated tour of an art museum. Adding narration at each stop on the tour would enhance the movie enormously. By placing cue points in the voice-over, you can pause the playback head at a specified frame that displays an exhibit in the museum, until the voice-over is finished giving the information about that exhibit. When the cue point is reached, the movie will continue to the next frame or exhibit. The cue points ensure that the timing for each scene in the movie matches the voice-over.

Incorporating Cue Points

1. Using SoundEdit 16, place the cue points in your audio or digital video file.
2. Import the sound into your movie, and place it in the Score at the frame in which you want the sound to begin (see Figure 7-10).

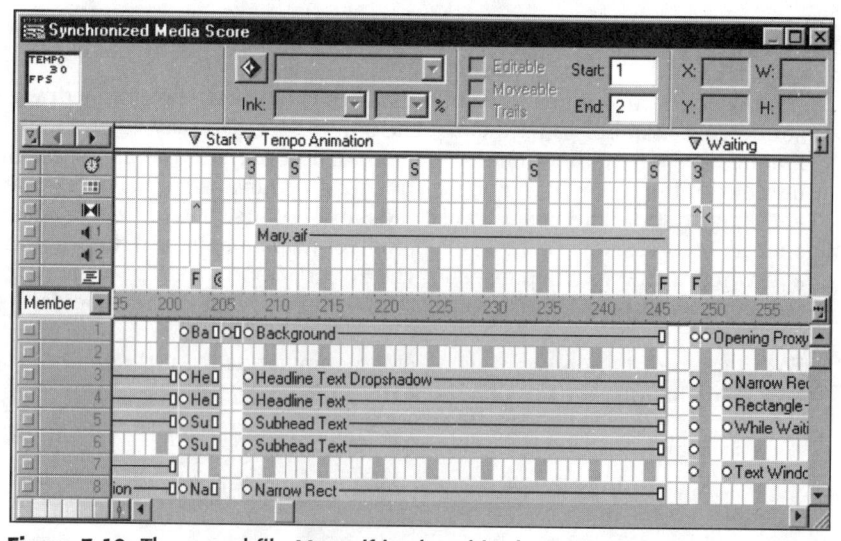

Figure 7-10: The sound file Mary.aif is placed in the Score at frame 209, which is where you want the sound to begin.

3. Click and drag to extend the sound through all the frames in which you want the sound to play.

4. Determine the first frame where you want the movie to pause, and double-click the Tempo channel for that frame. The Frame Properties: Tempo dialog box appears (Figure 7-11).

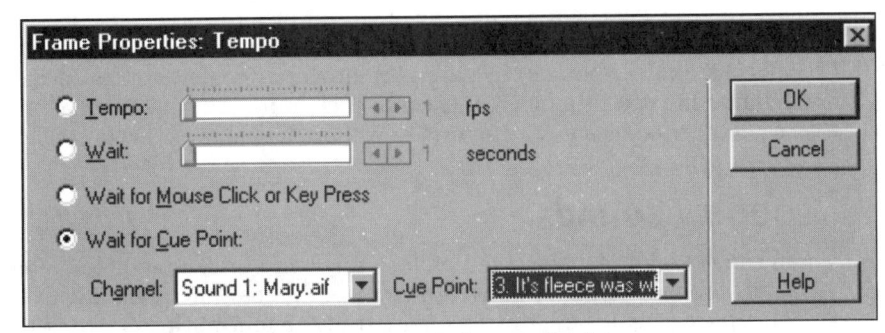

Figure 7-11: Specifying the pause to wait for a cue point

5. Click the Wait for Cue Point option.

6. Open the Channel list and select the sound file.

7. In the Cue Point list, select the cue point for which you want the movie to pause. You can choose {Start}, {End}, {Next}, or any named or numbered cue point.

   Note: If the frame does not include a sound file with cue points, the only option on the Cue Point pop-up list is {No Cue Points}.

Tip: For ease of navigation, place a marker at the frame where you specify a tempo cue point, and give it a name. This will help you identify sections of your movie later. You can also use these markers in conjunction with Lingo commands to navigate through your movie.

Tempo, sounds, and interactivity

Director allows you to place interactive elements such as forms, buttons, and other effects in your movies.

It's important to remember that once a sound begins to play, it plays to the end of its allotted frames. Though you can't stop the sound, you can control the other sprites and elements of your movie. Pausing a movie by specifying tempo settings will disable interactive elements such as buttons and animated sprites.

You can avoid conflicts between sound, tempo, and interactivity by using Lingo commands. Methods for using Lingo to control interactivity, sound, and animation are discussed in Part III of this book.

Tip: It's a good idea to avoid using the same frame for a sound or digital video cast member and several other effects sprites. The sound or digital video will take control over the movie, and it's difficult to predict the order in which the other effects will play. In addition to the problem of playing order, this arrangement can cause a brief but critical hit on the resources of low-end computers. To alleviate this conflict, duplicate the frame and specify a different effect to each frame. This helps you control the playing order and manage resources — without memory or effects conflicts.

Looping sounds

You can get a lot of mileage out of very small and brief sound files. Many of the sounds around us are repetitive: the roar of thunder, the pounding of surf, footsteps, a ringing bell, the din of city traffic, a murmuring crowd. With some careful editing, together with Director's ability to loop sound, you can add sounds without significantly increasing the file size of your movie.

Director offers you two non-Lingo methods of repeating a sound. You can specify that you want just the sound to loop, or you can include the sound in a film loop.

Note: You can't create a film loop with only sounds. You must include other sprites, or the Loop option will be unavailable. Later, you'll learn how to use sounds in film loops.

Setting a Sound to Loop

1. In the Cast window or Score, select the sound you want to loop. Be sure you have extended the sprites in the Score so that all of the sound will be played.
2. Select Modify ⇨ Cast Member ⇨ Properties using Command+I (Cntrl+I) to display the Sound Cast Member Properties dialog box (Figure 7-12).

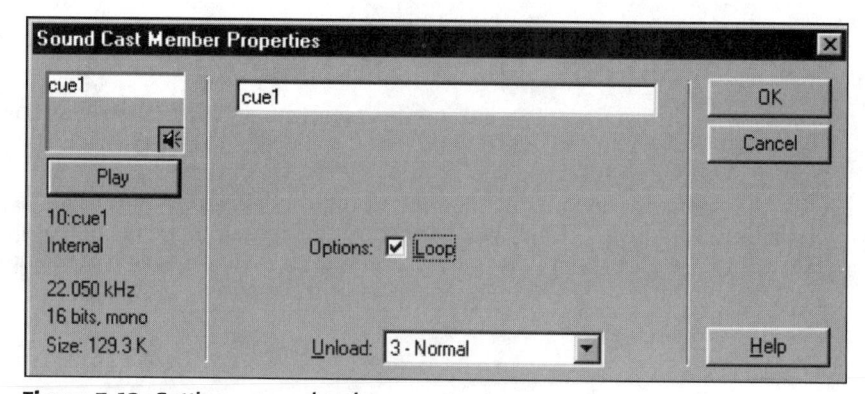

Figure 7-12: Setting a sound to loop

3. Mark the Loop check box, and click OK to complete the operation and return to Director's main window.

Looping sound is an effective means of getting the most from small sound files. If your sound is coordinated with a specific animation sequence, consider including the sound in a film loop with the animation.

Including a Sound in a Film Loop

1. In the Cast window or Score, select the sound you want to loop. Set up the loop as described in the preceding exercise.
2. Select the consecutive sprites you want to include in the film loop. Then press Command (Ctrl) and click the sound you want to include (see Figure 7-13).

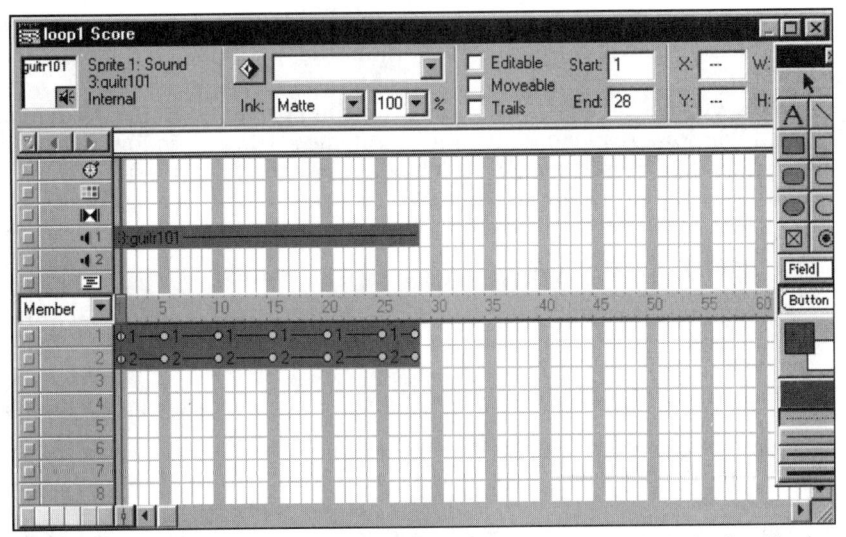

Figure 7-13: Selecting consecutive sprites and a sound to include in the film loop

3. Select Insert⌐Film Loop to create the film loop. Name the film loop, click OK, and it appears in the Cast window. Once you've created the film loop, you can delete the selected sprites from the Score (but *not* from the cast).
4. Click and drag the film loop from the Cast window to the Score and place it in a sprite channel.
5. Rewind your movie and play it.

> ### Back doors to sounds
>
> Earlier in this chapter, we stated that without Lingo you are restricted to using the two visible Sound channels to play one sound each. That's not exactly true. You can trick Director into playing more sounds — by using film loops that contain a different sound in each loop. This technique lets you have a unique sound in each film loop, and one in each of the Sound channels.
>
> The only limitation on using this trick is the availability of resources. In fact, this "back door" technique may be problematic for systems with limited resources. Note that if you include a digital video in a film loop, the sound attached to the video is disabled. The animation, however, isn't disabled.

Setting the volume for a movie

Director allows you to set the volume for your movie and save the volume settings both with the file and when the movie goes to distribution. As mentioned earlier in this chapter, you can't control the volume of *individual* elements such as sounds or digital videos within your movie without the use of Lingo (Chapter 15).

When you set the volume of a movie, it's important to remember that Macintosh and Windows respond differently to volume settings. Windows tends to distort sounds that are replayed at a high volume; Macintosh doesn't. If you are authoring for both platforms, it's a good idea to set the volume settings in the medium range, and presume users will adjust the volume to suit their computers and their individual tastes.

Setting the volume of your movie is done using the Control Panel or the Volume command:

- ✦ If you choose Control ⇨ Volume, select a volume level from the pop-up menu.
- ✦ If you use the Control Panel, click the Volume button and choose a volume level from the pop-up menu (Figure 7-14).

Tip When choosing a volume level, it's a good idea to take into account any sound editing you've done. The idea is to keep the median sound level consistent (with the exception of fades and effects). Your movie will have less impact if the volume is constantly changing.

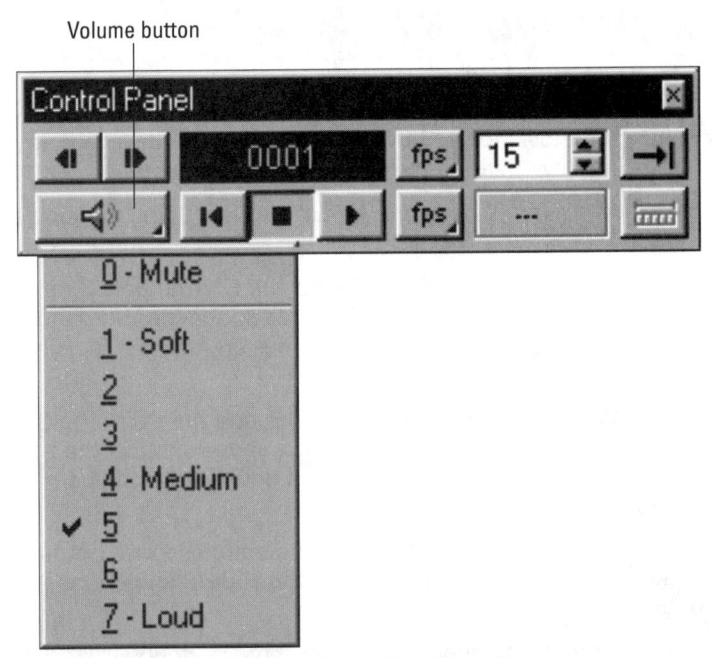

Figure 7-14: Click the Control Panel's Volume button to select a volume for your movie.

In this exercise, you can use the rain.dir movie to practice several of the skills you've learned in this chapter, such as importing sounds, placing sounds in your movie, adjusting the length of a sound, and looping sounds. The practice file, rain.dir, includes six cast members: Cover, Night Sky, Rabbit Front, Rabbit Back, Pole, the Hold on Current behavior, and the Go To Frame behavior. (The two behavior cast members are prescripted behaviors shipped with Director 6; see Chapter 6.) After completing this exercise, the rabbit will move across the screen to the pole and then return, between the sounds of rain, lightning, and thunder claps.

On the CD-ROM In this exercise you import three sound files into the rain.dir movie. The sound files are from Sonic Waves 3000, a two-CD collection of sounds, copyright 1993 by Innovative Media Corporation and used with permission. You'll find additional selections from Sonic Waves 3000 in Chapter 15. The original filenames have been changed to rain.aif (from 2608a.wav), thunder.aif (from 2601.wav), and wind.aif (from 0412.wav). All the files are on the companion CD-ROM in the exercise:ch07 (exercise\ch07) folder.

Adding Sound to a Movie

1. Open the rain.dir movie.

2. Rewind and play the movie to see how rain.dir appears in its incomplete form. You must click anywhere on the first screen to proceed.

3. Stop the movie and examine the Score Window. At this point, the movie includes no sound.

4. Click the Import button on the Toolbar or select the File➪Import command using Command+R (Ctrl+R), and import the three sound files from the exercise:ch07 (exercise\ch07) folder. The filenames are thunder.aif, rain.aif, and wind.aif.

5. In the Cast window, select the wind cast member and then click the Cast Member Properties button. When the dialog box appears, select the Loop check box. If you are anxious to hear the sound now, go ahead and play it and then close the dialog box.

6. To place the wind file in the Score, double-click Sound channel 1 in frame 1. (If the Sound channels are not visible, click the Hide/Show Effects Channels button.)

7. When the Frame Properties: Sound dialog box appears, double-click the wind cast member name in the Sound pane of the dialog box. This adds the sound to a single frame in the Score.

8. Save the movie as **rain1.dir** and play it. The wind sound should begin immediately.

9. Click anywhere in the Run Rabbit Run screen when you want to continue. When done, press Command+period (.) or Ctrl+period (.) or Esc to stop the movie. The wind sound continues even after the movie moves beyond frame 1. In the next step, you cause a different sound (rain) to begin playing as soon as the playback head hits frame 2.

10. Select the rain sound cast member in the Cast window and drag it to the Sound channel 1 in frame 2. By default, the rain sprite spans 28 frames.

11. Drag the end frame of the rain sprite until the sprite spans 121 frames. It should end in the same frame as the Rabbit Back and Pole sprites.

12. Save the movie again as rain1.dir, rewind, and play it. Click the Run Rabbit Run screen when you want to continue. When done, stop the movie. The wind sound stops when the playback head reaches frame 2, and the second sound (rain) begins to play.

13. The rain sound does not play through the entire animation. Use the Cast Member Properties dialog box to set it to be a looped sound.

14. Save the movie again as rain1.dir, rewind, and play it.

15. Stop the movie and drag the thunder cast member into Sound channel 2 in frame 30.

16. Extend the thunder sound sprite to fill all frames between frame 30 and 60 of Sound channel 2. This should cause the flash (produced by the absence of the NightSky bitmap cast member in frame 45), and the thunder sound to occur fairly soon thereafter.
17. Save the movie, rewind it, and play the movie.

Working with Sound Xtras

You already know a little about Xtras — small plug-in applications or scripts that enhance movies and expedite production by performing a series of tasks related to the selected sprite, frame, cast member, or movie. Xtras may come from a third-party developer or from Macromedia. Director includes a variety of Xtras for your use, such as Behaviors and Shockwave Audio (SWA). If you are a programmer, you can also develop your own Xtras for use with your movies. For more coverage of Xtras, see Chapter 19.

Using sound behaviors

Director allows you to alter the behavior of your movies by using Lingo scripting. The trade-off here is that Lingo can be a complex scripting language. If you aren't familiar with programming or scripting languages, adding Lingo scripts to your movies can be daunting. In response to this challenge, Macromedia added a new feature to Director 6 called *behaviors*. Behaviors are cast members that you can add to sprites and frames of your movie, to easily provide interactive functionality without complex scripting. Behaviors are collected together in the Behavior Library Cast.

Director 6 includes three behaviors in the sound category, two of which you used in Chapter 6. Each requires that you provide parameters such as the name of a sound, the channel assignment, and the event you want to use to start the behavior. Following are the sound behaviors:

- **Sound Beep** causes the system beep to play when a specified event occurs.
- **Sound Play Cast Member** plays a specified sound cast member when a specified event occurs. You specify the parameters, such as the cast member name and the channel from which you want the sound to play.
- **Sound Play File** plays an external sound file when a specified event occurs. You specify the parameters, such as the sound filename and the channel from which you want the sound to play.

When you add a behavior to a sprite or frame, the behavior is copied to the internal cast, to prevent the master cast member from being accidentally overwritten. Included in the Behavior Library Cast are a series of behaviors that are related to sound. For example, consider a movie that displays a series of musical instruments. By adding a behavior to each of the instrument sprites, you could play a sound file that made the sound of that instrument when an event occurred. In the case of the instruments, you might want the sound to play when the user clicks the instrument (see Figure 7-15). To display the Behavior library, select Xtras ⇨ Behavior Library.

As you become more adept with Director and write your own scripts, you can add script cast members to the Behavior library. Once you lean to create scripts (Chapter 10 and beyond) you simply drag your script cast member to the Behavior Library Cast window to place a copy there. Using a library of scripts can be an enormous time-saver when you're creating a movie.

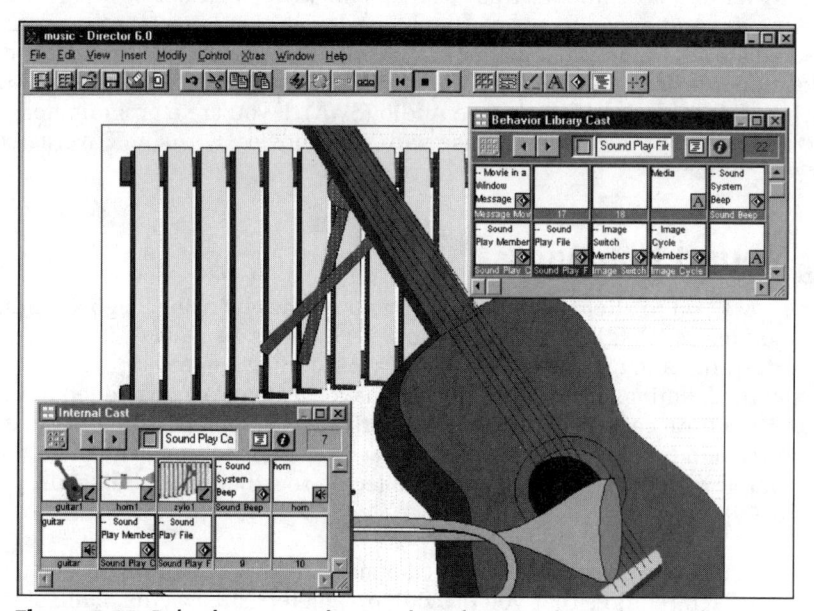

Figure 7-15: Behaviors are actions assigned to a sprite or frame. The action is triggered when the specified event occurs.

Assigning events to behaviors

An event is an action the user performs, such as a mouse click. All of the behaviors related to sound are *event oriented:* They occur in response to some action performed by the user. Table 6-2 in Chapter 6 lists the possible events you can assign to a sound-related behavior, and what they do.

Adding a Sound Behavior to a Sprite in Your Movie

1. Select Xtras ⇨ Behavior Library to open the Behavior library.
2. Scroll through the library to locate the sound-related behavior you want to use.
3. Click and drag the behavior onto the Stage, positioning it over the sprite to which you want to apply the behavior. Then release the mouse button. (Another option is to drag the behavior to a sprite in the Score window.) When you release the mouse button, the Parameters dialog box appears if the behavior you selected requires a parameter (see Figure 7-16).

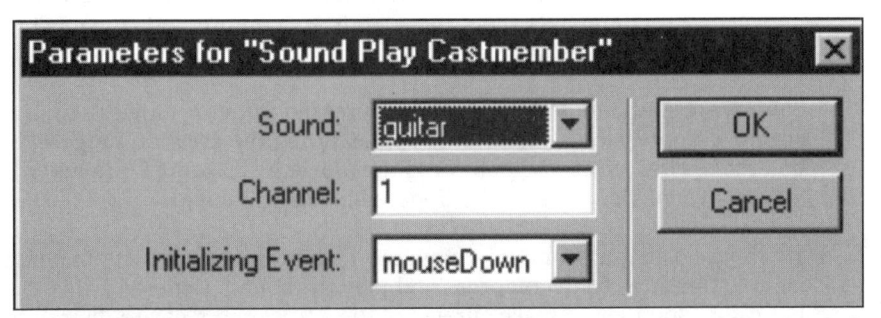

Figure 7-16: When you apply a behavior that requires a parameter, the associated Parameters dialog will appear.

4. Select or enter the information required. For the behavior shown in Figure 7-16, the required parameters are the name of the sound cast member, the channel assignment for the sound, and the event that will initiate the sound.

Behaviors are useful for quickly adding interactive elements to your movies. In addition, if you are unfamiliar with Lingo (Director's scripting language), behaviors provide a good introduction to scripting. By using, studying, and modifying behaviors, you can learn the basics of Lingo scripting.

Using Shockwave Audio (SWA)

Director 6 supports compression using *Shockwave Audio* (SWA). The SWA Xtra compresses both internal and external sound files, yielding much smaller file sizes than other compression routines. (Note that Shockwave Audio will not compress sounds that are already compressed using IMA compression routines.)

You can use Shockwave Audio to compress sound files to be used for the Internet and on disk:

- External sound files can be streamed. Streaming means that the sound file begins to play as it is downloading. You don't have to wait for the entire file to load before you hear sound. Streaming can be critical to the success of a Director project on the Internet, where you need to be conscious of file sizes and download times. Note that Shockwave Audio will not stream sounds compressed at values lower than 16 Kbps (kilobits per second).

- Although internal sounds can't be streamed, you can still enjoy a good rate of compression without degradation of quality. When you specify Shockwave Audio settings for internal sounds (using the Xtras ⇨ Shockwave for Audio Settings command), *all* of the sounds are compressed. You can't compress some sound files and not others.

Shockwave Audio only works with compressed Director movies. Although you can specify compression settings at any time during the creation process, they actually don't take effect until you compress the movie by creating a projector, a Shockwave movie, or using the Update Movies command.

Note

When you distribute a movie compressed using Shockwave Audio, you must include the Xtras to decompress and play the sound. Generally, this is automatic, but it's a good idea to make sure all of the associated files are distributed with your movie.

Understanding Shockwave compression

Shockwave Audio allows you to compress sound files up to a 176:1 ratio, which creates a much smaller file than other sound formats. The bit-rate scheme used by SWA is not related to the bit rate used to sample sound files, but rather to the speed of transmission. Therefore, the higher the compression rate, the faster the download, decompression, and playing of the sound.

Keep in mind the fact that some degradation of the sound quality occurs, as it does with most compression. SWA technology, however, changes the file as little as possible to achieve the desired compression. It's a good idea to try a variety of compression values and check the quality of the sound. Then choose the best quality that balances the type of sound, movie, and distribution you intend to use. For example, a voice-over doesn't require the same quality that is needed for music and can safely be compressed at a lower rate, between 8 and 16 Kbps transfer rate.

Table 7-2 shows the optimum compression ranges for Internet use. You should note that these rates are not for the user, but rather on the server end, for delivery.

Table 7-2
Optimum Shockwave Audio Compression Ranges

Delivery System	Compression Bit Rate	Quality Capability
T1	64 to 128 Kbps	Extremely high quality
ISDN or CD-ROM	32 to 56 Kbps	FM stereo to CD quality
28.8 modem	16 Kbps	FM mono or AM quality
14.4 modem	8 Kbps	Telephone quality

Note Any file with a compression rate below 48 Kbps is converted automatically by Director to mono.

Compressing Internal Shockwave Sound Cast Members

1. Select Xtras ⇨ Shockwave for Audio Settings, to display the Shockwave for Audio Settings dialog box (see Figure 7-17).

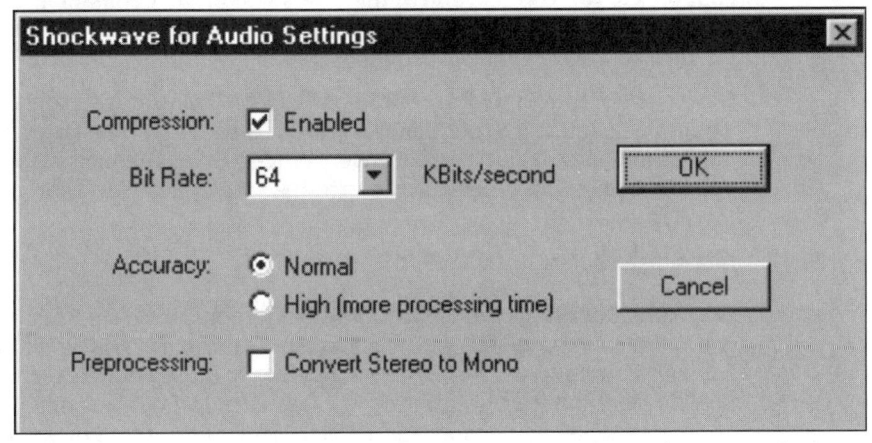

Figure 7-17: Specifying compression settings for internal sound cast members

2. Click the Compression check box to enable compression.
3. Click the Bit Rate field and choose the bit rate you want to use for compression.

4. Select the Accuracy level you want to achieve. Normal is fine for most purposes. High is best for CD-quality music or for sound at low bit rates, but it will require longer to process. See Table 7-3.

5. If you a want to convert the sound to mono from stereo, click the Preprocessing check box to enable this conversion.

6. Click OK to complete the operation and return to Director's main window.

Compression schemes are a bit like snowflakes in a blizzard. No two of them are identical, and there are many from which to choose. The sound industry is struggling to establish standards that provide commonality across platforms. Director supports — either directly or though the use of Xtras — a variety of compression types. The best idea is to choose the type that meets your platform needs, while providing the best quality for your movie.

Compressing and Streaming External Sound Cast Members

On the CD-ROM

To practice converting WAV files to SWA and linking them as external sound files, you can use any of the WAV files on the companion CD-ROM in the goodies:sonic (goodies\sonic), goodies:jjones (goodies\jjones), or goodies:kennerly (goodies\kennerly) folders.

1. Create an external Shockwave Audio file (SWA). Macintosh users can create this file using SoundEdit 16. Windows users can use Director's conversion command, Xtras ⇨ Convert WAV to SWA. The dialog box that appears allows you to specify the external sound files you want to convert (see Figure 7-18).

Note

Macintosh users can skip steps 2 through 7.

2. Check the bottom of the dialog. If the Folder for Converted Files indicated is not the location where you want to store your files, click Select New Folder. Navigate to a folder where you want to store your files, and click Select Folder to return to the Convert WAV files to SWA files dialog. (It's a good idea to keep all associated Director files in the same directory, especially if you intend to distribute your movies on the Internet.)

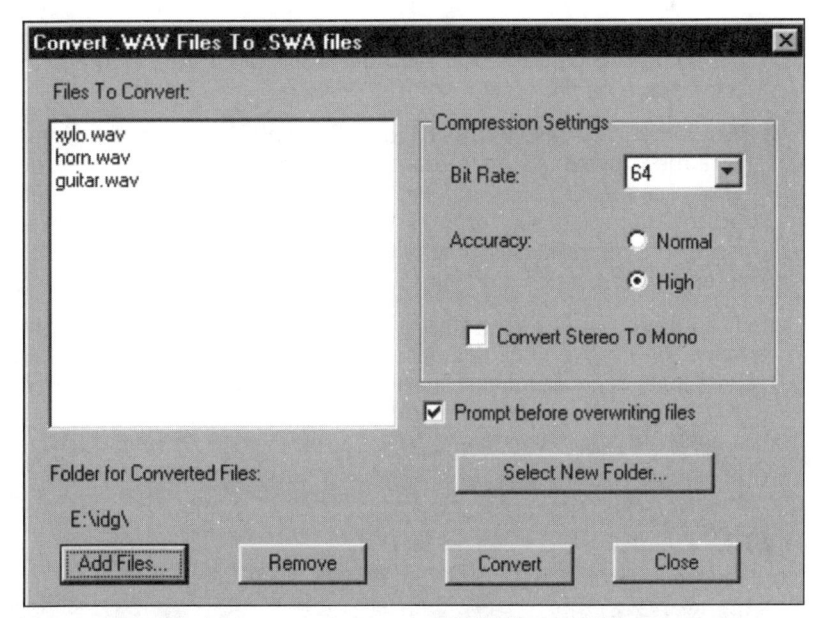

Figure 7-18: Windows users can convert WAV files to SWA.

3. Click the Add Files button, and then navigate to and select the files you want to convert. To select multiple files, press the Command (Ctrl) key and click each filename to highlight it. When all desired files are selected, click the Open button.

   If the files you need to convert are not in the same folder, you may have to repeat this step more than once. Selected files will be displayed in the Files To Convert list. To delete a file from the list, select it and click the Remove button.

4. Choose the Compression Settings you want to use. (For guidance, refer to the earlier instructions for compressing internal files.)

5. When you have added all the files to be converted and specified the compression settings, click the Convert button to begin the conversion. A progress bar appears, and you can watch as the compression occurs or go get a diet cola (it's less than a calorie and you'll burn that much going to the refrigerator).

6. When the compression is done, click the Close button to return to Director's main window.

Caution

7. The compressed files are still external to your movie, so now you must add the sounds to your internal cast. Select Insert ⇨ Media Element ⇨ Shockwave Audio.

8. When the SWA Cast Member Properties dialog box appears (Figure 7-19), click the Browse button, navigate to the location where you saved the Shockwave Audio files, and double-click the filename. The conversion process automatically compresses the movie and changes its extension to .swa, so look for files ending with this extension. You can use a URL (an Internet address) as the Link Address for the SWA file.

The location or link you specify for the SWA cast member must remain the same, or a broken link will occur and the movie will fail. To reduce the possibility of broken links, store *all* linked files in the same folder.

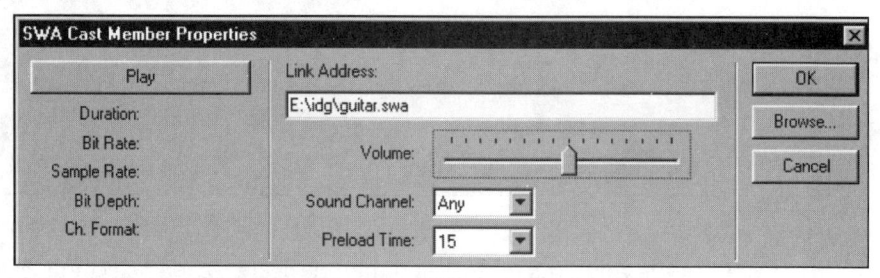

Figure 7-19: Specifying the options for SWA cast member Xtras

9. Specify a Sound channel. The default is Any, which lets Director assign a Sound channel based upon availability.

10. Choose a Preload Time from the pop-up. This represents the maximum amount of seconds that can lapse prior to streaming your sound. Since slow Internet connections can affect the transfer times, it's a good idea to choose a higher value than the 5 seconds Director uses as a default.

11. Specify the volume you want to use for your sound file. It's best to choose a medium volume as a compromise for all platforms.

12. Click the Play button to preview the sound. Click OK to return to Director's main window.

13. Repeat steps 8 through 12 for each of the SWA files you want to use.

14. Place each of the SWA cast members in a sprite channel (*not* a sound channel), and extend the sprite to ensure that the sound plays completely.

Shockwave movies are taking the Web by storm. They allow authors to showcase stunning animation and sound effects while keeping file download times within acceptable ranges. The potential audience for this media presents creative challenges to both the novice and expert Director user.

Summary

Sound enhances your movies, and adds the professional finishing touch to help make your movie a success. By understanding sound basics, you can easily add sounds to your movies. In this chapter you learned how to

- ✦ Choose sound file formats to meet your platform authoring needs.
- ✦ Add sound to your movie and control it with tempo settings.
- ✦ Link larger sound files as external files. Place smaller sound files in the Internal cast.
- ✦ Get the most out of sounds through repetition, by using looping and duplicating small sound files.
- ✦ Store Director files and linked files in the same location to prevent broken links and improve loading time.
- ✦ Use behaviors to give sounds interactive functionality.
- ✦ Employ the Shockwave Audio Xtra to get the maximum compression for your sound files, as well as to use streaming audio.
- ✦ Use sound cue points to control the pace of your movie.

✦ ✦ ✦

Video Advice

CHAPTER 8

In This Chapter

Understanding digital video

Adding digital videos to your movie

Managing video cast members

Exporting as digital video

Digital video is simply the result of capturing, storing, transmitting, and displaying a rapid succession of digitized images on a computer. The why of digital video is perhaps as important as the what. As mentioned earlier in this book, it is by appealing to multiple senses that multimedia enhances communications and increases the effective retention rate of the user. Digital video provides a superior means of transmitting images and sounds of real-world events and animations within your Director movies. The result, of course, is that the audience impact of your movies is increased.

Director movies containing digital video are appearing with increasing regularity in our world. Using digital video enables you to create

- Interactive kiosks
- Training CD-ROMs that display complex procedures
- High-impact sales presentations
- *Edutainment* titles (movies that entertain as well as educate)

The variety of movies you can create with Director is limited only by your imagination. Whether your movie will grace a boardroom or a home computer, that movie can be enhanced with digital video.

Two major kinds of video are in use today: analog and computerized digital video. Analog was one of the earliest means of transmitting images via video signals. When an analog signal was transmitted, it was represented by a fluctuating voltage signal known as an analog *waveform*. Each component — color, brightness, and sync — of a video frame is split and sent as a separate signal. The signals, used primarily for live broadcast, are then "recomposited" on the receiving end to create an image. In the process, color and clarity suffer. In addition, because of the tape storage method used, analog video suffers from generational loss. Each time an analog video is copied, the quality deteriorates slightly.

In contrast, the nature of computerized digital video is such that there is never a generational loss. Each copy is as crisp and clear as the original. The principal reason for this consistency has to do with the way computerized digital video is retrieved and stored. The data is retrieved, converted, and stored as bits of information on a hard disk, CD-ROM, or other computer storage media.

Another advantage of computerized digital video is that it does not have to be linear. This means it can support *branching*, which allows you to jump from one point in the video to another and then back again. When combined with sound, graphics, and animation to create an interactive video, the effect is powerful. The linear nature of analog video, on the other hand, makes it unsuitable for interactive applications.

Note

The topics in this chapter give you an introduction to working with digital video. Director is a robust program that offers features for all levels of users, and in Chapter 16 you'll work with digital video at a more advanced level, learning to manage this medium with Lingo.

Working with Digital Video

A series of factors are involved in the creation of any digital video. In terms of Director movies, the most important of these factors are frame rate, image dimensions, color depth, file size and compression, and image quality.

Determining an effective frame rate

Frame rate is the number of frames per second that are displayed on a screen. A rate of 30 fps represents high quality indeed, but it's unrealistic. Most computers don't have the resources to display video at that rate, and the amount of hard-drive space required to store such data is prohibitive.

In order for any system to display digital video without disruption to quality, it must be able to transfer data at a consistent rate of 150,000 bits per second, or 150K. And the amount of data contained in a digital video with a frame rate of 30 fps is enormous. As a result, lower-end computer systems are incapable of transferring and rendering this amount of data at the required rate to maintain quality.

A frame rate of 15 fps is much more realistic. Most computers can display this information without too much difficulty, allowing you to widen the range of your potential audience by choosing this lower rate.

Working with image dimensions

When you are planning a Director movie, one of the key considerations is the final resolution at which the movie will be displayed. Director offers a variety of preset stage sizes, or you can specify a custom size that meets your needs. Although larger Stage dimensions are possible, producing a movie at 640 x 480 pixels ensures that the broadest possible audience can view your movie.

Director displays digital video in a window placed upon the Stage. The default size of the window is equal to the exterior dimensions of the digital video frame. Although you can display a digital video at 640 x 480, the file size would be prohibitive and might cause resource problems on low-end computers. Most computers are capable of displaying digital video at one-fourth of the screen size, or 320 x 240 (the default size for a QuickTime movie), without any difficulty. You can also create your digital video at a smaller or custom frame size.

> **Note:** Director allows you to crop digital videos. For more information on cropping, see the later section "Scaling and cropping a digital video."

Considering color depth

By default, Director for Windows plays all video in Direct to Stage mode (discussed later in this chapter) at a 24-bit color depth. On Macintosh, the video is composited at either 8-bit or 24-bit. If your video is set for 8-bit or 16-bit color depth, Director has to recomposite the image to 24-bit. The result is a performance reduction in your movies. The digital video may appear jerky or slow. So for best results in Windows, use digital videos that are set at 24-bit. If you get jerkiness or slowness in your 8- or 16-bit digital video, you can improve performance by sequencing images using image and movie editors, or respecifying cast member settings. Let's take a look at both of these solutions.

Sequencing images to improve video performance

Editing 8-bit and 16-bit images to improve video performance in Director is a somewhat tedious task, but if performance is a critical issue, it's worth the effort. If the frames of the video are already stored as individual images, you are already one step into the process. If they are not, you need to break your video into individual frames.

> **Note:** The following instructions for sequencing are very general. For more precise instructions, consult the user manuals for your video and image editors.

Sequencing Images for Your Video

1. Import your video into a video editor, such as Adobe Premier (see Figure 8-1). If you already have the images set up as individual frames, skip to step 5.

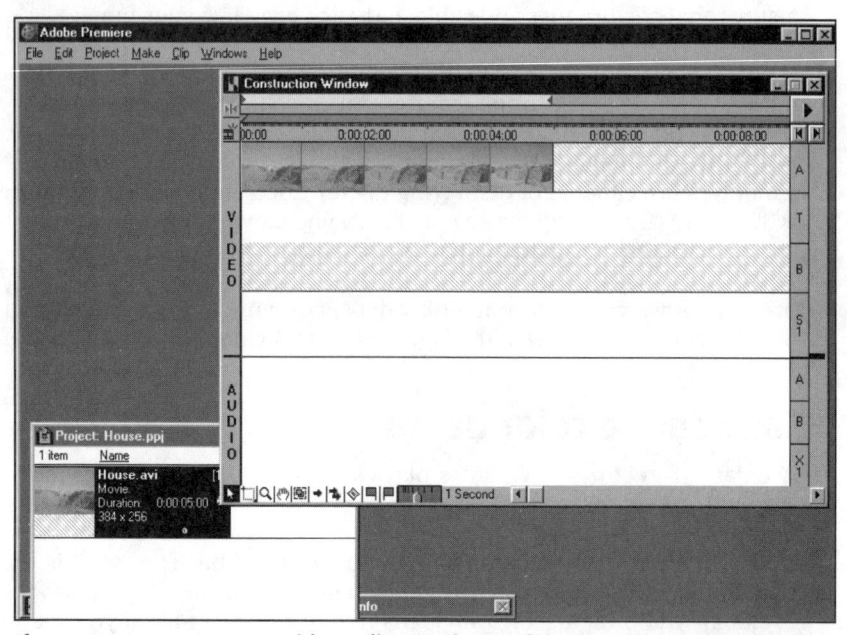

Figure 8-1: You can use a video editor such as Adobe Premier to convert an image into a sequence.

2. Export the video as a sequence of individual bitmap images or frames (see Figure 8-2). Windows users will find it easier to save the images as BMP files, and Macintosh users should save the images as PICT files.

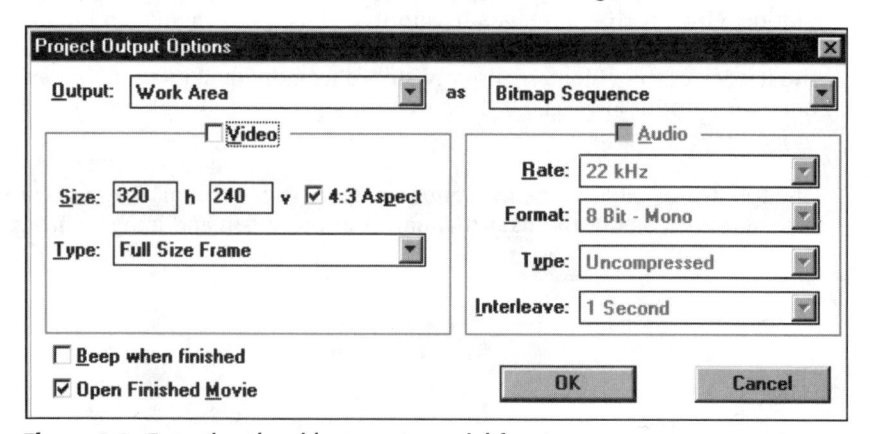

Figure 8-2: Exporting the video as sequential frames

3. Open the sequence of images in a bitmap image editor or image converter, such as Ulead's Multimedia Converter. (If your bitmap image editor or image converter allows for batch functions, this process will go more rapidly.)

4. Convert the images to RGB 24-bit images and save them.

5. Reimport the sequential images into your video editor.

6. Create a video file from the images. The video file is ready to import into Director.

Be aware that this method can be a formidable task if your image editor or converter doesn't support batch functions. For instance, sequencing 10 seconds of digital video that has a frame rate of 30 fps will require converting 300 frames!

Specifying Director settings to increase video performance

If your movie slows down or your resources are limited, digital video files may play slower than their assigned frame rate. This can be problematic, especially with 16-bit digital videos, which must be recomposited. You can specify the rate at which Director plays your video files, using settings in the Digital Video Cast Member Properties dialog box. If you specify a frame rate greater than the assigned frame rate of the digital video, it won't play faster than the assigned frame rate, but the increased setting *will* ensure that the video plays as fast as possible up to the limit of its frame rate.

Specifying a Frame Rate for a Digital Video Cast Member

1. Select the digital video cast member in the Cast window.

2. Select Modify ➪ Cast Member ➪ Properties, or press Command+I (Ctrl+I) to display the Digital Video Cast Member Properties dialog box (Figure 8-3).

3. If your video contains a sound track, and syncing is important, select Sync to Soundtrack from the Video list, and specify a frame rate of **60** fps. If syncing is not necessary, or your digital video doesn't have a soundtrack, choose Play Every Frame (No Sound) as the Video selection. In the Rate list, choose Maximum and enter **60** in the fps box.

4. Click OK to return to Director's main window.

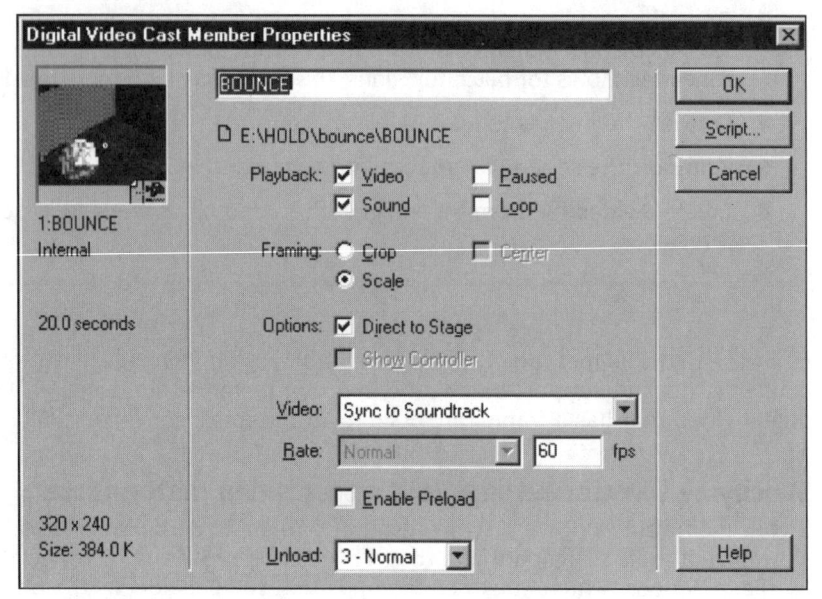

Figure 8-3: Specifying frame rate settings

Although it's best to use 24-bit movies in Windows, and 8-bit or 24-bit movies on the Macintosh, sometimes you can't select the bit depth of a digital video. This is especially true if you use stock footage or video clips from a third-party developer. By adjusting the frame rate of your movie, you can compensate for problems that might arise to ensure the best performance possible in your Director movies.

Note

Other options for controlling digital video in your Director movies are available through Lingo commands. See Chapter 16.

Getting the best performance from animated sprites

We all like to see the exotic. Sometimes, however, exotic animated sprites will cause a movie to slow down too much and play at less than the desired frame rate. Suppose your movie has a 24-bit sprite of a colorful parrot wildly flapping its wings. The bit depth of the color and the animation might reduce the performance of your movie, especially if other sprites are active at the same time. To adjust, you could reduce the color depth of the parrot or create a film loop. Neither of those options, however, will be as effective as exporting the animation sequence as a digital video. Once the digital video is created, you can import it and place it in your movie. The parrot will maintain its color, the animation will be smoother, and the performance of your movie will improve.

For more information on exporting frames as digital videos, see the section "Exporting Digital Video" at the end of this chapter.

Controlling file size and choosing compression

Like other graphics and sound files, digital video files tend to be on the large side. The average video that plays in your VCR requires 10 inches of videotape for each minute of play at 30 fps. An equivalent digital video file could take as much as 1.6GB of hard-drive space. The amount of space required varies depending on other factors in the creation of computer imagery, such as color depth and resolution. Even with the frame rate reduced to 15 fps, an uncompressed digital video file can consume 500MB.

The issue of file size has prompted substantial research to find a standardized means of compressing the data to an acceptable size. A variety of codec (compression/decompression) methods have become available. However, at the time of this writing, there is no standardized means of compressing files that works with every known platform. Director does support some file-compression techniques employed in conjunction with Apple's QuickTime and Microsoft's Video for Windows AVI (Audio Video Interleave) format. It's important, nevertheless, that you design your movie carefully if you intend to incorporate digital video files.

In order to achieve compression, most codecs reduce the amount of information stored with the file. Like the proverbial cutting room floor, bits and pieces of the original data are cut out to create a smaller file. There is a hierarchy that determines which data is cut. The human eye is extremely discerning of color but doesn't as readily perceive slight differences in brightness or motion. So compression schemes typically cut information that refers to minor changes in both brightness and motion. Many digital video files contain sound, and — again, since people tend to notice a disruption in sound before they notice a disruption in image quality — frames of the video may be sacrificed in order to maintain the sound quality.

MPEG format

Director doesn't directly support MPEG (Motion Picture Experts Group) format for digital video files. MPEG uses *interframe compression* to achieve compression rates up to 200:1. Interframe compression analyzes each frame of a video for redundancy, to create what are called *reference frames*. By comparing previous and subsequent frames in a video, only the difference between the frames is stored. Redundant information is removed, and the result is a smaller file.

Like most compression schemes, files compressed using MPEG can be lossy (as the compression ratio goes up, the quality of the video is reduced). MPEG is less lossy, however, than compression schemes employed by QuickTime or AVI formats. You can play MPEG in your Director movies with the assistance of any of the following: an Xtra, Lingo MCI messages, a Windows driver, or a Macintosh system extension designed for this purpose. The drawback with MPEG is that each type of software implements the compression differently, and this can make it difficult to control the quality of playback on all types and platforms of computers. (For more information on using MPEG format files, see Chapter 16.)

Selecting an image quality

Probably the most important factor in making decisions regarding digital video in Director is image quality. We've saved discussion of this final factor for the last because it determines your final decision. You must decide what look is acceptable for your movie given the constraints of file size and performance.

The decision on how you use digital video is subjective but should be influenced by your client's needs, the characteristics of the target audience, and the content of your end product. Ask yourself the following questions:

- Is there a truly valid need for the digital video to be full-screen and, if so, will the end-user's computer system support the required data transfer without choking?

- What content would be lost by using a smaller digital video window? Would there be a significant loss of clarity and/or detail?

- Is there supplemental content that should be concurrently displayed on screen with the digital video — which might necessitate less than a full-screen digital video window?

- How will the end-product be delivered (over the Internet, on CD-ROM, in a stand-alone kiosk format, etc.). Will that medium handle the quantity of digital video?

With the range of possibilities available (various codecs, frame rates, image size, and so on), only you can determine how much of your movie's resources should be dedicated to the delivery of digital video.

Note: Be sure to consider what's happening in the rest of the frames across which the digital video plays. In most cases, your movie and video will have more impact if you design the layout for the video to play in a smaller window.

Adding Digital Videos to Your Movies

Digital video files are imported and placed in the Cast window in the same manner as other files, but Director manages digital videos differently. By default, all digital videos are imported in Direct to Stage mode and linked rather than imported into your movie. When Director links a file to your movie, it places a thumbnail of the cast member into the internal cast, as it would for any other cast member. The thumbnail in reality doesn't represent the actual file, however. It is a pointer to the location where the file is stored. When you save the movie, the location is stored with the movie. If you move the file to another location, Director won't be able to find the file, and your movie won't run correctly. In order to avoid this problem it's a good idea to always store linked files, such as digital videos, in the same folder as your movie.

> **Note:** Unlike sound files, you can't include digital video sprites in a film loop. Although the video will appear at the appointed time in the film loop, it won't play.

Importing a Digital Video Cast Member

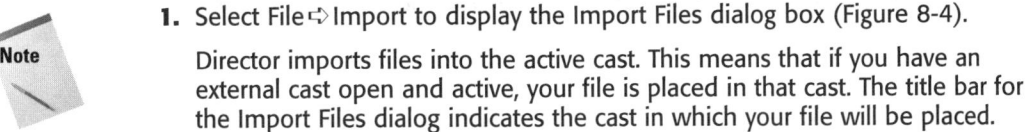

1. Select File ⇨ Import to display the Import Files dialog box (Figure 8-4).

   > **Note:** Director imports files into the active cast. This means that if you have an external cast open and active, your file is placed in that cast. The title bar for the Import Files dialog indicates the cast in which your file will be placed.

2. In the Files of Type list, choose QuickTime (Mac) or Video Clip (Windows). This restricts the File List to only those digital video files that are supported by Director.

3. In the Media list at the bottom, choose Include Original Data for Editing if you want Director to include a pointer back to the video editor you specified in the Editor Preferences dialog box. This allows you to quickly access your video editor by double-clicking the associated cast member in the Cast window. Otherwise, select the Link to External File option.

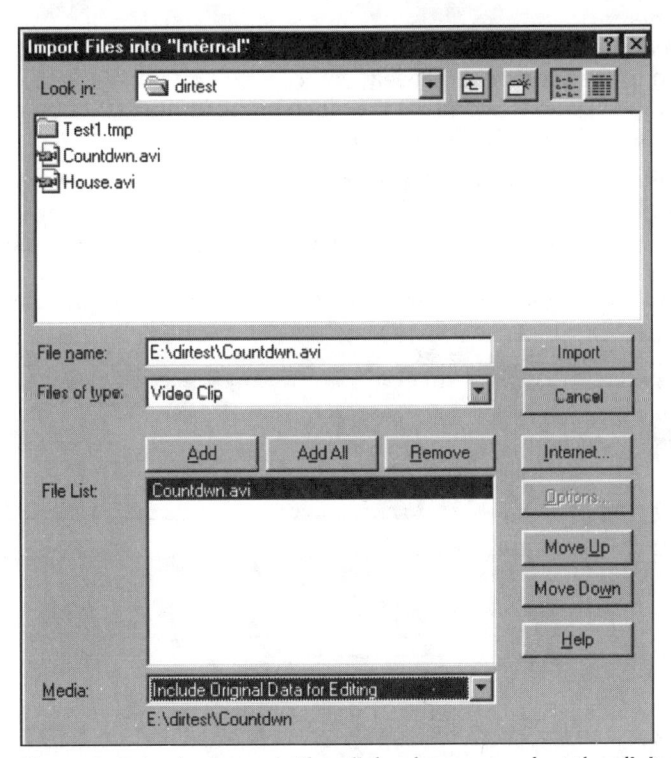

Figure 8-4: In the Import Files dialog box, you select the digital video files you want to place in your movie.

4. To import a single file, select it in the File List and then click the Import button. Or, if you want to choose more than one file or files from several folders, click the Add button instead and move the files one by one to the File List box. When you've finished selecting your files, click Import to complete the operation and return to Director's main window. The digital video cast members appear in the active cast.

Tip: If you make a mistake and import the files into the wrong cast, don't panic. Just select the files and drag them to the correct cast.

Once your files are placed in the cast, you can put the videos on the Stage and test their performance. Similar to other sprites, Director extends the video sprite across the number of frames you specified in the Sprite Preferences dialog box (displayed by selecting File ⇨ Preferences ⇨ Sprite).

Placing a Digital Video on Stage

1. In the Score window, click the frame where you want the digital video to start.

2. Click and drag the digital video from the Cast window to the location you selected in the Score. Alternatively, you can click and drag the digital video to the Stage. Director will place the video sprite in the first open channel of the active frame (see Figure 8-5).

   Notice that when you place the video into the Score and play the movie, the cast member appears on top of any other elements on Stage, regardless of its channel position. This is because Director, by default, places digital videos using the Direct to Stage option. The Macintosh version of Director allows you to turn off the direct to stage option, but Director for Windows does not.

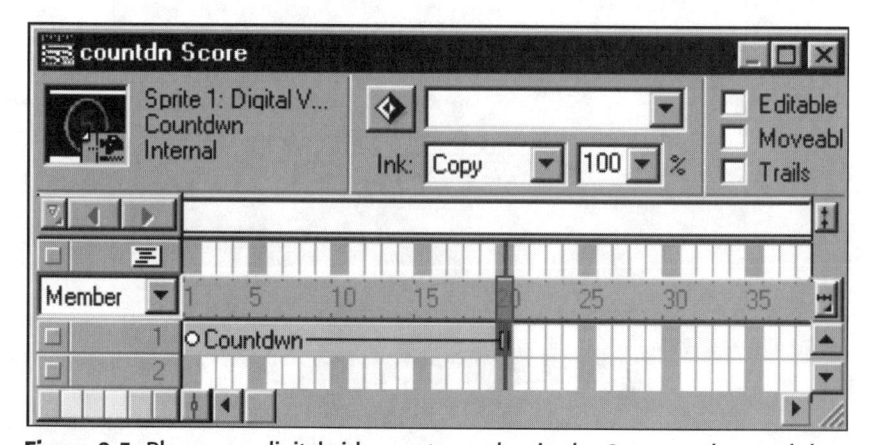

Figure 8-5: Place your digital video cast member in the Score, and extend the sprite to make sure the video plays completely.

3. Rewind your movie and play it. If the video doesn't play completely, click the end frame of the video sprite and drag it to the right to extend it. The sprite must extend through sufficient frames for it to play completely.

4. Rewind and play your movie again. Repeat step 3 as needed to ensure the video plays completely.

> **Tip**
> If you'd like to preview your video, you can choose Window⇨Video, or press Command+9 (Ctrl+9). Your video appears in the Video window. If the video is a QuickTime (.mov) file, a control bar appears at the bottom of the window, allowing you to play, stop, advance, or rewind the movie. When the movie is stopped, you can cut, copy, and paste frames from one video to another.

Understanding Direct to Stage mode

Director supports QuickTime movies for both Macintosh and Windows. You can also import Video for Windows (AVI) files for use in the Windows version of Director. Both QuickTime and AVI formats enable you to incorporate audio effects in the file. When you place videos on the Stage, Director displays them using the default Direct to Stage option. This option allows for the best speed and smoothest display of digital video in a Director movie.

Direct to Stage has both advantages and drawbacks, however. When this option is enabled, you can sync your video to the sound track, effectively modifying the speed with which frames are displayed. You can also specify that Director play every frame, and set the maximum speed for the playback of your video. As noted earlier in this chapter, if you specify a frame rate, the video will play at the fastest speed possible given resources and the frame rate of the video. It won't play faster than the embedded frame rate, though.

One of the drawbacks to the Direct to Stage option is that it places the digital video in front of every sprite on the stage, regardless of the channel where the video sprite is placed in the Score. Another limitation is that ink effects and transitions don't work. Without the use of ink effects, it's nearly impossible to conceal the perimeter rectangle that surrounds the movie window.

You can enable or disable the Direct to Stage option in the Digital Video Cast Member Properties dialog box (except in QuickTime movies in Windows, for which Direct to Stage is the only option).

Enabling or Disabling Direct to Stage

1. With the video cast member selected, select Modify ⇨ Cast Member ⇨ Properties or click the Cast Member Properties button on the Cast window to display the Digital Video Cast Member Properties dialog box (Figure 8-6).

2. Click the Direct to Stage check box to enable or disable the option. If a check mark appears in the box, the option is enabled.

3. Click OK to complete the operation and return to Director's main window.

Choosing whether to use Direct to Stage is a matter of assessing the needs of your movie. If the video has audio properties and you need to sync the video to the sound, leave Direct to Stage enabled. If it's more important that your video blend with the background, or if you have sprites that need to animate above the video, you'll want to disable Direct to Stage. Keep in mind that when this feature is disabled you'll be able to apply ink effects to your video and transitions to the frame.

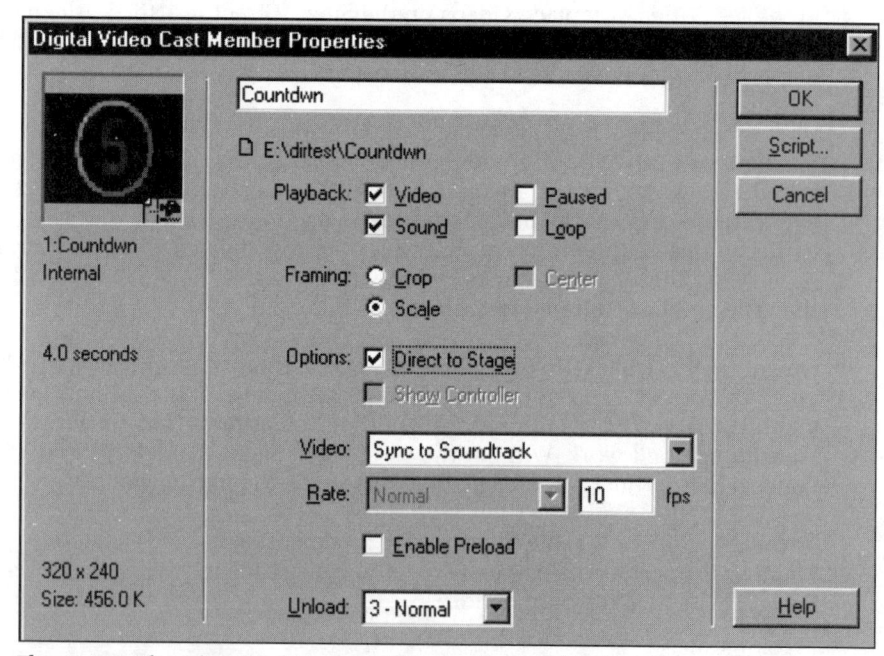

Figure 8-6: The Direct to Stage check box is in the Digital Video Cast Member Properties dialog box.

Syncing video to sound

If you are creating a video with sound for use in a Director movie, it's a good idea to map or sync the audio file to the video *before* importing it into Director. Adobe Premiere and other video editors provide the tools to ensure that the sound plays at the same frame rate as the associated video portion of the file.

Taking the time to sync your video and sound beforehand helps you manage the way Director processes such files. By default, Director syncs the frame rate of your video to match the embedded audio track. This syncing makes your movie appear more polished, but Director will skip playing frames in your video, if necessary, to achieve syncing. And skipping frames can produce undesirable results. You can avoid this by telling Director not to skip frames. Do this by choosing Play Every Frame for the Video selection in the cast member's Properties dialog. Be aware, however, that choosing Play Every Frame disables sound.

Scaling and cropping a digital video

Director lets you scale and crop digital video cast members. Because the scale and crop options are cast member options, they affect the entire sprite rather than a single frame.

Normally it's not a good idea to scale any type of bitmap image, even a digital video. It degrades the quality of the image, especially if you increase the size. Video editors don't always allow users to create custom frame sizes, though, and your movie might call for a size that fits a specific area of your movie. If you can live with some degradation of quality to get a custom fit, then try scaling and see what you get. First use your video editor to create the closest size for your needs. Then you can scale the video in small amounts to create the custom size, while minimizing the loss of quality.

Scaling a Digital Video

1. In the Cast window, select the video you want to scale. Alternatively, you can also select the cast member on Stage (see top of Figure 8-7).
2. Select Modify ⇨ Cast Member ⇨ Properties (Command+I or Ctrl+I) to display the Digital Video Cast Member Properties dialog box.
3. In the Framing section, click the Scale radio button to enable the option. Click OK to return to Director's main window.
4. On Stage, click and drag any of the handles to resize the video frame. The video appears scaled on Stage (bottom of Figure 8-7).

Figure 8-7: When Scale is enabled in the Digital Video Cast Member Properties dialog, you can scale a video by clicking and dragging the handles.

You can also crop a video. This is useful if you want to display a portion of the video within its bounding box. Although cropping has a similar appearance to scaling, it doesn't actually resize the image. It merely hides a portion of the image. If you stretch the bounding box of the video later, it will reveal portions of the image that were previously hidden.

> **Tip**
> By cropping your videos, you can reduce a distracting background. Cropping is also useful for creating special effects within your movies by allowing you to focus on a particular section of an image.

Cropping a Video

1. Select the cast member in the Cast window.
2. Select Modify ⇨ Cast Member ⇨ Properties, to display the Digital Video Cast Member Properties dialog box.
3. Under Framing, select the Crop radio button to enable the option. If you want Director to center the video inside the bounding box, check the Center option as well as Crop. Then click OK to return to Director's main window.
4. Select the video on the Stage.
5. On the Stage, click and drag any of the handles of the video's bounding box. Director displays that portion of the video that fits inside the bounding box (bottom of Figure 8-8).

Setting looping and controller preferences

The Digital Video Cast Member Properties dialog box also allows you to specify looping and whether you want a visible controller for the video. Both of these settings affect the behavior of your movie.

If you set a video to loop, the action repeats until the playback head goes beyond the number of frames you've allotted for your video. If looping is not enabled, the video plays to the end and then displays the last frame of the video until the playback head moves beyond the last frame you allotted for your video. To enable/disable looping, check the Loop check box in the Playback options.

If you enable Show Controller, a control bar appears below your movie that lets the user start, stop, and step through the movie. The Show Controller check box option is only available if Direct to Stage is enabled.

Figure 8-8: You can crop a digital video if you only want a portion of it to show.

Specifying an external video editor

When you specify an external editor for a video cast member, you can quickly jump to an editing application outside of Director. Double-click a cast member for which you've specified an external editor, and Director starts the editor and opens the video within it. Once you've modified your video, you save the changes, click Exit, and the video cast member is updated automatically with the modifications you made in the editor.

Specifying an External Video Editor

1. Select File ⇨ Preferences ⇨ Editors, to display the Editors Preferences dialog box.
2. Scroll through the file type list, and select Video Clip or QuickTime Movie (see Figure 8-9).

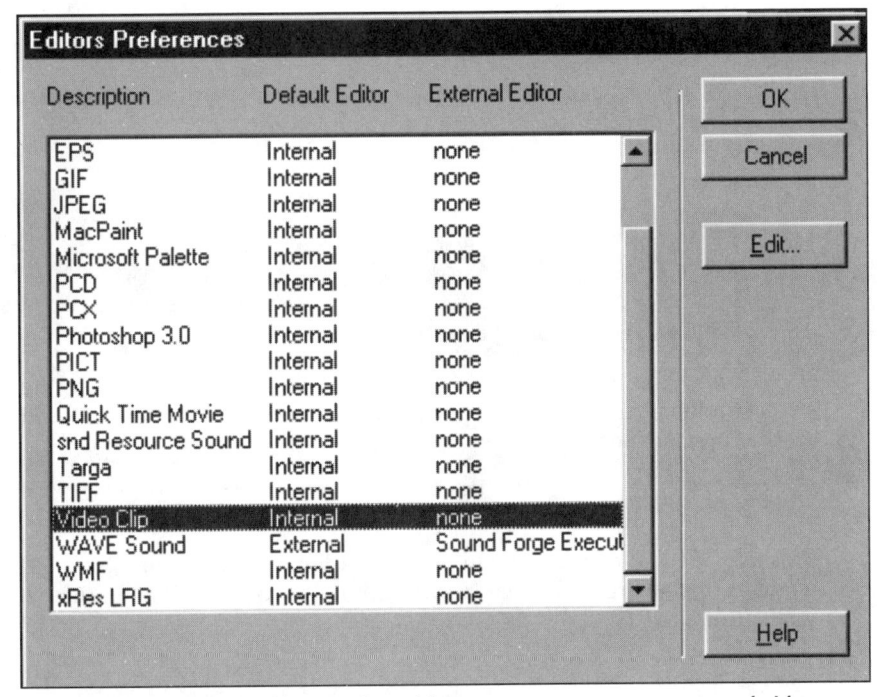

Figure 8-9: Choose the file type for which you want to use an external video editor.

3. Click the Edit button to display the Select Editor for Video Clip (or QuickTime) dialog box.
4. Select the Use External Editor option, and then click either the Browse or Scan button. If you click Browse, the Open dialog box appears, where you can navigate to the executable file that starts your video editor. If you click Scan, Director will scan your computer for possible editors by searching for program files, and present you with a list from which to choose.

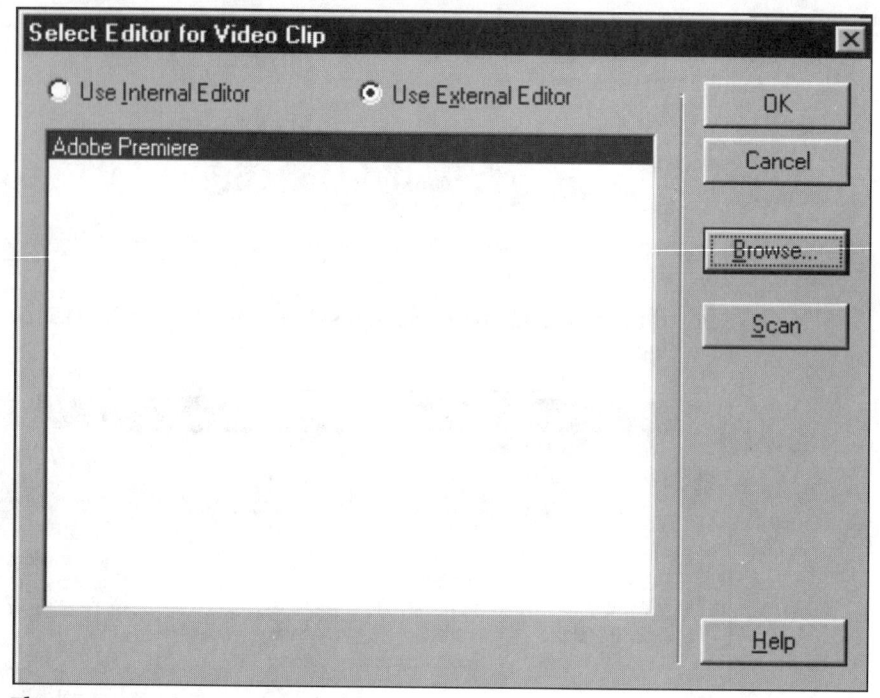

Figure 8-10: Choosing an external video editor

5. Select the Editor you want to use, and click Open to return to the Editors Preferences dialog. Click OK again to complete the operation and return to Director's main window.

Note: Normally, double-clicking would open the digital video in Director's Video window. If you assign an editor, however, this action opens your video in the external editor you specified.

Managing Video Cast Members

Director enables you to specify tempo settings that affect the behavior of digital video within your movie. These settings help you ensure that your video plays completely before moving forward in your movie. In addition to tempo settings, Director 6 comes packaged with two new features for enhancing your movies and video cast members: *behaviors* and *widgets*.

+ You've already been introduced to behaviors for sound, in Chapter 7. Behaviors are prepackaged Lingo scripts with which you can quickly and easily control cast members. You just select the behavior you want to use and drop it onto the sprite in the Score window or on Stage. Director then prompts you for the parameters that define the action you want to apply.

+ Video widgets are scripted buttons that you can place in your movies to control the action of your digital video.

The advantage of using these two new features is the ease with which you can quickly create scripts. For example, you can create a custom control bar for your QuickTime or Video for Windows cast member that allows the user to play, stop, or pause the video (see Chapter 16).

Working with behaviors

As discussed in Chapter 7, behaviors are small Lingo scripts that control interactivity and the behavior of sprites. If you want more information about a selected behavior, you can access the Behavior Inspector with the Window⇨Inspectors⇨Behavior command or by pressing Command+Option+; (Ctrl+Alt+;). When you apply a video behavior, a dialog box prompts you to enter parameters that control the behavior. Examples of parameters are the channel number of the video sprite, or the number of frames the video occupies.

Director comes packaged with five behaviors that apply to videos:

Behavior Name	Action
Video Rewind	Rewinds a video when the user clicks and releases the mouse button.
Video Play	Plays a video when the user clicks and releases the mouse button.
Video Stop	Stops a video when the user clicks and releases the mouse button.
Video Control	Supplies a set of video controllers to play, stop, rewind, pause, and step through a video.
Video Slider	Includes a time slider that tracks the progress of the video.

Behaviors are a quick way to add simple Lingo scripts to your sprites and cast members. They guide you through the process of applying a script by requesting the information required. You can attach as many behaviors to a sprite as you wish to get the effect you want. If you want to place visible controls in your movie, you can also add widgets.

Applying a Video Behavior

1. Select Xtras➪Behavior Library, to display the Behavior Library Cast window (Figure 8-11).

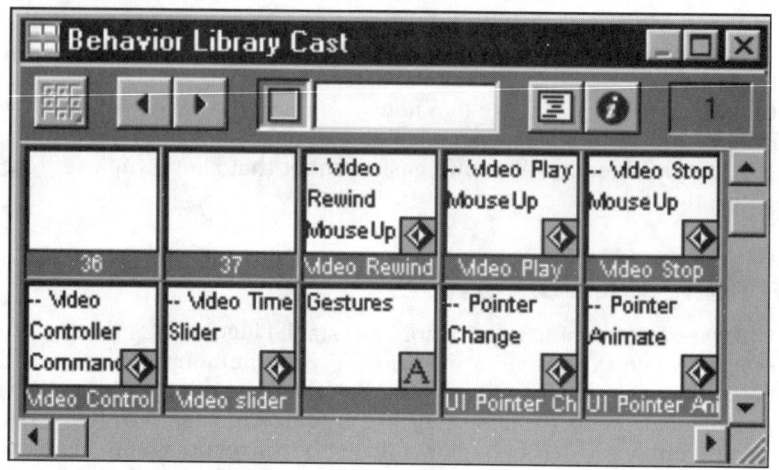

Figure 8-11: Available behaviors are in the Behavior Library Cast window.

2. Scroll through the library to find the behavior you want to use.

3. Click and drag the behavior onto a video sprite on Stage or in the Score. The Parameters dialog box appears. The name at the top of the Parameters dialog box reflects the name of the selected behavior (see Figure 8-12).

4. Enter the parameters for your video sprite. In Figure 8-12, the behavior was attached to a video sprite in channel 2, which extended for a total of 50 frames. The required parameters will vary, of course, according to the behavior you select.

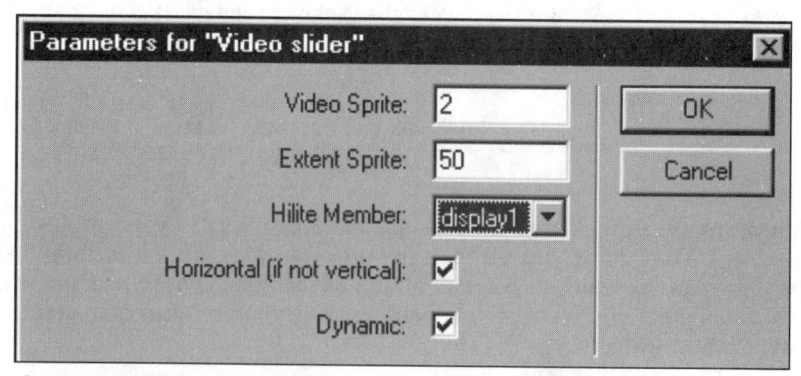

Figure 8-12: The parameters for a video slider behavior

5. Click OK to complete the operation and return to Director's main window.

> **Tip:** Use the Media Preload behavior to improve the performance of your movies. Place the behavior in the frame before the start of a video, or before a scene containing a video. When the playback head reaches the frame, the cast members of the next scene begin to load. Using Media Preload reduces lag that occurs frequently when large cast members are loaded into memory.

Using widgets

The dictionary defines a *widget* as a hypothetical mechanism or a control. Where Director 6 is concerned, it's the latter. Widgets are controls you can place in your movies to give the user interactive control over specified sprites or activities. Each widget is designed for a specific purpose and has an associated behavior. This doesn't restrict the widget. It just provides you with a quick means of adding a control to your movie. You can edit the scripts associated with a widget to customize it for your needs.

Director provides two ways of accessing and applying widgets. You can either use the Widget Wizard, which contains an assortment of the available widgets, or you can use widgets directly from the Widget library. You can also attach additional behaviors to a widget to customize its abilities. The Widget Wizard's collection of useful navigation, buttons, devices, and text effects are prescribed with instructions. They are easy and quick to use.

In this section you'll explore widgets that affect video behavior.

Inside the Widget Wizard

The Widget Wizard is a Director movie. When you select the wizard from the Xtras menu, you are actually playing a movie that allows you to interact with the movie you're creating. The Widget Wizard movie is located on the CD-ROM that came with Director. As you become more adept with creating your own movies, buttons, and behaviors, you can experiment with adding your own widgets to the Widget Wizard movie and the Widget library. If you decide to modify the movie, be sure to first use the Save As command to avoid overwriting the original movie.

Using a QuickTime Controller from the Widget Wizard

1. In the Score window, select a frame in which to place your wizard. If you neglect this step, you will be prompted to select a frame later.
2. Select Xtras ⇨ Widget Wizard ⇨ Widget Wizard, to display the Widget Wizard (similar to Figure 8-13).

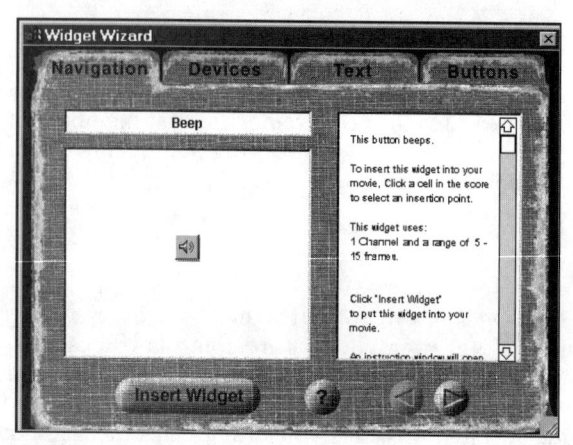

Figure 8-13: The Widget Wizard helps you to quickly insert widget controls into your movie.

3. Click the Devices tab at the top of the wizard to display the first device controller.

4. Click the right-arrow button near the bottom of the wizard, and scroll through the device controllers until you get to the QT Controller. The scrollable text box on the right provides you with information about the widget. A sample of the control itself appears on the left.

   Tip

   You can test most widgets in the Widget Wizard interactively, by trying the controls or clicking the object displayed in the sample box.

5. Click Insert Widget to place the widget both in the Score window and on the Stage. You should note that many widgets will occupy more than one channel and frame.

6. The QT Controller and some other widgets have extended instructions that appear automatically (see Figure 8-14). The instructions provide more information about the widget and how you can customize it for your use. Click the page curls at the bottom of the Instructions window to move forward and backward through the instructions. Note that the Widget Wizard has to remain open while you are flipping through the pages of the instructions.

7. The Widget Wizard window is really a movie in a window (MIAW; you'll learn how to create one in Chapter 21). You can drag it to the side, read the instructions, and work on your own movie on the Stage. When you're done with the instructions window, you can close it using the Close button (identified in Figure 8-14). On the Mac, the Close button is at the top-left of the window.

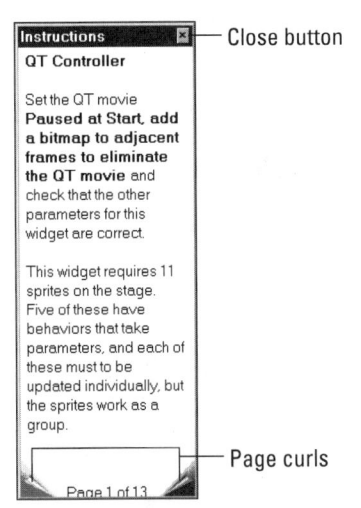

Figure 8-14: The Instructions window provides more information about the widget and how to customize it.

8. Once you click the Insert Widget button (see step 5), the sample movie and the controls are added to your movie. Check out the Cast window now. There, you can locate the sample video, delete it from the Cast, and import your own video into the same cast member slot.

On the CD-ROM

To practice these steps, use the digital video included on the CD-ROM that accompanies this book. The files brid063l.mov, mari007l.mov, rail051l.mov are on the companion CD-ROM in the goodies:4palms (goodies\4palms) folder and the files contrct.mov, everend.mov, and watrfall.mov are in the goodies:3digital (goodies\3digital) folder.

9. When you're done, you'll find that your video has replaced the sample video from the widget. If the size of your video window is different from the sample, you'll need to reposition your video on the Stage so it doesn't obscure the widget (video) controls.

10. Close the Widget Wizard window, save your movie, rewind, and test it.

Specifying tempo settings

Director allows you to specify tempo settings to control the way your movie interacts with video cast members. This is useful for pausing the movie while waiting for a video to finish playing.

You can also use tempo settings to control the video and interactive portions of the movie. By setting cue points in the digital video, you can have the Director movie pause until the video has reached the predetermined cue point. Once the digital video has reached the cue point, the Director movie continues. Before Director can recognize a cue point set within a video, however, you must first define the cue point in Macromedia's SoundEdit 16. Although SoundEdit 16 is only available for the Macintosh, you can use it to insert cue points into QuickTime digital videos, which can be used in both the Macintosh and Windows versions of Director.

Note: SoundEdit 16 is designed for the Macintosh platform, and has no Windows equivalent. For more information about placing cue points using SoundEdit 16, see the documentation for SoundEdit 16 and Chapter 15 of this book.

Pausing a Movie to Wait for a Video to Finish Playing

1. In the Score window, select the frame where you want the playback head to pause until the video finishes playing.

2. Double-click the Tempo channel in that frame to display the Frame Properties: Tempo dialog box (Figure 8-15).

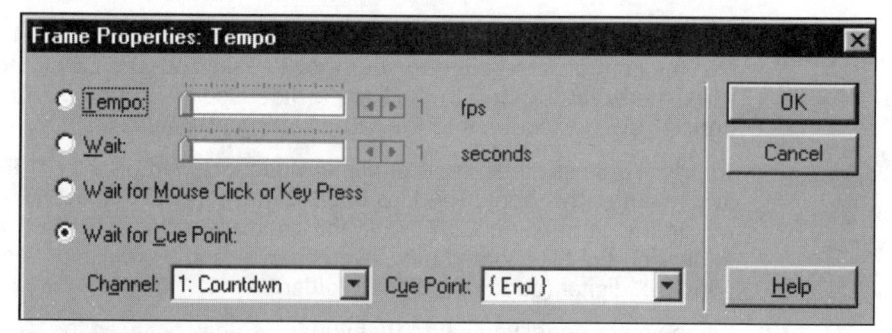

Figure 8-15: Choosing {End} as the Cue Point forces Director to wait for your video to finish before continuing to the next frame of your movie.

3. Click the Wait for Cue Point radio button to enable that option, and select the video from the Channel list.

4. In the Cue Point list, choose {End}. Click OK to return to Director's main window.

Even though you may not have any SoundEdit 16-specified cue points in your video, choosing {End} for the cue point setting causes Director to wait for the video to finish playing before continuing to the next frame of your movie.

Pausing a Movie to Wait for a Specific Cue Point in the Video

1. Using SoundEdit 16, you can define and name cue points for your digital video file.
2. Once cue points are in place, import the video into your movie, and place it in the cast.
3. Click and drag the video to the location in the Score where you want the video to begin.
4. Double-click the Tempo channel in the frame where you want to place the first pause. The Frame Properties: Tempo dialog box appears.
5. Click the Wait for Cue Point radio button to enable the option, and select the video from the Channel list.
6. Choose the name of your cue point from the Cue Point list, and click OK to return to Director's main window.

Using cue points enables you to pace your movie and coordinate video events. In order to stop or pause a video, however, you will need to add video controls using Director behaviors and widgets. The video behaviors as well as the video widget include controls to stop your movie and wait for the video to finish playing.

Note
More sophisticated integration of video, sound, and interactivity is accomplished by using Lingo statements within your movie, as discussed in Chapter 16.

Exporting Digital Video

Director allows you to export any range of frames as a digital video. Once you've exported the frames as a digital video, you can import that video back into Director as a single cast member. When you export a Director movie, it will retain tempo settings, palette effects, and transitions; however, any interactivity that is in the selected range of frames is lost. In addition, if you choose to export the frames as a Video for Windows (AVI) file, Director doesn't save any sounds with your video. Director only exports sounds when you export using the QuickTime for Macintosh file format. You cannot export a movie as a QuickTime for Windows file...yet!

Tip
To attach a sound file to a video, you can use a video editor such as Adobe Premier, which is available for both Macintosh and Windows platforms.

When you export a range of frames as a digital video, Director internally plays that portion of your movie, capturing the action as it would appear on Stage. Any scripts or other elements that have a visible effect during that playback time are captured, as well.

When you export a range of frames as a digital video, Director internally plays that portion of your movie, capturing the action as it would appear on Stage. Any scripts or other elements that have a visible effect during that playback time are captured, as well. Director 6 doesn't export transitions with digital video, however. If the selected range of frames contains a transition, it's a good idea to re-create this transition in your video editor.

It's important to remember that Director captures the entire Stage at its current size. If the action you want to save as a video is smaller than the current Stage size, you'll need to resize the Stage accordingly. Before resizing the stage, be sure to use the Save As command to save your movie using a new name. This way, you won't have to resize the Stage again before importing your digital video back into your movie. It also provides you with a back-up file of the original movie if the results of your export are unsatisfactory.

Exporting a Range of Frames as a Digital Video

1. Prepare your movie for export by checking and testing all media. Don't waste time by allowing a spelling error or a misplaced sprite to be discovered on the Stage after you've already exported to video!

   Note

   Before exporting frames as digital video, disable any screensavers that might be active. Exporting to digital video can take time, and if your screensaver comes on during the process, it will be included in your video.

2. Select the File ⇨ Export command by using Command+Shift+R (Ctrl+Shift+R). The Export dialog box is displayed. Figure 8-16 shows the Macintosh Export dialog box and Figure 8-17 shows the Windows Export dialog box.

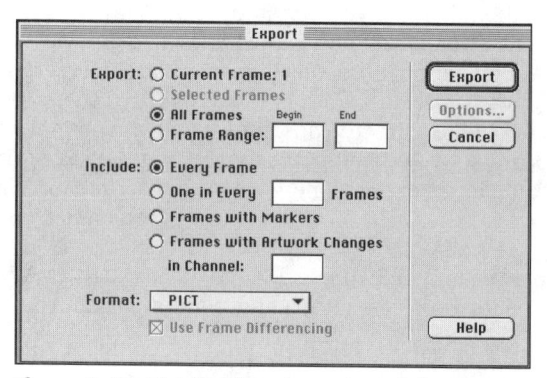

Figure 8-16: The Macintosh version of the Export dialog box

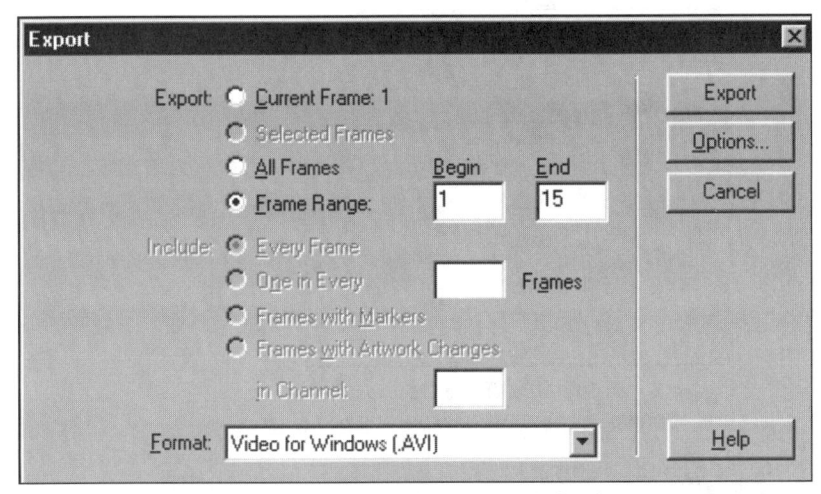

Figure 8-17: The Windows version of the Export dialog box

3. Set the Format field at the bottom of the dialog to the desired export format (Video for Windows, DIB File Sequence, PICT, Scrapbook, PICS, or QuickTime Movie).

4. Using the radio buttons at the top of the dialog box, indicate whether you want to export the current frame, selected frames (which you must have selected *before* you open the Export dialog box), all frames, or a frame range. If you choose the Frame Range option, enter the starting and ending frame numbers in the Begin and End fields next to the Frame Range radio button.

5. Click the Options button.

   ✦ If you are using Director for Windows and exporting to Video for Windows, the Video for Windows Export Options dialog box (Figure 8-18) appears.

   ✦ If you are using Director for the Macintosh and exporting to QuickTime, the QuickTime Options dialog box (Figure 8-19) appears.

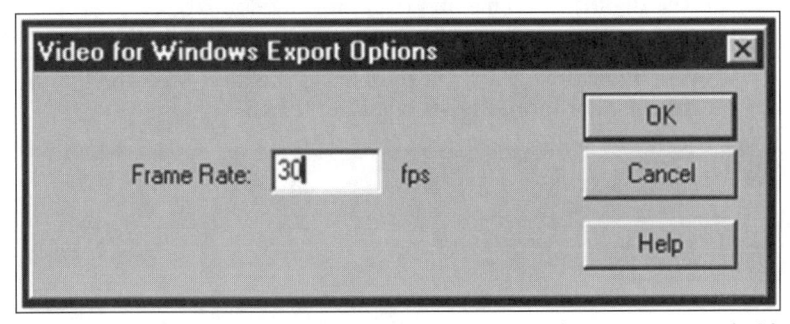

Figure 8-18: Windows users: Select the Frame Rate for your exported Video for Windows

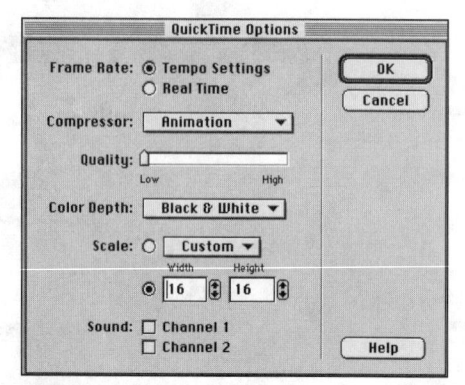

Figure 8-19: The QuickTime Options dialog box appears for Mac users exporting to QuickTime.

6. **For Windows users:**

   + Enter the fps (frames per second) in the Frame Rate field and click OK to close the dialog and return to the Export dialog box.

   + Click the Export button, and enter a filename for your video.

   + A Video Compression dialog box appears, in which you choose the codec to use, the compression quality, and the placement of keyframes. See Chapter 16 for more details on each of these settings.

   + Click OK and the movie is exported to video. Be prepared for a wait; video compression takes time.

   For Macintosh users:

   + Enter the compressor or codec type on the QuickTime Options dialog box (see Figure 8-19). In addition, choose the quality, color depth, scaling (such as 25%, 50%, 75%, or 100% of the movie's Stage size), and whether sound channels are to be exported. When done setting options, click OK.

   + In the Export dialog box, click the Export button. Enter a filename for the digital video file and click the Save button.

   + An Alert box reminds you that screensavers should be turned off during the file export. Click OK to dismiss the alert, and the export process begins. For more details see Chapter 16.

Exporting frames as a video is one way of keeping your movie compact, by replacing several sprites with a single sprite. Exporting frames of your Director movie as a digital video offers all the advantages — and the disadvantages — associated with including digital video in your movies. It can increase the file size of your movie, but it can also reduce the file size if the video is replacing several large cast members with a single, more compact cast member. You should consider the file sizes of the original cast members versus a digital video before deciding to export frames as a video.

Summary

Learning the basics of working with digital video enables you to easily enhance your movies. This chapter focused on the fundamental skills necessary to successfully incorporate imported animation sequences. In this chapter, you learned that

- ✦ Careful editing of digital video files is critical to the success of your Director movie.
- ✦ Considering the relationship between file size, frame rate, and color depth helps you create digital videos that are compact yet smooth and effective in appearance.
- ✦ Controlling the tempo allows you to pace your movie.
- ✦ Digital video cast members are always linked. Take care when moving the files and when distributing your movies; be sure to include the linked files.
- ✦ You can crop and scale digital video cast members.
- ✦ Widgets and behaviors enrich and add interactivity to your digital video cast members.
- ✦ You can export selected frames as digital video files.

✦ ✦ ✦

CHAPTER 9

Pulling It All Together

The creation of a Director movie requires advance planning for its success. In addition to ensuring success, planning ahead can reduce the amount of debugging and editing required throughout the development process. In this chapter, you'll examine the anatomy of a movie, from a planning point of view, by creating an interactive resume. The resume doesn't have many bells and whistles, but creating it requires a number of basic steps. These steps are broken down into a series of tasks to help you see how various actions are performed, as well as the workflow of developing a movie. (You have been learning most of these tasks as you've worked through Chapters 6, 7, and 8.)

The need to work in a team environment increases as a movie becomes more complex. Successfully addressing critical issues such as distributing the workload and maintaining a clear vision of the overall design will go a long way to ensure the success of your movies. Communication is a key factor.

In This Chapter

Designing an interface

Animating a portfolio

Applying navigation controls to your movie

Adding a background sound to a movie

Managing the creation of a movie

Creating an Interactive Resume

At one time, the process of obtaining employment was a matter of filling out an application and going through a brief interview. People typically sought jobs in their own local area. Today many companies advertise over a broad geographical area, and people frequently will relocate hundreds or thousands of miles to take advantage of career opportunities.

One thing that hasn't changed is the initial contact between an employer and a prospective employee: It's still the resume. Employers receive vast numbers of resumes for any given position and must sort through them to identify the best candidates. Because of the impersonal nature of the resume process, it's critical to the employer — but even more so to the prospective employee — that a resume grab the attention of the person reviewing it and leave an instant positive impression.

Multimedia resumes, particularly those that are interactive, need not be fancy to be effective. They help you capitalize on an environment that can be both informative and insightful for prospective employers. In this section you'll create a basic interactive resume, using elements already stored in a Director library cast. Although the finished resume doesn't contain any Lingo scripting per se, it takes advantage of a widget that is packaged with Director 6 to allow the user to navigate the movie.

On the CD-ROM The file resume.dir is stored on your companion CD-ROM, in the exercise:ch09 (exercise\ch09) folder.

You can replace the graphic elements in resume.dir with your own cast members, if you want to personalize this particular resume. Like any other Director project, planning and gathering resource files in advance will help ensure the success of the project. Once you've completed these initial stages, you're ready to start creating your interactive resume.

Designing the interface

A computer is a valuable tool. It provides the means of organizing and displaying information quickly and efficiently. To maximize its abilities, however, you need to effectively instruct the computer about what you want to do. In order to tell Director and your computer what you want, you design an interface for your resume.

A pencil and paper are probably the quickest and easiest means of tackling this task at the beginning. You don't have to be an artist or even a professional designer — the idea at this stage is just to block out the scenes of your resume (see Figure 9-1). You can add notes about the elements you want in each scene, the navigation between scenes, and any effects or transitions you want to use. Plotting your course of action helps you visualize the project and anticipate problems you might encounter as you create the resume.

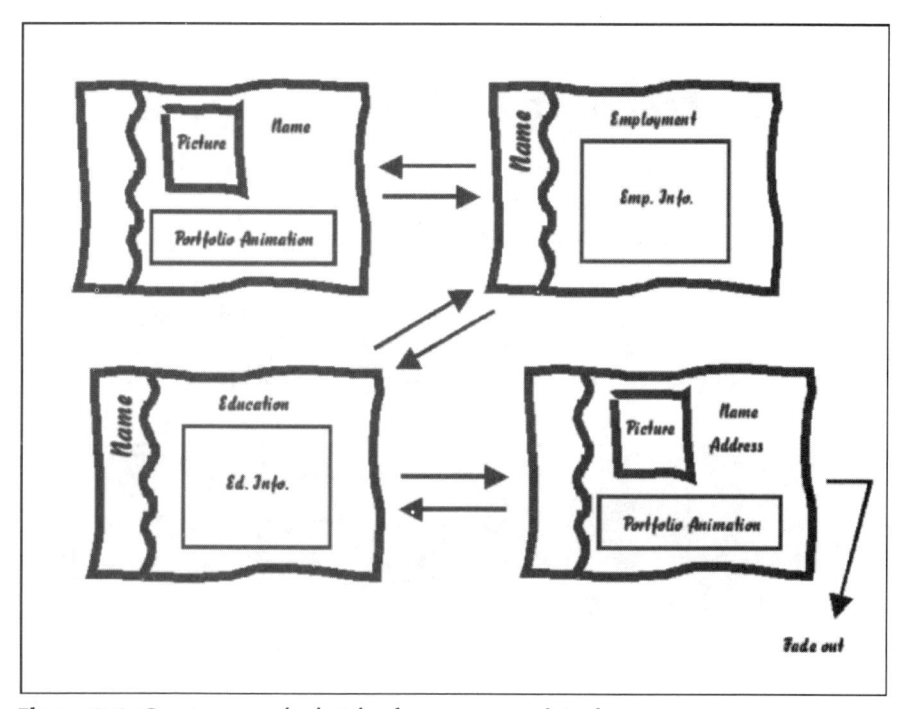

Figure 9-1: Create a rough sketch of your resume interface

Gathering the cast members

Create the cast members for your resume in Director, or use an external graphics package and then import them into Director. The resume.dir movie on the CD-ROM already contains all the cast members you'll need to create the sample resume. When you're creating a Director movie, it's easier if you work from the back to the front of each scene.

Tip Remember that you can shuffle the order in which elements appear in the Score (and on Stage). Just select the sprite you want to move in the Score window, and press Command+up arrow (Ctrl+up arrow) to move the sprite forward in the hierarchy, or Command+down arrow (Ctrl+down arrow) to move the sprite backward. These keystrokes may "feel wrong" to you because Command+up arrow (Ctrl+up arrow) does not move the sprite "up" to a lower-numbered channel.

Rather, it moves the sprite "down" to a higher-numbered channel — which moves it "up" toward the front of the Stage (ahead of objects in lower-numbered channels).

Adding a Background

1. Open resume.dir in Director, if it's not already open. It's on the CD-ROM in the exercise:ch09 (exercise\ch09) folder.
2. Open the Cast and Score windows, and select frame 1 of channel 1 in the Score.
3. Click and drag the cast member named *resume* to the location you selected in the Score. This image will be the background for every scene in the resume movie, and appears centered on the Stage (see Figure 9-2).

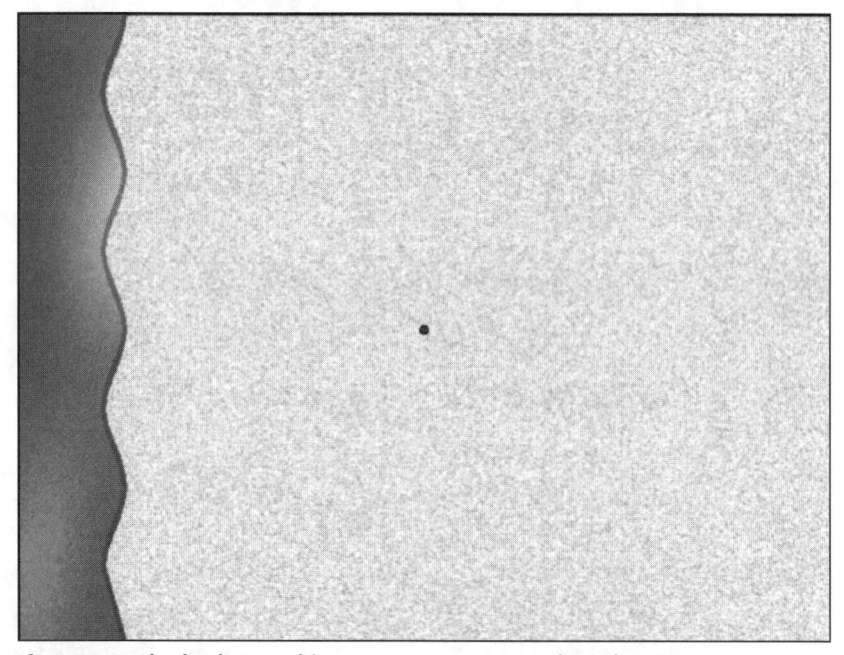

Figure 9-2: The background image appears centered on the Stage.

If you have specified the default frame span for a sprite in the Score, the background sprite will span 28 frames. Later you'll extend the sprite to span more frames, but for now 28 frames is fine. The first scene of the resume contains a photo, a title name, and an animated portfolio of thumbnail images. You'll add a mask and an ink effect to enhance the photo sprite. The Thumbnail portfolio scrolls from right to left, and employs two masks that enable the thumbnail sprites to appear and disappear at specific locations on the Stage.

Creating Scene 1

1. In the Score window, select frame 1 of channel 2.
2. In the Cast window, select Deb2, press the Shift key, and select mask1. Drag both images to the location you selected in the Score. Both images appear in the Score and centered on Stage. The photo isn't visible because it's directly below the mask.
3. With both sprites still selected, click and drag them up and to the left on Stage (see Figure 9-3).

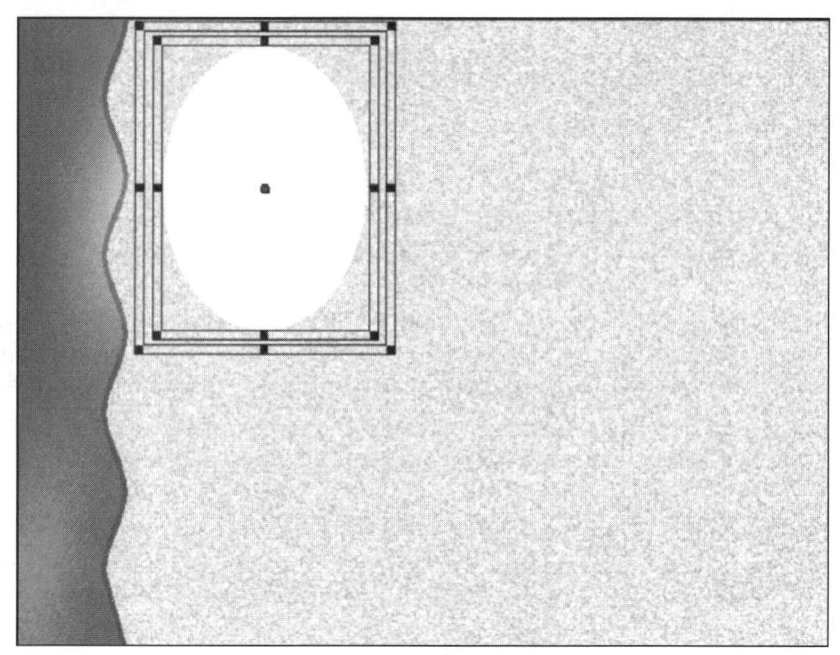

Figure 9-3: Both images appear centered on the Stage.

4. In the Score window, click the mask1 sprite in channel 3 to select it. From the ink pop-up, select Background Transparent. The white center of the mask disappears, and an elliptical frame appears around the visible photo (see Figure 9-4).

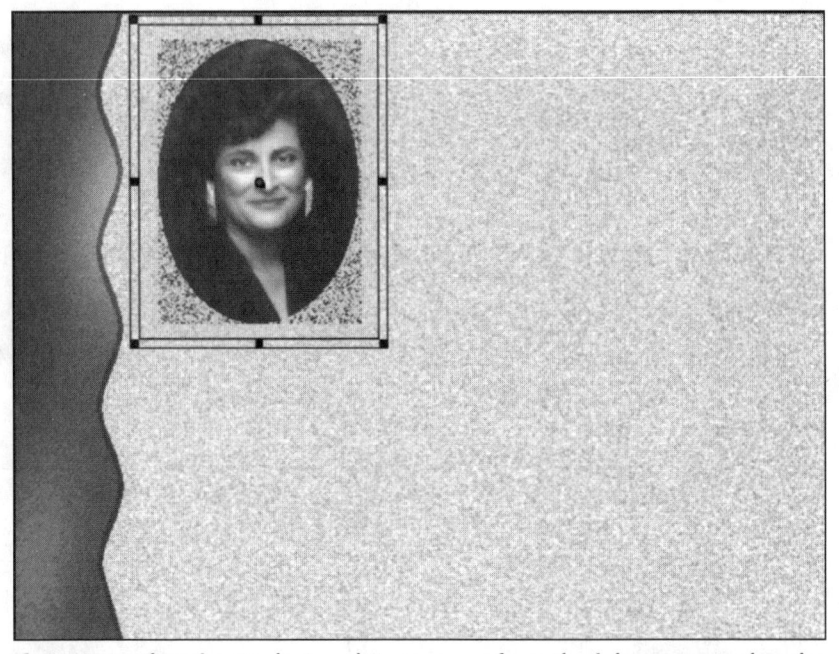

Figure 9-4: Choosing Background Transparent from the ink pop-up makes the photo visible beneath the mask.

5. Click frame 1, channel 4, and then select cast member 4 in the Cast window. Drag it onto the Stage, centering it between the photo and the right edge of the Stage. Be sure the sprite in channel 4 begins in frame 1.

Tip

Whenever you want to drag a cast member to the Stage, first select the frame on the frame bar where you want the sprite to begin. New cast members dragged to the Stage are always added to the Score beginning at the current location of the playback head.

6. With the sprite selected, select Background Transparent from the ink pop-up in the Score window. This removes the white bounding box behind the text.

7. Click in frame 1, channel5, and then drag mask2 from the Cast window to the Stage. Place it near the bottom-right corner. Click and drag another

copy of mask2 to the Stage, placing it near the bottom just to the right of the sidebar (Figure 9-5). Notice that these elements are difficult to see because they blend with the background image. Be sure the ink for the sprites in channels 5 and 6 is set to Copy.

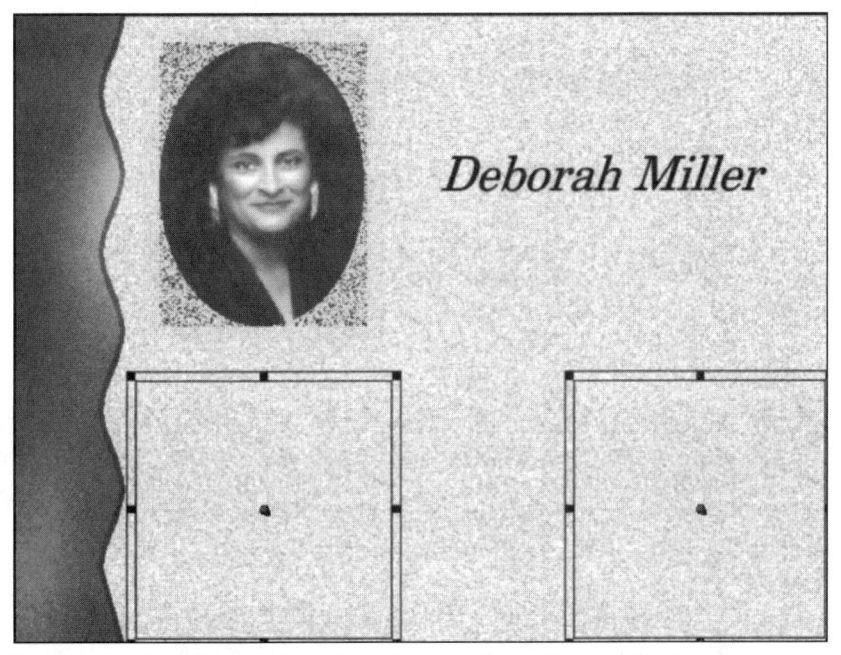

Figure 9-5: Place two copies of mask2 near the bottom of the Stage.

8. Select both sprites in the Score window, and select Modify➪Align to display the Align window. Choose Align Tops from the vertical alignment menu, and No Change from the horizontal alignment menu. Click Align. The tops of the two sprites are aligned.

9. Verify the location of each mask2 sprite. Select the sprite one at a time in the Score window. For each sprite, select Modify➪Sprite➪Properties to display the Sprite Properties dialog box. The mask2 sprite in channel 6 should be Left = 95, Top = 280. The mask2 sprite in channel 5 should be at Left = 450, Top = 280. Adjust the values in the Location boxes if needed (see Figure 9-6). After checking the properties of each sprite, click OK to complete the operation and return to Director's main window.

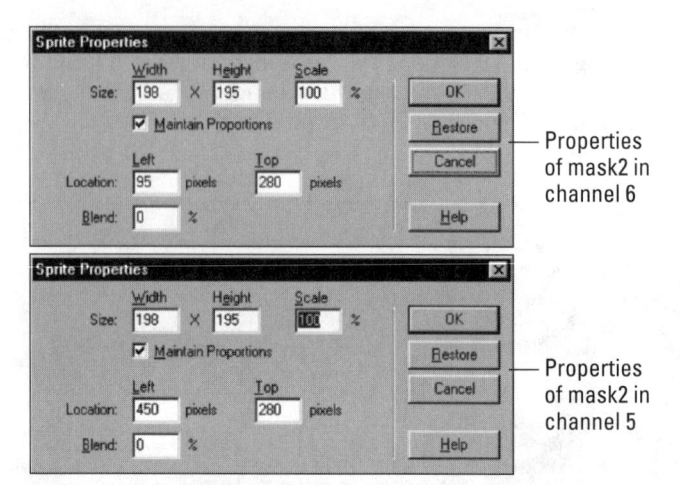

Figure 9-6: Adjust the Location values of the sprites in channels 5 and 6.

(Properties of mask2 in channel 6; Properties of mask2 in channel 5)

10. Select both sprites in the Score and press Command+up-arrow (Ctrl)+up arrow four times. As shown in Figure 9-7, this moves the two sprites forward in the Score, to channels 9 and 10, leaving four channels empty for the animated portfolio you'll add in the next exercise.

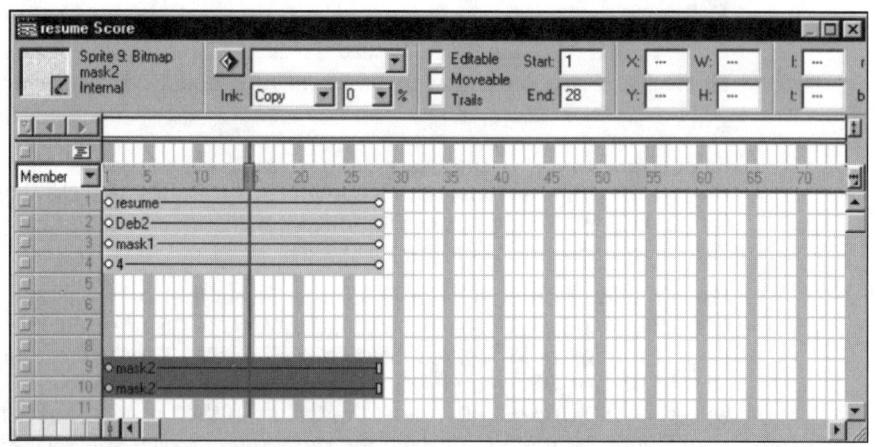

Figure 9-7: Shuffle the mask2 sprites up in the Score to move them forward four channels.

11. Save your movie to your hard disk as **resume1.dir**.

By establishing this first scene, you have created the foundation for the balance of the resume. The location of the mask2 sprites in the Score enables you to animate the series of thumbnail images behind them.

Animating a portfolio

When timing is critical, animating thumbnail images that aren't the same size can get tricky. Using the Sprite Properties dialog box to position the sprites makes the task a lot easier, however. In the next two exercises, you'll place the thumbnail sprites and animate them using the Score window and the Sprite Properties dialog box.

Each of the sprites is animated in the same way, by first extending the sprites in the Score. Then a keyframe is placed in the sprite being animated, to hold it in place for a specified frame span. At the appropriate frame, the tail frame of the sprite is repositioned using the Sprite Properties dialog box. With this method you can control the spacing between sprites as well as their precise beginning and finishing positions. Animating the portfolio is done in two exercises,to allow you to stop if needed and check the animation after the placement of the first sprite.

Tip When you are creating an animation sequence in Director that involves a number of steps, it's a good idea to stop long enough to save your file periodically. This gives you a saved version for reverting to if you aren't satisfied with the new results.

Animating the First Thumbnail Image in the Portfolio

1. Open resume1.dir in Director, if it's not already open.
2. Be sure the Score and Cast windows are open.
3. Press the Shift key and select cast members erud_t, hum_t, lake_t, and wnrose_t.
4. Drag the selected cast members to frame 1 of channel 5 in the Score. The sprites appear in the Score window, filling in the blank channels you created in the previous exercise (see Figure 9-8). They also appear centered on the Stage.

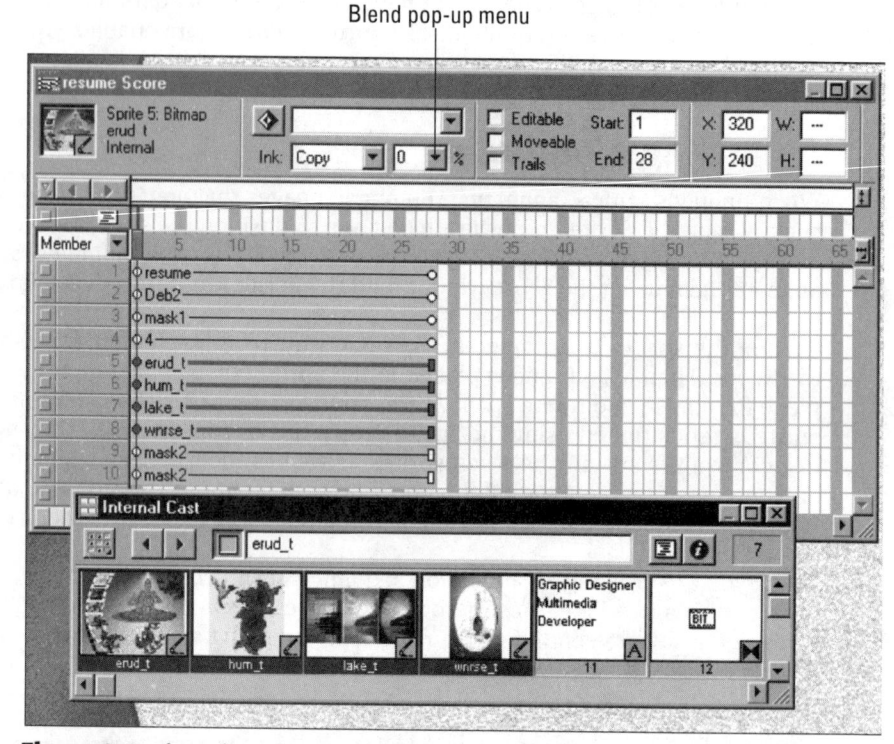

Figure 9-8: The selected cast members fill the blank channels in the Score.

5. With the sprites in channels 5–8 selected, select Modify ⇨ Sprite Properties. Enter Left = 450 and Top = 360 in the Location boxes. Click OK to complete the operation and return to Director's main window. The thumbnail sprites move behind mask2 and are aligned with the left side of the mask2 sprite (see Figure 9-9).

6. At this point, the four thumbnail sprites (erud_t, hum_t, lake_t, and wnrose_t) should be hidden by the mask2 sprite (bottom-right of the Stage). If you can see the four sprites, check that the ink for mask 2 is set to Copy (not Background Transparent) and that the Blend for all four objects is set at 100%.

> **Caution**
>
> Director has two nasty habits when using the Score window settings. First, the ink sometimes "sticks," and the default is not Copy, as it should be, when you drag new objects to the Stage. Second, the Blend setting mysteriously switches to 0% — which means your object is invisible on the Stage! So in step 6, if either copy of mask2 is set to an ink other than Copy, change it to Copy. If the Blend is set to something other than 100%, click the Blend pop-up menu button (identified in Figure 9-8) and change the blend to 100%.

7. Deselect all sprites in the Score. Then, select the tail frame of every sprite, by pressing the Command (Ctrl) key and click each tail frame. Then click the frame bar at frame 55. Press Command+B (Ctrl+B) to extend the sprites through frame 55.

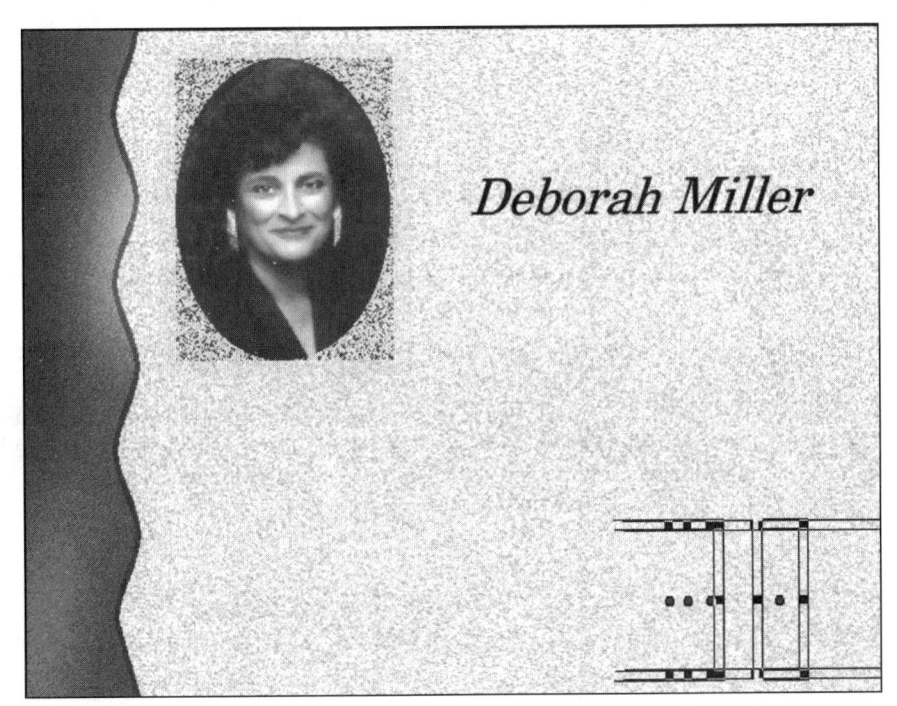

8. Click the sprite erud_t in frame 30, and select Insert ⇨ Keyframe (see Figure 9-10).

Figure 9-9: The aligned thumbnail sprites move behind the mask2 sprite.

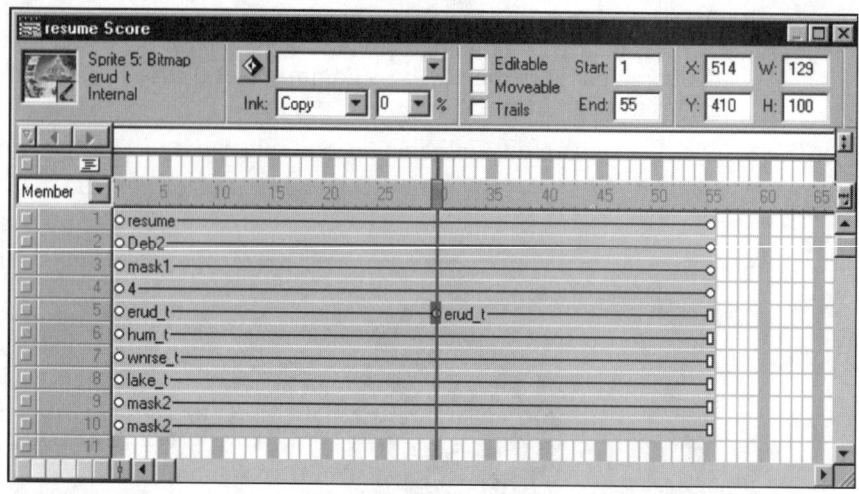

Figure 9-10: A keyframe inserted at frame 30 of the sprite erud_t in channel 5.

9. Select the tail frame of erud_t in the Score window, and set the location in the Sprite Properties dialog box to Left = 95. The Top setting is fine as is. Click OK to complete the operation and return to Director's main window. The sprite appears on Stage behind the first copy of mask2 on the left. An animation path indicates the movement the sprite will make over the span of frames (see Figure 9-11).

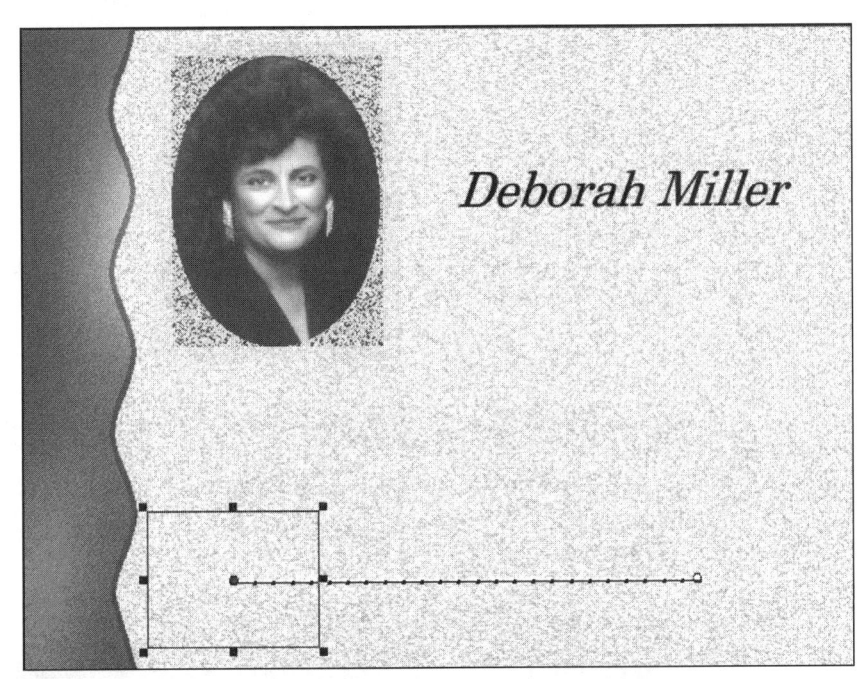

Figure 9-11: The animation path of the sprite

10. Rewind the movie, and click the Play button to check the animation sequence.

   Tip: If your sprites don't appear when you play your movie, check to make sure that the sprite's ink is set at 100% in the Score window.

11. Save your movie again as **resume1.dir**.

When you added a keyframe to the movie, you specified the starting point for the motion of the sprite. In the frames that precede the keyframe, the sprite is static and doesn't move, so the user has time to absorb the contents prior to the view changing. Each of the sprites starts moving at 25-frame intervals, which allows the appropriate amount of spacing between the sprites and gives the user time to view each thumbnail image. The life span of each animated sprite ends once it moves to the end of its designated path.

Next, you'll animate the remaining sprites.

Completing the Portfolio Animation

1. Open resume1.dir in Director, if it's not already open.
2. Open the Score window.
3. Press the Command (Ctrl) key and select the tail frame of each of the sprites *except* erud_t.
4. Click the frame bar at frame 80, and press Command+B (Ctrl+B) to extend the sprites through frame 80. Note that erud_t is not extended (see Figure 9-12).

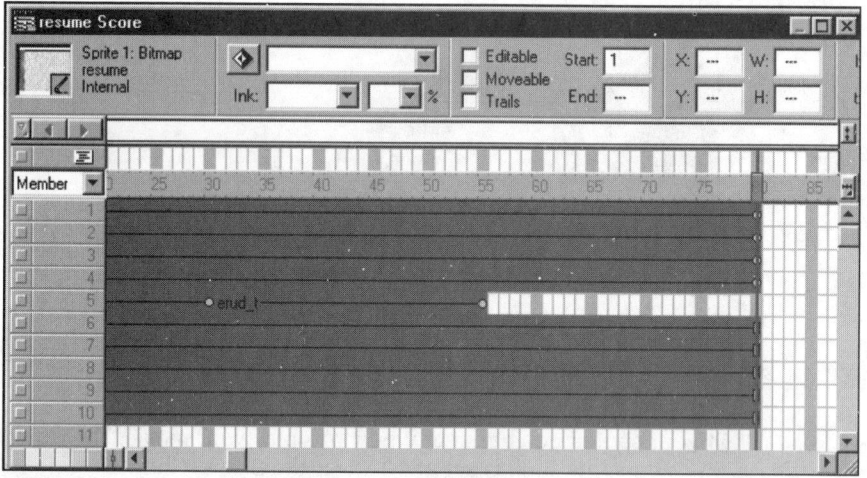

Figure 9-12: Extend the sprites through frame 80.

5. Click the sprite hum_t in frame 55, and select Insert ⇨ Keyframe. A keyframe appears in the Score at the specified location.
6. Select the tail frame of sprite hum_t and select Modify ⇨ Sprite ⇨ Properties. Set the location to Left = 95, and click OK to complete the operation and return to Director's main window. The animation path for the sprite appears on Stage.
7. Repeat steps 4 through 6 for each of the remaining two thumbnail sprites, extending the sprites 25 frames and adding a keyframe. When you complete the sequence of steps, your movie will end in frame 130 (see Figure 9-13).

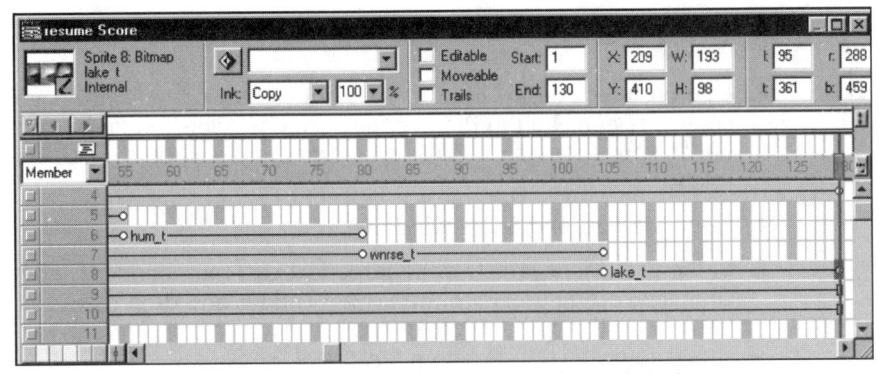

Figure 9-13: The animation sequence for the portfolio ends in frame 130.

8. Save your movie as **resume2.dir**.
9. Rewind the movie, and click the Play button to check the animation sequence.

The starting and ending point of the animation path for each of the thumbnail sprites is the same, which creates a consistent flow from one sprite to the next in the animation. The frame rate is a bit fast to really view the animation. In the section "Adding finishing touches," you'll adjust the frame rate for this movie.

Using navigation

The interactive resume in this chapter has three basic scenes. Each scene uses the same background for consistency and has a title with a highlight and drop shadow. In the following exercises, you'll create the other two scenes and add the navigation controls to make the resume interactive. With the exception of the background sprite in channel 1, the sprites have ended their life span in this movie. As you add the elements to create scenes featuring employment and educational backgrounds, you could place cast members in new channels after the existing sprites. Since you won't need the existing sprites in channels 2–10, however, it's easier and tidier to place the cast members in those channels as needed.

Adding Text to Your Resume

1. Open resume2.dir in Director, if it's not already open. If you haven't created resume2.dir in the previous exercises, you can find a copy of the file on your companion CD-ROM in the exercise:ch09 (exercise\ch09) folder.

2. Open the Cast and Score windows.

3. In the Cast window, select the three text cast members ed1, ed2, and ed3. Drag the cast members to the Score window, and drop them in channel 2, frame 131. The sprites appear in channels 2–4 (see Figure 9-14). These sprites form the title for the educational profile.

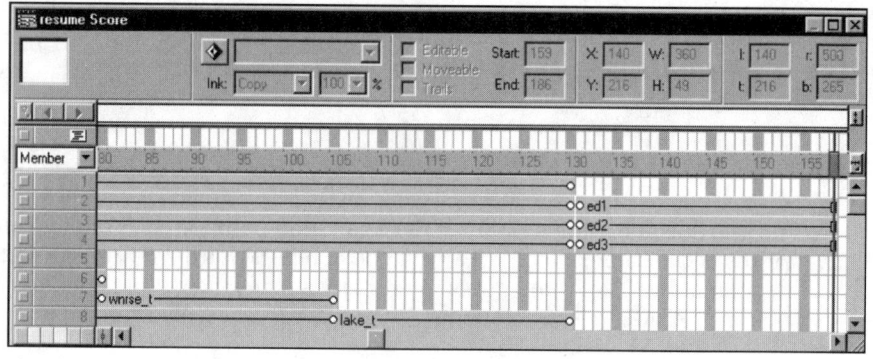

Figure 9-14: The sprites for the title in channels 2–4

4. With all three sprites selected in the Score, choose Background Transparent from the ink pop-up. The sprites are superimposed, so they will still appear as one sprite on Stage.

5. Select the tail frame of each of the new sprites; then click the frame bar in frame 135. Press Command+B (Ctrl+B) to reduce the frame span to five frames.

6. Select ed1 in channel 2. Press the down-arrow key twice and then the left-arrow key twice, to move the black drop shadow down and to the left.

7. Select ed2 in channel 3. Press the up-arrow key twice and then the right-arrow key twice, to move the orange highlight up and to the right.

8. Select all three new sprites in the Score. On Stage, click and drag them to a location near the top of the Stage (see Figure 9-15).

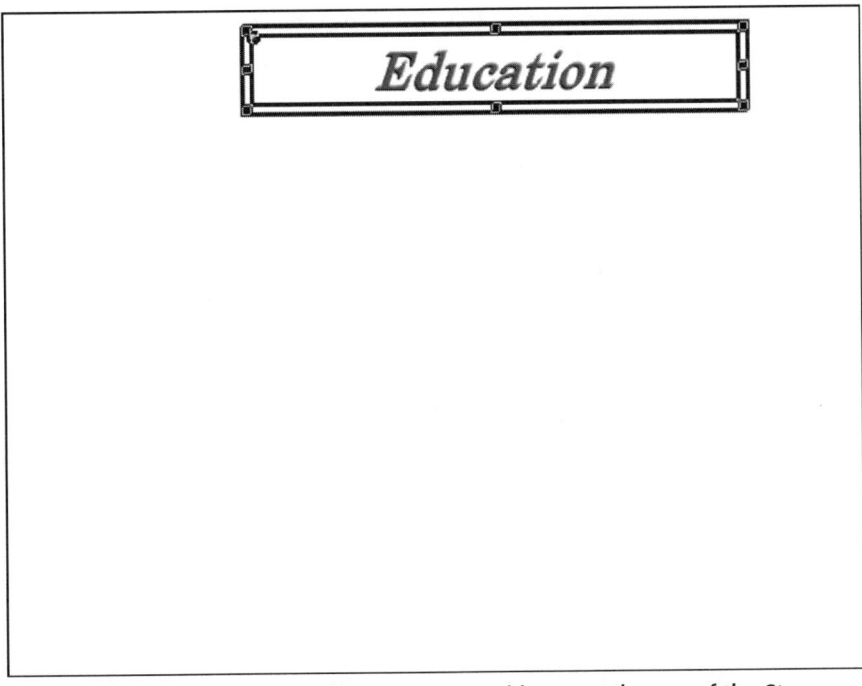

Figure 9-15: Click and drag the title up to a position near the top of the Stage.

9. Repeat steps 3–8 to place the cast members emp1, emp2, and emp3 in frames 136–140 of channels 2–4. Adjust the highlight and shadow as indicated.

10. Select the tail frame of the background in channel 1; then click the frame bar at frame 140. Press Command+B (Ctrl+B) to extend the background sprite.

11. Click and drag the cast member edstats from the Cast window to the Score. Place the sprite in frame 130 of channel 5. Adjust the sprite to span frames 130–135, and apply a Background Transparent ink in the Score window. Position the text so that it centers under the title.

12. Click and drag the cast member empstats from the Cast window to the Score. Place the sprite in frame 135 of channel 5. Adjust the sprite to span frames 135–140, and apply a Background Transparent ink in the Score window. Position the text so that it centers under the title.

13. Save your movie again as **resume2.dir**.

Using Lingo commands for precise control

If you rewind and play the movie at this point, it moves too quickly through the last two scenes to be read. You can slow the frame rate or add a tempo statement that pauses the movie for a specified period of time or a mouse click, but these options don't allow the user to review scenes without replaying the whole movie. The best option for providing navigation between scenes is the use of Lingo statements that enable you to control the playback head.

For those unfamiliar with Lingo scripting, Director provides a means of quickly adding a variety of navigational controls to your movies by using *widgets*. Widgets are small Lingo scripts with which you specify parameters to perform tasks such as navigation in your movies. The scripting has been done for you, so you only need to apply the widget and enter the parameters you want to use. The scripting and graphic elements of a widget are added to the cast of your movie.

In the following exercises, you'll apply a tempo statement and widgets to the interactive resume. The graphic element for the widget shows only backward movement. It needs to be edited in the Paint window to indicate bidirectional movement. When you first apply a widget, an instruction window tells you how to specify the parameters for the widget.

Adding a Widget to Your Movie

1. Open resume2.dir in Director, if it's not already open.
2. Open the Score window, and scroll until frame 130 is visible in the window.
3. Select Xtras ⇨ Widget Wizard ⇨ Widget Wizard to display the Widget Wizard window.

   Tip: You can get information about a widget by scrolling through the information box beside the active widget in the window. Most of the widgets are interactive, which means you can test them in the Widget Wizard to see what they do.

4. In the Widget Wizard, click to activate the Navigation tab (if necessary). Click the right-arrow button near the bottom of the Wizard window until the Go to Frame widget is visable, as shown in Figure 9-16.

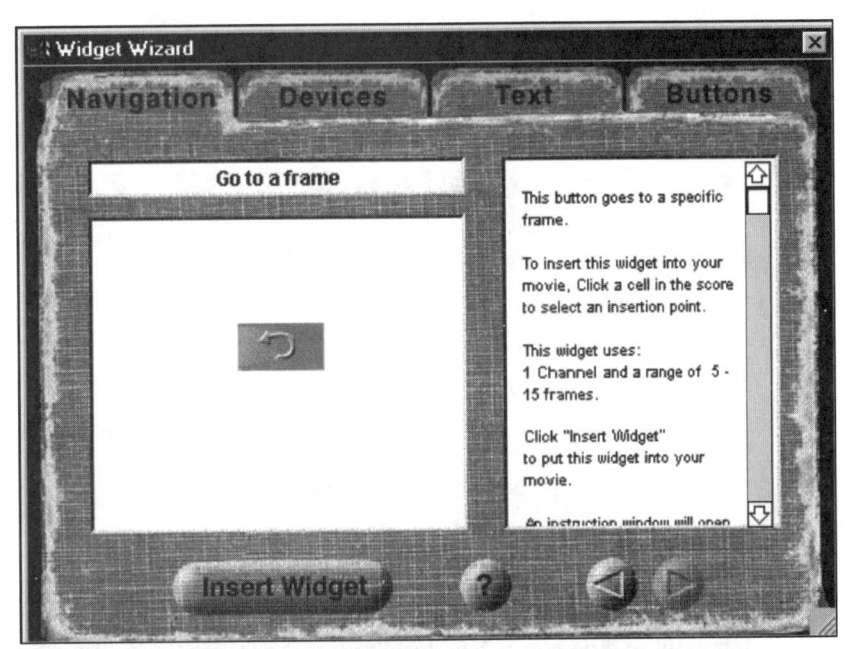

Figure 9-16: The Widget Wizard enables you to add elements such as navigational controls to your movies.

5. Drag the Wizard window to the side, and in the Score window click to select the cell at frame 131 in channel 6. Then click the Wizard window title bar to make it active, and click the Insert Widget button. The widget is inserted into the Score at the selected location (see Figure 9-17) and appears centered on the Stage.

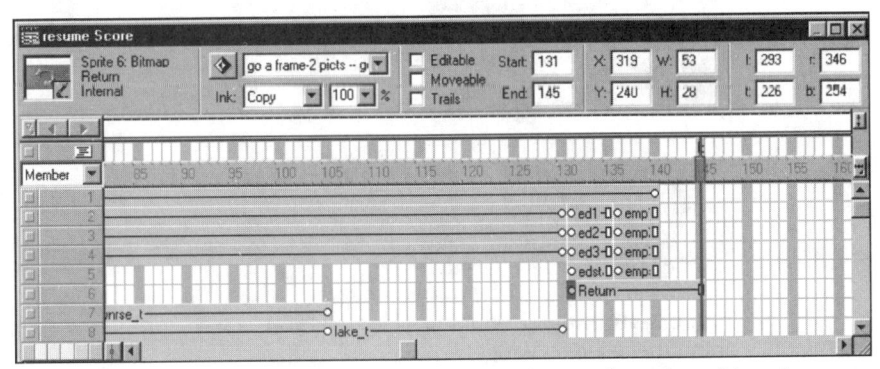

Figure 9-17: The Return widget in the Score window at the selected location.

6. In the Score, click the tail frame of the widget and drag it to the left until it spans frames 131–135 (see Figure 9-18). Move the script sprite in the script channel from frame 145 to frame 135.

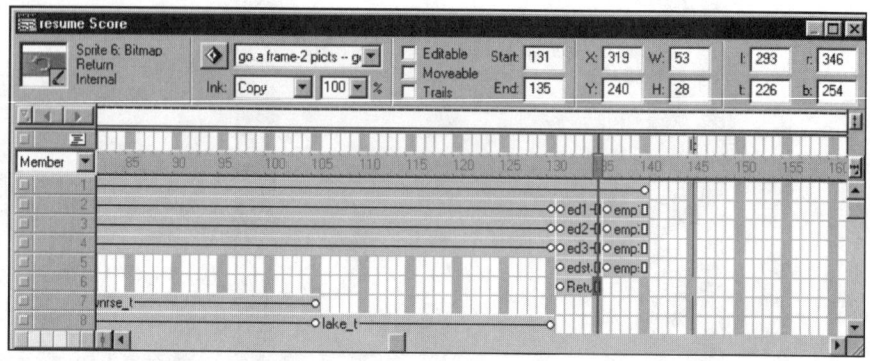

Figure 9-18: Adjust the frame span of the widget.

7. Select the entire widget sprite by clicking the center of the sprite in channel 6; then select Modify ⇨ Sprite ⇨ Properties. In the Location boxes, enter Left = **285** and Top = **435**, and click OK to complete the operation and return to Director's main window. The widget sprite moves to a location near the bottom of the Stage.

8. With the sprite still selected, select Window ⇨ Inspectors ⇨ Behavior. This displays the Behavior Inspector window (Figure 9-19), which provides information such as the widget's function or specific instructions attached to the widget.

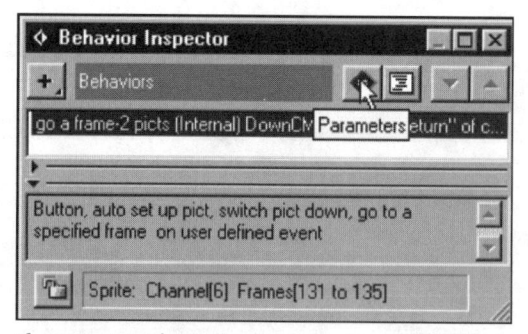

Figure 9-19: The Behavior Inspector tells you about the selected widget.

9. Click the Parameters button (note its position in Figure 9-19) to display the Parameters dialog box (Figure 9-20). Accept the default settings for the widget by clicking OK. If the movie is playing and you click the button in the last scene, the playback head returns to the beginning of the movie.

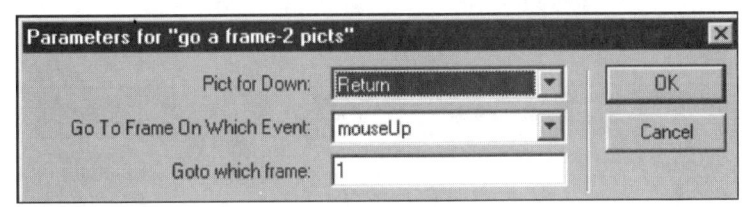

Figure 9-20: Entering the widget's parameters

10. Close the Instructions window for the widget, and close the Widget Wizard window.
11. Move the Behavior Inspector to the side of your screen by dragging its title bar. (You can close it, but you'll need it in the next exercise.)
12. Save the movie again as **resume2.dir**.

A widget, like a behavior, is considered a *scriptless* control that you can add to your movies. That's actually somewhat erroneous, because there *is* a script — in fact, sometimes the script is rather elaborate. A widget is considered scriptless because you don't have to write the script yourself. By choosing the parameters you want to use, you complete the instructions for the script, and it requires no further input from you as the author of the movie.

You can reuse a widget in other parts of your movie. By copying the widget sprite to another location, you can use the same parameters or choose new ones. The widget script is updated for the duplicate, without affecting the previous script, and added to the Cast window as a new cast member.

Duplicating and Modifying a Widget Sprite

1. Select the sprite in frames 131–135 of channel 6, and press Command+C (Ctrl+C) to copy it to the Scrapbook (Clipboard). Select frame 136 in channel 6, and press Command+V (Ctrl+V) to place a copy of the sprite in the last scene in your movie. Copy the script sprite in frame 135 of the script channel, as well, and paste it to frame 140.

2. Select the new sprite in channel 6, frames 136–140, and click the Parameters button in the Behavior Inspector. Enter frame **131** in the Goto Which Frame box, and click OK. If the movie is playing and you click the button in the last scene, the educational scene reappears.

3. In the Cast window, select the cast member Return. Press Command+5 (Ctrl+5) to display the cast member in the Paint window (see Figure 9-21).

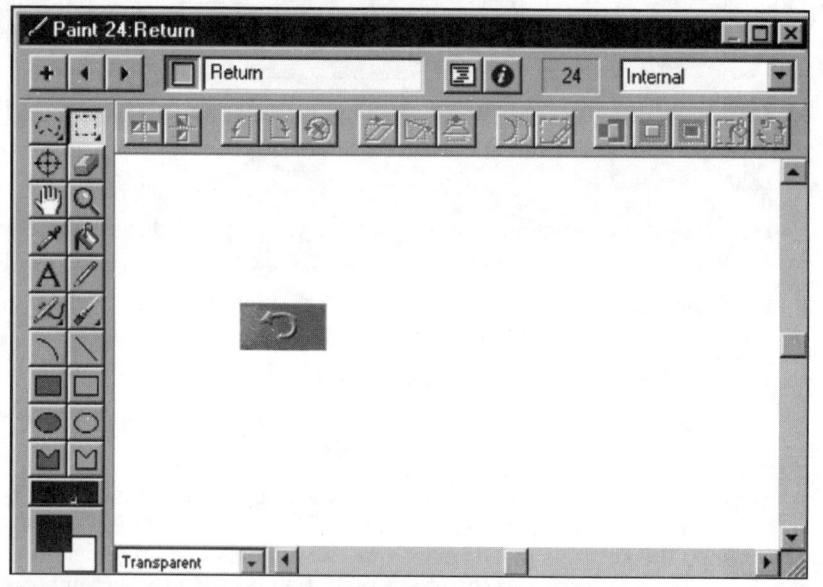

Figure 9-21: The cast member Return in the Paint window

4. Press Command+D (Ctrl+D) to duplicate the cast member in the Paint window.

5. Using the Marquee selection tool, set to Shrink select the Return button. Then click Flip Horizontal in the Effects toolbar, to flip the image horizontally. In the name box at the top of the Paint window, rename the button to **Forward**.

6. Use the Previous Cast Member button (see Figure 9-22) to locate the Return.Down button. Repeat step 4 to create a duplicate and mirrored image of the Return.Down button. Rename the new button **Forward.Down.**

7. Close the Paint window. The two new cast members appear in the Cast window (see Figure 9-22).

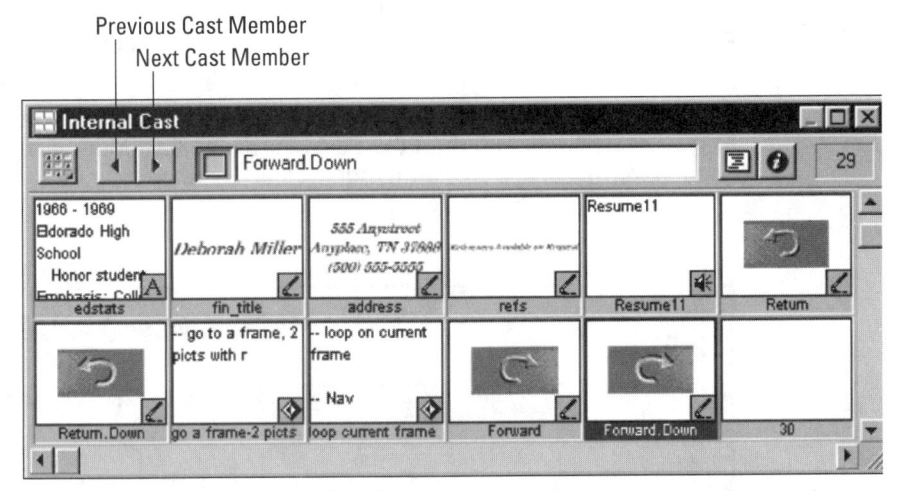

Figure 9-22: The new Forward and Forward.Down button cast members in the Cast window

8. Select the two Return sprites in channel 6 of the Score. Hold down the Option (Alt) key and drag them to channel 7. Duplicates of the sprites appear in the Score (see Figure 9-23).

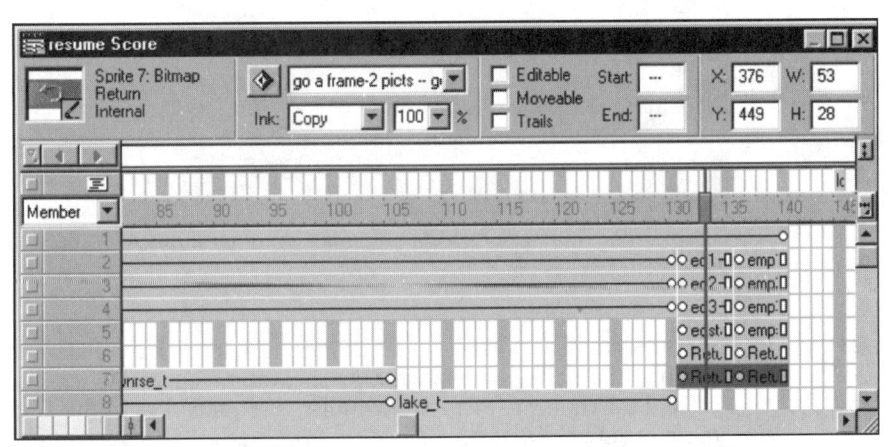

Figure 9-23: Click and drag the sprites while pressing the Option (Alt) key to create a duplicate of the sprites and place them in channel 7.

9. With the sprites still selected in the Score, select Modify ⇨ Sprite ⇨ Properties, and set the Left location to 350. The new sprites move to the right of the existing sprites on Stage.

10. With the sprites still selected in the Score, select the cast member Forward in the Cast window and then the Edit ⇨ Exchange Cast Members command. The Forward cast member replaces the existing image on Stage and in the Score (see Figure 9-24).

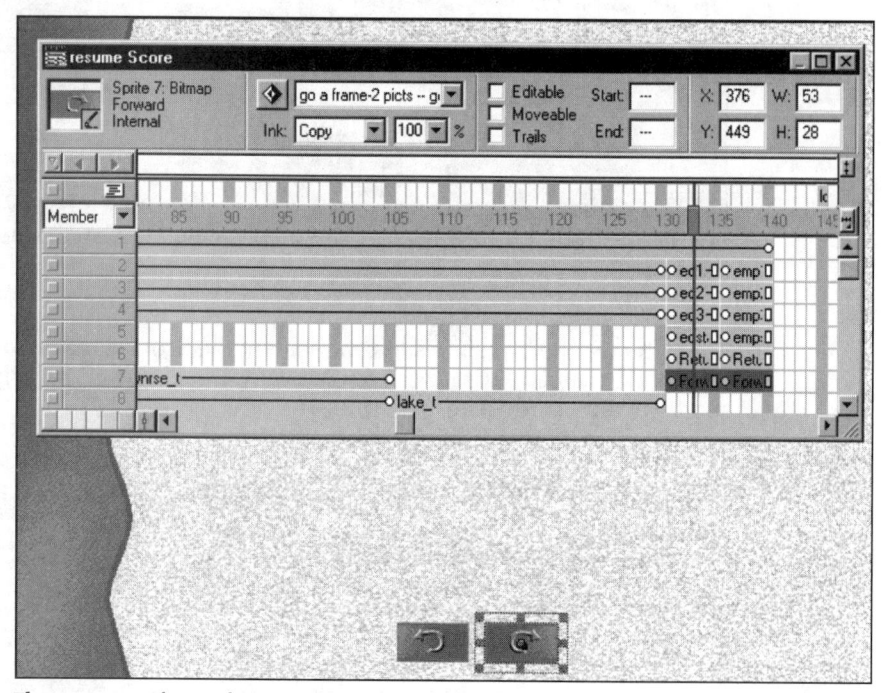

Figure 9-24: The Exchange Cast Member command has been used to replace the buttons.

11. Select the sprite in frame 131 of channel 7, and click the Parameters button in the Behavior Inspector. As shown in Figure 9-25, choose Forward.Down in the Pict for Down list, and enter **136** in the Goto Which Frame box. Click OK.

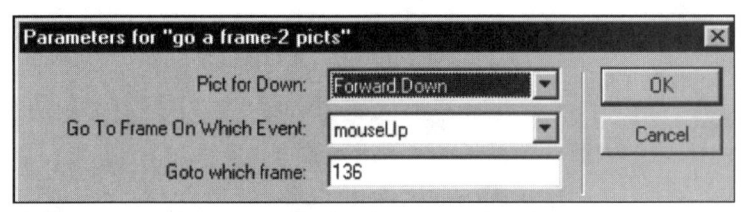

Figure 9-25: New parameters for the Forward sprite

12. Select the sprite in frame 136 of channel 7, and click the Parameters button in the Behavior Inspector. Choose Forward.Down in the Pict for Down list, and enter **141** in the Goto Which Frame box. Click OK. Then close the Behavior Inspector.
13. Save the movie again as resume2.dir.
14. Rewind the movie and play it. When the cursor changes to a clicking button, click to move the playback head to Scene 2. When the movie shifts to Scene 2, test the navigation controls.

The resume2.dir movie goes directly from the portfolio scene to the educational scene of the movie. This abrupt change is startling. By adding a transition and a tempo effect between the beginning portfolio scene and the educational scene, you can eliminate this problem. The transition effect is already in the cast library for your use. It uses a Bit Dissolve transition to move from one scene to the next.

Adding a Transition and a Tempo Effect

1. Open resume2.dir in Director, if it's not already open.
2. Open the Cast window and the Score; then scroll the Score until frame 130 is visible in the window. Expand the Score to display the Effects channels.
3. In the Cast window, select the transition cast member, number 11, and drag it to frame 131 of the Transition channel. The transition appears in the Score.
4. In the Score window, double-click the Tempo channel at frame 130 to display the Frame Properties: Tempo dialog box (Figure 9-26). Select the Wait for Mouse Click or Key Press option, and click OK to complete the operation and return to Director's main window.
5. Save the movie again as **resume2.dir**.
6. Rewind your movie and click the Play button to view the transition and test the tempo effects.

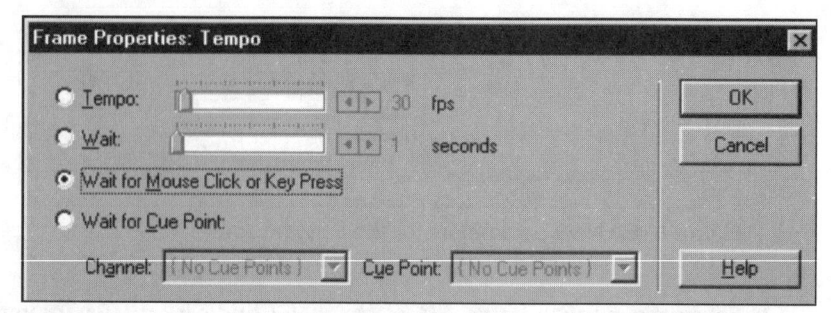

Figure 9-26: Select the Wait for Mouse Click or Key Press option to add a tempo effect.

Adding transitions smoothes the movement from one scene to the next, which gives your movies a professional appearance. Navigation controls that wait for user interaction allow the user to control the pace of the movie.

Adding finishing touches

The resume movie is nearly done. Although you could probably use it as it is, adding a few finishing touches will give it polish and help it leave a lasting impression. For instance, the name of the job applicant isn't visible during the two information scenes. In the following exercises, you'll add the name to the sidebar area of the movie so that it stays visible throughout the movie. Also, the frame rate of the animated portfolio needs to be adjusted to a slower pace and then set to resume a normal pace at the end of the portfolio. As a final touch, you'll add sound and a finishing scene that contains the name and address. The final scene fades to white using a blend effect.

Adding a Title Name, Sound, and a Tempo

1. Open resume2.dir in Director, if it's not already open.

2. Open the Cast window and Score. In the Score window, scroll until frame 131 is visible.

3. Click and drag cast member 6 to the sidebar area of the Stage, as shown in Figure 9-27.

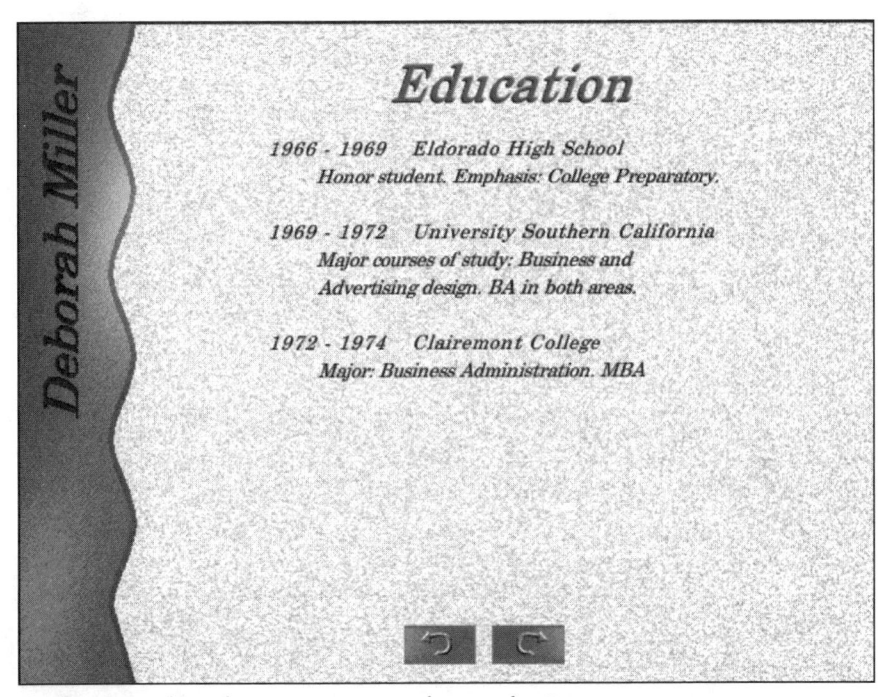

Figure 9-27: Place the name cast member on the Stage.

4. Select the tail frame of the name sprite and drag it to the left, placing the end of the sprite in frame 140.

5. Select resume11 from the Cast window, and place it in frame 1 of sound channel 1 to add background music to your movie.

6. Select the tail frame of the sound, and click the frame bar in frame 155. Press Command+B (Ctrl+B) to extend the sound sprite through frame 155. Press Command+I (Ctrl+I) to display the Cast Member Properties dialog box, and enable the Loop option. This ensures that the sound cast member will continue to play for the entire length of your movie.

7. Extend the background sprite, resume, in channel 1 to frame 155.

8. In the Score window, scroll to the beginning of the movie and double-click the Tempo channel in frame 1. Click the left arrow to adjust the Tempo value to 5 fps. This reduces the frame rate for the portfolio section of the movie.

9. In the Score window, scroll until frame 131 is visible, and double-click the Tempo channel in frame 131. Reset the Tempo value to 30 fps. This ensures that the movie will resume the maximum frame rate possible on the user's computer.

10. Save the movie again as **resume2.dir**.

Making minor adjustments like these and adding small details to your movie can mean the difference between a successful presentation and one that is blatantly unimpressive. One last touch is to add a final scene that fades — it gives your movie a nice graceful closure rather than an abrupt ending.

Adding the Final Scene

1. In the Cast window, select the fin_title, address, and refs cast members. Drag them to the Score, and drop them in frame 141 of channel 2. The sprites appear centered on the Stage, and in channels 2–4 of the Score.

2. With the sprites still selected in the Score, choose Background Transparent from the ink pop-up. This removes the white bounding box behind the text.

3. Adjust the tail frames of the new sprites to end in frame 155 (see Figure 9-28).

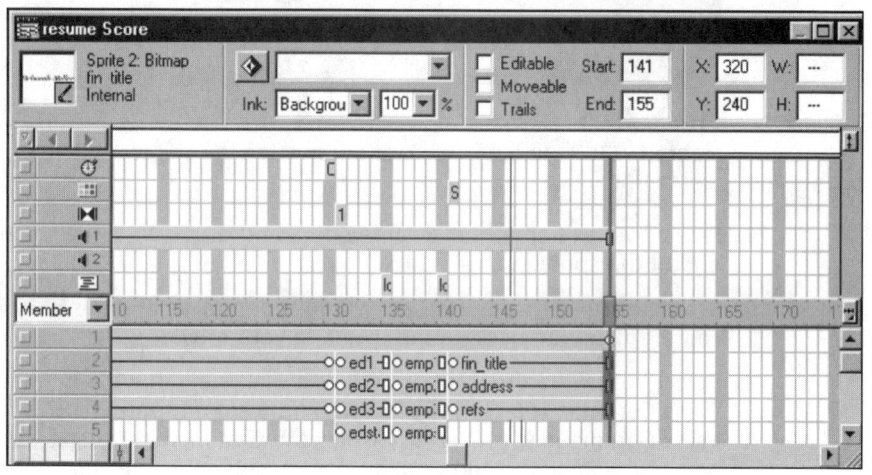

Figure 9-28: Adjust the tail frames of the new sprites to end in frame 155.

4. Select one of the three sprites in the Score and reposition it on the Stage as shown in Figure 9-29. Repeat this for the other two sprites.

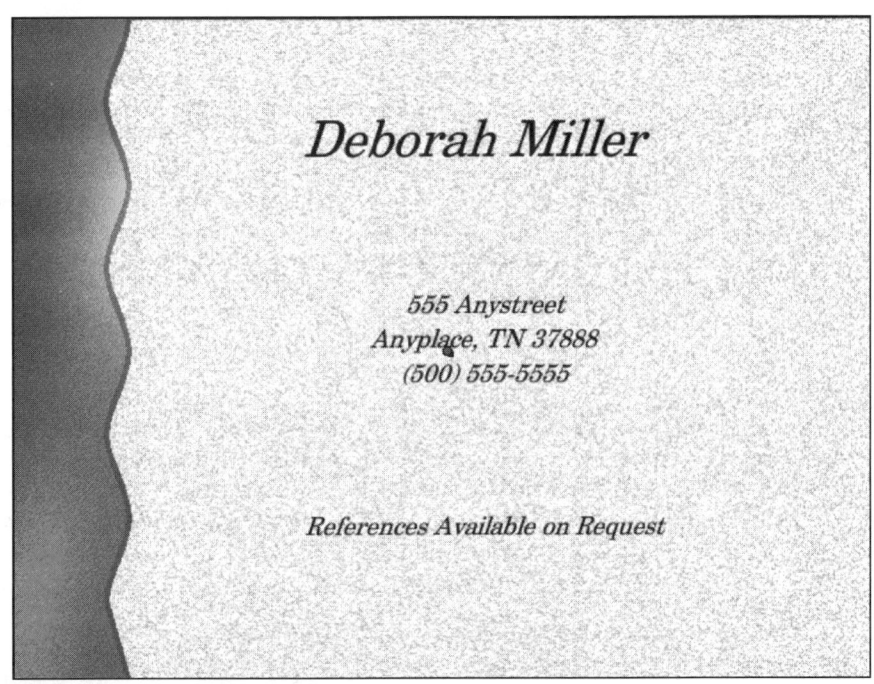

Figure 9-29: Reposition the sprites on the background to center them over the tan portion of the background.

5. Click frame 141 of the resume sprite in channel 1, and select Modify ⇨ Split Sprite. This creates a new sprite that you will use to add a fade at the end of the movie.

6. Select the tail frames of the sprites in frame 155 of channels 1–4, and select Insert ⇨ Keyframes to establish them as keyframes. Then select Modify ⇨ Sprite ⇨ Properties and set the Blend value at 0%. Click OK.

7. To select all four sprites in channels 1–4, press the Shift key and click between frames 141 and 155 of each sprite. Press Command+Shift+B (Ctrl+Shift+B), to display the Sprite Tweening dialog box, and select the Blend option. Click OK to complete the operation and return to Director's main window. This creates an effect that causes the movie to fade to white at the end.

8. Save the movie as **resume3.dir**.

9. Rewind the movie and click the Play button to test the movie.

The interactive resume movie is now complete and ready for distribution.

On the CD-ROM The resume movie is over 4MB in size; as a projector, it's approximately 2.5MB. A finished copy of both the movie and projector is on your companion CD-ROM in the exercise:ch09 (exercise\ch09) folder, under the filenames resume_f.dir for the movie and resume_f.exe for the projector. Obviously, both of these files exceed the capacity of a floppy disk. Ideally, movies that are larger than a single floppy disk should be distributed on CD-ROM. If you don't have access to a CD recorder, you can use a compression archive utility program such as StufFit or PKZip to create an archive file that spans disks.

Working as a Team

A popular stereotype of a programmer is a loner hid away in a cubicle, slaving away at creating the code that makes microchips sing and dance. Many newcomers do, in fact, approach interactive media production as a solitary activity, but it is not. Efficient programming, including the development of interactive media projects, requires a team effort.

The most successful multimedia development studios use a team approach that frequently includes the players described in Table 9-1. In some cases, a single person may wear several of these hats and fill several of these roles — not the ideal setup. In other cases, a specific role, such as graphic designer, may be shared by several people who form a subteam.

Table 9-1
Members of an Interactive Media Development Team

Player	Role
Project Manager	Also called Team Leader. Coordinates development activities and assignments, communicates with the client, establishes deadlines, and keeps the group "on task." In a small interactive media development shop, this role may be rotated among staff to avoid having one person as the Project Manager on all projects.
Graphic Artist/Designer	Develops the visual and interface design of the project.
Content Expert	Develops the project definition statement and learning objectives for the project. Responsible for identifying and collecting materials that form the informational core of the project. If the work is for hire, the Content Expert may be the client.

Table 9-1

Player	Role
Writer/Editor	Combines the content and supporting media into a single, unified project script. On a small development team, the Writer/Editor shares responsibility with the Programming Specialist for the development of documentation.
Programming Specialist	Codes the instructions for the project, based on the script, flowchart, and storyboards.
Audio Specialist	Coordinates the development of sound media; records, edits, digitizes, and collects the sound media required for the project.
Video Specialist	Coordinates the development of video media; records, edits, digitizes, and collects the video media required for the project.
Instructional Designer	Ensures that instructional outcomes are identified and are consistent with the project's learning objectives, learning activities, and assessments. Strives to ensure that the instructional activities are presented in an effective, efficient, and appealing way.

If your interactive media project does not have a complete team, the responsibilities for each aspect of development (content, graphics, audio, video, and instructional design) must be addressed by the existing team members. If you program alone, you are responsible for addressing all the needs of your project in all development areas; but you always have the option to hire services outside your "shop."

Using in-house versus contract sources

In addition to this bare-bones list, you are likely to need marketing, distribution, and sales people, or the means to accomplish these jobs. You'll also need someone to test the final product, checking it for errors or oversights. If you have the staff to accomplish all these tasks, or if you are a very versatile person, then fulfilling your production needs becomes less complicated.

When you have extremely tight deadlines to meet, distributing the workload can make the difference in your ability to meet a target date. Obviously, hiring outside contractors will help you in this effort, but it increases expenses. It's important to balance your needs, deadlines, and budget throughout the course of the project.

When you need to hire outside contractors to work on a project, it is critical to maintain a common focus and vision of the end results. Maintaining communication between the various individuals involved helps ensure the success of a team project. The coordinator or producer of the project generally has the ultimate responsibility for ensuring its consistency and flow.

Distributing the work

Managing a large Director project is much like conducting a symphony. Each instrument must play the correct music at the appointed time. Similarly, whenever a group of people work together on a single project, it's important to distribute the work so that the skills of the individuals are properly utilized, and so that each task is completed in the proper sequence.

It may not be possible for you to employ a team or even one or two other people. Take the artwork for a Director movie, for instance, which affects the overall appearance and design of the movie. Getting the artwork done is not simply a matter of designing it to fit the movie, however. Transitions and ink effects can alter the appearance or behavior of a graphic element. The designer, artist, and programmer all need to be aware of the limitations and possibilities that influence the final appearance of the movie. If tasks overlap, it's important that everyone involved in the project has a clear understanding of their role.

Understanding Copyright Issues

Copyright is a form of protection that is provided by the United States (and most foreign governments) to the author of an original work. An author can be an architect, artist, composer, photographer, publisher, singer, or writer. The copyright holder (that is, the author of a work) holds the exclusive right, according to the copyright law, to

- ✦ Reproduce the work
- ✦ Create derivative works based on the original
- ✦ Display the work in public
- ✦ Perform the work in public
- ✦ Distribute and sell copies of the original work

These rights must be specifically assigned, in writing, to you before you can duplicate a copyrighted image, sound, or text passage in any interactive media production.

A copyright notice is not required to assert the author's legal rights to original material. However, it is prudent to always include a notice of copyright; for example:

Copyright (C) 1997 by Jonathan Bacon, Deborah Miller, Kurt Cagle, and IDG Books, Inc. All rights reserved.

Ownership or possession of a work (book, fine art painting, limited-edition print, magazine, manuscript, photograph, sound recording, or video recording) does not give you permission to copy an item. For instance, if you purchase a limited-edition print, you do not have the right to scan the image and place it in an interactive media project. If you purchase a book from a bookstore, you do not have the right to use images and text from the book in a multimedia project. In both cases, you must seek permission from the copyright holder.

What can be protected by copyright?

Works that can be copyrighted include the following:

- Architectural drawings (blueprints, schematics)
- Audio visual works (films, video tapes)
- Dramatic works (pantomimes, musicals, plays, screenplays)
- Graphic images (cartoons, drawings, maps, paintings, photographs)
- Literature (articles, novels, poems, reports, short stories)
- Multimedia works (computer games, choreographic works, other products based on mixed media types)
- Music and lyrics
- Publications (books, journals, magazines)
- Sound recordings (cassette tapes, compact disks, phonograph records)

Publications of the United States government are not copyrightable and therefore are considered in the public domain; you can use these works without seeking copyright permission. This group does not include works belonging to the U.S. Postal Service, however. The Postal Service is an incorporated business and is entitled to copyright protection for the designs of its postage stamps.

Caution

Be extremely careful that you have not consciously or inadvertently included any information in your interactive media project that is the property of some other copyright holder. Obtain the required permissions if you want to use excerpts from textbooks, newspaper or magazine articles, material from other multimedia works, photographs, graphics, or other forms of media. The same restrictions and obligations that govern the use of print materials also apply in multimedia.

Copyright period

Copyright protection based on U.S. copyright law is limited to a specific period of time based on when the work was created. One of the following two formulas apply when determining the life of a copyright.

- If the work was created on or after January 1, 1978, it is protected from the moment of its creation until 50 years after the author's death.
- If the work was created prior to January 1, 1978, the life of the copyright is 28 years, and the author has the option to renew the copyright for an additional 47 years. Therefore, the maximum life span of the work is 75 years.

Fair use for educational purposes

Many colleges and universities have departments that product multimedia classroom materials for instructional purposes. In this regard, the following information describes guidelines for fair use of copyrighted materials in such productions.

The fair use provision of the Copyrights Act is found in Section 107. It states that the use of copyrighted materials for "criticism, comment, news reporting, teaching (including multiple copies for classroom use), scholarship, or research, is not an infringement of copyright." This provision was established at a time when the newest medium for copyrighted materials was the phonograph record. Further, the law predates the introduction of personal computer applications, including multimedia. Still, legal precedence suggests that the fair use doctrine (as a means whereby copyrighted works may be used for noncommercial, not-for-profit educational purposes) also applies to multimedia applications.

Note: If you intend to sell your work, read no further. Fair use guidelines do not apply to your application!

Although few written standards exists to cover the fair use of copyrighted nonprint media, most legal experts and students of copyright suggest that when you use materials to prepare multimedia courseware for instruction or classroom presentations, you should apply the same criteria as prescribed for the fair use of copyrighted print materials. The criteria includes the following characteristics:

- *Spontaneity*

The decision to use copyrighted material must be a spontaneous decision. For example, an instructor cannot use the same copyrighted material spontaneously for several semesters. The decision to use the material must be the instructor's and not dictated by management or administration (as a cost-saving measure, for instance).

✦ *Brevity*

When discussing print media, guidelines are very specific, even to the point of specifying the maximum length of an excerpt from poetry or prose. The intent is clearly to limit the use of copyrighted material to a small portion of the original work.

✦ *Cumulative Effect*

The fair use doctrine limits the copying or use of the copyrighted work in order to preserve the commercial or monetary value of the work to the author. Guidelines for copying print media limit the amount of information that can be used based on the fair use doctrine. For instance, the law restricts the educator from copying more than one short poem, article, story, or essay from the same author, or two excerpts from the same author in the same collective work or periodical. The limitation applies to using the material during any one class term. There are different considerations for integrated media; but in principle, the cumulative effect of any copying should not diminish the financial viability or rewards to the author.

As a developer, you can only claim fair use if the use of copyrighted material meets all three tests (spontaneity, brevity, and cumulative effect). In all other cases, you must procure a copyright release for the materials that you use.

The strongest argument for fair use involves use of the material in the following activities:

✦ The noncommercial use of copyrighted material for instructional purposes

✦ "Scholarly pursuits" (research and literary criticism)

✦ Copying modest portions of the copyrighted work for educational use

As a developer, what should you do?

First, when working with material that you, yourself have not personally created, maintain a record of each item you use in your project. Include the following information:

✦ The source of the asset (name of the book, magazine, publication, video)

✦ The author's name (artist, writer, cartoonist, illustrator, photographer)

✦ The copyright holder and any pertinent copyright information (address, phone number, year of copyright notice)

Note

Be aware that the author of a work may not be the copyright holder. Many authors create "works for hire" that belong to the publisher or their employer. Further, the copyright may be held jointly by two or more individuals, in which case permission must be sought from all owners.

Second, as soon as you know you plan to use a copyrighted work, seek permission from the copyright owner.

Finally, don't forget to protect your own creative works. Though not absolutely required, it is still wise to include a copyright notice in a prominent location on your work.

Note

Under the Berne Convention, any work you create is automatically protected even without the addition of the copyright notice. However, if an infringement against your work occurs, your case is strengthened when you enter litigation if the notice appears on your work.

Summary

The interactive resume in this chapter is rather simplistic. Despite its uncomplicated design, a number of steps are needed to create the finished movie. In a more complex design this process might seem daunting at first, but if you break a movie into a series of tasks, the creation process becomes much easier. Identifying the tasks is an important part of the design for any project. In this chapter you learned to

- ✦ Design an interface
- ✦ Logically approach the creation of a movie
- ✦ Add navigation controls to your movie
- ✦ Duplicate and modify a widget
- ✦ Animate thumbnail images
- ✦ Apply transitions
- ✦ Add tempo effects to a movie to adjust the frame rate
- ✦ Add interactive elements to a movie
- ✦ Duplicate and modify a cast member in the Paint window
- ✦ Create a fade-out effect
- ✦ Work in a team environment

✦ ✦ ✦

Speaking the Lingo

P A R T

III

◆ ◆ ◆ ◆

In This Part

Chapter 10
Scripting From Scratch

Chapter 11
Lingo Programming Building Blocks

Chapter 12
Writing Handlers

Chapter 13
Controlling Sprites from Lingo

Chapter 14
Text Manipulation with Lingo

Chapter 15
Sound Lingo

Chapter 16
Video Lingo

Scripting From Scratch

CHAPTER 10

In This Chapter

Explanations of events, messages, and handlers

Director's four script types

Composing your own scripts

Creating basic buttons

Using Lingo's fundamental navigational commands

To this point in the book, your exposure to Director 6 has been like visiting an unfinished furniture store. You can buy a nice deacon's bench or coffee table, take it home, then sand, stain, and varnish it, and finally use the object you've created. You know, however, that there's more to Director (and woodworking) than using objects other people have constructed and simply following the step-by-step assembly instructions. You know that the enormous toolbox called Director also contains a jigsaw, a table saw, and the ability to move beyond Score-based applications and prepackaged behaviors. This chapter opens the door to scripting your movies from scratch and escaping the confines of someone else's imagination. You're about to ease into the empowering world of Lingo scripting.

Event Handling for Fun and Profit

In the oldest version of Director, when it was still VideoWorks, the developer had no way to control the interaction between user and computer — the program was an animation engine, period. With the next iteration of Director, the engineers at Macromedia integrated into the program a primitive scripting language they called Lingo. The language didn't do a lot — indeed, the number of *keywords* in that version of Lingo numbered around 40 (keywords are the building blocks of the language). Today, five revisions of Director later, the keyword list has grown to something like 600+ commands, properties, methods, and events. This generous number isn't the only indicator of a language's power, but it does provide a benchmark for how much the language has improved since the earliest version.

For all that Lingo's dictionary of keywords has grown from a pamphlet to an encyclopedia, the basic model of how Lingo operates hasn't changed all that much over the years. Score-based Director movies are frame driven — the visible scene changes from one frame to the next. Lingo, on the other hand, is not. Lingo is *event driven*. Handling the events requires the creation of scripts that can be attached to the movie, to objects, and to specific frames.

Director uses four types of scripts, to which you can add functionality that is not available using the Score. Director supports *cast member scripts*, *movie scripts*, *parent scripts,* and *Score scripts* (which come in two varieties — *frame scripts* and *sprite scripts*). Beginning with Director 6, Score scripts are more commonly referred to as *behaviors* (see Chapter 6).

Director's Four Types of Scripts

Before you get your keyboard humming creating scripts, you need to understand the difference between the four types of scripts, the "effective domain" of each script, and how to create each variety of script. The best place to start is using Lingo's basic navigational commands to create a linear slideshow movie.

Note: Most of the navigational capabilities that you script in this chapter are available using behaviors. However, in this chapter, you gain a "behind-the-scenes" view that will free you from total reliance on Director's prepackaged behaviors.

Having four categories of Director scripts may seem unnecessarily complex until you discover how and why they are used. The primary differences among the four script types occur in the following areas:

- The script's *effective domain* (where it takes control)
- The placement of the script in a Director movie (whether it's attached to a frame, stored as a cast member, attached to a cast member, and so on)

- How the script is created (in the Cast window, Score window, or Script window)
- How the script is activated (by mouse action, system event, or playback head location)
- The system messages handled by the script (`mouseUp`, `exitFrame`, and so on)

In addition to creating these four types of scripts, you can use Lingo to define a *primary event handler*.

Scripting terminology

No matter what type of Director script you're discussing, three concepts are at issue: the event, the system message, and the handler. Let's examine what these terms mean.

An *event* is an incident in a movie that initiates the execution of a script. Examples of typical movie events include

- The start of a movie
- The point at which the playback head enters or exits from a frame
- The user's pressing of the left or right mouse button (on a two-button mouse)
- The user's release of the left or right mouse button
- The conclusion of a movie

Each of these events can cause the execution of a script. To signal the occurrence of an event and trigger the execution of a script, there must be a messenger, which is called a *system message*. A system message (usually shortened to just *message*) is a response generated by your computer system to a specific event.

The most frequently generated messages occur when the mouse button is clicked (pressed and released). Clicking a mouse button generates two messages, the `mouseDown` message (when the button is pressed) and the `mouseUp` message (when the button is released).

Note

Unless specifically stated otherwise, when we refer to a mouse click, we mean a click on the single mouse button on a Macintosh system, or a click on the left mouse button on a Windows system. For Windows users, if we refer to the right mouse button, we'll specifically call it *the right mouse button* and call the action a *right-click*. On the Macintosh, the right-click is simulated by holding down the Control key and then clicking the single mouse button. In this book, that action is also called a right-click.

Many events can generate messages, but unless they are intercepted Director will ignore them; the message is then passed on to the operating system and then to oblivion. Intercepted messages trigger specific actions as specified by one or more instructions stored in a *handler*. A handler is a series of commands (programming code) that together "handle" a message and invoke an action.

Handlers are stored in scripts. They begin with the keyword on and conclude with the keyword end. Following are two examples of handlers; the on mouseUp handler is listed first, and then the on click handler. (On click is a user-defined handler that plays an external sound; see the later sidebar "Building your own handlers.")

```
on mouseUp
      click
      go to the frame +1
end

on click
      puppetSound 1, "clickSnd.wav"
end
```

The on keyword tells Director that this is the handler for the mouseUp event in the first example and for a user-defined handler (click) in the second example.

The *body* of the first handler contains all of the code that will execute when the handler is called. In this case, the code calls another handler (click) and then includes the one-line go to statement.

The final line in a handler is the end statement. This acts as the end-bracket of the handler, telling Director that any code that follows it should be considered part of another routine. Note that this doesn't stop the Director program or projector that is running; terminating the program or projector is accomplished using a different keyword (two, actually — quit and halt). Instead, the end statement returns control to Director (or to the script that called the handler).

Figure 10-1 illustrates, in the form of a flowchart, a series of events within a Director movie. In this scenario:

- ✦ Events within a Director movie occur as the movie plays.
- ✦ Events generate messages.
- ✦ Scripts are composed of one or more handlers that respond to specific messages.

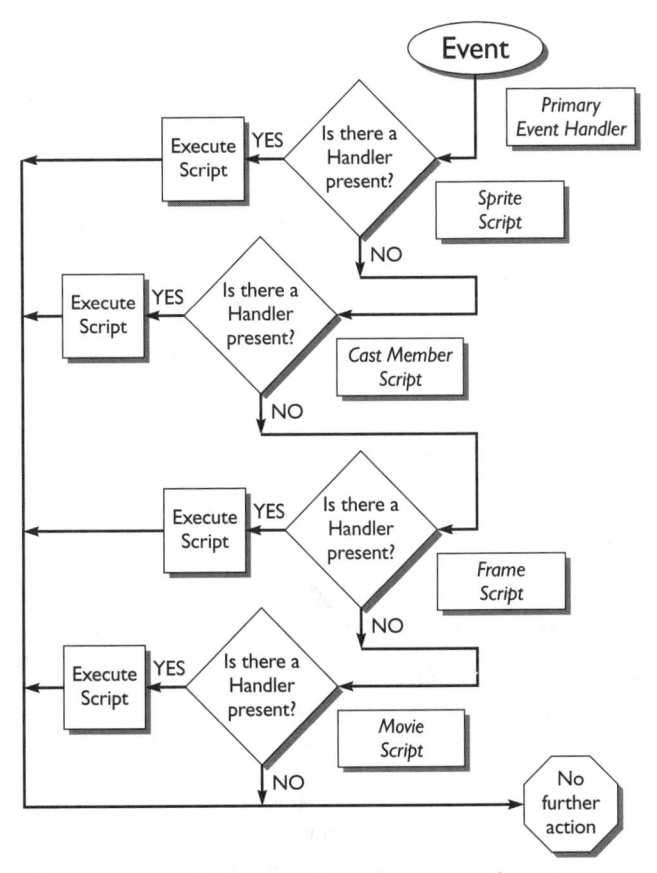

Figure 10-1: Path of events in a Director movie

As you examine Figure 10-1, you can refer to Table 10-1. It lists the system message in column one, the event that triggers it in column 2, and the type of script that can receive the message (in column 3).

Table 10-1
Messages, Related Events, and Script Types

Message	Event That Causes the Message to Occur	Script Type
activateWindow	A window is selected or becomes active.	Movie
closeWindow	A window is closed.	Movie
cuePassed	A cue point in a sprite or sound is passed.	All

(continued)

Table 10-1 *(continued)*

Message	Event That Causes the Message to Occur	Script Type
`deactivateWindow`	A window is deselected or becomes inactive.	Movie
`endSprite`	The playback head leaves the last frame of a sprite's span. An `on endSprite` handler is used to clean up after the sprite, restore properties, and compact memory.	Score
`enterFrame`	The playback head enters the frame, prior to the frame being drawn.	Frame, Movie
`exitFrame`	The frame has been drawn, but the playback head hasn't yet moved to the next frame. An `on exitFrame` handler frequently contains navigational information, telling where the playback head should go next.	Frame, Movie
`idle`	The movie has no other instructions.	Frame, Movie
`keyDown`	The user "presses" a keyboard key.	All*
`keyUp`	The user "releases" a keyboard key.	All*
`mouseDown`	The primary (left) mouse button is pressed. This message can be intercepted by the sprite or cast member over which the mouse pointer rests, or by the frame if you just want to capture a mouse click. For buttons, this can be used to change the button to a depressed state.	All
`mouseEnter`	The mouse moves into the *intercept region* of the sprite (usually the sprite's bounding box unless the sprite uses the Matte ink). For buttons, this can be used to change the button to a highlighted state. This event only occurs once, when the mouse first enters the sprite's intercept region and until a `mouseLeave` event occurs.	All
`mouseLeave`	The mouse pointer exits the intercept region of a sprite, regardless of whether the mouse button is pressed.	All
`mouseUp`	The mouse button is released. This event is sent only once, each time the primary (left) mouse button is released.	All

Message	Event That Causes the Message to Occur	Script Type
mouseUpOutside	The mouse button is released outside of a sprite's bounding box, after the mouse button was originally pressed while over the sprite. Similar to the mouseUp, this event only takes place once.	Sprite, Cast
mouseWithin	This event occurs repeatedly while the mouse pointer resides within the bounding box of a sprite. Use this event handler only when absolutely necessary, as the constant stream of mouseWithin messages intercepted by a handler can slow movie performance dramatically.	All
openWindow	A window opens.	Movie
resizeWindow	The user resizes a window.	Movie
rightMouseDown	The user "presses" the right mouse button.	All
rightMouseUp	The user "releases" the right mouse button.	All
spriteBegin	The playback head enters a frame containing the first cell of a sprite. (A cell is the intersection of a channel and frame. A sprite typically spans several cells.) Using the spriteBegin message is extremely useful, as it allows you to initialize sprite properties, make the sprite visible or invisible, and position it before it's drawn on the screen.	Frame
startMovie	A movie starts. Useful for initializing global variables and other moviewide resources.	Movie
stopMovie	A movie ends. Useful for cleaning up external resources and memory, storing information about the session, and otherwise putting everything away.	Movie
timeOut	Nothing is happening. This event measures a period of inactivity and is used to trigger another event.	Frame, Movie
zoomWindow	A window is maximized or minimized.	Movie

* If the keyUp or keyDown event occurs over an editable field, all types of scripts can intercept the message. If the event does not occur over an editable field, the message can only be intercepted by a frame or movie script.

Note: Director monitors a movie while it plays, watching for the `activateWindow`, `closeWindow`, `deactivateWindow`, `openWindow`, `resizeWindow`, and `zoomWindow` messages. Any of these events can be used to trigger the execution of a handler within a script.

Caution: The `startMovie` and `stopMovie` messages can only be intercepted in movie scripts. They should not be placed in any script other than a movie script.

Getting to know the script types

The four types of Director scripts are often confusing to the new programmer. If you focus on where scripts are created, what they're attached to, how they're activated, and which messages they are equipped to receive, the purpose and value of each type of script is easier to grasp.

Cast member scripts

A cast member script is attached to (stored with) the cast member. Cast member scripts include handlers that are executed in response to a message such as `mouseDown` (issued when the mouse button is depressed) or `mouseUp` (issued when the mouse button is released).

You create a cast member script by clicking the Cast Member Script button in the Cast window, identified in Figure 10-2. Once you click this button, the Script window opens (Figure 10-3). (Notice that the title bar at the top of the Script window indicates the type of script.) You can see that by default, when you create a cast member script, Director inserts the beginning and ending lines for an `on mouseUp` handler.

Note: If the Cast Member Properties dialog box is already open, you can access the Script window by selecting the Script button in that dialog box.

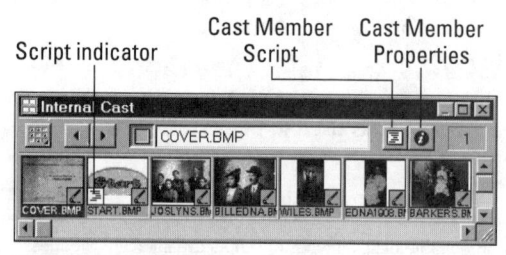

Figure 10-2: The Cast window

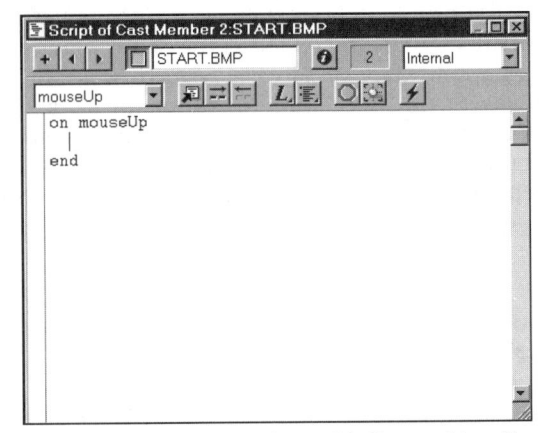

Figure 10-3: Script window with first and last lines of a mouseDown handler

You can see if a cast member has a script attached by looking at the cast slot that holds the cast member. The presence of a script indicator (as shown in Figure 10-2) indicates that a script is attached. The feature that displays the script indicator can be toggled on and off. Just select the File➪Preferences➪Cast command to display the Cast Window Preferences dialog box and use the check box for Show Cast Member Script Icons, as shown in Figure 10-4.

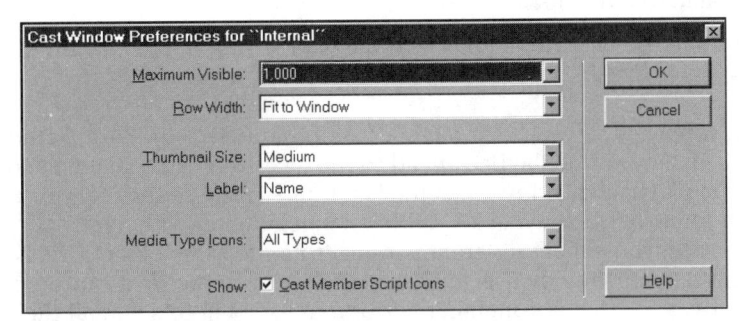

Figure 10-4: Cast Window Preferences dialog box

Score scripts

Director supports two types of Score scripts: the *sprite script* and the *frame script*. Both types are assigned to one or more cells in the Score window. As mentioned earlier, Score scripts are also called *behaviors* or *behavior scripts* beginning with Director 6.

Both frame scripts and sprite scripts (discussed in the following sections) are named Score scripts because they are created and edited in the Score window. (The Score window's title bar does not distinguish between a sprite script or a frame script.) When you create a new Score script, Director automatically assigns the script to the next available slot in the Cast window. The script number, which corresponds to its cast member number, appears on the Script pop-up when you open it in the Score window. When you edit a Score script, the changes take effect in every frame in which the original script appears.

Sprite scripts

A sprite script includes one or more handlers that are executed when a message is sent to the sprite to which the script is attached. The most common use of a sprite script is to check for a mouse click on the object and execute an action when the click is detected. If the cast member (from which the sprite was created) also has a script, the cast member script is ignored by Director.

Caution

It's very important to understand what happens when you attach a sprite script to an object that also has a cast member script. When both types of scripts are attached, the sprite script intercepts the system messages sent to the object. An attached sprite script, looking for the same system message as a cast member script (such as a `mouseUp`), always takes precedence.

A sprite script can be used to

- Script a different action in the same frame, for one or more sprites created from the same cast member.

- Override a specific occurrence of a cast member script, in the current frame only.

As an example, suppose there's a cast member script attached to a Next button that, when clicked, moves the playback head to the next frame in a sequence of frames. When the playback head reaches the last frame in the sequence, you want the Next button to move the playback head to an index frame (with a menu system). In this case, you expect different actions from the same object (the Next button). This is accomplished by assigning a sprite script to the Next button in the last frame — to override the cast member script that exists in this and all the other frames. You'll tackle this exact task in the later exercise, "Adding a Sprite Script That Overrides a Cast Member Script."

Note

A sprite is simply a cast member that has been dragged (placed) onto the Stage. The original cast member is simply a template for a sprite. Understanding the difference between a cast member (an imported or created object in the Cast window) and a sprite (an object on the Stage that is derived from the cast member) is crucial to understanding the difference between a cast member script and a sprite script.

As shown in Table 10-1, both cast member and sprite scripts accept the `mouseDown` and `mouseUp` messages. Sprite scripts can also accept the `keyDown` and `keyUp` messages if the sprite is an editable text field. The quickest way to create a new sprite script is to click the Script pop-up at the top of the Score window and select the New Script option (though you can also use the Script window to create or edit a Score script). By default, when you create a sprite script, Director inserts the beginning and ending lines for an `on mouseUp` handler.

Frame scripts

A frame script is attached to a specific frame in your Director movie. This type of Score script is executed when the playback head reads the script channel cell in a specific frame.

Though a frame script can receive and act upon most system messages, as shown in Table 10-1, the most common messages handled by a frame script are `enterFrame` and `exitFrame`. Frame scripts are created and edited in the Script channel of the Score window. By default, when you create a frame script, Director inserts the beginning and ending lines for an `on exitFrame` handler.

A typical frame script reads as follows:

```
on exitFrame
     go to the frame
end
```

This is one of the most common and useful frame scripts. It causes the playback head to "go to the current frame" (loop) until some other action is invoked (such as clicking a mouse button or pressing a key).

Note: Though the `go to the frame` statement loops through the current frame, it does not redraw the Stage unless objects change between each loop. In other words, Director only refreshes those areas of the Stage that change. Using the `go to the frame` instruction does not cause a loss in performance as other types of loops do — `repeat with` and `repeat while` statements, for instance, lock out any user interaction until they complete their work.

Movie scripts

A movie script is hardworking and robust — its effective domain is the entire movie. Any handler in a movie script can be executed or invoked from any frame within the movie. Further, movie scripts can include handlers that are automatically executed when the movie starts and stops. A movie script can accept and respond to all the events listed in Table 10-1. Movie scripts are also used to define and initialize global variables for use within your movie, and to store *user-defined handlers* (see sidebar, "Building your own handlers").

Movie scripts are created and edited in the Script window.

Building your own handlers

User-defined handlers are activated by a *calling statement* that may appear within any other script in your movie. You give the handler a name (such as `click`), and the handler is executed whenever called. For instance, the following cast member script causes the playback head to jump to the next frame and call the user-defined `click` handler:

```
on mouseUp
    click
    go to the frame +1
end
```

When the `click` handler is called, its instructions (stored in a movie script) are executed, causing Director to play a sound file named Click.wav in sound channel 1.

```
on click
    puppetSound 1, "Click.Wav"
end
```

Parent scripts

Parent scripts are special scripts used by Lingo to create child objects. Parent scripts are used in object-oriented programming and discussed in Chapter 18.

Tip: Frame, parent, sprite, and movie scripts appear in the Cast window as cast members while cast member scripts do not — they appear as an attachment to a cast member. Scripts that appear as cast members are accessible from the Script pop-up list on the Score window or by double-clicking the script cast member in the Cast window.

Which script has priority?

You may have noticed that all four script types can receive and act on some of the same messages (such as the `mouseDown` and `mouseUp` messages), and so you may be wondering what happens when handlers exist for the same event. What if a movie script has a handler that is meant to intercept a mouse click, as does the current frame script, cast member script, and sprite script? Which script gets control?

Messages generated by events in a Director movie follow a specific hierarchical path. There is no need to worry about duplicate handlers in overlapping scripts, because once a message is intercepted by one handler, it won't be passed to another handler unless specifically instructed to do so. The path of any event message is illustrated in Figure 10-5. In this example, the event is a mouse click, the message is `mouseUp`, and Director is seeking an `on mouseUp` handler to manage the event.

Handler

```
om mouseUp
    Do thisThing
    Do thatThing
    Beep
    Do someThing
end
```

mouseUp message

"Click" event

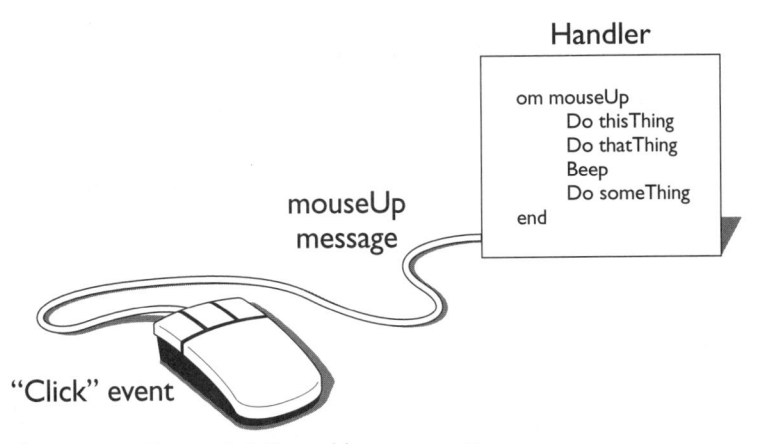

Figure 10-5: The path followed by a mouseUp message

Note

You can establish primary event handlers for four common events that generate messages in a Director movie (keyDown, mouseDown, mouseUp, or timeOut). If a primary event handler has been defined, the message is intercepted and the specific instructions in the primary event handler are executed instead of the handlers in the appropriate script in the message hierarchy.

Here's what happens when a mouse click occurs. This step-by-step explanation shows how messages are generated by events and passed to handlers.

- ✦ When the mouse button is clicked on the Stage, Director first checks to see if a primary event handler exists. If so, Director executes the instructions in the handler. No further action occurs unless the primary event handler instructions indicate another action.

- ✦ If no primary event handler exists, Director checks to see if there's a sprite at the clicked location. If so, Director looks for a Score script attached to the sprite. Remember, there are two varieties of Score scripts. In this case, Director checks for a sprite script that is attached to the cell that includes the sprite.

Note

If no sprite exists at the location of the mouse click, then Director immediately jumps to the frame script, to see if the frame includes a handler for the mouse click event. If no frame script exists, Director looks for a movie script.

- ✦ If a sprite script exists and it includes a handler for the event, control is passed to that handler. Director takes no further action unless instructed to by the sprite script. If no sprite script exists with a handler for the message, Director checks for a cast member script.

- If a cast member script is found and it includes a handler for the event, control is passed to that handler. Director takes no further action, unless instructed to by the cast member script. If no cast member script exists with a handler for the message, Director checks for a frame script.

- If a frame script is found and it includes a handler for the event, control is passed to that handler. Director takes no further action, unless instructed to by the frame script. If no frame script exists with a handler for the message, Director checks for a movie script.

- If a movie script is found and it includes a handler for the event, control is passed to that handler. Director takes no further action, unless instructed to by the movie script.

Tip

Visualize the script types as a series of safety nets, with the primary event handler being the first net, the sprite script being the second net, the cast member script being third, the frame script being fourth, and the movie script being the final net. If a script of a certain type exists, the net captures the event. If the script does not exist with a handler for the event, no net exists. The event jumps off a platform and keeps falling until it encounters a safety net. When a safety net is encountered, the event is grabbed by a handler that takes its message and executes a specific action.

Following are a few additional guidelines to help summarize the priority given to various scripts:

- If you click an object that has both a cast member script and a sprite script attached, the sprite script takes priority.

- If you click an object that has a cast member script and the current frame also has a script attached, the cast member script takes priority.

- If you click an object that has both a sprite script and a cast member script, and the current frame also has a script attached, the sprite script takes priority.

- If you click on an area of the Stage that does *not* have a sprite, the frame script takes priority.

- If you click on an area of the Stage that does *not* have a sprite and no frame script exists for the current frame, the movie script takes priority.

In the foregoing statements we used a mouse click as the event. The event could just as easily have been leaving a frame (exitFrame), entering a frame (enterFrame), no action (idle), the elapsing of a specified period of time (timeOut), or any of the other events listed in Table 10-1.

Whose territory is this, anyway?

The "safety net" analogy helps us understand which handler (in the case of multiple handlers) grabs the message and reacts to it. Another element of scripting you need to understand is which type of script to use so the script can receive appropriate messages. Every script has an effective domain — its "realm of control." Quite simply, a script attached to a cast member or sprite can only be called (executed) when the playback head reads the frame containing the object *and* the user interacts with the object. A frame script can only be called when the playback head reads the frame to which the script is attached (by "attached," we mean that the script appears in the frame's script channel).

On the other hand, movie scripts and their handlers are globally accessible from any sprite script, cast member script, frame script, event, or from any other movie scripts within the current movie. The beauty of this architecture is that you can define a handler in a movie script and then call that handler from any other script within your movie.

Tip

You can set up a user-defined handler to perform the same action when called from various handlers at different times during the playback of your movie. The instructions are the same each time the user-defined handler is called; only the variables change. This eliminates the need to create the same instructions over and over in the movie. See the "Building your own handlers" sidebar.

Composing Your Own Scripts

One of the most difficult steps in learning to use Director is to stop *reading* about creating scripts and start *doing* it. There is always that moment of confusion when you wonder what type of script is needed and where to start composing it. In the following sections, you'll learn the tasks required to create the various types of scripts, and review the situations that call for particular types of scripts.

Tip

To display the script in which a particular handler is defined, hold down the Option (Alt) key and click a handler's name in any script. Director will automatically open a new Script window with that handler. The original Script window remains open, but it may be totally or partially hidden by the newly opened Script window. If the target handler exists within the currently open script, a new window opens with the same script visible.

Creating a cast member script

The most common role for a cast member script is to make certain objects behave consistently throughout a movie. A perfect example of an object that needs this uniformity is the button — specifically, the navigational buttons (Forward, Backward, Home, Sound On, Sound Off, Index, and so on) in your movie. You'll want them to always behave the same, whenever and wherever they appear.

The steps required to create a cast member script include the following:

1. In the Cast window, select (click) the cast member to which you want to add a script.

2. Once the cast member's thumbnail is highlighted, indicating that it is selected (see Figure 10-6), click the Cast Member Script button.

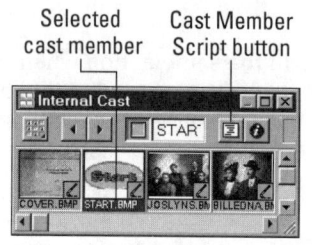

Figure 10-6: The start.bmp cast member has been selected.

3. When the Script window appears, type the text for the script. As you've already seen demonstrated, Director provides the first and last line of the new script. You can change the lines, but you'll often find that you only need to add the body of the handler.

   For example, the following cast member script is typical. It causes your computer to beep when the mouse button is pressed, and then to proceed to the next frame:

```
on mouseUp
    beep
    go to the frame +1
end
```

4. When the script is complete, press the Enter key on your keyboard's numeric keypad or click the Script window's Close button, identified in Figure 10-7.

Caution: Don't try to use the Macintosh Return key or the main Enter key on a Windows keyboard (the one just below the Backspace key) to close the Script window — it won't work. Instead, it adds a line break to the script in the window.

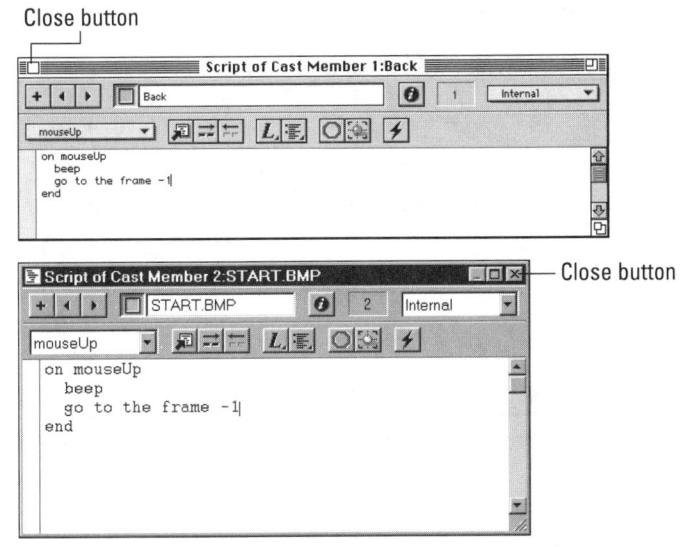

Figure 10-7: The Script window's Close button on the Macintosh (top) and on a Windows system (bottom).

Creating a sprite script

The most common role for a sprite script is to make a specific object behave differently in one frame than an identical object behaves in another frame of the movie. Sprite scripts enable you to handle the exceptions. When you want an object to behave the same way in all frames but one, attach a cast member script to the original object and then attach a sprite script to the object in the frame where you want a different behavior.

Tip Cast scripts are more efficient than sprite scripts when you want the same behavior for an object throughout the entire movie. Rather than attaching the same sprite script to multiple, identical sprites throughout your movie, attach a cast member script to the cast member on which the sprites are based.

To add a sprite script, complete these steps:

1. In the Score window, select the sprite to which you want to attach a script.
2. Locate the Script pop-up menu button at the top of the Score Window (see Figure 10-8) and click it to display available scripts plus the New Script option.

Script pop=up menu

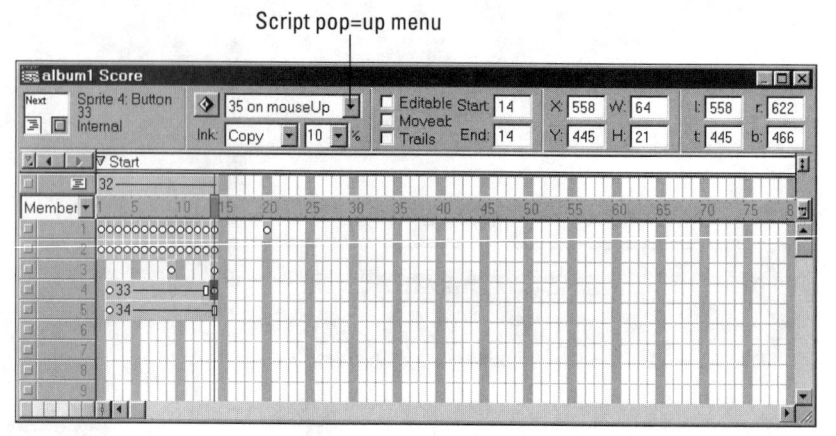

Figure 10-8: Click the Script pop-up menu to display a list of all scripts in your movie.

3. From the pop-up menu, select the desired script, or select New Script to create a script from scratch. For example, the following typical sprite script causes the playback head to move to the next marker in the movie when the mouse is clicked and released on the object:

```
on mouseUp
     go next
end
```

Tip

To delete or detach a script from the current sprite, select Clear Script from the Script pop-up.

4. When the script is complete, press the Enter key on your keyboard's numeric keypad, or click the Script window's Close button.

When you create a new Score script, Director automatically assigns a number to the new script. The number assigned to a new Score script corresponds to its cast member number. For example, if you create a new frame or sprite script and the next empty cast slot is slot 7, Director places the new script in slot 7 and assigns it that number on the Script pop-up menu.

Creating a frame script

The most common role for a frame script is to cause a specific event to occur when the playback head enters or exits a specific frame.

To add a frame script to a movie, complete these steps:

1. Locate the Script channel. Even if the Effects channels are hidden, the script channel is usually visible just above channel 1 (identified in Figure 10-9).

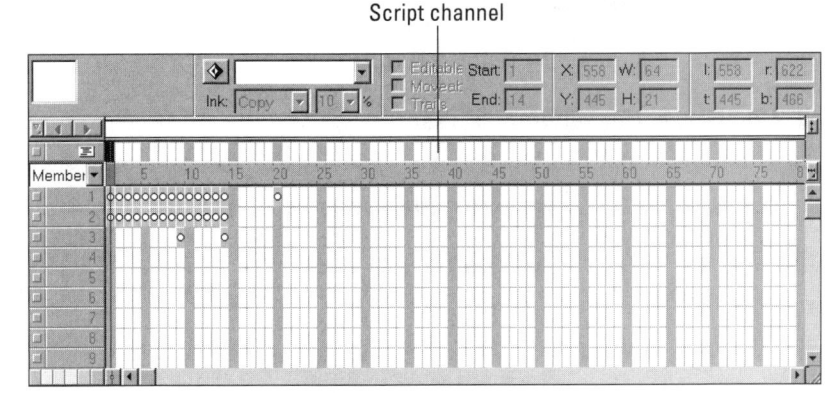

Figure 10-9: The script channel in the Score window

2. Select the script channel cell for the frame where you want to add a script.
3. At this point you can open the Script window using one of four methods:
    - ✦ In the Script pop-up menu (see Figure 10-9), click and drag until the New Script option is selected, and then release the mouse button.
    - ✦ Select the Window ⇨ Script command.
    - ✦ Press Command+0 (zero) or Ctrl+0.
    - ✦ Double-click the target script channel cell.
4. When the Script window appears, type the text for the script.

    For example, the following typical frame script causes the playback head to loop on the current frame until Director is instructed to do otherwise by another message. This other message might be to click an object (sprite) that includes a handler telling the playback head to move to another frame or marker.

    ```
    on exitFrame
         go to the frame
    end
    ```

5. When the script is complete, press Enter on the numeric keypad or click the Script window's Close button.

Creating a movie script

Movie scripts are commonly used

- ✦ To create a specific handler that can be *called* (accessed and run) from any frame in the movie
- ✦ To initialize variables

♦ To handle instructions that are executed only when the movie starts or ends

Here are the steps to create a movie script:

1. Open the Script window with Command+0 (zero) or Ctrl+0.
2. When the Script window appears, type the text for the movie script.

    For example, here's a typical movie script that creates a user-defined click handler that can be called from any script in the movie. This handler executes two commands (in pseudocode) called doThisThing and doThatThing:

    ```
    on click
          doThisThing
          doThatThing
    end click
    ```

3. When the script is complete, press Enter on the numeric keypad or click the Script window's Close button.

Creating an Interactive Movie

Multimedia typically features an integration of text, graphic images, sound, animation, and video in some combination. When navigating a multimedia application, the user expects to move freely from one segment of the program to another. This echoes the principles of *hypertext* and *hypermedia*.

Hypertext refers to a computer-based system that includes text-based links between related topics. The topics may be stored in several documents or within the sections of a single document. Hypertext enables the reader to access related information using nonlinear connections called *links*. The reader pursues topics of interest by selecting and jumping to and from linked blocks of text and linked documents. *Hypermedia* expands a hypertext document (or project) to include graphics, animation, digital video, and/or sound in addition to text.

Director can create hypermedia projects that enable the user to jump from one topic to any other topic within a movie. Yet you may want some of your presentation's content to retain its linear characteristic. Linear content may include credits, bibliographic sources, basic concepts (necessary to understand subsequent information), and operating instructions.

In this chapter, you'll construct a linear presentation. By using a minimal amount of Director's Lingo scripting language, you create a movie that can be explored frame by frame (sequentially) using navigational buttons.

Note

Before you start working at the keyboard, it is important to transfer your mental image of the project to paper using either pen, pencil, or the computer. On the computer, you can use tools to create a storyboard or flowchart.

A Director slideshow

The interactive movie covered in this chapter is a slideshow. In order to create even a simple movie with the capacity to move forward and backward one frame at a time, you must be able to do the following things:

- Import cast members such as graphics, audio, and so on (this is covered in Chapter 2)
- Place cast members on the Stage (also covered in Chapter 3)
- Create navigational buttons
- Assign scripts to buttons
- Save a movie to disk
- Open and run a movie

You already know how to accomplish all of these tasks — except for creating buttons and assigning scripts to them. We'll tackle that next.

Creating navigational buttons

There are several methods that you can use to create buttons (such as using an image editing program and importing the image). In this section, you learn to create standard Director buttons using the floating Tool Palette. Creating a button is only half the task. You must then assign a script to it if you expect it to do anything!

The steps required to create a button include the following:

1. If it's not already on the desktop, display the floating Tool Palette with Window ⇨ Tool Palette or by pressing Command+7 (Ctrl+7).

2. In the Score, move the playback head to the frame where you want to place the button. (To move the playback head to a frame, click any channel in the desired frame.)

3. Click the Button tool on the Tool Palette.

4. Move the mouse pointer to the location on the Stage where you want the button to appear. (Don't worry about the exact location; you can reposition it later, if needed.)

5. Click and drag horizontally to establish the width of the button. When it is properly sized, release the mouse button. (You'll be able to resize the button later, so just approximate the size.)

6. The button on the Stage is selected and looks like this:

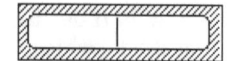

and you use it to type in the text you want to appear on the face of the button.

Note: The button's hash-mark border is the signal that you can edit the text on the face of the button. If handles appear around the button, it means you can move, resize, or delete it.

Resizing a button on the Stage

Once you create a button on the Stage, one of the most confusing tasks (until you get used to it) is trying to *resize* the button versus changing the text on the face of the button. What takes getting used to is determining when a button is selected for moving or resizing, as opposed to selected for modification of the text label.

Following are the steps for the easiest method of resizing a newly created button:

1. Deselect the button by clicking elsewhere on the Stage.
2. Click the button to reselect it. Figure 10-10 shows a selected button (with handles) and a deselected button. To enable you to clearly identify the selected button, we have turned off the Sprite Overlay display in Figure 10-10.

   When the button is selected, you can click and drag one of the handles to resize the button.

Stop — Deselected button

Go — Selected button with handles (the dark squares)

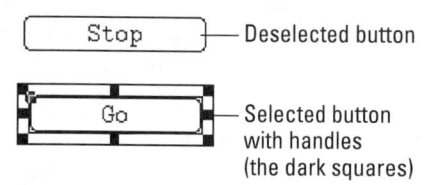

Figure 10-10: The selected button on the bottom displays the selection handles at the corners and on all four sides.

Changing the text on the face of a button

To edit the text label that appears on the face of the button, you must double-click the button. Once it's selected in this way, you can type over the text label to replace it.

Tip

It's important to remember that a single click selects the button so it can be moved or deleted, and a double-click selects it so you can modify its text label. If you are uncertain of the selected state of a button, click in an empty area of the Stage to deselect the button, and then do your single or double-click selection based on the task you want to perform.

You have a great deal of control over the text label on a button. For instance, you can split the text label over multiple lines by pressing Enter at the point where you want the text to wrap to the next line. You can also change the font, font size, font style, and font color for a button's text label. This is done by selecting the button and then executing the Modify ⇨ Font command from the menu bar. When the Font dialog box appears (Figure 10-11), you can change the properties of the text.

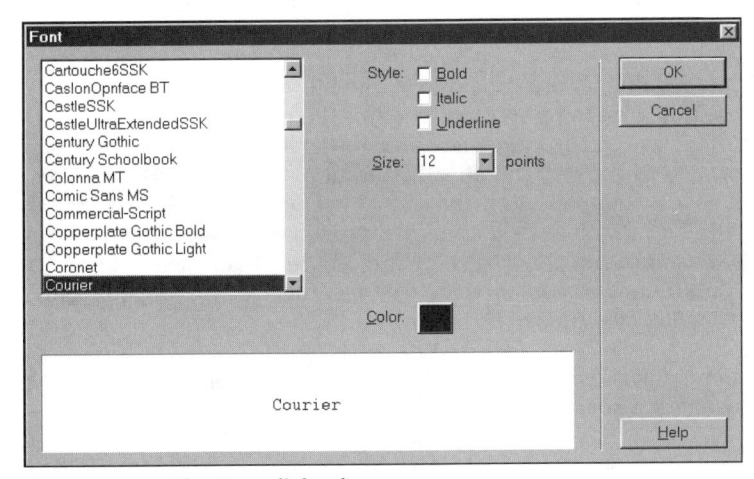

Figure 10-11: The Font dialog box

Tip

Another method of modifying a button's text attributes and properties is to Control+click (right-click) the button and then select the Font option from the pop-up menu. You'll see the Font dialog box as shown in Figure 10-11.

Changing other button properties

Some additional properties of a button can be set on the Button Cast Member Properties dialog box (Figure 10-12). To display this dialog box for a specific sprite on the Stage, move the mouse pointer over the sprite, Control-click (right-click), and select the Cast Member Properties option.

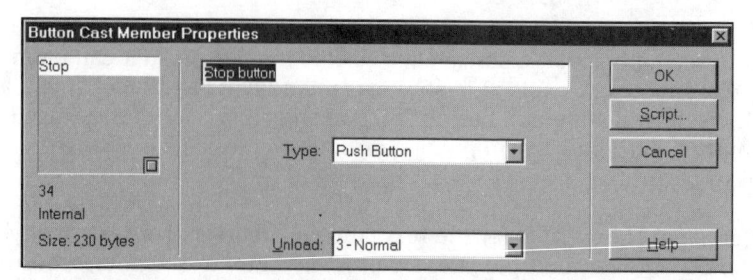

Figure 10-12: The Cast Member Properties dialog box for a button cast member

> **Tip:** If the Sprite Overlay for the button is visible, you can also display the Button Cast Member Properties dialog box by clicking the Cast Member Properties icon that is part of the Sprite Overlay.

In the Button Cast Member Properties dialog, the button is clearly identified by name and number, the size in bytes, and whether the button is stored in an internal or external cast. In the large view box on the left, you will see a script icon if a script is attached to the cast member. In addition, you'll see the name on the face of the icon — for example, "Stop" as shown in Figure 10-12. In this dialog box you can change the cast member's name, select a different type from the Type drop-down list (push button, check box, or radio button), and select an Unload setting (which determines when a specific cast member can be purged from memory in a low-memory situation).

> **Note:** The Cast Member Properties dialog box displays the properties of the cast member from which the sprite was derived.

Deleting a button

It's easy to delete a button (or any object) on the Stage. Make the Score Window the active window, select the cell that contains the object (or select the sprite in the Score), and then press Del or select the Edit ➪ Clear Sprites command.

Assigning scripts to buttons

We mentioned earlier that you have to assign a script to a button to make it interactive — that is, to make it do something.

> **Note:** Any object can serve as a button including objects created by the floating Tool Palette, imported bitmap images, backgrounds, and objects created in the Paint window. You can cause any object to act as a button by attaching an appropriate script to it.

Caution: It's best to identify buttons with text labels or symbols. Hidden or secret buttons are usually frustrating, not user friendly, and reserved for games of challenge.

Creating and Attaching a Script for a Button Cast Member

1. In the Cast window, click the button cast member to select it. The cast member's thumbnail will be highlighted in the Cast window to indicate it is selected.
2. In the Cast window, click the Cast Member Script button to display the Script window.
3. The first and last line of the default handler is provided for you in the Script window. Type the remaining code for the script.
4. When you're done typing the script, close the Script window. The cast member script is now attached to the cast member — wherever it is used throughout your movie.

Note: When you modify a cast member by adding a script, changing its appearance, or changing properties, the sprites created from that cast member are similarly changed. This linkage means that if you attach a cast member script to a button in the Cast window, that script is automatically attached to all current or future sprites based on that cast member.

Understanding Basic Navigation

One of the basic tasks of multimedia development is to give users the ability to navigate through a product. Navigation means *control*. As you plan and build your Director movie, you must consider how you want to enable and facilitate navigation.

Clicking a button to *go somewhere* within a project is familiar and well established as a traditional navigation action, but behind the scenes (in your script) how does that work? This section explains the fundamentals of this process.

When you play a movie, it runs continuously from the first frame to the last (this is Director's default approach to displaying objects in each frame). Just like projecting a film or playing a video, the movie runs continuously from the beginning to the end unless the film or tape breaks, the projector or VCR is turned off, or another event occurs (such as the Rewind or Fast Forward button being pressed).

If you want something other than the normal start-to-finish playback, you can cause the movie to loop within a specific frame until the user interacts with the movie. The most common type of event that breaks out of the loop is when the user clicks a button or an object on the Stage. A single click of the mouse button can cause the playback head to do any of these things:

- *Jump to another frame (using the* `go` *command).* The user clicks on a button or other object with a script attached, and the movie jumps to another frame where it loops until the user interacts with the movie (by clicking another button or object). Or the movie can simply continue running sequentially from the frame to which the playback head jumped, until the end of the movie.

- *Jump to another frame and then return to the original frame (using the* `play` *command (and optionally, the* `play done` *command).* In Director, this is called *branching.* The playback head jumps to a specific frame or sequence of frames. When that sequence completes, the playback head returns to the original frame (the frame where the user clicked the button). Programmers call this a *subroutine.* In Director, a subroutine can be one or more frames in length.

- *Jump to the previous frame containing a marker (using the* `go loop` *command).* In this case, a specific sequence of frames repeats until some other action is called for by the user. This is often used in kiosks, to display instructions or an opening animation while the system idles (waits for user interaction).

Why you should use markers instead of frames

Every developer has his or her own style, but there are certain techniques in working with Director that, in exchange for a little up-front work, will save you many headaches down the road. One of these techniques is *implementation independence.* This mouthful of a term describes a fairly simple concept: When you are designing your movies, behaviors, handlers, and Shockwave animations, you should create them so that you never rely directly on a specific sprite number, cast number, or frame number.

Frames and markers are a case in point. Suppose you have a button that jumps to a specific frame in the Score, using the navigation instruction `go to Frame 15`. If you ever need to add or delete frames in the Score, you will also have to change every reference to the old frame 15 and every other repositioned frame. For one or two buttons this might not be a problem, but a typical Director application can incorporate hundreds of buttons. It is better to identify the target of a navigation instruction as a marker rather than a frame, such as `go to "Boom"` rather than `go to frame 15`. The marker can then be moved as needed, and all of your references will change automatically when it does.

Chapter 6 tells you how to add, name, and delete markers.

Lingo navigation commands

Each of the "jump to" scenarios described in the preceding section uses one of two common navigational Lingo commands: `go` and `play`.

Using the `go` command

The various forms of the `go` command are listed in Table 10-2.

Note: In each of the command forms listed in Table 10-2, the word `to` is optional but frequently used for clarity.

Table 10-2
Forms of the `go` Command

Form of `go` Command	Action	Notes
`go to frame 100`	Jumps to frame 100 in the current movie.	The number is *not* relative to the current frame but rather refers to the absolute frame number. The command `go to frame 100` can be abbreviated `go 100`. The `to` and `frame` elements are both optional; `frame` is only required when using the `frame` function.
`go to the frame`	Loops to the current frame.	The `frame` function always returns a value representing the *current frame* displayed on the Stage. This command form is used to cause the playback head to loop on the current frame.
`go to the frame +1`	Moves the playback head to the next frame.	The number can be any positive value (to move toward the end of the movie) or any negative value (to move toward the beginning of the movie). For instance, `go to the frame +1` moves the playback head to the previous frame.

(continued)

Table 10-2 *(continued)*

Form of go **Command**	Action	Notes
`go to frame "Start"`	Jumps to the frame with the marker "Start."	Can be abbreviated to `go "Start"` because both `to` and `frame` are optional in this case
`go loop`	Jumps to the first marker previous to the current frame.	Caution: If frame 20 includes a script that tells the playback head to `go loop`, and frame 5 has a marker and there are no markers in frames 6 through 20, when the playback head reaches frame 20 it will jump to frame 5 and replay frames 5 through 20. When it hits frame 20 again, it will loop back to frame 5. This creates a continuous loop, which can be useful — unless you forget to include a handler that exits the loop!
`go to marker (+1)`	Jumps to the next marker not associated with the current frame.	The number can be positive (to move toward the end of the movie) or negative (to move toward the beginning of the movie).
`go previous`	Jumps to the previous marker not associated with the current frame.	`Previous` is a keyword that represents the previous marker in the current movie, *not* the previous frame.
`go movie "part2.dir"`	Jumps to a second movie and begins playing that movie.	The name of the target movie must be in double quotation marks. The filename extension is optional (if no other files exist in the target folder that might be mistaken for a movie file). Director makes the following assumptions about filename extensions: .dir = movie files (standard movie, uncompressed) .dcr = Shockwave movie .dxr = compressed, protected Director movie

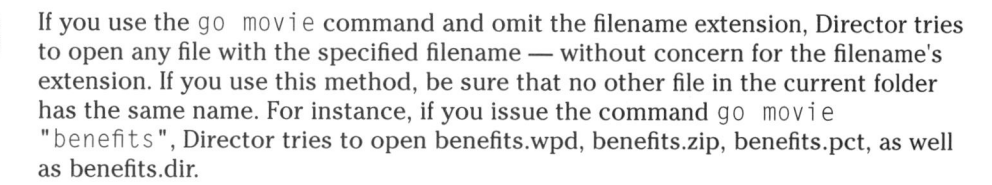

Caution: If you use the `go movie` command and omit the filename extension, Director tries to open any file with the specified filename — without concern for the filename's extension. If you use this method, be sure that no other file in the current folder has the same name. For instance, if you issue the command `go movie "benefits"`, Director tries to open benefits.wpd, benefits.zip, benefits.pct, as well as benefits.dir.

Note: Once you execute the `go movie` command (to jump from the first movie to another movie), the playback head does not automatically return to the first movie unless you specifically tell it to by using a `go movie` command at the end of the second movie.

Using the `play` command

The `go` command is a one-way street (unless you use a second `go` command to return to the original frame or movie). In contrast, the `play` and `play done` commands can be used for a complete round-trip. The `play` command sends the playback head to a specified frame. The playback head then continues playing frames from the target location to the end of the movie — or until the `play done` command is encountered in a script. The `play done` command sends the playback head back to the frame where the original `play` command was issued.

In addition to using the `play` command to send the playback head to a specific frame, you can use it to send the playback head to a specific marker, to another movie, or to a specific frame or marker within another movie.

Common forms of the `play` command are listed in Table 10-3.

Table 10-3
Common Forms of the `play` Command

Command Form	Action
`play frame "Glossary"`	Jumps to and starts playing the frame with the marker "Glossary."
`play frame 20`	Jumps to and starts playing frame 20.
`play "Credits"`	Jumps to and starts playing the frame with the marker "Credits."
`play movie "helps"`	Jumps to and starts playing the movie helps.dir.
`play frame "Glossary" of movie "helps"`	Jumps to and starts playing the frame with the marker "Glossary" in the helps.dir movie.

The `play done` form of the command is demonstrated in the following `on mouseUp` handler. Remember, it signals the end of the subroutine and causes the playback head to return to the frame where the `play` command was originally issued.

```
On mouseUp
        play done
end
```

When creating a Score-based animation, the `play` and `play done` command combination can be very helpful. It causes the playback head to jump from the current frame to a separate segment of the movie (operating like a subroutine) and then return to the "calling" frame.

In order to create a digital photo album (or any type of slideshow of sequential images), you must cause the playback head to pause after displaying sprites in the current frame. In the following exercise, you use the album.dir movie that initially runs from start to finish without pausing for you to read the text. If you press the Control Panel Loop button (turn it on), the movie continues repeating until you stop it by pressing Command+Period (.) on the Mac or Ctrl+Period (.) in Windows, or Esc.

In the following steps, you'll add a script to each frame (1 through 14), which causes the movie to loop on the current frame. You can create the required script in the first frame and then copy it to all other frames in the movie. When done, you'll be able to "page through" the album using the new navigational buttons.

On the CD-ROM The file album.dir can be found on your companion CD-ROM in the exercise:ch10 (exercise\ch10) folder. The movie includes several sepia-tone family history images with bitmap text.

Causing a Movie to Pause after Every Frame

1. Open the album.dir movie in Director.
2. Close all open windows, run the movie, and observe its behavior.
3. Stop the movie and open the Score window.
4. Double-click in the script channel cell in frame 1.
5. When the Script window opens, type **go to the frame**. Your screen will look like Figure 10-13.

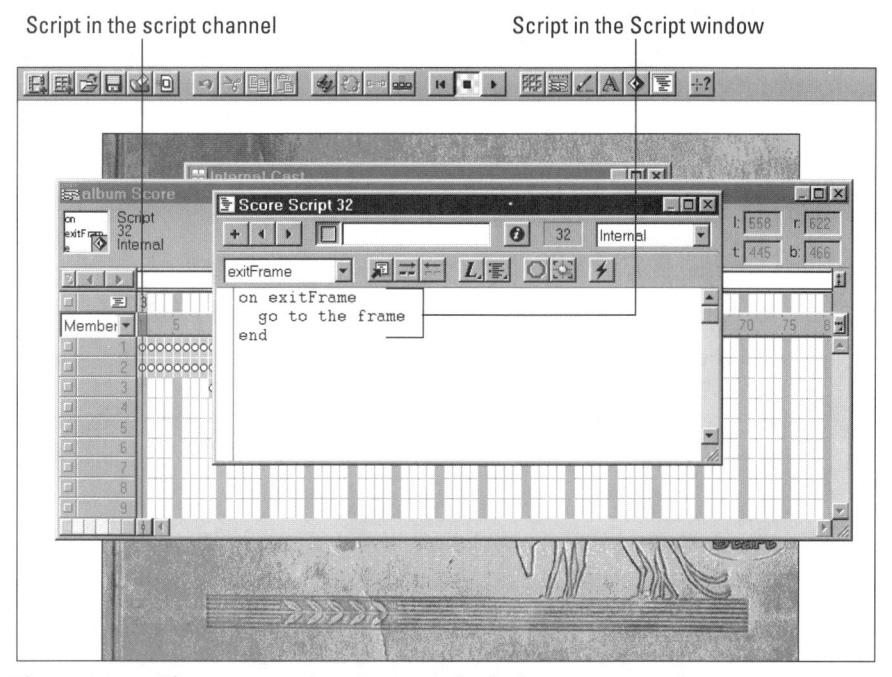

Figure 10-13: The `go to the frame` script in frame 1

6. Press Enter on the numeric pad to close the Script window. (The script channel cell in frame 1 should still be selected.)

7. Now you need to duplicate the script to the next 13 cells in the script channel. Press the Shift key and click the script channel cell in frame 14. All cells in the script channel, from frame 1 to 14, should be selected.

8. Select Modify⇨Extend Sprite or press Command+B (Ctrl+B) to extend the script sprite in frame 1 through the next 13 cells in the script channel.

9. Rewind the movie and play it. The movie stops at frame 1, because you have caused it to loop on frame 1 and have not provided a method for the movie to proceed beyond that frame in the movie.

10. Save the movie as **album1.dir** and use this file in the next exercise.

In the next exercise, you'll add a script to the Start button cast member (cast member 2). Because the sprite in frame 1 is based on cast member 2, the user will be able to click the Start button, and the playback head will move to the next frame in the movie.

Adding a Script to a Button to Move to the Next Frame

1. Open the album1.dir movie that you created in the previous exercise. You have already added the scripts that cause the playback head to loop on each frame.

2. If it's not already open, open the Cast window and select cast member 2 (start.bmp).

3. Click the Cast Member Script button in the Cast window.

4. The beginning and ending lines of an `on mouseUp` handler appear in the Script window. To complete the script, type

    ```
    go the frame +1
    ```

    between the two existing lines of the handler.

5. Close the Script window by pressing Enter on the numeric pad.

6. Save the movie again as album1.dir, and rewind the movie.

7. Play the movie. On the album cover, click the Start button. The movie proceeds to frame 2 and then stops.

8. Since no buttons are available in frame 2 to let you proceed or quit, you must press Esc to stop the movie.

9. Rewind the movie, start it again, and this time click anywhere on the album cover *except* the Start button. Nothing happens, because you have only attached the script (that moves the playback head to the next frame) to the Start button. Stop the movie again.

Now, in the next set of steps, you'll create the Next and Previous buttons for each frame in the movie. The Stage is arranged so that the bottom-right of each frame has space for these two buttons to reside side-by-side in the same location (in each frame).

By default, when you use the floating Tool Palette to create a button, the text appears in black with a black button outline on a white background. Since the target Stage color is black, we want the text to contrast, so in this exercise you will set the foreground color to white and the background color to black. The border for the button will be lost (black on black doesn't show), but that's okay in this case.

Creating Buttons Using the Tool Palette

1. Open the album1.dir movie you've been working with, which now has a Start button.
2. Click the empty cell at the intersection of channel 4 and frame 2.
3. If it's not already visible, open the Tool Palette by pressing Command+7 (Ctrl+7).
4. Using the Tool Palette color chips, set the foreground color to white and the background color to black.

   Tip: White is the first color on the System-Win and System-Mac palettes, and black is the last color.

5. Select the Button tool, and move the mouse pointer to the bottom-right corner of the Stage. (You may need to reposition some windows to have a clear view of that corner.) Click and drag to create a button slightly larger than one-half inch wide.
7. While the mouse pointer is over the new button, Control-click (right-click) to display the pop-up menu.
8. From the pop-up, choose the Font option. (Note: Mac users will need to drag down to the triangle at the bottom of the menu so it extends to show the Font option.)
9. In the Font dialog box, set the font to Arial (or Helvetica) and the font size to 14 points. Click OK.
10. Type **Next** as the text label for the button, and then click the Stage but away from the button to deselect it.
11. Click the Button tool again and create another button slightly to the left of the Next button. Label the new button **Previous,** as shown in Figure 10-14.
12. Be sure the two buttons do not overlap. To check, click the Next button, hold down the Shift key, and then click the Previous button. The bounding boxes for both buttons are displayed. If they overlap, deselect both buttons; then reselect one and drag it to a position where it does not overlap the other button.
13. If the buttons are too big (that is, overlarge for the text it contains), you can resize them. (This also helps keep the buttons from overlapping.)

   Note: Notice in the Score window in Figure 10-14 that each button sprite covers 28 frames. This is the default span for a sprite unless you change the settings (using the File⇨Preferences⇨Sprite command and the Sprite Preferences dialog).

15. Save the movie again as album1.dir.

(continued)

Figure 10-14: Frame 2 with the Next and Previous buttons added

In the following steps, you'll add a cast member script to the two buttons so that they act the same wherever they are encountered in the movie.

Adding Scripts to the New Buttons

1. Open the album1.dir movie, which now contains the Next and Previous buttons.

2. Select the Next button cast member in the Cast window, and click the Cast Member Script button. (The Next button is probably cast member number 33, and the Previous button is cast member 34. You may need to scroll through the Cast window to locate the two buttons.)

3. When the Script window appears, type

   ```
   go to the frame +1
   ```

   and then close the Script window.

4. Add the following script to the Previous button cast member:

   ```
   On mouseUp
         go to the frame -1
   end
   ```

5. Save the movie again as album1.dir.
6. Turn the Loop button off on the Control Panel.
7. Rewind the movie, close all open windows, and play the movie.
8. On the first frame (with the album cover), click the Start button.
9. Click the Next button to move to the wedding photo of Edna Belle Joslyn and William Bayes Barker.
10. Click the Previous button to return to the family photo of William with his five children. Because the button sprites span several frames, you already have added *almost* all the control you need to enable users to page through the movie.

    Note: You may find that in some frames the buttons overlap the photos. If this occurs, you can click and drag to reposition them.

11. Now click the Next button until you see the photo of Samuel Barker and Mary Littleworth Barker. When that screen appears, click the Next button again. The movie proceeds to an enlarged photo of Lyle Barker (a smaller version is in frame 8) and then stops.

You do not want the enlarged photo to appear, so you still have work to do on this project. In the following steps, you'll add a script to the Next button (in the frame that displays the image of Samuel and Mary) that causes the playback head to jump back to the album cover (frame 1 in the movie). In this particular frame, you want the Next button to behave differently from all other frames. You need to create and attach a sprite script that intercepts and overrides the `mouseDown` event for the Next button. Several steps are required to accomplish this task:

Note:

✦ Add a marker at frame 1 to serve as the target of the `go` command.

   You could tell the playback head to go to frame 1, but it's always better to name a frame (by adding a marker — discussed in Chapter 6) and then target the marker. By targeting a marker, you avoid potential conflicts when you add or delete frames that change the target frame number.

✦ Split the span of the Next button sprite so it becomes two sprites based on the same cast member.

✦ Because both sprites (after the split) will still have the same cast member script attached, you need a sprite script for the Next button sprite in frame 14. This script will override the cast member script attached to the Next button and send the playback head to the marker rather than to the next frame.

Adding a Sprite Script That Overrides a Cast Member Script

1. First, you must establish the marker. Open the album1.dir movie.

2. Locate frame 1 in the Marker channel and click once. The new marker appears as shown in Figure 10-15.

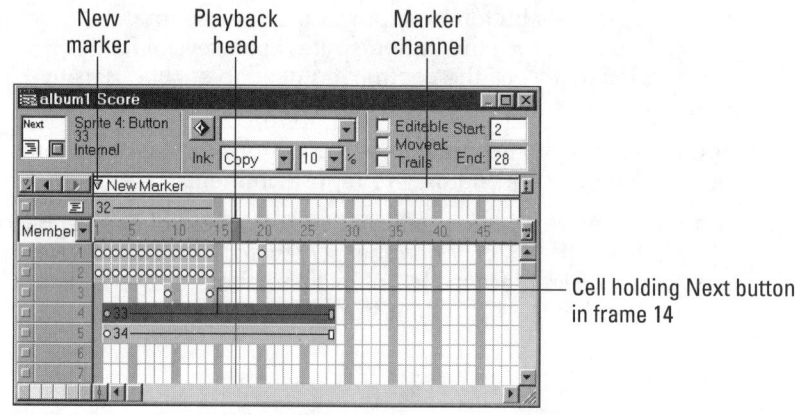

Figure 10-15: The new marker in the Marker channel

3. Type **Start** as the name for the marker and press Enter.

4. Next, you must split the sprite in channel 4 based on cast member 33 (the Next button). Once split, you can attach a sprite script to one sprite (that starts in frame 14) without affecting the other sprite spanning frames 1 through 13. Select the cell containing the Next button sprite (cast member 33) in frame 14 of the Score window (see Figure 10-18). It is in channel 4.

   Tip: Remember that you can tell when a sprite is selected on the Stage because it is highlighted. You can determine the current location of the playback head (which identifies the current frame) by looking for the playback head in the Score window, shown in Figure 10-15.

5. Select the Modify ⇨ Split Sprite command, or press Command+Shift+J (Ctrl+Shift+J) to split the sprite at the current frame. Now the Score Window shows two sprites based on cast member 33, as shown in Figure 10-16.

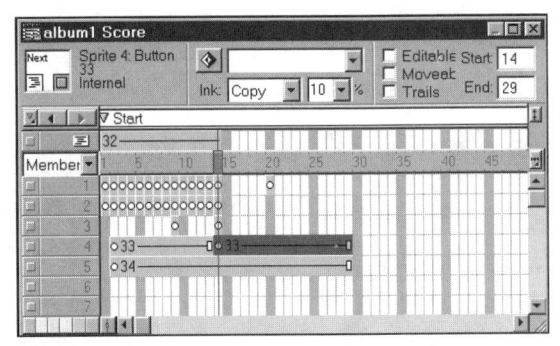

Figure 10-16: The split sprite in channel 4

6. Click and drag the end frame of the new sprite (see Figure 10-16) from frame 29 back to frame 14. This shortens the span of the sprite to a single frame. When you're all done, the Score window will look like Figure 10-17.

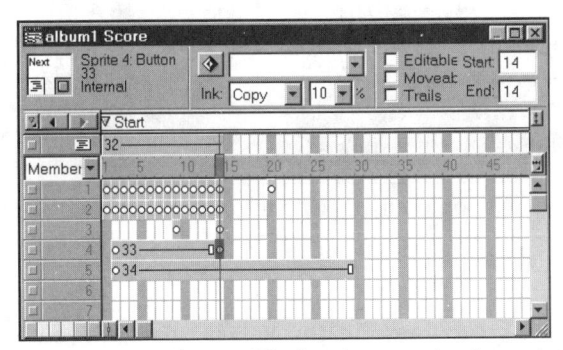

Figure 10-17: The modified sprite span in channel 4

7. Use the same technique (step 6) to shorten the sprite (number 34) in channel 5 until it spans only frames 2 through 14.

8. Finally, you can add a sprite script that causes the Next button in frame 14 to jump to the Start marker in frame 1. Select the sprite in channel 4, frame 14.

9. Click the Score window Script pop-up and drag the mouse pointer until the New Script option is highlighted, as shown in Figure 10-18. Release the mouse button to select the option.

10. When the Script window appears, type

    ```
    go frame "Start"
    ```

    and press the Enter key on the numeric pad to close the Script window.

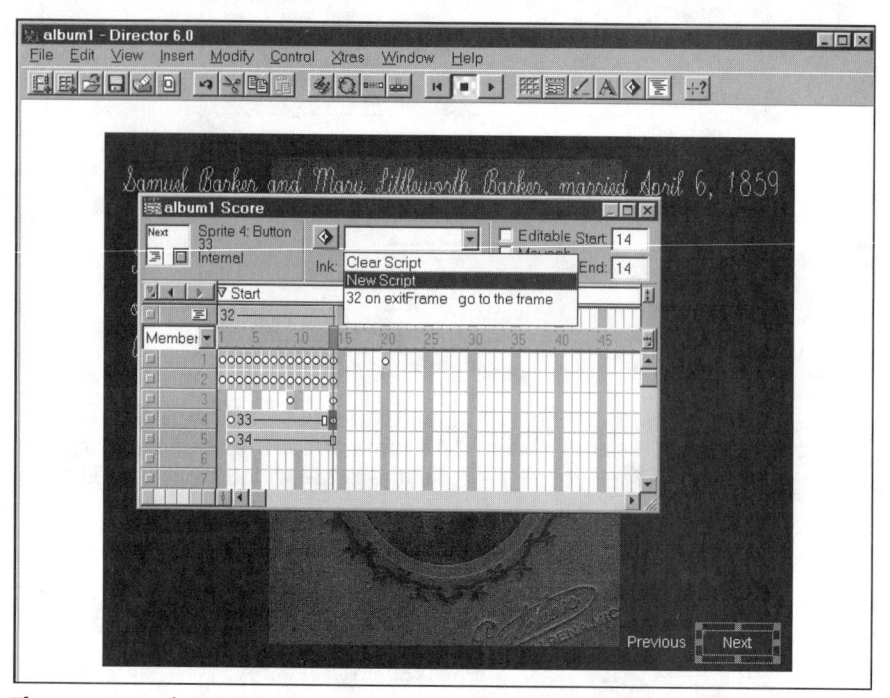

Figure 10-18: The Script pop-up menu with the New Script option selected

11. Save the movie again as album1.dir, rewind it, and play it. Try out all the buttons again.

    This time, when you get to frame 14, the Next button takes you back to the album cover. You cannot get to frame 20. You will cure that problem shortly, using the `play` command.

12. Stop the movie.

Side Dish: Notes on the album.dir movie

Each of the images in album.dir were scanned using a Hewlett-Packard Scanjet IIcx. Most of the original images were not sepia duotone images. To get that effect, Adobe Photoshop 4.0 was used. Each original scan was saved as an RGB Photoshop document (.psd) and then all existing color was removed using the Image⇨Adjust⇨Desaturate command. If needed, images were sharpened and lightened using the Image⇨Adjust command's various options. A new layer was added to the image and filled with a foreground color (using the color picker to set CMYK values to 24%, 62%, 84%, and 10%, respectively). Settings for the new layer include 100% opacity, and Overlay mode with Preserve Transparency turned off.

You can experiment with this process using the file wiles.psd found on your companion CD-ROM in the exercise:ch10 (exercise\ch10) folder.

To create an old photograph album motif, the Stage background color chip was set to black using the Modify ⇨ Movie ⇨ Properties command which displays the Stage Color chip on the Movie Properties dialog box. The cover image was scanned, shortened, edited, and the lettering added in Photoshop.

Using the `play` command to branch within the digital album

In the digital album, you still have an image (lurking in frame 20) that cannot be accessed by the navigational buttons added to the movie so far. Several modifications will be necessary to provide a button that causes the playback head to jump to frame 20, then loop on that frame to display an enlarged photo, and then give the user a button to return to the original frame. You must do the following to accomplish this:

- Add a script to frame 20 that causes the playback head to loop in that frame (using the `go to the frame` command).
- Add a marker named "Lyle" to frame 20 that is the target of the `play` command.
- Create two new cast members: the Zoom and Unzoom buttons.
- Add the Zoom button to frame 7 (with the photo of 15-year-old Lyle Barker).
- Add the Unzoom button to frame 20 (with the enlarged image).
- Add scripts to both buttons so that the Zoom button plays frame 20 and the Unzoom button signals that play is done.
- Save the movie and test it.

In the following exercises, you'll complete each of these tasks to prepare the album1.dir movie so that you can zoom to a larger version of one photograph.

On the CD-ROM The file album1.dir can be found on your companion CD-ROM in the exercise:ch10 (exercise\ch10) folder or you can use the file you created in the last exercise.

A Shortcut: Duplicating Existing Buttons

1. Open the album1.dir movie, and use the File➪Save As command to save the movie immediately as **album2.dir** on your hard drive.

2. In the Cast window, locate the `on exitFrame go to the frame` script (cast slot 32). Click and drag the script cast member until the mouse pointer is exactly over the script channel for frame 20, and release the mouse button. You are going to reuse an existing script to avoid creating another identical cast member.

3. Establish a marker at frame 20 and name it "Lyle."

4. Now you will duplicate a button and modify it. Go to the Cast window and select the Next button cast member (probably cast member 33).

5. Use the Edit➪Copy Cast Members command or press Command+C (Ctrl+C) to copy the cast member to the Clipboard.

6. Use the Edit➪Paste Button command or press Command+V (Ctrl+V) to paste the cast member from the Clipboard into the first open cast member slot (probably number 36).

7. Double-click on the new cast member to open the Button 36 dialog box.

8. Double-click the Next button's text to select it, and then type **Zoom** to overwrite it.

9. Close the dialog box. You now have a new button labeled "Zoom." When you duplicate a button, the script attached to the original button is copied to the duplicated button.

10. Repeat steps 4 through 9 to duplicate the Zoom button, and change its label to make it an Unzoom button.

11. Save the movie again as album2.dir.

Now, in this last exercise, you'll complete the modification of the album2.dir movie by adding scripts to the Zoom and Unzoom buttons. The `play` command is used in a script attached to the Zoom button, to jump to a specific frame. On the target frame, an Unzoom button is used to return the playback head to the original frame, using the `play done` form of the command. The same combination of buttons and scripts can be used to play a sequence of frames rather than just a single frame.

Adding Scripts Based on the `play` Command

1. Open the album2.dir movie that you created in the last exercise.
2. In the Cast window, select the Zoom button cast member and then click the Cast Member Script button.
3. Change the existing script to match the following:

   ```
   on mouseUp
        play "Lyle".
   end
   ```

4. Close the Script window.
5. Select the Unzoom button cast member in the Cast window and click the Cast Member Script button.
6. Change the existing script to match the following:

   ```
   on mouseUp
        play done.
   end
   ```

7. Close the Script window and save the movie again as album2.dir.

   Tip: Always save your work periodically. You don't want to lose more work than you care to re-create!

8. In the Score Window, move to frame 7 by clicking any cell in that frame. The Stage should display the photo of Lyle Barker with the Previous and Next buttons visible.

   Tip: Use the Step Forward and Step Backward buttons on the Control Panel to locate a specific frame. As you click these buttons, the Frame Counter displays the number of the current frame.

9. Select the Zoom button in the Cast window, hold down the Option (Alt) key, and drag the button to the Stage. Position the sprite above the Next and Previous buttons.
10. The button outline is too big, so resize it by dragging the handles to reduce its size. Make it match the size of the other two buttons on the Stage, and then center its text above the Previous and Next buttons.
11. Be sure the buttons do not overlap. Each one needs to occupy its own area of the Stage, so that when a button is clicked, there is no confusion over which sprite script is executed. When you're done, the Stage should appear similar to Figure 10-19.

Figure 10-19: The Stage with Zoom, Next, and Previous buttons

12. Move the playback head to frame 20. Use the same technique (from step 9) to place the Unzoom button, spanning one frame, in the bottom-right corner of the Stage.

13. Resize the button to be as small as possible while keeping the text visible on one line.

14. Place the button on Lyle's left sleeve at the shoulder, as shown in Figure 10-20.

Figure 10-20: The Stage with Unzoom button in position

15. Use the File➪Save and Compact command to reduce the movie's file size. Keep the name album2.dir, and rewind.

Note: After adding and deleting cast members from a movie, you should periodically save and compact it to reduce the file size.

16. Play the movie, testing the Zoom and Unzoom buttons. When you're done, press Esc or Command+Period (Ctrl+Period) to stop the movie.

A Few Closing Thoughts

You have learned a lot so far in this book about creating scripts in Director, yet there is always more to learn. Here are some additional guidelines that might prove helpful:

✦ If several scripts exist to handle the same message (such as the message generated by a `mouseUp` event) any existing sprite script gets first crack at executing its handlers. Next up is any existing cast script, frame script, and movie script. If a sprite has multiple behaviors attached (as explained in Chapter 6) the message is passed up the list of behaviors attached to the sprite before it is sent to the cast script, and so on.

✦ Another way to change the text properties for a standard button (created using the floating Tool Palette) is to use the Text Inspector (Figure 10-21). Select the button on the Stage and choose Window➪Inspectors➪Text or press Command+T (Ctrl+T). Then modify the font, font size, line spacing, attributes (bold, italic, underline), kerning, and alignment of the text. You can only use the Text Inspector to change the properties, not the text label, of a button.

Figure 10-21: You can change a button's properties with the Text Inspector.

✦ Now that you can import graphics, create text objects, and add basic navigational scripting, you are on your way to building Director movies. Even with simple projects, you should always test your movie on the "lowest-common-denominator" system on which you plan to run it. Test frequently and incrementally as you develop a project. Keep your projects simple and modular. Test each module as it develops rather than waiting for the completion of the entire project.

✦ To avoid confusion, remember that a sprite is defined by the channel it occupies. For instance, a sprite that occupies channel 3 — even though it may be based on cast member 5 — is referred to as sprite 3, not sprite 5.

✦ Use markers whenever you need to define a frame within a script. The relative number of a frame can (and usually does) change because you add or delete frames before it or after it. Markers always remain attached to the same frame, however — even if you add new frames or delete old frames around it. Therefore, it's better to reference a frame by a marker, such as "Lyle" in the album.dir movie, rather than a number (`go to frame 20`).

Summary

Director is an extremely powerful authoring environment. Don't let it intimidate you if you have limited programming experience. Take your learning one step at a time and master the simple script "stuff" before you plunge further into the world of Lingo scripting. In this chapter, you learned that

✦ Director uses four different types of scripts. Each script responds to messages issued by Director when an event occurs during the playback of a movie. The most common events include a mouse click; a keypress; the entering or exiting of the playback head into or from a frame; the start of the movie; and the end of the movie.

✦ A cast member script is attached in the Cast window to a specific cast member. The cast member script is executed when the user interacts with a sprite that is derived from the cast member.

✦ Score scripts or behavior scripts are created in the Score window and stored as cast members in the Cast window. Two types of Score scripts exist: Sprite scripts are attached to sprites on the Stage and supersede any instructions in the sprite's cast member script. Frame scripts are executed when the playback head enters or exits the frame that contains the script.

✦ Movie scripts can be accessed at any time during the playback of a movie. They can include instructions to be executed when a movie stops or starts and can be used to initialize global variables. Movie scripts are frequently used to store subroutines (user-defined handlers) that can be called from any handler in your movie.

✦ Parent scripts are used to create child objects and are discussed in Chapter 18.

✦ ✦ ✦

Lingo Programming Building Blocks

CHAPTER 11

In This Chapter

Definitions and examples of scripts, commands, expressions, functions, and properties

The difference between variables and constants

Local versus global variables

Assigning, initializing and naming variables

Using the Message window

Accessing system information

Using the Lingo Quick Reference

Arithmetic, comparison, logical, and other operators

Floating point numbers versus integers

Your house wasn't built with a hammer alone; other tools were put to work as well. It's important for you to understand that in Lingo, as in other forms of construction, a hammer is a great tool, but it doesn't replace a saw or a screwdriver. In Director's world, predefined behaviors are your hammers — but Director, too, provides other valuable, specialized tools.

Once you move beyond the simplest Director presentation, you need more control over your application, and you need the ability to fine-tune it. Lingo enables you to create and manage activities that are not readily available using behaviors — such as keeping track of Scores, monitoring the number of times a user passes through a scene, and discovering the name of a particular user. Director accomplishes these tasks and plenty more through the use of its specialized tools: Lingo commands, expressions, functions, variables, and properties. Together, they help you build a project.

Note To explore Lingo's tool set in this chapter, you will use the Message window — a great tool in itself.

This chapter introduces you to the fundamentals of the Lingo construction tools. Details on properties, another construction tool, will follow in Chapter 12.

Learning the Lingo

Lingo, like any authoring language, uses specific grammar to instruct the computer how to behave. Some Lingo terms you have already encountered include events, handlers, scripts, and system messages — covered in Chapter 10. Here in Chapter 11 you'll learn the meaning of commands, expressions, operators, properties, variables, and parameters.

Scripts

Any combination of words that, together, communicate instructions to Director is considered a *script*. A script can be very short (a single handler, or just two or three lines); or it may include numerous long-winded handlers containing line after line of instructions. As explained in Chapter 10, Director recognizes four types of scripts: cast member scripts, movie scripts, parent scripts, and Score (or behavior) scripts, which include sprite and frame scripts.

Commands

Commands are the basic building blocks of Lingo. You have already used commands such as `go to` and `play`, but that just scratches the surface. Two buttons in the Script window give you information about Lingo commands.

You can display a list of alphabetically arranged Lingo commands and keywords from the Script window by selecting the Alphabetical Lingo button:

Then highlight the alphabetical range within which the Lingo command falls (such as Pn to Q). An extended menu then appears. When you select a specific command from the extended menu, it is inserted into the open Script window along with placeholders (words) for each of the command's parameters.

You can also use the Categorized Lingo button:

to display the various categories of commands (such as Navigational, Casts, Fields, and Video). Once you highlight a category, an extended menu of the commands in the specified category appears. When you select a specific command from the extended menu, it is inserted into the open Script window.

For more information on these Lingo help features, see "Getting a jump start on Lingo syntax" later in this chapter.

Expressions

An *expression* is used to create a value, or *parameter,* in Lingo. Parameters are used by commands, handlers, and functions. A parameter clarifies the intended action of a command, and an expression can be used as a parameter. On the following command line, "Start" is a parameter:

    go to "Start"

"Start" is also an expression — specifically, a string expression. An expression can be a number (called an integer expression), a text string (called a string expression), or a formula.

> **Note**
> An expression can be used to perform a set of operations, either arithmetic or string manipulation.

You have already used several types of expressions. For instance, the following command line uses an integer expression (100), and go to is the command:

    go to 100

You have also used a formula as an expression, specifically as a parameter for the go to command. In the following example, the frame +1 is an expression (and a formula), and go to is the command:

    go to the frame +1

In Lingo, whenever a command calls for an expression, you can use an integer, string, formula, function, operator, or another expression.

Functions

Functions are keywords in Lingo that return a specific value. By using functions, you can build more complicated expressions and formulas.

A function is nothing more than a handler that returns a result when completed. Most functions take parameters; some do not. Director defines several dozen functions that perform a wide variety of operations.

You have already used functions. In Chapter 10 you encountered the frame function, which returns a value representing the frame where the playback head is currently located. Other common functions are listed in Table 11-1.

Table 11-1
Common Lingo Functions

Function	Description
the key	Returns the code for the last key pressed
random()	Returns a random number within a specified range
rollOver	Indicates if the mouse pointer is over a specified sprite
soundBusy	Indicates if sound is currently playing in a specified Sound channel
time	Returns the current time as stored by your computer system

Variables and constants

A *variable*, like a glass jar, is a container that "holds something." There's nothing mysterious about the jar. You can put things into the jar, take things out of it, fill it, and empty it. The jar can just as easily hold a number, text, lists of items, and even objects (buttons, pretty pictures, or scripts). Leaving the jar metaphor behind, a variable in Lingo can hold a value (number), a string (text), or an expression, such as the result of a formula or a function. It can also hold the name or number of a cast member, or the number or name of a sprite derived from a cast member.

Tip

In Lingo and other programming languages, you can easily see whether the content of a variable is a string or a variable: A string expression is surrounded by double-quotation marks; a variable is not.

When Director really doesn't care

In terms of the kinds of data (numbers or strings) that it handles, Lingo is a remarkably carefree language. With the exception of occasional glitches when you attempt to use the wrong type of operator when working with data, Director will usually convert numbers from one format to another without your needing to be aware of the distinctions. Further, a variable that you create can store integers, text, or an expression. Unlike other languages that carefully type variables, Lingo just doesn't care whether `myLittleVariable` stores a string, a floating point value, or an integer.

The only drawback to Lingo's carefree ways is that you can generate some problems by storing numeric data in a variable that should contain a string, or vice versa. This occurs when you try to manipulate data stored in a variable as if it contained an integer, when in fact it includes a string or a floating point value (or vice versa).

In contrast to a variable, which stores a value or string that changes as a movie is executed, a *constant* always represents an unchanging value. You can assign a new value or a new string to a variable each time the playback head moves to another frame. A variable can change when the user clicks a button or moves the mouse pointer across a sprite on the Stage. Constants, however, cannot and do not change.

Several frequently useful constants are `True`, `False`, `Empty`, `Quote`, and `Return`. Each of these constants has a set, unchanging value.

Variables come in two varieties. A *global variable* can be used anywhere within a movie. A *local variable* is only used within a specific handler. Once the handler completes execution, the local variable ceases to exist. Whether local or global, the first occurrence of a variable in your script creates it.

Global variable guidelines

The following guidelines are helpful when using a global variable:

- You can declare a global variable in any handler or any script in a movie.
- If you want to establish a global variable, use the `global` keyword followed by the name of the variable. You can declare more than one global variable on the same line. The following are examples of two global statements that declare, respectively, a single variable and multiple (three) variables:

    ```
    global gMyNewVariable

    global gCost gRetail gProfit
    ```

- To use a global variable in a specific script, *you must repeat the global statement* within that script. Once declared, the current value or string stored by a global variable is available for use and modification within the handler.
- Sometimes, to easily differentiate between local and global variables, Lingo programmers begin global variables with the lowercase letter *g*.
- To see a display of global variables and their current values, use the `showGlobals` command. The result appears in the Message window. (You'll see this later in the chapter.)

Local variable guidelines

The following guidelines are helpful when using a local variable:

- If you do not declare a variable as global, it becomes a local variable.
- A local variable can only be used within the handler where it is declared. When the handler completes, the variable ceases to exist.
- To see a display of local variables and their current values, use the `showLocals` command in the Message window.

Note: For the sake of comparison, a local variable is like a three-year-old child, and a global variable is like a teenager. The effective domain of a three-year-old (local variable) is limited to inside the house and a fenced backyard (the current handler). The effective domain of a teenager (global variable) is anywhere and everywhere he/she decides to go (the entire movie). Both global variables *and* teenagers will perform assigned tasks only when called by name (sometimes loudly), whenever and wherever they are needed.

Nonvariable variable nomenclature

A variable in Lingo can be named just about anything. However, as easygoing as Lingo is, there are limits to its patience:

- ✦ A variable cannot have more than 256 characters. Unless you are grandly verbose in your naming conventions, this shouldn't be a problem.

- ✦ A variable must start with a letter, but it can include letters, numbers, and the underscore character. For instance, `myBox`, `var32`, and `The_Book` are all legitimate variables, but `my Box`, `32var`, and `The-Book` are not.

- ✦ Variable names are *not* case sensitive. That's the same as saying they *are* case insensitive, but we don't want you to misread this rule. In other words, `myBox`, `mybox`, `MYBOX`, and `mYbOx` all refer to the same variable.

- ✦ Strive to keep your variable names descriptive. Both `i` and `index` are legitimate variable names, but the name `index` portrays much more. Even better choices would include `wordIndex` if the variable refers to a particular word in a string, and `spriteIndex` if the variable contains the number of a sprite channel.

- ✦ A favorite convention among Lingo programmers is to create variable names from several words strung together, with the first name of each word (except the first) capitalized. For example, `numberOfTimesInRoom` illustrates this point well; `numberoftimesinroom`, on the other hand, is harder to read.

Note: Some developers prefer to include a character prefix indicating the type of data that the variable contains. For example, the variable `sMyName` contain a string, and `iNumberOfEntrances` contains an integer value. We're not wild about such notation — we think a well-thought-out variable name should contain sufficient clues as to the variable's contents. Additionally, Lingo tends to be fairly loose about what type of contents a variable contains — unlike a language such as Visual Basic. Being aware of this specific type of naming convention may be useful when you examine code from other programmers, whether you decide to use the convention or not.

The primary rule about variable names is to exercise common sense. Choose a name that makes sense in the context of the situation, because at some point in the future you or someone else is likely to revisit your code in search of the purpose of each variable.

The life cycle of a local variable

Variables have a certain (albeit very limited) kind of "life." Within a script, a variable is born, lives out its life, and dies.

1. **Birth** — You write a `set` or `put` statement, with the variable being assigned a value. For example:

    ```
    set count=0
    ```

    In this case, Director creates space for the variable and reserves the variable name for as long as the variable shall live.

2. **Life** — The variable's contents can be accessed or changed. Within a routine, the variable retains its contents until such time as those contents are explicitly changed. For example:

    ```
    set count = count + 1
    ```

    updates the contents of the variable `count` every time the statement is evaluated (executed).

3. **Death** — Director removes the variable name from its references, the contents of the variable are discarded, and the variable ceases to exist. Death usually occurs only when the routine where the variable is defined ends. When this happens, the variable is said to "go out of scope."

Assigning a value or string to a variable

There are two methods of assigning a value or string to a variable. You can use either the `put` or the `set` command. The difference between the two commands is slight, and they generate identical results. You can `put` something *into* a variable, or you can `set` the contents of the variable *to* something.

The syntax for the set command is

```
put expression into variable
```

The *variable* can be a cast member name or number, or a local or global variable. In the following example, the value 100 is stored (`put`) into the variable named `cost`:

```
put 100 into cost
```

In Lingo, a field cast member that stores text is considered a field. In the following command, you place a specific text string ("too late") into a field cast member ("timeStatus"):

```
put "too late" into field "timeStatus"
```

The second method of assigning a value or string to a variable uses the `set` command. The syntax for the command is

```
set variable to expression
```

Let's look at the equivalent `set` commands for the `put` examples we just studied. You can `set` the value of the variable `cost` to 100 using the following command:

```
set cost to 100
```

You can set the "timeStatus" cast member to a specific text string ("too late") using the following command:

```
set the text of member "timeStatus" to "too late"
```

Note: The phrase `the text of member` is a property that represents the text string stored in a text cast member.

Tip: Even though the `set` and `put` commands are technically interchangeable, Lingo programmers typically use `put` to establish or change variables, and `set` to establish or change properties.

Initializing variables

A local variable is *declared* (created) and *initialized* (given an initial value) when it is first used in a handler. Global variables are often declared in a movie script and may not initially have a value. In that sense, a global variable is like an old penny found in a field. You don't know where it's been and you don't know its value!

It is good practice to initialize variables, especially when they may hold a value or string that you do not expect. Using an uninitialized variable can also cause problems if your script anticipates a numeric value and the variable holds a string. Further, if the numeric value is out of the expected range or contains no value (nothing), you can get some flaky results.

The following handler demonstrates one method of initializing a variable. The variable named `newVariable` is initialized to contain "something" if it holds a null value (no value):

```
On enterFrame
      if newVariable = nothing then
         put "something" into newVariable
      end if
end enterFrame
```

You can also initialize the value stored in a global value by following its declaration with a `put` statement, as in the following example. Just be sure the value assigned is appropriate for the intended use of the variable:

```
on startMovie
    global newVariable, anotherVariable
    put 10 into newVariable
    put "supplemental text" into anotherVariable
end startMovie
```

Getting to Know the Message Window

The Message window is your window into Lingo. It's the oldest of Director's scripting, testing, and debugging tools and still the most versatile.

Note: If you're familiar with other programming languages, you can consider the Message window an *immediate mode* window. It can interpret Lingo statements even when Director itself is stopped. You can immediately see the results of commands entered (and executed) in this window.

The Message window is a powerful learning tool, especially as you're beginning to work with Lingo. Using the Message window, you can

+ Execute Lingo statements, functions, and your own routines — even when your movie isn't playing.
+ Obtain information about your system.
+ Get help with Lingo syntax, using the Alphabetical Lingo and Categorized Lingo buttons.
+ Access several of Director's newer debugging tools (the Debugger window and the Watcher window, see Chapter 20).
+ Monitor values stored in variables during the playback of your movie.
+ Assign properties and values without having to create a whole movie.

Using the Message window

In the exercise coming up, you'll use the Message window to make variable assignments and to display values and strings held by variables. When you're writing scripts and troubleshooting, the Message window is a valuable tool because you can see how specific script instructions affect the values stored by variables.

Before you start, here are a few guidelines that will help you quickly learn to use the Message window. Keep them in mind as you continue working through the chapter.

- ✦ To open the Message window, select the Window ➪ Message command or press Command+M (Ctrl+M).

- ✦ When using the Message window, press the Return (Enter) key to execute an instruction. *Do not use the Enter key on the numeric keypad.* No instruction is executed until you press the Return (Enter) key.

- ✦ You can edit any instruction entered in the Message window before you execute it by pressing Return (Enter). If you mistype an instruction, simply correct it and then move the insertion point to the *end* of the instruction before pressing Return (Enter).

Tip

You can use the Home and End keys to quickly move to the beginning or end of a line of text in the Message window.

- ✦ To save yourself time and typing, you can use an existing instruction, make changes to it, and then execute it as usual. Move to the end of the instruction, press Return (Enter), and the modified instruction is executed. (If you are a hunt-and-peck typist like many of us, this can save you considerable effort.)

- ✦ The double-dash (--) indicates a comment line in Lingo. In the Message window, however, data that follows the double-dash is the result returned by the command line or instruction.

Instructions and their results in the Message window are a historical record of your actions. You can cut and paste from the Message window into a script. You can delete old results to clear the window. You can scroll back and edit previous instructions to make new ones. In the Message window you can do pretty much whatever you need to do to make your Lingo work. Once you execute an instruction and the result is returned, everything in the window is just text.

Working in the Message window

The Message window is a significant tool — versatile and helpful in many ways. The following notes can guide you in your understanding and use of the window:

- ✦ You can use the `put` statement along with an expression in the Message window to display the results of the expression in the Message window.

- ✦ You can use the `set` and `put` commands to assign values to variables in the Message window and then be able to immediately see the results.

- ✦ Any kind of data (numeric, string) can be assigned to a variable using the Message window and then changed by a new assignment.

- ✦ You can create a new cast member based solely on Lingo instructions issued in the Message window.

♦ To display the current value or string held by a variable, you can use the put command and the variable name alone on a line in the Message window.

In the following steps, you'll practice assigning a value to and storing strings in variables.

Assigning Values and Strings

1. Open a new Director movie.
2. To open the Message window, select the Window ⇨ Message command or press Command+M (Ctrl+M). You'll get a window that looks similar to Figure 11-1.

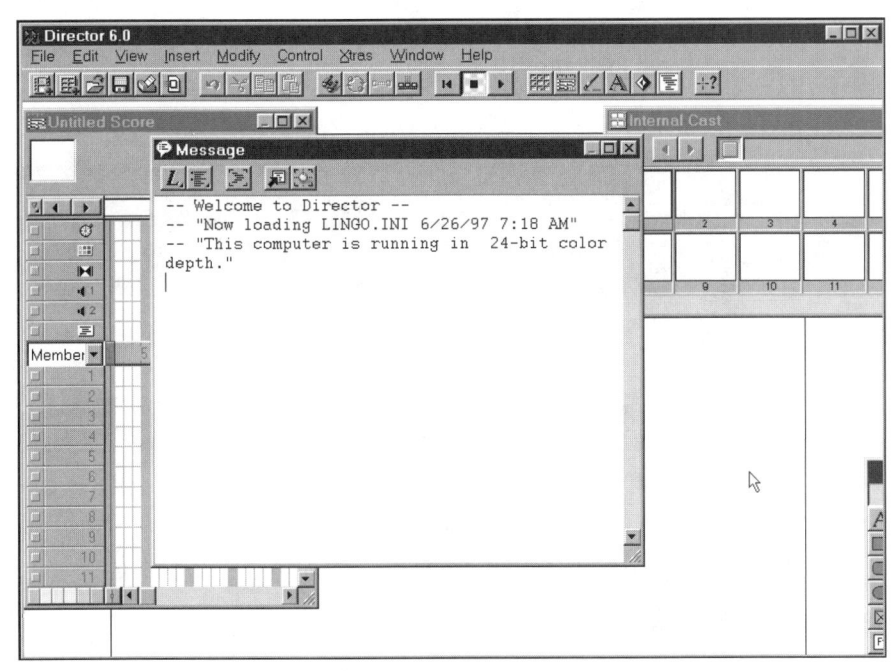

Figure 11-1: The Message window

3. In the Message window, type **put 100 into cost** and press Enter, and then type **put cost** and press Enter. The Message window displays the messages you have typed plus a response to the last line.

```
put 100 into cost
put cost
-- 100
```

4. In the next few steps, you set a variable to a specific value or string and then display the value or string. Type the following lines, pressing Enter after each one:

```
put "Alexander's Ragtime Band" into Name
put Name
```

5. Variables are containers, and you can change the values they hold. Type

```
put "Amusing Anecdotes" into Name
```

and press Enter. You have changed what was stored in the variable Name.

6. Type

```
put Name
```

and press Enter. The change in the string stored by the Name variable is displayed in Figure 11-2.

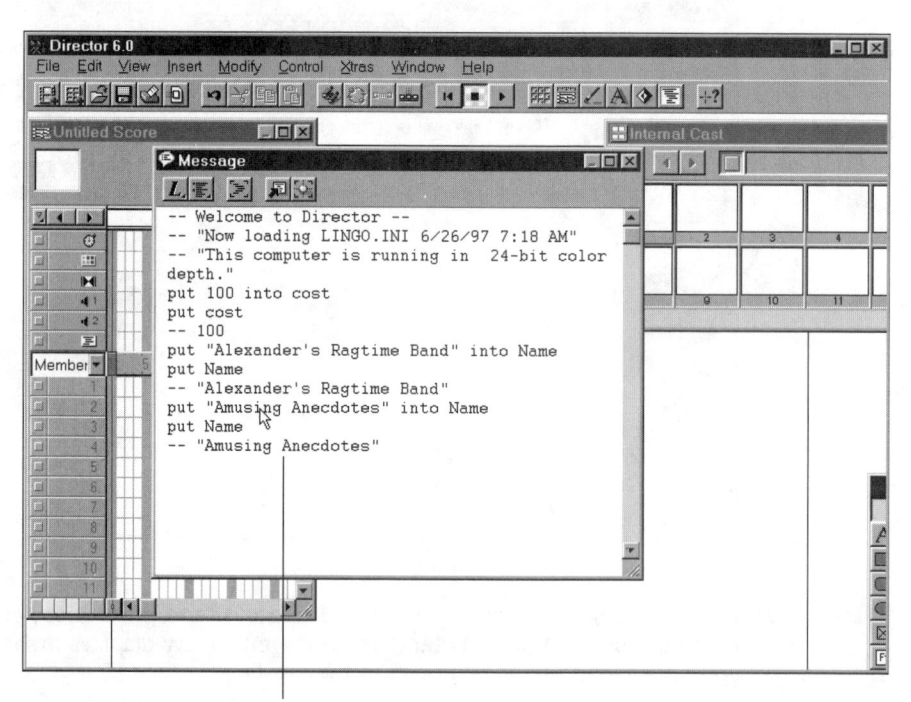

Figure 11-2: Changing the Name variable in the Message window

7. Notice that the cast of your new movie is empty. None of the cast slots holds cast members. Next, add a field cast member (storing a text string) using the `put` command, and then modify the cast member using the `set` command. (You could reverse this process, because either `put` or `set` can be used to change the cast member.) Type

   ```
   put "Absolutely Amazing Armadillos" into field 1
   ```

   and press Enter. Check the Cast window. Cast member 1 now stores the text "Absolutely Amazing Armadillos."

   Tip: Field 1 is equivalent to cast member 1.

8. Now change the string to "Beautiful Beetle Bugs." Type

   ```
   set the text of member 1 to "Beautiful Beetle Bugs"
   ```

   and press Enter.

Note: If you had given the cast member a name (using the Cast Member Properties dialog box), you could use that name, enclosed in double-quotes, instead of the cast member number in the command line. Lingo can refer to a cast member in one of three ways: by its literal cast number (cast member 1, 2, 3, and so on); by a relative cast number (such as cast member 10 + 5), and by the cast member name (such as "Beetle Bug").

Accessing system information

Using Lingo, you can access important data about the user's computer system. This information is stored by Director in a group of system variables, functions, and properties.

Note: *A word about properties*: We've referred several times in this chapter to *properties* in Lingo, without much explanation so far. In the next chapter, we'll focus on properties. For now, just think of them as attributes. If you are a woman with auburn hair and dark brown eyes, then two of your many properties are auburn hair and dark brown eyes. Properties in Lingo describe something, too — such as the platform a movie runs on, the color depth of the monitor in use, the ink effect applied to a sprite, and whether a sprite is visible or invisible on the Stage.

You can display the results of system properties, variables, and functions using the Message window, but a more important benefit is that you can use this data in your Lingo scripts and handlers. Each of the keywords in Table 11-2 can be included in a `put` statement that displays the result in the Message window.

Table 11-2
System Variables, Properties, and Functions

Keyword	Type	Purpose
`the colorDepth`	Property	Displays the current color depth of the monitor, such as 8-bit color.
`the machineType`	Function	Indicates by a numeric value whether the current system is an IBM PC-type or Macintosh system (`256` indicates an IBM PC-type).
`the maxInteger`	Property	Displays the largest whole number that is supported by the user's system.

`the platform`	System property	Displays the type of workstation. Possible values:
		`Macintosh,68k`
		`Macintosh,PowerPC`
		`Windows,16`
		`Windows,32`

`the runMode`	Function	Displays the run mode of Director; that is, whether the current movie is running in authoring mode (`author`), as a projector (`projector`), or as a Shockwave movie (`plugin`).
`version`	System variable	Displays the current version of Director.

In the following steps, you'll experiment with obtaining system information using the Message window.

Displaying System Information

1. In the Message window, type

   `put version`

   and press Enter. The Message window returns a value representing the current version of Director, like this:

   `-- "6.0"`

2. Type

   `put the machineType`

and press Enter. The value returned will be a number representing the type of machine (computer system) the user is using. Common results are as follows:

Numeric Code Returned	System Type Identified
24	Macintosh Quadra 950
45	PowerMac 7100/70
53	PowerComputing 8100/100
256	IBM PC-type machine

Caution

It is not wise to make assumptions about the user's system based on what is returned by the machineType function. Systems can vary greatly depending on RAM, hard-disk capacity, monitor size, attached peripherals, and the operating system. The only safe assumption is that IBM PC-type systems return a value of 256 while all other values returned indicate a Macintosh system. For a complete list of the machineType codes, check Director's online Help and search for "machineType function."

3. Type

    put the platform

and press Enter. The value returned indicates whether you are working on a 68K Macintosh, Macintosh PowerPC, Windows 3.x (16-bit system), or Windows 95/NT (32-bit system).

4. Type

    put the runMode

and press Enter. The Message window displays

    -- "Author"

Getting a jump start on Lingo syntax

At its heart, Lingo isn't a "large" language, but as the number and complexity of the Director-supported objects increases, so does the number of "special terms" that can be accessed using Lingo. There are currently over 600 of these commands, keywords, properties, and other elements within Lingo. And each has its own calling conventions, structures, and objects.

Two factors provide refuge for the sanity of both novice and experienced developers:

- ✦ Only about 80–100 of Lingo's terms are used on a regular basis. (You can now breathe a sigh of relief.)
- ✦ The Message window (as well as the Script window) includes a built-in Quick Reference utility for displaying the syntax of each Lingo command, property, function, and element.

As explained earlier in this chapter, you access the Lingo Quick Reference feature by clicking either the Alphabetical Lingo button or the Categorized Lingo button in the Message window. (These buttons are also available in the Script window.) Once you select the desired Lingo term from the pop-up menus displayed by these buttons, the keyword, as well as any parameters or other descriptive elements of the instruction, appears at the cursor location.

In the following steps, you can experiment with the Lingo Quick Reference feature using the Message window. You have just begun to learn a few Lingo commands (in this chapter and Chapter 10), but it's never too early to realize that online help is available when your brain freezes and the Lingo isn't flowing easily from your fingertips.

Get the Syntax Straight, Seymour!

1. Open the Message window using Command+M (Ctrl+M).
2. In the Message window, type **put** followed by a space.
3. Click the Alphabetical Lingo button. A menu pop-up appears with alphabetical ranges for Lingo commands, as shown in Figure 11-3.

   When you seek a specific command in the alphabetical listing, you should ignore words like `the` and `on` to get to the specific entry.
4. With the alphabetical pop-up menu visible, type **V**.
5. Move the mouse pointer over the Version option and click once. The keyword entry is inserted at the cursor and the menu disappears.
6. Press the Return (Enter) key, and the statement **put version** is evaluated.
7. Next you will retrieve a Lingo command using the Categorized Lingo button. In this case, the Lingo instruction requires parameters. If the Lingo keyword requires parameters, you are prompted for them by the appearance of placeholders. Click the Categorized Lingo button.
8. From the menu, select Strings (A to I), and then choose the Alert option from the submenu. See Figure 11-4.

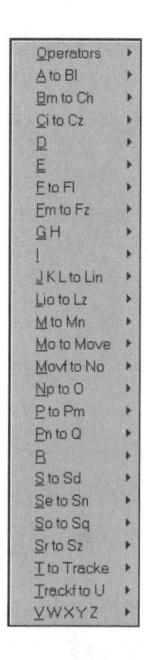

Figure 11-3: If you know the name of the property or the command, use the Alphabetical Lingo pop-up menu to look up the syntax of the command.

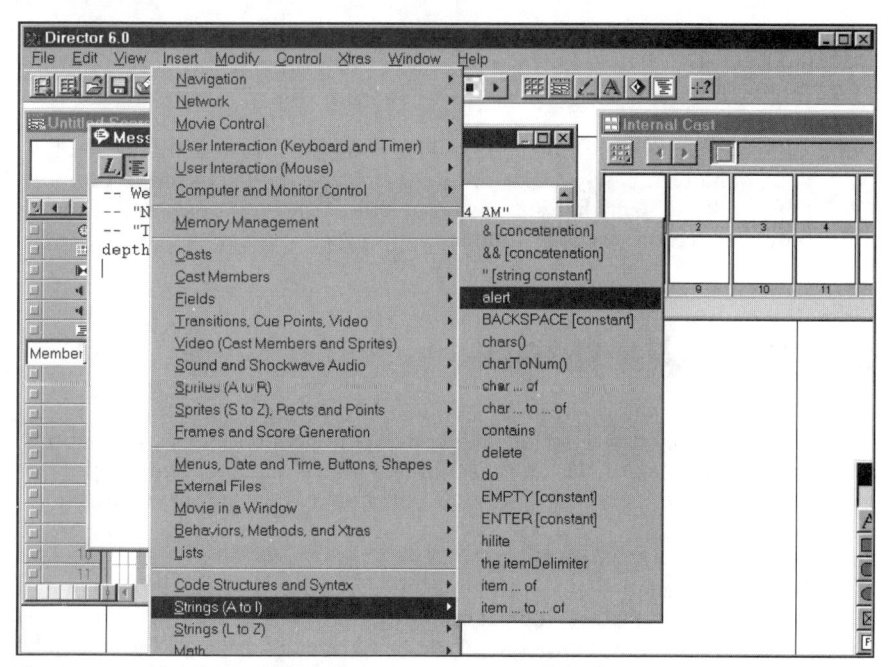

Figure 11-4: The Categorized Lingo menus are useful when you're not quite sure of the correct command but know generally what it does.

9. In the Message window, Director places the `alert message` instruction that needs to be modified. The word `message` is already highlighted (selected), so type the following, including the quotes:

   `"Warning! Warning!"`

   Press the Return (Enter) key, and a custom Alert box appears, displaying your message as shown in Figure 11-5.

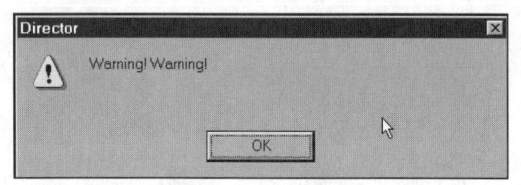

   Figure 11-5: The Alert box is a useful tool for debugging and prototyping, but it should generally never be present in the final product.

10. To close the Alert box, click the OK button.

The Alert box gives you a handy way to indicate that a section of your code is not implemented, that one of your variables or properties is corrupt or inappropriately set, or that something similarly dire is occurring.

Tip   Alert boxes are generally used only as a last resort in a final project, since Director now includes a vastly superior dialog box that is discussed in Chapter 22. Alert boxes tell the user that an error or problem situation exists, but they provide no option to fix it or work around it.

Smooth Operators

Like it or not, the operations involved in creating a Director movie can range from simple arithmetic to performing complex logical and string operations. Fortunately, Lingo provides you with a reasonably comprehensive suite of operators to work with. An *operator* is a symbol that tells how two (or more) expressions should be combined.

Lingo has essentially five different types of operators: arithmetic operators, comparison operators, logical operators, grouping operators, and a few miscellaneous operators. Each type has a specific role, and each can be used in expressions and formulas. Most of the operators are fairly self-explanatory, but it doesn't hurt to review the basics (after all, how long have *you* been out of school?).

Arithmetic operators

The most common operators are arithmetic operators (Table 11-3). Use them to perform basic addition, division, multiplication, and subtraction. These operators are positioned between the values or variables on which they act. In a formula using arithmetic operators, you can add, subtract, multiply, and divide values or the values represented by variables.

Caution

Addition, subtraction, and multiplication are straightforward in Lingo, but division can catch you by surprise. Lingo results when dividing values depend on whether the operands are integers or floating point numbers. See the upcoming section "When numbers aren't just numbers."

Table 11-3
Arithmetic Operators

Operator	Example	Result	Operation
Addition (+)	set a = 7 + 5	12	Adds the second number to the first.
Subtraction (–)	set a = 7 - 5	2	Subtracts the second number from the first.
Negation (–)	set a = -5	–5	Returns the negative of the number. This has only one argument.
Multiplication (×)	set a = 7 *5	35	Multiplies the first number by the second.
Integer division (/)	set a = 7 / 5	1	For two integers, finds the largest integer that evenly divides the first number by the second.
Float division (/)	set a = 7.0 / 5.0	1.4	For two floating point numbers, divides the first number by the second.
Modulus (MOD)	set a = 7 MOD 5	2	Returns the remainder that's left after an integer division.
Integer function	set a = integer(7.4)	7	Converts a floating point number (or a string representation of a number) to an integer.
Float function	set a=float(7)	7.0	Converts an integer (or a string representation of a number) to a floating point number.

Order of calculation

When you build a formula that includes more than one arithmetic operator, the order of calculation follows the rules of algebra:

- Equations are evaluated left to right.
- Multiplication and division are calculated first, followed by addition and subtraction.
- Any expressions included within parentheses are evaluated first.

The following example demonstrates the need to be aware of these rules. Both of the following formulas are accurate. Notice that the numbers used are the same and are presented in the same order. The only difference is in the presence of the parentheses in the second equation, which forces a change in the order of calculation.

```
30 × 10 - 6 = 294

30 × (10 - 6) = 120
```

Comparison operators

Much of programming is involved with the comparison of two items or conditions. Does the variable contain a value equal to zero? Is the current cast member number greater or less than three? Is the name of the current frame "EndReached"? Has a second (60 ticks) passed yet? All of these are comparisons, and Director has several operators that translate the comparisons into Lingo (see Table 11-4).

The result of a comparison can have only one of two values: True or False. *Comparison operators* compare the two expressions on either side of the operator and generate a value of 1 (True) if the test is True and 0 (False) if the test is False. Lingo also defines two constants (named, not surprisingly, True and False) which can be used in place of 1 and 0 to make your code a little more readable.

Note: The True and False constants are called Boolean values, after the nineteenth-century mathematician George Boole, the father of modern binary logic.

Table 11-4
Comparison Operators

Operator	Example	Result	Operation
(Equality) =	set a = (3 = 4)	a is False	Compares two values to see if they're identical.

Operator	Example	Result	Operation
(Inequality) <>	set a = (3<>4)	a is True	Returns True if the two compared values are not identical.
(Less than) <	set a = (3 < 4)	a is True	Returns True if the first number is less than the second number.
(Less than or equal to) <=	set a = (3 <= 4)	a is True	Returns True if the first number is less than or equal to the second number.
(Greater than) >	set a = (3 > 4)	a is False	Returns True if the first number is greater than the second number.
(Greater than or equal to) >=	set a = (3 >= 4)	a is False	Returns True if the first number is greater than or equal to the second number.
CONTAINS	A = "Jonathan" B = "Jon" A CONTAINS B	True	Compares two text strings and determines if the first expression includes the second expression.
STARTS	A = "Missouri" B = "Miss" B STARTS A	True	Compares two text strings and determines if the first expression begins with the second expression.

Comparison operators are frequently used in if...then statements, which evaluate a condition and then take one of two or more possible actions based on the result of the comparison. When you take a store coupon for cough syrup to the grocery story, and then compare the cost at the adjacent drug store (where the coupon is not accepted), you use an if...then statement. The statement would read:

> *If* the cost of the medication using the coupon (at the grocery store) is less than the regular cost of the medication at the drug store, *then* buy the medication at the grocery store; otherwise, buy the medication at the drug store.

A comparison is made (the cost of the medication at two stores with and without the coupon) and then an action occurs (you buy the medicine at the lowest price based on the comparison). Comparisons are made using one of the comparison operators in Table 11-4.

Logical operators

Often you will need to make more than one comparison or equality test. But comparison operators by themselves can only determine if two expressions or conditions are equal, not equal, and so on. To handle compound cases, you use *logical operators* (Table 11-5). When used with comparison operators, logical operators test more than one condition.

Note: Logical operators are frequently used in `if...then` statements.

Table 11-5
Logical Operators

Operator	When Both a and b Are False	When a Is False and b Is True, or Vice Versa	Both a and b Are True
AND	Result is False	Result is False	Result is True
OR	Result is False	Result is True	Result is True
NOT a	If a is False then NOT a is True	Not applicable	If a is True then NOT a is False

The `OR` operator tests the existence of either condition, and the `AND` operator tests the existence of both conditions. Let's look at an everyday example of using these logical operators. Framed within an `if...then` statement, the following statement tests to see if both conditions are True:

```
If you get off work early and I get off work early, we'll meet
at the mall and watch a 5 p.m. movie; otherwise, we'll meet at
6 p.m. for dinner.
```

For us to meet at 5 p.m. to see a movie, both situations must be True; you and I must both leave early from work. If either condition is False (if one of us doesn't escape work early), then we plan to meet for dinner at 6 p.m.

The decision can be similarly framed using an `OR` logical operator:

```
If you get off work late or I get off work late, we'll meet at
7 p.m. for dinner; otherwise, we'll meet at 6 p.m. for dinner.
```

In this example, if either situation is True, we'll meet at 7 p.m. for dinner. If neither condition is True, we'll meet earlier at 6 p.m. for dinner.

The decision can also be framed using the NOT logical operator:

```
If you do not get off work early or I do not get off early,
we'll meet at 7 p.m. for dinner, otherwise we'll meet at 6
p.m. for dinner.
```

In this example, if either situation is True (one of us does not get off early), or if both situations are True, we'll meet at 7 p.m. It's only when both situations are False (we do get off work early) that we'll meet at 6 p.m. for dinner.

Tip The NOT argument is typically the most difficult Boolean operation to interpret and understand. It's always safer to define conditions in terms of a positive statement rather than a negative statement (using NOT) — when you can.

When you use a logical operator, the operator itself is preceded and followed by the two conditions. The syntax for using a logical operator is as follows:

condition1 OR *condition2*

condition3 AND *condition4*

Other operators

This final group of operators serves a variety of functions (listed in Table 11-6).

Table 11-6
Grouping and Miscellaneous Operators

Operator	Example	Function
&	"More"&"Stuff" = "MoreStuff"	Concatenates (combines) two text expressions into a single expression. If one of the original expressions is a value, the result is converted to a text string.
&&	"More"&&"Stuff" = "More Stuff"	Concatenates (combines) two text expressions into a single expression and introduces a space character between the original two expressions. If one of the original expressions is a value, the result is converted to a text string.
( ) (Grouping)	(2 + 3)*4 = 20 2 + 3 * 4 = 14	Forces any portion of an expression (within the parentheses) to be calculated first.

(continued)

Table 11-6 *(continued)*

Operator	Example	Function
@ (Pathname)	`@\folder\folderWithinAFolder` `@:folder:folderWithinAFolder`	Specifies a pathname to a folder used in a movie. By using the pathname operator, the path is defined and understood on both Windows and Macintosh systems.
# (Symbol)	`#OkCancel`	Symbols are discussed later in this chapter. Defines and identifies a symbol. Director supports a symbol data type, in addition to integer, floating-point number, string, and object data types.
[ ] (List)	`set myNewList = [ ]`	Brackets the entries in a list. Lists are discussed in Chapter 17.

In the following steps, you'll get a chance to experiment using standard arithmetic operators. In this case, your computer with Director together serve as little more than a *very* high-priced digital calculator.

You'll also see how you can use the Message window to assign values to variables and then use the variables in your instructions. One variable (`profit`) is assigned a value solely based on the values stored by two other variables (`retail` and `cost`). In addition to using the arithmetic operators, you can use the grouping and concatenation operators to display a very readable message in the Message window.

Calculating Messages

1. If necessary, open the Message window.

2. Type **put 20+5** and press Return (Enter). You'll get the result as shown here:

   ```
   put 20+5
   -- 25
   ```

3. Type **put 100/10** and press Return (Enter), to get the result:

   ```
   put 100/10
   -- 10
   ```

4. So far you have only experimented with the arithmetic operators. Now you can assign a value to a variable and then modify the value stored. Type the following statements, pressing Return (Enter) after each statement:

```
put 100 into cost
put 140 into retail
put retail - cost into profit
put cost
put retail
put profit
```

When you're done, the Message window displays the values stored in each of the variables (cost, retail, and profit):

```
put cost
-- 100
put retail
-- 140
put profit
-- 40
```

5. One last little experiment demonstrates how the concatenation operators work. To assign a text string to the variable label, type

```
put "Net profit is" into label
```

and press Enter.

Tip: Text stored in variables (called *literal text strings*) must be entered within double-quotes on the command line.

6. Type

```
put label&profit
```

and press Enter. The result is

```
-- "Net profit is40"
```

Tip: You can enter the command as either put label&profit or put label & profit. The concatenation operator can be preceded and followed by no space or by a space — the result is the same.

7. In the result of your entry in step 6, there is no space between the string "Net profit is" and the value 40. You can cure the lack of readability and spacing using the following modified command form. Type

```
put label && profit
```

and press Enter. The result is

```
-- "Net profit is 40"
```

8. Finally, you can modify the output to add a dollar sign preceding the number 40 and add a period at the end of the sentence by using the following instruction. Type

   ```
   put label &&"$"&profit&"."
   ```

   and press Enter. The result is

   ```
   -- "Net profit is $40."
   ```

When numbers aren't just numbers

Director supports two different kinds of numbers: *integers* and *floating point numbers* (which we'll call *floats*, for short). Think of an integer as a "counting number" (1, 2, 3, and so on), or 0, or the negative of these numbers (–1, –2, –3, and so on). Integers are usually the preferred data type to express the *number* of a given item, such as

- The number of times you enter a frame
- The number of lines in a block of text
- The number of sprites that are currently on the Stage
- The number used to index a specific item within a group

When you talk about "sprite 3" or "sprite 12," both 3 and 12 are integers. When you loop a routine by counting from 1 to *n*, both 1 and the value stored by the variable *n* are integers.

Floats, on the other hand, are *decimal point numbers*. For example, the "normal" temperature for the human body is 98.6° Fahrenheit (although, in truth, the average temperature is really closer to 98.2° F, unless you're speaking in front of a large crowd or explaining why your project is three weeks late . . .). Floating point numbers are used to represent a continuum. One way of viewing the difference between integers and floats is that for any two floating point numbers, there is always a floating point number between them. In other words, between 3.1 and 3.2 is 3.15, between 3.1 and 3.15 is 3.14, and so forth. Integers don't obey this law. For example, there is no integer between 3 and 4.

Note

Any mathematical operation using two nonintegers or resulting in a noninteger value (but whose argument calls for an integer result) is rounded to the nearest integer. For example, an equation that adds 3.32 and 2.1 would return the value 5 if the result is specified as an integer (3.32 × 2.1 = 5.42, which is rounded down to 5). When an equation includes the addition of 3.32 and 2.3, the result is 6 (3.32 × 2.3 = 5.62, which rounds up to 6).

Why does Lingo need two different kinds of numbers? Only because they are used for two different purposes. Floating point numbers show up most often as the result of division. The average of several numbers (1, 2, 3, 4, 5, and 6, for example) is usually expressed in a decimal fraction form (in this case 3.5), which is a float, even when the numbers to be averaged are all integers. Furthermore, because of the way that integers are stored, an integer can only be as large as the maximum designated in the system property the maxInteger.

Now let's see how to use the maxInteger system property to determine the largest integer that your system can store.

What's the Largest Integer You Can Remember?

1. Open the Message window (if necessary).
2. Type

   put the MaxInteger

   and press Return (Enter), to get this result:

   -- 2147483647

On our system, this value is 2,147,483,647 — a little over two billion. Notice the use of the keyword the in step 2. As discussed earlier and listed in Table 11-2, the maxInteger is a system property, an attribute of either Director or your computer, and Lingo uses the to identify it as being different from a variable.

Will you need numbers greater than two billion? It's not likely — but if you were to ever build an application that showed the current national debt, you couldn't do it with just integers. (At last count, it was around $1.7 trillion, or about three orders of magnitude too large!) Floating point numbers, on the other hand, can go much higher. The largest floating point number (at least in Windows) has a 1 followed by 308 zeroes.

Entering a number that large is awkward, and Director adopts a shortcut notation (called *scientific notation*). A floating point number can be broken into a *mantissa* and an *exponent*. The mantissa is a regular floating point number (usually between 1.0000000 and 9.99999999). The exponent is a multiplier and is separated from the mantissa by the letter *E*. For example, 3.14E6 is the same as 3.14 times 1,000,000 (in other words, 1 followed by six 0's), or 3,140,000. Negative exponents indicate 1 divided by the equivalent positive amount, so 3.14E-6 is 3.14 times 1 / 1,000,000, or .00000314.

Fun with Floats and Figures

1. Open the Message window (if necessary) and click an empty line.
2. Type the following statement to convert a floating point number with an exponent, to a floating point number:

   put 3.14E6

   and press Return (Enter). The result is

   -- 3140000.0000

3. To display another floating point number, type

   put 3.14E20

   and press Return (Enter). The only difference is that the exponent has been increased from 6 to 20. The result displayed in the Message window is

   -- 314000000000000000000.0000

4. Type

   put 100/3.0

   and press Return (Enter). The result is

   -- 33.3333

Tip: For Lingo and the Message window to view a number as a float, the number must include at least one decimal place.

Let us be precise

In the last step of the preceding exercise, dividing an integer by a one-decimal-place float generated a number with four decimal places. This illustrates the conception of *precision*.

Internally, a floating point number is only an approximation of the "real" number because of the way the number is represented within the computer. Since the computer can only retain a certain amount of information about the number, it maintains a certain internal precision. Precision refers to the number of digits that are accurate when the value is represented. In Director's case, only the first 15 digits in the mantissa are guaranteed to be accurate, even if the number that's displayed exceeds that amount. Since most people don't really have a need for accuracy beyond 8 digits or so, this is actually precise enough for almost any project you may encounter.

Bear in mind that the *internal* precision provided by Director is different from the *display* precision. If you are working with dollars and cents, there's no need to display more than two digits past the decimal point; in fact, displaying more information than that can be confusing. However, if you attempt to display the dollar amount $4.25 as a string (which you'll have to do to show the dollar sign), Director may throw in more precision than you want. The solution is to set a property in Director called `the floatPrecision`. It affects the *displayed* precision only — nothing changes the *internal* precision.

Note

You're right — we're still throwing around the term *properties* without its having been defined. Remember, a property stores the description of an attribute. In this case, `the floatPrecision` property indicates the number of decimal places that are displayed by Director for a float.

Displaying Dollars and Cents

1. With the Message window open, click an empty line.
2. Type

   ```
   set myAmount = 4.25
   ```

   and press Return (Enter). No result is displayed, because you didn't use the `put` statement.
3. Type

   ```
   put "$" & myAmount
   ```

   and press Return (Enter). The result is

   ```
   -- "$4.2500"
   ```
4. Type

   ```
   put the floatPrecision
   ```

   and press Return (Enter). Unless you or someone else has already reset `the floatPrecision` **property, the result is**

   ```
   -- 4
   ```

5. Type

   ```
   set oldPrecision to the floatPrecision
   ```

   and press Return (Enter). This line creates a temporary variable called `oldPrecision` and puts the value of `the floatPrecision` property into that variable. (This step is necessary so that you'll be able to reset `the floatPrecision` at the end of this exercise.)

6. Type

   ```
   set the floatPrecision to 2
   ```

   and press Return (Enter). This sets the float precision to 2, which tells Lingo to display only two digits to the right of the decimal point.

7. Type

   ```
   set myAmount=4.25
   ```

   and press Return (Enter).

8. Type

   ```
   put "$" & myAmount
   ```

   in the Message window and press Return (Enter). After entering the last line of instruction, the result in the Message window is

   ```
   -- "$4.25"
   ```

   When Director displays the amount, it only uses two digits in the cents section of the string.

9. Type

   ```
   set the floatPrecision to oldPrecision
   ```

   and press Return (Enter). This final statement sets `the floatPrecision` back to its original value.

Summary

In the next chapter, you'll discover how to control sprites and set properties using Lingo. Before moving on, let's review some of the things you learned in Chapter 11.

- Like other programming languages, Lingo uses commands, expressions, functions, variables, and constants as code-building blocks.
- Variables can be *declared* (by their use) as local to a specific handler or global (available in all handlers within a movie).
- The Message window is your tool for assigning values and strings to a variable.
- Some Lingo commands are aimed at controlling the progression and navigation of a movie (`go to`, `play` as discussed in Chapter 10). Other commands are used to establish values and properties (`put` and `set`).
- The Lingo Quick Reference, available through the Alphabetical Lingo and Categorized Lingo buttons on the Message and Script windows, helps you check the syntax of Lingo commands, properties, functions, and keywords.
- Lingo includes system variables, properties, and functions that display system information.
- Operators are symbols that tell you how two or more expressions should be combined. Lingo includes arithmetic, comparison, logical, grouping, and a few miscellaneous operators.

✦ ✦ ✦

CHAPTER 12

Writing Handlers

In This Chapter

Setting and testing properties

Placing sprites under the control of Lingo

Swapping sprites on the Stage

Redrawing the Stage

Using the repeat loop, and if...then...else control structures

Determining the last sprite clicked

Creating user-defined handlers

Building better buttons

Using the mouseWithin, mouseEnter, and mouseLeave event handlers

---

Despite the extreme pleasure that can be derived from working in the Message window and with simple three-line handlers, I suspect you are ready to build something more concrete. If Chapters 10 and 11 enabled you to crawl, this chapter encourages you to take your first steps in Lingo programming.

The focus of this chapter is to help you create a series of handlers that build a well-behaved button without using prepackaged behaviors. The topics covered may seem widely divergent, but the real focus is on introducing you to basic programming structures. You'll study `repeat` loops and `if...then...else` statements, frequently used Lingo commands (`updateStage`, `puppetSprite`), functions (`the mouseDown`, `the rollOver`, `the mouseCast`, `the clickOn`), properties of sprites as well as system properties, and new event handlers (`mouseWithin`, `mouseEnter`, and `mouseLeave`) — all of which will enable you to take your first steps toward writing scripts.

A child never learns to walk by simply talking about walking, so in this chapter you'll get to *create something from scratch* — so you can learn by doing. First, we'll review properties, and then continue to a series of exercises in which you'll build (step-by-step) a button that responds to your every wish . . . almost.

There Go the Property Values

In Chapter 11, you learned that a property is an attribute of an object. If you have worked with a word processor, you know that the term *print attribute* describes the appearance of text. The attributes of a text string include the font (typeface), the font style (such as bold and italic), and the font size (12 points, 14 points, and so on). Print attributes are an example of the *properties* of text.

Any object (in Lingo and in life) has specific attributes called *properties* that determine how it behaves and how it looks. For instance, the properties of a billiard ball include a smooth, shiny surface, a small size, and a hard, impenetrable structure. On the other hand, the properties of a basketball include a dull, elastic surface with small bumps, and a larger, less dense structure as compared to the billiard ball. The properties affect both the type of ball and its use.

Each person you know has specific attributes or properties, too. (I am not talking about ownership). Blond hair is a property. A quick wit is a property. The amount of education completed is a property. Just as all human traits cannot all be set (such as skin color and height), not all properties in a Director movie can be set. Some properties can only be read.

Using Lingo, you can set and evaluate (*test*) properties. Properties are set using the `put` or `set` commands. A few of the properties that can be set using Lingo are listed in Table 12-1. The table includes examples of Lingo instructions using the listed properties. Notice that in some examples, the `set` command is used to establish a property value. In other cases, the `put` command is used (as you would enter it in the Message window) to display or indicate the current property value. These are examples only. Each of the properties in Table 12-1 can be set (using the `set` command) or displayed (using the `put` command).

Note

`Set` is a workhorse command in Director. Though it has a number of different uses, its primary purpose is to change the value of a Director property.

Table 12-1
Common Sprite Properties That Can Be Set Using Lingo

Property Name	Example	Description of Action
the cursor of sprite	set the cursor of sprite 2 to 4	Establishes the appearance of the mouse pointer over a specified sprite
the ink of sprite	set the ink of sprite 3 to 8	Establishes the ink effect applied to a specific sprite
the locH of sprite	put the locH of sprite 2	Indicates the horizontal location of a sprite on the Stage
the locV of sprite	put the locV of sprite 8	Indicates the vertical location of a sprite on the Stage
the stageColor	put the stageColor	Indicates the color setting for the movie's Stage

Property Name	Example	Description of Action
the visible of sprite	set the visible of sprite 3 to True	Establishes whether a sprite is visible or not
the member of sprite	put the member of sprite 10	Indicates the cast member and cast upon which the sprite is based
the current-SpriteNum	put the currentSpriteNum	Returns the highest channel number (or sprite number) in the Score over which the mouse is currently rolling

As you examine Table 12-1, notice that the is part of the *required* name of the property and is always used to signal a property. Sprite properties use the of sprite keywords (which follow the property name) to designate the sprite to which the property belongs.

Note

Not all properties are sprite properties. Some are system properties. Take the currentSpriteNum and the stageColor, for instance. Although you never write their "full" names, these properties are actually properties of the system or Director. Their more common "nicknames" are understood to equal the currentSpriteNum of Director or the stageColor of Director.

Properties do not stand alone in Lingo instructions. They are used in conjunction with commands. For instance, if you enter the following instruction:

    Put the ink of sprite 3

in the Message window, the result returned is the ink (designated by a number) of sprite 3. So if the sprite in channel 3 has the Matte ink applied, the result is 8:

    -- 8

In this next exercise, you set specific properties using instructions in the Message window. Later, you can include these instructions in a script that executes while a movie plays. For now, you can use the Message window to watch the result of modifying one or more properties.

Setting Properties Using Lingo

1. Open a new movie.
2. If necessary, press Command+M (Ctrl+M) to open the Message window.

(continued)

3. To create a text cast member, type

   put "For every rip, there is a patch" into field 1
   and press Enter.

4. Drag the text cast member (1) onto the Stage. Its position on the Stage does not matter.

5. In the Message window, type

   set the visible of sprite 1 to False

   and press Enter. The text of the field disappears from the Stage. In the next step, you'll make the sprite visible again.

6. Type

   set the visible of sprite 1 to True

   and press Enter. The text in the field reappears on the Stage.

7. Type

   set the stageColor to 255

   and press Enter. If your movie is using the System-Win or System-Mac palette, the background color of the Stage changes to black.

8. Issue the command in step 7 again, but change the 255 to any number between 1 and 254. Watch the results.

9. To reset the Stage color back to its default color (white), type

   set the stageColor to 0

10. Close the Message window.

Now that each Lingo structure or component has been defined (from scripts to properties and commands), you can proceed to build something more functional — a better navigational button.

Wanted: "Real" Navigational Buttons

Although the objective of this chapter is to study the control of sprites using Lingo, we find it's easier to learn when focusing on a real-world problem. In this case, you learn to add specific behaviors to a button while building those behaviors from scratch.

In Chapter 6, you attached several prepackaged behaviors to a button to make it behave like a well-designed interactive button. In Chapter 10, you took a step backward and attached a simple script to several cast members and caused them to act like buttons. The buttons were typical flat Director buttons that were created using the Tool Palette. They were functional buttons, but they did not provide users with very much feedback.

Throughout this chapter, you'll explore how Lingo commands can be used to enhance interactivity by providing visual feedback and standard responses. Every button behavior you learn to construct in this chapter can be accomplished using prepackaged behaviors — but it's time to bake your own apple pie, rather than always depending on Grandma to bake it.

The first step in your chapter-long project is to determine which actions you want incorporated into your well-behaved button.

What to expect from a polite button

When you click a button, certain specific behaviors are expected. You probably don't consciously think about what constitutes a well-behaved button, but you intuitively know that some specific, standard behaviors are expected.

As an end-user, you expect the following things from a polite button:

- ✦ When the mouse pointer is over a button and the mouse button is depressed, the appearance of the button changes (it highlights or flashes).

    Tip: Providing users with a visual clue that the "click was successful" is good design practice. Color changes are excellent visual clues.

- ✦ When you press and then release the mouse button over a button, the button on-screen reverts to its original appearance and an action (linked to the button) occurs.

- ✦ While holding down the mouse button over a screen button, if you move the mouse pointer off the button, the button reverts to its original appearance and whatever action is linked to the button does *not* occur.

- ✦ While the mouse button is still held down, if the mouse pointer moves back over the screen button, the button again changes (highlights or flashes).

- ✦ When you click the mouse button, an appropriate audio response occurs (a click or some other sound).

As you work through this chapter, you'll create a button script that includes all of these features — except for the sound feature. Adding a puppetSound will be covered in Chapter 14. Here you will walk through a trial-and-error approach to constructing an interactive button, so you can see what works and what does not work.

Creating Well-Behaved Buttons

You'll need to learn the following tasks to make your buttons functional:

- Placing the button sprites under control of Lingo
- Causing the button to change its appearance (by swapping one cast member for another)
- Determining the location of the mouse pointer, and causing the button to alter its appearance when it is rolled over

Using puppetSprites in Director

You know that a cast member placed on the Stage becomes a sprite. The sprite is derived from the cast member but can be modified on the Stage (without affecting the original cast member). Further, the sprite is under the control of the Score until you take control using Lingo. The Score can do some wonderful things with a sprite, but to get beyond the most basic forms of interactivity, the sprite must be *puppeted* (controlled) by Lingo. Just as a real puppet is under the control of the puppeteer, a puppetSprite is under the control of Lingo.

To puppet a specific sprite, you must issue the `puppetSprite` command followed by its two parameters. The first parameter designates the channel being placed under the control of Lingo. The second parameter establishes whether the `puppetSprite` property is turned on (using 1 or True) or off (using 0 or False). Either of the following two commands cause the sprite in channel 2 of the Score window to be puppeted:

```
puppetSprite 2, True

puppetSprite 2, 1
```

Tip Commands and variables in Lingo cannot include spaces. So to enhance readability, letters within the command are frequently capitalized, as in `puppetTransition`, `puppetSprite`, `mouseUp`, and `mouseDown`.

Either of the following two commands turn off the `puppetSprite` property for the sprite in channel 2.

```
puppetSprite 2, False

puppetSprite 2, 0
```

> **Tip:** The first parameter (2 in the above example) following the `puppetSprite` command refers to the channel to be puppeted — not to a cast member number. The second parameter (a constant) indicates if the `puppetSprite` property is turned on (1 or True) or off (0 or False).

A sprite is always controlled by either Lingo or by the Score. If the puppet property of a sprite is set to True, it is under the control of Lingo via the instructions in your scripts. If the puppet property of the sprite is set to False, the sprite is controlled by the directions in the Score. Any sprite, when first dragged to the Stage, has its puppet state set to False. In other words, all sprites are initially under the control of the Score.

Let's take a closer look at some guidelines for determining the puppet state of a sprite.

Knowing when to turn the puppet states on and off

Don't set the puppet state of a sprite to True until you want to transfer control to Lingo. In addition, don't forget to revert control back to the Score whenever you no longer need Lingo to control the sprite. In general, you should puppet a sprite only when absolutely required.

Following these guidelines will help you avoid unpredictable actions from puppeted sprites:

- ✦ You should "unpuppet" sprites before using the `go to` or `play` commands to jump to other sections of a movie — unless you are sure you want the channel puppeted in the new range of frames.
- ✦ Don't puppet a sprite if there is nothing for the sprite to do.
- ✦ Because you actually puppet a channel and not just a sprite, be sure to puppet a channel that has an object in it. You can puppet an empty channel, but the results may be unpredictable and can generate unexpected problems.
- ✦ Be sure to puppet a sprite for as long as you want the changes (introduced by puppeting the sprite) to endure. The puppet state of a sprite should only be turned off when you want the object to return to Score control.

Swapping cast members using Lingo

When you click a button in an application, you expect some visual response. This reaction can be a change in color, a change in brightness, a slight shifting of the button's on-Stage position, or a combination of visual cues. To create any of these changes in appearance, you can replace one sprite (the original button image) with a second sprite (the depressed button).

When you replace a sprite, the replacement image can be lighter, smaller, or darker. It depends on what you consider to be the most effective feedback for users in that situation. Whatever reaction you select, use it consistently throughout your movie.

To swap one sprite on the Stage for another, you use the `set` command along with a property called `the memberNum of sprite`. This property reflects the current cast member number upon which a sprite is based. The syntax of the statement is as follows:

```
set the memberNum of sprite x to y
```

The first parameter (*x*) refers to the channel number in which the affected sprite is stored in the current frame. The sprite is replaced by a sprite derived from cast member *y* (the second parameter). For instance, the following statement will replace the sprite in channel 1 with a sprite based on cast member 5:

```
set the memberNum of sprite 1 to 5
```

Caution

A sprite must first be puppeted, or Lingo cannot swap sprites using the `set` command.

Note

As a historical note, prior to Director 5, `the memberNum of sprite` property was called `the castNum of sprite x`. When Director 5 began to support multiple casts, it became necessary for most functions using the term `cast` to use the term `member`. Now you can specify `the member of cast`. Both terms are operational in Director 6, but the `castNum` keyword will become obsolete in the future.

In the following steps, you will modify an existing movie to provide a visual clue to users when a button is pressed or clicked. This task is accomplished by puppeting and then swapping one cast member (the initial undepressed button) for a second cast member (the depressed button).

Note in the following steps that we are using abbreviations to more easily identify and name cast members (buttons). The first character in the cast member's name refers to the color of the button (*B* for blue and *P* for purple). The second character describes the icon on the face of the button (*H* for horse and *G* for guitar). The third character identifies the direction of the icon (*L* for Left, *R* for right, and *N* for nondirectional). The final character in the code identifies whether the button represents an up or down state (*U* for up and *D* for down). We might have simply called each button by a longer name (such as "Blue Horse Facing Right in Down State") but the Cast window would truncate the display of the name, and several cast members would then appear to be called "Blue Horse" or "Purple Horse."

On the CD-ROM The file western.dir, used in the next exercise, is stored on your companion CD-ROM in the exercise:ch12 (exercise\ch12) folder.

Swapping Sprites on the Stage

1. Open the western.dir movie in Director.
2. Select cast member 5 (BHRU).
3. Select the Cast Member Script button to open the Script window.
4. When the Script window appears, press Command+Home (Ctrl+Home) to move the insertion point prior to the `on mouseUp` handler. Then add the following `on mouseDown` handler:

```
on mouseDown
     puppetSprite 3, True
     set the memberNum of sprite 3 to 6
end
```

The first instruction in the `on mouseDown` handler puppets the sprite in channel 3 (when the user clicks the mouse button). Frame 1 already includes a frame script that causes the playback head to cycle on the current frame until instructed otherwise.

5. Before leaving the Script window, change the `on mouseUp` handler to match the following code. (If the Script window is too small to view both the `on mouseDown` and the `on mouseUp` handlers, resize it so all the script code is visible.)

```
on mouseUp
     set the memberNum of sprite 3 to 5
     puppetSprite 3, False
end
```

The `on mouseDown` handler replaces the sprite in channel 3 with a sprite based on cast member 6. When the mouse button is released, the cast number reverts to 5 and the `puppetSprite` property is turned off. Notice that the `go to` statement in the earlier version of the `on mouseUp` handler has been deleted. At least initially, the movie has been modified so the playback head stays in frame 1.

6. Press Enter on the numeric keypad to close the Script window.
7. Save the movie as **western1.dir**, rewind, and play it.

8. Click the Blue Forward button (the rightmost button).

   The button changes, but does not change back. That's because the current sprite on the Stage is based on cast member BHRD (cast member 6) and it does not have a script attached. Even if you click it, no action is indicated without a script.

9. Stop the movie.

10. Add the following script to cast member 6 (BHRD):

    ```
    on mouseUp
          set the memberNum of sprite 3 to 5
          puppetSprite 3, False
    end
    ```

11. Close the Script window, rewind the movie, save it again as western1.dir, and play it.

    The Blue Forward button now changes when you click it, but its doesn't go anywhere. When you click the sprite based on cast member 5, it is replaced by a sprite based on cast member 6. When you release the button, based on the new script, the sprite based on cast member 6 changes back to a sprite based on cast member 5.

12. Click the Blue Forward button, hold down the mouse button, and drag the mouse pointer off the button. What happens? Release the mouse button. What happens?

    The button visually stays in the depressed state. You need to make some additional coding changes so the button returns to its natural appearance when the mouse pointer is no longer over the button.

13. Stop the movie.

Building bitmap buttons (with Photoshop)

The buttons in the western.dir movie were created using Adobe Photoshop. The icons on the face of each button were created using the Giddyup Thangs font. If you have Adobe Photoshop, you can use the following steps to create additional buttons of your own design:

1. In Photoshop, use the File➪New command to create a new document 50 pixels by 50 pixels with a white background. Resolution is set at 72 dpi and Mode at RGB.

2. Use the Elliptical Marquee tool to create a circle (hold down the Shift key while you click and drag). Turn on the anti-aliasing option and set the feather

option to 0. Start in the upper-left corner and drag to the bottom-right. Be sure the marching-ants marquee is entirely within the square area of the document.

You can also hold down the Alt+Shift keys (Windows) or Option+Shift (Macintosh) to drag and create a circle from the center out.

3. Set the foreground color to white and the background color to black.
4. Double-click the Gradient tool to open the Gradient Tool Options window. Set the gradient type to Radial and select the Foreground to Background style setting. Opacity should be 100% and ink set to Normal.
5. Click and drag from inside the selected circle, at the point where you want the highlight to appear, to the bottom opposite side of the circle. (To create the buttons used in the western.dir movie, we started inside the upper-left portion of the circle and dragged just outside the bottom-right portion of the circle.)
6. When satisfied with the sphere, create a new layer, and then switch the foreground color to Black and the background color to White.
7. Select the Edit ➪ Stroke command to add an outline to the sphere.
8. Set the Stroke Width pixels to 2, location to Outside, opacity to 100% and the Mode to Soft Light. Select the OK button.

The button is complete, except for text or an icon and some color. To achieve the embossed look, use these additional steps:

1. Create another layer with the Mode set to Normal. (Each layer enables you to delete the changes without starting from scratch.)
2. Set the foreground color to White.
3. Select the Text tool and click the face of the sphere.
4. In the Type Tool dialog box, select the desired font, font size, style, alignment, leading, and spacing. Then enter the desired text or symbol and select the OK button. (We used 42 point, Giddyup Thangs font to generate the symbols on the buttons. Other symbol type fonts include Marlett, Map Symbols, Monotype Sorts, Symbol, Wingdings, WP IconicSymbolsA and WP IconicSymbolsB, and WP Typographic Symbols.)
5. If needed, reposition the icon or text to appear centered on the sphere.

Tip

With Photoshop version 3.*x*, while the text or icon is selected you can use the arrow keys to adjust the object's position (pixel by pixel) on the canvas. With version 4, you must select the Move tool and then use the arrow keys to adjust the object's position.

6. With the text or icon still selected, select Filter ➪ Stylize ➪ Emboss. (We set the emboss angle to 135, the pixel depth to 3, and the amount to 100%. This makes the light source appear to shine from behind the viewer and highlight the upper-right corner of the object.)

7. Select the OK button and then, if satisfied with the result, deselect the text object or icon.

To add some color to the button:

1. Create another layer with the Mode set to Overlay.

2. Press Command+D (Ctrl+D) to deselect the sphere.

3. Set the foreground to a desired color and then use Edit ➪ Fill. In the Fill dialog, use the foreground color, set Opacity to 100%, and Mode to Overlay. Be sure the Preserve Transparency check box is *not* selected, and then click the OK button.

You are now ready to change the image's mode to indexed color, save it as a bitmap image, and then import it into Director.

If you save the original Photoshop document as a PSD file before changing its mode to indexed color, you can preserve the layers. Just be sure you do not save the indexed color version (which flattens all layers) as a PSD file. Layers are handy. You can hide or reveal them to create another button with different text from the same image file. All of the buttons in western.dir were created from the same PSD file. As we created each button, such as the Guitar button, we simply made the other, unwanted layers (with the right- and left-facing horse icons) invisible.

On the CD-ROM The file western.psd is stored on the companion CD-ROM in the exercise:ch12 (exercise\ch12) folder.

Adding expected button behaviors

Users want the ability to change their minds — frequently. One particular expected behavior for working with buttons is the ability to click a button, hold the mouse button down, move the mouse pointer off the button, and *not* have the action linked to the button occur. Another expected behavior is to be able to move the mouse (while holding down the mouse button) back over the on-screen button and have it highlight again. To accomplish these tasks, Director must

✦ Constantly check the location of the mouse pointer

✦ Display the replacement sprite only when the mouse button is down and the mouse pointer is over the original sprite

✦ Update the Stage as needed

You can accomplish these tasks using the `updateStage` command, the `repeat while` keyword, the `rollover()` function and the `mouseDown` function.

Adding repeat loops

To constantly check a condition — for example, the location of the mouse pointer — you create a `repeat` loop. The command syntax is

```
repeat while condition
     do-something
end repeat
```

The *do-something* statement can include any Lingo command that you want executed. The *condition* can be any Lingo-recognized event.

Note: In the above command syntax, the term *do-something* is of course not a Lingo command or statement. It is *pseudocode* — a placeholder for a real Lingo command or statement. Pseudocode is a way of writing out a program in English to get a better feel for what the final code will look like.

In the following example, Director uses `the mouseDown` function to check for a `mouseDown` event. This function evaluates whether the mouse button is currently being held down. Using the following handler, if the mouse button is depressed, the movie emits a double-beep:

```
repeat while the mouseDown
     beep 2
end repeat
```

Caution: Loops created using the `repeat while` command trap execution and force other events to wait until the current handler concludes. Use this kind of control structure cautiously.

Checking a state or condition

Director includes several functions, listed in Table 12-2, that check for a specific *state* or *condition*. Each of these binary functions returns a value of True (1) or False (0). When used with the `repeat while` command, the loop continues as long as the function returns a value of True.

A function is really just a Lingo built-in handler that returns a result when complete.

Table 12-2
Functions That Check for Specific Conditions

Function	What It Determines
`the controlDown`	If the Control key is being pressed
`the mouseUp`	If the mouse button is *not* being held down
`the pauseState`	If a movie is paused
`the shiftDown`	If the Shift key is being pressed
`the stillDown`	If the mouse button is still held down

Using the rollOver function

The `rollOver` function checks to see if the mouse pointer is located over a specified sprite. If it is, a value of True is returned; otherwise, the function returns a value of False. The syntax for the function is

`rollOver (x)`

The *x* parameter is the number of the sprite's channel — not the cast member's number. The parentheses are required.

To build a better, more responsive mouse button, the button's image needs to change when the mouse pointer is over the button. By using the `rollOver` function, you can cause the button to retain its original appearance when the mouse pointer is *not* located over the button, and then change to a different (highlighted) image of the button, when the mouse point *is* located over the button.

Updating the Stage

To change the appearance of a sprite on the Stage within a frame, you must force Director to update or refresh the Stage. Director only updates the Stage when the playback head exits a frame, at which time Director begins to draw the objects specified in the channels of the next frame.

If you need to redraw the Stage when the playback head does *not* exit the frame (as in a `repeat` loop), you must issue the `updateStage` command. The `updateStage` command has no parameters and redraws all objects on the Stage.

Using if...then statements

In Lingo and other authoring languages, the if...then statement is used to provide alternate courses of action. It is used to evaluate whether an expression is True or False. If the expression, called a *condition*, is True, then the statement or statements immediately following the then keyword are evaluated and executed. *If* a specific situation exists, *then* a specific action occurs. *If* the specified situation does not exist, *then* a specified action does not occur. (This type of statement was also briefly discussed in Chapter 11 in the section on comparison operators.)

You use if...then statements every day. *If* you have children, *then* you know how much doctor bills can cost. *If* you have a computer and modem at home, *then* you can access local bulletin board systems and the Internet. *If* you snore loudly at night, *then* your spouse needs ear plugs.

Here's the syntax for an if...then statement:

```
if condition then action
```

When the if...then statement contains an else clause, the statement must end with the keyword end if.

Caution

Some programming languages combine the end if into a single keyword (*endif*). In Lingo, you must use end if as two separate words.

An extension of the if...then statement is the if...then...else statement, in which the else can be interpreted as *otherwise*. For instance, *if* you pledge over $100, *then* you receive a bonus gift, *else* you only receive a receipt for your contribution.

Let's look at some examples. In this first example, you cause Director to switch sprites if the mouse pointer is not over the sprite that is stored in channel 3:

```
if rollover (3) = False then
     set the memberNum of sprite 3 to 5
end if
```

If...then...else statements can include several levels, as shown in the following example which evaluates the machineType of the user's workstation:

```
on mouseUp me
     if the machinetype=256 then
       set the member of sprite (the currentSpritenum)¬
       to "BtnBlue"
          if the platform="Windows,32" then
         go to movie "Movie2PC"
       else
          go to movie "Movie2Gen"
       end if
     else
       set the member of sprite (the currentSpritenum) to "BtnRed"
```

(continued)

```
            if the platform="Macintosh,PPC" then
               go to movie "Movie2Mac"
            else
               go to movie "Movie2Gen"
            end if
         end if
   end
```

Notice how the `if` statements are stacked within one another. This process is known as *nesting* and is common in complex logic statements. If statements can be nested up to 32 levels deep, although any more than four levels of `if` statements can become extremely difficult to debug.

The indentations in nested statements, by the way, are not just pedagogical devices. Director will automatically indent `if` statements, provided that they are syntactically correct (that is, you didn't misspell something or forget to put the `else` keyword at the end of the `if` statement). This automatic indenting can be quite useful, because it means any nested `if` statement can be visually matched with its corresponding `end if` statement. And when you're working with complex `if` statements, you can quite easily forget to write in an `end if` somewhere, which causes the code to execute incorrectly.

Taking the road less traveled

Nested `if` statements can be deceptively complex. You'll understand this complexity if you visualize the `if` statement as a branch in the road.

At the top level, the `if` statement is the first branch in the road, the place where you must choose to steer right or left. Your destination will be irrevocably altered depending on the choice you make (sorry, you can't back up and change your mind). The town at the end of one branch is the destination taken `if` a condition is True (you keep to the right), and the town at the end of the other branch is what you get to `if` the condition is False (you do not keep to the right).

In a single nested `if` statement, there's another fork in the road rather than a single destination, each fork having different towns at the end of the journey. You now have four possible destinations instead of two. Thus a branching structure eight layers deep can have up to 256 possible results (or actions or destinations), with the number doubling for every layer beyond that.

Remember the pseudocode presented earlier to show a `repeat while` loop? In the following step-by-step example, it is replaced with a statement that includes the `rollover` function. This statement checks the mouse pointer location to determine if it is over the sprite in channel 3. If so, Director replaces one sprite (the original button-up sprite) with a replacement sprite (the button-down image). Because control of the movie is trapped within a loop, Director does not redraw objects on the Stage. You must include an `updateStage` command.

As you modify the western1.dir movie, you alter the script so it instructs Director to replace the sprite in channel 3 with a sprite based on cast member 6. In the script, Lingo updates the Stage to display the new sprite. As long as the mouse button is down, Director evaluates the `if...then` statement. If the `rollover` function returns a value of False, a sprite based on the original cast member 5 appears in channel 3. Otherwise, the sprite in channel 3 is based on the replacement cast member 6.

When you finally release the mouse button, the `on mouseUp` handler is executed and the `puppetSprite` property is turned off.

Redrawing a Sprite When It Is Rolled Over

On the CD-ROM

1. Open the western1.dir movie in Director. You need the movie you modified earlier in this chapter, or the file western1.dir stored on your companion CD-ROM in the exercise:ch12 (exercise\ch12) folder.

2. Change the script attached to cast member 5 to match the following. (You can skip the comment lines that begin with a double-dash (--). These comments are present to help explain the code but are not executed by the program. See the upcoming section, "Commenting your code.")

```
on mouseDown
     puppetSprite 3, True
     set the memberNum of sprite 3 to 6
-- The next command redraws the Stage
     updateStage
     repeat while the mouseDown
-- As long as the mouse button is depressed
-- the statements within the repeat while
-- loop are executed again and again
          if rollOver(3) = False then
               set the memberNum of sprite 3 to 5
          end if
          UpdateStage
-- The updateStage command is needed so that
-- each time the if...then statement is evaluated
-- any action is updated on the Stage
     end repeat
end
```

(continued)

```
on mouseUp
     puppetSprite 3, False
end
```

Tip: After entering code in the Script window, you can press the Tab key and the script is automatically indented for easy reading. When you do this, Director lines up the `if` and `end if` keywords plus the `repeat while` and `end repeat` keywords. Each statement within a `repeat while` and `if...then` statement is indented one tab setting.

3. Close the Script window, save the movie as **western2.dir,** rewind, and play it.

4. Now you can test the Blue Forward button. Depress the mouse button over the Blue Forward button. Hold down the mouse button and slide the mouse pointer off the Blue Forward button. The button should return to its original state.

5. Click and hold the mouse button over the Blue Forward button. Hold down the mouse button, slide the pointer off the Blue Forward button, and then slide it back on. The button does not return to its depressed state, so you have another modification to make.

6. Stop the movie and open the script attached to cast member 5. Then make the following changes to the `if...then` statement:

```
if rollover(3) = False then
     set the memberNum of sprite 3 to 5
else
     set the memberNum of sprite 3 to 6
end if
```

Only the `else` clause in the `if...then` statement is added. The remainder of the script is still okay. The `else` clause tells Director that if the rollover condition is *not* False (in other words, True), the sprite stored in channel 3 should be based on cast member 6. Once you break through the double-negative, this statement tells Director to display the Blue Forward *depressed* button if the mouse pointer is over the sprite stored in channel 3 and the mouse button is down.

7. Close the Script window, save the movie again as western2.dir, rewind, and play the movie. Test the behavior of the button, and note that it finally behaves as you would expect it to — with one exception. When you click the button, the playback head remains on the current frame. Though the button now provides visual feedback, it still doesn't do anything.

8. Stop the movie.

9. Open the script attached to the BHRU cast member (5) and modify the on mouseUp handler as follows:

   ```
   on mouseUp
         if rollOver(3) = True then
               go to "Purple"
         end if
         puppetSprite 3, False
   end
   ```

   The new code indicates that if the mouse pointer is over the sprite in channel 3 when the mouseUp event occurs, then the playback head jumps to the marker Purple.

10. Save the movie again as western2.dir, rewind, and play it. Test the behavior of the Blue Forward button. The Blue Forward button moves the playback head to frame 30 (the Purple marker).

11. Click the Purple Back button.

12. Stop the movie.

Commenting your code

In the preceding steps, you encountered lines of text within the script that were identified using the comment symbol (--). The double-dash before a line of code indicates that the line is a *comment* and is not executed by Director. You can also comment part of a line, in which case everything to the right of the comment symbol is considered a comment.

Comments fall into two categories: They serve either as a note to the programmer, or to identify a line of code that you don't want executed. When you use a comment to disable code, the programming term for this is "commenting out the code."

You can comment your code by typing dashes, but if you're trying to disable an entire section or even a whole handler, this can be a tedious process. Fortunately, Director provides a shortcut. Here's how to comment out an entire block of code:

1. Click and drag the cursor across a selection of text in the Script window. (Another way to select text is to click in the white area at the left of the left margin and drag down.)

2. Press Command+Shift+> (Ctrl+Shift+>) to comment out the code. Or, to remove the comment status from the code, press Command+Shift+< (Ctrl+Shift+<).

There's currently a debate in programming circles as to whether commenting code is worth while. It's hard to deny, though, that for the most part it's helpful to place descriptive comments about what you're attempting to do in your code; the comments are sure to be of use to you and any other programmer who needs to modify your code in the future. Lingo is fairly self-descriptive, so make your comments focus on what you are attempting to do overall, rather than commenting each line individually.

Duplicating buttons and other stuff

When you finished running the western2.dir movie, the Purple Back button caused the playback head to jump to frame 1 (with the blue buttons), but it did not "flash" the same as the Blue Forward button. That's because the more detailed script was not added to cast member 7.

Director makes use of the cut and paste operations (using the Clipboard) that are common to Windows and Macintosh applications. In other words, you can

1. Select a cast member, sprite, script, text string, or other fragment of a movie.
2. Select the Edit ➪ Copy command using Command+C (Ctrl+C) to copy the object to the Clipboard.
3. Move to where you want the copied object inserted.
4. Select the Edit ➪ Paste command or press Command+V (Ctrl+V) to paste the object from the Clipboard to its target location in your movie.

You can use this technique to reduce the amount of typing you have to do, and to quickly duplicate a cast member script and attach it to another cast member.

Tip Rather than retyping an entire script from scratch, it is often easier to cut-and-paste a long similar script and then make the necessary modifications.

If you duplicate a script and it needs to be modified, you can quickly replace specific text strings within the script using the Edit ➪ Find ➪ Text command (Command+F or Ctrl+F). To do so, simply fill in the Find and Replace fields of the Find Text dialog box and then click the Replace or Replace All button.

In the following steps, you copy the script from cast member 5 to cast member 7 and then make a few modifications.

Copying and Modifying the rollover Button Script

On the CD-ROM

1. Open the western2.dir movie in Director. You need the movie you modified earlier in this chapter, or the file western2.dir stored on your companion CD-ROM in the exercise:ch12 (exercise\ch12) folder.
2. Open the script attached to cast member 5.
3. Triple-click in the Script window to select all the code.
4. Press Command+C (Ctrl+C) to copy the code to the Clipboard.
5. Select the Next Cast Member button twice, identified in Figure 12-1, until the script for cast member 7 appears.

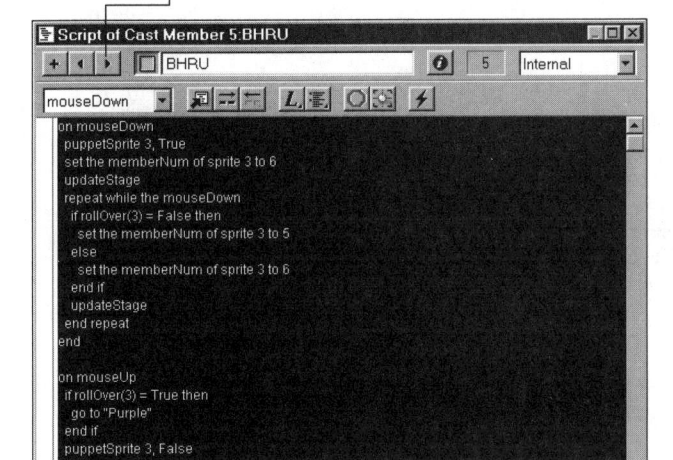

```
on mouseDown
  puppetSprite 3, True
  set the memberNum of sprite 3 to 6
  updateStage
  repeat while the mouseDown
    if rollOver(3) = False then
      set the memberNum of sprite 3 to 5
    else
      set the memberNum of sprite 3 to 6
    end if
    updateStage
  end repeat
end

on mouseUp
  if rollOver(3) = True then
    go to "Purple"
  end if
  puppetSprite 3, False
end
```

Figure 12-1: The selected script in cast member 5 that is copied to cast member 7

6. Triple-click to select all code in the current script, and then press Command+V (Ctrl+V) to paste the new script from the Clipboard into the Script window. Using this method, any selected text is overwritten.
7. Change all occurrences of the number 3 to 1 (this changes references to sprite or puppetSprite 3 to sprite or puppetSprite 1). There are seven occurrences.
8. Change the single occurrence of the number 5 to 7 (it is a cast member number). Be sure to change rollOver(3) to rollOver(1).

(continued)

9. Change all occurrences of the number 6 to 8 (the two occurrences refer to cast member numbers).

10. Change the one occurrence of the word Purple to Blue. The modified script is shown in Figure 12-2.

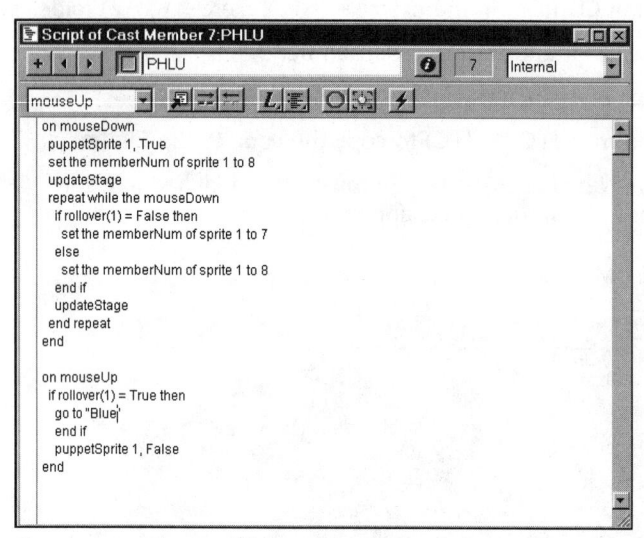

```
on mouseDown
  puppetSprite 1, True
  set the memberNum of sprite 1 to 8
  updateStage
  repeat while the mouseDown
    if rollover(1) = False then
      set the memberNum of sprite 1 to 7
    else
      set the memberNum of sprite 1 to 8
    end if
    updateStage
  end repeat
end

on mouseUp
  if rollover(1) = True then
    go to "Blue"
  end if
  puppetSprite 1, False
end
```

Figure 12-2: The modified script, now attached to cast member 7

11. Close the Script window, save the movie as **western3.dir**, rewind, play, and test the movie.

Now that you've learned how to script real navigational buttons, the next step is to add scripts to the remaining buttons. Because the new scripts have much in common with the existing scripts, it is time to figure out a way to reuse your code. Cutting, pasting, and modifying existing code does indeed save time, but there's a more efficient method available for duplicating code.

Reusing Code for Greater Efficiency

In this section you'll see how to cut and paste the script attached to cast member 5 into the other buttons that are not highlighted (cast members 1, 3, 9, and 11), and make some minor changes to the script at the same time — just as you did with cast member 7.

- References to channel 3 have to be changed to channel 1 or 2.
- References to cast members 5 and 6 have to be changed to one of these sets: 1 and 2, 3 and 4, 7 and 8, 9 and 10, or 11 and 12.

With all these changes to be made, already you can see the growing opportunity for typing errors and miscalculations. But by making the statements in the script more generic, then you can use the script over and over again. Lingo provides a vast array of functions and properties to accomplish this exact task. You can create your own *user-defined handlers* (often referred to as *routines* or *subroutines*) that can be called (executed) from any other handler or script in the movie.

Identifying the current cast member

You already know that every sprite is derived from a cast member. Once a cast member is dragged onto the Stage, it becomes a sprite. Using Lingo's `the mouseCast` function, you can ascertain the sprite over which the mouse pointer is located and in turn determine the number of the cast member from which the sprite is derived. In simpler terms, if the mouse pointer is over a sprite based on cast member number 10, `the mouseCast` function returns a value of 10.

Beginning with Director 6, you have access to a replacement for `the mouseCast` function; it's called `the mouseMember`. The `mouseCast` and `the mouseMember` serve similar functions, but they return different results. The `mouseCast` returns a number; `the mouseMember` returns an expression such as `member 1 of castLib 1`. You can perform arithmetic functions using the value returned by `the mouseCast` (as shown in the next exercise), but you cannot do so with the expression returned by `the mouseMember` function. For example, if the mouse pointer rests over a sprite derived from cast member 2 (from an internal cast), you can use the following instructions in the Message window and get the results shown:

```
put the mouseCast into underMouseNow
put underMouseNow
  -- 2
put the mouseMember into underMouseThen
put underMouseThen
  -- member 2 of castLib 1
put underMouseNow + 1
  -- 3
put underMouseThen + 1
  -- 0
```

As long as `the mouseCast` is still available, we'll use it to obtain a numerical value representing the cast member number in the Cast window.

In the following steps, you test `the mouseCast` function using the western3.dir movie and the Message window. By using `the mouseCast` function you can determine the number of the cast member on which the sprite is based and assign the value to a variable. The variable can be used in the button script to represent the current sprite. Further, the variable can be used in an instruction that swaps one cast member for another and changes the appearance of the button on the Stage.

Using the `MouseCast` Function in Your Button Script

On the CD-ROM

1. Open the western3.dir movie in Director. You need the movie you modified earlier in this chapter, or the file western3.dir stored on your companion CD-ROM in the exercise:ch12 (exercise\ch12) folder.
2. Open the Message window (Command+M or Ctrl+M).
3. Be sure the Message window is active and then move the mouse pointer over the Blue Guitar button (without clicking the mouse button).
4. In the Message window, type **put the mouseCast** and press Enter. Your Message window appears similar to Figure 12-3, indicating that the mouse pointer is over cast member number 3.
5. Now you can use this function to build a more generic button script. Open the script for cast member number 5.
6. First, you must edit the `on mouseDown` handler. Leave the existing text as is, but add the following statement immediately after the line of script that includes the `on mouseDown` keyword (see Figure 12-4).

   ```
   put the mouseCast into button
   ```

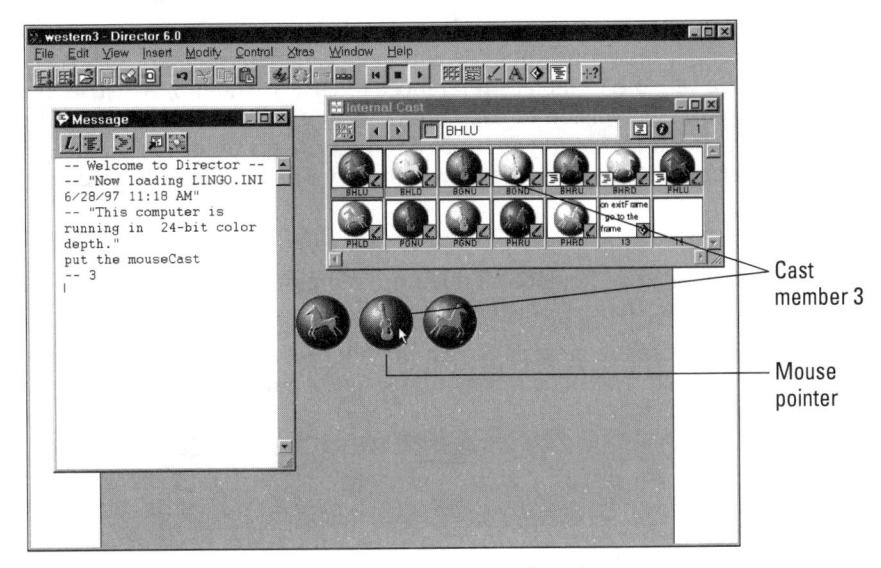

Figure 12-3: The response to the mouseCast function

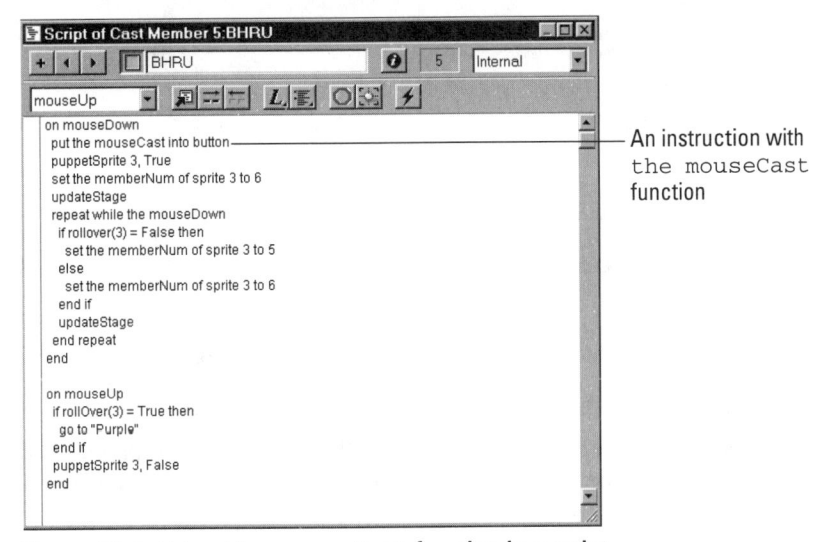

Figure 12-4: Using the mouseCast function in a script

7. Now that the statement places the Cast number of the current sprite (under the mouse pointer) into a local variable called `button`, you can use the variable to replace references to cast member 5. Because the depressed version of each button is in a Cast window slot numbered one higher than the original (not depressed) version of the button, you can also replace references to cast member 6 with the following expression:

   ```
   button +1
   ```

   Do this now. Replace all references to cast member 5 with the variable `button`. There is only one occurrence.

8. Replace all references to cast member 6 with the expression `button +1`. There are two occurrences. The script should appear similar to Figure 12-5.

```
on mouseDown
  put the mouseCast into button
  puppetSprite 3, True
  set the memberNum of sprite 3 to button +1
  updateStage
  repeat while the mouseDown
    if rollover(3) = False then
      set the memberNum of sprite 3 to button
    else
      set the memberNum of sprite 3 to button +1
    end if
    updateStage
  end repeat
end

on mouseUp
  if rollOver(3) = True then
    go to "Purple"
  end if
  puppetSprite 3, False
end
```

— Changes in the script

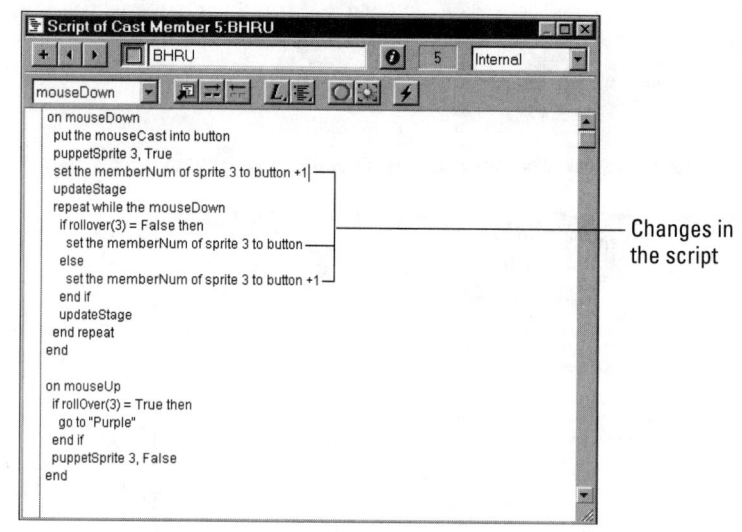

Figure 12-5: Modified script using the button variable

9. Close the Script window and save the movie as **western4.dir.**

10. Rewind the movie, play it, and test the buttons. The Blue Forward button should behave as it did before adding the `mouseCast` function and using the button variable.

11. Stop the movie.

Using the clickOn function to identify the current channel

The generic script you just created works fine if you are only concerned with sprites in channel 3, but that's an unrealistic expectation. You need a method of determining the channel in which a sprite is stored. Because you are clicking an object on the Stage, you can use the clickOn function. This function returns the number of the channel where *the last sprite clicked* is stored.

> **Caution**
>
> The clickOn function *only returns the channel number if the last sprite clicked has a script attached*. If no script is attached to the sprite, the function returns a value of 0.

In the following steps, you test the clickOn function using the western4.dir movie and the Message window. The clickOn function stores the number of the last sprite clicked on the Stage.

Determining the Last Sprite Clicked

On the CD-ROM

1. Open the western4.dir movie in Director. You need the movie you modified earlier in this chapter, or the file western4.dir stored on your companion CD-ROM in the exercise:ch12 (exercise\ch12) folder.

2. Open the Message window (Command+M or Ctrl+M). Play the movie without closing the Message window or the Score window, using Command+Option+P (Ctrl+Alt+P).

3. Click the Blue Guitar button.

4. Click the Message window title bar to activate that window, and type **put the clickOn.** Press Enter. The Message window displays a value of 0 because the Blue Guitar button is based on cast member 3, which has no script..

5. Click the Blue Forward button.

6. Activate the Message window and type **put the clickOn** and press Enter. The Message window returns the value 3.

7. Stop the movie and rewind it.

8. Open the script for cast member number 5.

9. First, you must edit the on mouseDown handler. Add the following two instructions (with each instruction on its own line) immediately following the on mouseDown keyword.

    ```
    global gchannel
    ```

(continued)

```
put the clickOn into gchannel
```

The first statement declares the existence of a global variable named `gchannel`. You can use the `gchannel` value in both the `on mouseDown` and the `on mouseUp` handlers. The second statement places the channel number of the last clicked sprite into the new global variable (`gchannel`) so the variable can replace references to channel 3. Your script should appear as shown in Figure 12-6.

```
Script of Cast Member 5:BHRU
BHRU                             5    Internal
mouseDown
on mouseDown
  global gchannel
  put the clickOn into gchannel          ← New instructions
  put the mouseCast into button             added to script
  puppetSprite 3, True
  set the memberNum of sprite 3 to button+1
  updateStage
  repeat while the mouseDown
    if rollover(3) = False then
      set the memberNum of sprite 3 to button
    else
      set the memberNum of sprite 3 to button+1
    end if
    updateStage
  end repeat
end

on mouseUp
  if rollOver(3) = True then
    go to "Purple"
  end if
  puppetSprite 3, False
end
```

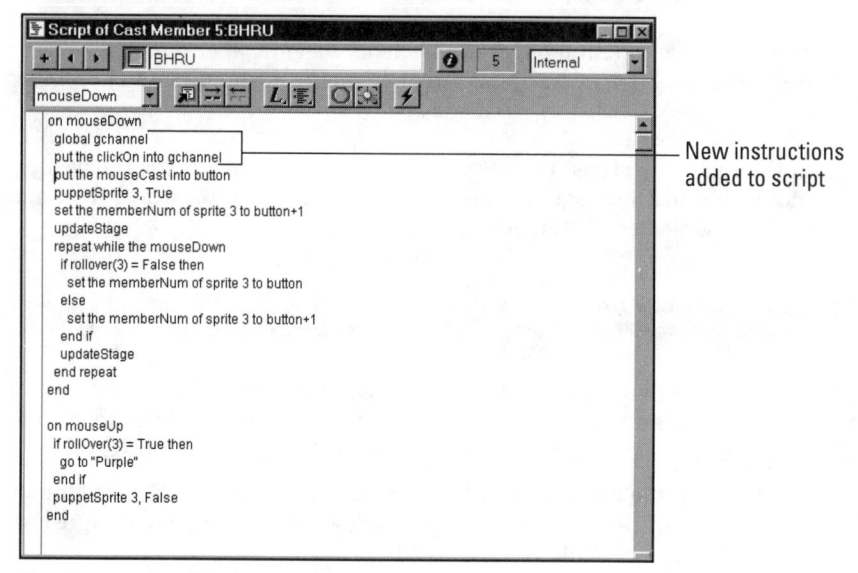

Figure 12-6: Modified script using the `clickOn` function

10. Replace all occurrences of the number 3 with the global variable **gchannel**. References to `sprite 3` should now read `sprite gchannel`. References to `puppetSprite 3` should now read `puppetSprite gchannel`. The script should appear similar to Figure 12-7. Be sure that you have changed `rollover(3)` to `rollover(gchannel)` and that you have also made the replacements in the `on mouseUp` handler.

Tip: To speed up the process of replacing all those occurrences of 3, double-click the `gchannel` variable name in the script, press Command+C or Ctrl+C to copy it to the Clipboard, double-click each occurrence of 3 and press Command+V or Ctrl+V to paste the variable name over the selected text. You can also use the Edit ⇨ Find ⇨ Text command (Command+F or Ctrl+F) to seek and replace one text string or character with another.

11. Close the Script window and save the movie as **western5.dir**.

```
on mouseDown
  global gchannel
  put the clickOn into gchannel
  put the mouseCast into button
  puppetSprite gchannel, True
  set the memberNum of sprite gchannel to button+1
  updateStage
  repeat while the mouseDown
    if rollover(gchannel) = False then
      set the memberNum of sprite gchannel to button
    else
      set the memberNum of sprite gchannel to button+1
    end if
    updateStage
  end repeat
end

on mouseUp
  if rollOver(gchannel) = True then
    go to "Purple"
  end if
  puppetSprite gchannel, False
end
```

— gchannel variables

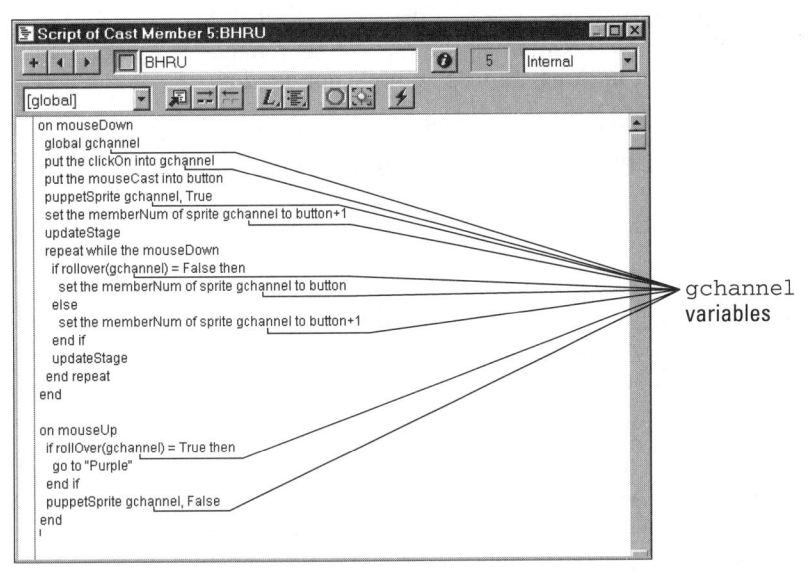

Figure 12-7: Modified script using the `gchannel` variable

12. Rewind the movie, play it, and test the buttons. The Blue Forward button behaves as it did before adding the `clickOn` function and using the `gchannel` variable. When done testing, stop the movie.

13. Now that you have modified the script attached to cast member 5, you can attach it to other buttons and it will work. Next, you need to copy the script from cast member 5 to cast member 7. With a single modification, it will work exactly the same when attached to either cast member. Start by opening the script attached to cast member 5.

14. Select all code in the script and copy it to the Clipboard.

15. Switch to the script attached to cast member 7. The current script has references to a specific channel and specific cast members.

16. Select all code in the script and then paste the script from the Clipboard into the Script window for cast member 7. The script attached to cast member 5 should overwrite the script attached to cast member 7.

17. Change the reference in the `on mouseUp` handler to Blue instead of Purple.

18. Close the Script window, save the movie again as western5.dir, rewind, and play the movie.

19. The script is now generic enough to manage the behavior of other buttons. The only modification needed is to specifically set the `go to` command in the `on mouseUp` handler. You can verify the practical application of this script in the next few steps. First, copy the script from cast member 5 or 7 to cast member 3 (the Blue Guitar button).

(continued)

20. After pasting the code into the Script window for cast member 3, delete the `go to` statement in the `on mouseUp` handler, replace it with the constant **nothing**, and close the Script window.
21. Save the movie again, rewind, and play.
22. Test the Blue Guitar button. The button flashes, but that is all.

Creating your own handlers

So far, you have used several standard handlers, including `on mouseUp`, `on mouseDown`, and `on exitFrame`. You can create user-defined handlers that can be reused time and time again within a movie without having to duplicate the code more than once.

So far in this chapter, you've used Lingo's commands, functions, and properties to create a generic button script. The only problem is that the *entire* script must be copied and attached to each cast member. You can save yourself the effort of copying and pasting the same script to multiple buttons, by creating a single user-defined handler that can be *called* from each button's script. By using this method, all changes to a user-defined script are made once, in one location, rather than in multiple scripts attached to multiple buttons.

User-defined handlers are typically placed in movie scripts so the routine is accessible from any part of the movie.

The following pseudocode illustrates how this technique can save you time, cause a movie to run more efficiently, and allow you to make changes and corrections in one location to affect several scripts. The `on mouseDown` script is attached to a sprite and includes a call to a handler (`doThisThing`) that invokes all instructions in a second handler (`on doThisThing`). The second handler has numerous actions, all of which would otherwise have to be listed in the `on mouseDown` handler.

```
on mouseDown
      doThisThing
end

on doThisThing
      tryThisThing
      tryThatThing
      doAnotherThing
      sitBackAndWatch
      tryItAllAgain
end doThisThing
```

In the following steps, you build a user-defined handler using the western5.dir movie. The calling of a user-defined handler eliminates the need for duplicate code in the movie. You no longer need the same duplicate handlers attached to several cast members.

Building a User-Defined Handler

On the CD-ROM

1. Open the western5.dir movie in Director. You need the movie you modified earlier in this chapter, or the file western5.dir stored on your companion CD-ROM in the exercise:ch12 (exercise\ch12) folder.
2. Open the Script window for either cast member 5 or 7 (it doesn't matter which one).
3. Click and drag to select only the `on mouseDown` handler.
4. Copy the selected text to the Clipboard.
5. Select the New Script button on the Script window, identified in Figure 12-8.
6. Paste the `on mouseDown` handler from the Clipboard to the new movie script.
7. Double-click the keyword `mouseDown` and type **click** to replace it.
8. Modify the last line of the handler to read **end click**. You have created a handler called `on click`. The script in the Script window should match the text in Figure 12-9.

New Script button

```
on mouseDown
  global gchannel
  put the clickOn into gchannel
  put the mouseCast into button
  puppetSprite gchannel, True
  set the memberNum of sprite gchannel to button+1
  updateStage
  repeat while the mouseDown
    if rollover(gchannel) = False then
      set the memberNum of sprite gchannel to button
    else
      set the memberNum of sprite gchannel to button+1
    end if
    updateStage
  end repeat
end

on mouseUp
  if rollOver(gchannel) = True then
    go to "Purple"
  end if
  puppetSprite gchannel, False
end
```

Selected `on mouseDown` handler text

Figure 12-8: The Script window with the New Script button

```
Movie Script 14
click
on click
  global gchannel
  put the clickOn into gchannel
  put the mouseCast into button
  puppetSprite gchannel, True
  set the memberNum of sprite gchannel to button+1
  updateStage
  repeat while the mouseDown
    if rollover(gchannel) = False then
      set the memberNum of sprite gchannel to button
    else
      set the memberNum of sprite gchannel to button+1
    end if
    updateStage
  end repeat
end click
```

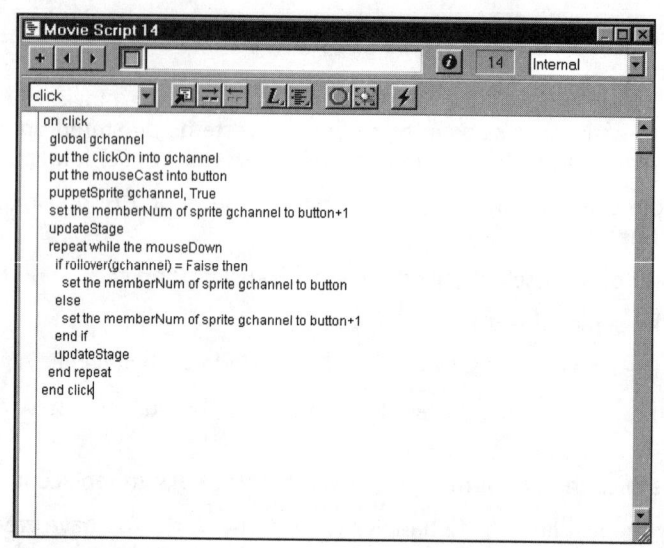

Figure 12-9: The `on click` handler

9. Close the Script window and save the movie as **western6.dir**.

10. You still need to modify the existing scripts (attached to cast members 3, 5 and 7) to *call* the new handler. So open the script attached to cast members 3, 5, and 7 and change the `on mouseDown` handler to match the following. While you make this change, you can delete almost all of the code in the `on mouseDown` handler. Do not change or delete the `on mouseUp` handler. Be sure to change the scripts for all three buttons.

```
on mouseDown
     click
end
```

11. Save the movie again as western6.dir, rewind, and play it.

12. All of the buttons react and provide visual feedback except for the Purple Guitar button. Add a script to cast member 9 that calls the `on click` handler. You want the button to change when clicked but not generate any other action. Hint: It should react just like the Blue Guitar button, which requires a second handler.

13. Once you have made the change, save the movie again as western6.dir.

Using Director 6's New Mouse Events

In Lingo — as in life — there's more than one trail to the end of your journey. Earlier in this chapter, you learned about the `rollOver` function. You learned that moving the mouse pointer over a specific sprite can trigger a desired action. Three new mouse events are introduced with Director 6, which can be tracked and used to trigger actions within your movies. These events, `mouseWith`, `mouseEnter`, and `mouseLeave`, can eliminate the need to use the `rollOver` function. (These three mouse events were initially mentioned in Chapter 11 along with the other events that generate system messages in Director.)

You can build a handler based on each of these events and then attach the script to specific cast members. Let's see how this works.

Note

The handlers for these three new mouse events affect the active area of a sprite. This is the area within its bounding box — *unless* the Matte ink is applied, in which case the active area is the visible area of the sprite.

Building an `on mouseWithin` handler

The instructions listed within an `on mouseWithin` handler are executed when the mouse pointer *is within* the active area of a sprite (to which the handler is attached). The handler is invoked whether or not the mouse button is pressed. In the following example, when the mouse pointer is within the active area of the sprite, the member number of the sprite changes and a different member is displayed:

```
on mouseWithin
     set the memberNum of sprite 3 to 6
     updateStage
end mouseWithin
```

Building an `on mouseEnter` handler

The instructions listed within an `on mouseEnter` handler are executed when the mouse pointer *enters* the active area of a sprite to which the handler is attached. The handler is invoked whether or not the mouse button is pressed. In the following example, when the mouse pointer first enters the active area of the sprite, a sound cast member (Tinkle) is played:

```
on mouseEnter
     puppetSound 1, "Tinkle"
     updateStage
end mouseWithin
```

Building an on mouseLeave handler

The instructions listed within an `on mouseLeave` handler are executed when the mouse pointer *leaves* the active area of a sprite to which the handler is attached. The handler is invoked whether or not the mouse button is pressed. In the following example, when the mouse pointer leaves the active area of the sprite, the member number of the sprite changes back to its original member number and a different member is displayed:

```
on mouseWithin
      set the memberNum of sprite 6 to 3
      updateStage
end mouseWithin
```

Uses for the New Mouse Event Handlers

The `mouseWithin`, `mouseEnter`, and `mouseLeave` handlers can serve a variety of functions:

- Displaying and erasing specific objects on the Stage (labels, help, callouts)
- Causing sound effects to play as the mouse moves over specific areas (sprites' bounding boxes) on the Stage
- Playing digital video or film loops
- Changing the appearance of button sprites or animating objects when the mouse moves over the object

Preparing sprites before the `enterFrame` event

As long as we're on the subject of new mouse events, Director 6 also has introduced a new event that occurs before the `enterFrame` message is sent. Now you can give Director instructions that you want it to execute as it prepares the next frame to display on the Stage. The `prepareFrame` event occurs before the frame is imaged on the Stage. Using an `on prepareFrame` handler, you can change sprite properties (such as the color or visibility of the sprite) before the sprite is drawn on the Stage.

As the list of events increases, keep in mind the following sequence as a guide to determining the order of events. This sequence applies whether you rewind and play a movie in authoring mode, run a projector, access a Shockwave movie, go to a movie (to the beginning or to a specific frame), play a movie (from the beginning or starting at a specific frame), or open a movie in a window (MIAW, discussed in Chapter 21).

1. The values from the Score are loaded into sprites.
2. The PrepareMovie message is sent.

3. The BeginSprite message is sent.

4. The StepFrame message is sent.

5. The PrepareFrame message is sent.

6. The frame is drawn.

7. The StartMovie message is sent.

8. The EnterFrame message is sent.

9. The PrepareFrame message is sent.

10. Instructions in the Tempo channel occur and idle events occur.

11. The ExitFrame message is sent.

12. The cycle continues until . . .

13. The StopMovie message is sent.

14. The EndSprite message is sent (the death of the sprite).

From the birth to the death of your movie, this order of execution applies.

In the following steps, you'll build an easier-to-construct, more responsive button using the `on mouseWithin` and `on mouseLeave` handlers.

Building Better Buttons Faster

1. Open the within.dir movie in Director. It's is stored on your companion CD-ROM in the exercise:ch12 (exercise\ch12) folder.

2. Notice the first three cast slots, shown in Figure 12-10. They hold three bitmap cast members: Normal, Hilite, and Pressed. The Normal cast member already appears centered on the Stage. These cast members represent the three "states" of a button. The cast also includes a bitmap cast member (cast slot 4) already placed in frame 2, and a `go to the frame` handler (cast slot 5). In this exercise, you will add a cast member script to each of the three buttons (Normal, Hilite, and Pressed).

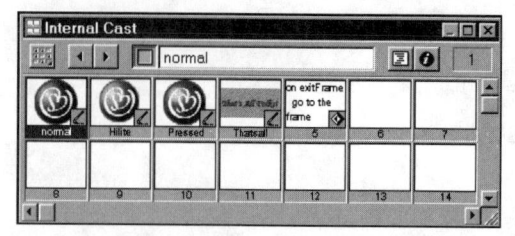

Figure 12-10: The Cast window for the within.dir movie

3. Change the Normal button's ink to Matte.
4. Attach the following handler to the Normal button:

```
on mouseWithin
      set the memberNum of sprite 1 to 2
      updateStage
end
```

5. Attach the following handlers to the Hilite button:

```
on mouseLeave
      set the memberNum of sprite 1 to 1
      updateStage
end


on mouseDown
      set the memberNum of sprite 1 to 3
      updateStage
end
```

6. Attach the following handlers to the Pressed button:

```
on mouseUp
      go to the frame +1
end


on mouseLeave
      set the memberNum of sprite 1 to 1
end
```

7. Save the movie as **within1.dir** and rewind it.
8. In the remaining steps, you'll test the movie. Play the movie, and move the mouse pointer over the button. It should change to the Hilite button.

9. Click the button, but do not release the mouse button. The Pressed button should appear.
10. Slide the mouse off the Pressed button. It reverts back to the Normal button.
11. Click and release the mouse button on the Normal button, and the playback head moves to frame 2.

That's all, folks! Don't you wish we had started with the new mouse events?

Summary

Before you discover how to control sprites in the next chapter, let's review some of the things you learned in this chapter.

- ✦ An object has specific attributes, called properties, that can be set and tested using Lingo.
- ✦ Common sprite properties are used to set the ink of a sprite, set the location of a sprite, set the movie's Stage color, and set the visibility of a sprite.
- ✦ Users expect specific, predictable behaviors from navigation buttons. You can program these behaviors *without* using Lingo's predefined behaviors.
- ✦ Lingo uses standard programming structures such as handlers (which are really routines and subroutines) and control structures (if…then…else statements and repeat loops).
- ✦ Some Lingo commands are aimed at controlling the progression of the movie (go to, play). Others are used to establish values and properties (put and set), place sprites under the control of Lingo (puppetSprite), redraw objects on the Stage (updateStage), and provide decision points within your movie (repeat while, if…then).
- ✦ Director 6 has added some new mouse events, such as mouseWithin, mouseEnter, and mouseLeave, that reduce the need to use the rollOver function and make it easier to program responsive buttons.

✦ ✦ ✦

Controlling Sprites from Lingo

CHAPTER 13

In This Chapter

Making sprites moveable using Lingo

Checking for intersecting sprites

Using global variables to shorten a handler

Constraining a sprite

Assigning a sprite the same location as the mouse pointer

Using Lingo to control transitions

Changing the cursor of a designated sprite

Creating a custom cursor in the Paint window

Making a sprite invisible on the Stage

When you drag a cast member on to the Stage, a wonderful transformation occurs. The cast member becomes an actor who sings, dances, and changes moods as directed by the script. And in this case it happens in *both* traditional theater and Director. The only difference is that in Director, the actor is called a *sprite*. In this chapter, you learn to make sprites move, react when they intersect with another sprite, match the location of the cursor, become invisible, and generally "act up" on the Stage. You learn to constrain a wayward sprite, and to control transitions and the cursor's appearance — all this using Lingo.

Dancing with puppetSprites

You're no stranger to dancing with sprites. In Chapters 2 and 3, you learned to move a sprite across the Stage using the tweening feature, and in Chapter 12 you swapped sprites using `the memberNum of sprite` property and the `set` command. In both situations, you as the movie developer are choosing when and where sprites travel across the Stage. You can also give that control to the user — by making a sprite moveable.

Making a sprite moveable — as you learned in Chapter 4 — is as easy as selecting the desired sprite and then checking the Moveable check box on the Score window (see Figure 13-1).

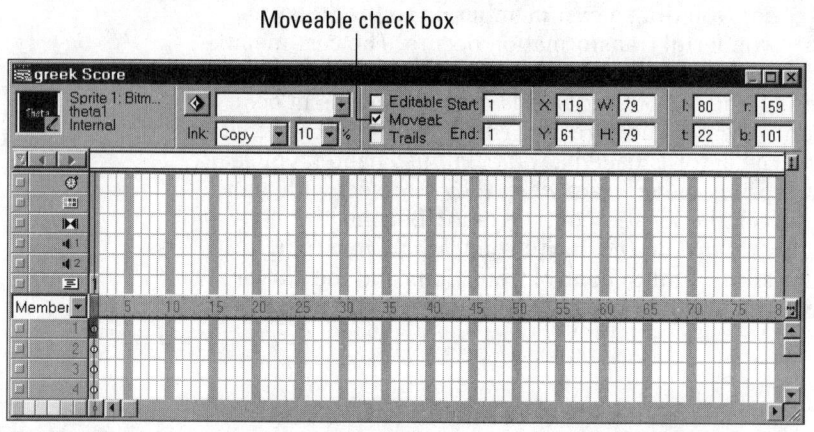

Figure 13-1: Check the Moveable option, and you enable the sprite to dance.

When using the Score window to set the sprite's moveable property, the sprite is moveable in all frames that it spans. A sprite can also be made moveable in a single frame if you make the frame a keyframe and set the sprite's moveable property. However, it is far easier to simply use Lingo to turn a sprite's moveable property on and off, as needed. In this chapter we'll find out how.

Using Lingo to make moveable sprites

The advantage of using Lingo to make a sprite moveable is that you can alter the property while the movie plays. You're not constrained to setting the property only in authoring mode. If you use the Score option, the property cannot be changed while the movie is playing — which is often too restrictive.

Enabling an object to be moveable using Lingo is a two-step process:

1. Puppet the sprite.
2. Set the moveableSprite property to True.

When the moveableSprite property is set to True, the user can move the sprite on the Stage while the movie plays. If the moveableSprite property is False, the sprite cannot be moved by the user. By default, all sprites are fixed in a specific location on the Stage.

The following handler puppets the sprite in channel 3 and then makes the object moveable:

```
on compare
    puppetSprite 3, True
    set the moveableSprite of sprite 3 to True
end compare
```

If you use a Score script, you can change the sprite's moveable property in a specific frame or when an event message (such as mouseUp or mouseDown) is received by the handler. For instance, the moveableSprite property can be set to True whenever the mouse button is clicked down on a specific sprite. Then, when the mouse button is released, the moveableSprite of sprite property can be reset to False.

Shortly, you will use a practice file and change the moveableSprite property of a group of sprites. But first, let's take a look at how to automatically set the property when a movie starts, and then how to set properties for a range of sprites more efficiently.

Using the on startMovie handler

You can use a user-defined handler to accomplish the task of automatically setting properties before the movie starts. The special on startMovie handler executes each time you play back a movie. Using this handler, you can initialize variables, puppet channels, and set properties (such as the moveableSprite property) before your movie starts playing.

Over the next several sections of this chapter, you'll use several versions of the greek.dir movie to explore properties. This simple little movie includes 17 cast members, as shown in Figure 13-2. The first eight cast members are Greek letters, the next eight are black squares containing the names of the letters, and the final cast member is a frame script with a go to the frame statement.

On the CD-ROM The files greek.dir, greek2.dir, greek3.dir, and greek4.dir are stored on your companion CD-ROM in the exercise:ch13 (exercise\ch13) folder.

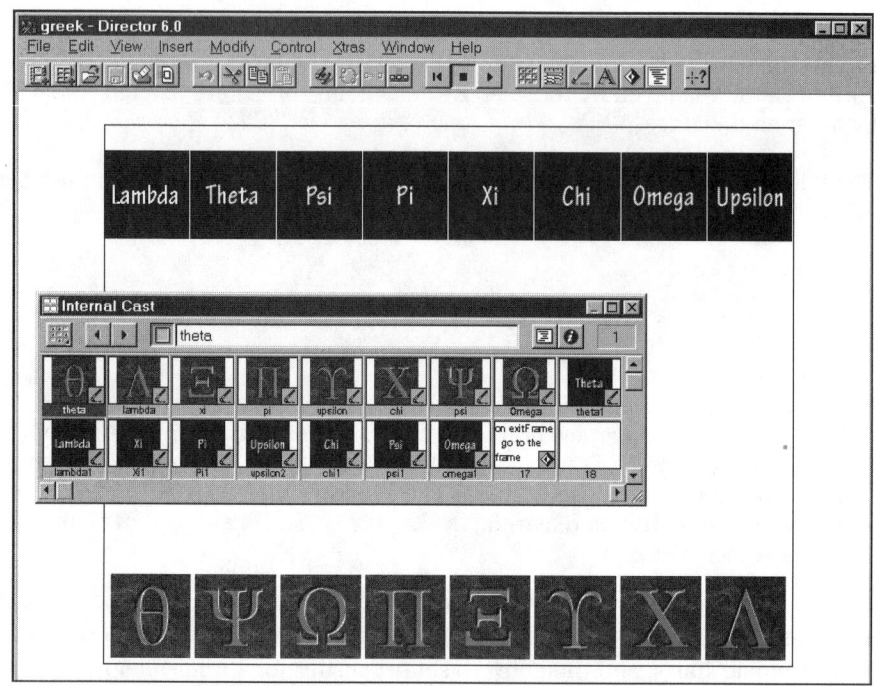

Figure 13-2: The cast and Stage setup for the greek.dir movie

The cast members have already been placed on the Stage, all in one frame. Channels 1 through 8 hold the black squares with the names of Greek letters (cast members 9 through 16), and channels 11 through 18 hold the corresponding cast members. By leaving two channels empty, each Greek letter and the black square with its name are exactly 10 channels apart. The positioning of the sprites in the Score window is planned, as you will see later in this chapter.

The single script is placed in the script channel for frame 1. At this point, none of the sprites are moveable, but that can be changed. After this next section on setting properties using a `repeat with` statement, you will modify the movie to puppet channels 11 through 18 (with the Greek letters) and set the `moveableSprite` property for each sprite in these channels to True.

Saving keystrokes and code with another type of loop

Based on what you know about puppeting sprites and setting the moveableSprite property, you will recognize that the following handler will accomplish the desired task — that is, to puppet each of the channels holding Greek letters (channels 11 through 18) and make the sprites in those channels moveable:

```
on startMovie
      puppetSprite 11, True
      puppetSprite 12, True
      puppetSprite 13, True
      puppetSprite 14, True
      puppetSprite 15, True
      puppetSprite 16, True
      puppetSprite 17, True
      puppetSprite 18, True
      set the moveableSprite of sprite 11 to True
      set the moveableSprite of sprite 12 to True
      set the moveableSprite of sprite 13 to True
      set the moveableSprite of sprite 14 to True
      set the moveableSprite of sprite 15 to True
      set the moveableSprite of sprite 16 to True
      set the moveableSprite of sprite 17 to True
      set the moveableSprite of sprite 18 to True
end startMovie
```

Certainly this handler will work, but it is unnecessarily long. You can abbreviate the code while achieving the same result using a repeat with statement with the following syntax:

```
repeat with variable = x to y
      doSomethingNeat
end repeat
```

Caution   A repeat with statement creates a loop that locks out other system messages and commands until the handler completes. Beware of creating unduly long loops that may slow down the responsiveness of your application.

Look at the following example. The variable used is called counter, and the repeat loop is repeated with the variable equal to every value from *x* to *y* (11 to 18). The action (the doSomethingNeat in the above syntax statement) puppets the sprite channels that are represented by the value contained in the counter variable. The second statement *within* the repeat loop changes the property of sprites 11 through 18 (represented by the counter variable) to moveable.

```
on startMovie
    repeat with counter = 11 to 18
        puppetSprite counter, True
        set the moveableSprite of sprite counter to True
    end repeat
end startMovie
```

By including this handler in the greek.dir movie, you cause the Greek letter sprites (not the black square blocks with Greek letter names) to be moveable.

In the following steps, you'll modify the greek.dir movie and create moveable sprites on the Stage using Lingo.

Making Sprites Moveable Using Lingo

On the CD-ROM

1. Open the greek.dir movie. (Remember, it's in the exercise:ch13 (exercise\ch13) folder on the CD-ROM.)

2. Play the movie and try to move any of the sprites on Stage. Click each one and try to drag it to a new location. Stop the movie.

3. Select the first empty Cast window slot, and click the Script window button on the toolbar, or press Command+0 (Ctrl+0).

4. Type the following on startMovie handler in the Script window and then close the window:

```
on startMovie
    repeat with counter = 11 to 18
        puppetSprite Counter, True
        set the moveableSprite of sprite counter to True
    end repeat
end startMovie
```

5. Save the movie as **greek2.dir** and play it. Click the Greek letters at the bottom of the screen and drag them around.

6. Try to drag any of the objects at the *top* of the screen. Why don't they move? (Answer: You didn't make them moveable.)

Next, to add a little interest in this project, you learn how to cause an action to occur when the Greek letter at the bottom of the Stage is properly placed over its namesake at the top of the Stage.

Where Are You Moving That Sprite?

Giving the user the ability to move a sprite is like a parent giving a son or daughter the keys to the car. Mom and Dad want to know where the kid's going and be able to react accordingly. However, it's easier to monitor the Stage than it is the destination of young people with cars!

By using specific functions, you can determine where a sprite is located on the Stage and have the program react accordingly. You can track the movement of a sprite and call for a specific action to execute when the following actions occur:

- ✦ When the moveable sprite is placed over another sprite on the Stage (using the `rollOver` function)
- ✦ When the moveable sprite touches another sprite on Stage (using the `intersect` function)
- ✦ When the moveable sprite moves outside the Stage area (using `the stageBottom, the stageLeft, the stageRight,` or `the stageTop` functions)
- ✦ When one side of the moveable sprite moves within specific coordinates on the Stage (by evaluating `the bottom of sprite, the left of sprite, the right of sprite,` or `the top of sprite` property)

What about those screen coordinates mentioned in that last item? To use the `rollOver` and `intersect` functions, you do not need to know about screen coordinates, but for the other Lingo sprite-tracking features, you do.

Understanding screen coordinates

Screen coordinates used by Lingo are based on x, y coordinates that can represent any point (pixel) on the Stage, as illustrated in Figure 13-3.

In Lingo, `the locH of sprite` property represents the horizontal location (x-axis) of the point. The `locV of sprite` property represents the vertical (y-axis) of the point. Based on this system, the upper-left corner of the Stage is location

```
0,0 (locH=0 and locV=0)
```

and the bottom-right corner of a VGA screen Stage is location

```
640,480 (locH=640 and locV=480)
```

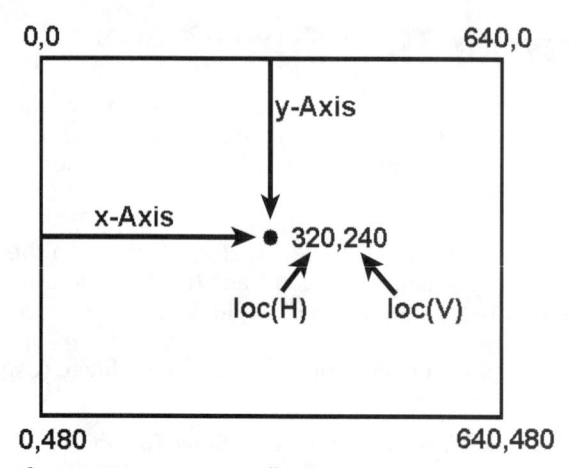

Figure 13-3: Stage coordinates

These two coordinates (locV and locH) represent the *registration point* of a sprite. Unless you change it, the registration point for a bitmap sprite (created in the Paint window) is its center point, and the registration point for a vector object (created with the floating Tool Palette) is the upper-left corner of the object. Registration points for bitmap cast members can be changed in the Paint window using the Registration Point tool.

Thus, if you have not changed the registration point for a bitmap sprite and you position the sprite exactly in the center of a standard VGA Stage (640 x 480), the locH of sprite property returns a value of 320 and the locV of sprite property returns a value of 240. The object's registration point is at 320,240.

The locH and locV properties of a sprite can be set or determined, respectively, using the locH of sprite x and the locV of sprite x functions.

Using the intersect function

The intersect function evaluates whether one sprite overlaps another sprite. In the Greek alphabet movie, you can cause a system beep to occur when the moveable sprite overlaps the nonmoveable or target sprite with the Greek letter's name. To accomplish this, you add the following if...then statement to the frame script in frame 1:

```
if sprite 12 intersects sprite 2 then
beep
end if
```

In the next practice exercise, you'll use a similar instruction to determine if sprite 12 overlaps sprite 2. If this situation occurs, you set the registration point of the moveable cast member to the registration point of the stationary cast member and then change the sprite to nonmoveable. As an example, if you were to add the above `if...then` instruction to the greek2.dir movie, you could test the script by dragging the Lambda letter (far-right bottom) over each of the sprites at the top of the screen. When the Lambda character overlapped its corresponding black name block, the system would beep.

Setting the location of a moveable sprite

After placing a moveable sprite over a specified location (such as another sprite), you can lock the moveable sprite to that location. This technique is used in games and educational programs to confirm that the moveable object is correctly placed. It works like this:

1. Determine if the moveable sprite intersects with the target sprite.
2. When the two sprites intersect, set the vertical location (`locV`) of the moveable sprite to the vertical location of the target sprite.
3. When the two sprites intersect, set the horizontal location (`locH`) of the moveable sprite to the horizontal location of the target sprite.
4. Change the moveable sprite to a nonmoveable sprite.

Simplifying with the `loc of sprite` property

When you want to change the horizontal and vertical location of a sprite to match the specific horizontal and vertical location of another sprite, you can eliminate the need to use both `the locV of sprite` and `the locH of sprite` functions. Instead, you can use `the loc of sprite` function. This function returns a value that represents both coordinates of a sprite (based on the sprite's registration point). Although there are times that you want to reference the `locH` and `locV` functions individually, `the loc of sprite` function is simpler and can help you shorten your code — and economy of code is always a virtue.

In the following steps, you'll create a new user-defined handler, `on compare`, for the Greek alphabet movie and call the handler in the frame script in frame 1. Each time the playback head exits frame 1 (it has a `go to the frame` script), the `on compare` handler is executed. The handler checks to see if the sprite in channel 12 `intersects` (that is, overlaps) the sprite in channel 2.

If sprite 12 (with the Lambda character) intersects sprite 2 (with the Lambda name block), then the registration point (`locV` and `locH`) of sprite 12 is set to the registration point of sprite 2. Further, `the moveableSprite` property is set to False and the Stage is redrawn (`updateStage`). Only the Lambda character "snaps to" when it encounters sprite 2 (the Lambda name block), because you will only create a handler that specifically targets the Lambda character. If you try moving other sprites around the Stage, they will move — but none of them locks on to the target sprite like the Lambda character.

Finally, after using the locH of sprite and the locH of sprite functions in the first version of the on compare handler, you will modify and simplify the handler to use just the loc of sprite function.

Checking for Intersecting Sprites

1. Open the greek2.dir movie in Director. You need the movie you modified earlier in this chapter, or the file greek2.dir stored on your companion CD-ROM in the exercise:ch13 (exercise\ch13) folder.

2. In this step, you'll create a new on compare handler and define the actions that occur when you call it. Select the next empty cast slot and click the ScriptWindow button on the toolbar to create a new script. Type the following script:

```
on compare
        if sprite 12 intersects sprite 2 then
                set the locV of sprite 12 to the locV of sprite 2
                set the locH of sprite 12 to the locH of sprite 2
                set the moveableSprite of sprite 12 to False
                updateStage
        end if
end compare
```

3. Close the Script window.

4. Edit Score script 17 to match the following:

```
on exitFrame
        compare
        go to the frame
end
```

> **Note:** The word compare is not a Lingo command, function, or keyword. It is the word used to call a user-defined handler. In essence, when you include a user-defined handler in your movie, you create a new (user-defined) Lingo command. The instructions within the user-defined handler stipulate the action to be executed when you call the new handler.

5. Save the movie as **greek3.dir** and test it.

Notice that you do not need to release the mouse button for the sprite to snap to its target sprite. If you want the user to consciously release the mouse button before the object locks in place, you must modify the handler to wait for the mouseUp function to return a True value.

6. Modify the `on compare` handler to read as follows:

   ```
   on compare
           if the mouseUp and sprite 12 intersects sprite 2 then
                   set the locV of sprite 12 to the locV of sprite 2
                   set the locH of sprite 12 to the locH of sprite 2
                   set the moveableSprite of sprite 12 to False
                   updateStage
           end if
   end compare
   ```

7. Save the movie again as greek3.dir and test it. When you test the new handler, you find that the user must release the mouse button while the Lambda character is over the Lambda black name box.

8. Next you'll shorten the script even further by using the `loc of sprite` function rather than both the `locV of sprite` and the `locH of sprite` functions. Modify the `on compare` handler to read

   ```
   on compare
           if the mouseUp and sprite 12 intersects sprite 2 then
                   set the loc of sprite 12 to the loc of sprite 2
                   set the moveableSprite of sprite 12 to False
                   updateStage
           end if
   end compare
   ```

9. Save the movie again as greek3.dir and test it.

To have all Greek characters behave as the Lambda character, you can duplicate the `if...then` statement within the `on compare` handler (once for each moveable sprite) and then change the sprite number references. But before you opt to use this approach, notice that your script is getting very long. Another option — using global variables — is available. Let's see how that works.

Substituting global variables to shorten code

By using variables, you can trim your code to a more manageable level. Look at Listing 13-1, which uses an `if...then` statement in the `on compare` handler. The code is getting very long.

Listing 13-1: **Handler that determines if the Greek letters and their names match**

```
on compare
      if the mouseUp and sprite 11 intersects sprite 1 then
          set the loc of sprite 11 to the loc of sprite 1
          set the moveableSprite of sprite 11 to False
          updateStage
      end if
  if the mouseUp and sprite 12 intersects sprite 2 then
          set the loc of sprite 12 to the loc of sprite 2
          set the moveableSprite of sprite 12 to False
          updateStage
      end if
  if the mouseUp and sprite 13 intersects sprite 3 then
          set the loc of sprite 13 to the loc of sprite 3
          set the moveableSprite of sprite 13 to False
          updateStage
      end if
  if the mouseUp and sprite 14 intersects sprite 4 then
          set the loc of sprite 14 to the loc of sprite 4
          set the moveableSprite of sprite 14 to False
          updateStage
      end if
  if the mouseUp and sprite 15 intersects sprite 5 then
          set the loc of sprite 15 to the loc of sprite 5
          set the moveableSprite of sprite 15 to False
          updateStage
      end if
  if the mouseUp and sprite 16 intersects sprite 6 then
          set the loc of sprite 16 to the loc of sprite 6
          set the moveableSprite of sprite 16 to False
          updateStage
      end if
  if the mouseUp and sprite 17 intersects sprite 7 then
          set the loc of sprite 17 to the loc of sprite 7
          set the moveableSprite of sprite 17 to False
          updateStage
      end if
  if the mouseUp and sprite 18 intersects sprite 8 then
          set the loc of sprite 18 to the loc of sprite 8
          set the moveableSprite of sprite 18 to False
          updateStage
      end if
end compare
```

Note: The moveable sprite and target channels are separated by ten channels, so that the target sprite for channel 11 is in channel 1, the target sprite for channel 12 is in channel 2, and so on. This is easier to keep straight — and it has another useful purpose that you will discover shortly.

In each occurrence of the if...then statement in the preceding example, the handler checks to see if the mouse button is up and if the corresponding Greek character sprite (such as sprite 18) intersects the Greek black name box (such as sprite 8). You can eliminate lines of code by using a variable that represents the current moveable sprite and the current target sprite. Of course these variables will change depending on which of the Greek letters is clicked.

Wanted: Short handlers

Writing short handlers instead of long ones is more than just an exercise in aesthetics. Yes, it is gratifying to write elegant, concise code. But the important rationale for writing short handlers is to enable your program to execute in a timely and responsive manner. When you write long handlers, you lock the user and the operating system out of the "action" until the handler completes executing. Long, elaborate if...then statements can burn up CPU cycles and contribute to an unresponsive application. In Director, only one handler can execute at a time. In addition, short handlers keep your coding simple and easier to understand and debug.

The first step in shortening your code is to create two variables called movingSprite and targetSprite. These variables will then be substituted in the on compare handler each time a reference is made to a specific sprite. For instance, the following snippet of code is one of a series of if...then statements from the handler in the long code listed above. Notice that all the other if...then statements are identical except for the sprite numbers:

```
if the mouseUp and sprite 14 intersects sprite 4 then
        set the loc of sprite 14 to the loc of sprite 4
        set the moveableSprite of sprite 14 to False
        updateStage
    end if
```

The script can be revised to use a variable instead of the actual sprite number. The revised handler reads as follows:

```
on compare
     if the mouseUp and sprite movingSprite intersects sprite¬
 targetSprite then
         set the loc of sprite movingSprite to the loc of¬
 sprite targetSprite
```

```
            set the moveableSprite of sprite movingSprite to False
            updateStage
        end if
end compare
```

> **Tip:** By using variable names that help identify the objects they represent, you make your code more readable.

Now you have substituted the variable names, but you have not assigned values to the variables. If you try to save the script or play the movie, you'll get the script error message in Figure 13-4. To avoid the error message, you declare a value for each of the local variables inside the on compare handler by using the put command:

```
put 11 into movingSprite
put 1 into targetSprite
```

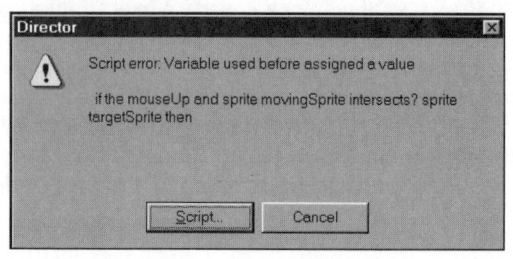

Figure 13-4: This alert box suggests that a variable is used before it is defined in the handler.

This works for a single case — the Lambda character and its name box. It still does not help set and identify matching sprites for the rest of the Greek letters. To finish this task, you must do the following to set up global variables:

> **Tip:**
> 1. Declare the two variables as global so they can be used throughout the movie.
>
>   Global variables must be declared in each handler that uses them.
>
> 2. Determine which sprite the mouse pointer is over (while it is dragging an object), using the rollOver function.
>
> 3. Assign sprite numbers to global variables so the variables can be reused each time the user selects a different sprite to move.

In the following steps, you'll substitute global variables (movingSprite and targetSprite) in place of specific values (sprite numbers) in a user-defined handler (on compare). This approach reduces the need to repeat the same if…then statement several times in the same handler.

The `movingSprite` and `targetSprite` variables are set to equal 99; this avoids having the initial value generate an action before you click and drag a sprite. The 99 value is used because it is clearly out of the range of values that can generate an action. (Later in this chapter, you learn to screen out values that are out of the desired range.) In this example, the desired ranges include sprite channels 1 to 8 and 11 to 18.

Using Global Variables to Shorten a Handler

On the CD-ROM

1. Open the greek3.dir movie in Director. You need the movie you modified earlier in this chapter, or the file greek3.dir stored on your companion CD-ROM in the exercise:ch13 (exercise\ch13) folder.

2. Modify the `on startMovie` handler (cast member 18) to match the following. The changes declare the global variables in the `on startMovie` handler. You do not need to include the comment lines:

```
on startMovie
      global movingSprite, targetSprite
      repeat with counter = 11 to 18
            puppetSprite Counter, True
            set the moveableSprite of sprite counter to True
      end repeat
      -- The next two statements initialize the global variables
      -- If you fail to do this, you will get a script error
      -- message when Director tries to execute the compare
        handler
      put 99 into movingSprite
      put 99 into targetSprite
end startMovie
```

Tip

You can declare more than one global variable after the *global* keyword, but each variable must be separated from the next by a comma.

3. Modify the `on compare` handler (cast member 19) to match the following script:

```
on compare
      global movingSprite, targetSprite
      if the mouseUp and sprite movingSprite intersects¬
sprite targetSprite then
            set the loc of sprite movingSprite to the loc¬
of sprite targetSprite
            set the moveableSprite of sprite movingSprite to¬
False
                updateStage
      end if
end compare
```

4. Save the movie as **greek4.dir**.

Tip: 5. Next, you must add a new handler called `on overlaps`. It identifies the current moveable sprite and specifies its target sprite (putting these values in the `movingSprite` and `targetSprite` variables). Select the next empty cast slot, open the Script window, and type the following code.

You can type the first `if...then...else` portion of the script, copy the lines to the Clipboard, paste the lines back into the script several times, and then make the necessary modifications. This technique reduces the amount of typing and lets you quickly edit the duplicated lines.

```
on overlaps
    global movingSprite, targetSprite
    if rollOver(11) then
        put 11 into movingSprite
        put 1 into targetSprite
    else if rollOver(12) then
        put 12 into movingSprite
        put 2 into targetSprite
    else if rollOver(13) then
        put 13 into movingSprite
        put 3 into targetSprite
    else if rollOver(14) then
        put 14 into movingSprite
        put 4 into targetSprite
    else if rollOver(15) then
        put 15 into movingSprite
        put 5 into targetSprite
    else if rollOver(16) then
        put 16 into movingSprite
        put 6 into targetSprite
    else if rollOver(17) then
        put 17 into movingSprite
        put 7 into targetSprite
    else if rollOver(18) then
        put 18 into movingSprite
        put 8 into targetSprite
    end if
end overlaps
```

6. Carefully check the script to be sure you did not type errors, and then save the movie as **greek4.dir**.

7. One more change before the movie works: Modify the `on exitFrame` handler in script 17 to match the following. You are adding a call to the `on overlaps` handler:

```
on exitFrame
    overlaps
    compare
    go to the frame
end
```

8. Save the movie again as greek4.dir, rewind, and play it.

Using cast placement to save code

Typing endless lines of code is never a joyful experience, so good programmers always look for ways to reduce the required lines of code. With one fairly small change, you can substantially shorten the `on overlaps` handler. The number (of the sprite) stored in `movingSprite` is identical to the number (parameter) used in the `rollOver` handler. How can we determine the sprite over which the mouse pointer passes?

To accomplish this objective we can use a roundabout technique. In Chapter 12, you used `the mouseCast` function that returns an integer representing the cast member number from which a rolled-over sprite was derived. If the sprite `MySprite` is created by placing cast member 10 on the Stage, then `the mouseCast` function will return a value of 10 when the mouse cursor is over the sprite.

By placing each moveable sprite and target sprite in a channel that corresponds to their respective cast member numbers, you can use `the mouseCast` function to replace the number of the sprite in a handler. Examine Table 13-1 and notice the relationship between moveable cast member numbers, the moving sprite channel, and the target sprite channel.

Table 13-1
Cast and Sprite Assignments

Cast Name	Cast Number	Moving Sprite Channel	Target Sprite Channel
Theta	1	11	1
Lambda	2	12	2
Xi	3	13	3
Pi	4	14	4
Upsilon	5	15	5
Chi	6	16	6
Psi	7	17	7
Omega	8	18	8

If you use this organization of cast names, numbers, and sprite channels, when the mouseCast function returns a value of 1 (meaning the mouse pointer is over the Theta character), then the same value represents the target sprite channel number. If you add ten (10) to the mouseCast value, it corresponds to the moving sprite channel number.

Watch out — this approach has one caveat. The mouseCast function returns a value of –1 when the mouse pointer is not over a sprite. To preclude the targetSprite from equaling a negative value, you must tell Director to only execute the on compare and on overlaps handlers when the value of the mouseCast is greater than zero and less than 9 (that is, 1 through 8). If you do not prevent the evaluation of a negative number in the on compare and on overlaps handlers, the error message in Figure 13-5 appears when you play your movie.

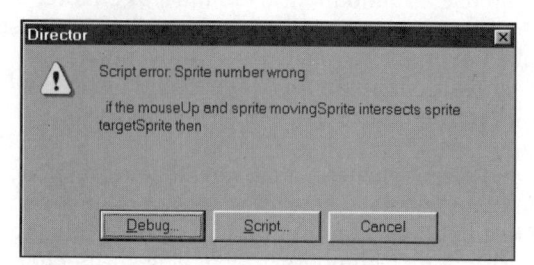

Figure 13-5: The sprite number is wrong because it is out of the acceptable range for a sprite channel.

In the following steps, you'll use the mouseCast function coupled with the movingSprite and targetSprite variables (and the placement of related cast members in the Cast window) to shorten the greek4.dir movie.

Shortening the Code for greek4.dir

1. Open the greek4.dir movie in Director. You need the movie you modified earlier in this chapter, or the file greek4.dir stored on your companion CD-ROM in the exercise:ch13 (exercise\ch13) folder.

2. Because of the placement of the matching cast members and the use of specific sprite channels, you can substitute the following code for the on overlaps handler (cast member 20):

```
on overlaps
    global movingSprite, targetSprite
    put the mouseCast + 10 into movingSprite
    put the mouseCast into targetSprite
    updateStage
end overlaps
```

3. Close the Script window, save the movie as **greek5.dir,** rewind, and play it. An error message will appear as soon as the mouse pointer is not over a sprite on the Stage.

4. Cancel the warning box, position the mouse pointer on top of a sprite at the bottom of the Stage, and play the movie again. The movie should play without the error message.

5. While the movie plays, drag the mouse pointer off the sprite and place it in an open area of the Stage. An error message appears again and stops execution of the movie.

6. Change the `on exitFrame` handler in cast member 17 to match the following:

```
on exitFrame
    if the mouseCast >0 and the mouseCast <9 then
        overlaps
        compare
    end if
    go to the frame
end
```

7. Save the movie again as greek5.dir, rewind, and play it.

> **Note**
>
> You can also trim back the `on startMovie` handler to eliminate the following two statements. The modification to the `on exitFrame` handler means the two global variables can never be equal to 0 or a negative number:
>
> ```
> put 99 into movingSprite
> put 99 into targetSprite
> ```

Dancing in Tight (Constrained) Shoes

In addition to helping you determine whether one sprite overlaps another or which sprite is currently under the mouse pointer, Lingo provides functions and properties that can control moveable sprites. The properties and functions listed in Table 13-2 can be used to limit the movement of sprites. Here are the most common reasons for constraining sprites:

✦ To restrict the movement of an object within a game to a specific portion of the Stage area

✦ To build a slider with an adjustable dial that adheres to the gauge portion of the slider

✦ To force a sprite to follow the movement of the mouse pointer

Keyword	Type	Action
the constraint of sprite	Property	Limits the movement of the specified sprite to within the bounding box of a second sprite.
constrainH	Function	Limits the movement of a designated sprite to within the left and right edges of a designated target sprite.
constrainV	Function	Limits the movement of a designated sprite to within the top and bottom edges of a designated target sprite.
mouseH	Function	Returns the horizontal position of the mouse pointer.
mouseV	Function	Returns the vertical position of the mouse pointer.

Table 13-2: Properties and Functions That Constrain Sprite Movement

Constraining movement within a specific area of the Stage

The gauge.dir practice movie, which you will use shortly, demonstrates how to restrict the movement of an object to a predefined area of the Stage. This restricted behavior is created using the constraint of sprite property. Examine the gauge.dir movie Stage, as shown in Figure 13-6, and you see several objects. Initially, let's focus on the planet in orbit around a sun that appears on the left.

To limit the movement of the planet sprite within the area of the sun sprite, you can use the following handler:

```
on startMovie
      puppetSprite 2, True
      set the moveableSprite of sprite 2 to True
      set the constraint of sprite 2 to 1
end
```

After puppeting the planet sprite in channel 2 and making it moveable, the handler constrains the planet's movement to within the area of the sun sprite in channel 1. Specifically, this forces the registration point for sprite 2 to be within the area of sprite 1.

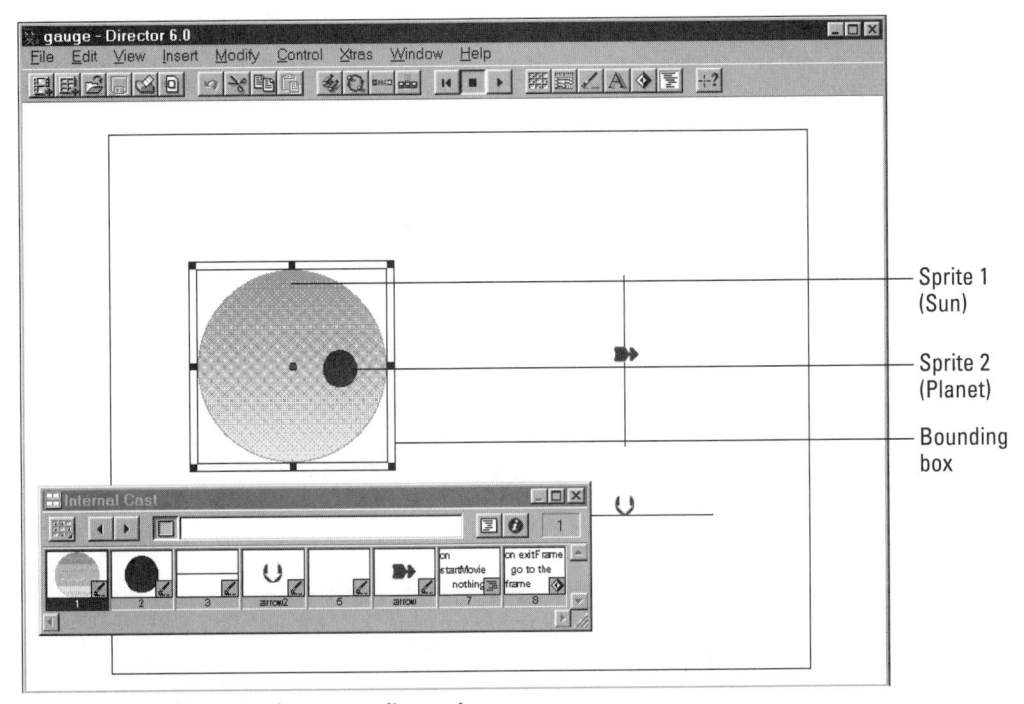

Figure 13-6: Objects in the gauge.dir movie

If you enter this script and test the movie, it appears that the planet moves outside the area of the sun. The actual constraint, however, is within the *bounding box* of the specified sprite. In this example, the constraint limits the movement of the planet (sprite 2) to an area within the bounding box (identified in Figure 13-6) of the sun (sprite 1). The boundaries for the moveable sprite are more obvious when the sun's ink is set to Copy and the Stage color is set to a color other than white. You can change the Stage color using the Stage Color chip in the Movie Properties dialog box by selecting Modify ⇨ Movie ⇨ Properties.

Once you constrain a sprite, you can remove the constraint by issuing the following instruction in a handler:

```
Set the constraint of sprite 2 to 0
```

Director does not use channel 0, so this instruction effectively constrains sprite 2 to the area of sprite 0 (a nonexistent sprite). This has the effect of turning off the constraint previously attached to sprite 2.

Note: By default, the registration point of a bitmap cast member is its center point. The registration point of a vector object (created using the Tool Palette) is the upper-left corner of the sprite.

In the following steps, you'll experiment with the constraint of sprite property. The end result is that the planet sprite is limited to moving only within the bounding box of the sun sprite. In these steps, you modify the movie script in cast slot 7. When you first open the script, notice the only instruction is the Lingo command nothing which, as you might expect, does nothing.

On the CD-ROM: The file gauge.dir, used in the following exercise, is stored on your companion CD-ROM in the exercise:ch13 (exercise\ch13) folder.

Constraining a Sprite

1. Open the gauge.dir movie in Director.
2. Open the movie script (cast member 7) and modify the on startMovie handler to match the following:

   ```
   on startMovie
        puppetSprite 2, True
        set the moveableSprite of sprite 2 to True
        set the constraint of sprite 2 to 1
   end
   ```

3. Save the movie as **gauge1.dir**, rewind, and test the movie by trying to drag the planet (sprite 2) away from the sun (sprite 1). As long as the constraint of sprite property is set to True, sprite 2 is locked within the bounding box of sprite 1.

Restricting the vertical or horizontal movement of a sprite

To create a slider requires that you take a slightly different approach to restricting the movement of a sprite. The two functions constrainH and constrainV are used to limit the movement of a sprite horizontally and vertically on the Stage, respectively. By using these Lingo functions in combination with the mouseH and mouseV functions, you can cause a sprite to follow the movement of the mouse pointer, while restricting its movement to either the horizontal or vertical area of another sprite. To build this little handler, you need a bit more information on these functions (listed initially in Table 13-2).

The syntax for the `constrainH` function is

`constrainH(spriteNumber, horizontalCoordinate)`

This function returns a value that indicates if the *horizontalCoordinate* is within the bounding box of the specified sprite (*spriteNumber*). If the *horizontalCoordinate* is within the bounding box, the function returns the value you enter as the *horizontalCoordinate*. It not, the function returns a horizontal coordinate that is within the bounding box.

Let's do a little experimentation in the Message window to clarify how this function works. Assume that sprite 3 is 100 pixels wide and its left edge is 200 pixels from the left edge of the Stage. That means the right edge is 300 pixels from the left edge of the Stage. So if you type

`constrainH(3, 100)`

the function evaluates the horizontal coordinate (100) and determines that it is outside the bounding box of sprite 3. The message window returns the following result:

`-- 200`

Notice that the value returned is the minimum integer required to place the horizontal coordinate within the bounding box. Since the coordinate entered in the instruction is beyond the left of the target sprite, the function returns a value that is the coordinate for the left edge.

Next, if you type

`constrainH(3, 220)`

the function evaluates the horizontal coordinate (220) and determines that it is inside the bounding box of sprite 3. In this case, the message window returns the value of the horizontal coordinate, with the following result:

`-- 220`

In this case, the horizontal coordinate is already within the bounding box, so Lingo echoes the integer as the function's result.

Finally, if you type

`constrainH(3, 438)`

the function evaluates the horizontal coordinate (438) and determines that it is outside the bounding box of sprite 3. The message window returns

`-- 300`

Notice that the value returned is again the minimum integer required to place the horizontal coordinate within the bounding box. Since the coordinate is beyond the right of the target sprite, the function returns a value that is the coordinate for the right edge of the sprite.

The `constrainV` function returns values similar to those returned by `constrainH`. The only difference is that the values are vertical coordinates and are measured from the top of the Stage.

Now that you have some background, here is the instruction to limit horizontal movement:

```
set the locH of sprite 4 to constrainH (3, the mouseH)
```

Let's evaluate the instruction. First you can assume the left and right horizontal coordinates for sprite 3 are still 200 and 300 respectively. The `mouseH` function returns the horizontal coordinate of the mouse pointer. Note that the `mouseH` function indicates the horizontal position of the mouse pointer on the Stage. The integer returned is actually the number of pixels from the left edge of the Stage to the mouse pointer.

Say the mouse pointer is at 425 (which is outside the area of sprite 3); then the function will return the value 300. The result is that `the locH of sprite 4` is set to 300 (the right edge of sprite 3). If the mouse pointer is at 245 (which is inside the area of sprite 3) then the function will return the value 245 — so sprite 4 matches the horizontal coordinate of the mouse pointer. Using this example, notice the following about the horizontal position of sprite 4 (such as the arrow outline in gauge.dir):

+ It can never be placed outside the right edge of sprite 3.
+ It can never be placed outside the left edge of sprite 3.
+ It will match the mouse pointer's horizontal location whenever sprite 4 is within the bounding box of sprite 3.

As you practice with the gauge.dir movie, you'll discover that only `the locH of sprite 4` is altered. To alter the vertical coordinates in a similar way, you use the `constrainV` function.

In summary, the `constrainH` function limits the movement of a sprite (in channel 4) to within the left and right edges of the sprite in channel 3. `The locHof sprite 4` (horizontal location) is constrained along the horizontal axis of the object's registration point and follows the horizontal movement (returned by `the mouseH` function) of the mouse. The movement of the slide lever is constrained to horizontal movement *along* and *within* the area of the slide gauge.

Tip: Because only the horizontal coordinate of the slider is affected, it is important for the gauge slider to be properly positioned on the Stage before the movie plays.

The same process can be used to cause the slide lever on a vertical gauge to follow the vertical movement of the mouse pointer (`the mouseV`), as in the following example:

```
set the locV of sprite 6 to constrainV (5, the mouseV)
```

Of course, `the mouseV` function indicates the vertical position of the mouse pointer on the Stage. The value returned is actually the number of pixels from the top edge of the Stage to the mouse pointer.

In this next stepped exercise, you'll modify a script by puppeting both slide levers. Then you'll use the `constrainH` and `constrainV` functions (in conjunction with `the mouseH` and `the mouseV` functions) to reposition a sprite on the Stage while restricting its movement along either the horizontal or vertical plane. The `mouseH` function is reevaluated each time the playback head exits the frame. Properties (such as `the moveableSprite` and `puppetSprite` properties) that do not change during the playback of the movie are set in the movie script.

Building a Basic Slider

On the CD-ROM

1. Open the gauge1.dir movie in Director. You need the movie you modified earlier in this chapter, or the file gauge1.dir stored on your companion CD-ROM in the exercise:ch13 (exercise\ch13) folder.

2. Open the movie script in cast slot 7 and puppet sprites 2, 4, and 6. The modified on `startMovie` handler appears as follows:

```
on startMovie
      puppetSprite 2, True
      puppetSprite 4, True
      puppetSprite 6, True
      set the moveableSprite of sprite 2 to True
      set the constraint of sprite 2 to 1
end
```

3. Open the frame script in cast member slot 8 and modify it to match the following:

```
on exitFrame
      set the locH of sprite 4 to constrainH (3, the mouseH)
      go to the frame
end
```

4. Save the movie as **gauge2.dir**, rewind, and play it. The horizontal slide lever (bottom-right of the Stage) follows the horizontal movement of the mouse pointer, even if you do not click and drag it.

5. In this step, you use the vertical location (`locV`) of the sprite in combination with the `constrainV` function to limit the sprite's vertical movement. Modify the `on exitFrame` handler (cast member 8) to match the following:

```
on exitFrame
    set the locV of sprite 6 to constrainV (5, the mouseV)
    go to the frame
end
```

6. Save the movie again as gauge2.dir, rewind, and play it. You do not need to click and drag the vertical slide lever. It follows the vertical movement of the mouse pointer.

The sliders that you've just created need some refinement. First, it would be nice to have the horizontal and vertical sliders working in the same frame. Second, you probably want the user to be able to click a slide lever and drag it to the desired location, rather than have the lever constantly track the mouse movement. The automatic tracking is irritating and frustrating, because you cannot permanently set the slide (to control volume, speed, or any other aspect of your movie).

To have the slider behave as a user expects, you must

1. Determine if the mouse pointer is over the appropriate sprite (using the `rollOver` function).

2. Determine if the mouse is in a down position (using `the mouseDown` function).

3. Update the Stage when the sprite moves (using the `updateStage` command).

In the following steps, you'll modify the slider into a well-behaved and useful tool.

Building a Better Slider

On the CD-ROM

1. Open the gauge2.dir movie in Director. You need the movie you modified earlier in this chapter, or the file gauge2.dir stored on your companion CD-ROM in the exercise:ch13 (exercise\ch13) folder.

2. Modify the `on frameExit` script located in cast member slot 8, as follows:

```
on exitFrame
    repeat while the mouseDown and rollOver(4) =True
        set the locH of sprite 4 to constrainH (3, the
            mouseH)
```

```
              updateStage
      end repeat
      repeat while the mouseDown and rollOver(6) = True
              set the locV of sprite 6 to constrainV (5, the
              mouseV)
              updateStage
      end repeat
      go to the frame
end
```

3. Save the movie as **gauge3.dir**, rewind, and play it.

Matching the sprite location to the mouse pointer location

While experimenting with the gauge.dir movie, you may have wondered if the functions `constrainH` and `constrainV`, used to restrict sprites' positions, can be used to force a sprite (on the Stage) to always follow the movement of the mouse pointer. Good observation! The answer is Yes.

To match the location of a sprite to the mouse pointer location, you must

- Make the sprite moveable so you can enable the user to drag it around the Stage
- Set the `locH` of a sprite to match the `mouseH` of the mouse pointer
- Set the `locV` of a sprite to match the `mouseV` of the mouse pointer

The net result is that the sprite "sticks" to the mouse pointer on the Stage without any user intervention.

In this case, you do not need to constrain the movement of a sprite. Instead, you constantly match the horizontal (`locH`) and vertical (`locV`) locations of the object's registration point to the horizontal (`the mouseH`) and vertical (`the mouseV`) location of the mouse pointer.

The following partial script includes the three important instructions to enable the sprite to move on the Stage, and then to match the vertical and horizontal coordinates of the sprite to the mouse pointer's location:

```
set the moveableSprite of sprite 1 to True
set the locV of sprite 1 to the mouseV
set the locH of sprite 1 to the mouseH
```

On the CD-ROM You can experiment with this code using the fish.dir movie in the next practice exercise. The file fish.dir is stored on your companion CD-ROM in the exercise:ch13 (exercise\ch13) folder. In these steps, you'll add a handler to the movie that causes the fish sprite to always follow the mouse pointer. Initially, the registration point for the fish sprite is at the center of the sprite.

In this exercise you will also alter the registration point in the Paint window, so the nose of the fish sticks to the location of the mouse pointer.

Sticky Sprite on the Mouse Pointer

1. Open the fish.dir movie in Director.
2. Double-click the script channel in frame 1 to open the Script window.
3. Type the following script. (You can omit the comments lines.)

   ```
   on enterFrame
        puppetSprite 1, True
        set the moveableSprite of sprite 1 to True
        set the locV of sprite 1 to the mouseV
        set the locH of sprite 1 to the mouseH
        --You do not need to include the updateStage command
        here.
        --Each time the playback head exits and reenters the
        current frame,
        --the Stage is redrawn.
   end

   on exitFrame
        go to the frame
   end
   ```

4. Close the Script window.
5. Save the movie as **fish1.dir**, rewind, and play it. Move the mouse pointer around the Stage and watch the effect. When you're done experimenting, stop the movie.
6. Double-click the Fish cast member (in the Cast window) to open the Paint window.
7. Select the Registration tool, identified in Figure 13-7, on the Tools palette.

   Note Notice that the Paint window's Tools palette is different from the floating Tool Palette that is displayed using the Window ⇨ Tool Palette command. These two sets of tools are not interchangeable in Director.

8. Click the nose of the fish.

9. Close the Paint window.
10. Save the movie again as fish1.dir, rewind, and play it.

Note: *Fish art*: The artwork for the fish.dir movie is based on an image (05449.eps) from the Designer's Club April 1996 CD-ROM (copyright 1996–97 by Dynamic Graphics, Inc. and used with permission). The black-and-white encapsulated postscript file was imported into Adobe Photoshop and colored. We also merged segments of the sea floor to create a wider image area.

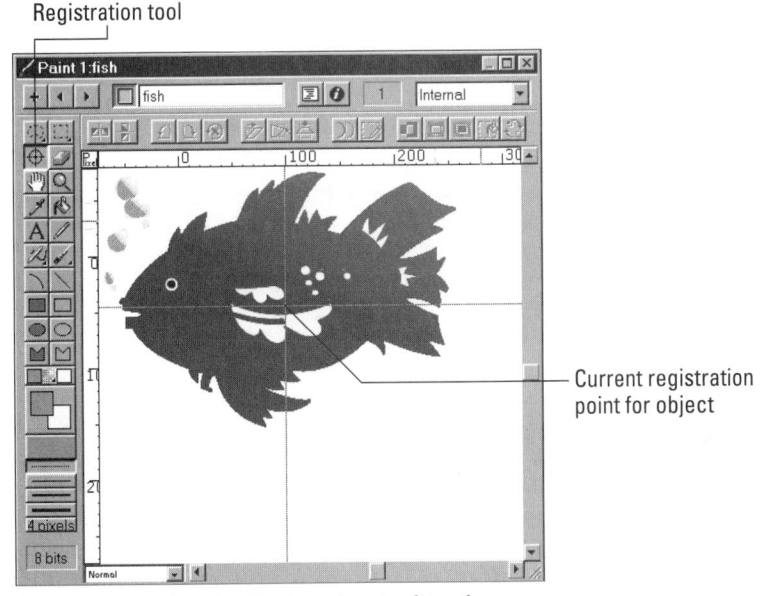

Figure 13-7: Using the Registration tool to change the registration point of a bitmap cast member

Moving sprites without using the moveableSprite property

There is always a second (and third and fourth) method of accomplishing the same task in Director. For instance, you don't necessarily have to set the sprite's moveableSprite property to True in order to move the sprite around the Stage. Instead, you can force the sprite's location to match the location of the mouse pointer. The following handler enables the user to click an object and drag it to a new location on the Stage. The object follows the mouse pointer only as long as the mouse button is still down. In fact, the handler uses a function called the stillDown. It returns a value of 1 (True) when the mouse button is depressed and a value of 0 (False) when the mouse button is *not* depressed.

The following handler can be used as a cast member script or a sprite script and attached to any object you want to be moveable:

```
on mouseDown
      set moveObject to the clickOn
      puppetSprite moveObject, True
      repeat while the stillDown
         set the locH of sprite moveObject to the mouseH
         set the locV of sprite moveObject to the mouseV
         updateStage
      end repeat
end
```

Note

If you turn off the `puppetSprite` property, the object reverts back to its original location on the Stage — that is, the location it occupied before the user started dragging the sprite around the Stage.

The `clickOn` function returns the channel number of the sprite clicked upon, if the sprite has a script attached. The channel number is then placed in the `moveObject` variable which is used to puppet the sprite. The same variable (`moveObject`) is then used to reset the `locH` and `locV` of the sprite to match the mouse pointer position (as returned by the `mouseH` and `mouseV` functions).

To effectively use this handler, the sprite must be in a frame with a `go to the frame` frame script.

Adding puppetTransitions

You have already discovered that Director movies can include transitions between frames. To designate the specific type of transition that you want, you use... surprise!... the Transition channel in the Score window. Once transitions are added to your movie, the transitions, too, are considered sprites — even though they reside in their own special channel and do not show up on the Stage.

Like other types of sprites, transitions can be placed under the control of Lingo. To do so, you use a special Lingo command, the `puppetTransition` command, with the following syntax:

```
puppetTransition code, time, chunkSize, changeArea
```

The *time, chunkSize,* and *changeArea* parameters are optional. For *code,* you use one of the codes representing the 52 possible transitions, listed in Table 13-3 and available "on line" using the Director Help function.

Table 13-3
Transitions and Transition Codes

Category	Transition Code	Description of Transition
Wipe	01	Wipe Right
Wipe	02	Wipe Left
Wipe	03	Wipe Down
Wipe	04	Wipe Up
Wipe	05	Center Out, Horizontal
Wipe	06	Edges In, Horizontal
Wipe	07	Center Out, Vertical
Wipe	08	Edges In, Vertical
Wipe	09	Center Out, Square
Wipe	10	Edges In, Square
Push	11	Push Left
Push	12	Push Right
Push	13	Push Down
Push	14	Push Up
Reveal	15	Reveal Up
Reveal	16	Reveal Up-Right
Reveal	17	Reveal Right
Reveal	18	Reveal Down-Right
Reveal	19	Reveal Down
Reveal	20	Reveal Down-Left
Reveal	21	Reveal Left
Reveal	22	Reveal Up-Left
Dissolve	23	Dissolve, Pixels Fast
Dissolve	24	Dissolve, Boxy Rectangles
Dissolve	25	Dissolve, Boxy Squares
Dissolve	26	Dissolve, Patterns
Dissolve	50	Dissolve, Bits Fast
Dissolve	51	Dissolve, Pixels
Dissolve	52	Dissolve, Bits

(continued)

Table 13-3 *(continued)*

Category	Transition Code	Description of Transition
Strips	39	Strips on Bottom, Build Left
Strips	40	Strips on Bottom, Build Right
Strips	41	Strips on Left, Build Down
Strips	42	Strips on Left, Build Up
Strips	43	Strips on Right, Build Down
Strips	44	Strips on Right, Build Up
Strips	45	Strips on Top, Build Left
Strips	46	Strips on Top, Build Right
Cover	29	Cover Down
Cover	30	Cover Down-Left
Cover	31	Cover Down-Right
Cover	32	Cover Left
Cover	33	Cover Right
Cover	34	Cover Up
Cover	35	Cover Up-Left
Cover	36	Cover Up-Right
Other	27	Random Rows
Other	28	Random Columns
Other	37	Venetian Blinds
Other	38	Checkerboard
Other	47	Zoom Open
Other	48	Zoom Close
Other	49	Vertical Blinds

When you add the `puppetTransition` command to a movie, the transition occurs between the current frame and the next one. The *time* parameter to the `puppetTransition` command establishes the duration of the transition in quarter seconds. In the following example, the value of 24 means the transition takes 6 seconds to complete:

```
puppetTransition 38, 24
```

The *chunkSize* is set in pixels, with smaller numbers generating a smoother transition than larger pixel values. The range of values is from 1 to 128.

The *changeArea* parameter is set to either True or False. False is the default value and causes the transition to occur only in areas of the Stage that change between the current frame and the next. If you use True, the transition appears over the entire Stage.

The following example is a typical puppetTransition. It occurs in an `on mouseUp` handler that uses the Dissolve, Pixels Fast transition (23) for one second (4 quarter-seconds), using a small pixel value (2) for a smooth transition. The transition applies only to the changing area. As the transition occurs, the playback head moves to the next frame.

```
On mouseUp
     PuppetTransition 23, 4, 2, False
     go to the frame +1
end
```

Each transition in Table 13-3 has its own default settings that control the duration, chunk size, and change area of the transition. If you like the default settings, simply add the transition code parameter and do not specify the time, chunk size, and change area values.

Note

Using Director's new Xtra capabilities, you can import a transition as a cast member and then access it using the following form of the `puppetTransition` command. The first form of the command uses the cast member's number (12), and the second example uses the cast member name ("newTransition"):

```
puppetTransition member 12
puppetTransition member "newTransition"
```

Transition Xtras are discussed in more detail in Chapter 19.

In the following steps, you'll add two different transitions to the ancestor.dir movie. Only the transition code parameter is used. The `puppetTransition` command is added to the cast member scripts for the Next and Previous buttons. When the user clicks either button, a transition is applied between the current frame and the next frame of the movie.

On the CD-ROM

The file ancestor.dir is stored on your companion CD-ROM in the exercise:ch13 (exercise\ch13) folder.

Controlling Transitions with Lingo

1. Open the ancestor.dir movie in Director.
2. Open the Cast window, select cast member number 33, and open the script attached to the Next button.
3. Modify the `on mouseUp` handler for cast number 33 to match the following script:

   ```
   on mouseUp
        puppetTransition 23
        go to the frame +1
   end
   ```

   The transition code 23 invokes the Dissolve, Pixels Fast transition.

4. Click the Next Cast Member button to display the Previous button's cast member script (number 34).
5. Modify the `on mouseUp` handler for cast number 34 to match the following script:

   ```
   on mouseUp
        puppetTransition 2
        go to the frame -1
   end
   ```

   The transition code 2 invokes the Wipe Left transition.

6. Close the Script window, and select the Control ➪ Recompile All Scripts command (Shift+Option+Command+C on the Macintosh or Shift+F8 in Windows).

   Note: The Control ➪ Recompile All Scripts command double-checks all scripts for correct syntax and then recompiles all scripts in the current movie. This command is helpful if you move from script to script using the Next or Previous Cast Member buttons. When you close a movie using the Enter key on the numeric keypad, Director recompiles the modified script. If you use the Next and Previous Cast Member buttons to move from one cast member to another, script cast members are not automatically recompiled.

7. Save the movie as **ancestor1.dir**.
8. Rewind the movie and play it. There is no transition attached to the Start button in the first frame (the album cover). However, once you get to the second frame and beyond, one of the two transitions occurs each time you press the Next or Previous keys.

   You can experiment and try Director's other transitions by changing the number code following the `puppetTransition` command in the script that is attached to cast members 33 and 34.

Using Standard Cursors

When you play any movie within Director or run an application, you'll encounter several standard cursors (what I've called "the mouse pointer" throughout this book). Most users take these standard cursors for granted unless something unusual occurs. Together, the operating system and each application control a cursor's shape. Common forms of cursors are listed in Table 13-4.

Table 13-4
Common Standard Cursors

Cursor Appearance	Function
I beam	Used when the mouse pointer is over a text entry area
Arrow	Used when the mouse pointer is over a menu bar or menu option
Hourglass or watch	Used when the operating system is saving or loading a file; signals that you must wait before proceeding

Within ancestor.dir and other Director movies, you have been limited to using the arrow cursor except when the operating system takes over. Director provides access to several cursors for use in your movies. The ability to change the appearance of the cursor is handled by `the cursor of sprite` property and the `cursor` command.

Choosing a cursor for a sprite

The `cursor of sprite` property is used to change the appearance of the cursor, but only when the mouse pointer is over a designated sprite. The syntax for the statement that is used to changed the cursor is

    set the cursor of sprite channel to type

In this statement, the *channel* refers to the channel that holds the sprite, and the *type* is replaced with a numeric value that represents one of the standard cursors available within Director. Cursor type codes are listed in Table 13-5.

Table 13-5
Cursor Codes

Cursor Code	Cursor Description
0	No cursor; uses the default system cursor
−1	Arrow or pointer
1	I beam
2	Crosshair
3	Crossbar
4	Watch
200	Invisible

Note: The standard arrow or pointer cursor is the default cursor. To reset the sprite cursor property back to the default, use the 0 type.

When you use `the cursor of sprite` property, the cursor changes when the mouse pointer is *over* the object. If the bounding box is visible, as with an object using the Copy ink, the bounding box is considered part of the area of the sprite. If Matte ink is used, only the visible portion of the object is considered part of the sprite.

In the following steps, you'll use various cursors over objects on the Stage. You can use Lingo to cause the mouse pointer (cursor) to take on designated cursor shapes when the mouse pointer rolls over specific sprites.

On the CD-ROM: The file objects.dir is stored on your companion CD-ROM in the exercise:ch13 (exercise\ch13) folder.

Changing the Cursor of a Designated Sprite

1. Open the objects.dir movie in Director.

   Notice that the sprite in channel 1 is a billiard ball number 1 (on the left side of the Stage). The sprite in channel 2 is a billiard ball number 5 (on the right side of the Stage). Cast member 1 (Ball 1) in channel 1 uses the Matte ink effect. Cast member 2 (Ball 5) in channel 2 uses the Copy ink effect.

2. Open the movie script in cast member slot 4 and modify it to match the following:

   ```
   on startMovie
        set the cursor of sprite 1 to 2
        set the cursor of sprite 2 to 3
   end
   ```

3. Close the Script window, and save the movie as **objects1.dir**.

4. Rewind and play the movie.

5. Move the mouse pointer over Ball 1 and then over Ball 5. Observe how the cursor changes shape.

Changing the cursor for an entire movie

In addition to changing the appearance of the cursor (mouse pointer) while it is over a sprite, you can establish a specific cursor type for the entire movie. In the following handler, the cursor (2) that you specify (using the cursor command) dictates the mouse pointer that appears over the entire Stage area, throughout the entire movie:

```
on startMovie
     cursor 2
end
```

Tip You can use the cursor command to establish a default cursor for a movie, and still use the cursor of sprite property to modify the cursor when it moves over a specific sprite.

If you change the default cursor using the cursor 2 command, the cursor appears as a crosshair throughout the movie, unless you direct the cursor to change over a specific sprite or in a specific frame of the movie.

Using Custom Cursors

Although the ability to switch the standard cursor (using the codes in Table 13-5) allows you to expand the available cursors somewhat, the field of choices is still very limited. Fortunately, Director enables you to create and use *custom cursors*. Custom cursors are based on bitmap cast members stored in the Cast window and accessed using the cursor command and the cursor of sprite property.

Creating custom cursors

The artwork that you use for a custom cursor can be any bitmap image that you draw or import, as long as it conforms to these guidelines:

- ✦ Black-and-white (1-bit color depth)
- ✦ 16 x 16 pixels in size (though it can be larger)

Caution: If you use an image that is larger than 16 x 16 pixels for a custom cursor, Director will crop it to 16 x 16 pixels starting in the upper-left corner of the image. Choose your image with this in mind.

You can also create a custom cursor from two overlaid 16 x 16 pixel bitmaps. When you do this, the second image (cast member) is called a *mask*. We'll examine mask creation later in the chapter. A custom cursor *without* a mask takes the following behavior:

- ✦ Appears black when over white
- ✦ Appears white when over black
- ✦ Blends and almost disappears when over gray

This is normal mouse pointer/cursor behavior. You can verify this behavior when you use the mouse in most Macintosh or Windows applications.

A custom cursor *with* a mask maintains a solid black color, and the cursor disappears over solid black areas on the Stage.

The cursor and the mask artwork are stored in the Cast window. Typically they are placed in adjacent cast member slots. Once the artwork for the custom cursor is in place, you can use the `cursor` command or `the cursor of sprite` property to access it.

Invoking a custom cursor

The following snippet of code switches to a custom cursor (stored in cast member slot 10) in the `on startMovie` handler (located in a movie script):

```
on startMovie
      cursor [10]
end startMovie
```

The following handler, which uses both the custom cursor (cast member 10) and a mask (cast member 11), causes the cursor to stay black over all areas of the Stage:

```
on startMovie
      cursor [10, 11]
end startMovie
```

You can also use the cursor of sprite property with custom cursors. In this next example, the custom cursor (cast member 10) and the mask (cast member 11) appear when the mouse pointer is over the sprite in channel 2:

```
set the cursor of sprite 2 to [10, 11]
```

Note: The cast member numbers in square brackets constitute a *list*. Lists are discussed in Chapter 17. For now, just be aware that a custom cursor utilizes a list that includes the cast member numbers of the cursor and its mask, respectively.

When you set a custom cursor in a movie script, it means you want the custom cursor used throughout the movie as the default cursor. You can also arrange for the custom cursor to be used only when the mouse pointer rolls over a specific sprite in a specific frame. For this, you use an on enterFrame handler like the following:

```
on enterFrame
      if rollover (1) then
          set the cursor of sprite 1 to [4]
      end if
end
```

You can also have the custom cursor appear in a selected frame (and not make it contingent on rolling over a specific sprite). Add the following script to the script channel as appropriate:

```
on enterFrame
      set mouseCursor to [4]
      set the cursor of sprite 1 to mouseCursor
end
```

In this example, a variable (mouseCursor) is assigned the cast member number for the custom cursor.

Creating custom cursors in the Paint window

It's possible to create custom cursor artwork in the Paint window, but it is often easier in Adobe Photoshop or Macromedia Freehand because of the editing features available. You can create custom cursors in the Paint window by using the "artwork" already available in some icon-oriented or symbolic fonts. Examples of this type of font include Monotype Sorts, Symbol, Wingdings, WP Iconic Symbols A and B, and Zapf Dingbats.

A word about Wingdings

Wingdings is a TrueType font available on both Macintosh and Windows systems. It includes icons that you can use to create attractive custom cursors. Unless you have a hardcopy printout that maps the correlation between the numbers and letters on your keyboard and the icons in the Wingdings font, you'll have to experiment to figure this out. Be sure to try each keyboard character (1, 2, 3, a, b, c, and so on) by itself, as well as in conjunction with the Shift key. Some of our favorite Wingding icons are listed in Table 13-6.

Table 13-6
Wingding Fonts and Equivalent Keystrokes

Keystroke	Icon Created Using the Wingding Font
5	Two-drawer file cabinet
6	Hourglass
8	Computer mouse
Shift+1	Pencil
Shift+4	Reading glasses
Shift+7	Open book
Shift +Plus (+)	Stamped letter
Shift+J	Smiley face
Shift+T	Snowflake

On the CD-ROM In the following steps, you'll create a custom cursor and then use it in the zoom.dir movie. The file zoom.dir is stored on your companion CD-ROM in the exercise:ch13 (exercise\ch13) folder.

Creating a Custom Cursor in the Paint Window

1. Open the zoom.dir movie and play it.

   Notice that clicking the thumbnail image zooms it to the full-screen image. If you click the zoomed, full-screen image, the playback head returns to the thumbnail image. However, the movie provides no clue as to what to do and when. Let's change the cursor to be a hint that a click is needed.

2. Stop the movie.

3. Select the first open cast member slot in the Cast window and then click the PaintWindow button on the toolbar (Command+5 or Ctrl+5).

4. Set the foreground color to black and the background color to white.

5. Set the ink effect to Normal, if it is set otherwise.

6. Select the Text tool on the Tools palette.

7. Click anywhere on the Paint window canvas, and then Control-click (right-click) to display the pop-up menu.

8. Select the second Font option on the menu to display the Font dialog box.

9. Scroll until you find the Wingdings font and select it.

   Tip for Windows users: When the font list is visible, you can type the first letter of the font you want to locate. The highlighter jumps to the first font beginning with the letter you type.

10. Set the Size option to 24 points, be sure the color swatch is set to black, and click the OK button.

11. When the Font dialog box closes, type **8** to enter a mouse icon on the Stage.

12. Set the Marquee tool to No Shrink, and then click and drag to select a square area around the mouse icon. Make the selection area as close to the edges of the icon and as square as possible.

13. Double-click the Color Depth indicator, shown in Figure 13-8, on the Tools palette, which you can use to verify the color depth of an image.

14. When the Transform Bitmap dialog box appears, set the Color Depth to 1 bit. If the Maintain Proportions check box is deselected, select it. Set either the Width or Height text box (whichever lists the larger size in the Size area) to 16. Turn on the Remap Colors radio button, and then click the Transform button.

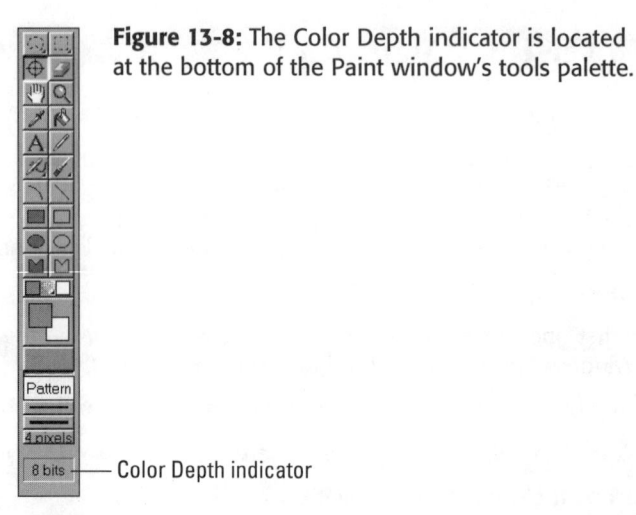

Figure 13-8: The Color Depth indicator is located at the bottom of the Paint window's tools palette.

Color Depth indicator

15. A message box warns you that the transformation to a different color depth is not reversible (Figure 13-9). Select the OK button to dismiss the message. The image is now 16 x 16 pixels in size, and black-and-white only (1-bit color depth).

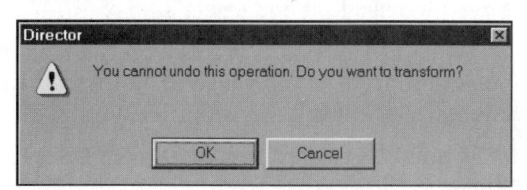

Figure 13-9: Director displays a warning message before the transformation begins.

16. To be sure the object's registration point is properly placed, click the Registration Point tool.

17. If the registration point is not centered on the mouse icon, double-click the Registration Point tool.

    Note that you can click and drag the registration point to whatever location you desire. However, in this case you want the registration point centered on the object.

18. Close the Paint window. Now you are ready to add a movie script that invokes the new custom cursor.

19. Select cast member slot 6 (skip slot 5) and click the ScriptWindow button on the toolbar (Command+0 or Ctrl+0). When the Script window opens, type the following handler:

```
on startMovie
    set the cursor of sprite 1 to [4]
end startMovie
```

20. Close the Script window, save the movie as **zoom1.dir,** rewind, and play the movie. As the mouse pointer moves over the thumbnail image, the cursor changes to the custom mouse cursor you created in the previous steps.

21. Click the thumbnail. When the playback head moves to frame 10 with the zoomed view, the custom cursor is still in use because the sprite based on the zoomed image is also in channel 1.

22. Click anywhere on the photo to return to frame 1 and the thumbnail. When you move the mouse pointer off of the thumbnail, it returns to the default arrow cursor.

Creating a mask for a custom cursor

The difference between the cursor artwork and the mask is simple: All black areas in the cursor artwork should be white in the map image, and all white areas of the cursor artwork should be black in the mask. But when you create a mask for a custom cursor, you want it to also be a 1-bit black-and-white image. Though it is somewhat tricky, you can create a mask for a custom cursor in the Paint window. The difficulty of using this method includes the following challenges:

+ It's hard to get the mask set to *exactly* 16 x 16 pixels and still have the reverse image of cursor artwork placed in exactly the same location within the area of the cursor artwork. And if the mask and cursor image are offset, your custom cursor will appear blurred and indistinct.

+ Sometimes when you double-click with the Marquee tool (with the Shrink option enabled) to select the cursor artwork and then cut-and-paste it into a new cast member slot, part of the artwork is clipped.

With those cautions in mind, here is the process of creating a mask:

1. In the Paint window, select the entire custom cursor image (double-click the Marquee tool).

2. Copy the image to the Clipboard and then paste it into a new, adjacent cast member slot. You can practice with the zoom1.dir movie, in which cast member slot 5 was left open for the mask.

3. Change the new object's ink effect to Transparent.

4. Change the new object's color depth to 1-bit.

5. Modify the Lingo instruction to use the mask. In the following example, you place the mask in cast member slot 5, and the custom cursor is in cast member slot 4:

```
on startMovie
     set the cursor of sprite 1 to [4, 5]
end startMovie
```

6. Save your movie, rewind, and play it.

Changing the Visible to Invisible

You can cause sprites on the Stage to appear and disappear using `the visible of sprite` property. To set the visible property, a sprite must first be under the control of Lingo; that is, it must be puppeted. Here are two examples of the visible statement:

```
set the visible of sprite 4 to True
```

```
set the visible of sprite 3 to False
```

In the first example, the sprite in channel 4 is made visible (True). In the second example, the sprite in channel 3 is made invisible.

At times, when you switch a sprite to invisible in an `on exitFrame` handler, the user sees a brief flash of the sprite before it disappears. You can cure this anomaly by using the `go to` command in the *calling* frame, and then changing the sprite to invisible within the same handler. The following example, which changes sprite 2 to invisible, illustrates the technique:

```
on exitFrame
     go to "FrameWhereSpriteBecomesInvisible"
     puppetSprite 2, True
     set the visible of sprite 2 to False
     updateStage
end
```

Tip: If you find that sprites appear momentarily in the first frame of your movie, even when you use the `on startMovie` or `on prepareFrame` handlers to make them invisible, then start your movie in frame 2. It is frequently useful to leave the Stage empty in frame 1 and then begin adding sprites in frame 2.

In this next exercise, you'll change the visible property of a sprite from visible (True) to invisible (False) using the dinner.dir movie. In the `on startMovie` handler (in the cast member 5 script), all three sprites (in channels 1 through 3) are puppeted. Next, they are made moveable objects and their visible property is set to True (visible). This handler initializes the movie each time it begins playing.

On the CD-ROM The file dinner.dir is stored on your companion CD-ROM in the exercise:ch13 (exercise\ch13) folder.

Making a Sprite Invisible on the Stage

1. Open the dinner.dir movie in Director.

   Notice the placement and numbering of the cast members. Cast member 1 is Worm, cast member 2 is Hook & Line, and cast member 3 is Fish. The script that you are going to enter will indicate that if the Worm (sprite 1) intersects with the Fish (sprite 3) then the Worm becomes invisible. If the Hook & Line (sprite 2) intersects with the Fish (sprite 3), then the Fish becomes invisible.

2. Select the movie script in cast member slot 5, and open the Script window.

3. Modify the existing script to match the following:

   ```
   on startMovie
       repeat with count = 1 to 3
           puppetSprite count, True
           set the moveableSprite of sprite count to True
           set the visible of sprite count to True
           updateStage
       end repeat
   end
   ```

4. With the Script window still open, select the Next Cast Member button to display the Score script in cast member slot 4.

5. Modify the existing script to match the following:

   ```
   on exitFrame
       if sprite 1 intersects sprite 3 then
           set the visible of sprite 1 to False
           updateStage
       end if
       if sprite 2 intersects sprite 3 then
           set the visible of sprite 3 to False
           updateStage
       end if
       go to the frame
   end
   ```

6. Close the Script window.

7. Save the movie as **dinner1.dir,** rewind, and play the movie.

8. Drag the Fish to the other objects, or drag the other objects to the Fish. When you're done testing, stop the movie.

Fine-tuning the fish

The dinner.dir movie in its current state still needs some fine-tuning. Did you notice any of the following situations? Let's look at why each one is happening.

✦ Even after the Fish is invisible, you can drag the Worm to the former location of the Fish and it disappears — eaten by the ghost of the Fish!

Though a sprite (the Fish) is invisible, it is still on the Stage and can still be intersected by another sprite. The cure is to check and see if the target sprite (the Fish) is already invisible. If the Fish is already invisible, then it won't disappear when the Worm sprite intersects it.

✦ If the Worm and the Hook & Line get too close together, it becomes difficult to grab the Worm.

This situation occurs because the bounding boxes of the Hook & Line and the Worm sprites overlap. The Hook & Line sprite is in a higher-numbered channel (it's on top), so you cannot click and select the Worm sprite.

✦ If the Hook & Line gets anywhere near the Fish, the Fish disappears.

Both of the previous problems are caused by the ink effect in use. When you attempt to move a sprite, you can grab it by any point within its bounding box — unless it uses the Matte ink. When this movie was first created, the designer did not want the loop at the top of the hook to appear in white; so the ink effect was changed to Transparent. Unfortunately, using the Transparent ink means you can click anywhere within the sprite's bounding box. Also, unless you use Matte ink, an intersection occurs when any point within the moving sprite's bounding box encounters the bounding box of the target sprite. By changing each of the objects to Matte ink, it's easier to grab either the Hook & Line or the Worm sprite without accidentally grabbing the other object. Further, greater accuracy is required before an intersection occurs.

The cure for the white within the loop at the top of the hook is to ignore it, or color it the same color as the blue background. Neither solution is entirely satisfying, however, because the loop may pass over either a nonwhite or a nonblue area.

Making a sprite invisible with the click of a mouse

You can also make a sprite appear or disappear when the user clicks an object. For instance, to make the Worm in the dinner.dir movie vanish when it's clicked, attach the following script to cast member 1:

```
on mouseUp
      puppetSprite 1, True
      set the visible of sprite 1 to False
      updateStage
end
```

Once you add this cast member script, you can no longer drag the Worm without it disappearing. Try it — whenever you release the mouse button, the Worm disappears, even if it is not intersecting the Fish.

Making a sprite visible on rollover

Another option is to make a sprite visible or invisible when the mouse pointer rolls over the sprite. You can also make one sprite appear or disappear when the mouse pointer moves over a second sprite. This technique can be used, for example, to display help information or a glossary listing.

The following frame script makes sprite 3 automatically appear when the mouse pointer rolls over it. Conversely, when the mouse pointer is no longer over sprite 3, it disappears:

```
On exitFrame
      if rollover(3) then
         set the visible of sprite 3 to True
      else
         set the visible of sprite 3 to False
      end if
      go to the frame
end exitFrame
```

You can test this script by opening the dinner.dir movie and replacing the current frame script (cast member 4) with the handler listed above. When you've made this change, the Fish disappears if you move the mouse pointer away from it. If you move the mouse pointer over the Fish, it comes back.

Summary

Before you discover how to add hypertext features to your movies in the next chapter, let's review some of the things you learned in this chapter.

- Objects in your movie can be placed under the control of Lingo using the `puppetSprite` command. Once puppeted, you can swap one sprite for another on Stage (`set the memberNum`), make a sprite moveable during playback (`set the moveableSprite of sprite`), constrain the movement of a sprite (`set the constraint of sprite`), cause a sprite to follow the movement of the mouse pointer (`set the loc of sprite`), and make an object visible or invisible (`set the visible of sprite`).

- Using Lingo, you can also add transitions between frames in your movie, and create and use custom cursors.

- Lingo includes commands to check for the intersection of one sprite with another. Once the intersection is determined, you can cause specific actions to occur.

- By using global variables, you can create a more generic handler that responds to a variety of values. This technique enables you to shorten a handler because you no longer have to write code to handle every distinct value that might occur when the movie plays.

✦ ✦ ✦

CHAPTER 14

Text Manipulation with Lingo

Even in the world of multimedia where pictures and sounds reign supreme, creating and manipulating strings of text is a large part of programming with Director. With a little bit of Lingo, you can control the properties of a text field in the Cast window or on your Stage. The properties of text extend beyond the traditional print attributes that you set in your word processor documents. In this chapter you'll see how to use *chunk expressions* to access and change specific portions of text (called *chunks*). Using Lingo, you can control all the text field attributes listed in Table 14-1.

In This Chapter

Setting the font, font color, font style, and font size using Lingo

Working with chunk expressions

Transferring text between field cast members

Sizing and positioning a text field

Incorporating hypertext into a movie

Resetting text to the top of the text box

Table 14-1
Text Field Attributes

Property Name	Can Chunk?	Range of Values	Attributes Set
the fontStyle of member	Yes	"plain", "bold", "italic", "underline", "condense", "extend" Macintosh only: "shadow", "outline"	Style of the font. Style "plain" causes font to lose all other styles, but otherwise font styles are additive; for example, setting bold followed by italic makes selection both bold and italic. Correct syntax requires that these parameters be enclosed within parentheses, and the font style names enclosed within quotes.
the fontSize of member	Yes	1 to 1,000	Size of the font in *points*. Most body text will be in the 12–14 point range.
the font of member	Yes	Any font on the current system can be entered as a string.	Specific font used by the field. The font names must be enclosed within quotes.
the foreColor of member	Yes	0 to 255; the entries in the current color palette.	Color of the text; values are from the current color palette. If no palette is currently specified, this function the default system palette.
the backColor of member	Yes	0 to 255; the entries in the current color palette.	Background color for the text in a field. Has no effect if field's ink is set to Background Transparent.
the alignment of member	No	"left", "center", "right"	Alignment of field to left, centered, or right-justified. Alignment parameters must be enclosed within quotes.
the border of member	No	0 to 127	Width of border surrounding text field.

Property Name	Can Chunk?	Range of Values	Attributes Set
the boxDropShadow of member	No	0 to 127	Offset distance in pixels for a duplicate copy of rectangular text box. Offset is down and to the right of text box, which adds a drop shadow effect to text box (not the text it contains).
the dropShadow of member	No	0 to 127	Offset distance in pixels for a drop shadow copy of the text. Drop shadow appears beneath text in the text field, giving illusion that text is casting a shadow. A typical text drop shadow is offset by 2 to 4 pixels.
the margin of member	No	0 to 127	Minimum distance between text and insides of the text box.

Note When setting the field properties, you can use either the `member` or `field` keyword, but the trend (initiated by Macromedia) is away from `field` and toward `member`. Our opinion is that `field` is more descriptive, but be prepared for its eventual phase-out in favor of `member`.

Tip You cannot change the properties (such as color, size, font, or style) of an empty field. You can control the properties of an *apparently* empty text field by including one or more space characters in it.

Understanding the Properties of Text

Note To avoid confusion when you begin working with text properties, remember the basic difference that exists between a text cast member and a field cast member (as discussed in Chapter 4). That is, both text and field cast members contain characters that comprise text. But during playback the text cast member becomes a bitmap image of the text it contains, and the text contained in a field cast member remains editable and changeable. For that reason, the properties discussed in this section only apply to fields, not text cast members. Once a text cast member is placed on the Stage or displayed during playback, you cannot change its color, style, font, or size.

The following sections contain specific information on the most commonly used field properties, such as `the foreground of color`, `the fontSize of member`, `the font of member`, and `the fontStyle of member`. After introducing these properties, we'll explore Lingo *chunk expressions*. A chunk expression is used to parse (subdivide) strings into smaller component parts (characters, words, items, and lines). Column 2 of Table 14-1 indicates which field properties are used with chunk expressions.

Setting the foreground color

You can change the foreground color of a text string in a field using `the foreColor of member` property. The syntax of the statement is

```
set the foreColor of member targetMember to colorNumber
```

Note that the foreground color of the text *is* the color of the text.

In this statement, *targetMember* is replaced with either the cast member name or number. The *colorNumber* is replaced with an index number representing a color from the current color palette. Acceptable values for the index number depend on the color depth of the current palette. If you are working with 8-bit color, the palette includes 256 colors and index numbers range from 0 to 255. A 4-bit color depth uses a 16-color palette and the index numbers range from 0 to 15.

In the following example, the cast member named "MyTextEntry" is set to index color 35 (the color red in both the Windows System and the Macintosh System palette).

```
set the foreColor of member "MyTextEntry" to 35
```

If the field cast member number is 3, the statement can also be entered as

```
set the foreColor of member 3 to 35
```

In the following steps, you'll experiment with Lingo's ability to set the color of text stored in a field cast member using `the foreColor of member` property. As you work through this exercise, keep the Color Palettes window open so you can identify the index number that matches the color you want to use. Index numbers can represent various colors, based on the color palette in use.

Setting Font Color Using Lingo

1. With Director open, select File ⇨ New ⇨ Movie or press Command+N (Ctrl+N) to open a new movie.

2. Open the Cast window (Command+3 or Ctrl+3), the Color Palettes window (Command+Option+7 or Ctrl+Alt+7), and the Message window (Command+M or Ctrl+M). Your screen should appear similar to Figure 14-1.

3. Open the Field window (Command+8 or Ctrl+8), and type

   Get your facts first, then you can distort them as you please.

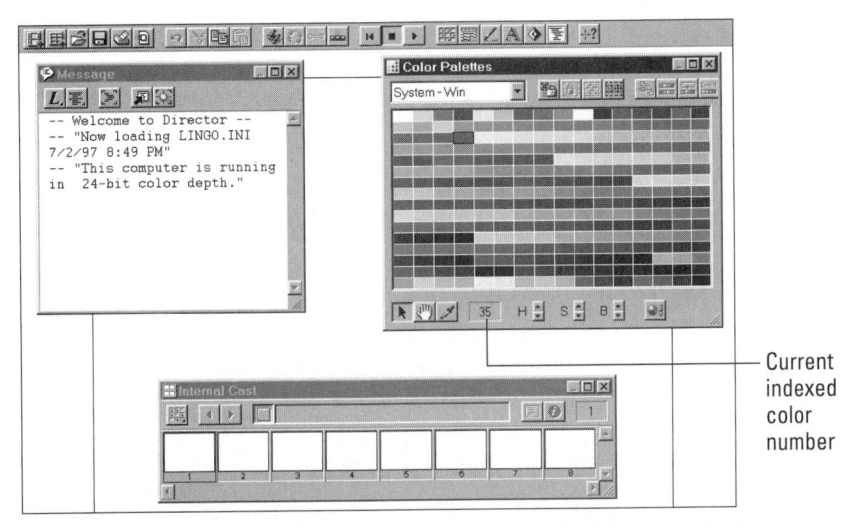

Figure 14-1: Getting ready to do some work on text attributes with Lingo

4. Press Enter twice and then type

   --Mark Twain

5. Click in the Name box at the top of the Field window, as identified in Figure 14-2, and type **Twain**.

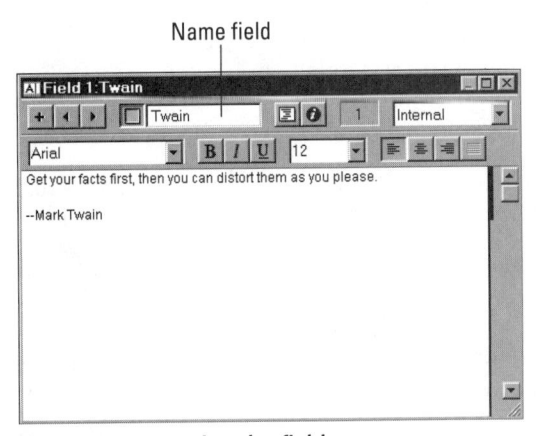

Figure 14-2: Naming the field

6. Close the Field window. The Mark Twain quotation appears as your first cast member.

7. Drag the Twain cast member onto the Stage and position it so you can see it between the open windows.

8. In the Color Palettes window, locate a red color chip (such as 35 on both the Windows and Macintosh System palettes) and click it. The color's index number appears at the bottom of the Color Palettes window (see Figure 14-1).

9. Select the Message window. Type

   set the foreColor of member "Twain" to 35

   and press Enter. The color of the text on the Stage and in the Cast window changes to red (corresponding to the color chip number you specified).

10. Locate an orange color chip in the Color Palettes window and select it, to see the index number for the color. On the System-Mac palette you can select color 23, or choose color 25 on the System-Win palette.

11. In the Message window, double-click the number 35 (or whatever color number you entered), type **23** (or **25**) to overwrite it, and press Enter. The text color changes to orange.

    You can reexecute a command in the Message window without completely retyping the instruction. Simply edit the command, move the insertion point to the end of the instruction, and press Enter.

12. Save the movie as **twain.dir.** Close the Color Palettes window.

Setting the font size

To change the type size of the text stored in a field, you use `the fontSize of member` property. The syntax of the statement is

```
set the fontSize of member targetMember to size
```

In this statement, *targetMember* is replaced with either the cast member name or number. The *size* parameter is replaced with the desired font size in points.

The value entered for the size parameter represents the point size of the font. A 72-point character is approximately one inch high.

Readability is a major issue when you're determining the font size for on-screen text. In print media (books and newspapers), type sizes are usually in the 11- to 12-point range for body text. Headlines range between 18 and 36 points and sometimes larger. By default, Director uses 12-point type, but you may want to use a slightly larger font size to ensure readability. We often use 14-or 16-point type to improve the readability of text on the screen, with headline text set larger still (often 24 points and larger).

In the following example, the cast member named "MyTextEntry" is set to a font size of 24 points:

```
set the fontSize of member "MyTextEntry" to 24 (this is the
example)
```

The results of `the fontSize of member` property can be tested and demonstrated using the Message window. This is true of all the text-field related properties covered in this chapter.

> **Tip**
>
> When working on a Director movie, it's a good idea to experiment with font sizes in order to maximize readability while minimizing the amount of Stage area consumed by text. It is always a balancing act.

Setting Font Size Using Lingo

On the CD-ROM

1. Open the twain.dir movie in Director, if it is not already open. You need the movie you created earlier in this chapter, or the file twain.dir on your companion CD-ROM in the exercise:ch14 (exercise\ch14) folder.

2. Select the Message window. Type

   set the fontSize of member "Twain" to 24

   and press Enter to execute the command. The text on the Stage changes to a larger font size.

3. Double-click 24 in the Message window, type **36**, and press Enter to again increase the size of the text.

4. Save the movie as **twain1.dir**.

Setting the typeface

You can change the typeface of text in a field using `the font of member` property. The syntax of the statement is

```
set the font of member targetMember to fontName
```

In this statement, *targetMember* is replaced with either the cast member name or number. The *fontName* parameter is replaced with the desired typeface name.

Note: The *fontName* parameter is the actual name of the font and must be entered as a string (inside double quotation marks). If you specify a font that is not available on the workstation, Director substitutes an available typeface.

In the following example, the cast member named "MyTextEntry" has the text set to use the Times New Roman font:

```
Set the font of member "MyTextEntry" to "Times New Roman"
```

The results of the font property can be demonstrated using the Message window. When working on a Director movie, don't hesitate to experiment with fonts to find the desired look and feel for field cast members.

Tip: When working with text cast members (as opposed to field cast members), you can still experiment with various typefaces, styles, sizes, and colors. You simply need to experiment in the Text window rather than modify these properties on the fly using Lingo.

Setting Font Using Lingo

On the CD-ROM

1. Open the twain1.dir movie in Director, if it is not already open. You need the movie you created earlier in this chapter, or the file twain1.dir on your companion CD-ROM in the exercise:ch14 (exercise\ch14) folder.

2. Select the Message window, and type

   set the font of member "Twain" to "Arial"

   If you do not have Arial, try any of the following sans serif fonts: Helv, Helvetica, Swiss, or Geneva. Or you can leave the Arial font name in the command and see what your system substitutes for it.

3. Press Enter to execute the command in the Message window. If the text in the text box was already set to Arial, you will see no change; otherwise, the text on the Stage changes to the new (Arial) typeface.

4. Double-click the font name (Arial) in the Message window and type **Times New Roman**.

5. *Be sure the cursor is placed after the double quote at the end of the instruction* in the Message window, and press Enter to execute the modified instruction.

6. Save the movie as **twain2.dir.**

If you like, you can experiment with other fonts such as Bookman, Chicago, Zapf Chancery, and so on.

Setting the style

To change the style (print attribute) assigned to text in a field, use `the fontStyle of member` property. The syntax of the statement is

```
set the fontStyle of member targetMember to styleName
```

In this statement, *targetMember* is replaced with either the cast member name or number. The *styleName* parameter is replaced with the desired style name, as shown in Table 14-2.

Table 14-2
Style Name Options in Director

Name of Font Style	Displayed Results
`plain`	plain (text using the plain font style, with no attributes such as italic, bold, or underline)
`italics`	*italic* (text using the italic font style)
`bold`	**bold** (text using the bold font style)
`underline`	underline (text using the underline or underscore font style)

In the following example, the cast member named "MyTextEntry" is set to a font style of bold:

```
Set the fontStyle of member "MyTextEntry" to "bold"
```

These font styles can be combined in a single instruction. In the first of the following examples, the cast member named "MyTextEntry" is set to a font style of bold and italic. In the second example, cast member 3 is set to use bold and underline styles.

```
Set the fontStyle of member "MyTextEntry" to "bold, italic"
Set the fontStyle of member 3 to "bold, underline"
```

The results of the font property can be demonstrated using the Message window.

Setting Font Style Using Lingo

On the CD-ROM

1. Open the twain2.dir movie in Director, if it is not already open. You need the movie you created earlier in this chapter, or the file twain2.dir on your companion CD-ROM in the exercise:ch14 (exercise\ch14) folder.

2. Select the Message window. Type

   set the fontStyle of member "Twain" to "bold"

   and press Enter. The text on the Stage is displayed with the bold property turned on.

3. Double-click the fontStyle name (`bold`) in the Message window and type **italic**.

4. Be sure the cursor is positioned *after* the double quote at the end of the instruction in the Message window, and then press Enter to execute the modified instruction.

5. Change the font style back to plain.

6. Save the movie again as twain2.dir.

Using Chunk Expressions to Change Parts of the Whole

So far you have used the properties of text to change the entire contents of a field cast member. By using Director's *chunk expressions,* you can take a "bite" out of a field and manipulate that chunk without changing the entire contents of the field. In word processing, you can change or modify a specific character, word, line, or paragraph of text. In Director, you can also control a chunk of text, such as a specific character, word, item, or line.

Understanding text strings

Except for bitmap text, your computer considers text a *string* of characters. For instance, the following string of characters makes up a quote:

```
"They are ill discoverers that think there is no land, when
they can see nothing but sea." Sir Francis Bacon (from
Advancement of Learning)
```

This sample text string includes not only alphabetical characters (*A, a, B, b, C, c,* and so on) but also punctuation (quotation marks, period, and comma) and special characters (left and right parentheses) plus spaces that separate words. When you work with chunk expressions, don't forget that spaces, punctuation, and special characters are all counted as part of a field cast member.

Guidelines for working with text strings

This section contains some helpful rules to keep in mind when you're working with text strings in Director.

To work effectively with text strings, you must remember that

- ✦ Text strings are always surrounded by quotation marks.
- ✦ You can insert a text string into a field cast member or into a variable using the `put` command.

The following line can be entered in the Message window, to add the text inside the quotation marks to field 1:

```
put "Too soon old, too late smart" into field 1
```

Note that `field 1` here refers to cast member 1. You can use this command to insert text into an empty cast member slot (in the Cast window) or to replace existing text in a field cast member. However, if cast member 1 is something other than a field — such as a text, bitmap, sound, or script cast member — the instruction will not work and the contents of the cast member remain unchanged.

A slightly different form of the `put` command can be used to place text in a field cast member:

```
put "Too soon old, too late smart" into member 1
```

In this arrangement, when you use the `put` command to place a text string in a *member* or *field*, you create a text field in the cast. This applies whether you use a cast member name or a number in the syntax of the command.

You can use a similar syntax to place a text string into either a local or global variable:

```
put "You can't tell how deep a puddle is until you step into it." into Proverbs
```

To initialize a variable (that is, to establish what the variable represents before any processing occurs), you can use an empty text string — called a *null entry* by programmers. This is done by placing an empty text string in a cast member with either of the following commands:

```
put "" into field 1
```

```
put EMPTY into member 1
```

Tip: You can use the word NULL instead of EMPTY in a Lingo command. Either is acceptable.

EMPTY is a character constant and always has the same value: nothing. Character constants are not case sensitive, so the constant can be entered as EMPTY, Empty, or empty.

When referring to a field cast member, you can use the cast member's name or the field number. If you use a field name, you must enclose it within quotation marks.

For the sake of clarity, it is better to use a cast member's name rather than its number — assuming that you have given the cast member a meaningful name. If you have a cast member named OldQuote, for instance, you can use either of the following instructions to add the text string (in quotes) to the field cast member:

```
put "You're never too old to learn." into field "OldQuote"

put "You can't teach an old dog new tricks." into member
"OldQuote"
```

If punctuation is inside the quotation marks, like the period in the preceding examples, it is part of the text string and is added to the text field.

Note: Lingo uses quotation marks to identify the beginning and end of a text string. To include quotation marks within a string, you must use the QUOTE constant as shown in the following example:

```
Put "T. S. Eliot once said,"&&QUOTE&"Only those who risk going
too far can possibly find out how far one can go."&QUOTE into
member "quoteField"
```

If the field into which you place a text string is not on the Stage, the text is stored in the Cast window but not displayed on the Stage. This may seem obvious, but it is useful to point out because you can change a text string before it is displayed in a subsequent frame of your movie.

If you do not use the `updateStage` command, changes to the text fields placed on the Stage are not displayed. Director builds the Stage when it enters a frame. If you manipulate text (or any object) while keeping the playback head within a frame, you must use the `updateStage` command to display the changes. If the playback head leaves the frame and keeps reentering the same frame (as when you use the `go to the frame` instruction), the Stage is updated automatically whenever the frame is entered.

Using chunk expressions

Chunk expressions are used to select a portion of a text string (that is, break it up into smaller parts). Chunk expressions can be used with field cast members and variables that contain strings. However, chunk expressions do not work with bitmap text cast members. To access standard "chunks" of text, you must use the chunk expression keywords listed in Table 14-3.

Table 14-3
Chunking Levels in Text

Level	Keyword	Example
Characters	Char	`put char 5 of "the grey man rises" -- "g"`
Words	Word	`put word 2 of "the grey man rises" -- "grey"`
Items	Item	`put item 3 of "red,green,blue,orange" -- "blue"`
Lines	Line	`put line 2 of "red,green,blue,orange"&return &"pink,wine,maroon,sepia" -- "pink, wine,maroon,sepia"`

The following sections provide specific information on using the chunk expressions to retrieve specific characters, words, items, and lines of text from fields and variables.

Using the `char` keyword

The `char` keyword is used to identify and retrieve one or more characters in a text string, including alphabetic and numeric characters, punctuation, and special characters. You can retrieve a single character or a range of characters using the following syntax:

```
char n of targetSprite
char n to m of targetSprite
```

In each example, *n* is replaced with a numeric value representing the character position within the field or variable. If you use a range of characters, *m* represents the last character in the range. The `targetSprite` parameter identifies the field name (if preceded by the keyword `field`) or the variable name that holds the text string to be searched.

The results of the `char` chunk expression can be demonstrated using the Message window.

Retrieving Characters from a Field with char

1. Open a new movie in Director and then open the Message window (Command+M or Ctrl+M).

2. In the Message window, type

   put "You can't tell how deep a puddle is until you step into it." into field 1

   and press Enter. The Cast window displays the new text field in cast member slot 1.

3. Type

   put char 1 of field 1

   and press Enter. The Message window displays the instruction and the first character in cast member number 1, as follows:

   ```
   put char 1 of field 1
   -- "Y"
   ```

4. With the field selected in the Cast window, select the Cast Member Properties button.

5. On the Field Cast Member Properties dialog box, type **Proverb** and click OK. You have assigned a name to the cast member, which you can now use in Lingo statements and commands.

6. Make the Message window active, and then type

   put char 1 to 3 of field "Proverb"

   and press Enter. The Message window displays the instruction and the result as follows:

   ```
   put char 1 to 3 of field "Proverb"
   -- "You"
   ```

7. Save the movie as **nuggets.dir**, so you can use it as you explore the remaining chunk expression keywords.

Retrieving Characters from a Variable Using char

1. In the Message window, type

   put "Anger is as a stone cast into a wasp's nest." into Malabar

   and press Enter.

2. Type **put Malabar** and press Enter. The instruction and the result appear in the Message window as follows:

   ```
   put "Anger is as a stone cast into a wasp's nest." into Malabar
   put Malabar
   -- "Anger is as a stone cast into a wasp's nest."
   ```

3. Check to be sure the quote is accurate. Then type

   put char 13 of Malabar

   and press Enter. The Message window displays the character *a*, which is the 13th character (including spaces) in the quote.

4. Type

   put char 15 to 24 of Malabar

   and press Enter. The Message window displays the instruction and the result as follows:

   ```
   put char 15 to 24 of Malabar
   -- "stone cast"
   ```

5. Type

   put char 14 of Malabar

   and press Enter. The Message window displays the instruction and the result as follows:

   ```
   put char 14 of Malabar
   -- " "
   ```

   The character stored in character position 14 is a space.

Using the word keyword

The word chunk expression retrieves one or more words in a text string. In Director, a *word* is a continuous string of characters separated from other characters in the text string by specific characters such as spaces, tabs, and return characters. Note that the separator between words (such as the space) is not considered part of the word.

You can retrieve a single word or a range of words using the following chunk expression statements:

```
word n of targetSprite

word n to m of targetSprite
```

In each example, *n* is replaced with a numeric value representing the word position within the field or variable. If you use a range of words, *m* represents the last word in the range. The *targetSprite* parameter identifies the field name (if preceded by the keyword field) or the variable name that holds the text string to be searched.

Tip: The word chunk expression can also be used to retrieve words from a variable that contains a text string.

The results of the word chunk expression can be demonstrated using the Message window.

Retrieving Words from a Field with word

On the CD-ROM

1. With the nuggets.dir movie open in Director, be sure the Message and Cast windows are open. You need the movie you created in the preceding exercise, or the file nuggets.dir on your companion CD-ROM in the exercise:ch14 (exercise\ch14) folder.

2. In the Message window, type

   put "The first man to raise his voice has lost the argument" into member 2

   and press Enter.

3. Type

   put word 1 of field 2

   and press Enter. The Message window displays the instruction and the result as follows:

   ```
   put "The first man to raise his voice has lost the argument"
   into member 2
   put word 1 of field 2
   -- "The"
   ```

4. Type

   put word 5 to 7 of field 2

   and press Enter. The Message window displays the instruction and the result as follows:

   ```
   put word 5 to 7 of field 2
   -- "raise his voice"
   ```

5. Save the movie as **nuggets1.dir**.

Using the `item` keyword

The `item` chunk expression retrieves one or more strings of characters that are *delimited* (separated) by commas in a text string. If you are familiar with database structures, you may have heard of *comma-delimited fields*. In Director, comma-delimited fields are considered *items*. Note that the separator (in this case, the comma character) is not considered part of the item.

You can retrieve a single item (field) or a range of fields using the following chunk expression statements:

```
item n of targetSprite

item n to m of targetSprite
```

In each example, *n* is replaced with a numeric value representing the item position within the text field or variable. If you use a range of items, *m* represents the last item in the range. The *targetSprite* parameter identifies the field name (if preceded by the keyword `field`) or the variable name that holds the text string to be searched.

Tip: The `item` chunk expression can also be used to retrieve items from a variable that contains a text string.

The results of the `item` chunk expression can be demonstrated using the Message window.

Retrieving Items from a Field Using `item`

On the CD-ROM

1. With the nuggets1.dir movie open in Director, be sure the Message and Cast windows are open. You need the movie you created earlier in this chapter, or the file nuggets1.dir on your companion CD-ROM in the exercise:ch14 (exercise\ch14) folder.

2. In the Message window, type

   put "Paper Clips,Pencils,Notebook Paper,Clasp Envelopes,Toner Cartridges" into member 3

   and press Enter.

3. Type

   put item 4 of field 3

(continued)

and press Enter. The Message window displays the instruction and the result as follows:

```
put "Paper Clips,Pencils,Notebook Paper,Clasp
Envelopes,Toner Cartridges" into member 3
put item 4 of field 3
-- "Clasp Envelopes"
```

If you had included a space after each comma in the text you entered in step 2, then step 3 would return the string

```
"Clasp Envelopes"
```

which includes a space prior to the letter *C*. Lingo assumes the item includes every text character between the commas including spaces.

4. Type

   put item 4 to 7 of field 3

   and press Enter. The Message window displays the instruction and the result as follows:

   ```
   put item 4 to 7 of field 3
   -- "Clasp Envelopes,Toner Cartridges"
   ```

   Because the field does not include an item 6 and 7, Lingo returns just the available items (4 and 5).

5. Save the movie as **nuggets2.dir**.

Using the `line` keyword

The `line` chunk expression retrieves a string of characters that is preceded and followed by a return character in a text string. Note that the separator (such as the return character) is not considered part of the line.

You can retrieve a single line or a range of lines using the following chunk expression statements:

```
line n of targetSprite

line n to m of targetSprite
```

In each example, *n* is replaced with a numeric value representing the first line position within the text field or variable. If you use a range of lines, *m* is a numeric value representing the last line number in the range. The *targetSprite* parameter identifies the field name (if preceded by the keyword `field`) or the variable name that holds the text string to be searched.

The `line` chunk expression can also be used to retrieve lines of text from a variable that contains a text string.

The results of the line chunk expression can be demonstrated using the Message window. In this case, however, pressing the Enter key when working in the Message window executes the line of text you have entered, so you need another method of entering a return character. The solution is to use the RETURN constant. It represents the Return key character and places it in the field. You must concatenate the text in line 1 with the Return key and then concatenate it to the text in line 2, and so on. The concatenation operator is the ampersand (&).

Retrieving Lines of Text from a Field using line

1. With the nuggets2.dir movie open in Director, be sure the Message and Cast windows are open. You need the movie you created in the preceding chapter, or the file nuggets2.dir on your companion CD-ROM in the exercise:ch14 (exercise\ch14) folder.

2. In the Message window, type

   put "Slow"&RETURN&"is every foot"&RETURN&"on an unknown path"&RETURN&"—Irish Proverb" into member 4

   and press Enter.

3. Type

   put line 2 of field 4

   and press Enter. The Message window displays the instruction and the result as follows:

   ```
   put "Slow"&RETURN&"is every foot"&RETURN&"on an unknown
   path"&RETURN&"--Irish Proverb" into member 4
   put line 2 of field 4
   -- "is every foot"
   ```

4. Type

   put line 1 to 2 of field 4

   and press Enter. The Message window displays the instruction and the result as follows:

   ```
   put line 1 to 2 of field 4
   -- "Slow
   is every foot"
   ```

   Notice that the word "Slow" and the string "is every foot" are on separate lines.

5. Save the movie as **nuggets3.dir**.

Using Other Chunky Activities

You can manipulate text strings in fields using numerous other Lingo commands, functions, and properties. For instance, you can

- ✦ Enter or update the text string in a field using the text of field property.

> **Tip:** When using the text of field property, you can include the keyword field, or member, or cast or cast member. Any of these terms still work in Director 6, but the preferred keyword is either field or member. The term "cast member" is being phased out in favor of the simpler "member."

- ✦ Count the number of words in a field using the number of words function.
- ✦ Transfer text from one field to another.
- ✦ Erase text from a field using the delete command.
- ✦ Combine text from two or more fields using the concatenation (&) operator.

Establishing the text string in a field

Earlier in this chapter, you used the put command to place a text string in a field. If the field already exists in the cast, you can accomplish this task using the text of field property. In the following example, the text string "Experience is the best teacher" is placed into an *existing field* 6:

```
set the text of field 6 to "Experience is the best teacher"
```

To create *a new* cast member, use the put command. The set command can only be used to establish the text in an *existing* field. The benefit of the text of field property is in your ability to use Lingo to change text strings during the playback of a movie.

Example: a movie with a word game

In the next exercise, you'll modify a small movie (only one frame long) to create a simple word game. The game movie sayings.dir places a text string in a field and then changes the font to Symbol so the text string is indecipherable. As the user clicks the Change Word button, the font of one word at a time is randomly switched from Symbol to Helvetica.

To better understand the changes you make, you need to understand the *objective* for the little sayings.dir movie. The objective is to build a simple Director movie that displays a familiar saying ("If the shoe fits, wear it") in an unrecognizable font (Symbol). As the player clicks a button (Change Word), a randomly selected word is changed from the unrecognizable font to Helvetica (or Arial or a similar sans serif font). The player attempts to guess the text of the proverb in the fewest tries (one attempt after each click of the mouse button). The project also includes a button to exit (Quit) the movie.

There are three tasks needed to finish building the movie:

Task 1 is to attach a script to the Quit button that halts the movie. The script also sets the contents of the Proverb cast member to a single space character, and then sets the font of field 1 (Proverb) to Symbol (in preparation for when the movie is run again).

Tip If you use the EMPTY or NULL constant to place "nothing" in field 1, then the field does not retain any formatting (such as a specified font or style). To retain the formatting properties of the text, you must leave at least one character (such as the space character) in the field.

Task 2 is to attach a script to the Change Word button that randomly changes one word to a different font. In the script, you use the random function to "capriciously" change text properties. In additional to changing the font, you can randomly select a color for a word in the text string, like this:

```
set the forecolor of word random(6) of field "Proverb" to
random(255)
```

The random(255) refers to the available index numbers for colors in an 8-bit color palette.

You can also randomly modify the font style of a randomly selected word in the "Proverb" field by adding the following statement to the handler:

```
set the fontStyle of word random(6) of field "Proverb" to
random(3) of "italic bold plain"
```

Task 3 is to add a movie script that places the text string in the field.

Working with Chunk Expressions in a Movie

On the CD-ROM

1. Open the sayings.dir movie in Director. The file sayings.dir is on your companion CD-ROM in the exercise:ch14 (exercise\ch14) folder.

   The movie includes two buttons on the Stage (Change Word and Quit), a text cast member named "Proverb" in the Cast window, and a go to the frame script (already placed in the script channel in frame 1). The cast members in the Cast window and the initial appearance of the Stage are shown in Figure 14-3.

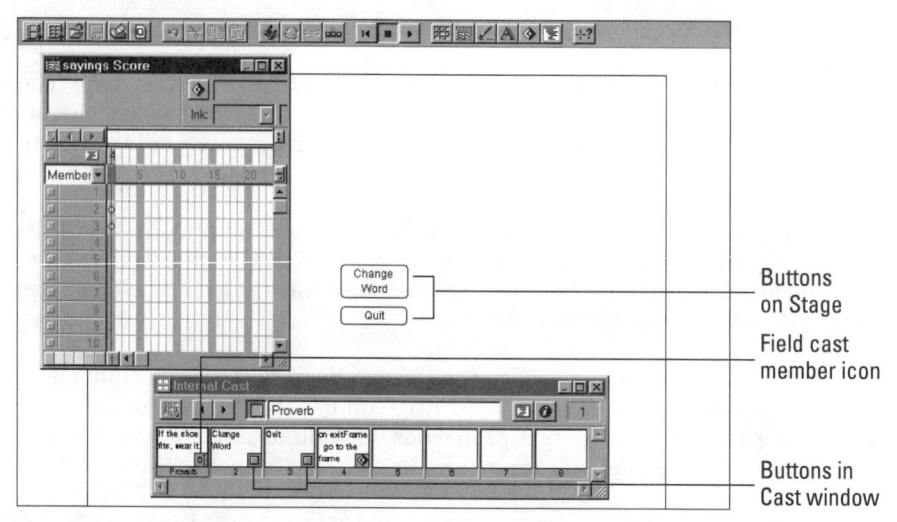

Figure 14-3: The Stage, Cast window, and Score window for the initial sayings.dir movie

2. With the Cast and Score windows open, drag the "Proverb" cast member on to the Stage. Put it any place where it does not cover up the two buttons — but be sure it spans only a single frame in the Score.

   You can accomplish this by dragging the end frame of the sprite on top of the beginning frame of the sprite (after placing the cast member on the Stage); or by holding down the Option (Alt) key as you drag the "Proverb" cast member onto the Stage. The end result is that the text stored in "Proverb" is placed on the Stage, centered in the text box and displayed in the Times or Times New Roman font.

3. Select the Quit (button) cast member in the Cast window and attach the following script to it. You do not need to type the comment lines that begin with a double-dash (--).

```
on mouseUp
      set the font of field "Proverb" to "symbol"
--The previous line resets the text back to the symbol font
--before you quit the movie
      set the text of field "Proverb" to " "
      --Be sure to include a space between the two quotation
      --marks.
      halt
--This causes Director to exit the movie without exiting
--Director, so you don't
--have to keep re-launching Director each time you use the
--Quit button
end
```

4. Close the Script window and save the movie as **sayings1.dir**.
5. Play the movie and select the Quit button.

   As soon as you click the Quit button, the text on the Stage disappears (replaced by a single space character) and then it is set to Symbol font.

6. Start the movie again and you'll see the blank Stage (except for the two buttons). Stop the movie again using the Quit button.

7. Select the Change Word button in the Cast window, and attach the following script to the button. You can omit the comment lines that begin with a double-dash (--).

   ```
   on mouseUp
         set the font of word random(6) of field "Proverb" to "helvetica"
         --the text in "Proverb" is six words in length.
         --The random(6) function returns a value between 1 and 6
         --which changes the font of the word identified by the
         --random function.
   end
   ```

8. Close the Script window.
9. Select empty slot 5 in the Cast window.
10. Select the Window⇨Script command (Command+0 or Ctrl+0). When the Script window opens, the title bar says "Movie Script 5."
11. Type the following `on startMovie` handler:

    ```
    on startMovie
          set the text of field "Proverb" to "If the shoe fits,¬
          wear it."
    end startMovie
    ```

    This script is executed when the movie starts; it replaces the space character in the Proverb field with the specified text ("If the shoe fits, wear it.").

12. Close the Script window.
13. Save the movie again as sayings1.dir, rewind it, and play it.

Note that the script does not check to see if the `random` function returns the same value more than once. So when you play the word game, you might click the Change Word button and nothing will happen. This occurs when the word selected by the random function has *already* been previously selected.

Counting words in a field

Using `the number of` function, you can count the characters, words, lines, or items in a text string. If you want to display or store the number of words in a specific field (such as "MyTextField") in a variable (such as "wordCount"), you can use the `put` command in combination with `the number of` function.

```
put the number of words in field "myTextField" into field
"wordCount"
```

You can substitute any field cast member's name, number, or variable (containing text) for `field "wordCount"`.

Caution The number function does not work with rich-text cast members.

Similar syntax is used to count other chunk expressions. Let's say that you want to count the number of specific chunks of text in a field named "Paragraph." The following statements, which count characters, words, items, and lines, respectively, place the result in a field named "Total."

```
Put the number of chars in field "Paragraph" into field "Total"
Put the number of words in field "Paragraph" into field "Total"
Put the number of items in field "Paragraph" into field "Total"
Put the number of lines in field "Paragraph" into field "Total"
```

Tip Did you notice the `chars` function in the first `put` line just above? The `chars` function counts spaces and punctuation, not just numbers and letters.

Transferring text from one field to another

Lingo also enables you to retrieve (and use) specific chunk expressions in a specific field. For example, you can identify and then use the first word in a paragraph stored in a field cast member. To identify the first word in field 5, the statement would be

```
word 1 of field 5
```

To place the first word in field "Statement" into another field named "FirstWord," you'd use the following instruction:

```
put word 1 of field "Statement" into field "FirstWord"
```

You can use the same approach to place a specific line from a text field in another field or into a variable. In each case, you are able to display and use a range of characters, words, lines, or items. For example, in each of the following examples, the instruction places the specified chunk expression in a field named "Result":

```
put char 5 of field 1 into field "Result"
put line 5 of field 1 into field "Result"
```

```
put item 5 of field 1 into field "Result"
```

This next example demonstrates that you can also access a range of words (or characters, lines, or items) from a field and then place the resulting text in a second field:

```
put word 3 to 5 of field 1 into field "Result"
```

Similar examples, using other chunk expressions, are

```
put item 1 to 10 of field 5 into field "Result"
put char 5 to 10 of field 4 into field "Result"
put line 1 to 2 of field "MyText" into field "Result"
```

Let's see how to use chunk expressions in our word game. With its single proverb, the sayings1.dir game quickly becomes predictable and boring. In the next exercise, you'll add additional quotations into a single text field (named "Source") and then modify the `on startMovie` script to randomly select a line from the field and place it in the Proverb field on the Stage.

When you create the new field, notice that the quotations placed in the "Source" field range from five to eight words in length. Earlier in this chapter, when you created the script for the Change Word button, you instructed Director to randomly select a word numbered 1 through 6 and change it from Symbol to Helvetica font. To adjust the range of random numbers to match the number of words in a specific quotation, you must determine the number of words transferred into the Proverb field, using `the number of words` function. As you'll discover in the following steps, you can substitute `the number of words` function for the value within parentheses after the `random` function.

Transferring Text Between Fields

On the CD-ROM

1. Open the sayings1.dir movie. You need the movie you created earlier in this chapter, or the file sayings1.dir on your companion CD-ROM in the exercise:ch14 (exercise\ch14) folder.

2. Select empty cast slot 6. Then select the Window ⇨ Field command using Command+8 (Ctrl+8).

3. In the Field window, type

   Experience is the best teacher.

   and press Enter.

4. With the Field window and cast member 6 still open, type

   You're never too old to learn.

   and press Enter.

5. Your field now has two lines of text. Let's add three more. Type the following lines, pressing Enter after each one:

   Two is company, three is a crowd.

   If it ain't broke, don't fix it.

   You can't teach an old dog new tricks.

6. Click in the Name field of the Field 6 dialog box, and type **Source** as the field name.

7. Close the Field window.

8. Open the movie script (cast member 5) and modify it to match the following:

   ```
   on startMovie
           put line random(5) of field "Source" into field "Proverb"
   end startMovie
   ```

9. Use the Next Cast Member button in the Script window to move to the script attached to the Change Word button (cast member 2).

10. Modify the handler to match the following:

    ```
    on mouseUp
            set the font of word random (the number of words in¬
    field "Proverb") of field "Proverb" to "helvetica"
    end
    ```

11. Close the Script window, save the movie as **thoughts.dir,** and play it. The quote displayed is one of the five in the "Source" field and appears in Symbol font.

12. Click the Change Word button to play the word game.

13. When done, select the Quit button. This stops the movie and replaces the text in the Proverb cast member with a space character. You need another button on the screen to reset the puzzle phrase, without quitting the word game. You'll do that next.

14. Stop the movie and use the Tool Palette to create another button. For the text on the face of the button, type **Restart**.

15. Place the button immediately under the Change Word button (spanning one frame only) and above the Quit button. To do this, you need to drag the Quit button lower on the screen. You can use the Modify⇨Align command (Command+K or Ctrl+K) to align the buttons on the Stage.

16. Be sure the text on the Restart button is centered and the width of the button is 75 pixels — the same as the width of the Change Word and Quit buttons.

17. Attach a script to the new button that includes the following handler:

```
on mouseUp
     set the font of field "Proverb" to "symbol"
     put line random(5) of field "Source" into field "Proverb"
end
```

18. Close the Script window and save the modified movie again as thoughts.dir.

19. Rewind and play the movie.

Creating uniform buttons

There are a few techniques that you'll find helpful when you create a new button (using the Tool Palette) and want it to match the size, alignment, and appearance of an existing button.

The first two techniques use the Sprite Properties dialog box (Figure 14-4) to change the size and placement of a new button. To access this dialog, Ctrl-click (right-click) the button sprite on the Stage. When the pop-up menu appears, choose Properties.

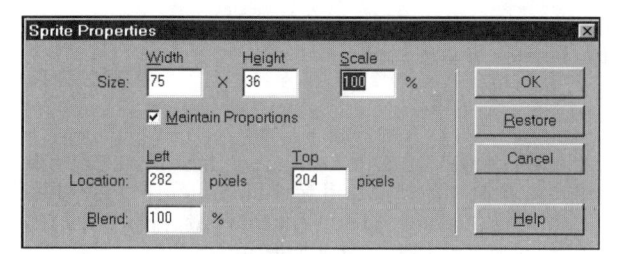

Figure 14-4: The Sprite Properties dialog box

Matching the size

Check the Sprite Properties dialog box for the dimensions of the existing button. Notice the Size values (Height and Width) of the object. These are the same dimensions you want to set for the new button. To match the dimensions, you must deselect the Maintain Proportions check box. If the original button has two lines of text and the new button has one (or visa versa), you cannot force the heights to be identical. You can, however, make the Width settings match — unless the text on the first button is significantly longer than the text on the second button (or vice versa). In that case, you may not be able to create identical Width settings.

Matching the location

If you want the buttons to line up on the Stage, either the Top or Left settings for Location in the Properties dialog must match. For instance, in the sayings.dir movie, we wanted the buttons to appear an equal distance from the left edge of the screen (centered on the screen), so we made sure that each button had the same value for the Left Location setting (in pixels). This works if you want buttons stacked on top of each other. If you want buttons positioned in a row across the bottom of the Stage, you would establish the same Top Location setting (in pixels) for each button.

Matching the font and alignment

The last technique is for setting the text on the face of a new button to match the font and alignment of an existing button. This technique uses the Button dialog box (Figure 14-5). To get to this dialog, you can either double-click the button cast member in the Cast window, or select the Edit ⇨ Edit Cast Member command after selecting the button or sprite on the Stage.

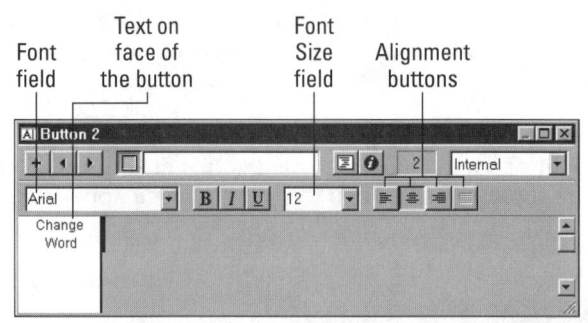

Figure 14-5: The Button dialog box for working with the text on Button 2

To match the font and alignment of an existing button label, first check the Button dialog for the original button and note the font and text alignment. Close the dialog and then open the Button dialog for the new button (in this case, Button 2). Set the font and alignment to match the settings of the first button.

The button's text alignment is set using the four alignment buttons to the right of the Font Size box. These options — probably quite familiar to you — are Align Left, Align Center, Align Right, and Justify. The font name and size used for the button label are displayed in their respective boxes in the Button dialog, and you can change these by clicking the drop-down list buttons. The available fonts will be the fonts installed on your system (see Figure 14-6).

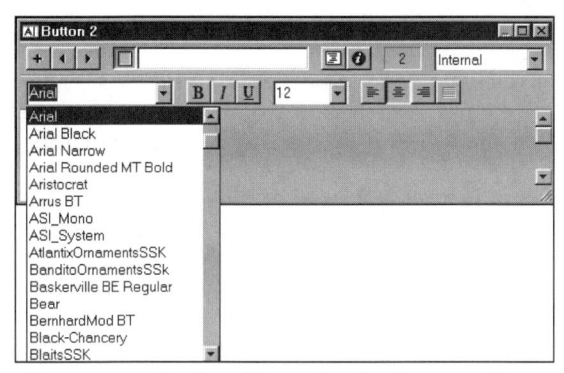

Figure 14-6: The list of fonts for the button will contain the fonts on your system.

Deleting text from text fields

By using the `delete` command in combination with a chunk expression, you can erase specific chunks of text from a field. For example, if you want to remove the third word in a text string (field 2), you can use the instruction

```
delete word 3 of field 2
```

In the following examples, text in the field named "OldText" is modified. In the first case, characters 3 through 5 are deleted. In the subsequent two examples, line 1 and then item 5 are deleted, respectively:

```
delete char 3 to 5 of field "OldText"
delete line 1 of field "OldText"
delete item 5 of field "OldText"
```

Instead of using the delete function, you can put EMPTY (or NULL) in the desired chunk location. The result is the same. For instance, the preceding three commands could be entered as

```
put EMPTY into char 3 to 5 of field "OldText"
put NULL into line 1 of field "OldText"
put EMPTY into item 5 of field "OldText"
```

Caution

When you delete any chunk of text, the remaining text changes its position. So in the above example, if field "OldText" has six lines of text and you delete line 1, then the original line 2 becomes the new line 1. The original line 3 becomes the new line 2, and so on.

Joining text strings

You have already learned about the concatenation operators that enable you to join strings together. After you use chunk expressions to break apart a text string, you can use those chunks in combination with the concatenation characters to join and form a new string.

As an example, suppose you have a movie that provides a self-paced assessment for a student. When the student answers a question correctly, you want to provide positive feedback, but you want that feedback to vary. The positive statements are stored as separate lines in a field called "Positive." The movie also includes a field cast member ("Student") that includes the current user's name. You can place the combined text from both field cast members in a third cast member ("OnStage") that is displayed on the Stage. Here is the instruction (which should be entered as a single line of code).

```
put field "Student" &","&& line (random(the number of lines in
field "Positive")) of field "Positive" into field "OnStage"
```

Tip Remember that a single concatenation operator joins any text (from variables or fields) with no space added between the text strings. The double-concatenation operator (&&) adds a single space between the joined text strings.

The concatenation operators are also helpful when you need to use special characters in text and the characters have special functions within Lingo. To include these characters in a text string, Lingo provides several character constants (listed in Table 14-4).

Table 14-4
Character Constants Available in Lingo

Constant	Represents
BACKSPACE	The Backspace key on a Windows system and the Delete key on a Macintosh system
EMPTY	An empty or null string, such as " "
ENTER	The Enter key on the Macintosh keyboard and the numeric keypad Enter key on PCs
QUOTE	The double-quotation mark (")
RETURN	The Return key on the Macintosh
SPACE	A space character generated by pressing the spacebar
TAB	The Tab key
VOID	No value

Let's look at an example. Lingo uses double-quotes (") to set off text strings, so you cannot use that character inside a text string unless you use the QUOTE constant. The following `put` statement shows how you might attempt to type a text string that includes quotation marks around a word. The example is not correct and will generate a scripting error message.

```
put "He who tells the "truth" should have one foot in the
stirrup." into Arabian
```

"Arabian" is a variable in this example. The correct method of storing the quotation (including the double-quotation marks around the word "truth") is shown in the following statement, which uses both the concatenation operator and the QUOTE constant:

```
put "He who tells the"&&Quote&"truth"&Quote&&"should have one
foot in the stirrup." into Arabian
```

If you type this statement in the Message window (without errors), you can see the results by typing **put Arabian** and then pressing Enter.

Simulating Hypertext in Director

A common feature in interactive media is the *hot word* or *hypertext link*. The World Wide Web is based on hypertext links; you click one word or phrase and you are transported to another Web page or another location within the current document, or you launch an application. It is also common for interactive multimedia products to include hot words (usually set apart from other text with underlining or a different font color). When you select (click) a hot word, you get a help message, definition, or glossary entry.

Director does not easily offer access to hypertext features, but you can simulate hypertext with a little programming and a little trickery.

Why would you want to use hypertext in your movie? Hypertext can enhance your multimedia application by

- ✦ Giving the user freedom to navigate through textual information based on his or her specific interests
- ✦ Providing easy access to related, supporting textual information without forcing the reader to read the material sequentially
- ✦ Enabling the reader to ignore supplemental material (by choosing not to follow specific links) and instead read only the main thread of information

How can you incorporate hypertext links into a Director movie? You can establish links (from a specific word, phrase, line, or item) to

- Play another frame in the movie or another Director movie
- Modify a sprite on the Stage
- Display a new sprite on the Stage

Planning for a hypertext field

The steps required to add hypertext capabilities to a movie include the following:

1. Create a text field that contains the desired text. The text can be in a scrolling text box or a fixed-size text box.
2. Place the text box on the Stage.
3. Identify the character, word, item, or line that is to serve as a hypertext link. The most common text element used to form a link is a word. Using this scenario, you can script an action to occur when the mouse pointer rests on or rolls over a specific word in a text box.
4. Add a script to the scrolling field that tells Director what action you want executed based on a mouse action over selected text in the text box.
5. If the specified action is to jump to another frame, or to display a different cast member, prepare the target object for the desired action.

You already know how to handle each of these steps, except for identifying the character, word, item, or line. Let's see how that's done.

Identifying characters, words, lines, and items in a field

The easiest method of adding hypertext to a movie is to use one of four functions that enable you to identify the text string under the mouse pointer. Once you identify the text, you can execute the desired action when the mouse pointer rolls over a specific text string, or when the user clicks a specific text string.

The four functions you can use for this identification task make use of the chunk expressions discussed earlier. The four functions are `the mouseChar`, `the mouseWord`, `the mouseLine`, and `the mouseItem`, listed in Table 14-5. The `mouseWord` function is the most commonly used function in a Director hypertext application.

Each of these functions returns a numeric value representing its position within the field cast member. The function identifies the specified chunk expression by counting from the beginning of the field. When the mouse pointer is *not* over a specified chunk expression, each of the integer functions returns a value of –1.

Table 14-5
The Four Integer Functions That Identify Text under the Mouse Pointer

Function	Description
the mouseChar	Starts counting at the beginning of the field and returns the sequential number that represents the current character under the mouse pointer
the mouseWord	Returns the number of the current word in the field that is under the mouse pointer
the mouseItem	Returns the number of the current item in the field that is under the mouse pointer
the mouseLine	Returns the number of the current line under the mouse pointer in a field sprite

Before you can implement any hypertext scheme, you must properly position the field on the Stage, which is exactly what you do in the following steps. In this exercise you will work with an incomplete Director movie (story.dir) to set up a scrolling text field on the Stage, and properly position the field on the Stage.

Typically, the reason you import text (rich text format or text files) into Director is because you want to avoid retyping the text. When you import text, you often create large text fields that you must resize and reposition after they're placed on the Stage. The techniques used in the following exercise help you create a scrolling text field from an imported field, resize the field so it appears completely on the Stage, and then position the field around existing graphic elements.

Sizing and Positioning a Text Field

On the CD-ROM

1. Open the story.dir movie. You'll find it on your companion CD-ROM in the exercise:ch14 (exercise\ch14) folder. This movie has three cast members:
    + A field cast member ("Storytext") in cast member slot 1
    + A bitmap image in cast member slot 2 ("Storytelling")
    + A `go to the frame` script in cast member slot 3

2. To place the field cast member in a scrolling text box, select cast member 1 and then click the Cast Member Properties button.

3. On the Field Cast Member Properties dialog box, set the Framing pop-up list to Scrolling. The dialog box should match the settings in Figure 14-7. Then click OK.

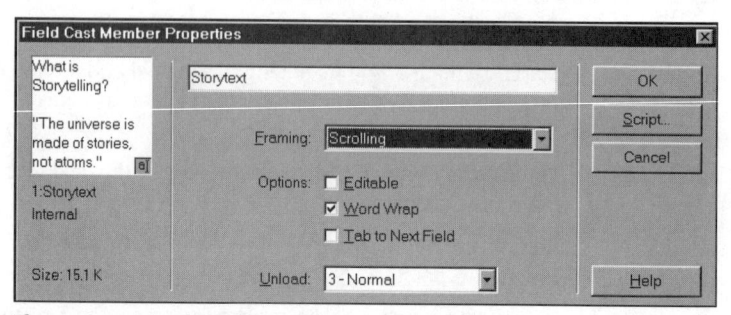

Figure 14-7: Settings for a scrolling text field

4. Select the "Storytext" cast member, hold down the Option (Alt) key and drag the cast member on to the Stage.

5. To position and size the text box, Ctrl-click (right-click) the field sprite on the Stage and select the Properties option.

6. The Location setting for the top of the scrolling field is probably a negative value as shown in Figure 14-8. This means the top of the object is *above* the top of the Stage. Double-click the negative number in the Top field and replace it with the number **185**. This sets the top of the field to 185 pixels from the top of the Stage.

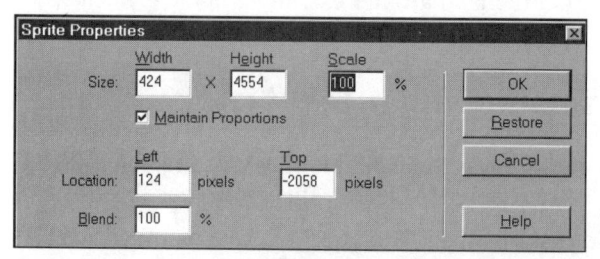

Figure 14-8: Sprite Properties dialog box settings for a scrolling text field

7. Deselect the Maintain Proportions check box so you can vary the height or the width of the field without adjusting the other dimension.

8. The Stage is set to 640 pixels wide, and you want to center the field within that area. To do so, you must first resize the text box and then position it horizontally on the Stage. Use the following settings to adjust the field's size on the Stage: Width=440 and Height=220.

9. To center the field horizontally on the Stage, set the Left Location field to **100**. Click OK to close the dialog box.

10. Save the movie as **story1.dir,** rewind, and play it. Use the scroll bar and you can move through the text. Notice that the upper-right corner of the text box overlaps and obscures part of the bitmap artwork on the Stage. You will fix this design faux pas in the next few steps.

11. Stop the movie.

12. On the Stage or in the Score window, select the scrolling text box (cast member 1 in sprite channel 2).

13. In the Score window, set the ink effect to Background Transparent. The bitmap image now shows through the text box.

14. Save the movie again and play it.

Creating hot links over bitmap text

The functions described in the section on identifying elements in a field only work with fields, not with rich-text or bitmap-text cast members. You can accomplish the same hypertext functionality when using bitmap text — using an invisible button with either an `on mouseUp` event handler (to react to a click) or the `mouseWithin` event handler (to react to a rollover). To create an invisible button, use the Tool Palette and the following steps:

1. On the Tool Palette, set the foreground color to white and the background color to black. This is the reverse of the default settings.

2. Select one of the shape tools (Round Rectangle, Rectangle, or Ellipse). Do *not* select any of the Filled versions of these tools.

3. Set the line width to No Line.

4. Click and drag over the object (the bitmap text sprite) on the Stage that you want to serve as a hot word or link. This action draws an invisible shape that is placed on top of the bitmap text image. Because the new object is invisible, the user sees only the bitmap text object that's underneath.

5. Set the ink effect for the new object to Matte.

6. Select the invisible shape in the Cast window.

(continued)

> *(continued)*
>
> **7.** Now you can attach a handler to the cast member — either an `on mouseWithin` or an `on mouseUp`:
>
> ```
> on mouseWithin
>     doSomeThing
> end mouseWithin
> ```
>
> ```
> on mouseUp
>     dosomethingElse
> end mouseUp
> ```
>
> In the on mouseWithin example, when the user moves the mouse over the invisible button (which covers the specified text), the instructions within the handler are executed. In the on mouseUp example, a mouse click is required to execute the instructions in the handler.

Determining a word's position within a field

To simulate hypertext in your movie requires a little planning. You can cause a specific action (such as jumping to a frame or displaying an invisible sprite) to occur when the mouse pointer rolls over or is clicked on a specific word. To do so, however, you have to be able to identify the word. There are two methods available, both using `the mouseWord` function. You can identify a word in a field

- By its position or word number within the field
- By the actual text string that composes the word or phrase (that is, the text you want to serve as a hypertext link)

Whichever method you choose, during the construction of your movie it can be very helpful to create a temporary field that displays the number of the specific word or the text that you want to use. In the later section, "Translating the text or position of a word into action," you'll use `the mouseWord` function to identify the word (by its number in the text field) that you want to use as a hypertext link. The temporary field ("wordNum") that you'll create in the next exercise displays the value returned by `the mouseWord` function when the user clicks a specific word.

Later in a movie's development process, you can remove the temporary field and cause other actions to occur based on the number generated by `the mouseWord` function. For instance, if the mouse pointer is clicked on the word *gleeman*, you can display an invisible sprite on the Stage with the glossary entry for *gleeman*.

When appropriate, you can use the other mouse functions, too — `the mouseChar`, `the mouseItem`, or `the mouseLine` — to identify text strings to use as hypertext links.

Setting a nonwhite background color for a text field

By using the Background Transparent ink, the colors and image of any object beneath the text box show through. If there are no sprites in lower-numbered channels, then the Stage color shows through. In some cases, you may want to set off the text box with a color different from the Stage color. You can accomplish this by creating an appropriately sized bitmap cast-member and placing it in the channel one number lower than the field sprite.

To accomplish this task, you'll need to

✦ Create a text field and set the sprite's ink effect to Background Transparent

✦ Create a rectangular block of color (in the Paint window) large enough to serve as a backdrop for the text box

✦ Place the text field sprite in a channel with a higher number than that of the rectangular bitmap sprite (lower-numbered channels are placed behind objects in higher-numbered channels)

✦ Align the two sprites so the text appears within the rectangular area of the bitmap sprite

To display the value returned by `the mouseWord` function in a field named "wordNum," you include the following instruction in a cast member script attached to the field cast member:

```
put the mouseWord into member "wordNum"
```

To display the text that corresponds with `the mouseWord` value, you use `the word of field` function in combination with `the mouseWord` function to display the text. In the following instruction, `the mouseWord` function returns the position of the word within the field, which in turn uses `the word of field` function to determine and display the actual text string:

```
put word(the mouseWord) of field 1 into member "wordText"
```

Caution When you use the `put word(the mouseWord) of field` statement and seek to match the returned text string to generate an action, be aware that the text strings followed by punctuation are different from text strings without the punctuation. For instance, each of the following are different text strings and would be evaluated as unequal strings:

myths

myths,

myths.

In the following steps, you'll create a dummy field (which can be removed later) that enables you to calculate the sequential position of a word within the field.

Determining the Number of a Word

On the CD-ROM

1. Open the story1.dir movie in Director, if it is not already open. You need the movie you created earlier in this chapter, or the file story1.dir on your companion CD-ROM in the exercise:ch14 (exercise\ch14) folder.

2. Select cast member slot 4, and then select Window ⇨ Field (Command+8 or Ctrl+8).

3. In the text area of the Field window, select 12-point Times New Roman as the font and font size. Press the spacebar twice to add text to the field.

4. Click in the Name field, and type **wordNum** to name the new field cast member. The Field 4 window should appear as shown in Figure 14-9.

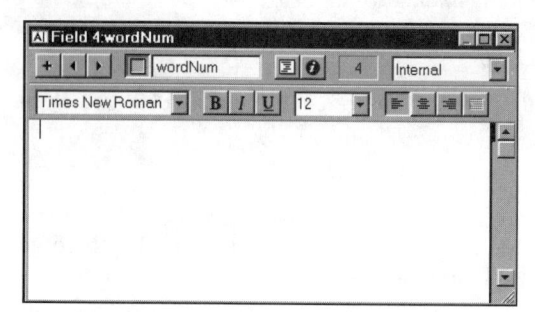

Figure 14-9: Settings for the "wordNum" field

5. Close the Field window.

6. Drag the new cast member, "wordNum," to the upper-right corner of the Stage. The sprite should span only a single frame. Because the text box is too large, you must resize it. You can do this by clicking and dragging the object's handles on the Stage, or use the Sprite Properties dialog box (this is the preferred approach and is used in the following steps).

7. Ctrl+click (right-click) the "wordNum" sprite on the Stage, and choose Properties from the pop-up menu.

8. Deselect the Maintain Proportions check box so you can freely resize the field.

9. Set the Size Width option to **32** and the Size Height option to **16** pixels.

10. Set the Left Location setting to **595** and Top Location setting to **30** pixels. Click OK to close the dialog box.

11. Add the following script to the Storytext cast member:

```
on mouseUp
    put the mouseWord into member "wordNum"
end
```

12. Save the movie as **story2.dir** and play it.
13. Be sure the scroll bar is scrolled to the top of the field.
14. Click the first word in the scrolling text field. The number 1 appears in the upper-right corner (that's the "wordNum" field).
15. Click the word *divergent* (the 2nd word in the 4th paragraph in the text box; the 75th word in the field). Watch as you click different words in the scrolling field; the number of the word appears in the "wordNum" field.
16. When you're done experimenting, stop the movie.

Determining the Text of a Word

On the CD-ROM

1. With a minor change to the story2.dir movie, you can display the actual text of the word selected. Open the story2.dir movie in Director, if it is not already open. You'll need the movie you created earlier or the file story2.dir on your companion CD-ROM in the exercise:ch14 (exercise\ch14) folder.
2. Select cast member slot 5, and then select the Window ⇨ Field command (Command+8 or Ctrl+8).
3. Set the Field's settings to 12-point Times New Roman; then press the spacebar twice to add text to the field.
4. Click in the Name field, type **wordText,** and then close the window. You have named the new field cast member.
5. Drag the new cast member, "wordText," onto the upper-left corner of the Stage and set it to span a single frame.
6. Using the Sprite Properties dialog box, resize the "wordText" field to 74 pixels wide by 16 pixels high.
7. Set the Location settings to Left = 15 and Top = 30 pixels and then close the dialog box.
8. Set the "wordText" sprite's ink effect to Background Transparent.
9. Modify the script for the Storytext cast member to match the following:

```
on mouseUp
     put the mouseWord into member "wordNum"
     put word(the mouseWord) of field 1 into member¬
     "wordText"
end
```

10. Save the movie as **story3.dir** and play it. Click various words in the scrolling field. Notice as you click a word that the text of the word appears at the top-left of the Stage (in the "wordText" field); and the number of the word within the field appears at the top-right of the Stage (in the "wordNum" field).

11. In the scrolling text box, click a word that is followed by punctuation. Because `the mouseWord` function includes *every* character in the text string that is surrounded by nonprinting characters (such as the space, tab, and return characters), the displayed word (upper-left corner of the Stage) includes the punctuation.

12. Stop the movie.

Translating the text or position of a word into action

You can use one of several approaches to translate the number of a word (within a field) or the actual text of the word into an action. In the following examples, you'll see how to use a hypertext link to

+ Play another frame in the movie

+ Display a definition for a word in the text field

+ Change the visible property of a sprite

In each of these examples, it is important to set off the hypertext link using a font style (underline, italic, bold) or a different font color. You must signal to the user that the hypertext link is different from other words in the field.

Using hypertext to jump to another frame in a movie

A click on a hypertext link can cause the playback head to jump to a specified frame. This approach is best handled in a cast member script that does the following:

1. Use the `rollOver` function or the `mouseWord` function to determine if the mouse is over or clicked on a designated field. If the `rollOver` returns a value of False or `the mouseWord` returns a value of –1, the mouse pointer is not over a field.

2. Determine the frame to jump to; and decide whether to use the `go to` command or the `play` command.

The following frame script determines if the mouse is clicked over the 75th word in the field. If it is, the playback head jumps to frame "FilmLoop."

```
on mouseUp
     if the mouseWord <> -1 then
        if the mouseWord = 75 then
```

```
            go to "FilmLoop"
        end if
    else
        exit
    end if
end
```

Using hypertext to display a definition

You can cause a definition to appear when the mouse pointer moves over a specific word in a field. In the following frame script, the definition for the word *divergent* appears in the "Definition" field whenever the mouse moves over word 75 (sprite 2). When the mouse pointer moves off the 75th word, the "Definition" field is filled with a space character.

```
on enterFrame
    if rollover(2) and the mouseWord = 75 then
        put field "Divergent" into member "Definition"
    else
        put " " into field "Definition"
    end if
end enterFrame

on exitFrame
    go to the frame
end
```

> **Tip**
> In the preceding example, the `put " " into field "Definition"` statement preserves any formatting you add to the field (such as font, font size, and font style). If you use the `put EMPTY into field "Definition"` statement, the field is devoid of any text and formatting.

You've just seen how the text in the "Definition" field is replaced by the text from the "Divergent" field. Another method is to swap cast members, rather than overwrite the text in one cast member with text from another cast member. In the next example, when the mouse pointer rolls over word 75 of the sprite in channel 2, the puppetSprite property is turned on for the sprite in channel 5. Next, cast member 7 is swapped for the object in channel 5:

```
on enterFrame
    if rollover(2) and the mouseWord = 75 then
        puppetSprite 5, True
        set the memberNum of sprite 5 to 7
    else
        puppetSprite 5, False
    end if
end enterFrame

on exitFrame
    go to the frame
end
```

Using hypertext to make a sprite visible

When the user clicks (or the mouse pointer rolls over) a hypertext link, you can cause a sprite to become visible or invisible on the Stage. This technique is used to make definitions, help screens, or images suddenly appear when a specific word is selected. Once again, be sure to highlight the hypertext link so the user can identify the word to click.

The following example uses a cast member script. The sprite in channel 5 is puppeted and its invisible property is set to False in a movie script (using the `on startMovie` handler).

```
on mouseUp
      if the visible of sprite 5 = False and the mouseWord = 75 then
         set the visible of sprite 5 to True
      else
         set the visible of sprite 5 to False
      end if
end
```

When the user clicks word 75, sprite 5 becomes visible. That sprite could be an illustration of the term, a definition, or other supplemental material. If the sprite is already visible, a click *anywhere* on the Stage causes sprite 5 to become invisible.

More Control of Text Fields

In this chapter, we have only scratched the surface of what you can do with text fields in Director. Lingo enables you to control a variety of properties and actions. You can automatically scroll the text in a field, add highlighting to selected words, lines, or items, plus make a text field editable — all using Lingo.

Scrolling through a field

Creating a text field for a movie is just the first step. You can use Lingo to scroll through the text string contained in the field either line by line or page by page. You can also force text in a scrolling field to reset itself to its beginning.

Resetting scrolling fields to the beginning of the text

When users move from frame to frame within a movie, they may discover that a scrolling field does *not* automatically reset itself to the top of the text box. This idiosyncrasy can be confusing and annoying. Users expect to arrive at a new frame with the scrolling field displaying the beginning of the text. With a little Lingo, you can cure this problem.

Of course, you may not always want to reset the scrolling field to the beginning each time the user leaves the frame. The user may be in the middle of reviewing text, then may decide to jump to another frame, and return and resume reading where they left off. Resetting the field is best handled in the `on startMovie` script — so each new user starts with text fields appropriately displaying the beginning of the text.

To reset the text in a field to the beginning, use the following handler:

```
on startMovie
    set the scrollTop of member "Storytext" to 0
end
```

Tip You can use `the scrollTop of member` function with a text cast member or a field.

To understand `the scrollTop of member` function, think of a scrolling text field as two entities: the border for the text box (which is your window on the text) and the text itself. The `scrollTop` function does not reposition the border on the Stage, but it does adjust the text that appears within the border.

If you set `the scrollTop of member to 0`, as in the previous example, you instruct Lingo to place the top of the text string at the top of the scroll box. If you increase the value in the statement to 100, you tell Lingo to display the text that begins 100 pixels from the top of the text string at the top of the scroll box. The value in `the scrollTop` function statement represents the distance, measured in pixels, from the top of the text string.

Note If you do reset the text in a field to the top, be sure to include the `updateStage` command. The `updateStage` command is only required if you want to redraw the Stage while the playback head stays within the same frame.

Here's another technique: You can create a button on a frame with a scrolling text field and attach a script that resets the scrolling text field to the top. The following cast member script added to a movie will cause the field to reset itself:

```
on mouseUp
    set the scrollTop of member "Storytext" to 0
    updateStage
end
```

Resetting Text to the Top of the Text Box

On the CD-ROM

1. Open the story3.dir movie and play it. You need the movie you created earlier in this chapter, or the file story3.dir on your companion CD-ROM in the exercise:ch14 (exercise\ch14) folder.
2. Scroll down several paragraphs in the scrolling field.
3. Stop the movie.
4. Rewind and then play the movie again. The text is positioned as you left it when you quit the movie. It has not reset itself to the top of the field.
5. Stop the movie.
6. Create a movie script using the following handler.

   ```
   on startMovie
         set the scrollTop of member "Storytext" to 0
   end
   ```

7. Save the movie as **story4.dir,** rewind it and play it.
8. Scroll down several paragraphs within the text field and then stop the movie.
9. Start the movie again and notice that the text is reset back to the top of the field.

Scrolling line by line

Using Lingo, you can scroll up or down through a field. The `scrollByLine` command is the tool for making this happen: The field will scroll one line at a time through the text string that's contained in the field. The syntax for the command is

```
scrollByLine member castMember, numberOfLines
```

The *castMember* can be either the cast member name or number. The *numberOfLines* parameter can be a positive value (to scroll down in the field) or a negative number (to scroll up in a field).

Note

The `scrollByLine` command can only be used with a field cast member, not a text cast member.

Here's a script that can be attached to a ScrollUp button on the Stage. As the user holds down the mouse button over the ScrollUp button, the text in the field scrolls up (toward the beginning of the text string).

```
on mouseDown —This is a mouseDown not a mouseUp handler!
    repeat while the mouseDown
--The negative 1 parameter in the next statement moves the text up.
        scrollByLine member 1, -1
        updateStage
    end repeat
end
```

This next script can be attached to a ScrollDown button on the Stage. As the user holds down the mouse button over the ScrollDown button, the text in the field scrolls down (toward the end of the text string).

```
on mouseDown —This is a mouseDown not a mouseUp handler!
    repeat while the mouseDown
--The plus 1 parameter in the next statement moves the text down.
        scrollByLine member 1, 1
        updateStage
    end repeat
end
```

> **Tip:** Lingo includes a `scrollByPage` command that functions exactly like `scrollByLine`, except it causes the text to scroll one page at a time rather than one line at a time.

Highlighting selected text

Users like visual feedback. They like to know that *something* has occurred in response to a mouse click or other user action. Highlighting selected text or a text option is one form of visual feedback. As the user clicks a chunk expression, you can highlight the character, word, item, or line using the `Hilite` command. The syntax for the command is

```
hilite chunkExpression
```

The following handler highlights any word under the mouse, when the mouse button is clicked:

```
on mouseUp
    put the mouseCast into currentField
    hilite word(the mouseWord) of field currentField
end
```

You can also highlight a specific chunk expression (such as a line) when the mouse pointer rolls over it. The following movie script causes the line under the pointer to be highlighted. This occurs only when the system is idle (no mouse clicks, frame exits, and so on) and when the mouse is over sprite 2 (the "StoryText" field).

```
on idle
    if rollover(2) then
        hilite line(the mouseLine) of field "StoryText"
    end if
end
```

Caution: As you create a script using `the mouseChar`, `the mouseWord`, `the mouseLine`, or `the mouseItem` function, you must check to be sure the mouse pointer is over a field. If not, these functions return a –1 value, which can cause the script to abort. The above handler checks first to ensure that the mouse pointer is over sprite channel 2, which holds the field.

Making fields editable

Have you scored high on a computer game that prompted you for your name? Or maybe you completed a computer-based educational assessment that required you to type your answers online. In Director, you can create a movie that includes data entry by the user. Examples of such data are demographic information, personal data, and answers to other types of questions in an editable field.

Only fields can be made editable. Rich-text and bitmap-text cast members cannot be made editable, so they cannot accept text entry from the user.

Note: Once a field is editable, you cannot use it for hypertext links. When you click in an editable field, Director assumes you are placing the cursor for editing purposes. Typically this causes no real difficulty, because you probably do not want long blocks of text that contain hypertext links to be edited by the user.

Fields in Director can be set to accept text entry (including the modification of existing text in the field) using `the editable of member` property. You can set this property using any of three methods:

+ Check the Editable check box on the Score window (see Figure 14-10).
+ Turn on the Editable option in the Field Cast Member Properties dialog box.
+ Use Lingo to turn `the editable of member` property on and off during the playback of a movie (this method provides the greatest flexibility).

The Editable property, like most properties, is easily established using the `set` command, as in the following example:

```
on startMovie
    puppetSprite 2, True
    set the editable of member "StoryText" = True
end
```

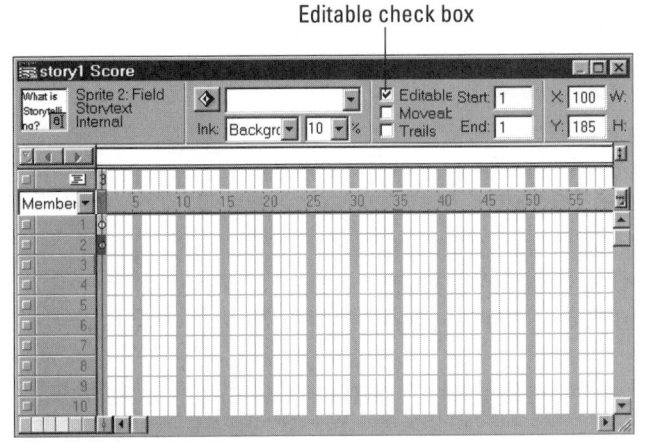

Figure 14-10: Turning on the Editable property for a field

Before you can make a sprite field editable, you must first set the field's puppet property to True. Once you've done this, the specified field can be edited during playback. If the property is set to False, the user cannot edit or type text into the field during playback.

> **Note:** By default, fields are not editable. You must explicitly designate a field as editable.

Controlling font substitutions

In several cases, we've have mentioned that if the playback system for your movie does not have the same fonts as your development workstation, Director substitutes the most similar font that is available. What we've not mentioned is that for cross-platform uniformity, you can control this font substitution using the fontmap.txt file. You create a font translation table (using the fontmap.txt file) that determines which fonts Director considers as equivalent when it is playing a Macintosh Director movie on a Windows playback system, and vice versa.

By now, you know that font, font size and style, and other text properties are stored with the field or text cast member. What you may not realize is that

+ The same fonts are not always available on both Macintosh and Windows systems.

+ If the font is not available on the playback system, Director substitutes another available font, which may change the look and size of the font and the text box. This can alter your screen layout in unexpected and undesirable ways.

+ Font sizes, as well, can differ between a Macintosh and Windows system. A specific font size on a Macintosh may appear smaller than the same font size on a Windows system.

The cure for these discrepancies is to use the fontmap.txt file to map the translation of each font on the PC to a specific font on the Macintosh — and vice versa. A standard fontmap.txt file is shipped with Director and installed in the same folder as the Director application.

The fontmap.txt file guidelines

To effectively use the fontmap.txt file, keep the following in mind:

✦ When you create a new movie, Director looks for the fontmap.txt file in the same folder as the Director application. If the file is not found, Director does not create an internal font map for the movie.

✦ If a cross-platform movie does not have an internal font map, Director still substitutes an available font when the stipulated font is not available. However, using an internal font map gives you greater control over the substitution.

✦ Director automatically uses the font map stored in the fontmap.txt file only when you create a new movie. For this reason, when establishing font mapping for a cross-platform movie, it is more efficient to edit the fontmap.txt file prior to creating the movie.

✦ If you change the font mapping in the fontmap.txt file, the change does not automatically affect existing movies. It is used only for any new movies you create. To change the internal font map to match an edited fontmap.txt file, you can use the Modify➪Movie➪Properties command. The steps for this process are explained later in the section on "Changing the font map for an existing movie."

✦ Whenever you open a movie that was created on the "other" platform, Director uses the movie's internal font map to establish the font substitution for text cast members.

✦ When font substitutions occur, even if you're using a font map, your text boxes may change slightly in appearance and size. The only way to ensure identical fonts for cross-platform movies is to use rich text or text cast members. These two cast member types are stored as bitmaps, so the designated font need not be available on the target playback system.

Caution: Although bitmap text images appear identical on both platforms, the text of a rich text or text cast member cannot be edited by the user during playback, and the bitmap text uses more disk space (when the movie is stored on the hard drive of the playback system or distributed on a CD-ROM or other media).

✦ If you plan to edit the same movie on both a Macintosh and a Windows system, be sure that the internal font map lists *only* a one-to-one font mapping for each font you plan to use. This ensures that the desired font is used when editing on either platform. It's an important step because, when you edit a text, field, or button cast member on one platform (such as the Macintosh) that was created on a different platform (such as Windows), the font established on the original platform is replaced by the equivalent font (based on the font mapping) on the current system.

✦ The fontmap.txt file can be edited using any text editor, such as SimpleText on the Macintosh or Notepad on a Windows system.

Dissecting the fontmap.txt file

The fontmap.txt file is a simple text file. Following are the key elements of a sample file. The semicolon (;) encountered at any point on a line indicates that the text following it is a comment, which is not executed.

```
; Basic Mac to Windows Font Mappings:
Mac:Chicago         => Win:System
Mac:Courier         => Win:"Courier New"
Mac:Geneva          => Win:"MS Sans Serif"
Mac:Helvetica       => Win:Arial
Mac:Monaco          => Win:Terminal
Mac:"New York"      => Win:"MS Serif"
Mac:Symbol          => Win:Symbol   Map None
Mac:Times           => Win:"Times New Roman" 14=>12 18=>14¬
24=>18 30=>24
Mac:Palatino        => Win:"Times New Roman"; Basic Character
Mappings:
Mac: => Win: 128=>196 129=>197 130=>199 131=>201 132=>209¬
133=>214 134=>220
; Basic Windows to Mac Font Mappings:
Win:Arial              => Mac:Helvetica
Win:"Courier"          => Mac:Courier
Win:"Courier New"      => Mac:Courier
Win:"MS Serif"         => Mac:"New York"
Win:"MS Sans Serif"    => Mac:Geneva
Win:Symbol             => Mac:Symbol   Map None
Win:System             => Mac:Chicago
Win:Terminal           => Mac:Monaco
Win:"Times New Roman" => Mac:"Times" 12=>14 14=>18 18=>24¬
24=>30
Win: => Mac: 128=>222 129=>223 130=>226 131=>196 132=>227¬
133=>201 134=>160
```

Each line in the fontmap.txt file represents a separate font substitution. This is not just for reading convenience: *You cannot declare more than one font-mapping definition per line.* The syntax is as follows:

```
OriginalPlatform:OriginalFontName => TargetPlatform:TargetFontName
```

The first font mapping in the sample file presented here converts the Courier font on the Macintosh to Courier New on a Windows system. Notice that there is a corresponding font mapping from the Windows Courier New to the Macintosh Courier.

> **Note**
>
> In the fontmap.txt file, a font name is surrounded by double-quotation marks only if the name is composed of more than a single word (such as "Times New Roman" or "Courier New"). Single-word font names (such as Arial) do not require the surrounding quotation marks.

The font-mapping definition can also include two additional arguments. Any arguments used must be separated by a space or a tab.

The first argument indicates whether special characters are remapped or ignored. Your options are

MAP ALL	Remaps all characters with ASCII values greater than 127
MAP NONE	Remaps none of the characters with ASCII values greater than 127

Using the second argument, you can adjust the font size to compensate for the fact that font sizes established on a Macintosh appear smaller than the same font size established on a Windows system. The following two font-mapping definitions equate the Windows Times New Roman font to the Macintosh Times font. In addition, the old font size (listed first) is mapped to a new font size (listed second).

```
Win:"Times New Roman" => Mac:"Times" 12=>14 14=>18 18=>24 24=>30

Mac:Times => Win:"Times New Roman" 14=>12 18=>14 24=>18 30=>24
```

In the second example, the Macintosh 14-point Times font (the original font used when the movie was created on a Macintosh system) is mapped to the 12-point Times New Roman font (when played on a Windows system).

You can also map specific characters using their ASCII value. For example, common mappings for the bullet character are

```
Mac: => Win: 165=>149

Win: => Win: 149=>165
```

You can add multiple character-mappings on a single line, like this:

```
Win: => Mac: 128=>222 129=>223 130=>226 131=>196 132=>227¬
133=>201 134=>160
```

Defining a font map for a new movie

To create a new fontmap.txt file, you can edit the standard file that accompanies Director, or you can create the file from scratch. Follow these steps.

First, check to see if the fontmap.txt file is in the same folder as the Director application. If it exists, open it with Notepad, SimpleText, or any text editor. If the file does not exist, you can create it from scratch.

> **Caution**: Be sure to create a backup of the original fontmap.txt file in case you want to revert to the original version.

Next, type a font mapping entry for each font substitution. Remember:

- ◆ Be sure to include no more than one remapping statement per line.
- ◆ Don't forget to remap in *both* directions: from Mac to Windows, and from Windows to Mac.

Add the MAP and font size parameters, if appropriate. Because font sizes appear smaller on a PC, you can map Macintosh font sizes to larger Windows font sizes.

If you use the MAP ALL parameter with any of the font-mapping definitions, add the desired character mappings for commonly used special characters. Remember to use the ASCII value for the special character. Next you can include several different font size remapping pairs for a single font on each line, but each pair (mapping the font size from Macintosh to Windows or vice versa) must be separated from the next pair by a space.

> **Note**: Only characters whose ASCII value is greater than 127 and less than 255 can be remapped.

Save the revised fontmap.txt file as an ASCII text file in the same folder with the Director application. Then open a new movie in Director. The new movie will include an internal font map based on the font-mapping definitions in the new fontmap.txt file.

Changing the font map for an existing movie

Existing movies continue to use the internal font map that was established (based on the fontmap.txt file) when the movie was originally created. You can change the font mapping for an existing movie by completing the following steps.

First, use Notepad, SimpleText, or any text editor to edit the fontmap.txt file. Make the needed changes, including the desired font, font size, and character-mapping definitions. (See the preceding section for details on making these changes.) Then save the file, using any filename you choose. It does not have to be saved as fontmap.txt. If you do save it as fontmap.txt, however, then any new movie you create will use the same (new) font, font size, and character-mapping definitions.

Open the existing movie whose internal font map you want to change, and select the Modify ⇨ Movie ⇨ Properties command. In the Movie Properties dialog box that appears, click the Load Font Map button (see Figure 14-11).

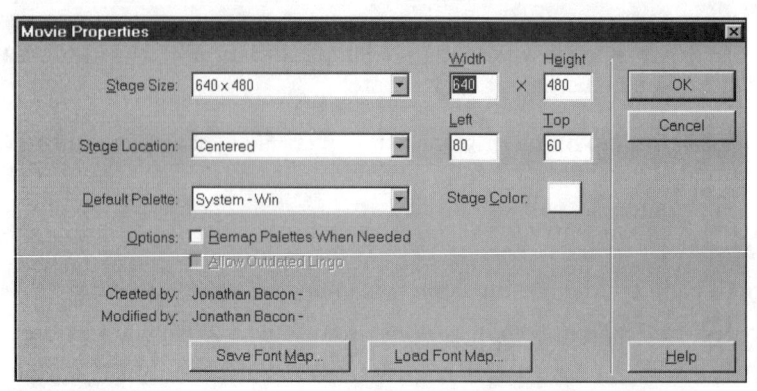

Figure 14-11: Loading a new font-mapping file from the Movie Properties dialog box

When prompted to specify the font-mapping file to load, select the file you just edited and click the Open button. Back in the Movie Properties dialog, click OK, and save the movie. Close the movie and then reopen it, and the new internal font map will be in effect.

Some Final Thoughts on Fields and Hypertext

You have learned a lot in this long chapter about working with text fields and hypertext in your Director movies. Yet there is always more to learn. Always explore new features in light of what you already know about other features in Director.

Pop-up Text Sprites. For instance, you know how to use `set the memberNum of sprite x to y` instruction to swap one sprite for another on the Stage. You also know how to create transparent buttons or invisible sprites (`set the visible of sprite x to False`). And you can use the `on mouseWithin` and `on mouseLeave` handlers to perform an action when the mouse pointer moves into (or rolls over) the bounding box or visible part of a sprite. You can use these techniques together to create pop-up text sprites that identify features or provide online help in your Director movies.

Locating the Registration Point for a Text Field. In Chapter 13, you used the Registration tool in the Paint window to alter a bitmap cast member's registration point. A text field or shape (created with the Tool Palette) also has a registration point, but by default it is the top-left corner of the object. A cast member's registration point can be determined using `the regPoint of member` property. To determine `the regPoint`, you can use the following instruction in the Message window:

```
put the regPoint of member "castMemberName"
```

Note: The `regPoint` property identifies the registration point for a cast member. The `loc of sprite` property identifies the location on the Stage of the sprite's registration point.

Setting Text Attributes for Lingo Scripts. Beginning with Director 6, you can set the font, font size, font style, and color of the text *in your scripts* using Lingo. The syntax parallels the syntax that you use to set these properties in a field. The following examples demonstrate how you can set these text properties for a script:

```
set the font of script 45 to "Helvetica"

set the fontsize of script "startMovie" to 33

set the fontStyle of script 45 to "bold"

set the foreColor of word 10 of script "start" of castLib
"Behaviors" to 55
```

Summary

Before you move on to Chapter 15 and the Lingo commands for controlling sound, let's review some of the things you learned in this chapter.

- ✦ Text properties (such as font, font size, and font style) are stored with the field cast member. These properties, which determine the appearance of text, can be controlled using Lingo.
- ✦ The foreground color of text is set using `the foreColor` property.
- ✦ The font or typeface of text is set using `the font` property.
- ✦ The type size of text is set using `the fontSize` property.
- ✦ The type style of text is set using `the fontStyle` property.
- ✦ Each of these properties can be set for a "chunk" of text that includes one or more characters, words, lines, or items.
- ✦ You can even add, delete, and modify part or all of the text stored in a field, using Lingo and `the text of field` property.
- ✦ You can use several workarounds in Director to simulate hypertext features for identifying, highlighting, and responding to actions over a specific character, word, line, or item in a field.
- ✦ By using Lingo, you can reset a scrolling text field to the top of the text box, scroll through line by line, and make field text editable.
- ✦ By editing the fontmap.txt file, you can control the font substitutions used by Director for cross-platform movies.

✦ ✦ ✦

Sound Lingo

CHAPTER 15

John Mason Brown once called television "chewing gum for the eyes." To paraphrase Brown's pithy statement, we think *audio* is chewing gum for the *ears*. Sound can add a distinctive or an unobtrusive flavor to any multimedia production. Like gum, sound can add emphasis by focusing the user's attention with a sudden burst of flavor. Or, like chewing gum while you're working, it can be "background" to the important tasks at hand.

Using the sound-related Lingo commands frees you from the limitations of just two audio channels in the Score. In this chapter, you learn to play linked and embedded sound files, start and stop the playback of a sound, trigger an event upon the completion of an event, and control sound volume.

Controlling Sound Using Lingo

Digital audio is used to add narration, special effects, and background music to an interactive media project. Sound in your movie can be triggered by a variety of events, including

- ✦ When the user clicks a button or other sprite
- ✦ When the mouse pointer rolls over a specific sprite
- ✦ When the playback head plays a specific series of frames
- ✦ While the playback head loops through a single frame

Two Lingo commands are used to play a sound file in your movie. You can use the `puppetSound` command to play an embedded sound cast member, or you can play an external (linked) sound file using the `sound playFile` command.

In This Chapter

Triggering and controlling sound using Lingo

Playing random sounds from the cast

Creating a self-repeating action in response to no mouse or keyboard activity

Setting the volume level of sound

Creating and using cue points in sound files

Preloading digital sounds

There's a third way, too, to introduce sound into your movie: by including the sound in the Score window's sound channel, as described in Chapter 7.

We'll take a look at puppet sounds in the first part of this chapter. A later section discusses linked sound files.

> ### Some cautions if you're using Director for Windows
>
> For users of Director for Windows, sounds appear to break up if the DirectX (especially DirectX 3) DirectSound drivers are not installed properly, or if they are damaged by a partial uninstall. This situation can occur when another program (such as a game) is partially installed and the installation program terminates unexpectedly. The problem is readily resolved by installing or reinstalling the DirectX drivers. You can download the required DirectX drivers from Microsoft's Web site at
>
> ```
> http://www.microsoft.com/directx/
> ```
>
> At least in the current release, there also appears to be a conflict when Director and the RealPlayer 4.xx are installed on the same system. Uninstalling the RealPlayer resolves the problem.

Using puppet sounds

The most common method of adding sound to your movie is to use the `puppetSound` command. The command's syntax is very simple:

```
puppetSound channelNumber, castSound
```

The *channelNumber* parameter determines which channel the sound plays in. Your options are channel 1 and channel 2, and you can play two different sounds in the two channels concurrently.

Although the Score window has only two sound channels, you can access additional *virtual sound channels* using Lingo. In the following statement, the sound "musicBed" is played in channel 4:

```
puppetSound 4, "musicBed"
```

Channels numbered higher than channel 2 are the virtual channels. The `puppetSound` command can support a maximum of eight sound channels on a Macintosh system and four on a Windows system.

The *castSound* parameter is the cast member name or number of the sound cast member. If you use the cast member name, it must be enclosed within double quotation marks. For instance, the following instruction plays a sound in the cast named siren.wav or siren.aiff, in channel 1:

```
puppetSound 1, "Siren"
```

Notice that you don't need to include the sound file's extension when using the `puppetSound` command.

If the "Siren" cast member is in cast slot 5, the following command form can be used:

```
puppetSound 1, 5
```

Note: When you issue the puppetSound command, any sounds in the Score's two sound channels are overwritten because Lingo takes control.

Mechanically speaking, within Director sounds play only at the following times:

✦ When the playback head moves, as in a `go to the frame` handler, or when the playback head moves through a series of frames that each have the sound in the sound channel

✦ Whenever the `updateStage` command is issued

Tip: When a sound fails to play, the most common cause is the programmer's failure to follow the `puppetSound` command with the `updateStage` command.

Sources of sounds

To effectively add music and special effects to a multimedia presentation does not require that you create the sound files from scratch. A large body of clip media exists that can be purchased and used royalty-free in your productions.

Always check the licensing agreement that accompanies any clip media you buy. Some clips can be used only for personal use or for internal use within your company. Others are royalty-free in all cases. However, almost every publisher of clip media prohibits the user from repackaging some or all of the media clips for resale as a clip-media collection.

Throughout this chapter you'll encounter sidebars that describe the clips we've used to bring you the movies for the exercises in this chapter. We've listed the names of the clips, how we've changed them (if appropriate), and given you information about their producers.

Sonic Waves 3000 clips

All sounds in the noise.dir movie used in this chapter's exercises are from a two-disc, CD-ROM collection called *Sonic Waves 3000*. The *Sonic Waves 3000* sound clips are copyright 1993–1996 by Innovative Media Corp. (631 East Allen Street, Springfield, IL 62703, phone 217-544-4614) and used with permission.

The clips used have been renamed for ease of use. The following table lists the filename assigned in Sonic Waves 3000, a description of the audio, and the cast member name used in the noise.dir movie.

Sonic Waves 3000 Filename	Description of Sound and Duration	Cast Member Name
2830.WAV	1920s-style ringing phone, 12.5 seconds	"Ringing"
0139.WAV	Ticking alarm clock, 3.0 seconds	"Ticking"
2820.WAV	Shortwave radio, 10.7 seconds	"Static"
0959.WAV	Manual typewriter, 11.2 seconds	"Typing"
1601.WAV	Franklin Roosevelt speech, 28.1 seconds	"Speech"

Triggering sound using Lingo

In the following steps, you'll modify the noise.dir movie to play sounds when the user clicks a sprite on the Stage.

The noise.dir movie includes five cast members that are bitmap images, beginning with cast member slot 1: "Clock," "Phone," "Radio," "Mike," and "Typer." Sequentially in the Cast window, the next two cast members are bitmap text objects used for the movie's title on the Stage (Classical Noise). The next five cast members are all digital sound cast members named "Ticking," "Ringing," "Static," "Speech," and "Typing." Cast member 13 is a frame script that contains a `go to the frame` handler that is already present in the script channel for frame 1.

To complete the movie, you'll add cast member scripts (using the `puppetSound` command) to play the appropriate sound file when the user clicks an object. All of the sounds are internal to the movie; that is, they are embedded and not linked external files.

On the CD-ROM The file noise.dir can be found on your companion CD-ROM in the exercise:ch15 (exercise\ch15) folder.

Adding Sounds to noise.dir Using Lingo

1. Open the noise.dir movie in Director.
2. Select the "Clock" cast member in the Cast window.
3. Select the Cast Member Script button to open the Script window.
4. Modify the script to match the following:

   ```
   on mouseUp
        puppetSound 1, "Ticking"
   end
   ```

5. Close the Script window and save the movie as **noise1.dir.**
6. Play the movie and test it by clicking the image of the clock. You should hear a ticking sound. (If you hear no sound, check to be sure your speakers are attached, turned on, and that the volume control for your system and speakers is turned up. The ticking sound should play and then stops when the sound file finishes.)
7. Select the "Phone" cast member in the Cast window and add a cast member script as follows:

   ```
   on mouseUp
        puppetSound 1, "Ringing"
   end
   ```

8. Select the "Radio" cast member in the Cast window and add a cast member script as follows:

   ```
   on mouseUp
        puppetSound 1, "Static"
   end
   ```

9. Select the "Mike" cast member in the Cast window and add a cast member script as follows:

   ```
   on mouseUp
        puppetSound 1, "Speech"
   end
   ```

(continued)

10. Select the "Typer" cast member in the Cast window and add a cast member script as follows:

```
on mouseUp
     puppetSound 1, "Typing"
end
```

11. Save the movie again as noise1.dir and play it. Test each object to be sure that each sound plays.

12. After clicking an object to generate a sound, click a second object. Director stops the first sound and plays the second, because all cast member sounds in this movie use the same channel (channel 1).

Note: Notice that we gave the sound cast members different names from those of the bitmap cast members. If they had the same names, Director would play or use the lowest-numbered cast member when the cast member's name is referenced in a Lingo command. As a result, if cast members 3 and 10 were called by the same name ("Radio"), the sound would not play when you click the Radio image on the Stage.

Review: Attaching sound to sprites and buttons

Before you continue working with digital sound, let's review some of your earlier Director discoveries — it may save you some time and effort. First, you can add visual feedback to confirm that a button has been clicked. Simply select the bitmap cast member (such as "Clock" in the noise.dir movie), select the Cast Member Properties button, and when the Properties dialog appears, check the Highlight When Clicked check box. When you play the movie, a click on the bitmap cast member displays a flash. Even when you add audio feedback to a button, don't forget the importance of having visual feedback, too.

Second, to make sound play continuously (or until another sound or action interrupts it), select the sound cast member in the Cast window (*not* the sprite that you click to play the sound, such as the "Clock"). Then click the Cast Member Properties button and be sure the Loop check box is checked.

Finally, if you set a sound file to loop, be sure that the clip's beginning and end blend well. For example, in order for the ticking sound in the "Ticking" cast member to maintain the proper beat, you must edit the sound in a digital sound editor and clip the pause at the end of the sound file. As it plays now, there is a noticeable pause as the ticking repeats. Can you hear it?

Side Dish: The pictures in noise.dir

To create the images for use in noise.dir, we used images from Classic PIO Partners (87 East Green Street, Suite 309, Pasadena, CA 91105, phone 800-370-2746). The objects used in noise.dir include clock02fl.tif (alarm clock) and type01sl.tif (antique typewriter) from the *Classic Sampler* CD, micro3sl.tif from the *Classic Microphones* CD, phone03sl.tif (antique telephone) from the *Classic Telephones* CD, and radi13fl.tif from the *Classic Radios* CD.

Each of these images was pasted into a new Photoshop document (with a transparent background) and resized to around 150 pixels for the longest side of the object (using Photoshop's Image ⇨ Image Size command). The document size was increased to approximately 200 x 250 or 250 x 200 pixels (using the Image ⇨ Canvas Size command). Then it was given a pastel oval background and saved as a PICT or BMP file.

Stopping sound

Once a sound has started, you may not always want it to finish playing. Lingo provides you with at least two methods to terminate the playback of a sound. First, you can issue the `puppetSound` command with the 0 (zero) parameter:

```
puppetSound 0
```

This command causes Lingo to relinquish control of the sound channels and return that control to the Score.

You can also stop the sound that's currently playing by using the `sound stop` command. In the following example, the sound playing in channel 2 is turned off:

```
sound stop 2
```

Another method of stopping one sound is to begin playing another sound in the same sound channel. Each sound channel can only play one sound at a time, as demonstrated at the end of the exercise "Adding Sounds to noise.dir Using Lingo."

In the next series of steps, you'll provide a mechanism for the user to stop the audio. As the noise1.dir movie is currently constructed, every sound that is played, plays to completion unless the user clicks another button to start another sound in the same channel. By modifying the noise1.dir movie as outlined in the exercise, you'll enable the following actions:

- ✦ Clicking the Stop Sound button will terminate the currently playing sound.
- ✦ The Sound Off button is displayed when a sound is stopped.
- ✦ Clicking any object on the Stage plays the sound and redisplays the Stop Sound button.

On the CD-ROM To complete the following steps, you need the noise1.dir movie or the movie you modified in the preceding exercise. You also need the stopsnd.pct and snd_off.pct files. All three of these files are on your companion CD-ROM in the exercise:ch15 (exercise\ch15) folder.

Adding a Button to Stop the Sound

1. With the noise1.dir movie open in Director, import the stopsnd.pct and snd_off.pct bitmap images, respectively, into cast member slots 14 and 15. *Note:* Be sure that you import the stopsnd.pct file into cast member slot 14 and the snd_off.pct image into slot 15. Import the new cast members as 8-bit color images, remap to the current palette, and dither.

2. Hold down the Option (Alt) key and drag the "stopsnd" cast member onto the Stage in channel 8. Position it at the bottom-center of the Stage as shown in Figure 15-1.

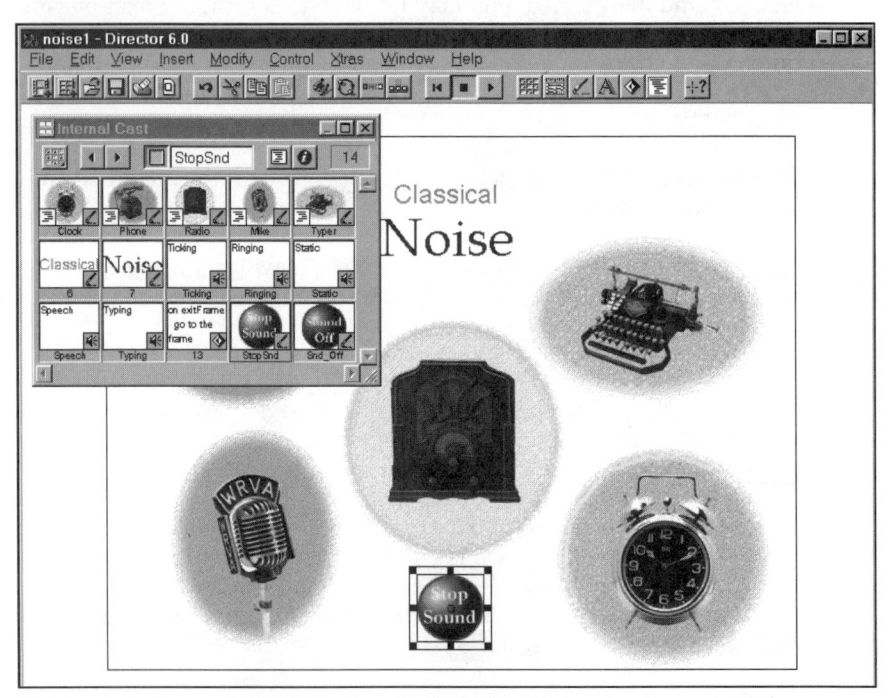

Figure 15-1: Stage after positioning the Stop Sound button

3. Because the Stop Sound button is 64 pixels wide and the Stage is 640 pixels wide, you can determine the exact center of the Stage by subtracting

64 from 640 and dividing the result (576) by 2. The result is 288. Place the button at 288 pixels from the left edge of the Stage. The button should be approximately 395 pixels from the top of the Stage.

4. Attach the following script to the Stop Sound button:

   ```
   on mouseUp
        set the memberNum of sprite 8 to 15
        sound stop 1
   end
   ```

5. Modify the script attached to the "Clock" cast member to read as follows:

   ```
   on mouseUp
        set the memberNum of sprite 8 to 14
        puppetSound 1, "Ticking"
   end
   ```

6. Add the `set the memberNum of sprite 8 to 14` instruction as the first statement in the `on mouseUp` handler for the other four cast members ("Phone," "Radio," "Mike," "Typer").

   Tip

   After typing the statement in one script, you can click and drag across the statement to highlight it, press Command+C (Ctrl+C) to copy the phrase to the Clipboard, use the Next Cast Member button to move to the next script, position the insertion point where the statement should be inserted, and then press Command+V (Ctrl+V) to paste it into the new script. Finally, press the Tab key to realign the indents in the script. Once you get the knack of this simple cut-and-paste operation, you can save yourself lots of typing.

   If you want to copy and paste the entire script, you can triple-click in the Script window to select the entire script, and then copy and paste the text of the script into a new cast member.

7. Modify the script in cast member 13 to read

   ```
   on exitFrame
        puppetSprite 8, True
        go to the frame
   end
   ```

8. Save the movie as **noise2.dir**.

9. Rewind and play the movie.

10. Click one of the buttons ("Clock," "Radio," or "Phone"). As soon as the sound plays, click the "Stop Sound" button. Each time you click the "Stop Sound" button, it is replaced with the "Sound Off" button and the sound stops. Click one of the other buttons ("Typer" or "Mike") and the "Stop Sound" button reappears. Whenever the "Stop Sound" Button appears, you can click it to stop the sound.

Additional Lingo controls for digital sound

With Lingo, you can do far more than just play and stop sounds. You can determine if a specific sound channel is busy, enable and disable sounds, control the sound's volume, and cause a sound to fade in or fade out. Let's take a look at how each of these controls is accomplished.

Determining whether a sound channel is busy

The soundBusy function determines if a sound channel is busy or not. If busy, the function returns the constant True. If the sound channel is not busy, the function returns the constant False.

Before you check whether a sound is playing, give Director sufficient time (a delay) to begin playing the sound, or the soundBusy function may return False. You can build in a delay using a small counting loop in the handler (after you start the sound), and then check to see if the channel is busy. The following *user-defined handler* employs this technique. It checks to see if a puppet sound has been started by another handler or by the Score.

Note: *About User-Defined Handlers:* Handlers that do *not* intercept standard Director events (mouseUp, mouseDown, startMovie, enterFrame, exitFrame, and so on) and are *not* named after those events are traditionally referred to as "user-defined." In the following example, the handler checkSound is a user-defined handler — because by creating this handler, you effectively create a new Lingo function called checkSound.

```
on checkSound
      repeat with counter = 1 to 5
      end repeat
      if soundBusy (1) then
          doSomething
      end if
end checkSound
```

Practical uses of the soundBusy function include the following:

- ✦ Looping within a frame until a sound finishes and then enabling the playback head to move to the next frame. This works very effectively for a self-advancing linear slideshow of sounds and images within your movie.
- ✦ Using a single object to toggle on and off a sound that is playing.

Using soundBusy to advance to the next frame

The silence that follows the completion of a sound can be used as the trigger to advance the playback head to the next frame. Such an approach is useful when you create a linear slideshow of images that are synchronized to specific sounds or breaks in narration. You can effectively use this technique in the following situations:

- ✦ When sounds or narration correspond to specific frames of a Director movie — that is, when a specific frame has an image on the Stage that corresponds to a given segment of digital sound
- ✦ When you check for the completion of a sound using the soundBusy command
- ✦ For sounds that have natural breakpoints that you can edit into separate sound cast members, which can then play and complete (triggering the next frame and the next sound)

You can also use a single sound track with *cue points,* and then have the playback head advance to the next frame as each cue point is encountered. Cue points are discussed in a later section.

The following handler demonstrates the soundBusy technique:

```
on exitFrame
        if soundBusy(1) then go to the frame
        else
        --This statement causes a transition to occur as the
        next frame is displayed.
        puppetTransition 2
        end if
end
```

Note The sound played for each frame is activated from an on enterFrame handler.

The net effect is to loop the playback head within the current frame (showing the desired image and playing the desired sound or narration). When the sound finishes, the playback head moves to next frame. If you repeat this script over a series of frames, you create a slideshow of images that advance whenever the narration for the current slide finishes.

Toggling sound on and off using a single object

You can use a single clickable object to turn sound off and then back on. In the following handler, when you click the sprite and release the mouse button, the soundBusy function checks to see if a sound is currently playing in the designated channel. If it is, the puppetSound 0 command is issued, which stops the sound. If the sound is not already playing, the click (on the sprite) causes the "Symphony" cast member to begin playing in sound channel 1. In summary, clicking the sprite toggles the sound on and then off.

```
on mouseUp
      if soundBusy (1) then puppetSound 0
         else puppetSound 1, "Symphony"
      updateStage
end
```

This handler is valuable when the sound you want to play or stop is long in duration. You would not use this handler to control a very brief sound effect or very short musical cut. If the sound is very short, it can conclude before Lingo evaluates the `soundBusy` function and cause the sound to repeat — even when you do not want the sound to play again.

In the following steps, you'll experiment with the `soundBusy` function to toggle the sound on and off in the dancin.dir movie. In its original form, the dancin.dir movie includes a film loop called "Beat" (cast member 13) based on the first 12 cast members, plus a `go to the frame` script (cast member 14) and two sound files. The sound files include "Circus" (cast member 15) and "Spike" (cast member 16). The script cast member has already been placed in the script channel of frame 1.

On the CD-ROM The file dancin.dir can be found on your companion CD-ROM in the exercise:ch15 (exercise\ch15) folder.

Using Lingo to Turn Sound On and Off

1. Open the dancin.dir movie in Director.

2. Hold down the Option key (Macintosh) or the Alt key (Windows) and drag cast member 1 to channel 1, frame 1 in the Score window. This causes the sprite to span a single frame and automatically centers the sprite on the Stage.

3. With the cartoon character (Spike) selected, set the ink effect for cast member 1 to Matte. *Note:* Without this step, a click anywhere inside the object's bounding box (the white square area that surrounds the object) would start the sound.

4. Attach the following cast member script to cast member 1:

   ```
   on mouseUp
        if soundBusy (1) then puppetSound 0
        else puppetSound 1, "Spike"
        updateStage
   end
   ```

5. Save the movie as **dancin1.dir**.

6. Be sure your speakers are turned on. Then go ahead and play the movie and click Spike. Once the music starts, click Spike again. The first click starts the sound and the second stops it.

When you click Spike, the music may not start immediately because Director must first load the entire audio clip into memory before it starts to play. To speed up this process, you can preload audio cast members by using the `preLoadMember` command in an `on startMovie` handler, like this:

```
on startMovie
  --You can use the cast member name rather than the
  number.
  preLoadMember 16
end
```

Preloading cast members is discussed further in the last section of this chapter.

Dancin' assets

The image used to create the character in dancin.dir is from the December 1995 Designer's Club CD. The Designer's Club ships a new CD to subscribers each month, containing black-and-white and color clip-art images. The image we incorporate here is 05236.EPS, copyright 1995 by Dynamic Graphics, Inc. (6000 N. Forest Drive, P.O. Box 1901, Peoria, IL 61656-190, phone 309-688-8800) and used with permission. After the image was imported into the dancin.dir movie, we used the Paint window and the Warp tool with the Auto-Distort command to create the animation. These tools are discussed in Chapter 3.

One of the two sound tracks initially imported and embedded in the movie's cast is Spike, a 60-second track from *Multimedia Soundtracks Volume One*. Spike is by Roger Kennerly of Kennerly Music Productions (400 Peachtree Industrial Boulevard, Suite 5, Suwanee, GA 30174, phone 770-271-2024), copyright 1995 and used with permission. You can visit the Kennerly Music Productions Web site at http://www.kenmusic.com.

The second track is M4555.WAV (renamed "Circus" in the movie) from *Sonic Waves 3000*. This 30-second track is by Innovative Media Corp. (631 East Allen Street, Springfield, IL 62703, phone 217-544-4614), copyright 1993–1996, and used with permission.

Later in this lesson, you'll add two more sounds to the dancin.dir movie. They are reg1.aif and pickin.aif, both created by Michael D. Miller of Miller Graphics Consulting (1108 Cove Lane, Oliver Springs, TN 37840, phone 423-435-9740) using Microsoft's Music Producer.

The sound tracks and the images in dancin.dir may only be used for the purpose of learning to import and use digital audio in a Director movie and may not be reproduced for any other purpose. To license the sound clips or images for other uses, please contact the copyright holder.

Adding a film loop and playing sound

In its current form, the dancin.dir movie does not use the film loop (cast member 13). It only uses a sprite based on cast member 1 (the stationary image of Spike) and the "Spike" sound cast member (number 14). In the next exercise, you'll add visual interest to the movie by switching a film loop for the stationary image of Spike. A film loop and sound together add a little more complexity to the project.

The best approach is to list what you want to occur in the movie and then convert the list into Lingo scripts. Here are the actions we want to occur in dancin.dir:

- Start new Spike music ("Circus") as soon as the user clicks the sprite in channel 1. Play the music in sound channel 1.
- When the user clicks the sprite based on cast member 1 (the stationary Spike), replace it with a sprite based on cast member 13 (the dancing Spike film loop named "Beat").
- As long as the sound plays, update the Stage so the film loop continues.
- If the user clicks again, replace the film loop with cast member 1 (the stationary Spike) and stop the sound.

To accomplish all this, you place a repeat loop within the on mouseUp handler, which constantly updates the Stage as long as the mouse button is up. The mouse button is down (after the handler begins) *only* if the user clicks a second time on the Stage.

Adding a Film Loop and Playing Sound in dancin.dir

On the CD-ROM

1. If it is not already open, open the dancin1.dir movie in Director. You need the movie you modified earlier in this chapter or the file dancin1.dir on your companion CD-ROM in the exercise:ch15 (exercise\ch15) folder.

2. Modify the script attached to cast member 1 to match the following:

```
on mouseUp
     puppetSound 1, "Circus"
     set the memberNum of sprite 1 to 13
     repeat while soundBusy(1)
          if the mouseUp then
               updateStage
          else
               puppetSound 0
               set the memberNum of sprite 1 to 1
          end if
     end repeat
end
```

3. Save the movie as **dancin2.dir** and test it. Spike should now play a different tune ("Circus") and dance!

If a `mouseDown` event is detected after the sound starts playing (meaning the mouse button has been pressed), the sound is turned off (`puppetSound 0`). This causes the repeat loop to end and swaps cast member 1 back into channel 1. When the loop ends, the `on mouseUp` handler terminates.

Creating sound on and sound off buttons

Though it is fun to watch Spike dance, it's time to move on to our next lesson: how to create a button that enables the user to turn sound on or off. Though you can use a single bitmap cast member, a more elegant approach involves two objects: Each button includes a symbol or text label that indicates whether the sound is on or off.

Note The button name stipulates the current *status* of the sound (on or off) — *not* the action to be taken (turn the sound off or turn the sound on).

As you work through the steps in the next section, you'll add two buttons to the dancin.dir movie: "nosound" and "soundon." You'll add scripts to these cast members so that the user can turn sound on/off in the dancin.dir movie. A click on the "soundon" button stops the audio and substitutes the second bitmap cast member image ("nosound") for the first. A click on the "nosound" sprite reverses the process, turning the sound on and displaying the first object.

The script for the "nosound" cast member is as follows:

```
on mouseUp
    puppetSprite 2, 1
    puppetSound 1, "Spike"
    set the memberNum of sprite 2 to 20
    updateStage
end
```

and here is the script for the "soundon" cast member:

```
on mouseUp
    puppetSound 0
    set the memberNum of sprite 2 to 19
    updateStage
end
```

When the "nosound" cast member script is executed, the sound "Spike" plays and the "soundon" cast member replaces the "nosound" cast member. To turn the sound off again, a script is attached to the "soundon" cast member.

Caution: When scripting buttons that replace each other, you must keep in mind which cast members are present on the Stage and attach the appropriate scripts to the visible object (not the original object that it replaced).

On the CD-ROM: The file dancin.dir and the nosound.pct and soundon.pct files can be found on your companion CD-ROM in the exercise:ch15 (exercise\ch15) folder.

Using a Button to Turn Sound On and Off

1. In Director, open the dancin.dir movie (*not* dancin2.dir).
2. Import the nosound.pct and soundon.pct images, respectively, into cast member slots 19 and 20. *Note:* Be sure that the nosound.pct image is imported into cast member slot 19 and soundon.pct is imported into slot 20. Import the images at the color depth of the Stage (probably 8-bit color), remap to the current palette, and dither.

   Note: Note that you are leaving two empty cast member slots (17 and 18). You'll use them later to add some additional sounds.

3. Drag the "Beat" film loop to a single frame on the Stage and center it. This places the dancing Spike in frame 1, channel 1.
4. Hold down the Option (Alt) key and drag the "nosound" cast member to the Stage, positioning it at the bottom-right as shown in Figure 15-2. This places the "nosound" button in channel 2, where it should only span one frame.

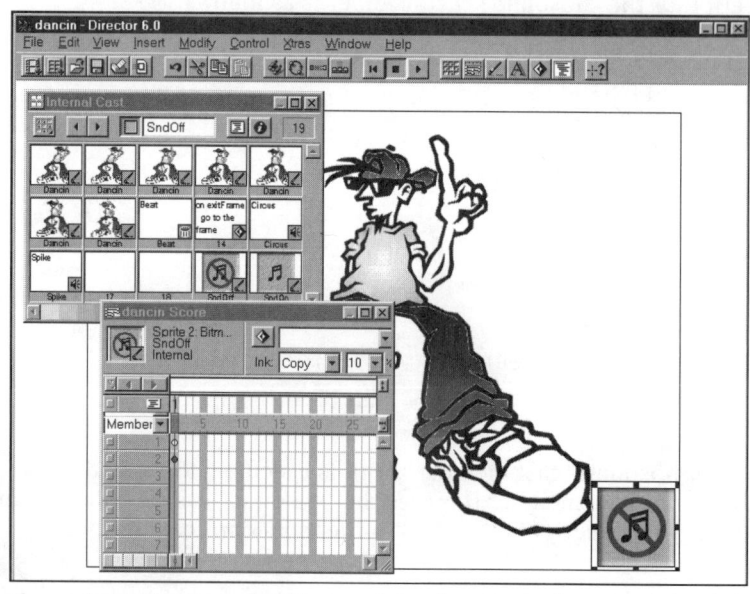

Figure 15-2: The Sound Off button is in place at the bottom-right of the Stage.

5. Attach the scripts (listed in the section just before this exercise) to the "soundon" and "nosound" cast members.
6. Save the movie as **dancin3.dir**.
7. Play and test the new buttons. When you first start the movie, no sound is playing. Click the "nosound" button (which indicates the current status of the sound). The audio begins to play and the no sound button is replaced with the "soundon" button. To turn off the sound, click the "soundon" button.
8. When you're done testing, stop the movie.

Playing sound while the mouse is down

Using Lingo-related sound commands, almost as many methods are available to control sound playback as there are digital sounds. So far, you have learned to turn sound off and/or on using a button or object. You can also cause a sound to play only as long as the mouse button is depressed over a specific cast member.

In the following handler, the sound cast member "Sunny" plays as long as the mouse button is depressed. As soon as the user releases the mouse button, the puppetSound 0 command is executed, which stops the music.

```
on mouseDown
      puppetSound 1, "Sunny"
      updateStage
      repeat while the mouseDown
      end repeat
      puppetSound 0
end
```

Playing sound on a rollover

Another technique is to have a distinctive sound play whenever the mouse pointer moves over a specific sprite. In the following handler, the Jazz sound is played when the mouse pointer moves over sprite channel 1 *and* no sound is playing.

```
on exitFrame
      if rollover(1) then
         if not soundBusy(1) then puppetSound 1, "Jazz"
            else nothing
      else
         puppetSound 0
      end if
      go to the frame
end
```

In the handler, when the mouse pointer moves over the sprite stored in channel 1, Director checks to see if a sound is playing. If not, then the `puppetSound` command plays the "Jazz" sound cast member. If a sound is playing, no action is invoked (`nothing`). Further, the `else` clause causes the sound to stop — if the mouse is *not* over the sprite in channel 1. The last command in the handler causes the playback head to loop on the current frame and reevaluate (on each pass) whether the mouse is over the sprite in channel 1.

> **More sound sources**
>
> The band.dir movie used in this chapter contains more selections from the *Sonic Waves 3000* collection described earlier: the sounds named Acoustic (abridged from M4454.wav), Drummin (2106.wav), and Softpiano (m1650.wav).
>
> Griff (renamed from griff3.wav) is from MediaBlitz version 3.0 from Asymetrix Corporation. Their royalty-free clip-media collection, part of the MediaBlitz studio, is copyright 1992–1993 by Asymetrix Corporation (110 110th Ave. NE, Suite 700, Bellevue, WA 98004-0692, phone 800-448-6543).
>
> And the itsbeen (itsbeen2.wav) sound clip is from *MusicBytes Volume 1*, copyright 1991 by Prosonus, a division of Big Fish Software (11003 Penrose Street, Suite C, Sun Valley, CA 91352, phone 800-717-3474). The collection includes royalty-free music, sound effects, and MIDI for production, education, and entertainment.
>
> The soundtracks as used on the CD may only be used for the purpose of learning to import and use digital audio in a Director movie and may not be reproduced for any other purpose. To license the sound clips for other uses, please contact the copyright holder.

In the following steps, you can practice activating a sound when the mouse pointer rolls over a specific sprite on the Stage. As currently constructed, the band.dir movie used in this exercise includes seven bitmap cast members, including "Band" (the complete image from which the other bitmap cast members are derived), "Stage," "Drums," "Keyboard," "Left Guitar," "Right Guitar," and "Singer." The next five cast members are sounds, including "Acoustic," "Drummin," "Griff," "Itsbeen," and "Softpiano."

On the CD-ROM The file band.dir can be found on your companion CD-ROM in the exercise:ch15 (exercise\ch15) folder.

Activating Sound When the Mouse Rolls Over a Sprite

1. Open the band.dir movie in Director.
2. Create the following frame script and place it in the script channel of frame 1:

```
on exitFrame
    if rollover(3) then
        if not soundBusy(1) then puppetSound 1, "Drummin"
        else nothing
    else
        puppetSound 0
    end if
    go to the frame
end
```

3. Save the movie as **band1.dir,** rewind, and play the movie. When you move the mouse pointer over any portion of the Drummer (cast member 3) in channel 3, the "Drummin" sound cast member plays.
4. With some modification, you can cause the movie to play a different sound cast member when the mouse pointer rolls over each of the on-Stage objects. Modify the script cast member (cast member 13) to match the following:

```
on enterFrame
    if rollover(3) then
        puppetSound 1, "Drummin"
        updateStage
        repeat while rollover(3)
        end repeat
        puppetSound 0
    else if rollover(4) then
        puppetSound 1, "Softpiano"
        updateStage
        repeat while rollover(4)
        end repeat
        puppetSound 0
    else if rollover(5) then
        puppetSound 1, "Acoustic"
        updateStage
        repeat while rollover(5)
        end repeat
        puppetSound 0
    else if rollover(6) then
        puppetSound 1, "Griff"
        updateStage
```

(continued)

```
                    repeat while rollover(6)
                    end repeat
                    puppetSound 0
            else if rollover(7) then
                    puppetSound 1, "ItsBeen"
                    updateStage
                    repeat while rollover(7)
                    end repeat
                    puppetSound 0
            end if
    end

    on exitFrame
            go to the frame
    end
```

5. Save the movie as **band2.dir**.
6. Play and test the movie.

Side Dish: Creating several buttons from one image

The artwork for the band.dir movie is based on an image (05071.eps) from the Designer's Club, September 1995-97 CD-ROM (copyright 1995-97 by Dynamic Graphics, Inc. and used with permission).

To create separate cast members (from a single image) that can serve as clickable buttons, we opened the black-and-white EPS file in Adobe Photoshop 4.0 and saved it as a Photoshop document (.psd). We created six different layers, each with a duplicate copy of the original image. We then used the Eraser tool to erase everything from the top layer except a single object (such as the keyboard player). The process was repeated until each layer retained only a single object (drummer, left guitarist, right guitarist, and singer). After resizing the image to its desired size, we hid all but one layer at a time, colored it, and then saved the document again in .psd format without merging the layers.

In Photoshop, you can save only the visible layers, so we did the following for each layer: We hid all layers except a single layer, and converted it to an indexed color image (using Photoshop's Image➪Mode➪Indexed Color command). Then we saved the image as a PICT or BMP image. After importing all the saved images into Director, we placed them on the Stage and aligned them. We also imported the original artwork in channel 1 and used it to line up the other bitmap cast members on the Stage. When done, we deleted the original image, now unneeded, to save bytes.

One final comment: All sprites were done using Matte ink except the bottom image (placed in the lowest-numbered channel), which causes only the solid portions of the image to react when the mouse clicks or rolls over the sprite.

Tidying up, using the `case` statement

This is a good point in the chapter to introduce the `case` statement. It is used to simplify and improve the readability of long `if...then...else` statements used in scripts (like those in the band2.dir movie listed in the preceding section).

The `case` statement is a *multiple branching logic* structure that allows you to list several alternative courses of action and choose one to be executed when the movie plays. A multiple branching logic structure is a selection mechanism similar to an `if...then...else` statement for making decisions based on a series of possible situations.

The selection of the action to be executed is made by matching the value of a *case expression* (also called the *case selector*) with a second expression (called a *label*) that is attached to a possible action. The use of a `case` statement is more efficient than the repeated use of parallel `if` statements or nested `if...then...else` statements.

The syntax and components of a typical `case` statement are as follows:

```
case caseExpression: of
      labelOne:
          statement1
          statement2
      labelTwo:
          statement3
      labelThree, labelFour:
          statement5
          statement6
      otherwise statement7
end case
```

In this syntax diagram, if the result of the *caseExpression* matches *labelOne*, then statement1 and statement2 execute. If the result matches *labelTwo*, then statement3 is executed. If you have multiple results for which you want the same statements to execute, you can place the results (separated by commas) on the same line of the case statement. In the example just given, if the result of the *caseExpression* matches *labelThree* or *labelFour*, statement5 and statement6 are executed. Finally, if the *caseExpression* results do not match any of the labels, statement7 (which follows the `otherwise` keyword) is executed.

Note: In the syntax diagram for the `case` statement, each label (such as *labelOne*, *labelTwo*, and so on) is an *expression*. An expression can be a value, text string, or formula.

When Lingo encounters a `case` statement (sometimes referred to as a *case structure*), Director searches through each label until an expression is found that matches the `case` expression. Once the match occurs, the statements linked to that label are executed. The `case` statement stops testing alternatives as soon as it encounters its first match.

On the CD-ROM To provide an example of the `case` structure, the script for cast member 13 in the band2.dir movie is rewritten in Listing 15-1 as a `case` statement. (This script is used in the bandx.dir movie on the companion CD-ROM.)

Listing 15-1: Revised Script for Cast Member 13 in band2.dir

```
On enterFrame
    case the rollover of
        3: puppetSound 1, "Drummin"
            updateStage
            repeat while rollover (3)
            end repeat
            puppetSound 0
        4: puppetSound 1, "Softpiano"
            updateStage
            repeat while rollover (4)
            end repeat
            puppetSound 0
        5: puppetSound 1, "Acoustic"
            updateStage
            repeat while rollover (5)
            end repeat
            puppetSound 0
        6: puppetSound 1, "Griff"
            updateStage
            repeat while rollover (6)
            end repeat
            puppetSound 0
        7: puppetSound 1, "ItsBeen"
            updateStage
            repeat while rollover (7)
            end repeat
            puppetSound 0
        otherwise: Nothing
    end case
end

on exitFrame
    go to the frame
end
```

Based on the `case` expression (`the rollover`), specific statements are executed when the rollover returns a value between 3 and 7. The statements determine which sound clip is played. Notice the use of the `otherwise` condition statement just before the `end case`. If the `rollover` function returns a value other than 3, 4, 5, 6, or 7, then no action occurs.

Whenever a case statement includes repetitive statements, you can pull out those statements and include them one time at the end of the case statement. The script in Listing 15-1 includes repetitive commands such as the puppetSound and updateStage commands (to play the music); the repeat while loop (to enable the sound to play out); and the puppetSound 0 command (to turn off the sound). Listing 15-2 is a rewritten, more concise version of the foregoing script.

Note

The major difference in the Listing 15-2 script is the use of two global variables: musicClip and bandNumber. The musicClip variable stores a string representing the desired sound's cast-member name, and the bandNumber variable holds a number representing the sprite channel returned by the rollover function. If the rollover returns a value other than a number from 3 through 7, the script sets the bandNumber variable's value to 1. When the value equals 1, the statements that play the sound are skipped.

Listing 15-2: Condensed Script for Cast Member 13, Using Global Variables

```
on enterFrame
global musicClip, bandNumber
    case the rollover of
        3: set musicClip to "Drummin"
            set bandNumber to 3
        4: set musicClip to "Softpiano"
            set bandNumber to 4
        5: set musicClip to "Acoustic"
            set bandNumber to 5
        6: set musicClip to "Griff"
            set bandNumber to 6
        7: set musicClip to "ItsBeen"
            set bandNumber to 7
        otherwise: set bandNumber to 1
    end case
    if bandNumber <> 1 then
        puppetSound 1, MusicClip
        updateStage
        repeat while rollover(bandNumber)
        end repeat
        puppetSound 0
    end if
end

on exitFrame
    go to the frame
end
```

Playing random sounds

Whenever possible, you want to add variety and a little friendly unpredictability to your movies. And although you want navigational buttons to always behave in the way the user expects them to, it doesn't hurt to add some surprises to the animation that occurs on the Stage or the sounds generated by specific objects.

Using the dancin3.dir movie, you can use the random function to randomly choose various sounds to play when the user clicks the sound button. The following script includes a slight modification to the script attached to cast member 19 (the "nosound" button). It generates a random number between 1 and 4. Next, a value of 14 is added to the random number, and the subsequent value is stored in a local variable (soundNumber), which corresponds to cast members 15 through 18.

```
on mouseUp
    puppetSprite 2, 1
    put random(4)+14 into soundNumber
    puppetSound 1, soundNumber
    set the memberNum of sprite 2 to 20
    updateStage
end
```

Earlier in this chapter, in the exercise "Using a Button to Turn Sound On and Off," you left cast member slots 17 and 18 empty. Now you can add sounds to those slots. To use the random function as described here, you want the sound cast members to occupy a continuous group of cast member slots.

In the following steps, you can practice with the random selection of a sound using the dancin3.dir movie.

On the CD-ROM To complete the following steps, you need the dancin3.dir movie or the movie you have been working with in earlier exercises. The file dancin3.dir can be found on your companion CD-ROM in the exercise:ch15 (exercise\ch15) folder. You will also need two sound files: pickin.aif (or pickin.wav) and reg1.aif (or reg1.wav). These files are also found on the CD-ROM in the exercise:ch15 (exercise\ch15) folder.

Playing Random Sounds from the Cast

1. In Director, open the dancin3.dir movie, if it's not already open.
2. Import two additional sound files into cast member slots 17 and 18. The recommended sounds are pickin.aif (or pickin.wav) as cast member 17 and reg1.aif (or reg1.wav) as cast member 18.
3. Modify the cast member script attached to the "nosound" button to match the script listed just above for playing random sounds.

4. Save the movie as **dancin4.dir,** rewind, and play it.

   Each time you click the "nosound" button (to start the sound again), the movie randomly selects a sound cast member to play. Because numbers are generated randomly (from 15 through 18) the same tune may be played more than once consecutively.

Playing a list of sounds in one frame

Another way to use sound is to play a series of sound clips sequentially in a single frame. Conceivably, you could combine the multiple sound clips into a single clip and play it in one frame or over several consecutive frames. However, because smaller sound clips load faster, it's often a good plan to play several sounds sequentially in a single channel. Here is one approach to the task.

In the following example, you create a frame script with both an `on enterFrame` and an `on exitFrame` handler in the same script. Within the `on enterFrame` handler, two user-defined handlers are called (`setTrackNumber` and `setSound`). The `on exitFrame` handler simply loops in the current frame.

```
on enterFrame
        global gsound
        if not soundBusy(1) then
        --Sets the gtrack global variable to 1, 2, or 3 and
        then recycles through these values.
        setSound --Equates a track number with a
        predetermined music track "One", "Two", or "Three".
        setTrackNumber
        --Plays the desired sound cast member.
        puppetSound 1, gsound           updateStage
        end if
end

on exitframe
      go to the frame
end
```

Two additional movie scripts are used, first to select the track (assigning a value between 1 and 3) and then to translate the track number to specify a specific music clip, as shown in the following `on setTrackNumber` and `on setSound` handlers.

Tip: If you arrange your multiple sound cast members in cast member slots 1, 2, and 3, you can combine the two handlers (`on setTrackNumber` and `on setSound`) into a single handler, in which the `gtrack` variable identifies the cast member number.

```
on setTrackNumber
      global gtrack
      if gtrack=3 then
         set gtrack =1
      else
         set gtrack= gtrack +1
      end if
end

on setSound
      global gsound, gtrack
      if gtrack =1 then
         set gsound ="sound 1"
      end if
      if gtrack =2 then
         set gsound ="sound 2"
      end if
      if gtrack =3 then
         set gsound ="sound 3"
      end if
end
```

The `on setSound` handler can be modified to use a `case` statement such as the following. (The results from using either script are identical.)

```
on setSound
      global gsound, gtrack
      case gtrack of
         1: set gsound ="sound 1"
         2: set gsound ="sound 2"
         3: set gsound ="sound 3"
         otherwise nothing
      end case
end
```

The first example script — the one using `if...then...else` instructions — is easier to read, but using the `case` statement greatly simplifies the handler and reduces the amount of code.

In the following steps, you'll create a small movie that plays three imported sounds sequentially in a single frame.

On the CD-ROM To complete this exercise, you can select any three sound files from the companion CD-ROM in the goodies:jjones (goodies\jjones) folder or the goodies:sonic (goodies\sonic) folder.

Playing Three Sounds Sequentially in One Frame

1. Open a new movie using the File➪New➪Movie command or press Command+N (Ctrl+N).
2. Import any three sound files.
3. Rename the imported sound cast members "sound 1," "sound 2," and "sound 3."
4. Double-click the script channel in frame 1 and type the following script:

```
on enterFrame
     global gsound
     if not soundBusy(1) then
          setTrackNumber
          setSound
          puppetSound 1, gsound
          updateStage
     end if
end

on exitframe
     go to the frame
end
```

5. Click the New Script button on the Script window and type the following script:

```
on setTrackNumber
     global gtrack
     if gtrack=3 then
          set gtrack =1
     else
          set gtrack= gtrack +1
     end if
end

on setSound
     global gsound, gtrack
     case gtrack of
          1: set gsound ="sound 1"
          2: set gsound ="sound 2"
          3: set gsound ="sound 3"
          otherwise nothing
     end case
end
```

6. Close the Script window.

7. Save the movie as **3sounds.dir,** rewind, and play it. Notice that nothing appears on the Stage when you play the movie, but the three sound clips play sequentially over and over again. (They won't stop until you stop the movie.)

8. Stop the movie.

Playing sound when the user goes to sleep

If you have ever used an interactive kiosk, you know that after a specified period of inactivity, the system prompts the user to take action or resets itself. Within Director you can use Lingo to determine the maximum amount of inactivity (in ticks) that can pass before some specified activity occurs.

This interval specification technique can be used to play a sound clip during the inactivity, as well as jump to a different frame or marker after the period of inactivity. The key is to wait for the absence of an event. In the following example, the playback head jumps to the "Start" marker (where the passive activity screen appears) if four seconds pass without a keystroke, mouse click, or mouse movement (rollover) occurring. This instruction uses the lastEvent function:

```
if the lastEvent > 4 * 60 then
      go to "Start"
end if
```

This handler can be used to automatically recycle an animation or opening instruction screen with or without sound.

In the next exercise, you'll simulate the behavior of a kiosk that jumps to a "passive activity" screen whenever four seconds pass without activity (mouse click, keypress, or mouse movement). In its current form, the kiosk.dir movie used in this exercise includes a sound cast member named "sound 1," four bitmap text cast members (cast member slots 2 through 5) and a transition (Dissolve Patterns). In these steps, you'll add several scripts to complete the movie.

On the CD-ROM The file kiosk.dir can be found on your companion CD-ROM in the exercise:ch15 (exercise\ch15) folder.

Creating a Mini-Kiosk

1. Open the kiosk.dir movie in Director.

2. Open the Score window and add the following script in the Script channel for frames 1, 5, and 10. The script causes the playback head to loop on the current frame after calling the `checkWait` handler that is created in the next step.

   ```
   on exitFrame
        checkwait
        go to the frame
   end
   ```

3. Add the following movie script. It is called by the frame scripts that you entered in step 2. The `checkWait` handler checks to determine if more than 4 seconds have elapsed since the last event (mouse click or keypress). If true, then the playback head jumps to the frame labeled "Start" and plays "sound 1."

   ```
   on checkWait
        if the lastEvent > 4 * 60 then
             go to "Start"
             puppetSound 1, "sound 1"
             repeat while the mouseUp
                  updateStage
             end repeat
             puppetSound 0
        end if
   end
   ```

4. Add the following movie script using the Script window. It is slightly different from most of the `on mouseUp` handlers you have used, because the handler is stored in a movie script and not attached to a specific cast member or sprite. The result is that when the mouse button is clicked anywhere on the Stage in any frame, the movie advances to the next frame.

   ```
   on mouseUp
        go to the frame +1
   end
   ```

5. Save the movie as **kiosk1.dir**, and rewind.

6. Play the movie. Click the first screen to move to the next frame. If you wait more than four seconds, the playback head jumps back to frame 1 and starts playing the sound cast member. The sound cast member only plays when the playback head is in frame 1.

7. Try clicking to move to the next page, and then wait to see if the playback head jumps back to frame 1 after slightly more than a four-second wait. Again, the playback head returns to frame 1 (with the "Start" label) and starts playing the sound clip.

8. Stop the movie.

Playing linked files with Lingo

At the beginning of the chapter, you learned that one of the ways to play a sound file in your movie — in addition to using the `puppetSound` command to play an embedded sound cast member — is to play an external (linked) sound file using the `sound playFile` Lingo command. Director can work with both AIFF files or wave sound (WAV) files on either a Macintosh or Windows system. On the Macintosh, the `sound playFile` command requires System 6.0.7 or higher.

To add linked media (such as sound files) to the Cast window, you use the File ➪ Import command or press Command+R (Ctrl+R), just as you do to import and embed media in a Director movie. There are two important differences between linked and embedded media:

♦ First, when you link an asset, you must select the Link to External File option in the Media list of the Import Files dialog, as shown in Figure 15-3. (For embedded files, you select the Standard Import option.)

♦ The second difference is that linked files are maintained as separate (external) files. To be available for use in a movie, linked files must be installed with the Director movie, preferably in the same folder or directory. (Embedded files, on the other hand, are stored within the Director movie, so they are automatically packaged with the movie.)

Once you've designated a linked sound file, to play it from within a movie you use the `sound playFile` command. The syntax for the command is

```
sound playFile channel, "externalSoundFileName"
```

The *channel* parameter is replaced with a channel number, and the name of the file to be played replaces the *externalSoundFileName* parameter.

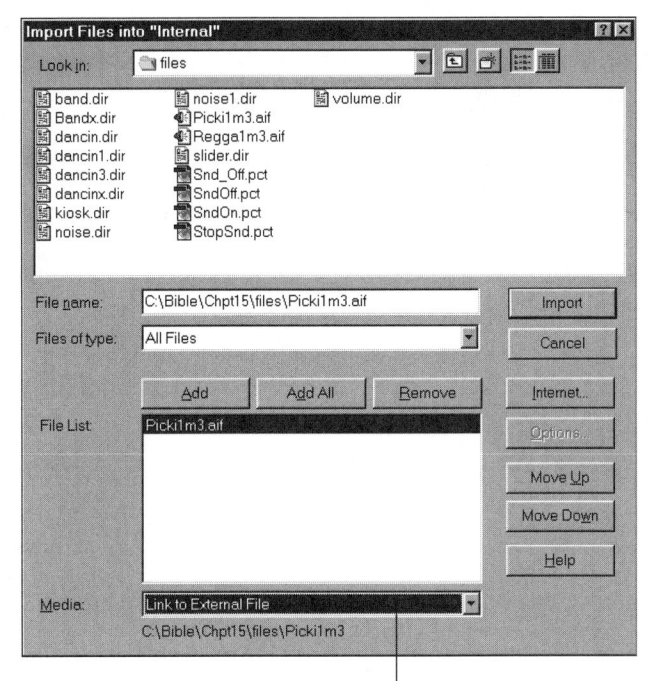

Figure 15-3: For linked assets, select Link to External File for the Media setting when you import the file.

> **Note**
>
> The sound playFile command cannot be used to play an embedded cast member.

For example, the following command plays the sound file "jazz" from an external sound file in channel 2:

    sound playFile 2, "jazz"

If you don't place the external sound file in the same folder or directory as the movie, you must include the file's path preceding its filename. For example, if the "jazz" sound file is in a folder called Sounds on your local hard drive, the sound playFile command requires one of the following pathname formats:

✦ On a Macintosh system, assuming the local hard drive is Macintosh HD, the pathname would be indicated like this:

    sound playFile 2, "Macintosh HD:sounds:jazz"

- On a Windows system (assuming the local hard drive is `C:`), the pathname would be indicated like this:

  ```
  sound playFile 2, "c:\sounds\jazz"
  ```

Caution: Using the `puppetSound` command loads the sound file into RAM and then begins playing it, but the `sound playFile` command streams the audio from disk and begins playing it immediately. Bear in mind that your computer cannot read two disk files simultaneously. If a Director movie is reading a sound file using the `sound playFile` command, the movie cannot concurrently play digital video, load cast members into memory, or conduct any other disk read/write activity.

Controlling the Sound Volume

You can control the sound in a movie in one of three ways:

- Adjusting the sound level for all sounds playing (using `the soundLevel` property)
- Adjusting the volume of a specific sound in a specific channel (using `the volume of sound` property)
- Causing a sound to fade in or fade out over a specific time period (using the `sound fadeIn` and `sound fadeOut` commands)

Using `the soundLevel` property

With `the soundLevel` property you can set or determine the volume of the sound that is played through your computer's speakers, from a value of 0 (muted) to 7 (maximum volume). By default, Director sets `the soundLevel` property to 7.

The syntax for setting the sound level (volume) is

```
set the soundLevel to n
```

where *n* is replaced with a value representing the sound volume.

For example, to set the volume to the maximum level, you can use the following instruction:

```
set the soundLevel to 7
```

In the following steps, you'll modify the volume.dir movie to set the volume of a sound cast member played through your computer's speakers.

On the CD-ROM The file volume.dir is on your companion CD-ROM in the exercise:ch15 (exercise\ch15) folder. This movie includes a sound track, 1–21am.aif from *Multimedia Soundtracks Volume One*. It is by Roger Kennerly of Kennerly Music Productions (400 Peachtree Industrial Boulevard, Suite 5, Suwanee, GA 30174, phone 770-271-2024), copyright 1995 and used with permission. Kennerly Music Productions has a web site at http://www.kenmusic.com.

The volume.dir movie includes two bitmap cast members (a Volume Up button and a Volume Down button), a sound cast member (the 1–21am.aif sound track), a go to the frame script (in cast member slot 4), and a Play Sound button (a push-button created in Director).

You need to add three scripts to the movie to make it functional. In the following steps, you'll add a script to the Play Sound button that causes the sound track to play (the soundLevel property is set to 4). You attach a script to the Volume Up button to increase the sound level by 1 level each time the user clicks the button, and a similar script to the Volume Down button that decreases the sound level by 1 level when the button is clicked. The current sound level setting appears in a field named Level (cast member 6) that appears on the Stage below the Play Sound button.

Setting the Volume Level of Sound

1. In Director, open the volume.dir movie (from the CD).
2. Select the Play Sound button in the Cast window and add the following script. (You can omit the comments.)

```
on mouseUp
      --Global variable that represents the current value
      of the soundLevel property
      global glevel
      if soundBusy (1) then puppetSound 0
      else puppetSound 1, 3
      put 4 into glevel
      set the soundLevel to glevel
      --Places the soundLevel property setting in the
      Level field.
      put glevel into field "Level"
      updateStage
end
```

3. Select the Volume Up button and attach the following cast member script:

```
on mouseUp
      global glevel
```

```
            if glevel <7 then
                set glevel to glevel +1 --Increases the soundLevel
                property value
                set the soundLevel to glevel
                put glevel into field "level"
                updateStage
            end if
end
```

4. Select the Volume Down button and attach the following cast member script:

```
on mouseUp
        global glevel
        if glevel >0 then
                set glevel to glevel -1 --Decreases the
                soundLevel property value
                set the soundLevel to glevel
                put glevel into field "level"
                updateStage
        end if
end
```

5. Save the movie as **volume1.dir**.

6. Play the movie, and test the Volume Up and Volume Down buttons. You should be able to hear the difference in volume as you adjust the sound level.

Using the volume of sound property

Like the soundLevel property, the volume of sound property enables you to control volume — in this case, the volume of a specific sound channel. Further, you can control the volume with a greater degree of precision because you have a wider range of acceptable values for this property: from 0 (muted) to 255 (the maximum volume).

In the following statement, the sound in channel 1 is set to the maximum volume:

```
set the volume of sound 1 to 255
```

The following statement mutes the sound that is playing in channel 2:

```
set the volume of sound 2 to 0
```

Since this property can be determined or set by the user, it is often adjusted using a slider to control the volume of sound in a movie. In the following steps, you'll modify the slider.dir movie so the user can control the volume of sound played in a specific sound channel.

On the CD-ROM The file slider.dir is on your companion CD-ROM in the exercise:ch15 (exercise\ch15) folder.

When you open the slider.dir movie and examine the cast, you can see that the slider comprises two sprites: Sprite 1 (the arrowhead) is constrained to sprite 2 (the line). As sprite 1 moves along the horizontal line, its right edge (the pointer on the arrow) ranges from 76 to 255 pixels from the left edge of the Stage (the Stage is 320 x 240 pixels in size). The handler stores the position of sprite 1, measured in pixels, in a variable (glocation) that is used to set the volume of the music clip. The position is also stored in the field cast member "Volume" and displayed on the Stage.

Tip When you use settings below 80 or 90 for the volume of sound property, the sound may be too soft to hear. This depends on the music clip's original recorded volume and the volume settings on your speakers. In this example, we are not concerned about settings below 76. Further, the line that makes the slider doesn't have to be 255 pixels long to use this technique. You can always mathematically modify the pixel value to place the result within the range used by the volume of sound property.

Setting the Volume Level for a Sound Channel

1. Open the slider.dir movie in Director.
2. Open the on startMovie script (cast member slot 7) and examine it. The script (in the movie) appears as follows, but without the comments:

```
on startMovie
      puppetSprite 1, 1 -- puppets sprite channel 1
      -- makes the sprite in channel 1 moveable
      -- constrains sprite 1 to the area of sprite 2
      set the moveableSprite of sprite 1 to true
      set the constraint of sprite 1 to 2
end

on idle
      global glocation
      -- identifies the right edge of the sprite
      put the right of sprite 1 into glocation
      -- places the glocation value in the Volume field
      put glocation into field "Volume"
```

```
            updateStage
            -- sets the sound volume to a value
            -- that matches the glocation variable
            set the volume of sound 1 to glocation
        end
```

Note: The `on idle` handler is executed when no other event occurs (such as `mouseUp`, `mouseDown`, `startMovie`, `stopMovie`, `exitFrame`, and `enterFrame`). For that reason, the volume is not adjusted until the user releases the mouse button after repositioning the slider control.

3. With the Cast window open, examine its contents. Notice that the slider is composed of cast members 1 and 2.
4. Play the movie, click the Play Sound button to start the musical clip, and then use the slider to adjust the volume.
5. Stop the movie.

Controlling fade-in/fade-out

The third way to control sound volume is to cause the sounds to fade in and fade out as needed. This feature is useful when you want to smooth an otherwise abrupt beginning to a musical clip, or to fade out background music at a specific point in your movie. Fade-outs can also reduce the volume in one channel while the volume of narration or sound effects increases in another channel.

You use two companion commands to handle the fade-in and fade-out of sound in a specific sound channel: `sound fadeIn` and `sound fadeOut`.

The `sound fadeIn` command increases the volume of a sound until it reaches an optimum level over a specified period of time. The time specified is measured in ticks, with 60 ticks equal to a second. Any fade-in you specify continues at the predetermined rate until the specified time has elapsed, or until the sound in the specified channel changes or stops.

To fade in a sound in channel 2 over a five-second period, for example, you use the following instruction:

```
sound fadeIn 2, 300
```

Here's another version of this instruction:

```
sound fadeIn 2, 5*60
```

The advantage of the second method is that you can easily (without any mathematical effort) determine the number of seconds (5) that the sound will use to fade in.

When you specify the number of ticks, the fade-in occurs smoothly over the specified period of time. However, if you do not specify the number of ticks, Director calculates the default number of ticks as follows:

15 × 60 ticks ÷ the Tempo setting in the first frame of the fade-in

The `sound fadeOut` command decreases the volume of a sound in a specified channel over a specified number of ticks. Similar to the `sound fadeIn` command, `sound fadeOut` fades the sound smoothly over the time period you specify. If you do not specify the number of ticks, Director calculates the default number of ticks as follows:

15 × 60 ticks ÷ the Tempo setting in the first frame of the fade-out

In the following example, the sound in channel 2 fades out over 3 seconds:

```
sound fadeOut 2, 180
```

Positioning the commands for fade-in and fade-out

Note that the `sound fadeIn` command should *precede* the `puppetSound` command, or the initial sound will be heard at the default volume, then drop to a muted level, and then fade in. The following cast member script for a button will fade in the sound as the sound starts:

```
on mouseUp
      sound fadeIn 1, 300
      puppetSound 1, "Waltz"
      updateStage
end
```

On the other hand, the `sound fadeOut` command should *follow* the `puppetSound` command so the initial sound is played at the current volume, which then drops (over the specified number of ticks) to a muted level. If you add a button that causes the fade-out to occur, the cast member script appears as shown here:

```
on mouseUp
      sound fadeOut 1, 300
      updateStage
end
```

This script assumes that the `puppetSound` command was issued in another handler and that the sound is current playing.

Using Cue Points Stored in Imported Sounds

Director 6 adds a new method of synchronizing sound (and video) with other media elements in your movies. Using Macromedia SoundEdit 16, you can define *cue points* in the following:

- AIFF sound files (cue points are referred to as *markers* in AIFF files)
- Shockwave for Audio (SWA) files
- QuickTime digital videos (discussed in Chapter 16)

Currently, Macromedia's SoundEdit 16 product is only available on the Macintosh platform. However, an AIFF file or QuickTime movie to which you add cue points (using SoundEdit 16) can be used in either a Macintosh or Windows Director movie.

Note: QuickTime for Windows 2.5 or later is required to use cue points on the Windows platform. Microsoft's AVI digital video format does not support cue points.

Cue points are helpful because you can use the Tempo channel to pause the playback head on the current frame (using the Tempo dialog box). When the specified cue point is encountered in the AIFF sound file or QuickTime movie that's playing, you can have the playback head proceed to the next frame.

Setting cue points in an AIFF sound file

When you insert cues in SoundEdit 16, the cue is attached to a specific point in time — that is, a specified number of milliseconds or seconds from the start of the sound track. The cue is *not* assigned to a specific point on the sound wave. If you add or delete information to the sound after assigning cues, the cues stick to the original point in time. Further, when you copy/cut and paste a segment of a sound file to a different sound file, the cue points are not transferred to the target file.

You can establish one or more cue points in an AIFF file by completing the following steps:

1. Load Macromedia SoundEdit 16.
2. Open the sound file to which you want to add one or more cue points.
3. Move the SoundEdit 16 insertion point to the location where you want to add a cue point.

   Tip: The easiest method to identify the position for placing a cue point is to use the VCR-style controls, play the sound, and stop it at the location where you want the cue point. Another method is to open the Insert Cue Point dialog box (see step 4) and enter a value representing the location of the cue point — but for this method you must know the numeric value representing the location.

4. Once the insertion point is properly positioned, select the Insert ⇨ Cue Point command or press Command+M to add a new cue point.

5. In the Insert Cue Point dialog (Figure 15-4), you can change the cue point's name and accept or change its location (in seconds, milliseconds, samples, frames, or time codes). By default, SoundEdit 16 sequentially numbers each new cue point (Cue 1, Cue 2, and so on). Cue point names are limited to 30 characters.

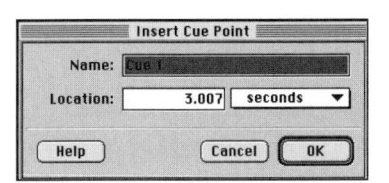

Figure 15-4: Specifying the location of the cue point

6. Click OK after you establish the desired settings. The cue point appears as a triangle (similar to a Director marker) just below the Time Ruler, as shown in Figure 15-5.

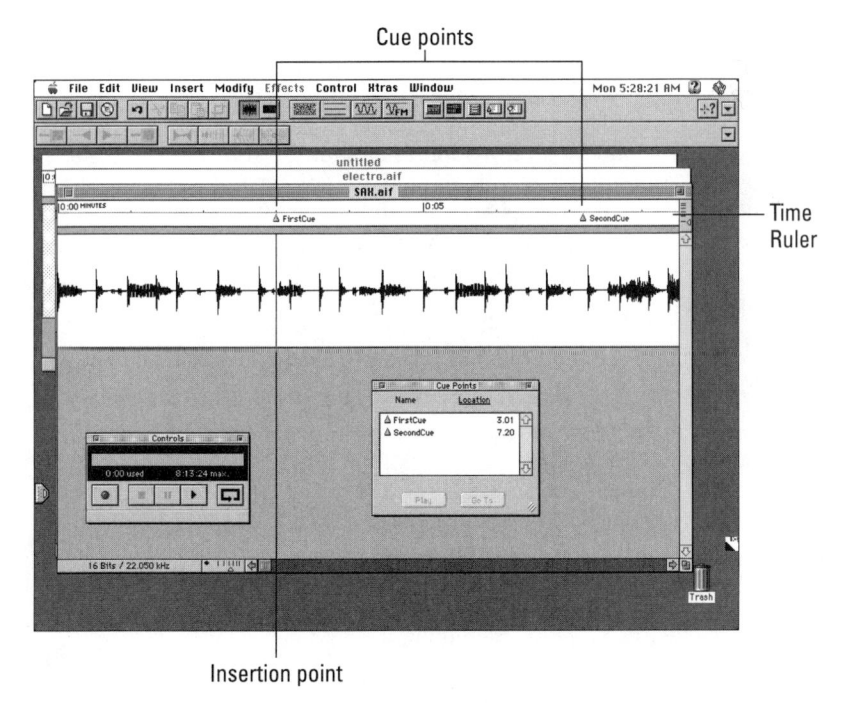

Figure 15-5: Cue points are designated just below the Time Ruler.

7. Change the cue points as desired. If the location of a cue point is not exactly where you want it, drag it to a new location. To delete a cue point, simply drag it off the bar under the Time Ruler. If you want to use a different cue point name, change it by clicking the default name and typing a new one.

8. To add additional cue points, move to a new location and repeat steps 3 through 7.

Caution: Director sometimes has problems recognizing the Option+space (ASCII character 202) that is used by SoundEdit 16 to insert a space between the word *Cue* and the cue number. To avoid any complications, you can rename the cue points using only alphabetical and numeric characters, without any spaces.

Using a cue point in the Tempo channel

Once you import an AIFF file (with cue points) into your Director movie, you can use the cue points to signal the places in the sound track where you want the playback head to move to the next frame.

Note: Every sound has an {End} cue point, even if you do not add it in SoundEdit 16. You can use this to cause the completion of a sound and move the playback head forward.

To use the AIFF file to synchronize sound and the movement through frames, complete the following steps:

1. Place the sound file in the Sound channel. Be sure to extend the sprite to cover all the frames in which you want any part of the sound to play. If you find that the sound does not play in the final frame, extend the sprite to the next frame beyond where you want it to play.

2. In the Tempo channel, select the frame where you want the sound to play *until* a cue point is encountered.

3. Double-click the target cell to open the Frame Properties: Tempo dialog box (Figure 15-6).

4. Select the Wait for Cue Point radio button, and in the Channel list choose the Sound channel in which the sound will play. If there is only one Sound channel (Sound 1: or Sound 2:) in use in the current frame, Director defaults to that channel.

5. If the sound cast member has more than one cue point, open the Cue Point list (see Figure 15-6). You can

    ✦ Select a cue point by highlighting its name in the list, or

    ✦ Select Next to tell the playback head to advance after the next cue point encountered, or

    ✦ Select End to tell the playback head to advance to the last cue point encountered in the sound cast member.

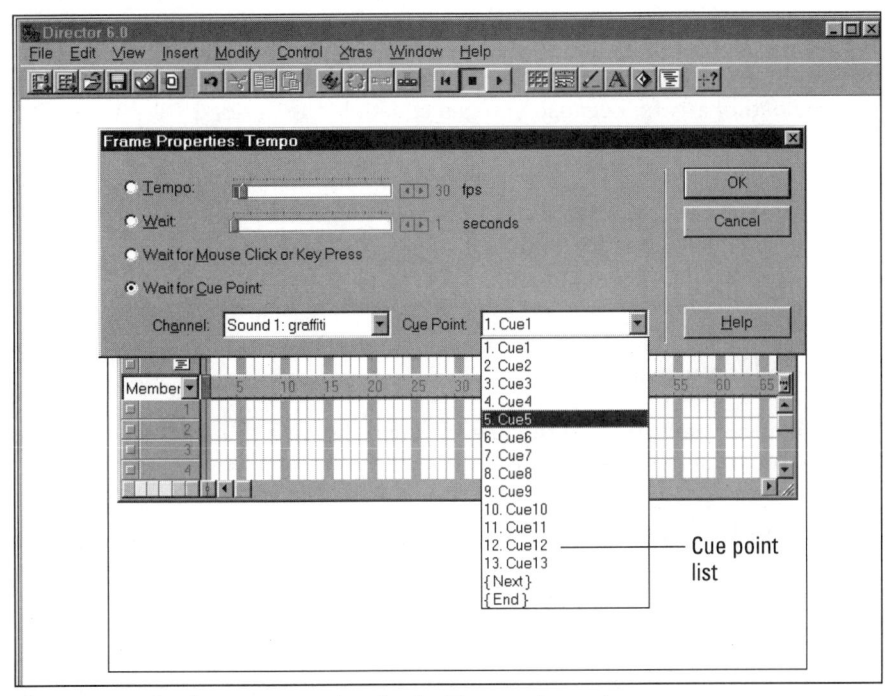

Figure 15-6: Setting up cue points in the Tempo channel

6. If the sound cast member has no cue points and you want the playback head to pause until the sound completes, select the Wait for Cue Point radio button and choose End in the Cue Point list.

7. Close the Frame Properties: Tempo dialog box.

8. If you have additional cue points in the sound cast member and you want subsequent frames to pause while the sound plays, repeat steps 2 through 7.

Preloading and Unloading Cast Members

The dancin.dir and band.dir movies used in this chapter's exercises both include some delay in playing sound when large sound files are involved. Both of those movies have imported sound files that must be loaded into RAM before the sound can be heard within the movies. Director enables you to control (somewhat) these delays by

✦ Preloading one or more specific cast members

✦ Preloading all cast members required in one or more frames

Preloading cast members still takes time, and the amount of time required is contingent on the amount of RAM available, plus the size and number of the cast members that you want to preload. Nevertheless, there are advantages to using a preload of assets, because you can schedule the preload

- While the system is normally idle
- When user interaction is not expected, such as while an instruction screen is displayed for the reader
- While a previously loaded animation is running

You can also add a screen message that alerts the user that work is going on behind the scenes.

Tip You never want to leave the user trying to figure out if a mouse click worked or if the program has locked up and gone into cyberspace.

Preloading specific cast members used in one or more frames

The `preLoad` command can be used to load all the cast members required for one or more frames in your movie. For example:

- You can preload all cast members used *in the current frame, to the end of the movie* by using the `preLoad` command without any parameters, as in

    `preLoad`

- To load all cast members used *in the current frame, through and including cast members used in frame 10*, use the command

    `preLoad 10`

- When you include a single parameter, the `preLoad` command preloads frames from the current frame through and including the frame designated by the parameter.

- To load all cast members used in frames 10 through 15, use the command

    `preLoad 10, 15`

- Note that this command does not preload *only* the cast members in frame 10 and 15. It preloads all cast members in frames 10 *through* 15.

The preloading process terminates when your system's RAM (working memory) is full or when the specified cast members are loaded.

You can use label names (markers) with the `preLoad` command. If you use one label, Director preloads from the current frame through the frame indicated by the marker. If you use two label names, all cast members between the two label names are preloaded. In the following example, all cast members in the frames labeled "Start" (cast slot 1) and "Midway" (cast slot 40) are preloaded into memory:

```
preLoad "Start", "Midway"
```

Another variation is to have the `preLoad` command load all cast members from the current frame to the next frame with a marker. The command form is entered as follows:

```
preLoad marker (1)
```

Preloading specific cast members

The `preLoadMember` command is used to load one or more cast members that you specify. Unlike the `preLoad` command, `preLoadMember` gives you greater control over selecting specific cast members that you want to place in RAM before they are normally loaded. This technique is used to load a cast member and then gain quicker display or playback of the member (sound, film loops, animation, and so on) at a specific point in the movie — without pausing to load the cast member. For example:

✦ You can preload all cast members in the entire movie by using the `preLoadMember` command without any parameters, as in

```
preLoadMember
```

✦ To load only cast member 20, use the command

```
preLoadMember 20
```

✦ To load all cast members (in the Cast window) beginning with cast member number 20 through 30, use the command

```
preLoadMember 20, 30
```

Note that this particular command form does not preload *only* the cast members 20 and 30. It preloads all cast members 20 *through* 30.

The preloading process terminates when your system's RAM (working memory) is full or when the specified cast members are loaded.

You can use cast member names, as well, with the `preLoadMember` command. If you name a specific cast member, it alone is preloaded into memory. If you use two cast member names, all cast members *between and including* the first- and last-named cast members are preloaded.

In the following example, all cast members between "Circus" (cast slot 15) and "Reg1" (cast slot 18) are preloaded into memory:

```
preLoad "Circus" "Reg1"
```

In the following steps, you'll modify the dancinx.dir movie to preload the four sound cast members.

On the CD-ROM The file dancinx.dir can be found on your companion CD-ROM in the exercise:ch15 (exercise\ch15) folder.

Preloading Digital Sounds

1. Open the dancinx.dir movie in Director.
2. Play the movie and click the sound button (no sound cast member).

   As you run the dancinx.dir movie, notice how quickly the movie jumps from the first frame (with the "Spike is Coming…" bitmap cast member) to the second frame (with the image of Spike). You will probably notice some delay between the time that you click the sound button and when the sound cast member starts playing, because no sound cast members have been preloaded. (The delay may not be very noticeable if you have a fast workstation. However, when you begin constructing large movies with dozens of frames and numerous cast members, the delay will become more and more obvious.)

3. After stopping and starting the sound several times to observe the delays, stop the movie.

4. Open the script attached to cast member 21. The script appears as follows. All of the code in cast member 21 is required whether you preload cast members or not.

```
on exitFrame
    puppetSprite 3, True --puppets channel 3
    put 10 into counter
    Repeat while counter >0
        -- places the value stored by the counter
        variable
        -- in a field named "countDown"
        put counter into field "countDown"
        updateStage
        delay 60
        -- reduces the value stored in counter by 1
        put counter-1 into counter
    end repeat
    put " " into field "countDown"
```

```
        -- Stores two spaces in the "countDown" field in order
        to hold the font and font size
        --turns off the puppet property
        puppetSprite 3, False
    end
```

Tip: The `delay` command halts the movie for the specified number of ticks; and 60 ticks equal one second, so the handler stops all movie action for one second (60 ticks). When using the `delay` command to stop action in your movie, you can make your code clearer by writing the instruction as `delay 3*60`. This clearly indicates that the pause is for three seconds (3 × 60 ticks).

5. Now you'll add a movie script that preloads cast members 22 through 25. Open the Script window and create the following movie script:

```
on startMovie
       preloadMember 22, 25
end
```

6. Close the Script window.

7. Play the movie and observe that the "Spike is Coming..." screen remains visible longer (the preload is occurring) and the sounds play sooner when you click the play sound button.

8. Save the movie as **dancinx1.dir**.

You can experiment with the dancinx.dir movie. Try preloading only the film loop ("Beat"). Then try preloading all the sound cast members *and* the film loop "Beat." Does your system have sufficient RAM to preload all the cast? If not, where do you prefer the time lag to occur?

Unloading cast members

Preloading cast members can help eliminate loading delays and provide smoother playback of a movie, but eventually every computer system runs out of memory. To free up memory for different cast members, use the `unLoad` command:

✦ You can unload all cast members in all frames except the current one, by executing the following instruction:

```
unload
```

✦ You can also instruct Director to unload files from a specific frame (frame 25 in this example) using the following instruction:

```
unLoad 25
```

✦ Similar to the `preLoad` command, you can unload all cast members in a range of files (say, 25 to 35) using this instruction:

```
unLoad 25, 35
```

You can use cast member names, as well, with the `unLoad` command. If you name a specific cast member, it alone is unloaded from memory. If you use two cast member names, all cast members between the first and last named cast members are unloaded. In the following example, all cast members between and including "Circus" (cast slot 15) and "Reg1" (cast slot 18) are unloaded from memory:

```
unLoad "Circus", "Reg1"
```

> **Note:** You do not need to routinely unload memory, because Director automatically unloads the least recently used cast members based on the cast member's Unload setting. The `unLoad` command is intended for special circumstances in which there is a lag in the startup of an animation, the redrawing of the Stage, the playback of a digital video, or the playback of a sound, due to the lack of sufficient working memory.

Summary

Before you move on to controlling digital video with Lingo in the next chapter, let's review some of the things you learned in this chapter.

✦ You can embed sound files in a Director movie and control the sound's playback using the Score or the `puppetSound` Lingo command.

✦ You can also link an external sound file to a Director movie and play back the sound using the `sound playFile` command.

✦ With Director 6, you can embed or link either AIFF (.aif on the Windows platform) sound files or wave (.wav) files.

✦ You can control the playback of a sound in several ways, by arranging for the sound to react to clicks on a stop/start button, to the mouse pointer's rolling over a specific object, and to the mouse button being depressed.

✦ The `puppetSound` and `sound stop` commands are used to terminate a sound that is currently playing.

✦ You can use the completion of a sound as the trigger to forward the playback head to the next frame in your movie (or to trigger other events).

✦ Lingo can control the fade-in and fade-out of a sound, adjust the volume, or preload and unload a sound.

✦ ✦ ✦

Video Lingo

CHAPTER 16

Digital video is still the overweight, finicky uncle in the multimedia household. Admittedly, digital video file sizes are typically large, and video must be linked as an external media to your movie. This chapter shows you how, with a few well-placed commands, you can tame the beast and control the digital video cast members in your movies. You'll also learn how to export Director movies to digital video and use utilities to convert among digital video formats.

Note: To work through this chapter, you need to have Director installed on your computer system as well as one of the following: QuickTime for Macintosh, QuickTime for Windows, or Video for Windows.

Understanding Digital Video

Digital video includes two very different varieties of video quality. In general, the term *desktop digital video* refers to video that can be displayed on your computer system's monitor. *High-end digital video* is what you see on television and in movie theaters. Certainly, computers are used for special effects and animation on the big screen and in television, but those computers are not your run-of-the-mill consumer-grade PCs. In this discussion, we will abbreviate the term desktop digital video to simply *digital video,* but keep in mind that it includes video that can be captured, manipulated, and displayed on a consumer-quality personal computer.

In This Chapter

Types of desktop digital video

Importing and using digital video in a Director movie

Preloading and unloading digital video

Controlling the properties of digital video

Building a custom video controller

Removing video artifacts from the Stage

Exporting Director movies to digital video

Cross-platform guidelines for using digital video

Digital video is far easier to watch than it is to explain. It is a stream of sights and sounds that together provide visual and auditory images to the viewer. If you have ever examined an 8mm or 16mm film, you know that what we see on the screen is really a series of still photos (coupled with a sound track) that race by fast enough to make us think we see natural motion. That "natural motion" is called *full motion* in video terminology. In full motion, people move around the screen without glitches or hiccups, and the sound is synchronized with the action we perceive. The human eye can be deceived into thinking it sees full motion if the still frames of a film or video are displayed at the rate of 24 to 30 frames per second (fps) — this phenomenon is called *persistence of vision*.

The number of frames per second is also known as the digital video clip's *frame rate*. Standard frame rates vary from 24 fps for film to 30 fps for NTSC television video (used in the Western Hemisphere) to 25 fps for SECAM and PAL video (the video standards used in the rest of the world). Slower frame rates can be used, but the results eventually deteriorate and become choppy. Further, the human ear must be considered. Video without sound is like breakfast cereal without milk. The best audio quality requires 44.1KHz, 16-bit, stereo sound. As you learned in Chapter 15's discussion of audio files, a higher quality of sound produces a proportionately larger audio file size.

The trade-off: file size vs. quality

The issue of file size is a problem because home computers typically do not have enough horsepower to manage a steady stream of 30 images per second (plus the accompanying sound). Here's the reason why:

30 [frames per second]

×

(640 x 480) [pixels per screen using SVGA graphics]

×

3 bytes [required for each pixel for 24-bit color]

=

27,648,000 bytes!

In other words, one second of full-screen, full-motion video at 640 x 480 screen resolution will require 27.6MB of storage. A full minute of the same quality video will require over 1.6GB of hard disk storage. Even with the rapidly decreasing cost of storage, that's a very substantial consumption of resources for one minute of video. Further, those storage requirements do not cover the audio component, which can easily require an additional 175K of storage per second.

In addition to hard disk or storage, these video requirements present another dilemma. The data transfer rate of an average hard drive is 300 kilobytes per second. To pump full-screen, full-motion video from your hard drive to your computer's CPU would require a data transfer rate of around 28MB per second — that's over 93 times more data than the average hard drive can handle.

Note

The average data transfer rate of the now obsolete single-speed CD-ROM drive is 150 kilobytes per second. A double-speed CD-ROM drive transfers data at 300 kilobytes per second. A quad-speed drive transfers data at 600 kilobytes per second, and a 6x drive can handle 900 kilobytes per second — which approaches the data transfer rate of an average hard drive.

How do your find an adequate compromise between what is ideal (full-screen, full-motion video with 24-bit color) and what your personal computer can handle? Consider the following concessions:

- ✦ Reduce the on-screen image size of the video. Rather than using a 640 x 480-pixel image, display the video at 160 x 120 or at 320 x 240 pixels.
- ✦ Reduce the number of frames per second. Rather than 30 fps, 10 to 15 fps will sometimes be adequate.
- ✦ Compress the image, eliminating unnecessary pixels and changes. Video compression is an integral aspect of both of the popular digital video technologies: QuickTime and Video for Windows.
- ✦ Reduce the quality of the audio track. For narration and music, something under 44.1 KHz audio may be enough to achieve what you want. (Refer to Chapter 15 for a discussion of sound.)

Caution

Be cautious when including audio in your compromises. Research has shown that humans are more tolerant of lower-quality video when they can understand the audio track. Thus if a production (movie, slideshow, multimedia project) includes clear and detailed graphics but uses poor-quality audio, you will lose your audience faster than if the image quality is mediocre while the audio is clearly understandable.

Director can import two digital video formats: Microsoft's Video for Windows and Apple's QuickTime. Both of these formats are based on a codec (compressor/decompressor) technology that enables your PC to compress video during a video capture session and decompress video during normal playback. Both QuickTime and Video for Windows can utilize more than one compression algorithm.

A Few Incarnations of Digital Video

Once the discussion turns to digital video, three prominent types of computer-based video are mentioned: QuickTime, Video for Windows, and MPEG video. The following sections take the mystery out of these terms.

What is QuickTime?

QuickTime is a multiplatform, industry-standard multimedia architecture that is used to create and deliver synchronized graphics, sound, video, text, and music. As a standard, QuickTime includes three elements: It is a system extension, a file format standard, and a set of compression algorithms.

It can be argued that QuickTime is also a series of human-interface standards that make the playback of digital video more intuitive. This is accomplished using a standard graphic controller with play, rewind, pause, and volume controls, plus a slider that provides a visual indication of how much of the current digital movie has been played and how much remains.

The current versions of QuickTime for Windows and QuickTime for the Macintosh can be downloaded from Apple's site at

    www.quicktime.apple.com

A system extension

QuickTime is a system extension (or, in plain English, an extension to the operating system) that enables you to create, compress, view, control, and edit time-based data, collectively known as a movie. Using QuickTime, you can edit the movie data just as you can edit text and graphic elements in a word processor.

QuickTime includes two system-level managers that extend the operating system and shield the end-user (and your applications) from the intricacies of transforming a desktop computer into a video playback machine. In addition, QuickTime includes utilities with which you can play movies and view picture files. Each of the QuickTime utilities is listed in Table 16-1.

Table 16-1
QuickTime Utilities

Utility Name	Function
MoviePlayer	Opens and plays QuickTime movies. The standard QuickTime installations for Mac and Windows include this utility.
MovieShop	An unsupported utility that converts existing QuickTime movies to other file formats. MovieShop 1.2.1, the most recent version, is shipped with earlier versions of the QuickTime Starter Kit. This utility is a replacement for the earlier Movie Converter.
Movie Recorder	No longer supported by Apple. Records digital video from external sources such as a video tape deck or video camera. Shipped with earlier versions of the QuickTime Starter Kit. (Currently, the most popular digital video recording and editing software on both the Mac and Windows platforms is Adobe Premiere.)
Picture Compressor	Applies QuickTime compression to any graphic stored in the PICT file format. Shipped with earlier versions of the QuickTime Starter Kit.
Picture Viewer	Views a picture (PICT) file in a window. Included in the standard installations of QuickTime for Mac and Windows.

A standard file format

QuickTime uses a standard file format that can contain multiple tracks of data. Simply stated, each track in a QuickTime movie can reference a single media type. QuickTime supports several media types, including

- Video tracks (including MPEG compressed video).
- Animation tracks (using sprites or moving objects).
- Sound tracks (common formats such as IMA 4:1, AIFF, WAV, or SND).
- Music tracks (a MIDI-like synthesizer track). QuickTime has an import feature that enables you to translate a MIDI track into a QuickTime music track. You can also use the MoviePlayer to export the audio from a QuickTime movie to an AIFF or standard MIDI file.
- Text tracks.
- High-quality compressed images.
- Three-dimensional (3D) objects.
- MPEG data streams.

A QuickTime movie can have more than one track of each media type. Data tracks include start and stop points on a time-based continuum for each element (sound, video, text, and so on) in the movie. QuickTime automatically synchronizes the data streams from each track during playback.

> **Note** Synchronization simply means that the data stored in the various data tracks is displayed at the proper time. For instance, narration from the sound track plays "in sync with" the talking head in the video track. Music in the sound or music track plays in sync with the appropriate credits in the text track.

Compression algorithms (codecs)

The third element of the QuickTime standard is a set of compression/decompression algorithms or schemes (*codecs*). A compression algorithm is a method of compressing images that together constitute a digital video sequence. The ultimate goal of compression is to reduce the movie's file size while retaining an appropriate level of quality for the media.

When exporting to QuickTime, several standard codecs are available, and more can be added. See Table 16-2.

Table 16-2
QuickTime Supported Codecs

Codec	Description
Animation codec	Uses run-time length encoding (RLE) for animation or computer-generated graphics. Avoids recording information about each pixel in an image by storing only new changes of color and the number of consecutive pixels of the same color. Works with all color depths.
Apple Video codec	Best utilized for compressing video from a video source (video deck, film recorder) as opposed to animation or computer-generated (synthetic) images. Slow to compress but offers rapid decompression (during video playback). Offers good results with up to a 95% compression ratio. Works with 16-bit color depth.
CinePak codec	First offered with QuickTime version 1.5. An asymmetrical codec — it encodes slowly (up to 20 minutes for a 10-second video clip) but decompresses quickly during playback. Frequently used for 16- and 24-bit video targeted for playback from a CD-ROM. CinePak compression is recommended when working with either QuickTime or Video for Windows files. Works best on raw, uncompressed video data that has not been previously compressed. Works with 24-bit color and grayscale images.

Codec	Description
Component Video codec	Also called YUV Codec. Best suited for archival storage. A symmetrical algorithm that takes just as long to compress as to inflate. Compression ratio is only 2:1, but is lossless (image is not degraded when video compression/decompression occurs multiple times). Works with 24-bit color depth.
Graphics codec	Exports a single frame of computer graphics. Targeted for use with 8-bit color images (256 colors). Can compress images twice as much as the animation compressor but takes twice as long to decompress. Excellent method for computer images but not for digital video. Works with 8-bit color and grayscale images.
Intel Indeo R3.2 codec	Similar to CinePak, but compresses in one-third the time. Image quality and compression are superior to CinePak, but more decompression time (CPU cycles) is required. Also, not as scalable as CinePak. (Scalability refers to optimizing the quality of video playback depending on the system resources available to play the video. Faster systems with more memory play back better-quality video than systems with less computing power.) Works with 24-bit color depth.
None codec	Supports the reduction of image file size by reducing the color depth of the image. For example, if you reduce a 24-bit color image to 8-bit color, you reduce the file size to one-third its original size without using any compression. Works with all color depths.
Photo codec	Often called the JPEG codec. Supports the Joint Photographic Expert Group standard and can be used to export continuous-tone grayscale or color still images. Best for continuous-tone images (photographs) as opposed to images with sharp lines (line art). Can compress file size by as much as 90–95%. One disadvantage: Image data lost during compression is not recoverable (lossy compression). Works with 8-bit grayscale and 24-bit color images.

In all, QuickTime is flexible and scalable. It can display a postage-stamp sized video window on a low-end Macintosh; 320 x 240-pixel playback on a Pentium with no hardware assist; or broadcast-quality video on high-end systems that have expensive video playback and digitizing boards. Digital video captured using QuickTime uses the .qt and .mov extensions. QuickTime movie files with the .mov extension can be played on either the Macintosh or Windows operating system.

Tip

To Windows, 16-bit and 32-bit dynamic link libraries (DLLs) are completely different resources. If you are developing on a Windows system, you'll be wise to install both the 16- and 32-bit versions of QuickTime for Windows 2.x.

> ## More information about QuickTime
>
> Anyone who begins working with digital video discovers quickly that it is a "double infinity" topic: The more you know, the more you know you don't know. We have found Charles Wiltgen's "The QuickTime FAQ" extremely helpful. Point your browser at
>
>   http://www.QuickTimeFAQ.org
>
> and be prepared for 70+ pages of bedtime reading. You will also want to get the Adobe Acrobat Reader to download, view, and print the document. See
>
>   www.adobe.com

What is Video for Windows?

Video for Windows is Microsoft's solution to full-motion digital video on a Windows-based computer system. Microsoft's video technology is built into Windows 95 but must be installed under Windows 3.1.

Digital video captured using Video for Windows is stored in a file with an .avi (Audio/Video Interleave) extension. Though not as mature a technology as Apple's QuickTime standard, Video for Windows provides some of the same capabilities, including

- ✦ Playback of digital video from a hard drive or CD-ROM
- ✦ Data streaming without using great amounts of RAM
- ✦ Parsing of digital video files and load/playback of a few frames at a time (as opposed to loading an entire video clip before playback can begin)
- ✦ Use of compression algorithms to reduce file size

AVI files do not support separate data tracks for text, music, and animation. Video for Windows interleaves audio and video data in order to maintain synchronization when the video is played.

Note Play Video is an Xtra from ImageMind Software that plays AVI files full screen with synchronized sound from a Director movie. You can download a copy of the Play Video demo from

    http://www.imagemind.com/develop.htm

ImageMind Software is at 5 Triad Center Suite 600, Salt Lake City, UT 84180, phone 800-321-5933, fax 800-355-5008, e-mail marcom@imagemind.com.

Video for Windows includes the Media Player applet that enables users to play AVI movies. (Although the Media Player and AVI support are included with Windows 95, they may not be installed on your system. If AVI files do not play, refer to your Windows 95 documentation for installation instructions.)

The Windows 3.1 installation of Video for Windows includes several utilities: VidCap to capture video, VidEdit to edit video sequences, and BitEdit, PalEdit, and WaveEdit to edit images, palettes, and sounds within an AVI movie.

The Windows 3.1 version of Video for Windows supports the Video 1, RLE, and Indeo compression algorithms. Under Windows 95, the AVI technology adds CinePak compression and provides MCI drivers for Sony ViSCA VCRs and LaserDisc players. Some third-party editing programs also install and support CinePak and other codecs under either Windows 95 or Windows 3.1.

What is MPEG?

MPEG stands for Motion Picture Experts Group. The acronym is commonly used to refer to the international standard for digital video and audio compression. Actually, however, MPEG is a collection of tools for compressing audio and video. The MPEG standard does not specify how to accomplish the specified video/audio compression. Rather, it describes a set of minimum requirements for an MPEG decoder — the device that plays back the compressed audio and video.

There are two versions of the MPEG standard, called *MPEG-1* and *MPEG-2*:

- ✦ MPEG-1 is a standard for "Coding of Moving Pictures and Associated Audio for Digital Storage Media at up to about 1.5 Megabits per second." This published standard provides playback quality that approximates the same picture quality or resolution you would get from a VHS tape played on your VCR. MPEG-1 was designed specifically to deliver video from a single-speed CD-ROM drive. This standard is sometimes called by its International Standards Organization (ISO)/IEC project number: 11172, parts 1 through 5.

- ✦ MPEG-2 provides a step up in video quality and has been chosen as the encoding standard for high-definition television (HDTV). It will be used for regular and interactive TV transmissions.

MPEG-1 and MPEG-2 are completely different standards, with different purposes. MPEG-1 (commonly called simply MPEG) was designed to compress video to improve playback on a desktop computer system, and MPEG-2 applies to the digital transmission or broadcast of video signals. MPEG-1 compresses video at a rate up to 200:1. It also enables full-screen, real-time, full-color, full-motion video playback as opposed to the frame-dropping (jerky) postage-stamp or postcard sized video that preceded the standard.

You can locate additional information on the MPEG standard at

    http://www.mpeg.org

> ### MPEG-4 on the horizon
>
> MPEG-4 is currently under development (current plans call for skipping MPEG-3). MPEG-4 will offer a common solution to the various technologies — TV, computer-based digital video, audio, the Internet, and so on — that converge in the "universal interactive audio/video terminal" (otherwise known as your TV or computer monitor). Plans for the new standard include new or improved functions and features in three areas: standardized content-based interactivity, compression, and universal access.
>
> MPEG-4 will provide efficient data access and organization based on the audio/visual content of the application. The characteristics of specific objects in an MPEG-4 movie can be accessed and changed. Natural and synthetic AV objects can be integrated into an MPEG-4 movie. And new methods will be available to randomly access a movie's data and objects within a limited time and with appropriate resolution.
>
> Better-quality images and sound at bit rates comparable to the current industry standards are also in store with MPEG-4. The new standard will support multiple streams of audio and video data that are sufficiently synchronized to foster stereoscopic and multiview applications (including efficient representations of 3D natural "objects" for virtual reality applications).
>
> Finally, the emerging MPEG-4 standard will offer a standard that promotes robustness in otherwise error-prone environments. The standard will support higher resolutions for objects in space and time, and the ability to prioritize (with better resolution) the principal objects in an MPEG-4 movie.

Using MPEG in Director movies

This chapter focuses primarily on the use of Video for Windows and QuickTime in Director. However, you can use MPEG video in your Director movies using two methods. One technique is to import MPEG video into a QuickTime format to provide easy control within Director. The second technique is to use an Xtra.

On the CD-ROM You may want to look into using the MpegXtra developed by Tabuleiro Da Baiana Multimedia (Rua Conego Eugenio Leite, 1089, Sao Paulo, Brazil 05414012, phone 55-11-9713342, fax 55-11-8142254, e-mail tbaiana@tbaiana.com). In addition to supporting the inclusion of full-screen, full-motion MPEG video in Director movies, this Xtra adds several new Lingo commands that offer precise control over MPEG digital video. MpegXtra Lite is available, as well, and is supplied on this book's CD in the goodies:tbaiana (goodies\tbaiana) folder. Or you can download it from

```
http://www.tbaiana.com
```

You can also order MpegXtra Pro from Tabuleiro Da Baiana Multimedia's Web site.

Xtras are discussed in Chapter 19. You can see a list of available Xtras at Macromedia's Web site:

```
http://www.macromedia.com/software/xtras
```

Adding a Digital Video Cast Member

Digital video, like sound, is a time-based medium — which means it changes over time. Early in this book, you discovered that a Director movie is frame-based — it changes frame by frame. Because of the need to incorporate time-based media (sound and video) into a frame-based product (Director), some of the same concerns when working with sound also apply to video.

The most obvious parallel is that to play sound or video, you must keep the playback head moving. This is accomplished by looping within a frame (using a `go to the frame` handler) or by copying the digital video sprite across multiple frames so that the entire video clip plays.

Adding digital video to a Director movie is a three-step process:

1. You import digital video into a Director movie using the File➪Import command (Command+R or Ctrl+R). This is the same method used for sound or graphic images. Digital video, however, is always an external cast member and cannot be embedded as digital sound or graphic images can.

2. Once imported, you use the Digital Video Cast Member Properties dialog box (Figure 16-1) to set the desired properties for the video clip.

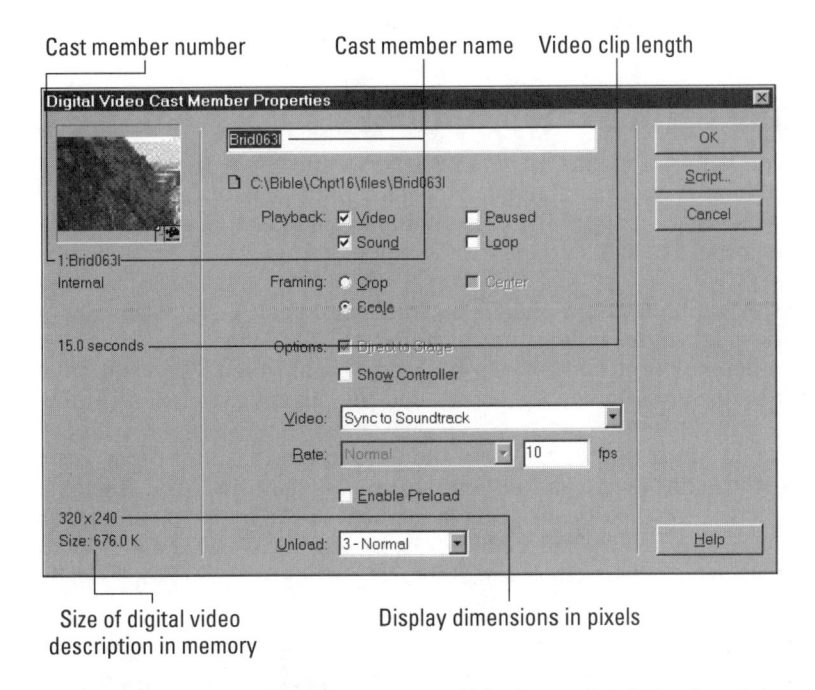

Figure 16-1: The Digital Video Cast Member Properties dialog box is headquarters for setting up your digital videos to play the way you want them to.

3. After placing the digital video cast member on the Stage, you must keep the playback head moving (even if it simply loops within the current frame) so the entire clip plays.

Importing digital video

Director for Windows can import either QuickTime for Windows or Video for Windows (AVI) files. Director for the Macintosh can only import QuickTime movies. If you work on both platforms, you may want to create and save all your digital video files using Apple's QuickTime format.

When you import digital video, whether it's in a QuickTime or AVI format, Director links the video rather than embedding it within the movie. This avoids adding substantially more bytes to the size of your movie; it also means you can edit the external video file without reimporting it. Changes will be automatically reflected in the Director movie, which reads from the external file whenever the movie plays.

There is a negative side to automatically linking rather than embedding digital video: You must keep track of the location where the digital video file is stored. To simplify matters, it's best to store the digital video in the same folder with your movie. This way, when you transfer the contents of the folder to another computer system, to a CD, or to other media, the video file and the movie will reside in the same folder, and the path from the movie to the video remains the same — which is necessary for the video to be accessible for playback.

Setting digital video options

Once you import a video clip, you need to set the clip's options in the Digital Video Cast Member Properties dialog box (Figure 16-1). This dialog can be used to display information about the current digital video cast member as well as to change properties and settings for the video.

Along the left-hand side of the dialog, you'll find basic information about the video clip. These attributes reflect the current state of the video cast member: name and number, length of the clip (in seconds), size of the video's description in memory (*which is different from the file's size*), and the display dimensions in pixels.

Note that these attributes are not edited in Director. To alter them, you must use a digital video editor such as Adobe Premiere. In Figure 16-1, the video clip is named Brid063l.mov, the file's description in memory is 676 bytes, it runs 15.0 seconds, and its size on-screen is 320 x 240 pixels. If your Stage size is 640 x 480 pixels, the video will cover one-fourth of the Stage.

Controlling playback

In the Playback area of the dialog box are four check boxes that affect the playback characteristics of the video clip:

- **Video** — Instructs Director to display the visual portion of a digital video clip.
- **Sound** — Instructs Director to play the audio portion of a digital video clip.
- **Pause** — Causes Director to display the first frame of the video clip, but the digital video is not played until Director is instructed to do so using Lingo.
- **Loop** — Instructs Director to play the video clip and then loop back to its beginning and replay it.

These four options are *not* mutually exclusive. You can select all or some of the options depending on the desired behavior for the movie. For example, you can turn off the Sound check box to play a digital video cast member without its audio portion. You might want to do this because the video clip doesn't include a sound track, or because you don't want to use the QuickTime movie's sound track in your Director movie.

Playing a sound-only video

By disabling the Video check box for a digital video cast member, you can play a sound-only video . This technique provides greater control over the synchronization of a sound clip with Director animation. Because Director 6 supports cue points within a digital audio file, however, using a sound-only QuickTime movie is not the best method of synchronizing sound to animation. (See also the section "Using Lingo to Control Digital Video Properties" later in this chapter.)

Caution: Using a sound-only digital video cast member includes a performance burden because Director links rather than imports digital video. A sound-only QuickTime movie must stream the sound off the local hard drive, so if your movie also is concurrently loading other multimedia assets, the movie may stutter. Your hard drive (or CD-ROM reader) cannot read two locations at the same time without choking. This problem does not exist if you use an imported sound cast member, because Director loads the sound into working memory. Your hard drive read/write head is thus free to tackle other tasks, such as loading other media from disk.

Working with the framing options

The Framing area of the Digital Video Cast Member Properties dialog lets you resize the video's bounding box (display area) on the Stage. You must choose either the Crop or Scale radio button:

- **Crop** — When you choose Crop, the display area in which the digital video plays becomes a window through which you view only a part of the video image, as shown in the example in Figure 16-2. This framing option retains the movie's original size when the video's bounding box is resized. If the bounding box is resized smaller than the cast member's original dimensions (in pixels), the outside edges of the video clip are cropped.
- **Center** — When you select the Crop option, you can also instruct Director to center the video clip within the resized bounding box. If you do not select the Center check box, the video within the bounding box is displayed in its

original location. Figure 16-2 demonstrates this; in the example on the lower-right, the video display area was resized to include only the upper-left corner of the original video window.

✦ **Scale** — Choose the Scale option when you want Director to adjust the digital video cast member's size (in pixels) to match the bounding box when you resize the video clip. In other words, if you choose this option, you can resize the video to play in a larger or smaller window. As shown in Figure 16-2, the digital video image is complete, but it plays in a smaller display area.

Figure 16-2: Examples of digital video framing

Stage options

In the Options area of the Digital Video Cast Member Properties dialog, you have two check boxes that control how digital video appears on the Stage and whether an on-Stage controller is displayed:

✦ **Direct to Stage** — Check the Direct to Stage option when you want to play the digital video clip in front of any other sprites on the Stage, without regard for the channel that holds the video sprite. When this setting is enabled, ink settings do not affect the video cast member. In most cases, the Direct to

Stage option offers the best playback performance and should be used unless you want to apply ink effects or compositing to the Stage.

Compositing is a technique by which objects are added to a digital video clip one at a time. In Director, the equivalent is to add several objects on top of one another to create the desired Stage appearance.

Under Windows 95, Director 6 only supports non-Direct to Stage playback when you develop and play back using a 32-bit projector (or authoring environment), and if you use AVI files. In all other cases, the Windows version of Director must play all video direct to the Stage. QuickTime for Windows can only play Direct to Stage.

✦ **Show Controller** — Check this option when you want to display a video controller like the one shown at the bottom of Figure 16-3. This controller lets the user play, pause, or step through a video clip and control the volume of the clip. While the video is playing, the Play button is replaced with a Pause button. This option is only available when video is played Direct to Stage and if you are using QuickTime (Macintosh or Windows).

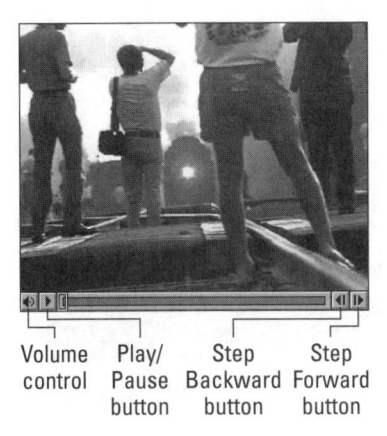

Figure 16-3: Digital video clip with the controller enabled

Volume control | Play/Pause button | Step Backward button | Step Forward button

Synchronization and frame rate settings

The Video options in the Digital Video Cast Member Properties dialog determine how the movie is synchronized. These options are only available when you select the Direct to Stage option:

✦ **Sync to SoundTrack** — Plays the sound while dropping frames as needed.

✦ **Play Every Frame** *(No Sound)* — Plays every frame of the movie but sound is disabled. This method guarantees that every frame of a video clip plays just as every frame in a Director movie plays. Without using this setting frames are "dropped" to maintain sound quality.

In the Rate boxes, you establish the rate at which the digital video sprite (not the Director movie) will play. This option is only available when you select Play Every Frame as the Video synchronization option. Rate field choices include

- **Normal** — Plays the digital video cast member at its normal rate (no frames are dropped).
- **Maximum** — Plays the digital video cast member as fast as possible while still playing every frame.
- **Fixed** — Plays the digital video cast member at a fixed rate, which you establish by entering a setting in the adjacent fps (frames per second) field. This option is used when you want every frame in a digital video played at the same rate.

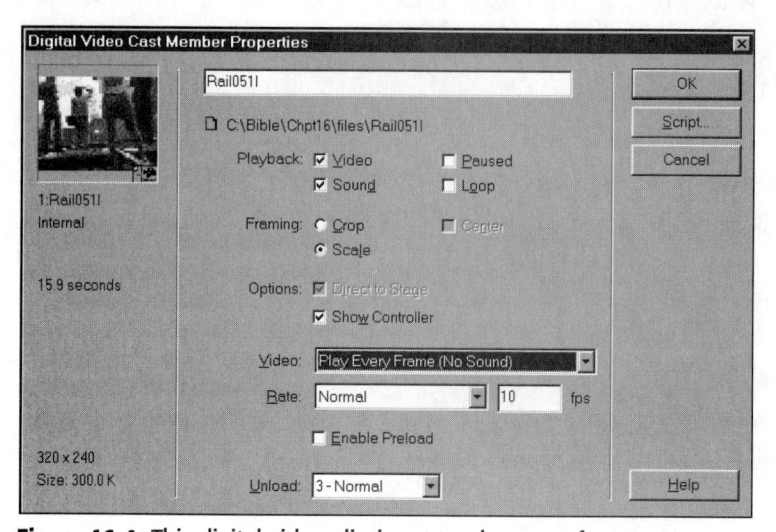

Figure 16-4: This digital video clip is set to play every frame.

Preloading and unloading a digital video cast member

The Enable Preload check box in the Digital Video Cast Member Properties dialog determines whether a digital video cast member can be preloaded into working memory (using the `preLoad` and `preLoadMember` Lingo commands), or that the file is read from disk during playback. If the Enable Preload option is selected (and you use Lingo to preload the cast member), Director will read as much of the video into memory as possible (constrained only by available RAM) and then will play the movie from memory. If you don't enable this option, the external video file will be read from disk frame by frame as the video plays. The `preLoad` and `preLoadMember` commands were discussed in Chapter 15.

What are the results of preloading a video clip?

- ✦ A potential increase in playback speed because frames don't have to be read from disk one at a time
- ✦ Fewer dropped frames
- ✦ Smoother video playback

The Unload field, at the bottom of the Properties dialog, determines when a cast member is removed from working memory. The options (Normal, Next, Last, and Never) are identical to the options available for other types of cast members.

Placing and playing a digital video cast member

The third step in using video in your Director movie is to place it on the Stage and play it. Placing a digital video cast member is no different from placing any other cast member — you click and drag it to the desired location on the Stage.

You have three choices for including digital video in a movie. Beginning with the *least* efficient method, your options for including a digital video clip in a movie are as follows:

- ✦ Drag the digital video cast member to the Stage, and then copy the sprite to a sufficient number of frames so the clip plays to completion. Remember that a cast member dragged to the Stage spans 28 frames by default.

   This method is very inefficient. The "sufficient" number of frames will vary depending on the speed of your computer and the playback system. You're essentially mixing apples and oranges: placing a time-based asset (the digital video) in a frame-based technology (the Director movie). It's highly unlikely that the video will play completely in a predetermined number of frames on all playback systems, and you will use an enormous number of frames to play even a short video clip.

- ✦ Use minimal Lingo to play the movie in a single frame. You'll only need one command: the `go to the frame` handler.

- ✦ Use Lingo commands that are specific to digital video for the best control over the video cast member, including play, pause, rewind, play backwards, and other operations.

Playing a video sprite using minimal Lingo

The simplest method of playing video in a movie, which uses a minimal amount of Lingo, is to

1. Place the video cast member in the desired frame.
2. Establish the desired settings in the Digital Video Cast Member Properties dialog.

> **Note:** If you want the digital video to begin playing as soon as the playback head reaches the frame containing the video, be sure to *turn off* the Paused check box in the Playback options. When Paused is turned on, you will have to either use Lingo to play the video clip, or include the controller and instruct the user to click the Play button to start the video.

3. Add a frame script with a `go to the frame` handler in the same frame as the video sprite.
4. Play the movie.

Playing a video sprite using Lingo for greater control

Though there are a couple dozen properties associated with digital video cast members, you only need a handful of them to control video playback using Lingo. Let's take a look at the two properties you'll set most often to control video cast members: `the movieRate of sprite` property and `the movieTime of sprite` property. Then we'll see how to set `StartTime` and `StopTime`. After that, we'll examine all the Lingo commands for setting the same properties that you encounter in the Digital Video Cast Member Properties dialog.

Note that `the movieRate of sprite` and `the movieTime of sprite` properties are sprite properties, not cast member properties. Digital video is only played on the Stage, and once a cast member is dragged to the Stage, it is a sprite.

Using `the movieRate` property

`The movieRate of sprite` property handles the most basic video function: playing the video clip. With this property you can determine or set the video sprite's speed (normal, double-time, and so on) and the direction (forward or backward). When used in a `set` command statement, the syntax is

```
set the movieRate of sprite spriteNumber to speedAndDirection
```

The *spriteNumber* parameter is simply the channel that holds the video sprite. The *speedAndDirection* parameter does a bit more work than that; it establishes the direction and speed of the playback. If the *speedAndDirection* setting is a positive number, the video plays forward. A negative number plays the video backward. If *speedAndDirection* is 1, the video sprite plays at normal speed, 2 means double-speed, and so on.

In the following example, the video sprite in channel 5 plays forward at normal speed:

```
set the movieRate of sprite 5 to 1
```

The same video clip (in sprite channel 5) plays backward at double-speed if you issue the following command:

```
set the movieRate of sprite 5 to -2
```

The `movieRate` property can also be used to stop a movie — that is, to freeze it on the current frame. In the following example, the `on mouseUp` handler causes the currently playing video sprite (in channel 2) to stop on the current frame of the video:

```
on mouseUp
        set the movieRate of sprite 2 to 0
end
```

Caution

Director frames vs. video frames: Don't get these confused. Frames in Director and digital video are similar concepts, but not synonymous. Director is a frame-based authoring tool. Each item in each frame is drawn to the Stage before the playback head moves forward. Frames are never dropped to maintain playback speed. They determine which objects appear on the Stage at a specific point in time. Keep in mind that although digital video uses the concept of frames, it is in a time-based medium. By displaying a series of still images over time, the human eye *perceives* motion. Unless you indicate otherwise in an application like Director, digital video *does* drop (skip) frames in order to maintain the desired pace and synchronization with the sound track, if there is one.

Using the `movieTime` property

The `movieTime of sprite` property is used to pinpoint a specific instant in a movie. Because digital video is time based, the `movieTime` property sets or identifies frames based on the number of ticks that have elapsed since the beginning of the video clip. For example, a frame that is 5 seconds into the video would be identified as 60 (ticks per second) times 5 seconds, or 300 ticks into the clip.

To jump to a frame 5 seconds into the video (assuming the video sprite is in channel 5), you would use this statement:

```
set the movieTime of sprite 5 to 300
```

Note that programmers commonly write the preceding statement as

```
set the movieTime of sprite 5 to 5*60
```

This makes it easier to recognize that the target frame is 5 seconds (60 ticks per second) into the video clip. The results are the same, whether you use the expression 5*60 or the value 300.

One of the most useful functions of the `movieTime` property is to rewind a video clip to its beginning frame. The following statement rewinds the video sprite in channel 4 to the beginning of the video clip:

```
set the movieTime of sprite 4 to 0
```

Combining the time and rate properties

You can combine the `movieTime` and the `movieRate` properties in a single handler that both rewinds and replays a video clip. The `on mouseUp` handler is an example of this approach. In the following, it is attached to a cast member button that serves a dual function (rewind and replay):

```
on mouseUp
        set the movieTime of sprite videoClip to 0
        set the movieRate of sprite videoClip to 1
end
```

Using the `StartTime` and the `StopTime` properties

By using the `startTime of sprite` and the `stopTime of sprite` properties, you achieve even greater control over the playing of a video. These properties tell Director to start/stop playing a digital video sprite at the specified number of ticks into the movie.

When combined with the `movieRate` property, as shown in the following handler, you can instruct Director to play a very specific segment of the digital video and then stop. The following handler can be attached to a button that plays only a six-second video segment (from 120 ticks to 480 ticks into the digital video), in sprite channel 6, at normal forward playback speed:

```
on mouseUp
        set the startTime of sprite 6 to 2*60
        set the movieRate of sprite 6 to 1
        set the stopTime of sprite 6 to 8*60
        updateStage
end
```

Note: The `updateStage` command in this handler is not required if you are using a frame script that includes the `go to the frame` statement. As long as the playback head is recycling back to the current frame (and not trapped within it), the Stage is redrawn automatically.

Caution: Be sure to set the `startTime of sprite` property *before* the `movieRate of sprite` instruction starts the video playing. The `stopTime of sprite` instruction must be issued *after* the video is playing, as shown just above in the code for the handler.

Exercise: Adding digital video to a movie

In the upcoming exercise, you'll add digital video to a Director movie called beware.dir.

On the CD-ROM: The files beware.dir and mari0071.mov can be found on your companion CD-ROM in the exercise:ch16 (exercise\ch16) folder. You'll also be using the file mari0071.mov, stored in the goodies:4palms (goodies\4palms) folder. Before you begin this exercise, be sure to copy these two files to a folder on your local hard drive.

As currently constructed, the beware.dir movie includes a `go to the frame` script in the script channel for frame 1. It also includes four VCR-like buttons named Back, Rewind, Stop, and Play, plus a bitmap text cast member (Beware of Steep Drops...). The buttons, frame script, and text cast member are already added to the Stage and Score, respectively. These files are back.pct, rewind.pct, stop.pct, and play.pct and are on the CD-ROM in the exercise:ch16 (exercise\ch16) folder.

In the beware1.dir movie, you will add scripts to four buttons in order to provide a controller for the video. As an alternative, you could simply select the Show Controller check box in the Digital Video Cast Member Properties dialog box. However, this function works only with QuickTime or QuickTime for Windows. The option to display the video controller is not available when you work with Windows AVI files. Further, although you can use the built-in controller with QuickTime movies, you may want to use your own buttons instead. This provides greater control over the design of your movie's user interface.

Importing and Controlling Digital Video in a Movie

1. Open the beware.dir movie. As mentioned just above, you'll find all the files needed for this exercise on the CD in the exercise:ch16 (exercise\ch16) folder.

2. Be sure the mari007l.mov file is in the same folder on your workstation as the beware.dir movie.

3. Import mari007l.mov into the beware.dir movie. The video cast member should be in cast member slot 7.

4. Click the Cast Member Properties button to display the Digital Video Cast Member Properties dialog box. As shown in Figure 16-5, select the Paused check box in the Playback options.

5. Be sure the other settings match Figure 16-5, and then close the Properties dialog.

6. Drag the mari0071 video cast member to the Stage. It should be in sprite channel 6.

7. Shorten the duration of the digital video sprite so it spans only frame 1 in channel 6.

8. Position it so the top of the sprite is 115 pixels from the top of the Stage, and the left edge is 50 pixels from the left edge of the Stage.

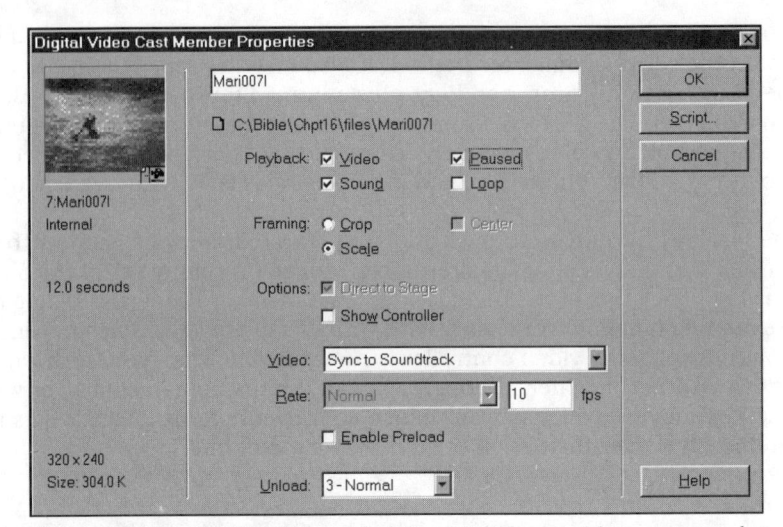

Figure 16-5: Properties dialog for the mari007l.mov video cast member

9. Attach the following scripts to the designated cast members. Notice that the following handlers do not require the use of the `updateStage` command because the frame script recycles through the current frame (which redraws the Stage). If you use digital video within a frame (and the playback head does not exit and reenter the frame) you would need to use the `updateStage` command to redraw the Stage and display the digital video clip.

The script for the Back button:

```
on mouseUp
    set the movieRate of sprite 6 to -1
end
```

The script for the Rewind button:

```
on mouseUp
    set the movieTime of sprite 6 to 0
end
```

The script for the Stop button:

```
on mouseUp
    set the movieRate of sprite 6 to 0
end
```

The script for the Play button:

```
on mouseUp
    set the movieRate of sprite 6 to 1
end
```

10. Save the movie as **beware1.dir,** rewind, and play it.

As you test the movie's buttons notice that the Play button plays the movie from the current frame forward, the Back button plays the movie in reverse, the Rewind button returns the movie to its first frame, and the Stop button pauses the movie on the current frame.

Some notes on button alignment

Aligning buttons on the Stage can be tricky. In the beware.dir movie, each of the buttons (Back, Rewind, Stop, and Play) are 35 x 35 pixels. After initially dragging the buttons to the Stage and visually placing them, we opened the Sprite Properties dialog to set each button's location from the left and top edges of the Stage. All buttons were fairly close to 400 pixels from the top of the Stage, so we set them to be exactly that distance from the top. The leftmost button appeared well placed at 400 pixels from the left edge of the Stage. So to leave a 5-pixel gap between each 35-pixel button, we placed the Back button at 400 pixels, the Rewind button at 440 pixels, the Stop (pause) button at 480 pixels, and the Forward button at 520 pixels from the left edge of the Stage. The main concern was to have the top of each button a uniform distance from the top of the Stage and to have a uniform gap between each button.

Digital videos from Four Palms

Three video clips from the Four Palms Royalty Free Digital Video Starter Kit are available on the CD-ROM in the goodies:fourpalm (goodies\fourpalm) folder. The video clips include brid063l "Approaching Royal Gorge Bridge" (2.94MB, 15 seconds), rail051l "Get Off The Tracks" (3.17MB, 16 seconds), and mari007l "Kayaker Going Over Falls" (2.36MB, 12 seconds). All three clips are copyright 1995 by Four Palms, Inc. and are used with permission.

In addition to Video for Windows versions of these clips, the Four Palms Royalty Free Digital Video Starter Kit contains QuickTime (Macintosh) versions. So that you can practice importing video into Director using these files, the AVI format files are on the CD, as well as a flattened QuickTime (.mov) version of each file that can be read by either the Macintosh or Windows version of Director.

Four Palms, Inc. offers royalty-free video in a variety of formats, including Windows AVI, Macintosh QuickTime, MPEG, and analog videotape. You can reach Four Palms at 11260 Roger Bacon Dr., Reston, VA 22090, phone 1-800-747-2567.

Using Lingo to Control Digital Video Properties

Most of the properties established on the Digital Video Cast Member Properties dialog box can also be set using Lingo. These properties can be set in frame or movie scripts as needed.

Setting the video of member property

Remember that even though you use a digital video clip, you don't have to display the video portion of the file. This can be helpful when you want to use a sound-only QuickTime movie in your project. To disable the display of video, use a statement like this:

```
set the video of member "MediaNews" to 0
```

To enable the display of video from a digital video cast member, use a statement like this:

```
set the video of member "MediaNews" to 1
```

The 1 and 0 values in the preceding examples can be replaced with `True` and `False`, respectively. This convention is consistent throughout Lingo. Using numeric values requires less typing, but the `True` and `False` keywords are more English-like and clearer to the casual Lingo reader. In the next two examples, we'll use these keywords.

Setting the sound of member property

Just as you might want to play a digital video clip without the video, you may want to skip the sound portion of the file and play only the video. The following statement disables the sound in a digital video cast member:

```
set the sound of member "NewsClip" to False
```

and this one enables the sound in a digital video cast member:

```
set the sound of member "NewsClip" to True
```

Pausing at the beginning of a video using Lingo

You can pause a digital video cast member on its first frame (which means you must use Lingo to play, rewind, and stop the video clip). This has the same effect as selecting the Paused check box option in the Digital Video Cast Member Properties dialog. Here's a statement that sets this property:

```
set the pausedAtStart of member "Talking Head" = True
```

and a statement that turns off the property:

```
set the pausedAtStart of member "Talking Head" = False
```

Setting the loop of member property

The following example statements show you how to cause a video clip to automatically loop and replay:

```
set the loop of member "Teaser" to True
```

and how to turn off the automatic looping of a video clip:

```
set the loop of member "Teaser" to False
```

Cropping and centering video using Lingo

The following statements show you how to enable a resized video clip to be cropped:

```
set the crop of member "NewsClip" to 1
```

and to disable the cropping of a resized video clip:

```
set the crop of member "NewsClip" to 0
```

To center a cropped video clip within its resized bounding box, use a statement like this:

```
set the center of member "MoreNews" to True
```

To disable this centering for the cropped video clip, use a statement like this:

```
set the center of member "MoreNews" to False
```

Playing a video direct to the Stage using Lingo

When working with QuickTime video on a Macintosh computer system, you can cause the digital video to be displayed direct to the Stage. In the following statement, we do this with a QuickTime video named "JumpStart":

```
set the directToStage of member "JumpStart" to True
```

And here's the statement to turn off this property:

```
set the directToStage of member "JumpStart" to 0
```

Remember, digital video on a Windows system is always displayed direct to the Stage, unless you are running the Windows 95 version of Director in a 32-bit environment.

Displaying a controller using Lingo

You can use Lingo to display or hide a controller when using QuickTime movies on either the Windows or Macintosh operating system. To display the digital video controller:

```
set the controller of member "Ceremony" to True
```

To hide the digital video controller:

```
set the controller of member "Ceremony" to False
```

Note If you try to set `the controller of member` property for a Video for Windows movie, a False condition is returned. Setting this property for an AVI movie has no effect.

Establishing the frame rate for digital video using Lingo

`The frame rate of member` property establishes the frame rate at which a digital video cast member plays. The settings you establish with this property correspond to the settings in the Rate and fps boxes in the Digital Video Cast Member Properties dialog. These settings are only available if you elect to play every frame, as opposed to selecting the Sync to SoundTrack option. When the Rate field is set to Fixed, Director uses the value in the fps field to establish the frame rate.

To set these values using Lingo, you can use a statement like this:

```
set the frameRate of member "Graduation" to 30
```

When you set the frame rate to a value between 0 and 255, Director equates this with a Fixed setting in the Rate field and assumes the numeric value is for frames per second. Although `the frameRate of member` property can range all the way to 255, in most cases you will only use values in the 10-to-30 fps range.

You can also use `the frameRate of member` property to simulate the selection of the Normal rate setting in the cast member's Properties dialog by using the following statement:

```
set the frameRate of member "Graduation" to -1
```

Another option is to use `the frameRate of member` property to simulate the Maximum rate setting in the Properties dialog, which plays every frame as fast as possible, by using the following statement:

```
set the frameRate of member "Graduation" to -2
```

Enabling the preload of video using Lingo

The following statement enables a video clip to be preloaded into memory:

```
set the preLoad of member "Remodeling" to True
```

and this statement disables the preload:

```
set the preLoad of member "Remodeling" to 0
```

Using Lingo to Create Other Controls

The controller that you created for the beware.dir movie handles most standard video control functions. On occasion, you may want to provide additional controls for volume, stepping forward and backward, and fast forward. Handlers for each of these functions can be attached to a cast member such as a button or other object that serves as part of your movie's control panel.

Setting the volume

Digital video uses `the volume of sprite` property to control the sound level of the sound track. This property is similar to `the volume of sound` property that was introduced and explained in Chapter 15.

You can set the volume of sprite to any value between –256 and 256, but any value lower than 0 mutes the sound. The following statement sets the volume at its highest level:

```
set the volume of sprite 6 to 256
```

The following statement sets the volume to mute (no sound):

```
set the volume of sprite 6 to 0
```

Adding step-forward and step-backward controls

The handlers required to create step-forward and step-backward controls are very similar. Both use `the movieTime` property and add or subtract a specified number of ticks to the current playback location within the movie.

In the following handler, the current frame is evaluated based on the location of the playback head. The value returned by `the movieTime` property is the number of ticks since the start of the movie. This example assumes a playback speed of 15 fps. Because each second is equal to 60 ticks, 4 ticks are required to move forward one frame. If your digital video plays at 30 fps, it takes two ticks (2/60th of a second) to move the movie forward one frame.

```
on mouseUp
     set the movieTime of sprite 6 to (the movieTime of¬
sprite 6) +4
end
```

This handler does the following:

- Determines the number of ticks since the start of the movie — `the movieTime of sprite 6`
- Adds 4 ticks to that value — `(the movieTime of sprite 6) +4`
- Sets `the movieTime` property to be equal to the new value (current ticks plus 4)

To create a step-backward control, you need to make one small change: Decrease the number of ticks by four, as shown here:

```
on mouseUp
     set the movieTime of sprite 6 to (the movieTime of¬
sprite 6) -4
end
```

The number of variations on these two handlers is near infinite. For instance, rather than forwarding frame by frame, you could rewind or forward by one second (60 ticks). The following handler would accomplish this task:

```
on mouseUp
     set the movieTime of sprite 6 to (the movieTime of¬
sprite 6) +60
end
```

Creating a fast-forward control

You can create a fast-forward button using `the movieRate` property. The following handler can be attached to an object (button) that will cause the digital video sprite to play forward at triple the normal forward speed.

```
On mouseUp
     set the movieRate of sprite 6 to 3
end
```

> **Note:** Always include a button or control that resets the playback speed back to normal. The following instruction can accomplish this task:
>
> ```
> set the movieRate of sprite x to 1
> ```

Now that you've seen examples of all these Lingo commands for working with digital videos, let's put them to work. Based on your reading in Chapter 12, you know how to use the `rollOver` function to determine which sprite the mouse pointer is currently over. With that information, you can tell Director to play a specific digital sound clip when the mouse pointer rests over a specific sprite on the Stage. The same technique can be used to play a specific digital video clip.

> **On the CD-ROM:** The file bend.dir and two digital video clips used in the following exercise are on your companion CD-ROM in the exercise:ch16 (exercise\ch16) folder. The movie includes two linked video clips (brid063l.mov and rail051l.mov). Both clips are included by permission and are also available in the goodies:4palms (goodies\4palms) folder on the companion CD. (See earlier sidebar on Four Palms.)

Using Rollovers to Activate Video in a Movie

1. Be sure the bend.dir movie and the two video clips (brid063l.mov and rail051l.mov) are in the same folder on your hard drive.

2. Open the bend.dir movie in Director.

3. In the following steps, you'll add two scripts to the cast to enable the `rollOver` function in the movie. Select cast member slot 2 in the Cast window, open the Script window, and add the following frame script to the movie. (You can omit the comment lines.)

   ```
   on exitFrame
        whichVideo --this calls a user-defined handler that
         --determines which video sprite the mouse cursor is over
        go to the frame
   end
   ```

4. Click the Script window's Cast Member Properties button and set the Type setting to Score (you do not want to create a movie script). Click OK to close the Properties dialog and then close the Script window.

5. The new script cast member (2) should automatically appear in the script channel of frame 1. If not, drag it to frame 1.

6. Add the following movie script as cast member 3 to the movie (again, you can omit the comment lines). This new movie script contains the user-defined handler: `whichVideo`. Within the handler, the value of `currentVideo` varies between 2 and 3, because those are the sprite channels containing the digital video sprites.

```
on whichVideo
     repeat with currentVideo = 2 to 3
          if rollover (currentVideo) then
               set the movieRate of sprite currentVideo¬
               to 1
-- The following statement places a numeric value in the¬
SecondsInto field. The value
-- indicates how much of the video (in seconds) has played.¬
As you rollover the two video sprites,
-- the value represents the seconds elapsed for that sprite.
               put     (the    movieTime    of    sprite¬
                    currentVideo)/60 into field "SecondsInto"
--The SecondsInto field is displayed at the bottom right cor¬
ner of the Stage when the movie plays.
               updateStage
          else
               set the movieRate of sprite currentVideo¬
               to 0
          end if
     end repeat
end
```

7. Close the Script window, save the movie as **bend1.dir,** rewind, and play it.

8. Move the mouse pointer over each of the two video display areas and watch the reaction. When you're done experimenting, stop the movie.

Depending on the speed of your computer, there may be a short delay before each video starts (as you move the mouse pointer to trigger a new video clip). Depending on the amount of RAM available on your playback system (and what is already in memory), each time the mouse cursor moves from one sprite to the other, Director may need to reload one of the video clips into memory.

By using the `rollOver` function and combining it with `the movieTime` and `the movieRate` properties, you have created a video controller that plays, stops, rewinds, steps forward, steps back, and fast forwards without a mouse click!

In the beware.dir movie you worked with earlier in this chapter, you used Lingo to control the playback of a digital video cast member using scripts attached to a series of buttons. In that case, the playback head continued cycling through the same frame. Now let's look at the situation where you want something to occur after the digital video clip finishes playing.

In the following example, you'll cause the playback head to cycle on a specific frame while the video cast member is paused (so the buttons can be used). When the user clicks to start the digital video, the playback head continues to loop on the current frame until the video finishes playing. When finished, the playback head jumps to the "Text" label. You'll use the Paused option in the Digital Video Cast Member Properties dialog to make the video pause and wait for user interaction. (You can also use the `pausedAtStart` property in a handler to accomplish the same task.)

The script that you add to the movie in this exercise causes Director to test and determine whether the current `the movieTime of sprite` property returns a value that is greater than the value returned by `the duration of member` property. As long as this is so (the expression tests True), the playback head will loop back to the same frame. When the expression no longer tests True, the playback head moves to the marker "Text." You can also cause the playback head to jump to the next frame (`go to the frame +1`), a designated frame (`go to frame 100`), or another movie (`go to movie "Glossary"`).

Caution

The `movieTime of sprite` property returns a value that indicates how much time (in ticks) has elapsed since the video sprite began playing. When you use this property, you need to reference *the sprite channel*. The `duration of member` property, on the other hand, returns a value determined by the length (in ticks) of the video cast member. When using this property, you must reference the *cast member name* or *number*. Don't get these two mixed up.

On the CD-ROM

The file bewarex.dir is on your companion CD-ROM in the exercise:ch16 (exercise\ch16) folder.

Jumping to a New Frame After the Video Ends

1. Be sure both the bewarex.dir and the mari007l.mov digital video files are in the same folder on your local hard drive.

2. Open the bewarex.dir movie in Director, and add the following frame script into the script channel of frame 1:

   ```
   on exitFrame
       if the movieTime of sprite 6 < the duration of member¬
   7 then
           go to the frame
       else
           go to "Text"
       end if
   end
   ```

3. Select the Mari007l cast member and then open the Digital Video Cast Member Properties dialog box. In the Playback options section, select the Paused check box. Unless you turn on the Paused option, the movie begins to play immediately. You want the video clip to pause until the user clicks the Play button.

4. Save the movie again as **bewarex1.dir,** rewind, and test it. The digital video clip plays once (after you click the Play button). When it's done, the playback head jumps to frame 5.

5. Stop the movie, open the Properties dialog again, and turn off the Paused option.

6. Save the movie again as bewarex1.dir, rewind, and test it again to see what happens.

Getting rid of annoying artifacts

As you played the bewarex1.dir in the preceding exercise, you probably noticed that when the bitmap text cast member appears in frame 5, a portion of the video image "persists" on the Stage. This persistence is associated with the Direct to Stage property. The image you see is an *artifact* (a leftover, unwanted image), and it's annoying and frustrating if you don't understand why it's there and how to remove it.

When Director plays a digital video clip direct to the Stage, control of that area of the Stage is handed to QuickTime or Video for Windows. Simply including the `updateStage` command or jumping to another frame without the video clip is not enough to effectively obliterate the artifact. Director does not control that area and so does not realize that it needs to be "redrawn."

One way to eliminate the artifact and enable Director to regain control of that area of the Stage is to reset the Stage color to the current Stage color, which causes Director to overwrite the entire Stage area. In the bewarex1.dir movie, you can accomplish this task using the `set the stageColor` instruction.

Three additional methods can be employed to eliminate the video artifact from the Stage after a video sprite finishes playing:

+ Create one or more objects that overwrite the area previously used by the digital video clip. The objects are placed in the frame that plays immediately after the video clip finishes.

> **Tip**
> For instance, you can use the Tool Palette to create a hollow rectangular object that is slightly larger than the display area of the video clip, change the object's ink to Matte or Transparent, and then position it in the area where the artifact appears. The object is placed in the frame that plays immediately after the video clip finishes, not in the same frame as the digital video clip.

- Attach a full-Stage transition to the frame that plays immediately after the digital video clip. Ideally, you want to make the transition occur quickly (set a minimum transition time) and use large areas of the Stage (set the chunk size to maximum).
- Create a handler that sets the visible of the sprite property (of the digital video) to invisible *or* moves the visible sprite off Stage. In either case, be sure to include an updateStage command.

In the following steps, you'll eliminate the video artifact on the Stage by resetting the Stage color using Lingo.

Removing Video Artifacts from the Stage

1. Open the bewarex1.dir movie in Director. You'll need the movie you modified in the preceding exercise, or the file bewarex1.dir from the CD-ROM in the exercise:ch16 (exercise\ch16) folder.
2. Rename the digital video cast member to **Kayake**.
3. Edit the frame script in cast member slot 1 to match the following:

```
on exitFrame
     -- In the next instruction, change member number (7)
to member name ("Kayake")
     if the movieTime of sprite 6 < the duration of member¬
"Kayake" then
          go to the frame
     else
          go to "Text"
          -- This is the instruction to add. set the
stageColor to the stageColor
     end if
end
```

4. Save the movie as **bewarex2.dir,** rewind, and test it.

From Director to Digital Video

Use the File ⇨ Export command to export your movies. You can export a Director movie in Video for Windows format using Director for Windows, or in QuickTime format using Director for the Macintosh.

Tip: The Macintosh version of Director 6 can export a movie as a QuickTime movie, a series of PICS or PICT images, or it can export to the Scrapbook. The Windows version can export as an AVI file or as a DIB file sequence (a series of bitmap images).

Advantages: Exporting a Director movie to digital video can be helpful if you want to

- Import your Director movie into another application that supports the import of digital video but not Director movies
- Export your Director movie to videotape
- Export your Director movie as a sound-only QuickTime movie (Macintosh only)

Note: The Windows version of Director is purported to gain the ability to export in QuickTime format as soon as QuickTime for Windows 3.0 is released. The release (originally announced in April 1997) is rumored to be imminent.

- Take advantage of digital video's frame-dropping capability in order to synchronize sound and animation in your application.
- Export the Director animation so it can be imported into another Director movie as a digital video sequence. A digital video clip is a single cast member, whereas the same animation sequence in Director can require numerous cast members. It is more efficient to load a single cast member than multiple cast members in Director. Furthermore, you have tighter control over the playback of digital video in Director by using Lingo and the settings of the Digital Video Cast Member Properties dialog box.

Disadvantages: The shortcomings of exporting a Director movie to digital video (either QuickTime or Video for Windows) include the following:

- Loss of interactivity (actions scripted in cast member, sprite, and frame scripts are lost).

Tip:
- The possible loss of transitions between frames. Many of the transitions used by Director do not export at all, and others fail to export depending on the Duration and Smoothness settings. You can try to increase these settings if transitions are lost. If you lose transitions, use a video editing program such as Adobe Premiere to add transitions back into the video.
- Loss of sound if exporting to the AVI format under Windows.

Exporting Director movies to digital video

When you select the File ⇨ Export command, the Export dialog box shown in Figure 16-6 appears.

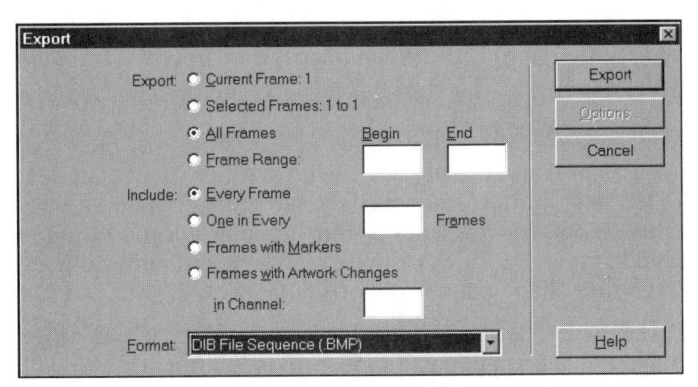

Figure 16-6: Export dialog box (for Windows users)

The items in the Windows and Macintosh dialog boxes for exporting differ slightly, but the information you must enter is roughly the same. On either platform, before the export occurs, you must indicate the following information in the Export dialog appropriate for your system:

- ✦ The range of frames in the movie that you want to export. You can export a single frame, all frames in the movie, or a range of sequential frames.

- ✦ The interval between each frame that you want included in the export. For example, you can specify that you want every frame, frames with markers, or only frames with artwork changes exported. You can also specify that you want all frames between a set interval dropped — for instance, you might want to export only every tenth frame. If you select the Frames with Artwork Changes option, frames are exported only when the artwork changes in the channel you specify.

- ✦ The file format desired for the exported file (QuickTime, AVI, BMP, PICT or PICS).

Additionally, when you want to export your movie to QuickTime format (only available using the Macintosh version of Director) or AVI format (only available using the Windows version of Director), you'll need to select the Options button in the Export dialog.

QuickTime export options

The QuickTime Options dialog (Figure 16-7) offers the following settings:

- ✦ **Frame Rate** — Determines whether the video created by the export uses the Tempo channel settings (Tempo Settings) or creates video frames to match the performance of your movie as it plays in Director (Real Time). This setting is only available when exporting to QuickTime.

- ✦ **Compressor** — Select the compressor for use in reducing the file size. (See Caution later in this section.)

♦ **Quality** — Move the slide bar to set the video quality from Low to High. The higher the quality you select for the video image, the larger the file will be. The reverse is also true.

♦ **Color Depth** — Select the color depth (QuickTime only).

♦ **Scale** — Here you establish the scale or resizing settings (QuickTime only). If you click the Scale radio button and specify a percentage, the Stage is kept proportional when exported to a digital video. If you select the Pixel radio button (identified in Figure 16-7), depending on the height and width values you select, the movie's shape may be distorted or warped.

♦ **Sound** — Mark one or both sound channels to export (QuickTime only). Note that you can only export embedded sounds into digital movies.

Tip   If your Director movie has a Stage size of 640 x 480 pixels or larger, you may want to use the Scale option to reduce the size of the exported QuickTime video. Large movies require the lion's share of your system's resources to play. In addition, if the area of the video is too large, there may not be room for the controller — which means users cannot control the playing of the video on the movie's Stage.

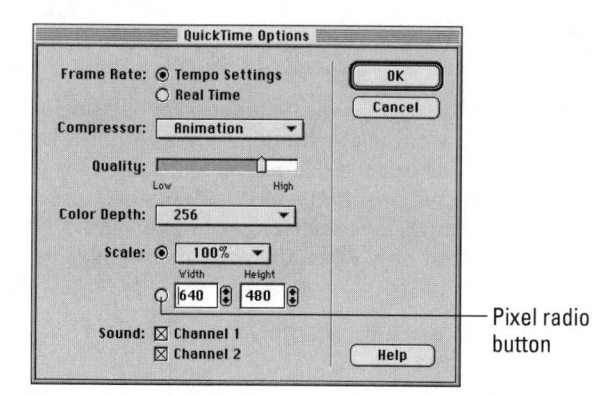

Figure 16-7: Options for exporting to QuickTime

Once you have established all the desired options, click OK to return to the Export dialog box. Click the Export button, assign a filename to the exported file in the Save As dialog box, and click the Save button.

Windows export options

When you're using the Windows version of Director, clicking the Options button in the Export dialog produces only one option: the frame rate for the digital video. Once you specify this, you return to the Export dialog. After clicking the Export button and stipulating the desired filename, you see the Video Compression dialog box (Figure 16-8).

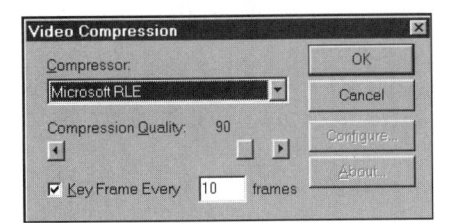

Figure 16-8: Video compression in Director for Windows

In the Video Compression dialog box, select one of these codecs:

- ✦ CinePak Codec by Radius
- ✦ Intel Indeo R3.2
- ✦ Microsoft Video 1
- ✦ Microsoft RLE
- ✦ Intel Indeo Video Raw [16]
- ✦ Full Frames Uncompressed

Note: Depending on the device drives and peripherals installed on your Windows system, you may find other compression options in this list, including the ATI RLE Video Compressor [16].

The Compression Quality slider lets you select a value from 0 (low quality) to 100 (high quality). The higher the quality for the video image, the larger the file will be. The reverse is also true.

You can also choose the location of keyframes. Mark the check box and enter a number of frames.

Once you click the OK button, the export occurs.

Caution: The export and compression of a digital movie — whether for Windows or Macintosh — is not instantaneous. Be prepared to wait. Depending on the codec used, it may take several minutes to export even a small Director movie (with a limited number of sprites and frames).

Digital Video for Cross-Platform Projects

More and more programmers develop for a cross-platform environment; that is, they want their products to run on both Macintosh and Windows systems. If you plan to develop Director movies for cross-platform distribution, you'll want to stick to QuickTime digital video for your movies.

To make QuickTime videos deliverable across platforms (Macintosh, Windows, and Internet), they must be

✦ Flattened

✦ Prepared for cross-platform use

Flattening QuickTime movies for playback on Windows

When you *flatten* a QuickTime movie, you make it self-contained. QuickTime on the Macintosh supports files that allow dependencies; that is, they reference data stored outside the movie file. When you flatten a QT movie, you consolidate all of its audio, video, and other media elements into a single file.

To make a QT movie cross-platform, you must save it using the Playable On Non-Apple Computers option. This option, in the QuickTime MoviePlayer utility's Save As dialog box, combines the movie's resource fork with its data fork so that other platforms (such as Windows) can read the data.

Your Mac will still be able to read the QT file after you flatten it and make it playable on non-Apple computers.

Following is a summary of the steps to prepare your QuickTime movie for cross-platform use:

1. Open the QuickTime movie on the Macintosh, using the MoviePlayer applet. (MoviePlayer is probably stored on your hard drive in a QuickTime folder.)
2. Select the File ➪ Save As command.
3. At the bottom of the dialog (see Figure 16-9), turn on the Make Movie Self-Contained option, and check the Playable on Non-Apple Computers check box. Then click the Save button.

A tool to improve QuickTime

Using the MoviePlayer utility, you can flatten only one QuickTime movie at a time. However, you can use third-party tools such as Media Cleaner Pro 2.0, a dedicated QuickTime MacOS production tool by Terran Interactive, Inc., to batch flatten, optimize, and compress your movies for desktop playback. With Media Cleaner Pro (formerly called Movie Cleaner Pro) you can preprocess and compress your movies using any of the available QuickTime codecs. A full-featured demo of Media Cleaner Pro 2.0 (Macintosh only) is available in the goodies:terran folder on this book's companion CD, or you can contact Terran Interactive, Inc., at 2 North First Street, Suite 215, San Jose, CA 95113, phone 800-577-3443. Terran's Web site is at

http://www.terran-int.com

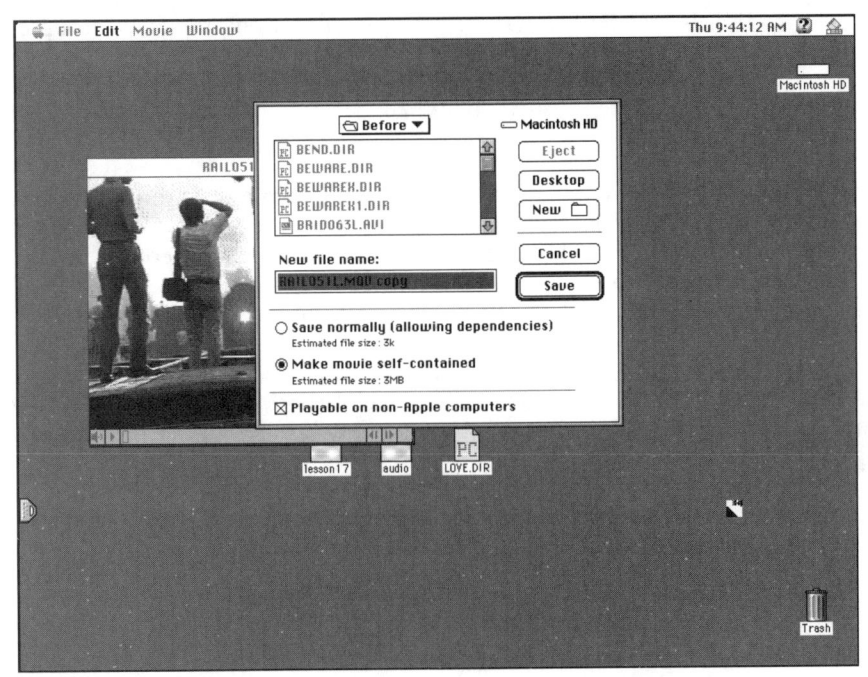

Figure 16-9: Flattening a video, using MoviePlayer's Save As dialog box

When creating a cross-platform digital video clip, it is wise to test it on a variety of Windows-based systems (386, 486, and Pentium; Windows 3.1, 3.11, and 95) and on several Macintosh systems (LC to Quadra to PowerMac). Cross-platform projects and assets should be tested on an actual PC, not on a Macintosh running a Windows emulation.

Tip

In the unlikely event you haven't picked up this tidbit of wisdom earlier in this book, here's one more reminder: Test early, test often, and test on *all* target systems. Digital videos developed for cross-platform projects are no exception. Test them early and often.

Converting digital video between QuickTime and AVI

At some point, you may want to convert digital video files from one format (such as Video for Windows) to another format (such as QuickTime). Numerous shareware, freeware, and commercial utilities are available to convert from QuickTime (.mov) files to Video for Windows (.avi) files.

Intel's SmartVid: The Windows-based SmartVid utility from Intel converts .avi files to .mov files and vice versa. However, SmartVid does not reinterleave the audio and video tracks in a movie. This utility is available at Intel's World Wide Web site at

```
http://www.intel.com/pc-supp/multimed/indeo/smartvid.htm
```

Microsoft's Utilities for Mac Users: Microsoft Corporation provides a group of Video for Windows version 1.1 utilities for Macintosh users at

    ftp://ftp.microsoft.com/developr/drg/Multimedia/Jumpstart/VfW11-Mac/

When you download these Mac utilities, be sure to obtain both the readme.txt file and the vfw11.sit file (in Mac StuffIt format). The readme.txt file includes installation instructions and hints for creating AVI files for later conversion to QuickTime. The Microsoft utilities enable you to convert an AVI file to the QuickTime environment (and vice versa) on a Macintosh running System 7 and QuickTime 1.5 or higher.

> **Note**
>
> The conversion from AVI file format to the Macintosh does not alter the source file's data. Instead, it adds a resource fork, so that AVI files can be recognized by the QuickTime environment.

The Windows-based run-time version of Video for Windows is available at the following ftp site:

    ftp://ftp.microsoft.com/softlib/mslfiles/WV1160.EXE

Horizons Technology: Available from Horizons Technology are the Power!Video Movie Translator that converts .avi files to .mov files and vice versa. The translators can be downloaded and purchased on the Web at

    http://www.horizons.com

Follow the link to Video Compression Services and Products. Power!Video Movie Translators work with most codecs, including Cinepak, TrueMotion-S, Indeo, and Power!Video. Information at the Horizons Technology Web site includes a list of additional digital video tools available from the company.

> **Tip**
>
> You can locate additional information on currently available codecs at Codec Central, a site sponsored by Terran Interactive. Point your browser at
>
>   http://www.terran-int.com/CodecCentral/

Adobe Premiere: Versions 4.2 and higher support the conversion of .avi to .mov or the reverse.

Don't forget that Media Cleaner Pro is available on the companion CD in the goodies:terran folder. It's a reg-ware utility (you only need to register to use the product) from Terran Interactive; see the sidebar, "A tool to improve QuickTime." These tools can be used to compress QuickTime video for playback from CD-ROM, the Web, and so on.

Other new tools are constantly surfacing that can improve compression and assist with creating cross-platform QuickTime movies. To visit one of the best sites for current QuickTime news (updated weekly), go to

    http://www.bmug.org/Services/qt/

This is the location of "Judy's and Robert's Little QuickTime Page" hosted at the Boston Multimedia Users Group (BMUG) site.

Other Resources for Digital Video Information

The Internet includes numerous excellent resources covering current developments related to digital video. Favorites of many are the digital video and QuickTime electronic mailing lists (sometimes referred to as list servers). As a subscriber to an electronic mailing list, you get a copy of any e-mail sent to the list. Likewise, if you send a message to the list, it goes to everyone subscribed to the list. The activity on some of these lists gets pretty heavy, so be prepared for a drastic increase in the mail hitting your mailbox. Also, an electronic mailing list to which you subscribe may be very active for a while and then drop to minimal activity. Or the reverse can be true. Expect anything.

Tip It's a good idea to save the welcome message that arrives shortly after you subscribe to a list. The message usually includes instructions on how to send mail to the list, how to unsubscribe if it doesn't meet your needs, how to switch to Digest mode (all messages arrive in a single daily message in your mailbox), and other information that you should review before participating in the list's discussion.

For QuickTime developers, an excellent list is QUICKTIME-DEV. To subscribe, go to

    http://www.lists.apple.com/quicktime-dev.html

Select the "How to subscribe to the lists" link, and follow the on-screen directions. If the Web page registration doesn't work, send a message to majordomo@public.lists.apple.com. Leave the subject line blank and in the body of the message, type **Subscribe QUICKTIME-DEV**. Whether you subscribe using the Web or an e-mail message, you will receive an e-mail confirmation that you must answer before your subscription is complete.

Another list that carries just QuickTime-related announcements is QUICKTIME-ANNOUNCE. To subscribe, go to

    http://www.lists.apple.com/Quicktime-Announce.html

Select the "How to subscribe to the lists" link, and follow the on-screen directions. If the Web page registration doesn't work, send a message to majordomo@public.lists.apple.com. Leave the subject line blank and in the body of the message, type **Subscribe QUICKTIME-ANNOUNCE**. Whether you subscribe using the Web or an e-mail message, you will receive an e-mail confirmation that you must answer before your subscription is complete.

QUICKTIME-ANNOUNCE is a moderated announcement-only list, meaning that it is used primarily by Apple to broadcast announcements regarding new Apple software releases (QuickTime for Macintosh, QuickTime for Windows, QuickTime VR, QuickTime plug-ins, and so on). You can send an announcement to

Quicktime-Announce-Moderator@public.lists.apple.com

for possible distribution to the entire list, but your message will first be reviewed by the list owner for relevance and appropriateness.

For digital video, check out DIGVID-L. To subscribe, send a message to listproc@ucdavis.edu. Leave the subject line blank and in the body of the message, type **Subscribe DIGVID-L** followed by your first and last name.

Closing Thoughts on Digital Video

You have learned a lot about incorporating digital video into your Director movies, but there is always more to learn. The following tips will be useful as you continue to explore:

- ✦ We often use removable cartridges (Syquest, Jaz, or Zip) to store large digital video files and transfer them between platforms.

- ✦ One of the most useful tools on the Windows side is DataViz's MacOpener for Windows. It assists in the reading, writing, and formatting of Macintosh disks and cartridges on the PC. The current version of MacOpener supports 1.44MB floppy disks, CD-ROMs, optical disks, plus Syquest, Bernoulli, Jaz, and Zip cartridges.

- ✦ DataViz's counterpart is PC Exchange for Macintosh users. It helps you to format, read, and write to and from Windows/DOS media.

- ✦ You can view digital video cast members using the Video window in Director. To open the Video window, double-click the digital video cast member and select Video ⇨ Window or press Command+9 (Ctrl+9).

Summary

Before moving on to Chapter 17's discussion of linear and property lists, let's review some of the things you learned in this chapter about Lingo commands for digital video:

- ✦ You can import and control the playback of digital video in a Director movie, but you cannot embed video in your Director movie. Digital video is always a linked external asset.
- ✦ You can build a custom controller for your video sprite rather than using the default QuickTime controller.
- ✦ You can use Lingo rollovers to control the playback of digital video.
- ✦ When a digital video clip plays in Direct to Stage mode, it will leave a video artifact that persists on the Stage. You can eliminate the artifact by changing the Stage color to the current Stage color using Lingo.
- ✦ You can export an animation from Director as a digital video clip.
- ✦ Numerous utilities exist for converting digital video between the two primary formats: QuickTime and Video for Windows.

✦ ✦ ✦

Behavioral Science

PART IV

In This Part

Chapter 17
Linear Lists and Property Lists

Chapter 18
Parent Scripts and Child Objects

Chapter 19
Xtras and File Manipulation

Chapter 20
Lingo Troubleshooting

Chapter 21
Movies in a Window (MIAWs)

Chapter 22
In Your Interface: Menus and Dialogs

Chapter 23
Designing for Memory Management

Linear Lists and Property Lists

CHAPTER 17

In This Chapter

Working with linear lists

Working with property lists

Creating a menu using a list

Sometimes the data you manage in a movie doesn't fit into a neat single value or string, but instead must be stored and manipulated as a collection of objects. Lingo responds to this need with *lists*. From collections of numbers to collections of windows and objects, the list is a tool for working with aggregate information. In this chapter, you learn how to build both linear and property lists and how lists can be useful when constructing a movie.

Using Lists

Lists are complex data structures that can store more than one piece of data per variable and treat the entire collection as a single item. If you have ever sorted mail in an office, you quickly learned to place and retrieve mail based on its position within the rows of mailboxes. In a similar fashion, you store and retrieve data in a list based on the data's position within the container (and we call the container a *variable*).

Lingo supports four types of lists:

- ✦ Unsorted linear list
- ✦ Sorted linear list
- ✦ Unsorted property list
- ✦ Sorted property list

Note Lists are valuable when you need to create an undetermined number of variables while the movie runs. Unlike variables that can hold only a single value or string at one time, lists are by definition variables that can store multiple values or strings at the same time.

You can add an item to a list, retrieve an item from a given position in the list, delete an item in a list, and even step through the list one item at a time. The list is actually one of the more useful structures in programming, because it provides a way to put items in order, to transport a lot of items at once, and to treat all the items within the list in a similar fashion without establishing a separate variable for each item individually.

A list can hold any data type that a simple variable can — an integer, a string, a reference to a cast member, even another list. There is nothing that says you can't have items of different data types within a list, although in practice you probably won't run into a lot of lists that have disparate data.

What Is a Linear List?

Like other variables, a list must have a name and must be initialized either with or without data. You declare or initialize a list when you use it. Two forms can be used to declare a linear list. The more common syntax is to use the `set` command:

```
set NameOfTheList to [item1, item2, item3...]
```

NameOfTheList is replaced with the list's name; and *item1*, *item2*, and so on, are replaced with the data that you want stored in the list. The square brackets signal to Director that the enclosed data is a list.

The other method of declaring a linear list, less frequently used, is

```
set NameOfTheList = list(item1, item2, item3...)
```

This second method uses the `list` keyword to clearly identify the data within the parentheses as a list.

Note

The first syntax saves keystrokes, but it assumes that whoever reviews your code will recognize the square brackets as defining a list of data.

In the following example, you initialize (create) a linear list with four entries:

```
set products to ["motherboard", "chip set", "keyboard", "mouse"]
```

You could accomplish the same task using any of the following instructions:

```
set products = ["motherboard", "chip set", "keyboard", "mouse"]
set products to list("motherboard", "chip set", "keyboard",¬
"mouse")
```

```
set products = list("motherboard", "chip set", "keyboard",¬
"mouse")
```

In addition to strings, lists can include values, as in

```
set playerScores to [50, 27, 33, 66]
```

To initialize an empty linear list (playerScores), you can use the `set` command as demonstrated here:

```
set products to []
```

Tip: The best place to initialize a list is in the `on startMovie` script.

Understanding the List-Related Commands

Lingo offers several commands to manage and manipulate data within lists. They enable you to

- Add data at the beginning of or at a specific location in a list
- Append data at the end of a list
- Remove data from a list
- Access data from a specific location in a list
- Edit data stored in a list
- Sort data in a list
- Count the number of data items in a list

Keep in mind the following rules about list commands:

- In all cases, the `nameOfTheList` argument refers to the list you are modifying.
- If the data you add is a string, be sure to enclose it within double quotation marks. If the data is numeric, quotation marks are not used.

The most important list-related Lingo commands are identified in Table 17-1.

Note: Notice that some commands can be used with either a linear or a property list (property lists are discussed later in the chapter).

Table 17-1
List-Related Commands

Command Syntax	Parentheses Required/ Optional	Purpose	Used In
`add (nameOfTheList, data)`	Optional	Adds a new entry to the list. If the list is unsorted, the new entry appears at the end of the list. If the list is sorted, the new entry appears in alphabetical order.	Linear lists
`addAt (nameOfTheList, position, data)`	Optional	Adds the specified data at the position indicated. Data in that position is shifted to the next position. No data is overwritten.	Linear lists
`append (nameOfTheList, data)`	Optional	Adds the specified data to the end of the list. This command generates a scripting error when used with a property list.	Linear lists
`deleteAt (nameOfTheList, position)`	Optional	Removes the data at the specified position from the list.	Both linear and property lists
`getAt (nameOfTheList, position)`	Required	Returns the data stored at the specified position in the list.	Both linear and property lists
`getLast (nameOfTheList)`	Required	Returns the last piece of data stored in the list.	Both linear and property lists
`getOne (nameOfTheList, data)`	Required	Returns the position of the specified data in the list.	Both linear and property lists

Command Syntax	Parentheses Required/ Optional	Purpose	Used In
`getPos (nameOfTheList, data)`	Required	Returns the position within the list where the data is stored.	Linear lists
`setAt (nameOfTheList, position, data)`	Required	Replaces the data item at the position specified with the data specified.	Linear lists
`sort (nameOfTheList)`	Optional	Alphabetizes all entries in the list.	Both linear and property lists

Retrieving list items

You can use several different methods to retrieve or set list information (22 different ways at last count, to be precise). The most basic methods use the `getAt` and `setAt` commands.

The `getAt` command takes the list as an argument, as well as the position within the list from which you want to get data. For example, to retrieve the name of the third day of the week (assuming Sunday is the first day) you'd use the `getAt` command. The following instruction can be entered in the Message window or in a Lingo handler. It sets the list `daysOfWeek` to the names of the days (Sunday, Monday, and so on):

```
set daysOfWeek=["Sunday","Monday","Tuesday","Wednesday","Thursday",¬
"Friday","Saturday"]
```

This next instruction sets the variable `thirdDay` to be equal to the third item in the `daysOfWeek` list:

```
set thirdDay to getAt(daysOfWeek,3)
```

If you type `put thirdDay` in the Message window, the result is as shown here:

```
put thirdDay
-- "Tuesday"
```

Caution: All of the list functions work on the assumption that the first element in the list is item number 1, the second is item number 2, and so forth. If you've learned programming in the C arena, this can throw you, because C-based languages (including C++ and Java) usually start counting from zero.

As you might expect, when using the `getAt` command you have to be careful about specifying the position within the list from which you want to get data. If you request a position that's greater than the number of items the list holds, Director will display the Alert message shown in Figure 17-1.

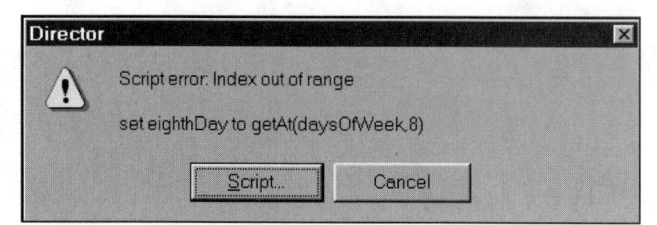

Figure 17-1: Director complains if the requested position exceeds the number of items in the list.

Using list-related functions

By counting in advance the total number of items in the list, you can avoid accidentally exceeding that number in commands such as `getAt`. Let's take a look at the `count` function, and the other list functions listed in Table 17-2. Like Table 17-1, the table of functions indicates which ones can be used with both linear and property lists.

Table 17-2
Functions That Can Be Used with Lists

Function	Parentheses Required/ Optional	Description	Used In
count (nameOfTheList)	Required	Returns a value representing the number of items in the list.	Both linear and property lists

Function	Parentheses Required/ Optional	Description	Used In
`ilk (nameOfTheList)`	Required	Returns a string indicating whether the `nameOfTheList` is a linear list or a property list. If the list identified by `nameOfTheList` is a linear list, this function returns the string `#list`. If the list is a property list, `ilk` returns the string `#propList`.	Both linear and property lists
`max (nameOfTheList)`	Required	Returns the maximum value in the list. When working with strings, the result is based on the ASCII value of the string, evaluated character by character, left to right.	Both linear and property lists
`min (nameOfTheList)`	Required	Returns the minimum value in the list.	Both linear and property lists

Using the `count` function, you can restrict the `getAt` command to a value that is not less than 1 (item 1 in the list) and that does not exceed the total number of items in the list, thereby avoiding the ugly Alert box. The following handler returns the name of a specific day of the week, contained in the parameter `whichDay` and based on its position in the list. The handler effectively limits the value used by the `getAt` command to a valid range (no more than the actual number of entries in the list).

```
on getDayOfWeek whichDay
    set daysOfWeek=["Sunday","Monday","Tuesday","Wednesday",¬
    "Thursday","Friday","Saturday"]
    if whichDay<1 or whichDay>count(daysOfWeek) then
        alert "The day requested ("&whichDay&") is invalid."
        halt
```

(continued)

```
        else
            set Day=getAt(daysOfWeek,whichDay)
        end if
        return Day
end
```

In this example, the `getDaysOfWeek` routine defines the `daysOfWeek` list and then checks to make sure that the day entered (`whichDay`) falls between 1 and the `count` of the number of items in the list, in this case 7. If it doesn't, the routine displays a dialog box reflecting the bad day (and yes, I've had bad days like that, too) and then quits the program. Otherwise, the handler uses the `getAt` command to return the correct day of the week.

> **Tip:** You might wonder if you can use this same technique using chunk expressions and items in a text string. The answer is yes, you can, quite easily. String operations, however are typically slower than the equivalent list functions — in some cases, an order of magnitude slower. Moreover, while this can be done with relatively simple text items, the more complex operations would get bogged down in chunk references. Whenever you see an operation that can be handled with text items, think about whether the actions can be transformed into list operations instead.

Retrieving a list item's position

Suppose you know the day of the week but not the corresponding numeric date. For example, you want a routine that takes the current date, parses out the day of the week, and then tells you which calendar day of the week that corresponds to, relative to Sunday.

The `long date` completely describes the current day. For example, the `long date` returns "Wednesday, December 31, 1997" for the last day in December, 1997. By parsing the date using the default comma as the delimiter, you can get the day of the week by requesting `item 1 of the long date`. Once you have this, you can use another Director list command: `getPos`. The `getPos` uses as an argument the list name and the contents of any item within the list. If the item is found within the list, then `getPos` returns the position of the item. Otherwise it returns a value of zero. With this information, you can create the inverse function `getCurrentDayOfWeek`:

```
on getCurrentDayOfWeek
    set daysOfWeek=["Sunday","Monday","Tuesday","Wednesday",¬
      "Thursday","Friday","Saturday"]
    set weekday to item 1 of the long date -- this gets name ¬
      of day
    set currentDay=getPos(daysOfWeek,weekDay)
    return currentDay
end
```

Running this function for a specific day (say Monday, September 22, 1997) returns a value of 2, since Monday is the second day of the week and the second item in the list.

Since most of the list commands by default put new items at the end of the list, Lingo also includes a shortcut command, `getLast`. For any given list,

```
getLast(myList)
```

is equivalent to

```
getAt(myList,count(myList))
```

Adding items to a list

You can add an item to a list by way of the `add` keyword. Add places the item into the list at the end — unless the list is sorted. See "Sorting lists" later in the chapter for the exceptions to this rule. The `append` command does the same thing. If you use either `add` or `append` followed by the required parameters (the name of the list and the item to be added), the results are the same as shown here:

```
set macromediaProducts=[]
add macromediaProducts, "Director"
add macromediaProducts, "Freehand"
add macromediaProducts, "XRes"
append macromediaProducts, "Authorware"
put macromediaProducts
-- ["Director", "Freehand", "XRes","Authorware"]
```

Tip: If the data you add is a string, be sure to enclose it within double quotation marks. If the data is numeric, do not use the quotation marks.

Setting list values

If you want to change an entry in a list, the simplest way is by using the `setAt` command, which mirrors the `getAt` command. The `setAt` command passes the name of the list, the position that you want to change, and the value you want to change as parameters. As an example, from a collection of pets you can create a list with the following animals:

```
set pets=["dog","cat","fish"]
```

Here's how to change the third entry ("fish") to a hamster, using the `setAt` command:

```
setAt pets,3,"hamster"
put pets
-- ["dog", "cat", "hamster"]
```

Be careful about passing the `setAt` command a number outside of its range. The results may surprise you:

```
setAt pets,7,"snake"
put pets
-- ["dog", "cat", "hamster", 0, 0, 0, "snake"]
```

When the index to the `setAt` command falls outside of the range of the list, Lingo pads the list, inserting zeroes for items that have not been defined. While this approach may be useful in some (unusual) circumstances, in general it should be avoided because it can introduce spurious data into your lists.

The `addAt` handler works similarly to `setAt`. Where `setAt` replaces the value at a given position, `addAt` *inserts* the value at that position, shifting all subsequent items back one position.

```
set mylist=["fish","dog","cat","hamster"]
addAt mylist,3,"bird"
put mylist
-- ["fish", "dog", "bird", "cat", "hamster"]
```

As with `setAt`, if you specify an index position outside of the range of the list with `addAt`, Lingo will pad the list with zeroes to fill the undefined locations in the list.

Deleting items from lists

To remove a specific item from a linear list, use the `deleteAt` command. This eliminates the item at a specified position and then collapses the list by one. For example, to delete the second item in this list:

```
pets=["cat","dog","fish","hamster"]
```

you'd use the following Lingo code:

```
set pets=["cat","dog","fish","hamster"]
deleteAt pets,2
put pets
-- ["cat", "fish", "hamster"]
```

Director's `deleteAt` function doesn't support removing a specific item based on its contents (such as "fish") from a list. Rather, it deletes an item based on its position within the list. However, a simple handler can be written that accomplishes this task:

```
on deleteItem myList,whichItem
    set pos=getPos(myList,whichItem)
    set itemDeleted=void()
    if pos>0 then
```

```
            deleteAt myList,pos
            set itemDeleted=whichItem
        end if
        return itemDeleted
    end
```

If you enter the above script as a cast member in a movie, you can call the `deleteItem` handler (in the Message window) to remove an item from the list. Here's an example:

```
set pets=["cat","dog","fish","hamster"]
deleteItem pets,"fish"
put pets
-- ["cat", "dog", "hamster"]
```

The return value from the function passes the item that is deleted (if found). Otherwise, the function returns the value `void`, indicating that the action didn't find anything to delete. This makes the `deleteItem` function work consistently with certain other list properties, such as the `getAProp` command used with property lists (discussed later in this chapter). You can test this to see if the operation was successful or not:

```
set pets=["cat","dog","fish","hamster"]
if voidP(deleteItem(pets,"rhinoceros")) then
      alert "A rhinoceros does not make a good pet."
end if
```

On the CD-ROM The `deleteItem` handler is contained in the cast member "listUtils" in the cast library genutils.cst, as are several other list-related utilities discussed in this chapter. The file genutils is on the companion CD-ROM in the exercise: ch06 (exercise\ch06) folder.

Sorting lists

Using the `sort` command, you can sort the items in a list:

```
set animals=["horse","dog","cat","snake","turtle","bat"]
sort animals
put animals
-- ["bat", "cat", "dog", "horse", "snake", "turtle"]
```

The `sort` command performs two types of sorts, depending on the type of data contained in the list. If the list contains numbers (integers or floats), the list is sorted in strictly numeric fashion. The following example can be tested in the Message window (notice that after the sort, the list is in numerical order):

```
set numList=[100,3,4,2.5,2.15,1,12]
sort numList
put numList
-- [1, 2.1500, 2.5000, 3, 4, 12, 100]
```

On the other hand, if the list contains strings, even if those strings are representations of numbers, then the sort command orders the list alphabetically. Alphabetical sorts are based on standard ASCII comparisons, using the ASCII value for any character in the list. In an ASCII sort, the string "11" will be evaluated as being *less than* the string "2" (since ASCII string comparisons run from left to right, not from right to left as numeric comparisons do).

It may happen that you anticipate a numeric sort and instead receive an alphabetical sort, as shown in the following example:

```
set stringList=["3","4","2.5","2.15","1","12","100"]
sort stringList
put stringList
-- ["1", "100", "12", "2.15", "2.5", "3", "4"]
```

This result is "correct" as far as Lingo is concerned, but it won't do if you were expecting the strings to be sorted numerically. The following two guidelines will help you avoid the unexpected:

✦ If you have numeric data, make sure it is converted to a numeric type before you sort the list.

✦ Never mix string representations of numbers with actual numbers in a list to be sorted — it is an open invitation to disaster because the sorting algorithm gets confused.

You may wonder why Lingo has *two* keywords for adding items to the end of a list. The reason has to do with sorted lists. If you use the add command to add an element to a sorted list, then the element is sorted into the list, rather than placed at the end:

```
set macromediaProducts=["Authorware","Extreme3D","Flash","Freehand",¬
"XRes"]
sort macromediaProducts
add macromediaProducts, "Director"
put macromediaProducts
-- ["Authorware", "Director", "Extreme3D", "Flash", "Freehand",¬
"XRes"]
```

On the other hand, the append command forces the item to the end of the list regardless of its alphabetic or numeric order. By using the append command, you also turn off the sort property, freezing the current order until the sort command is applied to the list again:

```
set macromediaProducts=["Authorware","Extreme3D","Flash","Freehand",¬
"XRes"]
sort macromediaProducts
append macromediaProducts, "Director"
```

```
put macromediaProducts
-- ["Authorware", "Extreme3D", "Flash", "Freehand", "XRes",¬
"Director"]
add macromediaProducts, "Shockwave"
put macromediaProducts
-- ["Authorware", "Extreme3D", "Flash", "Freehand", "XRes",¬
"Director", "Shockwave"]
```

Similarly, the `setAt` property turns off sorting within a list. If you want to understand how and why Director does this, check out the "How director handles lists" sidebar.

How Director handles lists

A list in Director changes its structure depending upon its contents and whether or not you sort it. In its simplest unsorted form, when you initially create a list, Director assigns it a block of memory and establishes a pointer to that block. Whenever you add a new element to the list, Lingo puts the data into the block of memory reserved for the list and creates a pointer from the existing list item to the new item. (The pointer actually points to the *next* block of memory allocated to the list.)

Consider the unsorted list as a train. The variable containing the list is the engine, and the coupler behind the engine is a pointer. If the list is empty, the coupler connects directly to the caboose. The caboose serves as a terminator and indicates that you have arrived at the end of the train (the end of the list). If you add an item to the list, it's like adding a boxcar behind the engine. One of the boxcar's couplers becomes a pointer back to the engine and the other coupler points to the caboose.

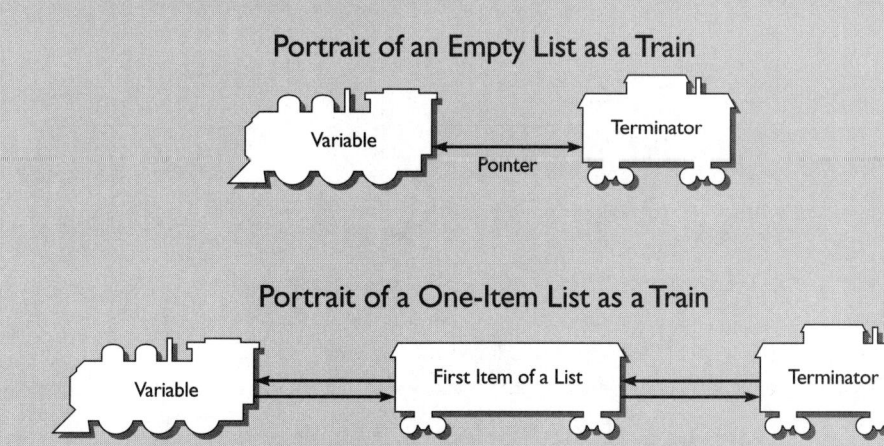

Portrait of an Empty List as a Train

Portrait of a One-Item List as a Train

(continued)

(continued)

Each time you add a new boxcar (item) to the train (list), it can go after the engine or after an existing boxcar. Deleting a boxcar means it must be uncoupled from the cars that precede and follow it, and moved aside so the remaining cars can be joined. This is just what happens when an item is deleted from a list — the previous item changes its pointer from the deleted item to the next item in the list. The deleted item's pointer is added to a stack of memory items to be purged during garbage collection (that's a programming term for clearing unused and unwanted data and variables from memory).

You have to change the metaphor, however, when a list is sorted. Rather than a string of boxcars, you have a spreading treelike structure, as illustrated just below. (Actually it looks more like a root, but that's part of the tree too!) Each data node (which equates to a position for an item in the list) has no more than two links (or two branches): a left link and a right link. When you add a new item to the structure, the item is compared to the *root node* in the tree. If the new data item is less than the current node, then Lingo moves it down to the left node of the tree structure and places the new item there if nothing currently occupies that spot. Or, if a previous node already exists at that location, Lingo compares the new item with *that* node, and if the new data item is greater, it is moved to the right — and so on and so forth. Ultimately every new item added to the list is placed so that the *binary tree* structure is preserved. Each *parent node* will be of lesser value than its right child node, and will be greater in value than its left child node.

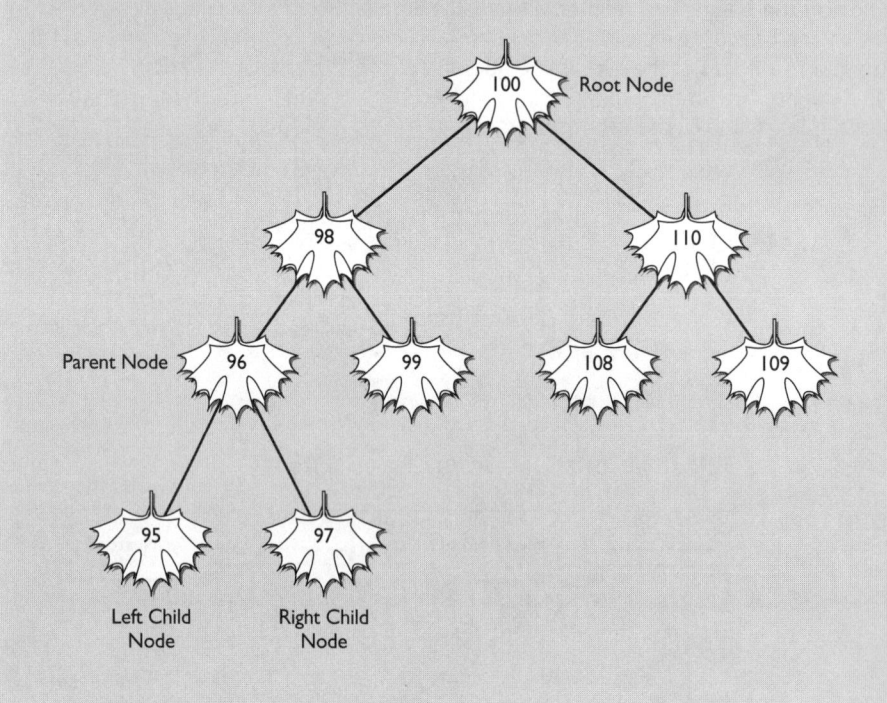

The binary tree is an efficient way of adding and sorting items because it can present a linear interface (a straight list) simply by walking the branches of this tree from left to right. When you sort a list, you are switching to this binary tree structure. That's why it is faster to sort an empty list first and then add items to it, instead of adding items and *then* sorting. Likewise, when the `append` or `setAt` statement is used in the binary tree structure, the tree is converted internally back to a linear list because a binary tree cannot support unsorted data.

You can observe the behavior of a list using the Message window. In the following steps, you'll establish a list called States, add new data to the list, sort it, and display the results.

Working with a Linear List

1. Open a new movie in Director and open the Message window.

2. In the Message window, type

   ```
   set States to ["Michigan", "Iowa", "Kansas", "West¬
   Virginia"]
   ```

   and press Enter.

   Tip: In the command in step 2, the spaces after each comma are optional. Also, if you want, you can use the `set States =` form of the statement rather than `set States to`. For example, the same results would be achieved with

   ```
   set States = ["Michigan","Iowa","Kansas","West Virginia"]
   ```

3. In the Message window, type **showGlobals** and press Enter to display the list you entered. You'll see something similar to Figure 17-2.

4. Type **add (States, "Missouri")** and press Enter to add the new data to the end of the list.

5. Type **showGlobals** and press Enter to display the enlarged list. Notice that "Missouri" is now added as the last element in the linear list.

6. Type **put getAt (States,3)** and press Enter. "Kansas" is displayed in response to the instruction. The `put` command displays the results of the instruction in the Message window.

```
-- Welcome to Director --
-- "Now loading LINGO.INI 7/12/97 4:05 PM"
-- "This computer is running in  24-bit color depth."
set States to ["Michigan", "Iowa", "Kansas", "West Virginia"]
showGlobals

-- Global Variables --
version = "6.0"
States = ["Michigan", "Iowa", "Kansas", "West Virginia"]
```

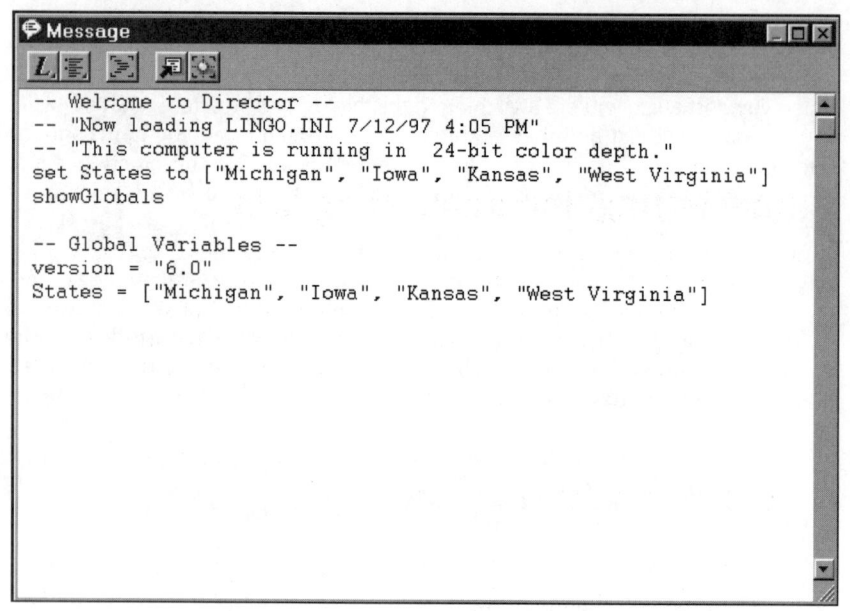

Figure 17-2: The Message window showing a list in memory

7. Type **put getOne (States, "West Virginia")** and press Enter. The position of the item ("West Virginia") within the list (States) is displayed in the Message window as

   ```
   put getOne (States, "West Virginia")
   -- 4I
   ```

8. Type **sort (States)** and press Enter to order all the state names alphabetically in the list.

9. Type **showGlobals** and press Enter to display the revised list.

10. Type **append (States, "Nevada")** and press Enter to add one more state to the list.

11. Type **showGlobals** and press Enter to display the revised list.

    Take a moment to observe what has happened. Until you *appended* Nevada to the end of the list, it was a sorted list. The `append` command *always* adds an item to the end of the list. If you had sorted the list and then used the `add` command, the list would retain its alphabetical order. Try that next.

12. Again in the Message window, type **sort (States)** and press Enter.

13. Type **showGlobals** and press Enter to display the revised list.

14. Type **add (States, "Louisiana")** and press Enter to add the new state to the list.

15. Type **showGlobals** and press Enter to display the list of items in alphabetical order.

Transferring and duplicating lists

The nature of Director's list structure (both the straight *linked list* and the *binary tree*) has one other implication. Because a list is kept internally as a pointer to a structure, if you assign one variable (which contains a list) to another variable, then the only thing transferred is the pointer, not the list itself. In other words, if you set listB to equal listA and change the contents of listB (or listA), the changes are reflected in both lists. That's because both variables point to the same list.

This can best be demonstrated in the following example. Again, we're using the Message window:

```
set listA=[1,2,3,4,5]
set listB=listA
add listB,6
put listB
-- [1, 2, 3, 4, 5, 6]
put listA
-- [1, 2, 3, 4, 5, 6] - They're the SAME!
```

This may not be the behavior you desire. Typically, when you copy a list you want to create a new list containing all of the components of the old list but that can also be changed. Beginning with Director 5 and the introduction of the `duplicate` function, you have the ability to create a copy of a list and modify it separately from the list upon which it was originally based. The `duplicate` function copies the entire list into a new block of memory and then assigns a new pointer to that block:

```
set listA=[1,2,3,4,5]
set listB=duplicate(listA)
add listB,6
put listB
-- [1, 2, 3, 4, 5, 6]
put listA
-- [1, 2, 3, 4, 5] -- the lists are no longer coupled or
identical.
```

Caution

When you copy a pointer, it happens in an instant: within tenths of milliseconds. On the other hand, copying the entire contents of a large list (and lists can get *very* large) may take a noticeable amount of time, perhaps even seconds (an eternity!). For this reason, as you design your project, try to minimize the amount of actual list duplication. It can have a profound impact on performance.

Processing with Lists

Lists can take a certain amount of effort to understand, but the work is generally worth it. Lists play a big part in any kind of database design, and many of the more useful properties in Director (such as `the actorList`, `the windowList`, and `the scriptInstanceList of sprite`) are linear lists. Because lists process much faster than strings, they can be used to make shadow structures of text blocks or item sequences; these can then be processed and transferred back to strings or text field entries. In this section, we'll demonstrate several useful routines for converting, processing, and otherwise manipulating lists.

Checking whether an item exists

A frequent problem when working with lists is determining if a given item has already been added to a list. The `getPos()` command tells you where an item is located, or returns 0 if the item does not exist in the list. Though it isn't especially obvious, the syntax

```
GetPos(mylist,myItem)=0
```

is another way of saying that the item isn't located in the list. A small handler can greatly improve the legibility of this code:

```
on IsWithin myList,myItem
    return (GetPos(mylist,myItem)>0)
end
```

The expression

```
getPos(mylist, myItem)>0
```

evaluates to True if the item is found inside the list, and False otherwise:

```
set pets=["cat","dog","horse","fish"]
if not IsWithin(pets,"rabbit") then
    add pets, "rabbit"
end if
```

Converting a list to a string

The `string()` function has to be one of the most versatile functions in Lingo. With lists, the `string()` function can convert even a very large and complex list structure into a string, making it useful for intermediate-term storage of lists beyond the scope of the movie. The converted information retains a certain amount of type information — for example, if you have a list of symbols, the function will retain the symbol notation:

```
set daysOfWeek=[#Sunday,#Monday,#Tuesday,#Wednesday,#Thurday,¬
#Friday,#Saturday]
put string(daysOfWeek)
-- "[#Sunday, #Monday, #Tuesday, #Wednesday, #Thursday,¬
#Friday, #Saturday]"
```

The `string()` function performs a little magic on lists that contain strings. The function retains the quotation marks inside of the list string, and the quotation marks therefore don't wind up breaking up the string and generating an error:

```
set pets=["cat","dog","fish","hamster"]
put string(pets)
-- "["cat", "dog", "fish", "hamster"]"
```

The `value()` function works in reverse of the `string()` — if you have a string in the shape of a list, the `value()` function converts it back into a list. This can be very handy for storing list data, as long as the list data itself is relatively simple (that is, no lists within lists or objects within lists):

```
set pets=["cat","dog","fish","hamster"]
set petString=string(pets)
put string(pets)
-- "["cat", "dog", "fish", "hamster"]"
put value(petString)
-- ["cat", "dog", "fish", "hamster"]
```

Caution

You can get away with storing lists within lists as strings, but this is a less reliable operation. Often, lists that *should* convert to strings and back to lists get corrupted unpredictably, while other seemingly improbable candidates go through the conversion process just fine. In general, you're better off saving the data in some other format and then loading the lists later, rather than attempting to save a string-converted list for reconstitution later.

Keep in mind that when you convert lists to strings in this manner, the outcome may not be quite what you were hoping for. We have frequently found it necessary to take a multiple-line or multiple-item selection in a text field and convert it into a list, or vice versa. Though there are no explicit Director routines to do this, writing your own is fairly simple.

Converting items to a list

In order to implement a *list box* — a staple of both Macintosh and Windows GUIs — your tasks include a lot of list-type activities, such as

+ Inserting items into a list
+ Retrieving an item at a specific position
+ Finding the position of an item in the list

A *shadow list* is a list that contains the contents of the list box, and in which you can do many of the operations needed to implement the list box. Shadow lists work faster than using chunking functions, and you have a flexibility you can't achieve using only string functions.

Two functions that are indispensable when working with shadow lists are the `textToList` and `listToText` routines.

The `textToList()` function takes as parameters a string or text field reference, and an optional delimiter. The delimiter is included so you can pull data out of a sequence of items as well as from lines of text. Normally, the routine defaults to the system item delimiter, typically a comma. You can convert lines of text into items in a list by passing RETURN as the delimiter. The code for the handler is relatively simple:

```
on textToList source,delimiter
    if voidP(delimiter) then  -- if no delimiter is specified
        set delimiter=the itemdelimiter  -- use the default¬
delimiter
    end if
    set olddelimiter=the itemdelimiter  -- save the item¬
delimiter
    set the itemdelimiter=delimiter  -- switch to the new¬
delimiter
    -- fill the list
    set templist=[]  -- create an empty list
    -- iterate through each of the items in the source
    repeat with index=1 to the number of items in source
        add templist, item index of source  -- add items to¬
the list
    end repeat
    -- restore the delimiter
    set the itemdelimiter=olddelimiter
    return templist  -- return the now filled list
end
```

Almost all of the code in the `textToList()` function is devoted to making sure that the right delimiter is used. The code that reads items from a string or text field and adds them to a list takes up maybe five lines. Thus, to convert a sequence of items — say, animals at a pet store — into a list, all you need do is write

```
set myAnimalStr="fish,cat,dog,hamster,snake,bird"
set animalList=textToList(myAnimalStr)
put animalList
-- ["fish", "cat", "dog", "hamster", "snake", "bird"]
```

As a more practical example, you can convert a file path into a list of folders:

```
on getFolderList filepath
-- determine the file delimiter character
case the platform of
      "Macintosh,68K","Macintosh,PPC":
           set fileDelimiter=":"
      "Windows,32","Windows,16":
           set fileDelimiter="\"
otherwise
      set fileDelimiter="/"
end case
-- use the file delimiter to parse the filepath
set folderlist=textToList(filepath,fileDelimiter)
-- return the list of folders
return folderlist
end
```

This can be tested in the Message window using the following instructions (minus the lines of comments):

```
-- I'm assuming I'm on a Macintosh here
set myPath="Hard Drive:Applications:SuperLingo:Myfile"
put getFolderList(myPath)
-- ["Hard Drive", "Applications", "SuperLingo", "Myfile"]
```

Converting a list to items

The inverse function, listToText(), is a little more complex. Because it is most often used to output a list as a series of lines, the RETURN token is the default delimiter:

```
on listToText sourcelist,delimiter
      if voidP(delimiter) then
          set delimiter=RETURN
      end if
      set buffer=""
      repeat with entry in sourcelist
          set buffer=buffer&entry&delimiter
      end repeat
      set numchars=length(buffer)
      delete char numchars-length(delimiter)+1 to numchars of¬
buffer
      return buffer
end
```

This routine illustrates yet another variation on the repeat loop. The statement repeat with entry in sourcelist sets entry to each list item in turn. It is the equivalent of two statements:

```
repeat with index=1 to count(sourcelist)
      set entry=getAt(sourcelist,index)
```

What we are doing in the `repeat` loop is adding the entry to a buffer, then adding the delimiter. This works fine until the last entry: The disadvantage of the `repeat with ... in` loop is that there is no way to know when you have reached the last entry without comparing the entry, and that's something that can add to the time it takes for the routine to run. As a consequence, once all the entries have been added to the buffer, we remove the delimiter from the end of the buffer and then output the buffer as a string.

Let's return to the list box concept. The following lines of code might be found in a button that reads the contents of one text box (field "Name") and then adds the contents, sorted, into the list of a second text box (field "AllNames"):

```
on mouseDown
    set entry=the text of field "Name"
    set namesList=textToList(field "AllNames",RETURN)
    sort namesList
    add namesList,entry
    set namesText=listToText(namesList,RETURN)
    put namesText into field "AllNames"
end
```

The sort algorithm that Director provides for lists is easily a couple of orders of magnitude faster than anything you could write to process text in Lingo — so much so that the time to convert to a list, sort the list, and convert back to text is negligible in comparison. Indeed, we use this particular routine so often that we've actually converted it into a standard handler:

```
on addFieldTextToSortedField entryFieldName,listFieldName
    -- get the entry from the entry field
    set entry=the text of field entryFieldName
    -- convert to list field into a linear list
    set namesList=textToList(field listFieldName,RETURN)
    -- sort the list
    sort namesList
    -- add the entry into the list
    add namesList,entry
    -- convert the list back to text
    set namesText=listToText(namesList,RETURN)
    -- put the text back into the field
    put namesText into field listFieldName
end
```

The routine is then called from a `mouseDown` or `mouseUp` script of a button sprite with the field names as parameters:

```
on mouseDown me
    addFieldTextToSortedField "Name","AllNames"
end
```

> **Note:** There is no reason why the delimiter has to be a single character. If you want to output a list as a series of paragraphs with a line between each paragraph, you can call the function using the instruction
>
> ```
> listToText(myList,RETURN&"-------------------------"&RETURN)
> ```

> **On the CD-ROM:** The routines `textToList`, `getFolderList`, `listToText`, and `addFieldTextToSortedField`, as well as several other list-related utilities from this chapter, are available on the CD for this book. They're in the cast member "listUtils" in the cast library exercise:ch06:genutils.cst (exercise\ch06\genutils.cst).

The Principles of Property Lists

Properties — of sprites, of cast members, of the system itself — form the core of Director Lingo programming. Through Lingo, you can also create your own *property lists*, thus opening the door for database processing, advanced programming in behaviors, and even object-oriented objects.

Consider the following situation: You are developing an application in Director that displays a catalog of merchandise. Each "page" of the catalog contains the name of a product, a picture showing the merchandise, a category that describes the type of merchandise, a description of the merchandise, a unique ID, and a price. To make things more complicated, every week the catalog is updated and distributed via the Internet to thousands of customers, who don't take kindly to long downloads. In other words, you don't have the luxury of creating a frame-based solution in which each page of the catalog is a separate frame or the new catalog is downloaded each week to all customers.

Does this sound like an impossible challenge? Actually, it's a scenario typical of many product-related environments, thanks to Internet-fostered changes that make hybrid CD-Web products feasible. Back to the point at hand, this example illustrates the principle of properties in a big way. If you think of a product in the catalog as an *object* in the same vein as a cast member or a sprite, then the page has several distinct *properties*. These properties are the nouns that quantify the page, describing what the page is made up of. We might come up with several properties just from the description of the application, as shown in Table 17-3.

Table 17-3
Properties of the Catalog Product Object

Property	What It Describes
The Name of Product	The name of the merchandise
The Picture of Product	A picture (or at least the filename of a picture)
The ID of Product	A unique identifying number for the product to help expedite processing
The Category of Product	A string specifying a given product category (for example, a book might be in the *fiction* category)
The Description of Product	A text description of the product
The Price of Product	The price of the product (which we'll assume is a floating point number)

Why are these characteristics described as properties of an object, rather than just generic variables? In a catalog, there may be hundreds of different products with various prices, descriptions, names, and so forth — but the important thing is that *each* item has *its own* description, name, price, and even maybe an ID.

If you could create a generic product and then customize it to uniquely describe this widget or that gadget, you could make routines that worked with these properties without having to know any specifics about what the properties contain. Once again, the principle of separating the functionality of your code from the content of the data comes into play. And, of course, there *is* a way — in Lingo — to specify such a generic product: That's what the specialized *property list* is for. Although this list shares some of the same characteristics as a linear list, it also has some considerably expanded functionality.

What is a property list?

A property list includes two related components for each entry in the list. The first component, called a property, is linked to a second component, a data element. A property list is like a two-field database. Using this analogy, the first field is the key field (the property) and the second field contains linked data. When you sort a property list, it is ordered by the property.

The syntax for a property list is demonstrated in the following example of test scores. In this example, the names (strings such as "Pat," "Joan," and "Mary Ellen") are properties, and the scores (such as 1200, 1545, and 950) are data. Each name and its associated score is an item in the list:

```
set Scores to ["Pat":1200, "Joan":1545, "Mary Ellen":950]
```

You can initialize or create an empty property list named Scores by using the following syntax:

```
set Scores [:]
```

In the following (slightly more complex) example, the property list is made up of a collection of entries, each referenced by the property name given as a *symbol*. For example, the following code segment represents a property list for a paperback book in a catalog application. Note that the following handler is all one logical line, with the continuation character (¬) used to split a single, very long line into several smaller lines. When Director evaluates this instruction, it assembles the smaller parts together before interpreting the entire line.

```
set Product1=[ #Name:"The Novaenglian Chronicles",¬
        #Picture:"NovChron1.jpg",¬
        #ID:"BKSTR123NC12",¬
        #Category:"Science Fiction",¬
        #Price:5.95,¬
        #Description:"The rise of civilization in post-¬
          apocalyptic England."¬
        ]
```

Tip

To enter the continuation character (¬), press Option+Enter (Alt+Enter).

Each list entry is given a label, using a symbol, that describes the property. Like a linear list, this property list is marked by square brackets. In contrast to a linear list, however, each entry uses a symbol followed by a colon (:).

Once you define a property list as shown above, you can refer to the properties of the list as if the list were an object. For example, after the above code fragment is encountered, you can write this code and get the result as shown:

```
put "The price of "&(the Name of Product1)&" is $"&(the Price¬
of Product1)&"."
-- "The price of The Novaenglian Chronicles is $5.95."
```

Note

If the Price of Product1 property on your system displays as 5.9500, it's because the floatPrecision property is set to 4, the default value. This property, which establishes the number of digits that a floating point number displays after the decimal point, can use a value between 0 and 15.

For all intents and purposes, Lingo will now treat Product1 as an object, in much the same vein as a cast member or sprite. This works in assignments as well. You can alter the price (the book is remaindered) using the following instruction:

```
set the Price of Product1 to 3.95
put "The price of "&(the Name of Product1)&" is $"&(the Price¬
of Product1)&"."
-- "The price of The Novaenglian Chronicles is $3.95."
```

Note

The use of symbols as labels in a property list is not required — you can use numbers, strings, even lists. However, if you don't use symbols, you cannot use the property syntax (`the Price of Product`), and several other operations with property lists become less efficient. Unless you have a compelling reason to do otherwise, stick with symbols as property labels.

Property list commands

Table 17-4 presents the property list commands.

Note

Some of the commands listed in Table 17-4 also work with linear lists. In other cases, parallel but not identical commands are used with both property lists and linear lists.

Table 17-4
Property List Commands

Property	Parentheses Required/ Optional	Description	Used With
addProp (nameOfTheList, property, data)	Optional	Adds a new entry to the property list. If the list is unsorted, the entry appears at the end of the list. If the list is sorted, the new entry appears in alphabetical order.	Property lists
deleteProp (nameOfTheList, property)	Optional	Removes the data associated with the specified property. When using property names, Lingo is case-sensitive.	Both linear and property lists

Property	Parentheses Required/ Optional	Description	Used With
findPos (nameOfTheList, property)	Optional	Returns a value representing the position in the list where the specified property appears. If the specified property is not in the list, the function returns a value of False. The property name is case-sensitive.	Property lists
findPos (nameOfTheList, property)	Optional	Returns a value representing the position in the list where the specified property appears. If the specified property is not in the list, the function returns a value of False. The property name is case-sensitive.	Property lists
findPosNear (nameOfTheList, property)	Required	Returns the same result as the findPos function, except when the specified property does not appear in the list. When that occurs, findPosNear returns a value representing the closest position in the list based on the sort order.	Both linear and property lists

(continued)

Table 17-4 *(continued)*

Property	Parentheses Required/ Optional	Description	Used With
`getPropAt (nameOfTheList, position)`	Required	Returns the property name stored at the specified position in the property list.	Property lists
`getAt (nameOfTheList, position)`	Required	Returns the data associated with the property at the specified position in the list.	Both linear and property lists
`getOne (nameOfTheList, data)`	Required	Returns the property name associated with the specified data.	Both linear and property lists
`setProp (nameOfTheList, property, newdata)`	Optional	Replaces the existing data stored by the specified property with the newdata specified.	Property lists

Duplicating property lists

As mentioned previously, a property list shares some of the attributes of a linear list. One of these attributes can be seen at work if we attempt to make a copy of the book object. (Warning: Copying books is a violation of copyright laws, unless done for solely educational purposes...oops, sorry, never mind).

```
-- make a copy of the book
set product2=product1
-- change the name of the new product
set the name of product2 to "The Aelvan Wars"
-- display product2's name
put "The name of the second product is "&(the name of product2)
-- "The name of the second product is The Aelvan Wars"
-- display product1's name...it's the same as the second
put "The name of the first product is "&(the name of product1)
-- "The name of the first product is The Aelvan Wars"
```

Construction of a property list is similar to that of a linear list. The variable containing the list is actually just a pointer to the list. If you set the reference for the new list to the value of the old list, then only the pointer gets passed, not the entire data structure. The moral of the story is that you must use the `duplicate` function to create a distinct copy of the whole list, whether you're copying a linear or property list.

```
-- make a duplicate of the book
set product2=duplicate(product1)
-- change the name of the new product
set the name of product2 to "The Aelvan Wars"
-- display product2's name
put "The name of the second product is "&(the name of product2)
-- "The name of the second product is The Aelvan Wars"
-- display product1's name...it's the same as the second
put "The name of the first product is "&(the name of product1)
-- "The name of the first product is The Novaenglian Chronicles"
```

Duplication is especially useful with property lists because their definitions often are very long. Consider the statement that defined Product1 above; that particular definition extended over eight lines, and it wasn't even a very large list.

Tip One technique that Lingo developers use is to create *template* property lists that contain default values. Whenever a working list is needed, that template can simply be duplicated and the properties changed as needed. This method is especially handy when the information comes from an external data source (such as a list of products for a catalog).

Working with Property List Attributes

Although property lists can be viewed as objects, they also have many of the same characteristics as linear lists — to the extent that a property list is like a "superset" of linear lists (which, to be honest, is pretty close to the way that linear lists work internally).

Both linear and property lists share a common set of commands and functions, which were summarized in Tables 17-1 and 17-2. In general, when a linear list function is used on a property list, it acts on the property list's *entries*, not on the properties themselves. For example, the command `getAt(product1,4)` retrieves the data associated with the fourth entry in the product1 list (the value 4) — as opposed to the property name of the fourth entry (product1). The primary benefit of using a property list is that you don't *need* to know where a given property is in the list. You only need to know that the property list contains the property. Don't waste this primary benefit of a property list — avoid relying on positional references for accessing entries unless you are retrieving all of the properties from the list.

Caution: The `sort` command is the only exception to the rule that functions common to linear and property lists work exclusively on the entries of the list (the data elements), not on the properties. The `sort` command sorts the properties alphabetically, instead of sorting the data elements. This idiosyncrasy can be a source of errors, because it may seem more logical to sort the entries.

The functions and commands in Table 17-1 that are associated only with linear lists do not work with property lists. When you try to use a linear list command with a property list, an Alert message (saying the handler is not defined) is generated. Because linear and property lists are constructed differently, the commands that modify or add an item to a list will vary.

Adding an item to a property list

In order to add an item to a list, you use the `addProp` handler, passing to it the list, the property name (preferably as a symbol), and the entry:

```
set myList=[:]
addProp myList,#Version,6.0
put myList
-- [#Version:6.0]
addProp myList,#ProductName,"Director"
put myList
-- [#Version:6.0, #ProductName:"Director"]
```

Tip: If the `put myList` instruction displays

`-- [#Version:6.0000, #ProductName:"Director"]`

(with four digits after the decimal point), issue the instruction `set the floatPrecision to 2` and then issue the `put myList` instruction again. The new result will be

`-- [#Version:6.0, #ProductName:"Director"]`

There is a theoretical limit to the number of items you can add to a list (something on the order of 32,000), but in general, memory considerations become a factor long before the limit is reached.

What about the `append` function?

The `append` function has no counterpart in property lists, since the order of the entries is secondary to the property being contained within the list.

Tip: This actually serves as a good benchmark for deciding whether to use linear lists or property lists. If the positions of the items within the object are more important, as they would be in a trivia contest or card game, then use linear lists. If the characteristics of the object — the object's name or description, for example — are more important, then your object should probably be defined as a property list. In cases where you have a collection of objects, then you may want to consider nested lists.

Setting and retrieving, revisited

We've already studied one way of getting or setting the contents of a list, by referring to `the property of mylist`. This works best when you know the name of the object's properties, but sometimes you may be in the dark about what the list contains. This is especially true as the Director program has become more sophisticated, since it is possible to use lists that are defined by third-party routines or Xtras. In this case, a better syntax to use is the `getProp()` and `setProp()` commands.

The `getProp()` command takes a property list and a property as arguments, and retrieves the value associated with that property. For example, using Product1 defined earlier in the chapter, we can get the name by using the `getProp()` command:

```
set ProductName=getProp(Product1,#Name)
put ProductName
-- "The Novaenglian Chronicles"
put the Name of Product1
-- "The Novaenglian Chronicles"
```

If you attempt to retrieve a nonexistent property, then Director generates an error. Since you will frequently encounter situations where you need to test to see if a property *is* in a list, you can get around this error by using the `getAProp()` command. It has an identical syntax to `getProp`, but instead of displaying an Alert box the command returns the value `void`, which can then be tested. Let's say you need to know the manufacturer of a product. Since that field hasn't been defined yet, you'll generate an error; if you use `getAProp`, however, you can trap the error and handle it yourself.

```
-- The next instruction displays an alert box and stops the
program
set ProductManufacturer=getProp(Product1,#Manufacturer)
-- The next instruction doesn't display an alert box
-- but does set ProductManufacturer to void
set ProductManufacturer=getAProp(Product1,#Manufacturer)
-- Using the second example, you can test the result:
if voidP(ProductManufacturer) then
       -- error code for handling the missing manufacturer
       put "This manufacturer hasn't been specified yet."
else
       -- use the ProductManufacturer
end if
```

The handler `setProp` works in the same fashion, changing the value of the specified property but generating an error if the property is not found. The `setAProp` handler, on the other hand, will create the new property if it doesn't exist.

```
-- The following instruction will generate an error
setProp Product1,#Manufacturer,"Calimari Books"
-- The following instruction doesn't display an
error...instead, it adds manufacturer to the list
setAProp Product1,#Manufacturer,"Calimari Books"
put the Manufacturer of Product1
-- "Calimari Books"
```

Caution Alert boxes serve a very real purpose for the developer — they indicate that a problem exists. If you accidentally misspell the name of a property when using `setProp`, Director will alert you that something is wrong. If you use `setAProp` instead, then the misspelled property name is blithely added to the list and you are none the wiser until the misspelling generates a syntax error down the line or a value is not properly updated. Unless you have a strong reason for using the `addAProp` routine to create a property, you should use `setProp` instead.

Getting property information

As mentioned earlier, it's not generally recommended to use positional information to retrieve entries in a property list. Nevertheless, sometimes you need a list of the properties in a property list. Since the `repeat with...in` syntax pulls out only values, not properties, you actually have to request the property at a specific position in the list in order to retrieve the property name.

The `getPropAt` command takes two parameters: the property list name and the position within the list. It returns the property and associated data element located at that position. If you want to output all of the properties and their associated values to the Message window (frequently a useful technique for debugging problems in property lists), here is the `dumpList` handler to use for that task:

```
on dumpList myPropList
    -- loop over the count of items in the list
    repeat with index=1 to count(myPropList)
        -- retrieve the property at the current position
        set prop to getPropAt(myPropList,index)
        -- retrieve the data element belonging to that¬
        property
        set entry=getProp(myPropList,prop)
        -- output the property and the data element to the¬
        Message window
        put prop&":"&entry
    end repeat
end
```

You can use this to get a "dump" of the contents of the Product1 list in the Message window:

```
dumpList Product1
-- "Name:The Novaenglian Chronicles"
-- "Picture:NovChron1.jpg"
-- "ID:BKSTR123NC12"
-- "Category:Science Fiction"
-- "Price:5.95"
-- "Description:The rise of civilization in post-apocalyptic¬
England."
-- "Manufacturer:Calimari Books"
```

Note The Manufacturer data is present only if you added it, using the Message window, as instructed in the "Setting and retrieving, revisited" section.

You may wonder why the `dumpList` handler doesn't just reference the entry from its position, rather than from the property. Surprisingly, the answer is because it's faster to do it from the property. The entries are internally referenced by property, and if we used the position, Lingo would have had to find the property corresponding to that position, and then retrieve the entry from the property. By using the property to get the entry, we cut down on a step that Director would have done otherwise. See the sidebar, "Making a hash of property lists," for more information.

Removing properties

Removing a property from a list involves calling the `deleteProp` command, which takes a property list and the property name (or symbol) as arguments, and removes the specified property. For instance, if you wish to delete the Category property from Product1, you can use the following syntax:

```
put the category of Product1
-- "Science Fiction"
deleteProp Product1,#Category
put the category of Product1
-- This puts up an alert box "Script Error: Property not found"
```

Warning Because attempting to remove a nonexistent property from a list *will* crash your system, the `deleteProp` command generates an Alert box if you try to do this. Thus there is no corresponding function that quietly ignores the attempted deletion of a nonexistent property. In general, you should test (with the `findPos` command) to make sure a given property exists before attempting to deleting it.

Let's use the Message window to observe the behavior of a property list. In the following steps, you'll establish a list called Scores, add new data to the list, sort it, and display the results.

Working with a Property List

1. Open a new movie in Director and open the Message window.

2. Type **clearGlobals** in the Message window and press Enter to purge any variables. Then type **showGlobals** and press Enter. Only the version of Director in use is listed. All other variables, such as the States list, have disappeared.

3. Continuing in the Message window, type **set Scores to [:]** and press Enter. You have created an empty property list with no data stored in it.

4. Type **showGlobals** and press Enter to display the empty list:
   ```
   -- Global Variables --
   version = "6.0"
   Scores = [:]
   ```

5. Type

   addProp (Scores, "Elizabeth", 125)

   and press Enter to add the new data to the end of the property list.

6. Type **showGlobals** and press Enter to display the property list with the new entry.

7. Type

   addProp (Scores, "Joan", 122)

   and press Enter to add the new data to the end of the property list.

8. Type

   addProp (Scores, "Anne", 126)

   and press Enter to add the new data to the end of the property list.

9. Type

   addProp (Scores, "Paul", 99)

   and press Enter to add the new data to the end of the property list.

10. Type **showGlobals** and press Enter to display the revised property list. The Message window should display the following response:
    ```
    Scores = ["Elizabeth": 125, "Joan": 122, "Anne": 126,¬
    "Paul": 99]
    ```

    From a list of scores like this, it's likely you'd want to determine the highest score. To accomplish this task, you first use the `max` function (to get the highest value) and then the `getOne` command to obtain the property name (player's name) that matches the specified score.

11. Type **put max (Scores)** and press Enter. The Message window displays the value 126, representing the largest value stored in the property list.

12. Type

    put getOne (Scores, 126)

    and press Enter. The Message window displays one property name (Anne) as matching the high score of 126. In the next step, you replace Joan's score (she played the game again and bested her previous score).

13. Type

    setaProp(Scores, "Joan", 153)

    and press Enter.

14. Type **showGlobals** and press Enter to display the current list of scores.

    Now you can repeat the earlier steps and determine which player has the highest score using the `max` function and the `getOne` command. However, you can also combine this two-step process, as shown next.

15. In the Message window, type the following `put` command:

    put getOne(Scores, (Max(Scores)))

    and press Enter. In the previous step, you substituted the statement that generated the high score (`put max(Scores)` for the value in the second instruction, so `put getOne(Scores, 125)` becomes `put getOne(Scores, (Max(Scores)))`.

16. Now concatenate the results with a text string to provide a better "descriptive" response indicating the person with the highest score. Type

    **put getOne(Scores, (Max(Scores))) &&"has the high score of"&& ¬
    max(Scores)**

    and press Enter. The Message window displays the current high score and the player who achieved that score.

Searching a dictionary list

The property list has a complementary concept in other programming languages: the *dictionary*. With the dictionary approach, each property of an object or list is like a term in a dictionary. Properties equate to the words that are defined in a dictionary, and data elements equate to the definitions of those words in a dictionary. It is with this view in mind that the engineers at Macromedia created the `FindPos` and `FindPosNear` commands.

The `FindPos` command requires two parameters: a property list and a symbol. It returns the position of that property within the list. If it doesn't find the property, then the command returns a value of Void. This is analogous to the `GetPos` command for entries. Here is `FindPos` at work:

```
put FindPos(Product1,#Category)
-- 4 -- since category is the fourth property in the list
put FindPos(Product1,#Author)
-- Void -- since author isn't a property in the list
```

`FindPosNear` is a little more intriguing. In a sorted list, `FindPosNear` compares the passed symbol with all of the other symbols, and indicates what position the passed symbol would take if it were sorted into the list. The result implies that the property currently occupying that position would be the closest "match" to the passed symbol. This works especially well with "type-ahead" projects such as a Help File Index, where the user of the product types in a string expression and the program returns the closest match.

Note

To use `FindPosNear`, you must first sort the property list. If the property list is not sorted, both functions return 0 regardless of whether a requested item is in the list or not.

Making a hash of property lists

Property lists are not just handy freebies that the Macromedia engineers decided to bestow upon users. In truth, property lists are at the heart of nearly everything that Director does. List structures are actually what give you access to capabilities that make Director work.

When Director creates a property list, it makes a *look-up* or *hash table.* When a property is added to the list, the symbol for that property is added to the look-up table, along with a pointer to the information that it references — that is, to the entry in the list. This is one of the reasons why you should generally access an entry in a property list using the property name. If you reference it by position, Director has to find the property that corresponds to that number in the list and then retrieve the information from the property, adding several steps to the process of getting the data.

Understanding this structure also tells you why sorting a list sorts the properties rather than the entries. When you sort a list, you convert it from a linked list to a binary tree. It's far more economical to sort the look-up table than it is to retrieve the entries from each property, sort them, and then rearrange the look-up table to reflect this new order.

Director keeps nearly all of its own internal objects in a similar look-up table that contains the property names of the objects, which in turn reference the actual data. The only difference is that Director's native objects (such as cast members and sprites) also retain pointers to functions within their look-up tables. A similar mechanism is used for the creation of behaviors and parent scripts. Still, in all but a couple of specialized cases, Director is built around the same structure that supports property lists.

Creating a Simple Menu System Using Objects in a List

In Chapter 10, you discovered how to use scripts (attached to Stage sprites such as buttons) to navigate from one frame in your movie to another. Each button sprite had a separate script and caused the button to respond to a click by moving the playback head to the next frame, to the previous frame, or to a specific marker in the movie.

By using a list, you can create a single generic script that establishes a navigation system. The system relies on placing a cast member (which serves as a "hot button") in a channel that corresponds to the position of a marker name (to which the playback head jumps) in the list. For example, examine the Score window in Figure 17-3 (from the travel.dir movie) and the names of the eight markers in the movie. From left to right the marker names are Start, China, Germany, Hong Kong, Japan, Singapore, Taiwan, and End.

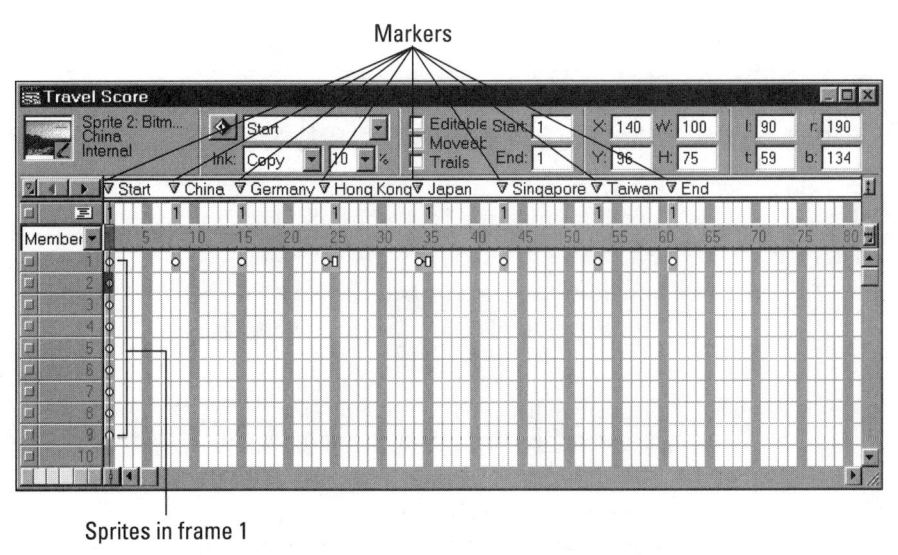

Figure 17-3: The travel.dir movie's Score window with markers

The cast member names for objects in slots 1 through 8 of the Cast window match the marker names, as shown in Figure 17-4.

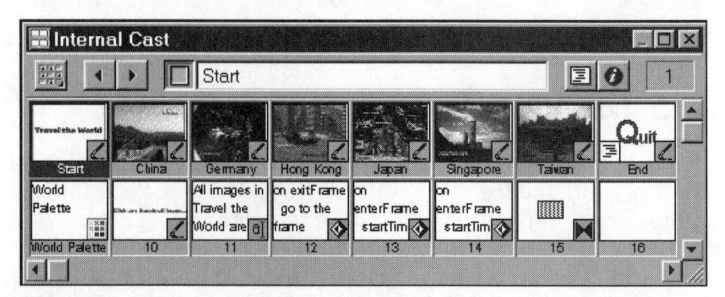

Figure 17-4: The travel.dir movie's Cast window

Figure 17-5 illustrates the sprites in channels 1 through 8 as they appear on the Stage, corresponding to the marker names. For example, the China thumbnail is in channel 2 and the China marker is the second marker; the Germany thumbnail is in channel 3 and the Germany marker is the third marker; and so on. The first marker is the Start marker, and in channel 1 is the bitmap text cast member "Travel the World." This is the image that is displayed on the Stage in frame 1, as shown in Figure 17-5.

Figure 17-5: Appearance of the travel.dir Stage in frame 1

The travel.dir movie is an example of this list-based menu scheme. In the on startMovie handler, a global variable menuOption is established and set to equal a list of all the markers in the movie, as shown here:

```
on startMovie
    global menuOption
    set menuOption to ["Start", "China", "Germany", "Hong¬
    Kong", "Japan", "Singapore", "Taiwan", "End"]
end
```

By carefully placing "button" sprites in channels that correspond to the order of the markers in the list, you can use the following generic script. When attached to each of the objects (used as buttons or links to another segment of the movie), the script tells the playback head to go to a frame. The frame is identified by the getAt(menuOption, the clickOn) expression:

```
on mouseUp
    global menuOption
    go to frame getAt(menuOption, the clickOn)
end
```

Tip

You must be extremely careful to include all sprite names (China, Germany, and so on) in the property list. If not, when you run the movie, you'll wonder if you're in the military, getting sent to places other than where you want to go. Click China, and you get a picture for Germany. Select Singapore, and you get Taiwan. The solution is to carefully double-check the startMovie handler to be sure the property list is complete and in the correct order.

GetAt retrieves an item from the list, as determined by the clickOn function. This function returns the number of the last active sprite clicked by the user. Remember: For a sprite to be considered active, it must have a sprite script attached to it. In the travel.dir movie, the sprites in channels 2 through 7 all have a script attached.

Caution

The clickOn function does not work in a repeat loop.

So if the user clicks the sprite in channel 3 of frame 1, the clickOn value is 3. The sprite script instruction began as

```
go to frame getAt(menuOption, the clickOn)
```

Now Director inserts the clickOn value and simplifies the instruction to read

```
go to frame getAt(menuOption, 3)
```

Look at the movie script where the menuOption list is declared, and you'll see that the third item in the variable is "Germany." Now Director simplifies the instruction further, to read

```
go to frame "Germany"
```

You can see how the same instruction using two variables and the `getAt` property attached to all objects in frame 1 can cause a mouse click to send the playback head to the appropriate marker based on a list. This single script eliminates the need for a series of different scripts, each attached to a specific object and with a specific `go to frame` instruction.

In the following steps, you'll use the travel.dir movie to create a menu system that relies on a list of markers. Depending on the object clicked in frame 1, the playback head jumps to a specific marker. In its current form, the movie includes a custom palette, six photographic images, three bitmap cast members, a text field, a transition, and three scripts. You'll add a movie script and a sprite (Score) script and then examine one of the existing scripts.

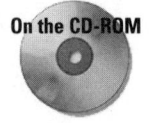

On the CD-ROM The file travel.dir is on your companion CD-ROM in the exercise:ch16 (exercise\ch16) folder.

Creating an Icon-Based Menu Using a List

1. Open the travel.dir movie in Director.

2. You're going to add a movie script that creates a list in memory. The order of the items in the list must correspond to the order of the markers in the movie. Select the first open cast member slot (slot 16) and then open the Script window.

3. Type the following movie script in the Script window:

   ```
   on startMovie
        global menuOption
        set menuOption to ["Start", "China", "Germany", "Hong¬
        Kong", "Japan", "Singapore", "Taiwan", "End"]
   end
   ```

   At the start of this movie, the script establishes a global variable named menuOption. The next instruction causes the variable to store a list of all the markers in the movie — in the order they appear in the movie.

4. When done, close the Script window.

5. Select the cells in frame 1 that include sprites. Shift+click to select only channels 2 through 7.

6. Click the Script (Behavior) drop-down list in the Score window and select the New Script option.

7. In the Script window that opens, type the following handler:

```
on mouseUp
    global menuOption
    go to frame getAt(menuOption, the clickOn)
end
```

8. Close the Script window. If you selected the sprites in channels 2 through 7 in frame 1 before you opened the Script window, the same sprite script is now attached to each of the sprites.

9. Save the movie as **travel1.dir,** rewind, and test the movie.

Before you quit the travel1.dir movie, examine the following handler. It appears in cast member slot 13:

```
on enterFrame
    startTimer
    repeat while the timer <180
    end repeat
    go to "Start"
end
```

In this project, we chose to give the user a limited amount of time to examine the various images; then, without requiring a mouse click, we return the playback head to the first frame. We accomplished this by building a delay into each frame with a photographic image, using the `startTimer` command and `the Timer` property. The `startTimer` command sets `the Timer` property to zero (0) and then begins incrementing by ticks (60 ticks per second).

Note: Just invoking the `startTimer` command resets `the Timer` property to zero!

In the `repeat while` loop, Director keeps looping as long as `the Timer` property is less than a value of 180 ticks or 3 seconds. When the property exceeds 180 ticks, the `repeat while` loop ends and the playback head jumps to the "Start" marker.

Note that the script cast member in slot 14 is identical to the script in slot 13, except there is no `go to frame "Start"` instruction. The result is that when the playback head hits frame 61 (with the End marker), the playback head pauses for three seconds and then ends the program. If the Control Panel Loop Indicator is turned on, the movie replays; otherwise, it terminates.

Side Dish: Creating cross-platform palettes

The images in travel.dir were originally scanned from color slides at millions of colors and then reduced to an 8-bit color depth (256 colors). Both Macintosh and Windows systems can use 256-color palettes. When importing a single image or a group of similar images (using a similar range of colors), it's not too difficult to get the images to reduce to a single 8-bit color palette. However, when you have a variety of photographic images using a wide range of colors, or when you create a movie that is targeted for a cross-platform audience, you must either import each image with its own distinctive color palette or you must generate a standard palette for all images. Adding to this challenge is the fact that Windows and the MacOS reserve different colors (in different positions in the color palette) for the standard interface elements (menus, scroll bars, and window borders). That's why Director includes a Macintosh system palette and a separate Windows system palette.

Your computer's monitor can only use one color palette at a time, so you cannot display two images using two different palettes simultaneously on the screen. If you try, one image will be controlled by its native palette and the other will not — resulting in one image appearing in psychedelic colors.

The solution to the multiple palette problem is to create a superpalette that includes the best colors in the best position within the palette. The tool of choice for this task is DeBabelizer Pro from Equilibrium Software. On this book's companion CD-ROM, you'll find DeBabelizer Lite Limited Edition (for the Macintosh) and DeBabelizer Pro for Windows Demo version. Look in the goodies:debablzr (goodies\debablzr) folder on the CD.

With DeBabelizer, you can create a batch list of images using the Select File ⇨ Batch ⇨ Superpalette command (Mac), or the File ⇨ New ⇨ Batchlist command (Windows). Then in one operation (using the Tools ⇨ Batch Automation ⇨ Create SuperPalette and Remap command) you can create a superpalette and remap all images to that.

After you remap the images, you can import them (as a group) into a Director movie using the File ⇨ Import command (Command+R or Ctrl+R). In the Image Options dialog, select the Image (8 bits) radio button and the Import radio button in the Palette area. This causes Director to import each 8-bit image and use the superpalette.

For more detailed information on the Macintosh or Windows versions of DeBabelizer, check Equilibrium's Web site:

    http://www.equilibrium.com

The site includes a comprehensive FAQ, as well as frequent free updates that add new features to the program. Equilibrium Software is at Three Harbor Drive, Suite 111, Sausalito, CA 94965, phone 415-332-43443

Summary

Before you continue on to creating parent scripts and child objects in the next chapter, let's review some of the things you learned here about lists.

- ✦ Lists are collections of data. Using various list access properties, you can sort and manipulate lists in a wide variety of ways.
- ✦ Lists can be used to augment text and field processing.
- ✦ The Message window can be used to experiment with creating and adding to a linear list or property list.
- ✦ Lists form the basis for many games and quiz-type programs, from card games to board games to computer-based training.
- ✦ Property lists are like objects or records, with the attributes described by properties.
- ✦ Property lists permeate Director but are especially useful in working with complex database structures.

✦ ✦ ✦

Parent Scripts and Child Objects

CHAPTER 18

In This Chapter

Lingo as an object-oriented programming tool

Relationships: parent scripts, child objects, and ancestors

Building child objects in memory

Using the `actorList`

Creating multiple child objects from a single parent script

Using an ancestor script

In this chapter, you explore a whole new approach to scripting a movie in Director: *object-oriented programming (OOP)*. If your experience with the principles of parent scripts and child objects in Director has been at all uncomfortable, that's about to change. By the time you've completed these pages you'll no longer shy away from these concepts. Rather than thinking of OOP as an esoteric art form, your eyes will be opened to this valuable programming approach: Object-oriented programming enables you to build reusable, self-contained objects that contain both instructions and data.

What Is Object Oriented Programming?

Suppose you have been charged with the creation of a model city for the future. You must build houses, office buildings, bridges, roads, sidewalks, vehicles, and all the other objects that populate the city. Although you could start building all structures simultaneously from the ground up, having all of them underway at the same time would cause great confusion, not good construction.

> *From the Author:* "When *I* first learned to program in BASIC, my own novice approach was to build everything simultaneously. BASIC programs are notorious for lacking structure."

Suppose you take a different path. As your model city develops, it will be more efficient to build specific, fundamental objects first, such as roadways, and conduits for water, electricity, and gas. Then you can move on to other objects, such as subdivisions of homes and office parks. This "graduated" method will help you to concentrate on a limited range of structures with common features (homes versus roads versus factories). It is more difficult to concentrate on building an excellent single-family dwelling if you are also building a power plant and a roadway system at the same time. A more organized approach lets you focus your attention and energy on one task at a time.

> *From the Author:* "When I learned to program in Pascal and COBOL, I was introduced to *structured programming,* in which routines and subroutines were created to handle specific tasks within the program. Within a single program, I would use one routine to sort data, another to provide error checking, and yet another to print the required hardcopy reports."

Imagine the efficiency you could capture and harness if you created a die or cast for a single-family home in the model city, and then used the cast to "punch out" all the other homes in the community. Imagine the savings in workhours and materials if you create a single office building die, from which all other office buildings could be cast. Of course, if all homes and all offices looked the same, the appearance of your city would be unnatural and monotonous. To add variety and imagination, your home die should have built-in options that can affect the appearance of the final product. If the home buyer wants "earth tones," then the carpets and walls can be done in shades of gold, brown, and off-white. Depending on the likes and dislikes of the owner, the house can be created using the desired color combinations.

> *From the Author:* "After mastering the basics of Lingo, I discovered that Director's scripting language supports object-oriented programming. With OOP, I could use a single *parent script* to create one or more objects. Each object from the same parent script inherits the same characteristics, but each object can also have traits that are distinctive to it alone."

These same principles of "organized duplication" are what make OOP your ticket to creating a single, self-contained object, such as a single-family dwelling, that knows how to *behave* like a single-family dwelling. When you need a second home, the same parent script can generate it. Furthermore, the parent script can be written to generate a slightly different home each time the script is invoked. The first home can have aluminum siding and an interior design using shades of blue and green. The second home can use cedar shingles, with an earth-tone interior and a bay window. Yet both home objects can be generated from the same parent script. They both have the basic attributes of a home (indoor plumbing, family room, central air, bedrooms, baths, and closets that are too small), but they also include distinctive properties (one house has three bedrooms while another has two).

Note

All instances of objects created from the same parent script use the same handlers, but the data stored by the objects can differ.

OOP in Lingo enables you to create an object that is totally self-contained — for example, a battleship in a game, an individual person's entry in a database, a spaceship firing lasers, an animated character, or a set of navigational buttons. *Encapsulation* (the ability to separate all handlers, variables, and instructions related to a single entity) is one of the key benefits of OOP.

> **Note** An *object* is a package that contains data and code; in traditional programming environments, the dichotomy is between data and function. In Lingo, that equates to variables that store data (values and strings), and handlers that contain the instructions that operate on the data.

You don't need OOP to create a single instance of an object. But once you begin creating multiple objects based on the same template, then OOP saves you substantial time, working memory, and programming efficiency.

How OOP and Director Work Together

Until you have worked with OOP, this approach to programming can be confusing and elusive. The best solution to achieving an understanding of OOP and its implementation in Director is to learn a few basic principles. This knowledge will provide the foundation you need to "get your hands dirty" and actually compose some parent scripts and child objects.

The basics: parent scripts and child objects

OOP is not a programming language but rather an approach to solving programming problems. Certainly you can create interactive media with Lingo and never once use OOP, but many programming tasks are best implemented using the self-contained objects of object-oriented programming.

In Lingo, OOP is implemented using *parent scripts* and *child objects.* You have already worked with objects in general and know how to use them. Indeed, throughout this book we have often used the terms *sprite* and *object* synonymously. Whenever you create a cast member, assign a script to it, or set its properties, you have created an object. When using OOP, you simply build more self-sufficient objects.

There is nothing mysterious about an object. It is a package capable of storing one or more handlers and global or local variables, and accepting messages. The cast members that you have placed on the Stage have these same features: handlers, variables, and the ability to react to messages.

When using the OOP conceptual approach to programming, the self-contained objects that you create enable you to break a complex system into specific, functional parts. In a Space Invaders-style game, for instance, you seek to create a single spaceship object that has established behaviors and knows how to interact with the other objects it encounters. Rather than having to create 50 or 100 spaceships, you create one — and then use that template to create 50 or 100 *instances* of the spaceship. Using the OOP mindset, you do not view a project as a single, complete structure. Instead, you intentionally seek to define the project as discrete units (objects) that can be created, tested, and modified independently of any other part of your movie.

Note: An *instance* is one occurrence of a class (child object) or, in other words, a *class instance*. You can create a new occurrence (instance) of a child object by sending a new message to the parent script.

Why use OOP with Director?

Lingo supports OOP, but Lingo is not necessarily an object-oriented language. You do not have to use OOP, but this method of programming has several advantages — when used in appropriate situations.

- ✦ You can build a project one object at a time. Returning to our model city metaphor, a home can be made fully functional without requiring that the office building down the street be complete also. With OOP you can build, test, and modify your project one object at a time. After all objects are complete, you can assemble the entire project using the various objects as building blocks.

- ✦ OOP can be used to create multiple, similar objects (even if some of them have different characteristics) without having to construct each object separately in the Cast window. OOP is an efficient method of creating multiple objects based on a single template. By creating child objects rather than separate cast members, you reduce the amount of code required and reduce the disk space required to store your movie.

- ✦ In Chapter 24, you'll discover how Director movies can be compressed and distributed on the World Wide Web. One of the most important rules for Web-distributed media is to keep the file size as small as possible. By using parent scripts and child objects, very complex movies can be created while keeping the file size relatively small.

- ✦ Because OOP conceptualizes an entire project as a series of objects, you can have several programmers concurrently working on different objects for the same movie. Modularity is one of the key benefits of OOP.

- ✦ Self-contained objects from one movie are frequently reusable in other movies. This reusability is another key benefit of OOP.

- ✦ You can create "intelligent objects" that contain instructions for reacting to and interacting with other objects in your movie.

- ✦ Objects with the same general characteristics (generated from the same parent script) and with the same inherited traits (based on handlers in the parent script) can be reused throughout a movie. At the same time, they can include specialized (distinctive) properties for each instance of the object.

✦ Objects can be used to interpret the same command in various ways, based on the instructions stored in the objects' handlers.

✦ Because their properties can be shared among movies, objects can be used to communicate among movies.

✦ During development or after the project is complete, small incremental changes can be made to specific objects without completely reworking the entire movie.

✦ Troubleshooting and debugging your movie is simplified because each object can be self-contained. Once you determine which particular object in the movie is misbehaving, you have instant access to the handlers for that object.

✦ OOP gives you the freedom to continually redesign and rework objects throughout the development cycle. When your project is composed of easily modified objects as opposed to a single, complex programming structure, you can more easily listen to the voices of perspiration and inspiration.

Getting the OOP into Lingo

With these OOP concepts under your belt, it's time to reduce them to a few pragmatic keywords in Lingo. To implement OOP in Lingo requires the use of just three keywords: `new`, `property`, and `ancestor`. Additionally, you need a solid understanding of variables, handlers, and scripts — as discussed in Chapters 10, 11, and 12.

Create a child object, using `new`

First, the `new` function (called the `birth` function in Director 4.*x* and earlier) is used to create an object based on the instructions contained in one or more handlers. The `new` function is part of a parent script, which you use to create child objects as a movie plays. Each time you call the parent script using the `new` function, you create a new instance of the child object. As an example, if your movie will include several identical butterflies, you can make a single parent script to create each instance of a butterfly. Once the parent script is created, you can birth (create) 1, 5, or 100 butterflies from that single script.

Note Parent scripts are the templates on which child objects are created.

> **Note:** The terms *birth* and *birthing* are considered dated. Current usage says "an *instance* of an object is *created*." However, in keeping with the parent-child metaphor, the term *birth* still has relevance and will occasionally be used in this chapter.

Send characteristics to the child from the parent, using `property`

Second, the `property` keyword enables you to send specific data to the parent script. This data is used to build child objects with unique characteristics. That's a different way of saying that you can send values or strings to a handler in the parent script to efficiently build similar objects with different characteristics. If your movie uses similar objects with different characteristics, such as various kinds of flowers, an effective way to create these sprites is to use parent scripts and child objects.

For example, the flowers include common characteristics such as stems and petals. Other characteristics may differ in each type of flower (such as the number and color of petals, and so on). It is inefficient to build separate cast members for each variety of flower when they are all similar. By using a parent script to birth each child object, you save many bytes of code. Further, when you make changes to the parent script, those changes are inherited by every flower cast member based on the parent script.

> **Note:** Property variables enable you to customize each instance of a child object.

Pass characteristics from another parent script to the child object, using `ancestor`

Third, the `ancestor` keyword enables you to establish another parent script for a child object and pass characteristics or messages from the ancestor object to a group of child objects. As a parallel, let's think in terms of a human family. A child object is *birthed* based on a parent script. The parent script can declare an ancestor (which is another parent script). Any instructions from the ancestor are passed through the parent script to all child objects it creates. The instructions become part of the child object, unless the object has specific instructions that contradict the instructions received from the ancestor script. If contradictory instructions exist for the child object, it disregards the inherited instructions.

Comparisons between Lingo OOP and C++

C++ is a programming language that supports OOP. If you are familiar with C++, the parallels between C++ and parent scripts/child objects in Director can be instructive. In Table 18-1, column two lists the C++ equivalent to the Lingo concept listed in column one. The third column includes notes that will help you understand Lingo's OOP concepts in light of your previous experience with Director.

Table 18-1
Lingo OOP and C++ Comparisons

Lingo	C++	Notes
Parent script	Class	A parent script is a special type of movie script. The parent script is different from other movie scripts because it *must* include a name (to be called by the new function) and a new handler with instructions for creating an object. It also can contain property declarations.
Child object	Class instance	A child object, like a sprite, is an object that can be used in your movie. Like a sprite, a child object can have properties and be controlled and modified using Lingo scripts. Unlike a sprite, child objects may exist only in memory and may not be present in the Cast window.
Property variable	Instance variable	A property variable is the parent script's equivalent to a global variable. Property variables persist after the parent script handler executes — just like global variables. Further, each child object can maintain its own values for each property variable. In other words, each child object (though created from the same parent script) can assign different data to the same property variables.
Handler	Method	A handler in a parent script is no different from a handler in a movie script. The structure, functions, keywords, commands, and instructions available are common to all Lingo handlers.
Ancestor script	Superclass	An ancestor script is just another special type of movie script. Once you understand the function of a parent script, just think of the ancestor script as "the parent script of a parent script."

The Components of OOP Programming in Director

The three keywords Lingo uses to implement OOP show up in three parts of your Director movie: parent scripts, child objects, and ancestors.

The parent

A parent script is used to create the desired child objects. It is basically a script that contains a set of handlers and any declaration of variables used by the handlers in the parent script. These shared variables are called *property variables*. The relationship of property variables to a parent script handler is analogous to the relationship of global variables to handlers in a movie script.

The following is an example of a parent script, in which the new keyword creates an instance of a child object:

```
on new me
      -- Add instructions here
      -- Add additional instructions here
      return me
end
```

The child object's address, as an identification number, is stored in a variable called me. Me is a keyword that by convention is used in parent scripts to refer to the script itself. In other terms, me refers to an instance of the parent script that is the child object. Although you can use any variable name to refer to the script, the use of me is a recognized convention and you should follow it.

In the preceding example, then, the instruction return me passes the child object's memory address back to the calling handler, where the instruction was issued to create a new instance of an object based on the parent script.

The child

A child object is an independent copy of the handlers and variables in a parent script. When a parent script is used to create an instance of itself, a child object is "birthed." In other words, an *instance* of a parent script results in a child object.

The handlers for each child object work the same as other handlers in a Director movie. The variables can be set or tested like any other variable in a movie. For example, when you create several child objects from the same parent script, each child object can include the same variable mycolor. For each child object, the value of the variable can be a different color.

The similarities and differences among a group of child objects are much the same as the similarities and differences among the members of a human family. Typically, each family member has certain traits in common: two eyes, two arms, two legs, similar facial features, and possibly the same bone structure and skin color. At the same time, each family member may exhibit differences in eye color, hair color, body weight, height, and personality. In a child object, these differences can be assigned based on values passed to the parent script (using property variables) or randomly assigned within the parent script's handlers.

We have already pointed out that using child objects allows you to create sets of objects with some similarities and some unique characteristics. For example, you might want to create a set of clickable buttons that look similar but behave differently when clicked. You might even want to hide or show buttons, or dispose of them as the movie plays.

Later in this chapter, you'll build a snowfall scene in a movie as an example of how child objects can be created and manipulated using OOP. Instead of having the same set of snowflakes fall repeatedly, your movie can create a new snowflake with slightly different characteristics (position on the Stage, color, and so on) each time a snowflake is required. Each snowflake can move at a different speed. As the snowflakes collide, one snowflake can engulf another that is smaller or in a "back-Stage" position. As the snowflakes fall off the Stage (out of view) they can be destroyed or made to pile up in snowdrifts.

It's possible to create a set of snowflakes without using parent scripts, but the number of handlers and global variables would soon become unwieldy. Trying to keep track of the state of each variable and handler would become impossible. If the movie is developed by more than one person, or you want to modify it at a later date, this level of complexity is difficult to manage.

Note

You can also create the snowflake scene using the Score, but the number of frames required would result in a large and unmanageable movie. By using OOP, you can create a one-frame snowstorm scene that is compact and easy to modify.

The ancestor

An ancestor is an additional parent script whose handlers are available to a child object. To do this, the `on new` handler in a parent script identifies another parent script as its ancestor by assigning the ancestor script's name to the ancestor property. To make sure we understand this relationship, let's look at the following example. In this instruction, the script "Ancestor Snowflake Script" is identified (set) as the ancestor for the child object created in the `on new` handler:

```
on new me, listPosition
      set ancestor to new(script "Ancestor Snowflake Script")
      Set the forecolor of sprite listPosition + 9 to random¬
(248) -1
      return me
end
```

In this case, it does not matter what characteristics are inherited from the "Ancestor Snowflake Script." It's only important that some characteristics are inherited. In addition, the second instruction within the handler sets the child object's foreground color to a random number (which indicates a specific color in Lingo).

A parent script can have only one ancestor at a time, but any ancestor can have its own ancestor. This allows for *inheritance* of characteristics from one or more generations of parent scripts, to the child object being birthed. In the most basic case, attaching an ancestor to a child object allows the object to use handlers that are not included in its parent script.

Later, when you create multiple child objects, it is often helpful to create sets of child objects that have different characteristics, but that also have some common characteristics. The beauty of parent-child scripting is that individual child objects can be similar and different at the same time. Using ancestor scripts enables child objects to inherit common characteristics from an ancestor (that is, from the parent script of the child object's parent script).

Creating a parent script

A parent script contains three types of Lingo handlers:

- ✦ A handler that creates a new child object and initializes the property variables for that child object.
- ✦ A statement declaring which variables are property variables. Each child object can maintain its own set of property variables.
- ✦ Optional handlers that control the child object's behavior and properties after the initial creation of the object.

The new handler

Every parent script must have a new handler in order to create child objects. The new handler creates the child object (a new instance of the parent script) and initializes any variables the child object might use.

The new handler always starts with the following syntax:

```
on new
```

The general form of the new handler is shown in the following example (items in square brackets are optional):

```
on new [me] [arguments being passed]
      set the width of sprite mySprite to 45 -- Line 2
      set the forecolor of sprite mySprite to 100 -- Line 3
      add(snowflakeList, new(script "Snowflake Parent Script",¬
count(snowflakeList) + 1))
      return me -- Line 5
end
```

The second and third lines of the handler set the width and the color of the snowflake. The fifth line returns the contents of me (the name of the child object) to the handler, which called the parent script.

Property variables

When a child object is created, any variables contained in the parent script are passed on to the child object. You can have each child object act differently based on the value of these variables. Each child object is capable of storing a different set of values for the same variables. This is accomplished by using the keyword property at the top of the parent script:

```
Property snowflakeWidth, forecolor, snowflakePosition
```

In this example, three variables are set using the property keyword. Each time a new snowflake is created, the three variables can contain different values for each child object. In this way, each new snowflake has a specific size, a specific color, and a specific position on the Stage.

In the above property statement, each instance of a child object stores a separate set of values for the same variables. This makes tracking the variables easier, because you only have three variables to track. If you were to create 100 snowflakes *without* using a parent script, each with three variables, you'd then have to track 300 separate variables. Using OOP, you need to track only three.

Property variables have two special characteristics that set them apart from normal variables. First, they persist beyond the handler in which they are declared and used. Second, each child object stores and maintains its own values for each property variable.

Tip *Before* writing your parent script, you should map out the behaviors each child object will have in common, and which properties will differ among the child objects.

Other parent script handlers

Other handlers (sometimes called *child scripts*) can be added to the parent script to specify behaviors for each child object. For example, in the snowing.dir movie used later in this chapter, the moveSnowflake handler moves snowflakes down the Stage, so they appear to fall. Here is the moveSnowflake handler:

```
on moveSnowflake
      global snowflakeList -- Line 2
      if count(snowflakeList) > 0 then -- Line 3
         repeat with snowflake = 1 to count(snowflakeList) --¬
  Line 4
            animateSnowflake getAt(snowflakeList, snowflake)
         end repeat -- Line 6
      end if
end
```

In this example, line 2 declares two global variables so that the handler can access their values. In line 3, an `if...then` statement checks to see if a list of child objects (`snowflakeList`) has at least one child object to move. As snowflakes are created and destroyed, the list changes. In lines 4 through 6, a `repeat` loop acts on each child object in the list by executing the `animateSnowflake` handler. Notice that the `snowflake` variable increments from 1 to the total number of snowflakes in the `snowflakeList` and causes the `animateSnowflake` handler to act on each child object in the list.

This example assumes that the child objects have been added to `snowflakeList` using an `on new` handler in the parent script.

Making a child object behave in a certain manner is accomplished by sending messages to the handlers in the parent script of a child object. By sending a `moveSnowflake` message to the parent script that includes the `on moveSnowflake` handler, you animate the snowflakes on the Stage. Messages to instances of child objects or to the parent script can be sent from anywhere in your Director movie.

Stepping through the creation of a parent script

Creating a parent script requires the following actions:

1. Open the Script window (Command+0 or Ctrl+0), and then open the Script Cast Member Properties dialog box (Command+I or Ctrl+I).

2. As shown in Figure 18-1, name the script and set the movie's Type field to Parent. You must assign each parent script a unique name so you can reference it using Lingo.

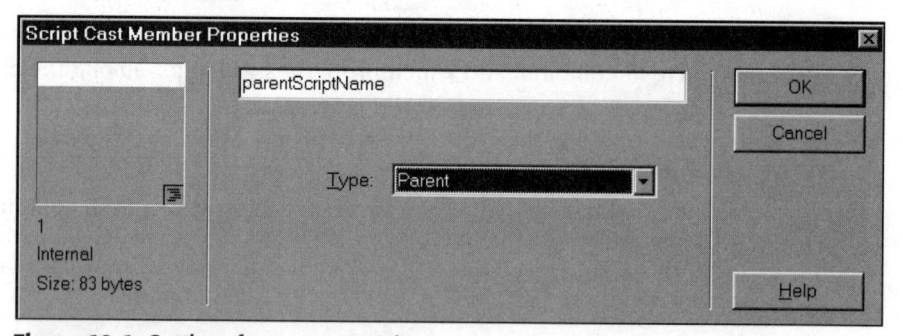

Figure 18-1: Settings for a parent script

3. Declare any property variables using the `property` keyword, like this:
   ```
   property variableOne, variableTwo, variableThree
   ```

4. Next, add an `on new` handler to the parent script. This is the handler that births (creates) a new instance of a child object each time it is called. The parent script must contain an `on new` handler in order to create new instances of the child objects. A typical `on new` handler looks like this:

   ```
   on new me
         --initialize the object here
         --and add properties or characteristics to the new¬
   child object
         return me
   end new
   ```

5. After the `new` handler instructions are entered, you can add additional handlers that contain instructions to tell the child object what to do. For example, if your child object is a space-invader ship, you would add additional handlers to tell each child object how to navigate on the Stage, how and when to fire weapons, and what to do if a ship encounters another object on the Stage. Each of these additional handlers (child scripts) is executed only when called — just like any other handler in a Director movie. Here is an example of a child script:

   ```
   on hitByLaserFire me
         --include self-destruct instructions here
   end hitByLaserFire
   ```

Creating child objects

Lingo creates a child object when you use the name of a parent script as an argument with the `new` command, as shown in the following syntax:

```
new(Script "scriptName", [argument1],[argument2])
```

By replacing *scriptName* with the name of the parent script (and adding any arguments to be passed) you create a child object. In the following example, a new child object based on the `snowflakeParentScript` is created, and two arguments (100 and 45) are passed to the child object. The arguments passed are values that establish the color and the width of the snowflake:

```
new(Script "SnowflakeParentScript" 100,45)
```

A new statement creates a single new child object but can be called as many times as you wish. Each call creates a new child object from the same parent script. This is one of the primary advantages of parent scripts. Each time a new child object is created, Director creates an identification number for the child object and a reference to the parent script, and stores these values in any property variables. The child object is stored in RAM.

Creation of child objects is restricted by two limitations:

+ The number of child objects that you can create is limited to the total amount of RAM available in your system.

+ The number of child objects is restricted to the number of sprite channels available.

Note

It's important to understand that a child object is a virtual entity, sometimes referred to as a "ghost in the machine." It is simply an object stored in memory (like a variable); it is not a physical element. You can include child scripts that cause a child object to control a visible element on the Stage, such as a sprite, but the child object itself is not a visible element. Although a child script can give the appearance of "creating" a physical, visible sprite, in fact the child object is only causing an existing cast member or sprite to appear on the Stage and behave in a manner proscribed by the child script.

The me variable

When a child object is created from a parent script, the new instance can be referred to as me. Any name can be used instead of the word me, but the standard convention among Lingo programmers is to use me. The term me is a *local variable* that contains the child object and provides a placeholder for the child object in Lingo commands. The me variable is not required, but is useful in two situations especially:

+ When one handler calls another handler and both handlers refer to the same child object, it is easier to use the term me to refer to the child object. This simplifies the task of passing messages to the child object.

+ Me is helpful when you refer to a property of the child object that is declared somewhere else in the child object's family of handlers — for example, in an ancestor property.

When me is used to create a new child object, the identification number and pointer to the parent script are assigned to the child object's version of the me variable. This is much like a family name that identifies several people as members of the same family. By using me, the calling of a handler is simplified because you don't have to specify the individual child object by name.

One last reason to use the me variable is because the term is quickly and easily recognizable by other Lingo programmers. If you are working as part of a product development team, it is helpful to make the scripts easily understood by all.

Removing a child object

Child objects persist in memory until you specifically remove them or until you write another value to the variable that stores the child object, as you will do in the "Creating Parent Scripts with Handlers" exercise. To remove a child object from memory, you can simply set its value to zero. The following instruction destroys (removes from memory) the child object "James":

```
set James=0
```

To be more specific, setting the child object to zero removes the parent properties from the variable, but the variable still exists in memory. It's a fine distinction. In the above example, setting "James" to zero destroys all the characteristics of the child object, but the variable named "James" persists in memory. To completely destroy both the characteristics of the child object and the variable, you can use the clearGlobals command.

Caution: Using clearGlobals wipes out *all* the global properties that exist in the movie. You cannot clear a single global without removing all globals from memory.

Building child objects in memory

In the following exercises, you'll create child objects in memory and watch how they respond to messages entered in the Message window. Each object takes on specific properties, depending on the parent script that is used to birth it.

Note: Child objects are *not* always associated with a sprite. In the following exercise, you create several child objects that have no "Stage presence" but still exist as a collection of code and data in memory.

In this example, each child object is an instance of a parent script based on an era (the Fifties, Early Sixties, Late Sixties, or Early Seventies). The child object inherits properties based on the era (parent script) that creates it.

Creating Parent Scripts with Handlers

1. Open Director and open a new movie. Use the default Stage size and color because none of the activity in this movie takes place on the Stage. You're going to add several new cast members.

2. Open the Script window with Command+0 (Ctrl+0) and type the following handlers:

   ```
   on Technology
        put "bomb shelters"
   end
   on Fads
        put "sock hops and duck tails"
   end
   on Politics
        put "Eisenhower, Korea, and McCarthy"
   end
   ```

3. Open the Script Cast Member Properties dialog box by clicking the Cast Member Properties button or pressing Command+I (Ctrl+I). Name the script **Fifties** and change the movie type to Parent. Close the dialog; the script appears as shown in Figure 18-2.

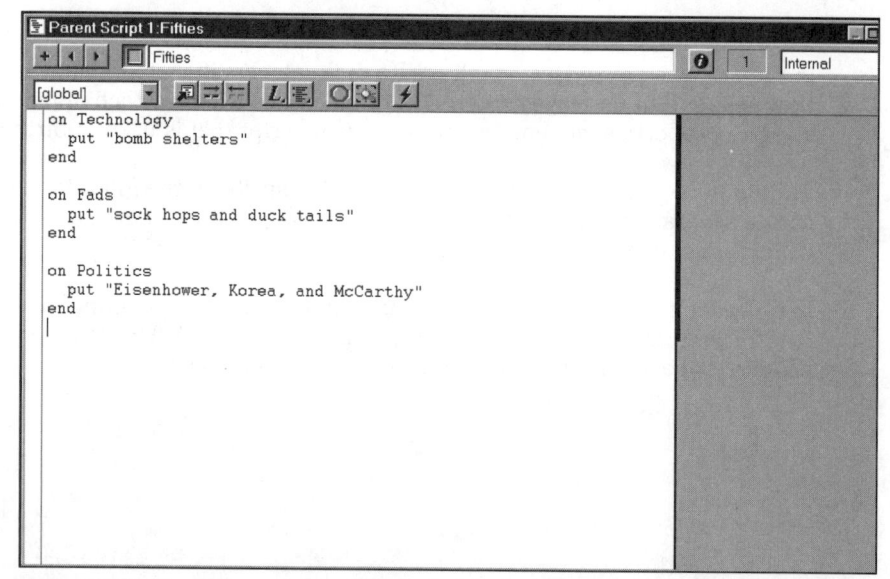

Figure 18-2: The Fifties parent script — definitely Baby Boomer in nature

4. Click the New Script button on the Script window to create a new script cast member with the following handlers:

   ```
   on Technology
         put "permanent press and color TV"
   end
   on Fads
         put "ratted hair and the British Invasion"
   end
   on Politics
         put "Kennedy, Bay of Pigs, and Cambodia"
   end
   ```

5. Display the Script Cast Member Properties dialog again, name the script **Early Sixties**, change the movie type to Parent, and close the dialog.

6. Add another script cast member with the following handlers:

   ```
   on Technology
         put "man on the moon and zip codes"
   end
   on Fads
         put "mini-skirts and spike heels"
   end
   on Politics
         put "Vietnam, Nixon, and Watts riots"
   end
   ```

7. Reopen the Script Cast Member Properties dialog, name the script **Late Sixties**, change the movie type to Parent, and close the dialog.

8. One more time — create a new script cast member with the following handlers:

   ```
   on Technology
         put "calculators and push button phones"
   end
   on Fads
         put "bell-bottoms, tie dye, and long hair"
   end
   on Politics
         put "Kent State, 18-year-old vote, and energy crisis"
   end
   ```

9. Open the Script Cast Member Properties dialog, name the script **Early Seventies**, change the movie type to Parent, and close the dialog.

10. Close the Script window and save the movie as **era1.dir**.

Now you have created parent scripts with handlers that assign properties to any child object associated with the script. The properties reflect technology, fads, and politics of the era associated with the child object. Next, you can create the child objects.

Creating Child Objects

1. With the era1.dir movie still open, in the Message window type the following instruction and press Enter. It creates a new child object called James:

   ```
   set James to new(script "Fifties")
   ```

   You have now created a single instance of the child object James. Nothing appears in the Message window, however, until you query the object.

2. Type **showGlobals** in the Message window and press Enter. A message similar to the following appears:

   ```
   -- Global Variables --
   James = <offspring "Fifties" 1 df037e>
   version = "6.0"
   ```

   This result indicates that James is an offspring (child object) of the Fifties script. The 1 means there is only one reference to the child object (the instance itself). The final hex number, which will depend on your computer system, is the identification number (the value of me). The identification number, which is the hex address for the object in memory, varies depending on the amount of RAM installed, other programs, device drivers, or objects stored in memory.

   Tip: The value 1 in the results of your showGlobals statement increments when other objects or variables reference the child object. For example, if you type **set MyFriend to James** in the Message window, you create a variable named MyFriend that references the child object. If you issue the showGlobals command again, the Message window displays the following:

   ```
   James = <offspring "Fifties" 2 df037e>
   ```

   Once again, the hex address at the end of the output varies depending on other programs, device drivers, and objects currently in memory.

3. To create additional objects in the Message window, type the following lines of instruction, one line at a time, pressing Enter at the end of each line. These instructions create three new child objects, each birthed from a different script.

```
set Joan to new(script "Early Sixties")
set Diane to new(script "Late Sixties")
set Mick to new(script "Early Seventies")
```

4. Type **showGlobals** in the Message window to see a list of all objects in memory. The Message window should look like Figure 18-3.

```
-- Welcome to Director --
-- "Now loading LINGO.INI 7/13/97 7:52 PM"
-- "This computer is running in  24-bit color depth."
set James to new(script "Fifties")
showGlobals

-- Global Variables --
James = <offspring "Fifties" 1 df037e>
version = "6.0"
set Joan to new(script "Early Sixties")
set Diane to new(script "Late Sixties")
set Mick to new(script "Early Seventies")
showGlobals

-- Global Variables --
James = <offspring "Fifties" 1 df037e>
Joan = <offspring "Early Sixties" 1 df034c>
Mick = <offspring "Early Seventies" 1 df0324>
version = "6.0"
Diane = <offspring "Late Sixties" 1 df0338>
```

Figure 18-3: Message window showing all global variables

To this point, you have created parent scripts that include handlers, which assign properties to child objects. You have also created four child objects, each an instance created from a different parent script. Now you can query the objects to see their differences.

Querying Child Objects

1. In the Message window, type **technology James** and press Enter. You have entered Lingo shorthand for saying "James, what do you remember about technology when you were a child?" His response is

   ```
   -- "bomb shelters"
   ```

2. In the Message window, type **technology Joan** and press Enter. The response is

   ```
   -- "permanent press and color TV"
   ```

3. You can also test Mick and Diane to see how they respond to technology. In the Message window, type **fads Joan** and press Enter. Joan responds with

   ```
   -- "ratted hair and the British Invasion"
   ```

4. Test the other child objects (James, Diane, and Mick) using the `fads` command, and then test all objects with the `politics` command.

5. When done, close the Message window.

> **Note**
>
> You have just experienced an example of *polymorphism*. Identical messages (such as `politics`, `technology`, or `fads`) produce divergent results based on the object that receives the message.

The fallacy of this script so far is that not all child objects born to the same parent script will necessarily have identical properties, just as not all children of the early 1960s have the same experiences, memories, and other "properties" as children born in other decades. In the following steps, you'll modify the Fifties parent script so that it randomly assigns a property in the technology handler.

Assigning Different Properties to Child Objects

1. Select the Fifties script in the Cast window.

2. Open the Script window and add the following instructions to the beginning of the Fifties parent script.

   > **Note**
   >
   > Note that the `on new` handler must list the `me` property first, or the results of the handler will not be what you expect.

   ```
   property Hero, Song, SocialValues
   on new me, MyHero, MySong, MyValues
        set Hero to MyHero
        set Song to MySong
        set SocialValues to MyValues
        return me
   end
   on WhatDoYouRemember
        put "My childhood hero was"&&Hero
        put "My favorite song was"&&Song
        put "Social attitudes dictated that"&&SocialValues
   end
   ```

The `on new` handler creates custom properties (`MyHero`, `MySong`, `MyValues`) at the birth of the child object. These custom properties are then set to the property values sent to the parent script.

3. Close the Script window and save the movie as **era2.dir.**

   Now when you create a new instance of a child object, you can send three values to the Parent script. Those values *add* custom properties and enable you to create instances that are birthed from the same parent script but have different properties.

4. In this step, you re-create an instance of the child object James (that is, you overwrite the earlier instance in memory). This time, James has three additional properties: a childhood hero, a favorite song, and a social value from his era (the Fifties). Type the following instruction in the Message window and then press Enter:

   ```
   set James to new(script "Fifties","Mickey Mantle","Purple¬
   People Eater","children respect all parents.")
   ```

5. In this step, you re-create an instance of the child object Joan. This time, Joan's parent script is the Fifties, not the Early Sixties. The old Joan no longer exists, and the new Joan now has a childhood hero, a favorite song, and a social value from her era. Type the following instruction in the Message window and then press Enter:

   ```
   set Joan to new(script "Fifties","Elvis","Hound¬
   Dog","girls never kiss on the first date.")
   ```

   You have just created two child objects from the same parent script but with different attributes.

6. Now prove the differences between James and Joan (both birthed from the same Fifties parent script). To see the values stored by Joan, type

   WhatDoYouRemember Joan

   in the Message window.

7. To see the values stored by James, type

   WhatDoYouRemember James

   in the Message window. Based on the `WhatDoYouRemember` handler, both James and Joan have different remembrances, which reflect their specific properties.

8. To destroy each child object, type the following instructions in the Message window. Be sure to type one line at a time and press Enter after each instruction.

   ```
   set James=0
   set Joan=0
   ```

(continued)

```
set Mick=0
set Diane=0
```

> **Tip** Setting the child object's name to zero destroys the child object but leaves the variable (James, Joan, and so on) in memory. You can remove the child objects in the Message window by typing the `clearGlobals` command and pressing Enter. This action also removes any other globals in memory.

Using the `actorList`

The `actorList` is a list of all child objects birthed in the current movie. Any object in the `actorList` receives an `enterFrame` message each time the playback head enters a frame. You can include a special handler called the `on stepFrame` handler each time the playback head enters a new frame in the movie. The `on stepFrame` handler is placed within the parent script for the object.

Since Director does not automatically clear the `actorList`, you can initialize it just as you would any other list by setting it to empty. Simply include the following instruction in a handler:

```
set the actorList to []
```

> **Caution** The contents of the `actorList` are not automatically cleared when you branch to another movie. To avoid unpredictable behavior in a new movie, be sure to set the `actorList` to empty in the `on startMovie` handler of the new movie.

To add a child object to the `actorList`, you can include a statement like the following that creates the new object and adds it to the list:

```
add the actorList, new(script "Bouncing Ball")
```

If the parent script requires property values, be sure to add them as shown here:

```
add the actorList, new(script "Bouncing Ball", 1, -45)
```

You can also add a new child object to the `actorList` by including the following instruction in the `on new me` handler:

```
add the actorList, me
```

This instruction treats the `actorList` as a list — which is exactly what it is.

To view a list of all existing child objects in the current movie, you can use the `put` command with the `actorList` property, like this:

```
put the actorList
```

To take full advantage of the actorList, be sure to include the special on stepFrame handler in the parent script. Each parent script can include a different on stepFrame handler that causes any of its child objects (in the actorList) to behave in a specified manner when the playback head enters a frame.

How far down is down?

In the bball.dir movie used in the two exercises of the "Using the actorList" section, the Floor cast member's placement is a little tricky. In the parent script, the falling object (based on cast member 2) falls until its registration point (locV) is at 400 pixels from the top of the Stage. The registration point is in the middle of the object unless you change it. Since the falling object is 90 pixels wide (according to its Sprite Properties dialog), when the registration point is at 400 pixels, the bottom edge of the object is at 445 pixels. To have the falling ball stop at the top edge of the sprite based on the Floor cast member, the top edge of the Floor object is set at 445 pixels from the top of the screen (again, using the Properties dialog). Figure 18-4 illustrates the distances and placement of the objects. All distances are from the top of the Stage.

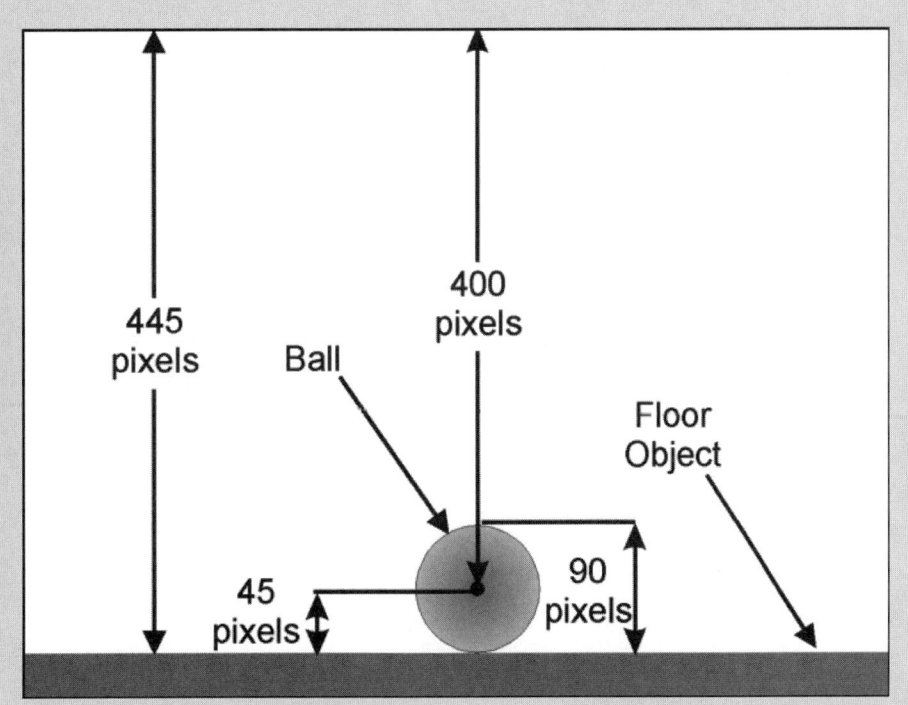

Figure 18-4: Placement of Floor sprite in relation to the registration point for the falling object at the bottom of the fall

In the era1.dir and era2.dir movies used in previous exercises, you sent text messages to a child object and received text responses. In the following steps, you'll use the bball.dir movie and add movement properties to a sprite on the Stage. By using property variables and instructions within the on new handler, you can create an object that exhibits specific behaviors without any outside influence.

On the CD-ROM The file bball.dir is on your companion CD-ROM in the exercise:ch18 (exercise\ch18) folder.

Creating a Child Object to Control a Sprite

1. Open the bball.dir movie in Director. In its current form, the bball.dir movie includes a `go to the frame` script in cast slot 1. There are round objects in cast slots 2 and 3 (you initially use only the object in slot 2), and a long black rectangular object in cast slot 4 (the floor on which the ball object bounces).

2. Select cast slot 5, open the Script window, and type the following comment line and list of properties:

   ```
   --Bouncing Ball
   property channel, newLocation, distanceTraveled, gravity,¬
   elasticity, floor
   ```

3. Press Enter twice to leave a blank line (for readability) and then type the on new handler. You can save some typing by skipping the comments, which simply tell you what each instruction accomplishes.

   ```
   on new me
        set channel = 1 --The child object uses channel 1
        set newLocation = -45 --Sets the initial registration¬
        point for the falling object
        set distanceTraveled = -50 --Indicates how many pix¬
        els the object moves in each frame
        set gravity = 5 --A larger value increases the force
        -- of gravity and the faster the object drops.
        set elasticity = -0.9 --The larger this number, the
        -- more the object bounces.
        set floor = 400 --The registration point of the
        -- falling object at the bottom of the fall.
        -- See the sidebar on How Far Down Is Down?
        puppetSprite channel, True --Puppets the object in¬
        channel 1
        return me
   end
   ```

```
on stepFrame me -- A special handler that affects all¬
--objects in the actorList each time the playback head
--enters a frame.
     --The following instructions cause the ball to move
--toward the floor object and then bounce.
     set distanceTraveled = distanceTraveled + gravity
     set newLocation = newLocation + distanceTraveled
     if newLocation > floor then
          set newLocation = floor
          set distanceTraveled = distanceTraveled * ¬
elasticity
     end if
     set the locV of sprite channel = newLocation --Resets ¬
the location of the bouncing ball
     --whenever the playback head enters a frame
end
```

4. Open the Script Cast Member Properties dialog box (Command+I or Ctrl+I). Name the script **Bouncing Ball**, change the movie type to Parent, and then close the Properties dialog.

5. In the Script window, click the New Script button to add a new script cast member in slot 6.

6. Type the following `on startMovie` handler:

```
on startMovie
     set the actorList to [new(script "Bouncing Ball")]
end
```

7. Close the Script window, save the movie as **bball1.dir,** rewind, and play it. When you run the movie, the bouncing ball drops from the top of the Stage and then bounces up and down, gaining less altitude with each bounce until it rests on the Floor object.

8. You can cause the falling object (cast member 2) to bounce more or bounce less by adjusting the elasticity setting in the `on new` handler. With a setting of –0.9, the bouncing ball has a high level of elasticity and bounces like a rubber ball. A basketball has less elasticity. Properly inflated, a basketball bounces back two-thirds of the distance from which it is dropped. Change the elasticity instruction to match the following, and then play the movie again.

```
set elasticity = -0.66
```

In the following steps, you'll modify the bball1.dir movie on-the-fly, to create a bouncing ball object. You will add a button (Drop Ball) and a cast member script for the button that will create an instance of the Bouncing Ball object.

Creating a Child Object On-the-Fly

On the CD-ROM

1. Open the bball1.dir movie. You need the bball1.dir movie you created earlier in this chapter, or the file bball1.dir from the companion CD-ROM in the exercise:ch18 (exercise\ch18) folder.

2. Use the Tool Palette to add a Drop Ball button to the bottom-right corner of the Stage, as shown in Figure 18-5.

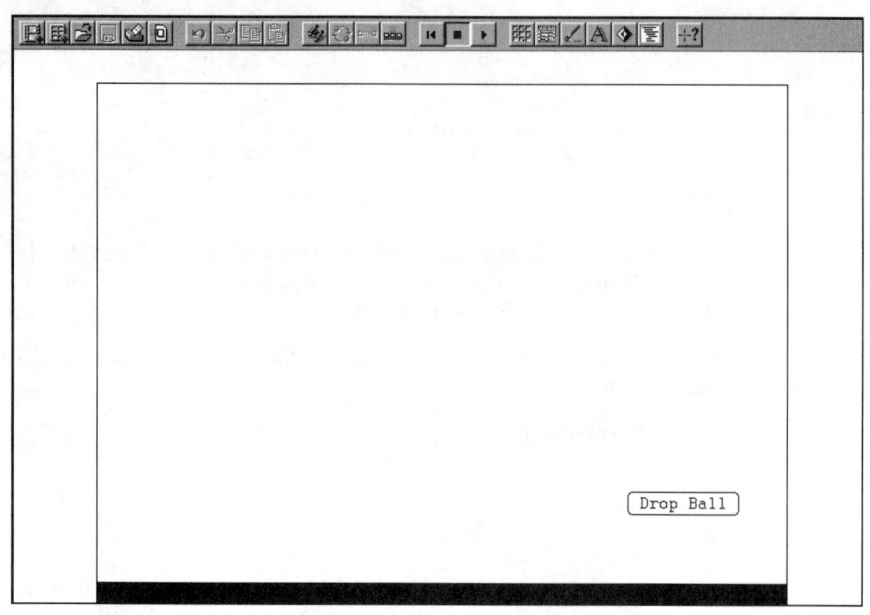

Figure 18-5: Position of Drop Ball button

3. Attach the following script to the new button:

```
on mouseUp
     set the visible of sprite 1 to False -- Line 2
     updateStage
     set the castNum of sprite 1 to random(2)+1 -- Line 4
     set the locV of sprite 1 to -50
     set the locH of sprite 1 to random(640) -- Line 6
     set temp to new(script "Bouncing Ball") -- Line 7
     append(the actorList, temp) -- Line 8
     set the visible of sprite 1 to True -- Line 9
end
```

In this handler, the bouncing ball object is set to be invisible in line 2, so it does not appear until properly positioned for the drop. In line 4, the cast number of the falling object is set randomly to either 2 or 3 (the locations where the ball objects are stored). Next, the handler places the object at 50 pixels above the top of the Stage (–50). In line 6, the handler randomly places the object's locH at a location ranging from 1 to 640 pixels from the left edge of the Stage. Line 7 creates a new instance of the bouncing ball child object, and line 8 adds it to the actorList, before making the object visible in line 9.

4. Go to the Score window and delete the bouncing ball object from channel 1. In the modified movie, you do not need to place the object on the Stage. Lingo does that for you. Channel 1 should be empty.

5. Because the on mouseUp handler uses channel 1 and positions the object, you can eliminate some of the instructions in the Bouncing Ball parent script. Open cast member 5 and modify it to match the following handler:

```
--Bouncing Ball
property newLocation, distanceTraveled, gravity, elastic¬
ity, floor
on new me
    set newLocation = -45
    set distanceTraveled = -50
    set gravity = 5
    set elasticity = -0.9
    set floor = 400
    return me
end
on stepFrame me
    set distanceTraveled = distanceTraveled + gravity
    set newLocation = newLocation + distanceTraveled
    if newLocation > floor then
        set newLocation = floor
        set distanceTraveled = distanceTraveled *¬
elasticity
    end if
    set the locV of sprite 1 = newLocation
end
```

Note

Notice the elimination of these instructions:

```
set channel = 1
puppetSprite channel, True
```

in the on new me handler. And note the changing of

```
set the locV of sprite channel = newLocation
```

to

```
set the locV of sprite 1 = newLocation.
```

6. Finally, go to cast member 6 and modify the on startMovie handler to match the following:

```
on startMovie
    set the actorList to []
    puppetSprite 1, True
    set the visible of sprite 1 to False
end
```

7. Close the Script window, save the movie as **bball2.dir,** rewind, and play it.

Each time you click the Drop Ball button, a new child object is created. The appearance of the object varies between the ball in cast slot 2 and the ball in cast slot 3. In addition, the horizontal position where the ball is dropped changes randomly each time you click the button.

Creating Multiple Child Objects

When creating multiple child objects, it is important to keep track of each instance of a new child object. This is accomplished by creating a list of child objects. Line 4 in the following example creates a new child object and adds it to a list named snowflakeList:

```
on new [me] [arguments being passed]
    set the width of sprite mySprite to 45
    set the forecolor of sprite mySprite to 100
    add(snowflakeList, new(script "Snowflake Parent Script",¬
count(snowflakeList) + 1))  -- Line 4
    set mySprite to count(snowflakeList) + 5  -- Line 5
    return me
end
```

If you want the child object to appear on Stage, you first must assign it a sprite channel. This is demonstrated in line 5.

In the next example, line 2 checks to see if the list contains the limit of 100 items. If less than a hundred snowflakes have been created, then a new snowflake is created.

```
on new me
    if count(snowflakeList) < 100 then -- Line 2
        add(snowflakeList, new(script "Snowflake Parent¬
Script", count(snowflakeList) + 1))
    end if
end
```

When you use a list to track child objects, be sure to initialize it, preferably in the `on startMovie` handler. To create a list using the snowflake example, you type the indented lines in a movie script for the movie:

```
on startMovie
    global snowflakeList
    set snowflakeList to []
end startMovie
```

Notice the variable `snowflakeList` is declared with the `global` keyword so that it is available to all handlers in the movie. Since a list is essentially an array, the list can be initialized with the following statement:

```
set snowflakelist to [ ]
```

The empty square brackets create an empty list.

In the following steps, you'll create multiple occurrences of a single object using an ancestor script that passes properties to the descendants.

On the CD-ROM The file snowing.dir can be found on your companion CD-ROM in the exercise:ch18 (exercise\ch18) folder.

In its current form, illustrated in Figure 18-6, the snowing.dir movie includes six cast members. Cast members 1 through 3 are movie scripts, but only the `on startMovie` handler in slot 1 is complete. In the following steps, you'll complete a parent script in cast member slot 3 and an ancestor script in cast slot 2. The bitmap cast member (Snow) is in slot 4, and slot 5 includes a `go to the frame` instruction that is executed after a call to the `animate` handler (in the Movie script in cast slot 1). Finally, cast member slot 6 holds a push button with a script that creates a new instance of the snowflake object each time the user clicks the button.

Figure 18-6: The snowing.dir Cast window

In the `on startMovie` handler (which you type in), `the stretch of sprite` property is set to True. When set to True, you can stretch a bitmap sprite using the `spriteBox` command or `the width of sprite` and `the height of sprite` properties. To prevent a bitmap sprite from being stretched, you set the property to False. The snowflake sprite is actually "stretched" in the `on new` handler in the parent script (cast member 2).

Using an Ancestor Script

1. In Director, open the file snowing.dir. It's on the CD in exercise:ch18 (exercise\ch18).
2. Open the Cast window if it is not already open. Following is the `on startMovie` script in cast member slot 1. The script initializes the `snowflakeList` list using a null string. Channels 10 through 19 are prepared (puppeted) to accept the child objects. The script also includes the `createSnowflake` and `animate` handlers.

```
--Main Movie Script

on startMovie
    global snowflakeList
    set snowflakeList to []
    repeat with currentChannel = 10 to 19
        puppetSprite currentChannel, TRUE
        set the stretch of sprite currentChannel to TRUE
    end repeat
end

on createSnowflake
    global snowflakeList
    if count(snowflakeList) >=10 then
        beep
    else
        add(snowflakeList, new(script "Snowflake¬
        Parent", count(snowflakeList) + 1))
    end if
end

on animate
    global snowflakeList
    if count(snowflakeList) > 0 then
        repeat with snowflake = 1 to count(snowflakeList)
            moveSnowflake getAt(snowflakeList, snowflake)
        end repeat
    end if
end
```

3. Examine the script in cast member 5. In this handler, a loop is set up using the `go to the frame` command. The `animate` instruction starts the animation process (contained in the `on animate` handler). Since this call occurs in a loop (established by the `go to the frame` instruction), the animation is continuous. Here's the handler:

```
-- Frame 1
on exitFrame
     animate
     go to the frame
end
```

4. With the Script window displaying cast member 5, click the Previous Cast Member button twice until the script attached to the cast member in slot 2 is displayed. The script window displays a single comment line:

```
--Ancestor for Snowflakes
```

5. Now add the following Lingo commands to cast member 2 after the existing comment line:

```
property velocity, mySprite -- Line 2

on new me, listPosition -- Line 3
     set myListPosition to listPosition
     set mySprite to myListPosition + 9
     set velocity to 10
     set the castNum of sprite mySprite to the number of¬
     cast "Snow" -- Line 6
     set the width of sprite mySprite to random(56) -- ¬
     Line 7
     if the width of sprite mySprite < 10 then -- Line 8
          set the width of sprite mySprite to the width¬
          of sprite mySprite * 5 -- Line 9
     end if
     set the height of sprite mySprite to the width of¬
     sprite mySprite
     set the locV of sprite mySprite to 100
     set the locH of sprite mySprite to random (599) + 40
     return me
end -- Line 16

on moveSnowflake me -- Line 17
     set currentPosition to the locV of sprite mySprite +¬
     velocity
     if currentPosition < 30 then
          set velocity to -1 * velocity
```

(continued)

```
            set currentPosition to 30
        end if
        if currentPosition > 480 then
            set currentPosition to -30 + (currentPosition¬
 - 480)
        end if
        set the locV of sprite mySprite to currentPosition
end -- Line 27
```

Let's analyze what's happening:

- Line 2 establishes the property variables (`velocity` and `mySprite`) for each new child object.

- Line 3 is the beginning of the `on new` handler and includes a `listPosition` variable that is used within the handler. The entire handler, lines 3–16, contains instructions for creating a new child object. For instance, line 6 assigns the bitmap image "Snow" to the child object.

- Next, line 7 sets the size (width) of the child object to a random size, and then line 8 checks to see if the random number is less than 10. If the size is less than 10 pixels, the sprite width is multiplied by 5 (in line 9) to keep the snowflake from being too small to see.

- Lines 17 through 27 contain the `on moveSnowflake` handler. This handler moves the child object after it has been created. The call to this handler is made in the frame script placed in frame 1.

6. Close the Script window for cast member 2.

7. Double-click cast member 3. The Script window displays a single comment line that reads

```
--Parent Script for Snowflake
```

8. Add the following Lingo statements to cast member 3 after the existing comment line:

```
property ancestor -- Line 2

on new me, listPosition -- Line 3
    set ancestor to new(script"Ancestor Snowflake",¬
listPosition) -- Line 4
    set the forecolor of sprite listPosition + 9 to ran¬
dom (248) - 1 -- Line 5
    return me
end -- Line 7
```

In this handler, line 2 includes the keyword `property` to make the variable (ancestor) specific to this child object. Lines 3 through 7 contain the `new` handler in this parent script. When a new child object is created using this parent script, line 4 sets the ancestor qualities and line 5 changes the color of the bitmap image "Snow." Line 6 makes the child object (`me`) available to the movie script.

9. Close the Script window.
10. Save the movie as **snowing1.dir.** Rewind and play the movie.
11. With the movie running, click the Add a Snowflake button repeatedly to add new snowflakes to the scene. After using the Add a Snowflake button ten times, your screen will look similar to Figure 18-7.
12. Stop the movie.

Note: You can only add ten snowflakes to the scene because the if...then statement checking for the count property of snowflakeList imposes this restriction. After you add ten snowflakes, the Add a Snowflake button generates a beep rather than a new snowflake.

Figure 18-7: The snowing1.dir movie after creating ten instances of snowflake objects

Summary

In the next chapter, you'll discover how to use Xtras. Before moving on, let's review some of the things you learned in this chapter.

- Lingo supports an object-oriented programming approach (OOP).
- OOP is implemented in Lingo by using parent scripts and child objects.
- Using OOP in Lingo requires the use of three keywords: `new`, `property`, and `ancestor`.
- A parent script includes an `on new` handler that creates a new instance of a child object.
- Using parent scripts and child objects is the best way to create multiple objects with similar characteristics in Director movies.
- With OOP methods, you reduce the complexity of your Lingo scripts because modifying a single parent script can change all child objects birthed from that common parent script. This approach simplifies debugging, adding new properties, and changing instructions for all related child objects.
- Making changes to the behavior of the child objects is centralized in the parent script. Because of this encapsulation, changing the behavior or even adding a behavior is a much simpler task.

✦ ✦ ✦

Xtras and File Manipulation

CHAPTER 19

◆ ◆ ◆ ◆

In This Chapter

Determining which Xtras are available

Opening a file using the fileIO Xtra

Saving a file using the fileIO Xtra

Packaging Xtras in a projector

◆ ◆ ◆ ◆

Macromedia Director is an extremely powerful authoring system — but no matter how many bells and whistles a product has, someone somewhere will want it to do more. Using Xtras, you can extend the already considerable capabilities of Director.

Xtending the Power of Director

The capacity to extend the features of an application is called *extensibility*. Two familiar examples of extensibility are the plug-ins used by Web browsers (such as Netscape Navigator and Microsoft Internet Explorer) and the plug-in filters supported by Adobe Photoshop. In both cases, the base product is enhanced by using small modules of code that enrich the product's feature set.

Director is extensible using plug-in modules of code called *Xtras* developed by Macromedia as well as third parties. Xtras are written in a language (often C or C++) that produces machine language code. Prior to Director 5, programmers could write XObjects using C or other programming languages to enhance the capabilities of Director. Just as XObjects are extensions to the Lingo programming language, Xtras are more powerful extensions to Macromedia programs. Most of the XObjects available before the advent of Director 5 are now available as scripting Xtras (see the discussion of scripting Xtras later in this chapter).

Caution Where possible, you should use Xtras rather than their XObject predecessors. XObjects are no longer supported by Macromedia. They have been replaced with Xtras that serve as cast members and transitions, provide additional authoring tools, expand the range of commands available in Director, and assist with importing and exporting specific types of media.

> ### Macromedia Open Architecture
>
> Xtras are the most common implementation of Macromedia's new Macromedia Open Architecture (MOA). As its name implies, MOA opens the architecture of Macromedia products to third-party vendors that develop and market tools (XObjects and Xtras) to enhance the power of Director and other Macromedia applications.
>
> Visual C/C++ on the Windows platform and Metrowerks CodeWarrior on the Macintosh platform are fully supported development environments for Macromedia Xtras. Developers can access the MOA Xtra Development Kit (XDK) from Macromedia's Web site at
>
>   www.macromedia.com

What Is an Xtra?

The software routines in Xtras (and their predecessors, XObjects) are written in C, C++, or another programming language. Director supports four kinds of Xtras that you can call, as you would a Lingo command, or access from a Director menu. Either way, you extend the capabilities and functionality of your Director movie. As the *X* in its name implies, an Xtra's code is external to Director.

Note: Every Xtra comes with its own internal documentation and command set.

Since Xtras interact at a low level with the operating system, they are platform specific. So an Xtra written for the Macintosh OS cannot be used on a Windows system, and vice versa. Most developers compile and provide Xtra code for both platforms as separate externals.

Why use Xtras?

When you first begin programming with Director, you will be overwhelmed with the application's native capabilities. However, once you gain a foothold in the learning curve and start building your own projects, you may wind up wanting "More! Now!" Director and Lingo cannot possibly include all the tricks and treats that every one of 250,000 developers wants and requires — and Xtras are what fill these "feature gaps." Xtras provide additional functionality in specific areas where Director is lacking. More commonly, an Xtra may fill the bill when Director "twists" but the developer also wants it to "shout."

Here are some of the things you can accomplish by using Xtras:

On the CD-ROM

- Add database functionality to your Director movie, using the FileFlex or the V12 Xtra. The V12 Database Engine Xtra is available on your companion CD-ROM in the goodies:v12 (goodies\v12) folder.

- Handle file input/output routines, using the fileIO Xtra.
- Add run-time print capabilities to a movie, using the PrintOMatic Xtra.
- Record and play back sound, using the Sound Xtra.
- Add new transitions, using the Killer Transitions Xtra.
- Include 3D modeling within a movie, using the 3D Dreams or the QuickDraw 3D Xtras.
- Play MIDI files, using the MIDXTRA Xtra.
- Import and export media into a movie.
- Add new transitions to a movie.

Xtras also add new tools to Director's tools set — similar to plug-in filters in Photoshop or OCXs in Visual Basic.

Xtra resources

The number of Xtras available for use with Director seems to grow almost daily. Three Web sites are especially helpful in tracking down Xtras that meet your specific programming needs. The first place to check is Macromedia's Web site at

www.macromedia.com/software/xtras/director

Second, you can check out the Penworks Publishing site at

www.penworks.com/xtras/home.html

Penworks (P.O. Box 531, Holderness, NH 03245, USA) publishes the *Lingo User's Journal*.

Another excellent resource for locating Xtras (and other Director-related tools) is Gretchen MacDowell's Mile-High Table of Products for Director at

www.updatestage.com/products.html

Types of Xtras

Director Xtras fall into five general categories: transition Xtras, cast member Xtras, scripting Xtras, tool Xtras, and importing Xtras.

Transition Xtras

Director has over 50 predefined, built-in transitions. You can enlarge the number and type of transitions available even further by installing one or more *transition Xtras*.

Transition Xtras control and customize frame-to-frame Stage changes. A transition Xtra can include its own custom properties, a properties dialog box, an animated thumbnail, a Cast window icon, and an About box. It can use a combination of visual change, sounds, and other media to handle the changes between frames in your movie.

To access the new transition Xtra after it is installed, you'll follow this general procedure:

1. Locate the frame where you want the transition to occur.
2. Double-click the Score's Transition channel cell in the desired frame.
3. When the Frame Properties: Transition dialog box appears (Figure 19-1), select a transition group from the Categories list and then choose a specific transition from the Transitions list.

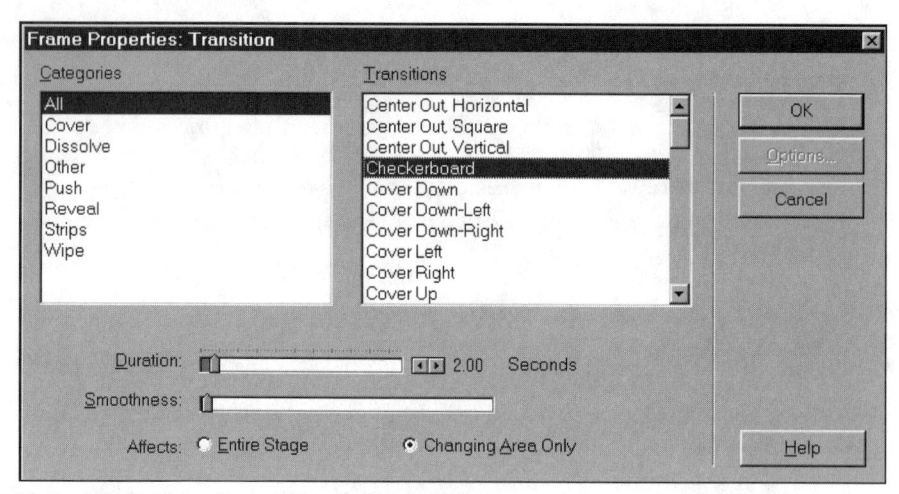

Figure 19-1: Choosing an installed transition Xtra

4. If desired, select the Options button to set properties for the transition Xtra.
5. Click the OK button to close the dialog box.

As soon as you use a transition Xtra in the Score's Transition channel, it appears in the Cast window, just like any other cast member.

To be accessible during playback, a transition Xtra must be distributed with the movie. Typically, packaging a transition Xtra is handled automatically when you activate the Check Movies for Xtras option in the Projector Options dialog box.

Cast member Xtras

Cast member Xtras are similar to other objects that you include in the cast of your movie. They add functionality such as database engines, text processing engines, and graphics engines. Once installed, the cast member Xtra appears on the Insert menu. Depending on how it is designed, a single cast member Xtra can add one or more menu items to the Insert menu.

Cast member Xtras are sometimes referred to as *sprite Xtras* (because they operate as sprites on the Stage after assignment to the Score) or *asset Xtras* (because they increase the assets available to the movie). Two examples of cast member Xtras include the Button Editor, discussed in Chapter 6, and the QuickDraw 3D Xtra, discussed in Chapter 26.

Just like other Director sprites, the cast member Xtra is displayed on the Stage, receives and reacts to user actions (mouse clicks, keypresses, and movement of the playback head), and responds to standard and custom Lingo commands. Similar to a transition Xtra, a cast member Xtra may include its own custom properties, a properties dialog box, a media editor, an animated thumbnail, a Cast window icon, and an About box.

Here's the general procedure for using a cast member Xtra:

1. Select a location in the Cast window.
2. Select the cast member Xtra from the Insert menu. The cast member Xtra appears in the Cast window and can be assigned to the Score.
3. To set the Xtra's properties, select the object in the Cast window, open the Cast Member Properties dialog box, and click the Options button.
4. You can open the Xtra's media editor by double-clicking the cast member's thumbnail in the Cast window.

To be accessible during playback, a cast member Xtra must be distributed with the movie. Typically, packaging a cast member Xtra is handled automatically when you activate the Check Movies for Xtras option in the Projector Options dialog box.

Scripting Xtras

Scripting Xtras enhance Director's scripting language by adding new commands and new capabilities to Lingo. To access the functions provided by a scripting Xtra, you must use the Xtra's built-in methods (which are discussed later in this chapter). Scripting Xtras can control movies, internal and external casts, cast members, Scores, media, and almost any Director feature. The fileIO Xtra, shipped with Director and available on Macromedia's Web site, is an example of a scripting Xtra. It enables you to open, close, save, and append data to an external file.

Scripting Xtras on the Windows platform take the form of dynamic link libraries (DLLs). For Director to have access to the "power" of the Xtra, the file ending with the .dll extension must be placed in the Xtras folder or included in the same folder as your projector. Placement of the Xtra file is covered in the later section, "How does Director know an xtra exists?"

For a scripting Xtra's methods to be accessible during playback, the Xtra must be distributed with your movie. This type of Xtra must be manually added to the list of Xtras that can be packaged in a projector. To add a scripting Xtra, select the Modify⇨Movie⇨Xtras command and then click Add. Once the scripting Xtra appears on the list of movie Xtras, it is automatically packaged with the projector if you activate the Check Movies for Xtras option in the Projector Options dialog box.

Tool Xtras

Tool Xtras add custom tools that you can use to create or modify cast members and sprites. Tool Xtras can take the form of

- Bitmap filters (such as Photoshop filters)
- External casts (such as the Behavior Library, stored as Behavior Library.CST)
- Director movies (open as a MIAW in authoring mode)

The Animation wizard, which you can use to create banners, rolling credits, and zoomed text, is an example of a tool Xtra that is stored as a movie in the Xtras folder.

The tool Xtra is only useful when you are creating and editing a movie. As such, this type of Xtra is only available in authoring mode and not useful or available when a movie plays. Tool Xtras are not packaged in projectors for distribution to the end-user.

Tool Xtras are placed in the Xtras folder (or in subfolders within the Xtras folder) and are accessible from the Xtras menu, as illustrated in Figure 19-2.

Look in the Xtras folder within the Director 6 folder on your hard drive, and you'll find the Behavior Library (Behavior Library.CST in Windows). In the Wizard folder (within the Xtras folder), you'll find the Animation Wizard movie (Animation Wizard.dir movie in Windows). Photoshop filters can be stored within the Xtras folder or in one of its subfolders.

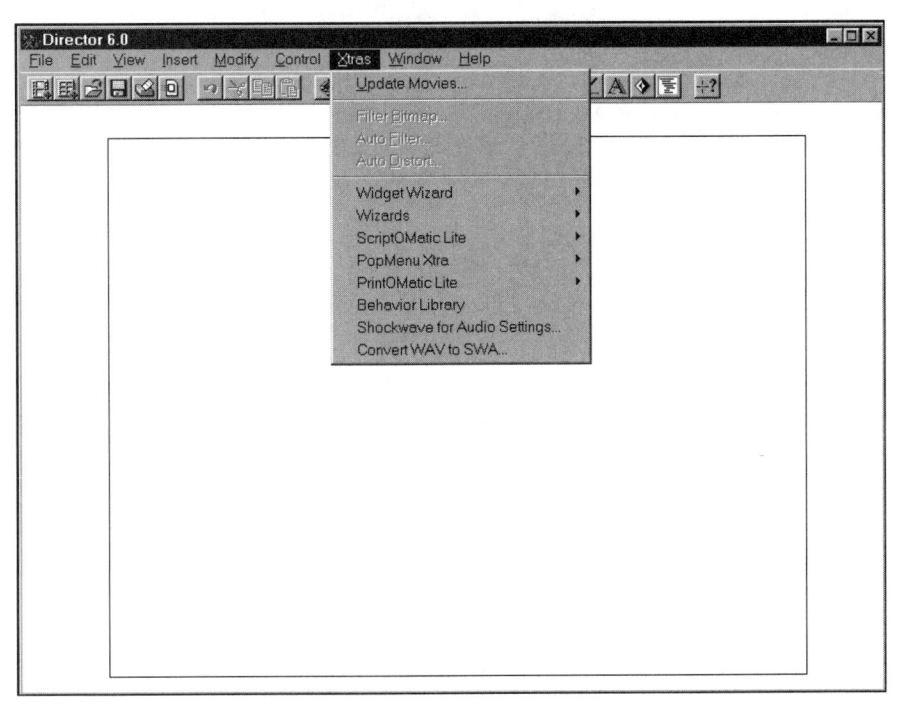

Figure 19-2: Xtras menu showing installed tool Xtras

Importing Xtras

An *importing Xtra* includes the code required to import various types of assets (media) into Director. Director uses an importing Xtra to access external media when the movie plays. If the Xtra is not available, Director cannot import the specified type of media. When you create a projector with the Check Movies for Xtras option enabled (in the Projector Options dialog box), Director automatically adds the importing Xtras required to access any media within your movie.

> **Note:** By default, when the Check Movies for Xtras option is enabled, Director includes the following Xtras in the projector: Sound Import Export, SWA Decompression, SWA Streaming, and MIX Services (Mix32.x32 in Windows 95).

Xtras that come with Director 6

Although by definition Xtras are created by third-party developers, Macromedia distributes over 100 Xtras with Director 6. Some of the Xtras available on the Director installation CD (and from Macromedia's Web site) include fileIO and PrintOMatic Lite:

✦ PrintOMatic Lite is a full-featured printing engine with which you can provide custom print output from your movies. You can generate order forms, data sheets, and other printed material. More information on PrintOMatic Lite — and the upgrade to PrintOMatic — is available from Gray Matter Design at 300 Brannan Street, Suite 210, San Francisco, CA 94101, telephone 800-933-6223, or by contacting their Web site at

www.gmatter.com

✦ The fileIO Xtra gives you the ability to read and write to external files from within Director movies. The fileIO Xtra is used as the vehicle to explain the use of Xtras within Director, in the upcoming sections.

Using Xtras in Director

To effectively use an Xtra, you must

- ✦ Know where to install the Xtra so Director can find it, if it is not already installed.
- ✦ Install the Xtra, if it is not automatically installed by Director.
- ✦ Know how to use specific Lingo commands to access and use Xtras (for scripting Xtras only).
- ✦ Identify and use commands that are specific to the Xtra (for scripting Xtras only).
- ✦ Know how to access Xtras using the Director menu system (for cast member, transition, and tool Xtras).
- ✦ Know how to package Xtras in projectors (for all Xtras except tools Xtras).

When three's a *welcome* crowd

Ever wonder where the term third-party originated? When you deal with the developer and publisher of a product such as Macromedia, the company is the "party of the first part," and you (the developer who pays a fee to use the product provided by the company) are the "party of the second part." Any person or company who creates and sells to you add-on tools, utilities, or services to help you better utilize the original product is the "party of the third part."

How does Director know an Xtra exists?

For Director to recognize and use an Xtra during authoring, the Xtra must be installed in one specific location. Director will always look in the Xtras folder within the Director folder, or in a subfolder *within* the Xtras folder.

When Director 6 is installed, several folders are automatically created within the Xtras folder. They include the following:

- Wizard, which includes the Animation Wizard.dir movie
- Net Support, with NetLingo extensions to Lingo that are discussed in Chapter 24
- MIX Readers, which stores the MIX Services (Mix32.x32 on Windows) file and all other Xtras for importing and exporting various types of media
- Media Support, with the fileIO and Shockwave for Audio Xtras
- GrayMatter, with ScriptOMatic Lite and PrintOMatic Lite Xtras
- MMX, with Windows MMX support
- Help Support

If you have more than one Macromedia application on your development workstation, Xtras for other Macromedia applications may be installed in a *common folder* where *all* Macromedia applications can locate them. Note, however, that Director *does not* look for Xtras in this common Xtra folder. Table 19-1 lists each operating system's location for the common folder.

Table 19-1
Locations of Common Folders

System	Location of Common Folder
Windows 95 or Windows NT	Program Files\Common Files\Macromedia\Xtras
Windows 3.1	Windows\Macromed\Xtras
Macintosh OS	System Folder:Macromedia:Xtras

When you create a projector that requires an Xtra to run, the Xtra should be included in the same folder with the projector. If the Xtra is stored elsewhere, you must provide the path to the file each time the Xtra is called within your movie. The topic of packaging Xtras is discussed in more detail later in this chapter.

Note: Director lets you place Xtras up to five levels deep within the Xtras folder, and it will still locate and automatically open the Xtra when it's needed. This feature enables you to group Xtras by function or vendor in the Xtra folder's subfolders.

If you run a movie or projector that references an Xtra that Director cannot find, the program issues you one of three types of warnings:

- ✦ If the missing Xtra is a transition Xtra, Director substitutes a simple Cut transition.
- ✦ For missing cast member Xtras, Director displays a red "X" character on the Stage. This serves as both a warning and a placeholder for the missing cast member Xtra.
- ✦ In all other cases when an Xtra is missing, Director displays an Alert box similar to Figure 19-3.

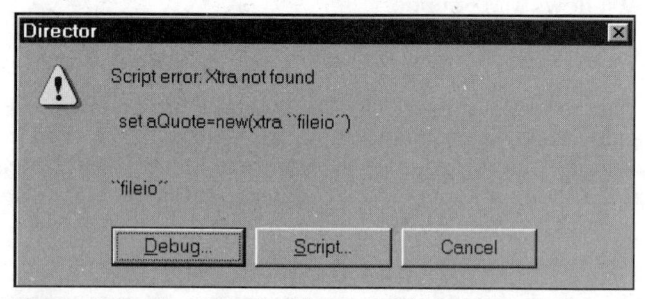

Figure 19-3: Alert box identifying missing Xtra

Installing new Xtras

If you are installing a new Xtra, make sure it is copied to the Xtras folder or to a subfolder within the Xtras folder on your hard drive. When properly placed, Xtras are automatically opened when Director is loaded and automatically closed when you exit the program. "Properly placed" means installed in the folders that Director checks, as described in the preceding section.

Note: If you install a new Xtra by copying it to the Xtras folder, you must exit Director and then reopen the application before the new Xtra is recognized.

Although the actual implementation of a new Xtra depends on the type of Xtra installed, Director always does the following things once it recognizes a new Xtra:

- ✦ Adds the Xtra to the Insert menu
- ✦ Adds the Xtra to the Xtras menu
- ✦ Makes the Xtra accessible using Lingo

♦ Adds the Xtra to the list of transitions available from the Frame Properties: Transition dialog box

Using the `openXlib` and `closeXlib` commands

Xtras in the Xtra folder are automatically opened when Director starts. If you choose to store new Xtras (or the older obsolete XObjects) in a different folder, you must use the `openXlib` command to open the Xtra and make it accessible for use in your movie.

Xtras and XObjects, as well as HyperCard XCMDs and XFCNs, are stored in Xlibrary files, which are opened using the `openXlib` command. The syntax for the `openXlib` command is simple. You follow the command with the Xlibrary file name that you want to open, like this:

```
openXlib "fileIO"
```

After using the `openXlib` command to open an Xlibrary, you must manually close the Xlibrary by using the `closeXlib` command, like this:

```
closeXlib "fileIO"
```

Note: When you're opening and closing the Xlibrary under Windows, the .dll extension is optional. You do not need to include it in the command.

Warning: If you do not indicate a specific Xlibrary filename in the `closeXlib` command, all open Xlibrary files are closed. You'll do well to develop the habit of closing Xlibraries as soon as you are done using them.

Before you proceed to use Xtras in the construction of your movies, you must know which ones are installed on your system. The easiest way to find out is to issue the `showXlib` command in the Message window.

Determining Which Xtras Are Available

1. With Director open, open the Message window.
2. Type **showXlib** and press Enter.

   On the Macintosh, the Message window looks similar to Figure 19-4. Notice that both Xtras and XObjects are listed.

```
-- Welcome to Director --
showXlib
-- XLibraries:
--    Xtra: ScriptColor
--    Xtra: PrintOMatic_Lite
--    Xtra: NetLingo
--    Xtra: QTVRXtra
--    Xtra: Mui
--    Xtra: fileio
-- "*Standard.xlib"
--    XObject: SerialPort      Id:200
--    XObject: XCMDGlue        Id:2020
```

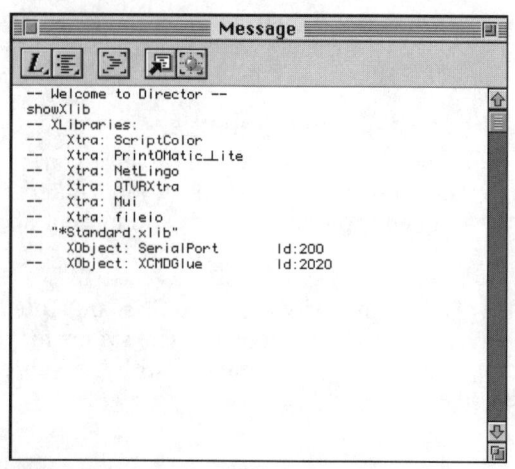

Figure 19-4: Message window showing installed Xtras on a Macintosh system

On a Windows system, the Message window looks similar to Figure 19-5. Several Xtras are listed in this example, including NetLingo, fileIO, and PrintOMatic_Lite.

```
-- Welcome to Director --
-- "Now loading LINGO.INI 7/22/97 8:47 PM"
-- "This computer is running in  24-bit color depth."
showXlib
-- XLibraries:
--    Xtra: NetLingo
--    Xtra: DirMMX
--    Xtra: fileio
--    Xtra: QTVRXtra
--    Xtra: Mui
--    Xtra: ScriptColor
--    Xtra: PrintOMatic_Lite
```

Figure 19-5: Message window showing installed Xtras on a Windows system

Note: Keep in mind that some Xtras (the scripting Xtras) are accessed using Lingo. Other types of Xtras appear as part of the Director user interface — menu choices or cast members or both.

Using Xtra-Related Lingo Commands

Lingo includes some commands that are specific to the use of Xtras. You have already read about three of these commands: `closeXlib`, `openXlib`, and `showXlib`. In addition, you can use Lingo to create a new instance of an Xtra (similar to creating an instance of a child object, as covered in Chapter 18). Because Xtras include their own command set, you need a *method* to discover which commands are available for use with each Xtra.

Creating a new instance of an Xtra

To use an installed Xtra in your movie, you still need to create an instance of the Xtra. The way in which you create an instance varies depending on the type of Xtra. For example, the method that you use to create a scripting Xtra is different from the method you use to create a transition, tool, or cast member Xtra. Because the latter three types can be created using Director's user interface (menu choices and so on), we'll focus here on the procedure for creating an instance of a scripting Xtra.

First, each instance of an Xtra is created using the `xtra` function, as follows:

    xtra nameOfTheXtra

You replace *nameOfTheXtra* with the Xtra's name inside quotation marks.

Next, to create the new instance of the scripting Xtra, you use the `new` function, with the keyword `xtra` as the first parameter and the name of the Xtra as the second parameter, like this:

    new (xtra nameOfTheXtra)

To effectively use the newly created instance, you assign the instance to a variable. In the following example, an instance of the fileIO Xtra is assigned to the variable `aQuote` using the `set` command:

    set aQuote = new(xtra "fileIO")

Like a child object, when you are done using an instance of an Xtra, you should remove the instance from memory. To do so, simply set the variable representing the instance to zero. The following example removes from memory the `aQuote` instance of the fileIO Xtra:

    Set aQuote =0

Listing the messages you can send to an Xtra

Each Xtra can receive messages that cause a specific action to occur. Earlier, we loosely referred to these messages as "commands." In reality, each Xtra includes specific handlers (just like the scripts you have created in this book), but you cannot see them. These invisible handlers are called *methods*. When you send a message to the Xtra, the method is executed.

Obviously, since they're invisible, you'll need a method to determine the methods available for an Xtra. That's where the `mMessageList` command comes in. The following instruction displays the Xtra's command set in the Message window, as shown in Figure 19-6, about the fileIO Xtra:

```
put mMessageList(xtra "fileIO")
```

```
put mMessageList (xtra "fileIO")
-- "xtra fileio -- CH 18apr97
new object me -- create a new child instance
-- FILEIO --
fileName object me -- return fileName string of the open file
status object me -- return the error code of the last method called
error object me, int error -- return the error string of the error
setFilterMask object me, string mask -- set the filter mask for dialogs
openFile object me, string fileName, int mode -- opens named file. valid modes:
0=r/w 1=r 2=w
closeFile object me -- close the file
displayOpen object me -- displays an open dialog and returns the selected fileName
to lingo
displaySave object me, string title, string defaultFileName -- displays save dialog
and returns selected fileName to lingo
createFile object me, string fileName -- creates a new file called fileName
setPosition object me, int position -- set the file position
getPosition object me -- get the file position
getLength object me -- get the length of the open file
writeChar object me, string theChar -- write a single character (by ASCII code) to
the file
writeString object me, string theString -- write a null-terminated string to the
file
readChar object me -- read the next character of the file and return it as an ASCII
code value
readLine object me -- read the next line of the file (including the next RETURN)
and return as a string
```

Figure 19-6: Using the `mMessageList` command to get a list of fileIO methods in Message window

Tip

Well-documented Xtras also include a readme.txt file that lists a glossary or list of methods available through the Xtra. Additionally, the readme.txt file includes error messages and additional notes on the Xtra and its features.

Using Xtra-Specific Methods

Once you know the specific methods available with an Xtra, you can incorporate them into your movie and access the features of the Xtra. Shortly you'll see how to use the fileIO Xtra, but first let's review a few of the methods available and displayed in Figure 19-6.

The fileIO Xtra provides file-management services that Director itself does not offer. With fileIO, you can open, close, save, create, and delete a disk file. You can also display an Open dialog box, save it, and filter (restrict) the files that appear in the dialog box. This Xtra also enables you to read and write a character, string, line, word, or the entire file.

Caution

Note that the commands covered in the following sections are not Lingo commands. They are specific to the fileIO Xtra. If the Xtra is not available, the commands are not available. When you rely on methods available through an Xtra, it's easy to forget that these methods or commands are not native to Director and Lingo. For a project that relies on one or more scripting Xtras, you *must* distribute the Xtra(s) with the project. Because Xtras are typically developed by third-party developers, be sure you are licensed to distribute the Xtra with your product.

Opening a file using the fileIO Xtra

Before you can read or write to a file, the file must be opened using the `openFile()` method, as follows:

```
openFile (instance, nameOfFile, mode)
```

The *instance* refers to the instance of the fileIO Xtra. In the following example, the instance is set to a variable named `aQuote`:

```
set aQuote = new(xtra "fileIO")
```

Note

A single instance of fileIO can reference a single open file. To open more than one file at a time, you must create multiple instances of fileIO.

If you use this instruction in a movie, you would substitute `aQuote` for *instance* in the syntax of the instruction.

The *nameOfFile* parameter is replaced with the filename of the disk file you want to open. If this parameter refers to an actual filename (rather than a variable name), the filename must be enclosed in quotation marks. The filename can be qualified using the path to the file on the local computer system. If the file to open is in the same folder as the Director movie or the projector, you can use a relative pathname or list just the filename itself.

Tip: Lingo provides a pathname operator, the @ sign, that can substitute for the typical pathname delimiters used by the Macintosh OS (:) or the Windows operating system (\ ).

The last parameter for the `openFile()` command is *mode*. Files are opened in one of three modes. You replace the *mode* parameter with one of the following numeric codes. To open a file

- ✦ In read-only mode, use the numeric code 1
- ✦ In write-only mode, use the numeric code 2
- ✦ In read-and-write mode, use the numeric code 0

Caution: After you set the mode to write or read/write, you can write to a disk file. Everything after the current position in the file will be overwritten by the write operation.

In the following example, Director uses the fileIO Xtra to create an instance of the Xtra called `aQuote`, and to open a file named `ReadThis.Txt` in read-only mode:

```
openFile(aQuote, "ReadThis.Txt", 1)
```

Closing a file using the fileIO Xtra

When you have finished working with the data in a file, you must close it. You cannot close a file unless it has been previously opened using the `openFile()` method. Here is the syntax for the instruction to close a file:

```
closeFile (instance)
```

In the following instruction, the `aQuote` instance of the fileIO Xtra is closed:

```
closeFile (aQuote)
```

Displaying an Open dialog box

Users are accustomed to seeing an Open dialog box when it comes time to load a file. The fileIO Xtra includes a method that displays a platform-specific Open dialog box, with which the user can select a file to open.

This method does more than just display the dialog box. It returns a fully qualified path and filename, which can then be used in your Lingo scripts and handlers. To access the method, use the following syntax:

```
displayOpen (instance)
```

To use the path and filename in your Lingo handlers, you can use an instruction similar to the following:

```
set fileName = displayOpen (instance)
```

In this example, the `fileName` variable now stores the path and filename returned by the `displayOpen` method.

Using the fileIO Xtra filterMask

You can limit the files visible in an Open dialog box by using the fileIO Xtra's `setFilterMask` method. (This method is also used with the Save dialog box discussed later in the chapter.)

```
setFilterMask(instance, filterMask)
```

The *filterMask* parameter is replaced with a text string identifying the file type (Windows only) and an associated file extension (Windows and Macintosh). Together, these values restrict the type of files that will appear in the dialog box. By default, when you create a new instance of the fileIO Xtra, *filterMask* is set to all files (*.* or "").

Note: The `setFilterMask()` method must be issued prior to using the `displayOpen` or `displaySave` method.

Setting *filterMask* under Windows

The *filterMask* parameter differs slightly depending on whether you're using a Windows or Macintosh platform. When you create a filter mask for use on a Windows system, you must stipulate the type of files using a text string (such as "Text Files") followed by the file's extension (such as *.txt or *.doc) The *filterMask* value is limited to 256 characters under Windows.

On a Windows system, the following instruction will display only text files in the Open dialog box:

```
setFilterMask(aQuote, "Text Files, *.txt")
```

On the Windows platform, you can offer users the ability to access more than one filter by listing multiple file types in the filter mask. For instance, the following instruction creates two filters:

```
setFilterMask(aQuote, "Document Files, *.doc, Text Files,¬
*.txt")
```

Each specified type is not displayed simultaneously; instead, the user has an opportunity to select one of the listed filter masks from a drop-down list, as shown in Figure 19-7. The first filter you list in the instruction becomes the default selection when the Open or Save dialog box is displayed.

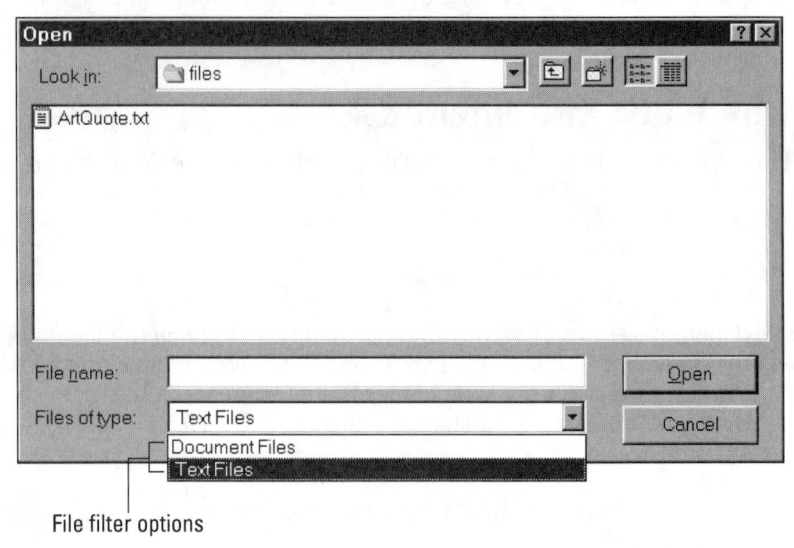

Figure 19-7: Drop-down list of file filter options

Setting *filterMask* under the Mac OS

When you create a filter mask on a Macintosh system, you do *not* use a text string to describe the type of file. You only include a string of files types, using four-character case-sensitive codes (such as TEXT or PICT) in the filter mask. On the Macintosh, you are limited to four sets of four-character filename extensions.

In the following example, only text files will be displayed:

    setFilterMask(aQuote, "Text Files, TEXT")

> **Note:** Using this filter, the fileIO Xtra displays *any* file it considers a text file, including MS-DOS text files and Director movie files with the .dir extension. This filter ignores the extension (since most Macintosh files do not include an extension) and interprets the file based on its header.

You can include additional file types (maximum of four) by stringing them together. For example, this command displays only text files and bitmap (PICT) files:

    setFilterMask(aQuote, "Text Files, TEXTPICT")

The following table lists some of the four-character codes that you can use with the `setFilterMask` method on the Mac.

File Type Codes for `setFilterMask`	File Type
MV95	Director movie
PICT	Bitmap image file
TEXT	Text file
W6BN	Microsoft Word file
WPD3	Corel WordPerfect file

Resetting *filterMask* to all files

You may need to reset the drop-down list back to All Files. To reset the filter mask to display All Files, use the following instruction:

```
setFilterMask(aQuote, "")
```

Accessing data in a file

The fileIO Xtra has several methods available for you to read data from a file. Each method reads a specific chunk of data, as identified in Table 19-2. To use any of these methods, the file must be open in read or read/write mode.

Table 19-2
Methods for Use with the fileIO Xtra to Read Chunks of Text

fileIO Xtra "Chunk" Methods	Result
`readChar(instance)`	Reads the character (either single or double-byte) at the current position of the pointer. Next, the method increments the position and returns the character to Lingo as a string.
`ReadWord(instance)`	Reads the next word starting at the current pointer position. Next, the method returns the string to Lingo.
`ReadLine(instance)`	Reads from the current position, up to and including the next carriage-return in the file. Next, the method increments the pointer's position and returns the string to Lingo.
`readFile(instance)`	Reads from the current position of the pointer to the end-of-file (EOF) character. Next, the method returns the file to Lingo as a string.

Once you access the data from a file, you need to assign it to a variable, so the data can be used by your movie. In the following snippet of code, the contents of the entire file are assigned to the `contents` variable. In the second line of code, the data stored in `contents` is placed in the field cast member named `Today's Quote`:

```
set contents = readFile(aQuote)
set the text of field "Today's Quote" to contents
```

On the CD-ROM In the next exercise, you will use a text file (artquote.txt) and a partially complete Director movie (artquote.dir). The files artquote.dir and artquote.txt are on your companion CD-ROM in the exercise:ch19 (exercise\ch19) folder. In its current condition and as shown in Figure 19-8, artquote.dir includes a bitmap cast member called "Art" (cast member 1) and a frame script (to cycle the movie on frame 1).

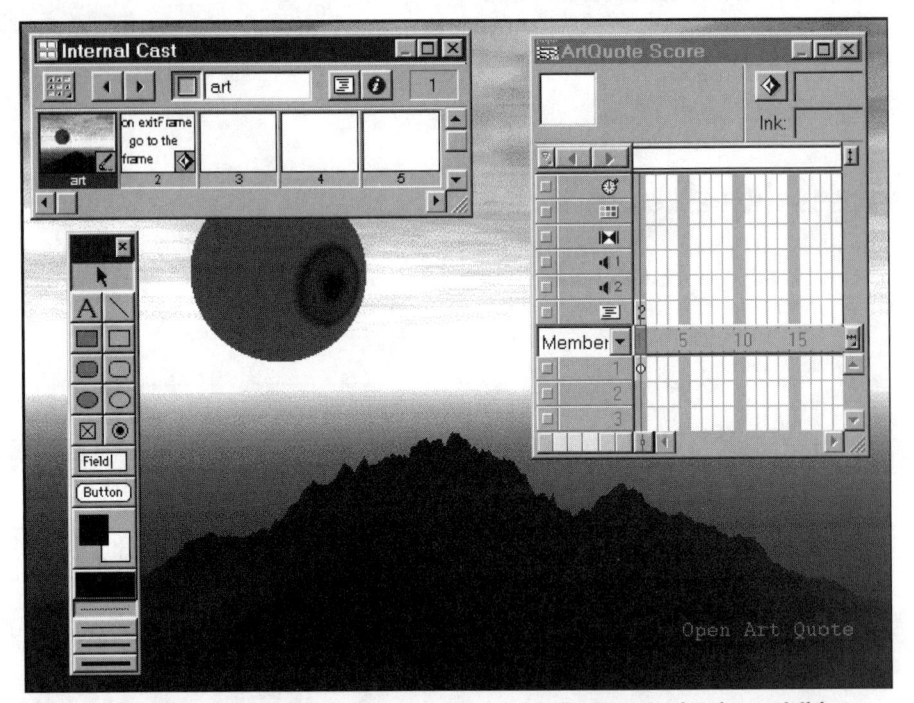

Figure 19-8: The artquote.dir movie on Stage, with floating Tool Palette visible

Notice the text "Open Art Quote" in the bottom-right corner of the Stage. In the following steps, you'll create a transparent button (with a script attached) to appear over that text. When the user clicks this button, the attached cast member script will be executed. The script then opens an external text file and reads its contents into a field on the Stage.

Because of the platform-specific parameters required, the instruction that calls the `setFilterMask` method will differ based on whether your movie runs on Macintosh or Windows. You select the instruction to execute by using the `machineType` function. This function returns a value of 256 if the system is an IBM PC-type system. All other values returned by the function indicate Macintosh systems. As a result, you can use an if...then...else statement similar to the following when you need to use one instruction for Macintosh systems and a different instruction for Windows systems:

```
if the machineType = 256 then
        --Instructions for Windows Systems
else
        --Instructions for Macintosh Systems
end if
```

In the script you add to the movie, you'll use the bits of example code from the preceding discussion of the fileIO Xtra. Examine the code, and you can see that the script creates an instance of the fileIO Xtra, sets a filter mask, displays the Open dialog box (using the filter mask) with only text files visible, opens the file selected by the user, reads the data into a variable named `contents`, places the text into a field called `Today's Quote`, and then closes the disk file. At the end of the handler, the instance of the fileIO Xtra is eliminated.

Opening a File Using the fileIO Xtra

1. Open the artquote.dir movie in Director. It's on the CD-ROM in the exercise:ch19 (exercise\ch19) folder.

2. If the Tool Palette is not displayed, open it (Command+7 or Ctrl+7).

3. At the bottom of the Tool Palette, set the border to No Line.

4. Be sure the foreground color chip is set to black and the background color chip is set to white.

5. Select the Rectangle tool (*not* the Filled Rectangle tool).

6. Click and drag to create a rectangle that surrounds the "Open Art Quote" text on the Stage, as shown in Figure 19-9.

7. With the rectangular area still selected, shorten the sprite to span a single frame (frame 1) and set the ink effect to Matte.

8. Select the new shape cast member in Cast window slot 3.

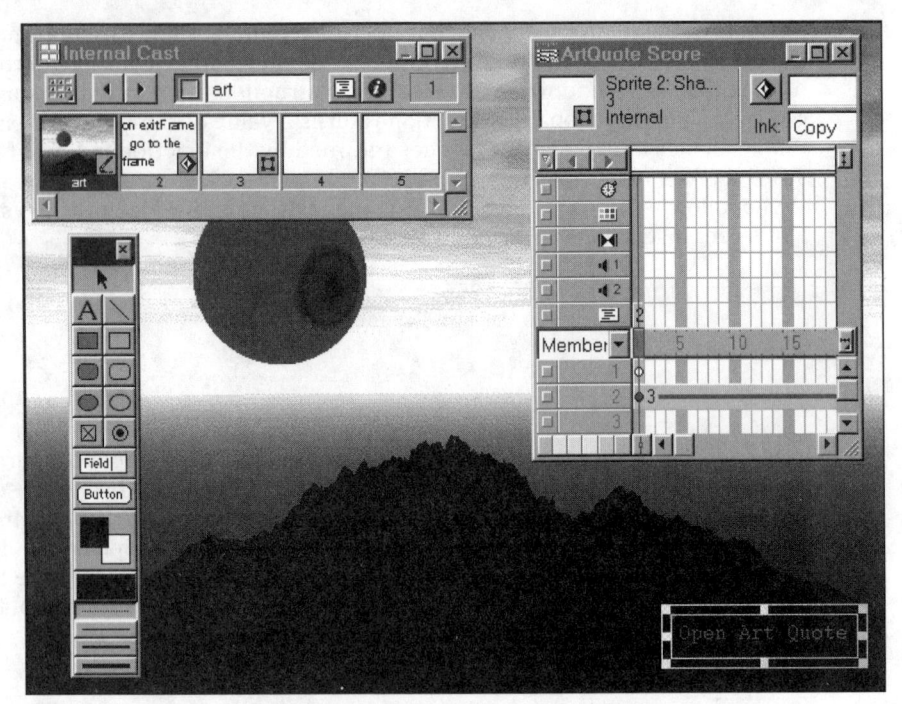

Figure 19-9: A rectangle area drawn for the transparent button

9. Attach the following script to the new shape cast member:

```
on mouseUp
     set aQuote=new(xtra "fileio")
     if the machineType = 256 then
          setFilterMask(aQuote,"Text Files, *.txt")
     else
          setFilterMask(aQuote,"TEXT")
     end if
     set fileName=displayOpen(aQuote)
     openFile(aQuote,fileName,1)
     set contents = readFile(aQuote)
     set the text of field "Today's Quote" to contents
     closeFile(aQuote)
     set aQuote=0
end
```

10. Close the Script window.
11. Select the Field tool on the Tool Palette.

12. Click and drag in the white area of the Stage image (as shown in Figure 19-10) to build a new field.

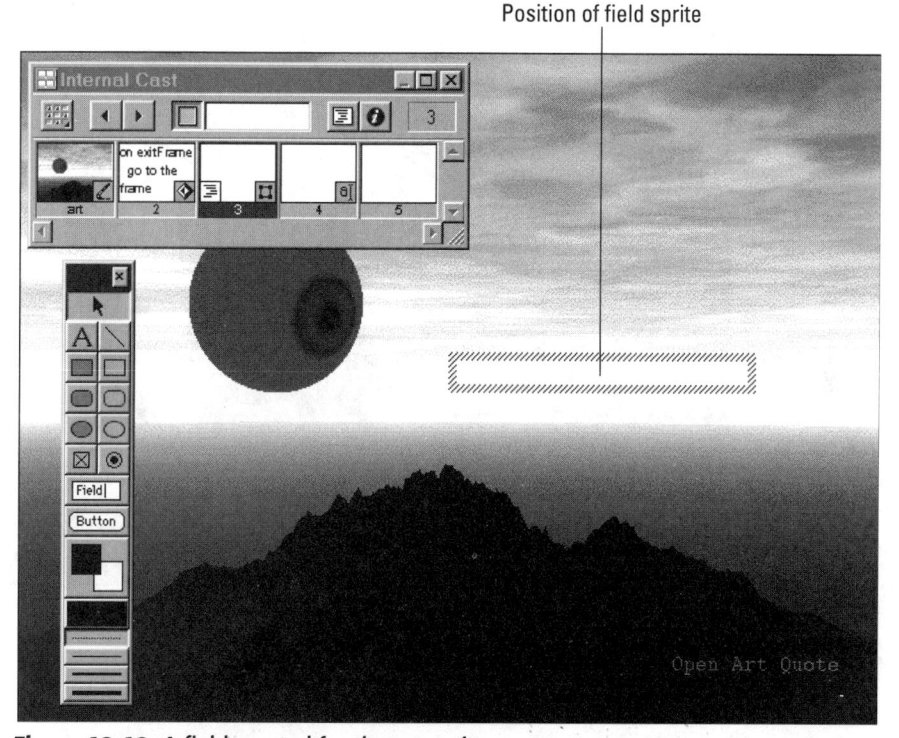

Figure 19-10: A field created for the quotation

13. Shorten the new field sprite to span one frame and set the ink to Background Transparent.
14. Select the field cast member (slot 4) in the Cast window.
15. Change the field cast member name to **Today's Quote**.
16. Save the movie as **artquot1.dir,** rewind, and play it.
17. With the movie running, click the Open Art Quote (transparent) button.
18. When the Open File dialog box appears, navigate to the folder on your local hard drive where you store your practice files. Locate and select the artquote.txt file, and click the Open button.

    Your Stage now appears similar to Figure 19-11. If you stop the movie and check the Today's Quote field, it contains the text of the artquote.txt file.

Figure 19-11: Completed artquote.dir movie

19. Save the movie again as artquot1.dir and close it.

More fileIO Methods

In addition to what you've used so far, there are several other methods available through the fileIO Xtra. You still need to learn how to open a Save dialog box, create a new disk file, and save data to it from your movie.

Displaying a Save dialog box

Users are accustomed to seeing a Save dialog box when it comes time to save a file. The fileIO Xtra includes a method, `displaySave`, that displays a platform-specific Save dialog box that allows the user to type the path and filename of a file to save.

> **Note**
> You use the `setFilterMask()` method to determine which file types are displayed in the Save dialog box. In order for it to affect the files displayed, `setFilterMask()` must be issued prior to using the `displaySave` method. The `setFilterMask()` does more than just display the dialog box. It returns a fully qualified path and filename (indicating where the file is saved), which can then be used in your Lingo scripts and handlers.

To access the `displaySave()` method, use the following syntax:

```
displaySave(instance, titleName, defaultFileName)
```

The *titleName* parameter is used to set the text that appears on the title bar of the Save dialog box. If you want the data to be stored in a specific file by default, you can use the *defaultFileName* parameter to establish the path and filename. To save game scores, for instance, in a file called scores.txt in the same folder as your movie's projector, you would use the following instruction:

```
displaySave(saveScores,"Save Game Scores","scores.txt")
```

This instruction designates the string "Save Game Scores" as the text to appear on the Save dialog box's title bar.

To use the path and filename in your Lingo handlers, you can use the `set` command to store the information in a variable. The following instruction is an example of this technique:

```
set fileName = displaySave (saveScores,"Save Game¬
Scores","scores.txt")
```

In this example, the `fileName` variable stores the path and filename returned by the `displaySave` method.

Creating a new disk file

Using the `createFile` method from the fileIO Xtra, you can create a new disk file in the current directory, or in a different folder if you specify the path. The syntax for this method is

```
createFile(instance, newFileName)
```

If the *newFileName* parameter is an actual filename, it must be surrounded by quotation marks. If it is a variable name, no quotation marks are required.

> **Caution:** When specifying a specific filename, you must use the Macintosh delimiter (:) or the Windows delimiter (\ ) between folders in the pathname. The Lingo @ pathname operator and relative paths are not supported by this method.

Creating a new file does not automatically open it. You must open it before you can read or write data to the new file, just as you did in the "Opening a File Using the fileIO Xtra" exercise.

Codes for Macintosh file types

For Macintosh users, after you create and open the new file, you must tell the Finder the type of file that you want to write to. You use another fileIO Xtra method called `setFinderInfo` to do this. The syntax for this method is

```
setFinderInfo(instance, "fileType creator")
```

The *fileType* parameter is replaced with a four-character code representing the file type (such as TEXT, APPL, or PICT). The *creator* parameter is replaced with a four-character code representing the application that created the file (such as XCEL for Excel, ttxt for TeachText or SimpleText, and MSWD for Microsoft Word). Using these codes has no effect on a Windows system.

> **Caution:** The four-character codes for the file type and the application that creates the file *are* case sensitive!

Table 19-3 lists a few of the codes that can be used with the `setFinderInfo` method.

Table 19-3
File Types and Creator Codes for the `setFinderInfo` Method

File Type Code	Creator Code	Source Application
ttro	CARO	Acrobat Reader (read-only file)
sWWP	BOBO	ClarisWorks text file
MV95	MD95	Director movie
APPL	XCEL	Excel spreadsheet
TEXT	MWPR	MacWrite Pro
TEXT	8BIM	Photoshop text file
PICT	DAD2	Bitmap image file

File Type Code	Creator Code	Source Application
TEXT	stxt	ReadMe
TEXT	ttxt	SimpleText or TeachText
TEXT	ANON	Text file from unknown application
W6BN	MSWD	Microsoft Word 6 document
TEXT	MSWD	Microsoft Word text file
WPD3	WPC2	Corel WordPerfect 3.5 document
TEXT	WPC2	Corel WordPerfect Text file

The fileIO Xtra also includes a `getFinderInfo` method that returns file type and creator codes for an existing file. Both methods (`getFinderInfo` and `setFinderInfo`) only work when a file has been opened using the `openFile` method.

Writing a disk file

Once you have created and opened a new file, the next logical step is to write something to it. The fileIO Xtra includes two similar methods for accomplishing this task. After using the keyword (either `writeString` or `writeChar`), you identify the instance of the fileIO Xtra in use, and then specify the text string to write.

Here's the syntax for the `writeString` method:

    writeString (instance, theTextString)

In this method, a text string is substituted for *theTextString* parameter and written to the open file. The string written to the file is a null-terminated string. For instance, to write a score of 12 to an instance of the fileIO Xtra called diceThrow, you can use the following instruction:

    writeString(diceThrow, "12")

The other option is to write a single character to the current pointer position in the file using the `writeChar` method. The syntax is

    writeChar(instance, theChar)

Note: To use either of these write operations, the file must be open in write or read/write mode. All writes are to the current pointer position within the file.

Knowing the current position within a file

In the foregoing discussion of reading and writing to a disk file, we've used the concept of *current position*. If you are familiar with database management, you know that applications use pointers to identify positions within a file. A pointer *points to* a specific record, the beginning of a file, or the end of a file. The pointer indicates the current position within the file. That location is where you can read or write data to the file. The same principle applies when you use the fileIO Xtra to read or write to a disk file. The Xtra includes several methods that enable you to determine or set the current position:

To establish (or set) the file pointer position for the current open file, use the following method syntax:

    setPosition(instance, position)

To identify the current pointer position in an open file, use the getPosition method. It returns an integer representing the number of bytes from the beginning of the file to the current pointer position:

    getPosition(instance)

The getLength method returns an integer that is the length of the file in bytes. This method's syntax is

    getLength(instance)

Note Each of these position-related methods works only on an open file.

By using a combination of these methods, you can write to the end of an open file. This enables you to append data rather than overwriting existing data. When a file is initially opened, the current position is the beginning of the file. You can start reading or writing at the end of a file by using the following combination of the setPosition and getLength methods:

    setPosition(instance, (getLength(instance)))

On the CD-ROM In the following exercise, you'll use a partially complete Director movie, score.dir, from your companion CD-ROM in the exercise:ch19 (exercise\ch19) folder. In its current state, the score.dir movie includes a bitmap cast member called Column (cast member 1) and a frame script to cycle the movie on frame 1. To complete the movie, you add a button that saves text (a name and score) to a disk file. The name and score are typed by the user in an editable field.

Saving a File Using the fileIO Xtra

1. Open the score.dir movie in Director.

2. On the Tool Palette, set the foreground color to white and the background color to black.
3. Select the Button tool on the Tool Palette.
4. Click and drag to build a button centered on the column (center Stage).
5. Add a caption. With the button still selected, type **Save**, press Enter, and then type **Score**. The caption on the button will appear similar to Figure 19-12.

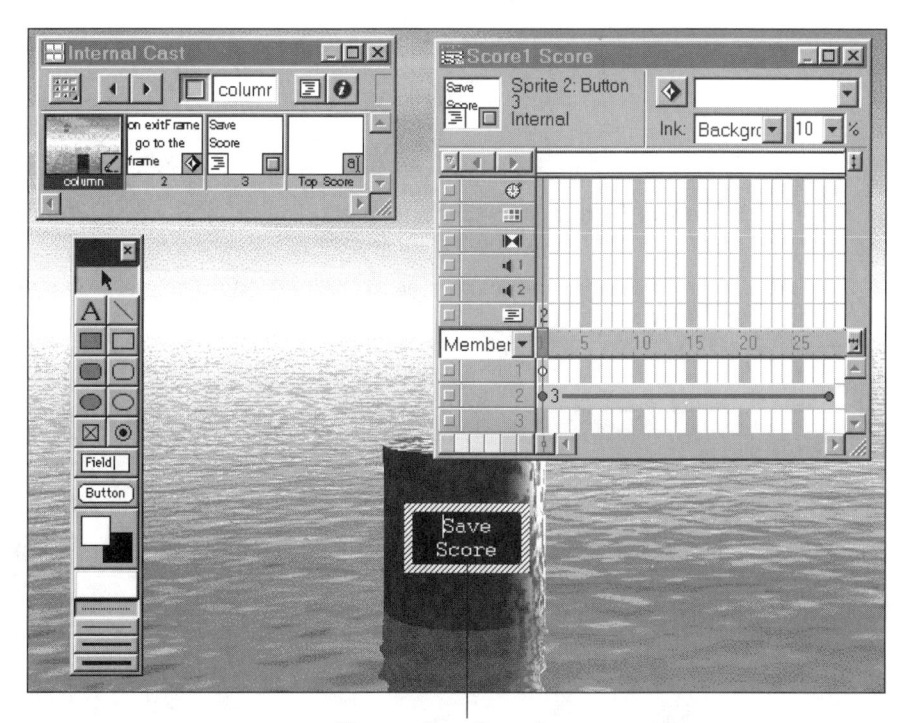

The new Save Score button

Figure 19-12: Button caption added to column

6. With the button still selected, shrink the sprite to span a single frame (frame 1) and set the ink to Background Transparent.
7. Select the newly created button cast member (slot 3) and add the following cast member script:

```
on mouseUp
    set scoreFile = new(xtra "fileio")
    set    fileName   =   displaySave(scoreFile,"Savescores¬
to:","Scores.txt")
      If fileName <> "" then
          createFile(scoreFile,fileName)
          openFile(scoreFile, fileName, 2)
```

(continued)

```
                if the machineType = 256 then
                    nothing
                else
                    setFinderInfo(scoreFile, "TEXT ttxt") -- ¬
                        This line is case sensitive.
                end if
                writeString(scoreFile, the text of field "Top ¬
                Score")
                CloseFile(scoreFile)
                set scoreFile=0
            end if
    end
```

8. When you're finished typing the script, close the Script window.
9. Select the Field tool on the tool Palette, and reset the foreground color to black and the background color to white.
10. Click and drag in the white area at the horizon, to create a new field as shown in Figure 19-13.

Figure 19-13: The field for the scores

11. Select the newly created field cast member (slot 4) in the Cast window and open the Field Cast Member Properties dialog box.

12. As shown in Figure 19-14, name the field cast member **Top Score**, select the Editable check box, and set the Framing option to Scrolling. Click OK.

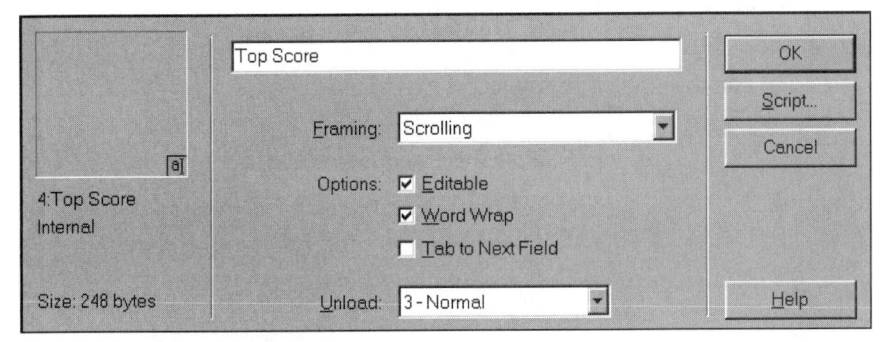

Figure 19-14: Field Cast Member Properties dialog box

13. Save the movie as **score1.dir,** rewind, and play it.

14. In the field, type your name followed by a number for your score.

15. Click the Save Score button.

16. When the Save Scores To dialog box appears, it defaults to saving scores.txt in the same folder in which you have placed the scores1.dir movie. Although you can save the file elsewhere by typing in a different filename, in this case leave the filename as is and click the Save button to save your name and score. (If a file with this name already exists in the target folder, you will be warned by the operating system, in which case you can either replace the file or cancel the Save operation.)

17. Stop the movie, go to the folder from which you played the score1.dir movie, and locate the scores.txt file. Double-click it to start SimpleText (Macintosh users) or NotePad (Windows users). When the file opens, you should see the text you typed on the Stage in the field.

Packaging Xtras in Your Projectors

Because Xtras contain extra code or resources for your Director movies, in order to use them in a movie you must package them in your projector or ship them with the movie (in the same folder). If you fail to do so, you lose the functionality of the Xtras.

Fortunately, with the exception of scripting Xtras, Director automatically registers any cast member Xtras you've used. To see the Xtras that are automatically packaged with your movie (when you create a projector), select Modify⇨Movie⇨Xtras to display the Movie Xtras dialog box (Figure 19-15). As soon as you click the Add button, the Movie Xtras dialog box shows you a list of available Xtras. It will include specific scripting Xtras you have added to the current movie.

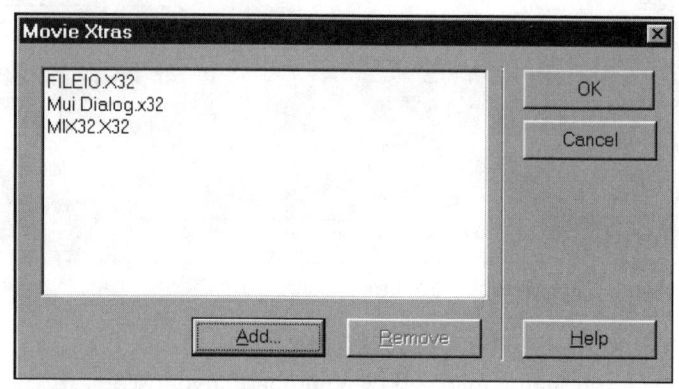

Figure 19-15: This dialog box shows you the Xtras automatically packaged with a movie.

Xtras available in Director 6

Director ships with a large number of installed Xtras that are needed for import operations. In most cases, the filenames listed in Table 19-4 correspond to the standard types of media that the Xtra imports. If the filename of the Xtra includes the word *Agent*, the Xtra is used to link and enable editing of external media, rather than to import embedded cast members.

<table>
<tr><th colspan="3">Table 19-4
Xtras Required to Import Media into Movies</th></tr>
<tr><th>Macintosh</th><th>Windows NT/95</th><th>Windows 3.x</th></tr>
<tr><td>AIFF Import Export</td><td>AIFF Import Export</td><td>mixaiff.x16</td></tr>
<tr><td></td><td>AVI Agent.x32</td><td></td></tr>
<tr><td>BMP Import Export</td><td>BMP Import Export.x32</td><td>mixbmp.x16</td></tr>
<tr><td>GIF Import Export and GIF Import 68k</td><td>GIF Import.x32</td><td>mixgif.x16</td></tr>
<tr><td></td><td>ImageMark Import.x32</td><td></td></tr>
</table>

(continued)

Macintosh	Windows NT/95	Windows 3.x
JPEG Import and JPEG Import 68k	JPEG Import.x32	mixjpeg.x16
LRG Import Export	LRG Import Export.x32	mixlrg.x16
MacPaint Import	MacPaint Import.x32	mixmcpnt.x16
MIX Services	Mix32.x32	mix16.x16
Palette Import	Palette Import.x32	mixpal.x16
Photoshop 3.0 Import	Photoshop 3.0 Import.x32	mixps30.x16
Photoshop CLUT Import (new with Director 6.01)	Photoshop CLUT Import.x32	mixclut.x16
PICT Agent	PICT Agent.x32	
PNG Import Export	PNG Import Export.x32	mixpng.x16
Quick Time Agent	Quick Time Agent.x32	
Sound Import Export	Sound Import Export.x32	mixsound.x16
Targa Import Export	Targa Import Export.x32	mixtarga.x16
TIFF Import Export	TIFF Import Export.x32	mixtiff.x16
WAVE Import Export	WAVE Import Export.x32	mixwave.x16
xRes Agent	Xresagt.x32	

The MIX Services Xtra (called MIX32.x32 on Windows) listed in Table 19-4 is the Macromedia Information Xchange Xtra. It is required to enable Director to import and export various media. Despite the abbreviation (MIX) included in its filename, this Xtra is used for reading and writing sound formats, *not* for mixing sounds.

Speaking of sound, Director 6.0 ships with a variety of sound Xtras collapsed into a single file: the Sound Import Export Xtra. This Xtra is needed during authoring to import and export sound files, *and* during playback to play compressed sound files. Sounds that are not compressed are stored in a standard format inside the movie, and the Xtras in the MIX Readers folder are not required for playback. In order to maintain their compression, compressed sounds are stored in that format within Director. As a result, both the Sound Import Export Xtra and MIX Services Xtra are required to play back compressed sounds.

Note Shockwave for Audio (SWA) compressed internal sounds are an exception to the rule. SWA only requires the SWA decompressor to play back sounds. The MIX Services Xtra in the MIX Readers folder is not required.

Selecting Xtras to package

Because Director may not be able to automatically detect scripting Xtras, you can add them to the projector (for the current movie) using the Movie Xtras dialog box, as shown in the next exercise.

You can also add one or more specific Xtras when you create a projector. In the Create Projector dialog box (Figure 19-16), you select an Xtra the same way you would select a movie or cast to include in the projector.

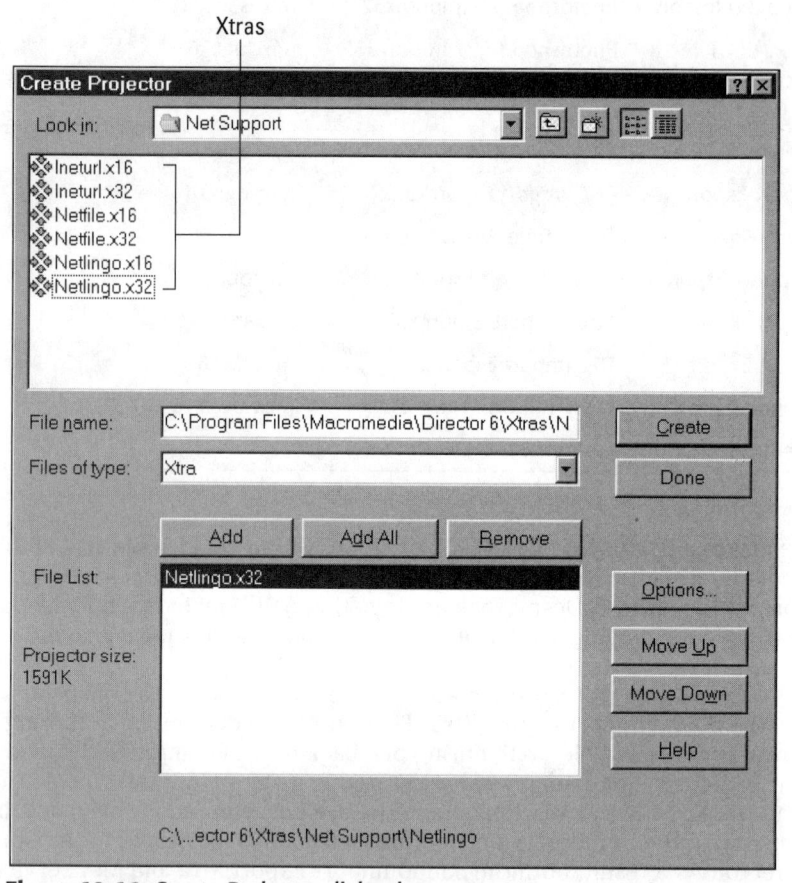

Figure 19-16: Create Projector dialog box

Tip If you are trying to trim your projector to a bare-minimum size, you can turn off the Check Movies for Xtras and the Include Network Xtras options in the Projector Options dialog box. As a result, no Xtras will be included in the projector by default. Be sure to also select the Compress (Shockwave format) check box to compress the movie files in the projector. Be aware, however, that turning off all these options means Director will *not* package any Xtras in the projector. So if any feature in your movie requires the presence of an Xtra and you've chosen not to embed it, the feature won't work unless the playback computer includes the required Xtra in the Xtras folder or the projector's folder.

When the Check Movies for Xtras option is selected for the projector, Director checks the file xtrainfo.txt to determine which Xtras should be automatically included in the projector. If the Include Network Xtras check box is selected, the xtrainfo.txt file is examined to determine which Xtras are needed for the projector to support network access. You can edit the xtrainfo.txt file, but do so judiciously.

Caution
You may think that specific Xtras are not required for your movie, but your assumption may be wrong. For instance, the `goToNetPage` NetLingo command requires the presence of the NetLingo.x32 Xtra, as well as the INetUrl and the NetFile Xtras.

You can package Xtras into projectors that are distributed via disk, CD, and cartridge. However, if a movie is run from a CD (and not installed to a read/write medium such as a hard drive), you should create an Xtras folder on the CD, place all necessary Xtras in the folder, and not worry about packaging the Xtras in the projector. Whenever Director runs a projector, it tries to create an Xtras folder and place any Xtras packaged within the projector in the folder. If the projector runs from a read-only medium such as a CD-ROM, it may not be able to create a virtual or real folder (depending on memory available) and the movie may not run satisfactorily.

In the next exercise, you'll use the Director movie from the last exercise (score1.dir) and create a projector. Initially, you package it without Xtras; then you modify the Projector Options dialog box to include the fileIO Xtra. The Modify ⇨ Movie ⇨ Xtras command works in conjunction with the Check Movies for Xtras option. You'll see in this exercise how they can be used together to instruct Director to package the fileIO Xtra (or any other Xtra) with the current movie.

Packaging Xtras in a Projector

On the CD-ROM

1. Select the File ⇨ Create Projector command. (It doesn't yet matter if the movie is open or closed.) To complete these steps, you'll need the score1.dir movie you modified earlier in this chapter, or the file score1.dir from the companion CD-ROM in the exercise:ch19 (exercise\ch19) folder.

2. Add the score1.dir movie to the File List of movies to include in the projector.

3. Select the Options button and deselect the Include Network Xtras and Check Movies for Xtras check boxes.

(continued)

4. Click OK and then click the Create button.

5. Indicate the folder where you want the movie saved, type **score1** in the File Name field, and then click the Save button.

6. After the projector is created, use the Finder or Microsoft Explorer and run the score1 projector.

7. Type **Wizard King 1000** in the editable field and then click the Save Score button. An Alert message tells you "Script error: Xtra not found." The fileIO Xtra is not available, so the movie cannot save the Score to a text file.

8. Click the Stop button to close the score1 projector and then return to Director.

9. Repeat steps 1 to 5 to create a projector. Name it **score2,** and this time select the Check Movies for Xtras check box in the Projector Options dialog box.

10. After the projector is created, use the Finder or Microsoft Explorer and run the score2 projector.

11. Type **Wizard King 1100** in the field and then click the Save Score button. An Alert message appears again: "Script error: Xtra not found." The fileIO Xtra is still not available, so the movie cannot save the Score to a text file. The reason is that scripting or Lingo Xtras are typically not detected when you select the Check Movies for Xtras check box.

12. Click the Stop button to close the score2.exe projector. Then return to Director.

13. With the score1.dir movie open, select Modify ⇨ Movie ⇨ Xtras.

14. Click the Add button; a list of all available Xtras appears as shown in Figure 19-17.

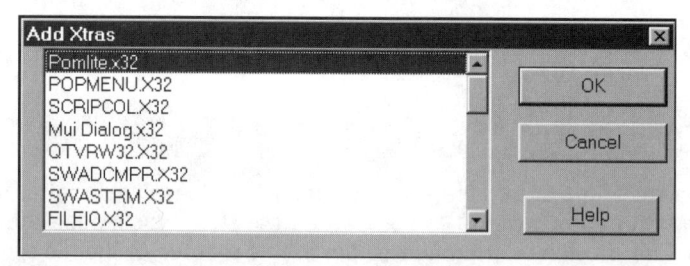

Figure 19-17: List of available Xtras in Movie Xtras dialog box

15. Select the fileIO Xtra from the list and click OK. The Movie Xtras dialog box now lists the fileIO Xtra. Click OK to close this dialog.

16. Save the movie as **score3.dir**.

17. Repeat steps 1 to 5 to create another projector, named **score3** (based on movie score3.dir). Make sure the Check Movies for Xtras check box is selected in the Projector Options dialog box.

18. After the projector is created, use the Finder or Microsoft Explorer and run the score3 projector.

19. Type **Wizard King 1200** in the field and click the Save Score button.

20. When the Save Scores To dialog box appears, leave the default filename (scores.txt) and click the Save button.

21. If you completed all the exercises earlier in this chapter, a scores.txt file already exists, so you'll see a "Replace Existing File" message. Click Yes to proceed. This time, the save to disk should be successful.

Summary

Before you move on to discovering how to troubleshoot your scripts and handlers in the next chapter, let's review some of the things you learned here in Chapter 19.

- Xtras are extensions to the functionality of Director. These code modules are developed by third-party vendors to enhance Director.

- The Macromedia Open Architecture (MOA) supports five types of Xtras: transition Xtras, cast member Xtras, scripting Xtras, tool Xtras, and importing Xtras.

- By placing Xtras in the Xtra folder or in the same folder with your movie or projector, Director can automatically open the code module when the application starts.

- The `showXlib` command returns a list of available installed Xtras.

- Each Xtra has its own set of methods that can be accessed. You can display the list of methods using the `mMessageList` command.

- The fileIO Xtra is used to create, open, close, read, and write to an external disk file from within a Director movie.

✦ ✦ ✦

CHAPTER 20

Lingo Troubleshooting

In This Chapter

Tracing script actions in the Message window

Executing instructions and handlers in the Message window

Tracking variables in the Watcher window

Checking handlers using the Debugger window

Have you ever had a really bad code day? If not, you will. When that happens, Director includes a variety of built-in troubleshooting tools. Paraphrasing two common themes, it's important to realize that "bad things happen to good programmers" and "where your problem is (in the script) is where you can fix it."

Programming errors happen to everyone. Director helps by

- ✦ Alerting you to syntax errors when you close the Script window
- ✦ Providing troubleshooting tools — the Watcher window, breakpoints, and the Debugger window — to help you locate errors in logic

Troubleshooting Your Scripts

When your Lingo script does not work the way you expect it to, the first thing to do is identify the problem. What is not working the way you expected it to? Is a button click not playing a sound? Is the movie not branching to the correct frame? Does the movie quit unexpectedly?

If you are working on a team project, read and understand the comments inserted by the other team programmers. If you are writing Lingo script as part of a team effort, make sure you are adequately commenting your own scripts. Valuable time is wasted when you or someone else must decipher the scripts from scratch.

Troubleshooting involves three techniques that are useful when identifying and solving problems within your coding. Director provides tools to help you with each of the three techniques:

- Locating the problem
- Identifying syntax and spelling errors
- Correcting errors of logic

Each technique, covered in the following sections, will bring you closer to creating bug-free, efficient code.

Locating the problem

Sometimes finding the problem really means locating where the problem begins. The debugging tools provided by Director can assist you in locating the origin of the problem. For example, watching the frames as they are executed in the Message window can be helpful. You can also execute Lingo scripts from the Message window to find out if the problem resides in a particular script.

Asking the following questions will help:

Does the problem occur only on specific computers or only on computers with certain display settings?

Is the error occurring with a sprite and the way it displays?

Is the error occurring only with certain keystrokes or combinations of keystrokes?

Identifying syntax and spelling errors

The most common Lingo error occurs when you mistype a command or use the wrong syntax for a command or property. Each time you close the Script window, Director automatically looks for syntax errors or errors resulting from misspelling a word. For example, if you type the following command in a script and close the Script window, you'll get the error message shown in Figure 20-1:

```
set the visible of sprte 6 to true
```

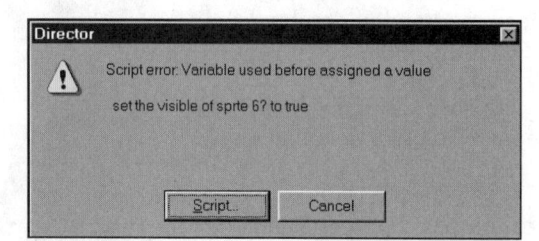

Figure 20-1: A script error message

The error message offers Director's view of the potential problem. In this case, Director assumes that a "variable (has been) used before (it was) assigned a value." The error message also displays a question mark after the portion of the script that Director cannot execute. In this case, Lingo is interpreting *sprte* as a variable name. Since no value has been assigned to the variable, Director cannot execute the instruction. The real problem, of course, is that a specific keyword in the instruction (*sprite*) is misspelled. The movie does not contain a variable named *sprte,* so an error is generated.

Note Director's capabilities do not include the intelligence to recognize that a simple misspelled word is the problem, as opposed to the error of a variable's being used before it is assigned a value. When debugging a script, your job is to examine the error message and interpret it in the context of the remainder of the Lingo script.

Checking for spelling errors

When checking for syntax errors (the most frequent type of error), you should always check the spelling of commands, functions, and properties. Be sure variable names are used consistently and that spaces and other punctuation are included when necessary. Director can only respond to your script as you typed it, not what you intended to type.

Checking for missing quotation marks

Another common syntax error results when you omit quotation marks. Make sure you've used the required quotation marks (" ") around the names of cast members, markers, and strings.

Checking for missing command parameters

Lingo commands, properties, and other instructions may need required parameters in order for Lingo to know how to interpret the instruction. Always check for missing parameters or arguments that are required by a command or instruction.

Checking for the correct command syntax

When you are not sure of a Lingo command's syntax and required parameters, you have three tools available to assist you: the Alphabetical Lingo button, the Categorized Lingo button, and the Director Help command.

Note The two Lingo buttons are available on the Script window toolbar (see Figure 20-2) and in the Message window toolbar.

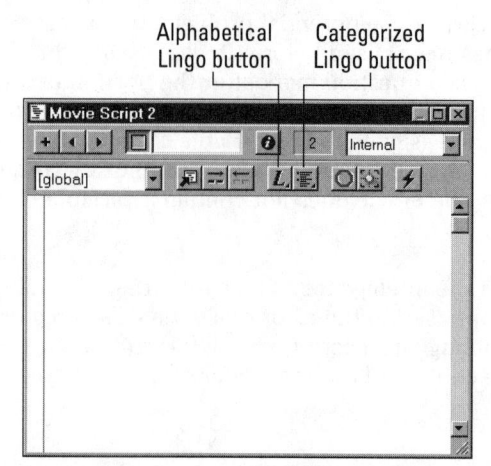

Figure 20-2: The Script window contains two tools to help you with Lingo syntax.

To use the Alphabetical list, place the cursor at the location in your script where you need help. Click the Alphabetical Lingo button, and search the list to locate the desired command. Select it, and the command's correct syntax and placeholders for required parameters will be added to the Script. The command is added to the Script window at the current cursor location.

To use the Categorized list, place the cursor at the location in your script where you need help. Click the Categorized Lingo button, and search the groups of commands (Navigation, Network, User Interaction, and so on) to locate the desired command. When you locate the command and select it, the command's correct syntax and placeholders for required parameters are added to the Script. The command is added to the Script window at the current cursor location.

The third tool for fixing up your Lingo syntax is Director's online help. Access the Director Help command (F1) from the menu bar on a Windows system; or select the Help button (upper-right end of the menu bar on a Macintosh) and then select the Director Help option on the menu that appears. Once the Help screen appears (Figure 20-3), you can select from a variety of help categories. In this case, you'll be interested in categories such as Scripting, Troubleshooting, and How To (Common Tasks).

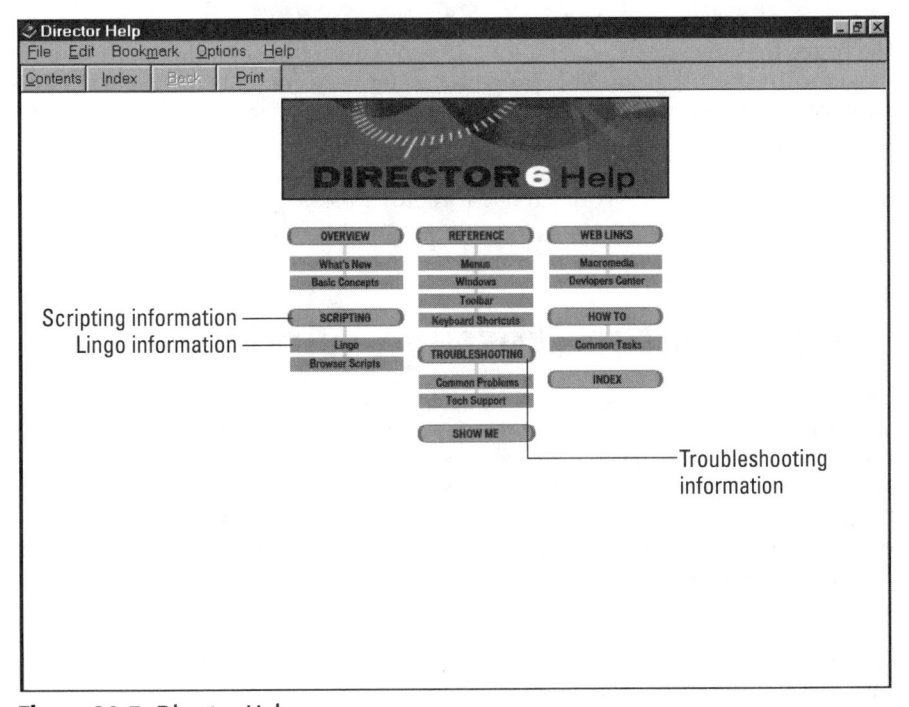

Figure 20-3: Director Help

Correcting errors of logic

Always keep in mind that just because the Script window may close without displaying an Alert window, it's no guarantee that your Lingo script is error free. It only indicates that the syntax checker did not locate or recognize errors in your script. As a parallel, consider that a word processor's spelling checker classifies a word as misspelled if the word is not contained in the speller's dictionary file. Proper names, even when they're spelled correctly, are often flagged as misspelled. The spelling checker only highlights words it does not find in its dictionary file. Any word not found is flagged as possibly incorrect.

The syntax checker in Director operates on a similar principle. It can only locate problems that appear to violate the patterns established in Lingo's rules file. The syntax checker that works with the Script window can only identify syntax errors; *it cannot identify errors of logic.*

Logic errors result when you assign incorrect values to variables or parameters. The Lingo command that uses or assigns values to a variable may be absolutely correct in its syntax, yet the value stored by the variable may still be the problem.

To troubleshoot errors of logic requires that you step through each line of code, in the order they are executed, and look for unexpected results that in turn play havoc with your program. This process can be very complex, because variables may store different values (or strings) depending on which events and actions occur as the movie plays.

To tackle errors of logic, you can use Director's Message window (with its debugging buttons), the Debugger window, and the Watcher window.

Debugging in the Message Window

The first line of defense against most script problems is to use the Message window. To open the Message window, use the Window ⇨ Message command or press Command+M (Ctrl+M). The Message window is used to observe the instructions contained in the handlers of a movie as it plays. The debugging buttons on the Message window's toolbar, identified in Figure 20-4, are used to provide access to debugging tools. Each button and its function are listed in Table 20-1. Notice that some of these buttons are also available in the Script window and the Debugger window.

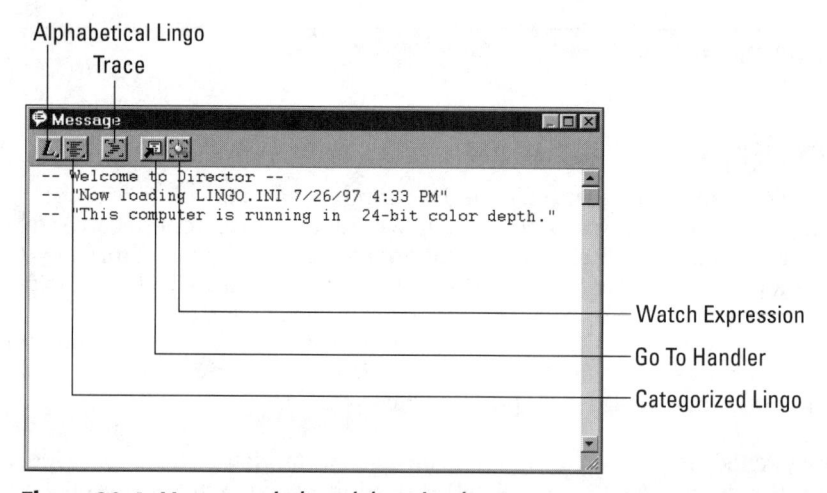

Figure 20-4: Message window debugging buttons

Table 20-1
Lingo Troubleshooting Tools

Button Name	Function and Purpose	Location
Alphabetical Lingo	Displays an alphabetical listing of all Lingo commands. Locate the desired command on the menu, and select it to insert the command and placeholders for all required parameters.	Message window Script window
Categorized Lingo	Displays a list of all Lingo commands, sorted by function. Locate the desired command on the menu, and select it to insert the command and placeholders for all required parameters.	Message window Script window
Trace	Toggles on/off the display of currently executing Lingo scripts.	Message window
Go To Handler	Opens the Script window and displays the handler referenced in the current instruction. Places the insertion point at that location in the script.	Message window Debugger window
Watch Expression	Adds the currently selected variable or expression to the "watch list" tracked by the Watcher window.	Debugger window Message window Script window

Each of these troubleshooting tools gains you access to fix-it features within Director. As you create scripts in Director, you'll probably find that the most useful tools are the Alphabetical Lingo and Categorized Lingo buttons. With both, you can type an instruction in the Message window and observe Director's reaction to the command, there in the Message window or on the Stage.

In the following steps, you'll use the Message window to trace the execution of commands in a movie and to locate a logic error. Using the Trace button, you can watch the execution of all instructions (in any script) as they are displayed in the Message window. In its current state, the movie includes a button (cast member 1), a field (cast member 2), two behaviors (cast members 3 and 4), and a movie script (cast member 5). The Count to 10 button has a behavior attached to it. The behavior is stored in cast member slot 4.

On the CD-ROM The file count.dir can be found on your companion CD-ROM in the exercise:ch20 (exercise\ch20) folder.

Tracing Script Actions in the Message Window

1. Open the file count.dir in Director. Open the Cast window and examine the cast members. Then open the Message window (Command+M or Ctrl+M).

2. Click the Trace button in the Message window, identified in Figure 20-4. This turns on the trace function.

3. Arrange the open Cast window and Message window so you can see the field (cast member 2) and the Count to 10 button on the Stage.

4. Use the Play button on the toolbar to play the movie. The movie stops almost immediately and displays the error message shown in Figure 20-5. In addition to the error, the Message window shows the last instruction executed before the movie stopped. The three buttons at the bottom are for opening the Debugger window (discussed later), opening the Script window so you can correct the error, and closing the Script Error message box.

Last instruction executed

Opens the Script window

Opens the Debugger window

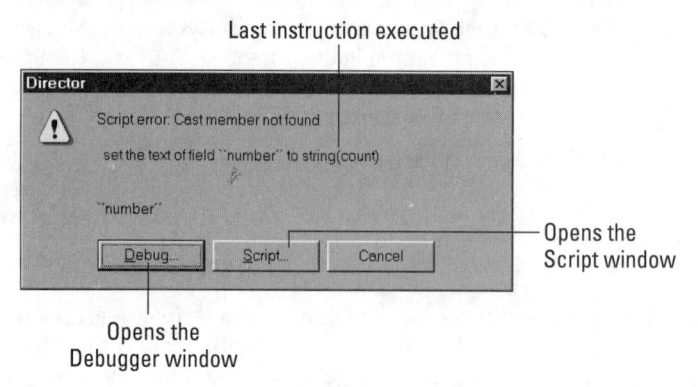

Figure 20-5: "Cast member not found" script error message

5. Click the Script button. When the Script window opens, examine the script and try to identify any errors or problems. If you don't see anything obvious, don't worry. Go ahead and close the Script window.

   Director now closes the window without issuing a syntax-error warning, which indicates that the problem is not related to a syntax error in the script. The real problem is that the script refers to a cast member ("number") which does not exist.

6. Select the field cast member (slot 2) in the Cast window, click in the Name field, and type **number**. Press Enter to apply the new cast member name to the field.

7. Save the movie as **count1.dir**.

8. Leave the Message window open, and play the movie. As soon as you start the movie, `go to the frame` instructions scroll down the Message window.

9. Click the Count to 10 button, and you'll notice that each instruction from script cast member 4 is displayed in the Message window — after you click the button and while the movie plays.

10. Stop the movie.

11. Use the Message window scroll bar to scroll back to the point where you clicked the Count to 10 button.

Now let's take a look at what you've found. At the point where you click the Count to 10 button, the Message window displays the following information. Notice that the Message window constantly updates the value of the variable count. At each step, you can examine the program's flow and see which handler and instructions are executed. Take a look at the first few cycles, as the count variable is incremented from 0 to 3:

```
== Clickon Script for sprite: 1
== Script: 4 Handler: mouseUp
-> set count =0
== count = 0
-> repeat while count <11
-> set the text of field "number" to string(count)
-> set count=count+1
== count = 1
-> end repeat
-> repeat while count <11
-> set the text of field "number" to string(count)
-> set count=count+1
== count = 2
-> end repeat
-> repeat while count <11
-> set the text of field "number" to string(count)
-> set count=count+1
== count = 3
```

If you scroll back to the beginning of the Message window listings, you'll see text similar to the following:

```
== Movie: C:\Personal Folder\exer20\count1.dir Frame: 1 Script: 5 Handler: startMovie
-> set count =0
== count = 0
-> set the text of field "number" to string(count)
-> end
== Script: 3 Handler: exitFrame
-> go to the frame
-> end
```

The Message window lists the filename and path for the movie, the frame number being executed, and the current handler (`on startMovie`). After the `on startMovie` handler finishes (which establishes the initial value of the variable `count` and places it in the number field), the cast member script 3 with an `on exitFrame` handler runs. It includes a `go to the frame` instruction.

Testing commands directly in the Message window

You can also type and test scripts in the Message window (you have already done this in earlier chapters). The Message window enables you to prototype and test specific instructions, to determine if the actual results match your anticipated results:

- ✦ To test a single line of code that you suspect may be causing a problem, type it directly into the Message window. If the command works in the Message window, some other part of your program must be causing the error.

- ✦ To test a handler in the Message window, type the name of the handler and press Enter. The handler is immediately executed, and if any errors occur you'll see an Alert message.

Executing Instructions and Handlers in the Message Window

On the CD-ROM

1. Open the change.dir movie. It's on your companion CD-ROM in the exercise:ch20 (exercise\ch20) folder.

2. In the Message window, click the Trace button and be sure the Trace feature is turned off.

3. In the Message window, type

   ```
   set the visible of sprite 1 to false
   ```

   and press the Enter key. The button (sprite 1) disappears.

4. Type

   ```
   set the visible of sprite 1 to true
   ```

   and press the Enter key. The button reappears.

5. The movie also has another handler in cast member slot 50, named `on change`. In the Message window, type **change** and press Enter. The script error message shown in Figure 20-6 appears, telling you that `the forecolor` property can only be set for a text cast member (field or rich text field).

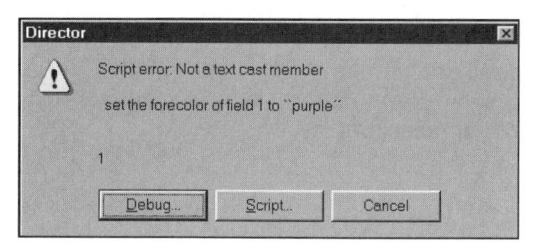

Figure 20-6: "Not a text cast member" script error message

6. Click the Script button in the error box. Three lines in the script refer to field 1. Because there is a mismatch between the type of cast member in slot 1 and the type of cast member specified in the command (field), you must change the instruction.

7. Change all three references in the on change handler from field 1 to field 2.

8. Close the Script window, and save the movie as **change1.dir.**

9. Type **change** in the Message window again and press Enter. Director displays a script error indicating that an integer (whole number) is expected, as shown in Figure 20-7. The word "purple" in the script is listed as the culprit. The foreColor property must be set using a numeric value (not a color name) that represents the color in the current palette.

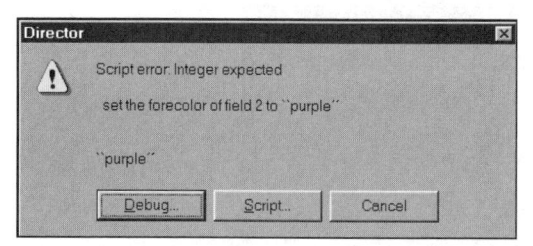

Figure 20-7: "Integer expected" script error message

10. In the error box, click the Script button to open the Script window.

11. Delete the word purple and the double quotation marks that surround it. Change the instruction to read as follows:

    set the forecolor of field 2 to 54

Note The color 54 is purple when using either the System-Win or the System-Mac palette.

12. Close the Script window, and save the movie again as change1.dir.
13. In the Message window, execute the `on change` handler by typing **change** and pressing Enter. The number 0 increases in size, switches to purple, and changes to an italic font style.

Using the `showGlobals` command

Another useful purpose for the Message window is to display variables that are currently available as globals. This can be helpful in your debugging efforts for two reasons:

- ✦ You may expect a variable to be global and it is not (that is, you did not declare it as a global variable).
- ✦ You want to know the value currently stored by a global variable.

To determine which variables are currently declared as globals, you open the Message window and type `showGlobals`. You'll get a list of all current global variables like the one shown in Figure 20-8.

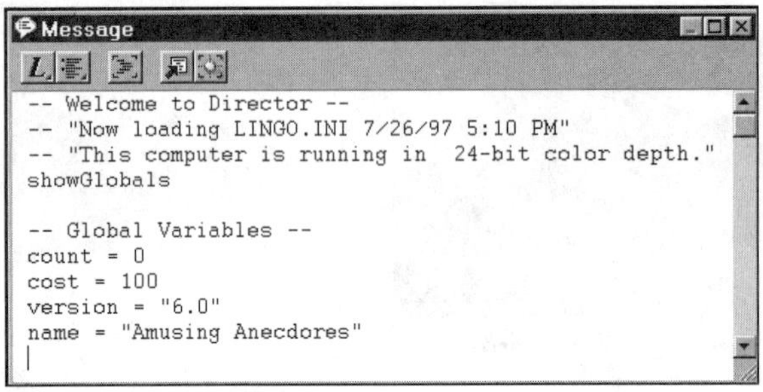

```
-- Welcome to Director --
-- "Now loading LINGO.INI 7/26/97 5:10 PM"
-- "This computer is running in  24-bit color depth."
showGlobals

-- Global Variables --
count = 0
cost = 100
version = "6.0"
name = "Amusing Anecdores"
```

Figure 20-8: Currently available global variables and their values

Using the Watcher Window

The Watcher window (Figure 20-9) displays the values stored in selected variables, while a movie plays. To open the Watcher window, use the Window➪Watcher command or press Command+Shift+` (Ctrl+Shift+`). The ` character is the one that shares a key with the tilde character on the keyboard.

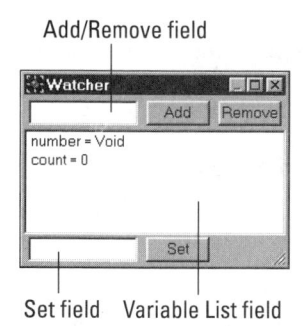

Figure 20-9: Watcher window

Designating variables to watch

Before you can use the Watcher window, you must establish the variables that you want "watched." To do this, you identify the variables using the Debugger window, the Message window, the Script window, or the Watcher window. In each case except the last, you use the Watch Expression button to identify the variables to watch. Figure 20-10 identifies the Watch Expression button in the Script window.

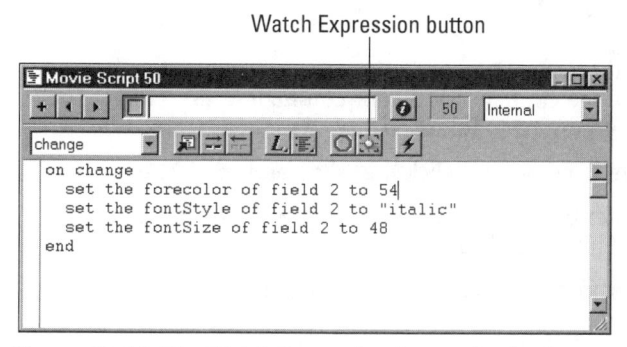

Figure 20-10: The Watch Expression button looks the same in the Debugger and Message windows as it does here in the Script window's toolbar.

Adding and removing variables to/from the watch list

To add a variable to the watch list using the Debugger window, the Message window, or the Script window:

1. Select the variable in the window.
2. Click the Watch Expression button or press Shift+F9.

You can tell Director to watch more than one expression at a time. As the data stored in a variable changes, the Watcher window displays the current value.

It's easy to add and remove variables from the watch list in the Watcher window:

1. Type the variable's name in the Add/Remove field (identified in Figure 20-9).
2. Click the Add button to add the variable, or the Remove button to remove it.

Establishing values for variables on the watch list

When debugging a script, you may want to establish an initial value for a variable. This can be helpful when determining if a specific value generates an error. To set the value of a variable, you type the value or string in the Set field of the Watcher window (identified earlier in Figure 20-9), and click the Set button.

In this next exercise, you'll use the Watcher window to track a variable. If you examine Score script 4 in the count1.dir movie, you'll find that the count variable increments until its value is greater than 10. By watching the value stored by the count variable, you can see this occur.

Tracking the count Variable in the Watcher Window

1. Open the count1.dir movie. You need the movie you modified earlier in this chapter, or the file count1.dir on your companion CD-ROM in the exercise:ch20 (exercise\ch20) folder.
2. Open the Message window and click the Trace button.
3. To open the Watcher window, select the Window ⇨ Watcher command or press Command+Shift+` (Ctrl+Shift+`).
4. Select the Add/Remove field (top-left corner of the Watcher window) and type **count**.
5. Click the Add button. The count variable is listed in the Variable List field located in the middle of the Watcher window. The variable's initial value may be <void> or zero (0). It doesn't matter until you play the movie.
6. In the Director toolbar, click the Rewind button and then the Play button to start the movie. Leave the windows open.
7. The count value in the Watch window first appears as follows:

   count=0

This is based on the initial value set in the `on startMovie` handler. As the movie plays, the Watcher window displays the current value of the variable `count`.

8. Click the Count to 10 button. After the script finishes running, the field on the Stage displays the value 10, and the line in the Watcher window Variable List field reads

   `count=11`

9. Now you'll reset the value of the `count` variable using the Watcher window. With the movie still playing, select the variable `count` in the Variable List field.

10. Select the Set field, type **33,** and click the Set button. The new value for the variable appears in the Watcher window.

11. While the movie is playing, click the Count to 10 button. This causes the handler to execute, and the value for the variable changes again to 11.

12. Stop the movie.

13. Now let's add another variable to the watch list, but this time using the Message window. Click the Message window to activate it.

14. Scroll up in the Message window until you locate the following expression:

    `set the text of field "number" to string(count)`

15. Click and drag across the following portion of the expression:

    `the text of field "number"`

16. Click the Watch Expression button on the Message window toolbar. The Watcher window now lists a second entry that displays the text stored in the field named `number`.

17. Run the movie, and click the Count to 10 button. When the script finishes running, the Watcher window updates the values for `count` and `the text of field number`.

18. Now you'll remove a variable from the watch list. Select `the text of field number` entry in the Variable List field of the Watcher window.

19. Click the Remove button on the Watcher window. The Watcher window no longer displays a value for the `number` field.

20. Stop the movie.

Using the Debugger Window

The Debugger window is illustrated in Figure 20-11. You can open this window manually: select the Window⇨Debugger command or press Command+` (Ctrl+`). This window also opens automatically when the playback head encounters a breakpoint. (Breakpoints are usually set in the Script window and will be discussed shortly.)

From the Debugger window toolbar you can open the Watcher window (using the Watcher window button), add an expression or variable to the Watcher window (using the Watch Expression button), and open the Script window and jump to a specific handler (using the Go To Handler button). Each of these features is also available from the Message window or the Script window, as discussed earlier in this chapter.

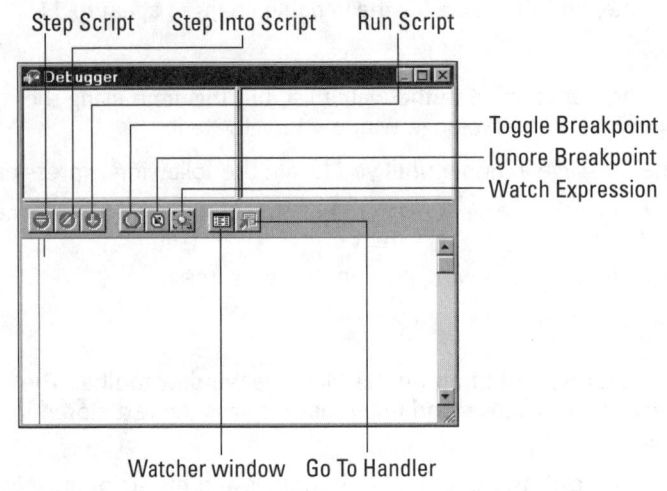

Figure 20-11: Debugger window

The Debugger window contains several controls for debugging complex scripts. In the Debugger window you can

- ✦ Examine the current line of Lingo as it executes.
- ✦ Play the current handler line by line.
- ✦ Walk through the sequence of handlers as they are called by the current handler.
- ✦ Debug errant code by examining the values stored in local variables, global variables, and properties as the movie executes.
- ✦ Access the Watcher and Script windows, for additional troubleshooting.

Note: To actually edit or correct an error in a script, you must open the Script window. You cannot edit in the Debugger window.

Setting breakpoints within your scripts

In order to use the full capabilities of the Debugger window, you need to set *breakpoints* in your handlers. Then you can use the Debugger window to watch the breakpoints within your scripts. Setting breakpoints is a good way to determine the state of variables within scripts, and handlers at specific points during the execution of a movie.

One way to set breakpoints in a Script window is to click a Lingo command and then the Toggle Breakpoint button, identified in Figure 20-12. You can also add a breakpoint using the Control⇨Toggle Breakpoint command (F9). When you set a breakpoint in the Script window, a red dot appears in the left column of the window (see Figure 20-12).

Tip: The fastest method, however, of setting a breakpoint in the Script window is to click in the left column adjacent to the line of code where you want the breakpoint to occur. To remove the breakpoint, click the red breakpoint symbol.

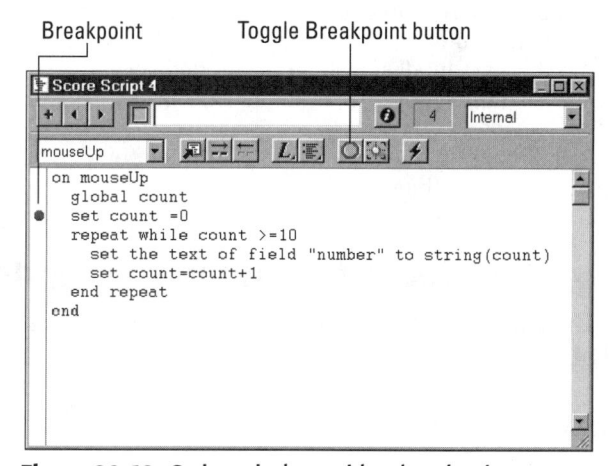

Figure 20-12: Script window with a breakpoint

Ignoring all breakpoints

When necessary, you can tell Director to temporarily ignore breakpoints during your troubleshooting activities. Simply click the Ignore Breakpoints button, identified in Figure 20-11, or select the Control⇨Ignore Breakpoints command (Alt+F9).

When the Ignore Breakpoints button is selected (or you use the Control➪Ignore Breakpoints command), the breakpoint symbol will still appear in the left column of the Script window, but it will be grayed out. This indicates that the breakpoint will be ignored in the Debugger window.

Tip: After successfully finding the problem in a script and fixing it, you should run the script one more time to verify that it is error free. The easiest way to test a corrected script is to temporarily disable the breakpoints.

Removing a single breakpoint

To remove a single breakpoint, click anywhere in the line containing the breakpoint and then press F9. You can also click the Toggle Breakpoint button or select the Control➪Toggle Breakpoint command to remove a single breakpoint. This method retains all other breakpoints whether they are in the same handler or another handler within the movie.

Tip: The fastest way to remove a breakpoint is to click once on the breakpoint symbol in the left column of the Script window. The breakpoint is erased when the red breakpoint symbol disappears.

Removing all breakpoints

After you troubleshoot and fix your scripts, you can quickly and painlessly remove all breakpoints that have been set. There's no need to open each script and toggle off the breakpoints individually. All you do is select the Control ➪ Remove All Breakpoints command. All breakpoints in all scripts are removed (not just disabled, as they are when you use the Ignore Breakpoints button).

Tip: If you want to reuse a previous breakpoint after removing all breakpoints, you must reset it in the appropriate script or handler.

Running through your script in the Debugger window

The Debugger window has three additional buttons that are used to run your movie while troubleshooting each handler.

"Stepping" through the script

The Step Script button runs the current line of Lingo and any handlers it calls. In essence, this lets you "walk through" your script, executing it line by line.

You can also use the Control➪Step Script command or press F10 to execute one line of code at a time.

Running the script through the next breakpoint

The Run Script button exits debugging mode and continues execution of the handlers in your movie. In the case of the count.dir movie, pressing the Run Script button continues the `repeat` loop until the breakpoint in the `repeat` loop is encountered again.

The basic difference between the Run Script button and the Step Script button is that the Run Script button executes all lines of code until the line with the breakpoint is encountered again, whereas the Step Script button executes one line of code at a time. Using the Run Script button is useful when you are confident that certain parts of the script are performing accurately and you only want to pause at specific lines of code with breakpoints. This saves you time and effort because it eliminates the need to repeatedly click the Step Script button to move forward one line of code at a time.

Instead of using the Run Script button, you can select the Control➪Run Script command or press F5.

Running the whole script

The Step Into Script button follows Lingo's normal execution flow. It executes each line of code and follows, line by line, each nested handler that the line calls. Step Into Script is handy when you're debugging errors in nested logic. For example, if you have a Lingo command that plays another Director movie, using the Step Into Script button executes the current line of Lingo that calls the other movie and then jumps to that movie and executes it line by line.

The Step Into Script button also works effectively for troubleshooting nested `repeat` loops or other control structures that use nesting.

The equivalent command for the Step Into Script button is Control➪Step Into Script or F8.

An exercise with the Debugger window

In the following steps, you'll use the countup.dir movie from the CD-ROM to set breakpoints in the Script window, and then debug the script using the Debugger window.

As you troubleshoot the countup.dir movie, the problem appears to be on the line that reads

```
repeat while count >=10
```

The greater-than symbol (>) rather than the less-than symbol (<) has been used. The lines that increment the count variable are never executed because 0 (the initial value) is never greater than or equal to 10.

Repeating an action until a value is less than or equal to a specific value (such as 10) is more efficiently accomplished by stipulating that the loop continue while the count is *less than one number larger* than your target value. The proper method of repeating actions until the `count` variable is equal to or less than 10 is to use the following instruction:

```
repeat while count <11
```

While you run the practice movie, watch the position of the green arrow at the left margin. The green arrow shows which line of the Lingo script is to be executed next. This is a helpful method of testing the logic of your control structures, such as a loop. By monitoring the state of the loop and the value of the conditional variables in the loop, you can thoroughly test the logic of the loop.

Checking Handlers Using the Debugger Window

On the CD-ROM

1. Open the countup.dir movie and play it. The file countup.dir is on your companion CD-ROM in the exercise:ch20 (exercise\ch20) folder.

2. Once the movie is playing, click the Count to 10 button. The value in the field on the Stage remains set to zero (0).

3. Stop the movie.

4. Open the script cast member stored in cast slot 4. This is the behavior attached to the Count to 10 button.

5. Click once in the left column of the Script window parallel to the line of code that reads `set count=0`. A red breakpoint symbol appears in the left column, identifying the location of the new breakpoint within the handler.

6. Close the Script window (and the Behavior Inspector, too, if it's open). This should catch any syntax or spelling errors, if they exist.

7. Play the movie and click the Count to 10 button. As soon as the line of code with the breakpoint is reached, the Debugger window automatically opens, as shown in Figure 20-13.

   Notice that the top-left pane of the Debugger window displays the name of the current handler (`mouseUp`). The top-right pane displays all variables and their values. Only the `count` variable is listed with a value set to zero. The bottom pane displays the script for the current handler. The green arrow in the left column of the bottom pane sits on top of the breakpoint symbol. It identifies the point within the script where the movie has temporarily stopped. You might not be able to see this in the screenshot of Figure 20-13.

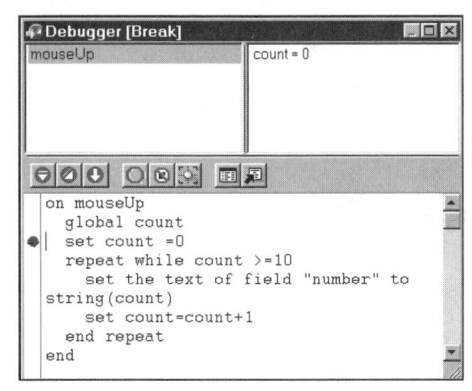

Figure 20-13: Debugger window opens when breakpoint is reached.

8. Click the Step Script button (F10) to move the Lingo script to the next command, which is `repeat while count >=10`.

9. Click the Step Script button again, and the green arrow jumps to the `end` keyword at the end of the `on mouseUp` handler. It skips the next two lines, which increment the value of the variable count.

10. Click the Step Script button one more time. The Debugger window goes blank because the playback head is no longer in the handler that contains the breakpoint.

11. Click the Count to 10 button on the Stage again. The Debugger window becomes active again because the playback head hits the line of code that includes the breakpoint.

12. To open the Script window and make the necessary change, click the Go To Handler button on the Debugger window (far-left button on the Debugger's toolbar).

13. In the Script window, change the handler to match the following:

```
on mouseUp
    global count
    set count =0
    repeat while count <11
        set the text of field "number" to string(count)
        set count=count+1
    end repeat
end
```

14. Leave the breakpoint on the `set count=0` instruction, so you can watch the values increment in the Debugger window.

15. Close the Script window.

16. Play the movie and then click the Count to 10 button.

17. Because you have edited the movie without saving it, an Alert message (shown in Figure 20-14) informs you that the script must be recompiled before debugging. The message does not appear if you save the movie or recompile the scripts. If the Alert message is displayed, click OK to close it.

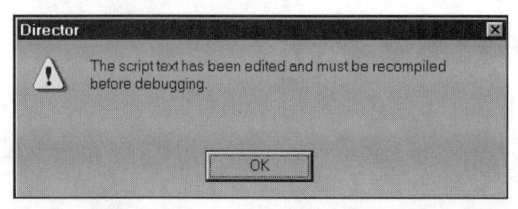

Figure 20-14: Alert message instructing you to recompile all scripts in your movie

18. Save the movie as **countup1.dir** using the File ⇨ Save and Compact command, or recompile all scripts in the movie using the Control ⇨ Recompile All Scripts command.

19. Play the movie and click the Count 1 to 10 button.

20. Click the Step Script button to step through the handler and watch the `repeat while` loop execute. To completely step through the handler will require four clicks on the Step Script button (before the `count` variable increases to 1). You can watch the variable `count` change values in the top-right pane of the Debugger window.

21. Continue to step through the script until the `repeat while` loop finishes and the value of `count` reaches 11. At that point, if you keep clicking the Step Script button, the Debugger window will go blank because the playback head exits the `on mouseUp` handler.

22. Now you'll test the corrected script but cause the playback head to stop only at the breakpoint and not at each line of code. With the countup1.dir movie still open, click the Rewind button on the main Director toolbar.

23. Click the Play button and then click the Count to 10 button. The Debugger window displays the script with the breakpoint as before.

24. This time, when the playback head pauses at the breakpoint, click the Run Script button. Instead of stopping on each line of Lingo script, the script runs until the breakpoint is encountered again. The `count` variable is still updated, as you can see by examining the field on the Stage that displays the value 10 when the handler finishes.

25. Stop the movie.

On the CD-ROM If you want to practice troubleshooting files, you can use the following three practice files: matchit.dir, orient.dir, and virgil.dir on your companion CD-ROM in the exercise:ch20 (exercise\ch20) folder.

Summary

Before you move on to exploring Director's movie in a window feature in the next chapter, let's review some of the things you learned here in Chapter 20.

- ✦ Director includes several tools that aid you in locating syntax, spelling, and logic errors in your scripts.

- ✦ Syntax and spelling errors are the most common problems that you'll encounter as you write Lingo scripts. You can always use the Alphabetical Lingo and Categorized Lingo buttons (in the Script window and the Message window) to assist in typing the correct syntax and spelling for a command, property, or function.

- ✦ In the Message window, you can test a single instruction or a single line of code. You can also run any handler within the current movie by just typing the handler's name into the Message window.

- ✦ To help you identify errant code, you can track variables and their values using the Watcher window. You can track one variable or many by adding the variable's name to the Variable List pane in the Watcher window. You can also specify a value for a variable while the movie is running, and watch the results as the movie plays.

- ✦ Identifying errors of logic is more difficult than locating syntax and spelling errors. You do have a powerful tool in the Debugger window: breakpoints that help you step through the execution of a handler.

✦ ✦ ✦

Movies in a Window (MIAWs)

CHAPTER 21

In This Chapter

Understanding MIAWs (movies in a window)

Creating MIAWs

Controlling MIAWs

Managing MIAWs effectively

Director's movie in a window (MIAW) feature enables you to simultaneously play two or more movies in separate windows. This is especially useful when you have a large movie that has elements that change. Suppose you are designing an interactive tour of the facilities of a corporate entity that has numerous facilities sites. You can create the host movie, then make separate movies featuring an individual site, and play each site's movie in a window with the host movie. The modular nature of MIAWs lets you change elements easily without rewriting the entire movie.

Movies in a window are especially effective for use as dialog boxes, control panels, toolbars, menus, floating palettes, and movie-building utilities.

What's Different about MIAWs?

When you create a movie in a window (MIAW), you are running two or more Director movies at the same time that can interact. An MIAW is a separate and independent movie that can be started by your host movie, otherwise known as the Stage to reduce confusion. Unlike playing a movie *within* another movie, MIAWs are Lingo controlled. Because they exist in their own window, you don't add them to the cast of the Stage. MIAWs also have their own casts, Lingo, and attributes such as Stage size and location.

Note

You can't use a movie in a window in a Shockwave movie. Web browsers don't allow Shockwave to open new windows.

MIAWs versus imported movies

Director imports movies as either film loops or linked movies, and places them in the cast. As a cast member, an imported movie behaves like any other graphic cast member and is subject to the control of the Stage and Score. Depending upon your chosen settings for importing, you can edit a movie within a movie. When you import a movie into another Director movie, it must be positioned within the physical boundaries of the movie (see Figure 21-1).

Figure 21-1: Imported movies must fall within the physical boundaries of the Stage.

In contrast to an imported movie, a movie in a window is linked by Lingo to the Stage. MIAWs don't appear in the Score or Cast window. They are represented by a movie script that controls them. Movie scripts do appear as cast members in the Cast window, however. The independent nature of an MIAW offers you several advantages over imported movies. You specify the size, orientation, and location of each MIAW (see Figure 21-2). You aren't constrained by the boundaries of the Stage.

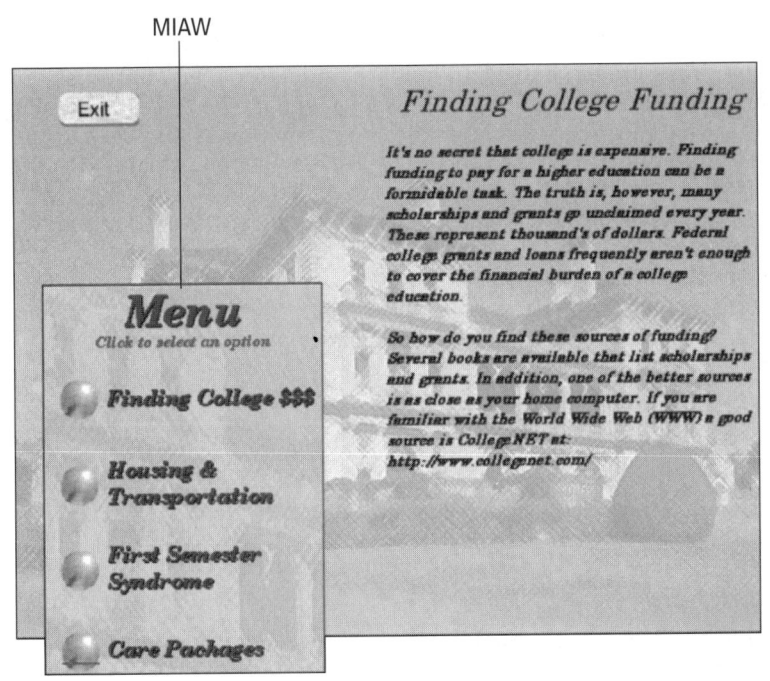

Figure 21-2: You control the location and size of an MIAW.

Each MIAW is opened in a window as needed and has the life span you specify using Lingo. When the movie is done playing, it can either be retained in memory if you'll need it later, or you can close it and remove it from memory. Because you don't need to extend sprites within the Score, you can pace the loading and unloading of data into memory. Using memory only on demand lets you create larger and more complex movies that operate faster and animate more smoothly.

> **Note:** A movie in a window is always in play mode. It starts playing immediately after it's opened, even if it's not part of a projector. You can't edit an MIAW when it's opened by another movie. If you need to edit the MIAW, you need to open it separately in Director. In fact, during development of movies with MIAWs, you can reasonably expect to go back and forth between the movies. You might want to open the MIAW in another copy of Director (by starting Director twice). Although you can open multiple copies of Director, you can't call a linked file to play while it's open in another copy.

Achieving interactivity between windows

The symbiotic relationship between the Stage and associated MIAWs is such that they can communicate and interact. This allows one movie to send instructions to another movie. The Stage is considered the parent (host) movie, and the MIAW is considered the child movie. The Stage specifies the start and end of MIAWs, as well as the attributes of the window in which each movie plays. Communication between the parent Stage and the child MIAW is not necessarily one way, however. The MIAW can return information to the Stage, or return the movie back to the Stage.

For example, suppose you wrote a cast member script in your MIAW that contained the following instruction:

```
on mouseDown
   tell the stage to go to "tips"
end
```

This instruction would send the playback head to the marker "tips" on the Stage, when the user clicks the associated cast member in the MIAW.

Using variables and global variables

By this point in the book you're familiar with how Director uses local variables and global variables to create values that appear throughout a movie. Local variables are those you use within the active window only. In addition to working in the active movie, global variables can be shared between movies. Both types of variables help you to maintain consistency within your movies. For example, suppose you are creating an interactive brochure describing a line of furniture products that could be purchased separately or as packaged sets. By describing each product as a variable, you can use the names throughout your movie in a variety of situations, without having to rewrite large portions of your Lingo script.

In the following statement, for instance, a product is specified as a variable:

```
set theProduct1 to "end&&table"
```

When you use this variable within your movie, the statement will specify that you want Director to return the value of "end table" whenever it encounters theProduct1 in your script. The phrase "end table" will appear on the Stage. The two ampersands (&&) in the statement tell Director to take the two words enclosed by quotes and set them together with a space in between.

If you wanted to specify the preceding example's product information as a global variable that can be shared between movies, you would use the following statement:

```
global theProduct1
set theProduct1 = "end&&table"
```

Once you create a variable, you can use it in other expressions and statements to send instructions throughout your movie. In this case, when you use `theProduct1` or `gProduct1` elsewhere in your scripts, Director automatically enters the text string `end table` in that location, regardless of whether it is in an MIAW or on the Stage.

Note: Remember that if you change the value associated with a variable, that value stays changed for the remainder of the movie, or until you change it again.

As you explore the guide.dir and menu.dir movies in the following sections, you'll see that we've used this technique (assigning the name of the MIAW to a variable). Once this is set up, you can refer to the variable name and not worry about the filename or the path to it. This method enables you to change a filename in one place — when it's assigned to a variable — and it affects the entire movie. No more searching every script for every occurrence of a filename if you decide to change it!

Creating a Movie with an MIAW

The first step to creating an MIAW is to plan and create the elements you want to include in the project. If you have a clear idea of what you want to do, the creation process will go more smoothly. Create your host movie (Stage) and the individual movies you want to play in a window. You can include any desired Lingo, interactive element, sound, and animation into an MIAW. Note that palette, transition, and tempo settings you make are ignored when your movie is played in a window. These elements are under control of the Stage.

Tip: The Stage remaps your MIAW to match its active palette. It's a good idea to create MIAWs using the Stage's palette to ensure that remapping doesn't cause undesirable effects.

Writing scripts to create an MIAW

An MIAW needs two scripts for it to work: a frame script telling the MIAW when to start, and a movie script that sets the parameters for the MIAW. Both scripts are created in the host movie (Stage).

The next step in creating your MIAW is to write a start script for the frame in which the movie will begin. This small script calls a larger movie script that contains information about your MIAW.

On the CD-ROM To supplement your work in the next few exercises, examine the guide.dir and menu.dir movies that are available on your companion CD-ROM in the exercise:ch21 (exercise\ch21) folder. These movies are complete, so you don't need to do anything to them — simply dissect the scripts to understand what's happening. The guide.dir movie is the host movie, and menu.dir is the MIAW.

Creating the Start Frame Script

1. Open the host movie (guide.dir).

2. Double-click the Script channel cell for the frame in which you placed the marker for beginning the MIAW (this is frame 281 in the guide.dir movie). The Score Script window appears.

3. In the Script window, enter the following:

   ```
   on enterFrame
      begin myMovie
   end
   ```

4. Close the Script window. Your script appears in the Score and Cast windows. In guide.dir, look at Cast member 16.

You don't need to specify the endpoint of an MIAW in the host movie. Nevertheless, it's a good idea to add a frame script controlling the playback head of your host movie while the MIAW is playing. You can hold the host movie in either a frame or loop between markers, pending instructions or the completion of the MIAW. If you don't create a frame script to control the playback head in the host movie, the movie continues to play until it finishes. Looping the host movie can be very important if your MIAW is intended as a controller for the host movie, as is the case with guide.dir.

In the next exercise, you'll create a frame script that holds the host movie in a frame until it receives instructions to continue.

Holding a Movie in a Frame

1. Open your host movie (guide.dir) in Director, if it's not already open.

2. In the Score window, double-click the Script channel in the next frame after the beginning of your MIAW, to display the Script window. In guide.dir, this is frame 289 — the end of the sprite based on the College4 cast member.

3. In the Script window, enter the following:

```
on exitFrame
   go to the frame
end
```

4. Close the Script window. In guide.dir, this script appears in cast member slot 24 and is added to frames 289, 294, 299, 304, and 309.

The frame script that begins your MIAW calls a movie script that contains the parameters for the MIAW. Movie scripts are global scripts that appear in the Cast window but not in the Score. In the case of an MIAW, the movie script contains information about the following:

- The size of the window in which the MIAW plays
- The location of the window in relationship to the upper-left corner of the Stage
- The name of the MIAW
- The filename of the MIAW
- The location of the file (if it's not in the same folder as your host movie)
- The type of window
- Whether or not the MIAW window has a visible title bar
- Instructions that close the MIAW when it's finished playing
- Instructions that remove the MIAW from memory

When you create an MIAW, you start by writing a movie script that creates a window in which the movie can play. After creating the window, you need to tell Director what movie to play and the path to the movie, if it's not stored in the same folder as the host movie. In the next exercise you'll create part of the movie script that starts a movie in an MIAW.

Tip Although it's not required that you enter comments in your scripts, these guideposts are useful if you are new to Lingo scripting. They provide a reference point for every developer when it's time to edit or debug the script.

Writing a Movie Script to Start an MIAW

1. Open your host movie guide.dir in Director, if it's not already open.

2. Select Window⇨Script to display the Script window (see Figure 21-3). Note that the title bar indicates this is a Movie Script window and shows the handler as being global. In guide.dir, this movie script is in cast member slot 14.

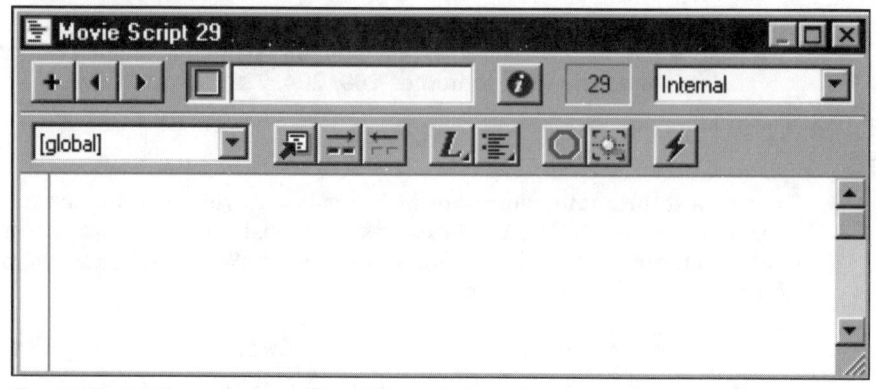

Figure 21-3: When you open the Script window from the Window menu, it opens as a Movie Script window, with the handler designated as global.

3. Enter the following lines in the Movie Script window. You can omit the lines beginning with two hyphens (--); they are comments that tell you what is happening in the script.

```
-- specifies the opening of a window for an MIAW checks to
see if the object (myWindow) is an object produced by a Xtra
or parent script, in which case the window won't open.

on begin myMovie
    global myWindow
    if objectP(myWindow) then
       forget myWindow
end if

-- specifies the horizontal and vertical location of the win-
dow, in relationship to the upper left-hand corner of the
host movie. The location is specified in pixels.

-- specifies the horizontal and vertical dimensions in pix-
els of the window. These properties are discussed later in
this chapter.
```

```
        set horzOrigin to the stageLeft + 25
        set vertOrigin to the stageTop + 180
        set myWindowRect to¬
        rect(horzOrigin, vertOrigin, ¬
        horzOrigin + 240, vertOrigin + 320)

    -- specifies the name of the window
    -- assigns the dimensions of the window to the window
    -- tells the MIAW window that it can respond to instructions
    from another movie
    -- specifies that the window has no title bar
    -- opens the window and completes the script

        set myWindow to window "windowOne"
        set the rect of myWindow to myWindowRect
        set the modal of myWindow = FALSE
        set the fileName of myWindow to "menu.dir"
        set the titleVisible of myWindow = FALSE
        open myWindow
    end
```

4. Close the Script window.
5. Rewind your movie and test it by clicking the Play button.

You've just created the basic script for playing an MIAW. The script in guide.dir contains several entries that might change depending upon your particular project. For example, the script presumes that both the host movie and MIAW reside in the same directory. If they didn't, you would need to insert a search path statement after the filename line, telling Director where to look for your files. The inability to find files is one of the most common reasons a Director movie or projector fails. If you intend to distribute your MIAW project on CD-ROM, you might want to insert a search path line into the movie script pointing toward the location of the files.

One of the following lines can be inserted to enable Director to find your files. For the Macintosh:

```
set the searchPath = ["hard drive: miaw"]
```

and for Windows:

```
set the searchPath = ["d:\miaw"]
```

Of course, you'll need to change the drive and folder names in these statements as appropriate. The location, dimensions, window name, and filename of your MIAW will also probably be different. Enter the correct information for those elements to specify the values that meet your particular needs.

Specifying window types

When you write the movie script that creates a window for your MIAW, you can specify one of the window types in Table 21-1, or create a custom window as shown in the previous exercise. Specifying window types is useful when you are creating an MIAW that is going to serve as a dialog box, menu, or other control box, and you want it to conform to the platform standard. For example, if you wanted to create a standard Macintosh dialog box, you'd specify window type 1. For Windows users, the window types have the same values, but their appearance will be consistent with the Windows platform.

Note: On a Windows system, the zoom capability included in Table 21-1 is equated to minimizing, maximizing, and restoring the window size.

Table 21-1
Window Types

Type Number	Window Description
0	Standard document window with title bar. Can be closed, moved, and resized. No zoom box.
1	Alert window or modal dialog box without title bar, with thick border. Cannot be closed, moved, resized, or zoomed.
2	Plain window without title bar, with thin border. Cannot be closed, moved, resized, or zoomed.
3	Plain window without title bar, with thin border and drop shadow (same as type 2 for Windows users, without drop shadow). Cannot be closed, moved, resized, or zoomed.
4	Document window with title bar that can be closed and moved for Macintosh users. Windows users can also minimize and maximize this type of window.
5	Movable Alert window or modal dialog box with title bar on Macintosh. The Windows version matches type 2.
8	Standard document window with title bar. Can be closed, moved, resized, and zoomed.
12	Document window with title bar. Can be closed, moved, and zoomed. Cannot be resized.
16	Rounded-corner window (on Macintosh); can be closed and moved. Square corners (on Windows system); can be closed and moved.
49	Floating palette in authoring mode. In a Macintosh projector, this type of window is stationary.

> **Note:** Some of the standard window types don't allow you to specify custom dimensions. They expand in prescribed, specific increments to fit the window size you designate in the movie script of your host movie. Director tries to match your specifications as closely as possible, but the precise window size is predetermined consistent with your platform.

Visibility of title

You can choose whether your MIAW has a title bar or not. In the movie script shown earlier in "Writing a Movie script to Start create an MIAW," the title was set as False. This setting tells Director that the MIAW should be displayed without a title bar. If you specify a visible title bar, Director displays the name of your movie window as the title. The following line tells Director to display a title bar:

```
set the titleVisible of myWindow = TRUE
```

Specifying a visible title bar is useful if you are using an MIAW as a control window, such as a dialog box or floating palette, for an application. If you're creating an MIAW for an informational or entertainment project, the title bar can be unattractive. For best results, specify the setting that meets the needs of your project.

Specifying a Window Type

1. Open your host movie (guide.dir) in Director, if it's not already open.
2. In the Cast window, double-click the movie script to open it in the Script window.
3. Insert a new line in the script, right after the line specifying the window dimensions (see Figure 21-4). This change is not reflected in guide.dir, so go ahead and make the change.

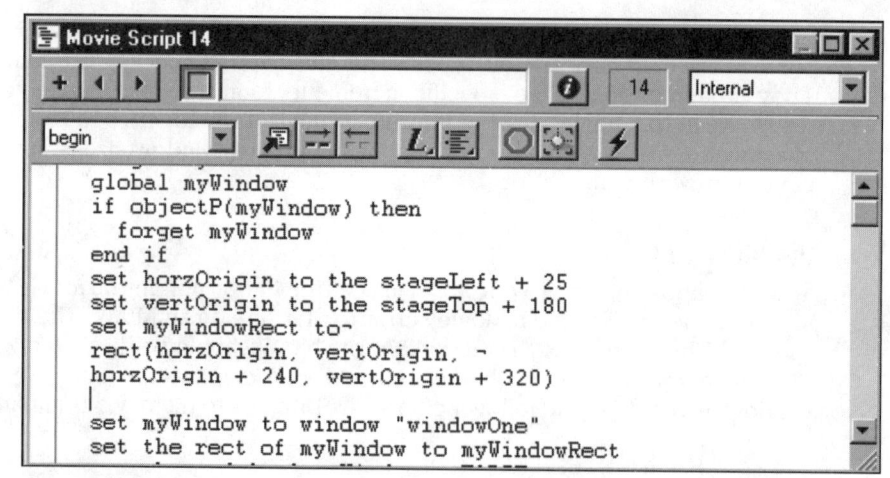

```
global myWindow
if objectP(myWindow) then
  forget myWindow
end if
set horzOrigin to the stageLeft + 25
set vertOrigin to the stageTop + 180
set myWindowRect to ¬
rect(horzOrigin, vertOrigin, ¬
horzOrigin + 240, vertOrigin + 320)

set myWindow to window "windowOne"
set the rect of myWindow to myWindowRect
```

Figure 21-4: Insert a new line after the line specifying the window dimensions.

4. Enter the following statement on the blank line you inserted:

```
set the windowType of window "menu" to 8
```

> **Note:** The name of your window in step 4 should be that of your MIAW. The value at the end of the statement is determined by the window type you want to use, as shown in Table 21-1.

5. Close the Script window, rewind your movie, and click the Play button to view the movie.

Controlling MIAWs

An essential part of creating a project that contains a movie in a window is creating Lingo scripts that pass information and instructions between the movies. For example, your MIAW can instruct the host movie to play another movie, go to a marker in a movie, or move to the front or back. The Lingo `tell` statement is used to send instructions between movies. You can place a `tell` statement in a cast member, frame, or sprite script.

For example, the menu that appears in Figure 21-5 is an MIAW. When the user clicks one of the menu choices, the action of the movie goes to a marker in the host movie and displays informational text. Each menu choice has an associated marker in the host movie. The `tell` statement is a cast member script in the MIAW movie.

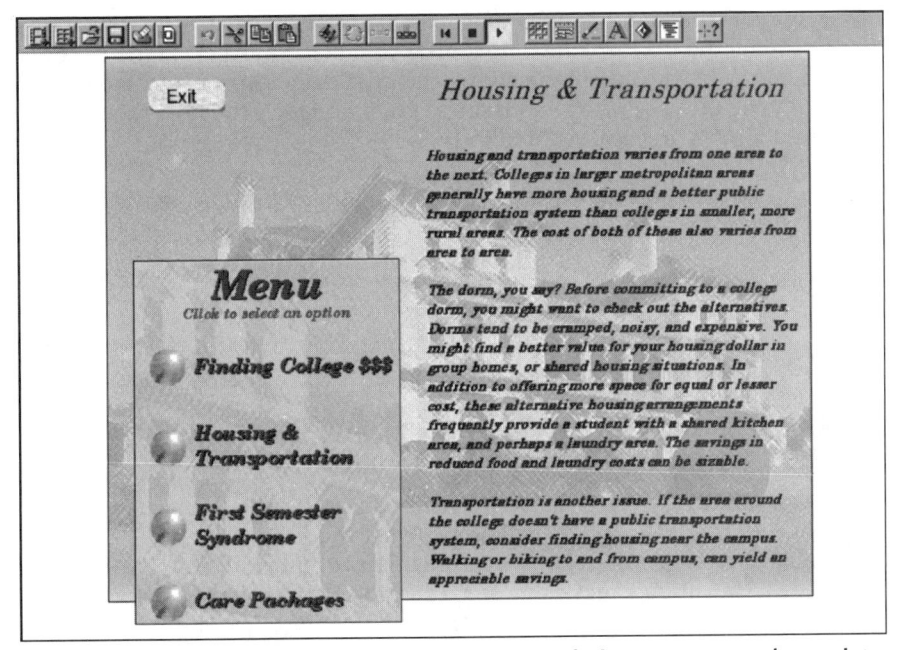

Figure 21-5: When the user clicks one of the menu choices, a cast member script tells the Stage to go to a marker in the host movie.

Attaching a `tell` Statement to a Cast Member

1. Open your MIAW movie (menu.dir) in Director, if it's not already open.
2. In the Cast window, select the cast member to which you want to attach the script (in this case, cast member 6 or "house"), and click the Script button at the top of the Cast window.
3. When the Script window appears, enter the following:

```
on mouseDown
     tell the stage to go to "housing"
end
```

4. Close the Script window and save your movie. Similar scripts are attached to cast members "Col_fund," "first_sem," and "care_pkg."
5. Open the host movie in Director, and click the Play button to test the movie.

The script you added in the preceding exercise was an instruction issued by the MIAW, sending the playback head to a marker called "housing" in the host movie. By changing the `tell` line of the script, the MIAW can tell the host movie to play another movie or quit. When you issue a quit statement, the host movie and its associated MIAWs are stopped and the windows are closed.

The following examples show the `tell` statements for playing another movie and quitting the movie, respectively:

```
tell the stage to play "homebound"

tell the stage to quit
```

Specifying transitions with MIAWs

The Stage controls transitions in addition to palettes. As a result, if your MIAW has a transition effect, the effect is ignored. That doesn't mean you have to do without transitions, however. If you are willing to invest the time, there are a couple of ways you can re-create the effect of a transition within your MIAW. You can either reproduce a transition effect using sprites, or create a digital video of the transition effect between two frames, and import it into the MIAW.

Re-creating a transition effect using sprites can be tedious and time-consuming. For example, you could create the illusion of a strip transition from one cast member to another, using the Paint window. Your first step would be to create several cast members from the first cast member. Each of the new cast members would be a strip of the original (as shown in the Cast window of Figure 21-6). You'd then align them over the second cast member on the Stage. By creating an animation sequence that moved the strips and made them disappear, the second cast member would be revealed.

The second method — creating a digital video to simulate a transition — is easier and faster than using a sprite animation. It involves exporting as bitmap images the two frames where you want the transition to occur, then creating the transition in a video editor, and importing the resulting digital video into the MIAW.

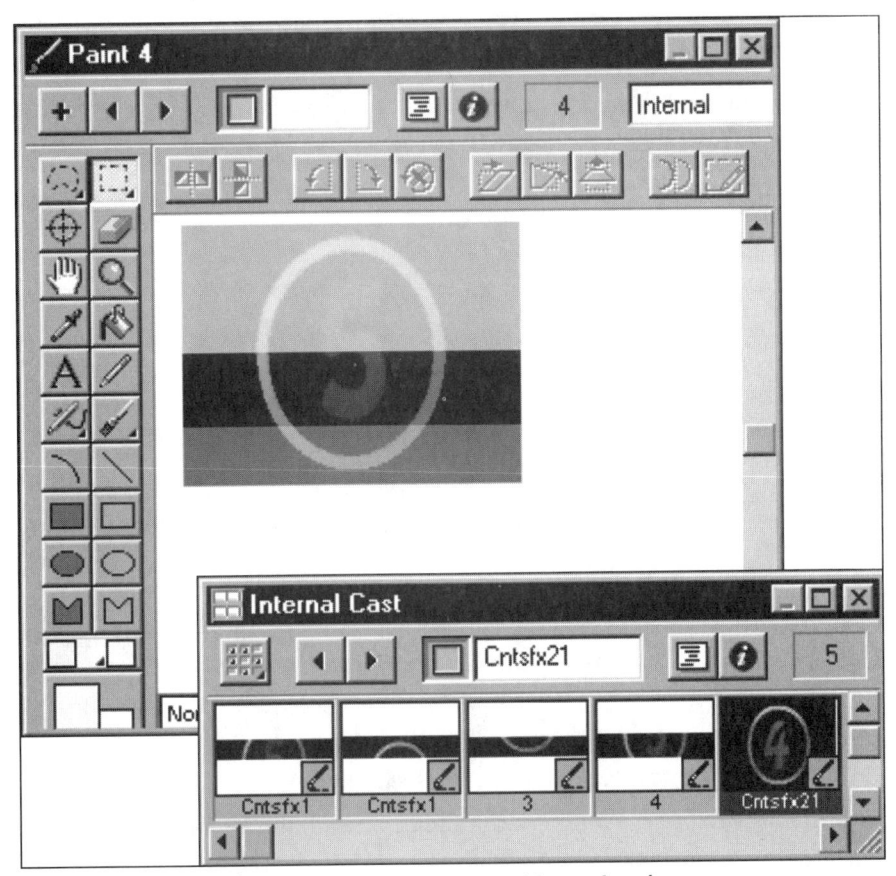

Figure 21-6: Creating the illusion of a strip transition using the Paint window takes some time and effort.

Creating a Digital Video Transition

1. Open your MIAW in Director, if it's not already open.
2. In the Score, select the two frames where you want the transition to occur.
3. Select File ⇨ Export.
4. In the Export dialog box (Figure 21-7), enable the Selected Frames option and choose a bitmap format from the list at the bottom of the dialog. Click the Export button.

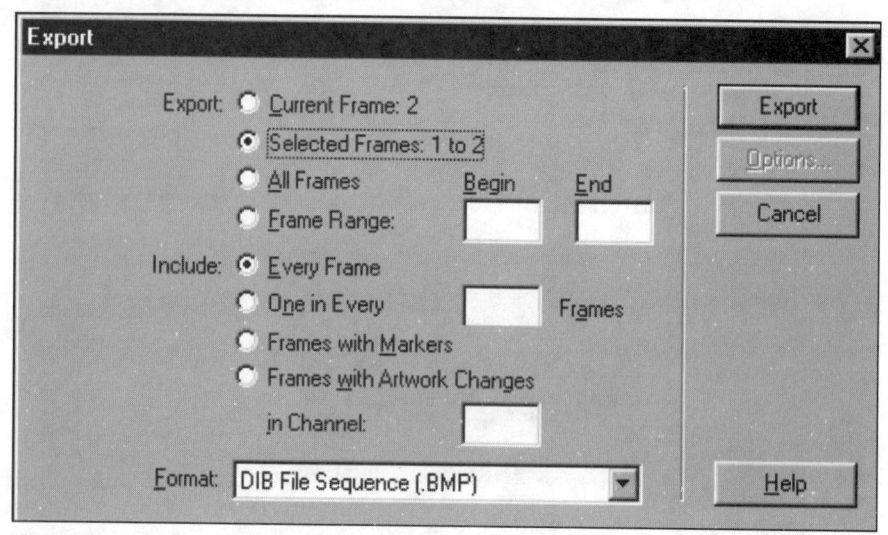

Figure 21-7: Export the two frames where you want to create a transition as bitmap images.

5. Open the two images in your video editor, and create the video transition between the two images. (Check the user's manual for your video editor for specific instructions on how to create a video transition.)
6. Save the video file as a QuickTime or Microsoft Video for Windows file.
7. Import the digital video into your MIAW.
8. Replace the transition frames in the Score with the digital video.
9. Save the MIAW file.

By creating the illusion of a transition in your MIAW, you'll be able to smooth the change from one frame of your movie to the next.

Tip

After creating such transition-type effects, you might want to reopen the host movie and check to make sure the results are what you wanted. You may need to extend the digital video sprites in the Score to ensure that it plays completely.

Working with palettes

Although the Stage controls the palettes when you have an MIAW, you can send instructions from the MIAW to the Stage to change the palette.

Caution: You should approach this task with caution, however. If you have multiple MIAWs playing at the same time, changing the palette can cause unpredictable results between the movies. For example, let's say you want the Stage to change to the metallic palette. The following statement makes this happen:

```
tell the Stage to puppetPalette "metallic"
```

If you do tell the Stage to change the palette, be sure to check all your MIAWs to ensure that the palette change didn't cause undesirable color shifts.

Adjusting the tempo with an MIAW

Like palettes and transitions, the Stage controls the tempo of your movies. Your MIAWs default to the tempo of the host movie. You can tell the host movie to change the tempo, however. The following statement changes the tempo in the host movie and any associated MIAWs to 15 fps:

```
tell the stage to puppetTempo 15
```

Changing the tempo in the Stage is useful if the MIAW contains a digital video or sound file and the animation isn't smooth. By increasing the tempo to play the frames as fast as possible, you can improve the performance of your movie.

Sound and tempo in MIAWs

You can include sound in your MIAWs, but you might want to place the sound in the host movie instead. Normally, Director synchronizes the animation of a movie to the sound. In the case of an MIAW, however, the tempo is under the control of the Stage, which takes precedence over sounds that might be in the MIAW. If the animation in your MIAW doesn't seem smooth or doesn't animate in sync with the sound, moving the sound to the host movie can improve the animation.

Setting the visibility of a window

The visibility of a window can be an important factor in the design of an MIAW project. If you have a project that contains multiple MIAWs (a control panel and a floating palette, for instance), you might want certain movies to disappear temporarily while others play. You could close the movie you want to be "hidden," but then you'd have to reload it if you need it again — and that can affect the performance of your project. To avoid this problem, you can create a script that sets the visibility of a window. Visibility settings are either True (visible) or False (invisible).

> **Note:** Bear in mind that, even when you specify that the visibility of the window is False, the movie is still there and using memory.

Setting a Window's Visibility

1. Open the movie for which you want to set visibility.
2. In the Score, go to the frame where you want to change the visibility, and double-click the script channel in that frame.
3. In the Script window, enter the following:

   ```
   on exitFrame
        set the visible of window "sndcntrl" to FALSE
   end
   ```

   This makes a sound control panel named "sndcntrl" disappear when the playback head exits the specified frame. (You could also place this script in a frame of the host movie, even if you are controlling the visibility of an MIAW.)

4. Close the Script window.

Managing MIAWs

So far you've learned how to create a window for an MIAW, play the movie, and create interactive events between movies. When you do have multiple MIAWs, or when your MIAW is a large file, good management becomes essential to the success of the project. Director gives you the following MIAW management tools. You can

- Preload larger files
- Remove MIAWs from memory when appropriate
- Move a window to the front or back

Creating multiple MIAWs

You can create multiple windows for MIAWs in the host movie's movie script. The example of the movie script shown earlier, in "Creating an MIAW," had only one MIAW. You can modify the same script to add more windows, however. To create multiple windows, each window needs to have a unique name and set of parameters.

For example, if you wanted to add the movie "sndcntrl" to the movie script, you would append the script as follows:

```
-- specifies the opening of a window for an MIAW -- checks to see
-- if the object (myWindow2) is an object produces by a Xtra or
-- parent script, in which case the window won't open. This sets
-- up the window for the first MIAW.

on begin myMovie2
  global myWindow2
  if objectP(myWindow2) then
      forget myWindow2
  end if

-- specifies the horizontal and vertical location of the window,
in relationship to the upper left-hand corner of the host
movie. The location is specified in pixels.

-- specifies the horizontal and vertical dimensions in pixels of
the window

  set horzOrigin to the stageLeft + 60
  set vertOrigin to the stageTop + 220
  set myWindowRect to¬
  rect(horzOrigin, vertOrigin, ¬
  horzOrigin + 200, vertOrigin + 160)

  -- specifies the name of the window

  -- assigns the dimensions of the window to the window

  -- tells the MIAW window that it can respond to instructions
      from another movie

  -- specifies that the window has no title bar

  -- opens the window and completes the script

  set myWindow2 to window "sndcntrl"
  set the rect of myWindow2 to myWindowRect2
  set the modal of myWindow2 = FALSE
  set the fileName of myWindow2 to "sndcntrl.dir"
  set the titleVisible of myWindow = FALSE
  open myWindow
end
```

Basically, adding a second MIAW involves repeating the script for the first MIAW. You change the names and parameters to reflect a unique entity. In the Score of your host movie, you place a marker and a frame script to start the second movie.

> **Tip:** You can also use one MIAW to create another MIAW, by creating a movie script like the one just above and placing it in the originating MIAW. Note that this does not make the originating MIAW the host movie. Control of transitions, palettes, and tempo still belong to the Stage.

Preloading MIAWs

By default, an MIAW isn't loaded until the playback head reaches the specified starting point in the Stage. This can be problematic if you have a large MIAW, or an MIAW that contains digital video or sound. It's a good idea to assign a script to a frame in the host movie that preloads the MIAW.

Preloading an MIAW

1. Open your host movie in Director, if it's not already open.
2. In the Score, go to the frame before the start of your MIAW, and double-click the script channel to display the Script window. (If there is a script already in that frame, you can choose any frame that occurs prior to the start of the MIAW.)
3. In the Script window, enter the following:

   ```
   on enterFrame
     preLoadMovie "menu"
   end
   ```

4. Close the Script window.
5. Rewind your movie. Click the Play button to test the preload.
6. If the MIAW needs more preload time to create a smooth start, select the script sprite in the Score window, and drag it to an earlier frame of the host movie.

You can place the preload script in any frame prior to the start of your MIAW. To keep memory usage to a minimum, keep the script as close to the start of the MIAW as possible while still ensuring a smooth start of your MIAW.

Moving windows to the front or back

When you create an MIAW, Director automatically displays it in front of all other windows when it starts playing. You can move a window to the front or back, though — this is most often useful when you want the MIAW to come to the front when it's active and go to the back when it's inactive.

Moving a Window to the Front or Back

1. Open your host movie in Director, if it's not already open.
2. In the Score, select the frame where you want to move a window to the front or back, and double-click the script channel for that frame.
3. In the Script, window enter *one* of the following scripts:

   ```
   on enterFrame
     moveToFront window "sndcntrl"
   end
   ```

   or

   ```
   on enterFrame
     moveToBack window "sndcntrl"
   end
   ```

   These scripts move the window "sndcntrl" to the front or back, respectively. (These scripts can also be placed in the MIAW.)
4. Close the Script window.
5. Rewind your movie. Click the Play button to test the movie.

Removing an MIAW

It's important to remember that MIAWs don't automatically remove themselves from memory or close the window when they finish playing. Unless you remove them from memory, you may get unpredictable results if the user decides to rewind and replay the movie. Parts of the movie may appear and others may not, or nothing may appear but the sound files will play. Perhaps more importantly, the movie is still residing in the computer's memory, and may cause the computer to lock up.

Caution

Remember — simply closing the window does not remove the movie from the computer's memory.

Removing an MIAW

1. Open your host movie (guide.dir) in Director, if it's not already open.
2. In the Cast window, double-click the movie script that controls your MIAW to open it in the Script window.
3. In the Script window, scroll to the bottom of the script and enter the following handlers. In the movie guide.dir, these handlers are added to cast member 14.

   ```
   -- checks to see if an action has stopped the movie
   
   on stopMovie
     finishMovie
   end
   
   -- if the movie has stopped, the window is forgotten, the
      stage is updated, and the window is closed
   
   on finishMovie
     global myWindow
       if objectP(myWindow) then
       forget myWindow
     end if
     updateStage
   end
   ```

4. Close the Script window.
5. Rewind your movie, and click the Play button to test the movie.

Removing a movie from memory is more than good housekeeping — it's critical to the success of your movie. In addition to causing the problems described above, if you don't remove the movie, stray bits and pieces of it may remain on-screen.

In this exercise, you'll pull together everything you've discovered in this chapter about MIAWs. In the MIAW you're about to construct, the host (Stage) movie stops and starts the MIAW using the `tell` command.

Remember that an MIAW is simply a movie like any other movie. You can create and edit it just like any other Director movie. The only difference is that the MIAW plays inside a window on the Stage and operates independently of the parent movie.

In its simplest form, the MIAW can be thought of as a movie with a small Stage area playing on top of a movie with a large Stage area. You can reverse this arrangement, but the end result is that you are back to displaying a single movie on the Stage, since the movie with the small Stage would be obscured by the movie with the large Stage.

On the CD-ROM The afrikmov.dir and africa.dir files used in this exercise are on your companion CD-ROM in the exercise:ch21 (exercise\ch21) folder.

From Dogon to Ivory Coast Art

The africa.dir movie uses clip media images from WorldBeat Africa. The icons and images are part of the Image Club DigitArt Clip Art Library, copyright 1996 by Image Club Graphics, a division of Adobe Systems Incorporated. The WorldBeat Africa images are inspired by artist Kari Lehr's exploration into traditional African Art — from the Kalahari Bushmen, to the iron work of the Dogon people on the Ivory Coast, to the hieroglyphs of Egyptian artists.

Opening and Controlling a MIAW

1. Open the africa.dir movie and play it so you know how it works. The movie cycles through five images that illustrate African proverbs.

2. Stop the movie (Command+period or Ctrl+period) and open afrikmov.dir. The movie includes two graphics that can be used as Pause and Continue buttons.

3. Attach the following script to the Pause button (cast member 1). The Pause command stops the playback head.

   Watch out — as you enter the scripts that follow, it's easy to get confused and type the word `movie` instead of `window`. Even though you are building a project with an MIAW, you are opening a *window,* not a *movie,* in these steps.

   ```
   on mouseUp
         tell window "africa.dir" to pause
   end
   ```

4. Attach the following script to the Continue button (cast member 2):

   ```
   on mouseUp
         tell window "africa.dir" to continue
   end
   ```

5. Select the next empty cast slot in the Cast window, and open the Script window to create the following on startMovie script:

   ```
   on startMovie
        open window "africa.dir"
   end
   ```

6. Close the Script window and save the movie as **afrika2**.

7. Play the movie, try out both buttons, and notice the window type used by the MIAW.

8. When you're ready to continue, stop the movie (Command+period or Ctrl+Period). Notice you did not close or remove the MIAW from memory, so it continues running even after the parent movie terminates.

9. Next you need to do some housekeeping (closing windows and removing the MIAW from memory). Create the following movie script in the next open cast member slot:

   ```
   on stopMovie
        close window "africa.dir"
        forget window "africa.dir"
   end
   ```

10. Save the movie again as afrika2.dir, play it, and test it. You may need to click the Continue button to restart the MIAW, depending on what state you left it in.

11. Stop the movie and notice that the MIAW closes and disappears.

12. Next, you'll experiment with changing the window type for the MIAW. The africa.dir MIAW does not need to be resized, closed, or zoomed, so you can set its window type to 5. Modify the on startMovie handler to match the following:

    ```
    on startMovie
         open window "africa.dir"
         set the windowType of window "africa.dir" to 5
    end
    ```

13. Save the movie again as afrika2.dir, rewind, and play it. The title bar has disappeared, and the window is a modal (Alert-type) window.

Note: To finish this movie, you would probably add a Start Movie (MIAW) and Stop Movie button, add sound to the movie, add sound controls, and add a Quit button (using the `halt` or `quit` command). Don't forget to provide these important controls for your users.

Selecting the location on Stage for the MIAW

When you open an MIAW, the default placement of the window is the center of the Stage. You can modify this placement using the `rect()` function in combination with `the rect of window` property. In the following example, the MIAW is set to appear in the bottom-left corner of the desktop. The "desktop" refers to the entire visible area on your monitor's screen. This statement assumes the MIAW is 100 x 100 pixels and that the Stage size for the parent movie is 640 x 480 pixels.

    set the rect of window "help" to rect (0,380,100,480)

The `rect()` function returns or sets the coordinates of a rectangular area on the desktop. The values inside parentheses in the `rect()` function follow this format:

    rect(leftEdge, topEdge, rightEdge, bottomEdge)

Tip: When you establish the location for a MIAW, you are also specifying its size in pixels.

Director's documentation and online help are a bit confusing in their discussion of the `rect()` function. The discussion refers to the points (left, top, right, and bottom) as being a specified number of pixels from the edge of the Stage. Actually, the function locates points based on their distance from the upperhleft corner of the desktop.

Caution: If you set `the rect of window` to a rectangular area such as

    rect(0,380,100,480)

then the MIAW appears *outside* the area of the Stage if either of the following situations exist:

- ✦ The Stage is centered on the desktop, Director is in authoring mode, and the Stage size is smaller (such as 640 x 480) than the area of the desktop (such as 1,024 x 768).

- ✦ You create a projector with the Full Screen option selected. The movie has the Stage centered on the desktop, and the Stage size is smaller (such as 640 x 480) than the desktop area (such as 1,024 x 768).

The same 640 x 480 movie, if made into a projector with the Full Screen setting deselected, does display the MIAW within the Stage area.

The only time the `rect()` function coordinates are identical for both the Stage and the desktop is when the Stage and the desktop are identical in size. Because of the number of Director windows that must be juggled in authoring mode, the Stage and desktop will rarely be equal in size — especially if you have a large monitor (17 to 20 inches) and your Stage dimensions are set for the typical VGA (640 x 480) monitor.

Consider the following example:

```
set the rect of window "help" to rect (0,380,100,480)
```

Here the window for the MIAW appears with its

- Left edge 0 pixels from the left edge of the desktop
- Top edge 380 pixels from the top of the desktop
- Right edge 100 pixels from the left edge of the desktop
- Bottom edge 480 pixels from the top of the desktop

The location of an object is based on the same coordinate system that begins with 0,0 in the upper-left corner of the Stage or desktop. The only difference is that `locV` and `locH` are based on the distance from the upper-left corner of the Stage, while the `rect()` function locations are based on the distance from the upper-left edge of the desktop.

The `rect of window` property can be determined or set. When placing an MIAW on the Stage, you are setting this property to match a location identified by the four coordinates in the `rect()` function.

Tip

You should know the size in pixels of the Stage for your MIAW. Knowing the size enables you to determine the `rect()` function coordinate values. You can determine the Stage size of the movie (to be played in the window) using the Modify ⇨ Movie ⇨ Properties command (Command+Shift+D or Ctrl+Shift+D). The width and height information is stored in the Width and Height fields on the Movie Properties dialog box.

Setting an absolute location for an MIAW

In the following example, you'll see how to calculate the placement of an MIAW. The location is absolute, in that the `rect()` function indicates the location in pixels from the upper-left corner of the desktop. With a little arithmetic, you can place the movie in a window just about anywhere you want on the Stage.

Let's work with an MIAW that is 100 pixels wide and 80 pixels high. The Stage is 640 x 480 pixels, and you want to place the MIAW at the exact bottom-center of the Stage.

1. First, center the MIAW horizontally. Subtract the width of the MIAW (100 pixels) from the width of the Stage (640). The result is 540.

2. Divide the difference by 2; this indicates the number of pixels on either side of the MIAW. The result is 290. Now you know the left coordinate for the `rect()` function is 290.

3. Add to the left coordinate (290) the width of the MIAW (100). The result — 390 — is the right coordinate for the `rect()` function.

4. Now you'll calculate how to place the MIAW at the bottom edge of the Stage. The coordinate for the bottom edge of the Stage is 480; your screen is set to 640 x 480, so no calculation is needed. Now you know the bottom coordinate for the `rect()` function is 480.

5. Subtract the height of the MIAW (80) from the height of the Stage (480). The result is 400. Now you know the top coordinate for the `rect()` function is 400.

Based on these calculations, the statement required to place the MIAW at the bottom center of the Stage (assuming the Stage and desktop sizes match) is as follows:

```
set the rect of window "help" to rect(290,400,390,480)
```

Caution

If you set `the rect of the window` property to be smaller than the actual Stage size, the view of the MIAW is cropped. If you set `the rect of the window` property too large, the movie is surrounded on the bottom and right sides with a solid fill based on the movie's background color.

Setting a relative location for an MIAW

The previous example works only if the Stage and desktop are the same size. Yes, we know we've already said that several times already, but remembering this fact will save you some frustration if you cannot figure out why your best efforts show the MIAW outside the Stage — and that's not where you want it to be.

It's highly likely you will be authoring on a monitor of a different size from what your users will have. So it's important to figure out how to force the MIAW's location to always be exactly where you want it. The trick is to use some simple arithmetic and calculate the relative address for the MIAW. Fortunately, Lingo includes four functions that help.

the stageBottom	Returns a value in pixels that is the distance from the top edge of the desktop to the bottom edge of the Stage.
the stageLeft	Returns a value in pixels that is the distance from the left edge of the desktop to the left edge of the Stage.
the stageRight	Returns a value in pixels that is the distance from the left edge of the desktop to the right edge of the Stage.
the stageTop	Returns a value in pixels that is the distance from the top edge of the desktop to the top edge of the Stage.

If you know the size of your MIAW (such as 144 x 100 pixels), you can use `the stageBottom`, `the stageLeft`, `the stageRight`, and `the stageTop` functions to center the MIAW at the bottom of the Stage, even if the desktop is a different size from the Stage. Here is where the arithmetic (and a little algebra) come in handy. Examine Figure 21-8 as you work through these expressions.

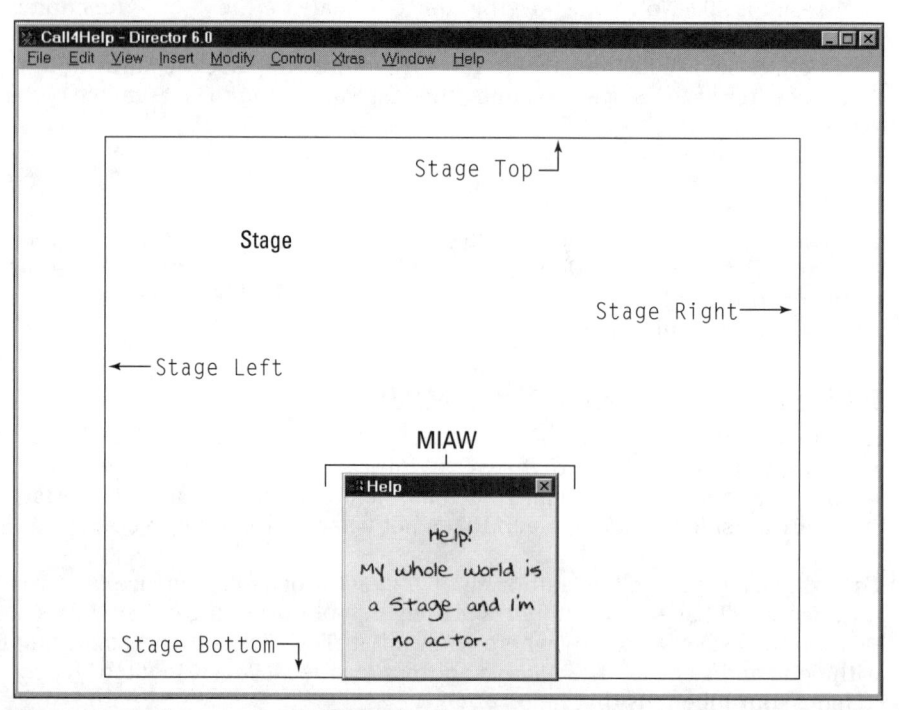

Figure 21-8: Diagram of an MIAW with `the stageBottom`, `the stageRight`, `the stageLeft`, **and** `the stageTop` **dimensions identified**

The left edge
First, you must determine the desired location for the left edge of the MIAW.

1. To center the window, determine the width of the Stage:

    ```
    the stageRight - the stageLeft
    ```

2. Subtract the width of the MIAW (stored in a variable named `miawW`) from the width of the Stage to determine how much space is on either side of the MIAW if it is centered:

    ```
    (the stageRight- the stageLeft)- miawW
    ```

3. Divide the buffer space by 2 to determine how much of the buffer is on the left side of the centered MIAW:

    ```
    ((the stageRight- the stageLeft)- miawW)/2
    ```

4. Add to the left buffer the distance from the edge of the desktop to the left edge of the Stage (the `stageLeft` function returns the second value):

    ```
    (((the stageRight- the stageLeft)- miawW)/2) + the stageLeft
    ```

    Although you can use this expression in the `rect()` function, it is more readable and easier to use if you assign the value to a variable, such as `leftEdge`, so the statement reads

    ```
    set leftEdge to (((the stageRight- the stageLeft)- miawW)/2)
    + the stageLeft
    ```

The top edge
The top edge of the MIAW is easier to figure. It is calculated by subtracting the height of the MIAW (stored in `miawH`) from the value returned by `the stageBottom` function. To store this value in the `topEdge` variable, you can use the following statement:

```
set topEdge to the stageBottom - miawH
```

The right edge
To determine the right edge of the MIAW (to be stored in the `rightEdge` variable), you must determine the buffer on either side of the centered MIAW and then subtract that value from the `stageRight` value. You calculated the buffer when you determined the left edge of the MIAW. This time, you simply subtract the expression from the `stageRight` rather than adding it to the `stageLeft` value. The expression is

```
set rightEdge to the stageRight - (((the stageRight- the
stageLeft)- miawW)/2)
```

The bottom edge

The final point in the rect( ) function is the easiest to determine. You want the bottom of the MIAW to match the bottom of the Stage, so you can use the statement

```
set bottomEdge to the stageBottom
```

The whole ball of wax

The entire handler is listed below. This handler appears in a movie script that is executed when the parent movie starts playing.

```
On startMovie
      set the windowtype of window "Help" to 4
      set miawW to 100
      set miawH to 80
      set leftEdge to (((the stageRight- the stageLeft)- ¬
miawW)/2) + the stageLeft
      set topEdge to the stageBottom - miawH
      set rightEdge to the stageRight - (((the stageRight- ¬
the stageLeft)- miawW)/2)
      set bottomEdge to the stageBottom
      set the rect of window "Help" to ¬
rect(leftEdge,topEdge,rightEdge,bottomEdge)
      open window "Help"
end
```

A similar handler could be attached to a button (on mouseUp) to cause the MIAW to appear at the bottom center of the Stage when the button is clicked.

Tip — If you want to place the MIAW at a different location, draw a diagram like Figure 21-8. Assume the Stage area is smaller than the desktop. Try to figure what combination of values can be used to arrive at the desired location.

Notice that the actual MIAW shown in Figure 21-8 is larger than 100 x 80 pixels (it's actually 192 pixels wide by 160 pixels high). In the previous example, we've used 100 x 80 pixels to keep the arithmetic simple, but Director will actually automatically alter your specified Stage dimensions to be increments of 16 pixels. Furthermore, you'd typically want a larger MIAW if it includes controls or anything at all more than a simple animation.

Hiding an MIAW

There is one more location for an MIAW that we have not discussed: off-Stage, where it is not visible (for the moment) by the user. Placing the MIAW off-Stage enables you to quickly display the MIAW (and the sprites it contains) when needed, without loading it from scratch. For instance, the following statement places the MIAW off stage (notice the negative numbers):

```
set the rect of window "help" to rect(-200,-200,-100,-100)
```

When you want the MIAW to appear, you can make it visible on the Stage using the following handler:

```
on mouseUp
      set the rect of window "help" to rect(290,380,390,480)
end
```

You can also hide a MIAW by using `the visible of window` property. It operates just like `the visible of member` property discussed in Chapter 12. The following statement causes our little Help window to disappear from the Stage:

```
set the visible of window "Help" to False
```

Now you can put some of this "`rect` power" to use. In the afrika2.dir movie, you have so far allowed Director to determine where the africa.dir MIAW will appear on the Stage. In the following exercise, you'll explicitly control the position of the MIAW.

Controlling Stage Position for the MIAW

1. Open the afrika2.dir movie that you modified in the last exercise.

2. Modify the `on startMovie` handler in the movie script to match the following. This handler calculates the center of the Stage and places the MIAW at that location, no matter what size monitor the end-user uses to view the movie.

```
On startMovie
      set the windowtype of window "africa.dir" to 5
      set miawH to 110
      set miawW to 288
      set leftEdge to (((the stageRight- the stageLeft)- ¬
miawW)/2) + the stageLeft
      set topEdge to (((the stageBottom- the stageTop)- ¬
miawH)/2) + the stageTop
      set rightEdge to the stageRight - (((the stageRight- ¬
the stageLeft)- miawW)/2)
      set bottomEdge to the stageBottom - (((the ¬
stageBottom- the stageTop)- miawH)/2)
      set the rect of window "Africa.dir" to ¬
rect(leftEdge,topEdge,rightEdge,bottomEdge)
      open window "africa.dir"
end
```

3. To test this, select Modify ⇨ Movie ⇨ Properties and set the left edge to 0. This throws your Stage off-center, flush left on your desktop. Close the dialog box.

4. Save again as afrika2.dir, rewind, and test the movie.

Summary

Here's a summary of what we covered in this chapter:

✦ An MIAW is an independent and distinct movie with its own Score, cast, and Lingo. It is not confined to the physical boundaries of the host movie.

✦ MIAWs enable you to pace the loading and unloading of movies into memory, so that you can create larger and more complex movies without straining resources.

✦ MIAWs can interact. Global variables can be shared between movies and handlers, reducing the amount of scripting necessary for the success of your movie.

✦ Movie scripts are used to specify the parameters for an MIAW.

✦ You can change the appearance of your MIAW by specifying a window type, a visible title bar, and telling the host movie to change palettes and tempos. You can also simulate transitions.

✦ You can create multiple MIAWs by specifying unique parameters for each one.

✦ Preloading an MIAW smoothes the flow of the movie. You can also move an MIAW in front of or behind the host movie.

✦ Be sure to remove an MIAW from memory when your movie is finished playing.

✦ ✦ ✦

In Your Interface: Menus and Dialogs

CHAPTER 22

In This Chapter

Learn to create and manipulate menus

Build simple dialogs with the MUI Xtra

Build not so simple dialogs with the MUI Xtra

Director by nature encourages a free-form interface design: buttons that come alive when the mouse rolls over them, animations that dance across the screen, whole toolbars that appear and disappear effortlessly. However, even in the most dynamic environment there is a place for menu bars and dialogs — the staples of more traditional programs on any platform. This chapter explores creation of menus and dialogs using Lingo.

Making Manic Menus

In the history of computing, the menu bar was a major step forward. It presented options to the user that previously had only been available through the use of terse (and frequently poorly documented) command-line arguments. The menu bar evolved into powerful and intuitive graphical user interfaces such as those of the Macintosh OS and Microsoft Windows. Today's menu interface is vastly more complex than the first menus — some say too complex — but there is no denying the importance of the fundamental principles that make menus useful:

- ✦ Menus group commands by functionality, providing a quick and logical path to performing a specific action.

- ✦ Similar common menus make it easier to work with several programs running on the same operating system. The beginning user doesn't have to learn a completely different paradigm when exploring every new application. An application's interface is typically more similar than dissimilar from those of other applications using the same operating system.

+ Menus act as reminders for common keyboard equivalents. When the shortcut operation to save a file is Command+S (or Ctrl+S in Windows), that shortcut is usually displayed with the menu option File ➪ Save. Until a user becomes familiar with the keyboard shortcuts, menus provide easy access to all features and list the shortcuts while remaining unobtrusive.

+ Menus frequently serve as a gateway to dialog boxes in a manner that would be difficult to implement with buttons and other more graphical elements. That's because each entry in a menu portrays an instant explanation of the action it is to perform (at least it *should*, although in poorly designed menus this isn't always true).

+ Menus are easy to localize, unlike bitmap graphics that need to be re-created every time the language changes. By switching a cast member, you can make a Director menu change the language it displays.

Tip

Menus are most useful to beginners — people who aren't familiar with the product. As users become more proficient, they tend to rely more on shortcut keys or, if they're available, button bar icons to get things done. Keep this in mind as you work on your own design. When you're putting together a menu, aim it toward the novice and you can't go wrong.

Creating Your Own Pull-down Menu System

You may not have given much thought yet to including a pull-down or drop-down menu in your Director movie, but you won't want to neglect this feature. Most off-the-shelf applications include some sort of pull-down menu system. In fact, menus are so commonplace that nobody even thinks about them — until they're not available.

Fortunately, menu systems are fairly easy to implement in Director. You can build a menu system to handle tasks such as these:

+ Executing commands and accessing features
+ Navigating within the application
+ Controlling system settings (such as audio volume)

To build a pull-down menu requires a few easy steps:

1. Create a field cast member that includes specific keywords that construct the menu and its options.
2. Install the movie using the `installMenu` command.
3. Create a movie projector.
4. Play and test the projector.

Creating a menu using a field cast member

Menus are created using a field cast member that begins with the `menu` keyword followed by the name of the menu. For instance, to create a File menu like the one found in nearly every application, you type the following text as the first line in a field:

```
menu: File
```

On subsequent lines in the field, you type the options that you want to appear on the menu. You add options to the menu using the following syntax:

```
menuItem | lingoInstruction
```

The vertical bar (|) character (known as a *pipe* in most programming languages) separates the text of the menu option from the Lingo instruction that is executed when the option is selected by the user. On most keyboards, the pipe or vertical bar character is generated by pressing Shift+\.

Director does not support a direct method of executing multiple commands from a single menu item on a user-defined menu. However, you can create a workaround. To implement this arrangement on the user-defined menu, create a menu option to call a user-defined handler that you construct with the desired instructions.

A typical File menu (on a Windows or Macintosh system) includes a Save option and an Exit option. Let's see how to add these options to the File menu. It requires the addition of two lines of instructions. The entire field cast member with the two options added looks like this:

```
menu: File
Save | saveMovie "Genealogy"
Exit | quit
```

Tip A space before and after the vertical bar character is optional. Your script may be more readable, however, if you add these extra spaces.

In this example, the `saveMovie` command saves the current movie using the filename specified inside quotation marks. This movie is saved as "Genealogy." Figure 22-1 demonstrates how this menu appears when the movie is played back in authoring mode. Notice that the menu appears in the upper-left corner of the screen, not on the Stage area.

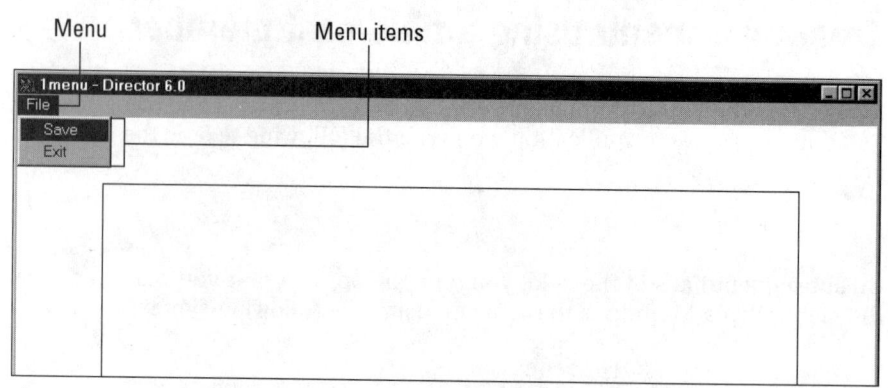

Figure 22-1: Custom File menu as it appears in authoring mode

Tip

When you add menus and menu options, be sure to use the capitalization that you want displayed. Capitalization for the Lingo instructions is not important because Lingo is not case sensitive. For the menus and their contents, however, what you type is what you get displayed on-screen.

In authoring mode, when you add a user-defined menu to a movie using the Windows version of Director, the menu bar appears immediately under the title bar, not on the Stage. This occurs only in authoring mode (that is, when you play the movie from within Director). When you create a Windows projector, the menu bar *consumes* part of the Stage area. Graphics and other objects on the Stage are shifted down because the menu bar occupies a 24-pixel band across the top of the Stage, as shown in Figure 22-2.

You'll need to keep this in mind when you add a menu to a movie. To avoid screen layout problems, you must

- Shift everything on the Stage down 24 pixels from where you would normally place the sprites
- Leave the blank bottom 24-pixel band across the screen.

Menu bar consumes part of the Stage

Figure 22-2: A Windows pull-down menu as it appears during playback from a projector

Caution

This downward shift of objects on the Stage does not increase the Stage size; it just pushes the bottom 24-pixel band into never-never land.

You can display more than one pull-down menu at a time on the Stage. To do so, you simply define the first menu (as described above), and then sequentially define each additional menu in the same field cast member. Each new menu and each new menu option within the field must start on a new line.

The following field cast member creates a menu bar with two command menus (Music Selections and Volume Control). The instructions for both menus are stored in the same field, one after the other.

```
menu: Music Selections
Beatles | puppetSound 1,"Beatles"
Brahms | puppetSound 1,"Brahms"
Elton John | puppetSound 1,"EJohn"
Mozart | puppetSound 1,"Mozart"
menu: Volume Control
Sound Off | set the soundLevel to 0
Low | set the soundLevel to 1
Medium | set the soundLevel to 4
Loud | set the soundLevel to 7
```

Figure 22-3 shows you what the menus will look like in authoring mode on a Macintosh system.

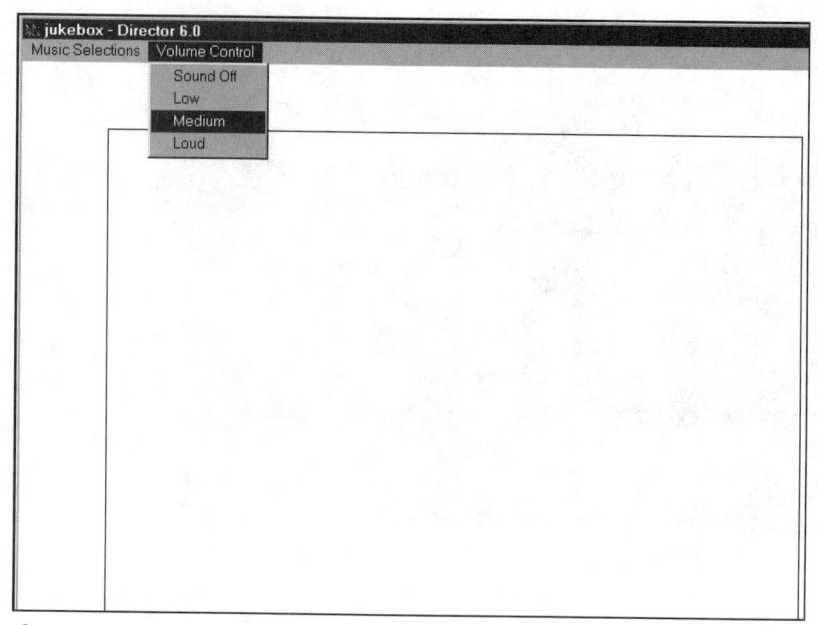

Figure 22-3: User-defined menus for Music Selections and Volume Control

Tip Macintosh users can add the Apple menu symbol using the following line in a menu definition:

```
menu:@
```

This instruction only adds the menu, not any options. You must create the desired options just as you would for any other menu that you want included in your movie. By convention, the Apple menu is always the first menu on the menu bar (starting at the upper-left edge of the screen), so the `menu: @` instruction (followed by the options you want available) should always be listed as the first menu entry in the field cast member.

Installing a menu

Once you have created the menu, you must install it using the Lingo `installMenu` command as follows:

```
installMenu castIdentifier
```

Replace the *castIdentifier* parameter with the number or name of the field cast member that contains the menu instructions. In the following `on startMovie` handler, the menu is stored in a field that is cast member 3:

```
On startMovie
      installMenu 3
end
```

In this next example, the menu is stored in a field cast member named "Volume Control."

```
On startMovie
      installMenu "Volume Control"
end
```

The initial installation of a menu is typically handled from within a movie script, but you can also install a menu from a cast, sprite, or frame script. For instance, you can attach a cast member script to a button that, when clicked, switches from one menu to another. You simply issue the `installMenu` command and name a new field cast member that includes the new menu.

To disable an installed menu, use the following form of the `installMenu` command:

```
installMenu 0
```

On the CD-ROM In the next exercise, you'll use the groovy.dir movie and add a field cast member that includes the menu instructions and a movie script that installs the menu. The file groovy.dir can be found on your companion CD-ROM in the exercise:ch22 (exercise\ch22) folder. In its current form, the movie includes one bitmap image, a script cast member with a `go to the frame` handler, and a sound cast member called groovy (composed by Jeffrey E. Jones, copyright 1997; all rights reserved).

Creating a Sound Volume Menu

1. Open the groovy.dir movie in Director.
2. Select the first open cast member slot (slot 4).
3. Open the Field window (Command+8 or Ctrl+8) and type the following text. Be sure to include the line breaks exactly as shown.

   ```
   menu: Play
   Groovy | puppetSound 1, "Groovy"
   Sound Off | puppetSound 1, 0
   menu: Volume Control
   ```

(continued)

```
Low   | set the soundLevel to 1
Medium | set the soundLevel to 4
Loud  | set the soundLevel to 7
```

4. Change the new cast member's name to **soundMenu**.
5. Close the Field window.
6. Select the next open cast member slot (5).
7. Open the Script window (Command+0 or Ctrl+0) and type the following script:

    ```
    on startMovie
          installMenu "soundMenu"
    end
    ```

8. Close the Script window. Save the movie in your personal folder as **groovy1.dir,** rewind, and play it.
9. Select the Play ⇨ Groovy menu option to start the sound and adjust your speakers so you can easily hear the music.
10. Experiment with the options on the Volume Control menu. Test the Low, Medium, and Loud options.
11. Turn off the sound using the Play ⇨ Sound Off command.
12. Stop the movie.

Finishing the job

To finish the project, you need to save the movie and create a projector, play it, and test it. Be sure that

- The menu options work as expected
- The area used by the menu bar does not shift Stage objects down and hide important text or images
- You have provided all necessary menu options

Additionally, you may want to enhance your menu, by adding such features as

- Keyboard shortcuts
- Check marks that indicate the currently selected options
- Grayed-out (disabled) options
- Formatting (boldface, underline, or shadow) for menu options

Adding keyboard shortcuts to a menu

Most applications provide keyboard shortcuts or quick keys to access frequently used features. These keyboard shortcuts perform the same function as choosing a menu option. You can easily add keyboard shortcuts to each menu item in your Director movie.

On a Macintosh system, keyboard shortcuts are typically assigned to the Command key plus a letter; on a Windows system, a combination of the Ctrl key plus a letter is used. To add the shortcut, you simply edit the field that contains your menu's instructions and add the slash (/) character, which represents the Command (Ctrl) key, followed by the name of the key you want to use in this key-combination to invoke the menu option.

For example, using the earlier File menu example, you can add shortcuts by changing the menu instructions to match the following:

```
menu: File
Save/S | saveMovie "Genealogy"
Exit/E | quit
```

In this example, either Command+S on a Macintosh or Ctrl+S on a Windows system invokes the File⇨Save command. Command+E on a Macintosh or Ctrl+E on Windows invokes the File⇨Exit command. These shortcuts are illustrated in Figure 22-4.

Figure 22-4: Menu with keyboard shortcuts

Make it intuitive!

When you select quick keys or keyboard shortcuts, use commonly accepted intuitive combinations. Users of Macintosh and Windows workstations *expect* consistency from application to application. The following quick-key conventions will look familiar to your users:

Command+C (Ctrl+C) invokes the Copy command.

Command+N (Ctrl+N) invokes the New Document command.

Command+P (Ctrl+P) invokes the Print command.

Command+S (Ctrl+S) invokes the Save command.

Command+V (Ctrl+V) invokes the Paste command.

Command+X (Ctrl+X) invokes the Cut command.

Adding check marks

To add a check mark to a menu item, use the checkMark of menuItem property. To display the check mark, you can issue an instruction that uses the following syntax:

```
set the checkMark of menuItem itemName of menu menuName to¬
True
```

In this instruction, *itemName* is replaced with the menu item's name or number that you want preceded by a check mark. If you use a number to identify the menu item, you must start counting with the first item on the menu. The *menuName* parameter is replaced with the menu's name or number. The menu number is based on the menu's position, counting left to right on the menu bar.

Caution On the Macintosh, the Apple Menu is menu 1. Be sure to include it when you determine the menu number.

Using the earlier example of the Music Selection menu, you can display a check mark in front of the Brahms option by issuing the following instruction:

```
set the checkMark of menuItem "Brahms" of menu "Music¬
Selection" to True
```

You get the same result with the following instruction, which uses menu and menu item numbers rather than names:

```
set the checkMark of menuItem 2 of menu 1 to True
```

To remove the check mark from the Brahms option, you issue the following instruction:

```
set the checkMark of menuItem "Brahms" of menu " Music¬
Selection" to False
```

Disabling menu items

By adding the left parenthesis (character after the menu item name, you can display a menu option as *disabled*. Disabled menu items appear grayed out and cannot be selected with a mouse click. In the following example, the Sound Off option is disabled on the Volume Control menu, as shown in Figure 22-5. The user will be able to adjust the volume of the audio track, but won't be able to turn it off — appropriate when the movie includes verbal instructions that you want all users to hear.

```
menu: Volume Control
Sound Off ( ¦ set the soundLevel to 0
Low ¦ set the soundLevel to 1
Medium ¦ set the soundLevel to 4
Loud ¦ set the soundLevel to 7
```

Figure 22-5: The Sound Off option is disabled.

You can also use `the enabled of menuItem` property to enable or disable a menu item. In fact, using Lingo to reset `the enabled of menuItem` property while a movie is running is really a better solution than creating multiple field cast members to enable and disable menu options.

> **Caution:** Even if you disable or enable a menu item by "hard coding" the instructions in the field cast member, you can use Lingo to change the property's setting.

The full Lingo syntax to enable or disable a menu entry is as follows:

```
set the enabled of menuItem itemName of menu menuName to state
```

In this instruction, the *itemName* is replaced with the menu item's name or number. If you use a number to identify the menu item, you must start counting with the first item on the menu. The *menuName* parameter is replaced with the menu's name or number. The menu number is based on the menu's position, counting left to right on the menu bar.

The last parameter, *state*, is either True or False depending on whether you want the menu item enabled or disabled, respectively.

Let's stay with our Volume Control menu, and disable the Loud menu item using the following instruction:

```
set the enabled of menuItem "Loud" of menu "Volume Control" to¬
False
```

The following instruction generates the same result, but uses menu and menu item numbers rather than names:

```
set the enabled of menuItem 4 of menu 1 to False
```

And here is the instruction to enable the Loud menu item:

```
set the enabled of menuItem "Loud" of menu "Volume Control" to¬
True
```

It is possible to use Lingo to disable a menu item with a visible check mark, but it doesn't make much sense to do so. In general, for any given menu item you should decide whether you want it to switch between the enabled and disabled state, or between the checked and unchecked state.

The best way of assigning the correct behavior is to question whether it makes sense to display the menu item's "state" as turned on or off. If it does, use a check mark. On the other hand, if you want to indicate whether a menu item is currently available or not, use the enabled/disabled pair. For example, a menu item that saves work in progress makes no sense as a toggle — either you can save the file or you can't, and if you can't (because you have not made changes to the file) then the menu item should be disabled. On the other hand, a menu item that turns background music on or off is a perfect toggle, and you should use a check mark to visibly indicate if the music is audible or inaudible.

Adding text formatting to a menu item

You can add some formatting to your menu, but because the Macintosh and Windows operating systems have their own idiosyncrasies, the menus you create for a Macintosh system may not be supported under Windows (and vice versa). We recommend creating two versions of your menus, one for each platform. Prior to actually installing a menu, you'll need to check which platform the user is running and then install the Macintosh or Windows menu as appropriate.

Tables 22-1 and 22-2 show the options that are supported on the Macintosh and Windows platforms, respectively. If you notice the brevity of the Windows table and wonder about the scarcity of options for this environment, don't fret or feel neglected. Though more options are available for Macintosh programs, few of the formatting options are really usable. Most of the formatting doesn't add much information; and a few of the formats — such as outline and shadow — tend to look a bit cheesy when used in a menu setting.

Caution: In Table 22-1, the letters in the menu formatting codes (column 1) must be entered in uppercase. The codes can precede or follow the text of the item to be formatted. Unless noted otherwise, the space character that separates the code from the item's text is optional.

Table 22-1
Macintosh Menu Formatting Options

Formatting Code	Example Usage	Results
@	`Menu:@`	Creates the Apple Menu character in the menu bar. By convention, if you include the Apple Menu it should be the first menu on the menu bar.

Formatting Code	Example Usage	Results
(	`( Save`	Displays the menu item (option) in a disabled state.
(-	`(-`	Adds a line break or disabled line between menu items. This is useful for separating sections within a given menu. Do not include a space between the left parenthesis and the dash characters.
!√	`!√ Music`	Creates a check mark in front of the entry. This is one way of indicating a mode switch (that is, the current setting for an item that can be toggled on and off). The √ is created by typing Option-v.
<B	`<B Database Controls`	Displays the menu item in **boldface**.
<I	`<I Save As`	Displays the menu item in *italic*.
<U	`<U Navigation`	Displays the menu item in <u>underlined</u> text.
<O	`<O Trace`	Displays the menu item in an outline font.
<S	`<S Float Selection`	Displays the menu item in a shadow font.

Table 22-2
Windows Menu Formatting Options

Formatting Code	Example Usage	Results
(	`( Save`	Displays the menu item (option) in a disabled state. A space is required between the left parenthesis and the entry name. If you omit the space, the first letter of the item name disappears.
(-	`(-`	Adds a line break or disabled line between menu items. This is particularly useful for separating sections within a given menu. Do not include a space between the left parenthesis and the dash.
&	`E&xit`	Creates an accelerator key (to speed up access to a menu item) using a combination of the Alt key, the first letter of the menu name, and the key that follows the ampersand. For example, in most Windows programs Alt+F+X selects the E<u>x</u>it option on the File menu to terminate the program.

As an example, the following instructions cause the Elton John menu item to appear in boldface. Further, a line break appears between the Mozart and the Sound Off menu items, as shown in Figure 22-6.

```
menu: Audition
Beatles | puppetSound 1,"Beatles"
Brahms | puppetSound 1,"Brahms"
Elton John <B | puppetSound 1,"EJohn"
Mozart | puppetSound 1,"Mozart"
(-
Sound Off | set the soundLevel to 0
Low | set the soundLevel to 1
Medium | set the soundLevel to 4
Loud | set the soundLevel to 7
```

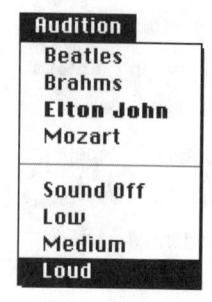

Figure 22-6: Menu on the Macintosh with a boldface-formatted option and a line break

A menu by any other name is still a menu

Two additional menu-related properties can be useful when you need to determine the name of a menu or the name of a menu item. In fact, you can even use one of these properties to modify an existing menu during the playback of your movie. The two properties, the name of menu property and the name of menuItem property, serve parallel functions.

Determining the name of a menu

With the name of menu property, you can determine the name of a specific menu. For instance, assume that you have three menus in your movie (File, Edit, and View). If you type the following instruction in the Message window (to determine the name of the second menu), you'll get the result shown:

```
put the name of menu 2
-- "Edit"
```

Note: You cannot change the name of a menu using `the name of menu` property; you can only identify the name of an existing menu.

Setting and changing the name of a menu item

With `the name of menuItem` property, you can set or determine the name of a specific menu item. For instance, assume that you have three entries under the File menu in your movie (Save, Export, Import). If you type the following instruction in the Message window (to determine the name of the second menu item), you get the result shown:

```
put the name of menuItem 2 of menu "File"
-- "Export"
```

Similarly, you can change the name of the third menu item from Import to Exit (in the Message window or from a handler) using the following instruction:

```
set the name of menuItem 3 of menu "File" to "Exit"
```

Note: You cannot create a menu item from scratch using `the name of menu` property. The menu item *position* must already exist.

Caution: When using the `menuItem` number, always count the number of menu items *including* disabled items and disabled lines (line breaks in your menu).

In the next exercise, you'll use the graffiti.dir movie from the CD-ROM and add a field cast member that includes the menu instructions and a movie script that installs the menu. In its current form, the movie includes several photographic images, transitions, text cast members, digital sounds, and scripts. Notice that none of the sprites in the movie includes any navigational scripts. All navigation is accomplished using the menu that you create.

Tip: In a production situation, you should provide a variety of methods for navigating through a movie. In addition to a menu system, you can include an interface with navigational buttons and clickable objects.

Creating a Navigational Menu

On the CD-ROM

1. Open the graffiti.dir movie in Director. This file can be found on your companion CD-ROM in the exercise:ch22 (exercise\ch22) folder.
2. Select the first open cast member slot (slot 33).

(continued)

3. Open the Field window (Command+8 or Ctrl+8) and type the following text. Be sure to include the line breaks as shown.

   ```
   menu:Explore
   Background/B | go to "Background"
   Little Sax/S | go to "LittleSax"
   Big Sax/D | go to "BigSax"
   Kaboom/K | go to "Gun"
   Graveyard/G | go to "Kelly"
   Credits/C | go to "Credits"
   Quit/Q | go to "End"
   ```

4. Change the new cast member's name to **ExploreMenu**.

5. Close the Field window.

6. Select the next open cast member slot (34).

7. Open the Script window (Command+0 or Ctrl+0) and type the following script:

   ```
   on startMovie
          installMenu "ExploreMenu"
   end
   ```

8. Close the Script window. Save the movie in your personal folder as **graffit2.dir,** rewind, and play it.

9. Once the movie operates correctly and you have created the field cast member and the movie script, create a projector for the movie (File ⇨ Create Projector command). Be sure to create a full-screen projector, or the custom menu will not be displayed. If you use Shockwave compression and include the appropriate Xtras, the file size of the graffit2.dir movie is shrunk by about 80%.

10. Go to the desktop, locate the projector's icon or its filename (in Finder or the Explorer) and play the projector. Test the movie to see how the menu system works.

Graffiti Gallery assets

The images included in graffiti.dir (Graffiti Gallery) are photographs by Kansas City photo journalist Dale Monaghen (copyright 1997 and used with permission; all rights reserved). Dale is a freelance photographer and photo editor for *New Times*. Portions of the narration for Graffiti Gallery are based on information from *Spraycan Art* by Henry Chalfant and James Prigoff, published by Thames and Hudson, New York, copyright 1987; all rights reserved. The musical score for Graffiti Gallery was composed by Jeffrey E. Jones (jjones@johnco.cc.ks.us), copyright 1997; all rights reserved.

On the CD-ROM The next exercise shows you how to attach a script to a button that issues the `installMenu` command and switches from an English-language menu to a French-language menu. You'll use the file french.dir from your companion CD-ROM in the exercise:ch22 (exercise\ch22) folder.

In its current form, the movie includes

- Two button cast members (French Version and English Version) in cast slots 1 and 2
- A field cast member that defines the English-language menu, in cast slot 3
- A field cast member that defines the French-language menu, in cast slot 4
- A movie script that installs the English menu and fills the Definition field on the Stage with nonsensical text, in slot 5
- A `go to the frame` script in cast slot 6
- The Definition field with nonsensical text, in cast slot 7

In the following steps, you'll add a cast member script to both buttons in the movie. You'll attach a script to the French Version button that installs the French menu and switches the English Version button for the French Version button. To the English Version button, you'll attach a script that installs the English menu and switches the French Version button for the English Version button.

Switching the Menu On-the-Fly

1. Open the french.dir movie in Director.

2. Select the French Version button in cast slot 1 and attach the following cast member script:

   ```
   on mouseUp
        installMenu "French"
        set the memberNum of sprite 2 to 2
   end
   ```

3. Select the English Version button in cast slot 2 and attach the following cast member script:

   ```
   on mouseUp
        installMenu "English"
        set the memberNum of sprite 2 to 1
   end
   ```

4. Save the movie as **french1.dir**, rewind, and play it.

Part IV ✦ Behavioral Science

5. Test both buttons and both menus. When you select the French Version button, the drop-down menu options appear as shown in Figure 22-7.
6. Stop the movie.

Figure 22-7: The French version of the menu

French art

The artwork for the french.dir movie is based on image 42 from the Planet Art *Architecture: Selected Works* CD-ROM (copyright 1996 by DiverseWorks). The Kodak photo CD file was imported into Adobe Photoshop and then modified using the fresco filter. For more information on the Planet Art clip media collection, call 1-888-526-4255 or visit the DiverseWorks Web site at

```
http://www.diverseworks.com.
```

Establishing a Dialog

Back in the good old days of Director 3.0, Macromedia introduced an XObject that let users create their own custom windows. This precursor of today's Xtras never really worked well, was for the most part undocumented, and when Director introduced the Windows Gaffer for converting Mac files to Windows, was quietly dropped from the available sites.

Movies in a window (MIAWs), a part of Director since version 4.0, were supposed to replace the persisting need that developers had for the occasional dialog box to get information from users. MIAWs (see Chapter 21) have a few critical flaws, however:

- They are memory hungry, since they are essentially separate instances of Director that run in their own windows.

- In order to create a simple dialog box that returns a value, you must arrange for another Director movie to already be available, and you spend a lot of time coding that movie from both the calling side and the dialog side.

- They take a long time to instantiate, which gives the impression that Director applications are slow. They aren't, comparatively speaking, but if it takes 20 seconds for a simple Yes/No dialog box to come up, then that will reflect badly on your application.

Macromedia again addressed the problem of dialog boxes in Director 6, and the solution, though still a little too complex, comes much closer to providing developers with the means to use dialogs. The latest incarnation of Director's dialog handlers is the MUI (Macromedia User Interface) Dialog Xtra that you can use to create general-purpose, OS-compliant dialog boxes. The Xtra creates dialog boxes that look like Macromedia products. You get the grayscale controls that are expected by Macintosh users when a movie plays on the Mac, and the typical controls expected by Windows users when a movie plays on a Windows system.

The MUI Dialog Xtra makes direct calls to the same engine within Director that creates most standard dialog boxes. In other words, the Xtra can be used to draw dialog boxes that are appropriate for either Macintosh and Windows movies with the same set of code. Indeed, the dialog boxes that are created to set Director behavior properties, as shown in Figure 22-8, are generated internally with the Xtra. It's not terribly friendly, but the Xtra offers the capability of integrating editable text, slider bars, list boxes, and other interface devices directly into your dialogs. Macromedia may even enable ActiveX and Java controls within these dialogs at some future time.

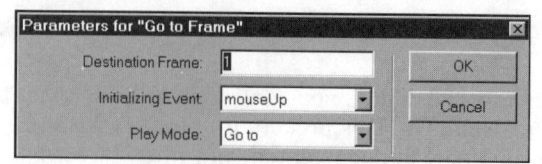

Figure 22-8: Director's behavior properties dialog boxes are internally created with the MUI dialog Xtra.

Getting basic information with MUI

The MUI Xtra is located in the Director Xtras folder. The filename for the Macintosh version of the Xtra is called Mui Dialog; the Windows filename is Mui Dialog.X32. There is no 16-bit version of the Xtra, since it is designed for use in authoring mode and a Windows 3.x version of Director 6 is not available.

Note: If you plan to use the MUI Dialog Xtra in your own application, make sure the Xtra is copied to your application's own Xtras folder.

Once the MUI Xtra is installed, create an instance of the Xtra using an instruction similar to the following (with the new keyword):

```
set muiInstance = new(Xtra "mui")
```

Dialogs that open, save, and target

The MUI Xtra usually makes you work to obtain any meaningful information, but it does offer a few freebies. If you need to load or save a file, or if you want the user to enter an Internet address, the MUI Xtra provides access to three functions for these situations: FileOpen, FileSave, and getURL. The first two functions display standard, system dialog boxes for loading and saving files, respectively, and they return the full pathname of the file that the user opens or saves. The getURL dialog simply prompts the user to enter or accept a default URL.

Displaying the File Open dialog box

The syntax for the FileOpen function is

```
FileOpen (muiInstance, filename)
```

The *muiInstance* parameter refers to the name you use when an instance of the Xtra is created. The *filename* parameter stores and returns the filename (of the file to be opened) that is supplied by the user. The following example creates an instance of the Xtra named messageBox and displays the File Open dialog box using textfile.txt as the default filename, as shown in Figure 22-9. The second instruction returns the result of the entry in the File Open editable text field and stores that string in the dialogResult variable.

```
set messageBox = new(Xtra "mui")
set dialogResult = FileOpen(messageBox,"textfile.txt")
```

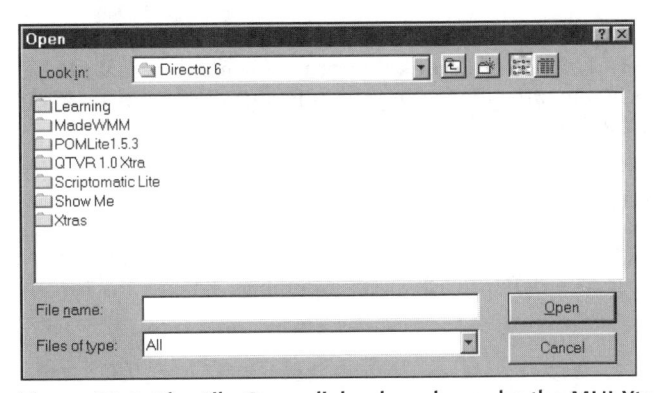

Figure 22-9: The File Open dialog box drawn by the MUI Xtra

Displaying the File Save dialog box
The syntax for the `FileSave` function is

```
FileSave (muiInstance, filename, prompt)
```

As in `FileOpen`, the *muiInstance* parameter refers to the name you use when an instance of the Xtra is created. The *filename* parameter is the default name supplied for the user. In other words, when using the `FileSave` function, the text string you substitute for the *filename* parameter appears as the default entry in the editable field on the File Open dialog box. The *prompt* parameter establishes the text that appears on the dialog box's title bar.

In the following example (Figure 22-10), the instance of the Xtra is called `saveMessage`, the default filename to use when saving a file is `textfile.txt`, and the title bar on the File Save dialog box displays the text `"Save the file as"`.

```
set saveMessage = new(Xtra "MUI")
set result = fileSave(saveMessage,"textfile.txt","Save the file¬
as" )
```

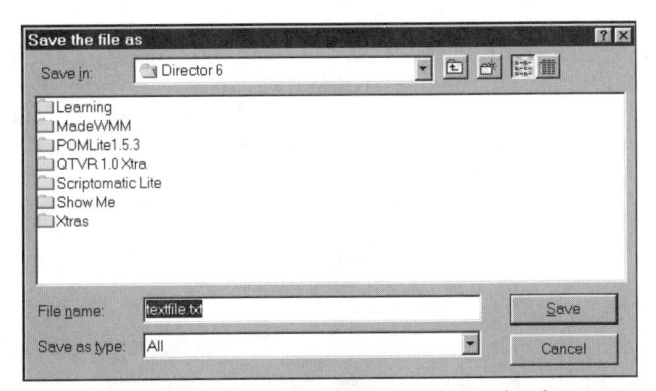

Figure 22-10: The File Save dialog box drawn by the MUI Xtra

> **Note:** The `FileOpen` and the `FileSave` functions do not perform any actual file I/O. They simply return a filename after displaying the relevant dialog box — it's up to you to save or load the file itself.

Getting an Internet URL from the user

The MUI Xtra also enables you to prompt the user for an Internet address — a handy and useful function. The `GetUrl` function pops up a dialog box that requests a URL and can pass a default URL as an argument. The syntax for the instruction is

```
getURL(muiInstance,defaultURL,booleanMoveable)
```

The `defaultURL` is replaced with the URL that appears in the dialog box by default. The `booleanMoveable` parameter is used to determine whether the dialog itself can be moved. A `true` setting makes the dialog box moveable and a `false` setting makes it nonmoveable. However, this parameter only works on a Macintosh system. The dialog box is always moveable in a Windows movie.

In the following example (demonstrated in Figure 22-11), the GetURL dialog box appears (with the Macromedia site as the default entry) when the user clicks a button to which the script is attached:

```
on mouseUp
      set getNetURL = new(xtra "MUI")
      set URL=getURL(getNetURL,"http://www.macromedia.com",true)
end
```

Figure 22-11: The URL dialog box drawn by the MUI Xtra

The instance of the Xtra is named `getNetURL`. When the pop-up appears, the user can then select the OK button to use the preexisting URL, or type in a specific URL. If the end user decides to click the Cancel button, the `getURL` function returns an empty string (""), so you should always check to see if the entry is a blank:

```
set URL=getURL(getNetURL,"http://www.macromedia.com",true)
if URL="" then
      alert "You didn't select a URL. The whole system will¬
now explode."
end if
```

Abort, retry, or ignore

The basic Alert box available through Director is useful only for one thing — enabling the developer to track what is happening in the system in real time. From an interface standpoint, however, a dialog box with only one button typically annoys the user. It stops the flow of the program without offering the user any options for handling the situation. This is like telling your neighbor that her house is on fire, her car has just been stolen, and would she like to organize the upcoming block party — and offering no response for her to select other than OK.

In the MUI Xtra, Director supplies a *super-Alert* box that provides many more capabilities than the fundamental OK. A typical situation for this usage is when you need to put up a dialog box before quitting, asking users if they want to save a file before quitting. You can create an Alert box with the buttons Yes, No, and Cancel (for aborting the quit process altogether). You can also display an Alert icon similar to system dialogs. Table 22-3 summarizes the various options for putting together a custom Alert box.

Table 22-3
MUI Alert Box Options

Property	Possible Values	Results
#buttons	#Ok, #OkCancel, #AbortRetryIgnore, #YesNoCancel, #YesNo, #RetryCancel	Establishes which buttons are displayed in the Alert box.
#default	0, 1, 2, or 3	If the default is greater than 0, then the indicated button (the first, second, or third) is set as the default, and is the button selected if the user presses the Return (Enter) key. A default of 0 means there is no default.
#title	String (for example, "File Save")	Establishes the text that appears on the title bar of the Alert box. Used in a Macintosh movie only when the Alert box is moveable. If not stipulated, a <Null> entry appears on the Windows title bar.
#message	String (e.g., "Save Before Quitting?")	Establishes the text that appears within the dialog box itself.
#icon	#stop, #note, #caution, #question, #error	Sets the icon that is displayed in the Alert box. If you want a custom icon, you'll have to create the dialog from scratch.

(continued)

Table 22-3 *(continued)*

Property	Possible Values	Results
#movable or #moveable	True, False	Indicates whether the Alert box is moveable or not. All Alert boxes in a Windows movie are moveable regardless of this setting.

Creating an Alert dialog is only slightly more complicated than making a GetURL dialog. You need to pass both the MUI instance and a property list containing the appropriate values for the Alert box. In other words, you must explicitly establish each of the properties for the Alert box. The MUI Xtra does not assume any default values; you must set them. For example, to create a Save Before Quitting dialog and attach the script to a Save button, you can use the following instructions:

```
On mouseUp
    set mui=new(Xtra "mui")
    set response=alert(mui,[#buttons:#YesNoCancel, ¬
        #default:1,¬
        #title: "File Save",¬
        #message:"Save Before Quitting?", ¬
        #icon:#caution])
    if response=#Yes then
        SaveFile
        -- Add other instructions
        quit
    end if
end
```

The `alert` method returns the symbol of the button that was pressed. Here, for instance, if the Yes button was pressed, the response would be #Yes.

Caution: Keep in mind that, unlike string comparisons, symbols are case sensitive: #Yes is not the same as #yes.

As you'll discover in the upcoming exercise, the MUI Xtra also returns a value corresponding to the position of the button clicked. For instance, in the above example (based on the use of the #YesNoCancel symbol), the Yes button is button 1, the No button is button 2, and the Cancel button is button 3. A click on button 3 returns a value of 3.

In the following steps, you'll use the alert.dir movie from the CD-ROM and add a cast member script that displays a super-Alert dialog box when the user clicks the Danger Button on the Stage. In its current form, the movie includes a Danger Button in cast slot 1, a `go to the frame` script in cast slot 2, three sounds (yesSound, noSound, and cancelSound) in slots 3 through 5, and two text cast members (Alert and Alerts) in cast slots 6 and 7, respectively. The Stage looks like Figure 22-12 and the movie is complete, except for adding a cast member script to the button in cast slot 1.

Figure 22-12: The alert.dir movie Stage

The cast member script causes an Alert box to appear each time the button is clicked. Based on the response to the three buttons, shown in Figure 22-13, a different sound is played. In the following steps, you'll also open the Message window to display the results of the `put` command (within the handler). The `put buttonResult` instruction displays a numeric value representing which of the three buttons is pressed. The first button (counting from the left in the dialog box) generates a value of 1. The second button generates a value of 2, and so on.

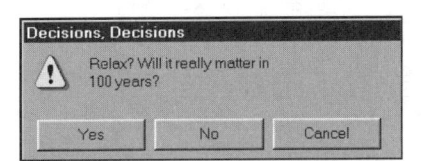

Figure 22-13: The Alert dialog box from the alert.dir movie

> **Note**
>
> *Improving line breaks*: In the cast member script, each of the properties in the `alertInitList` property list is on a separate line in the handler; yet each is considered part of the same instruction. This technique improves the readability of the script. However, if you press Enter at the end of each line the Lingo compiler assumes each line is a separate command. To solve this, use the *line continuation character* (¬), and split the property list over several lines. You'll improve its readability while signaling that the text on several lines constitutes a single instruction. Press Option+Enter on the Macintosh or Alt+Enter on a Windows system to add the line break.

Creating Your Own Dialog Box with the MUI Xtra

On the CD-ROM

1. Open the alert.dir movie in Director. The file alert.dir can be found on your companion CD-ROM in the exercise:ch22 (exercise\ch22) folder.

2. Attach the following script to the button in cast slot 1. You can omit the lines of comments. Use the line continuation character (¬) at the end of each line that lists a symbol in the `set alertInitList` instruction (#buttons, #title, and so on).

```
on mouseUp
    set alertBox = new(xtra "MUI")
    -- alertBox variable is set to an instance of the MUI¬
    xtra
    if objectP (alertBox) then
            -- if the object "alertBox" exists, then the
            -- buttons, Alert box title, message, icon,
            -- default button, and moveability of the dialog
            -- box are set using the alertInitList property
            -- list
        set alertInitList = [ #buttons : #YesNoCancel,¬
        #title    : "Decisions, Decisions",¬
        #message : "Relax? Will it really matter in 100¬
        years?",¬
        #icon : #caution,¬
        #default : 1,¬
        #movable : False]
            -- sets the properties for the MUI dialog box
        set buttonResult = alert(alertBox,alertInitList)
        case buttonResult of
                1 : puppetSound "yesSound"
                2 : puppetSound "noSound"
                3 : puppetSound "cancelSound"
```

```
                    otherwise : nothing
                end case
                put buttonResult -- displays the numeric value
                of the button clicked in Message Window
            end if
        end
```

3. Save the movie as **relax.dir,** rewind, and play it. The Alert dialog box appears as shown in Figure 22-13.

4. Test each of the buttons: Yes, No, and Cancel.

5. Stop the movie.

6. Open the cast member script for the Danger button.

7. Change the #buttons property to #AbortRetryIgnore.

8. Change the #default property to **3,** which causes button 3 (Ignore) to be the default or selected button.

9. Change the #message string to **Can't find any peace of mind!**

10. Change the #icon property to #Note.

11. Save the movie as **retry.dir,** rewind, and play it. Now the Alert box looks like Figure 22-14.

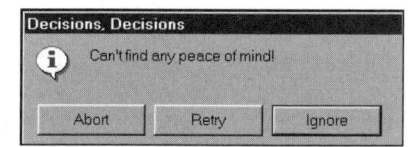

Figure 22-14: The revised Alert box

12. Test the buttons and then stop the movie.

Production clips used in alert.dir

The alert.dir movie includes sound clips from the Fresh Music Library, a full-buyout library of over 40 compact discs of production music. When you purchase and license buyout music, you own the right to synchronize any and all themes, as many times as you need, forever. You do not need to pay license or "drop" fees, and you never have to report usage. (Be sure to check the license from each vendor to make sure you are actually licensing buy-out music.)

(continued)

(continued)

The alert.dir movie includes Harp Gliss I, a two-second sound clip renamed (in the movie) as "yesSound," Orchestra Hit VIII Finale, a two-second clip renamed "noSound," and Electro - Stab I - low, a one-second clip renamed as "cancelSound." All three sounds are from the *Production Elements* CD which is available from Fresh, The Music Library (34 S. Main Street, Hanover, NH 03755, phone 800-545-0688); copyright 1997 by Fresh Music Library and the exclusive property of Fresh Music Library. Fresh is at

```
www.freshmusic.com
```

on the Web. The sound clips may only be used by the owner of this book for practice/learning activities and cannot be used in other productions unless licensed from the Fresh Music Library. Other CDs available from Fresh include *Alternative Rock, Classic Rock, Corporate Power, Hearts & Flowers, New Age Pop, Sports & Action*, and *Techno Industrial*. The Fresh Music Library also offers "SearchTrack," a searchable CD-ROM index containing essential versions of every theme in the 45 disc Fresh Music Library. "SearchTrack" allows users to quickly search and preview themes by emotion, style, and usage attributes. "SearchTrack" is available for Power Macintosh and Windows 95, and is free from Fresh Music.

Getting Fancy

On the CD-ROM The MUI Xtra features covered in this chapter represent only a fraction of the Xtra's capabilities. To implement anything of substance with the MUI Xtra requires some fairly serious programming and is outside the scope of this book. However, as you use Director you'll discover that there are a couple of basic dialog boxes that you need from time to time. I've included several dialogs built using the MUI Xtra in the genutils.cst on the companion CD. Take a look at the scripts RequestText, SelectCastMembers, and ObjectBrowser to get an idea about how the MUI Xtra is used in practice.

Before You Exit This Chapter

As in other chapters, we have a few parting thoughts for you about adding menus to your movies.

Using `exitLock`

You may want to force the user to exit your program through a menu system that properly closes files and clears memory. Also, you can prevent the user from quitting a self-running kiosk application, allowing the movie to recycle for the next user rather than falling back to the operating system. You can also prevent an "untimely" exit, so you can record specific information about the user and the user's activity. Do this by forcing the playback head to an "exit frame" rather than allowing the movie to terminate at any point. The exit block can be set using the following instruction in a movie script:

```
set the exitLock = True
```

The `exitLock` is a property that by default is set to `False`. A `False` setting enables the user to quit a projector using Command+Period (Ctrl+Period), Command+Q (Ctrl+Q), or Command+W (Ctrl+W). These keys do not work if the property is set to True.

Running a program or opening a file from the movie

From within a Director movie, you can run an external executable program. For instance, you can create a menu with a menu item that triggers the playing of an external file. The script for the menu (using Macintosh pathname notation) might look something like this:

```
Menu Item | open "Macintosh hard drive name:pathname:filename"
```

Using Windows pathname notation, you would use the following instruction:

```
Menu Item | open "C:\pathname\filename.exe"
```

You must include the full pathname and filename plus the extension for the executable file, unless it is stored in the same folder (directory) as your Director projector.

You can also open a data file using another application, with an instruction similar to the following:

```
Menu Item | open "Glossary.pdf" with "acroread.exe"
```

When the external program runs, all the commands and features of that program are available. Further, the user must know and use that application, not the interface you built using Director. After the user exits from the external program (or after it automatically terminates), control returns to the calling frame — that is, the frame from which the external application was called.

Caution Many programs, such as acroread.exe (Adobe's Acrobat Reader), require more than just the executable file; they may also need dynamic link libraries (DLLs), configuration or setup files, and so on. If you copy these files to the same folder as your projector (to avoid using the pathname in the `open` command), be sure you include *all* related files. And be sure you have permission to use and distribute the files!

Including this instruction to open an external application and file within a menu can be a handy method to provide your users menu-style access to appropriate external programs.

Watch out for pathnames

When you access external programs, it is important to recognize that the pathname is different on a Macintosh vs. a Windows system. Windows uses the backslash (\) to represent the root directory and as a delimiter between folder names. The Macintosh operating system uses the colon as a delimiter between folder names.

For example, under Windows the path from the root directory on drive C: through a Director directory to a Projects subdirectory to a file named glossary.txt is indicated using the following notation:

```
C:\Director\Projects\glossary.txt
```

Windows 3.1, 3.11, Windows 95, and Windows NT are not case sensitive.

For the Macintosh OS, the path from a hard drive (named Macintosh HD) to a file named glossary.txt in a Projects folder with the Director folder is indicated using the following notation:

```
Macintosh HD:Director:Projects:glossary.txt
```

Swapping cast members

You can use Lingo to rearrange cast members within the Cast window using the `move` command. In most cases, you will want to swap sprites on the Stage rather than move cast members, but at least you can do the move if needed. To move cast member 27 to cast member slot 30, for instance, you'd execute the following instruction:

```
move member 27, 30
```

Caution: The `move` command performs a destructive move. Any cast member in the target slot is deleted by the cast member moved into the slot.

Using the `move` command, you can replace a menu in a field cast member slot with another menu. It may be just as easy to swap sprites on the Stage rather than moving around cast members, but this command can be useful as you are displaying different menus for the segments of a movie.

Summary

Before you discover how to best manage memory useage in your Director movies in the next chapter, let's review some of the things you learned in this chapter.

- You can create a pull-down menu using a field cast member and the `installMenu` command.
- Menus provide an easy way for beginners to access features in your program.
- You may want to create unique menus for each platform (Macintosh and Windows) because some Macintosh formatting is not available in a Windows movie.
- You can modify menu items or swap menus on-the-fly using Lingo.
- The MUI Xtra is built into Director, and can be used to add more powerful dialog boxes.
- You can use MUI Xtras to create sophisticated dialog boxes that are essentially identical to behavior property boxes.

✦ ✦ ✦

CHAPTER 23

Designing for Memory Management

In This Chapter

Understanding and controlling memory usage

Preloading cast members

Setting purge priorities

Designing movies with memory usage in mind

Outputting to CD-ROM

Director is an enormously flexible authoring tool, enabling you to create movies for a broad variety of uses. With Director, you can design movies for playback on a variety of computers or other output devices capable of digital display. Certainly, on the authoring side of life, you need a powerful computer to create professional-quality Director movies in a production environment. There may be a vast difference, however, between an authoring computer and that of the end-user.

One of the most critical elements in designing a movie is to assess your audience and the capabilities of the computers they will use. In most cases it would a serious mistake to presume that the end-user's computer is equal to the machine you use to author your Director movies. Memory management is more than just good sense; it's essential for the success of your movies. For a movie to be successful, you need to design it for the viewer. In this chapter, you'll explore memory considerations both for authoring and the end-user.

Understanding Memory

Casual computer users frequently confuse memory with hard disk space. Part of this misunderstanding arises from the fact that many software programs use virtual memory created from hard disk space to supplement physical memory or RAM. Adding the concept of video memory can increase the confusion. All three of these types of memory are considered part of a computer's resources and are interrelated.

For any discussion of resources to be helpful, you must have an understanding of what the different types of memory do and, in the case of Director, what their combined impact is when you are authoring or playing a movie:

- **RAM** — RAM (Random-Access Memory) is hardware installed on your computer. Depending on the computer you use, these memory chipsets can be hard-socketed (permanently soldered) to your motherboard, or installable (plugged into special slots) on your motherboard. Some computers have a base amount of RAM hard-socketed on the board, plus sockets for expanding the amount of physical memory. How fast your computer operates and its power are determined by the speed of the CPU (central processing unit) and the amount of physical memory or RAM.

- **Virtual Memory** — Virtual memory is pseudomemory. You create virtual memory by allotting a portion of your hard disk to serve as temporary auxiliary memory for software programs to use. Unlike RAM, virtual memory does not affect the base speed of your computer. Rather, it is utilized by programs as needed to increase the amount of memory available to those programs. Virtual memory is slower than RAM because your computer's CPU must page to and from a physical device (the hard drive) to use the virtual memory.

- **Video Memory** — Video memory is also hardware-related memory. This memory is installed on your video display adapter, and its configuration can vary from one video board to another. Most video boards today have a minimum of 1MB of memory on the board. Some video cards are expandable, allowing you to add more memory as your needs increase. The more video memory you have, the more displayable color depth your monitor has. In addition to controlling the displayable color depth, video memory also affects the screen refresh rate. Performance and faster screen refresh rates increase proportionately with the amount of video memory on board.

Director works with your computer to use a combination of these resources when you author and play back a movie.

Special-effects inks and transitions can increase the amount of resources required for playback of a movie (although there is no hard data supporting this relationship). The amount of resources required depends on the effect, as well as the size of the area being affected.

> ### Preventing auto-syncing
>
> It's logical to presume that the more virtual memory you have, the better off you are. In other words, if you have a large hard disk and you allow the software to use as much of that space as needed for virtual memory, you might think that your software and computer will perform better. This is not true, however.
>
> Allowing large amounts of virtual memory creates a situation known as *auto-syncing to disk*, and can actually reduce the performance of your computer. When a software program uses virtual memory, it stores information temporarily on the hard disk for use, by swapping chunks of data to the disk. As virtual memory increases, the amount of data being swapped to the hard disk increases, and more chunks are stored to the disk before they are purged from the virtual memory.
>
> Your computer uses RAM to manage virtual memory. The increased amount of disk swapping (auto-syncing) uses more RAM strictly for the purpose of managing the virtual memory rather than for running software . As a result, performance decreases as more RAM is being dedicated to this use. In some cases you can actually see and hear the problem. If your hard disk sounds unusually busy or you see that light blinking on more and more often, there is an unusually high amount of activity going on and an auto-syncing problem probably exists.
>
> This is not to say that you shouldn't use virtual memory — but for best results, you should control virtual memory usage. Both Macintosh and Windows platforms allow you to do so. (For instructions on how to specify virtual memory, see the user's guide for your operating system.) As the amount of RAM in your computer increases, your needs for virtual memory decrease. A general rule of thumb is that virtual memory should never exceed the amount of RAM in your computer. Ideally, if you have a large amount of RAM (64MB or more), virtual memory should be set at one-half or less of the amount of RAM.

Determining memory requirements

Like most powerful programs, Director requires substantial resources for authoring. The amount of resources required is determined by the basic needs of the program, plus those of the movie you're creating. Obviously, movies that are more complex require increased resources. Director provides you with the tools to check the requirements of your movie, the available system resources, and information about the various cast members in your movies.

In the following exercise you'll learn how to use the Message window to check system resources, a movie's memory requirements, and the amount of contiguous memory available.

Checking System Resources and Requirements

On the CD-ROM

1. Open kiosk1.dir in Director. This file is located on your companion CD-ROM in the exercise:ch09 (exercise/ch09) folder.

2. Select Window⇨Message to display the Message window.

3. In the Message window, enter **put the memorySize** and press the Enter key. The amount of memory (RAM) installed on your computer is displayed in the window (see Figure 23-1).

4. In the Message window, enter **put ramNeeded (1, 62)** and press the Enter key. The amount of memory required for kiosk1.dir is displayed in the window.

5. In the Message window, enter **put the freeblock** and press the Enter key. The amount of contiguous free memory is displayed in the window.

```
-- Welcome to Director --
-- "Now loading LINGO.INI 11/24/97 11:03 AM"
-- "This computer is running in  8-bit color depth."

put the memorySize
-- 49727136
put ramNeeded(1,62)
-- 4106819
put the freeblock
-- 47814408
```

Figure 23-1: The Message window allows you to view memory information.

The memory values are shown in bytes; to convert bytes to kilobytes, divide by 1,024. Figure 23-1 shows that the computer used for this example has 48MB of RAM. The kiosk1.dir file requires 4,106,819 bytes of RAM, or a little over 4MB.

In order to load a cast member, you need a freeblock at least as large as the cast member. (As mentioned in step 5 of the preceding exercise, a freeblock is a contiguous chunk of available memory in bytes.) For example, you could add a Lingo statement to a movie script that identified a freeblock large enough to load your largest cast member. If your cast member required 500KB, the statement shown in Figure 23-2 would alert the user that memory needed to be freed up to run your movie.

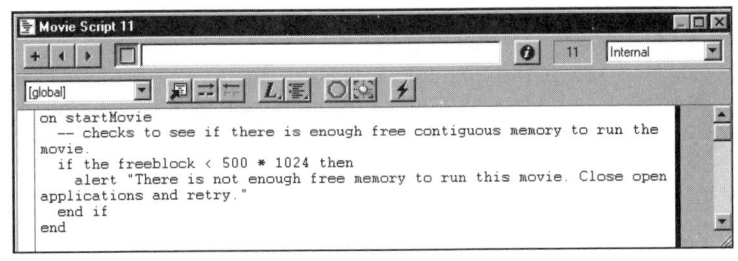

```
Movie Script 11
on startMovie
  -- checks to see if there is enough free contiguous memory to run the
movie.
  if the freeblock < 500 * 1024 then
    alert "There is not enough free memory to run this movie. Close open
applications and retry."
  end if
end
```

Figure 23-2: You can add statements to a movie script that allow you to check memory and warn users of potential memory problems.

Testing to avoid memory problems

The importance of testing should be a mantra. Most multimedia designers don't have the luxury of knowing the precise hardware configuration of the end-user's computer. The amount of resources, type of video adapters, and speed of the computer can vary widely.

It is critical that you test your movie, during development, on a variety of systems. This wise practice will prevent unpleasant surprises later. If you are creating a movie for cross-platform use, testing is even more critical. The movie that looks and plays wonderfully on the Macintosh may crash in Windows or vice versa. Although you can build a lot of safeguards into a movie, nothing replaces testing to ensure the success of your project.

Preloading Cast Members

Preloading large cast members, such as sound and digital video cast members, smoothes the performance of a movie. By default, Director loads cast members as needed. If you have a number of large cast members loading at the same time, this can create memory problems. In addition to smoothing the performance of your movie, preloading some of the larger cast members enables you to balance the memory load.

Caution

Take care when selecting the cast members you want to preload, however, if memory constraints are an issue. Preloading too many cast members at a time can cause memory problems, as well.

Lingo can play a significant role in preloading. It can be used to preload cast members, markers, and frames of a movie. Streaming audio files (SWA) can be preloaded either in the SWA Cast Member Properties dialog box or using Lingo. When you use Lingo to preload cast members, you can specify different preload times for each instance of the cast member. This is particularly useful if you need to swap between large cast members that appear more than once in a movie.

Specifying SWA preload values

In the following exercise, you'll add a Shockwave audio file (SWA) to kiosk1.dir and specify the preload time for the file. SWA files offer advantages not available with WAV, AIFF, and other sound files. The SWA files are much smaller, and they allow for streaming, which means they can start playing while they are loading. You can use SWA files in your movies whether they are being produced for the Internet or for running from a local disk. These sound files are linked rather than embedded, so you need to make sure that the SWA file is included when you transport your movies.

Note

It's a good idea to link sound files, regardless of their format, rather than embedding them into your Director movies. Linking sound files enables you to specify preloads and purge properties to conserve memory. Director lets you convert sound files to SWA format for inclusion in your movies (see Chapter 15).

Specifying a Preload Setting in the SWA Cast Member Properties Dialog Box

1. Open kiosk1.dir in Director, if it's not already open.

2. Select Insert ⇨ Media Element ⇨ Shockwave Audio, to display the SWA Cast Member Properties dialog box (Figure 23-3).

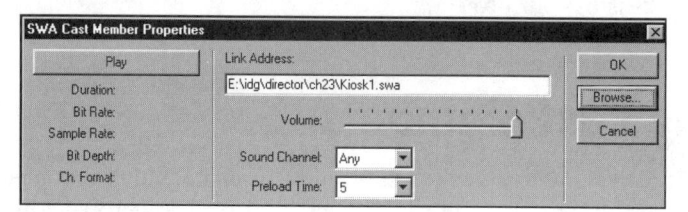

Figure 23-3: Specifying the preload setting

3. Click the Browse button, and select kiosk1.swa from the exercise:ch23 (exercise\ch23) folder.

4. The Preload Time value specifies the number of seconds ahead of the cast member's appearance in the movie, when you want the file to start loading. Choose 5 from the list; this is the default setting.

5. Click the Play button to hear the audio. When you're done, click Stop.

6. Click OK to complete the operation, and return to Director's main window. The SWA file appears in the first empty slot of the Cast window.

7. Save your movie as **kiosk2.dir** on your hard disk.

> **Note:** You can specify SWA files using either a URL or local disk location.

Unlike other sound files, SWA files are placed in the sprite channels of the Score rather than in a sound channel. Because SWA files are controlled by Lingo, they can use any of the sound channels during playback, including those not visible in the Score window. You can specify a sound channel when you insert the SWA file into your movie, or you can let Director use any available channel during playback.

Placing the SWA File in the Score

1. From the Cast window, click and drag the cast member to frame 1 of channel 22 in the Score.
2. Select the tail frame of the sprite; then click the frame bar at frame 77.
3. Press Command+B (Ctrl+B) to extend the sprite to frame 77 (see Figure 23-4).

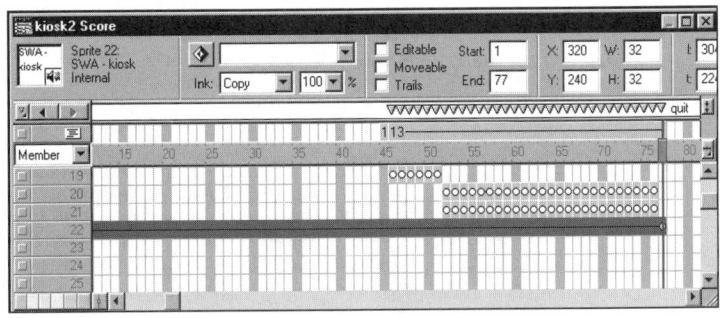

Figure 23-4: The SWA sprite is extended through frame 77 of channel 22.

4. Save the movie again as kiosk2.dir.
5. Rewind the movie, and click the Play button to test the movie.

SWA files play on both the Macintosh and in Windows. Using this format offers you the ability to play a movie containing sound on both platforms, even if you don't have utilities to convert the sounds from the native format of one platform to the other. In addition, the small file size of SWAs helps you to control the amount of RAM and hard disk space required for the storage of your movie.

Using Lingo to specify preload values

You can use Lingo to specify the preloading of individual cast members, a cast library, your movie, a marker, or a range of frames. This is especially useful if you are working with a movie in a window (MIAW), digital video, or sound cast members. Table 23-1 lists Lingo preload commands, their uses, and shows an example of the usage.

Table 23-1
Lingo Preload Commands

Command	Application	Usage Example
preLoad	Preloads cast members from a range of frames into memory. This is useful for loading cast members that animate. Note that if no parameter is specified, Director continues to load the entire movie, stopping only when memory is full.	preLoad marker ("finance"): Loads the marker named finance into memory. preLoad 20, 32: Preloads frames 20 through 32 into memory.
preLoadBuffer member	Preloads an SWA file or portion of an SWA file into memory. Only works if the SWA is is stopped.	preLoadBuffer (member "kiosk1"): Preloads the SWA file kiosk1 into memory.
preLoadMember	Preloads a specific cast member or range of cast members from the cast library into memory.	preLoadMember "seq01", "seq38": Preloads the cast members from seq01 through seq38 into memory.
preLoadMode of CastLib	Specifies when to preload a cast library. Options inclue the values 0 (when needed), 1 (before frame 1), 2 (afterframe 1).	set the preLoadMode of castLib "sounds" = 1: Preloads the Cast Library named "sounds" into memory before frame 1 of your movie.
preLoadMovie	Preloads the specified movie by preloading its cast members. Prevents delays when the current movie opens another movie or an MIAW.	preLoadMovie "menu": Preloads the movie named menu into memory.

Command	Application	Usage Example
preLoadNetThing	Preloads a file from the Internet. This is useful if you have multiple movies on a Web site, by preloading the next movie while the current movie is playing.	PreLoadNetThing ("http://www.mymovie.com/playit"): Preloads the movie named playit into memory while the current movie is playing.
preLoadRAM	Allocates limited memory for digital video, while allowing other cast members to load normally.	set the preLoadRAM to 2 (the size of member "cycling"): Specifies that the amount of RAM available for preloading equals twice the size of the digital video cast member named cycling. If preLoadRAM= False, all memory available can be used to preload digital video.
preLoadTime of member	Specifies the amount of a SWA file to download before it starts playing. The amount is limited by seconds, rather than a number of bytes. Note that the SWA file must be stopped for this command to work.	set the preLoadTime of member "kiosk1" = 6: Preloads the sound cast member named kiosk1, 6 seconds before it starts playing.

Setting Purge Priorities

You can set the purge priorities of the cast members in your movies. By default, Director purges cast members at random, as needed to free up memory when it's full. If the size of the movie exceeds the available memory, setting purge priorities enables you to control which cast members are purged from memory and which are retained. When Director needs to reload a cast member frequently, it puts a strain on the resources of the user's computer. For example, a bitmap used as a background throughout a movie should be retained in memory for the entire movie, to prevent repeated pauses for reloading the image.

To specify purge priorities, you specify a value that indicates when a cast member should be removed. The higher the priority value, the more likely a cast member will be purged if memory runs low. The following values are available for purge priority settings:

0 = Never Purge

1 = Purge Last

2 = Purge Next

3 = Purge Normal

Specifying Purge Properties in a Movie Script

1. Open kiosk2.dir in Director, if it's not already open.
2. In the Cast window, double-click cast member 11, "movie script," to open it in the Script window (see Figure 23-5).

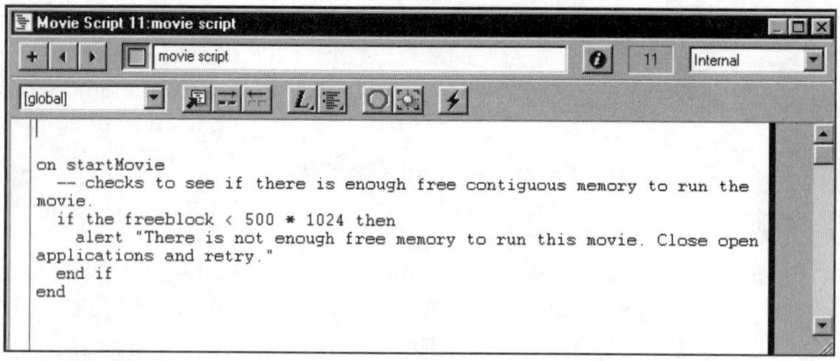

Figure 23-5: Adding purge priorities in a movie script

3. At the top of the script, enter the following lines:
   ```
   on prepareMovie
      set the purgePriority of member "background1" to 1
   end
   ```
4. Close the Script window, and save your movie.

Director doesn't purge cast members from memory unless it needs the memory to run a movie. On computers with substantial resources, purging cast members is rarely a problem. If you're designing an application for use on a broad range of computers, you should pay close attention to specifying the way cast members are purged from memory, to ensure the success of your movie.

Designing Movies for Memory Considerations

When designing Director movies, it's important to remember your audience. Where memory is concerned, designing for the least common denominator is a key issue if you want to reach the broadest audience. You need to decide on whom you want to see your movies and the computer resources at their disposal.

Clearly, if you are designing a project for the WWW, you can anticipate an enormous variety of users and hardware. Since it's impossible to design for every variable, it's a good idea to consider the average computer for most home users. As a general rule, you can consider the following to be a fairly common average system:

- ✦ A PowerMac 5500 with 16MB of RAM and a 14.4 modem; or for Windows users, a 486 DX2/66 with 8MB of RAM and a 14.4 modem.
- ✦ In addition, you can safely assume that both systems will have a video adapter with 1MB of RAM, capable of displaying at least 640 x 480 at an 8-bit color depth.
- ✦ Hard disk space can vary greatly, but generally these systems have between 540MB and 1.2GB of total hard disk space.

It's no secret that you wouldn't want to author a Director movie on such a machine, unless you had no choice. Your movies should play acceptably on these computers, however — especially if you are creating a movie for use on the Internet.

Bitmap memory considerations

It's a good idea to keep memory requirements in mind when you create bitmap images for use in your movies. Bitmaps can account for a rather large chunk of your final movie size. And if you add sounds and other effects in addition to large bitmaps, your movie may exceed the resources of the end-user's computer. You can use the following formula to predict the amount of memory required to display a bitmap:

(the width of the bitmap in pixels) x (the height of the bitmap in pixels) x (the color depth in bits) / 8 = the number of bytes of memory required

For example: a 200 x 200-pixel, 8-bit bitmap would require 40,000 bytes of memory, or (200 x 200 x 8) / 8 = 40,000.

Guidelines for saving memory

Director helps you to control memory usage. In addition, you can cultivate the success and improve the performance of your movies by keeping the following considerations in mind when you are designing your movies:

- Use the lowest possible color depth for bitmapped cast members that have only a few colors. The higher the color depth, the more resources Director has to use to render the cast member and refresh the screen.

- Create composite images of bitmap cast members that appear as static images on the Stage. This reduces the number of cells and channels that Director has to read and process, allowing your movie to run more smoothly.

- Use the floating Tool Palette to draw and fill simple geometric shapes instead of employing bitmap images. Objects drawn with tools from the Tool Palette are vector images and require less time and resources to render to the screen. *However*, don't use vector graphics for animation, because they will slow down your movie enormously.

- Keep the use of gradient fills to a minimum. Gradients require more resources to render to the screen.

- Try not to use memory-intensive inks with complex or large bitmaps. This can bring a movie to almost a dead stop on most computers, even if they possess significant resources.

- Use film loops for repetitive animation sequences. A film loop will play as a single cast member in a frame while Director is processing other cast members in the frame.

- Reduce the sampling rate of sound files, or consider using SWA files to improve performance.

- Get the most from small sound bites, such as knocks, beeps, and clicks, by setting them to loop.

- Link rather than embed your sound files, so that Director doesn't have to load the files until they're needed in your movie. Remember when you link files to make sure the file is included when you transport your movie from one location to another.

- Use Lingo preload and purge commands to control the memory usage of your movies. This prevents bottlenecks that will slow or halt a movie if too many cast members are loading at the same time.

- Consider using MIAWs when your movie contains multiple branches of movies that could be designed to run independently. Note, however, that you can't use MIAWs on the Internet.

Observing good memory-conservation practices can increase the performance of your movies and make troubleshooting easier. Frequently, as in the case of using film loops, memory conservation produces a tighter, more compact Score. And that makes it easier for you to find elements within your movies and edit them.

Optimizing for CD-ROM

Director movies are large. It's not uncommon for a single movie to be well over 4MB. If you are creating a project where multiple movies play in succession and have MIAWs, sounds, and perhaps digital video, the amount of space required for storage can mushroom almost geometrically. CD-ROMs have become the distribution media of choice for most Director projects that aren't being published on the Internet. CD-ROM disks have a number of advantages over floppy disks. They are durable, they can't be damaged by magnetic fields, they hold large amounts of data, and they can be recorded to play on multiple platforms.

The transfer rate of a CD-ROM drive can have an impact on the performance of a movie. As a general rule of thumb, the transfer rate of a CD-ROM drive is 150K per second × the speed of the CD-ROM. Thus a 4X CD-ROM would have a 600K-per-second transfer rate. Slower drives (below 4X) may cause a performance problem with your movies. Be sure to test your movie thoroughly before distributing it.

Building a virtual image

The first step in recording a CD-ROM is to build a *virtual image*. A virtual image is a database of pointers telling the mastering software where to find the files you want to include. When you create the virtual image, you are not actually moving any files. You are telling the mastering software how you want the CD-ROM organized, by setting up directories and allocating files to those directories.

Before recording your CD-ROM, it's a good idea to do a little housekeeping to organize your files. By organizing your files into folders, keeping related files together, you improve performance of your movies in the long run by reducing the amount of time the computer has to spend looking for files. In addition, you reap the short-term benefits of simplifying the task of creating a virtual image and improving your chances of a successful recording session. When you put the files in order on your hard disk prior to starting, you'll be prompted to remove files that will not be included on the CD-ROM, and will more easily recognize a logical order for your files. Remember: You are dealing with almost 650MB of information.

When it's time to move linked files, such as digital movies, sound files, and external casts, you should open and resave your Director 6 movies to update the location of those linked files.

Tip: Although most mastering software permits a directory tree of folders and subfolders eight deep, it's a good idea to limit the folder depth to three or four levels. This reduces the seek and transfer times from your CD-ROM to your computer — yet another way to improve the performance of your movies.

CD-ROM basics

There are two basic recording standards for CD-ROMs: ISO 9660 and HFS (Hierarchical File System). Macintoshes can read both formats but prefer the HFS standard; Windows-based machines can read only files that have been encoded using the ISO (International Standards Organization) 9660 standard.

It is possible to record both formats on a single CD-ROM. You should be aware, however, that recording your movies in both formats on a single compact disk cuts the amount of available storage space in half. This is the result of including two copies of a movie or projector (one for each platform). If you find that you need to record more than 300MB of data for each format, you'll either have to use some form of data compression or reevaluate your decision to put both formats on the same disk. Decompression takes time. And it may result in degraded performance during the playback of your movies, or require that the user store the decompressed data on a hard disk. If you want your project to play from the CD-ROM, it may be advisable for you to record separate disks for each platform.

Because of its audio origin, the CD-ROM blank medium is measured in *minutes:seconds:sectors*. It comes in two sizes: 63 minutes or 74 minutes. This works out to be 553MB and 650MB, respectively. The 650MB discs are the most common.

Note that it's not a good idea to run too close to the maximum storage amount on a disk. Both the ISO 9660 and HFS standards require approximately 1MB of overhead space for root files, resource forks, and other data required by the operating systems of both platforms.

Understanding logical blocks

Data is stored on a CD-ROM in *logical blocks,* rather than as the total number of bytes of all the files. A logical block is the smallest recordable unit on a CD-ROM. This means that files occupy more space than their original size. Logical blocks can be 512, 1,024, 2,048, or 4,096 bytes in size.

MSCDEX (Microsoft CD Extensions) and HFS can only read a 2,048-byte block. As a result, each file occupies a space equal to the nearest multiple of the next higher block. For example, if a file contains 16,000 bytes, it will require 8 blocks (16,000 / 2,048 = 7.812 blocks).

Simply totaling the number of bytes for all the files you want to record won't yield an accurate estimate of the space required. Most CD-ROM mastering software calculates the amount of space required for your files, but you should already have an estimate of your space requirements *before* you start recording a CD-ROM. Keep in mind that directories, like files, require space on the disc. As a general rule you can record up to 600MB of raw data on a CD-ROM. Under most circumstances, this amount leaves ample space for overhead while taking logical blocks into consideration.

Caution: If you are including data from multiple sources, be certain that you observe copyright laws and restrictions. You must obtain licenses to include any files, including sound and digital movie files. If you are using clip-media sounds, digital movies, text, or artwork, be sure the license rights allow for redistribution of the files. See Chapter 9 for more information about copyright law.

Single or multisession recording?

When you record a CD-ROM, you can choose between two modes: single session or multisession. Your choice will depend on the media you choose, the CD-R (CD-ROM recorder), and the recording software.

Two types of CD-ROM media are available today: CD-ROM (Mode 1) and CD-ROM XA (Mode 2). The difference between the two types is frequently misunderstood — due in part to the history of compact disk media. Early CD-ROMs were recorded in a single session, even though the standard made provisions for recording in multiple sessions. Kodak's Photo CD medium was one of the first to make use of multisession recording, but it did not use the standard CD-ROM format. These early multisession disks used the CD-ROM XA format, so the manufacturers of CD-

ROM drives assumed that all multisession CD-ROM media would also be CD-ROM XA format. The reality is that both formats can be used for multisession recording.

Because of the misconceptions arising from the two CD-ROM media formats, you cannot assume that a CD-ROM recorded in multiple sessions will be read correctly. If you anticipate recording in more than one session, you would do well to either premaster the CD-ROM on a hard drive, or make sure that data is recorded in the CD-ROM XA format.

The choice of whether to record in a single or multisession format requires taking a close look at your needs. Each recording format offers distinct advantages and disadvantages. To begin, bear in mind that when multiple people are involved in the production of a single movie project, sometimes it's difficult to gather all the data into a single location simultaneously. If you want to record a single-session CD-ROM, it's essential that the virtual image contains all of the files, organized precisely as they will be placed on the CD-ROM. If you are working on a network, or are including data from remote sources, a single recording session might not be practical.

Multisession recording offers the advantage of being able to add data at a later time, from a variety of sources or locations. If you are creating a CD-ROM for multiple platforms, it's necessary to create a multisession CD-ROM to accommodate the differences in the operating systems of the two platforms. On the other hand, multisession recording requires more headroom on the CD-ROM, which means it cannot hold as much data.

Summary

Employing memory management techniques helps trim the size of your movies while maintaining a high quality of performance for your projects. As your movies become larger and more complex, good memory management makes a noticeable difference in movie performance. In this chapter, you learned how to

- ✦ Use SWA files in your movies, and specify the preload times to ensure they play smoothly
- ✦ Calculate the amount of memory required for bitmap images.
- ✦ Set purge priorities
- ✦ Use the Message window to obtain information about memory and your movie
- ✦ Design movies with memory considerations in mind
- ✦ Organize your projects for CD-ROM output

✦ ✦ ✦

Onto the Web

PART V

In This Part

Chapter 24
Incorporating NetLingo and Shockwave

Chapter 25
Into the Third Dimension

Incorporating NetLingo and Shockwave

CHAPTER 24

In This Chapter

A brief history of the Internet

Clients and servers

Creating a Shockwave movie

Shockwave movies on and off the Web

Setting access rights for your documents on the Web

NetLingo for network operations

NetLingo that interacts with a browser

O n December 4, 1995, the World Wide Web (WWW) changed dramatically forever. Static graphics and text were replaced with animation and kiosk-like interactivity. This new technology was called Shockwave, and the key players were no less than Netscape, the creators of the Netscape Navigator Web browser, and Macromedia, developers of Director.

In this chapter, you'll explore a new class of Director movie — the Shockwave movie — that can be distributed to users across the globe over the World Wide Web. To build Shockwave movies requires some effort, but creating Shockwave movies from your Director movies is extremely easy. This chapter takes you through the Internet-related Lingo commands (NetLingo), the Hypertext Markup Language (HTML) tags, and the methods for building efficient and effective Shockwave movies. But first, a little history.

Director and the Internet

It wasn't that long ago that the Internet was a fairly obscure set of university and research networks familiar only to a small group of computer science nerds and physics professors. The Internet was outside the attention of most everyday people. Navigating the Net meant using odd tools like "gophers" and "fingers." While the Net was only this collection of obscure pockets of information, locating anything of significance could easily be a day-long task — and that's if you knew what you were doing.

Then around 1990 a brilliant guy by the name of Tim Berners-Lee came up with the idea of the http protocol, HTML, and the World Wide Web. The idea was simplicity itself: Take a preexisting template for page layout structures (SGML), throw in hypertext referencing capability, provide a protocol for transferring graphical information, and wham — suddenly the entire worldwide network of interconnected computers became one gigantic document library.

The Web was an instant hit among scientists who had been looking for a way to organize and display scientific information, and among grad students who had been trying to find a way to play arcane word games while pretending to focus on dissertation-related research. At the National Center for Super Computing of the University of Illinois, several research students developed Mosaic, a program that enabled graphical navigation of the information on the World Wide Web. This new program, called a browser, transformed the way the Net was viewed. Armed with this highly graphical viewpoint of the Web's information, the creators of Mosaic headed into industry to establish Netscape Communications Corporation and make Netscape Navigator one of the most successful browsers of all time.

Clients and servers

Netscape Navigator and other browsers are known in the networking industry as a *client*. The information it retrieves comes from a machine called a *server*. The term client comprises the machine that requests the information as well as the specific program on the machine that makes the formal request.

Think of the client as a patron at a restaurant. She is not a part of the restaurant, but simply visits it on occasion (if the food, ambiance, and service are agreeable). When she arrives, she is seated at a table and offered a menu by a waiter, who is the server. The client must talk to the server to make requests — in an effective setting, there is communication both ways. Once the client orders, the server takes stock of what the client requests. If the request is simple (she needs a cup of coffee), he handles the request himself and fetches some coffee. Likewise, an electronic server checks to see if it has the needed files locally, and then serves them back to the client. On the other hand, if the restaurant patron orders a full dinner, the server wouldn't be able to handle the request himself. He is taking care of too many other people and can't take time to do the cooking, too. Instead he goes to the kitchen and tells the cook what's needed. In Internet terms, the server sends a request to its *server hub,* which consists of many other computers storing data.

The cook can then do one of several things. If the request is one that she frequently receives, the cook probably has the ingredients stockpiled, and can turn the order out quickly (this is the Chef's Special). On the other hand, if this particular dish doesn't get ordered very often (the Tofu Surprise, for example), then the cook might dispatch someone to get the tofu from the nearby supermarket. Finally, if some component of the order isn't available (no tofu, even at the supermarket), the cook sends a response back to the server. "Tofu Surprise is not available today, and would the customer accept a substitute?" The response is delivered to the client, who either accepts the substitute or tells the server to cancel her entree.

In the client/server environment, the functions of the hub (a server to the server) may include

- Sending back frequently cached files (like the daily Chef's Special)
- Requesting files from other hubs (the hub is now a client to other hubs — like the restaurant's using the supermarket backup)
- Returning an error message if the requested file or some component of it isn't available ("Sorry, we're out of blueberry pie today.")
- In this model, the client and the server may keep switching roles (even as occurs in client/server computing environments):
    - The patron is the client to the waiter's server
    - The waiter is the client to the patron's server
    - The waiter is the client to the cook's server
    - The cook is the client to the supermarket's server

Back to computers, in general the client is the computer that is requesting the media, while the server is the computer that is providing the media. As in life, the roles played are not always clear-cut — the cook may request permission from the client for an item to be substituted, acting in this sense as the client.

Plug-ins, Java, and ActiveX

The Browser Wars arose shortly after Mosaic first appeared, as companies vied to create the best browsers with the most features. We use the term Browser Wars here in the plural, because the years since 1990 have seen waves of innovation and changes in available technologies and competitors, each marked by shifts in paradigms.

The first War, from 1990 to early 1992, was characterized by a proliferation of new browsers, each attempting to show off its own technology by controlling the direction of HTML. Spyglass and Mosaic were the first to market, but Netscape Navigator quickly rose to dominate almost all of the browsers on the planet. Netscape introduced many alterations to the HTML specification, to a great extent pushing the standards into the Netscape camp. Netscape HTML was generally considered more of a standard than the "officially sanctioned" HTML version set up by the oversight committee of developers, the World Wide Web (W3) Consortium.

As use of the Web grew, Web browsers increasingly fell short of meeting the needs of companies pushing their particular media toward the Web. If pictures and words could appear there, why not sound, video, animation, and spreadsheets? To accommodate an expansion of distributed media, Netscape looked around at what others in the industry were doing (especially Adobe and 3Dstudio with their active plug-in markets) and established a standard for designing *plug-ins*. These modules of code expand the browser's capabilities. Once a plug-in is downloaded and installed in a special folder for use by the browser, it can "host" a specialized media within the browser's window.

For example, the QuickTime plug-in grabs a portion of the browser window and uses it to display QuickTime movies. By using a specific filename extension or some internal mechanism, the media (QuickTime, Real Audio, Shockwave, and so on) identifies itself to the server, enabling the server to pave the way for the client. In terms of the restaurant metaphor, the waiter can bring the patron a bowl of soup — but until the server delivers a spoon, the soup is inaccessible (at least in polite company). The client is responsible for "consuming" the media, and if the plug-in doesn't exist, then the client is unable to figure out how to handle it. In both the computer and the restaurant, if the tool (plug-in or spoon) required to consume the media (QuickTime or soup) is unavailable, the client will probably ignore the media, fume a bit, and get on with the other aspects of the file/meal.

Note It is also possible for the client to complain (using the proper HTML tags), which might get assistance (an automatic download of the plug-in) from the server.

Shockwave is a plug-in, available from Macromedia, that allows Director movies to run within a browser window as part of a Web page. Actually, Shockwave is several different technologies under the same label. This multifaceted plug-in lets you integrate any of Macromedia's products into a Web page. Freehand, Extreme 3D, xRes, Authorware, Flash, and Director documents can all be repurposed for the Web, although for security and efficiency reasons there are some significant limitations to what can be done from within Shockwave — we'll go into all of these later in this chapter.

Note The name Shockwave may have been derived from John Brunner's visionary 1970s novel *Shockwave Rider*. This story of science fiction depicted one view of an Internet-type culture in the future. The term *shock wave* also refers to a compression wave that exceeds the speed of sound, so the "impact" reaches a stationary object before the sound of the "event" that created the wave. The Shockwave application is well named. As you will see, compression is definitely part of its raison d'être, and it has sent a "blast" throughout the rapidly evolving world of the Internet.

Plug-ins typify the second wave of the Browser Wars. Netscape emerged from the first war only to look up and see the Microsoft juggernaut in the distance.

Microsoft had pretty much ignored the first Browser War, although it did enter a combatant: Internet Explorer (IE) 1.0. This first Microsoft browser was barely adequate against even the second-rung armies in that war. Stung, Microsoft revised IE and reissued it. Like an exploratory probe, IE 2.0 came back similarly battered, and the word on the street (or at least that of the press) was that Microsoft had ceded the battle without really trying, and was doomed like IBM to be a desktop dinosaur.

But all that was before December 7, 1995. Nicknamed the Pearl Harbor Speech, the address on that day by Bill Gates signaled the start of the second Browser Wars. Microsoft's CEO announced that he was turning the juggernaut (Microsoft) into an Internet-based company. The pundits decried, "Too little, too late." But Gates proved them wrong.

The summer before, Sun Microsystems had released a new language. Originally designed for automating toasters, it was given the name Java and was designed as an interplatform development solution. It gained real currency, however, because as a language it was ideally suited for use on the Internet. In essence, Java enabled the construction of platform-independent code that could be run from within a browser window in a form called an *applet,* or mini-application. Developers rushed to play with it, and Netscape declared that Java would form the basis of a new plug-in language: A subset of Java called *JavaScript* was incorporated into the Navigator browser as an interpreted language. With Java and JavaScript, it became possible to automate Web pages, moving a lot of the processing work from the server (which was already fairly burdened as a fetcher of media) to the client (which was usually pretty inactive once the Web page itself was downloaded).

Microsoft was reexamining its current position and started leveraging technologies it had already developed. The first, *Object Linking and Embedding* (OLE) had originally been a means of embedding part of one application into another, but had evolved into an interapplication communication language. In March 1996, OLE was replaced with ActiveX, catching several developers by surprise. ActiveX is the physical manifestation of the Microsoft's *Component Object Model* (COM), a paradigm in which all applications are essentially nothing but components wrapped in a shell, and each component becomes a client responding to the server of the shell (sound familiar?) Then Microsoft released a perfect example of ActiveX technology: a browser consisting of a shell and an intelligent browser window. Released as Internet Explorer 3.0, this browser became Netscape's first true competition. The next iteration of Windows (subsequent to Windows 95) will incorporate this browser into the operating system.

Distributed object models

The second Browser War has shifted from the client side to the server side as the coalition surrounding Netscape (Sun, Netscape, Apple, IBM, and Oracle) sets up to do battle with the coalition surrounding Microsoft (principally Intel and Microsoft). Things are getting a little more exciting because both sides have created *distributed object models* (CORBA on the Sun/Netscape side and DCOM on the Intel/Microsoft side).

The esoteric-sounding distributed object models may seem far removed from Director, but once again the concepts involved are found in Director applications — especially applications built around the Web. In distributed computing, the actual code and resources needed by an application to operate don't all reside on the same machine. To a certain extent, any HTML page is a very limited version of this concept, but the difference is more subtle than it appears. In computer programming parlance, an object is a unit of code that is relatively independent of the code around it. Objects expose methods and properties that can be used to control it without having to know anything about what makes the object tick. Behaviors in Lingo are prime examples of logic in that they provide methods and properties, don't require other behaviors to operate (well, most of the time), and retain information about their state.

In a distributed environment, the components that make up an application could come from anywhere — the local machine, a server, a CD, a satellite transmission … from Mars, for that matter. Since objects retain state information, they can contain not only data but methods for interpreting that data. For example, within a distributed object model, a teacher could build a lesson object to be downloaded by a student's client. The lesson is run, a test is administered, and the answered test object is launched (already partially graded by the test object itself) back to both the human teacher and to a student database object. The teacher has a client application that reads the test results, displays the answers, notes patterns, and makes suggestions about how to proceed with each student. In essence, the test object becomes an agent shuttling back and forth between teacher and student.

Right now, the battle between DCOM and CORBA is still being waged, as each side attempts to make its model of distributed computing the de facto standard. The stakes are considerable — since more and more programs will comprise distributed components, the companies that control the friendliest operating system for those components will likely dominate the Internet (and intranet) markets.

Where is Macromedia in all of this?

So what does this have to do with Director? Actually, almost everything. Macromedia came to its current market dominance in the area of multimedia, which is at this point a fairly mature technology. With the rise of CDs, large multimedia applications became possible, and this arena is still Macromedia's mainstay. However, note the relationship in the previous section between "distributed" and "distribution." Specifically, CDs (and — once the legal niceties are taken care of — digital video disks or DVDs) are hampered by being real, physical objects that must go through a distribution channel that is better suited for books. The disks must be replicated by a CD plant, transported, and then must fight for shelf space with other CDs and face the dilemma of being inherently out-of-date before they hit the shelves. Today, effective shelf-life expectancy is measured in months or even less.

On the other hand, the Internet will in time become the ideal medium for electronic media, because it is an electronic distribution channel that obeys its own dynamic. The distribution costs drop dramatically when nothing physical has to be manufactured. Information can be kept as current as needed. What's more, when a distributed model is applied to multimedia development, it means that, say, a game can be upgraded with new technologies on-the-fly. A presentation can replace an obsolete product with a current one, with the only needed intervention by the user being an Internet feed. Lessons in an educational package can be tailored to an individual user's needs.

Director 6 has most of the tools needed to take advantage of this model, and the use of Xtras can add the rest of the capability. Behaviors can be encapsulated in cast libraries, which can then be distributed via the Internet, or can be extracted wholesale from HTML source code listings. Graphics, sounds, and movies can be retrieved from the Net. It is even possible to create three-dimensional worlds, controlled by Director, that originate from the Web or are transmitted to the Web from Director.

The beauty of Director is that, in this scheme, any product can function regardless of which distributed architecture wins the Wars. If an instructor creates a lesson with Shockwave, students can work with the lesson whether they are using Internet Explorer or Netscape Navigator or the instructor's own custom browser written in Director. Unlike Java, which requires a fairly strong understanding of OOP techniques, Director can make powerful, sophisticated applications without your writing a line of code.

What Is Shockwave?

Shockwave is a technology that enables you to transform static (text and graphics) Web pages into Web *documents* that include animation, audio, and interactivity. Shockwave takes advantage of Macromedia's existing tools (Authorware, Director, Flash, FreeHand, and xRes) to create and package a full range of multimedia products for Web distribution. Shockwave enables you to use everything you already know about authoring in Director and apply it to creating interactive media for the World Wide Web.

Shockwave technology is composed of two distinct elements:

✦ The compression engine
✦ The Shockwave plug-in for Netscape-compatible browsers, and the Shockwave ActiveX control for Microsoft Internet Explorer

The compression engine was originally released as a stand-alone applet called the Afterburner. Now the capability to create a "Shocked" movie is integrated into Director's menu system and is accessed using the File ⇨ Save As Shockwave Movie command. After you create a Director movie, it is only a few mouse clicks away from being transformed into a Shockwave movie.

The Shockwave plug-in operates as an ActiveX control for IE 3.0 and higher. The Shockwave ActiveX controller can be automatically installed by IE when the browser locates a Web page that includes a Shockwave movie. For Netscape users, the plug-in installation program can be downloaded, decompressed, and run to install the Shockwave plug-in in the Netscape Plug-ins folder.

Since the birth of Shockwave, millions of copies of the plug-in have been downloaded from Macromedia's Web site. Shockwave is currently used on thousands of interactive Web sites to provide banners, interactive games, advertising, training materials, and much more. Shockwave can provide on-demand streaming audio for live concerts and special effects, and create interactive news, sports, gaming, and information Web sites.

The Shockwave compression engine

Shockwave's compression engine (formerly called the Afterburner) is a post-processor for Director movies. It compresses your Director movie using a lossless compression algorithm. Shockwave reduces the file size of your movie without degrading the original content. Compression prepares your Director movie for faster downloading from a Hypertext Transport Protocol (http) server, commonly called a Web server. Once Web pages are created, they must be stored on a Web server, which then makes the pages available to Web browsers. To deliver Shockwave movies over the Web, the movie and its associated Web page must be stored on a Web server.

Although it's possible to deliver an uncompressed Director (DIR) movie or a protected (DXR) movie over the Web, download times are problematic. Just about any Web user will be impatient with downloading a large graphic image — especially if they're using a 14.4 or 28.8 Kbps modem (the typical device used to access the Web today). Smaller images mean faster download times, which means happier users. And the same holds true of delivering any media over the Web. That's why Macromedia developed Shockwave. It compresses a Director movie to its smallest possible size, often to 50% or less. When you can cut the file size of a movie in half, you also cut the download time in half.

After Director movies are compressed, Director adds a .dcr extension, which identifies the file as a Director CompRessed file.

The Shockwave plug-in

The second part of Shockwave technology is the Shockwave plug-in (for Netscape and compatible browsers) and the Shockwave ActiveX control (for Microsoft's Internet Explorer). The plug-in and ActiveX control both extend the capabilities of your Web browser to interpret and display Shockwave movies that are distributed on the Web. The Shockwave plug-in and ActiveX control interpret the HTML <EMBED> or <OBJECT> tags and display the compressed (or even an uncompressed) Director movie in your browser's window:

- The Shockwave plug-in for Netscape Navigator (version 2.0 or later) installs on a Macintosh PowerPC, a 68K Macintosh, a Windows 3.1, or a Windows 95/NT system.

- The ActiveX control is available for the Windows 95/NT version of Microsoft Internet Explorer 3.0 and 4.0.

The new Shockwave Player released in November 1997 is drastically reduced in size and plays streaming Shockwave movies created with either Director or Flash. Shockwave for AOL is also available; it works with the America Online browser. Currently under development is Shockwave for Marimba Castinet for Windows 95/NT only.

Installing the Shockwave plug-in for Netscape

The current plug-in for Netscape Navigator is available from Macromedia's Shockwave Central Web site at

```
www.macromedia.com/shockwave
```

The site includes installation notes, but you'll find the process is simple and straightforward:

1. Locate the Get Shockwave link and click it.

2. Follow the on-screen instructions, which include completing a form by entering your name and e-mail address.

    The Macromedia site automatically determines your computer's operating system and your Web browser and downloads the correct version of the plug-in for your system. If the operating system (Macintosh, Windows, UNIX) and browser (Netscape Navigator or Internet Explorer) selected by the site are incorrect, look for the Need a Different Shockwave link and follow it.

3. Click the Download Now button to download the plug-in to your system's local hard drive.

A download progress bar appears. You can watch it inch forward or just go get a cup of coffee. Depending on your connection, it may take several minutes or longer to download.

> **Tip:** Be sure to make a note of the folder on your hard drive where you save the file. You will need to locate it in the upcoming step 4. Also write down the name of the file that you download. You'll need this information to use the installation program.

> **Caution:** If you save the installer program on a Novell network server, the installer program filename is automatically shortened because Novell networks use the 8.3 file-naming conventions. The filename will appear as !Shockwa~.exe. The installation program will run okay with the shorter name.

4. After the download is complete, close your browser and any open applications. Locate the downloaded file on your desktop (Macintosh) or hard drive (Windows), and run it (It's an executable file that installs the plug-in).

5. When you're ready to run the installation, double-click the installer program icon.

> **On the CD-ROM:** *Attention Macintosh users*: If you have a compressed installation file that ends with the .sea.hqx extension and no Shockwave installer program, it means you do not have a decompression helper application available to decompress the downloaded file. You'll need to get StuffIt Expander, which is available on this book's companion CD-ROM in the goodies:aladdin folder or from Aladdin's site at
>
> `www.aladdinsys.com`

6. Once the Shockwave Installer program starts, follow the on-screen instructions.

   The program tries to locate the folder where your primary Web browser (Netscape Navigator) is located, and to place the Shockwave plug-in files in the browser's Plug-ins folder. If you have more than one browser installed, be sure to install Shockwave for *each* browser. In most cases, if you have a single installation of Netscape Navigator or Communicator, the installation program can accurately determine the location where plug-ins should be installed.

7. Once the installation is complete, you'll be asked by the program if you want to connect to the Internet and test some "Shocked" pages at the Macromedia Web site. If you agree, the installer automatically loads your browser and jumps to theShockwave ShockZone.

> **Tip:** The Shockwave ShockZone at
>
> `http://www.macromedia.com/shockzone`

is a good place to start, with its Spot Lights, Site of the Day, Arcade, Jukebox, Staff Picks, and more.

A note about cache space

Be sure that Navigator's disk cache is set to a minimum size of 10MB. If the disk cache is set smaller, you may not be able to view Shockwave movies. If, with the 10MB setting, you still have problems viewing Shocked sites, set the cache to 15MB.

You can check or adjust the disk cache setting by selecting Options⇨Network Preferences from the Netscape Navigator 3.0 menu bar, or Edit⇨Preferences⇨Advanced⇨Cache in Netscape Communicator 4. The Disk Cache setting in the Preferences dialog box appears as shown in Figure 24-1.

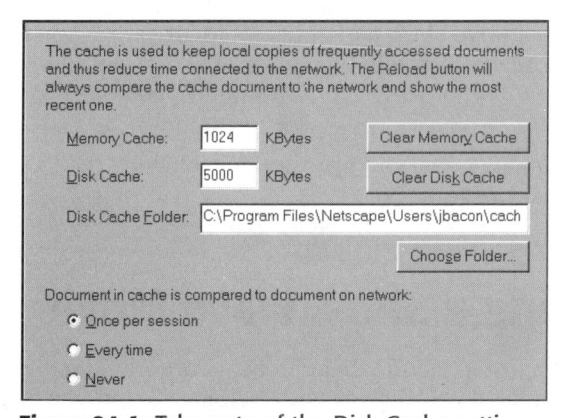

Figure 24-1: Take note of the Disk Cache setting.

Installing the Shockwave ActiveX Control for Internet Explorer

The current ActiveX Control for Internet Explorer is available from Macromedia's Shockwave Central Web site at

    www.macromedia.com/shockwave/download

Note: Some Shocked sites use HTML tags to automatically load the ActiveX control in the background while you're viewing other information on the site. For the details, see the "Using the CODEBASE parameter" section later in this chapter.

To acquire and install the control, complete the following steps:

1. Open Microsoft Internet Explorer (version 3.0 or later).

2. Go to the Macromedia Web site at

    www.macromedia.com/shockwave/download/

The Shockwave Download page is designed to automatically install the Shockwave for Director and Shockwave for Flash ActiveX Controls in Microsoft Internet Explorer. This ActiveX control plays Director, Flash, and Flash 2 media.

3. Complete the on-screen form by entering your name and e-mail address.
4. Click the Autoinstall Now button.
5. IE displays the Shockwave ActiveX Controls page, and the ActiveX controls are automatically installed. When the installation successfully finishes, sample Flash and Director Shockwave movies appear and play the page. Be sure to turn on your system's speakers to hear the audio.

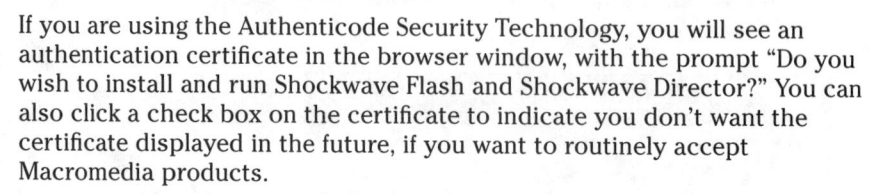

   If you are using the Authenticode Security Technology, you will see an authentication certificate in the browser window, with the prompt "Do you wish to install and run Shockwave Flash and Shockwave Director?" You can also click a check box on the certificate to indicate you don't want the certificate displayed in the future, if you want to routinely accept Macromedia products.

6. Once the installation is complete, you can proceed to explore all the "Shocked" sites on the World Wide Web.

Overview for Creating a Shockwave Movie

Director includes specific NetLingo commands that can be incorporated into your Shockwave movies (see the later section "Working with NetLingo"). But you can create a Shockwave movie right now, using the commands and skills you have already learned. With a few exceptions, and we'll get to those later, almost any Director movie can be converted to a Shockwave movie and distributed over the Web.

First, some general information:

♦ You probably have the same natural tendency as others to organize documents into separate folders. However, it is easier to create, test, and upload all related Web document files (HTML documents, GIF and JPEG files, Shockwave movies, and so on) to the server if you keep all files associated with a specific Web page in a single folder. This enables you to refer to various media files by their filenames rather than having to include pathnames, which can sometimes be long and complex.

♦ You create Shockwave movies using two menu commands in Director. To create a Shockwave movie from a single Director movie, use File➪Save As Shockwave Movie. If you need to convert more than one movie, use Xtras➪Update Movies. The latter command is typically used to batch-compress a complete folder of movies all in one operation.

♦ If protecting your movies from reverse engineering is a concern, keep in mind that DCR (Shockwave) movies have protection similar to DXR (protected) movies. The DCR movies are just as safe as DXR movies — and they have the added benefit of being compressed.

♦ When Director compresses your movie, it does not change the movie's content or appearance. The compression engine's role is simply to decrease the movie's download time.

Placement of movie elements in a Shockwave movie

Director tries to optimize a movie when you save it with File➪Save and Compact or File➪Save As Shockwave Movie. In both cases, the content of the movie is unchanged, but the compression engine does reorder the elements of the movie to expedite the playback and downloading over a network. The two Director commands place the Score, all scripts, shapes created with the Tool Palette, and cast member information at the beginning of the movie. Next, all additional cast members — text, field, shape, and bitmap, irrespective of size — are saved to the movie file in the same order as they are in the Score. Any cast members that do not appear in the Score are stored in Cast window order; that is, in their cast order.

This order is important because, when you play a movie over a network, the elements of the movie are downloaded in the same order they are saved. For instance, the Score is downloaded first, followed by all scripts, shapes created from the Tool Palette, and cast member information (not the cast member itself). Next, all scripts, shapes, and cast member information from *any external cast* used by the movie are downloaded, followed by any Xtras required for the movie's playback.

You can help optimize a Shockwave movie or a projector by placing cast members in the cast according to when the cast member is used in the movie. In other words, cast members used early in a movie should be placed in low-numbered cast member slots.

Make that streaming, please

The capability of creating a streaming Shockwave movie, which begins playing before it is fully downloaded, is now available with Director 6. All Director 6 movies are by default set to completely download before the movie begins playing. (This is the only setting available for Director 4 and 5 movies.) With Director 6, however, you can also change the streaming options for a movie using the Modify➪Movie➪Playback command. When you execute this command, the Movie Playback

Properties dialog box appears, as shown in Figure 24-2. The choices available for streaming movies in this dialog are listed in Table 24-1.

The streaming setting you establish in the Movie Playback Properties dialog box affects the current movie only. This setting is stored in the Director movie itself and must be set prior to saving your movie as a Shockwave movie.

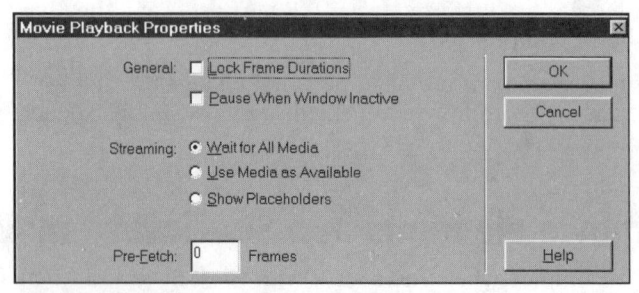

Figure 24-2: The streaming playback settings in the Movie Playback Properties dialog box

Table 24-1
Streaming Movie Options

Option	Effect If Selected
Wait for All Media	Waits for the entire movie to download before it begins playing. This is the default behavior for Director 6 movies and the only option available for Director 4 and 5 movies.
Use Media as Available	Causes the movie to play as soon as a sufficient portion of it has been downloaded, or as soon as the number of pre-Fetch frames have been downloaded, as specified in the Pre-Fetch box at the bottom of the Movie Playback Properties dialog box.
Show Placeholders	Displays rectangular outlines called placeholders on the Stage until the required images are downloaded from the Internet. This is standard browser behavior, except in this case it applies to Shockwave movies.

The following steps provide an overview of the process required to build and distribute a Shockwave movie.

The Shocking Steps to Shockwave

1. Create a movie using the basic commands and features available within Director.

   Caution: Avoid using commands and features that are not supported by Shockwave, as indicated in the upcoming section, "Director Authoring Issues and Constraints."

2. Test your movie as you normally would. Check all features, look for spelling and grammatical errors, and generally be sure your move is "clean" before proceeding.

3. Once the movie is complete and tested, select the Modify ⇨ Movie ⇨ Playback command and establish the streaming settings in the Movie Playback Properties dialog box (Figure 24-2).

4. Save the movie using the File ⇨ Save and Compact command.

5. If you have modified your Director movie since it was last saved or have edited a script but not recompiled it, Director displays an error message at this point. It is good practice (and saves time) to always recompile scripts and save movies just prior to saving a movie as a Shockwave movie. To recompile all scripts, use the Control ⇨ Recompile All Scripts (Shift+F8) command. Then save your movie again with File ⇨ Save and Compact.

6. Once your movie is compacted, select the File ⇨ Save As Shockwave Movie command. In the Save Shockwave Movie As dialog box (Figure 24-3), you indicate where you want the Shockwave movie saved and the filename to use. By default, a Shockwave movie uses the source movie's filename, with a new filename extension.dcr.

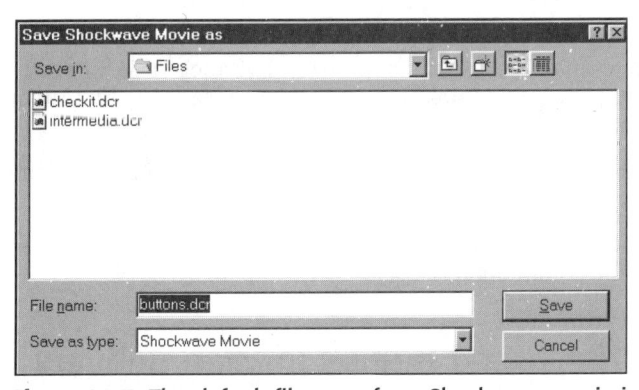

Figure 24-3: The default filename for a Shockwave movie is based on the filename of the movie being compressed.

7. Embed your Shockwave movie in an HTML document using the HTML <EMBED> and <OBJECT> tags.

   Tip: You can also find out, using Javascript as explained in Chapter 5, which type of browser is employed by the user. Then, based on the browser in use, display a Web page with the appropriate tag (<OBJECT> or <EMBED>) that best displays your Shockwave movie.

8. Place the compressed file and the HTML document that calls it on an http server that has been configured for the Shockwave MIME type.

   Your Shockwave movie is now ready to be downloaded across the Web. Each of these tasks is covered in greater detail later in this lesson.

Director Authoring Issues and Constraints

Authoring a Director movie for use on the Web is almost the same as creating multimedia for any other delivery system — with some added burden. Most Director features and Lingo commands are available for use in Web-bound movies, but there are a few exceptions.

The differences between authoring for the Web and authoring Director movies for other kinds of distribution (CD-ROM, kiosk, and so on) include the following requirements:

+ The need to minimize file size to reduce download times across the Internet
+ Avoiding Lingo commands and Director features that are *not* supported by Shockwave

  Note: Some Lingo commands are not supported in Shockwave for security reasons — that is, to prevent a Shockwave movie from maliciously destroying data or inappropriately retrieving data from the end-user's system.

+ Facing the limitations as well as the opportunities offered by using Director movies on the Web
+ Learning the new Lingo commands designed specifically for Web delivery (called *NetLingo* commands)

Beware of the speed bumps in Web delivery

Though cable modems are available, most Internet users today are accessing the Web using 14.4 and 28.8 Kbps modems. We live in an impatient era. At 14.4 Kbps, your typical modem user is receiving about a kilobyte of data per second of throughput. Depending on server performance, network traffic, and modem overhead, the rate drops even lower.

The issue is speed. Will the user who accesses your "Shocked site" tolerate long download times? The most beautiful image or the most intriguing animation must be viewed to be appreciated. If the end-user bails out before the download is complete, you have wasted your time and effort. As a gauge for your development efforts, keep in mind that theoretically it takes 25–30 seconds to download a small (30K) animation at 14.4 Kbps. If you are delivering a small movie (100–200K), the download time can run from 1.4 to almost 3 minutes or longer.

Table 24-2 lists some typical download times, but these times are based on a "best-case scenario." The amount of traffic on all systems between your server and the user's browser, as well as the type of Internet connection (modem, ISDN line, T1 line, and so on) all influence the time it takes to download a file.

Table 24-2
Approximate Times for Downloading Files Over the Internet

File Size	14.4 Kbps	28.8 Kbps	64 Kbps	1.5 mbps
30K	35 sec.	12 sec.	1 sec.	1 sec.
100K	1.4 min.	40 sec.	5 sec.	1 sec.
200K	2.8 min.	80 sec.	10 sec.	2 sec.
500K	6.9 min.	3.3 min.	25 sec.	5 sec.
1MB	13.9 min.	6.7 min.	50 sec.	10 sec.

Note: An ISDN line delivers approximately 64–128 Kbps. A T1 (high-speed access line) can deliver up to 1.5 mbps (million bytes per second).

Losing some Director features

When you author Director movies for distribution on the Web using Shockwave technology, you have access to most of Director's features. However, there are some exceptions. Shockwave was designed to distribute multimedia over a very unique environment: the Internet. Some Director features are not available because Web-based documents are downloaded one at a time, and for reasons of user security. The following limitations apply when you build Shockwave movies:

+ You cannot change the color depth of the end-user's monitor (using `the colorDepth` property).

+ You cannot include Director commands that save the movie to disk (`saveMovie`), and print the visible sprites on the Stage (`printFrom`).

+ You cannot use custom menus.

- The `open window` and `close window` Lingo commands are not available, so you cannot include movies in a window (MIAWs).

- Most system-related Director commands are disabled, including terminating or starting external applications (`Quit` and `Open`), turning off or restarting the user's computer system (`Restart` and `Shutdown`), and locating files or setting search paths for files on the end-user's system (`getNthFileNameInFolder`, `searchCurrentFolder`, and `searchPath`). These restrictions prevent anyone from creating a Shockwave movie that unexpectedly tampers with the user's system or the files stored on it.

- Director commands that control resource files (`OpenResFile` and `CloseResFile`) located outside a Director movie are disabled.

- The `pasteFromClipboard` command that can enter media from the Clipboard is disabled.

- The `MCI` command that sends specific control strings to the Windows media controller is disabled.

- Shockwave movies cannot access the Tempo channel settings such as the Wait for… options, or looping playback set by the Control Panel. (This latter restriction can be overcome by using Lingo scripts to cause a pause or loop within your movie.)

- Linked media referenced by a Shockwave movie must be available in either the Shockwave support folder or the Director Shockwave Media folder. Otherwise, the linked media cannot be accessed by the movie. This restriction is directly related to safety concerns for the end-user's system. Restricting access to the support and media folders protects users from a maliciously designed Shockwave movie that might cause serious system damage.

Note: The location of the Shockwave support folder (for linked media) varies depending on the platform and browser used. For Microsoft Internet Explorer, the Xtras, linked media, and external cast libraries are stored in the \Windows\System folder. For Netscape users, the Shockwave support folder is located in the Netscape Plug-ins folder. Beginning with version 6.01, your Shockwave movies can access local files on a hard drive using the `gotoNetMovie` and `gotoNetPage` commands. However, the linked media (such as digital video) must be stored in a folder named DswMedia or one of its subfolders. You can also link to digital video using a URL.

Limitations and opportunities of Web-delivered movies

Consider what you can do in a *regular* Director movie: You can include text, graphic images, sound, animation, and digital video. You can enable the user to interact with your movie by including editable text fields, hot spots, rollovers, and navigational buttons. All this is also true of Web-delivered movies. Each of these features can be included in your Shockwave movies. You can even include multiple movies in a single HTML document and access information from several Web sites as part of a Director movie.

The good news is that almost everything you have learned to do in Director can be used in Shockwave movies. The bad news is that, with Web movies, you're programming for a more limited environment where access time is crucial, and where you can never be sure of the capabilities of your *client's* playback system. Keep the following guidelines in mind as you design your movies targeted for Web delivery:

♦ Compressed Director movies should generally be kept to 50–200K. For the sake of your downloading public, use several small movies that call other movies, rather than using a single large Shockwave movie.

Note

Though the Open command cannot be used to call other movies, the `goToNetMovie` NetLingo command can call and display another Shockwave movie; and the `getNetText` command can display text from another Web document or file.

♦ Prior to Director 6.01, Macromedia suggested limiting Shockwave movies to about three per page, especially on the Windows platform. With version 6.01, the suggested limit was raised to around 12 movies on a single Web page, but we recommend you exercise some restraint. In addition to the RAM required to play your movie (based on its file size), an additional 50–100K of RAM is required for the Shockwave plug-in. Users with limited RAM may experience difficulties when trying to play back a page with several embedded movies. Because the Shockwave plug-in frees RAM when another page is loaded, it may be prudent to place movies on a sequence of separate Web pages rather than grouping them on a single HTML document.

♦ Always be aware that the load time for a Web document is based on all components of the page. That includes graphic images, length of the text portion of the document, and any Director movies it contains. Large graphic images coupled with Shockwave movies in a single document can greatly tax your user's patience.

♦ If you include more than one movie with audio on a single page, the browser may have problems sorting out the sound tracks. It is suggested that you only include a single movie with sound on each Web document. As an alternative, consider having sounds that are activated with a mouse click rather than automatically played as the movie starts.

♦ Beware of programming movies with continual loops. They tie up the end-user's processor and can cause other problems as well, such as slowed access to the network. Try to either program the movie to run for a predetermined number of loops, or enable the user to stop the movie with a mouse click on a button or other identifiable object.

Tip

If you choose to include a repeating loop in your Shockwave movie, at least don't loop an obnoxious sound without providing a method to turn off the sound. And remember that all sounds *become* obnoxious when repeated often enough.

Adding a Director Movie to Your Web Document

To add a Shockwave or Director movie to your Web page, you must first create a Web document using standard HTML tags. A number of excellent products exist to help you with this task, including HTML converters and editors such as Front Page 97, HotDog Pro, Pagemill, and Netscape Gold or Netscape Communicator 4. You can also create a Web document using any text editor (such as NotePad or SimpleText).

An HTML document is simply a text file that includes appropriate HTML tags. The tags surround (*mark up*) the text for special treatment (such as bold, italic, headline fonts, and so on). Other tags insert or embed graphics, audio, animation, and other media objects. An HTML document may include a few tags (primarily to format text) or may be greatly complex.

To embed a Shockwave movie in a Web document requires that you create a Web document and use the <EMBED> or <OBJECT> tags. The <EMBED> tag, introduced with the HTML 3.0 specification, is the original tag defined by Netscape Navigator for the inclusion of embedded media in a Web page. Any Netscape-compatible browser can interpret the <EMBED> tag. The tag used by Microsoft Internet Explorer to embed media objects is the <OBJECT> tag.

Rather than joining one camp or the other, you can straddle the fence and include both tags within your HTML document — enabling browsers compatible with either Internet Explorer or Netscape Navigator to view your Shockwave movie.

The two tags separately or jointly place a Shockwave movie directly on an HTML page, the same as if you placed a graphic image (such as a GIF file) on a Web page. The only difference is that the Shockwave movie can include animation, sound, and other interactivity, whereas the GIF file is static.

Note: Of course, you can use an animated GIF, which provides a flip-book approach to providing animation on your Web page. An animated GIF cannot, however, add the sound and interactivity that Shockwave movies can support.

Using the <EMBED> tag

The HTML <EMBED> tag includes several parameters, but only three are essential. You must include these three:

- Filename for the Shockwave movie
- Height of the Stage area (image)
- Width of the Stage area (image)

Following is the syntax of the tag, with these three required parameters and several optional parameters:

```
<EMBED SRC="pathname/filename.ext" WIDTH=imageWidth
HEIGHT=imageHeight PALETTE=whichGround BGCOLOR=color
PLUGINSPAGE="URL">
```

Using the SRC parameter

The SRC keyword is followed by an equal sign and then the *pathname* and *filename* to the Shockwave movie. The *filename* is the name of your shocked movie and the *pathname* indicates where the file can be found on your Web server.

Note

You can actually play a regular Director .dir movie or a protected .dxr movie from a Web document, but these types of movies are not compressed and download more slowly because of their size. To expedite downloading, you should use only movies that have been saved as Shockwave movies (DCR).

Using the HEIGHT and WIDTH parameters

The HEIGHT and WIDTH arguments in the <EMBED> tag indicate the height and width of the movie's Stage area in pixels. If the parameters you specify are smaller than the movie's Stage size, the Web browser will crop the movie to the size you specify.

Tip

If you plan to specify a smaller image area, it makes more sense to plan for a smaller Stage area when you author the movie. Don't download data that you don't intend to use.

The following is an example of an <EMBED> tag that plays a Director movie named logo.dcr. The movie is 320 x 240 pixels:

```
<EMBED SRC="http://www.shockserver.edu/movies/logo.dcr"
WIDTH=320 HEIGHT=240>
```

Using the PALETTE parameter

In addition to the required SRC, WIDTH, and HEIGHT parameters, the <EMBED> tag accepts three additional parameters: PALETTE, NAME, and PLUGINSPAGE.

The PALETTE parameter has two possible settings. If it is set to foreground, then the Shockwave movie's palette is loaded and applied to the user's system. The result is that the operating system's interface (scroll bars, desktop, and so on) as well as the Web browser's appearance all change to use the movie's color palette. In this case, the parameter appears as follows:

```
<EMBED SRC="http://www.shockedsite.edu/movies/logo.dcr"
WIDTH=320 HEIGHT=240 PALETTE=foreground>
```

> **Note:** The PALETTE=foreground setting is not supported by Microsoft Internet Explorer.

If the PALETTE parameter is set to background, the movie uses the current system palette, and the Shockwave movie's palette is prevented from loading. In this case, the parameter appears as follows:

```
<EMBED SRC="http://www.shockedsite.edu/movies/logo.dcr"
WIDTH=320 HEIGHT=240 PALETTE=background>
```

> **Caution:** If you set the embedded Shockwave movie to use the movie's palette, you may wind up shifting the colors used for the browser window and the operating system's interface to unfamiliar color combinations. If the palette you select matches the end-user's system palette, you don't need to worry. The problem, however, is that the Mac and Windows operating systems use different colors in different positions for their standard system palettes. The result is that your movie's colors can vary depending on its viewing platform.

If you use a custom palette, you should include a return to the original system palette in the final frame of the movie.

Using the NAME parameter

The NAME parameter is used for browsers that support forms and determines whether an object within a FORM block should be included in the submit process. The NAME parameter can be used by your browser or objects in your Web document to communicate with your Shockwave movie. For example:

```
<EMBED SRC="http://www.shockedsite.edu/movies/logo.dcr"
WIDTH=320 HEIGHT=240 NAME="LogoForm">
```

Using the PLUGINSPAGE parameter

The final <EMBED> parameter, PLUGINSPAGE, assists the user in locating the plug-in required to view unidentified media on the current Web page. For example, if the user is trying to view a page with a Shockwave movie, using a browser that doesn't have the Shockwave plug-in installed, then the PLUGINSPAGE parameter takes users directly to the Macromedia download site — or whatever Web address you specify in the parameter. (See the section "Some notes on Web terminology.") If the user already has the Shockwave plug-in installed, this parameter has no effect.

In your <EMBED> tag for a Shockwave movie, you should use the Web address for the Macromedia Shockwave Center, in which case the parameter appears as shown here:

```
<EMBED SRC="http://www.shockedsite.edu/movies/logo.dcr"
WIDTH=320 HEIGHT=240
PLUGINSPAGE="http://www.macromedia.com/shockwave/>
```

No Shocked files allowed

For browsers that do not support Shockwave movies, you can use the <NOEMBED> tag. This prevents the user from seeing the broken image icon:

The syntax for using the NOEMBED code is as follows:

```
<NOEMBED> <IMG SRC="pathname/filename.ext">   </NOEMBED>
```

Note Note that the NOEMBED tag requires both a start tag (<NOEMBED>) and an "off" or stop tag (</NOEMBED>). Tags that stop or turn off features in HTML are always preceded with a forward slash.

The image source (IMG SRC) parameter in the above syntax can be any HTML source, such as a GIF or JPEG image file.

In the following example, the <NOEMBED> code causes the sorry.gif file (in the movies folder on the www.shockedsite.edu Web server) to appear if the user's browser does not support or include the Shockwave plug-In. The <EMBED> tag is included in this example so you can visualize the placement of these tags in your HTML document:

```
<NOEMBED><EMBED
SRC="http://www.shockedsite.edu/movies/logo.dcr" WIDTH=320
HEIGHT=240 PLUGINSPAGE="http://www.macromedia.com/shockwave/>
</EMBED>
</NOEMBED>
<IMG SRC="http://www. shockedsite.edu/movies/sorry.gif" ALT=
Sorry, but you need the Shockwave Plug-in to fully enjoy this
site.">
</NOEMBED>
```

Note When Navigator 2.0 or later encounters a <NOEMBED></NOEMBED> pair, all HTML tags, instructions, and text between these tags are ignored. Other browsers that do not understand the <NOEMBED> tag will ignore it and execute the HTML between those tags.

Using the <OBJECT> tag

The HTML <OBJECT> tag includes several parameters, most of which you simply copy verbatim into your HTML document. Some of the parameters (such as WIDTH, HEIGHT, and NAME) are identical to the parameters used in the <EMBED> tag. The remaining parameters to discuss include CLASSID, CODEBASE, and PARAM NAME (a slightly different form for the SRC parameter used in the <EMBED> tag).

Using the CLASSID parameter

The CLASSID parameter is very specific and does not change. The identification number identifies the Shockwave ActiveX control. This parameter must be entered in the <OBJECT> tag as shown here:

```
CLASSID="clsid:166B1BCA-3F9C-11CF-8075-444553540000"
```

Using the CODEBASE parameter

The CODEBASE parameter identifies the URL where the user's browser can locate the Shockwave ActiveX control if it not already installed, or if the user has an older version of the ActiveX control installed. This parameter must be entered exactly as shown here:

```
CODEBASE="http://active.macromedia.com/director/cabs/sw.cab#ver¬
sion=6,0,0,0"
```

Note

If your Shockwave movie takes advantage of the enhancements added with Director 6.01, you should change the end of the CODEBASE parameter to match the following:

```
#version=6,0,1,0
```

This causes the browser to force a background download of the Shockwave 6.01 ActiveX control.

Using <PARAM NAME>

The <PARAM NAME> tag includes the <OBJECT> tag's equivalent of the <EMBED> tag's SRC parameter. It identifies the *pathname,* if needed, to the Shockwave movie's folder on your Web server, and the *filename* is the name of your Shocked movie. Here's an example of the <PARAM NAME> tag (which must fall inside the <OBJECT> tag):

```
<PARAM NAME="SRC"
VALUE="http://www.yourserver/movies/ShockedMovie.dcr">
```

You simply substitute the pathname to your own Shockwave movie, and the filename for the ShockedMovie.dcr. If your Shockwave movie is in the same folder on your Web server as the HTML document with the <OBJECT> tag (and this is the recommended practice), you can omit the pathname.

Putting it all together

The following example demonstrates how you can use the <OBJECT> tag and embed within it the <EMBED> tag, so that both Navigator- and Explorer-compatible browsers can view your Shockwave movie:

```
<OBJECT CLASSID="clsid:166B1BCA-3F9C-11CF-8075-444553540000"
CODEBASE="http://active.macromedia.com/director/cabs/sw.cab#ver¬
sion=6,0,1,0"
WIDTH="320"
HEIGHT="240"
<PARAM NAME="SRC" VALUE="
http://www.shockedsite.edu/movies/logo.dcr ">
<EMBED SRC="http://www.shockedsite.edu/movies/logo.dcr"
WIDTH=320 HEIGHT=240 PALETTE=foreground>
</OBJECT>
```

To modify this tag for use in your own Web document, you only need to change the WIDTH, HEIGHT, VALUE, SRC, and PALETTE parameters. If you use the system palette on the user's system, you can drop the PALETTE parameter and "fill in the blanks" on the other four parameters.

Some notes on Web terminology

Before we continue to the next exercise, in which you'll get a chance to see all this HTTP stuff in action, we need to make an important side trip into the Internet's "standards and practices." If you are new to the role of programmer or designer in the world of the Net and the Web, the following information is not so easy to locate.

To locate Web pages and other resources on the Internet, you must use a *Uniform Resource Locator (URL)*. Every URL consists of four components:

- The name of the Internet protocol (for example, `FTP`, `gopher`, or `http`). FTP is an abbreviation for *File Transfer Protocol*; *gopher* is a search engine that can be used to access resources on the Internet; and http stands for *Hypertext Transport Protocol*.

- The Internet host name (for example, `www.macromedia.com` for a Web site or `ftp.johnco.cc.ks.us` for an FTP site).

- The folder (directory) where the file is located (such as `/movies`). This is also called the pathname for the file; that is, the name of the path through folders, directories, and subdirectories to the desired file.

- The filename under which the resource is stored (such as `MyMovie.dcr`).

Each Web site includes an http server; that is, a computer that delivers World Wide Web data (pages) across the Internet. When your browser requests access to a specific URL, the http server sends back a block of data and specifies the type of data being delivered. The data type is called a *MIME* (Multi-purpose Internet Mail Extensions) type, which identifies the type of data that is returned from a server. Typical MIME types include text files (HTML), graphics files (GIF and JPEG), sound files (RA, RAM, or SWA), and Director movies (DCR, DIR, and DXR).

The MIME type for data on the Internet includes two identifiers: the content type and the content subtype. Common content types include application, audio, image, text, and video. The content subtype identifies a specific data subtype within the content type, such as a MIME type of `image/GIF` or `video/QuickTime`. The content type for a Director movie is `application`, and the content subtype is `x-director`.

To distribute Shockwave movies from your Web site, you or your system administrator must modify your http server's configuration file to recognize Shockwave movies. To do this, you or your system administrator must create an entry in the configuration file that lists the Shockwave MIME types. Usually, http servers are already set up to accept MIME types such as GIF and JPEG files. Remember, the MIME type is application, the subtype is x-director, and the acceptable extensions for this MIME type are .dcr, .dir, and .dxr.

The actual entry in your Web server's configuration file follows this form for a MacHTTP server:

```
BINARY .DCR TEXT * application/x-director
BINARY .DIR TEXT * application/x-director
BINARY .DXR TEXT * application/x-director
BINARY FGD TEXT * application/x-director
```

For an NCSA HTTPD server you should use the AddTypes directive to add new MIME types to the srm.conf file. The directives are issued as shown below:

```
AddType application/x-director dcr
AddType application/x-director dir
AddType application/x-director dxr
AddType application/x-director fgd
```

For a Netscape server, you manually edit the mime.types file in the CONFIG directory. For Shocked Director movies, you add the following line to the mime.types file:

```
type=application/x-director   exts=dir,fgd,dxr,dcr
```

After modifying the configuration file, your system administrator usually must shut down and then restart the Web server.

In addition to reading MIME types from your Web server's central configuration file (called .htaccess), your server may read MIME types from other files (also called .htaccess) that are placed in a user's home directory. This can be helpful if your Internet Service Provider (ISP) does not add the Shockwave MIME types to its server.

Note: Your system's administrator can configure your site's server to ignore .htaccess files located in end-users' home directories, or can require that the configuration file be named differently. If that is the case, establishing access using an .htaccess file in your user's folder will not work at your site.

To create an individual .htaccess file, complete these steps:

1. Make a file with the following text:
   ```
   AddType application/x-director dcr
   AddType application/x-director dir
   AddType application/x-director dxr
   AddType application/x-director fgd
   ```

2. Save the file as a text file using the filename **.htaccess.**

3. Upload the text file (typically using an FTP program) to the directory or folder on the server where your HTML files are stored. This folder is typically named public_html and resides in your personal mail folder.

4. Change the file's access to read by using the following UNIX command line:
   ```
   chmod 644 .htaccess
   ```

5. Test the success of this configuration by trying to access your Shockwave movie using your Web Browser.

The MIME type directive varies from server to server. If you are not familiar with configuring your Web server, contact the administrator for your Web site. If you are managing the Web server, be sure to check the Web server documentation under the heading "Configuring MIME types."

Some other MIME-type mappings for Macromedia applications include the following:

For Authorware	For Flash	For Freehand
application/x-authorware-map aam	application/futuresplash spl	image/x-freehand fh4
application/x-authorware-seg aas	application/x-shockwave-flash	image/x-freehand fh5
application/x-authorware-map aam		image/x-freehand fh7
application/x-authorware-bin aab		image/x-freehand fhc image/x-freehand fh

Exercise: Putting a movie in a Web page

You can create simple Shockwave movies without learning any of the special Lingo network extensions (NetLingo). By using the skills you have already acquired, you can create Director movies and then compress them for Web distribution.

Creating a Simple Shockwave Movie

On the CD-ROM

1. Open the checkit.dir movie. The file checkit.dir is on your companion CD-ROM in the exercise:ch24 (exercise\ch24) folder.

2. Examine the Cast window. It contains a yellow rectangular bitmap cast member in slot 1, followed by eight text cast members. Each text cast member (starting with slot 2) shows a bit more of the text phrase "Check It Out!"

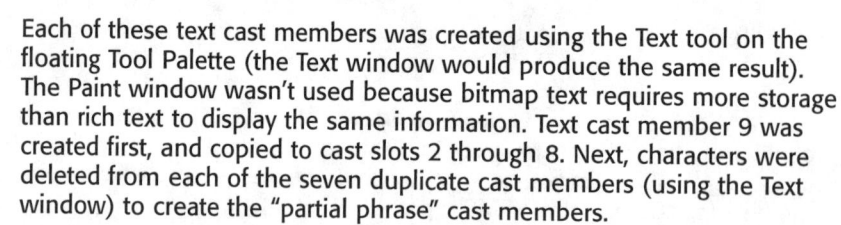

Tip

Each of these text cast members was created using the Text tool on the floating Tool Palette (the Text window would produce the same result). The Paint window wasn't used because bitmap text requires more storage than rich text to display the same information. Text cast member 9 was created first, and copied to cast slots 2 through 8. Next, characters were deleted from each of the seven duplicate cast members (using the Text window) to create the "partial phrase" cast members.

3. Be sure the Loop button on the Control Panel is disabled, and then play the movie. Observe its actions. The movie plays through once and then stops. For an animated icon on a Web page, however, you'll probably want the animation to repeat continually.

4. Double-click the script channel in frame 38 to open the Script window.

5. Type the following script in the Script window and then close the window

```
on exitFrame
     go to frame 1
end
```

6. Save and compact the movie.

7. Test the movie to be sure it loops.

8. Once the movie plays as you want, stop it and select the File ⇨ Save As Shockwave Movie command.

9. When the Save Shockwave Movie As dialog box appears (Figure 24-4), indicate the filename and the folder where you want the Shockwave movie to be saved. By default, the movie is saved in the current folder using its current filename (but with a .dcr extension). Then click the Save button.

It's that easy. You have now created a Shockwave movie from a Director movie.

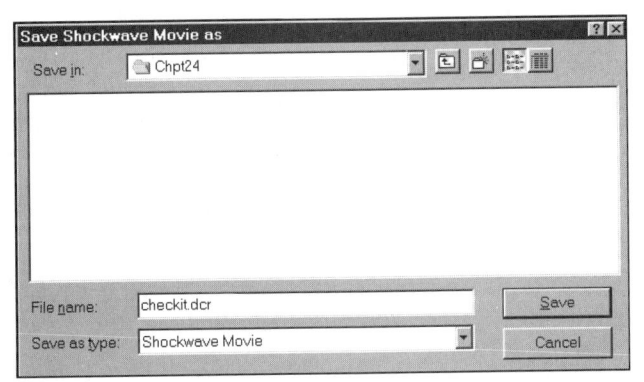

Figure 24-4: Saving checkit.dir as a Shockwave (DCR) movie

For testing purposes, you can use your Web browser off-line to view a Shockwave movie before placing it on a Web server. By previewing your Shockwave movie in this way, you can often save time by identifying problems and making corrections before you copy it to your Web server. It is not unusual for a movie to behave differently once loaded in your browser's window.

By "off-line," we mean your computer is not connected to the Internet. You do not need to be connected through a dial-up access number or through a network connection to view Shockwave movies and evaluate or test them — unless the movie links to other media on the Internet.

In the following exercise, you *do* need to have either Netscape Navigator (and the Shockwave plug-in) or Microsoft Internet Explorer (and the ActiveX control) installed on your workstation. You must also have access to the Shockwave version of the checkit movie (checkit.dcr).

On the CD-ROM

To complete the following steps, you need either the checkit.dcr Shockwave movie or the Shockwave movie you created in the preceding exercise. The file checkit.dcr is on your companion CD-ROM in the exercise:ch24 (exercise\ch24) folder.

Viewing Your Shocked Movie Off Line

1. Open Microsoft Internet Explorer or Netscape Navigator.

   When you first open your browser, it tries to dial up or connect to the Internet. Of course you can log on if you want, but it's not necessary for these steps. If you cancel the connection, the browser will either display an Alert box that says it is "unable to locate the server," or it will display the home page location that you established in your browser preferences. If you see the Alert box, click OK to ignore the message; then your browser will display a previously cached copy of your home page location.

2. Select one of the following Open commands: File➪Open (IE 4.0), File➪Open Page (Netscape 4.0), or File➪Open File in the Browser (Netscape 3.0).

   ✦ In IE 4.0, when the Open dialog box appears, click the Browse button.

   ✦ In Netscape Communicator 4.0, when the Open Page dialog box appears, click the Choose File button.

   ✦ In Netscape Navigator 3.0, when the Open dialog box appears, click the Open Location button.

3. By default, the Files of Type field in the Open dialog (Figure 24-5) is set to HTML files. You want to load and view Shocked Director movies, so click the drop-down list button for the Files of Type field, and select either

   ✦ All Files (for Internet Explorer)

   ✦ The Director (*.dir, *.dxr, *.dcr) option (for Navigator)

4. Click the drop-down list button for the Look In field and navigate to the folder where you are saving all your practice files.

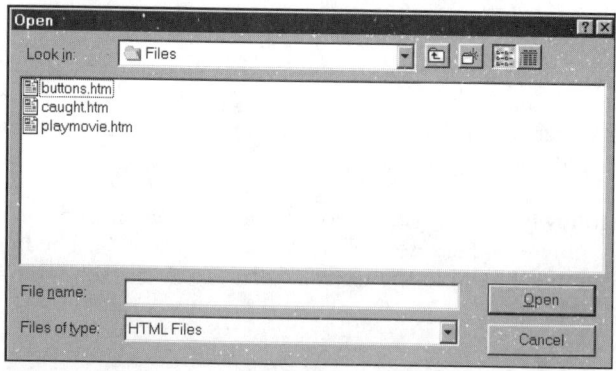

Figure 24-5: Navigator's File Open dialog

5. Locate the checkit.dcr file and double-click it. When the Open dialog box or Open Page dialog box reappears listing the pathname and filename (checkit.dcr), click the OK or Open button, and the Shockwave movie appears in the upper-left corner of your screen (Figure 24-6).

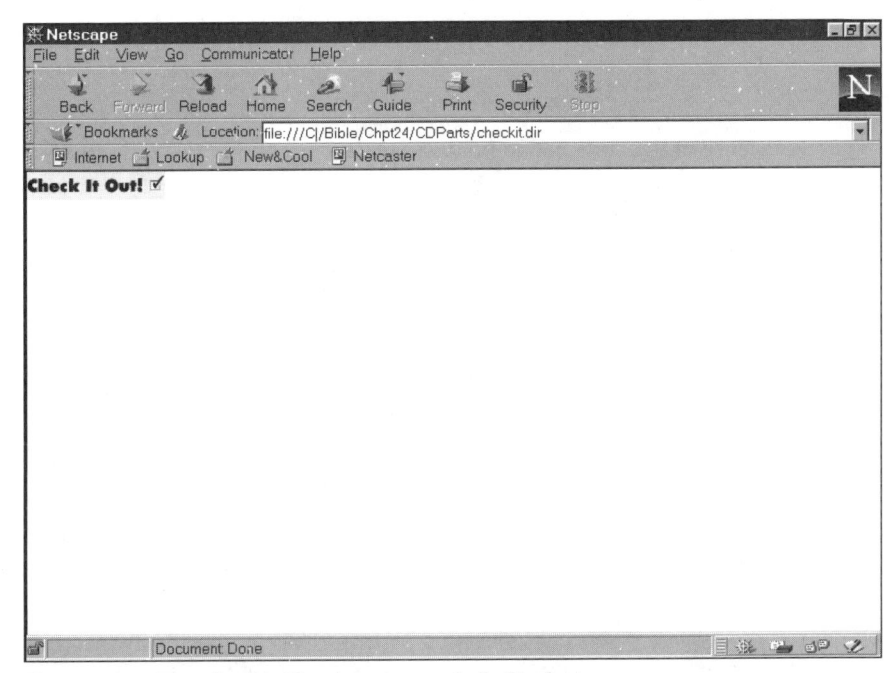

Figure 24-6: The checkit Shockwave movie in Navigator

6. To stop the movie, click the Back button to jump to the previous page viewed by your browser, or close the browser.

> **Caution**
>
> If you do not close the browser or move to another Web page, you may be locked out (by the operating system) of modifying the Shocked movie because "another application" (the browser) is accessing it. We have more work to do, so don't skip step 6.

Oh, what a tangled web we weave...

Macromedia is making a valiant effort to maintain compatibility between the different versions of Director, the Shockwave plug-ins and ActiveX controls, and the never-ending stream of new browser versions. We have experienced some idiosyncrasies while testing the November 1997 release of the Shockwave 6.01 Player and ActiveX control when it was installed in IE 3.0, IE 4.0, Netscape Navigator 3.0, and Netscape Communicator 4.0. We found that a Shockwave movie might fail to play in one browser, but that doesn't mean it won't play in another browser.

(continued)

(continued)

Following are our most significant findings:

- ✦ Because of tight integration between the browser and the Windows 95 OS, IE 4.0 does not support playing a Shockwave movie from a local drive. The Shockwave movie must be on a server to be played.

- ✦ IE 4.0 is sporadic in its ability to play embedded Shockwave movies from the Web. Sometimes the combined <OBJECT> and <EMBED> tags work, and sometimes they don't.

- ✦ Netscape Navigator 3.0 is able to play Shocked (DCR) movies from the Web or from a local drive, whether the movie is embedded in a Web document or not.

- ✦ Netscape Communicator 4.0 can play a Shocked movie created with Director 6.01, either from the Web or from a local drive. However, Shocked movies created with Director 6.0 cannot be played from a local drive.

- ✦ IE 3.0 can play a Shocked movie from a local drive if it's not embedded in a Web document. If the Shocked movie is embedded, you'll see a white Stage area but nothing more. The same problem may occur with files posted on a Web server.

- ✦ For testing your Shockwave movies, Netscape has the best track record — which is not reassuring if you want your movies to be viewed by everyone.

For the best results, always install the latest update for Director (officially 6.01 as of this writing, but a new "patch" is imminent), and install the most recent version of the plug-in or ActiveX control in your browser — and encourage your clients to do the same.

In the next exercise, you'll embed your Shockwave movie in an HTML or Web document and then view it off-line using your browser. To create and view the Web document, you need Navigator or Internet Explorer and the appropriate Shockwave application installed on your workstation. You'll also need an HTML editor (such as BackStage Designer, Front Page 97, HotDog, HoTMetaL, Netscape Gold, Pagemill, or the like) or any word or text processor that saves text as an ASCII text file.

On the CD-ROM To complete the following steps, you need the checkit.dcr Shockwave movie you've been working on in previous exercises, or the file checkit.dcr on your companion CD-ROM in the exercise:ch24 (exercise\ch24) folder. You'll also need caught.gif and caught.htm from the same folder. The arachnid pictured in the caught.gif file is from KPT Power Photos II, the Volume 8 (Bugs & Butterflies) CD. The KPT Power Photos series of clipart is published by MetaTools, 6303 Carpinteria Ave., Carpinteria, CA 93013, phone 805-566-6200.

Embedding a Shockwave Movie in an HTML Document

1. You must know the dimensions of your Shockwave movie in order to embed it in an HTML document. So in these first couple of steps, you'll determine the Stage dimensions. With the checkit.dir movie open, select Modify ⇨ Movie ⇨ Properties.

2. In the Movie Properties dialog box, look at the Width and Height fields. Figure 24-7 shows the dimensions of the checkit.dir movie; make a note of them. You'll need to use them as parameters in the <EMBED> and <OBJECT> tags. Then close the Properties dialog.

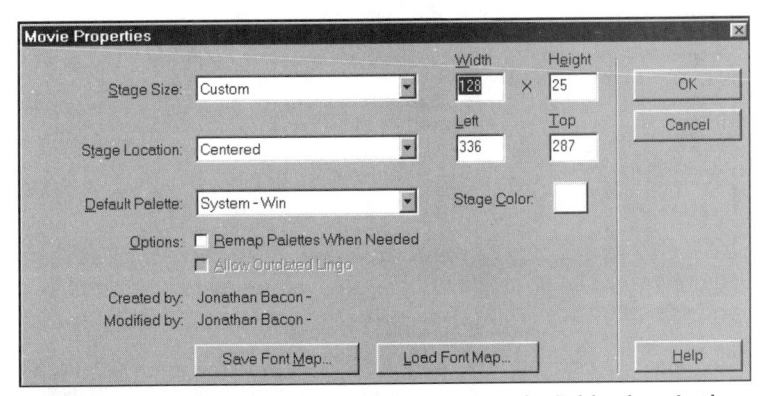

Figure 24-7: Make a note of the Width and Height field values in the checkit.dir Movie Properties dialog box.

3. Open caught.htm (on the CD-ROM in the exercise:ch24 (exercise\ch24) folder), using a text editor (SimpleText, NotePad, or whatever you like), or an HTML authoring program, or a word processor that stores files in either HTML or ASCII text format.

4. Type the following <OBJECT>/<EMBED> tag beginning on the eighth line of the file. The entry must be between the <TD> and </TD> tags. When you're done, the HTML document should appear as shown in Figure 24-8.

```
<OBJECT CLASSID="clsid:166B1BCA-3F9C-11CF-8075-444553540000"
CODEBASE="http://active.macromedia.com/director/cabs/sw.cab
#version=6,0,1,0"
WIDTH="128"
HEIGHT="25"
<PARAM NAME="SRC" VALUE="checkit.dcr">
<EMBED SRC="checkit.dcr" WIDTH=128 HEIGHT=25 PALETTE=fore¬
ground>
</OBJECT>
```

```
<HTML>
<HEAD>
<TITLE>Caught by the Web </TITLE>
</HEAD>
<BODY>
<IMG SRC="caught.gif" ALT="Caught by the Web Spider!"><P>
<TABLE COLSPEC="L20 L20">
<TR><TD><OBJECT CLASSID="clsid:166B1BCA-3F9C-11CF-8075-444553540000"
CODEBASE="http://active.macromedia.com/director/cabs/sw.cab#version=6,0,0,0"
WIDTH="128"
HEIGHT="25">
<PARAM NAME="SRC" VALUE="checkit.dcr">
<EMBED SRC="checkit.dcr" WIDTH=128 HEIGHT=25 PALETTE=foreground>
</OBJECT>
</TD>
<TD> Don't forget to check our Bug Report page.
It's full of news that will give you the creepy crawling willies.
With over one million insects for every human being on the planet,
You are in the minority! You need information before you're
"bitten by the bug." Check out our library of bugs with information
on potato bugs, ants, spiders, flies, beetles, bees, butterflies,
termites, wasps, catepillars, lady bugs, aphids, and more!</TD></TR>
</TABLE>

</BODY>
```

Figure 24-8: Text of caught.htm file after you've added the combined <OBJECT> and <EMBED> tag

5. Save the file *as a text file*, naming it **caught.htm** (don't forget the .htm extension).

   Because UNIX is case sensitive, you'll want to *create* your filenames in lowercase and always *reference* them in lowercase. Also, most Web servers recognize HTML documents by either the presence of .htm or .html as the filename extension. Because of the limitations of DOS and Windows 3.*x*, many developers consistently use just the three-character .htm extension.

6. The edited caught.htm file, plus caught.gif (a graphic banner for the page) and checkit.dcr (the Shocked movie) should all be in the same folder on your workstation. Open your browser, and select either the File ⇨ Open, File ⇨ Open File in Browser, or File ⇨ Open Page command.

   By default, the Open dialog box lists only HTML files in the Files of Type field, which is okay this time.

7. Navigate to your Personal folder (where you are saving all your practice files), locate the caught.htm file, and double-click it. The Browser window displays a Web document similar to Figure 24-9.

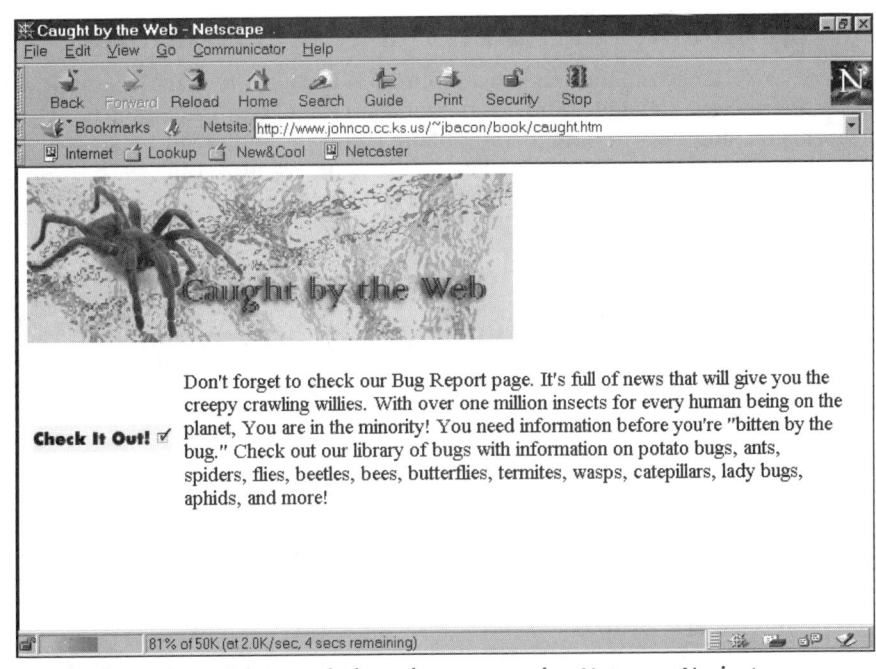

Figure 24-9: View of the caught.htm document using Netscape Navigator

Working with NetLingo

The Lingo Network Extensions are commands and functions specifically designed to extend the capabilities of Director movies to encompass network (Internet and intranet) operations. The most obvious use for NetLingo commands and functions is in Shockwave movies. However, NetLingo can also be used to create hybrid Director movies that are distributed in traditional ways (on disk and CD-ROM) but can interact with network media (URLs, Shockwave movies, network files, and so on).

NetLingo commands and functions fall into five general categories:

- ✦ Commands that start network operations
- ✦ Functions that evaluate the status of network operations
- ✦ Functions that retrieve the results of network operations
- ✦ Commands that cancel network operations
- ✦ Commands and functions that interact with the browser

Commands that start network operations

Five NetLingo commands (see Table 24-3) are used to start Internet-related operations: starting a Shockwave movie, getting text from an http server, preloading an http item, downloading a file, and jumping to a specific Web page. The *netAddress* parameter for each command identifies the path to the movie. Only the file, ftp, and http protocols are acceptable.

Table 24-3
Common NetLingo Commands

NetLingo Command	Function
`netAddress downLoadNetThing`	Downloads a file from the network to a file on the local workstation. Operates in the background; while the download occurs, the current movie continues playing. Once installed on the local user's workstation, the file can be loaded into memory without the normal delays on network traffic.
`getNetText netAddress`	Retrieves a file that is read by Lingo as text.
`goToNetMovie netAddress`	Downloads and runs a Shockwave movie from the network. The new movie occupies the same Stage area as the current movie.
`goToNetPage netAddress`	Opens a URL on the network. Equivalent to including an `<a href=http://netAddress> </a>` tag in an HTML document. It can display a Shockwave movie, an HTML document, or any other MIME type supported by the browser. The URL must be listed within quotation marks.
`preloadNetThing (netAddress)`	Preloads a file into the browser's local disk cache so the resource can run later without the normal download delay. Operates in the background; while the preload occurs, the current movie continues playing.

Going to a Net movie

When you use the `goToNetMovie` command, the current movie continues to run until the new movie is available — at which time the current movie is terminated without warning.

Caution: After issuing the command, be sure to keep the playback head moving. Your movie must be playing in order to make the file transfer.

In the following examples, the `goToNetMovie` command appears within an `on mouseUp` handler that is attached to a button. The first example includes a fully qualified URL that designates the path to the shocked movie. In the second example, the movie is located in the same folder as the calling Web page, so only the movie's filename is required.

```
on mouseUp
      goToNetMovie¬
"http://www.shockedsite.edu/movies/movie1.dcr"
end

on mouseUp
      goToNetMovie "movie1.dcr"
end
```

You can also use a marker or label in the *netAddress* parameter as shown in the following example. The marker or label is defined within the target HTML document using the `<a name="labelName"></a>` tag.

```
on mouseUp
      goToNetMovie http://www.¬
shockedsite.edu/movies/buttons.dcr#Contents
end
```

Going to a Net page

When you use the `goToNetPage` command, the current movie continues to run until the new page is available — at which time the current movie is terminated without warning.

In the following two examples, the `goToNetPage` command appears within an `on mouseUp` handler that is attached to a button. The first example includes a fully qualified URL that designates the path to a Web page. When the user clicks the button, the browser immediately jumps to the specified URL.

```
on mouseUp
      goToNetPage¬
"http://www.shockedsite.edu/~MyDocs/newText.html"
end
```

In the second example, the Web page is located in the same folder (on the server) as the calling Shockwave movie page, so only the HTML document's filename is required.

```
on mouseUp
      goToNetPage "newText.html"
end
```

The `goToNetPage` command also has an optional *target* parameter, as shown in the following example:

```
On mouseUp
        goToNetPage "targetPage.html", "topFrame"
end
```

The *target* parameter ("topFrame" in the above example) can be the frame or window name in which you want the page loaded. If the target frame or window does not exist, it is created and filled with the document specified.

Caution: Frame and window names are case sensitive.

The preload "thing"

Preloading a target URL enables your movie to read the item from the disk cache, which can make the movie far more responsive to the user and eliminate a potentially long download time. The `preLoadNetThing()` command can be used to preload a movie in the background while another movie continues to play. Used effectively, the command can greatly reduce normal network latency.

Tip: The `NetDone` command, discussed in the next section, is used to determine if the preload is complete. Be sure to include a short delay *after* issuing the `preLoadNetThing()` command and *before* issuing `NetDone` command to give the preload a chance to start.

The `preLoadNetThing()` command only loads one http item at a time. To preload a page that has several elements (graphics, movies, and so on), you must issue the `preLoadNetThing()` command once for each element to be downloaded. Embedded objects, such as Director movies and GIF images on the target Web page, are not automatically downloaded when the `preLoadNetThing()` command is issued to display the Web page.

In theory, a preloaded item can be seen by the user immediately, since it is already loaded from the Internet and can be accessed from a local disk cache. The catch is that you cannot determine if the local disk cache has been purged between the preload and the playback.

Note: Whether a preloaded item is available in the browser's disk cache is dependent on two factors: the browser's cache setting (the more kilobytes dedicated to the cache, the better chance that the item will persist in cache) and the user's activity.

Functions that evaluate the status of network operations

Network operations can include accessing a file, a Shockwave movie, or a URL on the Internet or an intranet. The functions, listed in Table 24-4, assist you in evaluating the progress made toward the completion of a network (asynchronous) operation. (Asynchronous operations return immediately — they do not block other processing from continuing.)

Table 24-4
NetLingo Functions That Report on Network Operations

NetLingo Function	Results
`NetDone()`	Determines if a network operation (started by `downLoadNetThing`, `getNetText`, `goToNetMovie`, `goToNetPage` or `preLoadNetThing`) has completed. Returns True (the default) if a network operation has successfully completed or if the operation was terminated by browser error. Returns False if the operation is incomplete.
`NetError()`	Returns a null or empty string until the specified network operation is complete. Upon completion, `NetError` returns an "OK" string if the operation was successful. If the operation is unsuccessful, the function returns an error number.

In the following handler, when the download is complete — that is, `netDone() = True` — the `netError()` function checks for an error (not "OK"). If an error occurs, an Alert box appears listing the error:

```
If netDone() = True then
     if netError() <> "OK"
         alert "Network Error:" && netError()
     end if
end if
```

Functions that retrieve the results of network operations

The three functions listed in Table 24-5 return results only after an asynchronous operation has completed. In each case, the function is available only *after* `netDone` or `netError` reports a complete operation and *prior* to the start of the next operation. In order to conserve memory, the Shockwave plug-in discards the results once the next asynchronous operation begins.

A Shockwave movie can include more than one active operation at one time. Under earlier versions of Shockwave, NetLingo uses the `getLatestNetID` function to return a unique ID for the last asynchronous operation begun. Because Net operations now return Net IDs, the `getLatestNetID` function is no longer needed.

Table 24-5
NetLingo Functions That Return Results of Network Operations

NetLingo Function	Results
netTextResult()	Returns the text result of the last network operation. If you use the getNetText command, netTextResult() returns the text of the http item accessed.
netMIME()	Returns the MIME type of the specified http item.
netLastModDate()	Returns a text string that indicates the last date a downloaded item (using the getNetText or preLoadNetThing command) was modified, based on the item's http header.

Canceling a partially complete network operation

NetLingo includes a command that can cancel a network operation that is in progress without waiting for completion or a result. To identify the operation to cancel, the NetAbort command can use the net ID for the operation or can reference the target URL of the operation. Using the net ID is always preferable. In the following handler, a Shockwave movie is preloaded, and the net ID for the operation is set to currentNetID:

```
On startMovie

preloadNetThing("http://www.myHomePlace/~jbacon/seaIsland.dcr")
     set currentNetID =¬
preloadNetThing("http://www.myHomePlace/~jbacon/seaIsland.dcr")
end startMovie
```

Because the operation's net ID has been set to currentNetID, you can attach the following handler to a button that, when clicked, will cancel the network operation:

```
On mouseUp
     netAbort(currentNetID)
end
```

The other form of the netAbort command would use a URL like the following:

```
netAbort("http://www.myHomePlace/~jbacon/seaIsland.dcr")
```

Commands and functions that interact with the browser

The latest version of Shockwave provides two commands and one function that interact with the end-user's Web browser. These items are listed in Table 24-6.

Table 24-6
NetLingo Commands and Functions That Interact with Browsers

Syntax	Function or Command	Function
`NetStatus message`	Command	Displays a message in the status bar area of the user's Web browser.
`setPref fileName, textString`	Command	Writes a text string (*textString*) to a file (*fileName*) on the user's local hard drive. This command can only write the file to a Prefs folder (which it creates) within the user's Plug-In Support folder. The *fileName* must be a valid filename, so avoid using more than eight alphanumeric characters. Though Macintosh and Windows 95 users can use longer filenames that include spaces and special characters, Windows 3.*x* users cannot. You should constrain filenames to the most limited environment of potential users.
`GetPref (fileName)`	Function	Returns the contents of the specified file (*fileName*) in the Prefs folder within the user's Plug-In Support folder. If the file does not exist or is empty, `getPref` returns a value of Void. The *fileName* parameter must be a valid filename on the user's operating system. (See cautions just above for the `setPref` command.)

Cluttering up the status bar

The netStatus command does not work with all browsers, but when it's available, it can be used to provide prompts to the user. In the following example, the status bar displays the message "Please click on a button." The message is displayed, in this case, as soon as the Shockwave movie loads and begins playing.

```
On startMovie
     netStatus "Please click on a button."
end
```

The netStatus command does not work with the Shockwave ActiveX control for Microsoft Internet Explorer 3.0.

Shockwave cookies, anyone?

The setPref command enables you to leave a tell-tale file (called a *cookie*) on the user's system. A cookie simply writes a small file on your local hard drive when you visit a Web site. The cookie can be retrieved by the Web server the next time you visit the site — to verify that you've been there before. Using the following handler, the setPref command leaves a file named Visited on the user's local drive. The file includes a text string based on today's date (using the long date function).

```
On startMovie
     set todaysDate to the long date
     setPref "Visited", todaysDate
end
```

In the handler, notice that the filename ("Visited") must be within double quotes. The Visited file is a text file, and it will be placed within the Prefs folder that is created by the setPref command within the browser's plug-in folder.

I want my Shockwave cookies back!

In the following handler, the text string stored in the Visited file is retrieved (returned by the getPref function) and stored in the variable lastVisit:

```
On startMovie
     set lastVisit to getPref("Visited")
end
```

If the file Visited does not exist, the getPref function returns a value of Void.

In the next exercise, you'll work with a partial Director movie, buttons.dir. You'll add scripts to the buttons (to jump to different Web addresses), attach a script that leaves behind a small cookie (a file with data), and then Shock the movie. You will also use a prebuilt HTML document called buttons.htm.

On the CD-ROM The files buttons.dir and button.htm are both on your companion CD-ROM in the exercise:ch24 (exercise\ch24) folder.

In its current form, the buttons.dir movie includes three buttons labeled 1, 2, and 3. The cast member names for these buttons are already set to Macromedia, Netscape, and Microsoft, respectively. Each button is already set to highlight when clicked, based on properties in the Bitmap Cast Member Properties dialog box.

Cast member 4 is a field cast member with a single space character (the font is set to 12-point Arial). You will add two new scripts in cast member slots 5 and 6. In slot 5, the script displays (to the right of the buttons) an identifying label as the mouse pointer rolls over each button. If the mouse pointer is not over a button, the label displayed is a single space character. In cast member slot 6, you use the `netStatus` command to display a message on the user's status bar and to save a file ("Visited") in the user's Prefs folder. This information can be retrieved later using the `getPrefs` function.

Finally, you'll attach a cast member script to each of the three buttons. The script uses the `goToNetPage` command to jump to a specific URL, for Macromedia, Netscape, and Microsoft, respectively. You can modify these URLs to jump to any Net address.

Incidentally, you don't create a streaming movie in this exercise because the movie is so small, there is no advantage to it.

Jumping to Another Net Address and Leaving Something Behind

On the CD-ROM

1. Open the buttons.dir movie from the exercise:ch24 (exercise\ch24) folder on the CD-ROM.

2. Select cast member slot 5, open the Script window, and enter the following script:

```
on exitFrame
     case rollover() of
          1: set the text of field 4 to¬
          "Visit"&return&"Macromedia"
          2: set the text of field 4 to¬
          "Visit"&return&"Netscape"
          3: set the text of field 4 to¬
          "Visit"&return&"Microsoft"
          otherwise set the text of field 4 to " "
     end case
     go to the frame
end
```

3. Click the New Script button and add the following script in cast member slot 6:

   ```
   on startMovie
       set todaysDate to the long date
       setPref "Visited", todaysDate
       netStatus "Click one of the three buttons, please."
   end
   ```

4. Close the Script window.

5. Go to cast member 1 (Macromedia) and attach the following cast member script:

   ```
   on mouseUp
       gotoNetPage "http://www.macromedia.com"
   end
   ```

6. Go to cast member 2 (Netscape) and attach the following cast member script:

   ```
   on mouseUp
       gotoNetPage "http://www.Netscape.com"
   end
   ```

7. Go to cast member 3 (Microsoft) and attach the following cast member script:

   ```
   on mouseUp
       gotoNetPage "http://www.microsoft.com"
   end
   ```

8. Save the movie as buttons.dir using the File ⇨ Save and Compact command.

9. Save the movie as a Shockwave movie using the File ⇨ Save As Shockwave Movie command. Use the default filename of buttons.dcr.

10. Be sure that the buttons.dcr and buttons.htm files are both together in a personal folder on your local hard drive. You can place these on your Web server if you wish, but it's not necessary to test the Shockwave movie.

11. Open your browser and connect to the Internet.

12. Use the File ⇨ Open or File ⇨ Open Page or File ⇨ Open File in Browser command, locate the button.htm document on your hard drive, and open it.

    It may take a few seconds, but the HTML document opens and displays the Shockwave movie (the button controls) as shown in Figure 24-10.

13. Move the mouse pointer over the three buttons; for each one, a text label appears as shown in Figure 24-10.

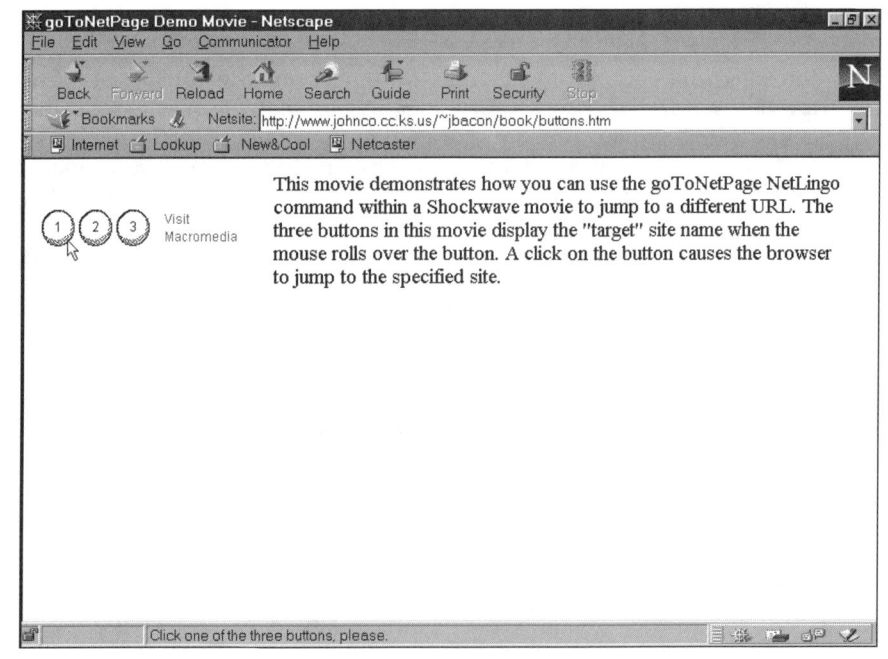

Figure 24-10: The buttons.htm Web document displays the button controls that are created using a Shockwave movie.

14. Click one of the buttons, and your browser will jump to the designated Web page.

15. Exit the browser. Go to the plugins:NP-PPC-Dir-Shockwave Folder:prefs (plugins\np32dsw\prefs) folder, locate the Visited file, and open it using SimpleText or NotePad (or another editor). It should include the long version of today's date.

Placing Your Movies on a Web Server

Shocked Director movies are not accessible to associated Web browsers until the movies (and any related HTML documents and files) are placed on your local Web server. An overview of the process includes these steps:

1. Start up your favorite FTP program (such as WS_FTP or Fetch).
2. Send the Director movie files, HTML files, and any related graphics files to your Web server.
3. From the UNIX prompt, set the file access rights.

Where to place your files

Knowing where to place your Director movies and the associated HTML documents is half the battle of successfully publishing on the Web. The most common practice is to create a public_html directory under your home directory (check with your system administrator or Webmeister for exact folder or directory names). For instance, on Jonathan Bacon's local server, his home directory is called /jbacon. He has control over what goes in that folder and who can view it. When he logs on to the local server, the current directory is typically his home directory: /jbacon.

With that background, here is the process required to create a new directory for your own Web pages.

Note: You only need to complete the following steps once to create the target directory. Once it exists, you do not need to re-create it.

1. Log on to your Web server and get to the UNIX prompt. On your server, the prompt will look like the following, with your own log-on name appearing in place of *username*:

    ```
    /u/username $
    ```

2. Create the public_html directory under your home directory using the following command:

    ```
    mkdir public_html
    ```

    To give other Web surfers visiting your site the ability to read your Web documents, you must set access rights to accommodate the "world."

3. Issue the following `chmod` command to make the target directory (public_html) read-accessible to other readers:

    ```
    chmod 755 public_html
    ```

Copying files to your Web server

Now you can copy files into your public_html directory, as the next step toward publishing your Shockwave movies (and other HTML documents) on the Web!

Tip: Web documents stored in

```
/username/public_html
```

can be accessed on the Web by using the

```
/~username
```

alias. The tilde is shorthand for the public_html directory located under the user's home directory. For instance, Jonathan Bacon has a /jbacon/public_html folder on a Web server. That folder can be accessed by using the ~jbacon alias.

You must complete the following steps each time you modify either a Web document (including the one with your movie embedded in it) or each time you modify your Director movie:

1. Launch your favorite FTP program (such as WS_FTP or Fetch).

2. Be sure that all the files associated with your Web pages are in the same directory.

3. Your FTP program should include selections (usually a series of radio buttons) for indicating whether files are sent in ASCII (text) or binary format. HTML documents (which are really text files) may be sent using the ASCII (text) setting. All other associated documents (movies, GIF, and JPEG files) must be sent as binary(or raw data on the Mac). So in theory, you can set the option to binary and send all files that way, as we do when we use WS_FTP.

Caution

If using Fetch on a Macintosh, use the Automatic setting. Using the binary setting actually is less reliable. Further, you need to use Fetch's Customize ⇨ Preferences command and select the Upload tab to set the Default Non-Text Format setting to RawData. Otherwise, your Web documents may appear to upload successfully, but they cannot be accessed via the Web.

4. Use your FTP program to set the source directory (the directory *to which* you are copying the documents and movies *from* your local drive) and the target directory (the public_html directory on the Web server).

Caution

Be careful: Do not copy the files to your home folder. For instance, copying to Jonathan's home folder would mean placing the files in \jbacon rather than in \jbacon\public_html. You must place all the files in your public_html folder. Your home folder is used to store your Internet e-mail, and you don't want to inadvertently set permissions on that folder that allow anyone to read your mail.

5. Once you have set the file transfer type to binary (or automatic if using Fetch) and indicated the source and target directories, click the Put File or Publish button, or choose the command to send the files to the server.

Changing access rights to the Web documents

After you have copied the movie and any associated files, you must change the file access rights so other people can read (view) your Web documents:

1. Log on to your Web server.

2. With the UNIX prompt visible, change to the public_html directory using the cd (change directory) command, like this:

   cd public_html

3. Use the following UNIX command to alter the access rights for all the files in the public_html directory:

   chmod 644 *

4. Close your FTP program, open your Web browser, and visit your pages to be sure you can read and view your Web documents. If you cannot access the pages, no one else can either!

Tip Once you place a file on the server and set the permissions for that file, you should not need to reset the permissions again — even if you overwrite the file with a new version later. Once permissions are assigned to a specific filename, they remain in effect unless you delete the file or remove the permissions.

Creating the Ideal Shockwave Movie

Creating a small, efficiently designed movie is always an important goal. When the aim is to distribute a movie over the Web, squeezing the maximum impact out of the smallest byte-size movie is even more important. The following guidelines can help you achieve this goal:

✦ Try to keep the size of all cast members as small as possible — which in turn minimizes the movie's size. You can use the Cast Info button on the Cast window to check the size of each cast member.

Tip To see the combined size of several cast members, Shift+click to select them and then select the Cast Info button. You'll get the "combined" Cast Member Properties dialog shown in Figure 24-12. This technique can be helpful when you are trying to break a single movie into multiple movies for faster Web distribution. It can also be used to help you locate the "fat" in the current movie, and which cast members might be modified to reduce the overall file size.

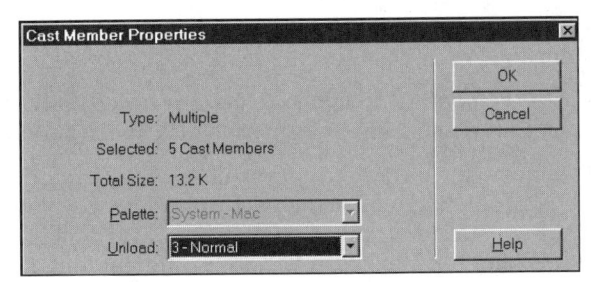

Figure 24-11: The Cast Member Properties dialog box

- Import or create small images, and then resize them on the Stage to make them appear larger. There will be degradation in your image — but, depending on how you use the graphic, the loss of quality may be acceptable. Keep in mind that if you use a bitmap cast member more than once in a Director movie, it is best to import it once at its largest size and then reduce it. This method lets you maintain the image's quality.

> **Tip**
>
> Integer scaling requires fewer, faster calculations than custom scaling. What that means is that you want to use the Sprite Info dialog box to scale an object on the Stage rather than clicking and dragging the sprite's bounding handles on the Stage.

- When you import images, choose the Remap option rather than the Dither option. Flat colors take less memory to display, and those objects will perform (animate or redraw) faster than dithered images.

- Keep the number of colors in your image as low as possible while still maintaining the image quality you desire. The number of colors used in an image is more important than color depth when compressing a movie. Don't transform images to less than 8-bit images — the size savings is in restricting the number of colors, not the bit depth.

- Another method of controlling your Director movie's size is to build backgrounds for the Stage using small images that you can tile. Tiles can be square or rectangular. The best size tile for creating backgrounds is 16 x 32 pixels, or 32 pixels square. Tiles (discussed in Chapters 2 and 4) enable you to create large areas of custom texture at a very small cost in memory by using and repeating a single small cast member.

- Remember that objects created by the floating Tool Palette are represented by their mathematical description. Bitmap images must be stored pixel by pixel. Whenever possible, use vector objects (buttons, geometric shapes, text, and tiles) that are created by the floating Tool Palette, rather than bitmap images that are created in the Paint window. Vector objects use very little memory or hard disk space as compared to bitmap images.

- ✦ To change the color of individual cast members, use the Color Palette in the Tools window rather than creating new palettes as cast members.

- ✦ Use text created with the floating Tool Palette (vector-based) rather than bitmap text (created in the Paint window) to save disk space and memory.

Tip: When developing a movie for Web distribution, choose a standard font for text created using the Tool Palette. For the user to see the font you specify, the same font must be installed on the user's system. If the font is not available, Windows 95 and the MacOS substitute a different font. Both operating systems try to match the font, but the results may be less than desirable. To play it safe, use the standard TrueType or Adobe fonts such as Arial, Courier New, Symbol, Times, Times New Roman, and Wingdings.

- ✦ If you want your movie to play well on the Web, test it at least on the two most common platforms: Windows 95 and Macintosh. Potentially, your Web pages will be viewed by users on the Macintosh and the Windows platform (not to mention UNIX, Windows 3.1, Windows NT, and others).

- ✦ Sound can dramatically increase the size of a movie, but it also adds impact and flavor to a project. Sound is often necessary to convey either content or mood. It is not unusual to allocate up to 20% of a movie's total bytes for sound. Try to use the lowest sampling rate possible while still maintaining the quality of the sound. For speech, the lowest recommended sampling rate is 11.025KHz. For quality music playback, you will probably need to use the 22.050KHz sampling rate.

- ✦ Consider using linked Shockwave Audio files rather then embedding large sound files in your Shockwave movie. SWA can stream across the network and begin playing as soon as a sufficient portion of the file has arrived at the user's workstation.

- ✦ When you need a long, background sound track, trying looping a shorter sound. You can check the byte size of a sound loop using the Cast window Info dialog box.

Tip: Repeated sounds, such as you find in a sound loop, can become annoying. If you use a sound loop, have it fade out or stop after playing a few times.

- ✦ Never make a visitor to your Web pages wait for a download without some indication that something is happening. Use screen text or a small Shockwave movie to alert the user that a movie is being downloaded. A small Shockwave movie with looping animation (using the `GoToNetMovie` command) is often a nice *cover* for the background download of a larger movie. In fact, the "pre-movie" can be as simple as a single `on startMovie` handler that sets the color of the Stage and then preloads or loads the second movie.

Tip: Remember that time is relative. Folks who are accessing your movie are probably more willing to wait for a game or the presentation of important information than for a banner or fancy bullet.

- Use `preLoadNetThing()` whenever possible to bring the next media object into disk cache. When properly timed, background preloading can greatly enhance the responsiveness of your application.

- Test your Shockwave movies initially from a single folder on your desktop before uploading them to your Web server. Open your pages from within your browser to be sure that all relative URLs work as desired. Make the necessary changes while the files are still local. If you're not careful about testing on your local drive, you can waste a lot of time transferring files that must then be fixed and transferred again. If your NetLingo doesn't work on the local drive, it probably won't work on the server.

- Unless you want the movie's sound track to go on forever (or until the user shuts down the browser) be sure to stop all sounds in the `on stopMovie` handler. The same caution applies when using `goToNetMovie` to jump to a second Shockwave movie. Be sure to shut down the sound.

- If using `preLoadNetThing()` and `goToNetMovie` cause the movie to be loaded twice, try calling the movie in the `goToNetMovie` instruction using just the filename, without the path.

Summary

Here are some of the things you learned in this chapter:

- Shockwave technology is composed of two distinct elements: the compression engine and the Shockwave plug-in and ActiveX control.

- Almost all Director features and commands can be incorporated into a Shockwave movie.

- To create a single Shockwave movie, use the File ⇨ Save As Shockwave Movie command. To convert more than one movie to Shockwave, use the Xtras ⇨ Update Movies command.

- Size is the most important constraint when creating a Shockwave movie. Because large movies take longer to download over the Internet or over an intranet, keeping files small is a major factor in creating responsive, efficient movies.

- Due to security concerns and the unique nature of network operations, some Director features are not available in Shockwave movies. For instance, access to the `saveMovie`, `printFrom`, `quit`, `restart`, `open`, `shutdown`, `pasteFromClipboard`, `open window` and `close window` commands is prohibited.

- A combination of the <OBJECT> and <EMBED> HTML tags can be used to place a Shockwave movie on a Web document that is accessible by users of either Netscape Navigator or Microsoft Internet Explorer.

✦ Before you can serve a Shockwave movie from your http Web server, the server's configuration file must be modified to recognize the Shockwave MIME type.

✦ You can view your Shockwave movies off-line by using Netscape's File ➪ Open Page command or Internet Explorer's File ➪ Open command.

✦ NetLingo commands are available to download (`downLoadNetThing`) or preload (`preLoadNetThing`) Shockwave movies or other network files, to retrieve text (`getNetText`) from a network file, and to play a Shockwave movie (`goToNetMovie`) or jump to a network address (`goToNetPage`).

✦ NetLingo includes two functions, `NetDone()` and `NetError()`, that determine the status of a network operation.

✦ The NetLingo `NetAbort` command interrupts a partially complete network operation.

✦ Three NetLingo functions are available to return the results of a network operation. The most commonly used NetLingo function is `netTextResult` which returns the result of a `getNetText` operation.

✦ The final three NetLingo commands communicate with the browser. The `netStatus` command displays text on the status line, while the `setPref` command and the `getPref` function write and retrieve information, respectively, to a file on the user's local drive.

✦ ✦ ✦

CHAPTER 25

Into the Third Dimension

In This Chapter

Making 3D come alive in 2D

Understanding 3D technologies

Using QuickDraw 3D sprites

Creating virtual reality

As graphics cards and 3D accelerator cards have improved in capabilities, they've launched a revolution in the way that multimedia products are developed. Fully rendered rooms, buildings, and even worlds serve as backdrops to three-dimensional characters moving around one another on the screen. While at its heart Director is built in two dimensions, a number of techniques can be used to simulate three dimensions within a Director program. In addition to that, with the aid of third-party Xtras, Director can also incorporate 3D sprites, scrollable virtual reality, and even completely embedded VRML worlds that can be controlled from Lingo.

Making 3D Come Alive in 2D

Computer programs started out flat. The screen was white, with buttons indicated by rounded rectangles, text within rectangles, scroll bars with black and white arrows, and a white box used for controlling the position of text, sitting within a rectangular border filled with alternating black and white pixels. For years this was *the* look in computer programming circles.

However, as color became available, odd things began to happen. Graphic designers began to integrate buttons that had beveled edges, and with one side lighter than the other as if to give the illusion that the button was lit from the top left. This simple device elicited changes elsewhere — text boxes were drawn embedded, scroll bars that had been flat now had a limited sense of depth. And the crowd went wild.

Why did something as simple as adding a lighter line and a darker line evoke such a strong reaction among users? The answer has to do with the way that we perceive computer interfaces. When everything was monochromatic, the viewer had to mentally assign a function to a given iconic form — a rounded rectangle represented a button, a square within a long rectangle represented a scroll bar, and so forth. This view meant that at some level, the mind was working overtime to translate these fairly abstract concepts into meaningful devices.

When even the most basic sense of depth was added, however, things suddenly became obvious. A surface with a surrounding indented bevel looks like it can be pressed — the mind fills in the mechanism without conscious thought. Depth perception is a critical part of the way that we handle the world, so by simulating three dimensions the interface designer converts a *schematic* view of the interface into a *tactile* one — even if the button being pressed is a mouse button rather than the "physical" button displayed on the screen.

Boxing at shadows

Shadows play an important part in our depth perception, and this particular fact forms the cornerstone of much of contemporary interface design. A button with a light and dark bevel will appear to have more depth than one without, and as a consequence will more readily make you want to press it. When the button is depressed, the bevel switches place — the lighter portions become dark, the dark portions light, and the button appears to recess into the screen. This simple illusion can be remarkably powerful, and it tends to reinforce the "reality" of the rest of the screen.

Drop shadows similarly can be used to add depth to your movies, though they should be applied judiciously. Director provides a simple drop shadow for rectangular text boxes with the `DropShadow of member` and the `BoxDropShadow of member` properties. Details on these properties are available in Chapter 14. However, these drop shadows have hard edges that don't accurately mimic the way shadows form in nature, and they appear extraordinarily harsh. Furthermore, there are no native drop-shadow controls for graphics. Because of this, you have to create your own.

The best way to make a drop shadow is to build one in a graphics program that supports layers, such as Adobe Photoshop, MetaCreations's Painter, or Macromedia xRes. While you can build drop shadows in Director, doing so takes a lot more work.

Making a Drop Shadow in Photoshop

1. Load, as a file, a copy of the background over which the graphic will float.
2. Load the graphic as a separate file.
3. Trace the perimeter of the graphic using the Lasso tool (or use the Magic Wand tool) to select just the graphic.
4. Copy it to the Clipboard. Select the background graphic.
5. Create a new layer and paste the graphic onto the layer.
6. Before deselecting the selection, save it as a channel.
7. Select the background layer and create another new layer that lays between the graphic and the background.
8. Load the selection you just created.
9. Feather the selection by three to ten pixels, depending upon the size of the graphic. The more you feather, the more diffuse the shadow becomes.
10. Fill the selection with black — this gives you a dark "halo" around the graphic.
11. Use the arrow keys to move the selection down and to the right by three or four pixels each.
12. Deselect the layer and then merge all three layers (see Figure 25-1).

Figure 25-1: Creating a faux 3D effect is fairly simple in Photoshop.

13. Save the portion of the newly created image that contains the graphic and the background.

Help with drop shadows: Alien Skin Software (http://www.alienskin.com/) has a cool collection of Photoshop filters. This collection, called Eye Candy, includes a drop-shadow filter that greatly simplifies the task of creating a drop shadow. Ulead Systems, Inc. (http://www.ulead.com/) provides a drop-shadow filter among several Web tools in its WebRazor for Photoshop offering.

Drop shadows should be used sparingly. Part of the reason for this (besides the novelty factor) is that an image that floats appears pressable, which may cause a momentary confusion to the people who use your software if the drop shadow graphic is just an ornament.

Using alpha channels

One of the primary problems with using this approach to drop shadows is that it forces the sprite in question to be located in exactly one place on the screen. This works fine for buttons, but sliders or free-floating elements ruin the illusion unless the background is completely without texture.

In 1996 the company Media Lab released AlphaMania, a sprite Xtra that lets you use the alpha channel of a graphic. To understand what this means, you need to reexamine the model used for displaying graphics in the first place. In 24-bit color mode, each of the three primary colors (red, green, and blue) has a channel that can hold a value from 0 to 255. Certain graphic formats (including TIF and Photoshop 3.0 or above) actually contain a fourth channel. This channel can likewise take a value from 0 to 255, and programs that are aware of that channel frequently use it to determine the level of transparency of a graphic with respect to the background, with 0 being completely transparent and 255 completely opaque. This is called the *alpha channel*, a term borrowed from the video industry to describe a transparency mask used to do video overlays.

Using a program like Photoshop, you can create a partially transparent graphic by painting on layers above the background layer, and then hiding the background layer before saving the image. Sprites that incorporate this form of drop shadow will appear to have a floating shadow. Similarly, you can create a halo effect by using a bright color with a partially transparent alpha channel. A demonstration version of the AlphaMania Xtra is located on the Macromedia Director 6.0 CD-ROM.

Prerendered worlds

Creating buttons, levers, and other interface elements with depth pushes the interface out of the flatness of the screen, but this design-oriented approach to 3D works best when you have a "control panel" type display. For a while, there was a craze for creating three-dimensional worlds as interfaces — an approach that works well for games, but that is not as effective when you're dealing with GUIs. Still, this approach has a great deal of merit and should be seriously examined if you want to give a "walking tour" of frequently abstract concepts or if you're targeting gamers.

With a prerendered approach, you build the world you want ahead of time using one of several rendering software packages available on the market today. Then you use each scene of the world as a background for prerendered characters and props that interact on the Stage. With all the other tools that are available, this is still the preferred method for creating 3D worlds for adventure games for a wide variety of reasons:

- The background can be highly detailed and rendered with a large number of textures. Most dynamic 3D rendering programs sacrifice level of detail for rendering speed.
- It's much easier to incorporate sprites into such a model — doors opening or monsters moving about can be controlled readily from within the scripting language.
- The game looks the same regardless of how high-powered (or low-powered) the host machine is.
- It becomes easier to incorporate text and "flat" interface elements into this kind of environment. As Xtras, Java applets, and ActiveX components become more readily integrated into Director, prerendering will become an important consideration.

For all this, however, there are some significant drawbacks to this approach:

- Everything must be prerendered, and furthermore must be rendered differently when lighting and perspective shifts.
- The number of cast members to create even the simplest animation can get to be staggering.
- You are limited in your points of view to those that are explicitly rendered. That is, if you want to turn around and see what's behind you, that option is only available if the designers decided to include it.

When you are evaluating your project, you should keep these advantages and disadvantages in mind. The 2D approach is probably the safest to pull off in terms of technology, but it doesn't have the "coolness" factor of many of the hot, true-3D games out today.

Rendering landscapes and environments

Hands down, one of the best tools for creating three-dimensional landscapes has to be Bryce — it's one of those programs that has generated a strong fan base of artists who do nothing but crank out Bryce worlds.

Bryce makes use of one of the most eclectic interfaces in computing, designed by UI poster child Kai Krause. You can add mountains, bodies of water, skies, and unusual geometric landscapes with the click of a button. The program makes heavy use of alpha channel technology to provide transparencies, bump maps, glowing elements, and shadows, letting you create some incredibly detailed images without a great deal of work. In addition to this, you can add "cardboard cutouts" — graphics that use alpha channels for transparency. In this way you could add a stoplight sticking out of a lake, a pet Allosaurus, or anything else that strikes your fancy (see Figure 25-2). Similarly, you can import 3D models that use the DXF format, which will then pick up lighting and shadows in exactly the same manner as the primitives contained within Bryce.

Figure 25-2: Bryce is indispensable for creating landscapes and other backgrounds.

If you are more experienced with 3D graphics tools, 3D Studio MAX is rapidly becoming the primary tool for sophisticated 3D development on the PC, and its making more than a few Mac users look longingly at Windows NT. It is a complex program — you should have a thorough understanding of working within a three-dimensional environment before you start playing with 3D Studio MAX — but for the high-end graphics professional, it's probably about the best for detailed environment generation. Caligari trueSpace is another remarkably effective environment generator and is a good midlevel tool for people who find 3D Studio MAX's price tag too rich to stomach.

On the Macintosh side, the technology is a little older and more seasoned. Strata Studio Pro has built a name for itself in this venue, and is at the heart of many commercials seen on television.

When you are creating your landscapes, you should keep several factors in mind:

✦ Work with a shallow depth of field. Think of a 3D environment as being a backdrop in a theater. The performers occupy a relatively narrow stage. If the perspective in the backdrop is too forced, the people toward the back of the stage can actually appear gigantic in comparison to the people closer to the front.

- Keep your lighting fairly neutral — work with a high amount of ambient light, rather than directional light. If a room's light source is obvious, it will force the characters and props to use the same light source, meaning that you need a different version of each sequence of animation for each changed light source.

- Be thinking about how foreground sprites are to be rendered against the background. A sprite of an arc lamp in a mad scientist's laboratory could be a set of rectangular cast members that incorporate the background, whereas a person moving about on the stage should be rendered independent of the background.

- Use bump maps, textures, and randomness (if available) in your graphics to break up the smoothness of most graphics primitives. In the real world, very few things are not dirty, pitted, or worn, and taking the time to add textures really adds to your production.

- On the other hand, be careful about incorporating reflective surfaces, especially if something will be moving in front of them. A highly detailed mirror looks great in a scene, but unless the character moving in front of it is a vampire, you should expect to see a reflection of that person as she walks past.

Flight of the avatar

Obviously, the details of putting together a series of such backgrounds is beyond the scope of this book. However, you should look at these elements as you would any other scenes you work with in Director. You can take a couple of different approaches when setting up such an environment, relating to the nature of the user's *avatar*.

Note: The term *avatar* comes from the Hindu culture and essentially refers to the mortal incarnation of an immortal being. In computer gaming and virtual reality parlance, on the other hand, an avatar is the representative of the player within the environment.

In some games, what could be termed *first-person* games, the world is displayed as if seen through your eyes. The avatar is implied in that sense. Flight and driving simulators, as well as games like Myst, make use of this perspective. It's the easiest to pull off, but you get much less feedback about how you are faring physically in this world.

In second-person games, your avatar has a limited "physical" presence in the world. For example, in games like Doom or Quake, you can see at least portions of your avatar in the arms holding the Nail Gun or Plasma Rifle, and when you get hit, you *know* it. These games are actually fairly difficult to do in a program like Director, because the implication is fairly strong that you have a great deal of freedom of movement.

With third-person games, you actually have several different variants. You control the motions of an autonomous sprite. This approach, which works well in strategy or adventure games where you may have a lot of interaction with other entities, is fairly easy to pull off in Director, but it loses a certain amount of the identification that the viewer may have with the avatar. Into this category also fall side-scroller games (where the background scrolls behind the character as she moves) and top-view games (in which you get a bird's-eye view of the action).

Creating avatars

Obviously, first- and second-person avatars are relatively simple to create. In the first instance the avatar is implied, while in the second you would need only to draw arms holding some massive piece of ordinance. Third-person avatars are a little trickier. In this case, you need to evaluate how many different views of the avatar need to be made.

In a variant of a trivia game completed by one of the authors, a mermaid moves along a pier, as viewed from what's traditionally called the three-quarters view: above the figures and slightly to one side, so that you see most of the character rather than just the top of her head. She moves in a sinuous motion with her tail propelling her. Since it is possible for her to move both forward and backward, four different sequences of animation were needed: one moving to the left, one to the right, one moving toward the viewer, and one moving away. Thus, since each stage of the "walk" took four frames, sixteen different frames of animation were needed, plus an additional four where she stood still for each direction (see Figure 25-3).

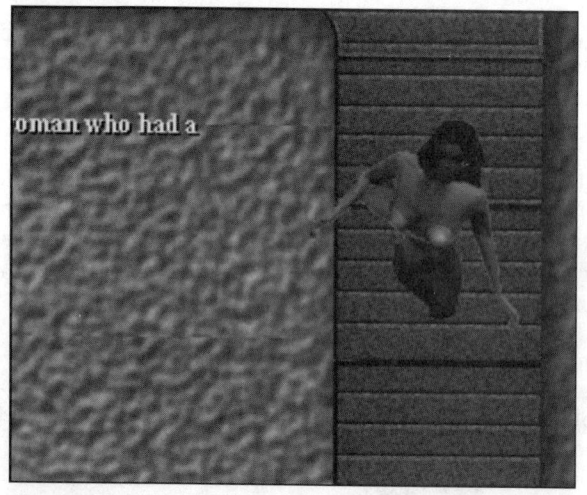

Figure 25-3: This alternate version of the trivia game demonstrates how three-dimensional realism doesn't always require a true 3D object.

For each avatar, you need to determine how many different actions they will perform, then multiply that by the number of frames it takes to accomplish each action, and then multiply *that* number by the number of directions that the character could face. If you had one avatar that could face in any of eight different directions and could walk, run, jump, crouch, stand and die, you could easily run into several hundred frames of animation. Multiply that by a couple dozen different foes, and you begin to see why it takes a full production staff to create a typical adventure game.

This is one of the reasons why three-dimensional programs have made such an impact on the gaming field. If you used a 3D program to model and render your avatar, rotating the avatar in space becomes almost trivial. This was, in fact, the technique used to create the trivia game. The initial avatar was created in Poser (see the upcoming sidebar), and then the camera was positioned above her and slighty to one side. From there, I rotated the character to keep lighting consistent, at 90° intervals. As the final step, each cell was imported into Photoshop to do some postproduction work (such as adding hair) and then into Director.

The power of Poser

Bryce and Poser, from MetaCreations, Inc., were made for one another. Poser is a specialized 3D program that lets you pose, animate, and render figures — men, women, children, mannequins, skeletons — the list is fairly extensive. Poser 2 is vastly superior in quality to the first version, offering better rendering, considerably more accurate models, inverse kinematics, and animation capabilities. Moreover, you can replace various body parts with imported three-dimensional models, making it ideal for making anthropomorphic animals, mythical beings, and cyborgs.

If you want more control over your characters, you should also check out Character Studio, a plug-in to 3D Studio MAX that lets you build characters with moving muscles, complex armatures, and rippling skin. Other add-ons let you animate faces, one of the hardest tasks to accomplish well in any 3D package.

Working with props

Certainly, making sophisticated backgrounds and characters takes some of the higher-end capabilities, but the best prop-making engines are also the least expensive. Macromedia Extreme 3D has some powerful resources for making inanimate objects, including the ability to link different objects together, build organic shapes using meta-balls, create particle systems, and edit meshes. It comes packaged with Macromedia Director Studio, making it an attractive option for quick-and-dirty objects. Moreover, it has a fairly powerful animation facility, given its price. The only drawback is that its renderer, the package that actually draws the model, is pretty mediocre. However, I'd recommend it highly for creating models for export.

MetaCreations's Ray Dream Studio package complements Extreme 3D's strengths and weaknesses pretty evenly. For an inexpensive modeling package, it has one of the better rendering engines on the market for PCs. It also lets you "paint" on your models, a feature unique to it until Fractal released Detailer, a specialized painting program that works on 3D models.

Almost all software packages let you import models from other packages, though in general, the most consistent standard seems to be DXF in Windows and RIB on the Macintosh. DXF is a three-dimensional standard in the same way that TIF is a two-dimensional standard — it defines varying levels of support for transferring data. In general, DXF doesn't retain linking or inverse kinematics information, and some DFX formats don't save the full complements of materials information from one program to the next. However, for props, which aren't likely to change from one program to another, DXF is a useful format to know about.

Putting 2D/3D presentations together

It's probably clear by now that putting together a faux three-dimensional world often involves skipping between various tools to find the ones that work best for a given situation. Virtual worlds and 3D objects can take time to put together — high-quality rendering, especially at higher resolutions, can take hours to accomplish on all but the fastest machines. If you plan on doing a lot of 3D work, you should invest in a good 3D graphics card for your computer. They are relatively inexpensive and can improve your rendering times dramatically.

Finally, don't neglect to take into account postprocessing time. Even after a scene or character is rendered, you may need to go in and touch it up — Poser, for example, doesn't yet handle hair. Especially with backgrounds, you are usually better off painting in intricate details after the fact than attempting to create hyper-realistic three-dimensional models that will slow down your render time without an appreciable gain in quality.

Once you do finish with these details, import them into Director, and treat them as you would any other graphic. In the trivia game mentioned earlier, for example, we made the mermaid's sinuous "walk" became a film loop. Any time she moved, the static image was replaced with the film loop using `the member of sprite` property.

There are some definite limitations to using two-dimensional technologies. A 2D world can only be viewed from one angle — like the set of a 1950s western, if you walk around to the side of the interface, and move away from the one favored angle, the three-dimensional view is exposed for the illusion that it is. Because there are some real benefits to being able to work with "real 3D," it's worth examining the underpinnings that make it happen.

Understanding 3D Technologies

It's easy to see how a computer can work in two dimensions — after all, the monitor is a two-dimensional plane, with a width and height that can be measured in pixels (or inches for that matter). Understanding how a computer works with three dimensions gets a little trickier.

Note: If you are already familiar with how three-dimensional objects are created inside a computer, skip ahead to "Using Quickdraw3D Sprites."

Concentrating on coordinates

From a computational standpoint, there's actually not much difference between a 2D point on a plane and a 3D point in space. The reason for this has to do with the fact that the computer actually works in only one dimension — memory starts at a certain location along a line, and ends at a different location farther along that line. When it refreshes the screen, from the standpoint of the central processor, it is simply spinning out a long continuous thread that the graphics card then translates into a coordinate on the screen. The computer sees a point in two dimensions as a pair of numbers in a data structure, nothing more. If a computer needed to work with a point in three dimensions, it would make up a triplet of numbers and work with them in a data structure. For that matter, if it wanted to work in four-dimensional space, it would make a quad of numbers, and . . . well, you get the idea. Your computer doesn't understand the notion of space except as it relates to a data structure and functions that act on that structure.

Traditionally, since modern algebra usually uses the letter x as the "width" dimension, and y as the "height" dimension, it's only logical to think of depth as the letter z. Furthermore, if the x (width) dimension goes from left to right, and the y (height) dimension goes from top to bottom on your computer screen, it is logical to assume that the z (depth) dimension goes into and out of your computer screen (see Figure 25-4).

Figure 25-4: Most computer 3D programs use the right hand rule.

One of the first questions that arises as a consequence of this is, which way does the arrow point — toward the user or away from her. The answer is not as clear-cut as it may seem. Analytical geometry (that subject you possibly studied, and probably loathed, before trigonometry) typically has the x direction increasing from left to right, and the y direction increasing from bottom to top. The z-axis then follows the *right-hand rule*: If the thumb pointing right indicates the x-axis and the index finger pointing up the y-axis, then the middle finger, pointed perpendicular to these two, would point in the positive z direction. By using this convention, since computers invert the y dimension (pixels go from top to bottom, not the other way around) a little fancy fingerwork will demonstrate that, if the right-hand rule is followed, the positive z-axis points away from the user, not toward her.

Most 3D graphics programs settled on the right-hand rule, simply because it is considered the standard orientation found in physics and mathematics. However, since most people tend to think of positive depth as coming toward them rather than vice versa, these same graphics programs usually define the positive y-axis as being toward the top of the screen, counter to the pixel direction, although even that isn't always the case.

Actually, most graphics programs don't have one single coordinate system. Instead, they may have three or four (or more). The *world coordinates* basically defines a standard of direction and distance for the whole object space. For the most part, world coordinates are fixed — they stay the same regardless of where the viewer (also known as the camera) is, or where any given object is. *Camera coordinates* are the coordinates with respect to a given viewpoint. Typically, you will have more than one view of your objects or environment, especially in the design phase, so camera coordinates provide a way to orient your world with respect to your viewpoint. Finally, *local coordinates* define a temporary coordinate system that may be oriented around a given object. For example, the local coordinates of a person may be defined by where her feet touch the ground, which direction she is facing, and the fact that she is standing perpendicular to the ground (see Figure 25-5).

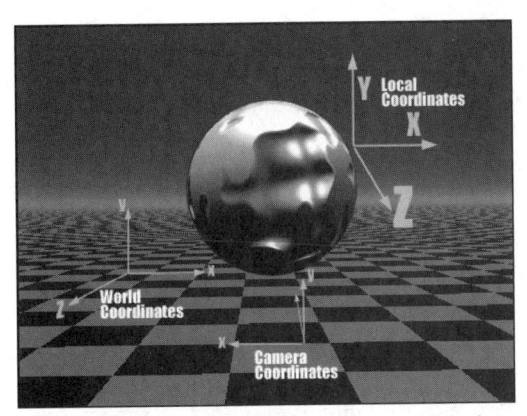

Figure 25-5: A given object can have several coordinate systems, depending on what needs to get done.

One of the earliest challenges 3D programmers had to face was the need to map the spatial coordinates of a scene onto the two-dimensional coordinates of the screen. The simplest mapping is called an *orthographic mapping* or *orthographic projection*. In this case, the program flattens out the object. Imagine a cube that sits slightly above the viewing plane but is otherwise parallel to it. In an orthographic mapping, the cube gets mapped as a square, with the rear part of the square exactly the same size as the front part when viewed from the screen. Orthographic mappings are typically used when designing an object, since you can easily see the scale of one side of an object with respect to the other.

However, the human eye doesn't see orthographic projections. Instead, objects farther away appear smaller than the same objects when close. In order to approximate this, a *perspective mapping* is used instead. With perspective, you create vanishing points, positions on the "horizon" where all parallel lines eventually seem to meet. The computer uses an approximation of this technique to create perspective, which is one of the things that gives objects the appearance of "depth" (see Figure 25-6).

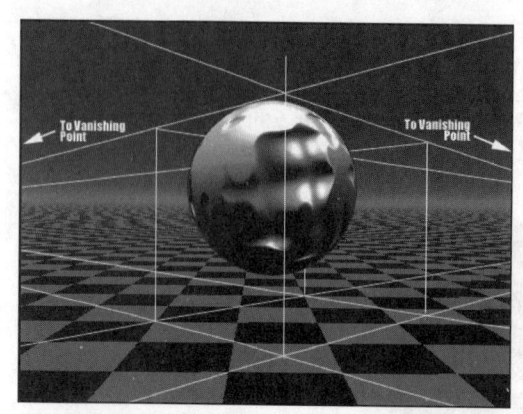

Figure 25-6: A perspective mapping makes the lines in an illustration converge at specific points of the horizon, called vanishing points.

Because internally the computer represents spatial points as operations on triplets of points, you actually have a certain amount of control over how extreme the sense of perspective is. Typically, computers define two points as the vanishing points. The closer these points are, the more noticeable the perspective, and the deeper the image appears as a consequence. The apparent depth is called the *depth of field*. Going back to the stage metaphor mentioned earlier, the depth of field of the backdrop would be increased (the vanishing points moved closer together) if you wanted to give the illusion of wide open space, cavernous buildings, or other large environments. On the other hand, if you decrease the depth of field, the world appears flatter, and things become more "intimate." Most graphics programs let you set your depth of field by using a target point, where the camera is focused. A few more advanced programs will actually blur distant objects to approximate haze and atmospheric effects, based principally on this same depth of field.

Rendering with meshes

When you move an object in some way, you are said to be applying a *transform* on the object. Typically, transforms include rotations, scaling (both universal and in a specific direction), and flipping. Internally, such a transform is accomplished using an array of 16 numbers, though the details of this are generally handled transparently.

Most objects are made up of a *mesh* of points and edges. The more detailed the mesh, the more the number of points in that mesh, and as a consequence the longer it takes to render. Mesh sizes can get big quickly — if you have a rectangular planar mesh that has four points on a side, there are 16 squares to that mesh. Doubling the density of the mesh will increase the number of squares to 64, doubling again will increase the number to 256. The denser the mesh, the smoother it will appear, but at the price of increased processing time. If you figure that rotating even one point in the mesh takes at least 16 multiplications and 9 additions, and multiply that number by 256 points in a single mesh, you might begin to appreciate why 3D graphics are so processor intensive (see Figure 25-7).

Figure 25-7: Doubling the dimensions of a mesh quadruples the number of points.

There are a number of ways that you can fool the *renderer* (that part of a 3D program that actually paints the final image on the screen) into making something smoother than it actually is. One of these techniques is to use a *shader*. Normally, with a given mesh, light hits each square (or frequently each triangle) in the mesh at a slightly different angle. This makes that square brighter or darker than the surrounding squares, and contributes to a fairly discontinuous view of the object. However, if you instruct the computer to paint any point on the square according to its distance from each of the four corner points, the resulting gradient will make the image appear smoother. The two primary shading algorithms in use today are *Phong* and *Giraud* shading. Phong shading tends to produce more intense highlights than Giraud, but in terms of time and quality, both give you comparable results.

For highly metallic objects, *ray tracing* can give remarkable reflections. With ray tracing, the renderer sends out a line parallel to the square (called a *normal*) which continues until it encounters something. Then the renderer uses the reflective properties of the hit object to see if the normal bounces, and the path is extended to the next object in the path (see Figure 25-8). Ray tracing can give you spectacular effects, but you should use it with caution, as it can dramatically lengthen your render time.

Figure 25-8: Ray tracing works by bouncing a line that emerges from a given face and averaging out the color at the beginning of that point, based upon what's hit.

Material witnesses

Another way to add detail to your objects is by use of materials. Most 3D packages now allow you to use *texture maps* to simulate texture on an object. A texture map is simply an image of some sort, although usually the image tiles left to right and top to bottom so that it appears seamless on your objects. Some higher-end packages let you specify the scale of the texture map to the object, giving you the ability to create what appears to be extremely detailed objects without a lot of extra modeling time.

A specialized form of texture map called a *bump map* can increase the illusion of texture further by making the rendering engine fill in shadows based upon the brightness of the map. For example, you can use a bump map to make a sphere appear to be a golf ball. Bump maps don't actually change the geometry of an object — the illusion breaks down a bit along the edges, since most renderers won't actually make the edges transparent where an apparent hole is. Since borders will typically have the least exposure to the viewer, however, this deception isn't all that obvious.

Most modern 3D engines support a variety of additional maps. Transparency maps cause the background to show through where the map is lightest (or darkest) in a manner comparable to alpha channels. Glow maps can be used to render lights or flames against a dark background. Reflectivity maps make objects reflect light at different intensities. In general, you can create almost any texture — from foliage to glass to city lights to fog against the moors — by the application (or combination) of texture maps (see Figure 25-9).

Figure 25-9: By using bump, glow, and reflectivity maps, you can add considerable texture to a model without needing to physically model.

Playing meta-balls

Almost every 3D technology that currently exists started out either in military flight simulators or came from Hollywood studios. Meta-balls are one of the more intriguing of the Hollywood special effects. Traditional meshes suffer a number of problems — a mesh is expensive computationally to transform, and because of this, it's difficult to make a good-looking skin out of a mesh.

One way around this particular conundrum was to turn to quantum effects in chemistry. (Huh!?) The jump is not as esoteric as it may seem. Most physicists and chemists recognize that atoms are best described according to an envelope of a given charge. When two of these envelopes exist, the two atoms merge together like two soap bubbles joining. This skin, describing the surface potential for the newly formed molecule, happens to have a lot of the same characteristics as soap bubbles, skin, and many other surfaces. By creating a "molecular" armature of such atoms, you can create very organic shapes. As 3D animators started playing with these, they dubbed the technology *meta-balls*.

Meta-balls figure prominently in movie special effects. The skin and musculature of the dinosaurs in *Jurassic Park* was created almost entirely with this effect. Incidentally, if you have the Macromedia Director Studio package, check out the meta-ball capability in Extreme 3D, a surprisingly advanced feature for such a basic 3D program.

A related technology can be found in *particle systems*. Certain effects, such as snow, swirling fog, fire, and hair are extremely difficult to create using traditional 3D primitives like spheres or cubes. However, by creating large numbers of tiny particles that have basic attributes such as transparency or brightness, you can imitate these effects surprisingly well. Such particle systems generally are found only in upper-3D packages. (Extreme 3D does have particle system capability, although it creates tiny clones of preexisting objects and as such is perhaps not as effective as those filters found in 3D Studio MAX or Lightwave 3D.) (See Figure 25-10.)

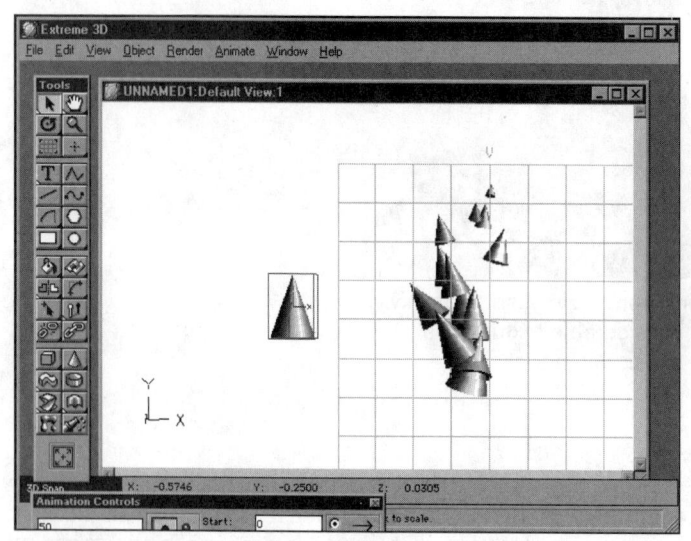

Figure 25-10: Particle systems consist of a cloud of points that change their positions and characteristics over time.

Implementing 3D systems

3D programs have always had an uneasy alliance with their host systems. The code is processor intensive, and for a while many such programs either had significant performance problems or could only run with specific graphics accelerator cards that were optimized for 3D. At about the same time (Apple was first by maybe six months) Apple and Microsoft began developing a set of standardized API calls for handling 3D graphics. On the Mac side, this technology was called QuickDraw 3D and is an offshoot of the earlier QuickDraw extensions. On the PC side, Microsoft introduced a host of new technologies to entice developers to move away from the DOS world. Under the general banner of DirectX, this suite included DirectDraw and Direct3D. In both cases the actual implementation is too complex to explain in any great detail.

Using QuickDraw 3D Sprites

Available only with the latest release of Director, QuickDraw 3D (QD3D) is an intriguing resource. With it, you can load in three-dimensional models, and then manipulate them either manually or from Lingo. In order to use the QuickDraw 3D Xtra, you need to install QuickDraw 3D onto your system.

The QD3D Xtra is only one file, but it performs two distinct functions: creating a 3D sprite cast-member type, and adding a number of properties to Lingo for handling the sprite. The QuickDraw 3D cast member is one of the most complicated cast members, to the extent that in order to define all of the attributes of the cast member the control has five distinct screens of information. However, in order to access these, it's necessary to create a QuickDraw 3D cast member in the first place.

When you install Apple's QuickDraw 3D system extension, the installer creates a folder on your hard drive named QuickDraw 3D (under Program Files on a Windows system). Within that folder is another folder named QuickDraw 3D Metafiles, which includes several subfolders with useful sample models. One of the folders, Model Masters, contains a teapot model (teapot.3dmf) that you can use in the following exercise.

Creating a QuickDraw 3D Cast Member

1. From the Director menu, select Insert ⇨ Media Element ⇨ QuickDraw 3D Model. If this option is not available, you have not installed either the QD3D Xtra, or Apple's QuickDraw 3D system extension, or both.

2. When the Open dialog box appears, as shown in Figure 25-11, navigate to a folder with 3D metafiles (such as QuickDraw 3D:QuickDraw 3D Metafiles:Model Masters or QuickDraw 3D\QuickDraw 3D Metafiles\Model Masters). Select a 3DMF file, such as teapot.3dmf.

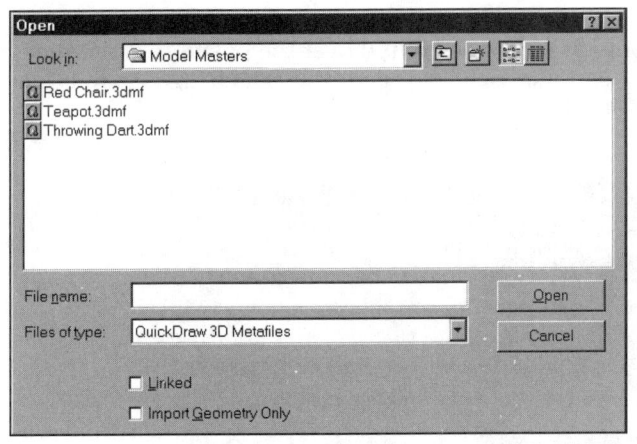

Figure 25-11: Selecting a 3D metafile to import into the cast

3. If you want to link to the 3DMF as an external cast member, select the Linked check box. If you want to import the object, leave the box unchecked. (A linked model becomes available at run-time but takes

longer to load initially. It can, however, be replaced with an alternative version without needing to reimport the object or re-create the projector.)

4. Select the Import Geometry Only check box if you only want to load the object's mesh. When you enable this option, Director does not load color information, textures, or any associated files.

5. Select OK to load. Once the file has been loaded into Director, a thumbnail image of the model will appear in the selected cast window.

You can't physically change the geometry of the model once you import it into Director, but you can alter the way that the model is displayed on the screen. This is accomplished through a series of five tabbed pages of settings that let you modify everything from the internal motion of the cast member to its lighting, rendering, and several other attributes. In order to access these settings, you will need to open the cast member information window for the QuickDraw 3D cast member.

6. Select the QuickDraw 3D cast member you want to modify, and press Command-I (Ctrl-I) to get the cast member information.

This model appears as a rotating thumbnail on the Xtra Cast Member Properties dialog box.

7. Click the Options button to display the QuickDraw 3D Xtra dialog box.

Modeling

The Modeling window gives you control over the position, orientation, and gross properties of the cast member. From here you can change the following properties (see Figure 25-12):

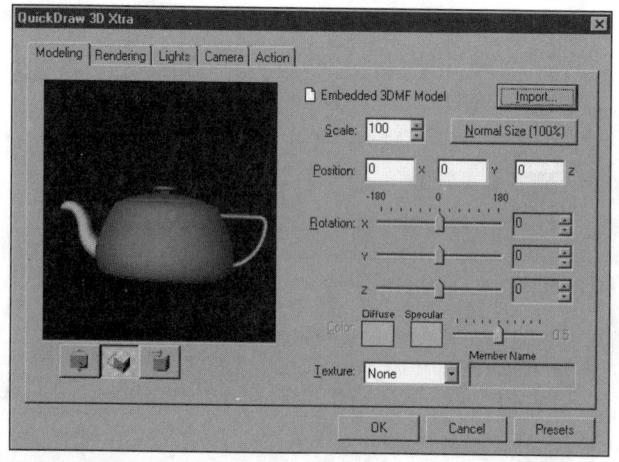

Figure 25-12: The Modeling tab dialog determines the source of the model.

- **File** — Selecting the Import button will give you a chance to switch the currently loaded model for a different model.

- **Scale** — Scale is relative to the width and height of the window. If you set the Scale to 50%, the object takes up only half the window's width. After adjusting the scale, you can revert to normal size by clicking the Normal Size button.

- **Position** — The position fields (x, y, and z) establish the object's position relative to world coordinates, *not* its position on the Director Stage. Values entered in these fields can be positive or negative. The x value moves the object to the right (if a positive number) or to the left (if a negative number) on the horizontal plane. The y value moves the object up (if a positive number) or down (if a negative number) on the vertical plane. The z value moves the object toward the viewer (if a positive number) or away from the viewer (if a negative number).

- **Rotation** — Rotation sliders adjust the rotation of the object in degrees about the axis. Both positive and negative numbers can be used for each rotation setting. The x slider rotates the object toward the viewer when the x value is increased or away from the viewer when the value is decreased. The y slider is best described by what you would see from a top view. That is, increasing the y value rotates the object counterclockwise, and decreasing the value rotates it clockwise. From the side view, the z slider spins the object counterclockwise as the value increases and clockwise as the value decreases.

- **Diffuse (Color)** — This option indicates the default diffuse color of the object, essentially the level of color that the object has if no internal color is defined for it.

- **Specular (Color)** — This gives the amount of reflective color. A dark specular color makes the image appear to be matte; a high color can make the object look very shiny. The midpoint on the Specular slider is the default value if the object doesn't have an internally defined specular color.

- **Texture** — This applies a texture to the model, either from a file or from a cast member. If you want to add a surface to the object based on a cast member, open the Texture drop-down list and select Cast Member.

On the CD-ROM

If you want to experiment with adding texture to a model, there are several graphic tiles on the CD-ROM that you can import. The files 16x32a.pct, 16x32b.pct, 64x32a.pct, 64x32b.pct, 64x32c.pct, and 64x32d.pct are in the exercise:ch02 (exercsie\ch02) folder. If you use a cast member, write down its name because that's what you'll need to type into the Member Name field. The current QD3D Xtra does not include a pop-up menu of available cast members.

> **Tip** The texture doesn't have to be a graphic, by the way. A digital video cast member can be applied to the model, making the texture appear to move. Before you do this, however, make sure that your host system has enough memory; applying a video will send your system scraping the barrel for every last kilobyte.

At any point, after experimenting with the Modeling tab settings, click the Preset button to return the object back to its original condition.

Rendering

To view the Rendering options, select the Rendering tab (Figure 25-13).

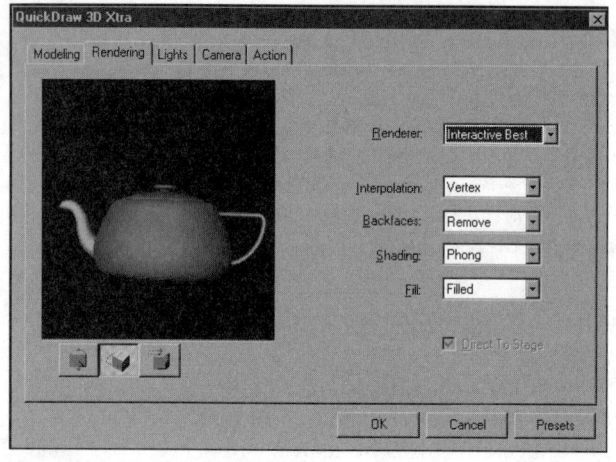

Figure 25-13: The Rendering tab controls how the model is drawn.

- ✦ **Renderer** — This drop-down list displays the options available for how an image is rendered. You can choose a 3D graphics video card, software drivers, or the QuickDraw drivers, which check to see if the appropriate hardware/software are available.

- ✦ **Interpolation** — Determines which method is used to determine the characteristics of each "square" in the mesh. Choose None, Vertex, or Pixel.

- ✦ **Backfaces** — Determines whether the renderer draws the back faces (surfaces that are away from the viewer or camera) before drawing the front faces, or whether instead the back faces are simply ignored. If the model has a hole in it (such as a donut), you may want to include the back faces, but normally this option should be set to ignore them.

- **Shading** — Sets the interpolation shading for faces of the mesh. The Lambert shader is a modification of the Giraud shader. For a quick preview of the graphic without shading, set this value to Flat. For the final version, set it back to either Phong or Lambert.

- **Fill** — Determines whether the model is drawn as a solid image (Filled), a wireframe model (Edges), or a point cloud (Vertices). Usually, you want this property set to Filled.

- **Direct To Stage** — The QuickDraw 3D sprite can be set so that the background is transparent (set the ink to Background Transparent), making the model appear to be lying on top of any background sprites. In order to do this, you need to make sure Direct To Stage is set to False (unchecked). On the other hand, if you are displaying the sprite in its own environment, set this property to True. Performance will improve considerably if Direct To Stage is enabled.

Lights

This tab of settings gives you control over the type and source of the light in the environment (see Figure 25-14):

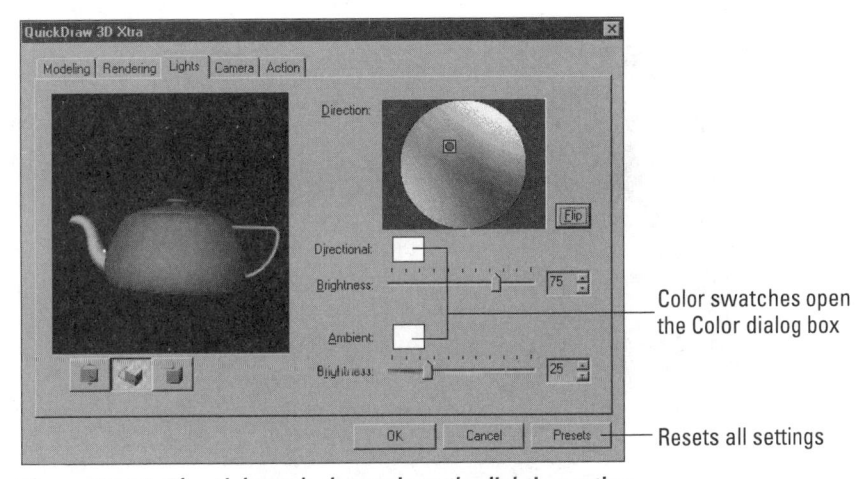

Figure 25-14: The Lights tab determines the lighting acting on the model.

✦ **Direction** — This is the direction from which the light source shines on the object. Click on a part of the globe to change the direction, or press the Flip button to move the light source so that it comes from behind the model.

✦ **Directional** — Indicates the color and intensity of the "spotlight" within the image. When you click this color swatch, the Color dialog box opens and you can select a color for the light source. If you don't want the model to have a spot, set the color to black or to a medium gray. Textures will react differently to the various colors, so you'll want to experiment. Also, you can use the Brightness slider to adjust the intensity of the light source.

✦ **Ambient** — Ambient light is the light that is present within the environment. Changing the color of the ambient light can be used to create a specific mood — a fish, for example, might work best in a light-blue ambient light that suggests water. The Ambient light, like the directional light, can be adjusted. You can change its brightness (using the Brightness slider) and its color (using the color swatch).

Camera

The settings on the Camera tab are used to establish the direction and other attributes of the viewing camera (see Figure 25-15):

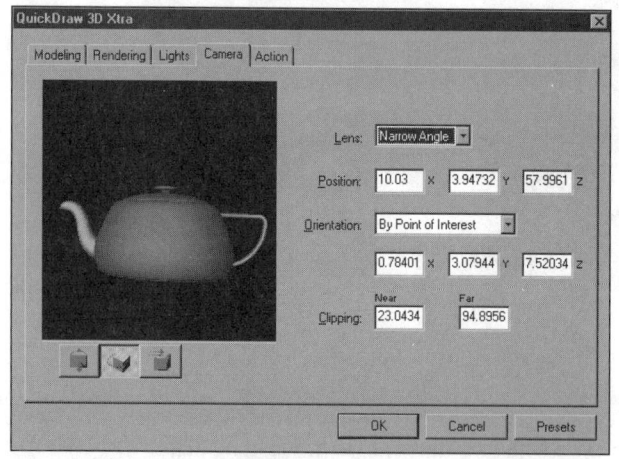

Figure 25-15: The Camera tab determines the position, direction, and field of view of the built-in camera type.

✦ **Lens** — Determines whether a narrow or wide-angle lens is used. This corresponds to the depth of field. A narrow lens will make the perspective seem limited and the model shallow, while a wide-angle lens will force the perspective and make the model seem deep.

✦ **Position** — This is the position of the camera in the world coordinates. You can type in new x, y, and z coordinates.

✦ **Orientation** — The direction in which the camera currently faces. It defaults to By Point of Interest, which is centered on the model, but can also be set to world coordinates.

✦ **Clipping** — Any vertices in which are closer than the first value or farther than the second will automatically be made invisible. This prevents the problem of an object being so close that it obscures the view.

Action

The options on the Action tab control whether (and how) the user can move the model (see Figure 25-16):

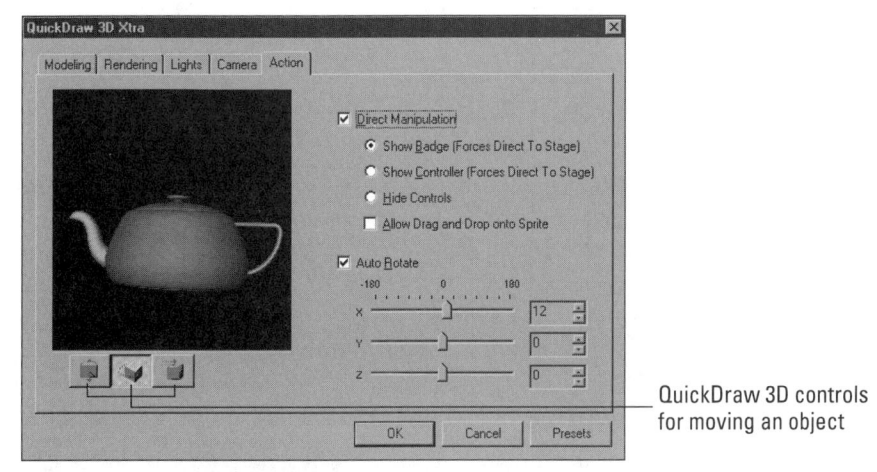

Figure 25-16: The Action tab controls how the model interacts with the Stage.

✦ **Direct Manipulation** — If this check box is selected, the user can move the model with the mouse.

✦ **Show Badge** — A badge is a small icon used to open up the QuickDraw 3D controls. If the badge is shown, the sprite is rendered as Direct To Stage, and as a consequence can't be transparent.

✦ **Show Controller** — If this option is selected, the three controls of the control panel are displayed on the Stage as shown in Figure 25-17. Again, this displays the model as Direct To Stage.

Figure 25-17: The control panel shows because Show Controler is enabled.

- **Hide Controls** — If this radio button is selected, the controls are hidden, and the object cannot be manipulated on the Stage.

- **Allow Drag and Drop** — This makes the control aware of drag-and-drop actions and passes events accordingly (normally, the sprite absorbs any mouse messages if Direct Manipulation is set).

- **AutoRotate** — If checked, this causes the model to rotate automatically without any code needing to be written. See the "Modeling" section earlier in this chapter for information about rotation angles.

QuickDraw 3D controls

All five tabbed windows show a live preview of the model. By selecting one of the three controls beneath the preview window (identified in Figure 25-16), you can control how the model is moved when you click it with the mouse:

- **Move In/Out** — The first button sets the move mode so that when you drag the object, it moves toward or away from you on the screen.

- **Rotate** — The second button sets the move mode to rotate. When you drag the model, it spins about on the axis that you create by the direction of the drag.

- **Move Up/Down/Left/Right** — The third button moves the object parallel to the viewing plane.

Tip: The bounding box for the sprite is resizable. When you drag the cast member onto the Stage, you may want to set it to fit within a given boundary and then adjust the position of the object from within the tabbed windows.

Manipulating QuickDraw 3D on the screen

Once you create a QuickDraw 3D cast member, you add it to your movie in exactly the same way that you would add a bitmap — you drag it onto the Stage. Once the cast member is on the Stage, you can control its position using traditional Lingo commands (in other words, locH, locV), set whether the background is transparent or not using the Background Transparent ink, and so forth.

Additionally, both within the QuickDraw 3D dialog and on the Stage, you can move the model around if the Direct Manipulation property is set within the QuickDraw 3D dialog (see the Action tab) or from Lingo. Once in this mode, clicking and dragging the model spins it around, moves it around within its display window, or zooms the model forward or backward, depending on which of the three control buttons is selected.

Tip

QuickDraw 3D is a memory hog, and it will perform sluggishly on slower machines. If your model is updated too slowly, you can optimize its performance by setting the shading mode to Lambert rendering (or even None) rather than Phong, by setting the Interpolation to Edges (or None), or by simplifying the model in a 3D program. Most 3D-modeling programs include some mechanism for reducing the number of polygons in the shape. Finally, if the model is displayed within a monochromatic rectangle, you can greatly improve performance by turning on Direct To Stage in the Rendering tab. This bypasses the Director buffering mechanism and draws directly to the Stage.

QuickDraw 3D and Lingo

Once your model is on the Stage, unless you're going for the gee whiz factor, you'll probably want to do something with the model. A static 3D image takes up far more processor activity than a traditional bitmap, so using such a model will have a significant impact upon what else you can with your program if the model doesn't move in some fashion.

As it turns out, the QuickDraw 3D Xtra adds a large number of useful commands to Lingo for free. These commands are expressed as properties of either the QuickDraw 3D cast member or the sprite that contains it (most are interchangeable in that regard). The commands can be used to duplicate any action that's possible to set within the QuickDraw 3D dialog box.

Because 3D graphics frequently need to refer to triplets of information, many of the values that these properties can hold are given as linear lists containing three values. For colors, this triplet is given as [red, green, blue] where each of the colors is represented as a byte holding a value between 0 (darkest) and 255 (brightest). Thus, the color yellow could be re-created as

```
set the diffuseColor of member m to [255,255,128]
```

while pure blue would be

```
[0,0,255]
```

You can determine the RGB color values to use with QD3D properties by opening the Color Palettes window (Command+Option+7 or Ctrl+Alt+7); then select the Color Picker button in the lower-right corner. When the Color dialog box appears, click anywhere in the color spectrum to display the RGB values in the Red, Green, and Blue fields. Some of the more common colors are listed in Table 25-1.

Table 25-1
Color Triplets for Use with QD3D Properties

Color	List of RGB values
black	[0,0,0]
blue	[0,0,255]
gray	[127,127,127]
green	[0,255,0]
purple	[255,0,255]
red	[255,0,0]
white	[255,255,255]
yellow	[255,255,0]

Positions, scale factors, and rotations are all given as a list triplet of floating point numbers. Thus scaling a model so that it is twice as wide as the original model but otherwise unchanged would be shown as

```
set the scale of sprite n to [2.0, 1.0, 1.0]
```

Tip

It is worth remembering that QuickDraw 3D sprites are worlds unto themselves. Thus, if you have two overlapping sprites, and the one with the lower sprite number has a z value that is closer to you than the higher sprite, it still appears behind the other since the two don't share the same internal space.

Table 25-2 is a summary of all of the QuickDraw 3D Lingo commands, along with short comments concerning their usage. You can find more information about these objects in the QuickDraw 3D documentation, which should be installed in the QD3D Authoring Xtra: Documentation (QD3DAuthoringXtra\Documentation) folder when you set up the QD3D Xtra.

Note: In Table 25-2, all QD3D properties that are preceded by an asterisk can be used on either a QD3D cast member or a sprite. If the property is not marked with an asterisk, it can only affect a cast member. Also, notice that in the first column, the information within parentheses indicates whether the property uses a Boolean operator (`True` or `False`), RGB colors (`[255,255,255]`) as listed in Table 25-1, a string, a floating point value (`float`), Cartesian coordinates (`XYZ`), or a special symbol (begins with the # character, such as #q3Video or #q3Filled).

Table 25-2
QuickDraw 3D Lingo Commands

Basic Properties	Example	Description
`modelFile (string)`	`Set the modelFile of member 3 to "c:\bin\newmodel.3dmf"`	The path to a 3DMF file. The cast member must have been specified as linked for this to have any effect.
`directToStage (Boolean)`	`Set the directToStage of member 3 to false`	Determines whether cast member is composited in its own window or integrated with other cast members. Corresponds to `directToStage` for digital video. Has no effect if controller or badge is turned on because these controls force Direct To Stage playback.
`*DirectManipulation (Boolean)`	`Set the directManipulation of member 3 to true`	Establishes whether user can move the model (True) or not (False) at run-time.
`diffuseColor (RGB)`	`Set the diffuseColor of member 3 to [0,0,255]` (Sets the diffuse color to light blue)	Sets base color of the object, if this is not set within the file itself. Uses an RGB triplet.
`specularColor (RGB)`	`Set the specularColor of member 3 to [255,128,255]` (Sets the diffuse color to a light brown)	Sets color of any highlight of the object, if this is not set within the file itself. Uses an RGB triplet.

(continued)

Table 25-2 (continued)

Basic Properties	Example	Description
`specularCoeff (float)`	Set the specularCoeff of member 3 to 7.5 (Makes the model fairly shiny)	Establishes how "shiny" the object is. A specular coefficient of 0.0 is completely matte; a coefficient of 1.0 is completely reflective.
`backColor (RGB)`	Set the backcolor of member 3 to [0,0,255] (Sets the color of the thumbnail's background to blue)	The color of only the background in the thumbnail; this has no effect at run-time.
`*modelCenter (XYZ)`	Put the modelCenter of member 3	Determines center of the object in world coordinates. (Read only.)
`*modelSize (XYZ)`	Put the modelSize of member 3. A [20,15,10] image is 20 units wide, 15 high, and 10 deep.	Determines dimensions of the object in world coordinates. (Read only.)

Transformations	Example	Description
`*scale`	Set the scale of sprite 4 to [2,1,0.5] (Makes sprite 4 twice as wide and half as deep, but retains the current height.)	Multiplies the dimension along each axis by the values in the list. First value in list affects the x-axis; second value affects y-axis; third value affects z-axis.
`*position`	Set the position of sprite 4 to [5,10,15] (Moves center of sprite to this position.)	Moves position of object, relative to its own container and not the Stage.
`*rotation`	Set the rotation of sprite 4 to [45,30,0] (Rotates the object by 45° around the x-axis, then rotates around the y-axis by 30°.)	Rotates model around axis defined by each of the list components.

Transformations	Example	Description
* autoRotate (Boolean)	Set the autoRotate of member 3 to true	Starts the model spinning, if auto-rotation angles are set.
* autoRotateAngle (XYZ)	Set the autoRotateAngle of member 3 to [15,30,45] (Starts model spinning at 15° per frame aound the x-axis, 30° per frame around the y-axis, etc.)	Sets angle of rotation of the object, along the three primary axes.

Lighting and Textures	Examples	Description
ambientColor (RGB)	Set the ambientColor of member 3 to [128,255,128] (Sets the ambient light to a bright green.)	Sets or retrieves color of ambient light (atmospheric light that illuminates model from all sides).
ambientBrightness (float, [0.0 - 1.0])	Set the ambientBrightness of member 3 to 0.20 (Sets intensity of ambient light to 20%.)	Sets intensity of ambient light to value specified. A value of 1.00 means object is completely illuminated by the ambient light; a value of 0 means object receives no light from surroundings.
lightDirection(XYZ)	Set the lightDirection of member 3 to [1,1,-1]	Determines direction of light source on x-, y-, and z-axis. Not applied to textured objects.
lightColor (RGB)	Set the lightColor of member 3 to [255,0,0] (Sets the color of directional light to bright red.)	Sets color of directional light source to the given color.
lightBrightness (float, [0.0 - 1.0)]	Set the lightBrightness of member 3 to 0.8 (Sets intensity of light on member 3 to 80%.)	Sets intensity of directional light source. Has no effect (in current version of QuickDraw 3D) if model has a texture.

(continued)

Table 25-2 (continued)

Lighting and Textures	Examples	Description
textureType (#q3Video, Mac only), #q3Member, #q3None)	Set the textureType of member 3 to #q3Member (Tells cast member the type of data cast member of live video used to "paint" it.)	esignates whether model Duses a bitmap (#q3Member), a video source (#q3Video, Mac Only), or nothing as the basis for a wrapping texture.
texture (member, or #q3Video)	Set the texture of member 3 to member 6 (Assigns bitmap in member 6 as the texture for member 3.)	Maps a bitmap cast member onto surface of model. Use textureType first to prepare proper texture format. If cast member changes after this statement is issued, change occurs only when movie is releaded or texture property is set again.

Rendering	Examples	Description
shading (#q3Phong, #q3Lambert, #q3None)	Set the shading of member 3 to #q3Phong	Sets shading algorithm used by model. #q3None indicates only flat shading is used; #q3Lambert creates gradient shading with no highlight; #q3Phong both shades and computes highlights.
interpolation (#q3None, #q3Vertex, #q3Pixel)	Set the interpolation of member 3 to #q3Vertext	If interpolation is #q3Vertex then shading is computed from points of each polygon in the mesh; #q3Pixel shades each pixel individually; #q3None produces flat shading in which each polygon in the mesh is a uniform color.

Rendering	Examples	Description
fillStyle (#q3Filled, #q3Edges, #q3Points)	Set the fillStyle of member 3 to #q3Edges	When fillStyle is #q3Filled, then each face is shown; for #q3Edges, a wireframe version of model is presented; #q3Points creates a point "cloud."
backfacing (#q3Both, #q3Remove, #q3Flip)	Set the backfacing of member 3 to #q3Remove	Specifies whether renderer should draw in faces that will be obscured by closer faces. #q3Both computes and draws both visible and "hidden" planes; #q3Remove removes hidden places; #q3Flip changes the normals for each polygon in the mesh, flipping the visible and hidden portions of the model so hidden polygons are rendered.

Camera	Examples	Description
*cameraPosition (XYZ)	Set the cameraPosition of sprite 4 to [100,0,0] (Sets camera at a point 100 units away from its origin along x-axis.)	Sets the position of the camera in world coordinates for the sprite
*cameraInterest (XYZ)	Set the cameraInterest of sprite 4 to the ModelCenter of sprite 4 (Sets camera at center of model.)	Makes camera always face toward a given point, even if camera itself moves. Overridden by setting cameraDirection and likewise overrides the cameraDirection value.

(continued)

Table 25-2 *(continued)*

Camera	Examples	Description
*cameraDirection (XYZ)	Set the cameraDirection of sprite 4 to [0,0,0] Aims camera at center of world coordinates.	Sets direction in which camera initially looks. If camera changes position, cameraDirection remains constant. Overridden by setting cameraInterest, and likewise overrides the cameraInterest value.
*cameraUpVector (XYZ)	Set the cameraUpVector of sprite 4 to [0,1,0]	Sets the Up direction for the camera.
*cameraHither (float)	Set the cameraHither of sprite 4 to 10.0	Sets distance to the near clipping plane (any part of a model that is nearer than this is not rendered).
*cameraYon (float)	Set the cameraYon of sprite 4 to 100.0	Sets distance to the far clipping plane (any part of a model that is farther away than this will not be rendered).
*cameraType (#q3Orthographic, #q3Perspective)	Set the cameraType of sprite 4 to #q3Perspective	Designates orthographic or perspective mapping. See "Concentrating on Coordinates" early in this chapter.
*cameraFOV (float)	Set the cameraFOV of sprite 4 to 45	Sets field of view, the angle seen by the camera of the total 360° (maximum FOV is 180°). Smaller FOV makes scene appear to zoom in; larger FOV "zooms out."
*cameraAspectRatio (float)	Set the cameraAspectRatio of sprite 4 to 1.6	Sets ratio of width to height. cameraAspectRatio is Izero, then this defaults to aspect ratio of the bounding rectangle. If nonzero, sprite is stretched to fit sprite's bounding rectangle.

Camera	Examples	Description
*cameraWidth (float)	Sets the cameraWidth of sprite 4 to 10	Sets width of camera's view plane in world coordinates (i.e., relative to size of model, not to any Lingo coordinates).
*cameraHeight (float)	Sets the cameraWidth of sprite 4 to 8	Sets height of camera's view plane in world coordinates.

Controls	Examples	Description
*badge (boolean)	Set the badge of sprite 4 to true	A badge is a small graphic displayed in the corner of the sprite. Clicking badge brings up controls. Set badge property to False to make it invisible.
*controller (boolean)	Set the controller of sprite 4 to true	The controller is a set of three buttons that determines which actions occur as result of dragging with mouse. Controller automatically forces directToStage mode.
*frame (boolean)	Set the frame of sprite 4 to true	If True, draws frame around sprite's bounding rectangle.
*dragAndDrop (boolean)	Set the dragAndDrop of sprite 4 to true	On Macintosh, allows a 3D model to be dragged to or from desktop from sprite container. On PC, allows dragging from sprite container to desktop. See QuickDraw 3D documentation for details.
*buttonDistance (boolean)	Set the buttonDistance of sprite 4 to true	Displays (True) or hides (False) Distance button (in controller) that moves object closer or farther away.
*buttonRotate (boolean)	Set the buttonRotate of sprite 4 to true	Displays/hides Rotate button (in controller) that enables user to rotate camera.

(continued)

Table 25-2 *(continued)*

Controls	Examples	Description
`*buttonZoom (boolean)`	`Set the buttonZoom of sprite 4 to true`	Displays/hides Zoom button (in controller) that alters camera's field of view.
`*buttonMove (boolean)`	`Set the buttonMove of sprite 4 to true`	Displays/hides the Move button (in controller) that moves camera right or left.

Uses for QuickDraw 3D

Three-dimensional sprites fall into a weird category. They are undeniably cool. When people think about computer graphics, the first things that usually come to mind are 3D models spinning about. However, given their processing requirements and the complexities involved in working with models, their real utility is often not immediately clear. Some useage suggestions include the following:

Games. While the most obvious usage, creating computer games using Director and the QuickDraw 3D Xtra isn't always as easy as it may seem. Unlike dedicated gaming environments that have full control over the screen, the QuickDraw 3D models are rendered within a window that has to share memory and programming space with Director and anything else that may be present at the time. Furthermore, QuickDraw 3D sprites can't efficiently be changed in real time (although take a look at RealSpace, discussed in the next section). They can be rotated or transformed, but the meshes involved can't be moved.

Because of this, games using QuickDraw 3D will likely work best if they are adventure games with 3D sprites on 2D backgrounds. Other games that might effectively use QD3D are ones like billiards, where the sprites are simple to create and can interact well with Director's collision detection, or chess, where the figures don't need to change form.

Product demonstrations. This is where the QuickDraw 3D Xtra shines. For example, let's say you are doing a promotional kiosk for an auto dealership (or car manufacturer). You can use QuickDraw 3D to rotate the car to show what it looks like from all angles, to selectively explode or alter parts (through the use of different models), and even to paint portions of the car, different colors so that you can show what a new paint job would look like.

Tip How would you pull off this last technique? Simple — when you create your model initially, don't assign any material to those portions of the model that will change. These, and only these parts will then reflect the color changes introduced through the `diffuseColor` property, as an example. You could even assign a texture to the model — set the texture property of the model to a cast member containing a picture of grass, and all of a sudden you have a Chia Pet Car!

Training and instructional materials. An early multimedia product one of the authors worked on, back in 1982, was a training video for General Motors on installing catalytic converters. If I only had today's technology back then! By combining a QuickDraw 3D model of a catalytic converter with a few well-placed callouts, the same part need not have been drawn from several different viewpoints — a technique that is often less illuminating because the reader has to figure out how the piece is oriented before it makes any sense. Since training pieces make up a significant part of any multimedia producer's work, you should explore this option, especially for mechanically significant operations.

CD-ROM titles. Combining digitized footage, 3D models, and rendered backgrounds into the same movie has some real potential, although the memory considerations and performance issues should make you examine this only for higher-end systems. You can simulate an on-screen track ball with a rotating icosohedron (a 20-sided polyhedron), or for that matter you create a set of dice that tumble and spin before settling on a given face.

Graphics generation. We've used QuickDraw 3D for avatar creation in games. If you have a game that involves multiple viewpoints of the same character, combine the QD3D Xtra with any of the screen-grabbing Xtras and then use Lingo to rotate the character at regular angular intervals, taking snapshots as you go. This can work especially well in conjunction with the technique described earlier for changing the diffuse color of the image only for selected portions of a model. For example, you could create a centaur figure with the human portion given a matte flesh tone and the horse part uncolored. Set the diffuse color of the model to reflect your tests, then rotate and snap.

From sprites to worlds

QuickDraw 3D is definitely a powerful technology, but it does have a number of limitations. It works best for objects — people, cars, buttons, and so on — but is next to useless for handling *virtual reality*. This singularly overused term actually means something: creating an immersive environment that a user can explore, not just a static world with rotating objects.

Creating Virtual Reality

"Virtual Reality!" The term conjures up images from a dozen cheesy science fiction movies — the sterile laser and neon of *Tron*, the metallic/organic frenzy of *The Lawnmower Man*, the rather astonishing video game sensibilities of the animated *Reboot* series, and even the virtual environs of the Starship *Enterprise's* Holodeck. Yet, for all of that, the state of the art in virtual reality can be more readily found in flight simulators, architectural walk-throughs and virtual studios — the last an amusing turnabout where television sets become blank walls that can be overlaid with live video, 3D-rendered sets, and floating graphics over which the commentators talk and move.

The rise of VRML

The rise of 3D graphics has been driven in great part by the desire to create worlds with which people can interact. Flight simulators, long a domain of the military, started to infect the commercial market as skilled engineers left the service or techniques became declassified. Architectural firms took computer-aided design to heart and trained a whole generation of computer-literate architects who could see their visions converted quickly and inexpensively into faux reality. Moreover, games like Doom raised everyone's awareness that convincing 3D could be accomplished in real time. However, this was tempered by the fact that several different "standards" existed for creating 3D worlds.

In 1996 a consortium of graphics software and hardware developers laid the foundation for the next link in 3D called *VRML*, for Virtual Reality Markup Language. The principle behind VRML was simple — create a nonproprietary 3D standard language that would be the equivalent of HTML in two dimensions, a standard for specifying models, lighting, cameras, and related parts of a 3D world, without relying on platform-specific features.

VRML 1.0 created environments that, with the proper "browser," would let you fly through various 3D worlds. It borrowed significantly from OpenGL, a modeling and rendering standard created by Silicon Graphics for architectural rendering. VRML 1.0 files were relatively compact, which made them ideal for Internet downloading.

The one problem that plagued most of these worlds was that, once the worlds were created, they held absolutely no interest for most people. Once the novelty wore off, quite a number of programmers and designers encountered the major paradox of 3D worlds — without some way to interact with it (and preferably with other people within it), most VRML worlds consisted of moving from one place to another with the occasional mouse click to enter a new region or return to a new HTML page.

The VRML consortium had been planning a 1.1 version of the technology that would add a few new features, but as the verdict came in about VRML 1.0, many realized that the next step would have to be fairly dramatic. Some way was needed to allow for individual motion of objects in the space, for hooks that accommodated external programming links, and for sensors that determined when a given action had taken place.

These changes became real in early 1997 as the VRML 2.0 standard was finalized. This version is considerably more dynamic — you can move items around (either programmatically or by "hand"), make events loop over time, respond to outside stimulus from the enclosing browser, and even play stereo music that will change in intensity as you move toward or away from an object (see Figure 25-18).

```
#VRML V2.0 utf8

DirectionalLight {
        direction -1 -1 1
}
DEF CoitTower Vista {
        type "SPHERE"
        filename "coit.jpg"
        vFov -0.785398 0.785398
        pitchRange -0.785398 0.785398
}
DEF MisslePos Transform {
        translation -650 -30 -650
        children [
                DEF MissleYaw Transform {
                        rotation 0 1 0 0
                        children [
                                DEF MisslePitch Transform {
                                        rotation 0 0 1 0
```

Figure 25-18: VRML includes support for stereo "surround" sound.

The next version of VRML is well underway, with its ultimate goals being shared communication, transference of objects, and the introduction of avatars. In this version, your 3D avatar can talk with someone else's avatar (to a certain extent literally, if both you and she have speech communication capabilities within your browsers). Further, your avatars can give and receive objects, feel the impact of gravity, and even battle monsters together (see Figure 25-19). There's a lot to work out yet, since much of what seems trivial is vastly more complicated when you have to literally create your universe from scratch. For example, in order for you to give someone else money in cyberspace, you have to create an encrypted data object, send the necessary protocols to a third-party e-money vendor, verify the transactions, pass the money from the hands (or claws) of one avatar to another, signal to the avatar's system that the e-money has arrived, and then dispose of the money avatar, all the while maintaining a high-level conversation.

Figure 25-19: VRML, short for Virtual Reality Modeling Language, lets you create interactive 3D worlds.

Reviewing the RealVR Xtra

In 1996 RealSpace created a VRML environment for Director. The first VRML Xtra was developed concurrently with the VRML 2.0 release, and offers a superset of commands for creating VRML 2.0 worlds that can also take advantage of *vistas*. A vista is a panoramic photograph that's wrapped around the whole world view, giving the impression that you are in a "real" world. The vista concept works remarkably well in conjunction with programs like Bryce 2 — you can generate a set of imaginary worlds that wrap completely around you and then set up hot spots that can take you to other vistas.

In a similar fashion, you can create virtual objects with transparency to give the illusion of a remote control (or if you're into Doom, a nail gun) or allow you to spin a photographic image completely around in space. Coupled with sensors and interpolators, your world can become remarkably complex and colorful. While its still not quite up to the standards of adding avatars into the world, the RealVR product is powerful enough to create dynamic walk-throughs and single-person adventure games. What's even better, you can actually communicate with the RealVR Xtra from Lingo. A demonstration of the RealVR Xtra can be found on the Macromedia Director 6 CD-ROM, under Xtra Partners/LivePicture/RealVR. While it includes both an authoring and a playback Xtra on the disk, the authoring module can only be activated via a password from Live Picture. Because of this, and the complexity of creating a VRML 2.0 world in general, any discussion about actually creating such a world falls outside the scope of this book.

Quizzing QuickTime VR

Apple has actually come up with two responses to the question of introducing three dimensionality onto the computer. The QuickDraw 3D Xtra focuses on the creation of live 3D entities, while QuickTimeVR (QTVR) is a method for creating interactive environments. With QuickTime VR, you can create a customized QuickTime file that — instead of playing as a traditional movie — lets you navigate through a panoramic world and work with interactive "sprites" and hot spots.

QuicktimeVR doesn't support VRML files or full three-dimensional objects; rather, it's a mechanism for working the "panoramic" three-dimensional worlds. In a panorama, either using Quicktime VR or RealVR, the background of the world is mapped around the viewer in one of two fashions:

- ✦ A cylindrical mapping in which the left side of the map meets the right side to form a continuous loop, and the tops and bottoms appear to extend into infinity above and below the user.

- ✦ A spherical mapping that wraps the background graphic around the rest of the "world," so that the viewer can see down to her feet or up to the "top of the sky" — an especially apt expression in this case.

Although the general quality of output is better for QuickTimeVR than for RealVR, Apple's product does suffer from some significant limitations. You need the QuickTime VR developer's kit to actually make QTVR files, and the kit is relatively expensive. In terms of complexity, QuickTime VR is probably about as complex as working with the XtraNet object.

Still, if you are concerned with getting the best, highest-quality 3D graphics and want the level of interactivity for the world to consist primarily of quick mouse clicks and other similar event handlers, you may want to look at QuickTime VR despite the cost. QuickTime VR and RealVR may appear to do similar things, but RealVR renders the world as a VRML environment, wrapping a JPEG image around either a cylinder or a sphere that in turn encapsulates the entire virtual reality world. QuickTime only controls the panorama, but returns Lingo handlers and provides Lingo methods and properties for direct manipulation of how that panorama is shown.

Summary

There can be no question that 3D technology is visually exciting, but it should be used sparingly and with care, especially if these tools are likely to be used in commercial products. The 3D arena is still evolving, especially with respect to Director.

- ✦ Simulating 3D with shadowed cast members is the least processor intensive way of pushing out of the screen, though it takes a fair amount of work to make the illusions appear real.
- ✦ The Alphamania Xtra can enhance the illusion of three dimensionality by casting shadows that affect sprites behind it.
- ✦ You can use three-dimensional tools such as Extreme 3D, Poser, KPT Bryce, Lightwave 3D, or Studio3D to create 2D cast members viewed from different angles.
- ✦ The QuickDraw 3D Xtra allows you to create true three-dimensional sprites on Stage. However, these objects use a great deal of processing power.
- ✦ Finally, QuickTime VR and RealVR can create moveable panoramas that can include hot spots and sprites. QuickTimeVR supports graphical "sprites," while RealVR makes use of VRML to create a complete, highly animated 3D environment.

✦ ✦ ✦

Appendixes

PART VI

In This Part

Appendix A
Installing and Configuring Director

Appendix B
Summary of Lingo Statements

Appendix C
Shortcuts

Appendix D
Resources

Appendix E
What's on the CD-ROM

Installing and Configuring Director

APPENDIX A

Installing Director is a reasonably straightforward process. The installation requires approximately 55–60MB of hard-disk space. Director offers you three installation options:

- ✦ The Compact option installs only those files required for Director's operation.

- ✦ The Typical option installs the entire program, with all of the options. Essentially, there is little difference in the amount of space required for the Compact and Typical installations.

- ✦ The Custom option allows you to choose which portions of the program you want to install. This installation option is useful when you need to reinstall a portion of the program. If you are performing the initial installation of Director using the Custom installation and you select all of the options, the amount of space required doesn't vary from a Typical installation.

Note The installation procedure outlined in this appendix uses the Custom installation, with all of the available options selected.

Director also offers you a variety of choices in the General and Network Preferences dialog boxes, which enable you to modify your work environment and control the way Director interfaces with the Internet. Using these options, you can custom-tailor the way Director uses system resources, displays your movies, and responds to commands. The preferences are described later in this appendix.

Using Access

On the CD-ROM — The Director CD-ROM has an Auto-Run feature called Access. When you insert the CD-ROM in the drive, Access starts, allowing you to install Director or explore the contents of the CD-ROM.

Tip — Director bundles a variety of useful utilities and applications that you can use to enhance your movies. Although they're not listed here, we recommend you take a few minutes to explore the CD-ROM. Click the Explore CD option on the Access main menu.

What to do when Auto-Run doesn't

Despite a software company's desire to make things as smooth and automatic as possible, one fact persists: Computers are somewhat like snowflakes, and no two have identical personalities. The result is that sometimes automatic run features don't automatically run. This may occur consistently or sporadically on any given computer. So, what do you do when Auto-Run doesn't?

You've got the CD-ROM in the drive. On the Macintosh, you've double-clicked the icon for your CD-ROM drive; on Windows, you've double-clicked the My Computer icon and then the CD-ROM drive icon. In most cases, this launches the Access Auto-Run program on the Director 6 CD-ROM, and the Access window appears. But if this doesn't work, in a few moments the contents for the root directory will appear in a window. To peruse the CD-ROM, double-click the Access icon. If you want to jump right into setting up Director 6, double-click the Setup icon.

Installing Director

1. Insert the Director CD-ROM into your CD-ROM drive. In a few moments the Access setup screen appears, displaying the choices available to you (see Figure A-1).

2. Click the Install Director 6 option to start the installation process. After the installation procedure initializes, a Welcome screen appears, displaying installation information.

3. Click the Next button to display the software licensing information. If you agree to the terms of the license, click Yes to continue the installation. You'll next see the Setup Type dialog box (Figure A-2).

Figure A-1: When the Access screen appears, you can choose to install Director or explore the CD-ROM.

4. Choose the setup option you want to use, and accept the default installation directory or choose a new location. Click Next to continue.
5. If you selected a Compact or Typical installation, the setup continues (you can skip step 6). If you selected Custom, the Select Components dialog box appears (Figure A-3).

Figure A-2: Choosing the type of installation you want for Director 6

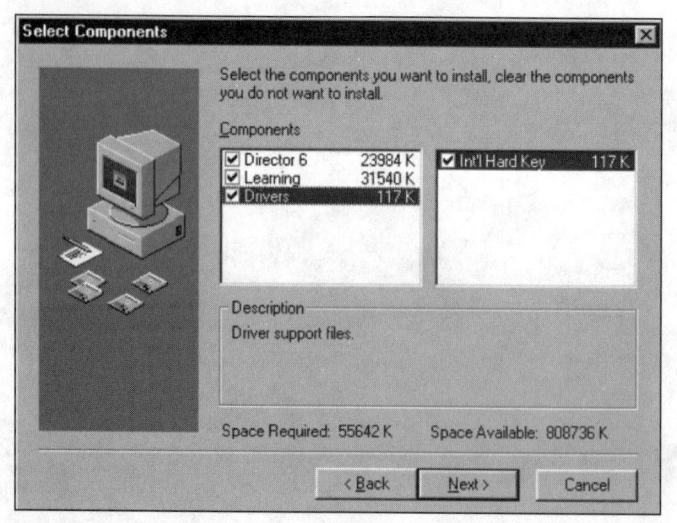

Figure A-3: Selecting the program components you want

6. Choose the components you want, and click Next to continue. If you are using Windows, you will be prompted to choose a Program Folder. Accept the default folder, or enter a new name in the Program Folders entry box. Click Next to continue.

7. When you have made your choices, the installer shows you a summary of them; click Next to continue or click Back to go back and make changes.

The installation now proceeds, transferring files to your hard disk from the CD-ROM. This can take some time. The amount of time depends on the resources available on your computer and the Director component options you selected. When the installation is done, the installer asks whether you want to view the Readme file. Always say yes! Next, you'll be prompted through several screens to register your copy of Director (you can do it now or later). Finally the Access screen reappears; you can exit or explore the Director 6 CD-ROM to locate the goodies it contains.

Tip

Before installing Director, it's a good idea to close any programs you have open and disable your screen saver. This allows your installation to proceed without interruption and reduces the amount of time required to install the program.

Currently Macromedia offers a single upgrade for Director 6: version 6.0.1. This upgrade is available from Macromedia's Web site (http://www.macromedia.com). To install it, download it to your hard drive and then double-click to select it. The installer then prompts you to locate the director.exe file on your computer. When you have you navigated to director.exe and double-clicked it, the installation proceeds without any need for your further intervention.

Configuring General and Network Preferences

The submenus found under the File⇨Preferences menu provide a variety of options and settings that affect the way Director performs. Many of the individual menus for specifying sprite, cast member, and other options appear throughout this book in conjunction with related topics. The General and Network Options on the File⇨Preferences menu are a bit different, however. In addition to determining the way Director itself performs, they also affect Director's interface with your system and the Internet.

Specifying general preferences

In the General Preferences dialog box, you specify settings that affect not only the current movie, but also Director's overall behavior. The settings you specify for User Interface and Memory will remain in effect until you change them. This lets you ensure consistency from one Director session to the next. Table A-1 lists the available general preference options and their effect on Director's behavior.

Table A-1
General Preferences

Option	Effect When Enabled
Classic Look (Monochrome)	Changes the current display interface, with the exception of the movie, to a monochrome display. This option saves system resources and prevents the appearance of the interface from changing when color palettes in the Score are altered.
Dialogs Appear at Mouse Position	Causes Director to display dialog boxes at the position of the mouse pointer. If this option is disabled, dialog boxes appear centered in the active window.
Save Window Positions on Exit	Causes Director to remember which windows were open and their location when you close the program. When you start Director for your next session, the dialog boxes open during the previous session are displayed in the same position as the previous session.

(continued)

Table A-1 (continued)

Option	Effect When Enabled
Message Window Recompiles Scripts	This option, which is enabled by default, causes your scripts to be recompiled when you open the Message window. If this option is disabled, you should recompile scripts prior to entering Lingo in the Message window.
Show Tooltips	Displays tags to identify the command or tool currently under the mouse pointer, whenever you pause momentarily over a tool or command. This option is especially useful when you are first learning your way around Director. This is the default setting.
Memory	Allows you to limit the amount of memory Director can use for operations. If you multitask and keep several applications open simultaneously, you might want to consider limiting the amount of resources available to Director. We recommend never lowering this amount below 16MB of RAM. If this option is disabled, you are specifying that Director can use as much of the available RAM as is needed, up to the amount indicated in the Limit Memory Size To box.

Setting General Preferences

1. Select File ➪ Preferences ➪ General Preferences to display the General Preferences dialog box (Figure A-4).
2. Click the check boxes for the options you want to use, and click OK to complete the operation and return to Director's main window.

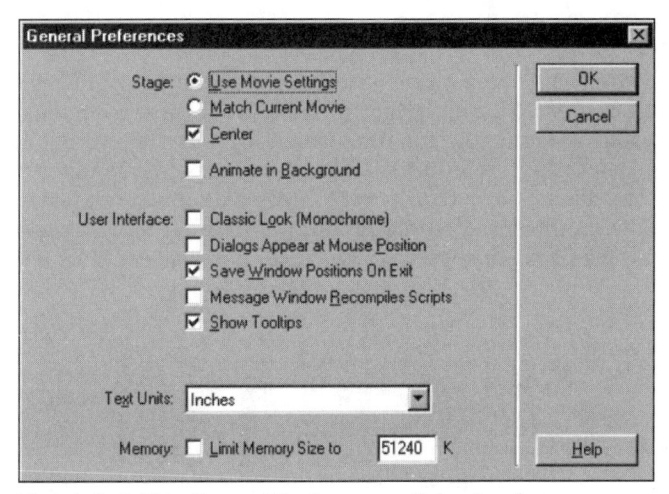

Figure A-4: The General Preferences dialog is where you specify the way you want Director to behave.

Configuring Director's general preferences to meet your needs enables you to work more efficiently. For example, if your movie contains a variety of palettes, each time the palette changes in the Score, Director's title bar, dialog boxes, and window change correspondingly. This occurs because you can't have more than one palette active at a given time in Director.

Projector palette changes don't affect the overall computer display when the movie is played back on a user's machine, but they do affect the display when you are developing a project. The result can be very distracting. For development, choosing a Classic Look not only reduces the distraction, but also decreases the resource demand Director places on your computer system. A monochrome display requires far less during refresh than do color palettes of greater depth.

Other settings in the General Preferences are matters of convenience, such as where dialog boxes appear and whether you save window positions when you exit the program. These settings can give you a little more screen real estate in which to work, and help you to be productive more quickly.

Specifying network preferences

Director allows you to link files on the Internet for use in your movies and projectors (see Chapter 24 for more information about Director, Shockwave, and the Internet). Using dynamically linked information from the Internet is useful when you want to incorporate information that changes frequently, such as stock quotes or weather data. The Network Preferences dialog box contains options that control communication between Director and the Internet (see Table A-2). You can specify settings such as the browser you want to use, disk caching, and proxy information.

Table A-2
Network Preference Options

Option	Description or Effect
Preferred Browser	Specify the location of the browser program that you want to use.
Launch When Needed	Causes Director to launch your preferred browser when an event requiring a browser is encountered by the program. If you don't specify a preferred browser, Director prompts you for the browser information or allows you to disable this option.
Disk Cache Size	Specify the amount of hard disk space you want to make available for disk caching.
Check Documents	Select Once Per Session if you want Director to verify and update dynamically linked media once per Director session or once per playback of a projector.
	Select Every Time if you want Director to verify and update dynamically linked media each time it encounters an instance requiring the information. This choice can slow the playback of a projector or movie.
Proxies	Select No Proxies to tell Director that you have a direct connection to the Internet, such as a private Internet Service Provider, that is not dependent on a local network server.
	Select Manual Configuration to tell Director that your machine is connected to a local network server that has security firewalls in place. If you choose this option, you need to enter the http or ftp URL and port number that provide your access to the Internet.

Setting Network Preferences

1. Select File ➪ Preferences ➪ Network Preferences to display the Network Preferences dialog box (Figure A-5).

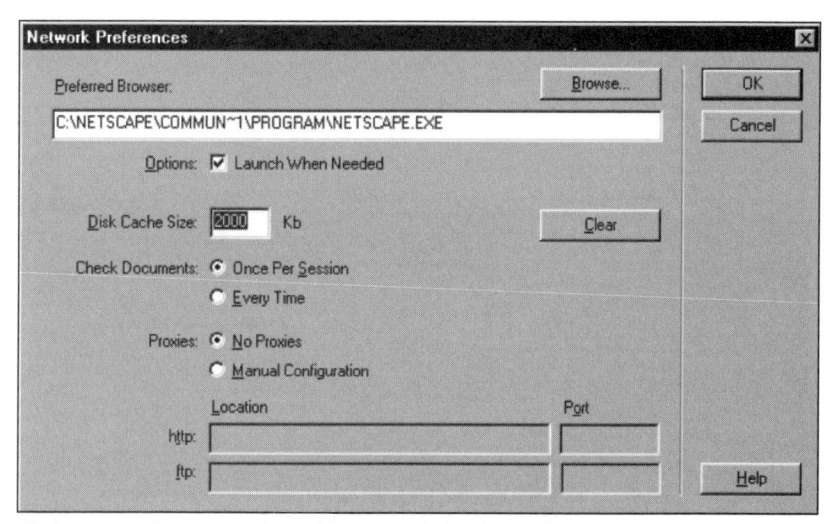

Figure A-5: The Network Preferences dialog box allows you to control the way Director interfaces with the Internet.

2. Set or enter information for the network options you want to use. Click OK to complete the operation and return to Director's main window.

Note When you are working with Director, you can clear the disk cache immediately by clicking the Clear button in the Network Preferences dialog box. Clearing the disk cache ensures that the dynamically linked media you see in a projector or movie is current.

✦ ✦ ✦

APPENDIX B

Summary of Lingo Statements

This appendix provides a quick reference to Lingo keywords and examples of how they can be used. It features the most common Lingo commands, functions, handlers, and properties available in Director 6.*x*; all Lingo elements used in this book's discussions are covered here.

Commands

Command Name	Syntax or Example	Description
abort	abort	Exits the current handler and any handler it called, without executing the remaining statements in the handler. Does not quit Director.
add	add (nameOf-TheList, data)	Adds a new entry to the list. If the list is unsorted, the new entry appears at the end of the list. If the list is sorted, the new entry appears in alphabetical order.
addAt	addAt (nameOf-TheList, position, data)	Adds the specified *data* at the *position* indicated. Data in that position is shifted to the next position. No data is overwritten.

(continued)

Command Name	Syntax or Example	Description
append	append (nameOfTheList, data)	Adds the specified *data* to the end of the list. This command generates a scripting error when used with a property list.
close window	close window "windowName"	Closes a window or movie in a window but does not remove it from memory.
closeXlib	closeXlib filename	Closes an Xlibrary file. Xtras or Xobjects are stored in Xlibraries.
deleteAt	deleteAt (nameOfTheList, position)	Removes the data at the specified *position* from the list.
downLoadNetThing	downLoadNetThing netAddress	Downloads a file from the network to a file on the local workstation. Operates in the background; while the download occurs, the current movie continues playing. Once installed on the local user's workstation, the file can be loaded into memory without the normal delays on network traffic.
forget window	forget window "windowName"	Closes a window or movie in a window and removes it from memory.
getAt	getAt (nameOfTheList, position)	Returns the data stored at the specified *position* in the list.
getLast	getLast (nameOfTheList)	Returns the last piece of data stored in the list.
getNetText	getNetText netAddress	Retrieves a file that is read by Lingo as text.
getOne	getOne (nameOfTheList, data)	Returns the position of the specified *data* in the list.
getPos	getPos (nameOfTheList, data)	Returns the position within the list where the *data* is stored.

Command Name	Syntax or Example	Description
`goToNetMovie`	`goToNetMovie netAddress`	Downloads and runs a Shockwave movie from the network. The new movie occupies the same Stage area as the current movie.
`goToNetPage`	`goToNetPage netAddress`	Opens a URL on the network. Equivalent to including an `<a href=http:// netAddress > </a>` tag in an HTML document. It can display a Shockwave movie, an HTML document, or any other MIME type supported by the browser. The URL must be listed within quotation marks.
`go to`	`go loop`	Jumps to the first marker previous to the current frame.
	`go next`	Jumps to the next marker not associated with the current frame.
	`go to frame frameNumber`	Jumps to specified frame in the current movie.
	`go to the frame`	Loops to the current frame.
	`go to the frame +1`	Moves the playback head to the next frame.
	`go to marker markerName`	Jumps to the specified marker.
	`go to movie movieName`	Jumps to a second movie and begins playing that movie.
	`go next`	Jumps to the next marker not associated with the current frame.
	`go previous`	Jumps to the previous marker not associated with the current frame.

`halt`	`on mouseUp`
	`halt`
	`end`
		Stops the current movie from playing but does not exit Directory.

`installMenu`	`installMenu castIdentifier`	Installs a custom menu based on a field cast member.

(continued)

Command Name	Syntax or Example	Description
	`InstallMenu 0`	Removes an installed custom menu.
`mMessageList`	`put mMessage-List(xtra xtraName)`	Lists all methods associated with an Xtra.
`move`	`move member oldCastLocation, newCastLocation`	Moves a cast member from one cast member slot to another.
`netStatus`	`netStatus message`	Displays a *message* in the status bar area of the user's Web browser.
`open window`	`open window "windowName"`	Opens a window or movie in a window and brings it to the front of the Stage.
`openXlib`	`openXlib filename`	Opens an Xlibrary file. Xtras or Xobjects are stored in Xlibraries.
`play`	`play markerName`	Jumps to and starts playing the frame with the specified marker.
	`play frame frameNumber`	Jumps to and starts playing the specified frame.
	`Play frame markerName`	Jumps to and starts playing the frame with the specified marker.
	`play frame markerName of movie movieName`	Jumps to and starts playing the specified frame with the named marker in the specified movie.
	`play movie movieName`	Jumps to and starts playing the specified movie.
`preloadNetThing`	`preloadNetThing (netAddress)`	Preloads a file into the browser's local disk cache, so the resource can run later without the normal download delay. Operates in the background; while the preload occurs, the current movie continues playing.
`put`	`put value into variable`	Assigns a value or string to a variable.

`quit`	`on mouseUp`
	`quit`
	`end`
		Stops a movie and exits Director.

`set`	`set property to state`	Assigns a value to a property or variable.

Command Name	Syntax or Example	Description
setAt	setAt (nameOfTheList, position, data)	Replaces the data item at the *position* specified, with the *data* specified.
setPref	setPref fileName, textString	Writes a text string (*textString*) to a file (*fileName*) on the user's local hard drive. The *fileName* must be a valid filename.
showXlib	showXlib	Displays a list of all Xtras installed on your system.
sort	sort (nameOfTheList)	Alphabetizes all entries in the list.

Functions

Function Name	Action
abs	Calculates the absolute value of a numerical expression.
constrainH	Limits the movement of a designated sprite to within the left and right edges of a designated target sprite.
constrainV	Limits the movement of a designated sprite to within the top and bottom edges of a designated target sprite.
the controlDown	Determines whether the Control (Ctrl) key is being pressed.
count (nameOfTheList)	Returns a value representing the number of items in the list.
getPref (fileName)	Returns the contents of the specified file (*fileName*) in the Prefs folder within the user's Plug-In Support folder. If the file does not exist or is empty, getPref returns a value of VOID. The *fileName* parameter must be a valid filename on the user's operating system.
ilk (nameOfTheList)	Returns a string indicating whether the *nameOfTheList* is a linear list or a property list. If the list identified by *nameOfTheList* is a linear list, this function returns the string #list. If the list is a property list, ilk returns the string #propList.

(continued)

Function Name	Action
`The key`	Returns the code for the last key pressed.
`the machineType`	Indicates by a numeric value whether the current system is an IBM PC-type or Macintosh system (`256` indicates an IBM PC-type).
`max (nameOfTheList)`	Returns the maximum value in the list. When working with strings, the result is based on the ASCII value of the string, evaluated character by character, left to right.
`min (nameOfTheList)`	Returns the minimum value in the list.
`the mouseChar`	Starts counting at the beginning of the field and returns the sequential number that represents the current character under the mouse pointer.
`mouseH`	Returns the horizontal position of the mouse pointer.
`the mouseItem`	Returns the number of the current item in the field that is under the mouse pointer.
`the mouseLine`	Returns the number of the current line under the mouse pointer in a field sprite.
`the mouseWord`	Returns the number of the current word in the field that is under the mouse pointer.
`the mouseUp`	Determines if the mouse button is *not* being held down.
`mouseV`	Returns the vertical position of the mouse pointer.
`netDone()`	Determines if a network operation (started by `downLoadNetThing`, `getNetText`, `goToNetMovie`, `goToNetPage` or `preLoadNetThing`) has completed. Returns True (the default) if a network operation has successfully completed or if the operation was terminated by browser error. Returns False if the operation is incomplete.
`netError()`	Returns a null or empty string until the specified network operation is complete. Upon completion, `netError()` returns an "OK" string if the operation was successful. If the operation is unsuccessful, the function returns an error number.
`netLastModDate()`	Returns a text string that indicates the last date a downloaded item (using the `getNetText` or `preLoadNetThing` command) was modified, based on the item's http header.
`netMIME()`	Returns the MIME type of the specified http item.

Function Name	Action
`netTextResult()`	Returns the text result of the last network operation. If you use the `getNetText` command, `netTextResult()` returns the text of the http item accessed.
`the pauseState`	Determines if a movie is paused.
`random()`	Returns a random number within a specified range.
`rollover`	Indicates if the mouse pointer is over a specified sprite.
`The runMode`	Displays the run mode of Director—that is, whether the current movie is running in authoring mode (`author`), as a projector (`projector`), or as a Shockwave movie (`plugin`).
`the shiftDown`	Determines whether the Shift key is being pressed.
`the stillDown`	Determines whether the mouse button is still held down.
`soundBusy`	Indicates if sound is currently playing in a specified sound channel.
`time`	Returns the current time as stored by your computer system.

Properties

Property Name	Example	Action
`the activeCastLib`	`set variable to the activeCastLib`	Returns the number of the most recently activated cast.
`the activeWindow`	`set variable to the activeWindow`	Returns the name of the currently active window in the movie. For the main movie, the active Window is the Stage. For an MIAW, the active Window is the MIAW.
`the actorList`	`set the actorList = []`	A list of child objects (explicitly added to the list) that receive the stepFrame message each time the playback head enters a new frame.

(continued)

Property Name	Example	Action
addProp	addProp (nameOfTheList, property, data)	Adds a new entry to the property list. If the list is unsorted, the entry appears at the end of the list. If the list is sorted, the new entry appears in alphabetical order.
the alignment of member	set the alignment of member to castMemberName Alignment	Sets alignment of the field to "left," "centered," or "right." The alignment parameters must be enclosed within quotes.
the backColor of member	set the backColor of member castMemberName to colorCode	Background color for the text in a field. Has no effect if the field's ink is set to Background Transparent.
the border of member	set the border of member castMemberName to pixels	Width of the border (in pixels) surrounding the text field.
the boxDropShadow of member	set the boxDropShadow of member castMember-Name to pixels	Offset distance in pixels for a duplicate copy of the rectangular text box. The offset is down and to the right of the text box, which adds a drop shadow effect to the text box (not the text it contains).
the checkMark of menuItem	set the checkMark of menuItem menuOption of menu menuName to state	Display (True) or hides (False) a check mark in front of the specified menu option.
the colorDepth	if the colorDepth = 8 then play movie movieName	Displays the current color depth of the monitor, such as 8-bit color.

Property Name	Example	Action
the constraint of sprite	set the constraint of sprite *spriteName1* to *spriteName2*	Limits the movement of the specified sprite to within the bounding box of a second sprite.
the current-SpriteNum	put the current-SpriteNum	Returns the highest channel number (or sprite number) in the Score over which the mouse is currently rolling.
the cursor of sprite	set the cursor of sprite *spriteNumber* to *cursorStyle*	Establishes the appearance of the mouse pointer over a specified sprite.
deleteProp	DeleteProp (*nameOfTheList, property*)	Removes the data associated with the specified property. When using property names, Lingo is case-sensitive.
the dropShadow of member	set the dropShadow of member *castMemberName* to *pixels*	Offset distance in pixels for a drop shadow copy of the text. The drop shadow appears beneath the text in the text field, giving the illusion that the text is casting a shadow. A typical text drop shadow is offset by 2 to 4 pixels.
the enabled of menuItem	set the enabled of menuItem *itemName* of menu *menuName* to *state*	Enables (TRUE) or disables (FALSE) a menu option.
findPos	findPos (*nameOfTheList, property*)	Returns a value representing the position in the list where the specified property appears. If the specified property is not in the list, the function returns a value of False. The property name is case-sensitive.

(continued)

Property Name	Example	Action
findPosNear	FindPosNear (nameOfTheList, property)	Returns the same result as the findPos function, except when the specified property does not appear in the list. When that occurs, findPosNear returns a value representing the closest position in the list based on the sort order. For instance, if the list is Scores = ["Joan": 1500, "Pat": 2000, "Patrick": 10000, "Quincy": 111], then issuing the findPosNear(Scores, "Patsy") command returns the value 4. If the property "Patsy" were in the list, it would hold position 4.
the float Precision	put the float Precision	Displaces the precision (number of decimal places beyond the decimal point) for floating-point numbers.
the font of member	set the font of member castMemberName to font	Specific font used by the field. The font names must be enclosed within quotes.
the fontSize of member	set the fontSize of member castMemberName to fontSize	Size of the font in *points*. Most body text will be in the 12–14 point range.
the fontStyle of member	set the fontStyle of member castMemberName to fontStyle	Style of the font. Setting the style to "plain" causes the font to lose all other styles, but otherwise font styles are additive (for example, setting bold followed by italic makes the selection both bold and italic). Correct syntax requires that these parameters be enclosed within parentheses, and the font style names must be enclosed within quotes.
the foreColor of member	set the foreColor of member castMemberNumber to foreColor	Color of the text; values are from the current color palette. If no palette is currently specified, this function uses the default system palette.

Property Name	Example	Action
getAt	getAt (nameOfTheList, position)	Returns the data associated with the property at the specified position in the list.
getOne	getOne (nameOfTheList, data)	Returns the property name associated with the specified data.
getPropAt	getPropAt (nameOfTheList, position)	Returns the property name stored at the specified position in the property list.
the ink of sprite	set the ink of sprite spriteName to 8	Establishes the ink effect applied to a specific sprite.
the locH of sprite	put the locH of sprite spriteName	Indicates the horizontal location of a sprite on the Stage.
the locV of sprite	put the locV of sprite spriteName	Indicates the vertical location of a sprite on the Stage.
the margin of member	set the margin of member marginName to value	Minimum distance between the text and the insides of the text box.
the maxInteger	put the maxInteger	Displays the largest whole number that is supported by the user's system.
the member of sprite	put the member of sprite spriteName	Indicates the cast member and cast upon which the sprite is based.
the name of menuItem	set the name of menuItem itemNumber of menu menuName	Establishes the name for an option on a custom menu.
the platform	put the platform	Displays the type of workstation. Possible values: Macintosh,68k Macintosh,PowerPC Windows,16 Windows,32
setProp	setProp (nameOfTheList, property, newdata)	Replaces the existing data stored by the specified property with the new data specified.
the stageColor	put the stageColor	Indicates the color setting for the movie's Stage.
the visible of sprite	set the visible of sprite 3 to True spriteName	Establishes whether a sprite is visible or not.

Constants

Constant	Represents
BACKSPACE	The Backspace key on a Windows system, and the Delete key on a Macintosh system.
EMPTY	An empty or null string, such as "".
ENTER	The Enter key on the Macintosh keyboard, and the numeric keypad Enter key on PCs.
TRUE	The statement, expression, or condition is true.
QUOTE	The double-quotation mark (").
RETURN	The Return key on the Macintosh; the Enter key on a Windows PC.
SPACE	A space character generated by pressing the spacebar.
TAB	The Tab key.
FALSE	The statement, expression, or condition is not true.
VOID	No value.

Shortcuts

APPENDIX C

Command	Macintosh Shortcut	Windows Shortcut	Description
Align	Command+K	Ctrl+K	Displays the Align window, where you can specify alignment options.
Cast	Command+3	Ctrl+3	Toggles the display of the Cast window.
Control ⇨ Ignore Breakpoints	Option+F9 Shift+Option+ Command+I	Alt+F9	Causes Lingo to ignore any breakpoints in the movie's scripts as the movie plays.
Control ⇨ Loop Playback	Command+ Option+L	Ctrl+Alt+L	Loops the playback of the active movie.
Control ⇨ Play	Command+ Option+P	Ctrl+Alt+P	Plays the active movie.
Control ⇨ Recompile All Scripts	Command+ Shift+Option+ C	Shift+F8	Recompiles all scripts and checks them for errors.
Control ⇨ Rewind	Command+ Option+R	Ctrl+Alt+R	Rewinds the active movie.
Control ⇨ Step Backward	Command+ Option+Left	Ctrl+Alt+Left	Moves the playhead back one frame.

(continued)

Command	Macintosh Shortcut	Windows Shortcut	Description
Control ⇨ Step Forward	Command+Option+Right	Ctrl+Alt+Right	Moves the playhead forward one frame.
Control ⇨ Stop	Command+Option+.	Ctrl+Alt+.	Stops the active movie.
Control ⇨ Toggle Breakpoint	Command+Shift+Option+K	F9	Inserts and removes breakpoints for the current line of Lingo in the Script window.
Control ⇨ Volume ⇨ Mute	Command+Option+M	Ctrl+Alt+M	Mutes the active sound.
Control ⇨ Watch Expression	Command+Shift+Option+W	Shift+F9	Adds to the Watcher window any expressions and variables in the current line of Lingo in the Script window (the line the text cursor is currently in).
Edit ⇨ Clear Cast Members or Edit ⇨ Clear Sprites or Edit ⇨ Clear Text	Del	Del	Clears the selected cast member, sprite, or text.
Edit ⇨ Copy Cast Members or Edit ⇨ Copy Sprites or Edit ⇨ Copy Text	Command+C	Ctrl+C	Copies the selected cast members, sprites, or text to the Scrapbook (Clipboard).
Edit ⇨ Cut Cast Members or Edit ⇨ Cut Sprites or Edit ⇨ Cut Text	Command+X	Ctrl+X	Removes the selected cast members, sprites, or text from the Score and places them in the Scrapbook (Clipboard).

Command	Macintosh Shortcut	Windows Shortcut	Description
Edit ⇨ Edit Entire Sprite	Command+Option+[	Ctrl+Alt+[	Allows you to edit an entire sprite as a unit.
Edit ⇨ Edit Sprite Frames	Command+Option+]	Ctrl+Alt+]	Allows you to edit individual frames in a sprite.
Edit ⇨ Exchange Cast Members	Command+E	Ctrl+E	Exchanges the selected sprite in the Score; selected cast member appears in the Cast window.
Edit ⇨ Find Again	Command+Option+F	Ctrl+Alt+F	Finds the next instance of the element you specified using the Find command.
Edit ⇨ Find Cast Member	Command+;	Ctrl+;	Finds the cast members you specify.
Edit ⇨ Find Handler	Command+Shift+;	Ctrl+Shift+;	Finds the handler you specify.
Edit ⇨ Find Selection	Command+H	Ctrl+H	Finds the selection you specify.
Edit ⇨ Find Text	Command+F	Ctrl+F	Finds the text that you specify.
Edit ⇨ Launch External Editor	Command+,	Ctrl+,	Launches the application you designated in Preferences as the external editor, for the selected cast member.
Edit ⇨ Paste	Command+V	Ctrl+V	Pastes the contents of the Scrapbook (Clipboard) into the active window. (Note: You can't paste objects on the Stage.)
Edit ⇨ Repeat	Command+Y	Ctrl+Y	Repeats the last action.
Edit ⇨ Replace Again	Command+Option+E	Ctrl+Alt+E	Replaces the element in the Find box with the element in the Replace box.
Edit ⇨ Undo	Command+Z	Ctrl+Z	Undoes the last action.
File ⇨ Close	Command+W	Ctrl+F4	Closes the active window.
File ⇨ Export	Command+Shift+R	Ctrl+Shift+R	Exports a range of frames as either a digital video or sequence of bitmap files.

(continued)

Command	Macintosh Shortcut	Windows Shortcut	Description
File ⇨ Import	Command+R	Ctrl+R	Imports files as cast members.
File ⇨ New Cast	Command+Option+N	Ctrl+Alt+N	Creates a new cast. You can choose an internal or external linked cast.
File ⇨ New Movie	Command+N	Ctrl+N	Starts a new movie. If you have a movie already open, you'll be prompted to save the movie.
File ⇨ Open	Command+O	Ctrl+O	Opens an existing file.
File ⇨ Page Setup	Command+Shift+P	Ctrl+Shift+P	Enables you to specify the printer setup.
File ⇨ Preferences ⇨ General	Command+U	Ctrl+U	Allows you to specify the General Preferences for your movie.
File ⇨ Print	Command+P	Ctrl+P	Prints the selected information about your movie.
File ⇨ Save	Command+S	Ctrl+S	Saves the existing file using the current name.
Help ⇨ Director Help	(none)	F1	Displays the Director help information.
Help ⇨ Help Pointer	Command+?	Shift+F1	Enables the Help Pointer; you can click on an element or menu item to get information.
Insert ⇨ Frames	Command+Shift+]	Ctrl+Shift+]	Inserts the specified number of frames into the Score at the selected location.
Insert ⇨ Keyframe	Command+Option+K	Ctrl+Option+K	Inserts a keyframe at the selected location in the Score.
Insert ⇨ Remove Frame	Command+[	Ctrl+[	Removes the selected frames from the Score.
Modify ⇨ Arrange ⇨ Bring to Front	Command+Shift+Up	Ctrl+Shift+Up	Brings the selected element to the front of the Stage.
Modify ⇨ Arrange ⇨ Move Backward	Command+Down	Ctrl+Down	Moves the selected element back one layer.

Command	Macintosh Shortcut	Windows Shortcut	Description
Modify ⇨ Arrange ⇨ Move Forward	Command+Up	Ctrl+Up	Brings the selected element forward one layer.
Modify ⇨ Arrange ⇨ Send to Back	Command+Shift+Down	Ctrl+Shift+Down	Moves the selected element to the back of the Stage.
Modify ⇨ Member ⇨ Properties	Command+I	Ctrl+I	Displays the cast member Cast properties of the selected cast member.
Modify ⇨ Cast Member ⇨ Script	Command+'	Ctrl+'	Displays scripts attached to the selected cast member.
Modify ⇨ Movie ⇨ Casts	Command+Shift+C	Ctrl+Shift+C	Displays a list of the casts associated with the active movie.
Modify ⇨ Movie ⇨ Properties	Command+Shift+D	Ctrl+Shift+D	Displays the movie properties.
Modify ⇨ Sprite ⇨ Properties	Command+Shift+I	Ctrl+Shift+I	Displays the properties of the selected sprite.
Modify ⇨ Sprite ⇨ Script	Command+Shift+'	Ctrl+Shift+'	Displays the scripts attached to the selected sprite.
Modify ⇨ Sprite ⇨ Tweening	Command+Shift+B	Ctrl+Shift+B	Displays the Tween dialog box, where you can specify tweening options for the selected sprites.
Modify ⇨ Tweak	Command+Shift+K	Ctrl+Shift+K	Displays the Tweak window, where you can move selected sprites with precision.
View ⇨ Grids ⇨ Show	Command+Shift+Option+G	Ctrl+Shift+Alt+G	Displays a grid on Stage.
View ⇨ Grids ⇨ Snap To	Command+Option+G	Ctrl+Alt+G	Causes elements on Stage to snap to the grid.
View ⇨ Marker ⇨ Next	Command+Right	Ctrl+Right	Moves the playhead to the next marker.
View ⇨ Marker ⇨ Previous	Command+Left	Ctrl+Left	Moves the playhead to the previous marker.
View ⇨ Sprite Overlay ⇨ Show Info	Command+Shift+Option+O	Ctrl+Shift+Alt+O	Displays the sprite information overlay on Stage.

(continued)

Command	Macintosh Shortcut	Windows Shortcut	Description
View ⇨ Sprite Overlay ⇨ Show Paths	Command+Shift+Option+H	Ctrl+Shift+Alt+H	Shows sprite paths on Stage.
View ⇨ Zoom ⇨ Narrower	Command+ -	Ctrl+ -	Reduces the view of the Score by making each frame narrower.
View ⇨ Zoom ⇨ Wider	Command++	Ctrl++	Enlarges the view of the Score by making each frame wider.
Window ⇨ Color Palettes	Command+Option+7	Ctrl+Alt+7	Toggles the display of the Color Palettes window.
Window ⇨ Control Panel	Command+2	Ctrl+2	Toggles the display of the Control Panel.
Window ⇨ Debugger	Command+`	Ctrl+`	Toggles the display of the Debugger window.
Window ⇨ Field	Command+8	Ctrl+8	Toggles the display of the Field window.
Window ⇨ Inspectors ⇨ Behavior	Command+Option+;	Ctrl+Alt+;	Displays the Behavior Inspector.
Window ⇨ Inspectors ⇨ Sprite	Command+Option+S	Ctrl+Alt+S	Displays the Sprite Inspector.
Window ⇨ Inspectors ⇨ Text	Command+T	Ctrl+T	Displays the Text Inspector.
Window ⇨ Markers	Command+Shift+M	Ctrl+Shift+M	Toggles the display of the markers in the movie.
Window ⇨ Message	Command+M	Ctrl+M	Toggles the display of the Message window.
Window ⇨ Paint	Command+5	Ctrl+5	Toggles the display of the Paint window.
Window ⇨ Score	Command+4	Ctrl+4	Toggles the display of the Score window.
Window ⇨ Script	Command+0	Ctrl+0	Toggles the display of the Script window.
Window ⇨ Stage	Command+1	Ctrl+1	Toggles the display of the Stage to the front.
Window ⇨ Text	Command+6	Ctrl+6	Toggles the display of the Text window.

Command	Macintosh Shortcut	Windows Shortcut	Description
Window ⇨ Tool Palette	Command+7	Ctrl+7	Displays the Tool Palette when selected.
Window ⇨ Toolbar	Command+Shift+Option+B	Ctrl+Shift+Alt+B	Displays the main toolbar when selected.
Window ⇨ Video	Command+9	Ctrl+9	Toggles the display of the Video window.
Window ⇨ Watcher	Command+Shift+`	Ctrl+Shift+`	Toggles the display of the Watcher window.

Resources

The following individuals and corporations contributed materials or services that were used in the Director 6 Bible. Where possible, e-mail addresses, World Wide Web sites, and telephone numbers have been included.

Aladdin Systems
165 Westridge Drive
Watsonville, CA 95076
Phone: 408-761-6200
FAX: 408-761-6206
E-mail: info@aladdinsys.com
URL: http://www.aladdinsys.com

Aris Entertainment
Phone: 310-821-0234
Fax: 310-821-6463

ArtBeats
2611 South Mrytle Road
Mrytle Creek, OR 97457
Phone: 800-444-9392
FAX: 541-863-4547
E-mail: facts@artbeats.com
URL: http://www.artbeats.com/

Asymetrix Corporation
110-110th Ave., NE
Bellevue, WA 98004
Phone: 800-448-6543
Fax: 206-637-1504
URL: http://www.asymetrix.com

Classic PIO Partners
87 East Green St., Suite 309
Pasadena, CA 91105
Phone: 800-370-2746
FAX: 818-564-8554
E-mail: cpio@best.com

Corel Corporation
1600 Carling Ave.
Ottawa, ONT, Canada K1Z 8R7
Phone: 800 772-6735
URL: http://www.corel.com

Digital Stock Corporation
750 Second Street
Encinitas, CA 92024
Phone: 760-634-6500
FAX: 760-634-6510
E-mail: sales@digitalstock.com
URL: http://www.digitalstock.com

Dynamic Graphics, Inc.
6000 N. Forest Park Drive
Peoria, IL 61614-3592
Phone: 309-687-0204
FAX: 309-688-8515
E-mail: service@dgusa.com
URL: http://www.dgusa.com

Equilibrium
Three Harbor Drive, Suite 111
Sausalito, CA 94965
Phone: 800-524-8651
FAX: 415-332-4433
E-mail: dave_pola@equil.com
URL: http://www.equilibrium.com

Four Palms
11260 Roger Bacon Drive, Suite 502
Reston, VA 22090-5023
Phone: 703-834-0200
FAX: 703-834-0219
URL: http://www.fourpalms.com

Fresh, The Music Library
34 South Main St.
Hanover, NH 03755
Phone: 800-545-0688
FAX: 603-643-1388
URL: http://www.freshmusic.com

Image Club Graphics
Adobe Systems, Inc.
1525 Greenview Drive
Grande Prairie, TX 75050
Phone: 800-661-9410
URL: http://www.imageclub.com

Image Farm, Inc.
110 Spadina Ave., Suite 309
Toronto, ONT, Canada M5V 2K4
Phone: 800-438-3276
FAX: 416-504-4163
E-mail: image-info@imagefarm.com
URL: http://www.imagefarm.com

Indigo Rose Corporation
123 Bannatyne Ave., Suite 230
Winnipeg, MAN, Canada R3B 0R3
Phone: 800-665-9668
FAX: 204-942-3421
E-mail: info@IndigiRose.com
URL: http://www.IndigoRose.com

Innovative Media Corp.
631 East Allen
Springfield, IL 62073
Phone: 217-544-4614

Integration New Media Inc.
1425 Rene-Levesque West, Suite 402
Montreal, Quebec, Canada H3G 1T7
Phone: 800-400-1772
FAX: 514-871-9251
E-mail: info@integration.qc.ca
URL: http://www.integration.qc.ca

JASC, Inc.
P.O. Box 44997
Eden Prairie, MN 55344-0997
Phone: 612-930-9800
FAX: 612-930-9172
E-mail: mattk@jasc.com
URL: http://www.jasc.com

Jones, Jeffrey E.
MIDI Music
8743 W. 121 Terrace #902
Overland Park, KS 66212
Phone: 913-338-4566
E-mail: jjones@johnco.cc.ks.us
URL: http://www.johnco.cc.ks.us/~jjones/

Kennerly Music Productions
400 Peachtree Industrial Blvd., Suite 5
Suwanne, GA 30174
Phone: 770-271-2024
FAX: 770-271-2123
E-mail: rek@mindspring.com
URL: http://www.kenmusic.com

Lovejoy, Pat and David
Photographic Images
E-mail: dlovejoy@ix.netcom.com

Macromedia
600 Townsend
San Francisco, CA 94103
Phone: 415-252-2000
FAX: 415-626-0554
E-mail: info@macromedia.com
URL: http://www.macromedia.com

MetaCreations Corporation
5550 Scotts Valley Dr.
P.O. Box 66959
Scotts Valley, CA 95067-6959
Phone: 408-430-4100
FAX: 408-438-9670
URL: http://www.metacreations.com

Miller Graphics Consulting
1108 Cove Lane
Oliver Springs, TN 37840
Phone: 423-435-9740
FAX: 423-435-1838
E-mail: berak@esper.com
URL: http://www.rainwatermedia.com

Monaghen, Dale
Photographic Images
2805 Gillham Road 1-N
Kansas City, MO 64108
Phone: 816-931-7812
E-mail: infrared@uit.net
URL: http://www.inf.net/~fotoman/

Mulvihill, Joe and Sherri
Photographic Images
E-mail: jmulvihill@waymark.net
          smulvihill@waymark.net

Nico Mak Computing, Inc.
P.O. Box 919
Bristol, CT 06011
Phone: 860-429-3539
FAX: 860-429-3542
E-mail: info@winzip.com
URL: http://www.winzip.com

Planet Art
Phone: 888-526-5255
E-mail: diverse@diverseworks.com
URL: http://www.diverseworks.com/

Prosonus/Big Fish Software
11003 Penrose Street, Suite C
Sun Valley, CA 91352
Phone: 800-717-3474
FAX: 818-768-4117

Robert Sindt Programming Support
E-mail: rsindt@johnco.cc.ks.us
URL: http://www.johnco.cc.ks.us/~rsindt/

Stuffy Room Productions
E-mail: stuffyroom@usa.net
URL: http://www.esper.com/bberak/dementia/dementia.html

Tabuleiro da Baiana Multimedia
1089 Pinheiros
Sao Paulo, SP, Brazil 05414-012
Phone: 55-11-8132547
FAX: 55-11-8142254
E-mail: atend@tbaiana.com
URL: http://www.tbaiana.com

Terran Interactive, Inc.
2 North First Street, Suite 215
San Jose, CA 95113
Phone: 800-577-3443
FAX: 408-278-9063
E-mail: dana@terran-int.com
URL: http://www.terran-int.com

Tri-Digital Software, Inc.
1800 Westlake Ave. North, #301
Seattle, WA 98109
Phone: 206-286-9402
FAX: 206-286-9442
E-mail: mjm@tri-digital.com
URL: http://www.tri-digital.com

APPENDIX E

What's on the CD-ROM

The CD-ROM that accompanies the *Director 6 Bible* contains all the files needed to do the exercises shown in the book.

The CD-ROM also includes a demonstration copy of Macromedia Director 6. In addition, there's a "goodies" folder that contains the following:

- ✦ Clip art
- ✦ Sound files
- ✦ Digital video clips
- ✦ Demonstration copies of commercial programs
- ✦ Essential shareware utilities

Using the CD-ROM

The CD-ROM is what is known as a *hybrid* CD-ROM, which means it contains files that will run on more than one computer platform — in this case, both Windows 95 and Macintosh computers.

Many of the files and programs on the CD-ROM have versions for both the Macintosh and Windows platforms. Although these files and programs may be essentially the same in content, the method used to install or access them may be different. You will find specific instructions on how to install the files and programs in the install.txt files found in each of the folders and in the movie on the CD-ROM. In addition, Appendix A describes the Auto-Run program stored on the CD-ROM.

Running the CD-ROM in Windows 95

The Windows 95 version of the CD-ROM contains an Auto-Run program that automatically starts the CD-ROM once it has been loaded in your CD-ROM drive.

Note: Auto-Run works only when the Auto Insertion Notification option is enabled in the properties for your CD-ROM drive. (Go to Settings⇨Control Panel. Select System⇨Device Manager. Double-click the CD-ROM drive icon and then the manufacturer's name of your drive. In the Properties dialog box, open the Settings tab to find the Auto Insertion Notification option.)

To run the CD-ROM, follow these steps:

1. Insert the CD-ROM into your CD-ROM drive.
2. Close the drawer. If Auto Insertion Notification is activated, the CD-ROM should begin playing a movie and no further action is required to start the movie.

If the movie does not automatically start playing, do the following:

1. From either My Computer or Windows Explorer, open the drive that corresponds with your CD-ROM drive.
2. Double-click d6bible.exe. This will start the movie.

Running the CD-ROM on a Macintosh

To start the CD-ROM, follow these steps:

1. Insert the CD-ROM into the CD-ROM drive.
2. Double-click the icon for the CD-ROM that is on the desktop.
3. Double-click the d6bible projector icon. This will start the movie.

The movie offers a brief description and installation instructions for the various files and programs found on the CD-ROM.

Files and Programs on the CD-ROM

The *Director 6 Bible* CD-ROM contains a sampling of clip media available from a variety of vendors, demonstration copies of programs useful in the preparation of Director movies, shareware utilities, and Xtras that enhance Director's capabilities. Following are descriptions of the files and programs you will find on the CD-ROM.

ArtBeats

ArtBeats develops and distributes libraries of quality background images and textures for prepress and multimedia users. These sample images were designed specifically for texture mapping. Whether placed side-by-side or top-to-bottom, they will not show a seam.

Classic PIO Partners

Classic PIO Partners offer a series of CD-ROMs with nostalgic images from bygone days. Included in the series are images of phones, radios, microphones, and all those quaint items you haven't seen since the '50s.

DeBabelizer Lite

With its 55-plus graphic readers and writers, DeBabelizer Lite is the perfect all-purpose graphics translation tool. For most digital graphic artists, it is a required utility for dealing with cross-platform color palettes and the easy translation of graphic files from one format to another. (Mac only, Windows users see DeBabelizer Pro for Windows).

DeBabelizer Pro for Windows Demo

The power of DeBabelizer, long a standard tool of Macintosh artists, is now available for Windows 95. This demo version lets you try out the power and versatility of this editing program for graphics and video.

Digital Stock

Digital Stock Corporation is a leading publisher of high-quality, royalty-free, stock photography on CD-ROM. They offer hundreds of images for developers of multimedia and interactive media.

DropStuff with Expander Enhancer

DropStuff with Expander Enhancer lets you easily create plain or self-extracting StuffIt archives from the Finder. DropStuff with Expander Enhancer will even BinHex files after stuffing.

Users of StuffIt Expander for Mac: You can add the Expander Enhancer that comes with DropStuff, and StuffIt Expander will be PowerPC accelerated, will expand more formats (including TAR), and will join StuffIt segments.

Dynamic Graphics, Inc.

Dynamic Graphics, Inc., is the company behind innovative art and idea products such as Clipper Creative Art Service, Print Media Service, Designer's Club, and Dynamic Graphics ArtWorks.

Four Palms

Four Palms is a producer of digital stock video. Their digital videos are available in a number of formats, including MPEG, ViVo, CinePak, and others.

Fresh, The Music Library

Fresh Music is a producer of contemporary production music that is easy to use, appropriate to the project, and crafted with the highest production values for broadcast, film, documentary, and multimedia productions. For each theme there is a full version, 60-second and 30-second versions, and alternate underscores where appropriate, to make your editing job as easy as possible. All sounds are provided as a full buyout library. You do not need to pay license or "drop" fees, and you never have to report usage.

Image Club

Founded in 1985 as an innovative graphic-design services company, Image Club Graphics has grown into what is now a wholly owned subsidiary of Adobe Systems Incorporated. It specializes in providing quality original clip art, brand-name display fonts, and stock photographic images at reasonable prices.

Image Farm, Inc.

Image Farm is a producer of high-quality stock photography.

Innovative Media Corp.

Innovative Media Corporation offers Sonic Waves 300, a comprehensive clip-audio library that includes over 2,800 sound effects (16-bit WAV files), over 200 stereo music clips (16-bit WAV format), and over 400 MIDI music files. The two-CD set includes a bound, easy-to-use index of the more than 3,000 audio tracks grouped by theme. All sounds are provided as a full buyout library. You do not need to pay license or "drop" fees, and you never have to report usage.

Kennerly Music Productions

Kennerly Music Productions is a producer of professional, royalty-free music clips and sound tracks. Their current collection, Multimedia Soundtracks, Volume One, is a brand-new collection of original music professionally written and recorded for use in multimedia, presentations, video, film, and broadcast.

Media Cleaner Pro

Media Cleaner Pro is a professional production tool that optimizes and compresses digital videos for desktop playback. It is a MacOS program that produces movies that can be played on both MacOS and Windows machines. Media Cleaner Pro allows you to preprocess and compress your movies using any of the available

QuickTime codecs, including CinePak and Indeo. You can also create RealMedia (RealVideo), RealAudio, VDOLive, and AIFF files. Media Cleaner Pro has powerful filters to improve video compression, and time-saving features to help you efficiently manage your compression jobs.

MPEGXtra Lite
The MPEG Xtra Lite allows you to use MPEG digital video clips in your Director movie.

PaintShop Pro
PaintShop Pro, from JASC, Inc., is a feature-rich image-editing program. PaintShop Pro has the tools found in expensive commercial image-editing programs, at a shareware price (Windows only).

Setup Factory
Create professional Windows installation programs for your finished product, without having to be a programming genius.

StuffIt Expander
This is Aladdin's award-winning freeware product. Use it, as is, to expand StuffIt, Compact Pro, BinHex, and MacBinary files. Add the Expander Enhancer from DropStuff with Expander Enhancer (described just below), and StuffIt Expander will be PowerPC accelerated, will expand more formats (including TAR), and will join StuffIt segments. Expander now handles segmented and multipart encoded files (BinHex and uuencoded files).

StuffIt Expander for Windows
StuffIt Expander for Windows, from Aladdin Systems, lets you expand files in Windows 95 that have been compressed on a Macintosh.

StuffIt InstallerMaker
InstallerMaker includes *all* the tools needed to install, uninstall, resource-compress, or update your software in one complete, easy-to-use package. With InstallerMaker you get the solution to the newest software distribution puzzle: electronic transaction processing. Create *trialware* (a time-locked demo) of your software quickly and easily with *no coding required*. Helps you safely distribute software on the Internet, online services, CD-ROMs, and floppy disks (Mac only).

Tri-Digital Software, Inc.

Tri-Digital Software, Inc., is a multimedia software company and service bureau with its headquarters in Seattle, Washington. Known for expertise in digital video compression and encoding, custom programming, graphics, and other elements of multimedia, Tri-Digital Software is committed to providing leading-edge products and services, always incorporating the latest technologies available.

WebXtra

Use Director to create a custom Web browser.

WinZip

WinZip, from Nico Mak Computing, Inc., is an indispensable utility that allows you to compress your files, making them easier to distribute on floppy disk or over the Internet (Windows only).

Installing from the CD-ROM

This section explains how to install the elements of the CD-ROM on your system.

Copying Clip Media

Most of the clip-media files on the *Director 6 Bible* CD-ROM are stored in an uncompressed format. This allows you to use the files either directly from the CD-ROM or to copy them into a folder on your hard drive. Unless otherwise specified for the specific item, use the following steps to copy clip-media files and folders to your hard drive.

Copying Clip-Media Files/Folders

1. Insert the *Director 6 Bible* CD-ROM into your CD-ROM drive.
2. Open the \goodies folder and select the folder for the item you want. (See Table E-1.)
3. If you wish to copy the entire folder to your hard drive, click and drag the folder from the CD-ROM to the hard drive.

   Macintosh users: Before dragging folders to your hard drive, first open the icon for the hard drive. Windows users: Open My Computer on the desktop and then double-click the icon for the CD-ROM. Then drag the clip media folder to the hard drive icon to which you want the folder copied.

4. To copy a specific file or files, open the folder that contains the desired files and drag them to a folder on your hard drive.

Table E-1
Clip Media on the CD-ROM

Vendor	Folder	Type	Notes
ArtBeats	artbeats	Clip art	PICT graphics (Macintosh) BMP graphics (Windows)
Classic PIO Partners	partners	Clip art	TIF graphics
Dynamic Graphics (Design Club)	design	Clip art	Placeable EPS files
Four Palms	4palms	Digital video	QuickTime and Video for Windows digital video clips
Image Club	imageclb	Clip art	TIF and Placeable EPS graphics
Image Farm, Inc.	imagefrm	Clip art	TIF graphics
Fresh, The Music Library	fresh	Sound clips	Sound clips in AIFF format
Innovative Media Corp.	sonic	Sound clips	Sound clips in WAV format
Kennerly Music Productions	kennerly	Sound clips	Sound clips in AIFF and WAV format
Tri-Digital Software, Inc.	3-digital	Digital video	Digital video in QuickTime and Video for Windows formats, in 240 x 180 and 320 x 240 pixel sizes

Installing Windows software

These sections give procedures for installing software from the CD-ROM on a Windows system.

Director 6 demo

Installing the Director Demo

1. Open the \macro folder on the CD.
2. Double-click the setup.exe file.
3. You may be prompted for a directory or program group in which to install. Either accept the defaults or enter another location and group.

WinZip

There are two methods of installing WinZip under Windows 95: directly from the CD-ROM, or through the taskbar Start menu.

Installing WinZip Directly from the CD-ROM

1. If necessary, insert the *Director 6 Bible* CD-ROM into the CD-ROM drive.
2. If Auto-Run starts the *Director 6 Bible* CD, click the Quit button and exit the movie.
3. From My Computer or Windows Explorer, select the drive letter for your CD-ROM drive.
4. Open the \goodies folder, and then open the winzip folder.
5. Double-click setup.exe. The Setup program will automatically detect which version of Windows you are running. (Both the 16-bit and 32-bit versions are included.)

Installing WinZip from the Taskbar Start Menu

1. In the taskbar, open the Start menu and select Run.
2. In the Run dialog box, type

   [D]:\goodies\winzip\setup.exe

replacing [D] with the letter of your CD-ROM drive. Press the Enter key. The Setup program will detect which version of Windows you are running.

WinZip upgrades

If you already have an older version of WinZip, follow the installation instructions just above. You can install this version of WinZip to the same location as a previously installed copy of WinZip.

Installing PaintShop Pro

To install this program, you will need WinZip or a similar compression/decompression program. If you do not already have an appropriate program for unzipping files, see the previously mentioned directions to install a copy of WinZip.

Installing PaintShop Pro

1. Using WinZip or a similar program, open the \goodies\jasc folder and open the file psp32bit.zip.

2. Extract all the files in the zip archive to a folder on your hard drive. Close WinZip. (Version 6.0 and later of WinZip will allow you to take files that have installation programs and install them directly from within WinZip, by either clicking the Install button or double-clicking on installer program.)

3. Locate the folder to which you extracted the PaintShop Pro files and double-click setup.exe. The installation process starts.

4. During the installation, you will be prompted for the folder and program group in which to install PaintShop Pro. Either accept the default selection or specify another location and group for the installation. The installer will do the rest.

Setup Factory

To install this program, you will need WinZip (or a compression/decompression program similiar to it). If you do not already have an appropriate program for unzipping files, see the earlier directions to install a copy of WinZip.

Installing Setup Factory

1. Using WinZip or a similar program, open the \goodies\indgrose folder and open the file named suf40.zip.
2. Extract all of the files in the archive to a folder on your hard drive. Close WinZip.
3. Locate the folder to which you extracted the archived files, and double-click setup.exe.
4. You may be prompted for a directory and group to which you want to install the program. Either accept the defaults or choose another folder and group for installing the program.

StuffIt Expander for Windows

Follow these steps to install StuffIt Expander.

Installing StuffIt Expander for Windows

1. Open the \goodies\aladdin folder on the CD-ROM.
2. Double-click the file sitex10.exe.
3. Enter the folder name and program group in which you wish to install the program, or accept the defaults shown in the dialog box.
4. Click the Installation button to begin the installation.

DeBabelizer Pro for Windows demo

Follow these steps to install the DeBabelizer Pro for Windows demo.

Installing the DeBabelizer Demo

1. Open the \goodies\debablzr folder.
2. Double-click the file setupex.exe.
3. When asked if you wish to continue, click Yes.

4. Click the Accept button to accept the terms of the licensing agreement and to continue installing the program.

5. You will be given the choices of typical, complete, and custom installations. Select Complete and then click the Next button.

6. Use browsing to locate and designate the folder to which you want the program installed, or click Next to accept the defaults.

7. Enter the name of the program group to which you want the program installed, or accept the default by clicking the Next button.

8. When notified that the installation is completed, click OK to return to the Windows desktop.

V12 DataBase Engine for Windows

To install this program, you will need WinZip or a similar compression/decompression program. If you do not already have an appropriate program for unzipping files, see the earlier directions to install a copy of WinZip.

Installing the V12 DataBase Engine for Windows

1. Using WinZip or another compression program, open the v12dbe32.zip file.

2. Extract the file v12-dbe.x32 into Director's Xtra folder. (It is recommended that you keep all Director Xtras in the Xtras subfolder. This folder is usually found in C:\PROGRAM FILES\MACROMEDIA\XTRAS.)

3. Extract v12-dbe.hlp into either the Windows folder, the Windows System folder, or the Windows Help folder.

   The next time you start Director, the V12 DataBase Engine for Windows Xtra will be found in the Xtras menu.

Note: The \goodies\v12 folder also contains documentation, a tutorial, and sample files. Extract these files to your hard drive using WinZip or another archive program.

MPEGXtra Lite

Follow these steps to install MPEGXtra Lite.

Installing MPEGXtra Lite

1. Open the folder \goodies\tbaiana on the CD-ROM.
2. Double-click the file named mpgxl2.exe.
3. Click Yes to accept the terms of the license agreement.
4. Select the folder in which to install the Xtra. (It is recommended that you keep all Director Xtras in the Xtras subfolder. This folder is usually found in C:\PROGRAM FILES\MACROMEDIA\XTRAS.)
5. If you wish, you can have a shortcut installed for this Xtra in an appropriate program group. Select the group you want to use.

WebXtra demo
Follow these steps to install the WebXtra demo version.

Installing the WebXtra Demo

1. Open the folder \goodies\tbaiana on the CD-ROM.
2. Double-click the file named webxdemo.exe.
3. Click Yes to continue with the installation, and Yes again to accept the terms of the license agreement.
4. Select the folder in which to install the demo files.
5. Select your Xtras folder. (This folder is usually found in c:\program files\macromedia\xtras.)
6. If you wish, you can have a shortcut installed for this Xtra in an appropriate program group. Just select the group you want to use.

Installing Macintosh Software from the CD-ROM

All of the programs in the Macintosh portion of the CD require a program that can expand MacBinary files (files with a .bin extension) or BinHex files (files with an .hqx extension). Aladdin System's StuffIt programs handle both formats.

If you do not already have a program that can unpack these files, a copy of Aladdin Systems StuffIt Expander is included on the CD-ROM and is described earlier in this appendix. You will need either StuffIt Lite or Fetch to expand the Expander files so they can be installed. If you have Fetch, proceed to the instructions on how to use Fetch to install StuffIt Expander. If not, check with your local Macintosh user group or search the Internet to obtain a copy of Fetch or StuffIt Lite.

Expanding StuffIt Expander Using Fetch

1. Open Fetch on your Macintosh.
2. Put the *Director 6 Bible* CD-ROM into your CD-ROM drive.
3. Open the CD-ROM and select the goodies:aladdin folder.
4. Use Fetch to copy either dropstuf.bin or dropstuf.hqx to a folder on your hard drive.
5. Fetch will ask you if you wish to unpack and save the file; tell it Yes.
6. Once Fetch has unpacked the file, you'll have a StuffIt Expander Installer file in the folder you selected. Double-click the file to install StuffIt Expander.

Once you have StuffIt Expander installed on your Macintosh, use the following steps to unpack and install the other software in the goodies folders.

Installing Software on the Macintosh

1. Double-click the desired MacBinary or BinHex files.
2. Tell StuffIt where to put the unpacked file on your hard drive.
3. Double-click the unpacked installer file.

✦ ✦ ✦

Glossary

ActiveX A type of Internet Explorer control.

AIFC Sound-file format readable by both Windows and Macintosh. Using this sound format enables you to create cross-platform movies, without needing to substitute sound cast members. *See also* WAV, AIFF.

AIFF Sound file format, readable by both Windows and Macintosh. Using this sound format enables you to create cross-platform movies, without needing to substitute sound cast members. *See also* WAV, AIFC.

align To adjust the position of two sprites in relationship to each other. You can align sprites at the top, bottom, left, right, center, or at their registration points.

ancestor An additional parent script whose handlers are available to a child object. A parent script makes another parent script its ancestor by assigning the script's name to the ancestor property.

animation A sequence of frames generally containing movement of a sprite. They can contain sound or digital video.

anti-aliasing A method by which the jagged edges of a bitmap are reduced by the use of interpolated pixels.

ASCII Text file format. Also known as "plain text."

Auto-Filter Applies selected filters incrementally to a series of cast members. This feature is part of Director's Xtras, and can be used to modify existing bitmap cast members or generate new cast members.

AVI Microsoft digital video format. This digital video format supports sound. *See also* QuickTime.

background color The secondary color that serves as the background for any graphic element or text in your movie.

behaviors Special cast members that define operations or procedures, providing for scriptless authoring.

bitmap A pixel-based image, generally created in a paint or image editing program.

blend In Director, a blend specifies a percentage of opacity between 0% and 100%.

BMP Bitmapped graphics file native to Windows. This is Director's preferred file format for imported bitmap images.

browser An application that allows you to view information on the WWW.

brush A tool in the Paint window that allows you to apply color to objects.

button A scripted graphic element for user interaction. When clicked, a task is performed as specified by the associated script.

cast member A graphic, text, movie, script, or other element that is a component of a Director movie; *see also* Score.

cast position The location of a cast member within the Cast window as indicated by a unique number assigned to every cast member.

Cast to Time Director command that allows you to place selected cast members from the Cast window on the Stage in sequential frames of the Score.

Cast window The window that contains all cast members.

cell A specific location in the Score; for example, frame 1: channel 1.

channel The rows in the Score. Channels can contain sprites, scripts, sound, color palettes, tempo statements, and transitions.

child An instance created by a parent script; a child shares the handlers of a parent but can have its own values for its variables; *see also* parent.

chunk expression Any character, word, item, or line in any source of text.

client applications In OLE, the client application receives files from originating server applications; *see also* OLE, server applications.

Clipboard A location in memory that serves as a temporary holding mechanism in Windows for holding information to be pasted into another location; *see also* Scrapbook.

color chip A representation of the current active color in the Paint window, the floating Tool Palette, or any other color palette.

color cycling The rotation through a palette of colors, or through a selected portion of a palette.

color depth The number of colors displayable at a given point in time or within a selected graphic image, using a specific palette.

color palette A collection of colors in a single grouping. Director 6 supports several color palettes.

comment A notation set off by two hyphens (--) that you place within Lingo scripts for your own reference.

Control Panel In Director, the Control Panel contains the command buttons for rewinding, playing, and other playback controls for your movie.

Copy To copy a selection to the Scrapbook (Clipboard).

courseware Software or a movie that is designed to teach a given topic.

cross-platform Refers to files that are readable by multiple types of computer systems, or issues that address concerns regarding the exchange of files among platforms.

.cst Filename extension of Director 6's native file format for cast files. Cast files are external and shared between movies. Internal casts are stored within the actual Director (.dir) movie.

cue point A point in a digital video or audio file that triggers an event in a movie.

Cut To remove the selection from the movie and place it on the Scrapbook (Clipboard).

destination color Used in gradient fills, switch inks, cycling colors or blends to specify the secondary color for those uses.

device-dependent Describes images whose final resolution is dependent on the output device rather than the creating application; generally vector images.

digital video Video animation files such as AVI or MOV files; may or may not include sound.

.dir Filename extension of Director 6 native file format for movies. DIR files are cross-platform. A DIR file created on the Macintosh can be read in Windows 95 and vice versa.

dither Mixing of colors to give the appearance of a another color or transition between colors.

DLL (Dynamic Link Library) These files provide the links and handlers to access programs, share information, and perform operations within a program.

dot size The size of dots sprayed by the Airbrush tool.

drawing program Vector-based graphics program used primarily for illustration.

elements A piece of information, data, or cast member contained in a movie.

Ellipse tool Creates curved closed objects, such as a circle.

EPS (Encapsulated PostScript) File format (filename extension .eps) supported by both Windows and Macintosh platforms. EPS files use a precision description language to send files to printers and other output devices.

event An activity, such as a mouse click or the start of a movie.

event handler A set of instructions that tell Director 6 what to do when an event occurs.

extended display Allows for enhanced display of cast member information in the Score; *see also* Score.

external cast Cast members stored in a separate file. Can be shared between movies or used in libraries of cast elements that are commonly used; *see also* internal cast.

Eyedropper tool Tool for picking up a color from an object on the Stage or in the Paint window.

field cast member Text that is editable or that can be formatted using Lingo.

film loop An animation sequence whose images are grouped together to create a single cast member.

FLC/FLI Multiple-image file format; *see also* PIC. FLC/FLI files are sequential images, much like digital video files, but can be edited as individual images.

flow rate Speed at which the Airbrush tool covers an area in the Paint window; *see also* Paint window.

fontmap A cross-platform font-conversion file that specifies the desired conversions between Windows and Macintosh fonts or vice versa.

foreground color The active primary color with which you paint, add text, or add any graphic element to your movie.

formatting Attributes assigned to text, such as font, font size, and font style.

fps Frames per second—the speed at which a movie plays; *see also* tempo.

frame counter Indicates the number of the frame at which the playback head is currently located.

GIF (Graphics Interchange Format) Compressed bitmapped graphics file format (filename extension .gif) supported by both Windows and Macintosh. GIF files are also supported on the Internet and allow for transparent backgrounds; *see also* bitmap.

global variables A variable that can be shared between multiple handlers and movies in a window; *see also* variable.

gradient A fill that is created by the transition between two colors.

handler A set of instructions that tell Director 6 what to do when an event occurs; *see also* event handler.

HTML (Hypertext Markup Language) HTML is the standard language used to create Web pages.

hypermedia The concept of manipulating multimedia in a way that allows nonsequential access to media.

image-editing programs Pixel-based graphics program used primarily for editing photo images and bitmaps.

import To add cast members, casts, movies or other assets to a movie.

ink effects Paint-like effects that can be applied in the Score or Paint window to graphic or text elements.

interactive Requiring user input. Interactive events include mouse clicks, typed entry of text, or other types of user input.

interface The front-end shell through which a user interacts with a movie or software application.

internal cast The default cast for a movie. You can have multiple internal and external casts. Internal casts are always linked, and updated with the movie. *See also* external cast.

Internet Global network that supports, among other things, the World Wide Web.

interpolate A method of creating a median color, and placing it between adjacent pixels to reduce jagged edges on bitmaps. *See also* bitmap, anti-aliasing.

ISP Internet Service Provider, an agency that provides a variety of services, from basic Internet access to full-range maintenance of domain Web servers.

jaggies A condition caused by using square pixels of color to create nonrectangular images; *see also* anti-aliasing, interpolate.

JPEG (Joint Photographic Experts Group) Format for compressing bitmapped graphics files, supported by both Windows and Macintosh platforms. JPEG is a popular format for presenting photographic images on the WWW; it allows a broad palette but supports a high degree of compression. *See also* bitmap.

kerning The space between pairs of characters in a text string.

kiosk A type of output or display for public locations. Kiosks are generally used for promotional or information presentations and may be interactive.

layers Objects placed in subsequent channels are layered; an object resides in the layer above or below another object, much like papers in a stack.

Lingo A powerful scripting language used with Director.

linked cast An internal or external cast containing the elements of a movie; *see also* internal casts, external casts.

linked files Files that can be stored separately from a movie, but which are opened with the movie each time the movie is opened for editing or playback; *see also* OLE, external casts.

logical block A chunk of data—the smallest recordable unit on a disk such as a CD-ROM.

lossless Describes a file format where the compression type, if any, does not result in a loss of information or reduced quality. *See also* lossy.

lossy Describes a file format that achieves compression by removing redundant information. Lossy file formats such as JPEG usually reduce image quality; *see also* lossless.

loop back Repeating of a selected animation sequence or movie.

MAC Macintosh Paint file format, bitmapped. Supported by both Windows and Macintosh platforms. MAC files are static bitmap files you can use in your Director movies.

marker A navigational point in the Score window.

Marquee selection tool Selects objects or portions of an image within the Paint window.

MCI (Media Control Interface) MCI provides the controls for media under the Windows 95 operating system.

media Data-storage methods that use particular devices and formats, such as CD-ROMs, floppy disks, or tape.

MIAW (movie in a window) A movie within a movie, playing concurrently with its host movie. The movies are interactive; they can exchange information and instructions.

MIDI (Musical Instrument Digital Interface) A digital audio recording. MIDI recordings are high-quality audio files; they have no direct support in Director. For use in Director, MIDI files require an Xtra or must be converted. *See also* WAV, AIFF, AIFC.

monochrome Black-and-white, 1-bit color; *see also* color depth, color palettes.

motion Movement from one location on the Stage to another.

movie A Director 6 animation project.

MPEG (Motion Picture Experts Group) A digital video format that supports a high degree of compression. This file format requires an MCI Lingo handler in Director.

multimedia An application or project that contains graphics, text, sound, interactivity, and animation.

non-linked cast An external cast, generally used as a library for several movies. Contains cast members used for those movies.

NTSC (National Television Standards Committee) Standardized palette for use with video presentations and broadcast media.

OLE (Object Linking and Embedding) A function of Windows that allows files to be linked between server and client applications.

onion-skinning Borrowed from traditional animation techniques, this feature allows the accurate placement and drawing of intermediate cast members.

output The method by which a finished movie will be stored or displayed. Some choices are CD-ROM, videotape, diskette, screen, or online.

Paint Bucket tool A fill tool; floods specified areas of an image with a solid, gradient, or pattern fill, using the selected active ink effects.

paint program A pixel-based graphics program used primarily for generating bitmapped graphics.

Paint window Editing window in Director for creating and editing bitmapped graphics.

palette A collection of colors or tools used within Director movies.

Palette channel Contains color-palette information, including color transition effects used within a movie.

pan To move through the Score or change the view of any window using the scroll bars.

parent object The original object from whose attributes child objects are created.

parent script A script capable of creating and controlling child scripts.

Paste To paste a selection contained on the Clipboard (Scrapbook) to a specified location.

Paste Special An OLE function that links a pasted element to the application that created it; changes are then updated automatically in the movie.

patterns Variable fills that are editable, comprising the foreground and background colors in the Paint window.

PCD Photo CD files; static photo images supported by Windows and Macintosh platforms. Normally, these files are available through third-party vendors such as Kodak.

PCX PC Paintbrush bitmapped graphic images supported by both Windows and Macintosh platforms. PCX files use an 8-bit (256-color) palette to represent color in bitmapped images.

PICT A Macintosh file format. This format can either be a single static image or a set of sequential images in an animation.

pixel A single dot of color or unit of measurement.

playback head Indicates the frame location in a movie.

plug-ins Filters and other effects files that are used to enhance your movies. Director 6 supports Photoshop and MetaCreations plug-ins.

Polygon tool A tool for drawing irregularly shaped, multisided objects; *see also* Paint window.

pop-up menu Any menu that appears as a result of clicking an arrow or option box, or of Option+clicking (right-clicking) on an object.

ppi (pixels per inch) Defines how smooth an object appears on the screen; see also anti-aliasing.

preload To load movie elements before they are required, to ensure the smoothness of an animation or movie.

projector A stand-alone version of a Director movie that does not require the end-user to have Director installed. Projectors are platform specific and can't be played on platforms other than the one on which they are authored.

puppet A sprite controlled by Lingo, not by the Score.

RAM (Random-Access Memory) The physical, electronic memory that each computer possesses; *see also* virtual memory.

real-time recording A type of animation that records the movement of an object moved by the mouse pointer, in real time, across the frames in the Score.

Rectangle tool Draws a closed rectangular shape such as a square.

redistributable files Files stored separately from a software program (often in the system folder) during the program's installation..

registration point An assignable location for a graphic element, used to align sprites.

rotation To turn an object around an axis.

RTF (Rich Text Format) A type of text file that retains its original formatting instructions.

Score One view of all of the components of a movie. Graphic images as well as all cast members are represented here, by number and other attributes that have been assigned to them.

Scrapbook A temporary holding mechanism on the Macintosh for holding information to be pasted into another location. *See also* Clipboard.

screen resolution The resolution of the display—generally 72 or 96 dpi. Macintosh generally displays graphics at 72 dpi; Windows-based machines display graphics at 96 dpi. Screen resolution is defined by pixels. *See also* pixels.

script A string of instructions written in Lingo for navigation or control of the elements of a movie.

script channel Contains script information associated with a specific frame in a movie. The script channel is part of the Effects channels accessed via the Score window.

seek time The amount of time it takes a computer to access information on a hard drive or other storage medium.

server application Allows you to create original files and share them with client applications. *See also* OLE, client applications.

shapes Geometric objects created using the Tool Palette. These are vector images as opposed to bitmapped images. *See also* Tool Palette.

Shockwave A player that allows the user to view Director movies on the World Wide Web.

shuffle backward Moves selected sprites toward the back in the hierarchy of channels in the Score window.

shuffle forward Moves selected sprites toward the front in the hierarchy of channels in the Score window.

sort Sorts the cast members in a cast, by the criteria you set. Also removes empty cast-member spaces at the end of a cast. *See also* Cast window.

Sound channels Contain the sound sprites associated with a movie. The sound channels are part of the Effects channels in the Score window.

Space to Time A Director command that allows you to move sequential sprites organized in multiple channels of a given frame to multiple sequential frames of the same channel.

spread In a gradient fill, the way the color is distributed between the foreground and destination colors.

sprite A copy of a cast member that is placed in the Score and on the Stage.

sprite channel Contains the individual sprites associated with a movie. The Score window supports 120 sprite channels.

Stage The location in Director where all of the visible cast members of a movie are placed.

static objects Objects that do not animate or move on Stage.

step recording An animation technique that allows the user to "step through," creating a motion sequence one frame at a time.

storyboard A rough sketch of sequential frames for an animation sequence.

streaming Allows a file to start playing before it is fully downloaded over a network.

sunburst A radial gradient fill; *see also* Paint window.

SWA Short for Shockwave Audio, which is a streaming Xtra. Streaming audio begins playing while it's still downloading; the end-user doesn't have to wait for the entire sound to download before it starts to play.

synchronize Causing the movie or animation to move at the pace of an associated sound file.

system message A message generated by the computer's operating system.

Tell Command to send messages between movies.

template A prototype movie created with cast members and placeholders for elements that will change from one movie to the next.

tempo The rate at which a movie plays—you can adjust the tempo, add delays, or insert wait states for interactivity.

Tempo channel Contains timing, delay, and wait statements associated with a movie. The Tempo channel is one of the Effects channels accessed through the Score window.

text field A type of on-Stage textobject that can store editable text; *see also* field cast member.

thumbnail A small bitmapped image of a cast member.

TIFF (Tagged Information File Format) A bitmapped graphics file format supported by both Windows and Macintosh platforms. This RGB (Red, Green, Blue) bitmap format is capable of supporting up to 32-bit color.

tiles Full-color patterns that are editable, created from bitmapped graphic images. Tile effects are available in the Paint window.

Tool Palette Also called the "floating Tool Palette," this is Director's collection of tools to draw on the Stage, create buttons and other interactive controls, add text, control colors of selected objects, and more.

toolbar Ribbon bar at the top of the main Director 6 screen, containing some of the most frequently used commands.

trails An effect in the Score that allows images from previous frames to remain on-screen as images from subsequent frames appear. The effect, when combined with motion, creates a stepped appearance of images.

Transform Bitmap Director 6 command that allows you to change the size, color depth, or palette of the selected cast member.

Transition channel Contains the transition cast members used to control the visual transition from one frame to the next in a movie. The Transition channel is part of the Effects channels found in the Score window. *See also* transition.

transition An effect between frames that allows for a smooth transformation from one frame to the next.

Transparent ink An ink effect, accessed through the Score window, that turns the background color of the object transparent.

TrueType fonts A font type common to Windows. These non-PostScript fonts come in a variety of font families, including several novelty fonts. They are ideal for representing text on-screen.

Tweak window Adjusts the position of a sprite, either one pixel at a time or by a specified number of pixels you select.

TXT ASCII text file format (filename extension .txt) supported by both Windows and Macintosh platforms.

Type 1 A font type, generally called Adobe Type 1 fonts. These fonts are PostScript fonts and produce the highest quality of printable font.

URL (Uniform Resource Locator) A specific address used to identify a document or file on the World Wide Web.

variables Expressions that allow you to use multiple values.

vector A type of mathematically precise, device-dependent graphic object created by a drawing package.

virtual memory Temporary memory created from hard disk space, generally used for the temporary storage of working files. Assigned by the computer or software, this is a working swap area; *see also* RAM.

WAV A sound file format common to Windows. Director provides direct support for WAV sound files within your movies. *See also* AIFF, AIFC.

WMF Windows Metafile Format. A graphics-file format (filename extension .wmf) supported by Windows. WMF files are vector format, which means they are object-based rather than bitmap images. Object-based images are device-dependent and can be output at any resolution without degrading their quality.

WWW (World Wide Web) A function of the Internet that allows integration and distribution of the information, images, sounds, and animation available on various servers.

x location Location of an object as determined by the number of pixels from the left-hand edge of the Stage to the edge of the object.

Xtras Prepared bodies of code used to extend the capabilities of Director movies.

y location Location of an object as determined by the number of pixels from the top edge of the Stage to the edge of the object.

Index

\ (backslash), 832
: (colon), 655
¬ (continuation character), 655
\> (greater-than symbol), 766
< (less-than symbol), 766
" (quotation marks), 740
; (semicolon), 533
| (vertical bar), 805

3D effects
    avatars and, 911–913
    basic description of, 905–946
    coordinates and, 915–918
    implementing, 922
    meshes and, 918–920
    presentations, assembling, 914–915
    props and, 913–914
    rendering landscapes/environments with, 909–911

A

access rights, 900
Action tab, 929–930
ActiveX components, 855–857, 883
actorList, 696–702
Add ink, 110
Add Pin ink, 110
Adjust to Fit option, 124
Adobe Photoshop, 408–409, 906–909
Adobe Premiere, 624
AIFF (Audio Interchange File Format), 227–228, 231, 568, 576–579
Air Brush tool, 28
Alert dialog box, 825–828
Align tool, 11
alignment
    of buttons, 607
    of text, 122, 512–513
alpha channels, 908
ancestor scripts, 680, 683–684, 704–705
anti-aliasing, 115, 124–125
append function, 660–661
Arc tool, 28
arithmetic operators, 385–386
Arrow tool, 12, 158
artifacts, getting rid of, 616–617

aspect ratio, 25
audio. *See also* SWA (Shockwave Audio)
    adding, 232–237, 310–312, 543–544
    AIFF (Audio Interchange File Format), 227–228, 231, 568, 576–579
    attaching, to sprites/buttons, 544–545
    basic description of, 223–254
    behaviors, 245–247
    channels, 236–237, 548–549, 568, 573–575, 578–579
    controls for, 548–552
    editing, 228–230, 232–237
    exporting digital video and, 620
    fade-in/fade-out controls, 574–575
    formats, choosing, 227–228
    importing, 224–226, 576–579
    linked, playing, 568–570
    lists of, playing, 563–564
    looping, 240–241
    managing, 237–245
    obtaining, for movies, 232
    on/off controls, 549–551, 553–556
    playing, during periods of inactivity, 566
    random, 562–563
    recording modes, 230–231
    sampling rates, 230–231
    sources of, 541, 551, 556
    stopping, 545–547, 549–551
    syncing video to, 267
    tempo, 239–240
    tracks, 551, 571
    triggering, 542–544
    using internal versus external, 226–227
    volume, 141, 242–243, 570–575, 611, 809–810
    WAV (Waveform Audio File) format, 227, 230–231, 568
    Xtras, 245–252
Audio Specialists, 315
authoring issues, 868–871
Auto-Distort
    creating an animation sequence with, 85–86
    generating cast members with, 84–87
auto-syncing, 837
avatars, 911–913
AVI (Video for Windows) format, 279. *See also* Video for Windows (Microsoft)

B

background(s)
  adding, 288–289
  nonwhite, 521
  for text fields, 521
  tracking, 90–94
  transparent ink for, 109
Background Transparent ink, 109
backslash (\), 832
behavior(s). *See also* Behavior Inspector
  applying, 274–275
  assigning events to, 246
  basic description of, 5, 175–222
  button, adding, 410–420
  creating basic, 196–200
  creating new, 200–203
  creating timers with, 210–213
  looping on the current frame with, 182–183
  predefined, 176–178
  properties, changing, 214–215
  reordering, 190
  sound, 245–247
  that swap one sprite for another, 194–195
  user-defined, adding actions to, 203–204
  video, 272–275
  viewing the script behind, 186–187
Behavior Inspector tool. *See also* behaviors
  adding behaviors with, 189, 191, 194–195
  attaching/deleting media-control behaviors with, 192–193
  basic description of, 11, 185–204
  changing behavior properties with, 214–215
  creating basic behaviors with, 196–200
  dragging and dropping media behaviors with, 193–194
  examining the Hold on Current Frame behavior with, 187–188
  removing behaviors with, 189–190
  reordering behaviors with, 190
  viewing the script behind a behavior with, 186–187
bitmap(s). *See also* graphics; images
  buttons, building, 408–409
  memory and, 845
  text, creating hotlinks over, 519–520
  transforming, 55–56, 83–84, 154–155
blends
  basic description of, 106–107
  Blend ink effect for, 34, 110
  Blend tool and, 158
Bold option, 122. *See also* fonts

breakpoints
  basic description of, 763–765
  deleting, 764
Brush tool
  basic description of, 28
  choosing brushes with, 42–43
  creating custom brushes with, 43–44
brushes
  choosing, 42–43
  custom, 43–44
button(s). *See also* Button Editor
  alignment of, 607
  assigning scripts to, 346–347, 354, 356–357
  attaching sounds to, 544–547
  basic description of, 180
  behavior, adding expected, 410–420
  building better, faster, 433–434
  changing text on, 344–345
  creating, 204–209, 355–356, 511
  custom, 204–209
  deleting, 346
  duplicating, 362, 418
  interactive, building, 217–221
  navigating with custom, 215–221
  "polite," what to expect from, 403
  properties, changing, 345–346
  resizing, 344
  uniform, 511
  using navigation behaviors to build, 181–182
  well-behaved, 403–420
Button Editor. *See also* buttons; Button tool
  basic description of, 204–209
  building buttons from scratch with, 205–206
  creating custom buttons with, 207–209
Button tool, 343–344. *See also* buttons

C

C++ programming, 680–681
Camera tab, 928–929
case statement, 559–560
case-sensitivity, 167, 372, 886
cast libraries
  basic description of, 16–17, 210
  linking, to movies, 211–212
cast member(s). *See also* cast member scripts; Cast window
  basic description of, 4, 9, 58–61
  creating tiles for, 31–33
  duplicating, 59–60
  exchanging, 102–104
  external, 209

Index ✦ C

field cast members, 113, 128, 805–808
  for film loops, 83–84
  positioning, 59–60, 601–605
  preloading, 579–584, 839–843
  sorting, 60–61
  sound, 233–234
  swapping, 405–410, 832
  unloading, 579–580, 583–584
  Xtras, 713
cast member scripts. *See also* cast members
  basic description of, 330–331
  creating, 338–339
Cast window
  basic description of, 9–11
  housekeeping, 97
CD-ROMs
  building virtual images for, 847–848
  optimizing for, 847–850
Center option, 162
centering
  digital video, 609
  movies, 162
cents, displaying, 395–396
channel(s)
  alpha channels, 908
  basic description of, 9
  identifying the current, 425
  sound, 236–237, 548–549, 568, 573–575, 578–579
  tempo, 578–579
char keyword, 497–500
Check Box tool, 13
check marks, 812
child objects. *See also* OOP (object-oriented programming)
  assigning properties to, 694–696
  basic description of, 675–708
  controlling sprites with, 698–699
  creating, 679–680, 687–707
  deleting, 689
  querying, 693–694
chunk expressions, 494–503, 504–507
CLASSID parameter, 876
CLASSID tag, 166
clickOn function, 425
client/server computing, 854–855
clip media, 541–542
Clipboard ink effect, 34, 35
closeXlib command, 719, 721
code
  -less development, 5
  reusing, 421–330
  substituting variables to shorten, 447–451
  using cast placement to shorten, 453–455
CODEBASE parameter, 876

CODEBASE tag, 166
codecs (compression algorithms), 590–591
colon (:), 655
color. *See also* color palettes
  3D effects and, 931–933
  adding fill, before adding fine detail, 50
  cycling, 160–161
  depth, 54–58, 151, 257–261, 620, 672, 846
  font, 488–490
  how Director handles, 54–55
  in the Paint window, 29–30
Color Depth option, 54
color palettes, 672, 786–787. *See also* color
  color theory and, 150–151
  creating effects with, 158
  mapping images to, 151–154
  modifying, 155–158
  Macintosh versus Windows, 152
Color Picker tool, 158
commands
  basic description of, 368
  closeXlib command, 719, 721
  delete command, 513
  go commands, 349–351, 368
  list-related commands, 633–647
  for navigation, 349–365
  openXlib command, 719, 721
  play command, 351–352, 361–364, 368
  preload commands, 842–843, 846
  put commands, 400
  set commands, 400
  showGlobals command, 758
  showXlib command, 721
  testing, 756–757
comments, 417
comparison operators, 386–387
compression, 163, 261–262, 589–591
  algorithms (codecs), 590–591
  export options and, 619
  interframe, 261
  Shockwave and, 859–860
  SWA (Shockwave Audio), 247–252, 576, 839–841
  streaming cast members and, 250–252
  understanding, 248–252
conditions, checking, 411–412
constants, 370–375
constrainH function, 456, 458–466
constrainV function, 456, 458–466
Content Experts, 314
continuation character (¬), 655
Control menu, 14
Control Panel
  functions, 141
  operating, 140–141

controller(s)
    displaying, 610
    preferences, for digital video, 269–272
cookies, 894–895
coordinates, 443–444, 915–918
copy ink effect, 73, 109
Copy tool, 11
copying. *See also* duplicating
    files to Web servers, 898–899
    graphics, 49
    widget sprites, 305–309
copyright law, 316–320, 849
    fair use issues, 318–319
    what can be protected by, 317–318
count variable, 760–761
counting words, 508
Cover transition effect, 147
Create For option, 162
Cropped option, 124
cropping
    digital video, 267–269, 609
    text, 124
cross-platform projects
    color palettes and, 672
    digital video and, 621–625
cue points
    basic description of, 238–239
    pausing a movie to wait for, 278
    sound and, 449, 576–579
cursors
    choosing, for sprites, 471–472
    creating masks for, 479–480
    custom, 473–480
    for designated sprites, changing, 472–473
    for entire movies, changing, 473
    invoking, 474–475
    using standard, 471–473
Cut tool, 11
cut and paste, 11, 49
Cycle ink effect, 34, 35
Cycle tool, 158

D

Darken action, 84
Darkest ink effect, 34, 111
debugging. *See also* troubleshooting
    basic description of, 752–758
    in the Debugger window, 762–770
    tracing script actions, 754–755
decimal point numbers, 392
delete command, 513
deleting
    breakpoints, 764

buttons, 346
child objects, 689
items from lists, 640–641
media-control behaviors, 192–193
objects, 689
properties, 663–665
text, 513
development teams, 314–316
dialog boxes
    Alert dialog box, 825–828
    creating, 803, 821–834
    File Open dialog box, 822–823
    File Save dialog box, 823–824
    Open dialog box, 724–725
    Save dialog box, 732–733
dictionary lists, searching, 665–666
Direct to Stage mode
    basic description of, 265–267
    enabling/disabling, 266–267
DirectX drivers, 540
Dissolve transition effect, 147
distributed object models, 857–858
Dither option, 54
dithered color, 54, 55
dollars, displaying, 395–396
drop shadow effects, 906–909
duplicating. *See also* copying
    buttons, 362, 418
    cast members, 59–60
    lists, 647, 658–659
    widgets, 305–309

E

Edit menu, 14
educational purposes, fair use for, 318–319.
    See also copyright law
Ellipse tool, 13, 28
<EMBED> tag, 861, 872–875, 876, 884, 885–886
Empty at End option, 61
enterFrame event, 432–433
Eraser tool, 27
errors. *See also* debugging
    logic, 751–752
    syntax/spelling, 748–751
event(s)
    basic description of, 325–326
    custom, responding to, 220–221
    handling, for fun and profit, 324
Exchange Cast Member tool, 11
Exit Frame event, 199
exitLock property, 830–831
exponents, 393
exporting data, 280–281, 617–621, 740–741

expressions
    basic description of, 369
    chunk expressions, 494–503, 504–507
extending sprites, 11, 79–82
Eyedropper tool, 28, 158

F

fade effects
    basic description of, 107–108, 159–160
    fade-in/fade-out controls, 574–575
    fade to black and white effect, 159–160
fair use, 318–319. *See also* copyright law
fast-forward controls, 612–613
field(s)
    cast members, 113, 128, 805–808
    hypertext, 516–526
Field tool, 13
figures, painting, 39–40
file(s)
    accessing data in, 727–732
    closing, 723–732
    disk, creating new, 733–734
    disk, writing, 735
    knowing the current position within, 736–739
    opening, 723–732, 831–832
    size, 261–262, 586–587
file compression, 163, 261–262, 589–591
    algorithms (codecs), 590–591
    export options and, 619
    interframe, 261
    Shockwave and, 859–860
    SWA (Shockwave Audio), 247–252, 576, 839–841
    streaming cast members and, 250–252
    understanding, 248–252
file formats
    AIFF (Audio Interchange File Format), 227–228, 231, 568, 576–579
    digital video, 261, 589–590, 593–594
    MPEG (Motion Picture Experts Group), 261, 593–594
    RTF (rich text format), 114–115, 120, 128
    sound, 227–228, 230–231, 568
    WAV (Waveform Audio File) format, 227, 230–231, 568
File menu, 14
File Open dialog box, 822–823
File Save dialog box, 823–824
fileIO Xtra, 723–739
Fill action, 84
Filled Ellipse tool, 13, 28

Filled Polygon tool, 29
Filled Rectangle tool, 13, 28, 43, 131–132
Filled Round Rectangle tool, 13
film loops. *See also* loops
    background tracking and, 90–94
    basic description of, 82–97
    creating, 94–97
    including sound in, 241–242
    onion skinning and, 87–94
    preparing cast members for, 83–84
    registration and, 87–94
    reverse sequence and, 95–96
filterMask parameter, 725–727
Find Cast Member tool, 11
flat models, 58
Flip Horizontal action, 83
Flip Vertical action, 83
floating point numbers, 392, 394–395
folders, storage of Xtras in, 717–718
Following Cast Members action, 89
font(s). *See also* text
    basic description of, 120
    for buttons, 512–513
    color, 488–490
    mapping, 114
    selecting, 122, 491–493
    size, 122, 490–491
    styles, 493–494
    substitutions, 531–536
Font Size option, 122
Foreground/Background Colors tool, 13
fork models, 58
frame(s). *See also* frame rates
    basic description of, 8, 64
    changing single, 106
    default number of, specifying, 69
    exporting, 280–281
    holding movies in, 776–777
    jumping to, 184, 348, 524–525, 615–616
    looping on current, 182–183
    moving to the next, 354
    options for text, 124
    pausing after every, 352–353
    playing a list of sounds in, 563–564
    playing three sound sequentially in, 565–566
    reference, 261
    scripts, 333, 340–341
    using markers instead of, 348
frame rates, 141, 143, 599–600, 610–611, 619
    determining effective, 256
    specifying, for video cast members, 259–260
Free Rotate action, 83

functions
    append function, 660–661
    basic description of, 369–370, 380
    clickOn function, 425
    constrainH function, 456, 458–466
    constrainV function, 456, 458–466
    intersect function, 444–445
    MouseCast function, 422–424
    mouseH function, 456, 463–466
    mouseV function, 456, 463–466
    new function, 679–680
    random() function, 370
    rollOver function, 370, 412
    soundBusy function, 370, 548–549
    the key function, 370
    time function, 370

G

Ghost ink effect, 34, 110
global variables. *See also* variables
    basic description of, 371
    MIAWs and, 774–775
    shortening handlers with, 447–452
    sound scripts and, 561
    substituting, to shorten code, 447–451
go commands, 349–351, 368
gradient bar, 30
Gradient ink effect, 34
gradients
    basic description of, 34, 41–42
    in the Paint window, 29–30
Graphic Artists/Designers, 314
graphics. *See also* bitmaps; color
    copying, 49
    creating concepts for, 24–25
    cutting, 49
    drawing, 36–37
    moving, 49
    pasting, 49
    techniques for selecting, 46–49
    working with, 23–62
greater-than symbol (>), 766

H

halos, tarnished, 57
Hand tool, 27, 158
handlers
    basic description of, 175, 326
    checking, 766–767
    creating moveable sprites with, 439–440
    creating parent scripts with, 684–687, 690–691
    creating your own, 428–430
    shortening, 447–452
    testing, 756–757
    user-defined, building, 429–430
    writing, 399–436
hash (look-up) tables, 66
HEIGHT parameter, 873
HEIGHT tag, 166
help
    accessing, 18
    basic description of, 17–18
    context-sensitive, 18–19
    surfing for, 19–20
Help menu, 14
Help Pointer tool, 11
hiding/displaying
    MIAWs, 800–801
    sprites, 480–483
highlighting text, 529–530
Horizons Technology, 624
horizontal movement, of sprites, 458–463
HTML (HyperText Markup Language), 853–857
    <EMBED> tag, 861, 872–875, 876, 884, 885–886
    <NOEMBED> tag, 875
    <OBJECT> tag, 861, 875–877, 884, 885–886
    <PARAM NAME> tag, 876
    plug-ins and, 855–857
    tags, for embedding movies, 166–169
hypermedia, 342. *See also* hypertext
hypertext. *See also* HTML (HyperText Markup Language); URLs (Uniform Resource Locators)
    basic description of, 342
    displaying definitions with, 525
    jumping to new frames with, 524–525
making sprites visible with, 526
    simulating, 515–526

I

icon-based menus, 670–672
ID tag, 166
If...then statements, 413–415
image(s). *See also* graphics
    artifacts, getting rid of, 616–617
    dimensions, video and, 257
    importing, 57–58, 153–154
    mapping, 151–154
    memory and, 846
    quality, selecting, 262
    sequencing, to improve video performance, 257–258
    thumbnail, 293–297

virtual, 847–848
immediate mode windows, 375. *See also*
    Message window
implementation independence, 348
importing
    basic description of, 51–55
    cast members, 263–264
    digital video, 263–264, 596, 605–607
    images, 57–58, 153–154
    media options for, 53
    movies, versus MIAWs, 772–773
    remapping when, 153–154
    sound, 224–226, 576–579
    text, 128
    Xtras, 715, 740–741
Import PICT File as PICT option, 53
Import tool, 11
Include Original Data for Editing option, 53
inks/ink effects. *See also* inks/ink effects
        (listed by name)
    basic description of, 4, 33–34, 106–111
    changing, 74–76
    using, 45–46
inks/ink effects (listed by name). *See also*
        inks/ink effects
    Add ink, 110
    Add Pin ink, 110
    Background Transparent ink, 109
    Blend ink effect, 34, 110
    Clipboard ink effect, 34, 35
    copy ink effect, 73, 109
    Cycle ink effect, 34, 35
    Darkest ink effect, 34, 111
    Ghost ink effect, 34, 110
    Gradient ink effect, 34
    Lighten ink effect, 34
    Lightest ink effect, 34, 111
    Mask ink, 110
    Matte ink, 110
    Normal ink effect, 33
    Not Copy ink, 110
    Not Ghost ink, 110
    Not Reverse ink, 110
    Not Transparent ink, 110
    Reveal ink effect, 34, 35
    Reverse ink effect, 33, 110
    Smear ink effect, 34
    Smooth ink effect, 34
    Smudge ink effect, 34
    Spread ink effect, 34
    Subtract Pin ink, 111
    Switch ink effect, 34
    Transparent ink effect, 33, 109
Insert menu, 14

installing
    menus, 808–809
    Shockwave, 861–864
    Xtras, 718–719
instances, 678, 683
Instructional Designer, 315
instructions, testing, 756–757
integers, 392–393
intersect function, 444–445
Invert action, 84
Invert Selection tool, 158
Italic option, 122. *See also* fonts
item keyword, 501–503

J

jaggies, 124–125
Java, 168, 855–857
JavaScript, 168
joining
    sprites, 79–82
    text strings, 514–515

K

kerning, 119–120, 123
Key Down event, 199
Key Up event, 199
keyboard shortcuts, adding, to menus, 811
keyframes
    basic description of, 68
    placement of, 75–76
    splitting sprites at, 81
    tweening and, 79
kiosks, 567–568

L

Lasso tool, 27, 47–48
leading, 119–120
less-than symbol (<), 766
Light tab, 927–928
Lighten action, 84
Lighten ink effect, 34
Lightest ink effect, 34, 111
line keyword, 502
Line Spacing option, 122
Line tool, 12, 28
Line Weight Selector tool, 13
line widths, 13, 32
linear lists. *See also* lists
    basic description of, 631–633
    working with, 645–646

Lingo. *See also* scripting
    basic description of, 4
    controlling sprites from, 437–484
    controlling transitions with, 470
    creating interactive movies with, 342–347
    digital video and, 585–628
    If...then statements and, 413–415
    making sprites moveable with, 442
    manipulating text with, 485–538
    OOP and, 676–677, 679–708
    preload commands, 842–843, 846
    programming, 367–398
    properties and, 379–380, 401–402
    QuickDraw 3D and, 931–940
    sound and, 236–237, 240, 242, 539–584
    swapping cast members with, 405–410
    syntax, 391–394
    troubleshooting, 747–770
Link to External File option, 53
links, basic description of, 342. *See also* hypertext
list(s)
    adding items to, 639, 660–661
    basic description of, 631–674
    converting, 648–463
    creating menu systems with, 667–772
    deleting items from, 640–641
    duplicating, 647
    how Director handles, 643–645
    items, checking for, 648
    items, retrieving, 635–636
    processing with, 648–653
    -related commands, 633–647
    -related functions, 636–638
    sorting, 641–645
    transferring, 647
    values, setting, 639–640
local variables. *See also* variables
    basic description of, 371–372
    life cycle of, 373
logical
    blocks, 849
    operators, 388–389
looping. *See also* film loops
    on the current frame, with behaviors, 182–183
    preferences for digital video, 269–272
loops. *See also* looping
    adding repeat, 411–412
    controlling sprites with, 441–442
    memory and, 846
    playing sound and, 552–553
    saving keystrokes and code with, 441–442

M

Macintosh
    color palettes, 152
    file types, codes for, 734–735
    filterMask and, 726–727
    menu formatting options, 814–815
    MIAWs and, 780–781
Macromedia Web site, 19
Magnifying Glass tool, 28, 46–47
mantissas, 393
mapping, 114, 153–154, 917
margins, 123
Maricopa Community College Web site, 19
markers, 215–216, 218–219, 348
Marquee tool
    basic description of, 27
    creating tween cast members with, 92
    selecting graphics with, 48–49
Mask ink, 110
Matte ink, 110
me variable, 688–680
Media: Compress (Shockwave Format) option, 163
Media Type option, 60
memory. *See also* RAM (Random-Access Memory)
    building child objects in, 689
    exitLock property and, 830–831
    guidelines for saving, 846–847
    management, 835–850
    MIAWs and, 791–793
    problems, testing to avoid, 839
    purge priorities for, 843–844, 846
    requirements, determining, 837–839
    types of, 835–836
    understanding, 835–839
menu(s)
    adding keyboard shortcuts to, 811
    bar, 14
    basic description of, 13–14
    creating, 803–820
    installing, 808–809
    items, disabling, 812–814
    pull-down, 804–820
    switching, 819–820
    systems, creating, 667–772
meshes, 918–920
Message window
    accessing system information in, 379–380
    assigning values/strings in, 377–379
    basic description of, 375–384
    calculating messages in, 390–381
    debugging in, 752–758

displaying dollars and cents with, 395–396
Lingo syntax and, 391–394
querying child objects in, 693–694
meta-balls, 921–922
MIAWs (movies in a window). *See also* movies
achieving interactivity between windows with, 774–775
basic description of, 771–802
controlling, 782–788, 793–794
creating multiple, 788–789
deleting, 791–793
dialog boxes and, 821
hiding, 800–801
imported movies versus, 772–773
managing, 788–802
memory and, 846
opening, 793–794
positioning, 795–802
preloading, 790
specifying window types for, 780–782
starting, writing scripts for, 778–782
Microsoft Web site, 540
MIME (Multipurpose Internet Mail Extensions), 877–879
mini-kiosks, 567–568
MOA (Macromedia Open Architecture), 710
modal dialog boxes, 8
modeless editors, 8
Modeling window, 924–926
modem speeds, 868–869
Modify menu, 14
motion paths, nonlinear, 76–78
mouse
making a sprites invisible with, 483
pointer location, matching sprite location to, 463–466
sound controls and, 555, 557
Mouse Down event, 198
Mouse Enter event, 199
Mouse Leave event, 199
Mouse Up event, 198
Mouse Within event, 198
MouseCast function, 422–424
mouseEnter handler, 431–432
mouseH function, 456, 463–466
mouseLeave handler, 432
mouseV function, 456, 463–466
mouseWithin handler, 431–432
movie(s). *See also* MIAWs (movies in a window); QuickTime
movies
activating digital video to, 262–272, 613–615
adding media behaviors to, 191

adding sound to, 244–245
basic description of, 4
building better, 179–184
chunk expressions in, 504–507
embedding, into Web pages, 166–167, 872–878, 880–887
interactive, 342–347
linking cast libraries to, 211–212
opening files from, 831–832
placing Text cast members in, 125–128
scripts, basic description of, 333–334
scripts, creating, 341–342
setting volume for, 242–243
streaming, 865–866
uploading, to servers, 897–900
using cue points in, 238–239
viewing, off-line, 882–884
MoviePlayer (QuickTime), 589, 622
MovieRecorder (QuickTime), 589
MovieShop (QuickTime), 589
MPEG (Motion Picture Experts Group) format, 261, 593–594
MUI (Macromedia User Interface) Dialog Xtra, 821b–820

N

Name option, 60
NAME parameter, 874
NAME tag, 166
navigation
basic description of, 347–348
buttons, 402–403, 343–344
controls for interactive movies, 343–344
controls for interactive resumes, 299–310
Lingo commands for, 349–365
menus, creating, 817–818
nesting statements, 414
NetLingo
basic description of, 887–897
commands, 888, 893
functions, 890–893
New Cast tool, 11
New Frame event, 199
new function, 679–680
new handler, 684–687
No Shrink option, 48
<NOEMBED> tag, 875
nonlinear motion paths, 76–78
Normal ink effect, 33
Not Copy ink, 110
Not Ghost ink, 110
Not Reverse ink, 110
Not Transparent ink, 110

O

<OBJECT> tag, 861, 875–877, 884, 885–886
objects, child. *See also* OOP (object-oriented programming)
    assigning properties to, 694–696
    basic description of, 675–708
    controlling sprites with, 698–699
    creating, 679–680, 687–707
    deleting, 689
    querying, 693–694
on startMovie handler, 439–440
onion skinning, 87–94
OOP (object-oriented programming)
    basic description of, 675–708
    C++ and, comparison of, 680–681
    components of, 682–692
    reasons to use, 678–679
open architecture, 15
Open dialog box, 724–725
Open tool, 11
opening
    files, 723–732, 831–832
    MIAWs, 793–794
openXlib command, 719, 721
operators
    basic description of, 384–396
    calculating messages with, 390–391
Options: Full Screen option, 162
Options: In a Window option, 162
order of calculation, 386
orthographic mapping, 917
outline drawings, creating, 36–37

P

Paint Bucket tool
    basic description of, 28
    creating gradients with, 41–42
    painting figures with, 39–40
Paint window. *See also* painting
    accessing, 26
    basic description of, 11, 26–35
    colors in, 29–30
    creating custom cursors in, 476–477
    gradients in, 29–30
    patterns in, 30
    tool palette, 27–28
painting. *See also* Paint window
    choosing brushes, 42–43
    creating outline drawings, 36–37
    drawing graphics, 36–37
    painting figures, 39–40
    techniques, 36–40, 46–50

PALETTE parameter, 873–874
PALETTE tag, 166
Palette:Import option, 54
Palette:Remap To option, 54
panning sprites, 71–72
<PARAM NAME> tag, 876
parameters
    basic description of, 369
    missing, 749
parent scripts. *See also* OOP (object oriented programming)
    basic description of, 675–708
    creating, 684–687, 690–691
    handlers and, 690–691
particle systems, 921–922
Paste tool, 11
pasting, 11, 49
pathnames, 832
Pattern tool, 13
patterns
    adding texture with, 50
    creating custom, 133–134
    creating shapes and, 130–134
    in the Paint window, 30
    within patterns, 132–133
    selecting, 13
    spotlights and, 134–136
    swatches, 30
pausing, 144–145, 278
    at the beginning of a video, 608–609
    after every frame, 352–353
    to wait for a cue point, 278
    to wait for a video to finish, 278
Pencil tool, 28, 37
perspective mapping, 917
Perspective action, 84
Photoshop (Adobe), 408–409, 906–909
Picture Compressor (QuickTime), 589
Picture Viewer (QuickTime), 589
Pinnacle Publishing Web site, 20
play command, 351–352, 361–364, 368
Play tool, 11
playback
    compensating for slow, 142
    controls, 596–597
    on Windows, flattening images for, 622–623
plug-ins, 855–864. *See also* Shockwave (Macromedia)
PLUGINSPAGE parameter, 874
PLUGINSPAGE tag, 166
point size, 120
Polygon tool, 29
pop-up list buttons, 75

pop-up text sprites, 536
portfolios, 293–299
Preceding Cast Members action, 89
precision, concept of, 394–395
Premiere (Adobe), 624
Prepare Frame event, 199
print attributes, 399–400
Print tool, 11
Programming Specialists, 315
Project Managers, 314
projectors
    basic description of, 139
    building, 161–165
    distributing, 165
    options for, 162
    packaging Xtras in, 739–745
properties. *See also* properties (listed by name)
    that constrain sprite movement, 456
    deleting, 663–665
    setting, using Lingo, 401–402
properties (listed by name). *See also* properties
    exitLock property, 830–831
    the constraint of sprite property, 456–458
    the loc of sprite property, 445–447
    the loop of member property, 609
    the moveableSprite property, 465–466
    the movieRate property, 602–603, 604
    the movieTime property, 603, 604
    the sound of member property, 608
    the soundLevel property, 570–571
    the StartTime property, 604
    the StopTime property, 604
    the video of member property, 608
    the visible of sprite property, 480–483
    the volume of sound property, 572–573
property keyword, 680
property lists
    attributes for, 659–666
    basic description of, 653–659
    commands for, 656–658
    duplicating, 658–659
property variables, 685
puppet sounds, 540–542
puppetSprites, 404–405, 438–442
puppetTransitions, 466–470
Push Button tool, 13
Push transition effect, 147
put commands, 400

Q

querying child objects, 693–694

QuickDraw 3D, 922–940, 944–945
QuickDraw 3D Xtra, 931–940
QuickTime movie(s), 576, 623–624
    basic description of, 588–592
    developers, resources for, 625–626
    export options, 619–620
    flattening, for playback on Windows, 622–623
QuickTime Controller, 275–277
" (quotation marks), 740

R

Radio Button tool, 13
RAM (Random-Access Memory), 226, 835–836. *See also* memory
    auto-syncing and, 837
    requirements, determining, 837–839
random() function, 370
RealVR Xtra, 944
recording
    modes, 230–231
    real-time, 97–102
    single versus multisession, 849–850
    step, 97–102
Rectangle tool, 13, 28
registration
    basic description of, 87–94
    creating tween cast members with, 91–92
    points, 27, 536–537
Registration Point tool, 27
Registration tool, 91–92
Rendering tab, 926–927
resumes, interactive
    adding backgrounds to, 288–289
    adding final scenes to, 312–314
    adding navigation controls to, 299–310
    adding tempo effects to, 309–310
    adding text to, 300–302
    adding transitions to, 309–310
    animating portfolios for, 293–299
    creating, 286–320
    designing interfaces for, 286–287
    gathering cast members for, 287–293
    scenes for, 289–290
reusing code, 421–430
Reveal ink effect, 34, 35
Reveal transition effect, 147
Reverse ink effect, 33, 110
Reverse Selected Colors tool, 158
reverse sequence, 95–96, 158
Reverse Sequence tool, 158
Right Mouse Down event, 199
Right Mouse Up event, 199

rollover(s)
    activation videos with, 613–615
    making sprites visible on, 483
    playing sound on, 555–556
rollOver function, 370, 412
Rotate Left action, 83
Rotate Right action, 83
RTF (rich text format), 114–115, 120, 128

S

sampling rates, 230–231
Save dialog box, 732–733
Save tool, 11
saving
    files, using the fileIO Xtra, 736–739
    keystrokes and code, with loops, 441–442
scaling video, 267–269
scientific notation, 393
Score window
    basic description of, 4, 8–9, 11, 67–69, 331–332
    editing in, 104–105
    opening, 68
    placing sounds in, 233–237
    placing SWA files in, 841
    scripts, 331–332
    specifying tempo settings in, 142–145
screen coordinates, 443–444
scripting. *See also* Lingo; scripts
    creating interactive movies with, 342–347
    from scratch, 323–398
    terminology, 325–330
    Xtras, 713–714
scripts. *See also* scripting
    ancestor, 680, 683–684, 704–705
    assigning, to buttons, 346–347, 354, 356–357
    basic description of, 4, 368
    behaviors and, 209
    composing your own, 337–342
    copying, 419–420
    effective domain on, 324, 337
    four types of, 324–337
    MIAWs and, 775–782
    parent, 675–708
    priority of, 334–336
    sprite, which override cast member scripts, 358–361
    stepping through, 764–765
    troubleshooting, 747–758
scrolling, 124, 528–529

Select Reserved Colors tool, 158
Select Used Colors tool, 158
semicolon (;), 533
servers
    basic description of, 854–855
    placing your movies on, 897–900
Set Background action, 90
set commands, 400
shadow effects, 906–909
shapes
    basic description of, 113–138
    creating, 129–130
    patterns and, 130–134
Shockwave (Macromedia). *See also* SWA (Shockwave Audio)
    basic description of, 165–169, 859–864
    creating movies with, 864–868
    implementation independence and, 348
    incorporating Netlingo and, 853–904
    installing, 861–864
    movies, saving Director movies as, 169
Show Title Bar option, 162
showGlobals command, 758
showXlib command, 721
Shrink option, 48
Size option, 61
Skew action, 83
slideshows, 343–347
sliders, 461–463
SmartVid, 623–624
Smear ink effect, 34
Smooth action, 84
Smooth ink effect, 34
Smudge ink effect, 34
Sort tool, 158
sorted linear lists, 631. *See also* lists
sorted property lists, 631. *See also* lists
sound(s). *See also* SWA (Shockwave Audio)
    adding, 232–237, 310–312, 543–544
    AIFF (Audio Interchange File Format), 227–228, 231, 568, 576–579
    attaching, to sprites/buttons, 544–545
    basic description of, 223–254
    behaviors, 245–247
    channels, 236–237, 548–549, 568, 573–575, 578–579
    controls for, 548–552
    editing, 228–230, 232–237
    exporting digital video and, 620
    fade-in/fade-out controls, 574–575
    formats, choosing, 227–228
    importing, 224–226, 576–579

linked, playing, 568–570
lists of, playing, 563–564
looping, 240–241
managing, 237–245
obtaining, for movies, 232
on/off controls, 549–551, 553–556
playing, during periods of inactivity, 566
random, 562–563
recording modes, 230–231
sampling rates, 230–231
sources of, 541, 551, 556
stopping, 545–547, 549–551
syncing video to, 267
tempo, 239–240
tracks, 551, 571
triggering, 542–544
using internal versus external, 226–227
volume, 141, 242–243, 570–575, 611, 809–810
WAV (Waveform Audio File) format, 227, 230–231, 568
Xtras, 245–252
soundBusy function, 370, 548–549
speed. *See also* tempo
of animation change, 78–79
modem, 868–869
playback, compensating for slow, 142
spelling errors, identifying, 748–751
splitting sprites, 79–82
spotlights, 134–136
Spread ink effect, 34
sprite(s)
adding sound behaviors to, 247
adjusting the length of, 234–236
anatomy of, 69–73
basic description of, 4, 10, 63–65, 69–73
changing single frames of, 106
copying, 305–309
creating moveable, 428–440
dragging/dropping media behaviors on, 193–194
drawing, on the Stage, 106–107
extending, 79–82
hiding/displaying, 480–483
inks, 109–111
intersecting, checking for, 446–447
joining, 79–82
last clicked, determining, 425–428
minimizing the number of, 64
panning, 71–72
positioning, 66–67, 443–455
preparing, before the enterFrame event, 432–433
properties, 400–401
redrawing, 415–417
removing behaviors from, 189–190
reordering behaviors attached to, 190
rolled over, 415–417
scripts, basic description of, 332–333
scripts, creating, 339–340
scripts, which override cast member scripts, 358–361
sound, 234–237
splitting, 79–82
swapping, 194–196, 407–408
SRC parameter, 873
SRC tag, 166
Stage
basic description of, 4, 65–67
digital video options for, 598–599
drawing sprites on, 106–107
making sprites invisible on, 481–482
playing digital video on, 264–265
placing sprites on, 66–67
positioning MIAWs on, 795–802
resizing buttons on, 344
size, 25, 65–67, 162
specific areas of, constraining sprite movement within, 456–458
swapping cast members on, 407–408
updating, 412
Standard Import option, 53
states, checking, 411–412
status bar, 894
step recording, 97–102
step-forward/step-backward controls, 611–612
Stop tool, 11
storyboarding, 25–26, 170–171
streaming movies, 865–866
strings, 494–505, 514–515
assigning, to variables, 373–374, 377–379
converting lists to, 648–649
Subtract Pin ink, 111
SWA (Shockwave Audio), 247–252, 576, 841
preload values, 839–841
Xtra, 247
swapping cast members, 405–410, 832
Switch Colors action, 84
Switch ink effect, 34
syntax errors, identifying, 748–751
system
extensions, 588-589
information, accessing, 379–380
messages, 325
variables, 379–380

T

tab characters, 123
tags
    <EMBED> tag, 861, 872–875, 876, 884, 885–886
    <NOEMBED> tag, 875
    <OBJECT> tag, 861, 875–877, 884, 885–886
    <PARAM NAME> tag, 876
teams, development, 314–316
tell statement, 782–784
tempo, 277–278, 787
    adding, to interactive resumes, 309–312
    basic description of, 8, 139–145
    channels, 578–579
    setting the base, 143–144
text. See also fonts; text fields; Text window
    adding, to interactive resumes, 300–302
    aligning, 122, 512–513
    anti-aliasing and, 115, 124–125
    basic description of, 113–138, 485–538
    on buttons, 344–345
    cast members, 113–120, 125–128
    field attributes, 486–487
    formatting, for menu items, 814–816
    importing, 128
    justifying, 122–123
    properties, 123–125, 487–488
    setting foreground color for, 488–490
    strings, 494–505
    terminology, 120
text field(s)
    attributes, 486–487
    basic description of, 485–538
    counting words in, 508
    deleting text from, 513
    editable, 530–531
    establishing text strings in, 504–505
    highlighting text in, 529–530
    positioning text in, 520–521, 528–529
    retrieving characters from, 498
    retrieving items from, 501–503
    retrieving lines of text from, 503
    retrieving words from, 500–501
    scrolling through, 526–527
    sizing/positioning, 517–521
    transferring text to/from, 508–513
Text Inspector, 365
Text tool, 12, 28, 116–120
Text window. See also text
    basic description of, 11, 120–127
    specifying formatting options in, 121–123
texture
    adding, with patterns, 50
    maps, 920–921

the constraint of sprite property, 456–458
the key function, 370
the loc of sprite property, 445–447
the loop of member property, 609
the moveableSprite property, 465–466
the movieRate property, 602–603, 604
the movieTime property, 603, 604
the sound of member property, 608
the soundLevel property, 570–571
the StartTime property, 604
the StopTime property, 604
the video of member property, 608
the visible of sprite property, 480–483
the volume of sound property, 572–573
3D effects
    avatars and, 911–913
    basic description of, 905–946
    coordinates and, 915–918
    implementing, 922
    meshes and, 918–920
    presentations, assembling, 914–915
    props and, 913–914
    rendering landscapes/environments with, 909–911
thumbnail images, 293–297. See also images
tiles
    basic description of, 30, 132–133
    creating, 31–33
    shapes and, 132–133
    spotlights and, 134–136
time function, 370
timers, creating, 210–213
titles, adding, 310–312
Toggle Onion Skinning action, 89
tool palette, 12–13, 355–356
Tool Xtras, 714
toolbar, 10–12
tools
    Air Brush tool, 28
    Align tool, 11
    Arc tool, 28
    Arrow tool, 12, 158
    Behavior Inspector tool, 11, 185–204, 214–215
    Blend tool, 158
    Brush tool, 28, 42–44
    Button tool, 343–344
    Cast Window tool, 11, 97
    Check Box tool, 13
    Color Picker tool, 158
    Copy tool, 11
    Cut tool, 11
    Cycle tool, 158
    Ellipse tool, 13, 28
    Eraser tool, 27

Exchange Cast Member tool, 11
Eyedropper tool, 28, 158
Field tool, 13
Filled Ellipse tool, 13, 28
Filled Polygon tool, 29
Filled Rectangle tool, 13, 28, 43, 131–132
Filled Round Rectangle tool, 13
Find Cast Member tool, 11
Foreground/Background Colors tool, 13
Hand tool, 27, 158
Help Pointer tool, 11
Import tool, 11
Invert Selection tool, 158
Lasso tool, 27, 47–48
Line tool, 12, 28
Line Weight Selector tool, 13
Magnifying Glass tool, 28, 46–47
Marquee tool, 27, 48–49, 92
New Cast tool, 11
Open tool, 11
Paint Bucket tool, 28, 39–42
Paste tool, 11
Pattern tool, 13
Pencil tool, 28, 37
Play tool, 11
Polygon tool, 29
Print tool, 11
Push Button tool, 13
Radio Button tool, 13
Rectangle tool, 13, 28
Registration Point tool, 27
Registration tool, 91–92
Reverse Selected Colors tool, 158
Reverse Sequence tool, 158
Save tool, 11
Select Reserved Colors tool, 158
Select Used Colors tool, 158
Sort tool, 158
Stop tool, 11
Text tool, 12, 28, 116–120
Undo tool, 11
tooltips, 10–12
Trace Edges action, 84
transition(s)
　applying, 148–150, 309–310
　basic description of, 145–150, 784–786
　choosing, 146–147
　controlling, 148–150, 470
　specifying, with MIAWs, 784–785
　Xtras, 711–712
Transparent ink effect, 33, 109
troubleshooting. *See also* debugging
　identifying syntax/spelling errors, 748–751
　locating problems, 748
Tweak window, 72

tweening, 79
typeface, setting, 491–492. *See also* font; text

U

Underline option, 122
Undo tool, 11
UNIX, 167
unsorted linear lists, 631. *See also* lists
updating, the Stage, 412
upgrading, versions of Director, 5–7
URLs (Uniform Resource Locators), 824, 877. *See also* hypertext
　jumping to, 895–897
　preloading, 890
Usage in Score option, 60
user intervention, waiting for, 145
Utilities for Mac Users (Microsoft), 624

V

variables
　assigning values/strings to, 373–374, 377–379
　basic description of, 370–375
　designation of, to watch, 759–761
　initializing, 374–375
　nomenclature, nonvariable, 372
　retrieving characters from, 498–500
　substituting, to shorten code, 447–451
versions, of Director, 5–7
vertical movement, of sprites, 458–463
vertical bar (|), 805
video
　adding, to movies, 262–272, 604–607
　basic description of, 255–284, 585–628
　cast members, adding, 595–607
　controller preferences for, 269–272
　cropping, 267–269
　editors, specifying external, 270–272
　exporting a range of frames as, 280–281
　framing options, 597–598
　looping settings, 269–272
　playback controls, 596–597
　preloading, 611
　properties, 608–611
　scaling, 267–269
　Stage options, 598–599
　synchronization, 599–600
　syncing, to sound, 267
Video for Windows (Microsoft), 279, 592–593, 623–624
video memory, 836
Video Specialists, 315

View menu, 14
virtual memory, 836
virtual reality, 941–945
volume, 242–243, 570–575, 611
    control, in the Control Panel, 141
        menus, creating, 809–810
VRML (Virtual Reality Modeling Language), 942–945

W

wait settings, 145
Warp action, 83
Watcher window, 758–761
WAV (Waveform Audio File) format, 227, 230–231, 568
Widget Wizard, 275–276
widgets, 272–273, 275–276
    adding, to interactive resumes, 302–305
    basic description of, 275–276
    duplicating, 305–309
    modifying, 305–309
WIDTH parameter, 873
WIDTH tag, 166
window(s)
    moving, to the front or back, 790–791
    types, 780–782
    visibility settings, 787–788
Windows (Microsoft)
    color palettes, 152
    export options, 620–621
    flattening QuickTime movies for playback on, 622–623
    menu formatting options, 814–816
    MIAWs and, 780–781
    setting filterMask under, 725–726
Wipe transition effect, 147
word games, 504–505
word keyword, 499–501
words
    counting, 508
    determining the number of, 522–523
    determining the text of, 523–525
Writers/Editors, 315

X

Xternal resources, 15–17
Xtra(s). *See also* Xtras (listed by type)
    adding, 15–17
    availability of, determining, 719–720
    basic description of, 16, 709–746
    that come with Director 6, 715–716
    creating new instances of, 721
    effective use of, 716–720
    four types of, 16
    installing, 718–719
    projectors and, 163, 739–745
    reasons to use, 710–711
    sound, 245–252
    -specific messages, 723–732
    storage of, in folders, 717–718
    types of, 711–715
Xtras (listed by type). *See also* Xtras
    Cast member Xtras, 713
    fileIO Xtra, 723–739
    Importing Xtras, 715, 740–741
    MUI (Macromedia User Interface) Dialog Xtra, 821–820
    QuickDraw 3D Xtra, 931–940
    RealVR Xtra, 944
    Scripting Xtras, 713–714
    Sound Xtras, 245–252
    SWA (Shockwave Audio) Xtra, 247
    Tool Xtras, 714
    Transition Xtras, 711–712

Z

zooming, 46–47

IDG BOOKS WORLDWIDE, INC. END-USER LICENSE AGREEMENT

READ THIS. You should carefully read these terms and conditions before opening the software packet(s) included with this book ("Book"). This is a license agreement ("Agreement") between you and IDG Books Worldwide, Inc. ("IDGB"). By opening the accompanying software packet(s), you acknowledge that you have read and accept the following terms and conditions. If you do not agree and do not want to be bound by such terms and conditions, promptly return the Book and the unopened software packet(s) to the place you obtained them for a full refund.

1. **License Grant.** IDGB grants to you (either an individual or entity) a nonexclusive license to use one copy of the enclosed software program(s) (collectively, the "Software") solely for your own personal or business purposes on a single computer (whether a standard computer or a workstation component of a multiuser network). The Software is in use on a computer when it is loaded into temporary memory (RAM) or installed into permanent memory (hard disk, CD-ROM, or other storage device). IDGB reserves all rights not expressly granted herein.

2. **Ownership.** IDGB is the owner of all right, title, and interest, including copyright, in and to the compilation of the Software recorded on the disk(s) or CD-ROM ("Software Media"). Copyright to the individual programs recorded on the Software Media is owned by the author or other authorized copyright owner of each program. Ownership of the Software and all proprietary rights relating thereto remain with IDGB and its licensers.

3. **Restrictions on Use and Transfer.**

    (a) You may only (i) make one copy of the Software for backup or archival purposes, or (ii) transfer the Software to a single hard disk, provided that you keep the original for backup or archival purposes. You may not (i) rent or lease the Software, (ii) copy or reproduce the Software through a LAN or other network system or through any computer subscriber system or bulletin-board system, or (iii) modify, adapt, or create derivative works based on the Software.

    (b) You may not reverse engineer, decompile, or disassemble the Software. You may transfer the Software and user documentation on a permanent basis, provided that the transferee agrees to accept the terms and conditions of this Agreement and you retain no copies. If the Software is an update or has been updated, any transfer must include the most recent update and all prior versions.

4. **Restrictions on Use of Individual Programs.** You must follow the individual requirements and restrictions detailed for each individual program in Appendix E, "Using the CD-ROM," of this Book. These limitations are also contained in the individual license agreements recorded on the Software Media. These limitations may include a requirement that after using the

program for a specified period of time, the user must pay a registration fee or discontinue use. By opening the Software packet(s), you will be agreeing to abide by the licenses and restrictions for these individual programs that are detailed in Appendix E, "What's on the CD-ROM," and on the Software Media. None of the material on this Software Media or listed in this Book may ever be redistributed, in original or modified form, for commercial purposes.

5. **Limited Warranty.**

   (a) IDGB warrants that the Software and Software Media are free from defects in materials and workmanship under normal use for a period of sixty (60) days from the date of purchase of this Book. If IDGB receives notification within the warranty period of defects in materials or workmanship, IDGB will replace the defective Software Media.

   (b) **IDGB AND THE AUTHOR OF THE BOOK DISCLAIM ALL OTHER WARRANTIES, EXPRESS OR IMPLIED, INCLUDING WITHOUT LIMITATION IMPLIED WARRANTIES OF MERCHANTABILITY AND FITNESS FOR A PARTICULAR PURPOSE, WITH RESPECT TO THE SOFTWARE, THE PROGRAMS, THE SOURCE CODE CONTAINED THEREIN, AND/OR THE TECHNIQUES DESCRIBED IN THIS BOOK. IDGB DOES NOT WARRANT THAT THE FUNCTIONS CONTAINED IN THE SOFTWARE WILL MEET YOUR REQUIREMENTS OR THAT THE OPERATION OF THE SOFTWARE WILL BE ERROR FREE.**

   (c) This limited warranty gives you specific legal rights, and you may have other rights that vary from jurisdiction to jurisdiction.

6. **Remedies.**

   (a) IDGB's entire liability and your exclusive remedy for defects in materials and workmanship shall be limited to replacement of the Software Media, which may be returned to IDGB with a copy of your receipt at the following address: Software Media Fulfillment Department, Attn.: *Director® 6 Bible,* IDG Books Worldwide, Inc., 7260 Shadeland Station, Ste. 100, Indianapolis, IN 46256, or call 1-800-762-2974. Please allow three to four weeks for delivery. This Limited Warranty is void if failure of the Software Media has resulted from accident, abuse, or misapplication. Any replacement Software Media will be warranted for the remainder of the original warranty period or thirty (30) days, whichever is longer.

   (b) In no event shall IDGB or the author be liable for any damages whatsoever (including without limitation damages for loss of business profits, business interruption, loss of business information, or any other pecuniary loss) arising from the use of or inability to use the Book or the Software, even if IDGB has been advised of the possibility of such damages.

   (c) Because some jurisdictions do not allow the exclusion or limitation of liability for consequential or incidental damages, the above limitation or exclusion may not apply to you.

7. **U.S. Government Restricted Rights.** Use, duplication, or disclosure of the Software by the U.S. Government is subject to restrictions stated in paragraph (c)(1)(ii) of the Rights in Technical Data and Computer Software clause of DFARS 252.227-7013, and in subparagraphs (a) through (d) of the Commercial Computer — Restricted Rights clause at FAR 52.227-19, and in similar clauses in the NASA FAR supplement, when applicable.

8. **General.** This Agreement constitutes the entire understanding of the parties and revokes and supersedes all prior agreements, oral or written, between them and may not be modified or amended except in a writing signed by both parties hereto that specifically refers to this Agreement. This Agreement shall take precedence over any other documents that may be in conflict herewith. If any one or more provisions contained in this Agreement are held by any court or tribunal to be invalid, illegal, or otherwise unenforceable, each and every other provision shall remain in full force and effect.

Save 25% On Additional Video Clips From Four Palms®

Save time and money on your next multimedia application with ready-to-use professional quality video clips from Four Palms. All Clips are royalty-free — our low, one-time fee is the buyout price so you can use the clips over and over again.

Choose From Thousands of Action-Packed Clips on More Than 12 CD-ROM Titles

Each CD-ROM comes with 80-120 clips, ranging from 4 to 40 seconds, each digitized and ready for immediate use with Macromedia Director. Plus, with Four Palms' unique browser so you can quickly and easily find the exact clip you want.

Titles	Windows .AVI (80+ clips)	Macintosh QuickTime (100+ clips)	TOTAL
Aviation	$ 99.99	$149.99	_____
Bridges	$ 99.99	$149.99	_____
Highways	$ 99.99	$149.99	_____
Sports	$ 99.99	$149.99	_____
Marine	$ 99.99	$149.99	_____
Occupations	$ 99.99	$149.99	_____
Professions	$ 99.99	$149.99	_____
U.S. Scenes	$ 99.99	$149.99	_____
Rail	$ 99.99	$149.99	_____
Recreation	$ 99.99	$149.99	_____
Relationships	$ 99.99	$149.99	_____
European Scenes	$ 99.99	$149.99	_____
Any 4 titles above	$299.99	$499.99	_____
Complete set of 12	$799.99	$1299.99	_____

Special Editors Edition $49.99
Includes 50 of our most memorable clips in both Windows and Macintosh file formats.

Starter Kit $24.99
Features 20 sample clips in both Windows or Macintosh format, plus a catalog with thumbnails of all clips in the Four Palms collection.

How to order:
Call: 800-747-2567 or 703-834-0200
Fax: 703-834-0219
Mail: Four Palms
11260 Roger Bacon Drive, 5th Floor
Reston, VA 20190
e-mail: info@fourpalms.com
Web: www.fourpalms.com

Subtotal _____
Less 25% Discount _____
VA residents add 4.5% tax _____
Shipping & Handling _____
(UPS Ground $10; outside US; Outside US add $30; overnight in US add $5)
Total Order _____

Method of Payment: ____ Check or purchase order enclosed. ____ Credit Card- VISA, Masercard, Amex (circle one)
Account#_____ Exp. Date _____ Signature _____
Name_____ Title _____ Company_____
Address_____ City_____ State_____ Zip_____
Telephone_____ Fax_____ e-mail_____

SETUP FACTORY 4.0

The Professional Setup Authoring Tool for Windows 95 • Windows NT • Windows 3.1

Now that your masterpiece is ready to go, the only thing left is a professional, bullet-proof installation. Well, you're in luck! By special arrangement, Setup Factory 4.0 is now available to owners of this book for only $199.95 (US)+ shipping. That's a savings of $30 off our regular retail price. But, in order to qualify you must order direct from Indigo Rose and quote offer #JB1022. Call us today at 1-800-665-9668! After all, what good is a masterpiece if nobody sees it?

SPECIAL OFFER!

NAME

COMPANY

ADDRESS

CITY/STATE   COUNTRY   ZIP/POSTAL CODE

PHONE   FAX   EMAIL

VISA / MC / AMEX #   EXPIRES

NAME ON CARD   SIGNATURE

P.O. Box 2159
Winnipeg, MB
Canada R3C 3R5
www.IndigoRose.mb.ca/indigo

IndigoRose
SOFTWARE DESIGN CORP.

Sales: (800) 665-9668
Phone: (204) 946-0263
Fax: (204) 942-3421
Support@IndigoRose.mb.ca

my2cents.idgbooks.com

Register This Book — And Win!

Visit **http://my2cents.idgbooks.com** to register this book and we'll automatically enter you in our monthly prize giveaway. It's also your opportunity to give us feedback: let us know what you thought of this book and how you would like to see other topics covered.

Discover IDG Books Online!

The IDG Books Online Web site is your online resource for tackling technology — at home and at the office.

Ten Productive and Career-Enhancing Things You Can Do at www.idgbooks.com

1. Nab source code for your own programming projects.
2. Download software.
3. Read Web exclusives: special articles and book excerpts by IDG Books Worldwide authors.
4. Take advantage of resources to help you advance your career as a Novell or Microsoft professional.
5. Buy IDG Books Worldwide titles or find a convenient bookstore that carries them.
6. Register your book and win a prize.
7. Chat live online with authors.
8. Sign up for regular e-mail updates about our latest books.
9. Suggest a book you'd like to read or write.
10. Give us your 2¢ about our books and about our Web site.

Not on the Web yet? It's easy to get started with *Discover the Internet,* at local retailers everywhere.

Using the CD-ROM

The CD-ROM is what is known as a *hybrid* CD-ROM, which means it contains files that will run on more than one computer platform — in this case, both Windows 95 and Macintosh computers.

Many files and programs on the CD-ROM have versions for both the Macintosh and Windows platforms. Although these files and programs may be essentially the same in content, the method used to install or access them may be different. You will find specific installation instructions in Appendix E, "What's on the CD-ROM," as well as in the install.txt files found in each of the folders and in the movie on the CD-ROM. In addition, Appendix A describes the Auto-Run program stored on the CD-ROM.

Running the CD-ROM in Windows 95

The Windows 95 version of the CD-ROM contains an Auto-Run program that automatically starts the CD-ROM once it has been loaded in your CD-ROM drive.

Note

Auto-Run will work only when the Auto Insertion Notification option is enabled in the properties for your CD-ROM drive. (Go to Settings ⇨ Control Panel. Select System ⇨ Device Manager. Double-click the CD-ROM drive icon and then the manufacturer's name of your drive. In the Properties dialog box, click the Settings tab to find the Auto Insertion Notification option.)

To run the CD-ROM, follow these steps:

1. Insert the CD-ROM into your CD-ROM drive.
2. Close the drawer. If the CD-ROM drive's Auto Insertion Notification option is enabled, the CD-ROM should begin playing a movie and no further action is required to start the movie.

If the movie does not automatically start playing, do the following:

1. From either My Computer or Windows Explorer, open the drive that corresponds with your CD-ROM drive.
2. Double-click d6bible.exe. This will start the movie.

Running the CD-ROM on a Macintosh

To start the CD-ROM, follow these steps:

1. Insert the CD-ROM into the CD-ROM drive.
2. Double-click the CD-ROM icon on the desktop.
3. Double-click the d6bible projector icon. Doing this will start running the movie.

The movie offers a brief description and installation instructions for the various files and programs found on the CD-ROM.